Teaching Tips—Provide suggestions on points to stress.

corp... ...is, are organi... ...y formally. Others, like... ...od basketball team, are more casually structured. But all organizations, formal or informal, have several elements in common.

Perhaps the most obvious of these basic elements is a *goal* or purpose. The goal will vary—to win a league championship, to entertain an audience, to sell a product—but without a goal no organization would have a reason to exist. All organizations also have some program or method for achieving their goals—to practice playing skills, to rehearse a certain number of times before each performance, to manufacture and advertise a product. Without some *plan* for what it must do, no organization is likely to be very effective. Organizations must also acquire and allocate the resources necessary to achieve their goals—a playing field or rehearsal hall must be available; money must be budgeted for wages. All organizations are made up of people and depend on other organizations for the resources they need—a team cannot play without the required equipment; manufacturers must maintain contracts with suppliers. Finally, all organizations have leaders or *managers* responsible ... their goals. T... ... a coach, a conduct...

Class Comments—Quotes, anecdotes, and factual data for emphasis.

issues, begin... ...pter.

The Need for Cultural Diversity

Our ethical concern for the fair and equitable treatment of employees reflects our culture's strong commitment to equal opportunity. It also reflects good management, for as the international economy increases competitive pressures, organizations must draw on their most talented employees—without regard for racial, cultural, or sexual differences. As Avon Chairman and CEO Jim Preston puts it, "Talent is color blind. Talent is gender blind. Talent has nothing to do with dialects, whether

...ialized field: surgeons, ...
skills in their respective fields. *Human skill* is the ability to work with, understand, and motivate other people, as individuals or in groups. *Conceptual skill* is the ability to coordinate and integrate all of an organization's interests and activities. It involves seeing the organization as a whole, understanding how its parts depend on one another, and anticipating how a change in any of its parts will affect the whole.

Katz suggests that although all three of these skills are essential to a manager, their relative importance depends mainly on the manager's rank in the organization. (See Fig. 1-2.) Technical skill is most important in the lower levels. Human skill, by contrast, is important for managers at every level: Because managers must work primarily through others, their ability to tap the technical skills of their subordinates is more important than their own technical proficiency. Finally, the importance of conceptual skill increases as one rises through the ranks of a management system based on hierarchical principles of authority and responsibility.

Discussion Questions—Prompt open discussion during class.

■ MANAGERIAL ROLES

Our working definition describes *managers* as organizational planners, organizers, leaders, and controllers. Actually, every manager—from the program director of a college club to the chief executive of a multinational corporation—takes on a much ...ange of roles... the ... ...stated... ...actl... ...broad

Thought Provokers—Questions for your students to consider on their own as they learn more about management.

Organizations such as universities, museums, and corporations are essential because they store and protect most of the important knowledge our civilization has gathered and recorded. In this way, organizations make that knowledge a continuous bridge between past, present, and future generations. In addition, organizations themselves add to our knowledge by developing new and more efficient ways of doing things.

ORGANIZATIONS PROVIDE CAREERS. Finally, organizations are important because they provide their employees with a source of livelihood and, depending on the style and effectiveness of their managers, perhaps even personal satisfaction and self-fulfillment. Most of us tend to associate career opportunities with business corporations, but in fact many other organizations, such as churches, government agencies, schools, and hospitals, also offer rewarding careers.

D1303402

Mary Coulter

Annotated Instructor's Edition

MANAGEMENT

Fifth Edition

James A. F. Stoner

Fordham University

R. Edward Freeman

University of Virginia

Prentice Hall, Englewood Cliffs, New Jersey 07632

Annotated Instructor's Edition

Acquisitions Editor: Alison Reeves
Development Editor: Linda Muterspaugh, Textbooks Plus
Production Editor: Eleanor Perz
Interior and Cover Designer: Suzanne Behnke
Prepress Buyer: Trudy Pisciotti
Manufacturing Buyer: Robert Anderson
Supplements Editor: David Scholder

Cover art: Raoul Dufy, Street Decked with Flags,
Le Havre. 1906. Oil on canvas 31 7/8 × 25 7/8″.
Musée National d'Art Moderne, Centre Georges Pompidou,
Paris.

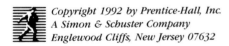

Printed in the United States of America
10 9 8 7 6 5 4 3 2 1

ISBN 0-13-544313-X

Prentice Hall International (UK) Limited, London
Prentice Hall of Australia Pty. Limited, Sydney
Prentice Hall Canada Inc., Toronto
Prentice Hall Hispanoamericana, S.A, Mexico
Prentice Hall of India Private Limited, New Delhi
Prentice Hall of Japan, Inc., Tokyo
Simon & Schuster Asia Pte. Ltd., Singapore
Editora Prentice Hall do Brasil, Ltda., Rio de Janeiro

PREFACE

■ *ABOUT THE TEXT*

We believe there has never been a more rewarding—or challenging—time to be a manager. The reward comes from knowing that effective, efficient managers can and are making a real difference in our world. The challenge comes from the globalization of the economy, which presents a constantly shifting kaleidoscope of competitive pressures and opportunities. Consider just a few facts. The Berlin Wall is rubble, and scores of U.S. and European companies have launched joint ventures within communist countries. Furthermore, the European Community is pointing the way for a new set of trade and political alliances. And while U.S. companies and foreign companies are competing for the same customers, they are just as likely to form joint ventures for research and production. Our goal for this edition then is to make students aware of these environmental changes and to show them how effective managers can and are adapting. To do this, we have adopted a three-pronged strategy.

First, we have grouped four chapters that discuss key aspects of the environment in the second part of the book, where they provide a framework for the traditional discussions of planning, organizing, leading, and controlling.

Second, we have supplemented the Fourth Edition's focus on business ethics with an emphasis on cultural diversity, one of the most prominent aspects of today's environment. If organizations are to meet the challenges of today's changing environment, they must draw on their most talented employees—without regard for racial, cultural, or sexual differences. Managers must also be sensitive to cultural differences as they deal with their counterparts, employees, and customers from other countries—an increasingly common event.

Third, we have placed an even greater emphasis on practical applications and examples drawn from real-world organizations. As always, we value theory and research for the insights they provide into the practice of management, but the real excitement comes from seeing these theories in action.

■ *ABOUT THE ANNOTATED INSTRUCTOR'S EDITION*

The Annotated Instructor's Edition is the text itself with various types of annotations in the margins and a brief overview of the textbook and package bound into the frontmatter.

The concept of the AIE puts into actual practice what professors have done for years—making brief notes in the margins of their lecture notes; jotting down thoughts on slips of paper and filing them away to enhance the teaching of a particular topic or chapter.

Three major changes have been made to the Fifth Edition AIE. The ABC News icon and Coordinated Resource annotations have been added, and we have moved the chapter-by-chapter materials into a separately bound *Instructor's Resource Manual* to make the AIE easier to carry.

Following is a more complete description of its features.

Chapter Annotations

Specific types of annotations in every chapter of the textbook include the following:

ABC NEWS ICON The ABC News icon appears in the margin of the textbook to alert instructors that a relevant ABC News video is available for that portion of the text.

COORDINATED RESOURCE These annotations provide a guide to the supplements in the Fifth Edition package by keying in the supplements to an appropriate portion of the text in each chapter.

HERE'S AN EXAMPLE Numerous and varied examples of management practices are provided. Each is tied to a certain concept presented in the chapter. In most chapters, several examples are presented, providing you with ample opportunities to pick and choose those that you want to use as you teach.

CLASS COMMENT These annotations provide anecdotes or factual data that you might want to emphasize for students as you lecture.

THOUGHT PROVOKERS These questions are designed to get students to think! Naturally there may be no easily available answer to every question, but at least the students will begin to appreciate the complexity and dynamics of the management process.

DISCUSSION QUESTIONS These questions are meant to prompt open discussion during class.

TEACHING TIPS Throughout most of the chapters, we have provided you with some suggestions for making the class more exciting and manageable.

Additional Supplementary Aids for the Instructor

INSTRUCTOR'S RESOURCE MANUAL The *Instructor's Resource Manual* provides chapter overviews, lecture outlines, detailed chapter outlines, answers to all of the review and case questions in the text, and teaching notes for the chapter-ending video cases.

 ABC NEWS/PRENTICE HALL VIDEO LIBRARY FOR *MANAGEMENT*, FIFTH EDITION
Prentice Hall and ABC News have joined forces to create the best and most comprehensive set of video materials available for any principles of management text. From its wide range of award-winning programs—*Nightline, Business World, On Business, This Week with David Brinkley, World News Tonight,* and *20/20*—we have assembled in the ABC News/Prentice Hall Video Library for *Management*, Fifth Edition, over 20 high-quality, relevant, and engaging feature and documentary videos directly related to the text. Each video is accompanied by a written video case at the end of each text chapter. All of the videos are supported by case commentaries and teaching suggestions in the *Instructor's Resource Manual* to help instructors effectively integrate the videos into their lectures.

LECTURE EXTRAS These have been updated and re-formatted so that they are easier to use as class handouts. Any necessary teaching materials, including transparency masters for the *Lecture Extras* activities, are included. The overview information for *Acumen* and teaching notes for integrating *Management Live!* with *Management,* Fifth Edition, are also included in the *Lecture Extras.*

TRANSPARENCY MASTERS This set of *Transparency Masters* includes full-page reproductions of all the figures in the book.

COLOR TRANSPARENCIES A set of 150 *Color Transparencies* is available to adopters of the text. The transparencies are a mix of artwork from the text itself and other applicable sources. An expanded caption accompanies each of the transparencies. The transparencies are keyed into the text in the Annotated Instructor's Edition under the Coordinated Resource annotations.

ATLAS TEST ITEM FILE To ensure the highest possible quality examinations, this *Atlas Test Item File* has been thoroughly reviewed by an expert in testing and measurement. The Test Item File contains 2000 multiple-choice, true/false, and essay questions.

PRENTICE HALL TEST MANAGER The Test Item File is supplemented by the *Prentice Hall Test Manager,* a computerized test bank. The Test Manager is a sophisticated and easy-to-use computerized testing system, providing individually tailored examinations. Test Manager allows you to edit, add, and delete questions. Tests may be generated manually or chosen randomly from the existing bank of questions. Test Manager is available in both 5.25″ and 3.5″ IBM formats.

TELEPHONE TEST PREPARATION SERVICE This service provides a letter-quality printed examination. Simply choose questions from the printed test bank, indicating your selections on the Computerized Testing Service Request Form, the number of questions you want, and the order in which they should appear. Within 48 hours you will receive the examination master.

Additional Supplements for the Student

STUDENT GUIDE On a chapter-by-chapter basis, the *Student Guide* contains pre-tests, overviews, learning objectives, key terms, fill-in reviews, post-tests, and application exercises.

The New York Times **THE NEW YORK TIMES: A CONTEMPORARY VIEW** *The New York Times* and Prentice Hall are sponsoring this program designed to enhance student access to current information relevant in the classroom. Through this program, the core subject matter in the text is supplemented by a collection of time-sensitive articles from *The New York Times.* These articles demonstrate the vital ongoing connection between what is learned in the classroom and what is happening in the world around us. To enjoy the wealth of information of *The New York Times* daily, a reduced subscription rate is available in deliverable areas. For information, call toll-free: 1-800-631-1222. Prentice Hall and *The New York Times* are proud to co-sponsor *A Contemporary View.* We hope it will make the reading of both textbooks and newspapers a more dynamic, involving process.

MANAGEMENT LIVE! THE VIDEO BOOK This video-based experiential management text is available at a discounted price when shrink-wrapped to *Management,* Fifth Edition. The corresponding video collection is available *one per department* upon adoption of the shrink-wrapped package. There is an *Instructor's Manual* to *Management Live!* that provides teaching notes for all of the exercises.

MANAGEMENT APPLICATIONS: EXERCISES, CASES, AND READINGS BY JOHN T. SAMARAS This collection of cases and student exercises extends and enhances many of the key issues in *Management,* Fifth Edition.

MICROMANAGING These Lotus-based software exercises have been designed to help students better understand and apply microcomputers to the process of management.

READINGS IN MANAGEMENT BY PHILIP B. DUBOSE   This text furnishes further background regarding classical management, planning and decision making, organizing, human resource management, controlling, and global management.

MODERN BUSINESS DECISIONS BY RICHARD V. COTTER AND DAVID J. FRITZSCHE   A computerized business simulation for the IBM PC. Consists of software, a *Player's Manual,* and an *Instructor's Manual.*

MANAGING AN ORGANIZATION: A WORKBOOK SIMULATION BY GARY R. ODDOU   A noncomputerized business simulation workbook.

HYPERCARD SIMULATIONS FOR MANAGEMENT   This is a Hypercard-based simulation on Desktop Order to be used with the Macintosh computer. Instructors receive a site-licensed disk to be copied for the students.

ACUMEN, EDUCATIONAL VERSION   *Acumen* is a computerized managerial assessment development program. Shrink-wrapped, it costs only a few dollars above the text price. It is available in 3.5″ and 5.25″ versions. *Acumen* has been revised to allow three assessments per disk and to work in "shared printer" environments.

We hope you will find all these teaching tools to be state of the art, interesting, exciting, and useful. We honestly believe that they will enhance and enrich your basic management courses.

MARY COULTER

What to look for in the new edition:

- increased emphasis on international management by moving the chapter to the front of the book.
- refocused chapter on entrepreneurship as an increasingly important dimension of the external environment.

- new Management and Diversity boxes incorporated throughout.
- new material on negotiation skills integrated into the communications chapter.

- separate chapters on control basics and financial control methods combined into one on "Effective Control."
- general tightening throughout to make the material shorter, clearer, and easier to teach and learn.

Women in the International Work Force

Since the 1950s, the United States has witnessed profound changes in women's prospects at work and in

Hong Kong's Most Powerful Woman. A Shanghai native, Berkeley-educated Dame Lydia Dunn, chairperson of the Hong Kong Trade Development Council, senior member of Hong Kong's inner cabinet, and director of several companies, is planning for 1997, when Hong Kong reverts to Chinese control.

> • **Management and Diversity boxes—**
>
> these new inserts are designed to help students become more aware of minority issues and challenges they will face as managers of tomorrow. The boxes also show how culturally diverse groups are being integrated into effective organizations and discuss how management styles differ throughout the world. Examples include: *Women in the International Work Force, Who Are the New Entrepreneurs?, The Disabled Bill of Rights,* and *Employing the Homeless.*

The Japanese attitude on this issue is especially significant because our economic interaction with them is vast and growing. A recent *New York Times* article recounts the experience of a major U.S. bank that was hosting a party for a Japanese firm. The bank decided to invite virtually no female employees because they felt the presence of businesswomen would make their guests uncomfortable.

Although the Japanese traditions do accord more respect to foreign women in a business setting that they would to Japanese women, it is widely acknowledged that "Japanese businessmen never negotiate anything important with a woman." Due in part

U.S. MNEs; organizational practices fav
acceptable to people from cultures at

Applying Japanese Approache
Synthesizing Differing Appro

While Hofstede has expressed seriou
management practices in other countr
cited about the effectiveness of Japane
ment has become almost a fad, in fact.
people refer to as "Japanese manageme
of companies, responsible for perhaps
Japan.

> *"The authors should be commended for their sensitive treatment of these issues. We need to keep reminding our students tha the labor force participatio rates of women, as well as racial minorities, continue to increase. Businesses nee to prepare for the changing 'face' of the traditional labor force."*
>
> —DEBORAH L. WELLS, *Creighton Universi*

INTERNATIONAL MANAGEMENT

Economic Experiments in the People's Republic of China

In 1980, the People's Republic of China launched a series of unique economic experiments—unique, that is, for a nation that had relied on a planned economy for 40 years. Under Mao Zedong, the govern- [owned ...ition. ..., not ...nage- ...n"; to ...often ...spite ...feed- ...on of]

> *'Like ethics, international management is an impor- ant topic. Multinationals ire a fact of life and leserve attention.*
>
> —JAMES C. SPEE, *The Claremont Graduate School*

on of leaders announced an ambitious new goal— economic growth—and a series of economic reforms to be phased into virtually all of China's state-owned enterprises. These reforms promoted entrepreneur-ship *within* state-owned businesses, permitted certain businesses to experiment with restructuring, and allowed entrepreneurs to start small, privately owned businesses.

Throughout the 1980s, China accelerated its reform program, hoping to become an increasingly viable player in the world economy. And companies such as Reebok, Nike, Squibb, and Ingersoll-Rand re-sponded by investing in joint ventures behind the Bamboo Curtain, attracted by untapped market op-portunities as well as by the productive capacities of an industrious, if not yet industrialized economy.

China's economic growth has created growing pains, however. To transform a predominantly peas-ant culture into one poised to reap the benefits of twentieth-century technology and innovation, Chi-na's leaders have chosen to *modify,* not abandon, its planned economy. This means trying to keep the economy from expanding too quickly, fearing the predictable effects of inflation—upward-spiraling wages and prices—which could be worsened by a planned economy that essentially violates the law of supply and demand. Many leaders believed the changes were coming too fast and were especially alarmed when university students agitated for demo-cratic reforms on top of the economic reforms.

In May 1989, tanks rumbled into Tiananmen Square, signaling an end to the period of liberaliza-tion. While the world watched, party hard-liners staged a bloody crackdown on the students, leaving many people in doubt about the future of economic experiments and foreign investment in China.

Wenzhou, site of China's most ambitious eco-nomic experiments and a hotbed of entrepreneurial ventures, was especially hard hit. These ventures are now under close government scrutiny, and tax rates have been increased—sometimes doubled in one year—to create more "reasonable" levels of profit. Anger and resentment among Wenzhou's entrepre-neurs have led to violence; one tax collector was killed and two others wounded in a clash in October 1989.

from and ac Office ingly techn ahead rule, amon; factor the C

> ## • International Management boxes—
>
> these reflect the fact that management has become a genuinely global activity encom-passing a vast range of cross-cultural encounters and problems. Examples include: *New Frontiers of U.S./Japanese Competition: The Race to Shape Our Brave New Biotechnological World, Economic Experiments in the People's Republic of China,* and *The Sullivan Principles in South Africa.*

*Sources Busine: na's Re Week, / nities," ham, "F pp. 117–118; Adi Ignatius, "A Tiny Chinese Venture into Capital-ism Feels Icy Chills in Wake of Crackdown," *The Wall Street Jour-nal,* March 8, 1990, p. A11; Kay M. Jones, "Westerners Learn to Read the Tea Leaves," *Management Review,* April 1990, pp. 46–49; Lora Western, "Hong Kong Deadline Doesn't Curb Deals," *Crain's Chicago Business,* March 18–24, 1991, p. 1.

ILLUSTRATIVE CASE STUDY

INTRODUCTION

Sumitomo: The Move to International Banking

Widely regarded as Japan's most efficient, aggressive, and innovative bank, Sumitomo is also Japan's most profitable bank. Net earnings for the fiscal year ending March 1989 were $1.5 billion—up 78 percent over the previous year. This is especially pleasing to

> • **Illustrative Case Studies**—every chapter opens with a case highlighting an actual company situation, problem, or challenge. The case is continued at a key point in the middle of the chapter, and then wrapped up at chapter's end.
> Examples include: *Sumitomo: The Move to International Banking, Image and Imaging Problems at Eastman Kodak,* and *The Apostle of Mass Production: Henry Ford.*

Japan's
fits has
and ra-
esident
y.

ssed in
s, as in-
-the-art
he first
on-line;
penser;
he bank
980s—
me per
employee in the same period. By 1985, Sumitomo had committed another $208 million to enhancing its information systems.

The second, more important expression of Sumitomo's profit orientation is its adaptation to the changing dynamics of the domestic and international banking environment. At one time, Japanese companies were important customers, but when Japanese economic growth slowed down, they turned to cheaper international sources for financing. In addition, a gradual program of bank deregulation launched by the Finance Ministry in 1982 intensified domestic competition and put more pressure on banks' profit margins.

To cope with these changes, Sumitomo has branched out internationally. The bank has been especially active in two areas recently: leveraged buyouts and merger and acquisition deals in the United States and Europe. It was the adviser to Yamanouchi for its $395 million takeover of San Francisco–based Shaklee, it arranged Japanese financing for Campeau's buyout of Federated Department Stores, and it got a loan commitment fee of $2.5 million from Paramount in its failed bid for Time, Inc. Sumitomo has also been important in pushing for greater Japanese involvement in shaping international fiscal policy. This was particularly evident in the presence of several Japanese banks at the international negotiations with Latin American debtor nations in February 1989.

In 1986, the bank made a large and aggressive acquisition of its own—12.5 percent of Goldman, Sachs & Company, a New York investment bank. Many bankers were intrigued by the move, since Sumitomo's role is strictly limited by the Federal Reserve Board. The Fed has already expressed concern that the arrangement might further erode the Glass-Steagall Act, which separates commercial banks from investment banks. Sumitomo may not increase its stake i
role or

H
not thi
yond t
simply
more f
force i

Sources:
Internat
Ikahata,
Business
Crock, "
ness We
Sumitom
pp. 297–
Charge o
Peter Tr
Wall Str
"The Ot
80–88;

> *"I particularly like the illustrative case studies at the beginning of each chapter. They grab students' interest and ground the chapter material that follows in reality. Subsequent referra* *to the opening mini-case is an excellent follow up that reinforces the reasons the case was presented in the first place."*
>
> —DEBORAH L. WELLS, *Creighton Universit*

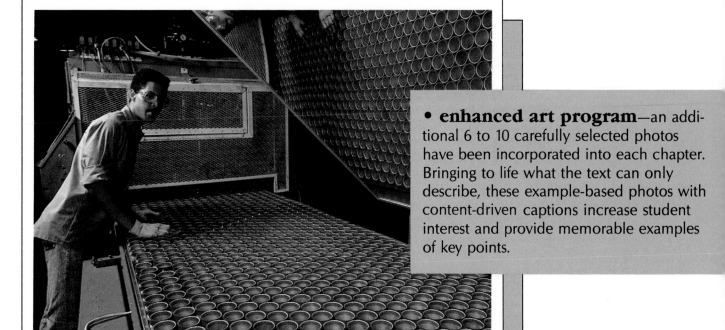

Nonprogrammed Decisions. Faced with deep Pentagon spending cuts, Ball Corp. CEO Richard M. Ringoen made a series of nonprogrammed decisions. He cut back the company's aerospace division, which depended on defense spending, and pumped money back into Ball's basic business—glass and metal containers. In other nonprogrammed decisions, Ball bought back part of the business it sold in 1987 and paid $1 billion for the European packaging operations of Continental Can Co., moves meant to prepare Ball to tap a European demand for beverage cans that is growing at twice the rate of demand in the United States.

Learning Teamwork. Students in the University of Chicago Graduate School of Business take part in required, noncredit Outward Bound exercises introduced, along with similar workshops in nonverbal communication and presentation skills, to improve their human skills and balance the school's quantitative emphasis.

VIDEO CASE STUDY

Managing the Environment at McDonald's

An aging population increasingly aware of the relationship between salt, dietary fat, and health, coupled with environmental concerns and a loss in sales momentum, are forcing McDonald's to take a new look at the fast-food marketplace it has dominated for so many years.

Consider the statistics on McDonald's, the nation's largest fast-food chain. Although 1990 sales exceeded $18 billion, almost one-third came from overseas operations. Domestic sales, in contrast, are flattening and percentage growth has slowed down for eight straight quarters. After a sluggish 1990 second quarter performance, security analysts at Prudential Bache downgraded McDonald's status from a hold to a sell even though the corporation ranks as [a] Dow-

• A video case for each chapter—

Every chapter concludes with a video case showing how an actual company has dealt with an issue covered in both the chapter and a corresponding ABC News video clip. Examples include: *Managing the Environment at McDonald's (World News Tonight/American Agenda); Workforce Literacy (On Business); Managing the U.S. Postal Service (Nightline);* and *Fetal Protection at Johnson Controls (World News Tonight/American Agenda).*

[hig]h, is [Reco]rd of [ ]em is [ ]-plus [ ]ate is [ ]'s, the [ ]phics [ ]rate a [ ] The [ ]rcent [ ] same [ ] kept [ ]naller [ ]nting with a 1950s diner concept for small towns and opened the first Golden Arch Cafe in Hartsville, Tennessee, in 1989. Not using the McDonald's name gives the company more freedom to experiment with new ideas, managers report. Another problem is the mounting competition from PepsiCo's Pizza Hut, Taco Bell, and Kentucky Fried Chicken, which offer more varied menus. In response, McDonald's is speeding up its introduction of new menu items. Traditionally, it test-marketed new menu items an average of five years before introducing them nationwide, but now it is testing a number of "healthier," non-burger menu items with plans to push the most promising into nationwide distribution as quickly as possible.

McDonald's has also had to deal with critics of the fat content of its menu. In response, McDonald's

switched to all-vegetable oil for its famous french fries and reduced the fat content of its hamburgers, introducing in April of 1991 the 91 percent fat-free McLean Deluxe. It reduced sodium in its breakfast pancakes by 30 percent and removed monosodium glutamate from Chicken McNuggets as well. Says McDonald's Chief Operating Officer Ed Rensi, "We let market conditions, the environment, and our customers lead us strategically."

The company is now in the process of following another environmental "lead" and phasing out its styrofoam packaging. The decision to switch to paper packaging was a difficult, expensive, and still controversial one for McDonald's.

The company has a history of environmental concern and initially switched from paper containers to styrofoam in the mid-1970s when researchers urged reducing the amount of paper used to prevent deforestation. In the 1980s, the firm reduced solid waste even more by decreasing the thickness of its straws and containers. McDonald's became the first company to sign a voluntary agreement, in 1987, to phase out the type of polystyrene (styrofoam) that is manufactured using chlorofluorocarbons (CFCs) deemed harmful to the ozone layer.

Still the company was criticized for the amount of solid waste it generated, including an annual 45 million pounds of polystyrene waste. McDonald's took the lead in polystyrene recycling, starting what was probably the world's largest program in Massachusetts. Here polystyrene from 450 New England McDonald's restaurants was converted to plastic resins and sold to companies that produced plastic products, including McDonald's own trays. The company committed to spend $100 million dollars a year over the next two years on recycling efforts.

Next the company embarked on a program to educate the American public about recycling polystyrene. Initial studies showed 70 percent participation by in-store customers. Critics charged, however, that the non-CFC styrofoam still might harm the atmosphere during the manufacturing process. In addition, they pointed out, recycling only worked for meals eaten in the stores; more than half of McDonald's business is carry-out.

In rebuttal, plastics manufacturers argued that McDonald's outside consultant had found that the material contained no toxic substances, took less

The ABC News/Prentice Hall Video Library

Prentice Hall and ABC have joined together to bring the most thoroughly integrated and comprehensive video libraries to the college market. These professional presentation packages offer both feature and documentary-style videos from a variety of ABC's award-winning news programs, including *World News Tonight, Nightline, 20/20, Primetime Live, This Week with David Brinkley,* and *Business World.*

In this Fifth Edition, you'll find a video clip that corresponds to a case in *every* chapter. To help you use the videos to their fullest advantage in your classroom, we provide you with an accompanying *Video Guide.* Following are just some of the elements you'll receive:

- **synopses** of the videos showing their relation to text chapters.

- **teaching notes** that outline strategic video use (i.e., when to show the video, how to wrap it up) to stimulate class discussions and support case studies and exercises.

- **discussion questions** that focus students on applying concepts/ theories to the real-life situations portrayed on video.

- **suggested activities** such as research paper topics, guest speakers, and additional references.

ABC News and Prentice Hall. Moving Images, Lasting Impressions.

Management Live! *The Video Book*

ROBERT MARX, *University of Massachusetts at Amherst*
TODD D. JICK, *Harvard University*
PETER J. FROST, *University of British Columbia*

"The marriage of video and management education has been slowly occurring in the last few years. With the publication of this new experiential video book, the full benefit and excitement of this marriage will surely be realized. It is a bold pedagogical innovation and one that many of us have awaited. And it has been put together with great teaching care by three instructors—Bob Marx, Todd Jick, and Peter Frost—who have dedicated much of their professional time to creating engaging and stimulating classroom experiences."

—from the Foreword by LEONARD SCHLESINGER, *Harvard Business School*

MANAGEMENT LIVE! THE VIDEO BOOK, the first book built around video segments, shows how to integrate the power of this visual medium with thoughtful exercises, readings, self-assessment and theory material. The clips chosen are sometimes very serious documents, but more often are segments of films and TV shows that creatively demonstrate key management issues. By watching managers in action, students get a first-hand look at real work situations revealing managerial behaviors that most

lectures and readings are alone unable to convey.

Within each module of the text you'll find learning activities specifically designed to prepare students for the video, focus them during the video, and help them retain the ideas following the video.

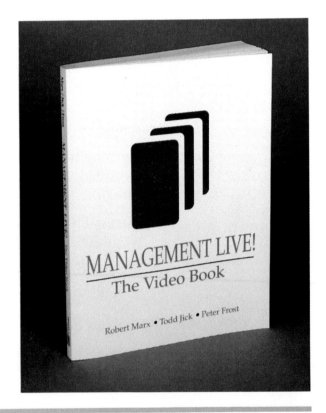

CHAPTERS:

1. Managing and Learning in the 21st Century
2. What Do Managers Do?
3. Organizational Culture
4. Organizational Theory
5. Power and Politics
6. Leadership
7. Decision Making
8. Teams and Groups
9. Communication in Organizations
10. Managing Information Systems
11. Operations and Control
12. Human Resources Management
13. Motivation
14. Gender and Race in the Work Place
15. Entrepreneurs
16. Ethics, Environment, and Social Responsibility
17. Going Global: International Management
18. Managing Change

VIDEOS:

2. Pat Carrigan, The Leadership Alliance (8:13); Rickover (*60 Minutes* 15:30)
3. Letterman, The GE Handshake (5:00)
4. *Modern Times* (full-length film)
5. *One Flew Over the Cuckoo's Nest* (full-length film)
6. Martin Luther King, I Have A Dream (full speech)
7. NASA *Challenger* (17:50)
8. The Israeli Air Force (*60 Minutes* 17:00)
9. Hyman Rickover (*60 Minutes* 15:30)
10. The Knowledge Navigator, Apple Computer (15:00)
11. *Broadcast News* (full-length film)
12. *Nine to Five* (full-length film)
13. Pat Carrigan (8:13)
14. Affirmative Action, (*Oprah Winfrey* 5:00); The Mommy Track (*Nightline* 10:00)
15. *Tucker* (full-length film)
16. Ben & Jerry's (7:00)
17. *Gung Ho* (full-length film)
18. *Broadcast News* (full-length film)

An *Instructor's Manual* with information on using the videos in class, as well as instructions for setting up and processing each exercise, is also available.

Prentice Hall/New York Times Contemporary View Program

No doubt, Stoner/Freeman's text is an excellent source for learning the basic principles and applications of management. However, nothing is as current as today's headlines. For this reason, Prentice Hall, the leading college textbook publisher, and *The New York Times,* the premier news publication, joined forces to bring the tempo of today's world into your classroom with the Contemporary View program. Now in its second year, this highly regarded program provides instructors and students who use Stoner/Freeman's MANAGEMENT 5/E with a carefully prepared "student supplement" containing recent articles that correspond directly to chapters and topics in the text. And to ensure timeliness, this complimentary "newspaper" is updated twice a year.

In addition, professors who adopt this text (in designated delivery areas) are eligible to receive a one-semester subscription of *The Times* for classroom use—free of charge. By offering students a view of all kinds of managers at work in today's society, *The Times* becomes not only a primary source of relevant information, but also the ideal complement to Stoner/Freeman's MANAGEMENT 5/E.

Keeping up with the times daily. Definitely a habit worth forming.

Photo Credit: Carl Baker

NOTES

MANAGEMENT

MANAGEMENT

Fifth Edition

James A. F. Stoner

Fordham University

R. Edward Freeman

University of Virginia

Prentice Hall, Englewood Cliffs, New Jersey 07632

Library of Congress Cataloging-in-Publication Data
Stoner, James Arthur Finch
  Management/James A.F. Stoner, R. Edward Freeman.—5th ed.
    p.   cm.
  Includes bibliographical references and indexes.
  ISBN 0-13-544305-9 (hard cover)
    1. Management.   I. Freeman, R. Edward.   II. Title.
HD31.S6963   1992
658—dc20   91-30891
                                                   CIP

Jim Stoner dedicates this edition with love to Alexandra, Barbara, and Carolyn, who helped him make the sensible decision at the right time.

R. Edward Freeman would like to dedicate this edition to Benjamin Wellen Freeman, Molly Wellen Freeman, and Emma Wellen Freeman.

Acquisitions Editor: Alison Reeves
Development Editor: Linda Muterspaugh, Textbooks Plus
Production Editor: Eleanor Perz
Copy Editor: Carole Freddo
Interior and Cover Designer: Suzanne Behnke
Photo Researcher: Christine A. Pullo
Prepress Buyer: Trudy Pisciotti
Manufacturing Buyer: Robert Anderson
Supplements Editor: David Scholder

Cover art: Raoul Dufy, *Street Decked with Flags,*
Le Havre. 1906. Oil on canvas 31⅞ × 25⅞".
Musée National d'Art Moderne, Centre Georges Pompidou, Paris.

 © 1992, 1989, 1986, 1982, 1978 by Prentice-Hall, Inc.
A Simon & Schuster Company
Englewood Cliffs, New Jersey 07632

Printed in the United States of America.
10 9 8 7 6 5 4 3 2 1

ISBN 0-13-544305-9

Prentice-Hall International (UK) Limited, *London*
Prentice-Hall of Australia Pty. Limited, *Sydney*
Prentice-Hall Canada Inc., *Toronto*
Prentice-Hall Hispanoamericana, S.A., *Mexico*
Prentice-Hall of India Private Limited, *New Delhi*
Prentice-Hall of Japan, Inc., *Tokyo*
Simon & Schuster Asia Pte. Ltd., *Singapore*
Editora Prentice-Hall do Brasil, Ltda., *Rio de Janeiro*

BRIEF CONTENTS

v

CONTENTS

PART TWO THE EXTERNAL ENVIRONMENT

3

THE EXTERNAL ENVIRONMENT OF
ORGANIZATIONS 59

PART THREE **PLANNING**

7

PLANNING AND STRATEGIC MANAGEMENT   183

12

AUTHORITY, DELEGATION, AND DECENTRALIZATION   341

13

HUMAN RESOURCE MANAGEMENT   371

14

MANAGING ORGANIZATIONAL CHANGE AND INNOVATION   405

15

MOTIVATION, PERFORMANCE, AND JOB SATISFACTION 437

16

LEADERSHIP 469

19

INDIVIDUAL CAREER MANAGEMENT 559

PART SIX CONTROLLING

20

EFFECTIVE CONTROL 597

PREFACE

Management was published in its first edition in 1978. Since then, the book has gained tenure as the most widely used and all-time best-seller in the Principles of Management field. The book has succeeded not only in the United States but also around the world, in its English edition as well as in its Portuguese, Spanish, Polish, Indonesian, and Bahasa Malayan translations.

We are humbled by this overwhelming show of trust and approached the fifth edition with renewed enthusiasm, determined to build on the solid foundation that made the first four editions such highly regarded teaching and learning tools.

As always, this book is about the job of the manager. It describes how men and women go about managing the people and activities of their organizations so that the goals of these organizations, as well as their own personal goals, can be achieved.

We have attempted in this book to convey the very positive view we have of the manager's job. We believe the job of a manager is among the most exciting, challenging, and rewarding careers a person can have. Individuals can, of course, make great contributions to society on their own. But it is also possible to realize major achievements in managed organizations—not only businesses but also universities, hospitals, research centers, government agencies, and other organizations. Such organizations bring together the talent and resources that such achievements require. A manager working within an organization has a far better chance to be involved in significant and far-reaching activities than would an individual working alone.

We also believe there has never been a more rewarding—or challenging—time to be a manager. The reward comes from knowing that effective, efficient managers can and are making a real difference in our world. The challenge comes from the globalization of the economy, which presents a constantly shifting kaleidoscope of competitive pressures and opportunities. Consider just a few facts. The Berlin Wall is rubble, and scores of U.S. and European companies have launched joint ventures within communist countries. Furthermore, the European Community is pointing the way to a new set of trade and political alliances. And while U.S. companies and foreign companies are vying for the same customers, they are just as likely to form joint ventures for research and production. One goal for this edition, then, is to make readers aware of these environmental changes and to show them how effective managers can and are adapting. A second goal is to help you, the reader, develop your own vital management skills.

In this text, we have chosen to address the reader as a potential manager. At times, in fact, we even adopt a tone that suggests the reader already *is* a manager. This is done intentionally: We want to encourage the reader to start thinking like a manager as soon as possible. Obviously, the earlier that one learns to think like a manager, the sooner one can develop managerial effectiveness. But there is another, more basic reason. All managers—but especially young managers just beginning their careers—are evaluated in large part on how effective they are as subordinates. The more successful an individual is as a subordinate, the more likely that his or her career will be successful. And one of the best ways of learning how to be an excellent subordinate is to learn how to think like a manager. Thus, addressing the reader as a manager (or at least a prospective manager) is meant to be a helpful way of improving the reader's chances for future managerial and career success.

■ DEVELOPING THE TEXT

As the Acknowledgments section of this Preface makes clear, we had the help of many people, beginning with a large and talented team at Prentice Hall—an acquisitions editor, a market-research specialist, a development editor, a book designer, a production editor, a supplements editor, a supplements coordinator, and many, many more people—united by experience and a commitment to producing effective teaching materials.

We began preparing the Fifth Edition of *Management* in the spring of 1990, when Prentice Hall developed a questionnaire specifically tailored to gather feedback from users of the Fourth Edition. When we had collected and collated all this information, we finalized our revision goals and plans, developed a comprehensive outline (which was also tested with reviewers), and began more focused work on individual chapters.

A key goal, based on the user feedback, was to streamline the text and focus on key concepts and research. Accordingly, a major part of our task was to analyze the reviews for guidance and then tighten both the organization and language. Drawing on years of experience developing texts in a number of fields, our development editor adopted the student's perspective and worked to ensure that we had succeeded in laying out for the student reader—interestingly and unambiguously—the fundamental topics in management theory and practice. In addition, our development editor worked to improve the illustration program, adding art that would clarify concepts and serve as additional study aids. This editorial procedure was applied to each of the drafts that finally became the Fifth Edition of *Management*.

The Fifth Edition of *Management* thus benefits from our years of teaching and writing experience as well as the many years of publishing experience represented by our support team at Prentice Hall. We feel strongly that the intensive process of development and the manifold resources of our publisher have enabled us to prepare a state-of-the-art revision that continues the book's tradition of being the standard by which other texts are judged.

■ ILLUSTRATIVE CASES AND CHAPTER FORMAT

Of course, the management case remains the favorite tool for giving future managers an idea of what it actually means to practice management on a day-to-day basis. Accordingly, we have provided more than seventy cases. However, the most important aspect of the cases is not their number, but the fact that they are good vehicles for applied learning, helping students develop their problem-solving and decision-making skills.

The **Illustrative Cases** that open each chapter focus on the efforts of such well-known organizations as Federal Express, Sony, Ford, Domino's Pizza, and Eastman Kodak to grapple with issues discussed in a particular chapter. At a strategic point within each chapter and again at the chapter end, we return to the Illustrative Case Study, showing how the profiled company's actions illustrate key concepts just discussed.

In addition, every chapter ends with a traditional management case and a video case, and every part ends with an integrative case, which ties together concepts discussed in that part.

The chapters, then, are organized as follows:

❑ A **Chapter Outline** (showing first- and second-level heads) is paired with **Learning Objectives,** to help students preview and plan their learning.

- ❏ The **Illustrative Case Study** presents a real-world dilemma faced by contemporary managers at some of the world's leading organizations.
- ❏ A **Chapter Introduction** previews, in prose, the chapter's main ideas and priorities.
- ❏ **Management and Diversity** boxes profile our growing awareness of our diverse population and of our obligation, as managers, to respect and even cultivate the rich talents people of different backgrounds bring to the workplace.
- ❏ **International Management** boxes, in keeping with the growing importance of international events, discuss how recent international developments are creating both opportunities and challenges for managers.
- ❏ **Ethics in Management** boxes highlight the ethical issues that affect every management decision, underscoring what we believe is one of the most important areas in management today.
- ❏ **Management Application** boxes add yet another example of how text theories and concepts are being used by practicing managers every day.
- ❏ Throughout the chapter, **marginal glossary entries** provide concise, complete definitions that clarify concepts and simplify review and study. These entries, of course, are supplemented by a complete glossary at the end of the book.
- ❏ A **Chapter Summary** provides a clear, succinct review of the chapter content, helping students reexamine the concepts they have just learned.
- ❏ **Review Questions,** keyed to the chapter's *learning objectives,* give students another opportunity to evaluate their understanding and pinpoint any areas they did not understand.
- ❏ A **Chapter-Ending Case** presents yet another management dilemma that is tied to the chapter content, giving students another opportunity to put themselves in the manager's shoes.
- ❏ A **Chapter-Ending Video Case** can be used by itself or with a corresponding video drawn from an ABC News program.

■ *IMPORTANT FEATURES OF THE FIFTH EDITION*

Increased Emphasis on the International Environment

International aspects of management continue to become increasingly important. Although we have expanded our coverage in each successive edition, we have in this edition moved our chapter on the international dimension from the end of the book to Part Two, where it provides a framework for many subsequent discussions. In keeping with the growing awareness of the global economy, many major examples are drawn from international management experiences, as are many of the chapter cases. Examples include Sumitomo Bank's effort to achieve worldwide leadership, Federal Express's push to expand worldwide, Lucky-Goldstar of Korea's experience in transplanting Korean management practices to U.S. plants, Harley-Davidson's attempts to stave off Japanese competitors, and Union Carbide's disastrous experience in Bhopal, India. This awareness is echoed, too, in the International Management boxes, which reflect the fact that management has become a truly global activity encompassing a vast range of cross-cultural encounters, activities, and problems.

Heightened Sensitivity to Diversity

As organizations increase their international activities, managers at all levels will have more opportunities to communicate, negotiate, and work with counterparts from other cultures. Even managers who never set foot beyond their home country will find themselves managing an increasingly diverse work force made up of employees from a wide variety of cultural, racial, and ethnic backgrounds. And, thanks to federal legislation, many more disabled individuals will be moving into the workplace and perhaps the executive suites of organizations of all sizes. Effective managers, then, need to be sensitive to this diversity and learn to work with many different types of people. In fact, many feel that the leaders of the global economy will be those organizations that learn to tap the talents of their best employees, without regard for diversity. To help readers develop their sensitivity to diversity issues, we have added several new Management and Diversity boxes to highlight these issues.

Continued Accent on the Practice of Management

As with the fourth edition, one of the most pervasive goals of this revision was to bring relevance to the student's learning experience. A prime example here is the chapter on individual career management. In addition, we have stressed relevance through examples, through cases, and through *video cases,* new to this edition.

Drawn from the activities of today's leading organizations, contemporary examples show how today's managers are applying text theories and concepts today. Although the majority of these examples are in the text, a great many are contained within the captions to four-color photographs showing the effects of management activities. And while many of the examples focus on Fortune 500 companies, a significant number feature smaller organizations, reminding readers that effective managers are found in organizations of all sizes.

Even a casual glance at the table of contents will give a good overview of the many practical examples contained in the Management Application, Ethics in Management, and International Management boxes, as well as the new Management and Diversity boxes.

New Program of Video Cases

Videos capture and hold students' attention, providing an easy and enjoyable way for them to learn and retain key concepts. Most importantly, the videos spark involvement, making students more willing and eager to enter into classroom discussions. This results in a lively, interesting, and productive class for everyone.

Prentice Hall and ABC News have joined forces to create the best and most comprehensive set of video materials available for any principles of management text. From its wide range of award-winning programs—*Nightline, Business World, On Business, This Week with David Brinkley, World News Tonight,* and *20/20*—we have assembled, in the ABC News/Prentice Hall Video Library for *Management,* Fifth Edition, over 20 high-quality, relevant, and engaging feature and documentary videos directly related to the text. The videos correspond to a video case at the end of each text chapter. In addition, all videos are supported by case commentaries and teaching suggestions in the *Instructor's Manual* to help instructors effectively integrate the videos into their lectures. Organizations profiled include the U.S. Postal Service, McDonald's, NASA, Avon, and Digital Equipment Company.

■ *SUPPLEMENTS PACKAGE*

We believe that even the most extensive supplements are useless if they don't work together. Based on that premise, we have compiled an extensive—and integrated—package of supplements, which feature these refinements and revisions.

ANNOTATED INSTRUCTOR'S EDITION (AIE).   To make the AIE a more handy, useful tool, we made two major changes to it. First, under the annotation category called *Coordinated Resources,* we have cross-referenced every element of every supplement in the package with the text, which makes the AIE a more complete resource reference guide. Secondly, to keep the AIE as close as possible to the size of the student text, we've moved the chapter-by-chapter lecture outlines, answers to review questions, and case analyses, including teaching notes for the video cases, to a separately bound *Instructor's Manual (IM)*.

LECTURE EXTRAS. These have been updated and reformatted so that they're easier to use as class handouts. Any necessary teaching materials, including transparency masters for the Lecture Extras activities, are included. The overview information for *Acumen,* as well as teaching notes for *Management Live!* (see below) are also included in the Lecture Extras.

PRENTICE HALL COLOR TRANSPARENCIES FOR MANAGEMENT SERIES C. We update our color transparency set every three years. It includes art from *Management,* Fifth Edition, as well as art from other sources. The box of color transparencies now includes a table of contents, which groups the transparencies under the categories "Introduction," "External Environment," "Planning," "Organizing," "Leading," and "Controlling." In addition, the Coordinated Resource annotation in the AIE provides specific cross-referencing of all the color transparencies with *Management,* Fifth Edition. Note, too, that the Transparency Masters that accompany this book are of all the text figures in this text, if you'd rather use overheads only from this text.

ABC NEWS/PRENTICE HALL VIDEO LIBRARY FOR MANAGEMENT, FIFTH EDITION. This video library contains all the videos to be used with the chapter-ending video cases. They are available free upon adoption. Contact your Prentice Hall representative for a demo tape ("Management Sample") of the ABC News/Prentice Hall Video Library.

MANAGEMENT LIVE! THE VIDEO BOOK. This innovative, video-based experiential workbook is available at a discounted price when shrinkwrapped to *Management,* Fifth Edition. The corresponding Video Collection is available (*one per department*) upon adoption of the shrinkwrapped package. There is an *Instructor's Manual* to *Management Live!* that gives complete teaching notes for all the exercises, while teaching notes tying it specifically to this text are in the Lecture Extras supplement.

PRENTICE HALL/NEW YORK TIMES CONTEMPORARY VIEW PROGRAM. *The New York Times* and Prentice Hall are sponsoring *A Contemporary View,* a program designed to enhance student access to current information of relevance in the classroom.

Through this program, the core subject matter provided in the text is supplemented by a collection of time-sensitive articles from one of the world's most distinguished newspapers, *The New York Times.* These articles demonstrate the vital, ongoing connection between what is learned in the classroom and what is happening in the world around us.

To enjoy the wealth of information of *The New York Times* daily, a reduced subscription rate is available in deliverable areas. (For information, call toll-free: 1–800–631–1222.)

Prentice Hall and *The New York Times* are proud to co-sponsor *A Contemporary View.* We hope it will make the reading of both textbooks and newspapers a more dynamic, involving process.

MANAGEMENT, FIFTH EDITION—ACUMEN EDITION. *Acumen* is a computerized managerial assessment development program. Shrinkwrapped, it costs only a few dollars above the text price. We now have both 3.5″ and 5.25″ versions available. Additionally, the software itself has been revised to allow three assessments per disk and to work in "shared printer" environments.

TEST ITEM FILE (TIF). The Atlas Test Item File has been designed in an effort to provide instructors with the highest quality examinations possible. In consultation with an expert in testing and measurement, this Atlas Test Item File is a comprehensive bank of 2,000 questions, thoroughly covering the topics discussed in the text.

The Test Item File contains 2,000 multiple-choice, true/false, and essay questions. We are pleased to offer what we believe is the finest test bank in the marketplace.

The Prentice Hall TestManager is a sophisticated and powerful computerized testing system. TestManager allows instructors to add and edit questions as well as to assemble and save tests. Examinations can be created manually or randomly generated from the provided bank of 2,000 questions. TestManager is available in either 5.25″ or 3.5″ IBM formats.

OTHER ADDITIONAL SUPPLEMENTS. We, of course, continue to offer the following supplements:

- ❏ *Student Guide to Note-Taking, Review, and Skills Practice*
- ❏ Samaras, *Management Applications* and *Instructor's Manual*
- ❏ Oddou, *Managing an Organization: A Workbook Simulation* and *Instructor's Manual*
- ❏ Cotter/Fritsche, *Modern Business Decisions: A Computerized Simulation and Software* and *Instructor's Manual*
- ❏ *Micromanaging Computer Exercise Template*/site license (Lotus-based)
- ❏ *Hypercard (Apple Macintosh) Simulations Template*/site license

■ *ACKNOWLEDGMENTS*

One of the most pleasant parts of writing a book is the opportunity to thank those who have contributed to it. Unfortunately, the list of expression of thanks—no matter how extensive—is always incomplete and inadequate. These acknowledgments are no exception.

Our first thanks must go to the editor of the First Edition of this book, Sheldon Czapnik. Sheldon's unflagging patience, constant good humor, and astounding capacity for creative work and long hours made the First Edition both possible and successful. Others who contributed greatly to earlier editions include Stuart Whalen, Robert DeFillippi, Peter Pfister, Samuel and Della Dekay, Arthur Mitchell, and Jim McDonald.

The following people also helped immensely with their reviews of the material for this edition: Aline Arnold, Eastern Illinois University; Chandler Wm. Atkins, Adirondack Community College; Allen Bluedorn, University of Missouri–Columbia; John F. Burgess, Concordia College; John J. Castellano, Suffolk University–Boston; Paul J. Champagne, Old Dominion University; Donald Conlon, University of Delaware; Roy A. Cook, Fort Lewis College; Patricia Feltes, Southwest Missouri State University; Diane L. Ferry, University of Delaware; James Gatza, American Institute for Property and Liability; John Hall, University of Florida; Phyllis G. Holland, Valdosta State College; John L. Kmetz, University of Delaware; K. B. Latham, Coastline College; Mary Lou Lockerby, College of Du Page; Ronald W. Maestas, New Mexico Highlands University; Harry J. Martin, Cleveland State University; Douglas M. McCabe, Georgetown University; Fekri Meziou, Augsburg College; Joseph F. Michlitsch, Southern Illinois University–Edwardsville; Alan N. Miller, University of Nevada–Las Vegas; Donald G. Muston, Elizabethtown College; Reed Nelson, Los Angeles Technical University; C. DeWitt Peterson, Burlington County College; William R. Soukup, Purdue University; James C. Spee, The Claremont Graduate School; Charlotte D. Sutton, Auburn University; Deborah L. Well, Creighton University; Gary L. Whaley, Norfolk State University; Linda C. Wicander, Central Michigan University; and Paul L. Wilkens, Florida State University.

Many people at Prentice Hall have contributed to the development of this revision: Dennis Hogan, former Publisher, Business and Vocational Books; Alison

Reeves, Executive Editor and Assistant Vice President; Jeanne Hoeting, Senior Managing Editor; Fran Russello, Managing Editor; Suzanne Behnke, Cover and Interior Designer; Lorinda Morris-Nantz, Director of Photo Archives; Christine A. Pullo, Photo Researcher; Liz Robertson, Scheduler; Trudy Pisciotti, Prepress Buyer; Robert Anderson, Manufacturing Buyer; David Scholder, Supplements Editor; Ray Mullaney, Vice President and Editor in Chief of College Book Editorial Development; and Asha Rohra, Editorial Assistant.

The production of the Fifth Edition was supervised by Eleanor Perz, whose professionalism and dedication to this project have been in evidence since the First Edition. The work of the following people in contributing to the content of this book have been invaluable: Professors Robert Behling (Bryant College), John Burgess (Concordia College), and Rick Hesse (Mercer University).

Without the untiring efforts of Development Editor Linda Muterspaugh, this edition simply would not exist. Andrew C. Wicks and Amy Gehman cheerfully prepared a number of cases and boxed inserts under the pressures of impossible deadlines. Karen Dickinson gave her usual superb support to everyone involved. The Sponsors of the Darden School and the Olsson Center for Applied Ethics provided resources and a wonderful environment in which to work. Maureen Wellen was again both critic and confidant.

MANAGEMENT

CHAPTER ONE

MANAGING AND MANAGERS

Detail from Jackson Pollock, *Convergence*

Upon completing this chapter, you should be able to:

1. Define the terms *organization* and *management* and explain why each is important.

2. Compare Drucker's concepts of "effectiveness" and "efficiency" and explain why each is important in measuring managerial performance.

3. Describe the basic activities in the management process and show how they are interrelated.

4. List and describe the duties of different types of managers.

5. Explain why managers at different levels need different mixes of technical, human, and conceptual skills.

6. Give examples of the different roles managers play in an organization.

7. Explain how vision, ethics, respect for cultural diversity, and training can help individuals meet the challenge of management.

Jackson Pollock, *Convergence,* 1952. 93½ × 155 inches. Oil on canvas. Albright-Knox Art Gallery, Buffalo, New York. Gift of Seymour H. Knox, 1956.

ILLUSTRATIVE CASE STUDY

INTRODUCTION

A Typical Day in the Life of Alison Reeves

Alison Reeves is a middle-level manager at Paramount Communications, a large conglomerate headquartered in New York. As she boards the train to go home to New Jersey, she reflects on a hectic day—the kind that is becoming routine for her.

She had arrived in the office at 7:45 to find a market research report on her desk. Bob Chang, the head of market research, had spent most of the week compiling the report, which had to be reviewed by Alison before it could be presented to her vice president. She spent 20 minutes talking with Bob over a cup of coffee and planning the logistics for having Word Processing and Graphics prepare a final copy of the report.

By the time Alison got back to her office, she had received three phone messages. She returned two calls, but only reached one person and scheduled a future meeting. She was now late for an 8:30 staff meeting, which lasted until 10:30. She returned to her office to find five *new* phone messages, including one from the person she had tried to reach *before* the staff meeting.

Next year's budget projections were due tomorrow, as were suggested revisions to the division objectives statement. Meanwhile, Alison had to meet with her boss at 2:00 today to explain why her department was over-budget in the current year. She considered working through lunch to prepare for the meeting, but decided it was unwise to cancel lunch with the new manager of a department that often competed with hers for the time and attention of her boss. Alison returned from lunch at 1:30 determined to plan her budget for the next year and to offer a good explanation of why she was currently over-budget.

Her 2:00 meeting went well. Alison's boss was pleased she was ahead of the game on next year's budget and gained a better appreciation of her plans for her department. They spent 15 minutes on their planned agenda and 45 minutes discussing the division, Alison's boss telling her he was considering reorganizing the division to eliminate some duplication of effort. At the end of the meeting, Alison mentioned the report she and Bob had prepared and commented on what a good job Bob had done.

At 3:00, Alison went for coffee and ran into one of the division's top salespeople, who was giving a

tour to a key customer. Alison mentioned the just-completed market report since it concerned a product the customer had bought. The three talked for 20 minutes and Alison gained some important illustrations for the marketing report.

At 3:30, Alison attended a meeting of the interdivisional task force established to coordinate the company's United Way campaign. By the time she returned to her office at 5:30, her desk was papered in pink telephone messages. She counted eight and began returning calls to time zones where callers might still be at work.

By 7:00, Alison left the office feeling tired but good. She had made some important progress on a number of issues. Her boss had taken her into his confidence for the first time and she felt a comfortable sense of security. Bob's report looked like a real winner, and the customer information she had gained this afternoon was going to help.

Now she could begin to think about a hiring decision she had to make. The interviewing process had yielded three well-qualified finalists—a white man, an Asian woman, and a black woman. Which, she wondered, would be best for the department and for meeting Paramount's commitment to developing a diverse work force? She headed for the train's smoking car, only to remember she had stopped smoking in response to a request that managers set a good example for employees. Oh well, she thought, maybe her health club would still be open by the time she reached home.

A lison is a typical manager in a large organization. Her days are hectic, and she spends more time in meetings and dealing with interruptions than she does working quietly at her desk. What is management and what do thousands of managers like Alison do every day for such long hours? In this chapter, we will begin to answer this question.

■ *ORGANIZATIONS AND THE NEED FOR MANAGEMENT*

organization Two or more people who work together in a structured way to achieve a specific goal or set of goals.

COORDINATED RESOURCE
The Application Exercise for Chapter 1 found in the Lecture Extras supplement has students interview managers.

COORDINATED RESOURCE
See Samaras Case 1.1, "Management?"

management The process of planning, organizing, leading, and controlling the work of organization members and of using all available organizational resources to reach stated organizational goals.

For most of our lives, we are members of one **organization** or another—a college, a sports team, a musical or theatrical group, a religious or civic organization, a branch of the armed forces, or a business. Some organizations, like the army and large corporations, are organized very formally. Others, like a neighborhood basketball team, are more casually structured. But all organizations, formal or informal, have several elements in common.

Perhaps the most obvious of these basic elements is a *goal* or purpose. The goal will vary—to win a league championship, to entertain an audience, to sell a product—but without a goal no organization would have a reason to exist. All organizations also have some program or method for achieving their goals—to practice playing skills, to rehearse a certain number of times before each performance, to manufacture and advertise a product. Without some *plan* for what it must do, no organization is likely to be very effective. Organizations must also acquire and allocate the resources necessary to achieve their goals—a playing field or rehearsal hall must be available; money must be budgeted for wages. All organizations are made up of people and depend on other organizations for the resources they need—a team cannot play without the required equipment; manufacturers must maintain contracts with suppliers. Finally, all organizations have leaders or *managers* responsible for helping them achieve their goals. These leaders—a coach, a conductor, a sales executive—may be more obvious in some organizations than in others, but without effective **management,** the organization is likely to founder.

This book is about how organizations are managed—more specifically, about how managers can best help their organizations set and achieve their goals. Our emphasis will be on the so-called *formal* organizations—such as businesses, religious organizations, government agencies, and hospitals—that provide goods or services to their customers or clients and offer career opportunities to their members. But regardless of how formal or informal their role, all managers in all organizations have the same basic responsibility: to help other members of the organization and the organization itself set and reach a series of goals and objectives.

Why Organizations and Managers Are Needed

Almost every day, it seems, headlines like these greet us from the front pages of our newspapers:

❑ "Auto Imports Gain Market Share"
❑ "Federal Budget Deficit Figures Revised Upward"
❑ "Dow Jones Falls for Third Straight Day"
❑ "EPA Levies Fines for Illegal Toxic Dumping"

The stories behind these headlines make us wonder whether our social organizations have failed us. Some Americans believe that government, business, and labor organizations have become too large to keep in touch with people's needs and that their leaders lack high ethical standards. Criticizing organizations is, of course, a time-honored American custom, but organizations are a necessary element of civilized life for several reasons: They serve society; they enable us to accomplish things that we could not do as well—or at all—as individuals; they provide a continuity of knowledge; and they are an important source of careers.

ORGANIZATIONS SERVE SOCIETY.   Organizations are important because they are social institutions that reflect certain culturally accepted values and needs. They allow us to live together in a civilized way and to accomplish goals as a society. From local police departments to large multinational corporations, organizations serve society by making the world a better, safer, cheaper, and more pleasant place to live. Without them, we would be little more than animals with unusually large brains.

ORGANIZATIONS ACCOMPLISH OBJECTIVES.   Consider for a moment how many organizations were involved in bringing us the paper on which this book is printed: loggers, a sawmill, manufacturers of various types of equipment and supplies, truckers, a paper mill, distributors, telephone and electric power companies, fuel producers, the postal service, banks and other financial institutions, and more. Even if an individual acting alone could do all the things that those organizations did to produce a ream of paper (which is doubtful), he or she could never do them as well or as quickly.

It is clear, then, that organizations and the people who manage them perform this essential function: By coordinating the efforts of different individuals, organizations enable us to reach goals that would otherwise be much harder or even impossible to achieve.

ORGANIZATIONS PRESERVE KNOWLEDGE.   We know from history that when recorded knowledge is destroyed on a large scale (as when the museum and library at Alexandria were burned in the third century A.D.), much of it is never regained. We depend on records of past accomplishments to provide a foundation of knowledge on which we can build to acquire more learning and achieve greater results. Without such records, science and other fields of knowledge would stand still.

Organizations Serve Society. Recyclable plastics (left) make up about 20 percent of the nation's bulging landfills. In response, many local governments are collecting and selling recyclables to middlemen, who then sell it to businesses such as Hammer's Plastic Recycling Corp. Using the patented process of founder Floyd Hammer (right), recycled plastic is converted into weather-resistant park benches, parking lot curbs, and landscaping timbers, of which the Chicago Park District ordered 40,000 in 1990. Hammer's company, based in Iowa Falls, had 1989 sales of $4.2 million from two plants in Iowa and Florida, and plans to build 16 more plants around the nation.

Organizations such as universities, museums, and corporations are essential because they store and protect most of the important knowledge our civilization has gathered and recorded. In this way, organizations make that knowledge a continuous bridge between past, present, and future generations. In addition, organizations themselves add to our knowledge by developing new and more efficient ways of doing things.

ORGANIZATIONS PROVIDE CAREERS. Finally, organizations are important because they provide their employees with a source of livelihood and, depending on the style and effectiveness of their managers, perhaps even personal satisfaction and self-fulfillment. Most of us tend to associate career opportunities with business corporations, but in fact many other organizations, such as churches, government agencies, schools, and hospitals, also offer rewarding careers.

Managerial and Organizational Performance

How successfully an organization achieves its objectives, satisfies social responsibilities, or both, depends, to a large extent, on its managers. If managers do their jobs well, the organization will probably achieve its goals. And if a nation's major organizations achieve their goals, the nation as a whole will prosper. The economic success of Japan is clear evidence of this fact. (See the Management Application box.)

How well managers do their jobs—**managerial performance**—is the subject of much debate, analysis, and confusion in the United States and many other countries,[1] as is organizational performance—the measure of how well organizations do *their* jobs.[2] Thus, we will be discussing many different criteria and concepts for evaluating managers and organizations.[3] Underlying many of these discussions are two concepts suggested by Peter Drucker, one of the most respected writers on management: efficiency and effectiveness.[4] As he puts it, *efficiency* means "doing things right," and *effectiveness* means "doing the right thing."

Efficiency—the ability to do things right—is an "input-output" concept. An efficient manager is one who achieves outputs, or results, that measure up to the inputs (labor, materials, and time) used to achieve them. Managers who are able to minimize the cost of the resources needed to achieve goals are acting efficiently.

Effectiveness, in contrast, involves choosing the *right* goals. A manager who selects an inappropriate goal—say, producing mainly large cars when demand for small cars is soaring—is an ineffective manager, even if the large cars are produced with maximum efficiency. No amount of efficiency can make up for a lack of effectiveness. In fact, Drucker says, effectiveness is the key to an organization's success. Thus, before we can focus on efficiency, we need to be sure we have found the right things to do.[5] We will have more to say about goal setting in Chapter 7, "Planning and Strategic Management."

■ *THE MANAGEMENT PROCESS*

Management has been called "the art of getting things done through people." This definition, by Mary Parker Follett, calls attention to the fact that managers achieve organizational goals by arranging for *others* to perform whatever tasks may be necessary—not by performing the tasks *themselves.*

Management is that, and more—so much more, in fact, that no one simple definition has been universally accepted. Moreover, definitions change as the environments of organizations change. Our discussion will start with a fairly complex definition so that we may call your attention to important aspects of managing:

> Management is the process of planning, organizing, leading, and controlling the efforts of organization members and of using all other organizational resources to achieve stated organizational goals.[6]

MANAGEMENT APPLICATION

From the Land of Opportunity to the Land of the Rising Sun

Japanese-manufactured goods were once proverbial for their shoddiness. (It's true—ask your teachers or parents.) When the Japanese realized they had a problem, they did not try to improve their "image." Instead, they strove to improve their manufacturing techniques. Today we know only too well that they succeeded.

What most of us don't know is that many of the products the Japanese now sell successfully were invented in America and manufactured according to standards set by an American. Here, in his own country, he is largely unknown—almost a prophet without honor. Yet in Japan, he is a national celebrity.

The man's name is W. Edwards Deming, and in books and articles he has preached the "quality crusade" for decades. Japan discovered him in 1950, when he went there to give a lecture on his ideas about quality control. A year later, Japan set up a nationwide quality-improvement contest whose winner was to receive what is now called the Deming Prize. It is one of the country's greatest honors.

Deming has set forth 14 points for top managers who want to promote quality:

1. Plan for the long-term future, not for the next month or year.
2. Never be complacent concerning the quality of your product.
3. Establish statistical control over your production processes and require your suppliers to do so as well.
4. Deal with the fewest number of suppliers—the best ones, of course.
5. Find out whether your problems are confined to particular parts of the production process or stem from the overall process itself.
6. Train workers for the job that you are asking them to perform.
7. Raise the quality of your line supervisors (see Chapter 12).
8. "Drive out fear."
9. Encourage departments to work closely together rather than to concentrate on departmental or divisional distinction.
10. Do not be sucked into adopting strictly numeri-

A National Commitment to Quality. Created by the U.S. Congress in 1987, the Malcolm Baldrige National Quality Award is the equivalent of Japan's Deming Prize. Past winners include Xerox, IBM, Federal Express, GM's Cadillac Division, and Wallace Co., a Houston pipemaker.

cal goals, including the widely popular formula of "zero defect" (see Chapter 21).
11. Require your workers to do quality work, not just to be at their stations from 9 to 5.
12. Train your employees to understand statistical methods.
13. Train your employees in new skills as the need arises.
14. Make top managers responsible for implementing these principles (see Chapter 8).

Some of these points make common sense; others will become clearer as you acquaint yourself with the material discussed throughout this book.

Source: W. Edwards Deming, "Improvement of Quality and Productivity Through Action by Management," *National Productivity Review* 1 (Winter 1981–1982):12–22.

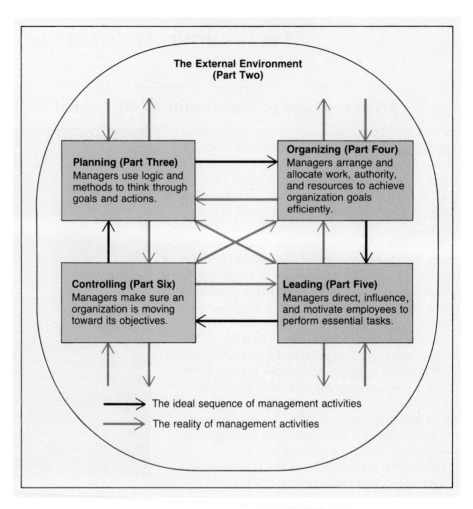

FIGURE 1-1 The Interactive Nature of the Management Process

A *process* is a systematic way of doing things. We define management as a process because all managers, regardless of their particular aptitudes or skills, engage in certain interrelated activities in order to achieve their desired goals. (See Fig. 1-1.)

It is easier to understand a process as complex as management when it is described as a series of separate parts. Descriptions of this kind, known as *models,* have been used by students and practitioners of management for decades. A model is a simplification of the real world used to convey complex relationships in easy-to-understand terms. In fact, we used a model—without identifying it as such—when we said that the major management activities were planning, organizing, leading, and controlling. This model of management was developed at the end of the nineteenth century and is still in use today.[7] In the rest of this section, we will briefly describe these four main management activities. Then we will describe the interactive nature of the management process.

Planning

Planning implies that managers think through their goals and actions in advance, that their actions are based on some method, plan, or logic rather than on a hunch. Plans give the organization its objectives and set up the best procedure for reaching them. In addition, plans are the guides by which (1) the organization obtains and commits the resources required to reach its objectives; (2) members of the organization carry on activities consistent with the chosen objectives and procedures; and (3) progress toward the objectives is monitored and measured so that corrective action can be taken if progress is unsatisfactory.

The first step in planning is the selection of goals for the organization. Then objectives are established for the organization's *subunits*—its divisions, departments, and so on. Once objectives are determined, programs are established for achieving them in a systematic manner. Of course, in selecting objectives and developing programs, the manager considers their feasibility and whether they will be acceptable to the organization's managers and employees.

Plans made by top management for the organization as a whole may cover periods as long as five or ten years. In a large organization, such as a multinational energy corporation, those plans may involve commitments of billions of dollars. Planning at the lower levels, by middle or first-line managers, covers much shorter periods. Such plans may be for the next day's work, for example, or for a two-hour meeting to take place in a week. Planning will be discussed in more detail in Part Three. The Illustrative Case for Chapter 7, for example, will show you how CEO Fred Smith planned for the future of Federal Express as an "information deliverer" to the world.

Organizing

THOUGHT PROVOKER
The flattened organizations of the 1990s are going to require teamwork and a free flow of information. (*Fortune,* 12/17/90, p. 115ff.)

Organizing is the process of arranging and allocating work, authority, and resources among an organization's members so they can achieve an organization's goals efficiently. Different goals, of course, require different structures. For example, an organization that aims to develop computer software needs a different structure than a manufacturer of blue jeans. Producing a standardized product like blue jeans requires efficient assembly-line techniques, whereas producing software requires organizing teams of professionals—systems analysts, programmers, and so on. Although these professionals must interact effectively, they cannot be organized like assembly-line workers. Thus, managers must match an organization's structure to its goals and resources, a process called *organizational design.* Organizing will be discussed in more detail in Part Four. In Chapter 11, for example, you will read an Illustrative Case showing how Hewlett-Packard reorganized to reflect its goal of providing better service to different types of customers.

Leading

CLASS COMMENT
A study by Russell Reynolds Associates, a headhunting firm, finds that leadership traits are more common in executive women than in executive men. (*Fortune,* 12/17/90, p. 115ff.)

Leading involves directing, influencing, and motivating employees to perform essential tasks. While planning and organizing deal with the more abstract aspects of the management process, the activity of leading is very concrete: It involves working with people. By establishing the proper atmosphere, managers help their employees do their best. Leading will be discussed in more detail in Part Five. In Chapter 17, for example, you will get a chance to decide if Jack Welch is an effective leader for General Electric.

Controlling

COORDINATED RESOURCE
Acumen: Those with high scores on 8 and 11 feel constrained when working in a highly controlled environment.

Finally, the manager must be sure the actions of the organization's members do in fact move the organization toward its stated goals. This is the controlling function of management, and it involves three main elements: (1) Establishing standards of performance; (2) Measuring current performance; (3) Comparing this performance to the established standards; and (4) If deviations are detected, taking corrective action. Through the controlling function, the manager keeps the organization on its chosen track. Controlling will be discussed in more detail in Part Six.

COORDINATED RESOURCE
Use Transparency 2, The
Interactive Nature of the
Management Process.

The Management Process in Practice

We have just presented a model of the management process. But the relationships we described are more interrelated than our model implies. For example, we said that standards and benchmarks are used to control employees' actions, but establishing such standards is obviously an inherent part of the planning process and an integral factor in motivating and leading subordinates. And taking corrective action, which we introduced as a control activity, often involves adjusting plans.

COORDINATED RESOURCE
See Study Guide Problem
Exercise 1, "Identifying
Management Functions
and Skills."

In practice, the management process does not involve four separate or loosely related sets of activities but a group of *interactive* functions. This interaction is summarized in Figure 1-1, in which the black lines indicate the ideal sequence. In reality, though, various combinations of these activities are usually going on simultaneously, a fact represented by the red lines. Furthermore, managers are limited by internal considerations—their place in the organization hierarchy, limited resources, and the need to coordinate their actions with others. Managers must also adapt to the environment in which their organization operates. For this reason, Part Two will focus on the external environment of organizations.

■ TYPES OF MANAGERS

COORDINATED RESOURCE
Use Transparency 1, Orga-
nizational Levels.

We have been using the term *manager* to mean anyone who is responsible for carrying out the four main activities of management. However, managers can be classified in two ways: by their *level* in the organization (so-called first-line, middle, and top managers) and by the *range* of organizational activities for which they are responsible (so-called functional and general managers).

Management Levels

first-line (or **first-level**) **managers** Managers who are responsible for the work of operating employees only and do not supervise other managers; they are the "first" or lowest level of managers in the organizational hierarchy.

middle managers Managers in the midrange of the organizational hierarchy; they are responsible for other managers and sometimes for some operating employees.

top management Managers responsible for the overall management of the organization. They establish operating policies and guide the organization's interactions with its environment.

FIRST-LINE MANAGERS. The lowest level in an organization at which individuals are responsible for the work of others is called **first-line** or **first-level management.** First-line managers direct operating employees only; they do not supervise other managers. Examples of first-line managers are the foreman or production supervisor in a manufacturing plant, the technical supervisor in a research department, and the clerical supervisor in a large office. First-level managers are often called "supervisors."

MIDDLE MANAGERS. The term **middle management** can include more than one level in an organization. Middle managers direct the activities of lower-level managers and sometimes those of operating employees as well. Middle managers' principal responsibilities are to direct the activities that implement their organizations' policies and to balance the demands of their superiors with the capacities of their subordinates.

TOP MANAGERS. Composed of a comparatively small group of executives, **top management** is responsible for the overall management of the organization. It establishes operating policies and guides the organization's interactions with its environment. Typical titles of top managers are "chief executive officer," "president," and "senior vice president." Actual titles vary from one organization to another and are not always a reliable guide to membership in the highest management classification.

Functional and General Managers

The other major classification of managers depends on the scope of the activities they manage.

A General Manager. "Think big because Coke is big!" William Hoffman tells French retailers displaying Coke products. As head of Coca-Cola's French bottling company, Hoffman oversees bottling operations, manages financing, underwrites promotions (such as a recent Georgia Week in Biarritz, complete with American football and a screening of *Gone with the Wind*), and oversees a staff of merchandisers who maintain retail displays.

functional manager A manager responsible for just one organizational activity, such as finance or human resource management.

FUNCTIONAL MANAGERS. The **functional manager** is responsible for only *one* organizational activity, such as production, marketing, *or* finance. The people and activities headed by a functional manager are engaged in a common set of activities.

general manager The individual responsible for all activities, such as production, sales, marketing, and finance, for an organization like a company or a subsidiary.

GENERAL MANAGERS. The **general manager,** on the other hand, oversees a complex unit, such as a company, a subsidiary, or an independent operating division. He or she is responsible for *all* the activities of that unit, such as its production, marketing, *and* finance.[8] A small company may have only one general manager—its president or executive vice president—but a large organization may have several, each heading a relatively independent division. In a large food company, for example, there may be a grocery-products division, a refrigerated-products division, and a frozen-food-products division, with a different general manager responsible for each. Like the chief executive of a small company, each of these divisional heads is responsible for all the activities of the unit.

ILLUSTRATIVE CASE STUDY

CONTINUED

A Typical Day in the Life of Alison Reeves

As a middle manager, Alison is responsible for directing the activities of first-line managers like Bob Chang, the head of market research, and responding to the direction of her boss, the vice president.

She is also responsible for all the management processes. She has to *plan* her budget for the next year, and she has to understand why she is currently spending more than she had been budgeted—she has to *control.* Alison talked with her boss about *reorganizing* the department, and giving up smoking showed her desire to *lead* by setting a good example.

Each of these activities is more subtle than at first appears. *Planning* isn't just figuring out the budget for the coming year: Alison is also planning when she decides what phone calls to return and whether or not to keep her lunch appointment. She has to decide what objectives are important, and she must do this almost routinely. Similarly, giving feedback to subordinates is a way of *controlling*—for example,

telling Bob that he is doing a good job or simply spending a few minutes casually talking to him. Talking with her boss is an obvious case of *organizing,* but equally important was Alison's lunch, where she *coordinated* the efforts of two departments, and her task force meeting, at which the company's United Way campaign was organized. Finally, leadership is more than symbolic behavior. When Alison spent time with the customer whom she met by accident in the hallway, she got important information that she could transmit both to Bob for his report and to her boss. Matching tasks and people, *motivating* and *communicating,* are also important parts of the leadership function.

As Alison considered her hiring decision, we can see how organizations serve society by honoring a commitment to equal employment opportunity for our diverse population. All of these activities are entailed in Alison's management responsibilities.

■ MANAGEMENT LEVEL AND SKILLS

Managers at every level plan, organize, lead, and control. But they differ in the amount of time they devote to each of these activities. Some of these differences depend on the kind of organization for which the manager works. Managers of small private clinics, for example, spend their time quite differently than the heads of large research hospitals. Managers of clinics spend comparatively more time practicing medicine, and less time actually managing, than do directors of large hospitals.

Other differences in the ways managers spend their time depend upon their levels in the organizational hierarchy. In the following sections, we will consider how management skills and activities differ at these various levels and look at the various roles managers perform.

Robert L. Katz, a teacher and business executive, has identified three basic kinds of skills: technical, human, and conceptual. Every manager needs all three. *Technical skill* is the ability to use the procedures, techniques, and knowledge of a specialized field. Surgeons, engineers, musicians, and accountants all have technical skills in their respective fields. *Human skill* is the ability to work with, understand, and motivate other people, as individuals or in groups. *Conceptual skill* is the ability to coordinate and integrate all of an organization's interests and activities. It involves seeing the organization as a whole, understanding how its parts depend on one another, and anticipating how a change in any of its parts will affect the whole.

Katz suggests that although all three of these skills are essential to a manager, their relative importance depends mainly on the manager's rank in the organization. (See Fig. 1-2.) Technical skill is most important in the lower levels. Human skill, by contrast, is important for managers at every level: Because managers must work primarily through others, their ability to tap the technical skills of their subordinates is more important than their own technical proficiency. Finally, the importance of conceptual skill increases as one rises through the ranks of a management system based on hierarchical principles of authority and responsibility.

■ MANAGERIAL ROLES

Our working definition describes *managers* as organizational planners, organizers, leaders, and controllers. Actually, every manager—from the program director of a college club to the chief executive of a multinational corporation—takes on a much wider range of roles to move the organization toward its stated objectives. In a broad sense, a "role" consists of the behavior patterns expected of an individual within a

FIGURE 1-2 Relative Skills Needed for Effective Performance at Different Levels of Management

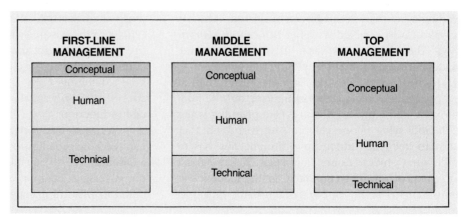

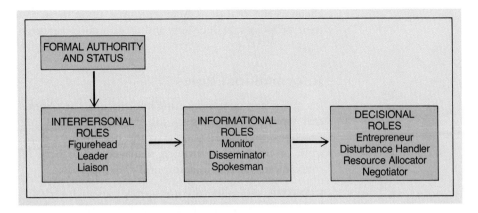

FIGURE 1-3 The Manager's Roles

Source: Reprinted by permission of the *Harvard Business Review.* An exhibit from "The Manager's Job: Folklore and Fact" by Henry Mintzberg (July–August 1975). Copyright © 1975 by the President and Fellows of Harvard College; all rights reserved.

COORDINATED RESOURCE

See Samaras Exercise 1.2, "Management Theory and Executive Practice."

COORDINATED RESOURCE

The Additional Lecture for Chapter 1 found in the Lecture Extras supplement is called "Mintzberg's Folklore and Fact."

COORDINATED RESOURCE

Acumen: Relate Mintzberg's managerial roles to the Humanistic-Helpful and Affiliation scales.

social unit. For the purposes of managerial thinking, a *role* is the behavioral pattern expected of someone within a functional unit. Roles are thus inherent in functions.

Henry Mintzberg made an extensive survey of existing research on the subject of managerial roles and integrated his findings with the results of a study of five chief executive officers.[9] In an effort to catalog and analyze the various roles of managers, the combined review covered all kinds and levels of managers—from street gang leaders to CEOs.

Mintzberg concluded that the jobs of many managers are quite similar. All managers, he argued, have formal authority over their own organizational units and derive status from that authority. This status causes all managers to be involved in interpersonal relationships with subordinates, peers, and superiors, who in turn provide managers with the information they need to make decisions. All managers thus play a series of interpersonal, informational, and decision-making roles that Mintzberg defined as "organized sets of behaviors." (See Fig. 1-3.) Here we will summarize Mintzberg's findings and theories about managerial roles.

Interpersonal Roles

Three sometimes routine interpersonal roles—figurehead, leader, and liaison—help managers keep their organizations running smoothly.

FIGUREHEAD. As a figurehead, the manager performs ceremonial duties as head of the unit: greeting visitors, attending subordinates' weddings, taking customers to lunch. More importantly, managers are symbols and personify, for both organizational members and outside observers, an organization's successes and failures. They are often held responsible for outcomes over which they have little or no control— thus the frequent dismissals of professional sports managers.[10]

COORDINATED RESOURCE

See *Management Live!* Chapter 2 Video 1, "Pat Carrigan (The Leadership Alliance)."

LEADER. Since managers work with and through other people, they are responsible and accountable for their subordinates' actions as well as for their own. In fact, their subordinates' success or failure is a direct measure of their own success or failure. Because managers have subordinates and other resources, they are able to accomplish more than nonmanagers—which means, of course, that they are *expected* to accomplish more than other organization members.

LIAISON. Like politicians, managers must learn to work with everyone inside or outside the organization who can help them achieve their organizational goals. All effective managers "play politics" in the sense that they develop networks of mutual obligations with other managers in the organization. They may also build or join alliances and coalitions. Managers draw upon these relationships to win support for their proposals or decisions and to gain cooperation in carrying out various activities.[11]

Informational Roles

Receiving and communicating information, Mintzberg suggests, are the most important aspects of a manager's job.[12] Managers need information to make intelligent decisions, and other people in the organization depend on information received from or transmitted through managers. Mintzberg identified three informational roles: monitor, disseminator, and spokesperson.

MONITOR. Managers are constantly looking for useful information both within and outside the organization. They question subordinates and collect unsolicited information, usually through their networks of contacts. The role of monitor often makes managers the best-informed members of their groups.

DISSEMINATOR. In this role, managers distribute important information to subordinates. Some of this is factual information conveyed in staff meetings and memos, but some is based on the manager's analysis and interpretation of events. In either case, it is the manager's responsibility to be sure subordinates have the information they need to carry out their duties.

SPOKESPERSON. Managers also transmit information to people outside their own work units. Keeping superiors well-informed is one important aspect of this role. Like diplomats, managers may also speak for their work unit within the organization or represent the entire organization in dealing with customers, contractors, or government officials.

Decision-Making Roles

HERE'S AN EXAMPLE
General Norman Schwarzkopf, commander of the Allied forces in the Persian Gulf, could find himself in hot demand by corporate America if and when he decided to leave the military. A "very unscientific" survey by the *Wall Street Journal* yielded a number of instantaneous offers for General Schwarzkopf! (*Wall Street Journal,* 3/1/91, p. B1ff.)

COORDINATED RESOURCE

Acumen: Low scores on the Dependence scale indicate an ability to take risks and try new approaches.

According to Mintzberg, information is the "basic input to decision making for managers," who play four decision-making roles.

ENTREPRENEUR. Managers try to improve their units. When, for example, managers get hold of a good idea, they might launch a development project to make it a reality. In this role, they initiate change of their own free will.

DISTURBANCE HANDLER. No organization runs smoothly all the time. There is almost no limit to the number and types of problems that may occur, from financial difficulties to strikes to a drop in earnings. Managers are expected to come up with solutions to difficult problems and to follow through—even on unpopular decisions.

To make these difficult decisions, managers must be able to think analytically and conceptually. *Analytical* thinking involves breaking a problem down into its components, analyzing those components, and then coming up with a feasible solution. Even more important is the ability to think conceptually, which means viewing the entire task in the abstract and relating it to other tasks. The ability to think about a decision's larger implications is essential if the manager is to meet the goals of both the work unit and the larger organization.

RESOURCE ALLOCATOR. Every manager faces a number of organizational goals, problems, and needs—all of which compete for his or her time and resources (both human and material). Because such resources are always limited, each manager must strike a balance between various goals and needs. Many managers, for example, arrange each day's tasks in order of priority, so the most important things are done right away and less important tasks are put off until later.

NEGOTIATOR. Managers spend a lot of their time negotiating because only they have the knowledge and authority this role demands. Some of these negotiations

Resource Allocators. Retail space at the three-story Woodfield Shopping Center in suburban Chicago is at a premium, and General Manager Jim Linowski and Marketing Director Betty Bryant are known for their toughness in enforcing mall standards designed to attract upscale shoppers in a highly competitive retail market. Stores must remodel at regular intervals, follow mall dictums about the merchandise they carry, and if they do not generate certain levels of sales revenue, move to smaller, less highly trafficked locations or leave when their leases expire, a fate that befell about 40 percent of the mall's tenants in recent years.

involve outside organizations. A company president, for example, may deal with a consulting firm; a production head may negotiate a contract with a supplier.

Managers also handle negotiations within the organization. People working for the same organization often disagree about goals or the most effective way of attaining them. Unresolved disputes can lower morale and productivity and may even drive away competent employees. For the reason, managers must take on the role of mediator and negotiate compromises as disputes occur. Settling quarrels requires skill and tact; clumsy negotiators may be dismayed to find they have only made matters worse.

Mintzberg's work calls attention to the uncertain, turbulent environment managers face in the real world. Reality is only partly predictable and controllable. According to Mintzberg, effective managers have neither the time nor the desire to be deep thinkers. They are, above all, *doers,* coping with life's dynamic parade of challenges and surprises. The ability to recognize the appropriate role to play in each situation and the flexibility to change roles readily are characteristics of the effective manager.

■ *THE CHALLENGE OF MANAGEMENT*

Being an effective manager is demanding under the best circumstances, but today's managers face special challenges. One of the most pressing is competition from foreign companies—each of them dedicated to bringing quality products to increasingly demanding customers around the world. As a result, managers need to think beyond local or even national concerns and try to picture their place in the interna-

CLASS COMMENT

The latest management theories that favor flatter organizations with authority less concentrated at the top simply represent the most effective way to run a business in an era of increasing global competition. (*Fortune,* 12/17/90, p. 115ff.)

tional economy—a fact highlighted by Chapter 5, "The International Dimension," and by the International Management boxes throughout the book.

The challenge of international competition has both managers and workers alike scrambling to find new ways of increasing *productivity*—the amount of quality work each employee creates. As a result, many managers are rethinking the manager-subordinate relationship and looking for new ways to tap the talents and resources of every employee. Throughout this book, you will read of companies who are putting aside their traditional structured hierarchies and experimenting with participative management and work teams—most with outstanding results. You'll also read of ethical issues, for we are becoming more and more aware that every management decision affects others—both in the present and in the future. To meet these challenges, effective managers need vision, they need ethics, they need respect for cultural diversity, and they need solid training.

The Need for Vision

HERE'S AN EXAMPLE

James Adamson, the executive who runs the ATM (automated teller machines) unit for NCR, oversaw the manufacturing plant that virtually ran IBM out of the business. His success story is one of principles of management and leadership that can work for anyone. He relied on personal energy and enthusiasm to get his people interested in doing better. (*Fortune,* 11/19/90, p. 165ff.)

In this and other courses, you will learn of *management science* tools—mathematical models that help managers analyze situations and make decisions. These tools are invaluable for helping managers make sense of data, but they have their drawbacks. For one thing, they tempt us to take the short view of problems that require long-term solutions. Thus, effective managers need to put aside their spreadsheets and listen to those around them. They need to recognize and even welcome change, trying to anticipate problems before they occur and, even more importantly, trying to see how change creates opportunities for growth and expansion. To do this, managers need to be flexible and they need to develop a vision—a long view of their company, its goals, and what it must do to achieve them. As you learn more about management, you will encounter hundreds of insightful managers—from Henry Ford of Ford Motor Company to Fred Smith of Federal Express—who looked beyond what *is* and saw what *could be,* and in so doing, reshaped our world.

The Need for Ethics

Our increasing alarm over industrial pollution is just one reminder that managers inevitably allocate advantages and disadvantages no matter what they do—or fail to do. Thus managers must be concerned with values and ethics.

ethics The study of rights and of who is—or should be—benefited or harmed by an action.

The study of who is—and should be—benefited or harmed by an action is called **ethics,** which also studies who does—and who should—have rights of any kind. Once you start to look for them (and often if you don't), ethical questions materialize at all levels of business.

On the surface, it is relatively simple to judge a business practice as ethically correct or incorrect. The hard part—especially when conventional rules don't seem to apply—is understanding the concepts and techniques of ethical decision making so that you can reach better moral judgments. Because business ethics is a major concern today, we will devote Chapter 4 to its study. In addition, every chapter includes an Ethics in Management box to help you become more aware of these issues, beginning with "Footing the Bill and Having a Heart" in this chapter.

The Need for Cultural Diversity

CLASS COMMENT

"Gone are the days of women succeeding by learning to play men's games. Instead the time has come for men on the move to learn to play women's games." (Tom Peters, *Fortune,* 12/17/90, p. 115ff.)

Our ethical concern for the fair and equitable treatment of employees reflects our culture's strong commitment to equal opportunity. It also reflects good management, for as the international economy increases competitive pressures, organizations must draw on their most talented employees—without regard for racial, cultural, or sexual differences. As Avon Chairman and CEO Jim Preston puts it, "Talent is color blind. Talent is gender blind. Talent has nothing to do with dialects, whether

ETHICS IN MANAGEMENT

Footing the Bill and Having a Heart

Ostensibly, the primary function of Reebok International is to outfit active people in athletic shoes for jogging, playing tennis, and attending casual get-togethers in fashionable sportswear. But Reebok has not lost sight of its other *stakeholders*—people who are directly or indirectly affected by its actions. Recently, Reebok assumed an ethical obligation to an unlikely stakeholder—an organization in the forefront of the human rights movement.

Reebok has underwritten—to the tune of $10 million—a five-continent tour sponsored by Amnesty International featuring such popular artists as Sting and Peter Gabriel. "Their objective dovetailed with our corporate philosophy about the right to live your life the way you want," explains company president Joseph LaBonte. Reebok encouraged retailers to participate, establishing a yearly $10,000 prize to reward the expression of the right to freedom, and merchandising such auxiliary items as T-shirts and jackets to promote the tour, all proceeds going to Amnesty International.

Pepsi-Cola Co. is also contributing to the cause. Both Pepsi and Reebok have invested substantial sums of money to support international human rights, to educate people about domestic violence, and to combat high dropout rates in urban schools.

Recently, the pharmaceutical company G. D. Searle gave away $10,000 worth of a costly hypertension drug to needy patients. The company plans to continue the program in subsequent years, when it will donate an unlimited supply of seven different medications manufactured for the treatment of heart diseases. A patient unable to reimburse a physician or

Reebok Supports Amnesty International. Peter Gabriel (left), Tracy Chapman, Youssou N'Dour, Sting, Joan Baez, and Bruce Springsteen perform at a 1988 Philadelphia concert underwritten by Reebok to raise money for Amnesty International.

clinic will be issued a certificate that Searle will then redeem. Searle believes one of the attributes of an excellent company is "a bias for action"—a preference for doing *something* in the interest of its customer community. Says Chairman Sheldon Gilgore, "We view it as the cost of doing business, making drugs available to the needy. We plan to make available every new drug that we introduce on the same basis."

Sources: "Reebok Foots the Bill for Human Rights," *Business Week,* April 25, 1988; "Free Heart Drugs for Needy," *USA Today,* April 6, 1988; Adam Shell, "Cause-Related Marketing: Big Risks, Big Potential," *Public Relations Journal,* July 1989, pp. 8, 13.

COORDINATED RESOURCE

See Samaras Reading "Should You Manage Like a Man?"

they're Hispanic or Irish or Polish or Chinese. And we need talent—all we can get. If America is to regain its competitive supremacy in the world, we won't do it just by restoking the blast furnaces in Pittsburgh, or cranking out more automobiles in Detroit. We'll do it by harnessing the human power of all the diverse groups that make up this country."[13]

Toyota showed that it recognized this fact when it made Guillermo L. Hysaw national sales manager for its Lexus Division. Hysaw, whose parents came from the Dominican Republic, grew up in California and has an MBA from Claremont Graduate School as well as 16½ years with General Motors in sales promotion, merchandising, and corporate resale. At Lexus, he used his knowledge of dealership operations, business management procedures, and marketing strategy to help Toyota break into the luxury market once dominated by European imports. Hysaw admits he came to Toyota with some misgivings, having heard the Japanese did not like blacks. After working closely with Toyota top management and even representing the company at international events, Hysaw now says "the only thing [the Japanese] expect of you is that you produce."[14] Throughout the book, Management and Diversity boxes will show you additional examples of organizations acting to tap the resources of previously neglected segments of our work force.

The Need for Training

HERE'S AN EXAMPLE
Some bad-boss characteristics: fuzzifies goals; can't delegate; wastes your day with meetings; has poor ethics; plays politics; never praises but always speaks up when you do something wrong; pushes people to be workaholics; pays little attention to detail. (*Springfield News Leader*, 1/24/91, p. 4D)

COORDINATED RESOURCE
See *Management Live!* Chapter 2 Video 2, "Hyman Rickover."

COORDINATED RESOURCE
See *Management Live!* Reading 1.1, "Day in the Life of Tomorrow's Manager."

To a great extent, effective managers are made, not born. That is, management skills can be and are learned by people of all backgrounds. However, J. Sterling Livingstone suggests that successful managers tend to share the following three qualities:

1. *The need to manage.* Only people who want to affect the performance of others and derive satisfaction from doing this are likely to become effective managers.
2. *The need for power.* Good managers have a healthy need to influence others. To do this, they rely on their superior knowledge and skill, rather than the authority of their positions.
3. *The capacity for empathy.* Effective managers are also able to understand and cope with the often unexpressed emotional reactions of others in the organization in order to win their cooperation.

As a potential manager you must ask yourself, Do I have these qualities?

Assuming the answer is yes, what can you do to develop your talent for management? One obvious answer is to take courses like this one. By itself, no course or textbook can teach you to be an effective manager. However, formal study can expose you to relevant information, theories, and research, presented in an orderly, systematic fashion. In addition, the case studies in this book will help you practice your decision-making skills.

Learning Teamwork. Students in the University of Chicago Graduate School of Business take part in required, noncredit Outward Bound exercises introduced, along with similar workshops in nonverbal communication and presentation skills, to improve their human skills and balance the school's quantitative emphasis.

Of course, this "book learning" needs to be supplemented by practical experience. Seek out skills-oriented courses that will help you develop the human skills Katz described. Look for opportunities to participate in experiential exercises, unstructured groups, and role playing. More importantly, try putting your managerial skills to work by assuming leadership roles in various organizations or by taking even a part-time job.

Often, the best way to learn to be an effective manager is to work with and observe managers. This means first learning to be a good subordinate—a task that should not be underestimated. Once you have learned your job, however, you can begin to view your own task in relation to others in the department and the relationship of your department to the rest of the organization. You'll also be able to analyze what your manager does and how things turn out—good preparation for becoming a manager yourself.

In all of this, you must realize that training yourself to become an effective manager is an ongoing task—a journey and not a destination. And although the challenges are great, we believe the effort will bring you satisfaction. Our goal, then, is to help you start this rewarding journey.

COORDINATED RESOURCE
See *Management Live!* Reading 2.1, "The Journey from Novice to Master Manager."

COORDINATED RESOURCE
See Study Guide Self-Learning Exercise 1, "Management Traits."

ILLUSTRATIVE CASE STUDY

WRAP-UP

A Typical Day in the Life of Alison Reeves

As a middle manager, Alison Reeves draws on technical skills (the ability to evaluate market research and devise budgets), human skills (the ability to motivate employees, communicate her plans to her boss, and build a working relationship with potential rivals), and conceptual skills (the ability to create departmental plans that will fit in with larger organizational goals). Moreover, Alison often has to be simultaneously analytical and people-oriented, as when she presents budget proposals to her manager.

Alison must also be able to switch roles quickly and without warning. When she meets with Bob, she is a leader, responsible for his motivation and results. When she plans her budget, she is a decision maker, looking for opportunities, allocating resources, and anticipating problems and their resolution. When she meets a customer, she becomes a figurehead and spokesperson for her department, and when she attends a United Way meeting, she switches to liaison. Finally, as the pile of pink telephone messages attests, Alison is a conduit for information within her department and within the organization.

As this case illustrates, management is not a methodical process of discrete and predictable steps. More often, it is an activity consisting of the miscellaneous accumulation of details and procedures. Alison has to keep half a dozen balls in the air at the same time and accomplish tasks through others, including her boss, subordinates, and peers. Some people have even described the world of managers like Alison as one of "chaos."* Clearly, management is a dynamic process without a beginning, middle, and end. If Alison is not in the proper frame of mind, her day will seem an endless series of frustrating interruptions and disconnected activities. But if she understands management as Mintzberg and others want us to—that is, as an important kind of social practice—she will be successful. On this particular day, Alison may well feel as if she has run a marathon—both tired and satisfied. ∎

*Thomas J. Peters, *Thriving on Chaos: A Handbook for Management Revolution* (New York: Alfred A. Knopf, 1988).

■ SUMMARY

Society needs organizations because they serve society, allow us to accomplish objectives individuals cannot achieve, preserve knowledge, and provide careers. How well organizations achieve their goals depends on managerial performance—the manager's effectiveness and efficiency. The management process itself includes the interrelated activities of planning, organizing, leading, and controlling.

Managers can be classified by level—first-line, middle, or top—or by organizational activity—functional managers, who are responsible for only one activity, or general managers, who are responsible for all the functions in an organizational unit. Managers at different levels need different types of skills. Lower-level managers need more technical skills than higher-level managers, who rely more on conceptual skills. Managers at all levels need human skills.

In moving organizations toward their goals, managers adopt a wide range of interpersonal, informational, and decision-making roles.

Today's managers face the challenge of meeting foreign competition, improving productivity, and making decisions that serve society. To meet these challenges, managers need to develop their long-term vision of the organization and its place in the world, they need to consider ethics and values in their decision making, and they need the talents of our culturally diverse population. Most importantly, they must develop their managerial potential through formal education and ongoing practice.

■ REVIEW QUESTIONS

1. Define the terms *organization* and *management* and explain why each is important.
2. Compare Drucker's concepts of managerial "effectiveness" and "efficiency" and explain why each is important to managerial performance.
3. Describe the basic activities in the management process and give examples of how they are interrelated.
4. List and describe the different types of managers discussed in this chapter.
5. According to Katz, what three basic skills do managers need? Discuss each of these skills in terms of management levels.
6. What roles does Mintzberg say a manager may assume in an organization? Give examples of each.
7. Why do managers need vision?
8. Why are managers often faced with ethical issues?
9. Why do managers need cultural diversity?
10. Compare the value of formal schooling and practical experience in the education of managers.

The Vice President, the Product Manager, and the Misunderstanding

Tom Brewster, one of the field sales managers of Major Tool Works, Inc., was promoted to his first headquarters assignment as an assistant product manager for a group of products with which he was relatively unfamiliar. Shortly after he undertook this new assignment, one of the company's vice presidents, Nick Smith, called a meeting of product managers and other staff to plan marketing strategies. Brewster's immediate superior, the product manager, was unable to attend, so the director of marketing, Jeff Reynolds, invited Brewster to the meeting to help orient him to his new job.

Because of the large number of people attending, Reynolds was rather brief in introducing Brewster to Smith, who, as vice president, was presiding over the meeting. After the meeting began, Smith—a crusty veteran with a reputation for bluntness—began asking a series of probing questions that most of the product managers were able to answer in detail. Suddenly he turned to Brewster and began to question him quite closely about his group of products. Somewhat confused, Brewster confessed that he really did not know the answers.

It was immediately apparent to Reynolds that Smith had forgotten or had failed to understand that Brewster was new to his job and was attending the meeting more for his own orientation than to contribute to it. He was about to offer a discreet explanation when Smith, visibly annoyed with what he took to be Brewster's lack of preparation, announced, "Gentlemen, you have just seen an example of sloppy staff work, and there is no excuse for it!"

Reynolds had to make a quick decision. He could interrupt Smith and point out that he had judged Brewster unfairly; but that course of action might embarrass both his superior and his subordinate. Alternatively, he could wait until after the meeting and offer an explanation in private. Inasmuch as Smith quickly became engrossed in another conversation, Reynolds decided to follow the second approach. Glancing at Brewster, Reynolds noted that his expression was one of mixed anger and dismay. After catching Brewster's eye, Reynolds winked at him as a discreet reassurance that he understood and that the damage could be repaired.

After an hour, Smith, evidently dissatisfied with what he termed the "inadequate planning" of the marketing department in general, abruptly declared the meeting over. As he did so, he turned to Reynolds and asked him to remain behind for a moment. To Reynold's surprise, Smith himself immediately raised the question of Brewster. In fact, it turned out to have been his main reason for asking Reynolds to remain behind. "Look," he said, "I want you to tell me frankly, do you think I was too rough with that kid?" Relieved, Reynolds said, "Yes, you were. I was going to speak to you about it."

Smith explained that the fact that Brewster was new to his job had not registered adequately when they had been introduced and that it was only some time after his own outburst that he had the nagging thought that what he had done was inappropriate and unfair. "How well do you know him?" he asked. "Do you think I hurt him?"

For a moment, Reynolds took the measure of his superior. Then he replied evenly, "I don't know him very well yet. But, yes, I think you hurt him."

"Damn, that's unforgivable," said Smith. He then telephoned his secretary to call Brewster and ask him to report to his office immediately. A few moments later, Brewster returned, looking perplexed and uneasy. As he entered, Smith came out from behind his desk and met him in the middle of the office. Standing face to face with Brewster, who was 20 years and four organization levels his junior, he said, "Look, I've done something stupid and I want to apologize. I had no right to treat you like that. I should have remembered that you were new to your job. I'm sorry."

Brewster was somewhat flustered but muttered his thanks for the apology.

"As long as you are here, young man," Smith continued, "I want to make a few things clear to you in the presence of your boss's boss. Your job is to make sure that people like myself don't make stupid decisions. Obviously we think you are qualified for your job or we would not have brought you in here. But it takes time to learn any job. Three months from now I will expect you to know the answers to any questions about your products. Until then," he said, thrusting out his hand for the younger man to shake, "you have my complete confidence. And thank you for letting me correct a really dumb mistake."

Source: From *Cases and Problems for Decisions in Management,* by Saul Gellerman. Copyright © 1984 by Saul Gellerman and published by McGraw-Hill, Inc. Reprinted by permission of McGraw-Hill, Inc.

Case Questions

1. What do you think was the effect on Brewster and the other managers of Smith's outburst at the meeting?

2. Was Smith right to apologize to Brewster or should he have left well enough alone?

3. What do you think the apology meant to Brewster?

4. What would it be like to have Nick Smith as a superior? As a subordinate?

5. How does Smith define Brewster's responsibilities as an assistant product manager? How does he define his own role as a top manager?

6. What is the most important aspect of the relations between management levels in this company?

VIDEO CASE STUDY

Raising Standards—The Will-Burt Company Challenge

In December 1985, the Will-Burt Company of Orrville, Ohio, was in terrible shape. A manufacturer of coal-fire heaters and pneumatically raised telescoping masts, the company also made metal parts for ladders, scaffolding, aircraft, and so on for the likes of Caterpillar, Parker-Hannifin, and AMC. Although sales were a respectable $20 million, product quality was so poor that employees spent nearly 25,000 hours reworking defective parts, at a cost of $800,000 a year. As a result, profitability had ranged between 1 and 5 percent over the past few years. Furthermore, the pre-World War II factories were outmoded and working conditions were miserable. Hourly wages were $2 lower than the area average, and the pension plan was so bad that a 35-year veteran could expect to collect only $80 to $120 a month upon retirement. No wonder employee turnover was approximately 30 percent.

As if that wasn't enough, the year before, Will-Burt had lost a product liability lawsuit involving a scaffold collapse that had killed one person and crippled another. The parts Will-Burt had made were not defective, but the manufacturer of the scaffold had declared bankruptcy. Under the doctrine of joint and several liability, therefore, Will-Burt had to pay the full award. Its insurer settled out of court for $6.2 million—and canceled the company's coverage. Moreover, the company faced two other product liability suits resulting from scaffolding accidents. Amidst these legal proceedings, Will-Burt's Chief Executive dropped dead of a heart attack, and the family that owned the company decided to sell it.

It was at this point that 55-year old Harry Featherstone stepped in as chief executive officer of the troubled company. Featherstone, a former accountant and engineer who had spent most of his working life with Ford Motor Company, had come to Will-Burt in 1978 as vice president. Now he wanted to preserve the company and the 350 jobs it provided.

He arranged for a leveraged buyout, borrowing $3.2 million from a bank, using the company and all of its assets as collateral. Then he established an employee stock ownership plan (ESOP), assuming employees who owned a part of the company would feel more committed and become more productive. In his rush to finance the buyout, though, Featherstone failed to prepare the employees. Instead of overseeing an easy transition to employee ownership, Featherstone confronted an atmosphere of suspicion, distrust, and fear. Employees in the small rural community didn't understand what an ESOP was. The workers' average educational level was tenth grade, but many were high-school dropouts, and some were functionally illiterate.

Featherstone began to hold meetings to explain what an ESOP was. He wrote about the plan in the company newsletter and included a quiz, complete with dinner-for-two for the employee who answered the most questions correctly. He also began posting profit-and-loss statements in an effort to explain Will-Burt's dire financial straits. Employees began to understand that they owned a company that was on the verge of bankruptcy. They also realized they had power. As owners, they wanted to elect the board of directors and the president and make all the major decisions. They also wanted raises for themselves. The situation bordered on anarchy. Featherstone needed a way to get the workers to focus on issues that would turn the company around.

Having spent many years in Japan as a Ford employee, Featherstone felt the Japanese success stemmed from their emphasis on education and training. Instead of looking at the skills the employees already possessed, Featherstone examined the skills the jobs required and then determined whether or not his employees actually had those skills. This process uncovered a major skills gap. Although most production employees needed to work from blueprints, few could read them. To correct this, Featherstone introduced a voluntary mathematics course taught on company time. Few employees attended, though, and all but three dropped out.

Clearly, people who had been out of school for twenty years were not comfortable with the idea of returning to the classroom and would avoid it if possible. So Featherstone made the training mandatory, but still on company time, and started with a basic blueprint reading course. He was beginning to discover that successful training programs focus directly on job-related skills. Later, he added other courses and enlisted the aid of the continuing education staff at the University of Akron.

Product quality improved immediately, and the number of rejects began to drop. Rather than trying to teach basic reading and math skills, Featherstone decided to concentrate on improving workplace literacy—knowledge of the skills needed to perform certain work tasks, with emphasis on state-of-the-art techniques. This was important, since employees' jobs had become more sophisticated over the years, but their training had not kept pace with the expanding requirements of those jobs.

Featherstone pressed on with his education and training programs, using industrial training specialists from the University of Akron as instructors. He added additional mathematics courses and introduced statistical process control, which reduced the rejection rate even more; the rejection rate of 35 percent in 1986 had dropped to below 10 percent in late 1988, and the cost of rework went from $800,000 to less that $180,000. Featherstone pushed for zero defects and perfect on-time delivery as a competitive edge against Japanese competition in the metal-working market. By 1988, on-time delivery was running at 98 percent.

In the interim, Will-Burt won one lawsuit; the other was dismissed. And with quality improvements and cost-cutting, the company was able to meet its first year loan obligation. Employees began to get comfortable with the idea of company ownership; they started to participate in production decisions and expanded their jobs in addition to their job skills. In Will-Burt's plant 9, for example, almost every worker can do every job. The people that do the work, design the work, and they make the purchasing decisions regarding the machinery they work with. Will-Burt is one employer that is discovering that productivity increases when workers are given more responsibilities for all aspects of production. Workers and office personnel now make up five out of the eight-member ESOP advisory committee. Decisions are made by simple majority.

Perhaps the most gratifying result of Featherstone's stress on education and training was the response to a two-year cross training program he's negotiating with the University of Akron, which can lead to an associate degree in manufacturing. He had anticipated that perhaps 15 people would be interested; 54 actually signed up.

With its emphasis on education and training, Will-Burt may be ahead of its time, but not by much. By the year 2000, it's estimated that nearly three-quarters of all workers will have to upgrade their skills. Advances in technology are demanding changes in the way managers view the workplace. Says *Business Week*'s John Hoerr, "If companies want to be continuously innovative to meet competition, they must engage in continuous, career-long training of all employees."

Sources: Joani Nelson-Horchler, "A Chewed-up Bill," *Industry Week*, February 15, 1988, p. 29; Robert W. Goddard, "Combating Illiteracy in the Workplace," *Management World*, March–April 1989, pp. 8–11; Leslie Brokaw et al., "Now Read This," *Inc.*, July 1989, p. 99; Jay Finegan, "The Education of Harry Featherstone," *Inc.*, July 1990, pp. 57–66; Stephanie Simon, "People Lagging as Machines Move to the Cutting Edge." *Chicago Tribune*, July 24, 1990. pp. 5, 6; John Hoerr, "With Job Training, A Little Dab Won't Do Ya," *Business Week*, September 24, 1990, p. 95.

Case Questions

1. Using Drucker's measure of managerial performance, look at Featherstone's initial approach to Will-Burt's problems. Was it effective or efficient? Did his approach change with time? Support your opinion.

2. Where were Featherstone's strengths as a manager? Where were his weaknesses?

3. Which of Featherstone's techniques or approaches would be applicable to workplace literacy problems in general? Which would need to be modified? Under what circumstances?

■ NOTES

[1] For a popular critique of American management practice, see Steve Lohr, "Overhauling America's Business Management." *The New York Times Magazine,* January 4, 1981, pp. 15ff.

[2] For a popular analysis of some of the apparent successes and possible failures of Japanese organizations, see Peter F. Drucker, "Behind Japan's Success," *Harvard Business Review* 59, no. 1 (January–February 1981):83–90.

[3] For a discussion of the complexity of evaluating organizational performance, see Terry Connolly, Edward J. Conlon, and Stuart Jay Deutsch, "Organizational Effectiveness: A Multiple-Constituency Approach," *Academy of Management Review* 5, no. 2 (April 1980):211–217.

[4] Peter F. Drucker, *The Effective Executive* (New York: Harper & Row, 1967).

[5] Peter F. Drucker, *Managing for Results* (New York: Harper & Row, 1964), p. 5. The pressures to focus on efficiency versus effectiveness are great in all organizations. Drucker also observed, in a seminar for federal executives during the Eisenhower administration, that "the greatest temptation is to work on doing better and better what should not be done at all."

[6] Michael H. Mescon, Michael Albert, and Franklin Khedouri, *Management: Individual and Organizational Effectiveness,* 2nd ed. (New York: Harper & Row, 1985), stress that "resources" should be defined to include not just general economic categories like labor and capital, but information and technology as well.

[7] See also Stephen J. Carroll and Dennis J. Gillen, "The Classical Management Functions: Are They Really Outdated?" *Proceedings of the Forty-Fourth Annual Meeting of the American Academy of Management* (August 1984):132–136.

[8] Because of their responsibilities for many diverse functions, it is increasingly important for top managers to have broad corporate experience. See W. Walker Lewis, "The CEO and Corporate Strategy in the Eighties: Back to Basics," *Interfaces* 14, no. 1 (January–February 1984):3–9.

[9] Henry Mintzberg, "The Manager's Job: Folklore and Fact, " *Harvard Business Review* 52, no. 4 (July–August 1975):49–61, and *The Nature of Managerial Work* (Englewood Cliffs, N.J.: Prentice Hall, 1973). Important precursors of Mintzberg's work include Sue Carlson, *Executive Behavior: A Study in the Work Load and Working Methods of Managing Directors* (Stockholm, Sweden: Stromberg Aktiebolag, 1951); Peter F. Drucker, *The Practice of Management* (New York: Harper & Row, 1954); and Rosemary Stewart, *Managers and Their Jobs: A Study of the Similarities and Differences in the Ways Managers Spend Their Time* (London: Macmillan, 1967). More recent studies of the manager's job include Colin P. Hales, "What Do Managers Do? A Critical Review of the Evidence, " *Journal of Management Studies* 23 (January 1986):88–115; and two articles by Hugh C. Willmott, "Images and Ideals of Managerial Work: A Critical Examination of Conceptual and Empirical Accounts," *Journal of Management Studies* 21 (1984):349–368, and "Studying Managerial Work: A Critique and a Proposal, " *Journal of Management Studies* 24 (May 1987):249–270.

[10] On the symbolic role of managers, see Jeffrey Pfeffer and Gerald R. Salancik, *The External Control of Organizations: A Resource Dependence Perspective* (New York: Harper & Row, 1978), pp. 16–18, 264–265.

[11] The importance of political skills in management is becoming increasingly apparent. See Rosabeth Moss Kanter, "Power Failure in Management Circuits," *Harvard Business Review* 57, no. 4 (July–August 1979):65–75; and Graham Astley and Paramjit S. Sachdeva, "Structural Sources of Intraorganizational Power: A Theoretical Synthesis," *Academy of Management Review* 9, no. 1 (January 1984):104–113.

[12] This suggestion has been supported by the work of John P. Kotter. See *The General Manager* (New York: Free Press, 1982) and "What Effective Managers Really Do," *Harvard Business Review* 60, no. 6 (November–December 1982):156–167.

[13] As quoted in Sheryl Hilliard Tucker and Kevin D. Thompson, "Will Diversity = Opportunity + Advancement for Blacks?" *Black Enterprise,* November 1990, p. 60.

[14] As quoted in Solomon J. Herbert, "The Making of a New Classic," *Black Enterprise,* November 1990, p. 66.

CHAPTER TWO

THE EVOLUTION OF MANAGEMENT THEORY

Detail from Paul Klee, *Monuments by G*

Why Study Management Theory?
Theories Guide Management Decisions
Theories Shape Our View of Organizations
Theories Make Us Aware of the Business Environment
Theories Are a Source of New Ideas

The Classical Management Theories
Forerunners of Scientific Management Theory
Scientific Management Theory
Classical Organization Theory
Transitional Theories: Becoming More People-Oriented

The Behavioral School: The Organization Is People
The Human Relations Movement
From Human Relations to the Behavioral Science Approach

The Quantitative School: Operations Research and Management Science

The Evolution of Management Theory
The Systems Approach
The Contingency Approach
The Neo-Human Relations Movement

Upon completing this chapter, you should be able to:

1. Explain why it is important to study management theory.

2. Discuss the environmental factors that enhanced the growth and development of the three major schools of management thought.

3. Describe some of the work methods and tools Frederick W. Taylor introduced to increase productivity.

4. Evaluate Taylor's assumptions about the relationship between management and labor.

5. Explain why Follett thought individuals could gain freedom and self-contol through group activities.

6. Evaluate the relevance of Fayol's principles to today's business environment.

7. Describe Elton Mayo's principal contribution to management and explain why it is controversial.

8. Distinguish between the "rational" and "social" models of human relations.

9. Explain what managers mean when they use the abbreviation OR and what it contributes to modern management.

10. Describe the systems approach and explain why it is appropriate to today's environment.

11. Discuss the manager's major task, according to contingency theory.

12. Explain the basic assumptions of the neo-human relations movement.

Paul Klee (1879–1940), *Monuments by G.* Gypsum and watercolor on canvas. H.69 cm. W.50 cm. The Metropolitan Museum of Art, The Berggruen Klee Collection, 1984. The pyramids were built by at least a hundred thousand people over a 20-year period. Although it's only within the last 100 years that Management has become a discipline, the pyramids are evidence that people have practiced managerial concepts of planning, organizing, leading, and controlling for thousands of years.

ILLUSTRATIVE CASE STUDY

INTRODUCTION

The Apostle of Mass Production

Henry Ford and the Model T have long been symbols of the modern industrial age. Even the subsequent growth and success of Ford's rival General Motors was due in large part to GM's need to find an innovative response to the Model T. In large measure, the managerial approach of Henry Ford, as well as his preferences in managerial theory, is a paradigm of much that was constructive—and much that was imperfect—in early approaches to management.

The son of a poor Irish immigrant, Henry Ford was born in 1863 and grew up on a farm in rural Michigan. He was fascinated by machinery and was quite skilled in repairing and improving almost any machine. He started the Ford Motor Company in 1903, and by 1908, the first Model T was built.

In the early part of the century when automobiles were first introduced, they were a symbol of status and wealth, the near-exclusive province of the rich. Ford intended to change that: The Model T was to be for the masses—a car that virtually anyone could afford. He understood that the only way to make such a car was to produce it at high volume and low cost. Ford focused his factory efforts on efficiency, mechanizing wherever possible and breaking down tasks into their smallest components. One worker would perform the same task over and over, producing not a finished part, but one of the operations necessary for the production of the whole; the incomplete part would then be passed on to another worker, who would contribute a successive operation. Ford was able to achieve remarkable efficiencies: Although the first Model T took over 12½ hours to produce, only 12 years later, in 1920, Ford was producing one Model T every minute. By 1925, at the peak of the car's popularity, a Model T was rolling off Ford's assembly lines every 5 seconds.

However, mechanization of the plant had some adverse effects. The faster Ford pushed his workers, the more disgruntled they became. In 1913, turnover was 380 percent, and Ford had to hire ten times more workers than he needed just to keep the line moving. In an action that at the time was unprecedented, Ford simply decided to double wages in order to get the best people and motivate them to work even harder. In the days following the announcement that wages were being doubled, thousands and thousands of men came to the Ford plant in search of work. Police had to be called in to control the crowds.

A Revolution Begins. Henry Ford takes a spin in his first auto.

Ford's management style was the darker side of his innovative personality, and it led to chaos in the ranks of management. Ford did not take criticism well, especially of the Model T. When his top engineers suggested changes, they were ignored, and some were even fired. As a result, competitors like Chevrolet were able to make a great deal of headway in the automobile market. Then, too, Ford liked to play his subordinates against each other, to the point of assigning two of them the same title and seeing which one (the weaker one, according to Ford) would back down first. Competent managers abandoned the firm, which remained overly dependent on the irascible Ford himself.

When he died in 1945, Ford was worth over $600 million. He left an indelible mark on both American industry and society. His name is synonymous with mass production and the development of modern management theory.

Source: Adaptation compiled from *The Reckoning* by David Halberstam. Copyright © 1986 by David Halberstam. By permission of William Morrow and Company, Inc.

Most people associate Henry Ford with the Model T, the affordable mass-produced automobile that changed society. But Ford is also important as a management *theorist,* someone who develops ideas about how organizations function. Moreover, Ford hired other theorists, such as Frederick Winslow Taylor, and gave them the chance to develop their management theories. In this chapter, we will see how different management theories developed and continue to evolve. But first, let's take a moment to look at the reasons studying management theory will help you become a more effective manager in today's complex organizations.

■ WHY STUDY MANAGEMENT THEORY?

Because management is an applied discipline concerned with practical results, you may be impatient with the idea of studying theories from the past. But this study is important for at least four reasons.

Theories Guide Management Decisions

theory Coherent group of assumptions put forth to explain the relationship between two or more observable facts and to provide a sound basis for predicting future events.

Studying theories helps us to understand underlying processes, and on that basis, choose an effective course of action. In essence, a **theory** is a coherent group of assumptions put forth to explain the relationship between two or more observable facts. Valid theories, then, let us predict what will happen under certain situations. With this knowledge, we can apply different management theories to different situations.

Theories Shape Our View of Organizations

Studying management theories also shows us where we get some of our ideas about organizations and the people in them. Take Henry Ford's assembly line, for instance. This is one very practical application of *scientific management theory,* the idea that managers can scientifically determine the best way to perform any task. This theory is based on the assumption that people don't like to work; instead, they need close supervision and the incentive of money rewards (a sensible assumption, given the dull, repetitious, and sometimes hazardous nature of assembly-line work). In recent years, though, many manufacturers faced a crisis in productivity, quality, and employee morale, forcing many employers—Ford Motor Co. among them—to rethink the assumptions of scientific management theory. As a result, Ford adopted a new set of assumptions about employees—that they care about their work and want a say in how it is organized and performed—ideas that underlie the *neoclassical approach.* These assumptions led Ford Motor Co. to experiment with a team approach in designing the acclaimed Ford Taurus (a process described in more detail in the Illustrative Case for Chapter 17).

Theories Make Us Aware of the Business Environment

As you study the various theories, you will come to see that each is the product of its environment—the social, economic, political, and technological forces present in a given time and locale. This knowledge will help you understand why certain theories are appropriate to different circumstances. At the beginning of the twentieth century, for example, skilled labor was in short supply, leading managers to concentrate on ways to make every worker more efficient. In this context, Henry Ford's approach makes sense. Today, though, when the general level of education is higher and we have an ample labor supply, different theories are more effective. (Because

Profiting from the Environment. Realizing busy two-career couples don't have time to cook, Safeway Chairman Peter Magowan upgraded in-store bakeries and added takeout counters like China Express.

environmental forces are so important to management, we will study them in more detail in the next chapter.)

Theories Are a Source of New Ideas

As you can see, theories give us a chance to take a different view of everyday situations. Even though you may feel more comfortable with one theory than another, it is important to realize that no general theory unifies or dominates the field. Instead, the eclectic approach—the practice of borrowing principles from different theories as required by circumstances—is the state of the art in management theory and practice.[1] Thus, you need to keep an open mind and become familiar with each of the major theories that currently coexist.

In this chapter, we will focus on three well-established schools of management thought:[2] the *classical school* (which has two branches—*scientific management* and *classical organization theory*), the *behavioral school,* and the *management science school.* Although these schools developed in historical sequence, later ideas have not *replaced* earlier ones. Instead, each new school has tended to complement or coexist with previous ones. At the same time, each school has continued to develop and even merge with others.[3] Thus, we will also discuss three recent integrative approaches: the *systems approach,* the *contingency approach,* and the *neo-human relations movement.* Figure 2-1 gives you an approximate idea of when each of these theoretical perspectives emerged.

FIGURE 2-1 Key Management Theories: An Overview
The dates on which each theory began are approximate.

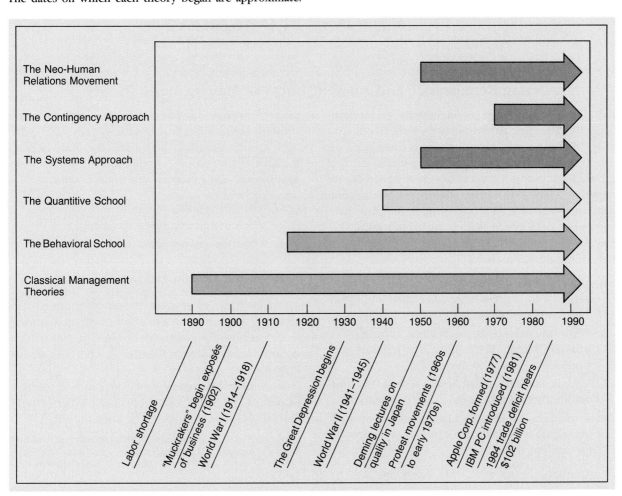

■ THE CLASSICAL MANAGEMENT THEORIES

TEACHING TIP
A good way to compare and contrast the various perspectives is to list on the board or prepared transparency the relative merits of each of the approaches to management. Emphasize to students that each approach contributes something of value to our knowledge of management.

COORDINATED RESOURCE
Use Transparency 7, Key Management Theories: An Overview.

People have been managed in groups and organizations since prehistoric times. Even the simplest hunting and gathering bands generally recognized and obeyed a leader or a group of decision makers responsible for the band's welfare. As societies grew larger and more complex, the need for managers became increasingly apparent, leading scholars of those times to ponder the nature of management in an intuitive fashion. (See the International Management box.)

Attempts to develop *theories* of management, however, are relatively recent, dating from the industrial revolution of the eighteenth and nineteenth centuries. The use of new technologies concentrated great quantities of raw materials and large numbers of workers in factories; goods were produced in quantity and had to be distributed widely. The need to coordinate all these elements gave rise to the systematic approach to management.

Forerunners of Scientific Management Theory

Imagine you are living in England in the early 1800s. The factory system has been spreading and the local entrepreneur has put you in charge of a new factory. What should your role be? Robert Owen, a manager of several cotton mills at New Lanark, Scotland, during the early 1800s, faced this question. At that time, working and living conditions for most workers were very poor. Men, women, and children (many as

INTERNATIONAL MANAGEMENT

Some Renaissance and Ancient Roots of Management Theory

Two classic works offer useful insights to modern managers. The first is by Niccolò Machiavelli. Although the adjective *Machiavellian* is often used to describe cunning and manipulative opportunists, the real Machiavelli was a great believer in the virtues of a republic, a fact shown in his *Discourses*. Machiavelli wrote the book in 1531 while living in the early Italian republic of Florence. With some paraphrasing, the principles he set forth can be applied to the management of organizations today:

1. An organization is more stable if members have the right to express their differences and solve their conflicts within it.

2. While one person can begin an organization, "it is lasting when it is left in the care of many and when many desire to maintain it."

3. A weak manager can follow a strong one, but not another weak one, and maintain authority.

4. A manager seeking to change an established organization "should retain at least a shadow of the ancient customs."

Another classic work that offers insights to

modern managers is *The Art of War,* written by the Chinese philosopher Sun Tzu more than 2,000 years ago. It was modified and used by Mao Zedong, founder of the People's Republic of China in 1949. Among Sun Tzu's dictums are the following:

1. When the enemy advances, we retreat!
2. When the enemy halts, we harass!
3. When the enemy seeks to avoid battle, we attack!
4. When the enemy retreats, we pursue!

Although these rules were meant to guide military strategy, they can be used when planning a strategy to defeat business competitors. (In fact, you will encounter similar ideas in Chapter 7, where we discuss Porter's view of strategy.)

Neither Machiavelli nor Sun Tzu was trying to develop a systematic view of management, of course. Nonetheless, their insights are still relevant.

Sources: The Portable Machiavelli, Peter Bondanella and Mark Musa, ed. and trans. (New York: Penguin, 1979); Sun Tzu, *The Art of War,* Samuel B. Griffith, trans. (London: Oxford University Press, 1963).

young as 5 or 6) worked up to 14 hours a day, six days a week. Wages were low and housing was crowded and unsanitary. Owen decided managers should play the role of *reformer.* He built better housing for his workers and operated a company store where goods could be purchased cheaply. He reduced the standard workday to 10½ hours and refused to hire children under the age of 10.

Owen argued that improving the condition of employees would inevitably lead to increased production and profits. Whereas other managers concentrated their investments in technical improvements, Owen believed that a manager's best investment was in the workers (or "vital machines," as he called them).

Aside from making general improvements in working conditions at his mills, Owen openly rated an employee's work on a daily basis, believing that open ratings let the manager identify problem areas and instilled pride and spurred competition among workers. In today's organizations, the practice of posting sales and production figures is based on the same psychological principle of *feedback*—letting workers know how they are performing.

At about the same time Owen was pursuing his reforms, a British professor of mathematics named Charles Babbage became convinced that the application of scientific principles to work processes would both increase productivity and lower expenses. Babbage was an early advocate of the division of labor, believing that each factory operation should be analyzed so that the various skills it involved could be isolated. In this way, expensive training time could be reduced, and the constant repetition of each operation would improve workers' skills and efficiency. Our modern assembly line, in which each worker is responsible for a different repetitive task, is partly based on Babbage's ideas.

Scientific Management Theory

Scientific management theory arose in part from the need to increase productivity. In the United States especially, skilled labor was in short supply at the beginning of the twentieth century. The only way to expand productivity was to raise the efficiency of workers. Thus, Frederick W. Taylor, Henry L. Gantt, and the Gilbreths—Frank and Lillian—devised the body of principles known as scientific management theory.

FREDERICK W. TAYLOR. Frederick W. Taylor (1856–1915) based his management system on production-line time studies. Instead of relying on traditional work methods, he analyzed and timed steel workers' movements on a series of jobs. Using time study as his base, he broke each job down into its components and designed the quickest and best methods of performing each component. Taylor thereby established how much workers should be able to do with the equipment and materials at hand. He also encouraged employers to pay more productive workers at a higher rate than others. The higher rate was carefully calculated and based on the greater profit that would result from increased production. Thus workers were urged to surpass their previous performance standards to earn more pay. Taylor called his plan the **differential rate system.** He believed that workers who met the higher standards need not fear layoffs because their companies benefited from their higher productivity. The higher payments were assured because they were "scientifically correct" rates set at a level that was best for both company and worker. He insisted that no one would be hurt by the differential system because those workers who fell below the standard would find other work "in a day or two" because of the existing labor shortage.

In 1893, Taylor decided he could best put his ideas into effect as a private consulting management engineer. He was soon able to report impressive improvements with one client, Simonds Rolling Machine Company. In one operation, Simonds employed 120 experienced women to inspect bicycle ball bearings. The work was tedious and the hours were long. There seemed little reason to believe

Scientific Management in Use. A General Electric engineer uses a teaching box to train an industrial robot to perform tasks that have been analyzed using motion studies.

THOUGHT PROVOKER

How did Taylor's ideas "protect" the worker?

TEACHING TIP

You might want to look ahead at Chapter 10 and share with your students the simplicity and richness of a Gantt chart.

improvements could be made. Taylor proved otherwise. First, he studied and timed the movements of the best workers. Then he trained the rest in the methods of their more effective co-workers. The least effective workers were transferred or laid off. He shortened the workday—from $10\frac{1}{2}$ to $8\frac{1}{2}$ hours—and introduced rest periods, the differential rate system, and other improvements. The results were impressive: 35 inspectors did the work formerly done by 120; accuracy improved by two-thirds; wages rose by 80 to 100 percent; and worker morale went up. Taylor reported equally impressive results for other clients, including Bethlehem Steel.

Although Taylor's methods led to dramatic increases in productivity and to higher pay in a number of instances, workers and unions began to oppose his approach because they feared that working harder or faster would exhaust whatever work was available, causing layoffs. The fact that workers had been laid off at Simonds and other organizations that adopted Taylor's methods encouraged this fear. As Taylor's ideas spread, so did the opposition to them.

By 1912, resistance to Taylorism had caused a strike at the Watertown Arsenal in Massachusetts, and hostile members of Congress called on Taylor to explain his ideas and techniques. Both in his testimony and in his two books, *Shop Management* and *The Principles of Scientific Management,*[4] Taylor rested his philosophy on four basic principles:

1. *The development of a true science of management,* so that the best method for performing each task could be determined.
2. *The scientific selection of workers,* so that each worker would be given responsibility for the task for which he or she was best suited.
3. *The scientific education and development of the worker.*
4. *Intimate, friendly cooperation between management and labor.*

Taylor contended that the success of these principles required "a complete mental revolution" on the part of management and labor. Rather than quarrel over whatever profits there were, both sides should try to increase production; by so doing, profits would rise to such an extent that labor and management would no longer have to fight over them. In short, Taylor believed that management and labor had a common interest in increasing productivity.

HENRY L. GANTT. Henry L. Gantt (1861–1919) had worked with Taylor on several projects, including Simonds and Bethlehem Steel. But when he went out on his own as a consulting industrial engineer, Gantt began to reconsider Taylor's incentive system.

Abandoning the differential rate system as having too little motivational impact, Gantt came up with a new idea. Every worker who finished a day's assigned work load would win a 50-cent bonus. Then he added a second motivation. The *supervisor* would earn a bonus for each worker who reached the daily standard, plus an extra bonus if all the workers reached it. This, Gantt reasoned, would spur supervisors to train their workers to do a better job.

Gantt also built upon Owen's idea of rating an employee's work publicly. Every worker's progress was recorded on individual bar charts—in black on days the worker made the standard, in red when he or she fell below it. Going beyond this, Gantt originated a charting system for production scheduling; the "Gantt chart" is still in use today. In Chapter 10, an illustration of a Gantt chart shows how it can be adapted to the process of planning and formally reviewing costs and progress.

THE GILBRETHS. Frank B. and Lillian M. Gilbreth (1868–1924 and 1878–1972) made their contribution to the scientific management movement as a husband-and-wife team. Lillian's doctoral dissertation, which later appeared in book form as *The Psychology of Management,* was first published in the magazine *Industrial Engi-*

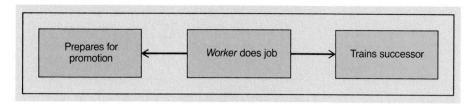

FIGURE 2-2 The Gilbreths' Three-Position Plan

neering in 1912.[5] Although she and Frank collaborated on fatigue and motion studies, Lillian also focused on ways of promoting the individual worker's welfare. To her, the ultimate aim of scientific management was to help workers reach their full potential as human beings.

COORDINATED RESOURCE

The Application Exercise for Chapter 2 found in the Lecture Extras supplement has students performing a task using time-motion study techniques.

Frank Gilbreth began work as an apprentice bricklayer and worked his way up the managerial ladder. Bricklayers, he noticed, used three different sets of motions: one for teaching apprentices, another for working fast, and a third for deliberately holding down the pace of their work. After careful study of the different motions, Frank was able to develop a technique that tripled the amount of work a bricklayer could do in a day. His success led him to make motion and fatigue study his life work.

In Frank Gilbreth's conception, motion and fatigue were intertwined—every motion that was eliminated reduced fatigue. Using motion picture cameras, he tried to find the most economical motions for each task in order to upgrade performance and reduce fatigue. Both Gilbreths argued that motion study would raise worker morale because of its obvious physical benefits and because it demonstrated management's concern for the worker.

The Gilbreths developed a *three-position plan* of promotion that was intended to serve as an employee-development program as well as a morale booster. (See Fig. 2-2.) According to this plan, a worker would do his or her present job, prepare for the next-highest one, and train his or her successor, all at the same time. Thus every worker would always be a doer, a learner, and a teacher, and would continually look forward to new opportunities.

CONTRIBUTIONS OF SCIENTIFIC MANAGEMENT THEORY. The modern assembly line pours out finished products faster than Taylor could ever have imagined. This production "miracle" is just one legacy of scientific management. In addition, its efficiency techniques have been applied to many organizations outside industry, ranging from fast-food service to the training of surgeons, making us aware that any task can be made more efficient and rational. Scientific management's influence can also be seen in the emphasis many organizations place on job design and the scientific selection and development of workers. Thus, scientific management fostered a rational approach to solving organizational problems. More importantly, it laid the groundwork for the professionalization of management.[6]

LIMITATIONS OF SCIENTIFIC MANAGEMENT THEORY. Scientific management was limited by its underlying assumptions about human beings. The then-popular model of human behavior held that people were "rational" and motivated primarily to satisfy their *economic* and *physical* needs.[7] However, this model overlooked the human desire for job satisfaction and the *social* needs of workers as a group, failing to consider the tensions created when these needs are frustrated.[8]

Furthermore, the emphasis on *productivity*—and, by extension, *profitability*—led some managers to exploit both workers and customers. As a result, more workers joined unions, reinforcing a pattern of suspicion and mistrust that colored labor-management relations for decades. In addition, the abuses of the "robber barons" sparked public outrage and the first wave of federal regulation of business. (See the Ethics in Management box.)

ETHICS IN MANAGEMENT

The Muckrakers and the Robber Barons

Applying "absolute rationality" to manufacturing left many American industrialists giddy with success and confidently searching for more. In this quest, they were encouraged by the prevalent economic philosophy of the time—laissez-faire, the idea that government should not interfere in business. It was widely believed that the free interplay of supply and demand in the marketplace would effect the best use of resources and promote steady economic growth. Wealth was considered a sign of merit and hard work; poverty a sign of idleness and wastefulness.

Too often, though, the industrialists' headlong pursuit of wealth led them to exploit their competitors, their workers, and their customers. During the era dominated by Theodore Roosevelt and the so-called Progressive Republicans (1902–1912), the press, particularly journalists who wrote for popular magazines, began to analyze the abuses of unchecked business power. Dubbed the "muckrakers" by Roose-

velt, these journalists detailed the corruption of such "captains of industry" as John D. Rockefeller, Andrew Carnegie, and Andrew Mellon. Historians looking at the records left by the muckrakers dubbed the industrialists the "Robber Barons."

Special objects of public wrath were the trusts and monopolies, which acted to limit competition and manipulate prices. Ida Tarbell's classic *History of Standard Oil,* detailing her four-year investigation into the monopolistic practices of that rapidly growing conglomerate, was published in 1904. Among other things, Tarbell discovered Standard Oil's purchase of illicit information about competitors and routine extortion of rebates and kickbacks from smaller companies dependent on it.[*]

In 1905, an investigation of the New York insurance and gas industries, led by the politician Charles Evans Hughes, uncovered such appalling corporate practices as bribes, payoffs, and large campaign con-

"A Nauseating Job, But It Must Be Done." In this 1905 political cartoon, President Teddy Roosevelt uses the "muck-rake" to probe the packing house scandal.

tributions.[†] And in 1906, David Graham Phillips published "The Treason of the Senate," a series in *Cosmopolitan* magazine, that led many people to reconsider the rightness of laissez-faire. If intense competition produced immoralities of one sort and monopolistic enterprises immoralities of another sort, then perhaps the federal government was duty-bound to intervene in the marketplace to protect the voiceless and to damp down the excesses of an unbridled free market.

This conviction grew with the 1906 publication of Upton Sinclair's famous novel *The Jungle,* an unsavory exposé of common practices in the meat-packing industry. Sinclair intended his book to be a powerful plea for socialist revolution; as he himself remarked, however, the book "aimed for the hearts of the American people and hit them instead in their stomachs." The following passage is a sample of the tale of filth and fraud that horrified the nation:

> There was never the least attention paid to what was cut up for sausage; there would come all the way back from Europe old sausages that had been rejected, and that was mouldy and white—it would be doused with borax and glycerine, and dumped into the hoppers, and made over again for home consumption. There would be meat that had tumbled out on the floor, in the dirt and sawdust, where the workers had tramped and spit uncounted billions of [tuberculosis] germs. There would be meat

stored in great piles in rooms: and the water from leaky roofs would drip over it, and thousands of rats would race about on it. It was too dark in these storage places to see well, but a man could run his hand over these piles of meat and sweep off handfuls of the dried dung of rats. These rats were nuisances, and the packers would put poisoned bread out for them: they would die, and then rats, bread, and meat would go into the hoppers together.[‡]

In another passage, Sinclair related how a worker who slipped to a lower level of the plant ended up shipped out to an unsuspecting public as "Durham's Pure Beef Lard"!

When President Theodore Roosevelt appointed a commission to investigate Sinclair's gruesome tale, the commission reported back that the author's story was essentially accurate, and Congress promptly enacted the Meat Inspection Act of 1906, followed in the same year by the Pure Food Act.

[*]Ida Tarbell, *History of Standard Oil Co.,* 2 vols. (Rpt. Lexington, Mass.: Peter Smith, 1904).

[†]Lewis J. Gould, *Reform and Regulations: American Politics, 1900–1916* (New York: Wiley, 1978).

[‡]Upton Sinclair, *The Jungle* (1906; rpt. Cambridge, Mass.: Bentley, 1971).

Source: Adapted from Donna J. Wood, *Strategic Uses of Public Policy: Business and Government in the Progressive Era.* Copyright © 1986 by Donna J. Wood. Reprinted by permission of Ballinger Publishing Company.

Classical Organization Theory

classical organization theory An early attempt, pioneered by Henri Fayol, to identify the principles and skills that underlie effective management.

CLASS COMMENT
Management theory and research originated in the lower operative levels of the organization and were subsequently applied to the upper administrative levels.

Scientific management was concerned with increasing the productivity of the shop and the individual worker. The other branch of classical management—**classical organization theory**—grew out of the need to find guidelines for managing such complex organizations as factories.

HENRI FAYOL. Henri Fayol (1841–1925) is generally hailed as the founder of the classical management school—not because he was the first to investigate managerial behavior, but because he was the first to systematize it. Fayol believed that sound management practice falls into certain patterns that can be identified and analyzed. From this basic insight, he drew up a blueprint for a cohesive doctrine of management, one that retains much of its force to this day.

Fayol believed that "with scientific forecasting and proper methods of management, satisfactory results were inevitable." In his faith in scientific methods, Fayol was like Taylor, his contemporary. While Taylor was basically concerned with *organizational functions,* however, Fayol was interested in the *total organization.*

Drawing on his many years as a manager, Fayol divided business operations into six interrelated activities: (1) technical—producing and manufacturing products; (2) commercial—buying raw materials and selling products; (3) financial—acquiring and using capital; (4) security—protecting employees and property; (5) accounting; and (6) management. Of these, he focused primarily on management, because he felt it had been the most neglected of business operations.

Bureaucracy + Scientific Management + Automation = Success. United Parcel Service (UPS) achieves efficiency through a bureaucratic organization marked by a clear division of labor, a fixed hierarchy of authority, and explicit rules and regulations for employee behavior. Industrial engineers establish performance standards, and mechanized and computerized equipment facilitate package processing and tracking.

Exhibit 2-1 lists the 14 principles of management Fayol "most frequently had to apply." Note that Fayol carefully chose the term *principles,* rather than *rules* or *laws:*

> I prefer the word principles in order to avoid any idea of rigidity, as there is nothing rigid or absolute in administrative matters; everything is a question of degree. The same principle is hardly ever applied twice in exactly the same way, because we have to allow for different and changing circumstances, for human beings who are equally different and changeable, and for many other variable elements. The principles, too, are flexible, and can be adapted to meet every need; it is just a question of knowing how to use them.[9]

Before Fayol, it was generally believed that "managers are born, not made." Fayol insisted, however, that management was a skill like any other—one that could be taught once its underlying principles were understood.

MAX WEBER. Reasoning that any goal-oriented organization consisting of thousands of individuals would require the carefully controlled regulation of its activities, the German sociologist Max Weber (1864–1920) developed a theory of bureaucratic management that stressed the need for a strictly defined hierarchy governed by clearly defined regulations and lines of authority.[10] For Weber, the ideal organization was a *bureaucracy* whose activities and objectives were rationally thought out and whose divisions of labor were explicitly spelled out. Weber also believed that technical competence should be emphasized and that performance evaluations should be made entirely on the basis of merit.

Today we often think of bureaucracies as vast, impersonal organizations that put impersonal efficiency ahead of human needs. We should be careful, though, not to apply our negative connotations of the word *bureaucracy* to the term as Weber used it. Like the scientific management theorists, Weber sought to improve the performance of socially important organizations by making their operations predictable and productive. Although we now value innovation and flexibility as much as efficiency and predictability, Weber's model of bureaucratic management clearly advanced the formation of huge corporations such as Coca-Cola and Exxon. Weber's contributions to the theory of organizational design are discussed further in Chapter 11.

CONTRIBUTIONS OF CLASSICAL ORGANIZATION THEORY. Much in classical organization theory has endured. For example, the concept that management skills apply to all types of group activity has, if anything, increased in importance. The concept that certain identifiable principles underlie effective managerial behavior and that these principles can be taught also continues to be valid. (For one thing, it is the justification for this book.)

Although classical organization theory has been criticized by other *theorists,* it has been well received by *practicing* managers for some time. This may be because classical organization theory helped isolate major areas of practical concern to the working manager. Above all, the classical organization school made managers aware of the basic kinds of problems they would face in any organization.

LIMITATIONS OF CLASSICAL ORGANIZATION THEORY. Classical organization theory has been criticized on the ground that it was more appropriate for the past, when organizations were in a relatively stable and predictable environment, than for the present, when organizational environments are more turbulent. For example, classical theorists insisted that managers maintain their formal authority, but today's better-educated employees are less accepting of formal authority, especially when it is applied arbitrarily.

TEACHING TIP

Make a point to go over Fayol's 14 principles and describe them. Engage students in discussion of examples of each principle in student organizations to which they belong.

EXHIBIT 2-1 Fayol's 14 Principles of Management

1. *Division of Labor.* The more people specialize, the more efficiently they can perform their work. This principle is epitomized by the modern assembly line.
2. *Authority.* Managers must give orders so that they can get things done. While their *formal* authority gives them the right to command, managers will not always compel obedience unless they have *personal* authority (such as relevant expertise) as well.
3. *Discipline.* Members in an organization need to respect the rules and agreements that govern the organization. To Fayol, discipline results from good leadership at all levels of the organization, fair agreements (such as provisions for rewarding superior performance), and judiciously enforced penalties for infractions.
4. *Unity of Command.* Each employee must receive instructions from only one person. Fayol believed that when an employee reported to more than one manager, conflicts in instructions and confusion of authority would result.
5. *Unity of Direction.* Those operations within the organization that have the same objective should be directed by only one manager using one plan. For example, the personnel department in a company should not have two directors, each with a different hiring policy.
6. *Subordination of Individual Interest to the Common Good.* In any undertaking, the interests of employees should not take precedence over the interests of the organization as a whole.
7. *Remuneration.* Compensation for work done should be fair to both employees and employers.
8. *Centralization.* Decreasing the role of subordinates in decision making is centralization; increasing their role is decentralization. Fayol believed that managers should retain final responsibility, but should at the same time give their subordinates enough authority to do their jobs properly. The problem is to find the proper degree of centralization in each case.
9. *The Hierarchy.* The line of authority in an organization—often represented today by the neat boxes and lines of the organization chart—runs in order of rank from top management to the lowest level of the enterprise.
10. *Order.* Materials and people should be in the right place at the right time. People, in particular, should be in the jobs or positions they are most suited to.
11. *Equity.* Managers should be both friendly and fair to their subordinates.
12. *Stability of Staff.* A high employee turnover rate undermines the efficient functioning of an organization.
13. *Initiative.* Subordinates should be given the freedom to conceive and carry out their plans, even though some mistakes may result.
14. *Esprit de Corps.* Promoting team spirit will give the organization a sense of unity. To Fayol, even small factors could help to develop the spirit. He suggested, for example, the use of verbal communication instead of formal, written communication whenever possible.

Source: Henri Fayol, *Industrial and General Administration*, J. A. Coubrough, trans. (Geneva: International Management Institute, 1930).

Classical organization guidelines have also been criticized as too general for today's complex organizations, where increased specialization has blurred the lines of authority. The maintenance engineer, for example, may take orders from the plant manager *and* the chief engineer. Thus we have a conflict between the classical principles of division of labor and unity of command.

Transitional Theories: Becoming More People-Oriented

Mary Parker Follett and Chester Barnard were among those who built on the basic framework of the classical school. However, they introduced many new elements, especially in the area of human relations and organizational structure. In this, they anticipated trends that would be further developed by the emerging behavioral and management science schools.

MARY PARKER FOLLETT. Follett (1868–1933) was convinced that no one could become a whole person except as a member of a group. Thus she took for granted Taylor's assertion that labor and management shared a common purpose as members of the same organization, but she believed that the artificial distinction between managers (order givers) and subordinates (order takers) obscured this natural partnership.[11] In her behavioral model of organizational control (see Fig. 2-3), control was sponsored by and oriented toward the group. Self-control (S) was exercised by both individuals and groups (G), with the result being shared control or power (P). Moreover, Follett took into account such factors as politics, economics, and biology (designated as E for environment in Fig. 2-4), which influenced the interactive or integrative nature of self-control groups (I). Because she saw this system as an integrated whole, Follett characterized it as a "holistic" model of control.

FIGURE 2-3 The Follett Behavioral Model of Control

Source: L. D. Parker, "Control in Organizational Life: The Contribution of Mary Parker Follett," *Academy of Management Review* (1984): 742.

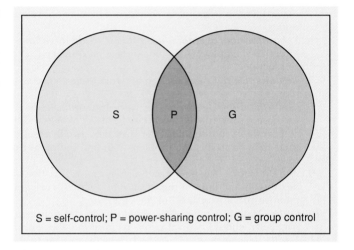

S = self-control; P = power-sharing control; G = group control

FIGURE 2-4 The Follett Holistic Model of Control

Source: L. D. Parker, "Control in Organizational Life: The Contribution of Mary Parker Follett," *Academy of Management Review* (1984):743.

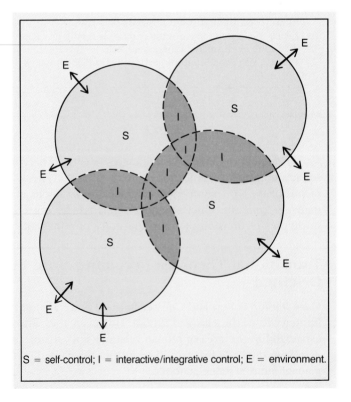

S = self-control; I = interactive/integrative control; E = environment.

ILLUSTRATIVE CASE STUDY

CONTINUED

The Apostle of Mass Production

[Taking the advice of efficiency expert Walter Flanders in 1908,] Ford bought grounds in Highland Park, where he intended to employ the most modern ideas about production, particularly those of Frederick Winslow Taylor. These would bring, as Taylor had prophesied, an absolute rationality to the industrial process. The idea was to break each function down into much smaller units so that each could be mechanized and speeded up and eventually flow into a straight-line production of little pieces becoming steadily larger—continuity above all. The process began to change in the spring of 1913. The first piece on the modern assembly line was the magneto coil assembly. In the past, a worker—and he had to be a skilled worker—had made a flywheel magneto from start to finish. A good employee could make 35 or 40 a day. Now, however, there was an assembly line for magnetos, divided into 29 different operations performed by 29 different men. In the old system it took 20 minutes to make a magneto; now it took 13.

Ford and his men soon moved to bring the same rationality to the rest of the factory. Quickly, they imposed a comparable system for the assembly of motors and transmissions. Then, in the summer of 1913, they took on the final assembly, which, as the rest of the process had speeded up, had become the great bottleneck. The workers [now maneuvered] as quickly as they could around a stationary metal object, the car they were putting together. If the men could remain stationary as the semifinished car moved up the line through them, less of the workers' time—Ford's time—would be wasted.

Charles Sorensen, who had become one of Ford's top production people, [initiated the assembly line by pulling] a Model T chassis slowly by a windlass across 250 feet of factory floor, timing the process all the while. Behind him walked six workers, picking up parts from carefully spaced piles on the floor and fitting them to the chassis. . . . [Soon,] the breakthroughs came even more rapidly. . . . [By installing an automatic conveyor belt,] Ford could eventually assemble a car in [93 minutes]. . . . Just a few years before, in the days of stationary chassis assembly, the best record for putting a car together had been 728 hours of one man's work. Ford's top executives celebrated their victory with a dinner at De-troit's Pontchartrain Hotel. Fittingly, they rigged a simple conveyor belt to a five-horsepower engine with a bicycle chain and used the conveyor to serve the food around the table. It typified the spirit, camaraderie, and confidence of the early days.

Nineteen years and more than fifteen million cars later, when Ford reluctantly came to the conclusion that he had to stop making the T, the company balance was $673 million. And this was not merely a company's success; it was the beginning of a social revolution. Ford himself [believed] he had achieved a breakthrough for the common man. "Mass production," he wrote later, "precedes mass consumption, and makes it possible by reducing costs and thus permitting both greater use-convenience and price-convenience."

[Not surprisingly,] the price of the Model T continued to come down, from $780 in the fiscal year 1910–11 to $690 the following year, then to $600, to $550, and, on the eve of World War I, to $360. At that price, Ford sold 730,041 cars, outproducing everyone in the world. . . .

Henry Ford, immigrant's son and one-time machinist's apprentice, had indeed become a very rich man. Obviously, he had become so by being a venturesome and successful theorist of industrial management. But both his practices and his personality drew fire from those who were critical of his implicit attitude toward those "masses" for whom he had originally perfected and priced the Model T. For example, his widely publicized doubling of wages for employees in 1914 was seen by some as a trailblazing maneuver in management-labor relations, by others as a scheme to solidify Ford's paternalistic power over those who depended upon him for a living. In addition, Ford stubbornly resisted the unionization of his employees long after his major competitors had made agreements with union organizations. Repression on the part of company police against union "agitators" was common on the company's grounds until, finally, having lost an election conducted by the National Labor Relations Board [a government agency established in 1935 to affirm labor's right to bargain collectively], Ford contracted with the United Auto Workers in 1941.

CHESTER I. BARNARD. Barnard (1886–1961), who became president of New Jersey Bell in 1927, used his work experience and his extensive readings in sociology and philosophy to formulate theories on organizational life. According to Barnard, people come together in formal organizations to achieve ends they could not accomplish working alone. But as they pursue the organization's goals, they must also satisfy their individual needs. And so Barnard arrived at his central thesis: An enterprise can operate efficiently and survive only when the organization's goals are kept in balance with the aims and needs of the individuals working for it.

For example, to meet their personal goals within the confines of the formal organization, people come together in informal groups such as cliques. To ensure its survival, the firm must use these informal groups effectively, even if they sometimes work at cross-purposes to management's objectives. Barnard's recognition of the importance and universality of the "informal organization" was a major contribution to management thought.

Barnard believed that individual and organizational purposes could be kept in balance if managers understood a subordinate's "zone of indifference" or "zone of acceptance"—that is, what the subordinate would do without questioning the manager's authority. Obviously, the more activities that fell within an employee's zone of acceptance, the smoother and more cooperative an organization would be. Barnard also believed that executives had a duty to instill a sense of moral purpose in their employees. To do this, they would have to learn to think beyond their narrow self-interest and make an ethical commitment to society. Although Barnard stressed the work of *executive* managers, he also focused considerable attention on the role of the individual worker as "the basic strategic factor in organization." When he went further to emphasize the organization as the cooperative enterprise of individuals working together as *groups,* he departed from the mainstream of classical management theory and set the stage for the development of a great deal of current management thinking.[12]

■ *THE BEHAVIORAL SCHOOL: THE ORGANIZATION IS PEOPLE*

behavioral school A group of management scholars trained in sociology, psychology, and related fields, who use their diverse knowledge to understand and more effectively manage people in organizations.

The **behavioral school** emerged partly because the classical approach did not achieve sufficient production efficiency and workplace harmony. To managers' frustration, people did not always follow predicted or expected patterns of behavior. Thus there was increased interest in helping managers deal more effectively with the "people side" of their organizations. Several theorists tried to strengthen classical organization theory with the insights of sociology and psychology. As we shall see in Chapter 15, many of these insights have contributed to our thinking about employee motivation.

The Human Relations Movement

Human relations is frequently used as a general term to describe the ways in which managers interact with their subordinates. When "employee management" stimulates more and better work, the organization has effective human relations; when morale and efficiency deteriorate, its human relations are said to be ineffective. The human relations movement grew out of early attempts to systematically discover the social and psychological factors that would create effective human relations.

THE HAWTHORNE EXPERIMENTS. The human relations movement grew out of a famous series of studies conducted at the Western Electric Company from 1924 to 1933. These eventually became known as the "Hawthorne Studies" because many of them were performed at Western Electric's Hawthorne plant near Chicago. The

Hawthorne Studies began as an attempt to investigate the relationship between the level of lighting in the workplace and worker productivity—the type of question Frederick Taylor and his colleagues might well have addressed.

In some of the early studies, the Western Electric researchers divided the employees into test groups, which were subjected to deliberate changes in lighting, and control groups, whose lighting remained constant throughout the experiments. The results of the experiments were ambiguous. When the test group's lighting was improved, productivity tended to increase, although erratically. But when lighting conditions were made worse, there was also a tendency for productivity to increase in the test group. To compound the mystery, the control group's output also rose over the course of the studies, even though it experienced no changes in illumination. Obviously, something besides lighting was influencing the workers' performance.

In a new set of experiments, a small group of workers was placed in a separate room and a number of variables were altered: Wages were increased; rest periods of varying lengths were introduced; the workday and workweek were shortened. The researchers, who now acted as supervisors, also allowed the groups to choose their own rest periods and to have a say in other suggested changes. Again, the results were ambiguous. Performance tended to increase over time, but it also rose and fell erratically. Partway through this set of experiments, Elton Mayo (1880–1949) and some associates from Harvard, including Fritz J. Roethlisberger and William J. Dickson, became involved.

In these and subsequent experiments, Mayo and his associates decided that a complex chain of attitudes had touched off the productivity increases. Because they had been singled out for special attention, the test and the control groups had developed a group pride that motivated them to improve their work performance. Sympathetic supervision had further reinforced their motivation. The researchers concluded that employees would work harder if they believed management was concerned about their welfare and supervisors paid special attention to them. This phenomenon, subsequently labeled the **Hawthorne effect,** has remained quite controversial to this day. Since the control group received no special supervisory treatment or enhancement of working conditions but still improved its performance, some people (including Mayo himself) speculated that the control group's productivity gains resulted from the special attention of the researchers themselves.

The researchers also concluded that informal work groups—the social environment of employees—have a positive influence on productivity. Many of Western Electric's employees found their work dull and meaningless, but their associations and friendships with co-workers, sometimes influenced by a shared antagonism toward the "bosses," imparted some meaning to their working lives and provided some protection from management. For these reasons, group pressure was frequently a stronger influence on worker productivity than management demands.

To Mayo, then, the concept of "social man"—motivated by social needs, wanting rewarding on-the-job relationships, and responding more to work-group pressures than to management control—was necessary to complement the old concept of "rational man" motivated by personal economic needs.[13]

CONTRIBUTIONS OF THE HUMAN RELATIONS APPROACH. By stressing social needs, the human relations movement improved on the classical approach, which treated productivity almost exclusively as an engineering problem. In a sense, Mayo had rediscovered Robert Owen's century-old dictum that a true concern for workers, those "vital machines," paid dividends.

In addition, these researchers spotlighted the importance of a manager's style and thereby revolutionized management training. More attention was focused on teaching people-management skills and less on teaching technical skills. Finally, their work led to a new interest in group dynamics. Instead of focusing just on the individual worker, managers began thinking about group processes and group rewards.

Hawthorne effect The possibility that workers who receive special attention will perform better simply because they received that attention: one interpretation of studies by Elton Mayo and his colleagues.

COORDINATED RESOURCE
See Samaras Case 1.2, "To Lead or Not to Lead."

LIMITATIONS OF THE HUMAN RELATIONS MOVEMENT.   Although the Hawthorne experiments profoundly influenced the way managers approached their jobs and how management research was subsequently conducted, the studies had many weaknesses of design, analysis, and interpretation. Whether Mayo and his colleagues' conclusions are consistent with their data is still the subject of lively debate and considerable confusion.[14]

The concept of "social man" was an important counterweight to the one-sided "rational-economic man" model, but it, too, failed to describe completely individuals in the workplace. Many managers and management writers assumed satisfied workers would be more productive workers. However, attempts to increase output during the 1950s by improving working conditions and employee satisfaction did not result in the dramatic productivity increases that had been expected.

Apparently, the social environment in the workplace is only one of several interacting factors that influence productivity. Salary levels, the interest levels of given tasks, organizational structure and culture, and labor-management relations also play a part. Thus the entire matter of productivity and worker satisfaction has turned out to be far more complex than originally thought.

For example, a rigorous study conducted by social psychologists P. Mirvis and E. E. Lawler in 1977 produced inconclusive findings about the relationship between job satisfaction and job performance.[15] In attempting to measure the performance of bank tellers in terms of cash shortages, Mirvis and Lawler proposed two arguments: (1) satisfied tellers were less likely to show shortages through either carelessness or dishonesty; (2) satisfied workers were less likely to leave their jobs, and so saved their employers the considerable expense of recruiting and training replacements. However, subsequent analysis of this study tends to support the contention that when the quantity of a worker's output is used to measure the relationship between satisfaction and performance, the correspondence is generally lower than expected. Such analysis raises a crucial question: Does a worker perform well because he or she is satisfied, or does the worker's perception that he or she is performing well lead to satisfaction?

Satisfaction does seem to lower absenteeism and job turnover, but analysis of the Mirvis-Lawler data shows that even this correspondence is lower than one might expect. Finally, even the correlation between dissatisfied workers and job turnover is smaller than one might assume.[16]

In conclusion, there seem to be at least two reasons why it is difficult to study the relationship between job satisfaction and performance or productivity. First, job satisfaction is largely an emotional response to one's work, and emotional factors, besides involving numerous variables, are notoriously hard to *measure* in terms precise enough to satisfy the requirements of social scientific study. Second, as we will see in Chapter 15, it is difficult to separate the issue of job *satisfaction* from the equally complex issue of job *motivation.*

From Human Relations to the Behavioral Science Approach

Mayo and his colleagues pioneered the use of the scientific method in their studies of people in the work environment. Later researchers, more rigorously trained in the social sciences (psychology, sociology, and anthropology), used more sophisticated research methods and became known as "behavioral scientists" rather than "human relations theorists."

Mayo and the human relations theorists introduced "social man," motivated by a desire to form relationships with others. Some behavioral scientists, such as Argyris, Maslow, and McGregor, believed that "self-actualizing man" was a more accurate concept for explaining human motivations.[17] (MacGregor's contributions will be discussed more fully in Chapter 15, Argyris's work in Chapter 11.)

According to Maslow, the needs people are motivated to satisfy fall into a hierarchy, at the bottom of which are physical and safety needs and at the top of which are ego needs (the need for respect, for example) and self-actualizing needs (such as the need for meaning and personal growth). In general, lower-level needs must be satisfied before higher-level needs can be met. Since many lower-level needs are routinely satisfied in contemporary society, most people are motivated more by the higher-level ego and self-actualizing needs. (The hierarchy of needs is discussed in greater detail in Chapter 15.)

Some later behavioral scientists feel that even this model cannot explain all the factors that may motivate people in the workplace. They argue that not everyone goes predictably from one need level to the next. For some people, work is only a means for meeting lower-level needs; others are satisfied with nothing less than the fulfillment of their highest-level needs and may even choose to work in jobs that threaten their safety if that means they can attain uniquely personal goals. To these behavioral scientists, the more realistic model of human motivation is "complex man." The effective manager is aware that no two people are exactly alike and tailors his or her attempts to influence workers according to their individual needs.

CONTRIBUTIONS OF THE BEHAVIORAL SCIENCE SCHOOL. Behavioral scientists have made enormous contributions to our understanding of individual motivation, group behavior, interpersonal relationships at work, and the importance of work to human beings. Their findings have enabled managers to become much more sensitive and sophisticated in dealing effectively with subordinates. Behavioral scientists continue to offer new insights in such important areas as leadership, conflict resolution, the acquisition and use of power, organizational change, and communication.

THOUGHT PROVOKER
What contributions of these early management theorists would still be applicable to today's organizations? Why?

LIMITATIONS OF THE BEHAVIORAL SCIENCE SCHOOL. Despite its impressive contributions, many management writers—including some behavioral scientists—believe the field's potential has not been fully realized. Because they do not like to admit they need help in dealing with people, managers may resist suggestions from behavioral scientists. Also, the models, theories, and jargon of behavioral scientists may seem too complicated and abstract to practicing managers. Finally, because human behavior is so complex, behavioral scientists often differ in their conclusions and recommendations, making it difficult for managers to decide whose advice to follow.[18]

■ THE QUANTITATIVE SCHOOL: OPERATIONS RESEARCH AND MANAGEMENT SCIENCE

At the beginning of World War II, Great Britain desperately needed to solve a number of new, complex problems in warfare. With their survival at stake, the British formed the first operational research (OR) teams. By pooling the expertise of mathematicians, physicists, and other scientists in OR teams, the British were able to achieve significant technological and tactical breakthroughs. When the Americans entered the war, they formed what they called *operations research* teams, based on the successful British model, to solve similar problems, using early computers to perform the thousands of calculations involved in mathematical modeling.

DISCUSSION QUESTION
Have students identify some organizational problems that could be solved by the management science approach. (Examples include reducing waiting time in a supermarket express lane checkout, reducing the number of rejects for unacceptable product quality, opening a new building on a college campus, etc.)

When the war was over, the applicability of OR to problems in industry gradually became apparent since new industrial technologies were being put into use and transportation and communication were becoming more complicated. These developments brought with them a host of problems that could not be solved easily by conventional means. Increasingly, OR specialists were called on to help managers come up with answers to these new problems. With the development of high-powered computers, OR procedures were formalized into what is now called the "management science school."[19]

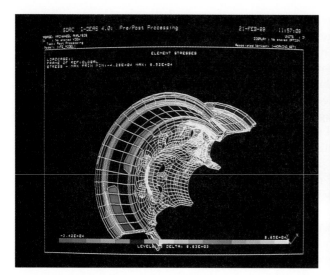

Management Science in Action. B.F. Goodrich engineers and managers used software from Structural Dynamics Research Corp. (SDRC) to model a wheel and brake assembly and avoid costly design and production mistakes. Fixing an error costs as little as $1 at the design stage but as much as $100,000 once production has begun.

management science (MS) Mathematical techniques for the modeling, analysis, and solution of management problems. Also called *operations research (OR)*.

Today the **management science** approach to solving a problem begins when a mixed team of specialists from relevant disciplines is called in to analyze the problem and propose a course of action to management. The team constructs a mathematical model that shows, in symbolic terms, all the relevant factors bearing on the problem and how they are interrelated. By changing the values of the variables in the model (such as increasing the cost of raw materials) and analyzing the different equations of the model with a computer, the team can determine the effects of each change. Eventually, the management science team presents management with an objective basis for making a decision.[20]

The techniques of management science are a well-established part of the problem-solving armory of most large organizations, including the civilian and military branches of government. As we will see, management science has made its greatest contributions in planning and control activities, including the development of product strategies, human resource development programs, production scheduling, capital budgeting, cash flow management, and the maintenance of optimal inventory levels.

Management science is limited in two ways, however. First, some managers feel the mathematical basis of management science is too complicated for ready understanding and use. Second, management science is inadequate for dealing with the psychological and behavioral components of workplace activities. Some practicing managers trace this to their limited involvement in developing management science techniques.[21] Management scientists themselves believe they have not achieved their full potential because they are too remote from the problems and constraints faced by actual managers.[22]

■ *THE EVOLUTION OF MANAGEMENT THEORY*

Although we have described the three major schools of management thought in terms of their chronological emergence, all continue to maintain their importance today. The behavioral science and the management science schools both represent vital approaches to researching, analyzing, and solving management problems. The classical school, too, continues to evolve, integrating newer developments from other schools into its basic framework of such traditional issues as division of labor,

CLASS COMMENT
A book by Theodore Levitt, *Thinking About Management* (Free Press, 1991), offers some thoughts about the evolution of management: "Entrepreneurship was the sacred mushroom of the 1980s. It seemed delusively greater and grander than it was." "Organizations exist to enable ordinary people to do extraordinary things." And "In some circles, after all is said and done, mostly all that's done is said." (*Business Week*, 2/25/91, p. 18)

authority and responsibility, and initiative. In fact, while each school retains its special focus, each tends to borrow insights and concepts from the others. Indeed, it often seems that the boundaries between the various schools are becoming progressively blurred.[23]

But the growing similarities among the schools should not be exaggerated. Although many individuals integrate the perspectives of all the schools, there are many others whose training and background are firmly in a single school. One benefit of studying the major theories is that you will understand the perspectives of your future colleagues in management and thus be prepared to work effectively with them.

Moreover, current management theory continues to generate exciting concepts. It is impossible to predict what future generations will be studying, but at this point we can identify at least three additional perspectives on management theory that will become important: the systems approach, the contingency approach, and a neo-human relations approach.

The Systems Approach

systems approach View of the organization as a unified, directed system of interrelated parts.

COORDINATED RESOURCE
Use Transparency 8, A General Systems View.

DISCUSSION QUESTION
How can an organization be viewed as a system? Demonstrate examples of organizations as systems on the board or with prepared transparencies.

Rather than dealing separately with the various segments of an organization, the **systems approach** to management views the organization as a unified, purposeful system composed of interrelated parts. This approach gives managers a way of looking at the organization as a whole and as a part of the larger, external environment. (See Chapter 3.) In so doing, systems theory tells us that the activity of any segment of an organization affects, in varying degrees, the activity of every other segment.[24]

Production managers in a manufacturing plant, for example, would like to have long uninterrupted production runs of standardized products in order to maintain maximum efficiency and low costs. Marketing managers, on the other hand, wanting to offer quick delivery of a wide range of products, would like a flexible manufacturing schedule that can fill special orders on short notice. *Systems-oriented* production managers would make scheduling decisions only after they have identified these decisions' impact on other departments and the entire organization. The point of the systems approach is that managers cannot function wholly within the confines of the traditional organization chart. They must mesh their department with the whole enterprise, and to do that they have to communicate with other employees and departments, and frequently with representatives of other organizations as well.[25]

subsystems Those parts making up the whole system.

synergy The situation in which the whole is greater than its parts. In organizational terms, synergy means that departments that interact cooperatively are more productive than they would be if they operated in isolation.

open system A system that interacts with its environment.

closed system A system that does not interact with its environment.

SOME KEY CONCEPTS. Many of the concepts of general systems theory are finding their way into the language of management. As managers, we need to be familiar with the systems vocabulary so we can keep pace with current developments.

Subsystems. The parts that make up the whole of a system are called **subsystems.** And each system in turn may be a subsystem of a still larger whole. Thus a department is a subsystem of a plant, which may be a subsystem of a company, which may be a subsystem of a conglomerate or an industry, which is a subsystem of the national economy, which is a subsystem of the world system.

Synergy. Synergy means that the whole is greater than the sum of its parts. In organizational terms, **synergy** means that as separate departments within an organization cooperate and interact, they become more productive than if each had acted in isolation. For example, in a small firm, it is more efficient for each department to deal with one financing department than for each department to have a separate financing department of its own.

Open and Closed Systems. A system is considered an **open system** if it interacts with its environment; it is considered a **closed system** if it does not. All organizations interact with their environment, but the extent to which they do so varies. An automobile plant, for example, is a far more open system than a monastery or a prison.

A Merger Creates Synergy. Kraft food scientists display some of the products developed when corporate parent Philip Morris Cos. merged their research efforts with those of another subsidiary, Entenmann's, Inc., which had been working since 1987 on Project Lightening (to create no-cholesterol bakery items) and Project Thunder (to create fat-free cakes and cookies). Three months after the first meeting with Kraft scientists, Entenmann's researchers made a breakthrough, and both Kraft and Entenmann's introduced no-fat, cholesterol-free products in October 1989.

system boundary The boundary that separates each system from its environment. It is rigid in a closed system, flexible in an open system.

flows Components such as information, material, and energy that enter and leave a system.

feedback (job-based) The part of system control in which the results of actions are returned to the individual, allowing work procedures to be analyzed and corrected.

System Boundary. Each system has a boundary that separates it from its environment. In a closed system, the **system boundary** is rigid; in an open system, the boundary is more flexible. The system boundaries of many organizations have become increasingly flexible in recent years. For example, oil companies wishing to engage in offshore drilling now must consider public concern for the environment.

Flow. A system has **flows** of information, materials, and energy (including human energy). These enter the system from the environment as *inputs* (raw materials, for example), undergo transformation processes within the system (operations that alter them), and exit the system as *outputs* (goods and services).

Feedback. **Feedback** is the key to system controls. As operations of the system proceed, information is fed back to the appropriate people or perhaps to a computer so that the work can be assessed and, if necessary, corrected.[26] Figure 2-5 shows the flows of information, materials, energy, and feedback in an open system.

Systems theory calls attention to the dynamic and interrelated nature of organizations and the management task. Thus it provides a framework within which we can plan actions and anticipate both immediate and far-reaching consequences, while allowing us to understand unanticipated consequences as they develop. With a systems perspective, general managers can more easily maintain a balance between the needs of the various parts of the enterprise and the needs and goals of the whole firm.

Its advocates believe systems theory will either absorb concepts of the other management schools until it becomes dominant or eventually develop into a well-defined school by itself. At present, though, it seems most likely that systems theory will be incorporated into the thinking of all the major schools. The systems approach has already permeated management thinking, and the concepts just described are an integral part of the thought processes and research designs of both on-the-job managers and academic theorists of all three major schools.

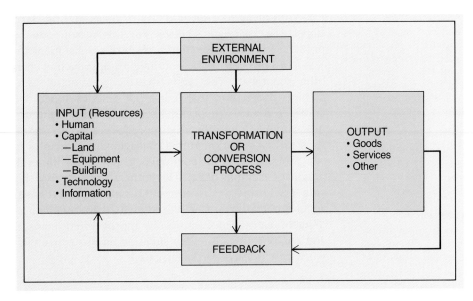

FIGURE 2-5 The Flows and Feedback in an Open System

The Contingency Approach

The well-known international economist Charles Kindleberger was fond of telling his students at MIT that the answer to any really engrossing question in economics is: "It depends." The task of the economist, Kindleberger would continue, is to specify *upon what* it depends, and *in what ways.*

"It depends" is an appropriate response to the important questions in management as well. Management theory attempts to determine the predictable relationships between situations, actions, and outcomes, so it is not surprising that a recent approach seeks to integrate the various schools of management thought by focusing on the interdependence of the many factors involved in the managerial situation.

contingency approach The view that the management technique that best contributes to the attainment of organizational goals might vary in different types of situations or circumstances.

DISCUSSION QUESTION

Assign individual students or groups of students the roles of Taylor, Fayol, Barnard, Follett, Maslow, Kast and Rosenzweig (systems), and Luthans (contingency). How would each of these scholars interpret and manage the following situations: the introduction of robots into the workplace, actual sales inconsistent with sales projections, employee dissatisfaction, product quality decline? Develop other examples.

The **contingency approach** (sometimes called the *situational approach*) was developed by managers, consultants, and researchers who tried to apply the concepts of the major schools to real-life situations. When methods highly effective in one situation failed to work in other situations, they sought an explanation. Why, for example, did an organizational development program work brilliantly in one situation and fail miserably in another? Advocates of the contingency approach had a logical answer to all such questions: Results differ because situations differ; a technique that works in one case will not necessarily work in all cases.

According to the contingency approach, the manager's task is to identify which technique will, *in a particular situation, under particular circumstances, and at a particular time,* best contribute to the attainment of management goals. Where workers need to be encouraged to increase productivity, for example, the classical theorist may prescribe a new work-simplification scheme. The behavioral scientist may instead seek to create a psychologically motivating climate and recommend some approach like *job enrichment*—the combination of tasks that are different in scope and responsibility and allow the worker greater autonomy in making decisions. (The relationship between such approaches and job satisfaction and motivation is discussed in more detail in Chapter 15.) But the manager trained in the contingency approach will ask, "Which method will *work best here?*" If the workers are unskilled and training opportunities and resources are limited, work simplification would be the best solution. However, with skilled workers driven by pride in their abilities, a job-enrichment program might be more effective.

The contingency approach builds upon the systems approach by focusing in detail on the relationships between system parts, by seeking to define those factors

HERE'S AN EXAMPLE
"Visionary thinkers are rejecting the by-the-numbers approach to enterprise and seeking a new paradigm for viewing the world." (*Fortune,* 10/8/90, p. 156ff.)

COORDINATED RESOURCE
See Study Guide Self-Learning Exercise 2, "Management School Preferences."

COORDINATED RESOURCE
See Study Guide Problem Exercise 2, "Identifying Management Theories."

neo-human relations movement An integrative approach to management theory that combines a positive view of human nature with the scientific study of organizations to prescribe how effective managers should act in most circumstances.

COORDINATED RESOURCE
The Additional Lecture for Chapter 2 found in the Lecture Extras supplement looks at Dr. W. Edwards Deming and the role he has played in the management discipline.

CLASS COMMENT
W. Edwards Deming, the man behind the quality movement, looks for quality in all aspects of business: what goes on in the factory, how products are sold, and how managers deal with workers. (*Business Week,* 1/28/91, p. 14)

that are crucial to a specific task or issue, and by clarifying the functional interactions between related factors. For this reason, advocates of the contingency approach see it as the leading branch of management thought today.[27]

The primacy of the contingency approach is challenged, however, by several other theorists.[28] They argue that this approach does not incorporate all aspects of systems theory and that it has not yet developed to the point where it can be considered a true theory by itself. Critics also contend that there really isn't much new about the contingency approach—that, for example, even classical theorists such as Fayol cautioned that management principles must be applied flexibly.

Supporters of the contingency approach counter that many theorists forgot the pragmatic cautions of Fayol and others and too often theorists tried to come up with "universal principles" that could be applied in every situation. When working managers applied these principles, though, they often had a rude encounter with unpredictable reality. The contingency approach tells managers to be aware of the shades and complications in every situation and to actively try to determine what would work best in each particular case.

The Neo-Human Relations Movement

The **neo-human relations movement** is an integrative approach that combines a positive view of human nature with the scientific study of organizations to prescribe how effective managers *should* act in most circumstances. This movement began in the 1950s and gained momentum in the 1960s.[29]

That the neo-human relations approach is indebted to the contingency approach is evident in Tom Burns and G. M. Stalker's declaration that "the beginning of administrative wisdom is the awareness that there is no optimum type of management system."[30] The neo-human relations movement goes beyond contingency theory, though, to propose how management should act in *most* circumstances.

W. Edwards Deming, Tom Peters, and others have combined scientific studies and clinical experience to devise a comprehensive and practical set of principles of management, much as Fayol did in the early part of the century. These principles focus on the concept of "quality" in work and in the individual worker's relationships with others. You have already seen some of these principles in Chapter 1, where we discussed how Deming's 14 principles helped the Japanese improve the quality of their manufactured goods.

The neo-human relations movement captured widespread public attention in 1982, when management consultants Thomas J. Peters and Robert H. Waterman published their study of 43 "excellently managed" U.S. companies.[31] These companies, which included IBM, Eastman Kodak, 3M, Boeing, Bechtel, Procter & Gamble, and McDonald's, had been consistently profitable over a 20-year period. In addition, they were unusually successful in responding to customer needs, provided a challenging and rewarding work environment for their employees, and met their social and environmental obligations effectively. Peters and Waterman concluded that these companies were "brilliant on the basics"—they simply did the most fundamental organizational tasks very well.

In a little-read chapter of their *In Search of Excellence,* Peters and Waterman describe the social science research on which they base their principles of management. This research, some of which will be discussed in the remainder of this book, is explicitly about human nature and the ways people interact in organizations. Instead of "rational man" or "man motivated by fear," the research reveals human beings to be emotional, intuitive, and creative social creatures. We all like to think of ourselves as winners and need to celebrate our victories, however small. Although we value self-control, we need and want the security and meaning of achieving goals through organizations. Peters and Waterman used conclusions like these to deduce some general rules for treating workers with the dignity and respect they require to do quality work.

DISCUSSION QUESTION

Read a corporate case study in a business periodical such as *Business Week* or *Fortune*. What management approaches can be identified? (You can either assign a specific reading or leave the assignment open-ended.)

COORDINATED RESOURCE

See Samaras Reading "Manager, Manage Thyself!".

One of these "rules" stresses the importance of values. According to Peters and Waterman, "The top performers create a broad, uplifting, shared culture, a coherent framework within which charged-up people search for appropriate adaptations."[32] As examples, they cite such strongly held managerial values as IBM's "respect for the individual" and Frito-Lay's commitment to a "99.5 percent" level of satisfactory service. Such values help employees work toward common goals and to adapt to inevitable changes in internal and external conditions.

No company can rest on its laurels, however, for a firm that embodies excellence one year may founder the next. As Peters notes, "IBM was declared dead in 1979, the best of the best in 1982, and dead again in 1986."[33] Companies must remain flexible if they are to survive in our increasingly competitive international economy. Indeed, Peter Drucker, writing as far back as 1965, envisioned an "entrepreneurial society" in which "Tradition, convention, and 'corporate policy' will be a hindrance rather than a help."[34]

In their subsequent research, Peters and Waterman (working separately) have stressed two principles. The first, as Peters says, is "a set of new basics: world-class quality and service, enhanced responsiveness through greatly increased flexibility, and continuous, short-cycle innovation and improvement" of all a company's products.[35] Companies must pursue what Waterman calls "informal opportunism"; they must respond to opportunities and challenges quickly, as they arise.

The second principle, as Waterman puts it, is to recognize that people are "the main engine" of any company, not just "interchangeable parts of the corporate machine."[36] Only a company's people can make it succeed and then help it defend its turf. Employees' loyalty must be won through a new sort of social contract. As Peters says:

COORDINATED RESOURCE

Acumen: Ouchi's Theory Z can offer information about the behaviors and attitudes associated with the Humanistic-Helpful scale.

> For managers this path means continuously retraining employees for more complex tasks, automating in ways that cut routine tasks and enhance worker flexibility and creativity, diffusing responsibility for innovation, taking seriously labor's concern for job security, and giving workers a stake in improved productivity via profit-linked bonuses and stock plans. For workers this . . . path means accepting flexible job classifications and work rules, agreeing to wage rates linked to profits and productivity improvements, and generally taking greater responsibility for the soundness and efficiency of the enterprise.[37]

If writers like Drucker, Peters, and others[38] are correct, the new emphasis on human relations management is an important step in the evolution of management thought—one that must be acknowledged in any integrative approach to management theory. One such effort has been made by William Ouchi, an American familiar with Japanese organizational practices.[39] Ouchi first observed that many of the most successful American companies "behaved" much like Japanese organizations. Since much of the Japanese managerial style was actually borrowed from Western models based primarily on scientific management principles, Ouchi has proposed a management model that *integrates* the successful practices of both Japanese and American cultures. In particular, he endorses greater emphasis on human relations management as a complement to the techniques of scientific management. The organization, he proposes, must devote more energy to satisfying the needs of its human resources, both as individuals and as groups. He suggests such goals can be attained if an organization focuses on changes in two crucial areas: *Decision making* should become a participatory activity for a greater number of employees; and *responsibility* should be considered a collaborative function, preferably the product of group or team processes.

COORDINATED RESOURCE

The Distinctive Discussions for Chapter 2 found in the Lecture Extras supplement include "Teaching Management in Business Schools" and "New Age Corporations."

THOUGHT PROVOKER

If you had the opportunity to sit down and talk with any one of the management theorists discussed, who would it be? What questions would you want to ask this person?

Whether the neo-human relations approach will turn out to be a major contributor to management theory or just another conceptual fad is impossible to say at this point, but it is certainly having a tremendous impact on management thinking in both universities and organizations.

ILLUSTRATIVE CASE STUDY

WRAP-UP

The Apostle of Mass Production

We have discovered two basic things in this chapter. First, theorists, whatever their fields of endeavor, tend to be people and products of their times. Second, management theories, like theories in all fields, tend to *evolve* to reflect everyday realities and changing circumstances. By the same token, managers must be sensitive to changing circumstances and equally willing to change. If they do not, they may be surpassed by more flexible competitors.

Both of these ideas apply to Henry Ford, the man who boldly embraced the ideas of scientific management, revolutionizing the auto industry and our society in the process.

Yet many of Ford's managerial practices were conservative or unresponsive to changing times, and his hold on the automotive market was eventually wrested from him by companies more farsighted in their managerial theories and practices. Hostile to the banking community, for example, Ford refused outside investments in his company throughout his lifetime, borrowing capital only when absolutely necessary and preferring to finance corporate activities solely through the company's own income. He was also inclined to ignore the dynamics of the industry that he had largely founded. Although he opened up branch factories to cater to a growing European market, he long failed to follow managerial advice to retool for both the hydraulic brake and the six- or eight-cylinder engine; he also resisted management counsel regarding advances in gearshift and transmission technology and even put off introducing color variety into his product line (Ford preferred his cars to be black). His disinterest in consumer demands for comfort and style ultimately cost him his industry's leadership, which passed to General Motors, a conglomerate assembled from over 20 diverse firms by founder William Durant and a second generation of American industrial organizers. ■

■ *SUMMARY*

Three well-established schools of management thought—classical, behavioral, and quantitative—have contributed to managers' understanding of organizations and to their ability to manage them. Each offers a different perspective for defining management problems and opportunities and for developing ways to deal with them. In their current state of evolution, however, each approach also overlooks or deals inadequately with important aspects of organizational life. The newer systems approach (based on general systems theory), the contingency approach, and the neo-human relations movement have already been developed to the point where they offer valuable insights for the practicing manager. Eventually, these most recently evolved perspectives may lead to the integration of the classical, behavioral, and quantitative schools; on the other hand, some new approach not yet on the horizon may accomplish this end.

It is also possible that the awaited theoretical breakthrough will never occur and managers will have to continue on their own to select the perspective or perspectives appropriate to a given situation.

■ *REVIEW QUESTIONS*

1. Why is it important to study the various management theories that have been developed?
2. What environmental factors enhanced the growth and development of each of the three major schools of thought?

3. What were some of the work methods and tools that Taylor introduced to increase productivity?

4. Was Taylor's assumption that management and labor had a common cause valid? Why or why not?

5. Why did Follett believe that individual freedom and self-control should come through the activities of the group?

6. Which of Fayol's principles and functions of management do you believe still apply today?

7. What was Mayo's principal contribution to management knowledge? What is the Hawthorne effect?

8. Distinguish between the "rational" and "social" models of human relations.

9. What is OR and how does it work?

10. Why is the systems approach more appropriate today than it would have been in Fayol's time?

11. What is the major task of the manager according to the contingency approach?

12. What are the basic assumptions of the neo-human relations movement?

13. Which approach or school of management thought makes the most sense to you? Why?

CASE STUDY

Theory and Policy Encounter Power and Motivation at Consolidated Automobile

On Tuesday morning at 6 A.M., two young automobile assembly-line workers, disgruntled over failing to get their supervisor transferred, shut off the electric power supply to an auto-assembly line and closed it down at Consolidated Automobile Manufacturers, Inc.

The electric power supply area, containing transformers, switches, and other high-voltage electrical equipment, was positioned near the center of the plant in a 6-by-7-foot area. Enclosing this area was a 10-foot-high chain-link fence with a locked gate of equal height that formed a protective cage around the facility and provided a measure of security.

The two assembly-line workers, William Strong and Larry Kane, gained access to the electric power supply area simply by scaling the fence. Once inside, they halted the assembly line by opening the switches and cutting off the electrical power.

Strong and Kane, who worked as spot welders, had taken matters into their hands when the union's grievance procedure had not worked fast enough to satisfy them. Co-workers, idled by the dramatic protest and the motionless assembly line, grouped themselves around the fenced area, shouting encouragement to the two men inside. In response, Strong and Kane were chanting, "When you cut the power you've got the power." They were in the process of becoming folk heroes to their co-workers.

Sam Winfare, who supervised Strong and Kane and who was the target of their protest, had been supervisor for only a short time. In explaining the events that led to the protest, Winfare said that production on the assembly line had been chronically below quota before he took charge, and the plant manager had plainly told him that his job was to improve the production rate. Production had improved markedly in the short time that Winfare had been supervisor.

Winfare advised the plant manager that his transfer would only set a serious long-term precedent. "The company's action to remove me would create a situation where the operations of the plant would be subject to the whims of any employee with a grudge," he argued. His contention was confirmed by the comments of a union steward, who said there were other conditions in the plant that needed improving—such as the cafeteria food and relief from the more than 100-degree heat in the metal shop. Moreover, the steward said, there was at least one other supervisor who should be removed. He implied that, if successful, the power cage protest would achieve two goals—namely, employees could dictate the company's problem-solving agenda and simultaneously undermine its power to determine decision-making priorities. The union steward's final comment was that two men on an unauthorized, wildcat strike might accomplish the same thing as a full-blown strike.

Each passing minute was costing the company a production loss of one automotive unit valued at $6,000; the cost of each lost production hour, therefore, was $360,000.

As he began a staff meeting to resolve the dilemma, the plant manager felt pressure to accomplish two objectives: (1) to restore production on the profitless assembly line (a solution about which he was uncertain), and (2) to develop policies for preventing future production interruptions by assembly-line workers.

Source: Adapted from John M. Champion and John H. James, *Critical Incidents in Management: Decisions and Policy Issues,* 5th ed. (Homewood, Ill.: Richard D. Irwin, 1985), pp. 36–37. Copyright 1985 by Richard D. Irwin, Inc.

Case Questions

1. What is the real problem in this case?
2. How would each of the approaches to management in this chapter analyze the case?
3. How should the plant manager restore production on the assembly line?
4. What policy, if any, should be developed to prevent future production interruptions?
5. If there is an underlying struggle for power in this situation, precisely where does it lie? Which theoretical approach to management policy is best suited to answer this question?

Managing the U.S. Postal Service

In recent years, the United States Postal Service (USPS) has come under a hail of crticism for its rates (too high) and its service (too slow and surly). As U.S. Postmaster General Anthony M. Frank admits, "Most people don't understand . . . the $500 billion that's needed to bail out the savings and loan industry. But they sure understand when you increase the postal rate from 25 to 29 cents."

Between 1789 and 1971, the uniform service provided by the government-run U.S. Post Office Department was deemed so important that Congress let it operate at a loss. In 1971, though, the USPS was created as an independent agency that was to become self-supporting by the mid-1980's and to make a specified contribution to the federal budget every year.

The transition has not been easy. James Miller, director of the Office of Management and Budget under Ronald Reagan, panned the USPS as a grossly inefficient bureaucracy, overstaffed with overpaid workers, which should lose its monopoly on first-class service or be sold to a private firm. However, Frank warns, a privitized service would probably cut rural delivery and other vital but low-profit services.

Unlike a private corporation, the USPS cannot set its own prices; rates are set by the Postal Rate Commission. Furthermore, Congress ordered the USPS to cut its budget by $2.1 billion in 1987, and in 1988 ordered a 74 percent cut in capital investments, which delayed plans to modernize facilities and mail-handling equipment. Meanwhile, mail volume increased by 5 billion pieces in 1990.

Furthermore, the USPS *is* a unionized bureaucracy. Workers are hired and promoted under a merit system, set up to reform the corrupt spoils system of the 1870s. Today, the average postal worker earns about 47 percent more than a comparable private-sector worker. Personnel costs alone make up 83 percent of the USPS budget.

Nevertheless, Frank, who became postmaster general in 1988, is on record as wanting to trim costs, increase productivity, and improve morale, using skills honed as chairman and CEO of one of the nation's largest thrift institutions.

A major priority is automation. One-third of all mail handling is now automated, with plans to complete automation by 1995. In addition, the USPS is experimenting with bar-coding systems to speed the handling of business mail, which accounts for 75 per-

cent of all mail. Because many mail-handling facilities are antiquated and inefficient, Frank has budgeted an annual $1 billion for new facilities.

Marjorie Stein, program director of operations research for USPS, has hired a private firm to build a computer model to analyze portions of the mail-delivery system. The model has identified situations where airline schedules have made timely deliveries impossible and helped managers assess the benefits of automation. The model is now used at about 20 regional centers, with plans to create a supermodel of the USPS within five years.

To boost employee motivation, the USPS is also initiating discretionary bonuses for divisions that score well on customer survey questionnaires. (The surveys, which sample 750,000 people every year, are also new.)

Even though Federal Express and similar services control 90 percent of the overnight market, the USPS has boosted advertising for its express service and expanded its philatelic (stamp collecting) service. Equally important, Frank is using marketing techniques to teach the public to address mail correctly. (One-third of all mail has some addressing flaw, slowing delivery and increasing costs.)

Postal rates will continue to go up, Frank admits, but over the last two years, the annual increase has dropped from twice the rate of inflation to half the rate of inflation. Nevertheless, he faces an uphill battle. Because labor costs are such a big part of the USPS budget, his success may ultimately depend, not on automation, but on his ability to work with the unions that represent his highly paid workers.

Sources: Janice Castro, "Charging More and Delivering Less," *Time,* March 28, 1988, p. 50; Albert G. Holzinger, "An Optimistic Captain at the Helm," *Nation's Business,* May 1990, p. 25; Jon Van, "Computer Models Make Mail Intricacy Visible," *Chicago Tribune,* July 30, 1990, Sect. 4, pp. 1, 4; Stanley Ziemba. "Postmaster Becoming Taskmaster on Service," *Chicago Tribune,* April 8, 1991, Sect. 4, pp. 1, 5.

Case Questions

1. Analyze the postal service as an application of the classical management theories.

2. Analyze the postal service from a systems viewpoint. How does Frank's management indicate he is aware of the USPS as a system?

3. What other management theories can be seen in Frank's management techniques?

■ NOTES

[1] For an excellent treatment of the process of change in theories, see Thomas S. Kuhn, *The Structure of Scientific Revolutions,* 2nd ed., enlarged (Chicago: University of Chicago Press, 1970). See also Richard G. Brandenberg, "The Usefulness of Management Thought for Management," in Joseph W. McGuire, ed., *Contemporary Management: Issues and Viewpoints* (Englewood Cliffs, N.J.: Prentice Hall, 1974), pp. 99–112.

[2] Much of the discussion in this chapter on the evolution of management theory is based on Claude S. George, Jr., *The History of Management Thought,* 2nd ed. (Englewood Cliffs, N.J.: Prentice Hall, 1972); and Daniel A. Wren, *The Evolution of Management Thought,* 2nd ed. (New York: Wiley, 1979).

[3] An excellent discussion of this evolutionary process appears in Harold J. Leavitt, "Structure, People, and Information Technology: Some Key Ideas and Where They Come From," *Managerial Psychology,* 4th ed. (Chicago: University of Chicago Press, 1978).

[4] Both books, in addition to Taylor's testimony before the Special House Committee, appear in Frederick W. Taylor, *Scientific Management* (New York: Harper & Brothers, 1947). For an assessment of Taylor's impact on contemporary management, see Edwin A. Locke, "The Ideas of Frederick W. Taylor: An Evaluation," *Academy of Management Review* 7, no. 11 (January 1982):14–24. See also Allen C. Bluedorn, Thomas L. Keon, and Nancy M. Carter, "Management History Research: Is Anyone Out There Listening?" in Richard B. Robinson and John A. Pearch, II, eds., *Proceedings of the Academy of Management* (Boston, 1985), pp. 130–133.

[5] Lillian M. Gilbreth, *The Psychology of Management* (New York: Sturgis & Walton, 1914).

[6] Another important contributor to scientific management was Harrington Emerson. See his book *The Twelve Principles of Efficiency,* published in 1913.

[7] For a rich discussion of "rational, economic, social, self-actualizing, and complex man," see Edgar H. Schein, *Organizational Psychology,* 3rd ed. (Englewood Cliffs, N.J.: Prentice Hall, 1980), pp. 52–72 and 93–101.

[8] One observer, reporting on an automobile plant, wrote, "Some assembly-line workers are so turned off, managers report in astonishment, that they just walk away in midshift and don't even come back to get their pay for the time they have worked." See Judson Gooding, "Blue Collar Blues on the Assembly Line," *Fortune,* July 1970, pp. 69–70.

[9] Henri Fayol, *Industrial and General Administration,* J. A. Coubrough, trans. (Geneva: International Management Institute, 1930). Fayol used the word *administration* for what we call *management.*

[10] Max Weber, *The Theory of Social and Economic Organizations,* Talcott Parsons, ed., A. M. Henderson and Parsons, trans. (New York: Free Press, 1947).

[11] See Mary P. Follett, *The New State* (Gloucester, Mass.: Peter Smith, 1918); Henry C. Metcalf and Lyndall Urwick, eds., *Dynamic Administration* (New York: Harper & Brothers, 1941); and L. D. Parker, "Control in Organizational Life: The Contribution of Mary Parker Follett," *Academy of Management Review* 9, no. 4 (October 1984):736–745.

[12] See Chester I. Barnard, *The Functions of the Executive* (Cambridge, Mass.: Harvard University Press, 1938).

[13] For extensive discussions of Mayo's work, see Elton Mayo, *The Human Problems of an Industrial Civilization* (New York: Macmillan, 1953); and F. J. Roethlisberger and W. J. Dickson, *Management and the Worker* (Cambridge, Mass.: Harvard University Press, 1939). Also see Roethlisberger's autobiography, *The Elusive Phenomena,* George F. F. Lombard, ed. (Boston: Division of Research, Graduate School of Business Administration, Harvard University, 1977). Analysis, criticism, and defense of the Hawthorne Studies can be found in George C. Homans, *The Human Group* (New York: Harcourt, Brace, 1950), pp. 48–155; Alex Carey, "The Hawthorne Studies: A Radical Criticism," *American Sociological Review* 32, no. 3 (June 1967); Henry A. Landsberger, *Hawthorne Revisited* (Ithaca, N.Y.: Cornell University Press, 1958); Jon M. Shepard, "On Carey's Radical Criticism of the Hawthorne Studies," *Academy of Management Journal* 14, no. 1 (March 1971):23–32; and Dana Bramel and Ronald Friend, "Hawthorne, the Myth of the Docile Worker, and Class Bias in Psychology," *American Psychologist* 36, no. 8 (August 1981):867–878.

[14] Personal communications with Gary Yunker and a paper by him were particularly helpful in clarifying some of the confusions associated with these experiments. See Gary Yunker, "The Hawthorne Studies: Facts and Myths," *Faculty Working Papers,* Department of Psychology, Jacksonville State University, Summer 1985. One example of the confusions associated with the research focuses on the fact that the Hawthorne effect suffers from many different definitions. Some researchers doubt that it actually exists, and many others feel its power to improve performance is greatly exaggerated. See Berkeley Rice, "The Hawthorne Defect: Persistence of a Flawed Theory," *Psychology Today,* February 1982, pp. 70, 72–74; and John G. Adair, "The Hawthorne Effect: A Reconsideration of the Methodological Artifact," *Journal of Applied Psychology* 69, no. 2 (1984):334–345.

[15] P. Mirvis and E. E. Lawler, "Measuring the Financial Impact of Employee Attitudes," *Journal of Applied Psychology* 62 (1977):1–8.

[16] P. M. Muchinsky, *Psychology Applied to Work* (Homewood, Ill.: Dorsey Press, 1983).

[17] Abraham H. Maslow, *Motivation and Personality* (New York: Harper & Row, 1964).

[18]See Edgar H. Schein, "Behavioral Sciences for Management," and Edwin B. Flippo, "The Underutilization of Behavioral Science by Management," in Joseph W. McGuire, ed., *Contemporary Management: Issues and Viewpoints* (Englewood Cliffs, N.J.: Prentice Hall, 1974), pp. 15–32 and pp. 36–41. See also James A. Lee, "Behavioral Theory vs. Reality," *Harvard Business Review* 49, no. 2 (March–April 1971):20–28 passim; and Jay W. Lorsch, "Making Behavioral Science More Useful," *Harvard Business Review* 57, no. 2 (March–April 1979):171–180.

[19]Larry M. Austin and James R. Burns, *Management Science* (New York: Macmillan, 1985); Robert J. Thierauf, *Management Science: A Model Formulation Approach with Computer Applications* (Columbus, Ohio: Merrill, 1985); and Kenneth R. Baker and Dean H. Kroop, *Management Science: An Introduction to Decision Models* (New York: Wiley, 1985).

[20]The management science approach has been applied to other uses besides industrial problem solving. Jay Forrester and his colleagues, for example, have pioneered attempts to simulate the operations of whole enterprises. He and others have also simulated economic activities of Third World nations and even of the world system as a whole. See Jay W. Forrester, *Industrial Dynamics* (Cambridge, Mass.: MIT Press, 1961), and *World Dynamics,* 2nd ed. (Cambridge, Mass.: MIT Press, 1979); Dennis H. Meadows et al., *The Limits to Growth* (New York: Universe Books, 1972); Dennis H. Meadows, ed., *Alternatives to Growth,* Vol. 1: *A Search for Sustainable Futures* (Cambridge, Mass.: Ballinger, 1977); and Mihajlo Mesarovic and Eduard Pestel, *Mankind at the Turning Point* (New York: Dutton, 1975).

[21]See James R. Miller and Howard Feldman, "Management Science—Theory, Relevance, and Practice in the 1980s," *Interfaces* 13, no. 5 (October 1983):56–60; and Leonard Adelman, "Involving Users in the Development of Decision-Analytic Aids: The Principal Factor in Successful Implementation," *Journal of the Operational Research Society* 33, no. 4 (1982):333–342.

[22]For a discussion of how management science should reorient itself to compete with other approaches, see A. M. Geoffrion, "Can MS/OR Evolve Fast Enough?" *Interfaces* 13, no. 1 (February 1983): 10–25.

[23]For an example of interaction among the various management theories, see Sang M. Lee, Fred Luthans, and David L. Olson, "A Management Science Approach to Contingency Models of Organizational Structure," *Academy of Management Journal* 25, no. 3 (September 1982):553–566.

[24]See Ludwig von Bertalanffy, Carl G. Hempel, Robert E. Bass, and Hans Jonas, "General System Theory: A New Approach to Unity of Science," I–VI, *Human Biology* 23, no. 4 (December 1951):302–361; and Kenneth E. Boulding, "General Systems Theory—The Skeleton of Science," *Management Science* 2, no. 3 (April 1956):197–208.

[25]See Seymour Tilles, "The Manager's Job—A Systems Approach," *Harvard Business Review* 41, no. 1 (January–February 1963):73–81.

[26]Fremont E. Kast and James E. Rosenzweig, "General Systems Theory: Applications for Organization and Management," *Academy of Management Journal* 15, no. 4 (December 1972):447–465. See also Arkalgud Ramaprasad, "On the Definition of Feedback," *Behavioral Science* 28, no. 1 (January 1983): 4–13.

[27]See Fred Luthans, "The Contingency Theory of Management: A Path Out of the Jungle," *Business Horizons* 16, no. 3 (June 1973):62–72; Fred Luthans and Todd I. Stewart, "A General Contingency Theory of Management," *Academy of Management Review* 2, no. 2 (April 1977):181–195; Jon M. Shepard and James G. Hougland, Jr., "Contingency Theory: 'Complex Man' or 'Complex Organization'?" *Academy of Management Review* 3, no. 3 (July 1978):413–427; Fred Luthans and Todd I. Stewart, "The Reality or Illusion of a General Contingency Theory of Management: A Response to the Longenecker and Pringle Critique," *Academy of Management Review* 3, no. 3 (July 1978):683–687; and Jay W. Lorsch, "Making Behavioral Science More Useful," *Harvard Business Review* 52, no. 2 (April 1979):171–180. A recent assessment of contingency theory can be found in Henry L. Tosi, Jr., and John W. Slocum, Jr., "Contingency Theory: Some Suggested Directions," *Journal of Management* 10, no. 1 (1984):9–26.

[28]Among the more outspoken critics of contingency theory are Harold Koontz ("The Management Theory Jungle Revisited") and Justin G. Longenecker and Charles D. Pringle ("The Illusion of Contingency Theory as a General Theory," *Academy of Management Review* 3, no. 3 [July 1978]:679–682).

[29]Joan Woodward, *Industrial Organization* (London: Oxford University Press, 1965).

[30]Tom Burns and G. M. Stalker, *The Management of Innovation* (London: Tavistock, 1961), p. 125.

[31]Thomas J. Peters and Robert H. Waterman, Jr., *In Search of Excellence* (New York: Harper & Row, 1982). The themes from this book are discussed further in Thomas J. Peters and Nancy Austin, *A Passion for Excellence* (New York: Random House, 1985); in Thomas J. Peters, *Thriving on Chaos: Handbook for a Management Revolution* (New York: Alfred A. Knopf, 1987); and in Robert H. Waterman, Jr., *The Renewal Factor: How the Best Get and Keep the Competitive Edge* (New York: Bantam Books, 1987).

[32]Peters, *In Search of Excellence,* p. 51.

[33]Peters, *Thriving on Chaos,* p. 3.

[34]Peter F. Drucker, *Innovation and Entrepreneurship: Practice and Principles* (New York: Harper & Row, 1985), pp. 11, 264.

[35]Peters, *Thriving on Chaos,* pp. 3–4.

[36]Robert J. Waterman, "The Renewal Factor," *Business Week,* September 14, 1987, p. 104.

[37]Peters, *Thriving on Chaos,* p. 22.

[38]See Rosabeth M. Kanter, "The Middle Manager as Innovator," *Harvard Business Review,* July–August 1982, pp. 95–105; "Shaping Corporate Change," *Productivity Brief,* no. 35 (April 1984):2–8; *The Change Masters* (New York: Simon & Schuster, 1983).

[39]William Ouchi, *Theory Z—How American Business Can Meet the Japanese Challenge* (Reading, Mass.: Addison-Wesley, 1981).

CASE ON INTRODUCTION TO MANAGEMENT

THE WOLVERINE FASTENER CO.

The Wolverine Fastener Co. was founded 20 years ago by Roger Gordon and Edwin Andrews in Detroit. Wolverine's early years were relatively unstable, and the company was on the verge of bankruptcy on more than one occasion. By 1983, however, Wolverine had blossomed into one of Michigan's most prosperous manufacturers' representative firms; in addition to many smaller product lines, Wolverine represented a major fastener corporation based in Chicago. The majority of Wolverine's annual orders of $10 million come from Detroit's auto industry, where the manufacture of every automobile requires hundreds of fasteners (screws, bolts, clips, latches, and customized metal and/or plastic connectors).

Both Roger Gordon and Edwin Andrews came from well-to-do Michigan families. Each had attended a Big Ten university, from which he graduated with honors. Soon after their graduation, both men were married in the same year to women who were sisters. Thus, their relationship began as brothers-in-law. About a year later, the two men, both manufacturers' representatives, decided to form a partnership, which they called The Wolverine Fastener Co.

Roger Gordon gave the impression of being a dynamic businessman. Always in a hurry, he consistently tried to squeeze 14 hours of work out of his 10-hour days. This often created a frantic sense of disorganization in the office. He had an uncanny ability to get things done "just under the wire." He was what is often called a "doer," never refusing a potential money-making venture because he lacked the time to give it the attention it deserved. Somehow he managed to get everything done.

Edwin Andrews was Roger's working partner, and they shared equally in its annual profits. The two men made all corporate decisions together, yet each was responsible for his own accounts. Thus, in their day-to-day work they went their own way and seemed quite independent of each other.

Just as the company reached its most prosperous point in 1976, the automobile market began to drop off rapidly. Wolverine soon followed the downward track. After about two years of steadily declining profits, Roger Gordon realized that he must somehow get an edge on the many other vendors competing for the automotive industry's limited business if his company was to survive. Because one of the Big Three automakers (which we will call Genchryford or GCF) accounted for most of the company's orders, he decided to concentrate on gaining an advantage with them.

Roger examined the process by which he obtained orders from the individual fastener buyer at GCF, Robert Jacobs. It had long been GCF's practice to accept only closed quotations (i.e., all quotes were privately submitted and the lowest group got a percentage of the order for that part). Roger knew that if he could find out the exact price, or even the range of the quotations, he would have the advantage he desired. He was sure that the fastener buyer himself would not disclose this type of information. However, Jacobs's secretary, Mary Swoboda, who was responsible for opening all the quotes, seemed a possible source of help. During 1979, Roger began to get to know her better.

Mary Swoboda was a pleasant woman in her mid-20's, unmarried, but with a steady boyfriend. She was very sharp and always eager to take care of any problems that might arise in her area. She was rather plain in appearance, very quiet, and seemed somewhat awed by the size and reputation of GCF. She was from a lower-middle class suburb of Detroit.

Roger Gordon began an extensive but subtle implementation of his "plan," as he told it to me. He started by taking Mary to lunch at frequent intervals. After this became an accepted practice, Roger began to take her out to dinner at posh Detroit establishments. Next he offered her various presents such as paintings and plane rides. (Roger flew his own plane.) The relationship, however, remained purely platonic to the best of my knowledge. Roger told me that whenever he took Mary out to dinner, he invariably included his wife. The Gordons were obviously a happily married couple. Once during the summer of 1983, Roger took me to dinner with Mary and Mrs. Gordon at the Grosse Pointe Country Club, and we all had a cordial time.

The results of this process were remarkable. After a short time, Mary began to tell Roger if his quotes were "warm or cold." That helped, but Roger realized that to maximize his profits he had to know the exact price he must beat. As his program to "win over" Mary Swoboda continued, he eventually realized his goal. Roger could be observed calling Mary late in the afternoon when a quote was due, to get the lowest price of the quotes she had to date. Then he would call Chicago to determine if he could undercut that price. If he found that he could, he would type his quotation and take it over to GCF for submission. Two weeks later he could receive an order for that part, which could amount to as much as $750,000. It is important to note that not every quote he submitted was the lowest because often Wolverine was not able to supply a particular product at a competitive price. As a result, no suspicion ever arose from Roger's practices, as far as I could tell.

I had intended to work for Citicorp in New York between my two MBA years at Tuck School, but a family illness required me to be at home for the summer. So in June 1983 I came to Wolverine Fastener as an assistant to Roger Gordon, who was a close friend of our family and a good friend of mine. My primary responsibility was to handle a number of the company's smaller product accounts, allowing Roger to devote more time and energy to his larger customers, the Big Three automakers. Within a few days of arriving at Wolverine, I realized there was a special relationship between Roger and Mary Swoboda and I understood its importance. During my summer at Wolverine, the number of part orders from GCF more than doubled. Edwin Andrews, Roger's partner, seemed to be well aware of the tremendous help Roger was getting from Mary, and although he never sought her aid himself, he never expressed any concern or objected to what Roger was doing either. Edwin's "mind-your-own-business" approach to Roger's tactics surely played a major role in the company's—and his personal—success.

One Friday afternoon late in August I returned from lunch to find a memo from Roger on my desk. The gist of it was that he was unable to return to the office for the rest of the day and he wanted me to submit a very important quote ("in the rough neighborhood of $125,000") to GCF by four o'clock. As I read on, I discovered that he also expected me to do what he himself did so often before submitting a major quotation: "Call Mary, find out the lowest quote she has received, call Chicago to get their OK for a slightly lower price, then type our quote and deliver it to Mary's office."

When I finished reading the memo, I sat back in my chair and looked out the window. Many different thoughts ran through my head. Was what I had been instructed to do ethical? Fair? I thought about the other vendors that were going to suffer because of the advantage we had. What we were doing, in effect, was cheating the system. If I did carry out my orders, could I be responsible for unethical conduct? I wondered why our system never seemed so bad in the past, but now . . . I also tried to diagnose why Mary Swoboda had chosen to supply Roger Gordon with this important information. Surely other vendors must have tried to get this kind of help from her. Perhaps she was up against it financially and appreciated his many gifts. Maybe she just liked him; after all, he was an extremely likable man. In addition, Roger did not come across as a cutthroat vendor, the way many others did, and Mary seemed to appreciate his manners.

I also thought of what Roger had told me about his arrangement with Mary—that it was not uncommon in business, that it broke no laws even if it violated GCF standard practice, and that if he hadn't "gotten the edge," a competitor would have. "After all," he told me one day, "I have had a lot of experience, and I really worked to get this advantage in bidding. The system owed that to me."

There I was, an MBA candidate who thought of himself as a responsible, professional person, and I was unsure what to do in a fairly simple summer job. The irony was that I felt confident discussing much more important ethical cases in my MBA courses. Yet I was really paralyzed by the dilemma before me. What should I do? I didn't have much time to think.

Source: This case was written by Lance Edson while he was a student at The Amos Tuck School of Business Administration, Dartmouth College, based on a summer employment experience with The Wolverine Fastener Co. Names have been disguised. © 1984.

Case Questions

1. What are the managerial issues in this case?
2. Why is ethics important in the day-to-day management of organizations?
3. What is the relationship between a company like Wolverine and the auto industry?
4. What should the casewriter do?

CHAPTER THREE

THE EXTERNAL ENVIRONMENT OF ORGANIZATIONS

Upon completing this chapter, you should be able to:

1. Explain the importance of the external environment.

2. List and discuss the elements of the direct-action and indirect-action environments.

3. Identify the stakeholders of an organization.

4. Explain how organizations can use stakeholder networks and coalitions to influence stakeholders.

5. Discuss the four variables that make up the indirect-action environment.

6. Identify examples of how recent changes in social variables have affected organizations.

7. Explain the difference between structural and cyclical economic change and what each means for organizations.

8. Discuss the way technology develops and what its development means for competition.

9. Give examples of some of the challenges and opportunities posed by the increase in international trade.

10. Summarize key theories of total-organization environment.

11. Explain some techniques managers can use to influence, monitor, and adjust to the external environment.

The Hennepin County Government Center, Minneapolis. John Warnecke and Associates.
Photo courtesy of the Hennepin County Public Affairs Dept.

ILLUSTRATIVE CASE STUDY

INTRODUCTION

Image and Imaging Problems at Eastman Kodak

Until the mid-1970s, the name *Kodak* was synonymous with the yellow boxes in which it marketed its products—boxes symbolizing quality film, simple but excellent cameras for amateur photographers, and continued profits for investors. The company was known for its determined self-reliance. (It even maintained a herd of cattle to provide gelatin for its film process.) As an employer, Kodak was a lifetime safe bet for recent high-school and college graduates, and its employees had the sort of company loyalty commonly associated with Japanese companies today. There were no strikes in the U.S. plants, and a familylike corporate culture—generous, hierarchical, conservative, fiscally sound—pervaded the company and spun off benefits for the entire Rochester, New York, community. But then the world changed very quickly for Kodak.

Kodak had been slow to respond to new markets in its business. Customer tastes had shifted from cheap but dependable standard products, like the familiar Brownie or instamatic camera, to sophisticated SLRs and feature-loaded instant cameras. The electronics revolution made many more options available to amateur photographers and radically altered the technology of the industry. The decline in the use of silver halide film and subsequent popularity of electronic image processes made Kodak aware of the profitability of the instant camera. But when Kodak ventured into the instant camera market, it found itself involved in an embarrassing legal battle with Polaroid over patents; on January 9, 1986, Kodak lost the court battle, and a week later laid off 500 employees.

At the same time, Kodak encountered serious foreign competition in both cameras and film. While Kodak still holds the lion's share of the U.S. color film market, one Japanese firm, Fuji, is moving up fast in quality and market share. In addition, high-end sophisticated equipment manufacturers like Nikon and Minolta came out with "point and shoot" cameras for the amateur market as soon as electronic advances made these developments possible.

In light of these troubles, Kodak has reorganized and trimmed its work force—by some 12,000

A Major Kodak Market. After a long period of being slow to respond to changing market conditions, Kodak rushed the disposable Fling camera to market in 1987, beating rival Fuji by a matter of hours.

people worldwide—and may have to close down facilities worth $230 million. Its managers have begun to pay more attention to the external environment. They have speeded up their product-development processes and have acquired some innovative companies. They have also begun to form partnerships in some businesses and have ventured into biotechnology and electronic publishing.

Sources: Subatra N. Chakravarty and Ruth Simon, "Has the World Passed Kodak By?" *Forbes,* November 5, 1984, pp. 184–192; Barbara Buell, "Kodak Is Trying to Break Out of Its Shell," *Business Week,* June 10, 1985, pp. 92–95; William B. Glaberson, Marilyn A. Harris, and James R. Norman, "Polaroid vs. Kodak: The Decisive Round," *Business Week,* January 13, 1986, p. 37; Alex Taylor III, "Kodak Scrambles to Refocus," *Fortune,* March 3, 1986, pp. 34–39; Leslie Helm and James Hurlock, "Kicking the Single-Product Habit at Kodak," *Business Week,* December 1, 1986, pp. 36–37.

*L*ike Kodak, many organizations have been caught off-guard by changes in the external environment. Indeed, an organization's survival often depends on its skill in adapting to the changes in the world around it. The purpose of this chapter is to analyze these changes and provide a framework for understanding them. Then, in Parts Three to Six, we will show how management concepts and practices can help organizations survive and even prosper despite changing environments.

■ THE EXTERNAL ENVIRONMENT AND ITS IMPORTANCE

If you look back over the Chapter 2 discussion of the classical, behavioral, and quantitative schools of management, you will see that they focused on events *within* the organization: how many subordinates managers should have, why managers should improve working conditions, and how they could use new technology in decision making. But in their concern with the *internal environment* of organizations, these theorists tended to downplay the importance of the *external environment.* They could do this because most organizations in the first half of this century were operating in a relatively stable and predictable environment.

The Challenge of Change

Today the external environment is undergoing continuous, rapid changes that are having far-reaching effects on organizations and their management strategies. Asian and European firms have emerged as strong competitors in a global marketplace; rapid and widespread technological change has become the norm. Indeed, new information-processing technologies have made it possible to eliminate thousands of middle-management jobs. In addition, the roles of the private and public sector are less clearcut; even in the United States, a stronghold of capitalism, the government intervened to save Chrysler from bankruptcy and exempted a joint research and development consortium from antitrust laws. Customer lifestyles, employee demographics, and government regulations are also in flux.

At the same time, the standards by which managers are judged have changed. Once it was enough for organizations to maximize profits; managers were judged by how well they furthered the interests of *stockholders.* Now organizations must hold themselves responsible not only to stockholders but also to the larger and more varied community of *stakeholders*—those groups or individuals who are affected directly or indirectly by the organization's pursuit of its goals.[1]

Today, more than ever, managers are under increasing pressure to anticipate and respond to this host of external forces and to think globally. As a result, many are using "strategic thinking" to respond to and capitalize on the rapidly changing environment. At R.R. Donnelley, one of the nation's largest printers, CEO John Walter sees the company as competing with all other mediums of communication. As a result, he has invested heavily in technology and overseas expansion, so that computer manuals can be printed simultaneously in several countries; on paper, magnetic disk, or CD; or even customized for certain users. "Probably 50 percent of our revenues by 1995 or 2000," he says, "will come from businesses that we weren't in ten years ago."[2]

The External Environment: An Overview

To understand the external environment and its effects on organizations, we must borrow some concepts from systems theory. As we saw in the previous chapter, one of the basic assumptions of systems theory is that organizations are neither self-sufficient nor self-contained. Rather, they exchange resources with and are dependent

external environment
All elements outside an organization that are relevant to its operation; includes direct-action and indirect-action elements.

inputs Resources from the environment, such as raw materials and labor, that may enter any organizational system.

outputs Transformed inputs that are returned to the external environment as products or services.

direct-action elements Elements of the environment that directly influence an organization's activities.

indirect-action elements Elements of the external environment that affect the climate in which an organization's activities take place, but do not affect the organization directly.

on the **external environment,** defined as all elements outside an organization that are relevant to its operation. Thus organizations take **inputs** (raw materials, money, labor, and energy) from the external environment, transform them into products or services, and then send them back as **outputs** to the external environment.

The external environment has both **direct-action** and **indirect-action elements.**[3] Stakeholders directly influence an organization, and so are elements of the direct-action environment. Some stakeholders, such as employees and shareholders, are considered *internal stakeholders,* while others, such as customers and competitors, are considered *external stakeholders.* Indirect-action elements, such as the technology, economy, and politics of a society, affect the climate in which an organization operates and have the potential to become direct-action elements. This happened in the United States, for example, when changes in public expectations concerning corporate behavior led to the creation of new governmental regulatory agencies. Direct-action elements may also disappear, as happened in the late 1970s and early 1980s, when budget pressures and public disenchantment with regulatory efforts led to the closing or shrinking of some government agencies.

An element's practical impact on an organization determines whether it is a stakeholder, and thus a part of the organization's direct-action environment. The same element may have different relationships with different organizations. For example, labor unions may have only a small, indirect impact on a nonunionized industry, such as book publishing, but a major and direct impact on a heavily unionized industry, such as automobile manufacturing. Labor unions would thus be stakeholders of an automaker but not of a book publisher. Figure 3-1 outlines an organization's environmental picture and shows the influence of both direct- and indirect-action elements. The roles of each type of element are discussed in the next two sections.

FIGURE 3-1 The Direct-Action and Indirect-Action Environments of an Organization

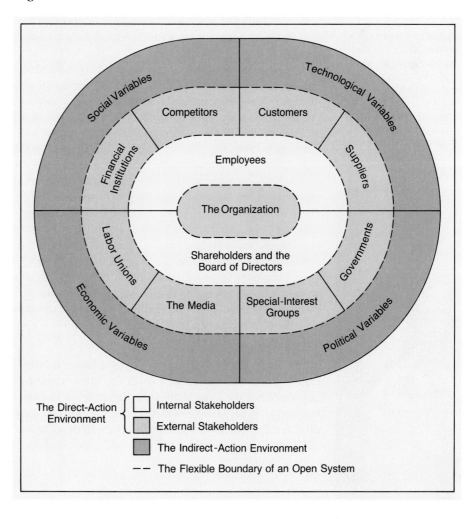

■ ELEMENTS OF THE DIRECT-ACTION ENVIRONMENT

The direct-action environment is made up of **stakeholders**, individuals or groups who are directly or indirectly affected by an organization's pursuit of its goals. Stakeholders fall into two categories. **External stakeholders** include such groups as unions, suppliers, competitors, customers, special-interest groups, and government agencies. **Internal stakeholders** include employees, shareholders, and the board of directors.

Before we discuss these two categories, we must stress one major point: The roles stakeholders play may *change* as organizational environments *evolve* and *develop*. Managers must be sensitive to this fact when they are tracing the various influences on an organization's behavior and recommending responses to environmental change. The importance of being sensitive to changes in the direct-action environment is shown in the Ethics in Management box, "Ethics and Ethnicity in Global Merchandising."

Both the internal and external stakeholder groups of most organizations have changed substantially over the past few years. In the rest of this section, we will outline the stake of each group and how it has shifted.

External Stakeholders

External stakeholders, which affect an organization's activities from outside the organization, include customers, suppliers, governments, special-interest groups, the media, labor unions, financial institutions, and competitors.

CUSTOMERS. Customers exchange resources, usually in the form of money, for an organization's products and services. A customer may be an institution, such as a school, hospital, or government agency; or another firm, such as a contractor, distributor, or manufacturer; or an individual. Selling tactics vary according to customer and market situations. Usually, a marketing manager analyzes the potential customers and market conditions and directs a marketing campaign based on that analysis.

The customer market may be highly competitive, with large numbers of potential buyers and sellers seeking the most congenial arrangements. In such markets, managers must be especially concerned about price, quality, service, and product availability if they want to keep old customers and attract new ones.

In recent years, as foreign firms have challenged the dominance of American business by offering customers more choices and setting new standards of quality, competition has begun to change customer relationships. For example, when Japanese television manufacturers found it difficult to set up service networks for their products in the United States, they responded by making televisions that were less likely to malfunction. Before, the customers' relationship with a television manufacturer was cemented by the local dealer and repair shop. Now customers are able to buy televisions at large discount retailers, without having to worry about service. A similar pattern has emerged in the U.S. auto industry.

Thanks to improved communications and transportation, people around the globe are now exposed to the latest and best products. As a result people in different countries have become potential customers for the same goods.[4] Manufacturers can now think in terms of a world car, for example, or a worldwide computer networking system.

SUPPLIERS. Every organization appropriates inputs—raw materials, services, energy, equipment, and labor—from the environment and uses them to produce its output. What the organization brings in from the environment—and what it *does* with what it brings in—will determine both the quality and the price of its final product. Every organization is therefore dependent upon suppliers of materials and

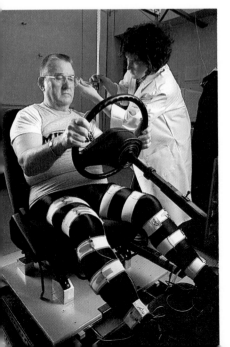

Taking the Customer's Measure. Because older drivers favor larger cars and safety features, Ford Motor Co. used tips from a "mature-driver's advisory committee" plus physical measurements to be sure Ford Taurus controls could be operated safely by drivers with arthritis.

Ethics and Ethnicity in Global Merchandising

After nearly two years of research and testing, Colgate-Palmolive Co. is still trying to satisfy critics of its Darkie toothpaste brand amid renewed charges that it's moving too slowly to jettison the "racist stereotype" of the Asian-marketed product.

Colgate has tried to find a way to quiet American critics of the product—whose logo is a grinning, top-hatted blackface minstrel—while sustaining the 60-year-old brand's appeal to Asians. But members of the Interfaith Center for Corporate Responsibility, a nonprofit New York organization of more than 240 church groups, remain dissatisfied with the pace of Colgate's efforts.

"Most people cannot believe . . . this racist stereotype is still in existence anywhere," says Dara Demmings, an Interfaith Center executive, who charges the company is dragging its feet.

Stung by such criticisms, Colgate began market research on new versions of Darkie, in which it acquired an interest when it bought a 50 percent stake in Darkie's maker, Hong Kong-based Hawley & Hazel Chemical Co., in 1985. "We've done an enormous amount of work on the logo, but it continues to be a problem," says Gavin Anderson, director of executive services for Colgate. "We thought the solution would be a lot easier," he adds. "Darkie is so ingrained in the culture, particularly in Taiwan."

The flap began when an American in Thailand sent a Darkie sample to the Interfaith Center, which has targeted other companies in the past for advertising or product packages its members considered racist or sexist. In Colgate's case, the Interfaith Center, the School Sisters of St. Francis (an order of nuns), and other religious shareholders complained.

Darkie is sold in Hong Kong, Taiwan, Malaysia, Thailand, and Singapore. Mr. Anderson says Hawley's Chinese founder chose the name after he traveled to the United States in the 1920s "and literally fell in love with Al Jolson." Darkie became a big seller and eventually an archrival of Colgate. By acquiring an interest, Colgate ended the fight and gained a new market in Taiwan, but made themselves the target of critics in this country. In choosing to sustain a brand name and packaging that perpetuate racial stereotyping and ethnic condescension, critics hold, Colgate is violating its social responsibility to both stakeholders and shareholders.

Meanwhile, critics say they're particularly disturbed that Colgate's Far Eastern partner is launching a new toothpaste in Japan, where Darkie has never had a presence. The tube, labeled "Mouth Jazz," also bears the logo of a smiling, top-hatted blackface. Though the Interfaith Center was frustrated by Colgate's pace, Ms. Demmings and the center's director, Timothy Smith, did praise Colgate Chairman Reuben Mark and other Colgate executives for their "moral sensitivity to the issue."

The protest has challenged New York-based Colgate, which has been forced to ask Hawley to change product packaging Asians apparently don't find offensive in order to satisfy American concerns. Colgate says the issue is further complicated by research showing that Asian consumers associate the logo with nothing more derogatory than clean white teeth. "We were concerned about the image all along, but after research we saw no racial connotations at all for those who buy it," says Mr. Anderson.

Tensions resurfaced when more than a year passed and Colgate still had not changed its Darkie logo. Several coalitions developed to protest the delay. In particular, Congresswoman Cardiss Collins (D., Ill.) is threatening to spearhead an American boycott of all Colgate products. This threat is worrisome because Colgate is the brand leader among blacks in the United States. Reuben Mark, the president and chairman of Colgate, has been in contact with Collins and promises to speed up the process of change.

Source: Based on Ann Hagedorn, "Colgate Still Seeking to Placate Critics of Its Darkie Brand," *The Wall Street Journal,* April 18, 1988, pp. 36–37; and Leon E. Wynter, "Business and Race," *The Wall Street Journal,* March 29, 1990, p. B1. Reprinted by permission of *The Wall Street Journal.* Copyright © 1988, 1990 Dow Jones & Company, Inc. All Rights Reserved Worldwide.

labor, and will try to take advantage of competition among suppliers to obtain lower prices, better-quality work, and faster deliveries.

Today, as organizations look overseas for more and more of their raw materials, their relationships with suppliers have changed, sometimes dramatically. For example, political considerations can be as important as those of price and quality. Witness the strategy used by the OPEC nations to quadruple the price of oil in 1973–1974, and then double it in 1979–1980.[5] From a manager's standpoint, the power in the relationship has shifted irrevocably from the oil refiners to the petroleum-exporting nations—that is, to the suppliers. This is a good example of the environmental complexity facing today's manager: Managers not only have to know which organizations affect them *directly,* but which organizations affect the organizations affecting them!

Advances in inventory control and information processing have also changed supplier relationships. Under the conventional system, the manufacturer was usually responsible for all of the inventory necessary for production capability. Today, however, some companies keep zero inventory, relying on several "just in time" deliveries each day. Suppliers such as Baxter Healthcare Corporation have used new information technology to put computer terminals on the customer's premises so that the customer can directly order a product whenever it is needed. Regular customers of Emery Air Freight receive personal computer systems that not only weigh packages, calculate charges, and generate air bills, but also consolidate shipments, give the customers a direct link to Emery's computer tracking system, and generate management reports about their shipping activity.

Finally, we should note the increasingly important role played by a particular group of suppliers called *vendors.* Vendors supply materials and services necessary to an organization's specific production activities (for example, parts, either finished or ready for assembly) or general operations. A company that produces airplanes will contract with a vendor that specializes in the design and production of guidance systems and another that specializes in flying-control systems. Automobile manufacturers rely on vendors for such items as windshields and tires. Purchasing managers must develop firm relationships with vendors and maintain constant, careful control over those relationships. Shortages, untimely deliveries, and fluctuating prices are only a few of the variables that can develop in an organization's relationship with its vendors.

HERE'S AN EXAMPLE
OSHA is becoming tougher. In the last 18 months, it has proposed a standard requiring workers to wear seatbelts if they drive as part of their jobs, prepared guidelines to prevent repetitive-motion disorders, proposed a rule to protect health-care workers from exposure to infectious diseases such as hepatitis B and AIDS, and levied large fines on companies for alleged violations of its rules. (*Business Week,* 8/20/90, p. 57)

GOVERNMENT. The doctrine of laissez-faire, developed in the eighteenth century, holds that government should exert no direct effects on business, but should limit itself to preserving law and order, allowing the free market to shape the economy. By the beginning of the twentieth century, however, abuses of business power led the U.S. government to take on the role of "watchdog," regulating organizations to protect the public interest and ensure adherence to free-market principles. As Exhibit 3-1 shows, Congress has passed many laws creating regulatory agencies, which establish and enforce the ground rules within which businesses must operate. In addition, court decisions have played a major role in shaping the strategies and policies of the modern business organization. State and local governments, too, have assumed the role of watchdog and passed laws concerning the operation of businesses within their boundaries.

The scope of government intervention in the economy has expanded since World War II. And as government intervention has grown, it has become increasingly controversial. On the one hand, it promises genuine social benefits, such as cleaner air and water, safer automobiles, and a general increase in the standard of living; it can also be argued that regulation benefits and protects the regulated industries themselves. On the other hand, regulation is costly and may inhibit free enterprise.

This debate became even more heated when the Reagan and Bush administrations began to reform regulatory law in the 1980s, claiming that deregulation would result in savings of $150 billion by 1990.[6] Supporters argued that regulation did not always achieve its goal and that free enterprise could do the job more cost-effectively[7]; opponents claimed that deregulation was a return to the law of the jungle.[8]

Whatever the merits of regulation as a specific government policy, managers must deal with a complex web of local, state, federal, foreign, and international

COORDINATED RESOURCE

Use Transparency 11, Business–Government Relationships in the United States.

EXHIBIT 3-1 Major Federal Regulatory Agencies

❏ *Consumer Product Safety Commission* Establishes and enforces federal safety standards for the content, construction, and performance of thousands of manufactured goods.

❏ *Environmental Protection Agency* Establishes and enforces federal standards for environmental protection, especially from industrial pollution.

❏ *Equal Employment Opportunity Commission* Administers and enforces Title VIII (the fair employment practices section) of the Civil Rights Act of 1964 and the Equal Employment Opportunity Act of 1972.

❏ *Federal Aviation Administration* Regulates and promotes air transportation safety; sets standards for the operation of airports and the licensing of pilots.

❏ *Federal Communications Commission* Regulates interstate and foreign communication by radio, television, telegraph, and telephone.

❏ *Federal Deposit Insurance Corporation* Insures bank deposits; has authority to examine bank practices and approve bank mergers.

❏ *Federal Reserve System* Regulates the nation's banking system; manages the nation's money supply.

❏ *Federal Trade Commission* Ensures free and fair competition in the economy and protects consumers from unfair or deceptive practices.

❏ *Food and Drug Administration* Administers federal laws regarding food purity, the safety and effectiveness of drugs and medical devices, the safety of cosmetics, and the safety and honesty of packaging.

❏ *Interstate Commerce Commission* Enforces federal laws concerning the transportation of goods and people across state lines.

❏ *National Labor Relations Board* Prevents or corrects unfair labor practices by either employers or unions.

❏ *Nuclear Regulatory Commission* Licenses and regulates the design, construction, and operation of nonmilitary nuclear facilities.

❏ *Occupational Safety and Health Administration* Develops and enforces federal standards and regulations ensuring safe and healthful working conditions.

❏ *Securities and Exchange Commission* Administers federal laws concerning the buying and selling of securities.

governments, each with the potential to affect an organization through legislative initiatives, judicial action, and executive regulation. (See Fig. 3-2.) For example, they must cope with contradictory regulations by different federal agencies. They also have to understand the working of foreign governments, which may be deliberately placing obstacles in their path to protect domestic organizations. They must deal with conflicting state laws, such as the tax and packaging requirements for beer. They have to fight product-liability, equal-opportunity, and antitrust suits in court. They must weigh state incentive plans when deciding on plant locations and plant closings. They even have to cope with citizen initiatives such as bottle deposit laws. Obviously, the cumulative effect of all this governmental activity is enormous.

Governments also act to aid and protect industries. For example, in 1980, the federal government bailed out Chrysler Corporation by guaranteeing its loans. Shortly thereafter, the government exempted a number of computer manufacturers from antitrust laws to allow them to perform joint research and development, and thereby increase their ability to compete with the Japanese. In Japan, of course, the Ministry of International Trade and Industry actively assists some industries.

SPECIAL-INTEREST GROUPS. "Special-interest groups" (SIGs) use the political process to further their position on some particular issue such as gun control, abortion, or prayer in the public schools. Managers can never be sure that an ad hoc group will not form to oppose the company on some issue—selling nonstandard infant formula in the Third World, for example, or investing in South Africa.

While special-interest politics is hardly a new phenomenon, modern communications technology and election financing have allowed SIGs to flourish in our time.[9] The media can give such groups instant national attention, and the political action committees (PACs) of the groups use campaign contributions to influence

CLASS COMMENT

U.S. companies are spending $1 billion a year to protect top executives and their families from terrorists and other attackers. (*Fortune*, 12/31/90, p. 88ff.)

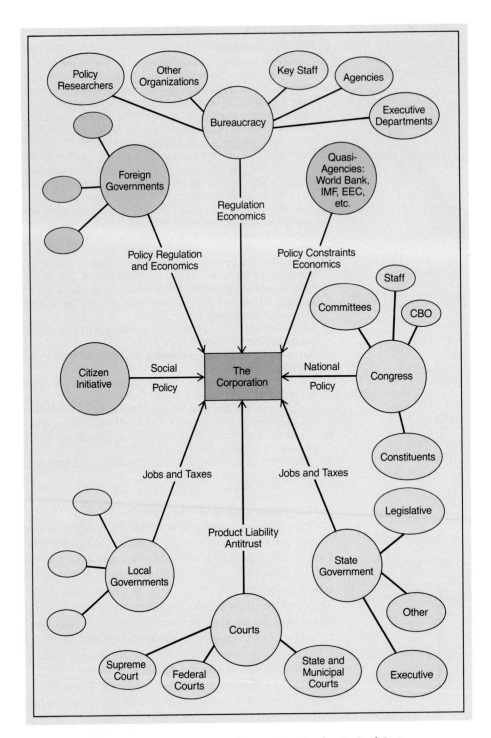

FIGURE 3-2 Business-Government Relationships in the United States

Source: R. Edward Freeman, *Strategic Management: A Stakeholder Approach* (Boston: Pitman, 1984), p. 15. Copyright 1984 by R. Edward Freeman.

legislators.[10] Managers must take both present and future special-interest groups into account when setting organizational strategy. Among the most important special-interest groups are *consumer advocates* and *environmentalists*.

The modern consumer movement dates from the early 1960s, with President Kennedy's announcement of a "Consumer Bill of Rights" and Ralph Nader's crusade against General Motors' Corvair. While government agencies became less of a factor in the Reagan era, consumer advocates are still powerful.

COORDINATED RESOURCE

See Study Guide Problem Exercise 3, "The Environment."

Hirschmann's model of exit, voice, and loyalty provides a framework for understanding the consumer movement.[11] Dissatisfied customers can choose either to *exit*—that is, to take their business elsewhere—or to *voice* their complaints; the customers' *loyalty* to the organization will determine which option is used. Exit, of course, can cripple an organization by removing its customer base without giving managers time to make changes. Voice, in contrast, is a political strategy designed to seek redress for grievance. Filing lawsuits requesting the intervention of a regulatory agency and lobbying a lawmaking body are examples of the exercise of voice.

In its use of voice, the consumer movement can be constructive rather than adversarial. Recognizing the costs of government intervention, consumer leaders often prefer negotiation, while progressive managers welcome voice as an opportunity to understand customer needs and to learn about changes in the marketplace. In fact, many successful companies, such as Procter & Gamble, make handling consumer complaints a high priority. AT&T has even formed consumer advisory panels (CAPs) to gain an understanding of consumer reactions to proposed changes in rates, products, and services.

The environmentalist movement also dates from the 1960s, when the public became aware of the threat some new technologies posed to the environment. The first national debate over the costs and benefits of a particular technology was inspired by the building of the supersonic transport (SST), a commercial aircraft designed to fly routinely faster than the speed of sound. Activists attacked the project as wasteful and argued that the sonic boom generated by SST aircraft would harm the ozone layer and the oceans. These and other environmental concerns led to the passage of the Clean Air and Water Acts and to the creation of the Environmental Protection Agency.

Not surprisingly, environmental regulations have imposed extra burdens on business. Emissions standards, for example, required the development of the catalytic converter as part of the automotive exhaust system, reduced engine performance by eliminating the use of leaded gasoline, and, of course, added to the overall purchase price of a car. In the chemical industry, the cleanup costs for generations of neglect have become staggering. Still, managers have no choice but to take into account the current climate of broad and genuine concern for the environment.

MEDIA. The economy and business activity have always been covered by the media, since these topics affect so many people. Today, though, mass communications allow increasingly extensive and sophisticated coverage, ranging from general news reports to feature articles to in-depth investigative exposés. The coverage is also more immediate, due to the increasing use of communication satellites. Consider Bhopal, India. This was the site of a 1984 industrial accident at a Union Carbide plant, which released clouds of poisonous gas over a poor neighborhood. The nightly news carried same-day coverage of the accident and its victims, making it much more than a mere news story about one company's safety policies in a remote part of the world. (See the Illustrative Case Study for Chapter 18.)

Today most large organizations realize they live in a fishbowl, where every action may be the subject of media scrutiny. To help them communicate with both internal and external audiences, they have developed sophisticated public relations and marketing departments. In addition, executives who regularly deal with the media often seek professional coaching, with the goal of presenting information and opinions clearly and effectively. United Airlines, for example, holds regular drills to prepare all employees—from emergency workers to media relations workers—to deal effectively with the aftermath of an airplane crash.

LABOR UNIONS. Personnel specialists generally deal with an organization's labor supply, sometimes supplemented by other managers with specific hiring and negotiating responsibilities. They use multiple channels to locate workers with the various skills and experience the organization needs. When an organization employs labor

COORDINATED RESOURCE
See Samaras Case 1.3, "As The Environment Turns."

HERE'S AN EXAMPLE
Recycling is becoming big business. For example, Eastman Kodak rounds up used disposable cameras, like the Kodak Fling 35, from photo processors and reuses them in new cameras. (*Fortune*, 8/13/90, p. 81ff.)

HERE'S AN EXAMPLE
Procter & Gamble has started shipping eight laundry and detergent products, including Spic 'n Span and Downy fabric softener, in plastic bottles recycled from milk jugs and soda bottles. (*Fortune*, 8/13/90, p. 81ff.)

Increasing Media Coverage. Television shows like ABC's "Nightline," hosted by Ted Koppel, reflect the public's increased interest in business activities.

collective bargaining
The process of negotiating and administering agreements between labor and management concerning wages, working conditions, and other aspects of the work environment.

union members, union and management normally engage in some form of **collective bargaining** to negotiate wages, working conditions, hours, and so on.

There have been dramatic changes in labor relations in recent decades. Both personnel and union management have been professionalized. Also, employers generally accept the collective bargaining process and cooperate with the unions to increase worker responsibility and participation. The sit-down strikes and violence that so often characterized the unions' early days are for the most part over. Instead, unions urge stock-ownership, profit-sharing, and gain-sharing programs that give the workers a stake in the organization, and quality-of-worklife programs that give them more control over what they do and how they do it.[12]

THOUGHT PROVOKER
More than 18,000 U.S. companies filed for Chapter 11 bankruptcy reorganization in 1989, and an estimated 20,500 in 1990. (*Fortune*, 2/11/91, p. 13)

FINANCIAL INSTITUTIONS. Organizations depend on a variety of financial institutions, including commercial banks, investment banks, and insurance companies, to supply funds for maintaining and expanding their activities. Both new and well-established organizations may rely on short-term loans to finance current operations and on long-term loans to build new facilities or acquire new equipment. Because effective working relationships with financial institutions are so vitally important, establishing and maintaining such relationships are normally the joint responsibility of the chief financial officer and the chief operating officer of the organization. That responsibility has been made considerably harder by the enormous changes that have taken place in the financial industry.

One change is that large full-service investment houses are replacing older partnership arrangements. For example, to broaden its financial services, American Express acquired international and investment banks, insurance companies, and mutual funds in the 1980s. Recent insider-trading charges against investment bankers caused turmoil in the industry, as did the 1987 stock market crash—which was linked in part to sophisticated computer trading programs. Similarly, arbitrage departments fueled the takeover and merger trend of the 1980s, and there are growing linkages among world stock and money markets. Moreover, deregulation of the banking industry is increasing competition at the same time that many banks have been weakened by loan failures here and abroad.

COMPETITORS. To increase its share of the market, a firm must take advantage of one of two opportunities: (1) it must gain additional customers, either by garnering a greater market share or by finding ways to increase the size of the market itself; or (2) it must beat its competitors in entering and exploiting an expanding market. In either case, the firm must analyze the competition and establish a clearly defined marketing strategy in order to provide superior customer satisfaction.[13]

Airline companies such as Eastern, American, Piedmont, TWA, and their foreign counterparts are clearly competitors in the American air-carrier market. But competition can also come from organizations that provide substitute products or services. In the northeast corridor, for example, Amtrak metroliners compete with airlines for intercity shuttling service. The world petroleum crisis that started in the 1970s drew attention to the competitive interrelationships in the energy industry. Although Texaco, Mobil, and Exxon compete against one another in the sale of petroleum, they share the common problem of competition from the coal, nuclear, solar, and geothermal industries, all of which provide energy-producing substitutes.

HERE'S AN EXAMPLE
From a $25 million start in 1985, laptop computers carved out a $6.4 billion market in 1989. The figure reached $8.4 billion in 1990. (*U.S. News & World Report,* 12/24/90, p. 46ff.)

Sometimes competition is limited. In an oligopolistic market, where relatively few sellers confront large numbers of buyers, the sellers may informally divide the market up among themselves and set prices. In a monopolistic market, every customer must buy from one available source, such as an electric utility. Sometimes a firm enjoys a temporary monopoly, as Xerox did when it introduced the electrostatic copier. (Monopolies, of course, are subject to government regulation.)

In recent years, the competition for U.S. organizations has broadened to include foreign firms. In the 1950s, "Made in Japan" meant "junk" or "cheap"; by the 1980s, it had become a hallmark of quality. The success of Japanese products, rang-

An American Dilemma. After years of neglecting consumer electronics, American managers find themselves unable to meet the needs of shoppers like Teamsters member Phil Gaspers (left), who wanted to buy an American-made camcorder but bought a Japanese model after Highland Superstore's Bret Lee (right) told him no United States company makes camcorders.

ing from cars to cameras, has been enormous. Many products, such as VCRs, are not even made in the United States today, and there is competition from abroad in almost every "U.S.-dominant" industry.

Foreign competition poses a special problem. As long as all significant competition is domestic, everyone must play by the same rules. Each competitor bears the burdens and shares the benefits of the same government, the same fickle consumer population, and the same special-interest groups. Firms within an industry can implicitly or explicitly coordinate their responses to various issues, and theoretically no one is at a competitive disadvantage. Not only does foreign competition upset this balance, but it is much more difficult to analyze because that entails learning about another culture.

COORDINATED RESOURCE
Use Transparency 12, Stakeholder Map of a Major Oil Company in the 1980s.

OTHER STAKEHOLDER GROUPS. Each individual organization will have a host of different stakeholders. For instance, a hospital will have to consider the American Hospital Association, groups of doctors, nurses, and other caregivers, and, of course, patients. Every organization will have a particular stakeholder map that will in essence be a picture of the direct-action component of its external environment. Figure 3-3 is the stakeholder map for one organization, a hypothetical "major oil company."

Internal Stakeholders

Even though, strictly speaking, internal stakeholders are not part of the *organization's* environment, they are a part of the environment for which an *individual manager* is responsible. While we will return to these stakeholders in other chapters, it is worth spending a few minutes here to complete the stakeholder picture.

COORDINATED RESOURCE
See DuBose Reading #30, "The 1995 Labor Force: A Second Look."

EMPLOYEES. The nature of the work force is changing in most organizations, partly because of demographic factors. The so-called baby-boom generation is getting

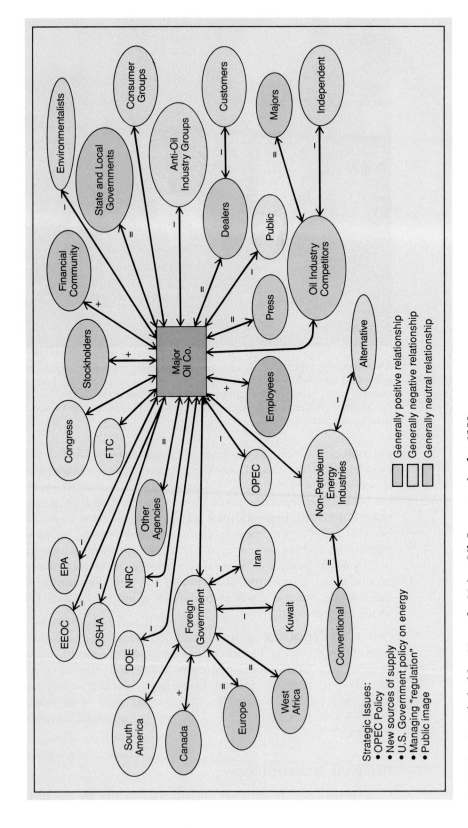

FIGURE 3-3 Stakeholder Map of a Major Oil Company in the 1980s

Strategic Issues:
• OPEC Policy
• New sources of supply
• U.S. Government policy on energy
• Managing "regulation"
• Public image

Generally positive relationship

Generally negative relationship

Generally neutral relationship

older, and the declining birth rate means that the United States will soon face a labor shortage. At the same time, the skills needed by employees are changing. As companies find it necessary to experiment with quality programs, team approaches, and self-managed work groups, they need employees who are better educated and more flexible.

Employee involvement paid off at an AMAX coal mine when the miners, not the engineers, thought of a way to keep the main operating face of the mine open at moderate expense. The miners also were able to reclaim cast-off equipment and make it among the best in the company's inventory.[14]

SHAREHOLDERS AND BOARDS OF DIRECTORS. The governing structure of large public corporations allows shareholders to influence a company by exercising their voting rights. Traditionally, however, shareholders have been interested primarily in the return on their investment and have left the actual operation of the organization to its managers.

In recent years, however, certain groups of social activists have begun purchasing small quantities of stock for the purpose of forcing votes on controversial issues at annual corporate meetings.[15] Ralph Nader pioneered the technique in 1969, when he launched "Campaign GM," whereby an ad hoc group bought two shares of General Motors stock with the intention of waging a proxy fight on social and business issues, including the need for public transportation, the rights of women and minorities, product design for safety, and emissions control.[16] A Securities and Exchange Commission ruling of 1983 made it more difficult to carry out this particular tactic,[17] but the tactic of buying up shares to seize control of entire companies continues to be common business policy. Although mergers and hostile takeovers are often spurred by the legitimate need to reorganize American manufacturing, they involve large expenditures of capital that are usually justified by cutting back operations and liquidating assets. In the 1980s, many managers were on the defensive; sometimes they harmed the long-term health of their organizations in their efforts to keep profits and stock prices up so as to discourage takeover attempts.[18]

Moreover, direct ownership of stocks by individuals is on the decline; individuals are now more likely to hold shares through investments in mutual funds, contributions to retirement plans, and membership in company pension plans. These large blocks of shares are managed by professionals who emphasize financial performance, putting greater pressure on managers to produce short-term results.

Finally, political pressures during the 1970s forced organizations to include more outsiders on their boards of directors. In fact, to be listed on the New York Stock Exchange, a company must have at least three outsiders serving on the board's audit committees. In principle, this is a sound idea, but finding willing and qualified outsiders can be difficult. Thus boards of directors are growing smaller, and although smaller boards seem to get more done, the job has become more time-consuming. Conflicts of interest have to be more carefully scrutinized, and committee responsibilities have been expanding.[19]

Multiple-Stakeholder Environments

TEACHING TIP
Emphasize the *balance* among key stakeholders and how this ensures organizational survival. Use a company example (such as McDonald's, Du Pont, or Chrysler) to illustrate how overemphasis on or ignorance of key stakeholders could harm the organization.

Each individual organization has a host of different stakeholders. For instance, a hospital manager will have to consider doctors, nurses, cleaning and kitchen staff, patients, the American Hospital Association, the state licensing board, medical insurers, and others. Every organization has a unique stakeholder map—a picture of the direct-action component of its external environment.

NETWORKS AND COALITIONS. A complex network of relationships links stakeholders with one another as well as with the organization. For example, consumer advocates may have contacts with an organization, its employees, and a government regulatory agency; in turn, the regulatory agency will affect both the organization and its competitors.

A particular issue may unite several stakeholders in support of or in opposition to organizational policy.[20] For example, special advocacy groups might join with labor unions, the media, and legislators to block a new technology that could cost workers jobs as well as pollute the environment. On occasion, such coalitions outlive the initial issue and continue to work together on others.

Organizations can use stakeholder networks and coalitions to influence stakeholders indirectly. For example, Marathon Oil used the courts and antitrust officials to delay a takeover bid from Mobil and give it time to search for another company to come to its rescue; other companies have even enlisted employees and stockholders in letter-writing campaigns. Such strategies have been known to work, but, as yet, little has been done to formulate their details.

COORDINATED RESOURCE
See Samaras Exercise 1.3, "Influence of Stakeholders."

MULTIPLE ROLES. A single individual or group may have multiple relationships with an organization.[21] A toy company employee, for example, may also be a parent who purchases the company's products, a shareholder with an investment in the company, a member of a consumer group lobbying for stricter safety codes for children's products, and a member of a political party with pronounced ideas about free trade and protectionism. Thus stakeholders may have to balance conflicting roles in determining what action they want the organization to take. This is especially true of management.

THE SPECIAL ROLE OF MANAGEMENT. Management has its own stake in the organization. All employees do, of course, but management is responsible for the organization as a whole, a responsibility that often requires dealing with multiple stakeholders and balancing conflicting claims. Shareholders, for example, want larger returns, while customers want more investment on research and development; employees want higher wages and better benefits, while local communities want parks and day-care facilities. To ensure the survival of the organization, management must keep the relationships among key stakeholders in balance over both the short and the long term.[22]

■ ELEMENTS OF THE INDIRECT-ACTION ENVIRONMENT

COORDINATED RESOURCE
The Distinctive Discussions for Chapter 3 found in the Lecture Extras supplement include "Locating for Lifestyle—Not Anymore" and "Big but Not Necessarily Best."

The indirect-action component of the external environment affects organizations in two ways. First, forces may dictate the formation of a group that eventually becomes a stakeholder. Second, indirect-action elements create a climate—rapidly changing technology, economic growth or decline, changes in attitudes toward work—in which the organization exists and to which it may ultimately have to respond. For example, today's computer technology makes possible the acquisition, storage, coordination, and transfer of large amounts of information about individuals, and banks and other business firms use this technology to maintain, store, process, and exchange information about the credit status of potential buyers. Individuals concerned about the misuse of such data might form a special-interest pressure group to seek voluntary changes in bank business practices. If this group were to organize a successful boycott of a particular bank, it would become a stakeholder of that bank and enter its direct-action environment.

Fahey and Narayanan have grouped these complex interactions into four broad factors that influence the organization and must be considered by its managers: social, economic, political, and technological.[23]

Social Variables

social variables Factors, such as demographics, lifestyle, and social values, that may influence an organization from its external environment.

Fahey and Narayanan divide **social variables** into three categories: demographics, lifestyle, and social values. Demographic and lifestyle changes affect the composition, location, and expectations of an organization's labor supply and customers. Values underlie all other social, political, technological, and economic changes and determine all the choices that people make in life. Social values also set the guidelines that determine how most organizations and managers will operate.

DEMOGRAPHICS. The demographics, or make-up, of the U.S. population has undergone major changes since World War II. The population as a whole is growing only slowly, but some segments of the population, such as Hispanics and blacks, are growing much faster than others.

Figure 3-4 shows the aging of the American population in terms of the number of people 65 years or older. Americans are also living longer; by 2010 the average life expectancy for men will be 74.4 years, as opposed to just 53.6 years in 1920. There have also been dramatic shifts in age structure—that is, the relative sizes of different age groups. The "baby boomers"—those people born between 1946 and 1964—account for more than a third of the country's population, and as this cohort has grown up, society has naturally reflected its interests and demands. Moreover, despite an increase in fertility since the baby boomers started to become parents, the median age of the population continues to rise. By 1986, it had grown to 32.7, compared with a postwar low of 28 in 1970.

COORDINATED RESOURCE
See *Management Live!* Chapter 14, Video 1, "The Mommy Track."

Why are these changes so important to managers? First, they affect the size of the labor supply. In recent years, for example, the relatively small number of teenagers has forced fast-food restaurants and other traditional employers of teenagers to turn to housewives and retirees to fill their part-time jobs. Meanwhile, the rising median age means that managers may face a shortage of skilled workers in the future, once the baby boomers start to retire.

Second, changes in the make-up of the population create social issues that affect managers. Today, for example, many employees are finding themselves in the "sandwich generation"—caught between the demands of caring for their own children and the need to help their aging parents. As a result, many major corporations,

FIGURE 3-4 The Aging Population: Percentage of the Population 65 Years and Over
Sources: Historical figures from the *Statistical Abstract of the United States,* 1981, 1990; projected figures from Allan & Brotman, 1981.

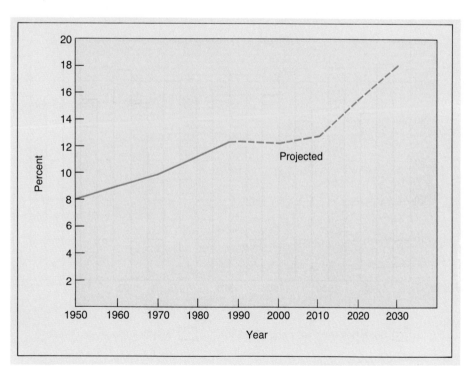

including IBM, Johnson & Johnson, and Mobil Corporation, have set up special programs to help their employees deal with elder care.[24] Third, demographics shape the markets for many products, as indicated by the baby boomers' influence.

Geographically, as Figure 3-5 demonstrates, the West and South have been growing more quickly than other parts of the country. This shift also affects the labor supply, as well as a state's tax base, which in turn affects its ability to offer tax incentives and other support to businesses. As a result, many corporations have moved their headquarters or located new facilities in the West or South. Nonmetropolitan areas within commuting distances of cities have also been growing more quickly than metropolitan areas. Though this represents the reversal of a long-time trend, it still leaves 73 percent of the nation's population in metropolitan areas. Economically, low growth and changes in the composition of families led to a 3 percent decline in median family income in real terms during the 1970s; by the mid-1980s, real family income had begun to rise once more.

CLASS COMMENT
Americans appear to be going back to the "simple life." They are rediscovering the joys of home life, basic values, and things that last. (*Time*, 4/8/91, p. 58ff.)

LIFESTYLES. According to Fahey and Narayanan, lifestyles are the "outward manifestations of people's attitudes and values."[25] In recent decades, change rather than stability has characterized Americans' lifestyles. For example, families account for a shrinking proportion of U.S. households, and fewer and fewer U.S. families include married couples; households consisting of single adults and one-parent families are becoming more numerous.

With respect to work, the most striking trend is the increasing participation of women in the labor force. More than half of all adult women now work. As a result, finding high-quality, reliable, and affordable day care is a major concern for many employees. In most countries, social barriers are still raised against women who seek managerial careers, so reaching the top may mean considerable personal sacrifice for women.[26] In the United States, however, women are penetrating this male strong-

FIGURE 3-5 Regional Population of the United States, 1940–2010
Sources: For 1940–1986; U.S. Bureau of the Census; for 1990–2010: *Statistical Abstract of the United States,* 1990.

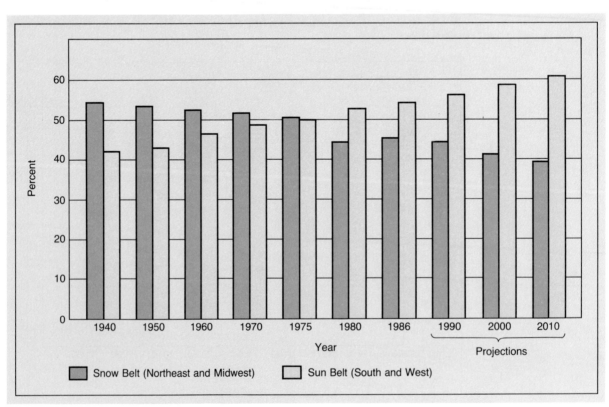

hold in increasing numbers: The number of women managers doubled from 1972 to 1980. (This is not to say that women are reaching "the top" at the same significant rate. In the United States as elsewhere, reaching the top ranks of management is generally a slow process for everyone.)

Other lifestyle changes include a trend toward better education: More people now complete high school and go on to college. Smaller cars, condominiums, diet soft drinks, and paid household help are only a few examples of new consumption patterns. Physical fitness has surged in popularity, and home-centered activities—notably cable TV and video recorders—are becoming more prevalent. At the same time, the gap between the wealthiest and poorest has increased, as evidenced by the emergence of the homeless and the underclass as social issues.

SOCIAL VALUES. In recent years, changing social values have weakened our commitment to equality of opportunity and the regulation of industry, altered our assessments of the costs and benefits of new technology such as life-support systems for the seriously ill, and increased the social and economic expectations of consumers, women, and minorities.

Perhaps most important for managers is the way in which values affect our attitudes toward organizations and work itself. For example, employee participation in managerial decision making was once seen as a means of improving worker morale and productivity; now it is regarded by some observers as an ethical imperative.[27]

Rescher has described five ways in which social values may change.[28] On rare occasions, a new value may emerge or an existing value may totally disappear. Such was the case in the wake of historic Supreme Court decisions about racial integration. In other instances, the distribution of a value throughout the population may become more or less widespread. This occurs when the values held by a special-interest group—a consumer bloc or a political movement, for example—spread into the population as a whole. A value may also move up or down in our hierarchy of values. Under the Reagan administration, for instance, national defense became a higher priority. Similarly, the scope of a particular value may be broadened or narrowed. Thus the values associated with civil rights were expanded to apply to employment and education as well as to voting. Finally, the standard by which a value is measured may change, as is constantly happening to our assessment of the minimum standard of living.

Naturally, social values vary from one country to another. In Japan, for example, where many employees work for the same company all their lives, low-level workers participate in policy and decision making more freely than American workers do. French organizations, which operate in a society where relationships are somewhat formal, tend to be more rigidly structured than their American and Japanese counterparts.

Economic Variables

COORDINATED RESOURCE
See DuBose Reading #32, "Productivity in America: Where It Went and How to Get It Back."

economic variables
General economic conditions and trends that may be factors in an organization's activities.

Obviously, general economic conditions and trends are critical to the success of an organization. Wages, prices charged by suppliers and competitors, and government fiscal policies affect both the costs of producing products or offering services and the market conditions under which they are sold. Each is an **economic variable.** For example, the 1984 devaluation of the peso and imposition of currency controls by the Mexican government benefited American-owned assembly plants on the Mexican side of the border but devastated wholesalers and retailers in the United States who catered to visiting Mexicans.

Common economic indicators measure national income and product, savings, investment, prices, wages, productivity, employment, government activities, and international transactions. (See Exhibit 3-2.) All these factors vary over time, and managers devote much of their organizations' time and resources to forecasting the

EXHIBIT 3-2 Common Economic Indicators

❑ National Income and Product	❑ Labor Force and Employment
Gross national product	Numbers employed by age/sex/class
Personal income	of work
Disposable personal income	Unemployment rate
Personal consumption expenditures	❑ Government Activities
Retail sales	Federal surplus/deficit
❑ Savings	Expenditures by type
Personal savings	Government purchases of goods and
Business savings	services
❑ Investment	State and local expenditures
Industry investment	Defense expenditures
Investment expenditures	Money supply changes
New equipment orders	❑ International Transactions
Inventory investment	Currency exchange rates
Housing starts	Exports by type
❑ Prices, Wages, and Productivity	Imports by type
Inflation rate	Balance of trade
Consumer price (index) changes	Merchandise
Producer price (index) changes	Goods and services
Raw material price (index) changes	Investment abroad
Average hourly earnings	
Output per hour per business sector	

Source: Reprinted by permission from *Macroenvironmental Analysis for Strategic Management* by Liam Fahey and V. K. Narayanan. Copyright © 1986 by West Publishing Company. All rights reserved.

CLASS COMMENT
A survey of CEOs showed that services and labor availability, not quality-of-life factors, determine where they locate manufacturing facilities. (*Newsweek*, 11/18/90, p. 18)

HERE'S AN EXAMPLE
In preparing for the recession, Corning Corporation devised a recession plan that would reduce costs significantly without layoffs. (*Fortune*, 11/5/90, p. 58ff.)

economy and anticipating changes. Since economic change is now the norm rather than the exception, this task has become more complicated.

There are two types of economic change. *Structural* changes in the economy are major alterations, whether permanent or temporary, in the relationships between different sectors of the economy and key economic variables; such changes challenge our basic assumptions about how the economy works. The shift from an industrial to a service economy and the rise in energy costs relative to the cost of other raw materials are examples of structural changes. In contrast, *cyclical* economic changes are periodic swings in the general level of economic activity. Examples are the rise and fall of interest rates, inflation, and housing starts.

Cyclical changes have far different implications for organizational strategies than structural changes because they are a function of normal economic volatility. The real problem lies in *distinguishing* cyclical from structural changes.

Political Variables

Will a government agency adopt a rigorous or a lenient stance toward the management of a company with which it is dealing? Will antitrust laws be rigidly enforced or ignored? Will government policy inhibit or encourage management's freedom to act? These sorts of questions concern **political variables,** and their answers depend largely on the nature of the political process and on the current political climate. The political process involves competition between different interest groups, each seeking to advance its own values and goals. Some of these interest groups are direct stakeholders in an organization, others are not, but since they all interact with one another, even the nonstakeholders may influence the organization.

In the United States, the political climate has ranged from strong support of corporate autonomy—epitomized by President Coolidge's dictum that "the business of America is business"—to the deep suspicion and distrust of business and government that surfaced in the 1960s. Both the number and activities of interest groups have increased, as has the diversity of the issues they bring into the courts

political variables Factors that may influence an organization's activities as a result of the political process or climate.

and legislatures for consideration. Despite the move to deregulation over the last decade or so, government responsibilities still include the protection of consumers, the preservation of the environment, and the ending of employment discrimination.

As interest groups, particularly special-interest groups, become more committed to their goals, political conflicts can grow more intense and last longer. Issues often bring groups into conflict with other groups, including business organizations. These conflicts can enter the legal system and come out with quite complex ramifications. Consider a business's right to free speech. This issue, together with related ethical and legal questions, has been raised more than once in the last 15 years and is not yet resolved despite several court rulings. Is it ethical for a business to take a stand on a public issue that is not directly related to its particular type of business activity? Is it legal? In 1980, in the case of *Consolidated Edison Company of New York* v. *Public Service Commission of New York,* the Supreme Court held that the New York Public Service Commission could not prohibit Consolidated Edison from including pro-nuclear energy brochures in its monthly statements. In such cases, ethical issues tend to remain even after legal ones have been decided. In the *Consolidated Edison* case, the Court took into consideration the argument that businesses have so much power and so much money at their disposal that their influence on both legislators and certain segments of society is inherently "unfair." Proponents of this position argue that this fact is especially important when the position of a business differs from what the interest group holds is the "public interest."

At the same time, the nature of the contemporary media permits interest groups to compete more effectively with well-financed organizations for national attention and resources. Thus the potential for interest groups to influence the political process is greater than ever.

Technological Variables

technological variables
New developments in products or processes, as well as advances in science, that may affect an organization's activities.

Technological variables include advances in basic sciences such as physics, as well as new developments in products, processes, and materials. The level of technology in a society or a particular industry determines to a large extent what products and services will be produced, what equipment will be used, and how operations will be managed.

THE COURSE OF DEVELOPMENT. Technological development begins with basic research, through which a scientist discovers some new phenomenon or advances some new theory. Other researchers then examine the breakthrough for its potential utility. If further development leads to a workable prototype and engineering refinements make commercial exploitation practical, then the technology is put to use and may be widely adopted.[29] Government institutions such as NASA, independent research establishments such as Bell Labs, universities, and large corporations all conduct basic research. Independent entrepreneurs, business firms and some government agencies carry the developments out of the laboratory and into the marketplace.

THOUGHT PROVOKER

Despite increased investment in high-tech office equipment during the 1980s, white-collar productivity has remained flat. (*U.S. News & World Report*, 12/24/90, p. 46ff.)

Technological change takes place in many directions at once—that is, it is *multifinial.* Bar codes, for example, are used to track items not only in grocery stores, but also in warehouses, assembly lines, shipping docks, libraries, and even the Department of Defense. Technological change is also *nonlinear.* Developments take place irregularly. There are many dead ends, and each highly visible advance may depend on a host of small developments (including failures). Thus the production of 100 percent solid-state televisions came only after five frustrating years of unsuccessful attempts.

LIFE CYCLES. As development proceeds and a specific technology moves through its life cycle, its functional performance characteristics improve. This change in performance characteristics often follows an S-shaped curve. Figure 3-6 indicates the

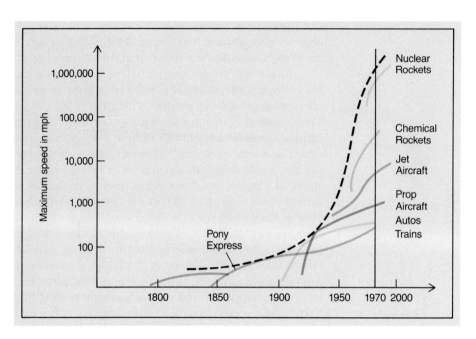

FIGURE 3-6 Technological Development and the Increase in the Speed of Travel
Source: S. C. Wheelwright and S. Makridakis, *Forecasting Methods for Management,* Third Edition. Copyright © 1980 by Ronald Press. Reprinted by permission of John Wiley & Sons, Inc.

increase in speed of travel due to improvements in transportation technology over the past two centuries.

Any single product or process will also contain many specific technologies in different phases of their life cycles. *Base* technologies are fully mature; their performance has peaked, and they are shared by all competitors. Although base technologies may pose an entry barrier to the industry, they are not the focus of competition. *Key* technologies, in contrast, are growing and changing rapidly; improvements in this area give firms a competitive edge. *Pacing* technologies are those that may eventually replace key technologies but whose potential use has not yet been proven. *Peripheral* technologies, which are not by their design intended to add much to a product's features, do not play a major role in competition.[30]

■ *THE INTERNATIONAL DIMENSION*

One of the most important changes to the external environment is the globalization of business, which has both direct and indirect effects on the environment. A growing number of companies operate production facilities outside the United States and market their products abroad; even companies with mainly domestic operations face international competition and rely on foreign suppliers. Thus managers must be aware that their companies may have both external and internal stakeholders in other nations.

The globalization of business also affects the indirect-action environment. The daily press is filled with reports of trade deficits, calls for protectionism or for free trade, and challenges to the command economies of communist nations, raising the possibility of new opportunities for international trade. Managers must be aware of social, economic, political, and technological variables in each country in which they wish to do business or anticipate competing.

HERE'S AN EXAMPLE

Avon Products Inc. got approval from the government of Czechoslovakia to begin direct sales there in October 1991. (*Wall Street Journal*, 3/14/91, p. A8)

INTERNATIONAL MANAGEMENT

New Frontiers of U.S./Japanese Competition: The Race to Shape Our Brave New Biotechnological World

Japanese industry's success in selling innovative, well-made consumer goods in the United States is well known. Now Japanese corporations are mounting a powerful new challenge to American dominance in biotechnology products. Although we are only beginning to see the applications of this new technology, it is already a multibillion-dollar industry, with products ranging from genetically improved farm animals and grains to cancer treatments and biodegradable plastics. The real focus in this rapidly growing field, however, is a battle between the Japan and the United States for prominence in research and development (R&D).

The United States has been at the forefront of biotechnology, but Japanese companies are quickly gaining ground. Drawing on a strategy that has served them well in other industries, the Japanese are heavily relying on "piggybacking." The key to this strategy is using their considerable financial assets to supply needed cash to biotechnology laboratories around the world, which grants the Japanese access to technological breakthroughs. By riding "piggyback" on basic research conducted in other countries, the Japanese companies, in effect, augment their own research budgets, freeing resources for perfecting products that have the best chance of dominating markets around the world. Takeda, for example, which has a joint venture with Abbott Labs and alliances in West Germany, France, and Italy, funds research at Harvard University. Fujisawa acquired LyphoMed and a former joint venture with SmithKline. Chugai bought Gen-Probe, Inc., for $110 million and has stakes in Genetics Institute, Inc., and British Bio-technology.

The speed with which the Japanese have moved is startling. Beginning essentially from scratch ten years ago, they have used their vast financial resources to gain access to American and European technology and to develop their own impressive bio-technology industry, which grossed over $9 billion in 1989. This push was unavoidable—Japanese drug companies had to expand beyond their own markets and develop new technologies because of fierce competition and declining domestic profits—but it was not accomplished alone. Three-quarters of their $2 billion research and development budget for 1990 did come from private sources (many outside the drug industry), but the rest came from the Japanese Ministry of International Trade and Industry, which is actively supporting a variety of promising new projects for the twenty-first century. The Japanese now dominate the American market in anticancer drugs and growth hormones and they are working on other biotech products such as anti-Alzheimer's drugs, cosmetics, biosensors, and agriculture.

The downside for the Japanese is that the United States is spending over $6 billion per year on biotech R&D (three times the Japanese investment) and still holds a considerable lead in most areas of research. In addition, Japan's drug imports are still three times greater than their exports. Despite their success in gaining access to several smaller companies and research facilities in the United States, Japanese interests appear unable to swallow the European and U.S. giants. Moreover, they are concerned about a potential market backlash, especially in the United States, to biotech foods (grains, fish, vegetables, fruits, etc.)—an area of biotechnology in which the Japanese have invested heavily.

Sources: Roger E. Shamel and Joseph J. Chow, "Biotechnology: On the Rebound and Heading for a Boom," *Chemical Week,* September 27, 1989, pp. 31–32; Jacob M. Schlesinger, "One High-Tech Race Where U.S. Leads: Personal Computers," *The Wall Street Journal,* October 31, 1989, pp. A1, A12; Neil Gross, "Japan's Next Battleground: The Medicine Chest," *Business Week,* March 12, 1990, pp. 68–72; "Strategic Challenges in Commercializing Biotechnology," *California Management Review,* Spring 1990, pp. 63–72; Barbara Buell, et al., "A Shopping Spree in the U.S.," *Business Week,* Innovation 1990 Issue, pp. 86–87.

The complexity added by the international dimension is so important that it is the subject of an entire chapter of this book (Chapter 5, "The International Dimension"). At this point, we can suggest this complexity with the International Management box.

ILLUSTRATIVE CASE STUDY

CONTINUED

Image and Imaging Problems at Eastman Kodak

By the mid-1970s, it was clear that Kodak's image of its external environment was out of focus. Consider Kodak's image of the amateur photographer—a major customer (external stakeholder). In the early days, customers were thrilled with the novelty of taking amateur-quality snapshots and home movies, and Kodak's basic strategy was to supply reliable, inexpensive, simple-to-use cameras that encouraged the use of Kodak film. Family pictures and home movies quickly became an integral part of the American lifestyle (indirect-action environment). Then other changes in the indirect-action environment, ranging from increased leisure and disposable income to exposure to high-quality photojournalism, combined to raise expectations of the humble snapshot. Now many customers wanted more professional results, like the photographs they saw in glossy magazines, without having to master the technical complexities of more sophisticated cameras. When Japanese manufacturers adapted new technology to create models with such features as automatic focus and built-in flash, customers were primed to buy them and to try new brands of film as well.

Failing to understand the significance of these changes, Kodak was slow to respond. By 1986, it was evident that Kodak had spent at least one decade perfecting the art of foot dragging. Between 1975 and 1985, Kodak had been unaccountably slow in marketing such products as 35mm cameras and SLRs—products that would seem to be natural extensions for a company that depends on photography-related business for about 80 percent of its over $10 billion in sales. When, in January of 1986, Kodak reentered the 35mm camera field after an absence of 17 years, it was obliged to manufacture its cameras not in its own once-vaunted facilities but in Japan.

Besides waking to discover vigorous competition from such formidable American rivals as RCA and GE in consumer electronics, IBM and Xerox in copiers and office-publishing equipment, and Memorex and 3M in floppy disks, Kodak found that it *shared* a problem with its American counterparts: In the fields of film, SLRs, and video cameras, Japanese concerns like Fuji, Konica, Nikon, Canon, Minolta, Sony, and Toshiba had made ominous inroads into both American technology and profits. Says Columbia University management professor E. Kirby Warren, who served as a consultant at Kodak for seven years, "Psychologically, I don't know whether some of those people in Rochester can get it into their heads that they got whooped by the Japanese, and they have to fight harder, tougher, and meaner."

After its long sluggishness in combating the Japanese in general, and Fuji's assault on the amateur photography market in particular, Kodak has begun to learn its lesson. In 1984, Fuji waltzed off with sponsorship rights to the 1984 Olympic Games—a major promotional vehicle—for $7 million after Kodak submitted an embarrassingly low bid. In 1988, though, Kodak bounced back, reclaiming the Olympic sponsorship with a $10 million bid.

Kodak has also vastly improved its market responsiveness. In the battle over disposable cameras designed to meet customer demands, Kodak introduced the Weekend 35 (a waterproof camera) and the Stretch 35 (with a lens that takes in twice the scenery width of other cameras). As *Business Week* analyst Leslie Helm notes, "Kodak already has become more quick-footed. Last spring [1987] the company rushed out an announcement of its first disposable, the Fling, to beat Fuji's U.S. invasion with its Fujicolor Quick Snap by a matter of hours. And this spring's entries [the Weekend 35 and the Stretch 35, released in 1989] demonstrate the Rochester (N.Y.) giant has cranked up new-product development."

Source: Leslie Helm and Neil Gross, "Playing Leapfrog in Disposable Cameras," *Business Week*, May 1, 1989, p. 34.

■ THEORIES OF TOTAL-ORGANIZATION ENVIRONMENTS

The Theory of Uncertainty and Dependence

uncertainty According to Hannan and Freeman, the theoretical problem posed to an organization by lack of information.

dependence According to Hannan and Freeman, the theoretical problem faced by an organization because of its need for vital resources from outside sources.

The environment as a whole may be viewed both as a source of information and as a stock of resources.[31] Depending on its approach to its environment, an organization therefore faces one of two theoretical problems: **uncertainty,** caused by a lack of information; and **dependence** on others for vital resources. M. T. Hannan and J. H. Freeman have described six environmental factors that affect an organization's level of uncertainty and dependence. (See Exhibit 3-3). Petroleum refiners, for example, became more dependent in the 1970s when crude oil supplies, concentrated in the Middle East, were suddenly less readily available. By the 1980s, the Iran-Iraq War, which embroiled the Persian Gulf, had rendered the supply of oil even less dependable, as had the web of uncertain alliances in the region. This area became even more unstable in 1990, when Iraq invaded Kuwait, touching off the Gulf War early in 1991.

EXHIBIT 3-3 Hannan and Freeman's Factors Affecting an Organization's Uncertainty and Dependence

The environment is more uncertain and less easy to understand when:
❑ It is more differentiated.
❑ It is changing.
❑ There are numerous interconnections among its various elements.

A manufacturing organization in an uncertain environment, for example, might have to contend with many different types of customers, the rapid introduction of new products, and connections with a large number of suppliers.

Organizations are more dependent in an environment where:
❑ Required resources are not widely available.
❑ Those resources are not evenly distributed.
❑ Increasing connectedness disturbs elements of the environment and the linkages among them.

Source: M. T. Hannan and J. H. Freeman, "The Population Ecology of Organizations," *American Journal of Sociology* 82 (1977):929–964.

Other Theories of Environments

Other theorists have developed strategic models of the environment in an effort to explain the relationships between organizations and the environment.

NATURAL SELECTION. This model is based on biological theories of population ecology and shares their emphasis on competition for resources.[32] In the variation stage, organizations make different responses to environmental pressures; error and chance are as important as problem-solving abilities in determining which organizations acquire information and resources most efficiently. In the selection stage, those organizations that best fit the constraints imposed by the environment survive. In the retention stage, the selected organizations persist until the environment changes or different organizations arise.

RESOURCE DEPENDENCE. This model assumes that organizations are dependent on the environment for resources, such as suppliers, customers, competitors, and regulators.[33] The organization may take action on its own to acquire and maintain those resources—for example, negotiating long-term contracts or adopting a technological innovation. It may also act collectively with other organizations—for example, by participating in trade associations that lobby government agencies and set informal industry norms. The organization's strategy will vary according to the relative importance of each of its dependencies.

■ MANAGING THE TOTAL ENVIRONMENT

THOUGHT PROVOKER

Why would environments tend to become more turbulent over time?

The external environment is more or less important to managers depending on the types and purposes of their organization, their own position and functions, and their place in the organizational hierarchy. Thus managers at Exxon may be more influenced by factors in the external environment than managers at A&P, pollution-control engineers more so than sales-division managers, and executives more so than clerical workers.

Because of their greater power and broader perspectives, managers at the higher levels bear greater responsibility for managing relations with the external environment than do lower-level managers. Top managers play key roles in balancing the interests of the various stakeholders in the organization and in forecasting and adjusting to trends in the indirect-action environment.

Influencing the Direct-Action Environment

COORDINATED RESOURCE

See Study Guide Self-Learning Exercise 3, "Priorities."

The direct-action environment is a known quantity with which the organization has regular and established patterns of interaction. For the most part, managers use such standard and reliable techniques as advertising, lobbying, and collective bargaining to influence an organization's stakeholders. The real challenge for managers is to determine the relative importance of each stakeholder and to balance managerial decisions accordingly.

Monitoring the Indirect-Action Environment

Managers monitor the indirect-action environment for early-warning signs of changes that will later affect their organization's activities. For example, rather than waiting for sales to fall, a savvy manager will reduce production of luxury items when he or she first spots a downward trend in general consumer spending.

Information about the indirect-action environment comes from many sources: an industry's grapevine, managers in other organizations, the data generated by an

Monitoring the Indirect-Action Environment. Businesses that want to appeal to affluent customers need to be aware of the yucas—young, upwardly mobile Cuban Americans—typified by business consultant Roberto Suarez and his wife, Anays Robles, of Miami. Unlike other ethnic groups who have sought to blend into the U.S. culture, the yucas switch between English and Spanish publications and media to find the best quality and remain actively involved in the mainstays of Cuban culture. Because young people tend to live at home until they are married, yucas can spend more on consumer goods such as clothing, cars, and consumer electronics.

organization's own activities, government reports and statistics, trade journals, general financial and business publications, on-line computer data-bank services, and others. Hints, predictions, statistics, gossip—any of these may alert a manager to a trend that should be monitored. The manager can then order further research to clarify potentially important developments. By using statistical *forecasting* techniques, managers can anticipate change in social, economic, political, and technological variables and so prepare alternate plans for the future.

Adjusting to the Environment

Managers generally adjust to the external environment through the planning process. They develop and implement strategic plans in order to guide the organization's attempts to influence the behavior of stakeholders and its adaptations to the indirect external environment.[34]

Another type of adjustment to the environment involves changes in the organization's formal structure—its work flows, authority patterns, reporting relationships among managers, and the like. This kind of "organizational design" implies a conscious structuring of the organization so that it will best meet the demands of the environment at a given time. Although few organizations operate according to such an ideal design, many are regularly reorganized and restructured in accord with environmental dictates (we will describe this process in Part Four of this book). In both cases, adjustment demands that the manager deal with a critical paradox: With the environment changing ever more rapidly and areas of "relevant uncertainty" increasing, strategic planning, fundamentally a process for *stabilizing* an organization's activities, must now be more *flexible* than ever before.

ILLUSTRATIVE CASE STUDY

WRAP-UP

Image and Imaging Problems at Eastman Kodak

Kodak has come a long way over the past five years; it has protected its healthy market share and has over $10 billion in assets. Still, the company is clearly struggling. A 60 percent plunge in profits in the first half of 1989 helped motivate Kodak's fourth major restructuring since 1984. In the latest set of changes, over 4,500 employees were cut and several "ailing" businesses were sold or consolidated to reduce costs. Although the move should produce savings in excess of $200 million, Wall Street shrugged off Kodak's latest restructuring and its stock price actually dropped. One problem is unusually stiff competition in the photo film and paper markets. But an equally important problem is doubts about Kodak's management and their ability to adjust to the external environment.

When 60-year-old Colby H. Chandler, a Kodak engineer for over 30 years, became chairman and CEO in 1983, he inherited a ponderous bureaucracy based on the outmoded managerial ideas laid down by Kodak founder George Eastman in 1880. Decision making was highly centralized and the company was organized along strictly functional lines. A marketing idea that affected manufacturing had to percolate to the top of the organizational bureaucracy and then dribble back down to the appropriate level. Under such conditions, decision making was sluggish and often faulty. For example, in the 1940s, Kodak rejected an instant-photography system offered it by Edwin Land, who went on to found Polaroid instead. When Kodak finally succeeded in duplicating the product 20 years and $94 billion later, Polaroid superseded it with an SX-70 camera that produced litter-free color prints—and successfully sued Kodak for patent infringements.

One of Chandler's first moves was to institute a decentralized organization that wrenched decision-making responsibilities from the executive level to the unit-manager level. For example, Chandler reorganized Kodak's core Photographic Division into 17 operational units in 1985.

There have been some drawbacks to reorganization, as when Bob Sharp, general manager of Kodak's U.S. Sales Division (USSD), was put in charge of restructuring the division and retraining its personnel. Customers (external stakeholders) were sometimes overrun by an "army of Kodak sales representatives and overwhelmed by 17 times the paperwork." Meanwhile, the morale of sales reps (internal stakeholders) dropped when they were grouped with people who had different training and their career paths were effectively cut by three-fourths. To boost morale, Sharp was careful to avoid retraining people in areas they already knew, and he gave them new titles—sales account executives—to generate enthusiasm and reflect the added responsibility of their new roles. The changes paid off. Sales per employee have jumped 25 percent since the creation of USSD and total sales were up 47 percent between 1986 and 1989.

Kodak has also instituted a new value system. "Historically this company has been risk-averse," understates Executive Vice President J. Phillip Samper. "Today," he explains, "we're saying 'Making a mistake isn't bad. Just don't make it twice.'" Chandler agreed, saying, "It's essential that we take more risks."

These internal changes have helped Kodak branch out into new technologies that supplement its strengths and prepare it for markets of the future. The Life Sciences Division applied film-coating techniques to the production of blood analyzers invaluable in the diagnosis of anemia and diabetes. Kodak's purchase of Fox Photo, Inc., in 1986 made it the nation's largest photo finisher and secured a huge customer for its products. Kodak has also been active in the field of electronic imaging—the use of computers to manipulate photos and graphics. The 1985 introduction of its Ektaprint Electronic Publishing System showed off the latest technology and demonstrated Kodak's willingness to use hardware and software from rival corporations. Between 1984 and 1988, Kodak invested close to $6 billion in new high-tech ventures.

Still, some of Kodak's acquisition risks have been questioned. In 1988, Kodak acquired Sterling Drug for $5.1 billion—a price many felt was far too high for a company whose staple money makers were losing ground (Bayer aspirin) or facing stiff new challenges (Omnipaque). Last year Sterling-related debt exceeded unit operating earnings by $50 million. But Kodak is still holding out hope for the acquisition. It has trimmed Sterling's work force and increased research funding for a targeted set of areas, even though the few promising drugs the company has produced are bogged down in the early stages of development and FDA testing. Meanwhile, Kodak's copier division—thought to be an up-and-comer a few years back—was cut back in the latest restructuring.

Moreover, Kodak faces some crushing fines. Nine chemical drums at its Kodak Park plant ruptured in September 1989, releasing hazardous fumes into the air. Kodak admitted to two criminal violations of New York antipollution laws in April 1990 and was fined $1.51 million. In addition, in October 1990 a federal judge ordered Kodak to pay $909.5 million for its violation of Polaroid's patent. This has kept the value of Kodak stock down, deterred investors, and dampened morale.

Kodak seems to be facing up to the challenges. CEO Colby Chandler has been succeeded by Kay Whitmore, and William Fowble has taken over as head of photographic products. Fowble has decided to get back to basics by cutting costs and milking more profits out of Kodak's current market share instead of trying to reclaim lost business. In addition, Eastman Chemicals has been a stabilizing influence and a solid performer—accounting for about 20 percent of Kodak's overall sales. Finally, Kodak has recently given workers a "parachute"—guaranteed severance pay, health and life insurance benefits, and outplacement service—if they lose their jobs in a corporate takeover. This guarantee is thought to be a powerful deterrent to a hostile takeover and has helped to generate some confidence and stability in Kodak's work force.

Notwithstanding, many observers agree with experts like Mark Hyde, a partner at Egon Zehndor International (a N.Y. recruiting firm), who says, "They [Kodak] don't know what it takes to be successful." Looking over the span of this case study, it is hard to understand how Kodak could lose sight of such basic values as competitiveness, risk taking, innovation, and customer responsiveness. Will Kodak's latest moves finally prove to their employees, Wall Street, and their customers that they do know "what it takes" to be successful? ■

Sources: Leslie Helm and Susan Benway, "Has Kodak Set Itself Up for a Fall?" *Business Week,* February 22, 1988, pp. 134–137; "Kodak Strategy: Sensible Retreat," *Business Month,* April 1989, p. 15; Peter Pae, "Kodak Is to Take $225 Million Charge, Signaling Bigger Restructuring Plans," *The Wall Street Journal,* July 15, 1989, p. A5; Clare Ansberry, "Kodak Plans to Cut Work Force by About 4,500, and to Sell Units," *The Wall Street Journal,* August 24, 1989, p. A3; "Kodak Says Drums of Chemicals Leaked, Releasing Hazy Cloud," *The Wall Street Journal,* September 8, 1989, p. C11; Keith H. Hammonds, "Kodak May Wish It Never Went to the Drugstore," *Business Week,* December 4, 1989, pp. 75–76; "Kodak Pays $2 Million in Environmental Fines," *The Wall Street Journal,* April 6, 1990, p. C16; Clare Ansberry, "Kodak Seems a Pretty Picture to One Analyst But Patent Suit by Polaroid Scares Off Others," *The Wall Street Journal,* April 12, 1990, p. C2.

The many rapid changes taking place in the external environment of organizations require increasing attention from managers. The direct-action component of the environment consists of the organization's stakeholders—that is, the groups with direct impact on the organization's activities. External stakeholders include customers, suppliers, governments, special-interest groups, the media, labor unions, financial institutions, and competitors. Internal stakeholders include employees, shareholders, and the board of directors.

Managers must balance the interests of the various stakeholders for the good of the organization as a whole. They may be able to use the network of relationships among the stakeholders and the organization to influence stakeholders individually. For their part, stakeholders may unite in coalitions to exert influence over the organization. Individual stakeholders may also hold conflicting stakes in an organization.

The indirect-action component of the environment consists of social, economic, political, and technological variables that influence the organization indirectly. These variables create a climate to which the organization must adjust, and they have the potential to move into the direct-action environment. Demographic and lifestyle variables mold an organization's labor supply and customer base, and changes in values are at the heart of every other social, economic, political, and technological change. Managers must distinguish between and adjust to structural and cyclical changes in the economy. In addition, they must contend with the growing influence of special-interest groups in politics and technological developments that fuel competition between organizations.

Technological advances in communications and transportation have made the international environment increasingly important. This fact has increased the complexity of both the direct-action and indirect-action components of the environment.

The environment determines both the amount of uncertainty an organization faces and the extent to which it is dependent on others for vital resources. In turbulent environments, organizations must devote more of their resources to monitoring the environment. The natural-selection and resource-dependence models provide alternative views of the relationship between organizations and the environment.

Managers—especially at higher levels—must monitor the external environment and try to forecast changes that will affect the organization. They may use strategic planning and organizational design to adjust to the environment.

■ REVIEW QUESTIONS

1. Distinguish between the direct-action and indirect-action elements of the environment, giving examples of each.
2. Who are the stakeholders of an organization and how have their stakes changed in recent years? What *new* categories of stakeholders are now developing?
3. What are stakeholder networks and coalitions? How can managers use them to influence stakeholders?
4. Discuss the four variables that make up the indirect-action environment of organizations.
5. Describe some recent changes in U.S. demographics, lifestyles, and social values and state how they affect organizations.
6. What is the difference between structural and cyclical economic change? What are the implications of both kinds of changes for organizations?
7. How does technological development proceed? At which stages in its life cycle is a technology critical to competition?

8. What management challenges and opportunities are posed by growing international trade?

9. Define uncertainty and dependence, and describe the environmental characteristics that affect them.

10. What techniques can managers use to influence the direct-action environment? To monitor the indirect-action environment? To adjust to the environment?

CASE STUDY

Tri-State Telephone

John Godwin, chief executive of Tri-State Telephone, leaned back in his chair and looked at the ceiling. How was he ever going to get out of this mess? At last night's public hearing, 150 angry customers had marched in to protest Tri-State's latest rate request. After the rancorous shouting was over and the acrimonious signs put away, the protesters had presented state regulators with some sophisticated economic analyses in support of their case. Additionally, there were a number of emotional appeals from elderly customers who regarded phone service their lifeline to the outside world.

Tri-State Telephone operated in three states and had sales of over $3 billion. During the last five years, the company had experienced a tremendous amount of change. In 1984, the AT&T divestiture sent shock waves throughout the industry, and Tri-State Telephone had felt the effects, as pricing for long-distance telephone service changed dramatically. The Federal Communications Commission instituted a charge to the effect that customers should have "access" to long-distance companies whether or not they were in the habit of making long distance calls. Consumer groups, including the Consumer Federation of America and the Congress of Consumer Organizations, had joined the protest, increasing their attention on the industry and intervening in regulatory proceedings wherever possible. The FCC was considering deregulating as much of the industry as possible, and Congress was looking over the commissioner's shoulder. Meanwhile, the Department of Justice and Judge Harold Greene (both of whom were responsible for the AT&T divestiture) continued to argue about what businesses companies like Tri-State should be engaged in.

In addition, technology was changing rapidly. Cellular telephones, primarily used in cars, were now hand-held and could be substituted for standard phones. Digital technology was going forward, leading to lower costs and requiring companies like Tri-State to invest to keep up with the state of the art. Meanwhile, rate increases negotiated during the inflationary 1970s were keeping earnings higher than regulators would authorize. New "intelligent" terminals and software developments gave rise to new uses for the phone network (such as using the phone for an alarm system), but as long as customers paid one flat fee, the phone company could not benefit from these new services.

Godwin's company has recently proposed a new pricing system whereby users of local telephone services would simply pay for what they used rather than a monthly flat fee. All of the senior managers were convinced that the plan was fairer, even though some groups who used the phone with notable frequency (like real estate agents) would pay more. It would give the company an incentive to bring new services to their customers, and customers would be able to choose which ones to buy. None of them had anticipated the hue and cry from the very customers who would save money under the new plan. For instance, Godwin's studies showed that the elderly were very light users of local service and could save as much as 20 percent under the new plan.

After the debacle at the hearing the previous night, Godwin was unsure how to proceed. If he backed off the new pricing plan, he would have to find a different way to meet the challenges of the future—maybe even different businesses to augment company income. Alternatively, the company could not stand the negative press from a protracted battle, even though Godwin thought that the regulators were favorably disposed toward his plan. In fact, Godwin himself believed the company should help its customers rather than fight with them.

Source: This case is based on an actual managerial situation but names have been changed to protect confidentiality.

Case Questions

1. Who are the stakeholders in this case?
2. Which stakeholders are most important?
3. What are the critical trends in Tri-State's environment?
4. Why do you think Tri-State's customers are so upset?
5. What should John Godwin do?

Managing the Environment at McDonald's

An aging population increasingly aware of the relationship between salt, dietary fat, and health, coupled with environmental concerns and a loss in sales momentum, are forcing McDonald's to take a new look at the fast-food marketplace it has dominated for so many years.

Consider the statistics on McDonald's, the nation's largest fast-food chain. Although 1990 sales exceeded $18 billion, almost one-third came from overseas operations. Domestic sales, in contrast, are flattening and percentage growth has slowed down for eight straight quarters. After a sluggish 1990 second quarter performance, security analysts at Prudential Bache downgraded McDonald's status from a hold to a sell even though the corporation ranks as one of the Fortune 500 and is listed on the Dow-Jones 30 Industrials.

What critics may be overlooking, though, is McDonald's tradition of resiliency, its track record of finding solutions to tough problems. One problem is meeting the traditional goal of opening 500-plus units a year at a time when well-located real estate is becoming scarce and expensive. (To McDonald's, the term *well-located* means they can use demographics and traffic patterns to forecast a site will generate a certain dollar amount of business each year.) The cost of opening a new outlet increased 10.2 percent in 1989, but sales rose only 1.6 percent in the same period. These considerations have long kept McDonald's from expanding into many smaller towns. The solution? The company is experimenting with a 1950s diner concept for small towns and opened the first Golden Arch Cafe in Hartsville, Tennessee, in 1989. Not using the McDonald's name gives the company more freedom to experiment with new ideas, managers report. Another problem is the mounting competition from PepsiCo's Pizza Hut, Taco Bell, and Kentucky Fried Chicken, which offer more varied menus. In response, McDonald's is speeding up its introduction of new menu items. Traditionally, it test-marketed new menu items an average of five years before introducing them nationwide, but now it is testing a number of "healthier," non-burger menu items with plans to push the most promising into nationwide distribution as quickly as possible.

McDonald's has also had to deal with critics of the fat content of its menu. In response, McDonald's switched to all-vegetable oil for its famous french fries and reduced the fat content of its hamburgers,

introducing in April 1991 the 91 percent fat-free McLean Deluxe. It reduced sodium in its breakfast pancakes by 30 percent and removed monosodium glutamate from Chicken McNuggets as well. Says McDonald's Chief Operating Officer Ed Rensi, "We let market conditions, the environment, and our customers lead us strategically."

The company is now in the process of following another environmental "lead" and phasing out its styrofoam packaging. The decision to switch to paper packaging was a difficult, expensive, and still controversial one for McDonald's.

The company has a history of environmental concern and initially switched from paper containers to styrofoam in the mid-1970s when researchers urged reducing the amount of paper used to prevent deforestation. In the 1980s, the firm reduced solid waste even more by decreasing the thickness of its straws and containers. McDonald's became the first company to sign a voluntary agreement, in 1987, to phase out the type of polystyrene (styrofoam) that is manufactured using chlorofluorocarbons (CFCs) deemed harmful to the ozone layer.

Still the company was criticized for the amount of solid waste it generated, including an annual 45 million pounds of polystyrene waste. McDonald's took the lead in polystyrene recycling, starting what was probably the world's largest program in Massachusetts. Here polystyrene from 450 New England McDonald's restaurants was converted to plastic resins and sold to companies that produced plastic products, including McDonald's own trays. The company committed to spend $100 million dollars a year over the next two years on recycling efforts.

Next the company embarked on a program to educate the American public about recycling polystyrene. Initial studies showed 70 percent participation by in-store customers. Critics charged, however, that the non-CFC styrofoam still might harm the atmosphere during the manufacturing process. In addition, they pointed out, recycling only worked for meals eaten in the stores; more than half of McDonald's business is carry-out.

In rebuttal, plastics manufacturers argued that McDonald's outside consultant had found that the material contained no toxic substances, took less energy to produce than paper, and didn't require the cutting down of any trees.

Still the protests continued. In October of 1990, Earth Action Network broke windows and vandalized an outlet in San Francisco. A schoolchildren's movement called Kids Against Polystyrene urged people to boycott McDonald's. A Send-It-Back campaign began, which encouraged customers to mail their used McDonald's styrofoam containers to the corporate headquarters in Oak Brook, Illinois.

In August 1990, the company announced a strategic alliance with the Washington, D.C.-based Environmental Defense Fund to produce the first joint study of the food service waste problem. The result was an ambitious program of 42 initiatives to reduce McDonald's waste and the environmental impact of certain practices, such as using bleached paper bags.

The most noticeable change was the dropping of McDonald's distinctive styrofoam clamshell in November 1990, in favor of paper containers. Ironically, the new paper sandwich containers can't be recycled. They will, however, reduce the volume of waste by 90 percent; the material will still sit in landfills, but it will take up less room. In addition, McDonald's is launching a recycling program to reduce its behind-the-counter waste, which accounts for 80 percent of the waste a McDonald's generates. (One-third of this is corrugated boxes used to ship supplies.)

McDonald's guiding philosophy, created by founder Ray Kroc, is that *the* customer is king. Today, though, this guidance seems less clear, since there is no "one voice" that speaks for the marketplace. Now-adays, McDonald's, along with other corporations, is finding that its decisions must reflect the opinions of many stakeholders.

Sources: Lisa Bertagnoli, "Company of the Quarter Century," *Restaurants & Institutions,* July 10, 1989, pp. 33–56; Lisa Bertagnoli, "Inside McDonald's," *Restaurants & Institutions*, August 21, 1989, pp. 44–70; Charles Bernstein, "McDonald's at 35: Unparalleled Success; Clouds on the Horizon," *Nation's Restaurant News,* August 27, 1990, pp. 60–76; Scott Hume, "Sales Flattening, McD's Scrambles to Grow," *Crain's Chicago Business,* September 10, 1990, p. 17; Brian Quinton, "The Greening of McDonald's," *Restaurants & Institutions,* December 20, 1990, pp. 28–42; Lois Thierren, "Restaurants: Doing Well by Being Big," *Business Week,* January 14, 1991, p. 92.

Case Questions

1. Did McDonald's make the "right" decision regarding recycling? If you were the decision-maker, what would you have chosen to do? Why?

2. Did McDonald's correctly interpret the environmental concerns it was hearing? Why were the company's initial education and recycling efforts not very successful?

3. Refer to the elements of the indirect-action environment. Which variable or variables played a major role in influencing McDonald's decisions? Has McDonald's responded to the right variable or variables?

■ *NOTES*

[1]For a more complete discussion of the stakeholder approach to management, see R. Edward Freeman, *Strategic Management: A Stakeholder Approach* (Boston: Pitman, 1984). See also Nancy C. Roberts and Paula J. King, "The Stakeholder Audit Goes Public," *Organizational Dynamics* 17 (Winter 1989):63–79.

[2]As quoted in Ronald Henkoff, "How to Plan for 1995," *Fortune,* December 31, 1990, pp. 70–77.

[3]See Alvar O. Elbing, "On the Applicability of Environmental Models," in Joseph W. McGuire, ed., *Contemporary Management: Issues and Viewpoints* (Englewood Cliffs, N.J.: Prentice Hall, 1974), pp. 283–289.

[4]Theodore Levitt, *The Marketing Imagination* (New York: Free Press, 1983), pp. 20–49.

[5]"Beware Cheap Oil," *The Economist,* March 12, 1988, pp. 12–13.

[6]Henry Eason, "Deregulation: Dream Deferred," *Nation's Business,* February 1984, pp. 24–26.

[7]See Robert A. Leone, "Examining Deregulation," *Harvard Business Review* 62, no. 4 (July–August 1984):56–58.

[8]Susan J. Tolchin and Martin Tolchin, *Dismantling America: The Rush to Deregulate* (Boston: Houghton-Mifflin, 1983).

[9]G. Wilson, *Interest Groups in the United States* (New York: Oxford University Press, 1981).

[10]E. Epstein, "Business Political Activity: Research Approaches and Analytical Issues," in L. Preston, ed., *Research in Corporate Responsibility and Social Policy,* Vol. 2 (Greenwich: JAI Press, 1980).

[11]A. Hirschmann, *Exit, Voice and Loyalty* (Cambridge: Harvard University Press, 1970).

[12]See David H. Rosenbloom and Jay M. Shafritz, *Essentials of Labor Relations* (Reston, Va.: Reston Publishing, 1985); and Arthur A. Sloane and Fred Witney, *Labor Relations,* 6th ed. (Englewood Cliffs, N.J.: Prentice Hall, 1988).

[13]See Lyn S. Wilson, "Managing in the Competitive Environment," *Long Range Planning* 17, no. 1 (February 1983):59–64.

[14]Tom Peters, *Thriving on Chaos* (New York: Alfred A. Knopf, 1988), p. 289.

[15]David Vogel, "Trends in Shareholder Activism: 1970–1982," *California Management Review* 25, no. 3 (Spring 1983):68–87.

[16]Ralph Nader, *Unsafe at Any Speed* (New York: Grossman Publishers, 1972).

[17]Richard L. Hudson, "SEC Tightens Annual Meeting Proposal Rules," *The Wall Street Journal,* August 17, 1983, p. 4.

[18]Edward L. Hennessy Jr., "The Raiders Make It Harder to Compete," *The New York Times,* March 13, 1988, p. F3.

[19]George Melloan, "A Good Director Is Getting Harder to Find," *The Wall Street Journal,* February 9, 1988, p. 39.

[20]W. Graham Astley, "Toward An Appreciation of Collective Strategy," *Academy of Management Review* 9 (1984):526–535; W. Graham Astley and Charles J. Fombrun, "Collective Strategy: Social Ecology of Organizational Environments," *Academy of Management Review* 8 (1983):576–587.

[21]R. Edward Freeman and Daniel R. Gilbert, Jr., "Managing Stakeholder Relationships," in *Business and Society: Dimensions of Conflict and Cooperation,* S. Prakash Sethi and Cecilia M. Falbe, eds. (Lexington, Mass.: Lexington Books, 1987).

[22]William M. Evan and R. Edward Freeman, "A Stakeholder Theory of the Modern Corporation: Kantian Capitalism," in *Ethical Theory and Business,* 3rd ed., Tom L. Beauchamp and Norman E. Bowie, eds. (Englewood Cliffs, N.J.: Prentice Hall, 1988), pp. 102–103.

[23]Our discussion of the indirect-action variables in the following sections is largely drawn from Liam Fahey and V. K. Narayanan, *Macroenvironmental Analysis for Strategic Management* (St. Paul: West Publishing, 1986).

[24]Arsenio Oloroso, Jr., "Elder Care Comes of Age," *Crain's Chicago Business,* July 9, 1990, pp. 17, 19–20.

[25]Fahey and Narayanan, *Macroenvironmental Analysis,* p. 73. The remainder of this section is based on Fahey and Narayanan, pp. 74–78.

[26]Frank Taylor, "Women Grab Management Power," *International Management* 39, no. 2 (February 1984):24, 25ff.

[27]Marshall Sashkin, "Participative Management Is an Ethical Imperative," *Organizational Dynamics* 12, no. 4 (Spring 1984):5–22.

[28]N. Rescher, "What Is a Value Change? A Framework for Research," in *Values and the Future,* K. Baier and N. Rescher, eds. (New York: Free Press, 1969).

[29]J. B. Quinn and J. A. Mueller, "Transferring Research Results to Operations," *Harvard Business Review* 41 (January–February 1963).

[30]Arthur D. Little and Co., "Strategic Management of Technology." Paper presented at the European Forum, 1981.

[31]H.E. Aldrich and S. Mindlin, "Uncertainty and Dependence: Two Perspectives on Environment," in *Organization and Environment,* L. Karpik, ed. (Beverly Hills, Calif.: Sage, 1978), pp. 149–170.

[32]Aldrich and Mindlen, *Organization and Environment;* M. T. Hannan and J. H. Freeman, "The Population Ecology of Organizations," *American Journal of Sociology* 82 (1977):929–964.

[33]M. E. Porter, *Competitive Strategy* (New York: Free Press, 1980).

[34]A useful discussion of how managers respond to the challenges of the environment is found in Rosemary Stewart, "Managerial Agendas—Reactive or Proactive?" *Organizational Dynamics* 8, no. 2 (Autumn 1979):34–47. According to Stewart, *reactive* managers respond to events after they have taken place, while *proactive* managers provide for future eventualities in their plans and programs.

CHAPTER FOUR

SOCIAL RESPONSIBILITY AND ETHICS

Upon completing this chapter, you should be able to:

1. Discuss the basic principles of Andrew Carnegie's *The Gospel of Wealth*.

2. Evaluate the criticisms of Carnegie's gospel.

3. Explain Milton Friedman's position on corporate social responsibility.

4. Compare and contrast Carnegie's views with those of Friedman.

5. Discuss the main models of corporate social responsiveness.

6. Evaluate corporate social responsiveness as a guide to organizational action.

7. Explain the difference between *social responsibility* and *business ethics*.

8. List and define the key terms used in ethics.

9. Explain the basic tenets of common morality.

10. Compare the "justice" and "care" perspectives on moral reasoning.

11. Discuss the issues a manager must consider in applying ethics.

12. Explain how managers can institutionalize ethics.

13. Evaluate the challenge of relativism to moral reasoning.

Lewis Hines, *Carolina Cotton Mill.* 1900–1909. Photo courtesy of the Library of Congress. Like ethical insights, compelling artistic images frequently refuse to remain confined to the realm of the abstract or aesthetic: Some of Hines's photographic images were so powerful that they helped prompt laws prohibiting child labor.

ILLUSTRATIVE CASE STUDY

INTRODUCTION

The *Exxon Valdez:* Corporate Responsibility and the Environment

Just after midnight on March 24, 1989, the oil tanker *Exxon Valdez,* carrying more than 1.2 million barrels of oil, struck Bligh Reef in Prince William Sound, Alaska. For the next several days, the tanker lay precariously grounded on the reef, threatening to break apart. More than 300,000 barrels of oil spilled into the water, coating over a thousand miles of shoreline with a poisonous slick that killed thousands of birds, fish, and sea creatures and endangered everyone who depended on the sound.

The response to the oil spill was a managerial nightmare. No one was certain who should take action: Was it Alyeska? (Alyeska, the consortium of six oil companies that own the Trans-Alaska pipeline, did have a clean-up team stationed in the sound.) Or was it Exxon, the Coast Guard, or some combination of federal, state, and local government officials?

Whenever one of these groups did advocate decisive action—for instance, using chemical dispersants to burn off large parts of the slick—others would object. Critical hours and days were lost as decision making became bogged down in committee. By all accounts, clean-up efforts came far too late to prevent the worst damage and were well short of what was projected in Alyeska's contingency plan.

What took place was inevitable, critics charged. As far back as 1982, Alyeska had dismantled its team devoted to round-the-clock oil-spill response— "without permission," according to Alyeska managing engineer William Howitt. Since then, steady cutbacks by oil companies and politicians on equipment, personnel, and funds had made a significant, prompt response to a spill unlikely. In fact, the first Alyeska response team did not arrive on the scene until 14 hours after the spill was reported, and Exxon did not have the proper equipment on location or even at hand. Transportation Secretary Samuel Skinner claimed that, on a scale of 1 to 10, response was a zero.

Exxon's management was also faulted for *causing* the spill. It was later revealed that veteran Captain Joseph Hazelwood was not on the bridge at the time of the grounding, but had left the ship in the hands of a third mate who was not licensed to steer the tanker. Critics were incensed to learn that Hazelwood, who disappeared immediately after the acci-

dent, had been drinking the evening of March 24. When he was finally tested *nine* hours after the grounding, his blood alcohol level was .06 (.10 is considered legally intoxicated in most states). Furthermore, Hazelwood was known to have a history of drinking problems and his driver's license had been revoked three times since 1984; indeed, his driver's license was suspended at the time of the accident. Nonetheless, Exxon had continued to employ Hazelwood as a captain on its huge supertankers, an act critics labeled highly irresponsible.

For months, the media were filled with pictures of paid and volunteer efforts to clean the beaches and to rescue sick and dying birds and animals. This was perhaps the most ingrained media image in the minds of Americans in 1989. While the spill helped catapult a grass-roots environmental movement onto the American political agenda, it gave Exxon and the oil industry a black eye and raised lingering questions about corporate social responsibility and ethics.

Sources: Martha Peak, "The Alaskan Oil Spill: Lessons in Crisis Management," *Management Review,* April 1990, pp. 12–21; Ben Yagoda, "Cleaning Up a Dirty Image," *Business Month,* April 1990, pp. 48–51; Art Davidson, *In the Wake of the* Exxon Valdez (Sierra Club Books, 1990); Don Phillips, "Safety Board Spreads Blame for *Exxon Valdez* Oil Spill," *The Washington Post,* August 1,1990, p. A2; Casey Burko, "Cleanup Worse Than Oil Spill, Expert Says," *Chicago Tribune,* September 17, 1990, p. 1.

TEACHING TIP
Start this chapter off by
asking students to write
down what a "socially re-
sponsible organization"
would be like. Write some
of the answers on the
board. Compare and con-
trast the responses. Ask
students to write down
what an "ethical manager"
would be like. Again use
the responses as a basis
for comparing and con-
trasting.

Exxon's dilemma typifies, albeit on a massive scale, the moral dilemma all managers face every day. At one time, it was enough to determine an organization's *responsibility* to specific internal and external stakeholders. Exxon's managers, for instance, complied with government regulations (an external stakeholder). However, they cut back on the equipment and personnel needed to respond to an oil spill to satisfy customers (external stakeholders), who wanted "low" prices, and stockholders (internal stakeholders), who expected a certain return on their investment. As the organizational environment grows more complex, it becomes harder and harder to identify stakeholders and sort out an organization's conflicting obligations. In the case of a massive oil spill or a nuclear incident, for instance, an organization may find itself with millions of stakeholders who are directly affected by managerial decisions. For this reason, the earlier emphasis on corporate social responsibility has given way to an emphasis on the broader guidelines of *ethics*. In this chapter, we will trace this evolution of thought, including the challenge of relativism.[1]

■ THE CHANGING CONCEPT OF SOCIAL RESPONSIBILITY

HERE'S AN EXAMPLE
Xerox was cited by the
Council on Economic Pri-
orities for its long history
of community involve-
ment. For example,
Xerox's social service
leave program allows eligible employees to take one
year's leave, at full pay, to
perform community ser-
vice. (*Newsweek*, 5/28/90,
p. 3)

HERE'S AN EXAMPLE
The Council on Economic
Priorities cited Pitney
Bowes for its strong af-
firmative action practices
as well as for its benefits
program, which includes
profit sharing, a suggestion
program, and a generous
child-care leave. (*News-
week*, 5/28/90, p. 3)

charity principle Doctrine of social responsibility requiring more fortu-
nate individuals to assist
less fortunate members of
society.

stewardship principle
Biblical doctrine that requires businesses and
wealthy individuals to
view themselves as stew-
ards, or caretakers, holding
their property in trust for
the benefit of the whole
society.

Big businesses has always been criticized, beginning around the turn of the century, when crusading journalists—the "muckrakers"—shocked the nation with exposés of corrupt business practices, touching off a wave of government regulation. (See Chapter 2.) Another wave of government regulation was created in the wake of the Great Depression of the 1930s and then again in the 1960s and 1970s, when the civil rights and consumer movements held corporations responsible for a growing list of social problems.

These regulations provide some ground rules for managers, but they do not answer more pressing questions: Where does an organization's social responsibility begin? Where does it end? To answer these questions, we need to take a closer look at different views of corporate social responsibility and responsiveness that have developed over the past century.

Andrew Carnegie and the Gospel of Wealth

In 1899, Andrew Carnegie (1835–1919), founder of the conglomerate U.S. Steel corporation, published a book called *The Gospel of Wealth,* which set forth the classic statement of *corporate social responsibility.* Carnegie's view was based on two principles: the charity principle and the stewardship principle. Both were frankly paternalistic; they saw business owners as parents to childlike employees and customers who lacked the capacity to act in their own best interests.[2]

The **charity principle** required the more fortunate members of society to assist its less fortunate members, including the unemployed, the handicapped, the sick, and the elderly. These unfortunates could be aided either directly or indirectly, through such institutions as churches, settlement houses, and (from the 1920s onward) the Community Chest movement. Of course, well-to-do people themselves decided how much to contribute, and charity was considered an obligation of individuals, not of business itself. By the 1920s, however, "community needs outgrew the wealth of even the most generous wealthy individuals,"[3] and business was expected to contribute its resources to charities aiding the unfortunate. Carnegie himself practiced what he preached by giving away millions of dollars for charitable and civil purposes.

The **stewardship principle,** derived from the Bible, required businesses and wealthy individuals to view themselves as the stewards, or caretakers, of their property. Carnegie's idea was that the rich hold their money "in trust" for the rest of

COORDINATED RESOURCE

See *Management Live!* Reading 16.2, "Stinky B.C. Pulp Mill Clears the Air."

society and can use it for any purpose that society deems legitimate. However, it is also a function of business to multiply society's wealth by increasing its own through prudent investments of the resources under its stewardship.[4]

U.S. Steel, acting on Carnegie's ideas, embarked upon an active program of philanthropy. Admittedly, it was the exception rather than the rule; between the Civil War and the Great Depression, most management commitments to social welfare were encouraged either by law or by labor-movement pressure.[5]

Not until the Great Depression of the 1930s did large numbers of executives take an independent interest in the social impact of business. In 1936, for example, Robert Wood (the CEO of Sears, Roebuck) pointed proudly to his "stewardship" of "those general broad social responsibilities which cannot be presented mathematically and yet are of prime importance."[6] Such views were the starting point for a new vision of the social responsibilities of business.

THOUGHT PROVOKER

Ask your students if their attitudes toward work are any different from their parents' attitudes. How? Ask them if their lifestyles are any different from their parents' lifestyles. How? How do these changes affect the changing concept of responsibilities?

By the 1950s and 1960s, the charity and stewardship principles were widely accepted in American business as more and more companies came to recognize that "power begets responsibility." Even companies that did not subscribe to these principles realized that if business did not accept social responsibilities of its own free will, it would be forced to accept them by the government. Many others believed that acknowledging social responsibilities was a matter of "enlightened self-interest." Dayton Hudson in Minneapolis, a leader in corporate philanthropy, supports a group of companies called "the 5% club," which give 5 percent of their pre-tax earnings to charity. After a number of years of giving to the community, Dayton Hudson was in a position to get an anti-takeover law passed by the Minnesota legislature when it needed it.

But even at the high point of concern for corporate social responsibility, in the 1950s and 1960s, doubts began to undermine it. In 1953, H. R. Bowen insisted that business managers are morally bound to "pursue those policies, to make those deci-

The Stewardship Principle. Protestors helped close many nuclear plants in the 1970s, claiming utilities were more interested in profits than in the future safety of the planet. However, a few plants, like the San Onofre nuclear plant in southern California (right), have shown that nuclear plants can operate without jeopardizing the environment or their human neighbors. Meanwhile, GE and Westinghouse are both developing nuclear plants with standardized modular designs that can be built more simply and operated more safely than previous designs. Ultimately, these plants may reduce dependence on oil shipments and the risk of *Valdez*-type spills.

sions, or to follow those lines of action which are desirable in terms of the objectives and values of our society."[7] This rather different concept of the social responsibilities of business—one that saw business both as a reflection of social "objectives and values" and as an agency for promoting them—inspired much new thinking on the subject.

The charity and stewardship principles appealed chiefly to those who had a vested interest in preserving the free enterprise system with its assurance of freedom from other forms of social pressure. Thus it attracted "an odd coalition of critics" that included just about everyone who was skeptical of the corporate commitment to balancing social needs with economic needs:

> Included among the opponents were leftist critics ("It's a capitalist smokescreen hiding profits and greed"); free-market advocates ("It reduces market efficiency"); liberal critics ("Its impact is marginal"); and a large but unknown number of hard-nosed business executives ("It's impractical, too costly, and unworkable").[8]

One problem had to do with the meaning of the term *social responsibility.* Some critics suggested that the concept of "social responsibility" did not indicate the appropriate magnitude of corporate concern, nor did it suggest how a company should weigh its social responsibilities against its other responsibilities. For example, when Ford was developing the Pinto model, the company discovered that the gas tank was unusually prone to catching fire in crashes. The company undertook a cost-benefit analysis to see if fixing the problem would be worthwhile. The analysis showed that the company could make the car much safer by installing an $11 shield for the gas tank, but Ford decided not to do this. In effect, it decided that the human lives disrupted and destroyed by the faulty gas tanks were worth less than $11 per Pinto.[9]

TEACHING TIP

You might want to set up a debate format with one group for social responsibility and one group taking Milton Friedman's point of view.

Finally, some critics charged that the notion of "social responsibility" permitted business executives to choose their corporations' social obligations according to their own lights. In this sense, the notion of corporate responsibility became a smokescreen for the personal values of a few powerful individuals.

Milton Friedman's Argument

In the 1970s and 1980s, the convergence of a number of economic forces led some scholars to reexamine the notion of corporate social responsibility. Business was reeling from the one-two punch of rising energy costs and the expense of complying with legislation designed to reduce pollution, protect consumers, and ensure equal opportunity. In addition, inflation and the national debt were soaring—a legacy of the Vietnam War, the Great Society programs of the 1960s, and the shifting balance of trade. Many held that if businesses were to survive, they must be relieved of inappropriate social responsibilities and allowed to get back to basics: making money. This is not a new idea. In fact, *caveat emptor* ("let the buyer beware") goes back to the Roman Empire. In our own time, the economist Milton Friedman has been the leading proponent of the idea that a business's primary responsibility is to maximize profits.

DISCUSSION QUESTION

Who should be expected to bear the costs of corporate social activities? (Responses will usually be the consumer, the company, perhaps employees, etc.)

According to Friedman, "There is one and only one social responsibility of business: to use its resources and energy in activities designed to increase its profits so long as it stays within the rules of the game . . . [and] engages in open and free competition, without deception and fraud. . . ." Friedman contends that corporate officials are in no position to determine the relative urgency of social problems or the amount of organizational resources that should be committed to a given problem.[10] He also insists that managers who devote corporate resources to pursue personal, and perhaps misguided, notions of the social good unfairly tax their own shareholders, employees, and customers. In short, businesses should produce goods

DISCUSSION QUESTION
Is a company behaving in a socially responsible manner if it refuses to make necessary changes that will keep it in business? (This question will stir up some interesting discussion.)

TEACHING TIP
Have students look in current business periodicals for examples of socially responsible actions taken by organizations, and bring them to class.

and services efficiently and leave the solution of social problems to concerned individuals and government agencies.

More recently, Friedman has argued that government intervention is also often undesirable.[11] He charges that bureaucratic officials responsible for implementing programs actually have little incentive to solve the problems their organizations were created to deal with.

Friedman favors eliminating Social Security and other government benefits and adopting in their place a limited set of government policies to influence national income. Citing growing productivity problems, he believes that our present system discourages work, and he wants to give individuals greater freedom to make their own economic decisions, without government controls. He believes that this freedom would lead to less waste and greater productivity.

Friedman's views represent one extreme on a continuum that recognizes some division of social responsibility among the various segments of society, including government and the business community. Most managers and other people believe that both the government and the business community do have some responsibility to act in the interest of society. As the two most powerful institutions in the country, their sheer size obliges them to address problems of public concern. Both corporations and government depend upon acceptance by the society to which they belong. For them to ignore social problems might in the long run be destructive. In any case, if business does not amend its public image voluntarily, it will almost inevitably be subjected to increased government regulation.

Government Responsibility. Gerard F. Scannell heads the Occupational Safety and Health Administration (OSHA), the federal agency charged with ensuring safe and healthful working conditions. The former head of safety at Johnson & Johnson, Scannell has proposed standards that require all people who drive as part of their job to wear a seat belt and prepared guidelines to eliminate repetitive-motion disorders, the cause of half of all workplace illnesses and disabilities. In a show of force, Scannell levied fines of $7.3 million against USX for safety, health, and record-keeping violations, and pushed Ford Motor Co. to institute a company-wide program to reduce repetitive-motion hazards on the assembly line.

COORDINATED RESOURCE
See Samaras Reading and DuBose Reading #28, "The Four Faces of Social Responsibility."

COORDINATED RESOURCE
Use Transparency 13, The Theory of Corporate Social Responsiveness.

corporate social responsiveness A theory of social responsibility that focuses on how companies respond to issues, rather than trying to determine their ultimate social responsibility.

HERE'S AN EXAMPLE
Kentucky Fried Chicken is missing something—the word "fried." From now on, the chicken company will be known as KFC. Their senior VP of marketing says, "It is equally important to us to be cool and contemporary as to be nutritionally relevant." (*Newsweek*, 4/8/91, p. 44)

Keith Davis has said that there is "an iron law of responsibility which states that in the long run those who do not use power in a manner that society considers responsible will tend to lose it."[12] Procter & Gamble's quick action in voluntarily removing from the market the Rely tampon, which may have been responsible for toxic shock syndrome in the early 1980s, is an example of one company's awareness of this "law."[13] In a January 1988 survey by *Fortune,* Procter & Gamble was ranked third behind Johnson & Johnson and Eastman Kodak as corporations most admired for their community and environmental responsibility; in *Fortune's* February 1991 survey, Procter & Gamble was still ranked third (behind Merck and Rubbermaid) in a listing of America's most admired corporations.

Corporate Social Responsiveness

Philosophical debates about social responsibility tend to raise more questions than they answer, frustrating managers who are primarily interested in practical guidelines and concrete results. For this reason, many managers and theorists turned to **corporate social responsiveness,** which studies how organizations become aware of and then respond to social issues.

Corporate social responsiveness takes two basic approaches. On the microlevel, it analyzes how individual companies respond to social issues. This approach is represented by Robert Ackerman's model. On the macrolevel, the theory studies the forces that determine the social issues to which businesses should respond. This approach is represented by Preston and Post's model. Archie Carroll's theory combines the micro and macro approach to classify the ways in which corporations can and do respond to specific social issues. (See Fig. 4-1.) In the rest of this section, we will see how these three models build upon one another.

ACKERMAN'S MODEL. Robert Ackerman was among the first to suggest that responsiveness, not responsibility, should be the goal of corporate social endeavors. Ackerman described three phases through which companies commonly pass in developing a response to social issues.[14]

In phase 1, a corporation's top managers learn of an existing social problem. At this stage, no one asks the company to deal with it. The chief executive officer merely acknowledges the problem by making a written or oral statement of the company's policy toward it.

FIGURE 4-1 The Theory of Corporate Social Responsiveness

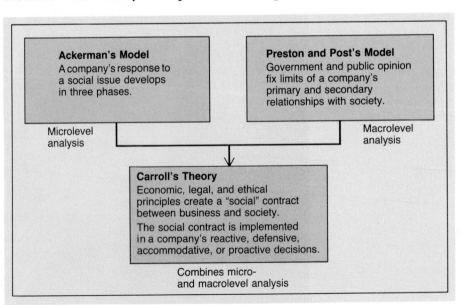

In phase 2, the company hires staff specialists or engages outside consultants to study the problem and to suggest ways of dealing with it. Up to this point, the company has limited itself to declaring its intentions and formulating its plans.

Phase 3 is implementation. The company now integrates the policy into its ongoing operations. Unfortunately, implementation often comes slowly—often only after the government or public opinion forces the company to act. By that time, the company has lost the initiative. Ackerman advises managers to "act early in the life cycle of any social issue in order to enjoy the largest amount of managerial discretion over the outcome."[15]

For example, it has recently been suggested that women who spend a great deal of time working at video display terminals stand a higher-than-average chance of having problem pregnancies. The research is confusing and disputed by some investigators. Ackerman's point is that as this issue unfolds, and as more actors and competing interests become involved, managers could lose the power to handle the issue at their own discretion. We can easily imagine several studies confirming these early indications and the resulting drama of congressional hearings, work stoppages, lawsuits, and bureaucratic regulation. In Ackerman's model, options are developed early in the life cycle of such an issue. "Enlightened" companies would make the best information available to their employees, encourage them to ask questions, and even give transfers or retraining to workers who request them. Being responsive may well be the only responsible course of action.

PRESTON AND POST'S MODEL. As Ackerman well knew, companies tend to react slowly to just about any social problem. Even the most responsive of them take up to eight years to reach the third and highest stage of response. By the late 1960s, many social activists had concluded that business would act decisively on social problems only if prodded by the government.[16]

Lee Preston and James Post presented one of the first definitive statements of the macro approach to the concept of corporate responsiveness.[17] In this model, business and society interact in two distinct ways. The **primary relations** of business—with customers, employees, shareholders, and creditors—are market-oriented. When these relations create social problems, **secondary** (or nonmarket) **relations,** such as with the law and morality, come into play.

Government and public opinion, claim Preston and Post, fix the limits of both market and nonmarket relations. When managers encounter a social problem, they do not merely examine their own consciences in deciding what to do about it. They also have to examine the law—federal, state, and local, including rulings by courts and regulatory agencies. And they have to consider public opinion.

For example, a company may decide to institute an affirmative action program to broaden its employee base by including more women and minorities. But even noble sentiments should not be embodied in policy without a clear knowledge of the law. Before Procter & Gamble took the Rely tampon off the market, it studied the regulatory climate and was quite aware of the risk of continuing to market Rely if there were liability suits from victims of toxic shock syndrome.

CARROLL'S THEORY. In 1979, Archie Carroll tried to combine the philosophical ideas of social responsibility and the earlier models of social responsiveness into a single theory of corporate social action called **corporate social performance.**[18]

The macrolevel—the arena of social responsibility debates—is shaped by economic, legal, and ethical principles. In this country, for example, we support free enterprise (an economic principle), the public's right to a safe workplace (a legal principle), and equal employment opportunity (an ethical principle). Together, these principles create a "social contract" between business and society, permitting companies to act as moral agents.

On the microlevel, companies try to implement the *principles* of the social contract in their decision-making *processes* and in their company *policies.* These decisions and policies may be *reactive* (the company only responds to a social issue *after* it has challenged company goals), *defensive* (the company acts to ward off a challenge), *accommodative* (the company brings itself into line with government requirements and public opinion), or *proactive* (the company anticipates demands that have not yet been made).[19]

What determines which position a specific company will take? To answer this question, we need to look at the interaction of the microlevel and the macrolevel. On the macrolevel, how strongly does the public feel about an issue? Is the government likely to be strict or relaxed in enforcing regulations? On the microlevel, how does the issue fit in with company's goals and policies? Does it strike at the heart of the company's activities or is it marginal? VDT safety, for example, would be a much more important issue for a newspaper, where almost every worker uses a VDT, than for a chain of health clubs, where only a few office workers use VDTs. *If* workers express concern or management *anticipates* rising health insurance claims, the newspaper might want to take a defensive, accommodative, or even proactive stance, depending on its interpretation of the real risk, government policy, and the issue's impact on employee health and morale.

THE LIMITATIONS OF CORPORATE SOCIAL RESPONSIVENESS MODELS. The shift from concern for "responsibility" to "responsiveness" and "performance" was an advance for several reasons. It gave business executives a more realistic framework for making decisions about social policy, shifting the focus of the debate from abstract speculation to concrete operational decisions.[20] But a practical and basic problem remains to be solved: Precisely which values should social responsiveness try to encourage? For example, should business be responsive to all social demands or only some of them? If only some, then which ones? Should companies change their social priorities when the government changes theirs? Or should companies hold fast to one set of priorities no matter what government does?

The meaning of social "responsiveness" is quite fluid, depending upon a given company's shifting attitude toward a particular issue. In fact, it seems to mean whatever the business community intends it to mean at a given time and in a given case.[21] When restaurants in racist towns refused to serve blacks, were they not being "responsive" to community sentiment? By contrast, when a company like Control Data tries to make a business out of inner-city redevelopment and train the hard-core unemployed, it is being technically "unresponsive" because it is striking out in a new direction. Similar ambiguities apply to companies that bolster political regimes in other countries. Who defines community or national interest in a country like South Africa? Is apartheid, maintained by the ruling white minority, in the interests of the total community? Many U.S. corporations have left South Africa because of its political situation; those that remain struggle with such dilemmas.

The real difficulty with all the models described in this section is that they provide no way of effectively managing a conflict in *values*. They offer little advice about how to solve disputes that represent fundamentally different visions of the world. What we need is a model that is more directly concerned with ethics.

■ *THE SHIFT TO ETHICS*

The changing concepts of responsibility, responsiveness, and performance are manifested in what some critics call the "ethics crisis." We see headlines that touch upon it daily. Wedtech and other companies have been accused of exerting improper influence upon the federal government in the awarding of contracts. Wall Street's already low reputation plunged still lower with the insider-trading scandal. More recently, the savings and loan crisis has shaken the public trust. Not surprisingly, pollster Louis Harris reported that 70 percent of the public answers no to the question, "Does business see to it that its executives behave legally and ethically?"[22]

ILLUSTRATIVE CASE STUDY

CONTINUED

The *Exxon Valdez:* Corporate Responsibility and the Environment

The theories of social responsibility and responsiveness provide a number of tools for evaluating the performance of Exxon and Alyeska. For example, many critics claimed that Exxon and Alyeska violated the public interest by being so grossly unprepared for the spill. The basis of this charge is, of course, Andrew Carnegie's stewardship principle.

Others pointed out that Exxon and Alyeska had cut back on the personnel and equipment needed to deal with oil spills. In this, of course, they were following Milton Friedman's directive to companies to do whatever maximizes profit.

In looking back at Exxon and Alyeska's efforts to clean up the spill, we can also see elements of social responsiveness. Once it was aware of the problem, Exxon initiated a number of *reactive* decisions. It promptly admitted responsibility for the accident and its clean-up response was as prompt and comprehensive as possible under the circumstances.

Bad weather slowed the transportation of needed materials and the use of chemical dispersants, while the confused chain of command initially paralyzed Exxon's efforts to tackle the problem. Still, many experts have hailed Exxon as one of the best-managed oil-shipping companies in the world and exonerated it from the most serious charges of negligence on the grounds that no single organization could adequately respond to a disaster the size of the *Exxon Valdez* spill.

Exxon claims the accident was the result of human error—a frustrating but inescapable part of life. It readily admitted that Hazelwood should have been on the bridge at the time of the grounding, and later gave this as a reason for firing him (another reactive decision). However, Exxon claimed that it could not have foreseen Hazelwood's error. True, the company was aware of the captain's drinking problem, but it had reason to believe that it was under control.

In this claim, we can see Exxon honoring an ethical commitment to an employee who had tried to overcome a personal problem. Furthermore, Exxon, aware that heavy drinking is common among seamen,

had instituted a random drug-testing policy to weed out drug-abusing employees. Even employees who have been successfully treated for drug abuse cannot hold "safety sensitive" positions, a policy affecting about 10 percent of Exxon's 20,000 jobs. In this, Exxon was *proactive*—anticipating future demands. And in a move that was both proactive and reactive, six major U.S. oil companies formed the Marine Spill Response Corporation in September 1990 to help clean up future major oil spills.

Despite all these efforts, Exxon suffered an immeasurable loss of public esteem. Indeed, the conglomerate sees itself as being unfairly punished for a tragic accident that it took every reasonable measure to prevent and then spent exhaustive energies and resources cleaning up. By the spring of 1991, Exxon estimated it had spent $2.5 billion on cleanup efforts during the summers of 1989 and 1990, pausing only for winter weather.

Exxon received another blow in April 1991. As part of a combined $1 billion civil and criminal settlement, Exxon had offered to pay a record $100 million fine to avoid felony charges. Although some influential environmental groups hailed this as a step in the right direction, many thought Exxon was getting off easy. Indeed, Exxon Chairman Lawrence Rawl assured stockholders the settlement would not affect company profits, giving support to an Associated Press analysis that Exxon could halve the real cost of the settlement by taking advantage of tax savings and by buying an annuity to make the required payments over 10 years.

Bowing to the ensuing letters of protest, U.S. District Judge H. Russell Holland rejected Exxon's offer, saying he did not want to send a message that such fines could be absorbed as a cost of doing business. (On that same day, Exxon had announced first quarter profits were up 75 percent.) This ruling, while satisfying to some, called into question the settlement of related civil claims, leaving many people outraged and worried that cleanup efforts would be stalled during subsequent renegotiations or litigation.

In a proactive move of its own, meanwhile, Congress passed the Oil Pollution Act in August 1990, setting up a $1 billion Oil Spill Liability Trust Fund and requiring all oil tankers to have double hulls. (Some experts claim the latter measure would have reduced the severity of the *Exxon Valdez* spill; others counter that double hulls would be of little value in a serious crash.) In this act, we can see the truth of the maxim that if a business does not amend its public image, it will almost always be subject to increased government regulation.

Source: Casey Burko, "Cleanup Worse Than Oil Spill, Expert Says," *Chicago Tribune,* September 17, 1990, Sect. 1, p. 1; William C. Symonds et al., "Is Business Bungling Its Battle with Booze?" *Business Week,* March 25, 1991, pp. 76–78; New York Times News Service, "Exxon: Spill Pay-Out Won't Hurt Company," *Chicago Tribune,* Sect. 1, p. 16; Chicago Tribune Wire Service, "Exxon Penalty Too Small, Judge Orders," *Chicago Tribune,* April 25, 1991, Sect. 1, pp. 1, 18.

COORDINATED RESOURCE
See Samaras Exercise 1.4, "The Iran-Contra Affair."

COORDINATED RESOURCE
See *Management Live!* Reading 16.1, "Ethical Managers Make Their Own Rules."

Gallup, another polling organization, reported similar findings from an earlier poll in 1983. According to that poll, almost 50 percent of all Americans thought that business ethics had declined during the previous ten years.[23] Executives themselves are unhappy about the current business climate: Close to 40 percent say "superiors have at some point asked them to do something they considered unethical."[24]

Although public opinion polls, especially different ones done at different points in time, cannot be taken as definitive reflections of business conditions, all recent polls point in the same direction: Public confidence in business ethics has declined. As a result, many theorists are calling for a broader examination of business ethics. Because every business decision has an ethical component, effective managers must add the ideas of ethics to their managerial tool kits.

What Is Ethics?

THOUGHT PROVOKER
"If an ATM gave you $200 too much, would you tell the bank?" More than half of the 7.4 million customers surveyed in 7-Eleven stores said they would keep the money. (*Wall Street Journal,* 3/14/91, p. A1)

Assessments of an organization's *social responsibility* cover its relationships with the external world; *ethics* is a more general term that covers both internal and external relationships. Some writers make a further distinction between "ethics" and "morals," but we believe that this is needlessly confusing, so we will define *ethics* broadly and simply as the study of how our decisions affect other people. It is also the study of people's rights and duties, the moral rules that people apply in making decisions, and the nature of the relationships among people.[25]

Four Levels of Ethical Questions in Business

COORDINATED RESOURCE
Use Transparency 14, The Four Levels of Ethical Questions.

CLASS COMMENT
"Always do right. This will surprise some people and astonish the rest"—Mark Twain.

CLASS COMMENT
Lawmakers are creating new enforcement tools and stiffer penalties to prevent corporate crime. For example, the Anti-Trust Amendment of 1990 increases the maximum penalties for price-fixing from $1 million to $10 million. (*Business Week,* 4/22/91, p. 102)

We cannot avoid ethical issues in business any more than we can avoid them in other areas of our lives. In business, most ethical questions fall into one of four levels, which are not mutually exclusive (see Fig. 4-2).

The first level might be called *societal.* At this level, we ask questions about the basic institutions in a society. The problem of apartheid in South Africa is a societal-level question: Is it ethically correct to have a social system in which a group of people—indeed, the majority—is systematically denied basic rights?

Another societal-level moral question concerns the merits of capitalism. Is capitalism a just system for allocating resources? What role should the government play in regulating the marketplace? Should we tolerate gross inequalities of wealth, status, and power?

Such societal-level questions usually represent an ongoing debate among major competing institutions. As managers and individuals, each of us can try to shape that debate. Andrew Carnegie (and other early theorists of corporate social responsibility) worked at this level by arguing that the proper role of a business such as his own U.S. Steel was to apply the principles of charity to assist the poor and unfortunate.

The second level of ethical questions concerns stakeholders—employees, suppliers, customers, shareholders, bondholders, and the rest. Here we ask questions

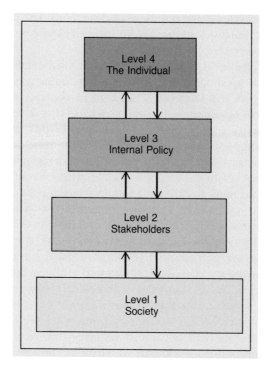

FIGURE 4-2 The Four Levels of Ethical Questions

HERE'S AN EXAMPLE

Mars Inc. is finding out the hard way that they shouldn't stereotype groups. Their commercial for Twix candy bars that pokes fun at all-girl schools was not viewed as funny by the Coalition of Girls' Schools, who demanded that the ad be scrapped. (*Wall Street Journal*, 4/1/91, p. B1)

about how a company should deal with the external groups affected by its decisions, as well as how the stakeholders should deal with the company.

There are many such issues. Insider trading is one; another is a company's obligation to inform its customers about the potential dangers of its products. What obligations does a company have to its suppliers? To the communities where it operates? To its stockholders? How should we attempt to decide such matters? No-

Levels of Ethics. When a fire destroyed family-owned Kidd & Co.'s Nevada marshmallow factory, vice president John Kidd (pictured) and his older brother Charlie decided to pay all 63 employees while they were rebuilding, honoring an obligation to employees and other stakeholders. In turn, the employees performed community service work. "Why pay them for staying at home?" asked John Kidd.

CLASS COMMENT

In a recent survey of corporate chief executives to determine the top four characteristics they most prefer in their employees, integrity was listed as number four in importance. (*Kwik-Copy Business Review,* Vol. 5 #1, p. 3)

TEACHING TIP

Have students identify business situations they might face where questions of ethics might arise. (For example, padding expense accounts like everyone else in the department; sending a secretary on a personal errand; knowing about a safety hazard in a work area, etc.)

tice that at this level, the questions deal with business policy. Stakeholder questions concern a company's relations with its key resources. Managers make decisions at this level every day.

The third level of moral discourse might be called "internal policy." At this level, we ask questions about the nature of a company's relations with its employees, both managers and workers. What kind of contract is fair? What are the mutual obligations of managers and workers? What rights do employees have? These question, too, pervade the workday of a manager. Layoffs, perks, work rules, motivation, and leadership are all ethical categories at the third level.

Finally, we come to the "personal" level of moral issues. At this fourth level we ask questions about how people should treat one another within a corporation. Should we be honest with one another, whatever the consequences? What obligations do we have—both as human beings and as workers who fill specific work roles—to our bosses, our subordinates, and our peers? These questions deal with the day-to-day issues of life in any organization. Behind them lie two broader issues: Do we have the right to treat other people as means to our ends? Can we avoid doing so?

Ethical questions must be confronted at all levels of business activity. Business ethics concern the ground rules of individual, company, and societal behavior. As philosophers such as Mark Pastin have argued, our behavior—on individual, company, and societal levels—implies ground rules we have already put in place.[26] "Doing ethics" is hard because it requires that we be critical of our own half-conscious ground rules and that we strive to improve them.

■ THE TOOLS OF ETHICS

Consciously or unconsciously, we engage in some kind of ethical reasoning every day of our lives; to improve our ethical reasoning, we must analyze it explicitly and practice it daily. Business will not overcome the moral uncertainties that now plague it until it learns to address ethical issues in ethical terms.

Ethical Language

Some companies, such as IBM, have an open-door policy that encourages employees to speak up about problems. Others, such as J. C. Penney, have spelled-out policies on conflicts of interest. (See the Management Application box entitled "A Code of Conduct at J. C. Penney.") Ethics uses terms that have been absent from a lot of management theory. The key terms of the ethical language are *values, rights, duties, rules,* and *relationships.* Let's consider each in turn.

VALUES. When you value something, you want it or you want it to happen. **Values** are relatively permanent desires that seem to be good in themselves, like peace or goodwill.

Values are the answers to the "why" questions. Why, for example, are you reading this book? You might reply that you want to learn about management. Why is that important? To be a better manager. Why do you want that? To be promoted and make more money sooner. Why do you need more money? To spend it on a VCR. Such questions go on and on, until you reach the point where you no longer want something for the sake of something else. At this point, you have arrived at a value. Corporations also have values, such as size or profitability or making a quality product.

THOUGHT PROVOKER

"The public tends to invest human life with infinite value and has little sympathy for businesses that profit from sustaining it. That puts pharmaceutical companies in a particularly tough bind." (*Fortune,* 11/5/90, p. 112ff.)

RIGHTS AND DUTIES. A **right** is a claim that entitles a person the "room" in which to take action. In more formal terms, one might call this room a person's "sphere of autonomy" or, more simply, his or her freedom. Rights are rarely absolute; most people would agree that the scope of individual rights is limited by the rights of

A Code of Conduct at J. C. Penney

J. C. Penney is one of many companies that have corporate codes of ethical conduct. Called "Conflicts of Interest," this code was meant to ensure that Penney's employees (whom it calls "Associates") do nothing that "could impair, or appear to impair, an Associate's ability to perform his or her Company duties or to exercise his or her judgment in a fair and unbiased manner."

The statement covers gifts, loans, and entertainments offered to Penney employees by people who do business with them. Penney recognizes in the statement that employees have a "right to conduct their personal affairs without interference." Nonetheless, the statement also points out that the company must also know if its employees have behaved in ways that are opposed to its own interests.

First, it must do so because some of the things that its employees could do—take bribes, for instance—are illegal. But what is a bribe? Let's suppose that a company doing business with Penney invites one of its employees to a lavish and expensive lunch. Does this constitute a "bribe"?

Not in principle, says the Penney statement, since attendance at "business-related functions, in-

cluding the acceptance of lunches or other meals . . . is a normal and permissible business practice." Penney merely advises its employees to make sure that "their value and frequency are not excessive." Dinners, theater tickets, hunting trips, and other kinds of business entertainment "may be accepted only if it is practical for the Associate to reciprocate." If employees cannot do so, they should take the problem to their supervisors.

The statement provides several such cases and the proper resolution of each. Suppose, for example, that another company were to invite a Penney employee to attend a two-day seminar at a fashionable resort. The seminar is the most important commercial event of the year in the employee's specialty, but she cannot reciprocate in any practical way. She therefore takes the problem to her supervisor, who should rule in favor of attendance, since it is "necessary or desirable at times in order that Associates remain current in their areas of responsibility for the Company."

Source: Ronald Berenbeim, *Corporate Ethics* (New York: The Conference Board, 1987), pp. 26–27.

---

others. Ordinarily, you have a right to speak your mind freely—until you make slanderous statements about another person.

Moreover, rights are correlated with duties. Whenever someone has a right, someone else has a duty to respect it. A **duty** is an obligation to take specific steps— to pay taxes, for example, and to obey the law in other respects.

duties Obligations to take specific steps or obey the law.

moral rules Rules for behavior that often become internalized as moral values.

MORAL RULES. **Moral rules** guide us through situations where competing interests collide. You might think of moral rules as "tie breakers"—guidelines that can resolve disagreements. Moral rules, which are rules for behavior, often become internalized as moral values.

RELATIONSHIPS. Every human being is connected to others in a web of relationships. These relationships exist because we need one another for mutual support and to accomplish our goals. From a small child's relationship with parents to a manager's relationship with an employee, relationships are a pervasive aspect of moral life. We constantly decide how to maintain and nurture them. These decisions reflect our values and our concern for ethics.

Common Morality

common morality The body of moral rules governing ordinary ethical problems.

Common morality is the body of moral rules governing ordinary ethical problems. These are the rules we live by most of the time. Let's briefly examine some basic principles of common morality to see how they work.

PROMISE KEEPING. Most of us want to have some assurance that other people will do what they say. Without the simple convention of promise keeping, social interaction would grind to a halt; business would be impossible. Every moral theory thus asserts, at the very least, that human beings should keep most of their promises most of the time. Insider trading became such a scandal in part because those who were caught had promised not to engage in such activities.

NONMALEVOLENCE. Among other things, rights and duties are a way of preventing violent conflict. If we constantly had to worry about our basic physical safety, we would be much less willing to trust other people and engage in more complex dealings with them in which disputes may arise that require resolution. Most moral theories thus require that most people, most of the time, refrain from harming other human beings.

There are, of course, exceptions: We allow the police to use force to subdue criminals; we accept wars that we regard as just; we let people defend themselves when they are attacked without cause. But morality requires us to avoid violence in settling disputes.

MUTUAL AID. Morality and moral codes regulate the behavior of human communities that include individuals who pursue both the group's common interests and their own separate interests. Just as we have a negative desire that these individuals refrain from harming us, we have a positive desire that they help us when we need help. From this desire we derive the principle that individuals should help one another if the cost of doing so is not great.

RESPECT FOR PERSONS. By and large, common morality also requires us to regard other people as ends in themselves, not as mere means to our own ends. Treating people as ends involves taking them seriously, accepting their interests as legitimate, and regarding their desires as important.

RESPECT FOR PROPERTY. The preceding principle, unlike those before it, is controversial. Even more controversial is the principle that most people, most of the time, should get the consent of others before using their property. If you think of people as owning their own bodies, respect for property is a corollary of respect for individuals.

The Morality of Care

Recent theorists such as Carol Gilligan and Nell Noddings have argued that common morality—the morality of rules and justice—is only one perspective for reasoning about morality. They have suggested an alternative mode of reasoning called "the ethics of care."[27] In this, they are reacting to moral-development theorists like Lawrence Kohlberg, who has suggested that there are seven stages of moral reasoning through which individuals normally progress as they pass from childhood to maturity. Women, he noticed, don't seem to reach the "higher" stages of moral reasoning that are concerned with such abstractions as justice and generalizable rules.

Refusing to accept Kohlberg's conclusion that women are morally immature, Gilligan argues instead that there are two strands of moral theory—the "justice" perspective and the "care" perspective—and that Kohlberg's theory represents the justice perspective typical of men. This should not be surprising, since Kohlberg studied only men when he was developing his theory. The care perspective, however, is more common among women.

People operating from the justice perspective emphasize separateness from others and an autonomous life. They see the solutions to moral problems as a balancing of competing rights in a formal and abstract manner. In contrast, the care perspective is characterized by a sense of connection to others, by a life of love and caring, and a view that moral problems arise from conflicting responsibilities, which require a contextual and narrative kind of thinking.

TABLE 4-1 Key Differences in the Justice and Care Perspectives

	Justice	Care
Orientation	Separation; autonomy	Attachment; interdependence
Mode of thinking	Formal; abstract	Contextual; narrative
Idea of morality	Fairness; rights; equality	Care; responsibility
	Primacy of individual	Primacy of relationship
	"Formal logic of fairness"	"Psychological logic of relationships"
	Separation justified by ethic of rights	Attachment required by ethic of care
Conflict resolution	Balancing rights; adversarial adjudication	Communication; protecting relationships
Responsibility	Limiting aggression and protecting rights	Extension of care and nurturing of relationships
Images of violence	Closeness	Isolation
Metaphor of relationship	Hierarchy or balance	Network or web

Source: Rebecca Villa, Andrew Wicks, and R. Edward Freeman, "A Note on the Ethics of Caring," (Charlottesville: The Darden School, UVA-E-068, 1990).

People who take the justice perspective fear entangling connections to others; they want to protect the rights that preserve separation. The care perspective, on the other hand, fears that morality of rights and noninterference will sanction indifference and unconcern. People who take the justice perspective criticize the care perspective as being inconclusive, ambiguous, and inconsistent because of its situational emphasis. Those who operate from the care perspective see the justice orientation as unfeeling, unemotional, and afraid of commitments. The main differences between these two perspectives are summarized in Table 4-1.

It is important to realize that both perspectives exist and that more comprehensive theories may someday integrate the two views. For now, we must be sure we work hard at understanding people coming from a different perspective than our own and that we try to reach mutually satisfactory solutions.[28]

Applying Ethics

COORDINATED RESOURCE

Use Transparency 15, Factors Affecting Ethical/ Unethical Behavior.

COORDINATED RESOURCE

The Application Exercise for Chapter 4 found in the Lecture Extras supplement asks students to describe a personal instance they have experienced regarding ethics in the workplace.

COORDINATED RESOURCE

See Samaras Case 1.4, "Images and Raindrops."

Like any other institution or organization—perhaps even more so—modern corporations establish certain rules that may conflict with the rules of common morality. For example, invoking the principle of mutual aid to assist a person who needs help might draw sneers from corporate managers if the distressed party is a competitor. We must know *how* to apply the principles of common morality and the language of ethics to business situations.

Let's consider one of the most important business events of recent history. On January 1, 1984, what had until then been the largest corporation in the world ceased to exist. The American Telephone and Telegraph Company (AT&T) was broken up into eight separate multimillion-dollar telephone-operating companies.

Why? Two years earlier, AT&T and the U.S. Justice Department had signed a consent decree in which the government agreed to drop its antitrust suit against the company and to permit AT&T to compete in the relatively unregulated computer business. In return, AT&T agreed to divest its large distribution network and local telephone business—seven Bell System operating companies.

The future of AT&T was up for grabs. Billions of dollars were at stake. But there were even more important issues. More than one million people worked for AT&T. Local communities throughout the United States depended on it for much of their employment base. Many smaller companies depended on sales to AT&T. Tens of

EXHIBIT 4-1 12 Questions for Examining the Ethics of a Business Decision

1. Have you defined the problem accurately?
2. How would you define the problem if you stood on the other side of the fence?
3. How did this situation occur in the first place?
4. To whom and to what do you give your loyalty as a person and as a member of the corporation?
5. What is your intention in making this decision?
6. How does this intention compare with the probable results?
7. Whom could your decision or action injure?
8. Can you discuss the problem with the affected parties before you make your decision?
9. Are you confident that your decision will be as valid over a long period of time as it seems now?
10. Could you disclose without qualm your decision or action to your boss, your CEO, the board of directors, your family, society as a whole?
11. What is the symbolic potential of your action if understood? If misunderstood?
12. Under what conditions would you allow exceptions to your stand?

Source: Laura L. Nash, "Ethics Without the Sermon," *Harvard Business Review* 59 (November–December 1981):78–90.

millions of people, in the United States and abroad, were customers. There were more than three million shareholders. Many people had come to expect that AT&T would provide everything from low-cost phone service to lifetime employment.

The AT&T divestiture was a matter of ethics because it distributed harms and benefits to various groups with a stake in the decision. Let us suppose that Charles Brown, then CEO of AT&T, decided to use the language of ethics in making this decision. To keep things simple, let's suppose that Mr. Brown had only two choices: to go on fighting the Justice Department or to accept the divestiture. Mr. Brown would then have to answer four questions. (Of course, these are not the only questions that might be asked. For another set of questions, see Exhibit 4-1.)

First, Mr. Brown must find out whom his decision will affect—for instance, stockholders, employees, customers, the government, suppliers, local communities, and competitors. He will also have to make an effort to see these groups as embodiments of real flesh-and-blood people, not as a mere faceless mass.

Second, Mr. Brown must know how his decision will affect the people in each group. The two strategic alternatives may yield different results. If AT&T decides to continue to fight the Justice Department, the outcome would be far from clear. Should AT&T prevail, its stockholders, its employees, its customers, its suppliers, its competitors, the government, and the local communities where it does business will all experience "business as usual." If the Justice Department prevails, the existing allocation of harms and benefits will change, and change differently for different groups.

Third, Mr. Brown needs to know the interests and desires of each group. He also needs to identify each group's rights. The stockholders have rights because they have risked their capital and are thus entitled to a return; employees have what they regarded as a virtual right to lifetime employment by AT&T, an expectation encouraged by the company; customers feel they have a right to the good low-priced service that the company has long provided.

Finally, Mr. Brown has to decide which rules to use and which relationships to maintain in making his decision. He might begin by examining the rules accepted by each stakeholding group. Traditionally, management has claimed to believe it should maximize the wealth of the stockholders. Mr. Brown could also view the decision from the standpoint of other stakeholders, and he must be prepared for the likelihood that these various standpoints will conflict. Whatever rules Mr. Brown decides to use, he will be allocating harms and benefits among the various stakeholders.

Institutionalizing Ethics

COORDINATED RESOURCE
See Study Guide Problem Exercise 4, "Ethics Score."

social audit Report describing a company's activities in a given area of social interest, such as environmental protection, workplace safety, or community involvement.

COORDINATED RESOURCE
Use Transparency 16, Social Responsibility and Ethics Over Time.

Mr. Brown and other CEOs do not have to confront these questions all alone. Instead, they can institutionalize the process of ethical decision making by ensuring that each moral decision builds upon preceding decisions. There are several ways of institutionalizing ethical policy, including corporate codes of conduct, ethics committees, ombudsman offices, judicial boards, ethics-training programs, and **social audits.**

One survey found that more than 90 percent of the companies that have tried to institutionalize ethics have created codes of ethics requiring and prohibiting specific practices. Although no more than 11 percent of these companies actually display their codes in offices and factories, most of them will dismiss, demote, or reprimand employees who intentionally violate those codes.[29] For one code that has become a model—especially given the company's trauma over the Tylenol-tampering disaster—see the box on "The Credo" at Johnson & Johnson.

Even though another survey reports that "codes have a limited effect in deterring the misbehavior of intentional wrong-doers," many companies feel that codes of ethics notify employees that business decisions should take account of ethical as well as economic considerations. "More importantly," the study concludes, codes of conduct remind employees "that the company is fully committed to stating its standards and is asking its work force to incorporate them into their daily activities."[30] Figure 4-3 indicates the groups to whom corporate ethics codes apply.

FIGURE 4-3 Groups to Whom Corporate Ethics Codes Apply (Survey of 225 Corporations)
Source: Ronald Berenbeim, *Corporate Ethics* (New York: The Conference Board, 1987), p. 15.

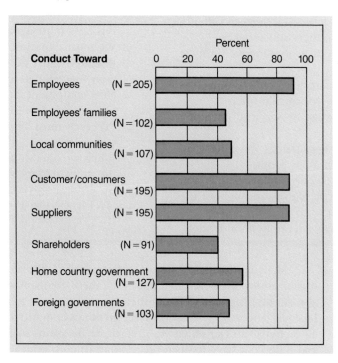

Ethics in Management

The Spirit of "The Credo" at Johnson & Johnson

In its beginnings, when it specialized in baby powder and bandage products, Johnson & Johnson was a highly centralized organization. Now it is both highly diversified, operating over 160 businesses in over 50 countries, and highly decentralized. The process of decentralization started under General Robert Wood Johnson, a son of one of the company's three founders, who took it over in 1932, and today each company has a president or managing director who reports to a company group chairperson but who generally manages his or her particular company with a fair amount of independence. Because Johnson & Johnson's decentralized structure depends so heavily on individual autonomy and decision making, the company established a "Credo" in 1945, not only to ensure its essential dedication to product quality, but also to encourage personal commitment to the goals of a loosely structured organization. "The Credo," says Chairman James Burke, "is our common denominator."

Our Credo

- We believe our first responsibility is to the doctors, nurses and patients, to mothers and all others who use our products and services.
- In meeting their needs everything we do must be of high quality.
- We must constantly strive to reduce our costs in order to maintain reasonable prices.
- Customers' orders must be serviced promptly and accurately.
- Our suppliers and distributors must have an opportunity to make a fair profit.
- We are responsible to our employees, the men and women who work with us throughout the world.
- Everyone must be considered as an individual.

- We must respect their dignity and recognize their merit.
- They must have a sense of security in their jobs.
- Compensation must be fair and adequate, and working conditions clean, orderly and safe.
- Employees must feel free to make suggestions and complaints.
- There must be equal opportunity for employment, development and advancement for those qualified.
- We must provide competent management, and their actions must be just and ethical.
- We are responsible to the communities in which we live and work and to the world community as well.
- We must be good citizens—support good works and charities and bear our fair share of taxes.
- We must encourage civic improvements and better health and education.
- We must maintain in good order the property we are privileged to use, protecting the environment and natural resources.
- Our final responsibility is to our stockholders.
- Business must make a sound profit.
- We must experiment with new ideas.
- Research must be carried on, innovative programs developed and mistakes paid for.
- New equipment must be purchased, new facilities provided and new products launched.
- Reserves must be created to provide for adverse times.
- When we operate according to these principles the stockholders should realize a fair return.

Source: Laura L. Nash, Nash Associates, Cambridge, Massachusetts, "Johnson & Johnson's Credo," in James Keogh, ed., *Corporate Ethics: A Prime Business Asset* (New York: The Business Roundtable, 1988), pp. 77–104.

Many companies trying to institutionalize ethical policy have created specific organizations to enforce that policy. Of these companies, more than 40 percent have also set up programs to teach their employees how to confront moral problems in business. Some 18 percent have set up ethics committees; 3 percent have appointed an ombudsman (an officer to investigate decisions from an ethical point of view); and 3 percent have judicial boards that rule on ethical questions.[31] Ethics training programs very often include discussion programs and workshops in which employees thrash out hypothetical moral problems. Participating companies report that "the give-and-take of these programs helps to sensitize employees to ethical issues, broaden and deepen employee awareness of code directives, and underscore the commitment of the company to its ethical principles."[32]

■ *THE CHALLENGE OF RELATIVISM*

HERE'S AN EXAMPLE
Judge Kimba Wood, in sentencing Michael Milken to ten years in prison, is sending a message that aims to deter white-collar crime. (*Time*, 12/3/90, p. 82)

Finally, we must confront the challenge of relativism to moral theory in general. There are many versions of moral relativism, but all of them hold that we cannot decide matters of right and wrong, good and evil, in any rational way.

Moral relativism seems to imply that since right and wrong are relative to whoever is making the decision, there are only individual answers to any moral question. It also suggests that constructive moral argument is impossible, for each person will do what is right for himself or herself. Though we may agonize over moral problems, we have no sure way of deciding that one decision is morally better than another.

Naive Relativism

naive relativism The idea that all human beings are themselves the standard by which their actions should be judged.

Perhaps the most widespread form of relativism might be called **naive relativism**—the idea that all human beings are themselves the standard by which their actions should be judged. The naive relativist believes that because ethical decisions are personal, important, and complex, only the decision maker's opinion is relevant.

However, it does not follow from the personal and serious nature of morality that we can't reason about it—quite the contrary. Precisely because morality is so vital to our lives, we must do our very best thinking in this area, and for this we need the help of people who are engaged in the process of moral reasoning. If we reject the idea that one's moral beliefs have to stand up to scrutiny and criticism, how will anyone get better at making moral choices? If there are no standards for deciding whether one moral decision is better or worse than another, how can we believe that morality is important?

Tolerance of others is necessary and good, but naive relativism takes tolerance too far. People often disagree about moral questions, but we should not therefore conclude that there can never be any reason for anything we do or that one course of action is always just as good as another. Instead, we must try to sort things out, because if we don't, we have admitted defeat in coming to terms with our own lives. Besides, the naive relativist's tolerance for all points of view is a contradiction in that it is itself an absolute point of view: "We must always be tolerant."

There is an even more compelling argument against naive relativism. In insisting that the moral test of any action is whether or not the agent believed it to be correct, naive relativism tells us that we need not check on the *content* of a particular action; we need only find out if the agent acted in accord with his or her beliefs. Therefore, any judgment about an action taken regarding such issues as abortion, infanticide, civil liberties, and capital punishment is necessarily suspended.

The real failing of naive relativism is its laziness: It is not a belief but rather an excuse for having no beliefs. It is hard to marshal facts and construct theories about many ethical questions, and the naive relativist just doesn't want to bother. Such moral laziness exacts a price. It requires giving up any hope of living in a better world or becoming a better human being.

Cultural Relativism

cultural relativism The idea that morality is relative to a particular culture, society, or community.

A second form of moral relativism, **cultural relativism,** claims that morality is relative to particular cultures, societies, or communities. It further asserts that no standards can help us *judge* the morality of a particular culture, and that the best anyone can hope to do is to *understand* the moral codes and customs of a given society.

Cultural relativism tells us to try to understand, for example, South African morality or Soviet morality, but not to judge them. If norms and customs are shared by the members of any society, what right do we have to criticize them from an external standpoint? Why should South Africans or Soviets be obliged to accept our ideas of morality?

The implications of cultural relativism for business are vast, since more and more corporations operate in a global marketplace today, with employees who maintain allegiances to many different nations, races, and creeds. Managers who have to do business in such dissimilar places as Japan, Korea, Saudi Arabia, France, Mexico, China, and Brazil confront a diversity of cultural norms, from different table manners to different religions and moral principles.

If the cultural relativists are right, the search for morals in the business arena is over. Managers are merely obligated to obey local customs, codes, and laws. But are the cultural relativists right? Can American managers in Saudi Arabia ethically treat Saudi women as the Saudis do, without a second thought? Can American managers in South Africa adopt white South African policies toward blacks without a qualm? (See the International Management box.) Or consider the People's Republic of China. Should a corporation operating there accept the denial of basic political freedoms? And what if companies find themselves torn between the requirements of two different governments and legal systems? For instance, the government of France once instructed the French subsidiary of U.S.-based Dresser Industries to sell the Soviet Union materials for a gas pipeline linking it to Western Europe while our own government was forbidding Dresser and all of its subsidiaries to sell such materials to the Soviets.[33]

When companies find themselves caught between conflicting moral and legal demands from more than one culture, the only advice a cultural relativist can offer is: Do whatever you like, because you will violate legal strictures whatever you do. So far from helping Dresser out of a difficult situation, cultural relativism would only confirm the realization that the company cannot possibly escape it.

The second problem with cultural relativism is that most cultures are fairly diverse. In South Africa, for instance, whose moral norms should be obeyed—those of the white minority or those of the black majority? It is all too easy to accept as norms what are merely the beliefs of a society's elite—beliefs that may be nothing more than an excuse for the strong to oppress the weak.

A Kernel of Truth

Relativism represents an admission that human reason cannot solve the most important of all questions: How shall we live as human beings? It tells us, on the contrary, that we *should* live in the way that we actually *do* live. In business, where ethical decisions are often regarded as separate from business decisions, relativism would prevent us from trying to find consistent moral principles that will help us solve our business problems. It would also make it impossible for us to resolve conflicting moral demands in any satisfactory way. This is a very high price to pay for a theory.

Relativism warns us that ours is a very big and complex world in which we must be tolerant of diversity. To be sure, a proper level of tolerance is a real virtue, but taken to extremes, tolerance can be an alibi for refusing to make judgments that must be made. Should we be tolerant of the white-majority regime in South Africa? Should we be tolerant of the regime in China? Should we be equally tolerant of both? Strictly speaking, relativism requires that we answer yes in all cases; it tells us to forgo the exercise of reasoned judgment.

To behave morally, of course we must believe we are acting correctly, but that belief is not a *sufficient* condition for morality. We must also take into account the community of individuals whose lives could be changed by our actions. And here, in the interplay between individuals and the community, is the kernel of truth in relativism.

INTERNATIONAL MANAGEMENT

The Sullivan Principles in South Africa

In an effort to change business practices in South Africa, a black minister from Philadelphia, Reverend Leon Sullivan, put forward a set of principles to guide U.S. firms who did business in South Africa. Sullivan, a member of the board of directors of General Motors, then lobbied corporations to sign the principles and to report on their progress in implementing them. Most of the major companies in the United States signed a statement promising to abide by the principles. Sullivan's six principles are:

❑ *Principle 1* Nonsegregation of the Races in All Eating, Comfort, Locker Rooms, and Work Facilities

❑ *Principle 2* Equal and Fair Employment Practices for All Employees

❑ *Principle 3* Equal Pay for All Employees Doing Equal or Comparable Work for the Same Period of Time

❑ *Principle 4* Initiation and Development of Training Programs That Will Prepare Blacks, Coloreds and Asians in Substantial Numbers for Supervisory, Administrative, Clerical and Technical Jobs

❑ *Principle 5* Increasing the Number of Blacks, Coloreds and Asians in Management and Supervisory Positions

❑ *Principle 6* Improving the Quality of Employees' Lives Outside the Work Environment in Such Areas as Housing, Transportation, Schooling, Recreation and Health Facilities

As innocuous as they may seem to us, these principles proved controversial. On the one hand, they require companies to disobey South African law. On the other hand, critics such as Bishop Desmond Tutu have argued that they do not go far enough.

Reverend Sullivan repudiated his principles when the controversy over business divestment in South Africa became a heated issue, admitting that

Reverend Leon Sullivan

although his principles may have made life better for some blacks in South Africa, they have not produced changes at a fast enough pace.

Although Reverend Sullivan has backed off his push for economic sanctions, the black South African political leader Nelson Mandela has not. Mandela was not placated by his release from prison, the opening of dialogue between the ANC (African National Congress), a black nationalist group, and the South African government, or statements by South African President F. W. deKlerk that apartheid can be abolished peacefully. Instead, he feels that the reforms have been too few and have come too slowly. In recent tours of England and the United States, Mandela argued strongly against a relaxation of economic sanctions, maintaining they are vitally needed to create enough pressure to dismantle apartheid.

Sources: Jonathan Kapstein et al., "South Africa: The Squeeze Is On," *Business Week,* September 11, 1989, pp. 44–48.

The notion of a broad human community is an important one, for it gives us the institutions that make relativism attractive, as well as the intuitions that defeat it as a theory. Human communities give rise to communication. Without a community, language itself would be impossible. In fact, we must all communicate through some language, and to communicate we must literally speak the same language. To speak

ILLUSTRATIVE CASE STUDY

WRAP-UP

The *Exxon Valdez:* Corporate Responsibility and the Environment

How can the resources of ethics guide Exxon executives in sorting out their own responsibility and in evaluating their policies on oil transportation and spill response? Who will be affected by the decisions they make and how will they be affected? Who ought to be involved in making those decisions? Which standard or standards ought Exxon executives to use in their decision making?

The guidance ethics gives us is much like a road map. Ethics is a useful, perhaps even indispensable, basis for acting, but it must be used critically, with constant attention to the contexts in which it is employed. In the present case, it is crucial that Exxon reexamine its most basic commitments and proceed with close attention to those values and their demonstration in daily business practice. ■

the same language is to share the same kinds of experience, to live together with a sense of solidarity. We must know the accepted and proper use of words or we cannot communicate. If we share the same kinds of experience—for example, the experience of learning a language, of enjoying family ties, and meaningful work—we have a common base from which to look for principles. If we have no basis for communication, we have no reason for morality and moral principles except as a way of codifying our beliefs about our obligations to "persons" or "things" with which we have no communication.

Suppose we encountered an alien society and that all attempts to communicate with it failed. If we could nevertheless infer that the aliens were living creatures, we would probably continue our efforts to communicate. If we could make no such inference, we would have very little, if anything, in common with the aliens, and there would be no basis for communication. We would see the aliens much as we see rocks and trees; morality would be irrelevant.

Although two sets of consistent and coherent cultural norms and legal systems can sometimes be equally justified, further investigation may clarify some of the key questions in dispute and may find important similarities where only differences were once perceived. What, for example, generally happens when two scientists or two conflicting schools of thought propose competing hypotheses? The fact that two hypotheses can be simultaneously conflicting and sensible suggests the need for further research to resolve the conflict. A moral theory should work the same way. Like other kinds of theories, it will always be incomplete and fallible, and therefore we will often find ourselves in need of a new theory. But such a need is an argument for further work, not for giving up.

■ SUMMARY

Since the Depression of the 1930s, business practices have come under increasing scrutiny. Today most people believe that managers have a responsibility to society as well as to their employers.

The classic statement of corporate social responsibility was created by Andrew Carnegie in his *The Gospel of Wealth* (1899). Carnegie's "gospel" was based on the charity principle (society's more fortunate members are obligated to help the less fortunate) and the stewardship principle (the rich are the caretakers of wealth and public property). Carnegie was a noted philanthropist, and his philosophy inspired a concern for corporate social responsibility between the 1930s and the 1960s. The drawbacks of Carnegie's gospel were that it preserved the status quo and protected business from other forms of pressure, and that the term *social responsibility* was so vague that it left too much to individual discretion.

In the 1960s, economist Milton Friedman asserted that a business's only social responsibility was to maximize profits, within the limits of the law. A company's contribution to the general welfare should be the efficient production of goods and services. Social problems should be left to concerned individuals and government agencies.

As early as the 1950s, but especially in the 1960s, other critics began to address the shortcomings of corporate social responsibility and to advocate replacing it with the concept of corporate social responsiveness. On the microlevel of analysis, this meant trying to show individual companies how to be more socially responsive. Macrolevel analysis assumed that government regulation and public opinion affect business decisions, which should be made with these considerations in mind.

But the models of social responsiveness could not provide practical guidelines for choosing one value over another. This shortcoming, along with public concern about the "ethics crisis," has prompted management scholars to focus on business ethics, the study of how business decisions affect others. Most ethical questions exist at one of four levels: society, stakeholders, internal policy, or the personal level.

To engage in ethical reasoning, we need to understand ethical language, including the terms *values, rights and duties, moral rules,* and *relationships.* We must also understand the basic tenets of common morality, ranging from promise keeping to respect for property. In addition, we need to comprehend the distinction between the justice perspective men commonly use and the care perspective women commonly use in making moral decisions.

To apply ethics, managers must weigh their options against the effects on different groups of stakeholders. To simplify ethical decision making, managers can also institutionalize ethics by creating corporate codes of conduct and ethics committees or by conducting ethics-training programs and social audits.

Managers must also be aware of and avoid the temptations of naive relativism—the idea that human beings are themselves the standard by which they should be judged—and cultural relativism—the idea that morality is relative to a particular culture. Relativism's main contribution to the debate on ethics in business is to remind us of the interplay between individuals and the community—a basic requirement for ethical thinking.

■ REVIEW QUESTIONS

1. Explain the basic tenets of Andrew Carnegie's *The Gospel of Wealth.*
2. What criticisms have been made of Carnegie's concept of corporate social responsibility?
3. What, according to Milton Friedman, is a corporation's primary responsibility? Why does he believe this?
4. How do Friedman's views differ from Carnegie's?
5. Describe the main models of corporate social responsiveness.
6. What is the main drawback to the models of corporate social responsiveness?
7. What is the difference between *social responsibility* and *business ethics*?
8. List and define the key terms you must be able to use in analyzing ethical issues.
9. What are the basic tenets of common morality?
10. Explain the differences between the "justice" and "care" perspectives on moral reasoning.
11. What must a manager consider in applying ethics?
12. How can a manager institutionalize ethics?
13. Why is relativism a challenge to moral reasoning?

CASE STUDY

Alexander Gavin's Dilemma: Cultural Relativism and Business as Usual

April 10, 1983

Dear Professor Hennessey:

I have not talked with you since my participation in The Executive Program at Tuck School in the summer of 1978. Many times I've hoped I might come back to visit but my life has been one surprise after the other, and I have been too busy to take any vacations in recent years.

I want to tell you about a situation that happened to me recently. I know you will be interested in it, and if you have time I'd like you to tell me what you would have done had you been in my position.

As I think you know, I am Senior Project Manager for the El Sahd Construction Company in Kuwait. The company is a prosperous one, with an excellent reputation for producing in a timely and cost-effective way on major construction projects in the Middle East. The Chairman and Chief Executive Officer is a well-known Kuwaiti and my direct boss is another American expatriate who is Senior Vice President for urban construction projects.

Two months ago, we put in a bid to be the principal subcontractor on a project in Iran. Our bid was $30 million, and we expected to bargain with Ajax, Ltd., the British-based company asking for the bids. We had built a heavy profit into the $30 million.

I was asked to go to Tehran on March 3rd to talk with the Ajax manager of the major project. That manager told me that we were going to get the job. I was delighted. The job meant a lot to us. We had put a great deal of planning into it, and it was exactly the kind of work that we do best.

Then came the surprise. I was told our bid had to be $33 million. My response was that we can always raise our price but that I would like to know why we were being asked to do so. The reply was, "Our way of doing business requires that because $1 million will go directly to the Managing Director of our Company in London. I will get $1 million and you, Alexander, will get $1 million in a numbered Swiss account." "Why me?" I asked. "Because we need to have you on the hook as insurance that you will never talk about this with anybody else."

I went back to Kuwait to ponder the matter. I was particularly disturbed because I had heard of cases like this in which, should the bidder fail to cooperate, the next message was that physical harm might be part of the exchange. I had been involved in "pay-offs" before. They are a common part of doing business in the Middle East, but I had never been in a situation where I was being coerced into taking a "cut" myself. I didn't like that. It went against my ethics.

At that point, I really didn't know what to do. I thought, among other things, how helpful it would have been to put my dilemma before a Tuck class and listen to the discussion.

Sincerely,

Alexander Gavin

Source: This case has been prepared for instructional purposes only. Copyright 1983 by John W. Hennessey, Jr., Provost, The University of Vermont. Most names have been disguised.

Case Questions

1. What rights are at stake in this case?
2. What decision rule should Mr. Gavin use?
3. Will this rule work in different cultures?

VIDEO CASE STUDY

Fetal Protection at Johnson Controls

In 1983, Gloyce Qualls's employer forced her to make one of the most difficult decisions of her life: Provide medical proof that she was sterile or transfer out of a job that exposed her to lead. The hazardous job paid $450 a week; the "safer" one paid just $200.

Her employer was Milwaukee, Wisconsin-based Johnson Controls, a member of the Fortune 500 and the nation's largest manufacturer of automobile batteries, as well as large industrial batteries. The ultimatum was part of the company's new "fetal-protection policy," a response to OSHA regulations that required companies to take "affirmative steps" to protect third parties—such as unborn children—from recognized workplace hazards.

Qualls, then 34, panicked. She had just bought a new car, moved to a new apartment, and would soon be marrying a man who already had four children. She needed the money. Even though her husband and friends tried to dissuade her, she underwent medical sterilization to keep her job in the "lead room," where molten lead and lead posts are installed in heavy industrial batteries.

Doris Stone, her friend and co-worker in the lead room, refused to be sterilized. After a temporary assignment in another department, and a lengthy lay-off, Stone was finally given a new job—at about half the pay.

Their dilemma was not unique. Thousands of women in Johnson Controls's 14 plants faced the same predicament, as did women employees at 15 other major corporations with similar policies. To them, the policies became an issue of sex discrimination, one that barred them from an estimated 20 million industrial jobs that offer higher pay and the opportunity to advance. Many were outraged at the unspoken assumption that women could not assess the risks of a job or make responsible decisions about their own fertility.

Besides, they said, if the working conditions were so hazardous, they probably weren't safe for male employees, either. In fact, OSHA regulations introduced in 1989 limit worker exposure to about 400 widely used hazardous substances, including lead. Over time, lead can build up in the body, causing lead poisoning, which damages the brain, kidneys, liver, and other organs of both men and women.

Qualls and Stone filed a grievance over the policy, which was turned over to arbitration. When they lost the arbitration, their union, the Allied Industrial Workers of America, took it to court. Meanwhile, the United Auto Workers, which represents workers in other Johnson Controls battery plants, also filed suit on behalf of women employees at other Johnson plants in the 7th U.S. Circuit Court—and lost. The judge upheld the policy as a valid way of promoting the company's interest in industrial safety.

Undaunted, a consortium of civil rights, women's, and labor organizations took the case to the Su-preme Court, on the grounds that the policy violated Title VII of the 1964 Civil Rights Act, which prohibits sex discrimination, and the Pregnancy Discrimination Act of 1978, which prohibits discrimination against women just because they can become pregnant, unless this prevents them from performing their jobs.

In a 9–0 decision, the Supreme Court struck down Johnson Controls's fetal-protection policy. Justice Henry Blackmun, writing for the court, wrote, "Women as capable of doing their jobs as their male counterparts may not be forced to choose between having a child and having a job."

Ironically, Johnson Controls, now associated in the public mind with sex discrimination and hazardous working conditions, is widely viewed as a "corporate good guy," according to Robin Conrad, vice president of the legal arm of the U.S. Chamber of Commerce, who says Johnson Controls has already spent $15 million to update its engineering technology and improve plant safety. Even more unsettling, it left managers uncertain about the best way to meet their ethical obligations to women employees and how to protect themselves from costly lawsuits over infants who were harmed because their pregnant mothers were exposed to hazardous chemicals on the job.

Gloyce Qualls is glad no other women will be forced to make the decision she made, but the larger ethical and legal issue—how best to ensure a safe workplace for both men and women—is far from settled.

Sources: Deborah Shalowitz, "OSHA Cracks Down: Rules Limit Toxic Exposures," *Business Insurance* 22 (June 13, 1988):1, 33, 34; "Johnson Controls: The Battle Over Fetal Protection," *Occupational Hazards,* May 1990, pp. 79–80; Carol Kleiman, "20 Million Industrial Jobs Hinge on Fetal Protection Court Case," *The Chicago Tribune,* August 27, 1990, Sect. 4, p. 2; Linda P. Campbell, "Supreme Court Invalidates Employers' Fetal-Protection Policies," *The Chicago Tribune,* March 21, 1991, Sect. 1, pp. 1, 18; Florence Estes, "Supreme Friends," *The Chicago Tribune,* April 28, 1991, Sect. 6, p. 3.

Case Questions

1. Use Caroll's theory to evaluate Johnson Controls's corporate social performance.
2. What rights are at stake in this case?
3. How would common morality evaluate Johnson Controls's actions?

■ *NOTES*

[1]This chapter as a whole is based on William C. Frederick, "Corporate Social Responsibility and Business Ethics," in S. Prakash Sethi and Cecilia M. Falbe, eds., *Business and Society* (Lexington, Mass.: Lexington Books, 1987), pp. 142–161; and R. Edward Freeman and Daniel Gilbert, Jr., *Corporate Strategy and the*

Search for Ethics (Englewood Cliffs, N.J.: Prentice Hall, 1988).

[2]This discussion is based upon William C. Frederick, "Corporate Social Responsibility and Business Ethics," in Sethi and Falbe, *Business and Society,* pp. 142–161.

[3]Ibid., p. 143.

[4]Ibid., p. 143.

[5]Lee E. Preston, *Social Issues and Public Policy in Business and Management: Retrospect and Prospect* (College Park: University of Maryland College of Business and Management, 1986), pp. 3–4.

[6]J. C. Worthy, *Shaping an American Institution: Robert E. Wood and Sears, Roebuck* (Urbana: University of Illinois Press, 1984), quoted in Preston, *Social Issues and Public Policy.*

[7]H. R. Bowen, *Social Responsibilities of the Businessman* (New York: Harper & Row, 1953), p. 6, quoted in Steven L. Wartick and Philip L. Cochran, "The Evolution of the Corporate Social Performance Model," *Academy of Management Review* 10 (1985): 758–759.

[8]Frederick, "Corporate Social Responsibility and Business Ethics," pp. 145–146.

[9]These issues were litigated in *Grimshaw* v. *Ford Motor Company,* 119 Cal. App. 3d 757 Cal. Rptr 348 (1981).

[10]Milton Friedman, *Capitalism and Freedom* (Chicago: University of Chicago Press, 1963), p. 133.

[11]Milton Friedman and Rose Friedman, *Free to Choose* (New York: Harcourt Brace Jovanovich, 1980).

[12]Keith Davis, "The Meaning and Scope of Social Responsibility," in Joseph W. McGuire, ed., *Contemporary Management* (Englewood Cliffs, N.J.: Prentice Hall, 1974), p. 631.

[13]Susan B. Foote, "Corporate Responsibility in a Changing Legal Environment," *California Management Review* 26, no. 3 (Spring 1984):217–228.

[14]Robert W. Ackerman, "How Companies Respond to Social Demands," *Harvard Business Review* 51, no. 4 (July–August 1973):88–98. See also Sandra L. Holmes, "Adapting Corporate Structure for Social Responsiveness," *California Management Review* 21, no. 1 (Fall 1978):45–54.

[15]Frederick, "Corporate Social Responsibility and Business Ethics," p. 150.

[16]Edwin M. Epstein, *The Corporation in American Politics* (Englewood Cliffs, N.J.: Prentice Hall, 1969).

[17]Lee E. Preston and James E. Post, *Private Management and Public Policy: The Principle of Public Responsibility* (Englewood Cliffs, N.J.: Prentice Hall, 1975).

[18]Archie B. Carroll, "A Three-Dimensional Conceptual Model of Corporate Social Performance," *Academy of Management Review* 4 (1979):497–506. See also Carroll, *Social Responsibility of Management* (Chicago: Science Research Associates, 1984); and Kenneth E. Aupperle, Archie B. Carroll, and John D. Hatfield, "An Empirical Examination of the Relationship Between Corporate Social Responsibility and Profitability," *Academy of Management Journal* 28 (1985):446–463.

[19]This account of corporate social performance is based chiefly on Wartick and Cochran, "The Evolution of the Corporate Social Performance Model," pp. 758–759.

[20]Frederick, "Corporate Social Responsibility and Business Ethics," p. 153.

[21]Ibid., p. 154.

[22]Louis Harris, *Inside America* (New York: Vintage Books, 1986), p. 236. See also Frederick Bird, Frances Westley, and James A. Waters, "The Uses of Moral Talk: Why Do Managers Talk Ethics," *Journal of Business Ethics* 8 (1989):75–89; John R. Boatright, "Ethics and the Role of the Manager," *Journal of Business Ethics* 7 (1988):303–312; and Ralph A. Mortensen, Jack E. Smith, and Gerald F. Cavanagh, "The Importance of Ethics to Job Performance," *Journal of Business Ethics* 8 (1989):253–260.

[23]Roger Ricklefs, "Executives and General Public Say Ethical Behavior Is Declining in U.S.," *The Wall Street Journal,* October 31, 1983, p. 33.

[24]Roger Ricklefs, "Public Gives Executives Low Marks for Honesty and Ethical Standards," *The Wall Street Journal,* November 2, 1983, p. 33.

[25]Our discussion of this issue is based on R. Edward Freeman (ed.), *Business Ethics: The State of the Art* (New York: Oxford University Press, 1991); and R. Edward Freeman, "Ethics in the Workplace: Recent Scholarship," in C.L. Cooper and I.T. Robertson (eds.), *International Review of Industrial and Organizational Psychology* 5 (1990):149–167.

[26]Mark Pastin, "Ethics as an Integrating Force in Management," *Journal of Business Ethics* 3 (November 1984):293–304; "Business Ethics, by the Book," *Business Horizons* 28 (1986):2–6; and Frederick B. Bird and James A. Waters, "The Moral Muteness of Managers," *California Management Review* 32 (Fall 1989):73–88.

[27]Carol Gilligan, *In a Different Voice* (Boston: Harvard University Press, 1982); Nell Noddings, *Caring* (Berkeley: University of California Press, 1984).

[28]Rebecca Villa, Andrew Wicks, and R. Edward Freeman, "A Note on the Ethics of Caring" (Charlottesville: The Darden School, UVA-E-068, 1990).

[29]The foregoing statistics about ethics codes come from the Center for Business Ethics, Bentley College, "Are Corporations Institutionalizing Ethics?" *Journal of Business Ethics* 5 (1986):86.

[30]Ronald Berenbeim, *Corporate Ethics* (New York: The Conference Board, 1987), p. 13.

[31]Center for Business Ethics, "Are Corporations Institutionalizing Ethics?" p. 87.

[32]Berenbeim, *Corporate Ethics,* p. 17.

[33]For an interesting view of the Dresser case, see B. Crawford and S. Lenway, "Decision Modes and International Regime Changes: Western Collaboration on East-West Trade," *World Politics* 37, no. 3 (1985):375–402.

CHAPTER FIVE

THE INTERNATIONAL DIMENSION

Detail from Dufy, *Street Decked with Flags.*

Upon completing this chapter you should be able to:

1. Discuss the history of the globalization of business.

2. Explain why companies go international.

3. Discuss the ways in which companies go international.

4. Describe the economic, political, and technological variables that managers need to be aware of in planning and managing direct investments in other countries.

5. Discuss the impact of MNEs on both host and home countries.

6. Explain how becoming aware of social variables in other countries can help international managers.

7. Compare and contrast the U.S. and Japanese approaches to management.

Raoul Dufy, *Street Decked with Flags, Le Havre*. 1906. Oil on canvas 31⅞×25⅞″. Musée
National d'Art Moderne, Centre Georges Pompidou, Paris.

ILLUSTRATIVE CASE STUDY

INTRODUCTION

Sumitomo: The Move to International Banking

Widely regarded as Japan's most efficient, aggressive, and innovative bank, Sumitomo is also Japan's most profitable bank. Net earnings for the fiscal year ending March 1989 were $1.5 billion—up 78 percent over the previous year. This is especially pleasing to Sumitomo, which likes to think of itself as "Japan's Citibank." Although Sumitomo's focus on profits has been criticized in Japan (as being "too cold and rational" or worse "un-Japanese"), bank President Sotoo Tatsumi dismisses this as mere jealousy.

Sumitomo's profit orientation is expressed in two ways. First, it emphasizes tight operations, as indicated by its early commitment to state-of-the-art electronic banking. In 1967, Sumitomo was the first Japanese bank to put all customer accounts on-line; in 1969, it installed the country's first cash dispenser; and in 1974, it launched automatic banking. The bank cut staff by 10 percent in the first half of the 1980s—a key ingredient in the quadrupling of net income per employee in the same period. By 1985, Sumitomo had committed another $208 million to enhancing its information systems.

The second, more important expression of Sumitomo's profit orientation is its adaptation to the changing dynamics of the domestic and international banking environment. At one time, Japanese companies were important customers, but when Japanese economic growth slowed down, they turned to cheaper international sources for financing. In addition, a gradual program of bank deregulation launched by the Finance Ministry in 1982 intensified domestic competition and put more pressure on banks' profit margins.

To cope with these changes, Sumitomo has branched out internationally. The bank has been especially active in two areas recently: leveraged buyouts and merger and acquisition deals in the United States and Europe. It was the adviser to Yamanouchi for its $395 million takeover of San Francisco–based Shaklee, it arranged Japanese financing for Campeau's buyout of Federated Department Stores, and it got a loan commitment fee of $2.5 million from Paramount in its failed bid for Time, Inc. Sumitomo has also been important in pushing for greater Japanese involvement in shaping international fiscal policy. This was particularly evident in the presence of several Japanese banks at the international negotiations with Latin American debtor nations in February 1989.

In 1986, the bank made a large and aggressive acquisition of its own—12.5 percent of Goldman, Sachs & Company, a New York investment bank. Many bankers were intrigued by the move, since Sumitomo's role is strictly limited by the Federal Reserve Board. The Fed has already expressed concern that the arrangement might further erode the Glass-Steagall Act, which separates commercial banks from investment banks. Sumitomo may not increase its stake in Goldman, Sachs nor have any management role or engage in joint venture with Goldman, Sachs.

However, as a Swiss banker notes, "Sumitomo is not thinking of the next quarterly returns but far beyond that—ten years, twenty, thirty." Sumitomo will simply bide its time until it can incorporate Goldman more fully into its corporate plan to become a major force in global merchant banking.

Sources: Robert Neff, "Leading Japan's Overseas Banking Drive," *International Management,* March 1985, pp. 52–53, 55; Takashi Ikahata, "Quality and Quantity Mark Sumitomo Bank's History," *Business Japan,* October 1986, pp. 30–36; Sarah Bartlett with Stan Crock, "U.S. Bankers Try to Capitalize on Sumitomo's Deal," *Business Week,* October 13, 1986, p. 50; Kevin Rafferty, "Probing the Sumitomo Culture," *The Institutional Investor,* November 1986, pp. 297–301, 303; Joel Dreyfuss, "A Japanese Survivor Leads the Charge on World Banking," *Fortune,* January 5, 1987, pp. 60–61; Peter Truell, "Japanese Banks Increase Role in Debt Talks," *The Wall Street Journal,* February 17, 1989, p. A11; Andrew Tanzer, "The Other Banks Feel Threatened," *Forbes,* October 2, 1989, pp. 80–88; "The Top Banks," *Fortune,* Fall 1989, pp. 135–136.

*T*he globalization of business is one of the most important changes in the external environment of most organizations. A growing number of companies operate production facilities outside the United States and market their products abroad; even companies with only ostensibly domestic operations face international competition and rely on foreign suppliers. The daily press is filled with reports of trade deficits, calls for protectionism or for free trade, and the latest-breaking news on China, the Soviet Union, and other countries that are experimenting with alternative market mechanisms and forming *joint ventures* with foreign firms. More and more foreign countries are not only investing in the U.S. stock and bond markets, but are purchasing American companies and establishing their own facilities in the United States. Today no American manager can afford to take an exclusively domestic point of view. In this chapter, we will trace the globalization of business and the economic, political, technological, and social variables that make up the international dimension.

■ THE GLOBALIZATION OF BUSINESS

Companies and individuals can own foreign assets in two fundamental ways. They can purchase shares in the companies that own those assets; foreign **portfolio investment** of this sort gives those companies and individuals a claim on profits, but no right to participate in management. Or they can engage in **direct investment,** the buying and management of foreign assets.[1]

Direct investment goes beyond *exporting,* the selling of domestically produced goods in foreign markets; *licensing,* the selling of rights to market brand-name products or use patented processes or copyrighted materials; and even *franchising,* a special type of licensing in which a company sells a package that contains a trademark, equipment, materials, and managerial guidelines. Direct investment is characterized by an active involvement in the management of foreign investments, typically through a **multinational enterprise (MNE),** a large corporation with operations and divisions spread over several countries but controlled by a central headquarters.[2]

Figure 5-1 gives an idea of just how large some multinational firms have grown. It shows the 1988 ranking of the world's 20 largest MNEs, based on total revenue. Although the United States, with monoliths like General Motors, Ford, Exxon, IBM, and Sears, accounts for more than half the world's largest MNEs, it does not have a monopoly on them.[3] Many of them are European, such as the Royal Dutch/Shell group, British Petroleum, and IRI (Italy). They are being joined by an increasing number of Japanese firms, including Toyota and Matsushita. In fact, General Motors' 1988 revenue was greater than the GNP of Saudi Arabia and the Philippines—combined. In the rest of this section, we will see where these enormously wealthy corporations came from and why and how companies go international.

A Brief History

International business has existed in some sense since prehistory, when flint blanks, ceramics, and other goods were traded across great distances. Even during the Roman Empire, traders carried goods to consumers around the world.

Multinational enterprises—as we know them today—were great rarities until the late nineteenth century. By then, U.S. companies like General Electric, International Telephone and Telegraph, and Singer Sewing Machine Company had started to invest in overseas manufacturing facilities, as had West European companies like Ciba, Imperial Chemicals, Nestlé, Siemens, and Unilever. Despite these preliminary explorations, the globalization of business did not get seriously under way until the end of World War II in 1945.

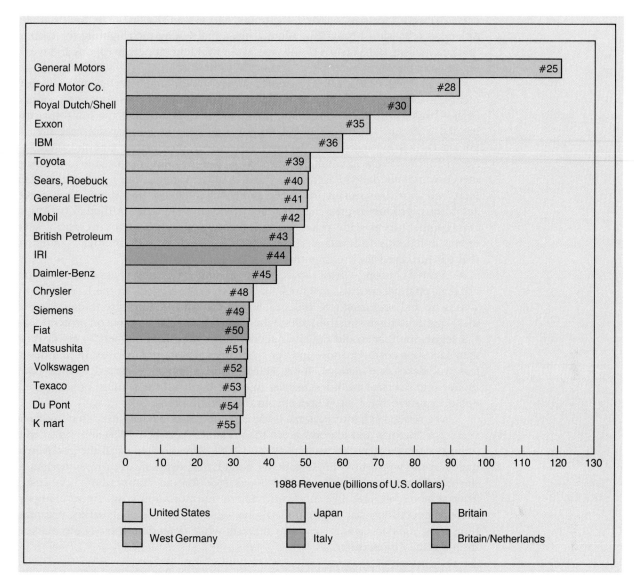

FIGURE 5-1 The World's Top 20 MNEs. Numbers on bars indicate MNE's rank when all nations and MNEs are ordered by either GNP or total revenue. By way of comparison, the U.S. GNP ranked #1; the Yugoslavian GNP ranked #21; the Saudi Arabian GNP ranked #32; and the Philippine GNP ranked #47.

Sources: *Handbook of Economic Statistics* (Central Intelligence Agency, 1989), pp. 30–31; "The 100 Largest U.S. Multinationals," *Forbes*, July 24, 1989, pp. 320, 324; Susan E. Kuhn and David J. Morrow, "The International 500," *Fortune*, July 31, 1989, pp. 290–318.

THE AFTERMATH OF WORLD WAR II. When World War II ended, the United States was the only major country that had not been devastated by the war. Quite the contrary, in fact: The size of our economy had almost doubled during the war, and we dominated the world economically, politically, and militarily. In this climate, many U.S. firms started making substantial direct investments in foreign primary industries. For the most part, though, technological development and product design remained at home, with American-owned multinationals generally viewing the rest of the world as a source of raw materials, cheap labor, and supplemental markets.

At the same time, technological advances radically reduced the costs of communication and transportation. Today radio and television bring the news simultaneously to people around the world. Even people in deserted corners of the globe crave Western clothing, movies, cigarettes, and Coca-Cola. In 1979, for example, American television brought us nightly images of young men fighting for Islamic fundamentalism and a return to the past while wielding modern weapons and wearing fashionable French-cut pants and open-body shirts.[4]

In the mid-1950s, U.S. companies started to make substantial direct investments in foreign manufacturing facilities. In the 1960s, it was American service firms—banks, insurance companies, marketing consultants, and the like—that expanded overseas. U.S. companies were so aggressive and successful that a well-known French journalist, Jean Jacques Servan-Schreiber, wrote a book called *The American Challenge,* in which he warned that Europe might not be able to maintain its economic independence from the United States. However, as purchasing power increased abroad, especially in Europe and Japan, indigenous production prospered and foreign producers grew beyond their national boundaries. Although these foreign competitors initially relied on U.S. technology, lower costs eventually gave them a competitive advantage, and today they have taken a technological initiative that has furthered their competitiveness.[5]

Western Europe's firms—particularly in such industries as chemicals, electrical gear, pharmaceuticals, and tires—started to counterattack in the late 1960s by setting up and acquiring U.S. affiliates. So did the gigantic Japanese trading companies—particularly during the 1980s, when they were trying to stave off protectionist U.S. legislation that would cut their access to the American market. To lower their manufacturing costs, Japanese and U.S. companies also started to invest in facilities in less well-developed nations. Even Third World companies started to sink their money into overseas facilities, usually to evade limits on the amount of goods they could export to the United States from their home bases.

As a result, both international trade and competition have intensified in recent years. U.S. imports and exports more than doubled between 1970 and 1981,[6] and imports doubled again between 1980 and 1989. One-quarter of all the goods produced in the world now cross national boundaries, while nearly three-quarters of the goods produced in the United States face foreign competition.[7] As Lester Thurow notes, we now live in a world where transportation costs are so unimportant that everything that can be traded soon will be.[8] In this global market, organizations must fight to capture overseas markets while defending their home markets from foreign competition.

DISCUSSION QUESTION
Are any other industries facing the problem of competitiveness? Which ones, and what are they doing about it?

COORDINATED RESOURCE
Use Transparency 18, Conceptual Trading Process.

COORDINATED RESOURCE
The Distinctive Discussions for Chapter 5 found in the Lecture Extras supplement include "Global Factory Designs" and "The Global Manager."

THE PROBLEM OF COMPETITIVENESS. The United States has been slow to recognize and respond to this rise in international competition. Japan has become our most visible competitor. For example, although home video technology was originally developed and patented in the United States, not one videocassette recorder has ever been manufactured in this country; Japan now controls the world's $15 billion market for VCRs. The Japanese have also taken over a large portion of the semiconductor market, once an American monopoly, and they have even assumed the lead in the development of new drugs.[9] The Japanese are not our only competitors, however. European products, such as the Airbus, are also taking market shares away from American organizations,[10] and other Asian countries are becoming strong competitors. Korean exports, for example, ranked thirteenth in the world in 1985 and are growing over 30 percent annually.[11]

The automobile market is a good example of the changes in international competition over the past three decades. American automakers initially had a stranglehold on the domestic market, but German and Japanese manufacturers eventually flooded the country with less expensive, well-built cars, putting American automakers on the defensive. Only government intervention kept Chrysler afloat. Today there is a world auto market, with firms from all countries locked into ever-closer competition—and cooperation. Toyota, Honda, and Nissan have assembly plants in the United States; other foreign manufacturers are following their lead. General Motors and Toyota actually alternate production in a California factory. Some "Chry-

A Lost Opportunity? Research scientists at MIT study high-definition television (HDTV), the center of a debate about how best to restore U.S. technological competitiveness. The traditional U.S. approach has been to give government funding to basic science research, like the space program, which eventually produces marketable technologies, but many economists now support the European and Japanese policy of investing in specific product-oriented technologies, coupled with government protection at strategic points. Because HDTV incorporates the computing power and memory of more sophisticated computers, it promises to have wide applications in computers and weaponry, as well as in lucrative consumer electronics.

sler" cars and trucks are designed and made by Mitsubishi, and Mazda engineered the 1991 Ford Escort. Meanwhile, the inexpensive end of the American market is being aggressively courted by Korean manufacturers.

John A. Young, chairman of the President's Commission on Industrial Competitiveness, has reported that the ability of the United States to compete in the world economy has declined over the past two decades.[12] Productivity is growing more slowly in the United States than among its major trading partners. Real hourly wages have been stalled for more than a decade, and the return on manufacturing assets has dropped since the mid-1960s to a point where investments in financial assets yield higher returns; trade deficits have been at record highs, and high-technology industries continue to lose world market share.

The commission concluded that both the public and private sectors need to place a higher priority on international competitiveness and made some specific recommendations. According to the commission, the responsibility for formulating international trade policy and encouraging exports, which is now fragmented among multiple government agencies, should be unified. The government also needs to cut its deficit, encourage savings, and stabilize its monetary policy in order to bring down the cost of capital. Civilian research and development, including university training and research programs, need more funding. The successful implementation of such policies, plus a renewed interest in manufacturing, may help overcome our disappointing track record in developing manufacturing applications. Finally, the private sector must use stock-purchase and profit-sharing plans to motivate its employees.

THE BLURRING OF PUBLIC AND PRIVATE SPHERES OF INFLUENCE. Because international competition has increased, government has played an increasingly active role in the post-World War II marketplace. In the United States, this role crystallized when the federal government bailed out the Chrysler Corporation in 1980 by guaranteeing its loans. Shortly thereafter, the government exempted a number of computer manufacturers from antitrust laws in order to allow them to perform joint research and development and to increase their ability to compete with the Japanese.

Under President Reagan, a major tax-reform bill led to an enormous influx of venture capital into the economy. The Reagan administration also actively promoted American business over international competitors in defense contracting. For example, a low foreign bid to install a glass cable between New York and Washington was rejected in favor of AT&T's bid on the grounds that the cable had "national defense" implications. Thus the American ideal of laissez-faire is today a fiction.

This blurring of public policy and private enterprise is not limited to the United States. In Japan, the Ministry of International Trade and Industry actively assists some industries rather than others, and government takes an active role in the economy. The Group of Five (the United States, West Germany, Japan, France, and the United Kingdom) routinely meet to plan their monetary policy in concert. And since the October 19, 1987, stock market crash, there have been suggestions to coordinate the stock markets in these nations.

Changes in government policy can help or hurt an industry or an organization overnight. Many organizations are therefore spending more time and resources trying to influence policy in governments around the world.

ECONOMIC EXPERIMENTS AMONG THE COMMUNISTS. At one time, the communist nations relied solely on a planned economy in which the government makes all major economic decisions. In more recent years, flagging productivity and other economic woes have led these nations to experiment with capitalist measures and foreign investment.

Catering to a Nation of "Little Emperors." China's policy of rewarding parents who have just one child has created a nation of 22 million only children—pampered, demanding "little emperors"—with parents anxious to buy them the best. Since 1986, this has included H.J. Heinz Co.'s instant, precooked rice cereal. Bilingual packaging and glitzy Hong Kong-produced television commercials have created a mystique that the Western cereal is more nutritious than Chinese products, and working parents—the norm in China—appreciate the convenience of the precooked foreign cereal, even though it is much more expensive than Chinese products that have to be cooked. Heinz's factory, a joint venture with two Chinese partners, is currently operating at capacity, with plans to open another factory soon.

This trend toward capitalism began in 1978, when China announced a new policy of "economic adjustment," allowing free-market forces to supplement the planned economy. The greatest changes took place in the countryside, where the "economic responsibility" system stopped just short of giving individual families title to their land. Private companies were allowed to grow; foreign investments included Volkswagen's $200 million assembly plant and over $5 billion of investment by McDonnell Douglas, Xerox, and other American corporations. Optimists hoped the entrenched bureaucracy of communism would gradually give way to a more democratic and capitalistic system.

Those hopes were dashed in 1989, when the Chinese government launched a bloody crackdown on prodemocracy students demonstrating in Tiananmen Square. Soon, private-sector efforts within China were being stifled by new high taxes and economic restrictions.[13] Although China continues to court foreign investment, the initial optimism of foreign investors is tempered by a more realistic appreciation of China's political instability and the restrictions it places on private business ventures, as well as the ethical problem of dealing with a repressive government that disregards human rights. Clearly, China is mainly seeking foreign help for very specific areas of its economy, as determined and regulated by its government.[14]

The picture is far more hopeful in the Eastern Bloc, where the tearing down of the Berlin Wall symbolized the bold moves toward democracy. German reunification has assured the restructuring of the economy in what was East Germany, and investments by General Electric and General Motors in Hungary and other projects in Poland have the entire Eastern Bloc in a flurry of economic activity.[15]

HERE'S AN EXAMPLE
Some enterprising U.S. universities are sponsoring campus programs for born-again Russian capitalists. (*Business Month*, September 1990, p. 29)

Meanwhile, *perestroika,* the Soviet version of economic restructuring announced by President Mikhail Gorbachev in 1988, calls for a gradual end to central economic coordination for the Soviet Union. When the Soviets showed an interest in embracing foreign investments, European, Japanese, and American companies were quick to respond. A consortium of top-notch U.S. companies—including Chevron, RJR Nabisco, Eastman Kodak, Johnson & Johnson, and Archer Daniels Midland—was formed to invest $5 billion to $10 billion in the U.S.S.R. over the next 15 years through a number of joint ventures.[16] McDonald's has already opened its doors in Moscow, and Pepsi is now a favorite Soviet beverage. Taken together, the 700-plus joint ventures exceed the $500 million mark.

Given the deteriorating state of the Soviet economy, however, some companies were hesitant to jump on the bandwagon. Some observers wondered how long Gorbachev could retain power and feared a hard-line backlash. These fears became reality when Gorbachev was toppled by a coup on August 19, 1991, and placed under house arrest. The coup leaders, dominated by the military and the secret police, appointed Vice President Gennadi I. Yanayev as acting president. Two days later, the coup collapsed in the face of popular opposition led by Boris Yeltsin, Gorbachev's main rival, a split in the military, and lack of support from a number of Soviet republics. Although these events are likely to hasten democratic reform, they are also sure to aggravate already serious economic problems.

HERE'S AN EXAMPLE
Corporations are beginning to put foreigners on their boards of directors. Chemical maker Hercules, of Wilmington, Delaware, recently recruited Manfred Caspari, an economist retired from German government and European Community positions. (*Wall Street Journal*, 12/27/90, p. B1)

THE COMING OF THE EUROPEAN COMMUNITY. The European clash of cultures, languages, and politics has been expressed on a business level as a gauntlet of regulations and tariffs designed to protect each nation's firms from foreign competitors. All of this will change in 1992, when the European Community (EC) goes into effect.[17] The EC's goal is to eliminate trade barriers among member nations, creating a single market of 300 million people and fostering political unity in Europe.

The EC is an evolution of the Common Market, which was created in 1957 by the Treaty of Rome. The original members—Belgium, France, Italy, Luxembourg, Netherlands, and West Germany—have been joined by Denmark, Great Britain, and Ireland (1973), by Greece (1981), and by Spain and Portugal (1986). (See Figure 5-2.) In theory, the Common Market would coordinate economic policies and eliminate trade barriers among member nations. In reality, the Common Market had little

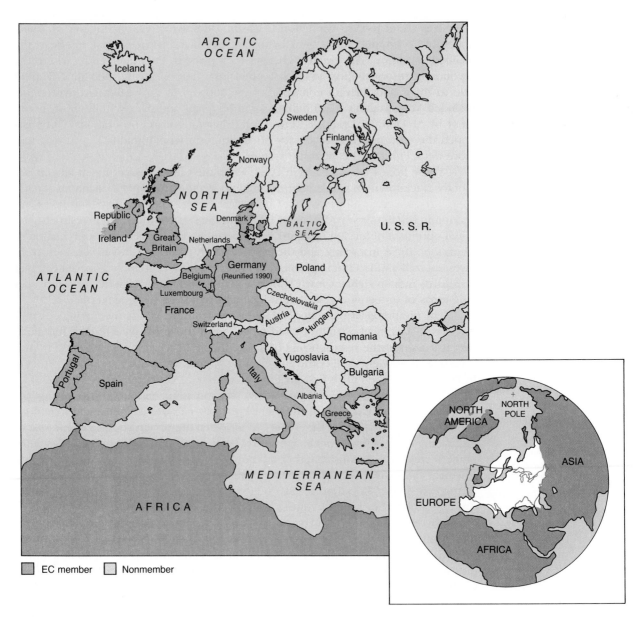

FIGURE 5-2 The European Community. Inset map shows the continent of Europe in relation to the rest of the world. Europe's area is about one-third larger than that of the United States (excluding Alaska and Hawaii) and its population is more than double that of the United States.

Source: (Inset map) *World Book Encyclopedia* (Chicago: World Book, 1985), Vol. 6, p. 310.

authority and trade barriers proliferated. Meanwhile, strong American and Japanese multinational companies threatened to leave Europe behind in the increasingly global economy.

Europe responded with the Single Europe Act of 1987, which amended the Treaty of Rome and created the EC, conferring real power on the largely symbolic European Parliament. Many areas of cooperation have been established, such as a commitment to eliminate trade barriers by 1992, end custom formalities by 1993, and create a central European bank by 1994, paving the way for a single European currency in the late 1990s.

The EC has a number of dramatic implications for business. First, it should increase efficiency. Under the Common Market, trade barriers sometimes forced firms to modify a product design or manufacturing facilities. Under the EC, these

CLASS COMMENT

European firms are trying to find business executives who are skilled at dealing with a variety of cultures and bringing a diverse team together. (*Wall Street Journal*, 1/25/91, p. B1ff.)

THOUGHT PROVOKER

"Either be prepared to deal with Koreans, Germans, or Americans—or opt out of world competition"—Roland Smith, CEO of British Aerospace. (*Fortune*, 12/17/90, p. 121ff.)

COORDINATED RESOURCE

See Samaras Exercise 6.3, "Going International."

TEACHING TIP

Find local company representatives that are doing business on an international level. Either invite them to speak to your class or send your students out to interview them about their opportunities and problems.

CLASS COMMENT

A recent survey by KPMG Peat Marwick found that international firms will be investing in global communications networks just to remain competitive. (*Business Perspectives*, Fall 1990, p. 20ff.)

HERE'S AN EXAMPLE

Federal Express is finding its formula for package delivery falling flat overseas. Although the company has poured more than $1.5 billion into expansion abroad since 1985, FedEx makes just one of every ten express deliveries within Europe, and its planes often fly half-empty from Europe to New York. (*Wall Street Journal*, 4/15/91, p. A1ff.)

barriers will be eliminated; firms will be able to create a single plan for Europe and to consolidate manufacturing in strategically located plants. Second, European companies should become more formidable competitors in the global economy, since they will be developing within a more cooperative system. In addition, the EC will unify European markets, and the increased profit potential should encourage innovation. Third, the EC will encourage businesses to focus on their relationship with the EC, rather than with domestic governments. This will heighten political unity in Europe, in keeping with the long-term goal of establishing a United States of Europe.

Many view the 1992 changes with alarm, claiming it will create a "Fortress Europa," in which the EC erects trade barriers to American and Japanese companies. Others claim that a united Europe will exist on paper only; it will take a great deal of time and effort to overcome so many differences. In fact, recent events show that both views have some validity.[18] Nevertheless, the emergence of the EC is one of the most significant international events of the 1990s, and many savvy American and Japanese firms are responding by increasing their direct investments in Europe.

Why Companies Go International

Political changes, like those in China and the Soviet Union, make direct investment risky, since new regimes sometimes take over foreign-owned business facilities with little or no compensation to the original owners. Political considerations aside, MNEs are more difficult to manage than purely domestic firms, simply because they are larger and require more coordination. Why, then, do companies go international? There are at least four reasons: to gain access to more reliable or cheaper resources, to increase return on investment, to increase market share, and to avoid foreign tariffs or import quotas.[19]

TO GAIN ACCESS TO MORE RELIABLE OR CHEAPER RESOURCES. Petroleum and mining companies often go international to get a more reliable or cheaper supply of raw materials than they can find at home; manufacturing companies venture overseas to find less-expensive labor. The quest for cheap labor has become more difficult and politically risky in recent years, though, because foreign workers are demanding higher wages and better job benefits. South Korea is a good example here. Companies may also invest in foreign facilities to escape political instability at home or to gain access to a larger pool of technological know-how.

TO INCREASE RETURN ON INVESTMENT. Businesses, like individuals, shift their funds "from areas where returns on capital are lower to those where they are higher."[20] During the 1980s, for example, a favorable exchange rate led the Japanese to invest heavily in commercial real estate in the United States.

By expanding overseas, companies also increase their chances for achieving a certain return on investment and stable or growing profits. Faced with a saturated U.S. market for home appliances, Whirlpool purchased a majority stake in a Canadian appliance maker and a 49 percent interest in a Mexican appliance maker in 1987, followed in 1989 by the purchase of a controlling interest in the appliance division of N.V. Philips, the Dutch electronics giant, with an option to purchase the rest.[21] In a similar fashion, Ford and GM can look to European sales to pull them through a domestic slump in auto sales. In the view of H. Levy and M. Sarrat, then, foreign direct investment lets a company "construct a 'portfolio' that has more optimal risk/return characteristics" than one containing income streams from just one nation.[22]

TO INCREASE MARKET SHARE. According to Steven Hymer, companies that expand internationally tend to be "oligopolistic"; that is, they tend to dominate their domestic market, either because their products are highly desirable or because their size lets them reap economies of scale. To continue growing, though, they have to expand into international markets.[23] Smaller companies, by comparison, may have to

ETHICS IN MANAGEMENT

Japanese Manufacturers in America

Between 1981 and 1987, the number of manufacturing plants owned by Japanese companies in the United States more than doubled as many large companies, especially car makers, established plants here. The weakening dollar made such investments attractive and they were a good way to avoid import quotas and tariffs while meeting the American demand for Japanese goods. Although the majority of Japanese ventures here have been successful, some plants are experiencing problems.

The greatest successes have been in the automobile industry. Japanese groups now have seven plants in the United States and three in Canada, and they are among the most efficient, technologically advanced, and least unionized plants in North America. While Chrysler, Ford, and GM were cutting their output by 18 percent in the fourth quarter of 1989, the Japanese increased production by 41 percent. Sales of Japanese cars in the United States are up 5.5 percent, despite a weak overall market.

Furthermore, in July 1989, workers at the Nissan plant in Smyrna, Tennessee, voted two to one not to unionize. This result is standard for the Japanese here. Four of their seven U.S. plants are nonunionized, and the other three are unionized only because they have ties to the Big Three automakers—Chrysler, Ford, and GM—an impressive record in an industry where workers have traditionally been heavily unionized.

Japanese plants are planned and organized to encourage managers and workers to see themselves as collaborators who aid one another in putting forth their best efforts. In contrast to their more bureaucratic and hierarchical American counterparts, Japanese managers strive to soften the chain of command and encourage an interactive, team-based approach to tasks. This focus, plus an emphasis on job security, seems to win employees' trust and loyalty.

This management philosophy pays important dividends in terms of efficiency. Because they have job security and feel connected to the company, workers have been willing to adopt the Japanese principle of *kaizen*—meaning "improvement." *Kaizen* pushes workers to continually improve their performance, both to increase quality and to reduce waste and inefficiency. This drive and intensity—not automation—accounts for the greater productivity of Japanese-managed workers. American employees have had a chance to experience this phenomenon at the NUMMI plant, in operation since 1984; located in Fremont, California, this plant is jointly owned and managed by Toyota and GM. According to a recent study, workers at a typical GM plant actually worked 48 seconds out of a minute; workers at the NUMMI

---

expand overseas just to survive. Ball Corp., the nation's No. 3 maker of beverage cans, recently bought the European packaging operation of Continental Can Co., so that it could meet the European demand for soft drink cans, which is growing twice as fast as the U.S. demand.[24]

product-cycle theory
According to Vernon, the process whereby products originally developed for home markets earn enough foreign demand to justify direct foreign investment in their production.

Of course, the decision to make a direct investment does not happen overnight. According to Raymond Vernon's **product-cycle theory,** companies that develop attractive new products sell them first in their home markets. Sooner or later, foreigners learn of these products, creating enough demand to justify exporting. If this demand continues to grow, it will eventually become more economical to invest in foreign manufacturing facilities. By building a factory in Germany, for example, Ford could save the considerable time and expense needed to ship finished autos from Detroit to Europe.

TO AVOID FOREIGN TARIFFS AND IMPORT QUOTAS. Governments often use tariffs or import quotas to protect domestic business concerns. Japan, for example, places high tariffs on rice and other agricultural goods imported from the United States. Similarly, U.S. manufacturers have sought government protection from imports, ranging from autos to electronics. (In 1983, for example, Harley-Davidson sought—

A Success Story. Jimmy Haynes selects bumper fascias at the Smyrna, Tennessee, Nissan factory, one of many Japanese auto plants that have rejected unionization.

plant worked 55 seconds per minute. In addition, the emphasis on team effort allows the Japanese to offer fewer promotions or other forms of individual distinction, which can undermine worker collaboration and increase bureaucracy.

Interestingly, the Sanyo factory in Forrest City, Arkansas, has not experienced the same sort of success as other Japanese plants here. Sanyo bought the factory from American owners and inherited their problems. Principal among these was a heavily unionized work force that has refused to adapt to the Japanese way of doing things. Quality circles—a team approach to solving problems and improving efficiency—have failed at Forrest City, as has the practice of consensus management. Part of the problem may have been that few of the Japanese managers

spoke fluent English; communication headaches were common. Plant production has been severely cut, and many local employees expect it will soon cease altogether.

Another problem that all Japanese companies in the United States encounter is unhappiness among their own managers. Japanese managers sent to oversee American plants find the transition difficult, and their families often fare even worse. Language and cultural barriers make integration into a community difficult, especially in larger cities where helpful behavior toward foreigners is not an everyday occurrence. Those families located in small towns often fare better, thanks to friendly neighbors, but the overall inferiority of American schools worries Japanese parents, since a good education is essential for success in Japan. The cultural and family stresses often make Japanese managers less effective.

Since Americans continue to demand Japanese goods and since American properties continue to be good investments, Japanese companies will continue to open factories and businesses here. Some of them will find success; others will not. The keys seem to be a cooperative labor force, helpful local populations, and managers able to make needed compromises.

Sources: Stewart Toy with Neil Gross and James B. Treece, "The Americanization of Honda," *Business Week,* April 25, 1988, pp. 90–96; John Schwartz with Jeanne Gordon and Mark Veverka, "The 'Salarymen' Blues," *Newsweek,* May 9, 1988, pp. 51–52; Ernest Beazley, "Battered Image: In Spite of Mystique, Japanese Plants in U.S. Find Problems Abound," *The Wall Street Journal,* June 22, 1988, pp. 1, 17; Nathaniel Gilbert, "Foreign Companies Use Democracy to Prosper in the U.S.," *Management Review,* July 1988, pp. 25–29; Wendy Zellner and Dean Foust, "Shaking Up Detroit," *Business Week,* August 14, 1989, pp. 74–80; "The Dilemma of Japanese Investment," *Directors and Boards,* Spring 1990, pp. 52–53.

and won—five years of tariff protection from Japanese imports; you can read more about this in the Chapter 11 case study, "Harley-Davidson Regroups for Success.")

Direct investment is a more secure solution to the threat of foreign tariffs and import quotas. Thus Sony, Honda, and Toyota all have created subsidiaries that are, in effect, American companies, and GE, Whirlpool, and the Big Three automakers all have foreign subsidiaries. In the case study at the end of this chapter, you will see how a fear of import quotas helped Lucky-Goldstar, the South Korean electronics maker, decide to open American facilities. In that case and in the Ethics box, you can also read of the management adjustments these moves require.

COORDINATED RESOURCE

Use Transparency 19, How Companies Go International.

COORDINATED RESOURCE

See DuBose Reading #27, "How Multinational Organizations Evolve."

COORDINATED RESOURCE

See Samaras Reading, "The Internationalization of Business: One Company's Response."

How Companies Go International

Few organizations start out multinational. More commonly, an organization proceeds through several stages of internationalization. (See Fig. 5-3.) Christopher Korth has broken this process down into four stages, or degrees, which apply both to manufacturing and to services.[25] Not all companies reach the fourth and last stage, and some companies that do reach it later recede, as Chrysler did in the early 1980s, when it sold much of its overseas manufacturing capacity.

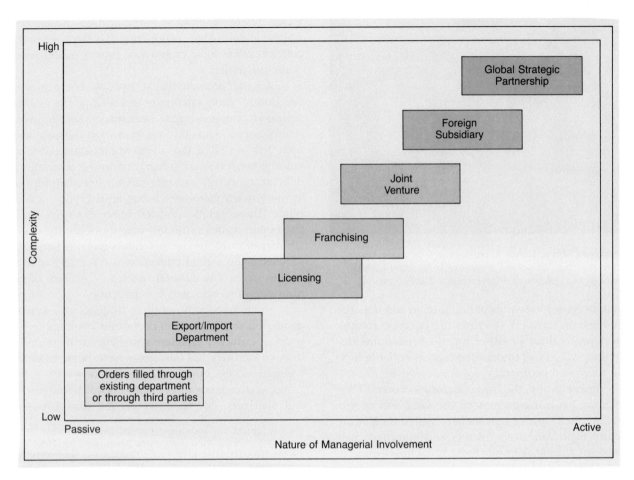

High

Complexity

Low

Passive ——————————————— Active

Nature of Managerial Involvement

Global Strategic Partnership

Foreign Subsidiary

Joint Venture

Franchising

Licensing

Export/Import Department

Orders filled through existing department or through third parties

FIGURE 5-3 How Companies Go International

COORDINATED RESOURCE
See Study Guide Problem Exercise 5, "Going Global."

licensing The selling of rights to market brand-name products or to use patented processes or copyrighted materials.

franchise A type of licensing arrangement in which a company sells a package containing a trademark, equipment, materials, and managerial guidelines.

joint venture Business undertaking in which foreign and domestic companies share the costs of building production or research facilities in foreign countries.

Companies at the first stage of internationalization have only passive dealings with foreign individuals and organizations. At this point, for example, a company may content itself with filling overseas orders that come in without any serious selling effort on its part. International contacts may be handled by an existing department. Third parties, such as agents and brokers, often act as go-betweens for companies at the first stage of internationalization.

In the second stage, companies deal directly with their overseas interests, though they may continue to use third parties also. At this point, most companies do not base employees abroad, but domestic employees regularly travel abroad on business. The company may decide to set up an import or export department.

In the third stage, international interests shape the company's overall makeup in an important way. Although still essentially domestic, the company has a direct hand in importing, exporting, and perhaps producing its goods and services abroad. In the final stage, the company sees its activities as essentially multinational and makes no distinction between domestic and foreign business activities.

In the third and fourth stages, organizations face a number of strategic options for exploiting foreign opportunities. They can use **licensing** or they can sell **franchises,** a special type of license. Franchising is the primary way McDonald's, Pizza Hut, and other fast-food chains have expanded into international markets.

Although licensing and franchises give corporations access to foreign revenue, their role in management is limited. To gain a greater say in management, organizations have to turn to direct investment, either by creating a foreign subsidiary or by buying a controlling interest in an existing foreign firm.

Another option is the **joint venture,** in which domestic and foreign companies share the cost of developing new products or building production facilities in a foreign country. A joint venture may be the only way to enter certain countries, where, by law, foreigners cannot own businesses. In other situations, joint ventures let companies pool technological knowledge and share the expense and risk of research that may not produce marketable goods. For example, Abbott Labs, an American pharmaceutical company, has a joint venture with Takeda, a Japanese company, to develop biotechnology products. Indeed, Howard V. Perlmutter and David A. Heenan, who have studied international cooperation,[26] argue that a true **global strategic partnership** among companies must be international, "extending beyond a few developed countries" to include newly industrializing, less-developed, and socialist nations.[27] Firms that forge these strategic alliances will try either to assume "leadership as low-cost suppliers" or to come forward with the best possible product or service, or both.

Consider the strategic alliances forged by Philips of the Netherlands, Europe's largest electronics company. Philips wanted to strengthen itself in two other markets: the United States and the Far East. In the United States, Philips allied itself with AT&T, the communications giant, which is giving the Dutch company access to its electronic components in return for Philips' global marketing expertise. In Japan, Philips joined forces with Matsushita. And "every Philips alliance has cost leadership and/or differentiated product superiority in at least one national market as its objective."[28]

To be successful, Perlmutter and Heenan think, global strategic partnerships must meet six conditions. First, "each partner must believe the other has something it needs."[29] Second, the partners must choose a strategy before they start to do business, not afterward. Third, they must share the same attitudes toward control of the new business. U.S. companies, the two researchers say, have traditionally felt that "power, not parity, should govern collaborative ventures," whereas Japanese and European companies "subscribe to management by consensus."[30]

The fourth condition, which Perlmutter and Heenan regard as the "most important factor in the endurance of a global alliance, is chemistry"—operating styles, corporate cultures, and moral values.[31] Fifth, joint ventures must agree to discard whatever organizational forms that do not work. Finally, there must be some ultimate decision maker and some way of making decisions stick. Otherwise, "the new venture suffers from unclear lines of authority, poor communication, and slow decision making.[32]

global strategic partnership Alliance formed by an organization with one or more foreign countries, generally with an eye toward exploiting the other countries' opportunities and toward assuming leadership in either supply or production.

HERE'S AN EXAMPLE
Chevrolet's best-selling Geo Metro was designed in Japan and built in Canada at a factory managed by Japan's Suzuki. (*Harvard Business Review,* March–April 1991, p. 79)

ILLUSTRATIVE CASE STUDY

CONTINUED

Sumitomo: The Move to International Banking

Sumitomo's stake in Goldman, Sachs is an example of portfolio investment, since U.S. law prevents Sumitomo from having any involvement in Goldman, Sachs's management. However, Sumitomo needs even a tentative toehold in the United States if it is to keep pace with the increasing globalization of business. Sumitomo's purchase also reflects a number of the reasons MNEs turn to international investments. Faced with a slow-growing and more competitive

domestic market, for example, Sumitomo has turned to international ventures to gain a higher rate of return on its investments and to increase its share of the world's banking market. In addition, even the partial acquisition of Goldman, Sachs signals Sumitomo's ambition to become a major force in international banking. Clearly, Sumitomo's managers envision a future in accord with Korth's fourth stage of development.

■ ECONOMIC, POLITICAL, AND TECHNOLOGICAL VARIABLES: THE INTERNATIONAL DIMENSION

When a firm plants a flag in a new country, it has to be especially aware of the economic, political, technological, and social variables that shape the business environment. In this section we will look at the economic, political, and technological variables an organization must consider in deciding to make a direct investment in another country. Then in the final section of the chapter, we will look at the social variables that play an important role in determining an organization's ultimate success in operating and managing a foreign subsidiary.

Economic Variables

To reduce the risk of any international venture, organizations must pay particular attention to such economic variables as foreign patterns of economic growth, investment, and inflation. Besides assessing current economic conditions, they need to forecast future conditions in any country they operate in, sell to, or purchase from. Large companies have their own staffs of economists; smaller ones tend to rely on the forecasts supplied by managers, private companies, governments, and banks.

Organizations must also concern themselves with various aspects of international trade, such as the value of a country's currency relative to other currencies (the foreign-exchange rate) and its balance of payments, as well as the type of controls placed on imports, exports, and foreign investors.

Of these, the exchange rate between its currency and the currencies of other nations may be the most important. When a company enters into a transaction with overseas customers or suppliers and it is not paid immediately, it is in effect gambling on the currency in which it will be paid. Say a U.S. firm agrees to buy 100,000 francs' worth of raw materials for its Swiss factory from a French supplier. The terms of the agreement state that the U.S. firm will pay within 90 days in French francs. If the exchange rate shifts from 10 francs to the dollar at the time of the sale to 9 francs to the dollar 90 days later, the U.S. company will have to pay $11,111 for its 100,000 francs, not the $10,000 they would have cost at the time of the sale. A shift in the other direction would make the U.S. company's payment cheaper.

When millions of dollars change hands, such fluctuations can be significant. As a result, many multinational companies "hedge" and "cover" their international financial transactions. (These terms refer to methods of protecting investors from possible fluctuations in currency exchange rates.[33]) Companies can try to cover themselves against losses by negotiating contracts that specify which currency will be used in payment, as well as by taking out and making loans in foreign currencies. Foreign-exchange-rate forecasting, hedging, and covering methods have become very sophisticated.

infrastructure Physical facilities needed to support economic activity; includes transportation and communication systems, schools, hospitals, power plants, and sanitary facilities.

Multinational managers must also evaluate a country's **infrastructure,** the facilities needed to support economic activity. The infrastructure includes transportation systems, communication systems, schools (important for providing workers with adequate skills), hospitals, power plants, and sanitary facilities. The state of a nation's infrastructure often reflects the strength of the nation's economy and the government's priorities.

Political Variables

Firms that want to expand into a foreign country must also analyze its political stability; the business attitudes of its government, ruling party, and opposition (legal and illegal); and the effectiveness of its government bureaucracy. Both a country's internal and foreign policies can powerfully influence the business environment. For

The Importance of Infrastructure. Broken pipelines and fires, like this one, plague the Soviet oil pipeline system, prompting Texaco's James Kinnear to sign an agreement to study the feasibility of developing a Soviet "elephant"—oil jargon for a giant field—near the Arctic Circle. Its appeal: oil could be exported by ship through the Barents Sea, bypassing the unreliable pipeline.

political risk Possibility that political changes, either in the short or long run, will affect the activities of an organization doing business in foreign countries.

this reason, MNEs must assess **political risk,** the possibility that political changes, either in the short or the long run, will affect its activities abroad. In recent years, political risk forecasting has become as sophisticated as economic forecasting.

A multinational company must also adjust to a multinational legal environment, which includes different laws and regulations concerning taxes, tariffs, quotas, copyright laws, and currency exchange.[34] Sometimes these differences are difficult to see; in other instances, outsiders spot lucrative opportunities that local businesses take for granted. For example, Japanese stock traders in the United States recently began to practice "dividend capture." They buy a large block of stock and then sell it in seconds—merely to go on record as having owned it, so that they can collect some of the dividends the company pays. The practice is perfectly legal but rarely used on such a large scale by American traders.

Home-country laws may also affect overseas operations. For example, the Foreign Corrupt Practices Act of 1977 makes it illegal for U.S. firms to bribe foreign political decision makers, an accepted practice in many countries. Critics charge that the act hampers U.S. business unduly, since ours is the only nation that has passed such a law.

Technological Variables

Multinational managers must be sensitive in introducing new technology to foreign cultures and adapt to the fact that levels of technology vary among countries. Production technologies that work well in the United States, with its fairly high technological level, might not work well in Ecuador. Moreover, the Ecuadorians and their government might resent being forced to adapt to new technology, a change that is often traumatic. Any technological change is difficult, and the support of the host government may be nearly essential.

Some experts argue that most multinational companies have failed to adjust their production methods to suit the varying levels of technological sophistication found throughout the world. Introducing automated production techniques to a culture whose technology depends on extensive manual labor may be neither appropriate nor successful. Yet other observers praise multinational companies for using high technology in less-developed countries, which thereby gain experience with it.

The Impact of MNE Operations

THOUGHT PROVOKER

The U.S. operations of Japanese companies are important American enterprises. During 1989 alone, Nissan produced $8.5 billion worth of cars and trucks for the American market in American factories with American workers. Is this good or bad? Why?

COORDINATED RESOURCE

Use Transparency 20, Host-Country Perspective of Advantages and Disadvantages of MNC Involvement.

Some early studies of the impact of MNEs on host and home countries showed the overall impact to be solidly favorable, but others reached the opposite conclusion.[35] It is fair to say that most studies indicate the effects are *relatively* favorable, though these findings are usually heavily dependent on key assumptions made by the researchers. And because there may be a mix of positive and negative effects, how the effects are weighted can influence the overall conclusion. For example, if an MNE had only two sources of influence—creating jobs and bribing government officials—its overall effect would be favorable if we care a great deal about jobs and don't mind bribery. Its effect would be negative if our preferences (weighting) are reversed.

THE IMPACT OF MNEs ON HOST COUNTRIES. Christopher Korth has identified some of the potential benefits and costs that the operations of an MNE may have on a host country.[36] Note that the benefits and costs listed below are *potential.* Whether they actually occur in a specific situation depends on the environment (including government actions) and the actual behavior of the MNE involved. Some of the major potential benefits are transfer of capital, technology, and entrepreneurship to the host country; improvement of the host country's balance of payments; creation of local job and career opportunities; improved competition in the local economy; and greater availability of products for local consumers.

These benefits may occur in any given situation; many MNE managers and some analysts believe that they usually do. But each potential benefit may incur a cost. For example, the MNE may use local financing, thereby absorbing capital that might have financed indigenous companies. Or a few well-advertised, standardized consumer products may drive many locally produced products from the market, thereby reducing consumer choice.

However, not all costs have analogous benefits. Generally, the potential negative effects, which are very emotional issues with some observers, can be placed into three broad categories: political interference by the MNE; social-cultural disruptions and changes (which are bound to have both advocates and opponents); and local economic dependence on decisions made outside the country.

THOUGHT PROVOKER

What are the implications of a company operating in a country whose GNP is smaller than the company's annual sales?

Clearly, there were abuses on the part of some MNEs in the past. United Fruit, for example, is generally acknowledged to have engaged in extensive political and economic interference in Latin America between the two World Wars. More recently, officials of ITT were accused of conspiring with the CIA to prevent the election of Salvador Allende Gossens, a Marxist, to the presidency of Chile.[37] And the Japanese electronics giant, Hitachi, has admitted stealing proprietary technology from IBM.

Generally, however, the ethics of MNEs are on a par with or above those of local companies. Today MNEs have high political visibility and, despite their size and power, are vulnerable to punitive actions by local governments. Under such conditions, few companies are likely to risk even the appearance of unethical behavior.

It is worth noting that although MNEs are viewed with suspicion by some host country government officials, they are actively courted by most countries rather than denied entry.

COORDINATED RESOURCE

Use Transparency 21, Home-Country Perspective of Advantages and Disadvantages of Multinational Business.

THE IMPACT OF MNEs ON HOME COUNTRIES. The debate over the impact of MNEs on their home countries is less intense, probably due to the absence of such highly charged emotional issues as political interference, cultural disruption, and economic dependence. We have already discussed the potential benefits that lead companies to go international, so we will focus here on the potential negative effects of MNEs on home countries.

One drawback is that the outflow of foreign investments, coupled with reduced income from exports, may weaken the national balance of payments. In the long run, these losses may be more than compensated for by the flow of income from dividends, licensing fees, royalties, and sales of components for foreign assembly. Still, there is the risk that the home country will suffer a loss of technological advantages, especially when joint ventures and global strategic partnerships are involved.[38]

The most volatile issue on the home front is whether an MNE's foreign investment (most obviously in manufacturing) causes the loss of domestic jobs. On the surface, moving factory production overseas would certainly seem to cause job loss at home, but some observers feel this job displacement is inevitable, whether or not organizations decide to invest overseas. Even if one organization ignores the possible cost benefits of moving its production overseas, its competitors will not. This will put the stay-at-home company at a competitive disadvantage, cause it to lose business, and eventually force it to reduce its work force anyway.[39] Other observers note that these dire conclusions depend heavily on the assumption that *all* local companies are prohibited from investing in overseas manufacturing. They also argue that many government, tax, political, and insurance policies and programs actually encourage companies to manufacture abroad rather than at home. Furthermore, any jobs a home country loses to foreign investment may be offset by the jobs created when foreigners make direct investments in the home country. As evidence, Harvard political economist Robert B. Reich notes that in 1989 foreign-owned factories created more new jobs in the United States than did U.S. manufacturers.[40]

As a final potential drawback, an MNE's actions abroad can have negative political effects at home. One example is the continuing protest some Americans raise over U.S. involvement and investment in South African businesses.

■ SOCIAL VARIABLES: THE INTERNATIONAL DIMENSION

Analyzing the demographics and lifestyles of people in different companies is vital to the successful marketing of products that will appeal to foreign customers. Whirlpool engineers, for example, were initially critical of the washers made by Philips, a Dutch company they had invested in, because the washers contained internal water heaters, making them more expensive and slower to operate. Their criticism disappeared once they realized that many European homes do not have central water heaters.[41]

However, an MNE's ultimate success often hinges on its skill in fitting into the social fabric created by another country's values and culture. This is especially important for managers who must motivate and lead employees from different cultures with varying concepts of formality and courtesy—even different ideas about when a 10 A.M. meeting should start.[42]

bureaucratic control
Method of control that employs strict regulations to ensure desired behavior by organizational units—often used by multinational enterprises to control subsidiaries.

culture control Method of control, often associated with large Japanese companies, that emphasizes implicit and informal direction based on a broad company culture.

Bureaucratic versus Clan Control

At one time, managers in foreign countries could use **bureaucratic controls,** the application of explicit rules and regulations to describe acceptable employee behavior and results. Bureaucratic companies usually spell out operational procedures for their managers and keep close tabs on their behavior. Today, managers are shifting to **culture control,** which uses implicit and informal direction based on a broad company culture.[43] This approach is characteristic of many Japanese firms. Companies that use culture control tend to train their managers extensively before they send them overseas and then give them more authority to adapt company procedures to local customs. These managers are encouraged to interest themselves in the host company's history and culture, with special emphasis on learning the language, the straight road to the heart of any culture.[44] Exhibit 5-1 contains excerpts from a pamphlet prepared for people about to encounter Americans for the first time. Do you think this presents a fair image of Americans?

EXHIBIT 5-1 What Americans Are Like

- ❑ Citizens of the United States often call themselves "Americans." Other "Americans"— citizens of Mexico, Central and South America—often find the term inappropriate. However, Americans have been calling themselves "Americans" for the more than 200 years of their brief history, and you will hear the term often.
- ❑ Americans are very informal. They like to dress informally, entertain informally, and they treat each other in a very informal way, even when there is a great difference in age or social standing. Foreign students may consider this informality disrespectful, even rude, but it is a part of U.S. culture.
- ❑ Americans are generally competitive. The American style of friendly joking or banter, of "getting the last word in," and the quick witty reply are subtle forms of competition. Although such behavior is natural to Americans, you may find it overbearing or disagreeable.
- ❑ Americans are achievers. They are obsessed with records of achievement in sports and they keep business achievement charts on their office walls and sports awards displayed in their homes.
- ❑ Americans ask a lot of questions, some of which may to you seem pointless, uninformed, or elementary. You may be asked very personal questions by someone you have just met. No impertinence is intended; the questions usually grow out of genuine interest.
- ❑ Americans value punctuality. They keep appointment calendars and live according to schedules. To foreign students, Americans seem "always in a hurry," and this often makes them appear brusque. Americans are generally efficient and get a great many things done, simply by rushing around.
- ❑ Silence makes Americans nervous. They would rather talk about the weather than deal with silence in a conversation.

Source: Excerpts from Margo Ernest, ed., *Predeparture Orientation Handbook: For Foreign Students and Scholars Planning to Study in the United States* (Washington, D.C.: U.S. Information Agency, Bureau of Educational and Cultural Affairs, 1984), pp. 103–105, as cited in "What Americans Are Like," *The New York Times,* April 16, 1985.

TEACHING TIP

Tell your students: "You are the manager in charge of selecting employees to be sent on international assignment. What qualities, experience, and characteristics would you look for in prospective employees?"

HERE'S AN EXAMPLE

The European division of Colgate-Palmolive quizzed all its top European managers about what kind of executive works best in an international setting. One of the main attributes mentioned was flexibility in managing. (*Wall Street Journal,* 1/25/91, p. B1ff.)

ethnocentric management Attitude that the home country's management practices are superior to those of other countries and can be exported along with the organization's goods and services.

polycentric management Attitude that since a foreign country's management policies are best understood by its own management personnel, the home organization should rely on foreign offices.

geocentric management Attitude that accepts both similarities and differences between domestic and foreign management policies and so attempts to strike a balance between those that are most effective.

With regard to staffing, there are both advantages and disadvantages to being a multinational firm. On the one hand, finding the right people for organizational positions is often more difficult for MNEs than for domestic operations, since talented employees may be unwilling to relocate to another country. On the other hand, an MNE literally has a whole world of talent to draw on. In fact, hiring local nationals for key management positions can ease political, social, and cultural frictions, helping the MNE fit more smoothly into a foreign society.

Managers and Prejudice

Dealing with employees from other countries often forces managers to confront their own prejudices. For example, many men (and some women) used to assume that women were unsuitable or not interested in international jobs, particularly in countries with patriarchal social structures. As the Management and Diversity box shows, the fallacy of this viewpoint is now generally recognized, although women remain a distinct minority among international managers.[45]

Howard Perlmutter and David A. Heenan have identified three primary attitudes among the managers of international companies: ethnocentric, polycentric, and geocentric.[46] **Ethnocentric managers** see foreign countries and their people as inferior to those of the home country. These managers believe that the practices of the home country can be exported along with its goods and services. A **polycentric manager** sees all countries as different and as hard to understand. Believing that a company's foreign offices are likely to understand their needs, such managers leave them alone. **Geocentric managers** recognize similarities as well as differences among countries. Such managers attempt to draw on the most effective techniques and practices, wherever they originate.

Firms with foreign interests are likely to have managers with each of these perspectives. Perlmutter and Heenan believe that polycentric attitudes are the most

DISCUSSION QUESTION
What problems could arise from hiring local people as managers?

HERE'S AN EXAMPLE
Both 3M Company and Colgate-Palmolive Corporation give young managers international experience without moving them out of their home country. They put managers on project teams with colleagues in other countries. (*Wall Street Journal*, 1/25/91, p. B1ff.)

COORDINATED RESOURCE
See *Management Live!* Reading 17.2, "The Chief Executives in the Year 2000 Will Be Experienced Abroad."

suitable kind for managers of multinational companies, but they are also the hardest to learn and accept.

Applying U.S. Approaches Abroad

Although polycentric attitudes may be the most effective, American managers have a natural tendency to favor U.S. approaches. How well do they work? There are at least two ways to view this question. On the one hand, U.S. companies plainly have a long record of successful overseas operations following the types of practices supported by U.S./Western-based theory. It was not too long ago, in fact, that some writers feared that U.S. MNEs would completely dominate world business.[47] Their management skills were seen as their key competitive advantage.

On the other hand, contingency theory states that what works managerially in a given situation depends on a number of factors. Therefore, it is logical to assume that, in the international arena, what works with some people won't work with others. An organization needs to plan wherever it has operations but the best way to go about planning might be quite different in India than in the United States.

THE HOFSTEDE STUDIES. The Dutch management scholar Geert Hofstede conducted studies in 40 countries in order to draw some conclusions about the relationship between national character and employee motivation.[48] He concluded that people vary a great deal and those variations seriously challenge the rules of effective managerial practice based on Western theories and peoples. Hofstede cites four dimensions he feels describe important aspects of a national culture.[49]

1. *Individualism versus collectivism* measures an individual's relationship with other people and the degree to which the desire for personal freedom is played off against the need for social ties.
2. *Power distance* evaluates the way a particular society handles inequality among people. On one end of the scale are countries and people that play down inequality as much as possible. At the other end are cultures that accept and support large imbalances in power, status, and wealth.
3. *Uncertainty avoidance* measures how a society deals with the uncertainty of the future. A weak uncertainty-avoidance society is one that does not feel threatened by the uncertainty of the future, but is generally tolerant and secure. A strong uncertainty-avoidance culture, on the other hand, tries to overcome future uncertainties by developing legal, technological, and religious institutions that create security and avoid risk.
4. *Masculinity versus femininity* refers to the rigidity of sex roles. Hofstede defines a society as masculine if there are extensive divisions of social roles by sex and as feminine if these divisions are relatively small.

In light of the differences he found between nations, Hofstede feels that it is unrealistic to expect any single management approach to be applicable worldwide. For example, U.S. theories on leadership are appropriate for cultures that are extremely high in individualism but inappropriate for the collectivist cultures found in most Third World nations. Western theories of motivation, he feels, are likewise flawed by a high individualism bias. In the United States, the strongest motivation is the internal need to gain self-respect or achieve personal goals. In collectivist societies, motivation is more externally directed. People feel obligations to their groups, such as their family, enterprise, or country, and are driven to seek "status" within these groups rather than self-realization.

Hofstede sees organizational structure and policies as ways to distribute power and avoid uncertainty. As such, they are affected by power distance and uncertainty avoidance. The United States placed very close to the middle of the scale in both these aspects in Hofstede's studies, which may account for some of the success of

MANAGEMENT AND DIVERSITY

Women in the International Work Force

Since the 1950s, the United States has witnessed profound changes in women's prospects at work and in society. Once our culture identified men predominantly with public or work life and linked women to private and home life. Slowly, the idea has taken hold that women should be allowed to seek fulfillment at work as well as at home. How far women have actually come is debatable, given their virtual absence from the upper echelons of management, but few would disagree that American women have many more options today than they did 40 years ago.

Yet in international management, women frequently encounter stifling reminders of a more patriarchal past. Dealing directly with Asian and Middle Eastern firms can be quite awkward for women executives. In these cultures, women are traditionally excluded from or thought incompetent to hold positions of authority outside the home. Many Asian and Middle Eastern business*men* view the presence of American business*women* at negotiations as an insult and refuse to work with them.

The Japanese attitude on this issue is especially significant because our economic interaction with them is vast and growing. A recent *New York Times* article recounts the experience of a major U.S. bank that was hosting a party for a Japanese firm. The bank decided to invite virtually no female employees because they felt the presence of businesswomen would make their guests uncomfortable.

Although the Japanese traditions do accord

Hong Kong's Most Powerful Woman. A Shanghai native, Berkeley-educated Dame Lydia Dunn, chairperson of the Hong Kong Trade Development Council, senior member of Hong Kong's inner cabinet, and director of several companies, is planning for 1997, when Hong Kong reverts to Chinese control.

more respect to foreign women in a business setting that they would to Japanese women, it is widely acknowledged that "Japanese businessmen never negotiate anything important with a woman." Due in part

---

COORDINATED RESOURCE

The Additional Lecture for Chapter 5 found in the Lecture Extras supplement examines Japanese management style.

COORDINATED RESOURCE

See Samaras Case 6.3, "Who Won the War?".

U.S. MNEs; organizational practices favored by U.S. managers may be reasonably acceptable to people from cultures at other ends of the scale.

Applying Japanese Approaches Abroad and Synthesizing Differing Approaches

While Hofstede has expressed serious doubts about applying American/Western management practices in other countries, some observers have become very excited about the effectiveness of Japanese practices. The study of Japanese management has become almost a fad, in fact. We should note, however, that what most people refer to as "Japanese management practices" are drawn from a select group of companies, responsible for perhaps as little as one-third of employment within Japan.

William G. Ouchi (see Chapter 2) is among those who have studied Japanese business in the hope that it might provide solutions to some American problems.[50]

to the influence of Confucianism, the Japanese have long maintained a high wall between the world of men and the world of women. Tradition dictates that a woman's primary responsibility is to take care of her working husband and to raise their children.

Sexism is common in Japanese culture. New women employees are routinely channeled into assistant-track positions, while male workers are put on the management track. At Japan's largest bank, Dai-Ichi Kangyo Bank, Ltd., only about 40 of the nearly 7,000 women employees are on the managerial track. Although a small percentage of women do make it into management, female executives are extremely rare. More typically, women who work are employed as "office ladies" who do clerical tasks and serve tea to their male "superiors." Women who try to buck the system often find themselves out of a job.

Although there is no Japanese phrase for sexual harassment, instances of violent abuse by superiors, forced sexual encounters, and other forms of harassment are not uncommon. Outside the workplace, female employees are often treated like bar hostesses by their bosses and colleagues.

There are signs of change, however. In April 1990, the first harassment case was brought to trial. Japanese women have also begun to take a more active role in politics and in consumer and domestic issues. In 1989, 146 women ran for office in the Japanese legislature, up 82 from 1986. Even though women occupy only 33 seats in the 252-seat Upper House and 7 in the 512-seat Lower House, women had their best-ever showing in the elections. In addition, women successfully pushed for the passage of antidiscrimination legislation. Unfortunately, this is seen as a token gesture, since the law provides no penalties or provisions for enforcement.

Despite their minimal substance, these changes represent profound symbolic gains, which are certain to be followed by more substantive changes in Japanese culture. If nothing else, demographics and international competition will force the Japanese to take a more open attitude toward sexual equality in the workplace. For every college graduate in a technical field, there are four jobs waiting with Japanese firms. Also, Japan's best and brightest women are flocking to foreign (especially U.S.) firms for better working conditions, fairer pay, and more chances for advancement. Japan may soon find that it cannot afford to ignore the potential contribution of women employees. Although these conclusions are encouraging, several commentators claim that Japanese culture is roughly 30 years behind the United States in the way it treats women, and it is not clear how fast real change will come.

Thus American managers in Japan face serious ethical and business problems. Should they alter their practices to accommodate Japanese clients? Should female executives adopt passive roles in dealing with Japanese colleagues? Our answers are profoundly important, says Diana Henriques. Because Japan is playing an increasingly important role in the U.S. and world economy, she argues, our acceptance of Japanese attitudes toward women may undo progress made by American women. In the pursuit of clients, corporations may revert to the ethos that women do not belong in the office unless they are serving coffee to men.

Sources: Flora Lewis, "Now Turn to Women," *The New York Times,* July 26, 1989, Sect. A, p. 23; Diana Henriques, "To American Women: Sayonara," *The New York Times,* August 27, 1989, Sect. 4, p. 19; Chieko Kuriki, "Empty Words," *Chicago Tribune,* November 5, 1989, Sect. 6, p. 8; Ronald E. Yates, "Stepping Out," *Chicago Tribune,* November 19, 1989, Sect. 6, pp. 1, 7; Chieko Kuriki, "Awakening," *Chicago Tribune,* March 4, 1990, Sect. 6, p. 7; Carol Kleiman, "Study Puts Japan, U.S. in Same Bias Boat," *Chicago Tribune,* March 5, 1990, Sect. 4, p. 6.

Table 5-1 lists some of the characteristics he noted that distinguish Japanese organizations from American ones.

TABLE 5-1 Characteristics of Japanese and American Organizations

JAPANESE ORGANIZATIONS	AMERICAN ORGANIZATIONS
Lifetime employment	Short-term employment
Slow evaluation and promotion	Rapid evaluation and promotion
Non-specialized career paths	Specialized career paths
Implicit control mechanisms	Explicit control mechanisms
Collective decision making	Individual decision making
Collective responsibility	Individual responsibility
Wholistic concern	Segmented concern

Source: William G. Ouchi, *Theory Z: How American Business Can Meet the Japanese Challenge* (Reading, Mass.: Addison-Wesley, 1981), p. 58.

These differences in organizational characteristics are associated with differences in managerial behavior. Naturally, there are wide variations in how individual Japanese managers act, yet there are a number of ways in which the *average* Japanese manager appears to differ from the average American manager. Overall, Japanese managers seem to be more concerned with the longer-term implications of their decisions and actions and more willing to make current sacrifices for future benefits. They are also more likely to encourage subordinates to participate in decision making and to welcome and acknowledge suggestions from subordinates. Partly because of this participation, they are less likely to make quick, unilateral decisions. In addition, communication between managers and subordinates is more indirect and subtle than in the United States. Managers try hard to avoid embarrassing co-workers in public or in private. They get to know their co-workers well as individuals and show concern for their welfare outside the workplace.

There is much controversy over Japanese management style. Some observers doubt that it is the key to the success of "Japan, Inc." Others challenge the "one big happy family" image of Japanese companies and argue that employee fear of punishment is a major factor in Japanese success. They also point out the restricted nature of some of the supposed employee benefits in Japanese firms. For example, the guarantee of "lifetime employment" is essentially restricted to males, since it is assumed that women will work for a few years, get married, and then leave the company. Moreover, the guaranteed employment terminates at age 55, when most individuals are forced to seek other, lower-paying jobs because of relatively modest pension benefits.[51]

In the overall analysis, however, Japanese companies do seem to do many things well. In fact, Pascale and Athos have noted that there is much similarity between well-managed Japanese firms and well-managed U.S. firms.[52] As managers "try, observe, adjust, and try again," the practices around the world should become more similar and any differences that are uncovered will probably look like "commonsense." Finally, those practices that do work will continue to change and evolve over time.[53]

CLASS COMMENT

The Japanese now own or have large investment stakes in at least 1,435 manufacturing plants in the United States, according to a new survey by the Japan External Trade Organization. The number of workers employed at such plants has increased from 200,000 to 300,000 since 1989. (*Fortune*, 4/22/91, p. 14)

COORDINATED RESOURCE

See DuBose Reading #20, "What Japanese Managers Know That American Managers Don't."

COORDINATED RESOURCE

See *Management Live!* Chapter 17 video, "Gung Ho."

ILLUSTRATIVE CASE STUDY

WRAP-UP

Sumitomo: The Move to International Banking

In making foreign investments, such as buying an interest in Goldman, Sachs or arranging the financing for the buyout of Federated Department Stores, Sumitomo must be aware of the economic, political, and technological variables of each country in which it does business. The best example here is the Glass-Steagall Act, which creates a "wall" between the lending activities of commercial banks and the deal-making and securities activities of investment banks. In turn, Sumitomo's investment in Goldman, Sachs affected regulators in its host country—the United States; to them Sumitomo's purchase represented a potentially worrisome challenge to the wall between commercial and investment banks.

Sumitomo's activities strongly suggest it believes that competitiveness will endure in the U.S. business culture and that the restrictions imposed on investment and commercial banks will be lifted in the future, heightening competition and creating more opportunities for profit. Recognizing the profit opportunities created as Europe moves toward economic and political unity, Sumitomo has increased its European investments as well. Ultimately, though, Sumitomo's success will depend on its ability to adapt its business practices to the social variables of the United States and of any other country in which it does business. ■

■ *SUMMARY*

Globalization is one of the most important changes to the external environment of most businesses. Individuals and companies can own foreign assets either through portfolio investment, which involves no role in management, or through direct investment, which involves a direct role in management.

The pace of internationalization began to quicken after World War II, when the strong U.S. economy and technological advances in communication and transportation made it feasible to buy and manage foreign assets. By the 1960s, though, economic growth in Europe and Japan had spawned competitors for American firms. The United States was slow to recognize this trend, though, and many worry that American firms are not competitive in international markets. Because international competition has stepped up and has wide-ranging ramifications, governments are taking a more active role in supporting domestic firms. More recently, communist nations have opened themselves to capitalist measures and foreign investment, and the European Community is working to eliminate trade barriers and increase political unity among members.

Companies go international to gain access to more reliable or cheaper resources, to increase the return on their investments, to increase their market share, and to avoid foreign tariffs and import quotas.

Korth holds that companies follow four stages in becoming an international firm. As the company moves from passively filling orders to establishing joint ventures or foreign subsidiaries, its complexity increases, as does its managerial involvement in other countries.

In making direct investments, organizations need to be aware of economic, political, technological, and social variables in other countries, since these variables will affect the organization's direct-action and indirect-action environments.

To reduce the risk of direct investment, organizations can turn to economic forecasts and assess other countries' foreign-exchange rates, balance of payments, and the controls placed on imports, exports, and foreign investors. Of these, the exchange rate is especially important. Multinational managers must also assess a country's infrastructure, the physical facilities needed to support business activity; these range from transportation to school systems.

Organizations must also assess the political climate of other countries—the government's business attitudes, say, and its stability. To help them do this, they can turn to sophisticated political risk analysts, who can make them more aware of laws and regulations affecting business activities.

In making a direct investment, MNE managers must be aware that levels of technology vary among countries, as do people's experience and comfort with technology. Although some criticize the way technology has been introduced into other cultures, others praise the MNEs for giving less-developed countries a chance to gain experience with it.

MNE operations can have other positive effects on host countries, including an improvement in their balance of payments, the creation of local jobs, improved competition, and a greater availability of goods. However, MNE investments may also absorb local financing and drive local producers out of business. In addition, some MNEs in the past were guilty of political and social-cultural interference. Today, though, most MNEs are sensitive to these issues and their investments are actively courted by host countries.

Although MNEs make direct investments to gain such benefits as increased market share and so forth, direct investment may weaken the home country's balance of payments, dilute its technological advantage, and cause the loss of domestic jobs.

Although an MNE's success in marketing products abroad hinges on its ability to analyze foreign demographics and lifestyles, its ultimate success depends on how well its foreign operations fit into the values and culture of its host country. MNE managers must be aware of the difference between bureaucratic and clan control and be sensitive in general to the culture of foreign employees. They must also be sensitive to their own attitudes, says Perlmutter and Heenan, who distinguish between ethnocentric, polycentric, and geocentric managers.

Selecting a managerial approach is a subject of much debate. Although U.S. firms have succeeded overseas, Hofstede's research indicates that no one approach is likely to be effective in every country. Intrigued by the success of Japanese management techniques, many are urging a synthesis of U.S. and Japanese management techniques.

■ REVIEW QUESTIONS

1. Explain the difference between portfolio investment and direct investment. Give examples of each.

2. What forces contributed to the current concern that U.S. firms are not competitive in the international marketplace?

3. Why do companies decide to go international?

4. Describe the four stages of corporate internationalization identified by Christopher Korth and explain how they affect organization complexity and managerial involvement abroad.

5. What economic variables should managers be aware of before they invest in other countries? Why?

6. Describe the political variables of the international dimension and explain why they concern managers.

7. What must managers be aware of in introducing technology into a foreign country?

8. What are the possible impacts of MNEs on their host countries? On their home countries?

9. How can familiarity with and responsiveness to foreign cultural characteristics aid international managers? What can managers do to develop this familiarity?

10. Discuss Hofstede's findings on variations in national character. How might these be relevant to managers?

11. How does Japanese management style differ from U.S. management style?

CASE STUDY

Lucky-Goldstar: Management, Korean Style

When Japanese companies first began manufacturing in the United States, many people smiled at certain of their corporate oddities, such as prework exercise, but analysts were also struck with the efficiency of the Japanese management style. Now the Koreans are coming, setting up their own factories, and bringing their version of management "harmony."

Dozens of South Korean corporations have already opened offices in the United States, and two have begun manufacturing operations. The Lucky-Goldstar Group opened a color television factory in Huntsville, Alabama, in 1983 and is now bustling with expansion plans. In 1985, the Samsung Group also began producing color televisions, at a factory in Roxbury Township, New Jersey.

In gambling that they can manufacture profitably in America, just when American manufacturers are bitterly complaining and even going abroad because of foreign competition, the Koreans are counting on being able to successfully blend their own traditional management style with American methods.

The Korean style is similar to the much better known Japanese approach, although experts say the Koreans are often more willing to marry their techniques to American methods. Korean management fosters a family atmosphere in which employees interact freely with executives and share a strong commitment to the company's success.

Acting more like a gentle patriarch than like the president of the Goldstar of America plant, P.W. Suh has taken charge of the delicate task of grafting Korean management principles onto Dixie. Mr. Suh concedes that there have been awkward moments—such as the reluctance of some American workers to wear uniforms—but employees and management generally appreciate the result.

"You wouldn't believe what Goldstar does for us," said Rachel Cothren, pausing from her job on the assembly line. "My husband was in the hospital for major surgery, and some of the management came and sat with me through that. Mr. Suh came and stayed with me in intensive care, and brought books and magazines."

This carefully cultivated image of a caring company that resembles a happy family typifies the Korean management style. But the care is not for nothing. It is intended to keep unions at bay and to foster the kind of loyalty and enthusiasm in the work force that will generate more televisions per hour than American management can. One measure of its success is that the daily absenteeism rate at Goldstar averages 1 percent, compared with 5 percent in American companies.

The idea is to import Korean management methods instead of Korean televisions. These methods are associated with an economic miracle that produced even faster economic growth in South Korea over the last 25 years than in Japan. The Korean growth was three times faster than that in the United States. The principal weapon in the Korean armory is its management philosophy, what the Koreans call *inhwa,* or harmony. In South Korea, Lucky-Goldstar is an exemplar of this philosophy.

"If we are in a hurry, we may ask employees for special consideration to do things differently," said D.H. Koo, president of overseas operations for the Lucky-Goldstar Group, explaining the Korean approach. "And they will oblige. But in the United States, maybe they do not care that there is a hurry."

Mr. Koo and his colleagues in the Lucky-Goldstar boardrooms want employees at the Huntsville plant to care, so they are trying to transplant *inhwa.* "I expect dedication and loyalty in the future, if we help our family," Mr. Suh said, using "family" to refer to his work force.

Telling employees about company goals and even asking for help are cardinal principles of Goldstar. "Family meetings" for all of the staff are held monthly, and quality discussions are scheduled every two weeks. In addition, bonuses are used to build enthusiasm. About three days a week, workers get a bonus—an hour of overtime pay—if their assembly line has increased output while maintaining quality levels. Employees also get $50 in cash if they do not miss a day of work for three months.

Similar management methods are used at Samsung's plant in Roxbury Township. There employees are also called a family, and interaction between workers and executives is stressed.

One reason the Koreans have begun to manufacture in the United States is their fear that protectionist rules will otherwise keep their products out of U.S. markets. On several occasions, Goldstar has found itself in U.S. courts, accused of "dumping" products in our markets (meaning they offered the goods for less than fair value). In the latest case, Goldstar was one of the major defendants in a suit alleging that $275 million worth of small-business telephone equipment was dumped in violation of U.S. law.

Despite its efforts, Goldstar is finding it particularly hard to make inroads here because the company lacks a recognizable brand name and customers have formed allegiances to American and Japanese products. In addition, volatile political change in South Korea is challenging the philosophy and economic viability of Goldstar and other *chaebol* (a Korean term for large family-owned and -run businesses). Once the *chaebol* were the country's pride and could rely on an authoritarian government to bankroll them, outlaw trade unions, keep wages low, and bar foreign competition. Today, though, South Korea is becoming more democratic and egalitarian, so the *chaebol* are out of favor. Labor strikes have helped raise Korean wages by 60 percent, undermining one of the key advantages Korean producers had over competitors. Government officials expect smaller, faster-moving businesses to lead Korea's economy into the future and have therefore cut aid to the *chaebol*.

These changes threaten the survival of the *chaebol*. Their common strategy has been to let American and Japanese firms develop new products, which they then copy and manufacture with cheap Korean labor, gaining a competitive price advantage. Given the speed of technological change today, though, companies face enormous pressure to be on the cutting edge of research, to specialize their products, and to respond to change quickly. Because Goldstar has a commitment to *inhwa* and a democratic approach to managing and decision making, it may be better equipped to meet these challenges than the more hierarchial *chaebol* that still reflect the founding family's interests. Ultimately, however, how well these companies respond will largely depend on how Korea's struggling economy fares.

All these forces will test the strength of Goldstar's management skills and corporate philosophy. By manufacturing in the United States, it gained important market advantages and more secure access to America's insatiable market for high-tech products. Nevertheless, it is Goldstar's ability to foster the spirit of *inhwa* at home that may well determine the company's survival.

Source: Nicholas D. Kristof, "Management, Korean Style," *The New York Times,* April 11, 1985, pp. D1ff. Copyright © 1985 by The New York Times Company. Reprinted by permission. Additional information taken from Mark Clifford, "Corporate Democracy Pays Dividends," *Far Eastern Economic Review,* November 19, 1987, pp. 84–85; Louis Kraan, "The Tigers Behind Korea's Prowess," *Fortune,* Fall 1989, pp. 36–40; Damon Darlin, "Korea's Goldstar Faces a Harsh New World Under Democracy," *The Wall Street Journal,* November 8, 1989, p. A1; Damon Darlin, "Do or Be Done For," *The Economist,* December 9, 1989, pp. 74–79; John T. Norman, "South Korean Firms Cited Over Exports of Phone Systems," *The Wall Street Journal,* December 20, 1989, p. A16.

Case Questions

1. Describe the Korean method of management. What advantages and disadvantages does it have over U.S. methods? How has it borrowed from U.S. methods?

2. Why are Korean manufacturers setting up manufacturing operations in the United States?

3. In your opinion, will the entry of foreign electronics manufacturers have a positive or a negative impact on the domestic electronics industry? Explain.

4. Can the recent success of Japanese and Korean MNEs be best explained by political, economic, or cultural factors?

VIDEO CASE STUDY

The Environment: Crisis in the Global Village

In March 1991, Iraqi troops withdrew from Kuwait, but not before soldiers opened pipelines that poured thousands of gallons of oil into the Persian Gulf, while others set fire to hundreds of oil wells. Experts predicted it would take at least a year to cap the fires and clear the air of the thick black smoke that turned day into night. While Kuwaiti parents worried about the health of their children, environmentalists tried to grasp the potential harm done to Kuwait, as well as to the earth.

Thanks to electronic technology, millions of people saw the damage on television—the rolling, oil-soaked waves, the sheep with sooty wool, the dead and dying seabirds—reminding everyone in the "electronic village" that our earth is truly small and its parts closely interrelated.

This was just the latest in a number of events that are making managers aware that their actions affect the planet's future and quite possibly the lives of their children's children.

Consider just a few other disasters: The *Exxon Valdez* oil spill; the explosion and fire at the Soviet nuclear reactor in Chernobyl, which spewed radioactive fallout over parts of the Soviet Union and the

Scandinavian countries; the acid rain that pours down upon the forests of the northern United States and parts of Europe; and the destruction of the rain forests in South America by developers, even though environmentalists warn that these vast rain forests are vital to clearing the air of pollution and are a rich source of potentially beneficial medicinal plants.

These events occur in addition to the daily abuse heaped upon the planet. Every hour over 150 million trees are cut down. In the United States, 2 million pounds of raw sewage are pumped into the ocean. The Soviets dump nearly 200,000 gallons of chemical waste into the Caspian Sea alone. Cars and trucks consume over 6 million gallons of fuel and spew 90,000 tons of carbon monoxide into the environment.

The combined pressure of environmental groups, governmental agencies, and concerned managers have led to a number of changes in the way corporations operate. Take, for example, the grave concern scientists and large segments of the public have expressed over the greenhouse effect, a warming of the earth's surface caused by a buildup of carbon dioxide and damage to the earth's ozone layer. In response, the United States, the Soviet Union, and several other countries have entered into an international agreement to phase out chlorofluorocarbons (CFCs) by the year 2000. CFC, a substance used in cars and building air conditioning and refrigeration units, has been shown to harm the ozone layer, which shields the earth from the sun's rays. Responding to pressure from scientists, Du Pont, the U.S.'s largest producer of CFCs, agreed to phase out their usage of CFCs, a lead voluntarily followed by a number of other major corporations.

Other international agreements involving the depletion of topsoil, the production and disposal of toxic wastes, and acid rain are all items on the international agenda.

More importantly, managers are beginning to change their priorities. They are trying to anticipate and prevent environmental problems in a proactive way—rather than just reacting *after* a crisis has happened.

Case Questions

1. Given the impact that business practices can have across the globe, what sorts of control or authority ought to influence or control business activities in a specific country?

2. If a company's managers realize that their operations have a potentially significant impact on the environment of a foreign country in which they plan to do business, what should they do?

3. If a company does business in a foreign country that has lower emission and pollution control standards than its home country, which standards should they follow?

■ NOTES

[1]This section is based upon William A. Dymsza, "Trends in Multinational Business and Global Environments: A Perspective," *Journal of International Business Studies* (Winter 1984):25–46. See also Isaiah Frank, "Meeting the Challenges of the 1990s: Trade and Investment Policies for a Changing World Economy," *Business in the Contemporary World* 5 (Spring 1990):63–76.

[2]Our definition is from Stefan H. Robock and Kenneth Simmonds, *International Business and Multinational Enterprises,* 3rd ed. (Homewood, Ill.: Irwin, 1983), p. 7. See also Yair Aharoni, "The Issue of Defining Transnational Corporations," in *Transnational Corporations in World Development: A Reexamination* (New York: United Nations, 1978), pp. 158–161, and "On the Definition of a Multinational Corporation," *Quarterly Review of Economics and Business* 11, no.3 (Autumn 1971):27–37.

[3]Reed Moyer, ed., *International Business: Issues and Concepts* (New York: Wiley, 1984), p. 137.

[4]Theodore Levitt, *The Marketing Imagination* (New York: Free Press, 1983), p. 22.

[5]Russell E. Palmer, "Trends in International Management: Toward Federations of Equals," *Business Quarterly* 152, no. 1 (Summer 1987):116–120.

[6]*Economic Report of the President,* 1984, p. 221.

[7]John A. Young, "Global Competition: The New Reality," *California Management Review* 37, no. 3 (Spring 1985):12.

[8]Lester Thurow, "Revitalizing American Industry: Managing in a Competitive World Economy," *California Management Review* 27, no. 1 (Fall 1984):10.

[9]Ibid., pp. 10–12. See also David Lei, "Strategies for Global Competition," *Long-Range Planning* 22, no. 1 (1989):102–109.

[10]Ibid., pp. 12.

[11]Sangjin Yoo and Sang M. Lee, "Management Style and Practice of Korean Chaebols," *California Management Review* 29, no. 4 (Summer 1987):95–110.

[12]Young, "Global Competition: The New Reality," p. 12.

[13]Adi Ignatius, "A Tiny Chinese Venture into Capitalism Feels Icy Chills in Wake of Crackdown," *The Wall Street Journal,* March 8, 1990, p. A11.

[14]Kay M. Jones, "Westerners Learn to Read the Tea Leaves," *Management Review,* April 1990, pp. 46–49; and Lawrence W. Foster and Lisa Tosi, "Business in China: A Year After Tiananmen," *The Journal of Business Strategy* 11 (May–June 1990):22–27.

[15]Martha H. Peak, "Revolutions Signal Opportunity for American Business," *Management Review,* March 1990, pp. 8–13.

[16]Louis Kraar, "Top U.S. Companies Move into Russia," *Fortune,* July 31, 1989, pp. 165–170.

[17]Our discussion is based on Robert Williams, Mark Teagan, and Jose Beneyto, *The World's Largest Market: A Business Guide to Europe 1992* (New York: AMACOM, 1990); and on Donald J. Puchala, "Will the Europeans Be Coming After 1992, or Have They Already Arrived?" *Business in the Contemporary World* 5 (Winter 1990):63–73.

[18]Shawn Tully, "Europe Hits the Brakes on 1992," *Fortune,* December 17, 1990, pp. 133–140.

[19]This section is based on Chapter 2, "Foreign Direct Investment and Multinational Firms," in Yoshi Tsurumi, *Multinational Management: Business Strategy and Government Policy* (Cambridge, Mass.: Ballinger Publishing, 1977), pp. 73–127.

[20]Ibid., p. 76.

[21]Steve Weiner, "Growing Pains," *Forbes,* October 29, 1990, pp. 40–41.

[22]Tsurumi, *Multinational Management: Business Strategy and Government Policy,* p. 82.

[23]Ibid., p. 76.

[24]Kevin Kelly, "From Glass Jars to Star Wars and Back Again," *Business Week,* August 20, 1990, pp. 62–63.

[25]Christopher M. Korth, *International Business, Environment and Management,* 2nd ed. (Englewood Cliffs, N.J.: Prentice Hall, 1985), p. 7.

[26]This section on global strategic partnerships is based upon their article, "Cooperate to Compete Globally," *Harvard Business Review* 64 (March–April 1986):136–152.

[27]Ibid., p. 137.

[28]Ibid., p. 137.

[29]Ibid., p. 145.

[30]Ibid., p. 146.

[31]Ibid., p. 146.

[32]Ibid., p. 150. See also Jeremy Main, "Making Global Alliances Work," *Fortune,* December 17, 1990, pp. 121–126.

[33]See Carl R. Beidleman, John J. Hilley, and James Greenleaf, "Alternatives in Hedging Long-Date Contractual Foreign Exchange Exposure," *Sloan Management Review* 24, no. 4 (Summer 1983):45–54.

[34]Donald A. Ball and Wendell H. McCulloch, *International Business: Introduction and Emotion,* 2nd ed. (Plano, Texas: Business Publications Essentials, 1985), pp. 242–267; see also Robock and Simmonds, *International Business and Multinational Enterprises,* p. 342.

[35]See, for example, Richard J. Barnet and Ronald E. Müller, *Global Reach: The Power of the Multinational Corporations* (New York: Simon & Schuster, 1974) for a popular critique of MNEs, widely cited by critics of MNEs in the 1970s. See also Joseph S. Nye, Jr., "Multinational Corporations in World Politics," *Foreign Affairs* 53, no.1 (October 1974):153–175; and Peter F. Drucker, "Multinationals and Developing Countries: Myths and Realities," *Foreign Affairs* 53, no. 1 (October 1974):121–143 (both reprinted in Moyer, *International Business*).

[36]This discussion is based on Korth, *International Business, Environment, and Management,* 2nd ed., pp. 277–297, 308–326.

[37]Robock and Simmonds, *International Business and Multinational Enterprises,* p. 233 (originally from "Dollar Diplomacy, 1972 Style," *Newsweek,* April 10, 1972).

[38]Lawrence G. Franko, "Foreign Direct Investment in Less Developed Countries; Impact on Home Countries," *Journal of International Business Studies* 9, no. 2 (Winter 1978):55–65; and Robert G. Hawkins and Bertram Finn, "Regulation of Multinational Firms' Foreign Activities: Home Country Policies and Concerns," *Journal of Contemporary Business* 6, no. 4 (Autumn 1977):14–30 (both reprinted in Moyer, *International Business*).

[39]Moyer, *International Business,* p. 138. For a discussion of the types of jobs U.S. MNEs might move overseas and the impacts of doing so on the U.S. economy and work force, see Robert A. Reich, *The New American Frontier* (New York: Times Books, 1983).

[40]Otis Port, "Why the U.S. Is Losing Its Lead," *Business Week,* Special Innovation 1990 Issue, pp. 34–39.

[41]Steve Seiner, "Growing Pains," *Forbes,* October 29, 1990, pp. 40–41.

[42]For an interesting early book that called managers' attention to these kinds of differences, see Edward T. Hall, *The Silent Language* (New York: Doubleday, 1959).

[43]B.R. Baliga and Alfred M. Jaeger, "Multinational Corporations: Control Systems and Delegation Issues," *Journal of International Business Studies* 15, no. 2 (Fall 1984):26–28. See also Alfred M. Jaeger, "The Transfer of Organizational Culture Overseas: An Approach to Control in the Multinational Corporation," *Journal of International Business Studies* 14, no. 2 (Fall 1983):101.

[44]Rosalie L. Tung reports that Japanese MNEs have better success rates with managers they send overseas than do U.S. MNEs. To read her recommendations for improving U.S. performance in this area, see her article, "Human Resource Planning in Japanese Multinationals: A Model for U.S. Firms?" *Journal of International Business Studies* 15, no. 2 (Fall 1984):139–149.

[45]Nancy J. Adler, "Women in International Management: Where Are They?" *California Management Review* 26, no. 4 (Summer 1984):81.

[46]Perlmutter and Heenan, "Cooperate to Compete Globally," pp. 136–152.

[47]See, for example, Jean Jacques Servan-Schreiber, *The Awakening Challenge* (New York: Atheneum, 1968).

[48]Geert Hofstede, "The Cultural Relativity of Organizational Practices and Theories," *Journal of International Business Studies* 14, no. 1 (Fall 1983):78–85, and *Culture's Consequences: International Differences in Work-Related Values* (Beverly Hills, Calif.: Sage Publications, 1980). For a rich debate on the applicability of Western management in other cultures, see Geert Hofstede, "Motivation, Leadership, and Organization: Do American Theories Apply Abroad?" *Organizational Dynamics* 9, no. 1 (Summer 1980):42–63, and "Do American Theories Apply Abroad? A Reply to Goodstein and Hunt," *Organizational Dynamics* 10, no. 1 (Summer 1981):63–68; and John W. Hunt, "Applying American Behavioral Science: Some Cross-Cultural Problems," *Organizational Dynamics* 10, no. 1 (Summer 1981):55–62.

[49]Geert Hofstede, "The Cultural Relativity of Organizational Practices and Theories," *Journal of International Business Studies* 14, no. 1 (Fall 1983); *Culture's Consequences: International Differences in Work-Related Values.*

[50]William G. Ouchi, *Theory Z: How American Business Can Meet the Japanese Challenge* (Reading, Mass.: Addison-Wesley, 1981). Other studies of note are Richard Pascale and Anthony Athos, *The Art of Japanese Management* (New York: Simon & Schuster, 1981); and N. Hatvany and V. Pucik, "An Integrated Management System: Lessons from the Japanese Experience," *Academy of Management Review* 6, no. 3 (July 1981):469–480.

[51]S. Prakash Sethi, Nobuaki Namiki, and Carl L. Swanson, *The Attack on Theory Z: The False Promise of the Japanese Miracle* (Marshfield, Mass.: Pitman, 1984).

[52]See Martin K. Starr and Nancy E. Bloom, *The Performance of Japanese-Owned Firms in America: Survey Report* (New York: Center for Operations, Graduate School of Business, Columbia University, 1985); Malcolm Trevor, "Does Japanese Management Work in Britain?" *Journal of General Management* 8, no. 4 (Summer 1983):28–43; and Satoshi Kamata, *Japan in the Passing Lane: An Insider's Account of Life in a Japanese Auto Factory* (New York: Pantheon, 1983). For a discussion of the extent to which some Japanese companies have introduced these techniques in U.S. subsidiaries, see Richard D. Robinson, *The Japan Syndrome: Is There One?* (Atlanta: Georgia State University, 1985). See also Pascale and Athos, *The Art of Japanese Management;* and J. Bernard Keys and Thomas R. Miller, "The Japanese Management Theory Jungle," *Academy of Management Review* 9, no. 2 (April 1984):345–346.

[53]Modesto A. Maidique, "Point of View: The New Management Thinkers," *California Management Review* 26, no. 1 (Fall 1983):151–161.

CHAPTER SIX

ENTREPRENEURSHIP

The Meaning of Entrepreneurship
Entrepreneurship versus Management
Entrepreneurship versus Intrapreneurship

The Importance of Entrepreneurship
The Benefits of Entrepreneurship
Environmental Variables Favoring Entrepreneurship

The Entrepreneur
Psychological and Sociological Factors
Distinctive Competence

The Entrepreneurial Process

Launching the Entrepreneurial Organization
Recognizing Barriers to Entry
Planning a Strategy
Choosing an Organization
Nurturing the Entrepreneurial Spirit

Upon completing this chapter, you should be able to:

1. Discuss the difference between entrepreneurship and management.
2. Explain the term *intrapreneuring*.
3. Describe the reasons entrepreneurship is currently a very popular topic among students of management.
4. Describe the three benefits entrepreneurship offers to society.
5. Explain the economic and noneconomic factors that account for the varying levels of entrepreneurship found in different societies.
6. Discuss the psychological and sociological factors that seem to motivate entrepreneurs.
7. Explain why entrepreneurs need a distinctive competence and how they can get it.
8. Describe the two basic stages of the entrepreneurial process.
9. Discuss the barriers to entry an entrepreneur faces in launching a new venture.
10. Describe various strategies an entrepreneur can use to compete against established firms.
11. Define the basic forms of legal organization and explain the ways an intrapreneurial venture can be organized.
12. Discuss the differences between entrepreneurial and administrative corporate cultures and explain why each is important.

Ad for Peerless Motor Car Co. from *Life,* October 21, 1909. (Hank Ehlbeck). Courtesy
Jones, Brakeley & Rockwell, Inc.

ILLUSTRATIVE CASE STUDY

INTRODUCTION

Start-Up Pains at Nova Pharmaceutical Corporation

It takes courage and conviction to break into the pharmaceutical industry, which is dominated by such giants as Eli Lilly, Merck, and Pfizer. Brand-name recognition and huge capital requirements pose significant barriers for a start-up entrepreneur wanting to join the big league. Moreover, the research-intensive nature of the business necessitates a large, steady infusion of capital, while the returns from these investments—which depend on the success of the firm's products—remain highly uncertain.

On the other hand, rewards from a successful product can be very attractive, catapulting a small, struggling start-up into enormous fame and fortune. This prospect was a sufficiently strong incentive for Donald J. Stark, a one-time high-school principal who left his lucrative job as president of Sterling Drug's Pharmaceutical Group to become CEO of Nova. Stark had observed one key fact about the drug industry—namely, that because of regulatory constraints and the tendency of major firms to emphasize growth over research, there was a dearth of new products.

Nova was founded in 1982 around the talents of three men. David Blech had been a stockbroker, his brother Isaac a public relations executive. Seeing how well some biotechnology companies were doing, the Blechs decided to quit their jobs and play the start-up game. In search of a scientific star to complete their team, they found Dr. Solomon Snyder, a biochemistry pioneer researcher into how the human body senses pain. The trio hit it off well; the Blech brothers provided the management expertise needed with investors, government, and other key external stakeholders, while Synder provided the medical expertise.

All of the senior managers, such as Donald Stark, were recruited from major drug companies. Each understood the risks of competing with the industry giants, but each believed that Nova had a competitive advantage that would help it succeed.

The substantial commitments in time and money needed to do laboratory work were difficult barriers for Nova, which based its research on a complex theory of receptor-cell behavior in the pain-response system of the human body. The key principle holds that critical processes taking place in the body—from the initial perception of pain to the production of antibodies that fight disease—are orches-

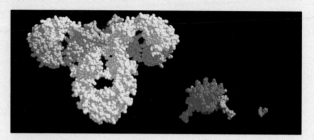

The Future of Research. Traditional drug research uses a hit-or-miss approach, screening 10,000 chemical compounds (far right) to find one drug that is effective. But in "rational drug design," scientists create genetically engineered proteins (left and center) that amplify the body's own disease-fighting mechanisms. The resulting drugs have fewer side effects and promise cures for such ills as cancer and AIDS. By the year 2000, "all drug companies will use these tools," says Nova's current president, Dr. Hans Mueller. In 1991 Nova licensed laboratory-grown brain cells from Johns Hopkins University with the hopes of creating genetically modified versions to treat Parkinson's and Alzheimer's diseases.

trated by chemical messengers that match corresponding receptors on nerve cells; drugs often work by turning these receptors on or, alternatively, blocking their action. Nova assumed that breakthroughs in receptor pharmacology would increase its ability to tailor drugs to specific receptor sites and ultimately determine the pace of evolution of new-drug development.

However, scientific breakthroughs cannot be ordered like room service. By 1986, Nova was nurturing 15 research projects, but had no guarantees that any would grow into the kind of success needed to start a family of recognizable products. Then, too, each stage of testing along the way to commercialization is closely monitored by a very cautious Food and Drug Administration, which must approve any final product. The slightest complication or side effect can ruin a product's chances of success before it ever meets its first commercial test.

Sources: William H. Miller, "Can Don Stark Mix Up a Winner?" *Industry Week,* September 30, 1985, pp. 76–77; "Dreams of Future Profits," *Financial World,* September 4–17, 1985, pp. 51–52; Emily T. Smith, "This Company Could Lead a Revolution in Drugs," *Business Week,* March 24, 1986, p. 100; "Celanese and Nova Form Joint Venture," *C&EN,* July 7, 1986, p. 8; Gene G. Marcial, "Pain Relief May Make Nova Feel Good Again," *Business Week,* June 1, 1987, p. 114.

THOUGHT PROVOKER
Companies with fewer than 100 employees bear the responsibility for 51 percent of the nation's 18.8 million uninsured workers and for more than two-thirds of those without retirement plans. What are the implications? (*U.S. News & World Report*, 6/3/91, p. 52ff.)

Nova's start-up symbolizes one of the major differences between managers and entrepreneurs. The managers at the pharmaceutical giants saw *problems* and reacted cautiously, but the entrepreneurs at Nova saw an *opportunity* to make money and they took the risk.

Our society has always had entrepreneurs, but today's rapidly changing environment has created a record number of opportunities and a corresponding number of entrepreneurs. Most, like the founders of Nova, first gain experience working for someone else, but a few launch small businesses while still in school. Others create entrepreneurial ventures without ever leaving the payroll, in a process known as *intrapreneurship* or corporate entrepreneurship. In this chapter, we will study the nature of entrepreneurship, its importance, the characteristics of the entrepreneur, and the key aspects of launching an entrepreneurial venture.

■ THE MEANING OF ENTREPRENEURSHIP

entrepreneur Either the originator of a new business venture or a manager who tries to improve an organizational unit by initiating productive changes.

The function that is specific to **entrepreneurs** is the ability to take the factors of production—land, labor, and capital—and use them to produce new goods or services. The entrepreneur perceives opportunities that other business executives do not see or do not care about.

Some entrepreneurs use information that is generally available to produce something new. Henry Ford, for example, invented neither the automobile nor the division of labor, but he applied the division of labor to the production of automobiles in a new way: the assembly line. Other entrepreneurs see new business opportunities. Akio Morita, the president of Sony, the Japanese consumer electronics giant, saw that his company's existing products could be adapted to create a new one: the Walkman personal stereo. "Basically, the entrepreneur sees a need and then brings together the manpower, materials, and capital required to meet that need."[1]

CLASS COMMENT
The most profitable companies in the United States are small firms that have been in business over ten years and employ fewer than 20 people, according to the Small Business Administration. (*Wall Street Journal*, 12/26/90, p. 11)

entrepreneurship The seemingly discontinuous process of combining resources to produce new goods or services.

Entrepreneurship versus Management

Entrepreneurship is different from management. As Paul H. Wilken notes:

> Entrepreneurship . . . involves combining *to initiate changes* in production where [management] involves combining *to produce*. Management therefore refers to the *ongoing coordination* of the production process, which can be visualized as a continual combining of the factors of production. But entrepreneurship is a discontinuous phenomenon, appearing to initiate changes in the production process . . . and then disappearing until it reappears to initiate another change.[2]

DISCUSSION QUESTION
What does it mean to be an entrepreneur?

COORDINATED RESOURCE
The Additional Lecture for Chapter 6 found in the Lecture Extras supplement looks at the "Corporate Brain Drain"—employees who are breaking away from corporate life to go into business for themselves.

As this definition suggests, even undoubted entrepreneurs do not always function in the entrepreneurial role. Entrepreneurs often play other roles, especially those of capitalist and manager, while people who primarily act as capitalists or managers may at times become entrepreneurs. Many people who want above all to be entrepreneurs find that they must eventually leave the ventures they created because they do not have the temperament to run an established business. Others, like Steve Jobs, leave to pursue new entrepreneurial goals. Jobs left Apple in 1985 and, with a few friends and $20 million in capital from Texas businessman H. Ross Perot, started a new company called Next, Inc., which was to produce a "fourth-wave microcomputer" ten times more powerful than the most popular IBM or Apple personal computers.[3]

Entrepreneurship is, above all, about change. "Entrepreneurs see change as the norm and as healthy. Usually, they do not bring about the change themselves [that is, they are usually not inventors]. But—and this defines entrepreneur and entrepreneurship—*the entrepreneur always searches for change, responds to it, and exploits it as an opportunity.*"[4]

Entrepreneurship versus Management. "Eric's the professional manager, not me," says Johnson Products Co. founder George Johnson about his son, Eric G. Johnson, who became chief executive in 1989. The nation's first black-managed public corporation, Johnson Products Co. dominated the black hair-care market until 1975, when federal-mandated warning labels opened the door to "no lye" competitors. Cosmetics giants Revlon Inc. and Alberto-Culver Co. followed, leaving Johnson Products just 6 percent of the highly competitive market. Enter son Eric, who worked as a sales representative for Procter & Gamble and earned an M.B.A. before joining the family firm in 1975, where he worked his way up through the ranks. Since 1989, Eric Johnson has acquired a competitor, cut payroll by 36 percent, increased factory output by 30 percent, used the proceeds from a real-estate sale to reduce debt, and launched two new brands, increasing sales by 20 percent.

CLASS COMMENT
According to John Macomber, chairman of the U.S. Export-Import Bank, only a third of American small businesses with export potential are currently shipping abroad. (*U.S. News & World Report*, 6/3/91, p. 52ff.)

These words were written by Peter Drucker, a well-known contemporary management writer, but they might just as easily have come from the pen of Joseph Schumpeter (1883–1950), the Austrian economist who popularized the term "entrepreneurship." For Schumpeter, indeed, the whole process of economic change hung on the person who makes it happen—the entrepreneur.[5]

Entrepreneurship versus Intrapreneurship

The typical entrepreneur starts small, with just a few part-time or full-time employees. (In the early stages, the entrepreneur may not even have employees.)

intrapreneuring Corporate entrepreneurship, whereby an organization seeks to expand by exploring new opportunities through new combinations of its existing resources.

Other new ventures are born within the confines of an existing corporation in a process called corporate entrepreneurship or **intrapreneuring**,[6] the process of "extending the firm's domain of competence and corresponding opportunity set through internally generated new resource combinations."[7] Consider Hyatt Hotels, which supplies its guests meeting rooms, food services, and help with planning parties and other events. When James E. Jones, director of sales development, noticed the impressive fees professional event planners were getting for these same services, he saw an opportunity. He considered going out on his own, drawing on his experience and contacts with professional sports teams, a major customer of event planners, but checked with Hyatt first. Hyatt's upper management helped him put together a *business plan* and in 1989 gave him $78,000 to launch Regency Productions by Hyatt. Jones's new venture managed the National Football League's corporate hospitality at the 1991 Super Bowl and provided catering for the 1991 U.S. Open Golf Tournament. Jones is exhilarated and Hyatt has a new income stream, drawing on resources it already possessed.[8] For another example of intrapreneurship, see the Management Application Box.

The Nurturing of Entrepreneurs at 3M

The development of entrepreneurs boils down to a fairly simple principle: Human beings are endowed with the urge to create—to bring into being something that has never existed or never worked so well before. It follows, then, that corporations can encourage profit-making innovations by encouraging employees to think like entrepreneurs. This has been a major goal at 3M.

3M CEO Allen Jacobson has worked tirelessly to ensure that new ideas and innovation are at the heart of the company's philosophy and its structure. Since he took over four years ago, 3M has pumped out 200 new products a year, including successful ventures in high-tech medical and diagnostic equipment and computer imaging systems. 3M has also targeted home repair as a new area of development. Their expanding DIY (Do It Yourself) division is prepared for a surging demand for home-repair products in the 1990s. 3M had already developed an impressive array of new easy-to-use and environmentally conscious products, among them Safest Stripper, a paint and varnish remover that contains no odor or harmful chemicals and can be used indoors.

3M spent 6.5 percent of its 1988 sales on R&D, twice the U.S. average, according to *Fortune* magazine. (Only Merck is rated more innovative.) This innovative and entrepreneurial spirit is manifest in 3M's new building in Texas. In the Minnesota headquarters, sales marketing, management, and research are in separate buildings several blocks apart. In Texas, all functions are in one building; despite its size, it takes only five minutes to walk from one end to the other. This physical proximity is crucial to a company whose innovation process depends on interaction and communication.

Employees are encouraged to spend 15 percent of their time working on projects that are not expected to enter the market for years. This long-term emphasis is balanced by Jacobson's requirement that 25 percent of each division's sales come from products developed in the last five years. Technical people are urged to share information in the halls, and a

A Commitment to Openness. 3M's new building in Austin, Texas, is designed to encourage communication.

corporate committee of scientists monitors all new research efforts to minimize duplication of effort and to facilitate the sharing of new discoveries. In addition, 3M's annual private "trade show" lets members of all 115 research labs display their latest work and for three days try to "sell" it to other 3M scientists and engineers. The corporate hierarchy and pay structure are also shaped to reward technical people. Researchers who prefer to stay in R&D can still rise to the equivalent of vice president in pay and benefits.

It is not hard to see that the commitment to entrepreneurship at 3M is more than a slogan. It emanates from the company's basic philosophy and shapes virtually every aspect of 3M—from pay scales and perks to management style and even the structure of the 3M building.

Sources: Lewis Lehr, "The Care and Flourishing of Entrepreneurs at 3M," *Directors and Boards,* Winter 1988, pp. 18–20; Brian Dumaine, "Ability to Innovate," *Fortune,* January 29, 1990, pp. 43–44; Warren Berger, "The 'Scotch Tape Company' Embraces Home Repair," *Adweek's Marketing Week,* February 5, 1990, p. 1.

■ *THE IMPORTANCE OF ENTREPRENEURSHIP*

start-up Business founded by individuals intending to change the environment of a given industry by the introduction of either a new product or a new production process.

Entrepreneurship is currently a very popular topic among students of management and economics. It was not always so. Before 1960, most economists understood its importance, but in the sixties, they tended to underrate it. To begin with, the attention then devoted to big companies obscured the fact that most new jobs are created by newer, smaller firms. Moreover, the function of the entrepreneur—organizing new productive resources to expand supply—seemed unimportant to the dominant school of economics, which was chiefly interested in managing consumer *demand*.

In the 1970s, the mood changed again when economics concerned primarily with consumer demand failed to prevent the constant inflation of that decade. Economists began to worry about the fact that our productivity was increasing much less rapidly than it had earlier—it had dropped from 2–3 percent annually in the good years of the 1950s and 1960s to almost nothing. This made them more interested in the *supply* of goods and services—the entrepreneur's sphere—and less interested in managing demand.

Slower growth in general made those sectors of the economy that were still growing quickly stand out: medical services, electronics, robotics, genetic engineering, and a few others. These are all high-tech industries in which many companies are small **start-ups** founded by people who wanted to change the business world—by entrepreneurs and by intrapreneurs. What George Wilder calls the "heroic creativity of entrepreneurs"[9] came to seem essential to our economic well-being, especially in a global economy. In this section, we want to look at the ways entrepreneurship benefits society; then we will look at the environmental variables that foster entrepreneurship and why different societies have different levels of entrepreneurship.

The Benefits of Entrepreneurship

Entrepreneurship has at least three benefits for society: it fosters economic growth, it increases productivity, and it creates new technologies, products, and services. We will discuss these benefits here. Then, when we discuss the entrepreneurial process, we will see how entrepreneurship addresses practical problems created by changes in the external environment.

ECONOMIC GROWTH. One reason economists started paying more attention to small new firms is that they seem to provide most of the new jobs in our economy. In an important U.S. industry, electronics, a trade association study showed that companies that have survived for 5 to 10 years hire more than 50 times as many people as do companies that have been around for more than 20 years.[10]

Moreover, one researcher, David Birch, has estimated that in the United States more than four-fifths of all new employment openings come from small businesses. Of these openings, upwards of 30 percent are provided by companies that are less than 5 years old. But Birch adds, "Not all small businesses are job creators. The job creators are the relatively few younger ones that start up and expand rapidly in their youth, outgrowing the 'small' designation in the process."[11] Birch has also found that new companies—and therefore the jobs they create—are increasingly found in the service sector of the economy rather than in the manufacturing sector.[12]

PRODUCTIVITY. *Productivity*—the ability to produce more goods and services with less labor and other inputs—increased much less rapidly in the United States during the 1970s than it had in the 1950s and 1960s. Many economists concluded, and still believe, that this is the most fundamental problem of our economy. One reason for the greater interest in entrepreneurship has been the growing recognition of its role in raising productivity.

research and development (R&D) Entrepreneurial function devoting organizational assets to the design, testing, and production of new products.

macroeconomic policy Decisions concerning such factors as taxation, development costs, regulatory control, and other external factors that might affect the development of a new product.

Higher productivity is chiefly a matter of improving production techniques, and this task, according to John Kendrick, is "the entrepreneurial function par excellence." Two keys to higher productivity are **research and development (R&D)** and investment in new plant and machinery. According to Kendrick, "there is a close link between R&D and investment programs, with a high entrepreneurial input into both."[13]

Another important influence on productivity growth is government regulation and **macroeconomic policy**—that is, taxation, spending, and money creation. Many economists believe that innovation—the essential precondition for high productivity growth—was (as Kendrick put it) "dampened by the developments of [the 1970s], especially by accelerating inflation and its consequences and by increasing governmental interventions in the business economy."[14] In this respect, entrepreneurs are important, says Kendrick, because they "help contain the negative impacts of regulations."[15]

NEW TECHNOLOGIES, PRODUCTS, AND SERVICES. Another consequence of the association between entrepreneurship and change is the role that entrepreneurs play in promoting innovative technologies, products, and services. Many people who have developed new technologies, products, and services—Gore-Tex fabric, for example—were employees of large corporations that refused to use them, forcing the inventors to become entrepreneurs. Take Gore-Tex, now a staple of winter sportswear. When Gore-Tex was first developed, no established garment manufacturer wanted to use it, and it was ignored until a struggling smaller firm decided to experiment with it. Exhibit 6-1 lists some other contributions, ranging from the zipper to titanium, that have resulted from the innovative efforts of entrepreneurs over the past several decades.

Other innovations—for example, Henry Ford's mass-production line—were pioneered by people who opted for independent product supply from the start. Yet as Ford's example shows, start-ups may eventually become so successful that they cease to be entrepreneurial in spirit or ownership.

Sometimes one entrepreneurial innovation gives rise to many others. The most famous and important case comes from the very start of the Industrial Revolution during the second half of the eighteenth century. Early in that century, imported cotton fabric from India gave some British entrepreneurs the idea of producing such fabric in Britain. At first, the raw cotton (mostly from the American South) was spun into yarn by hand-operated machines and then woven, also by hand-operated ma-

HERE'S AN EXAMPLE
Doug Kahn's software company, Easel Corporation, joined IBM's Business Partners program in 1989. Under their latest joint contract, IBM will market Easel's Workbench programming software, remitting the revenues to Easel, which will then pay its big partner a marketing fee. The contract guarantees Easel $4 million in 1991, plus a $3.5 milion licensing fee for the use of its software. (*U.S. News & World Report,* 6/3/91, p. 52ff.)

EXHIBIT 6-1 Some Contributions of Independent Inventors and Small Organizations

Digital computers	Ball-point pen	Cotton picker
Xerography	Tungsten carbide	Dacron polyester fiber
Laser	Velcro	Automatic transmission
Insulin	Fiberglass surfboards	Mercury dry cell
Turbojet engine	String trimmers	Power steering
Magnetic recording	Magnetic core memory	Color photography
Oxygen steelmaking process	Flexible soda straws	Polaroid camera
Gyrocompass	Vacuum tube	Cellophane
Rocketry	FM radio	Bakelite
Shell molding	Penicillin	Hovercraft
Shrink-proof knitwear	Petroleum catalytic cracking	Metal-laminated skis
Zipper	Fiber optics	Fiberglass snow skis
Self-winding wristwatch	Heterodyne radio	Prince tennis racket
Continuous hot-strip steel	Streptomycin	Geodesic domes
Helicopter	Cyclotron	
Air conditioning	Titanium	

Sources: Adapted from Jacob Rabinow, National Bureau of Standards. Reprinted from Karl H. Vesper, *Entrepreneurship and National Policy* (1983). Walter E. Heller International Corporation Institute for Small Business.

chines, into fabric. But a problem arose: The machines that did the spinning worked too slowly to produce enough yarn to keep all the weaving machines fully occupied. Spinning, therefore, was a bottleneck. Before long, inventors were working to unjam it. In the mid-1760s, James Hargreaves invented the spinning jenny, a machine that could produce up to 11 threads of cotton simultaneously. Later in the century, the spinning jenny was linked to the steam engine, so that it no longer had to be worked by the operator's foot. The overall effect of these innovations was to increase the amount of cotton thread still further. Now there was too much thread and not enough weaving capacity—exactly the opposite of the old problem. Again, inventors went to work. In 1785, an English clergyman invented the power loom, a weaving machine powered by a steam engine. Innovation had come full circle.

A similar process can be seen in California's Silicon Valley, where one study showed that as many as four-fifths of all companies had been started by exiles from larger companies. In fact, one researcher showed that Fairchild Semiconductors, founded in 1967 by exiles from Shockley Transistor Laboratories, spawned at least 35 other start-ups by 1970.

Environmental Variables Favoring Entrepreneurship

CLASS COMMENT
Each year, the National Federation of Independent Business surveys its members on a wide range of legislative and business issues. On several common issues, small-business owners broadly agree. They overwhelmingly oppose legislation to mandate such employee benefits as parental leave and health insurance coverage, and they strongly favor measures to pare worker compensation costs. (*Wall Street Journal,* 3/25/91, p. B2)

COORDINATED RESOURCE
See Geis & Kuhn, Chapter 10, "Venture Capital Expert System—Looking for Cash."

COORDINATED RESOURCE
Use Transparency 25, Barriers to Entrepreneurship.

Some societies—notably the United States, South Korea, and such Southeast Asian countries as Thailand, Indonesia, Malaysia, and Singapore—abound with entrepreneurs. In contrast, the Soviet Union and mainland China have far fewer entrepreneurs, although recent changes in their laws are meant to encourage entrepreneurship. To understand why different societies have different levels of entrepreneurship, we must examine both economic and noneconomic variables in the indirect-action environment of various societies.

ECONOMIC VARIABLES. Since entrepreneurship is essentially the promotion of economic change, "the same factors that promote economic growth and development account for the emergence of entrepreneurship."[16] Two kinds of economic factors are relevant here. The first is market incentives—new social needs the entrepreneur can attempt to satisfy in new ways. In England, for example, the government long operated steel companies, airlines, and automobile manufacturers, which dampened market incentives. In recent years, the government has begun to turn these firms over to private industry, creating opportunities that encourage entrepreneurship.

The second kind of economic factor relates to the stock of capital. There must be a sufficient stock of capital to fund new enterprises, and institutions (like banks) must be willing to direct capital to would-be entrepreneurs. (To some extent, old wealth is a precondition of new wealth.) Some nations—like Mexico—seek to increase their stock of capital by inviting partnerships with foreign firms.

SOCIAL VARIABLES. Though the Soviet Union is poorer today than the United States, it has more wealth than the United States had in the nineteenth century. Nonetheless, the Soviet Union has few entrepreneurs, while the United States has always had many. To understand this, we must look at social variables—cultural and social differences—in the indirect-action environment of each country.

In the United States, entrepreneurs and entrepreneurial behavior enjoy a legitimacy they have never had in the Soviet Union. In the mid-1980s, Mikhail Gorbachev sought to change Soviet laws to legalize and even encourage entrepreneurship, particularly by worker-owned collectives, but by early 1988, he was attacking co-ops that "take advantage of shortages" to raise their prices.[17] To an entrepreneur with capitalist values, this reaction is ludicrous, for a shortage represents a market incentive and a legitimate reason for raising prices. Thus it is easier to change laws than to change norms and values. In the United States, whole political and economic ideologies have been built around values central to entrepreneurship. Moreover, our legal structure is based on the values of free enterprise and protects individual rights

Building the Japanese Dream. Frustrated by a regimented, boring work life, over 500,000 Japanese have jumped ship for the entrepreneurial life of a sales representative for Amway (Japan) Ltd., one of Japan's largest and most profitable foreign businesses. Instead of selling door-to-door, Amway's new recruits rely on *giri*—the notion of obligation between family and friends—and on *kuchi-komi,* or word-of-mouth recommendations. Together, these two concepts have helped the U.S. purveyor of detergents, cosmetics, vitamins, and housewares work around Japan's restrictive distribution system.

much more than its Soviet counterpart, which is based on a socialist economic-legal structure. (As the International Management box shows, China's experiments with economic reforms have also run into social and cultural roadblocks.)

Cultural differences also help explain the different levels of entrepreneurship in Japan and the United States. The American culture stresses individualism, which encourages the innovations of entrepreneurs. Japan's traditions, in contrast, stress group action and cooperation, and business-government cooperation, which have not encouraged entrepreneurs (although there is evidence of a growing sentiment in favor of entrepreneurship).

Another factor that affects entrepreneurship is social mobility. In India, for example, most people are born into castes, social divisions that perform specific economic functions such as fishing or farming. Although the caste structure is not as rigid as it used to be, it is still fairly strict, especially in rural areas. As a result, it is harder for the child of an Indian carpenter to become an entrepreneur in some other field than it would be for a carpenter's child in the United States. Yet Indians who live in the United States are even more prone to engage in entrepreneurial activity than other Americans are. The reason is that caste boundaries are much weaker for Indians who live here than for Indians who stayed at home, where entrepreneurship is discouraged by heavy corporate and personal income taxes as well as personal-wealth and excise taxes. Currently, however, the Indian government is pursuing reforms that would permit more economic flexibility, which would encourage entrepreneurial ventures as well as increased domestic and foreign investment.[18]

Moreover, the Indians who live in the United States, like many entrepreneurs throughout the world, are "marginal." That is, they do not belong to any of the groups that make up the historical core of our population: white Protestants of British and European descent. Precisely because they are marginal, they can see certain opportunities more clearly than members of the core group, who are likely to take the facts of our society more for granted.

INTERNATIONAL MANAGEMENT

Economic Experiments in the People's Republic of China

In 1980, the People's Republic of China launched a series of unique economic experiments—unique, that is, for a nation that had relied on a planned economy for 40 years. Under Mao Zedong, the government had set the nation's economic goals and owned almost all the means of production and distribution. Managers were chosen for their devotion to Mao, not for their skill or experience. In fact, "sound management" was condemned as "bourgeois revisionism"; to reorient their thinking, educated people were often sent to work alongside peasants in the fields. Despite this antimanagement bias, China met its goal of feeding, housing, clothing, and educating a population of one billion people between 1950 and 1976.

After Mao's death, China's new generation of leaders announced an ambitious new goal—economic growth—and a series of economic reforms to be phased into virtually all of China's state-owned enterprises. These reforms promoted entrepreneurship *within* state-owned businesses, permitted certain businesses to experiment with restructuring, and allowed entrepreneurs to start small, privately owned businesses.

Throughout the 1980s, China accelerated its reform program, hoping to become an increasingly viable player in the world economy. And companies such as Reebok, Nike, Squibb, and Ingersoll-Rand responded by investing in joint ventures behind the Bamboo Curtain, attracted by untapped market opportunities as well as by the productive capacities of an industrious, if not yet industrialized economy.

China's economic growth has created growing pains, however. To transform a predominantly peasant culture into one poised to reap the benefits of twentieth-century technology and innovation, China's leaders have chosen to *modify,* not abandon, its planned economy. This means trying to keep the economy from expanding too quickly, fearing the predictable effects of inflation—upward-spiraling wages and prices—which could be worsened by a planned economy that essentially violates the law of supply and demand. Many leaders believed the changes were coming too fast and were especially alarmed when university students agitated for democratic reforms on top of the economic reforms.

In May 1989, tanks rumbled into Tiananmen Square, signaling an end to the period of liberalization. While the world watched, party hard-liners staged a bloody crackdown on the students, leaving many people in doubt about the future of economic experiments and foreign investment in China.

Wenzhou, site of China's most ambitious economic experiments and a hotbed of entrepreneurial ventures, was especially hard hit. These ventures are now under close government scrutiny, and tax rates have been increased—sometimes doubled in one year—to create more "reasonable" levels of profit. Anger and resentment among Wenzhou's entrepreneurs have led to violence; one tax collector was killed and two others wounded in a clash in October 1989.

Some fear this violence signals a lasting retreat from economic reforms. Others are more optimistic and accept the 1987 assessment of the Congressional Office of Technology that China will become increasingly important to the United States as its economic, technological, and military strength grows. Looking ahead to 1997, when Hong Kong reverts to Chinese rule, many U.S. firms continue to invest in China, among them Motorola, Inc., which has built a new factory outside Hong Kong and just 30 minutes from the Chinese border.

Sources: James O'Toole, "The Good Managers of Sichuan," *Harvard Business Review,* May–June 1981, pp. 28–40; Ted Holden, "China's Reformers Say: Let a Thousand Businesses Bloom," *Business Week,* April 1988, pp. 70–72; Susan Leshnover, "China's Opportunities," *Management Review* 77, no. 7 (1988):48–51; Alan Farnham, "Ready to Ride Out China's Turmoil," *Fortune,* July 3, 1989, pp. 117–118; Adi Ignatius, "A Tiny Chinese Venture into Capitalism Feels Icy Chills in Wake of Crackdown," *The Wall Street Journal,* March 8, 1990, p. A11; Kay M. Jones, "Westerners Learn to Read the Tea Leaves," *Management Review,* April 1990, pp. 46–49; Lora Western, "Hong Kong Deadline Doesn't Curb Deals," *Crain's Chicago Business,* March 18–24, 1991, p. 1.

ILLUSTRATIVE CASE STUDY

CONTINUED

Start-Up Pains at Nova Pharmaceutical Corporation

Nova's existence and continued survival depend on both economic and social variables. Nova has had severe problems with financing, since research efforts have demanded more and more ongoing resources. To keep up its momentum, Nova has had to seek outside help; it signed research contracts with Celanese, GAF, and Marion Laboratories in return for much-needed capital and marketing expertise.

In addition, Nova has tapped the entrepreneur-

ial spirit in a lot of people who risked their careers to create a company that will make their lives and their industry better. Eventually, society may benefit from Nova's new products and technologies. In the meantime, entrepreneurship requires more than a vision or good ideas. It requires hard work, superb management skills, and solid, dependable financing. So far, Nova is still in the game.

■ *THE ENTREPRENEUR*

COORDINATED RESOURCE

The Application Exercise for Chapter 6 found in the Lecture Extras supplement asks students to interview entrepreneurs about their experiences.

need-achievement According to McClelland, a social motive to excel that tends to characterize successful entrepreneurs, especially when reinforced by cultural factors.

TEACHING TIP

If there are any small-business "entrepreneurs" in your community, invite them to speak to your class about their experiences.

CLASS COMMENT

The typical franchisee is likely to be affluent, mature, and experienced, according to a recent report by Francorp Inc., a consulting firm. (*Business Week*, 5/6/91, p. 70)

Because they have the potential to contribute so much to society, researchers have tried to analyze entrepreneurs' personalities, skills, and attitudes, as well as the conditions that foster entrepreneurs. Research has shown that psychological and sociological factors, plus distinctive competencies, are characteristic of entrepreneurs.

Psychological and Sociological Factors

Entrepreneurs, like most people, are complex, and no one theory can explain all of their behavior. Perhaps the first and certainly the most important theory of entrepreneurship's psychological roots was put forward in the early 1960s by David McClelland, who found that people who pursued entrepreneur-like careers (such as sales) were high in **need-achievement,** the psychological need to achieve. People with high need-achievement like to take risks, but only reasonable ones, and such risks stimulate them to greater effort. Moreover, he found that certain societies tended to produce a larger percentage of people with high need-achievement. Other researchers have studied the entrepreneur's motives and goals, which seem to include wealth, power, prestige, security, self-esteem, and service to society.[19]

In the mid-1980s, Thomas Begley and David P. Boyd studied the psychological literature on entrepreneurship in an effort to distinguish between entrepreneurs and people who manage existing small businesses, ultimately identifying five dimensions.[20]

1. *Need-achievement.* Entrepreneurs are high in McClelland's concept of need-achievement.
2. *Locus of control,* the idea that individuals—not luck or fate—control their own lives. Entrepreneurs and managers both like to think they are pulling their own strings.
3. *Tolerance for risk.* Entrepreneurs who are willing to take moderate risks seem to earn higher return on assets than entrepreneurs who either take no risks or take extravagant risks.

164 *PART TWO / THE EXTERNAL ENVIRONMENT*

MANAGEMENT AND DIVERSITY

Who Are the New Entrepreneurs?

Too often, minorities feel employers discriminate against them—either directly or indirectly. To succeed in the corporate culture, some minorities feel they must "sell their souls" by giving up their racial, ethnic, or sexual identity. Others bump their heads against the "glass ceiling." (New studies indicate that less than 5 percent of the top executive jobs in the United States are held by minorities.) These frustrations have left many minorities thirsting for an environment that suits their needs and allows them the latitude to create and thrive. This desire, coupled with the perennial enticements of entrepreneurship, have made minority entrepreneurs common in today's business world.

One minority-owned business is the Artemis Capital Group, which deals in municipal bonds. Artemis is the creation of six women who left good positions at prestigious Wall Street firms to start their own business. Five of them worked at Goldman, Sachs & Co.; the sixth came from Citicorp. The group is made up of Phylis Esposito, Robin Wiessmann, Sandra Alworth, Aimee Brown, Deborah Buresh, and Toberta Connolly. They all share the title of "principal." Although they are young (mostly mid- to late-30s), they share a wide variety of experience, ranging from investment banking to debt restructuring, sales, and syndicate management.

The women say the "glass ceiling" had nothing to do with their decision to launch their own business (although only 1 out of 128 partners at Goldman, Sachs is a woman); their reasons were their skills and economic trends. Particularly important was the growing number of governments and municipalities with deficits, which make the market ripe for new and talented players who know how to make the most of the opportunity.

Despite the cutthroat competition in the municipal bonds business, many experts feel these women have what it takes to succeed. Carol Bellamy, a principal at Morgan Stanley & Co., who has worked with members of the Artemis firm, calls them "first rate"; Robert Downey, head of the municipal bond department at Goldman, Sachs, also has high praise for their abilities. Given that they took their name from the Greek goddess for hunting, the Artemis Group seems primed for the challenge of this volatile field.

Another of the "new entrepreneurs" is Bertram Lee, a successful black man who is president of B.M.L. Associates, Inc., a $26 million conglomerate in Boston; president of the Boston Chamber of Commerce; and a partner in several ventures, including a $400 million real estate project in downtown Boston. Lee served as the national finance chairman for Reverend Jesse Jackson's 1988 presidential campaign. Although his thriving business projects have made him a model of entrepreneurial success, he is perhaps happiest about his most recent venture. He and Peter Bynoe, a black Chicago lawyer and real estate developer, are joint owners of the Denver Nuggets, making them the first black owners of a major sports franchise.

Things weren't always so peachy for Lee. Fifteen years ago, he was filing for Chapter 11 after he and his partners failed to turn around a sagging printing business (Geneva Printing). Facing $400,000 of debt and $125,000 of taxes, he spent a good deal of time pulling himself out of a vat of red ink. But Lee, a true entrepreneur, never considered working for someone else or giving up the pursuit of new ventures. Using his own funds and borrowing from friends, he managed to free himself of all Geneva-related debt by 1986. Throughout this period, he pursued new ventures, especially in the communications area, which have paid off. Still, success hasn't spoiled Lee, who knows all too well that fortune can come and go for entrepreneurs. He jokes, "If you hear that Bert Lee jumped out of a window, then you know that somebody pushed me."

More and more larger firms are trying to make the workplace more sensitive to minority needs. Still, the challenge of beating the odds and creating their own firms will continue to convert many minorities into entrepreneurs.

Sources: Sharon R. King, "Back from the Brink," *Black Enterprise,* March 1988, pp. 40–43; Nathan McCall, "With M&M Buy, B.M.L. Moves into Hair-Care Business," *Black Enterprise,* August 1989, p. 17; Patricia Raybon, "Nuggets Buy Makes History: Will It Crumble Barrier?" *Black Enterprise,* September 1989, pp. 17–18; Leah J. Nathans, "What Do Women Want? A Piece of the Muni Business," *Business Week,* February 12, 1990, p. 66; Frank Swoboda, "Looking for a Way to Break the 'Glass Ceiling,'" *Washington Post,* August 28, 1990, p. A15.

4. *Tolerance for ambiguity.* To some extent, every manager needs this, since many decisions must be made with incomplete or unclear information. But entrepreneurs face more ambiguity, since they may be doing certain things for the first time—ever—and because they are risking their livelihood.

5. *Type A behavior.* This refers to the drive to get more done in less time, and if required to do so, despite the objections of others. Both founders and managers of small businesses tend to have much higher rates of Type A behavior than do other business executives.

Clearly, the entrepreneur needs self-confidence, drive, optimism, and courage to launch and operate a business, beyond the safety of a steady paycheck. Sometimes, entrepreneurs decide to launch a new venture because they cannot ignore their dream, their vision, and they are willing to risk security for financial gain. In other cases, they are pushed by circumstances beyond their control, such as a corporate cutback (an increasingly common phenomenon today) or frustrated by limited opportunities for advancement or the need to coordinate personal and professional goals. Faced with these circumstances, many individuals find the courage and confidence to take control of their professional fate. In the Management and Diversity box, you can read about some of these entrepreneurs.

distinctive competence
Entrepreneurial desire to
start a business coupled
with the ability or experience to compete effec-
tively once the enterprise
is initiated.

Distinctive Competence

Attitudes do not in themselves make an entrepreneur. As Karl Vesper observes, when Steve Wozniak and Steve Jobs were creating Apple Computer Incorporated in the mid-1970s, many other people may have wanted to be entrepreneurs even more than they did.[21] Besides desire, Wozniak and Jobs had a profitable business idea—"just the right product suited to a big market that others were not prepared to serve."[22]

The two friends also had the electronics and marketing skills to exploit their idea, as well as the modesty to reach out to executives with skills and experience they lacked. Would-be entrepreneurs, says Vesper, must also have access to capital and other production assets, personal contacts, and enough time to create a firm from scratch.

To date, there has been little research into why so many people want to start up businesses but so few do, despite the reasonably high attendance at seminars conducted by government agencies, universities, and private promoters. There are probably two reasons for this discrepancy. First, there is certainly no one-to-one correspondence between attendance figures for seminars and reasonably profitable ideas. Second, many entrepreneurial aspirants lack what some analysts call **distinctive competence.** In particular, as Figure 6-1 shows, there is a big difference between having a desire to start a business (even with a feasible idea) and possessing the competence to *compete* effectively. Of course, Wozniak and Jobs had the right idea at the right time, but their "distinctive competence" included an insightful analysis of the market and the managerial ability to outperform their competitors.

■ *THE ENTREPRENEURIAL PROCESS*

An organization is a living thing that is born, grows, ages, and sooner or later dies. Entrepreneurs are present at the birth of an organization, which unfolds in two basic stages.[23]

The first stage is some change in the real world. A war, for example, may destroy a country's manufacturing facilities but spare its trained work force; in an-

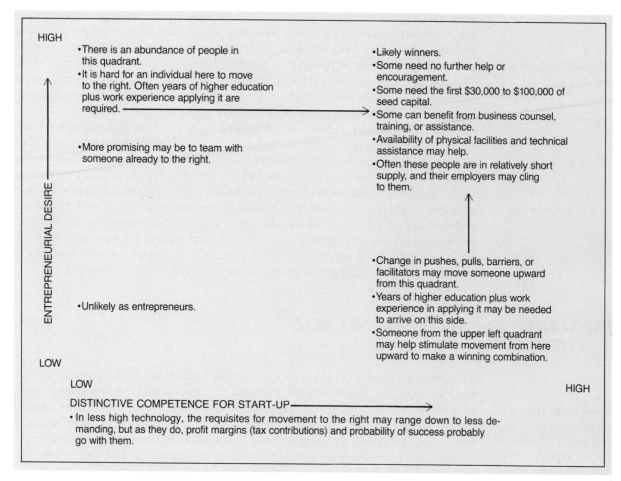

FIGURE 6-1 **Entrepreneurial Desire versus Capability**

Source: Karl H. Vesper, *Entrepreneurship and National Policy* (1983). Walter E. Heller International Corporation Institute for Small Business.

The Right Idea. Noting no established sportswear maker offered well-designed volleyball shorts and shirts, University of California junior Tom Knapp launched Club Sportswear out of his apartment in 1984. Now a millionaire, Knapp was named top graduate in USC's entrepreneur program in 1986.

other country, a large number of births may take place within a certain span of years. Changes like these affect every aspect of life.

Some changes create needs for substitute goods or for new services and goods. The destruction of Japan's prewar industry at the end of World War II allowed the Japanese to rebuild from scratch. A phenomenon like the American baby boom of the late 1940s and 1950s created a huge age-specific market for goods and services that shaped the 1970s and 1980s and will continue to be felt throughout the 1990s.

The second stage in the entrepreneurial process is "the idea." Where do entrepreneurs get their ideas? A lot of people draw on their work experience. They learn a certain field by working for someone else and then use their knowledge to search for new opportunities. (In this way, jobs are like schools—except that they pay.) Take the personal computer as a case in point. Steve Wozniak, then an employee of Hewlett-Packard, saw how the microprocessor, which had been on the market since the 1970s, could be used to create a personal computer. One would think the chairman of Hewlett-Packard would have gotten down on his knees and begged Wozniak to invent something just like this. Instead, Wozniak could not talk his employer into developing the product.

Note that the *idea* of a personal computer was not really Wozniak's. A company called Altair had already put out a computer that was so personal you had to put it together yourself. Yet it was Apple Computer, not Altair, that entered the ranks of the Fortune 500. Wozniak and Jobs perceived something that Altair had not: The personal computer market was potentially a lot bigger than the clique of hobbyists it was currently serving, but most consumers would care neither to put the thing together nor to write the software for it. Yet before personal computers actually existed, it was almost impossible to persuade people that they needed one. Thus Wozniak and Jobs helped create a new and expanding industry, allowing Apple Computer to acquire market share more cheaply, but more speculatively, than entrepreneurs who look for ideas in established industries.

In other cases, entrepreneurs' ideas draw them to established industries. If it is the cheapest way of getting the needed resources, an entrepreneur might even buy an existing company. Some entrepreneurs are drawn to franchising, which has become much more common during the last few decades. People who buy a franchise buy a brand name that enjoys name recognition among potential customers, yet at the same time, they own their own businesses and are their own bosses. Of course, franchise operators cannot run their businesses just as they please; they usually have to conform to the standards of the franchise, and sometimes they must buy the franchiser's goods or services. But it is precisely the popularity of a franchiser's goods or services that induces people to buy a franchise in the first place.

■ LAUNCHING THE ENTREPRENEURIAL ORGANIZATION

business plan Formal document containing a mission statement, description of the firm's goods or services, a market analysis, financial projections, and a description of management strategies for attaining goals.

Recognizing a need and having an idea of how to fill it are rarely a strong enough basis for launching a new venture, particularly if the would-be entrepreneur needs to borrow capital. Most successful entrepreneurs also create a **business plan,** a formal document that contains a mission statement, a description of the products or services to be offered, a market analysis, financial projections, and a description of management procedures designed to attain the firm's goals. Before they can write a business plan, though, entrepreneurs must be aware of the barriers to entry, plan a strategy, choose a legal form of organization, and consider the entrepreneurial culture.

Recognizing Barriers to Entry

TEACHING TIP

Have your students write a short paper on the role of women in developing new businesses.

Karl Vesper, whose work on the preconditions of entrepreneurship has already been mentioned, also studied the barriers to it.[24] Why do many entrepreneurs fail? The most common reason, says Vesper, is "lack of a viable concept." Another common one is a lack of market knowledge. Sometimes it is hard to attract the people with the best information because they already have attractive jobs, are chained to their present employers by "golden handcuffs," or are too complacent to feel a need to do truly first-rate or important work. Even a lack of technical skills can be a problem, says Vesper.

THOUGHT PROVOKER

Small-business owners report that they are having trouble finding employees with the necessary skills. Why do you think this is so? What can the small-business owner do about the situation?

Then, too, there is the difficulty of finding the $25,000 to $100,000 a start-up typically needs. A certain number of entrepreneurs fail after start-up because they lack general business know-how. Some would-be entrepreneurs are deterred from entering certain lines of work—for example, housecleaning—by what they see as a social stigma. Others are discouraged by the monopolies controlling certain professions, notably medicine and the law. Stiff competition from large, entrenched corporations can also present a formidable obstacle to the young start-up. (See the Ethics in Management box.)

In Figure 6-2, Vesper lists 12 common barriers; the arrows indicate how certain environmental "helps" can act to reduce the effect of these barriers.

ETHICS IN MANAGEMENT

"Competing with the Biggies"

Battle lines have been drawn in a modern version of David and Goliath: Ben & Jerry's Homemade and Häagen-Dazs are fighting over the market for super-premium ice cream, which has become big business. Over the last ten years, Americans have consumed the high-fat, low-air treat in ever-increasing amounts. Not surprisingly, this boom in demand has resulted in the introduction of numerous brands and fierce competition for market shares.

In the beginning was Häagen-Dazs, begun by a Brooklyn immigrant who sold his company to Pillsbury as the market was expanding. Before long, other brands emerged on the scene, including Ben & Jerry's, which was originally developed by Ben Cohen and Jerry Greenfield to cater to the college population in Vermont. Although there are several other brands on the market, these two are now the major competitors in one of the business world's fiercest battles for consumers.

As a subsidiary of a large company, Häagen-Dazs enjoys national distribution. Ben & Jerry's is currently distributed in 35 states. However, much of their distribution has been threatened by a Häagen-Dazs move to create exclusive distributionships: Häagen-Dazs would like to require that distributors and retailers who handle its product handle no other ice cream in the super-premium class. The practice is widespread in some segments of the food market—for example, Coke and Pepsi each require that its bottlers handle only one of the two. However, in market segments where there are only a few competitors, this practice can severely affect the competition and effectively lock the smaller company out of the market. In this case, the maneuver can also be interpreted as a violation of the Sherman and Clayton Acts, which mandate fair trade.

As Ben & Jerry's began to expand from local sales in Vermont to distribution throughout New England, Häagen-Dazs sent letters to the independent dealers who sold its product stating that they could not sell both Häagen-Dazs and Ben & Jerry's. Ben & Jerry's believed this ploy denied them the chance to compete and were ready to take Pillsbury to court over it. They also took their complaint to the public, distributing ads that told the story and printing bumper stickers that asked "What's the doughboy afraid of?" Eventually, Pillsbury and Ben & Jerry's reached an out-of-court settlement that prohibited exclusive dealership for two years in any new market into which Ben & Jerry's chooses to venture.

Another up-and-comer, San Francisco–based Double Rainbow, has not had the same luck fighting giant Häagen-Dazs. Double Rainbow has been battling Häagen-Dazs's exclusive dealership arrangement since 1985, but so far the courts have proved unsympathetic. Now owned by a British conglomerate, Häagen-Dazs has argued that it has only 2 percent of the highly competitive ice-cream market. Double Rainbow counters that the 2 percent figure is misleading because it represents Häagen-Dazs's share of the *total* ice-cream market, not of the smaller market segment of super-premium ice creams, where competition for freezer space is especially intense. Although Double Rainbow's critically acclaimed ice cream has been extremely successful in San Francisco, national sales have sagged because it is "frozen out" of many markets. Meanwhile, Häagen-Dazs's profits have soared nationally.

Who will win the next round in the super-premium ice-cream wars? No one can be certain, but the ethics of competition will continue to be an issue in the battle for America's sweet tooth.

Sources: Calvin Trillin, "Competitors," *The New Yorker,* July 8, 1985, pp. 31–32, 35–38, 41, 43–45; Len Strazewski, "Four Davids Reject Goliath-Like Path," *Advertising Age,* October 12, 1987, pp. S3, S4, S6, S8; Keith H. Hammonds, "Is Häagen-Dazs Trying to Freeze Out Ben & Jerry's?" *Business Week,* December 7, 1987, p. 65; Lawrence Ingrassia, "Ice Cream Makers Rivalry Heating Up," *The Wall Street Journal,* December 21, 1988, p. 1; Martha Groves, "Court Ruling Fails to Melt Double Rainbow's Resolve," *Los Angeles Times,* March 7, 1990, pp. D2, D14.

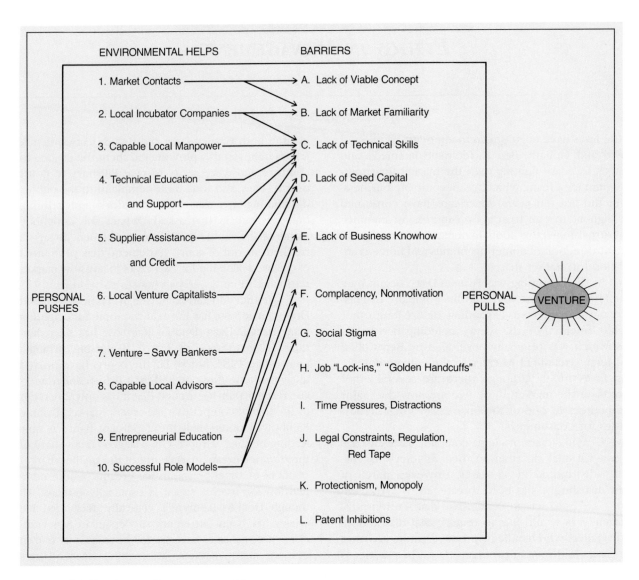

FIGURE 6-2 Barriers to Entrepreneurship

Source: Karl H. Vesper, *Entrepreneurship and National Policy* (1983). Walter E. Heller International Corporation Institute for Small Business.

Planning a Strategy

COORDINATED RESOURCE

The Distinctive Discussions for Chapter 6 found in the Lecture Extras supplement include "A Mother/Daughter Business" and "Abolishing the Perils of Growth."

COORDINATED RESOURCE

See Samaras Case 2.1, "The Home Plan."

There are several ways of trying to be an entrepreneur.[25] One strategy, as Peter Drucker puts it, is to there "fustest with the mostest." In this case, the entrepreneur tries to take the lead in a new line of business from the start. One rather interesting case of a company that followed this strategy, both as a small firm and then as an established one, is Hofmann-LaRoche, a leading drug maker based in Switzerland.

Hofmann-LaRoche started small. In the 1920s, it put all its resources into producing and marketing vitamins, which older drug companies, along with medical opinion, still regarded with skepticism. Even now, the company still supplies almost half of the world's gigantic demand for vitamins.

Hofmann-LaRoche bet its money against the medical establishment again during the 1930s, when, as Drucker says, it "went into the new sulfa drugs—even though most scientists of the time 'knew' that systemic drugs could not be effective against infections; and then, 20 years later, it went into the muscle-relaxing tranquil-

Getting There First.
When his three partners at Seagate Technology refused to develop his innovative ideas, Finis F. Conner left to found Conner Peripherals, whose compact hard disk drives helped spur the boom in laptop and notebook computers and made it the nation's fastest growing company.

HERE'S AN EXAMPLE
Cocodrie Tanner Inc. of Baton Rouge, Louisiana, is struggling to survive in a market that demands the quality of European-produced alligator leather. Says its owner, Chris Dumestre, "We're almost satisfied. We don't want to be the biggest. We just want to be the best." (*Wall Street Journal*, 3/28/91, p. B2)

COORDINATED RESOURCE
See Samaras Reading, "Making It on Main Street."

izers Librium and Valium—which at that time were equally 'heretical' and incompatible with what 'every scientist knew.'"[26]

This is a successful case, but naturally there are many unsuccessful ones. If at first you don't succeed by using the "fustest with the mostest" strategy, you may not succeed at all because you may have bet the whole company and lost.

Drucker calls another strategy "creative imitation"—a paradox that is far from absurd. Over the years, its most striking practitioner has been International Business Machines Corporation. In the 1930s, the last decade before the emergence of computers, IBM was the biggest firm in the adding machine business and had even designed what might be called the first real computer, which was finished in 1945. Yet IBM shelved it and started to build machines based upon a rival computer, ENIAC, designed at the University of Pennsylvania.

Moreover, the first company to market a business computer was Sperry with its Univac. IBM beat out Sperry in the long run because IBM understood the nature of the computer business better than anyone else. Computers, in the early 1950s, were rare and wonderful things. Hardly anyone had ever had anything to do with them, or even quite knew what they were. Sperry and other companies either in the business or thinking about entering it assumed these conditions would endure forever. But IBM understood that the market for computers was huge and that computers would have to be designed with this huge market in mind. (The founders of Apple Computer had this same insight in the mid-1970s.)

Drucker explicates his third and final category of entrepreneurial strategies, "entrepreneurial judo," by telling the story of the transistor.[27] What was then the AT&T Bell Telephone Company announced its discovery in 1947. Bell had developed the transistor specifically to replace old-fashioned vacuum tubes, which burned out at frequent and unpredictable intervals in the company's switching equipment. Tubes were also used in a great many other products—computers, radios, hi-fis, and televisions, for example—and it should have been obvious that transistors would replace tubes in each and every one of them.

In fact, it was obvious, and many companies had plans to convert to transistors with all deliberate speed—by 1970 or thereabouts. It did not happen that way because Sony's Akio Morita paid $25,000 for a license to incorporate transistors into his company's products. In the mid-1950s, Sony came out with a cheap transistor radio and proceeded to transistorize all its consumer electronics products, winning a market lead that it has never relinquished.

However, companies can be downed by entrepreneurial judo, says Drucker, because they are prone to certain vices. Take the *NIH* ("not invented here") *syndrome*—the "arrogance that leads a company or an industry to believe that something new cannot be any good unless they themselves thought of it." Another vice is what Drucker calls the "tendency to '*cream*' a market, that is, to get the high-profit part of it."[28] In gravitating toward the high end of a business, many companies ignore markets below it that may be much larger.

Drucker illustrates a third vice by pointing to the delusions of American radio manufacturers, who believed their vacuum-tube radios were better than Sony's transistorized models because the U.S. companies "had put 30 years of effort into making radio sets bigger, more complicated, and more expensive." The public preferred the small transistorized sets, and the public is always right in matters of this sort.

A fourth vice is succumbing to the temptation to charge a premium price, which "is always an invitation to the competitor."[29] A fifth bad habit is the tendency to "maximize rather than optimize"—to take a basic product and adapt it to different needs or many different applications until it becomes too complex and not exactly suited to *any* application. A company with such a product is always liable to be brought down by a competitor with products designed for specific applications.

TABLE 6-1 Basic Forms of Business

BUSINESS FORM	FEATURE				
	Liability	Continuity	Transferability	Management	Equity Investment
Proprietorship	Personal, unlimited	Ends with death or decision of owner	Free to sell at any time	Personal, unrestricted	Personal
Partnership—General	Personal and unlimited, joint and several	Ends with death or decision of any partner	Individual interest can be sold with consent of all partners	Unrestricted or depends upon partnership agreement	Personal by partner(s)
Partnership—Limited*	For limited partners, only invested capital; as above for general partners	Limited partners do not affect; as above for general partners	Limited partners free to sell; as above for general partners	Limited partners may not participate, dependent upon agreement	Personal by partner(s)
Corporation	Capital invested	As stated in charter, perpetual or specified period of years	Stock may be sold or traded without affecting other stock	Under control of board of directors, which is selected by stockholders	Purchase of stock

*Limited partnerships consist of both general and limited partners, with different rules for each.

Source: Melvin J. Stanford, *New Enterprise Management,* © 1982, p. 50. Reprinted by permission of Prentice Hall, Inc., Englewood Cliffs, N.J.

Choosing an Organization

DISCUSSION QUESTION

If you were starting your own business, what steps could you take to ensure its success?

COORDINATED RESOURCE

See Samaras Reading, "Succession Planning—A Blueprint for Your Company's Future.

COORDINATED RESOURCE

See Geis & Kuhn, Chapter 9, "Leveraged Buyout—Getting Rich."

Entrepreneurs who are starting a business need to choose a legal form of organization. (See Table 6-1.) A key consideration here is the entrepreneur's liability, especially if the business involves a product or service that could injure another party. Continuity and transferability are also important if the entrepreneur anticipates selling the firm or even offering franchises. And while sound management is important to any business, the corporate form of organization entails additional legal and managerial restrictions.

Launching an entrepreneurial venture within an established corporation also requires some thought, as the research by Robert A. Burgelman indicates.[30] Burgelman believes that the organizational form the entrepreneurial project takes should depend on the project's importance to the company sponsoring it. If it is very important but not related to a company's core business, it should be spun off as a special business unit. If it is partly related, it should be assigned to a new-product department. If the entrepreneurial project is strongly related to the company's core business, it should be directly integrated into existing business units.

For a project that is unimportant, Burgelman recommends different alternatives: Projects that are not related to a company's core activities should be spun off into separate businesses; partly related projects should be contracted out; and strongly related projects should be performed by subcontractors who receive some nurturing from the contracting company.

If a project's importance is both uncertain and unrelated to the company's main line of business, Burgelman suggests that it be implemented by an independent business unit. If it is partly related, the company should consider setting up a new-venture division. If the project is of uncertain importance but strongly related to the firm's core activities, the firm should establish what Burgelman calls "a micro new-ventures department." In a micro new-ventures department, managers are "allowed to develop a strategy within budget and time constraints but should otherwise not

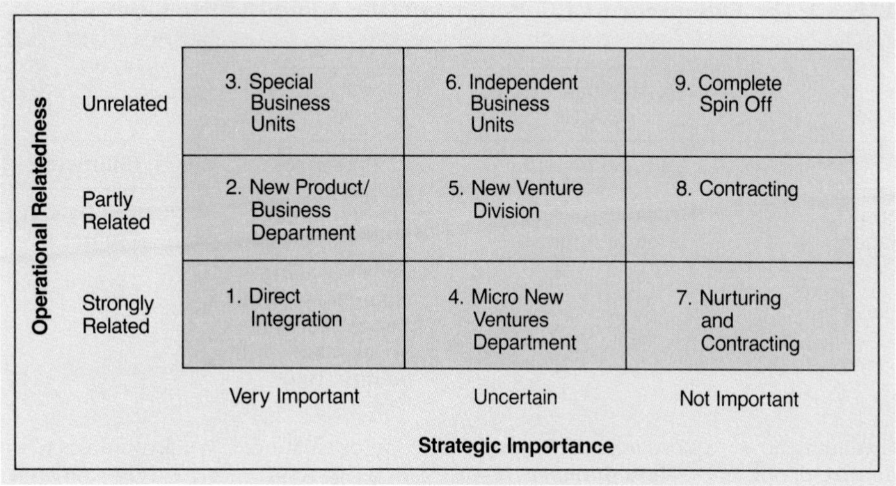

FIGURE 6-3 Organization Designs for Corporate Entrepreneurship

Source: Robert A. Burgelman, "Designs for Corporate Entrepreneurship in Established Firms," *California Management Review* 26, no. 3 (Spring 1984). Copyright © 1984 by The Regents of the University of California. Reprinted by permission of The Regents.

COORDINATED RESOURCE

Use Transparency 26, Organization Designs for Corporate Entrepreneurship.

COORDINATED RESOURCE

Use Transparency 24, Crises Entrepreneurs Face in New Venture Growth.

COORDINATED RESOURCE

Acumen: The Power scale measures an individual's tendency to be controlling. High scorers on this scale usually have little confidence in others. *Acumen* suggests that even those with average scores on this scale begin to delegate more authority to others.

entrepreneurial culture
According to Stevenson and Gumpert, corporate culture focusing on the emergence of new opportunities, the means of capitalizing on them, and the creation of the structure appropriate for pursuing them.

administrative culture
According to Stevenson and Gumpert, corporate culture focusing on existing opportunities, organizational structures, and control procedures.

be limited by current divisional or even corporate-level strategies. Operational linkages should be strong, to take advantage of the existing capabilities and skills and to facilitate transferring back newly developed ones."[31] (In Figure 6-3, Burgelman illustrates nine alternatives for the design of administrative and operational linkages between an organization's new and existing businesses.)

Drucker has a very definite view of how entrepreneurial ventures should be structured within larger companies, and it is radically different from Burgelman's. Says Drucker, "The entrepreneurial, the new, has to be organized separately from the old and existing. Whenever we have tried to make an existing unit the carrier of the entrepreneurial project, we have failed."[32] He believes this axiom is applicable to businesses of any size. Procter & Gamble, Johnson & Johnson, and 3M follow Drucker's strategy in their own well-known entrepreneurial ventures. (See the Management Application box describing 3M's success.) Finally, someone in the larger organization—perhaps the CEO—should be responsible for promoting innovation within it.

So much for the "dos." Now for the "don'ts." Companies should not innovate outside of their area of expertise. New ventures should not be required to show high short-term returns on investment. Finally, it is almost impossible for companies to buy their way into entrepreneurship by purchasing entrepreneurial firms. The people who worked for these independent businesses almost always get out when they are acquired, and the acquiring company rarely has people capable of taking over from the original group.

Nurturing the Entrepreneurial Spirit

Since companies may contain both entrepreneurial and established units, they must often embody two different, and even conflicting, corporate cultures. Howard H. Stevenson and David E. Gumpert call these **entrepreneurial cultures** and the **administrative cultures**.[33] They are ideal types—that is, collections of traits that make sense together and may be found, to a greater or lesser extent, in particular cases.

Stevenson and Gumpert say, for example, that an ideal administrator would ask such questions as "What resources do I control? What structure determines our organization's relationship to its market? How can I minimize the impact of others

TABLE 6-2 The Entrepreneurial Culture versus the Administrative Culture

	ENTREPRENEURIAL FOCUS		ADMINISTRATIVE FOCUS	
	Characteristics	**Pressures**	**Characteristics**	**Pressures**
A Strategic orientation	Driven by perception of opportunity	Diminishing opportunities Rapidly changing technology, consumer economics, social values, and political rules	Driven by controlled resources	Social contracts Performance measurement criteria Planning systems and cycles
B Commitment to seize opportunities	Revolutionary, with short duration	Action orientation Narrow decision windows Acceptance of reasonable risks Few decision constituencies	Evolutionary, with long duration	Acknowledgment of multiple constituencies Negotiation about strategic course Risk reduction Coordination with existing resource base
C Commitment of resources	Many stages, with minimal exposure at each stage	Lack of predictable resource needs Lack of control over the environment Social demands for appropriate use of resources Foreign competition Demands for more efficient resource use	A single stage, with complete commitment out of decision	Need to reduce risk Incentive compensation Turnover in managers Capital budgeting systems Formal planning systems
D Control of resources	Episodic use or rent of required resources	Increased resource specialization Long resource life compared with need Risk of obsolescence Risk inherent in the identified opportunity Inflexibility of permanent commitment to resources	Ownership or employment of required resources	Power, status, and financial rewards Coordination of activity Efficiency measures Inertia and cost of change Industry structures
E Management structure	Flat, with multiple informal networks	Coordination of key noncontrolled resources Challenge to hierarchy Employees' desire for independence	Hierarchy	Need for clearly defined authority and responsibility Organizational culture Reward systems Management theory

Source: Reprinted by permission of the *Harvard Business Review.* An exhibit from "The Heart of Entrepreneurship" by Howard H. Stevenson and David E. Gumpert (March–April 1985). Copyright © 1985 by the President and Fellows of Harvard College; all rights reserved.

on my ability to perform? What opportunity is appropriate?"[34] By contrast, an ideal entrepreneur would ask very different questions: "Where is the opportunity? How do I capitalize on it? What resources do I need? How do I gain control over them? What structure is best?"[35]

Table 6-2 lists certain dimensions of the entrepreneurial and administrative psychologies. In the first dimension, strategic orientation, the most entrepreneurial kind of managers will be driven by "perception of opportunity." The pressures they experience include diminishing opportunities as they age and changes in consumer economics, political rules, social values, or technology they cannot understand. At the other extreme, the strategic orientations of those managers with the most administrative kinds of personalities are driven by "controlled resources"—the amount of a company's money, skills, and other assets they can command. The pressures on them include social contracts with colleagues and subordinates, as well as performance-measurement criteria and planning systems and cycles. Stevenson and Gumpert also list the characteristics of each orientation on other dimensions. They believe that most managers' orientations can be properly described as falling between the entrepreneurial and administrative extremes.

Older, larger organizations that want to innovate, says Peter Drucker, must recognize, first of all, that it is easier to continue doing things as they have been doing them and that change always looks harder than it actually is.[36] Such organizations should require their subunits to justify their existence every few years and should follow "a systematic policy of abandoning whatever is outworn, obsolete, no longer productive, as well as the mistakes, failures, and misdirections of effort."[37]

Why, for example, did companies that knew transistors would sooner or later transform the whole electronics business fail to apply transistors themselves? Why was the actual breakthrough left to a small Japanese company? Because the managers of American electronics firms thought only about the *problems* of their existing business—not, says Drucker, about the *opportunities* it presented.

DISCUSSION QUESTION
What are the similarities of
managing a small business
and a large business? Differences?

For starters, attitudes must change. In entrepreneurial companies, entrepreneurs are role models: "Entrepreneurial companies always look for the people and units that do better and do differently. They single them out, feature them, and constantly ask them: 'What are you doing that explains your success? What are you doing that the rest of us aren't doing, and what are you not doing that the rest of us are?'" This open attitude helps keep the entrepreneurial spirit alive.

ILLUSTRATIVE CASE STUDY

WRAP-UP

Start-Up Pains at Nova Pharmaceutical Corporation

Managers at Nova must plan, organize, lead, and control, just like their counterparts in large organizations. The management process may be easier because there are fewer long-standing organizational barriers in place, but managerial efficiency may suffer from a lack of organizational experience. Operations that are routine at large organizations must be constantly reinvented or modified at smaller ones. To hasten the influx of experienced management personnel, Nova's founders have cleverly resorted to recruiting managerial talent from the same companies they hope to compete with. Too often, entrepreneurs fail to pay sufficient attention to the managerial process, trusting that innovation and technical ingenuity will carry the day. This route is littered with failures.

Nova's future is looking bright. While holding fast to its entrepreneurial spirit and technological know-how, Nova is relying on a corporate biggie to help it make the most of its ventures. To get a fresh infusion of cash and take advantage of the sophisticated sales and marketing of SmithKline, Nova entered into a joint venture involving its most promising new drug, the Bradykinin blocker. SmithKline gets a 60 percent stake in the venture and 19 percent of Nova's stock. In return, Nova receives over $70 million in cash and can use the expansive SmithKline marketing and sales divisions to publicize Nova inventions to consumers. Although there are several new drugs that look to be real money-makers for Nova, variations of the Bradykinin blocker appear to be most promising. According to initial tests, it should have a wide range of applications, including the relief of common cold symptoms, the extreme pain of severe burns, and the pain of arthritis and other chronic illnesses. Combined sales of these pain-blocking drugs are projected to range between $220 million and $300 million annually when they hit the market in the next few years. Other drugs, such as variations of Biodel (which treat brain cancer tumors, leukemia, and bone infections), should also be on the market in the next few years and bring in some hefty revenues (projections range from $60 million to $220 million per year). If everything proceeds according to plan, Nova could carve out a very large and important place for itself in the pharmaceutical industry. ■

Sources: "Latest Crop of Hot New Companies with High-Tech Drugs," *Drug Topics,* April 18, 1988, pp. 24–25; Gene Bylinsky, "What a Way to Start a Company!" *Fortune,* June 19, 1989, pp. 141–143.

■ SUMMARY

The entrepreneur, who sees environmental change as an opportunity, uses the factors of production to produce new goods and services. Entrepreneurship is different from management because it focuses on initiating change, although the entrepreneur must at times assume the functions of both manager and capitalist. Entrepreneurship can occur when an individual or group of individuals start a new business or it can occur within an existing corporation in a process called intrapreneuring.

Entrepreneurship is now an important area of study and contributes to a society's economic growth, its productivity, and to its supply of technologies, products, and services. A nation's level of entrepreneurship depends on both economic factors (the supply and availability of capital) and noneconomic factors (especially cultural and social differences that affect business).

The most important theory of entrepreneurship's psychological roots was put forward by McClelland, who found that certain types of people had high need-achievement and that certain types of societies tended to create high need-achievement. Begley and Boyd identified five dimensions—need-achievement, locus of control, tolerance for risk, tolerance for ambiguity, and Type A behavior—that seemed to distinguish the founders and managers of small businesses from the typical executive. In addition, social circumstances, such as lack of opportunity for advancement or salaried employment, tend to push certain individuals into entrepreneurship.

The entrepreneurial process is sparked by some environmental change, which gives the entrepreneur an idea for a new product or service. Many ideas grow out of the entrepreneur's work experience; others come from the entrepreneur's observation of established businesses or even franchises.

In preparing to launch an entrepreneurial organization, would-be entrepreneurs need to prepare a business plan. Before they can do this, they must recognize the barriers to entering certain areas, come up with a business strategy, and choose a form of organization. Most importantly, though, the entrepreneur must recognize the differences between the entrepreneurial and administrative cultures, choosing procedures that will tap the best both cultures have to offer.

■ REVIEW QUESTIONS

1. What function do entrepreneurs play in the productive process? How does this function relate to the functions of manager and capitalist?

2. What is "intrapreneuring"?

3. Why have scholarly attitudes toward entrepreneurship changed since 1960?

4. How does entrepreneurship contribute to economic growth, productivity, and innovation in products and services?

5. What economic conditions encourage entrepreneurship?

6. What noneconomic conditions *discourage* entrepreneurship?

7. How does David McClelland's theory of need-achievement account for the emergence of individual entrepreneurs? What other psychological and sociological factors seem to motivate entrepreneurs?

8. What is a "distinctive competence"? Why is it important?

9. Describe the entrepreneurial process.

10. What is a business plan?

11. What are the most important barriers to entrepreneurial success?

12. Identify Drucker's entrepreneurial strategies and describe the advantages and disadvantages of each.

13. List the common forms of legal business organization.

14. Compare Burgelman's suggestions for organizing entrepreneurial ventures within corporations to those of Drucker.

15. How do the "entrepreneurial and "administrative" corporate cultures differ? Why are each important?

CASE STUDY

Pro-Line Corporation Puts a New Face on an Old Industry

With $600 and a borrowed typewriter, Comer Cottrell entered the beauty business in 1970, marketing his own hair-care formula and building a company whose rapid growth once threatened its survival.

From a shoestring start in Los Angeles, Cottrell's Pro-Line Corporation has expanded into a $26 million company that has 175 employees. With headquarters now located in Dallas, Pro-Line has become the largest black-owned firm in the Southwest. It was ranked 39th in *Black Enterprise* magazine's 1987 list of the top 100 black businesses in the United States.

Pro-Line's beauty products sell well not only in the United States but also in the Caribbean, Europe, Africa, Saudi Arabia, and the Orient. Today, Comer Cottrell runs an empire of creams and gels that has become a major success. Nonetheless, some earlier ventures were disappointing. He struck out with a Chinese restaurant in a black section of Los Angeles, for example, and he sold his stable of race horses after he decided that the sport of kings was not for him. Cottrell has flourished by, as he puts it, "selling hope—that's all the beauty business is."

Cottrell's decision to get into the beauty business grew out of a discovery he made some years ago. "I managed an Air Force base exchange and noticed that there were no hair products for blacks," he says. "Twenty percent of the people on the base were black. I talked to the authorities, and they told me there was no need for such products." Cottrell then asked various chemical companies if their scientists could come up with products for the care of the then-popular "Afro" hairstyle. A successful formula was developed eight months later.

Since he could not afford to pay a company in advance to make the first batch of his new product, Cottrell persuaded a small manufacturing firm to gamble on him. The company made him a quantity of what he named Pro-Line Oil Sheen hair spray. He peddled his new product to black beauticians and barbers and paid the manufacturer within 20 days.

In 1975, when Pro-Line was five years old, Cottrell opened a distribution center in Birmingham, Alabama, but found it hard to obtain shelf space in area stores. The Chicago-based Johnson Products Company, the market leader for black cosmetics, had all the displays. Its hard-working area manager was Isabell Paulding, a former Miss Black Alabama and a onetime runner-up for the Miss Black America title. She became Cottrell's wife a year after they met.

In an interview in the *Dallas Morning News* in 1984, Cottrell said, "I got in touch with her and asked her to tell me how she did it. She wouldn't tell me anything. I couldn't hire her, so the only alternative was to marry her."

By 1980, Pro-Line was running out of space for expansion of its Los Angeles plant. Cottrell looked eastward, where his major markets had been developed. He decided to take the company to Dallas—a move that he says nearly killed Pro-Line.

As production lines were being shut down in Los Angeles, Pro-Line came out with its Curly Kit Home Permanent. Sales jumped $11 million in ten months. "Here we were moving our equipment from California to Texas, and we couldn't keep up with the orders," says Cottrell. "Competitors jumped in with similar products."

When the new $4 million, 127,000-square-foot Texas facility went into operation, Pro-Line fought back to keep its market share. It is now the fourth-largest ethnic beauty concern in the United States.

Strong competition from both general and ethnic firms has led Pro-Line to advertise on prime-time television shows such as ABC's *Monday Night Football.* Pro-Line purchased time in 20 of the show's markets around the country, says Rene Brown, the company's marketing director, in order to advertise a new product for black men. It is a comb-through hair relaxer for those with short hairstyles.

Cottrell has a group of scientists working on new products as well as ensuring the quality of those he is producing now. He is cautious, however, about expanding too fast. "We make about 18 percent profit," he says. "We're working on a five-year plan. We want steady growth."

Source: Michael Whittaker, *Nation's Business,* January 1988, p. 24. Reprinted by permission. Copyright © 1988, U.S. Chamber of Commerce.

Case Questions

1. How would you characterize Pro-Line's strategy?
2. What are the key factors in its success so far?
3. What are some potential problems? Do you think there is a worldwide market for Pro-Line's products?
4. What are the key factors of a five-year plan?
5. How can Mr. Cottrell ensure that the entrepreneurial spirit of Pro-Line stays alive?

VIDEO CASE STUDY

Prodigy—Intrapreneurship on a Large Scale

A $450 million joint venture shows how intrapreneurship can combine IBM's technical knowledge with Sears's retailing know-how to create what *The Wall Street Journal* called one of 66 enterprises "poised to lead business into the 1990s." Their brainchild, dubbed the Prodigy Service, is an interactive videotex service, which combines graphics and text to provide information and shopping services for busy owners of IBM-compatible personal computers.

After four years of planning, Prodigy debuted in 1988 in the San Francisco Bay area. In return for their comments, users got free access to Prodigy, which offered fifty daily columns by experts such as Gene Siskel on movies, as well as transactions through Dean Witter, weather updates, and stock quotations from the Dow Jones Retrieval Service.

Prodigy was not the first online information service, of course. H&R Block's CompuServe—its nearest U.S. competitor—has long offered access to many information databases, as well as electronic mail (e-mail), and shopping services. But CompuServe users must supply their own telecommunications software and be fairly sophisticated to navigate the CompuServe treasure trove. Moreover, they are charged for their connect time, which quickly mounts up.

Prodigy, in contrast, encourages usage by charging a low monthly fee for unlimited access. In addition, the Prodigy start-up kit includes specialized telecommunications software and simplified instructions for navigating the system.

Prodigy keeps its user costs down by selling advertising and electronic catalog time to retailers, who pay up to $25,000 as a one-time set-up fee, plus up to a third of their gross profit, based on a billing system called the measured response system. It works this way: teaser ads are flashed across the bottom of the screen. If the viewer accesses the ad for more information, the advertiser is charged for the number of screens of information the user watches. Otherwise the advertiser is billed only a flat rate for the teaser ad.

From the modest beginning of 40 advertisers, about 50,000 subscribers, and a handful of employees, Prodigy has grown to more than 200 advertisers, 800,000 users in 30 markets, and over 1,300 employees, with the goal of enrolling 15 million subscribers by the year 2000. It ranks second only to France's Minitel, the world's largest videotex system.

There are a few clouds on the horizon, though. Lack of consumer interest is an ongoing problem for all videotex services, as is low volume and irregular usage. Also, the home computer market is small and growing more slowly than predicted. Furthermore, Prodigy is not yet available to Apple and Macintosh computer users; also Prodigy says it is negotiating with Apple Computer. Some users complain about Prodigy's "cartoon" graphics and its slow response times.

Prodigy also alienated some users when it disconnected 12 of them without warning in 1990 for overusing and abusing Prodigy's e-mail, prompting a call from the American Civil Liberties Union (ACLU). Although Prodigy tried to clarify its policies, disgruntled users formed a group called PIG (Prodigy Improvement Group), which registered its complaints with CompuServe's Cooperative Defense Committee.

While analysts are awed by Prodigy's enormous financial resources and its aggressive advertising campaigns, they wonder how long IBM and Sears will be willing to fund the venture, which has yet to turn a profit. Prodigy's ultimate success, some marketers feel, will depend on its ability to adapt to whatever new home information appliances (such as voice-date telephones) become generally accepted in the years ahead.

Sources: Judith Graham, "Linkup: IBM, Sears Set Ads for Videotex Venture," *Advertising Age,* May 23, 1988, pp. 1, 93; Clifford Carlsen, "Online Service Tests Bay Area for Acceptance," *San Francisco Business Times,* September 5, 1988, p. 11; Alison Fahey, "Prodigy Sets Trade, Consumer Ads; PC Service Reaches Top 20 Markets," *Advertising Age,* October 23, 1989, p. 16; Alison Fahey, "Videotex Hard-Sell," *Advertising Age,* April 30, 1990, p. 54; "Prodigy Gains Subscribers, Vendors," *Chain Store Age Executive,* August 1990, p. 84; Jeffrey Rothfeder and Mark Lewyn, "How Long Will Prodigy Be a Problem Child?" *Business Week,* September 10, 1990, p. 75; Michael R. Zimmerman, "Prodigy Offers Olive Branch, of Sorts, to Protesting Users," *PC Week,* December 3, 1990, p. 13.

Case Questions

1. What are the strengths of this intrapreneurial relationship between IBM and Sears? What are the weaknesses?

2. What is Prodigy's distinctive competence in the videotex business?

3. Although many earlier videotex businesses failed, what environmental factors might make Prodigy more successful this time?

■ NOTES

[1]Jules Backman, ed., *Entrepreneurship and the Outlook for America* (New York: Free Press, 1983), p. 3.

[2]Paul H. Wilken, *Entrepreneurship: A Comparative and Historical Study* (Norwood, N.J.: Ablex Publishing, 1979), p. 60.

[3]"Steve Jobs Tries to Do It Again," *Fortune,* May 23, 1988, pp. 83–86.

[4]Peter F. Drucker, *Innovation and Entrepreneurship* (New York: Harper & Row, 1986), pp. 27–28.

[5]Wilken, *Entrepreneurship,* p. 57.

[6]Gifford Pinchot III, *Intrapreneuring* (New York: Harper & Row, 1985).

[7]Robert A. Burgelman, "Design for Corporate Entrepreneurship in Established Firms," *California Management Review* 26, no. 3 (Spring 1984):154.

[8]James E. Ellis, "Feeling Stuck at Hyatt? Create a New Business," *Business Week,* December 10, 1990, p. 195.

[9]George Gilder, *Wealth and Poverty* (New York: Basic Books, 1981).

[10]Karl H. Vesper, *Entrepreneurship and Public Policy* (Pittsburgh: Carnegie-Mellon University, The Graduate School of Industrial Administration, 1983), p. 14.

[11]David Birch, "Who Creates Jobs," *The Public Interest* 65 (Fall 1981).

[12]David Birch, *The Job Creation Process* (Cambridge, Mass.: MIT Program on Neighborhood and Regional Change, 1979), referred to in Sue Birley, "The Role of New Firms: Births, Deaths, and Job Generation," *Strategic Management Journal* 7 (1986):363. See also D. Littler and R. C. Sweeting, "The Management of New Technology-Based Businesses," *Omega* 18, no. 3 (1990):231–240.

[13]Backman, *Entrepreneurship and the Outlook for America,* p. 17.

[14]Ibid., p. 9.

[15]Ibid., p. 18.

[16]Wilken, *Entrepreneurship,* p. 7.

[17]Daniel Ford, "Rebirth of a Nation," *The New Yorker,* March 28, 1988, p. 78.

[18]William A. Stoever, "India: The Long, Slow Road to Liberalization," *Business Horizons,* January–February 1988, pp. 42–46.

[19]This discussion is drawn from Wilken, *Entrepreneurship,* p. 20.

[20]For example, Thomas Begley and David P. Boyd, "The Relationship of the Jenkins Activity Survey to Type A Behavior Among Business Executives," *Journal of Vocational Behavior* 27(1987):316–328; C. Borland, "Locus of Control, Need for Achievement, and Entrepreneurship," unpublished doctoral dissertation (Austin: University of Texas, 1974); David P. Boyd, "Type A Behavior, Financial Growth, and Organizational Growth in Small Business Firms," *Journal of Occupational Psychology* 57:137–140; J. A. Hornaday and J. Abboud, "Characteristics of Successful Entrepreneurs," *Personnel Psychology* 24:141–153; P. R. Liles, *New Business Ventures and the Entrepreneur* (Homewood, Ill.: Richard D. Irwin, 1974); J. A. Timmons, "Characteristics and Role Demands of Entrepreneurship," *American Journal of Small Business* 3(1987):5–17; J. A. Welsh and J. P. White, "Converging Characteristics of Entrepreneurs," in K. H. Vesper, ed., *Frontiers of Entrepreneurship Research* (Wellesley, Mass.: Babson Center for Entrepreneurial Studies, 1981), pp. 504–515. See also Thomas Begley and David P. Boyd, "Psychological Characteristics Associated with Performance in Entrepreneurial Firms and Smaller Businesses," *Journal of Business Venturing* 2 (1987):79–93.

[21]Vesper, *Entrepreneurship and Public Policy,* p. 42.

[22]Ibid., p. 43.

[23]This discussion is based on Joshua Ronen, "Some Insights into the Entrepreneurial Process," in Joshua Ronen, ed., *Entrepreneurship* (Lexington, Mass.: D. C. Heath, 1983), pp. 152–154; and Melvin J. Stanford, *New Enterprise Management* (Reston, Va.: Reston Publishing, 1982).

[24]Vesper, *Entrepreneurship and Public Policy,* pp. 59–68.

[25]This section is based on Peter Drucker, "Entrepreneurial Strategies," *California Management Review* 27, no. 2 (Winter 1985):9–25.

[26]Ibid., p. 10.

[27]Ibid., p. 19.

[28]Ibid., p. 21.

[29]Ibid., p. 22.

[30]Burgelman, "Designs for Corporate Entrepreneurship in Established Firms," pp. 154–166.

[31]Ibid., p. 162.

[32]Drucker, *Innovation and Entrepreneurship,* pp. 161–162.

[33]Howard H. Stevenson and David E. Gumpert, "The Heart of Entrepreneurship," *Harvard Business Review* 63 (March–April 1985):85–94.

[34]Ibid., p. 86.

[35]Ibid., p. 87.

[36]This section is based on Chapter 13, "The Entrepreneurial Business," of Peter Drucker's *Innovation and Entrepreneurship,* pp. 147–176.

[37]Ibid., p. 151.

CASE ON THE EXTERNAL ENVIRONMENT

SEAFOOD AMERICA: CORPORATE RESPONSE TO AIDS

Jack Mathews, CEO of Seafood America, returned the phone to its cradle and slowly shook his head. He had to give an answer to his restaurant managers in Cheyenne and St. Louis. Nothing that he had learned in business school or 25 years of industry experience had prepared him to deal with the issue facing him: AIDS.

Background. Jack Mathews had spent his entire business career with Amalgamated Foods. For the last eight years, he had been involved in Amalgamated's move into the restaurant business. Initially, he was a corporate planner responsible for designing the "restaurant strategy," but then he requested a chance to help actualize the plans. Starting as manager of a small chain of fast-food restaurants, Jack was now chief executive officer of Seafood America, a national chain of restaurants that catered to the 18-to-35-year-old upwardly mobile consumer and provided both a "meeting place" and "good but not gourmet" food at moderate prices. Entrees averaged $7.95, and were almost exclusively fresh seafood. Roughly 35 percent of revenue came from the bar business, as typical customers spent some time in the bar before being seated, or just came to Seafood America to graze on appetizers, drink, and meet friends. In 1985, sales had grown 24 percent to $100 million and net profits had increased 13 percent to $8 million. The prospects for growth were excellent, as the eating habits of Americans continued to change to "whiter and lighter" food.

Seafood America had been founded in 1975 by John Andrews of Cheyenne, Wyoming. The fourth son of a rancher, Andrews was vice president of a regional meat distributor. On several business trips to the East and West Coasts, Andrews had become convinced that the excellent seafood that he always ordered in restaurants would sell in Cheyenne. So he quit his job, sold his house to raise capital, and started Seafood America. At first, he struggled because he knew little about the restaurant business. However, at the end of the third year, the initial restaurants opened in Cheyenne, Albuquerque, and Phoenix had turned the corner, and he prepared to grow quickly. By 1983, Andrews had opened 25 restaurants in 22 cities in the western part of the country. Seafood America had become enormously successful, by providing fresh seafood at reasonable prices in a pleasant and sociable atmosphere.

At the end of 1983, Andrews decided to sell the business to Amalgamated Foods, a distinguished food-processing company that was increasing its presence in the restaurant business. By 1985, Amalgamated had doubled the number of restaurants and planned to add ten new "properties" every year for the next four years.

Employees at Seafood America fit the profile of the restaurant industry: Most were young and looking forward to the day when they would be doing something else. Few saw themselves in long-term careers as waiters, waitresses, bartenders, or buspersons. However, since Andrews tried to treat his employees "like family," Seafood America had a significantly lower turnover than the industry average. Each Seafood America restaurant employed an average of 40 people. In most large cities, at least half of Seafood America's employees were members of minorities or low-income groups, and the majority of them were single and male.

The AIDS Problem. AIDS (acquired immune deficiency syndrome) is now a household word.[1] As most of us know, the virus works by destroying the body's immune systems, making it vulnerable to a host of diseases. It incapacitates a special type of white blood cell that coordinates the activities of other immune cells. Without this "helper" cell, the body cannot respond effectively to many external challenges.

The latest reports from the Centers for Disease Control (CDC) indicate that more than one million Americans have already been infected with the virus. Well over half of these people do not know they are carriers and could infect others. A very few people who are HIV-positive never reach the AIDS stage, but the vast majority of those who are infected with the virus eventually develop fatal AIDS-related illnesses. Since there is a long lag between infection and the onset of AIDS (there have been reports of eight years or more) it is still extremely difficult to predict the disease's overall impact on the population. However,

[1]This section is based primarily on the Institute of Medicine and National Academy of Sciences report *Mobilizing Against AIDS* (Cambridge, Mass.: Harvard University Press, 1986).

approximately 57,000 Americans had developed full-blown AIDS in 1989, which brought the total number of AIDS cases in the United States to 122,000. The number who have died of AIDS is 42,000.[2]

Transmission is thought to be primarily through sexual contact or through the practice of passing unsterile needles from user to user, since the virus is present in blood, semen, and vaginal secretions. As a result, most blood is now routinely screened for the AIDS virus. However, because AIDS is such a deadly disease and because so little is known about it, public fear is widespread.

Demonstrators have tried to keep infected children out of the public schools. AIDS victims have lost their jobs, been ostracized, and had to cope with virtual isolation in addition to the knowledge of impending death. Rarely does a victim live longer than three years after onset of the disease.

The Institute of Medicine and National Academy of Sciences has tried to allay people's fears that AIDS can be transmitted by casual contact:

> It must be emphasized at the outset that there is no evidence that AIDS can be transmitted by "casual" contact. . . . Thus, the disease cannot be transmitted by a handshake, by a cough or sneeze, or by the consumption of food prepared by someone with AIDS.

Subsequent studies have shown that the virus is very rare in secretions such as tears and saliva, and even when it is present, the levels are probably too low to play a role in infection.

The economic impact of AIDS is difficult to calculate. One study estimates that the economic loss from the first 10,000 victims was over $4 billion. The medical costs for each AIDS victim is estimated to be between $42,000 and $147,000 for hospital care alone. Public health officials estimated that the cost of caring for AIDS patients in the United States was $16 billion in 1991. According to *Fortune,* most of

[2]"The AIDS Statistics," *The Washington Post Health Magazine,* April 3, 1990, p. 5.

this burden falls on corporations, since 70 percent of the population is covered by health insurance through their employers.

Although there is hope of a vaccine to prevent AIDS, it is far from certain that the AIDS virus will lend itself to the development of vaccines, since it seems to mutate into other forms rather quickly. Scientists have used or developed a number of drugs to alleviate the disease and, it is hoped, to prolong life, but for now no cure is in sight.

The Management Dilemma. The first case of AIDS at Seafood America was brought to the attention of the Cheyenne restaurant manager by the employee himself. The second case was more difficult to deal with. In St. Louis, a regular customer who happened to be a nurse came up to the restaurant manager and said, "You should know that your waiter, John, is being treated for AIDS at my clinic."

In keeping with the family tradition established by Mr. Andrews, the normal policy for Seafood America was to give a certain amount of sick leave and to pay the full cost of medical care for its employees.

Given the prognosis for the AIDS epidemic, especially among high-risk groups, Mathews knew that he needed a formal policy to help restaurant managers decide what to do in these tragic cases.

Source: This case was written by R. Edward Freeman, The Olsson Center for Applied Ethics. Copyright © 1986 by the Colgate Darden Graduate Business School Sponsors, University of Virginia, Charlottesville, Virginia. *Note:* Although this case is based on a factual situation, such particulars as industry, city, and proper names have, of course, been changed.

Case Questions

1. Who are the stakeholders of Seafood America?
2. Describe the indirect environment. What political, technological, and economic trends will affect Mathews's decision?
3. What is Mathews's responsibility to his employees? To his customers? To his employee with AIDS? To the employee accused of having AIDS?
4. What would you do if you were Mathews?

CHAPTER SEVEN

PLANNING AND STRATEGIC MANAGEMENT

**Upon completing this chapter, you should be
able to:**

1. Explain how Peter Drucker's criteria of effectiveness and efficiency are related to planning.

2. List and discuss four reasons goals are important to planning.

3. Evaluate the statement, "Of the four management functions, planning is the most important."

4. Describe the two types of plans and explain how they are related.

5. List and describe the nine steps that make up the formal planning process.

6. Distinguish between the two ways in which the term *strategy* is used.

7. Trace the evolution of the concept of strategy.

8. Compare and contrast the three levels of strategy.

9. Distinguish between the values-based and the corporate portfolio approach to corporate-level strategy.

10. Explain the BCG matrix and discuss its advantages and disadvantages.

11. Describe Porter's framework for business-unit strategy.

12. Describe functional-level strategy and suggest ways that functional-level conflicts can be resolved.

John Tenniel illustration colored by Fritz Kredel, *Alice and the Cheshire Cat.* Print courtesy of Historical Pictures Service, Chicago. Alice asked, "Cheshire-Puss . . . Would you tell me, please, which way I ought to go from here?" "That depends a good deal on where you want to get to," said the Cat.

ILLUSTRATIVE CASE STUDY

INTRODUCTION

Planning for the Future at Federal Express

The managers of Federal Express were concerned. They had grown from a small package-delivery service into the major force in overnight delivery. However, they needed to decide on directions for the future. Competition was closing in from several sides, and Federal Express felt the need to move quickly if it was to continue to grow and thrive.

Federal Express did not consider itself simply a package "delivery service." It saw itself as part of a larger, more complex industry that should be thought of as "information delivery." Although they competed with such traditional rivals as other overnight carriers like United Parcel Service and the United States Postal Service, they also worried about such information carriers as MCI, AT&T, and other telecommunication companies. Therefore, it was important for company managers to speculate on the future directions of all these companies.

Federal Express had a reputation for being at the forefront of trends, and it wanted to keep both its position and its reputation. The company had started long before anyone thought overnight-delivery service would be such an important part of doing business. Although it had taken over three years for the concept to catch on and make the company profitable, Federal Express was now the leader in the industry. The technology and the attitude of innovation that made it possible to go from handling 40 packages a night to 400,000 were important assets. The question now was: How should these assets be used?

The postal service was obviously impinging on Federal Express's overnight-delivery business, the "Express Mail" package being a direct and serious challenge. However, the post office was somewhat limited as to future directions. It could challenge in terms of price and service, but would probably continue to specialize in the same type of product. United Parcel Service (UPS) was also a direct challenger—one that priced its service considerably under Federal and was noticeably improving that service. Where would UPS go in the years to come?

Despite the obvious challenges of the package-delivery services, Federal Express was far more concerned about the competition from other methods of information transfer. MCI, for example, had recently introduced its MCI Mail System, which transferred documents from one computer to another in far fewer hours than Federal Express could promise. Was

A Strategic Decision. When the importance of foreign expansion became clear, Federal Express opened this facility in Anchorage, Alaska, which puts it within several hours of key markets around the world.

this what business in the information age wanted? If so, how should Federal react?

Since 1978, the mechanics of doing business have changed drastically; the rapid development of technology has changed business attitudes and expectations forever. It is no longer acceptable for a business letter to take a week to move from one coast to the other; for important documents, businesses now think in terms of hours instead of days. The development of a truly global marketplace has also affected the document-delivery business. As international business becomes more common, information-transfer systems have to keep pace.

The people at Federal Express knew they had to move forward in order to survive. Federal Express had to be ready to meet the needs of *tomorrow's* businesses, and to do this, they had to anticipate those needs today. Which needs were going to be the most important? What could they do to get ready now?

Sources: Larry Reibstein, "Turbulence Ahead: Federal Express Faces Challenges to Its Grip on Overnight Delivery," *The Wall Street Journal,* January 8, 1988, pp. 1, 10; Arthur M. Lewis, "The Great Electronic Mail Shootout," *Fortune,* August 20, 1984, pp. 167–169; Joan M. Feldman, "Federal Express: Big, Bigger and Biggest," *Air Transport World,* November 1985, pp. 46–48; John J. Keller with John W. Wilson, "Why Zapmail Finally Got Zapped," *Business Week,* October 13, 1986, pp. 48–49; David H. Freedman, "Redefining an Industry Through Integrated Automation," *Infosystems,* May 1985, pp. 26–27; Katie Hajner, "Fred Smith: The Entrepreneur Redux," *Inc,* June 1984, pp. 38, 40; John Merwin, "Anticipating the Evolution," *Forbes,* November 4, 1985, pp. 163–164.

Federal Express's success in recognizing and then tapping an unmet demand for overnight delivery is testimony to the value of *planning*. Planning, of course, is not a single event, with a clear beginning and end. Instead, it is an ongoing process that reflects and adapts to changes in both the direct-action and indirect-action environments. We can see this in the case of Federal Express, which entered the 1980s facing stiff competition and the rising expectations of customers (direct-action environment), as well as evolving technology (indirect-action environment). To stay on top, Federal Express had to reevaluate its plans and plot a new course into the future. In this chapter, we will take a closer look at the planning function and the way plans are created at various levels within the organization, concluding with a discussion of *strategic management,* whereby top management establishes a broad program of organizational goals and the means to achieve them.

■ PLANNING: AN OVERVIEW

Peter Drucker has proposed that a manager's performance be judged by the twin criteria of **effectiveness**—the ability to do the "right" things—and **efficiency**—the ability to do things "right." Of these two criteria, Drucker suggests, effectiveness is more important, for no amount of efficiency will ever make up for choosing the wrong goals.[1] These two criteria parallel the two aspects of **planning:** setting the "right" goals and then choosing the "right" means for attaining those goals. Both of these aspects of planning are vital to the process of management.

The Importance of Goals

All of us have dreams of finding fame and fortune and winning the respect and admiration of others. To make our dreams come true, though, we need to set specific, measurable goals with realistic, achievable deadlines. The same is true of organizations. Goals are important for at least four reasons.

1. *Goals provide a sense of direction.* Without a goal, individuals and organizations tend to muddle along, reacting to environmental changes without a clear sense of what they really want to achieve. By setting goals, people and organizations bolster their motivation and gain a source of inspiration that helps them overcome the inevitable obstacles they encounter.

2. *Goals focus our efforts.* Every person and every organization has limited resources, which can be used to achieve a variety of goals. By selecting just one or a set of related goals, we make a commitment about the way we will use our scarce resources and we begin to set priorities. This is especially important for an organization, which has to coordinate the actions of many individuals.

3. *Goals guide our plans and decisions.* Do you want to become a chess champion? Or a champion gymnast? The answers to such questions will shape both your short-term and long-term plans and help you make many key decisions. Organizations face similar decisions, which are simplified by asking, What is our goal? Will this action move the organization toward or away from its goal?

4. *Goals help us evaluate our progress.* A clearly stated, measurable goal with a specific deadline easily becomes a standard of performance that lets individuals and managers alike evaluate their progress. Thus, goals are an essential part of *controlling,* the processing of being sure that actions are in keeping with goals and the plans created to achieve them. If we find we are straying off course or if we encounter unforeseen contingencies, we can take corrective action by modifying our plan. "Replanning," in fact, is sometimes a key factor in an organization's ultimate success.

The Importance of Goals. "Ready-to-eat cereal is our thing," says Kellogg Co. Chairman William E. LaMothe, who oversees Monday-morning taste-tests of Kellogg cereals from around the world. Kellogg's long-range goal—controlling 50 percent of the U.S. cereal business—translates into plans for ongoing product innovation, clever marketing, and heavy investment in sophisticated and efficient factories.

COORDINATED RESOURCE

Acumen: High achievers enjoy challenges, encourage others to set realistic goals, and often have effective planning and goal-setting skills.

As evidence of the importance of goals, consider the case of Servus Rubber, which had as its original goal the manufacture of high-quality rubber boots worn by farmers, construction workers, electricians, military personnel, and industrial workers. When South Korean manufacturers introduced competing products that were considerably cheaper in price and lower in quality, the managers at Servus adopted a new goal: Rather than remaining in their niche as a high-quality bootmaker, they would try to compete with the Koreans on price. This new goal led Servus to use cheaper materials and to neglect equipment. Morale at the company declined, and by 1981 profits were down by 50 percent.

Enter two young entrepreneurs, Tommy Hewitt, 35, and Michael Cappy, 33, former employees of GE. They bought Servus and set yet another goal: Save the company and restore its former reputation. To carry out this goal, they decided to differentiate Servus from its competitors by offering products that represented the best value and a mix of price and quality. This led them to develop new products and markets, work with employees to improve morale, and replace ineffective managers. Because Hewitt and Cappy had a clear-cut set of goals, they could formulate plans and activities that moved the company from the brink of disaster to prosperity.[2]

The Importance of Planning

COORDINATED RESOURCE

The Additional Lecture for Chapter 7 found in the Lecture Extras supplement looks at the Oakland A's baseball team and the results of their strategic planning.

COORDINATED RESOURCE

See Samaras Exercise 2.1, "A Plan to Transport."

In Chapter 1, we showed planning as one of the four interacting functions of management. However, we could just as easily see planning as the initial management function. Even this statement does not begin to capture the magnitude of planning's importance to management, though. It might be better to think of planning as the locomotive that drives a train of organizing, leading, and controlling activities. Or maybe we should think of planning as the taproot of a magnificent oak tree, from which grow the branches of organizing, leading, and controlling.

Without plans, managers cannot know how they should organize people and resources; they may not even have a clear idea of *what* they need to organize.

strategic plans Plans designed to meet an organization's broad goals.

mission statement Broad organizational goal, based on planning premises, which justifies an organization's existence.

planning premises Basic assumptions about an organization's purpose, its values, distinctive competencies, and place in the world.

Without a plan, they cannot lead with confidence or expect others to follow them. And without a plan, managers and their followers have little chance of achieving their goals or knowing when and where they stray from their path. Controlling becomes an exercise in futility. Too often, faulty plans affect the health of the entire organization. That is why the business press (*The Wall Street Journal, Fortune,* and so on) devotes so much attention to organizational *strategies,* the plans top managers devise to meet an organization's broad goals. Their readers are stakeholders who use this information to judge the organization's current performance and chances for future success.

Types of Plans

The modern organization is extremely complex. A multinational enterprise like General Motors, for example, has to coordinate the actions of thousands of employees around the world. Thus it should come as no surprise that managers at all levels create plans to guide their subunits toward goals that will contribute to the organization's larger goals.

Organizations use two main types of plans. **Strategic plans** are designed by top and middle managers to meet the organization's broad goals, while *operational plans* (to be discussed in the next chapter) show how strategic plans will be implemented in day-to-day activities. As Figure 7-1 shows, these plans form a hierarchy of plans that are linked by interrelated goals.

At the top is the **mission statement,** a broad goal based on the organization's **planning premises,** basic assumptions about the organization's purpose, its values, its distinctive competencies, and its place in the world. A mission statement is a relatively permanent part of an organization's identity and can do much to unify and motivate its members. Consider the visionary mission described by a former chairman of AT&T some 80 years ago: "The dream of good, cheap, fast, worldwide telephone service . . . is not a speculation. It is a perfectly clear statement that you're going to do something."[3] Since its divestiture in 1984, of course, AT&T has altered its mission; the company now aims to be "a major factor in the worldwide move-

FIGURE 7-1 The Hierarchy of Plans

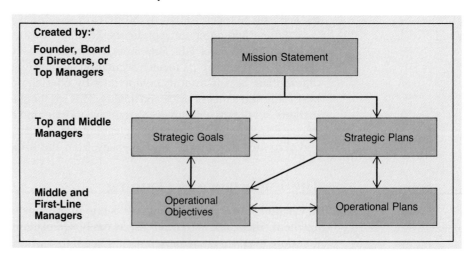

*This is an ideal scenario, but responsibility for planning varies widely in practice. Larger organizations often have a centralized or decentralized staff of professional planning specialists, while in smaller organizations, a committee of executives or even managers and a few key employees may meet to brainstorm about plans. Furthermore, the board of directors sometimes takes an active role in strategic goal-setting and planning.

objective A goal characterized by a comparatively short time span and specific, measurable achievements.

ment and management of information."[4] Although this mission statement lacks the drama of the earlier statement, it still highlights AT&T's new awareness of itself as a provider of information—not just telephone service—to customers in the United States and around the world. The mission statement then becomes the driving force behind both strategic goals and operational goals, which in turn shape strategic plans and operational plans.

Figure 7-1 gives you an idea of how operational plans evolve out of strategic plans and mission statements, but you need to be aware of at least four major differences between strategic and operational plans.[5]

1. *Time horizons.* Strategic plans tend to involve years or even decades. For example, Coca-Cola has adopted a continent-wide strategy for achieving its goal of making Europe its most profitable market in the 1990s. For at least five years, Coca-Cola has been building or buying joint interests in European bottling plants. In addition, Coca-Cola will be the exclusive soft drink at France's Euro Disneyland and aims to be a major presence at the Olympics in Barcelona and Albertville, France, the World's Fair in Seville, Spain, and other major European events. At the operational level, William Hoffman, head of bottling in France, enacted these strategic goals by hiring 350 "merchandisers," who were trained at the newly created Coca-Cola University and then dispatched to visit French retailers, where they schedule promotions and use tape measures, feather dusters, and glass cleaner to be sure Coke is displayed properly.[6]

2. *Scope.* Strategic plans affect a wide range of organizational activities, while operational plans have a more narrow and limited scope. For this reason, some management writers distinguish between strategic *goals* and operational **objectives.** (We will use the terms interchangeably, however, reflecting the fact that even strategic goals should be stated in specific, measurable terms that include a deadline. We'll have more to say about formulating objectives in the next chapter.) At the strategic level, Coca-Cola has enacted a broad program of building a network of reliable, strategically located bottlers and increasing Coca-Cola's visibility to European consumers. At the operational level, this strategy is transformed into a set of specific, short-term, measurable objectives for Coke's French merchandisers, such as visiting 15 retailers a week and scheduling eight in-store promotions each month.

3. *Complexity and impact.* Often strategic goals are broad and deceptively simple. Consider, for example, Coke's "simple" goal of making Europe its most profitable market in the 1990s. Yet this simple goal is forcing Coke to rethink some long-standing policies, among them its relationship to European bottlers, who previously bought Coke's syrup and then independently sold and promoted Coke to retailers. As a result, Coke's promotions—and sales—sometimes varied from region to region. To prevent this, Coca-Cola is taking greater control over its foreign bottlers. This strategy, in turn, supported another strategic goal of increasing Coke's visibility when Coca-Cola shipped thousands of cans of Coke from its new Dunkirk, England, bottling plant to the opening of the Berlin Wall, where the soda was given away to the celebrants. This operational plan was complex, but it would have been impossible if Coca-Cola's strategy had not laid the groundwork.

4. *Independence.* If the organization is to move forward effectively, operational goals and plans have to reflect strategic goals and plans, as well as the organization's larger mission. Thus, Coke's merchandisers receive specific training and guidelines about the company-approved way to display Coca-Cola.

■ THE FORMAL PLANNING PROCESS: AN EXAMPLE

strategic business-unit (SBU) planning Grouping business activities within a multibusiness corporation because they generate closely related products or services.

COORDINATED RESOURCE
See DuBose Reading #5, "A Look at Planning and Its Components."

THOUGHT PROVOKER
"Trying to predict the future is necessary but impossible" (*Fortune*, 4/23/90, p. 281ff.). Comment on this statement.

TEACHING TIP
Have your students formulate a post-graduation plan. Have them follow the planning steps.

COORDINATED RESOURCE
Use Transparency 30, Steps in the Formal Planning Process.

COORDINATED RESOURCE
See Samaras Exercise 2.4, "Start Up Your Own MBO."

CLASS COMMENT
Corporate vice presidents rank their bosses high on energy, self-confidence, and assertiveness, but low on being visionaries or open to new ideas. (*Wall Street Journal*, 5/15/90, p. A1)

COORDINATED RESOURCE
Acumen: Acumen scales compatible with cooperative goal setting and appraisal would be high scores on Humanistic-Helpful, Affiliation, and Achievement, and low scores on the Dependence, Apprehension, Oppositional, and Power scales.

Now that you have a clearer idea of what planning contributes to organizations, let's take a closer look at the formal planning process itself. Our example will be based on **strategic business-unit (SBU) planning,** a type of strategic planning, but it could easily be applied to any other type of organizational or individual planning.[7] The process itself is summarized in Figure 7-2. Although it looks formidable, it is surprisingly straightforward and easy to understand if we translate each step into a simple question or statement.

Step 1: What do we want?

Step 2: What are we now doing to get what we want?

Step 3: What's "out there" that needs doing?

Step 4: What are we able to do?

Step 5: What can we do that needs doing?

Step 6: Will continuing to do what we are now doing take us where we want to go?

Step 7: This is what we'll do to get what we want.

Step 8: Do it.

Step 9: Check frequently to make sure we're doing it right.

Let's consider each of these nine steps in more detail.

Step 1: Goal Formulation

Goal formulation involves reviewing and understanding the organization's mission and then establishing goals that translate the mission into concrete terms. Because the goals chosen will take up a large amount of the organization's resources and govern so many of its activities, this is a key step. Yet many managers hesitate—or fail—to carry it out (see Exhibit 7-1).

As Figure 7-2 indicates, the values managers hold will affect the kinds of goals they select. As we noted in Chapter 4, these values may be social or ethical, or they may involve practical matters, such as the size that managers would like their organization to be, the kind of product or service they would like to produce, or simply the way they prefer to operate.[8] Peters and Waterman, Pascale and Athos, and other researchers have concluded that many excellently managed companies are "value-driven"—that is, organizational values actually guide many managers' actions. The founder or another early leader of a value-driven organization usually plays a key role in creating these values.[9] The Walt Disney Company is an excellent example of this phenomenon.

EXHIBIT 7-1 Why Managers Fail to Set Goals

❑ They are unwilling to give up alternative goals.
❑ They are afraid of failing and endangering their self-esteem, losing the respect of others, or jeopardizing their job security.
❑ They lack organizational knowledge.
❑ They lack knowledge of the environment.
❑ They lack confidence.

Source: Adapted from David A. Kolb, Irwin M. Rubin, and James M. McIntyre, *Organizational Psychology: An Experiential Approach to Organizational Behavior,* 4th ed. (Englewood Cliffs, N.J.: Prentice Hall, 1984), p. 102.

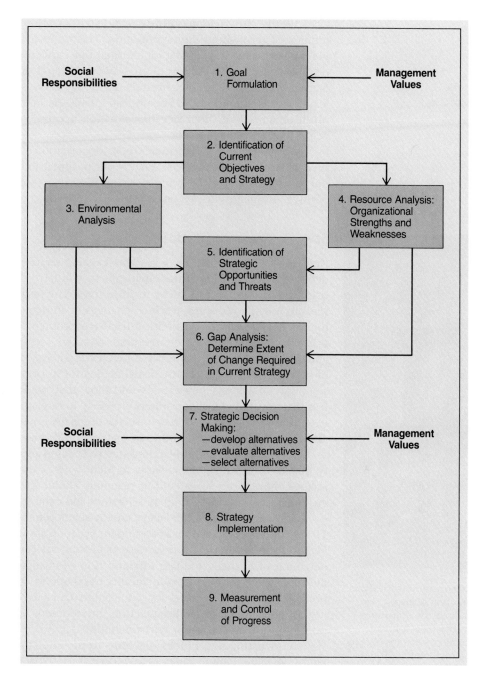

FIGURE 7-2 Steps in the Formal Planning Process

Source: Modified Figure 3.1, page 48, by permission from *Strategy Formulation* by Charles W. Hofer and Dan E. Schendel. Copyright © 1986 by West Publishing Company. All rights reserved.

Step 2: Identification of Current Objectives and Strategy

COORDINATED RESOURCE
See DuBose Reading #7, "The Ethics of MBO."

COORDINATED RESOURCE
Use Transparency 31, Cascading of Objectives.

Steps 2 through 6 provide the basis for determining what must be done differently to achieve organizational goals. The first step in this series is to identify the organization's existing objectives and strategy, which may be quite similar to its existing mission and objectives. Sometimes, however, the goal-formulation process yields a substantial change in mission and objectives; this is especially true if the organization has been failing to meet key objectives.[10]

Ideally, the existing objectives and strategy are well defined and clearly communicated throughout the organization. This optimal situation usually follows earlier formal strategic planning or informal but explicit strategy making by a strong organizational leader. All too often, however, Step 2 uncovers no explicit strategy; managers then have to infer from its day-to-day actions what the organization's top leadership is attempting to accomplish. Managers in small businesses and not-for-profit organizations often face this situation because such organizations rarely develop formal strategic plans.

Many managers determine their organization's current strategy by asking themselves such questions as: What is our business and what should it be? Who are our customers and who should they be? Where are we heading? What major competitive advantages do we enjoy? In what areas of competence do we excel?

Step 3: Environmental Analysis

Knowing the organization's goals and existing strategy provides a framework for defining which aspects of the environment will have the greatest influence on the organization's ability to achieve its objectives. The purpose of environmental analysis is to identify the ways in which changes in an organization's economic, technological, sociocultural, and political/legal environment can indirectly influence the organization and the ways competitors, suppliers, customers, government agencies, and others can directly influence it (see Chapter 3).[11] For example, a manufacturer of steel shelving might find the usual market for its product reduced during a recession. Careful analysis, however, would show that, while industrial users are buying less shelving, individual consumers are likely to buy more, since steel shelving costs less than wood shelving. In response, the company might make its product line more attractive for home use—and thus survive the recession.

It is important in this planning step to develop a list of just those factors judged to be truly crucial. No list is likely to identify all potentially relevant factors, but a serious effort to do so can aid in planning. Useful sources of information include customers and suppliers, trade publications and exhibitions, and technical meetings.

Forecasting and other management science methods (discussed in Chapter 10) are extremely useful for analyzing information about the environment. As James M. Utterback has noted, one key to successful environmental analysis is the early detection of changes, for late identification of changes in the environment often increases an organization's vulnerability to competitors.[12] Although forecasts rarely predict with complete accuracy, environmental analysis helps the organization adjust to changes in the indirect-action environment and anticipate and influence activity in the direct-action environment.

Anticipating stakeholder reactions to the implementation of a strategy is also important. For example, Ian C. MacMillan reported that one firm delayed launching a new product until the marketing manager of its main competitor had departed for an extended business trip and vacation. Its competitor was paralyzed while the absent manager's stand-in slowly grappled with this new threat and eventually acted too late, allowing the aggressive company to establish a dominant position in the marketplace.[13] This illustrates the value of systematically gathering information on competitors—a technique that, according to a recent study, is too little used in American business.[14]

Step 4: Resource Analysis

The organization's goals and existing strategy also provide a framework for analyzing its resources. This analysis is necessary to identify the organization's competitive advantages and disadvantages, its strengths and weaknesses relative to its present and likely future competitors.

Environmental Analysis. Marketing Manager Skip Gladfelter demonstrates the IBM PS/1, a home computer/software package designed for the 20 million households in which at least one person is computer literate. Tandy Corp., in contrast, designed its 1000 model package for the 30 to 40 million first-time users who mainly want to balance their checkbooks.

COORDINATED RESOURCE
See DuBose Reading #6, "Business Planning Is People Planning."

The question is not "What do we do well or poorly?" but rather "What are we doing better or worse than anyone else?" If all the universities in an area provide excellent teaching, then University X does not gain a competitive advantage in attracting students because its faculty performs well in the classroom. By contrast, if University X offers only good, but not excellent, teaching while the other universities do a poor job, it will have a competitive advantage in this dimension. Furthermore, relative strength depends on what an organization is trying to do. A strong sales force will be of little or no use to a firm that plans to shift to direct-mail selling.

Step 5: Identification of Strategic Opportunities and Threats

Identifying strategy, analyzing the environment, and analyzing the organization's resources (Steps 2, 3, and 4) come together in the fifth step: determining the opportunities available to the organization and the threats it faces. Opportunities and threats may arise from many factors: Land purchased for farming activities by a large agribusiness corporation may become so valuable that the company considers forming or acquiring a housing development division. In this instance, changed market conditions present a new opportunity.

In the 1960s, organizations that owed their success to expertise in designing and manufacturing complex electromechanical products, such as cash registers, found that advances in electronic technology rapidly made both their skills and their plants and equipment obsolete. Here technological changes were a clear threat. But firms that could move ahead rapidly with the new technology had the opportunity to do so. Thus, the same environment that posed a threat to some organizations offered opportunities to others.

Step 6: Determination of Extent of Required Strategic Change

After resources and the environment have been analyzed, the results of continuing the existing strategy can be forecast. The longer that strategy has been in place and the more stable the environment, the easier it will be to make this prediction. Then managers can decide whether or not to modify that strategy or its implementation. This decision should be based on whether **performance gaps** can be identified. A performance gap is the difference between the objectives established in the goal-formulation process and the results likely to be achieved if the existing strategy is continued. Performance gaps arise when organizations choose more difficult objectives or fail to meet former objectives because of effective responses by competitors, changes in the environment, or loss of resources—all amounting to a failure by the firm to properly implement the strategy—or because the strategy itself had not been well thought out.

Step 7: Strategic Decision Making

If it appears necessary to change the strategy to close the performance gap, the next step is to identify, evaluate, and select alternative strategic approaches. The process of decision making is discussed in detail in Chapter 9; our discussion here will highlight those aspects that concern strategic alternatives.

IDENTIFICATION OF STRATEGIC ALTERNATIVES. In a given instance, a variety of alternatives for closing the performance gap probably exist. New markets may be entered; key products may be redesigned to enhance quality or reduce cost; new investments may be undertaken or old ones terminated.

Side notes:

COORDINATED RESOURCE
See Study Guide Self-Learning Exercise 7, "Job Attitude and Strategy."

COORDINATED RESOURCE
Use Transparency 35, Components of the SWOT Analysis.

COORDINATED RESOURCE
Use Transparency 36, External Factors That Influence Strategic Decisions.

COORDINATED RESOURCE
Use Transparency 37, Internal Factors That Influence Strategic Decisions.

COORDINATED RESOURCE
The Application Exercise for Chapter 7 found in the Lecture Extras supplement has students performing a SWOT (strengths, weaknesses, opportunities, and threats) analysis for a company.

DISCUSSION QUESTION
How often do you think a SWOT analysis should be done? Why?

performance gaps The difference between the objectives established in the goal-formulation process and the results likely to be achieved if the existing strategy is continued.

CLASS COMMENT
The best-known method for translating blue-sky conjecture into practical business plans is scenario planning. (*Fortune*, 4/23/90, p. 281ff.)

A Dual Strategy. James G. Kaiser, senior vice president in charge of Corning's technical products division, has two strategies: Achieve total quality performance (his division was one of four finalists for the 1989 Malcolm Baldrige Award) and foster Corning's cultural diversity initiative, dedicated to retaining and promoting talented minority managers.

COORDINATED RESOURCE

Acumen: Those scoring high on the Perfectionism scale set very high performance standards to demonstrate competence, focus on the elimination of even the smallest mistakes, and then try doing even better in the future.

If only a minor change in the existing strategy is needed, the logical alternatives may be few. If, for example, a lag in new-product introduction has been identified as a major cause of dwindling sales, a program to improve the performance of the research and development department may be the obvious choice. But if a significant change in the strategic approach is required, more alternatives must be identified and greater care will be needed later to avoid attempting to blend incompatible options into a new strategic approach.

EVALUATION OF STRATEGIC ALTERNATIVES. Richard P. Rumelt has described four criteria for evaluating strategic alternatives: (1) The strategy and its component parts should have consistent goals, objectives, and policies; (2) It should focus resources and efforts on the critical issues identified in the strategy-formulation process and separate them from unimportant issues; (3) It should deal with subproblems capable of solution, given the organization's resources and skills; and (4) The strategy should be capable of producing the intended results—that is, it should show promise of actually working.[15] In evaluating alternatives, it is also important to focus on a particular product or service and on those competitors who are direct rivals in offering it. A strategy that does not create or exploit the organization's particular advantage over its rivals should be rejected.

SELECTION OF STRATEGIC ALTERNATIVES. In choosing among the available possibilities, successful managers select the alternatives that are best suited to the organization's capabilities. New capabilities can be acquired only through investment in human resources and/or equipment and cannot be built up quickly. Therefore, it is seldom advisable to embark on a strategic plan requiring resources or skills that are weak or nonexistent. Instead, recognized strengths should be fully exploited.

Step 8: Strategy Implementation

Once the strategy has been determined, it must be implemented, or incorporated into the daily operations of the organization. Even the most sophisticated and creative strategy will not benefit the organization unless it is carried out effectively. Whether or not the strategy is recorded in a formal and detailed strategic plan, it must be translated into the appropriate operational plans. This process will be discussed in the next chapter.

Step 9: Measurement and Control of Progress

As implementation proceeds, managers must check their progress at periodic or critical stages. Company controllers often play an important role in designing systems of *strategic control* (as this process is generally known). The two main questions relevant to strategic control are: (1) Is the strategy being implemented as planned? and (2) Is the strategy achieving the intended results?[16]

■ *THE EVOLUTION OF THE CONCEPT OF STRATEGY*

strategy The broad program for defining and achieving an organization's objectives; the organization's response to its environment over time.

The concept of **strategy** can be defined from at least two different perspectives: (1) from the perspective of what an organization *intends to do* and (2) from the perspective of what an organization eventually *does.*

From the first perspective, strategy is "the broad program for defining and achieving an organization's objectives and implementing its missions."[17] The word *program* in this definition implies that managers play an active, conscious, and rational role in formulating the organization's strategy.

From the second perspective, strategy is "the pattern of the organization's response to its environment over time." By this definition, every organization has a strategy—even if that strategy has never been explicitly formulated. This view of

ILLUSTRATIVE CASE STUDY

CONTINUED

Planning for the Future at Federal Express

Federal Express always had a clear sense of where it was going. The company wanted to be the leader in the information-delivery business. Yet as the business has become more complex and diverse, being the best has become more difficult. Take Federal Express's ZapMail facsimile service, which was intended to compete with MCI's Mail System. The move seemed a well-timed innovation and a way to stay ahead of the competition, but Federal Express didn't anticipate the number of businesses that would buy their own facsimile machines, effectively undermining the new service. They wisely discontinued ZapMail in 1986.

The ZapMail effort is simply one example of CEO Fred Smith's responsiveness to the rapidly changing world of information delivery. Having concluded that Federal Express had to become a global player if it wanted to stay on top, Smith has concentrated on foreign markets and acquisitions. Over the past few years, these efforts have been frustrated on several fronts. Difficulties in gaining access to specific foreign delivery routes and government restrictions favoring domestic services, coupled with the high cost of flying small packages in large planes, have created a spotty network of service running at high cost. (Federal Express lost $50 million for the 1988–1989 fiscal year.) Although their American rivals face the same obstacles, Federal Express has yet to gain a leg up on the competition.

This has not fazed Smith, who is noted for his highly driven and risk-taking nature; no move was too bold to get the international network he sought. To demonstrate his commitment to global information services and get beyond piecemeal acquisitions in France, Italy, and Britain, Smith made two key moves. First, he acquired Tiger International, the world's largest cargo hauler. This gave Federal Express access to the vast network of routes Tiger had won over the past 40 years and allowed Smith to mix Federal Express's small parcels in with Tiger's cargo, making more efficient use of space. As another bonus, acquiring Tiger's squadron of long-haul aircraft let Federal Express move its fleet of DC-10s back to the higher-volume parcel routes in the United States. The price was also right: $895 million, or eight times Tiger's 1989 profits.

To make the deal work, however, Smith must overcome a number of imposing obstacles. First, the merging of two companies' cultures has been described as "like mixing oil and water." The most daunting cultural difference is that Tiger is heavily unionized, while Smith is adamant about keeping unions out and maintaining an entrepreneurial, gung-ho spirit at Federal Express. Clashes about pilot seniority have already created rifts between workers and management, amid threats that Federal Express's pilots will also seek unionization. Second, a number of Tiger's biggest customers are some of Federal Express's most serious competitors. Several have already claimed they will stop using Tiger to avoid supporting Federal Express. Finally, the debt for the purchase will raise operating costs and make the company more vulnerable to swings in the economy.

Smith's other bold move was to build a new facility in Anchorage, Alaska. The plant fills out the center of a transportation triad and puts Federal Express within seven hours of key markets in Asia, Europe, and the United States. This move caught the competition off guard, forcing it to scramble to follow Smith's lead. One expert claims these two moves make Federal Express the "undisputed leader" in information delivery.

The decision to buy Tiger was a bold gamble. Thus far, it has set the company back, with after-tax losses for 1990 reaching $194 million in its foreign operations; analysts predict 1991 losses could exceed $200 million. If Federal Express's managers can turn the foreign operations around and solidify their global operation, they will have a clear edge over the competition and secure a thriving business through the turn of the century and beyond. If they can't, Federal Express could be paying the price for years.

Sources: Dean Foust et al., "Mr. Smith Goes Global," *Business Week,* February 13, 1989, pp. 68–72; Stephen W. Quickel, "Wisely, Fed Ex Opted to Join 'Em," *Business Month,* March 1989, pp. 17–18; Eugene Carlson, "Federal Express Wasn't an Overnight Success," *The Wall Street Journal,* June 6, 1989, p. B2; Peter Waldman, "Federal Express Pilots Upset by Handling of Seniority Issue in Merger with Tiger," *The Wall Street Journal,* August 4, 1989, p. A6; Glenn Ruffenbach, "Federal Express Earnings Plunge 79% But Firm, Others See Turnaround," *The Wall Street Journal,* March 20, 1990, p. A3; Chuck Hawkins, "Is Federal Express an Innocent Abroad?" *Business Week,* April 2, 1990, p. 34; Erik Calonius, "Federal Express's Battle Overseas," *Fortune,* December 3, 1990, pp. 137–140.

CLASS COMMENT

Strategic management is much more than just strategic planning. It involves formulating, implementing, and evaluating the strategy.

strategy applies to organizations whose managers are reactive—who passively respond and adjust to the environment only as the need arises.[18]

Although our discussion will use both definitions, we will emphasize the active role, known as *strategic planning* or *strategic management,* since both anecdotal evidence and research have demonstrated its value in preparing for and dealing with today's rapidly changing business environment.[19]

Strategy as the Grand Plan

THOUGHT PROVOKER

The environment is so uncertain that strategic planning is a waste of time. Agree or disagree and tell why.

CLASS COMMENT

As you can see, the concept of strategy has a long and colorful history. As pointed out in the management history chapter, the military has played a key role in the development of many management concepts.

The concept of strategy is ancient. The word itself comes from the Greek *strategeia,* which means the art or science of being a general. Effective Greek generals needed to lead an army, win and hold territory, protect a city from invasion, wipe out the enemy, and so forth. Each kind of objective required a different deployment of resources. Likewise, an army's strategy could be defined as the actual pattern of *actions* that it took in response to the enemy.

The Greeks also knew that strategy was more than fighting battles. Effective generals had to determine the right lines of supply, decide when to fight and when not to fight, and manage the army's relationships with citizens, politicians, and diplomats. Effective generals not only had to plan but to *act* as well. Dating back to the Greeks, then, the concept of strategy had both *planning* components and decision-making or *action* components.[20] Taken together, these two concepts form the basis for the "grand" strategy plan.

General Robert E. Wood, president of the giant mail-order house of Sears, Roebuck and Co., sounded a similar theme in the 1920s. Wood realized that the growing popularity of the automobile would give increasing numbers of people access to urban areas. A population no longer confined to the countryside, he reasoned, would abandon the mail-order catalog in favor of the retail store. So Sears embarked on the long-range strategy of converting to a retail chain. According to Wood, the company "made every mistake in the book" at first, but its carefully laid plans spelled success in the end. "Business is like war in one respect," the general wrote. "If its grand strategy is correct, any number of tactical errors can be made and yet the enterprise proves successful."[21]

The Rise of Strategic Management

Although effective managers have always plotted grand strategies, management scholars have only recently recognized strategy as a key factor in organizational success. The main reason for this belated recognition is the environmental changes occurring since World War II.

First, the *rate* of change in the environment has increased rapidly, partly because the greater interdependence of environmental factors has led to more complex demands on management operations and to a much more rapid birth-and-death cycle of innovative ideas. Second, there has been an obvious growth in the size and complexity of business organizations. For example, in 1949, the majority of Fortune 500 companies were single-product-line or single-key-idea organizations; by 1970, not only had a majority shifted to multi-industry organizations, but many had become multinational organizations as well.[22] Integrating the interests and needs of a diverse group of functional areas (and sometimes of different cultures) is a *strategic* enterprise, not least because it takes so much time to accomplish such an integration.

Today management scholars advocate the *strategic management approach.* This comprehensive approach to developing strategy did not appear overnight. As Dan Schendel and Charles Hofer have shown, it evolved out of the earlier policy-formulation and initial-strategy approaches.[23]

THE POLICY-FORMULATION APPROACH. When an individual entrepreneur offered one class of product to a restricted range of customers, the activities of the firm could be coordinated quite informally. But when the product was modified or supplemented or when sales territories were expanded, the number of the firm's functions increased. The task of integrating functions soon required more formal procedures so that the firm could coordinate activities both within and between functional areas. Thus the **policy-formulation approach** arose, based on the concept of implementing day-to-day rules that put boundaries around what a functional area could and could not do.

The concept of "business policy" soon became part of the country's educational curriculum, but by the 1950s and early 1960s, the policy-formulation approach had begun to prove inadequate. Organizations were increasing in size and complexity, and the magnitude and unpredictability of their environments presented them with problems the policy-formulation approach could not solve.

THE INITIAL-STRATEGY APPROACH. In 1962, business historian Alfred D. Chandler proposed that "strategy" be defined as

> the determination of the basic long-term goals and objectives of an enterprise, and the adoption of courses of action and the allocation of resources necessary for carrying out these goals.[24]

Chandler's formula, now recognized as the **initial-strategy approach,** embraced at least four key ideas. First, he was as interested in courses of *action* for attaining objectives as he was in the objectives themselves. Second, he emphasized the process of *seeking* key ideas rather than the routine principle of implementing policy based on a key idea that may or may not need reexamination. Third, Chandler was interested in *how* strategy was formulated, not just in *what* that strategy turned out to be. Fourth, Chandler abandoned the conventional notion that the relationship between a business and its environment was more or less stable and predictable. He developed his ideas using historical methods and by analyzing the growth and development of such classic American companies as DuPont; General Motors; Sears, Roebuck; and Standard Oil.

Chandler's definition of "strategy" was eventually refined by Kenneth Andrews, H. Igor Ansoff, and others, who brought the idea of strategy as *process* instead of fixed formula (policy) into the classroom. In the decade between 1965 and 1975, the term *strategy* came to replace the term *policy* in the nation's business schools.[25]

Two factors soon became evident: (1) *strategic planning* paid off in the world of real business activity, but (2) the role of the manager in the implementation of strategic planning had not yet been clarified. (See Chapter 8 for a more complete discussion of strategy implementation.) What could top management do to deal with the two major problems faced by modern organizations: rapid changes in the organization-environment interrelationship and the rapid growth in size and complexity of modern business organizations? In an effort to address this problem, the strategic-management paradigm began to take shape.

THE STRATEGIC MANAGEMENT APPROACH. Because many scholars have proposed different definitions and descriptions of strategy, Charles Hofer and Dan Schendel surveyed the resulting literature to create a composite definition and suggest a **strategic management approach,** based on the principle that the overall design of an organization can be described only if the attainment of *objectives* is added to *policy* and *strategy* as one of the key factors in the strategic management process.[26]

In their synthesis, Hofer and Schendel focused on four key aspects of strategic management. The first was goal setting. A second they call **strategy-formulation task,** a model that creates a strategy based on the organization's goals.[27] This leads to *strategy implementation,* and a shift from analysis to **administration,** the task of achieving predetermined goals.[28] Key factors are the organization's internal "politi-

---

policy-formulation approach The concept of implementing day-to-day rules that puts boundaries around what a functional area can and cannot do.

initial-strategy approach According to Alfred D. Chandler, "The determination of the basic long-term goals and objectives of an enterprise, and the adoption of courses of action and the allocation of resources necessary for carrying out these goals."

strategic management approach A pattern based on the principle that the overall design of the organization can be described only if the attainment of objectives is added to policy and strategy as one of the key factors in management's operation of the organization's activities.

strategy-formulation task A model of strategy formulation that takes into account the organization's goals and its strategy.

administration The performance of tasks needed to achieve predetermined goals.

strategic control The process of checking strategy implementation progress against the strategic plan at periodic or critical intervals to determine if the corporation is moving toward its strategic objectives.

cal" processes and individual reactions, which can force the revision of strategy. The final task, **strategic control,** gives managers feedback on their progress. Negative feedback, of course, can touch off a new cycle of strategic planning. Consider what happened to Clorox Co., the bleach king, when it tried to grow by introducing a line of detergents in 1988—a bid for a share of the $3.5 million detergent market dominated by such giants as Procter & Gamble and Colgate-Palmolive. Customer reaction was only so-so; most associate the Clorox brand with bleach. Also, the Clorox products were powders; liquid detergents are growing in popularity. Profits slumped, as did Clorox's stock price. Faced with this negative feedback, Clorox was forced to reconsider its strategy for assuring future growth.

■ LEVELS OF STRATEGY: SOME KEY DISTINCTIONS

COORDINATED RESOURCE
Use Transparency 32,
Three Levels of Strategy.

In discussing strategy, it is useful to distinguish between three levels of strategy: corporate-level, line-of-business or business-unit level, and functional-level strategy (see Fig. 7-3).[29]

Corporate-Level Strategy

corporate-level strategy Strategy formulated by top management to oversee the interests and operations of multiline corporations.

Corporate-level strategy is formulated by top management to oversee the interests and operations of organizations made up of more than one line of business. The major questions at this level are: What kinds of business should the company be engaged in? What are the goals and expectations for each business? How should resources be allocated to reach these goals?

THOUGHT PROVOKER
Single-mindedness by corporations (i.e., sticking to their core businesses) may spur innovation. Why?

In developing corporate-level goals, Peter Drucker suggests, corporations need to decide where they want to be in eight areas: market standing; innovation; productivity; physical and financial resources; profitability; managerial performance and development; worker performance and attitudes; and public responsibility.[30] In turbulent environments, however, a firm may strive for stability, simply drawing on existing strengths as a way of surviving until more favorable times. To do this, the corporation may have to retrench or make a strategic retreat from overambitious plans for growth. (To find out how Chrysler has used these goals to shape its strategy, see the Management Application box.)

FIGURE 7-3 Three Levels of Strategy
Source: Adapted from Robert H. Hayes and Steven C. Wheelwright, *Restoring Our Competitive Edge: Competing Through Manufacturing,* p. 28. Copyright 1984 by John Wiley & Sons, Inc.

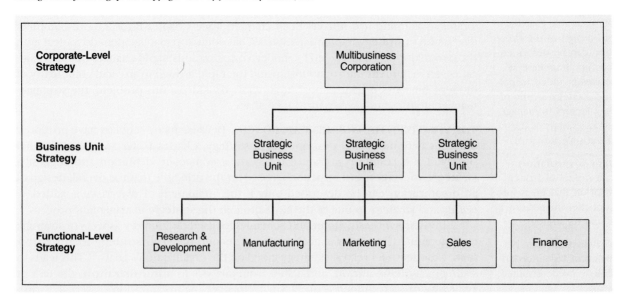

MANAGEMENT APPLICATION

Corporate Strategy at Chrysler

Lee Iacocca led Chrysler back from the brink. When he was brought in as chairman and CEO, Iacocca took the helm of a company that faced bankruptcy and had lost its direction. He cut costs, improved productivity, and shook up the company from senior management to advertising and operations, making Chrysler profitable and competitive once again.

Yet just as Iacocca was being hailed as a savior and Chrysler as the model of corporate success, the company found itself sinking back into the mire. Sales dropped 22.8 percent in 1987, competition increased, and demand shrank. After six fairly stable years, Chrysler's share of the domestic market fell from 12.1 percent to 10.6 percent in 1989. While sales in minivans and Jeeps were still solid, weak auto sales and high operating costs led to declining profits over the past five years—down to only 1 percent of Chrysler's $35 billion revenues in 1989. Meanwhile, Japanese car makers were opening new plants and increasing production. Chrysler is especially vulnerable to these changes; unlike other U.S. car makers who have hefty profits from European sales, the company sold its European connections during its last struggle for survival. Finally, Chrysler's new models have been criticized for years as being warmed-over versions of the K-car that lack the quality and innovation of competitors' models.

Iacocca has taken stock of these problems and forged a strategy to bring Chrysler back again. He is especially pessimistic about domestic demand, believing it will continue to shrink over the next few years. To take pressure off sagging U.S. sales, he has made a high priority of forging links to European markets. After unsuccessful negotiations with Fiat and other European groups, Chrysler established a joint venture with an Austrian firm, Steyr-Daimler-Puch AG, to build minivans (estimated at 25,000 per year). Other joint ventures are likely to follow.

Another key facet of Iacocca's plan has been to trim costs. Chrysler announced plans to cut $1.5 billion out of fixed costs. It has closed three U.S. plants since 1987, including the St. Louis plant in 1990. This greatly reduced operating costs, but left thousands of workers without jobs, increasing tensions between Chrysler and the UAW. In addition, Chrysler sold off the profitable Gulfstream Aerospace Corporation for $825 million to increase its cash holdings and to focus attention on the auto business.

A pensive Lee Iacocca.

To win back its share of the U.S. market, Chrysler has put much hope, energy, and funding into one key area: building "home run" or trend-setting autos like the Ford Taurus and the Chrysler minivan. The primary means of doing this have been restructuring Chrysler's much-maligned engineering division and pumping in more funding. Chrysler has also divided its engineers into new subgroups and introduced "simultaneous engineering," whereby teams of engineers from all divisions work together on a project.

Although sales continued to drop, Lee Iacocca remains confident. If the company survives the current recession, he holds, newly designed 1992 models should lift the company to new heights. At this point, only one thing is certain: Iacocca's decision to focus Chrysler's energies on developing trend-setting new cars will profoundly shape the company's success or failure over the next decade.

Sources: Edward K. Miller, "Chrysler Engineers Realign," *Ward's Auto World,* March 1989, p. 73; Doron P. Levin, "Chrysler's U-Turn in Car Design," *The New York Times,* May 7, 1989, Sect. 3, p. 1; Doron P. Levin, "Gulfstream to Be Sold by Chrysler," *The New York Times,* December 7, 1989, p. D1; Wendy Zellner, "Chrysler Heads Back to Earth," *Business Week,* December 18, 1989, p. 46; Joseph B. White, "Chrysler to Shut St. Louis Plant, Third Since '87," *The Wall Street Journal,* February 2, 1990, p. A3; Paul Ingrassia and Neal Templin, "Chrysler Corp. Posts Record Net Loss of $664 Million for the Fourth Quarter," *The Wall Street Journal,* February 14, 1990, p. A2; James B. Treece and David Woodruff, "Crunch Time Again for Chrysler," *Business Week,* March 25, 1991, pp. 92–94; Alex Taylor III, "Can Iacocca Fix Chrysler—Again?" *Fortune,* April 8, 1991, pp. 50–54.

Business-Unit Strategy

business-unit strategy
Strategy formulated to meet the goals of a particular business.

COORDINATED RESOURCE
Use Transparency 33, Strategic Business Units.

COORDINATED RESOURCE
See Study Guide Problem Exercise 7, "Strategic Business Unit Planning."

Business-unit strategy is concerned with managing the interests and operations of a particular business. It deals with such questions as: How will the business compete within its market? What products/services should it offer? Which customers does it seek to serve? How will resources be distributed within the business? Business-unit strategy attempts to determine what approach the business should take to its market and how it should conduct itself, given its resources and the conditions of the market.

Many corporations have extensive interests in different businesses, and top managers have difficulty organizing these corporations' complex and varied activities. One approach to dealing with this problem is to create strategic business units, each of which groups all business activities that produce a particular type of product or service and treats them as a single business unit. The corporate level provides a set of guidelines for the SBUs, which develop their own strategies on the business-unit level. The corporate level then reviews the SBU plans and negotiates changes if necessary. Single-business corporations use business-unit-level strategy unless they are contemplating expanding into other types of business. At that point, strategic planning on the corporate level becomes necessary.

Functional-Level Strategy

functional-level strategy
Strategy formulated by a specific functional area in an effort to carry out business-unit strategy.

Functional-level strategy creates the framework for the management of functions—such as finance, research and development, and marketing—so that they support the business-unit-level strategy. For example, if the business-unit strategy calls for the development of a new product, the R&D department will create plans on how to develop that product.

■ CORPORATE-LEVEL STRATEGY

COORDINATED RESOURCE
Use Transparency 34, The Strategic Management Process.

Steven Wheelwright describes two major approaches to corporate strategy: the values-based approach and the corporate portfolio approach.[31]

The Values-Based Approach

In this approach, the beliefs and convictions (values) of managers and workers about how the firm should conduct its business are the key to setting the organization's long-term direction. Values-based strategies tend to develop gradually and incrementally, providing general guidance rather than a narrowly focused plan. Consensus among organizational members is important; often there is a "company way" of doing things that shapes strategy. Firms such as Johnson & Johnson and Hewlett-Packard, as well as many Japanese companies, take this approach. Another example is Ben and Jerry's, the small New England maker of super-premium ice creams. It has rented billboards in South Boston to express its opposition to the Seabrook, New Hampshire, nuclear power plant and publicly advocates other causes. In addition, it conducts an annual evaluation of other companies' social responsibility, and recently promised that 7.5 percent of the pretax profits from a new flavor, Rainforest Crunch, would go toward saving the Amazon rain forests. (For additional insight on this approach, see the Ethics in Management box.)

The Corporate Portfolio Approach

In this approach, top management evaluates each of the corporation's various business units with respect to the marketplace and the corporation's internal makeup. When all business units have been evaluated, an appropriate strategic role is devel-

What Do You *Stand* For?

Peter Drucker and other management consultants and theorists used to argue that the most important question for managers to ask was: What's your business? The emphasis on clearly defining *what* business an organization was in captured the creative and intellectual imagination of an entire generation of management thinkers. The literature of the field is filled with stories about consultants who made a fortune by informing managers, "You aren't in the tin can business, you are in the packaging business." Theodore Leavitt's famous article, "Marketing Myopia," which sought to broaden the production and marketing horizon of managers, became a bible for a generation seeking to define their businesses more broadly.

But another question lurks at the heart of strategic management decisions: What do you *stand* for? This question calls for a statement of values and principles, for an answer to questions about *why* a company did what it did. The critic who asks, "Why did AT&T agree to divest the Bell operating companies?" may want to know *what* options were available to AT&T, but it is even more likely that the critic wants to know what values and principles lay behind AT&T's decision. Drucker and others call such a statement of values and principles "Enterprise Strategy" ("E-Strategy" for short).

At least seven different Enterprise Strategies have been identified in the literature concerned with this issue:

1. *Stockholder E-Strategy:* The corporation should maximize the interests of stockholders.

2. *Managerial Prerogative E-Strategy:* The corporation should maximize the interests of management.

3. *Restricted Stakeholder E-Strategy:* The corporation should maximize the interests of a narrow set of stakeholders, such as customers, employees, and stockholders.

4. *Unrestricted Stakeholder E-Strategy:* The corporation should maximize the interest of all stakeholders.

5. *Social Harmony E-Strategy:* The corporation should maximize social harmony.

6. *Rawlsian E-Strategy:* The corporation should promote inequality among stakeholders only if inequality results in raising the level of the worst-off stakeholder.

7. *Personal Projects E-Strategy:* The corporation should maximize its ability to enable corporate members to carry out their personal projects.

Although these brief statements become immensely more complicated when any organization attempts to put them into practice, the trend toward looking at the ethical foundations of strategy is likely to continue—especially given the uncertain environment of today's organizations and the increasingly critical eye with which its decisions are being examined.

Source: R. Edward Freeman and Daniel J. Gilbert, Jr., *Corporate Strategy and the Search for Ethics* (Englewood Cliffs, N.J.: Prentice Hall, 1988).

COORDINATED RESOURCE
Use Transparency 38, The BCG Matrix.

portfolio framework An approach to corporate-level strategy advocated by the Boston Consulting Group; also known as the BCG matrix.

oped for each unit with the goal of improving the overall performance of the organization. The corporate portfolio approach is rational and analytical, is guided primarily by market opportunities, and tends to be initiated and controlled by top management only. Texas Instruments is one company that has used the corporate portfolio approach extensively.

THE BCG MATRIX. One of the best-known examples of the corporate portfolio approach is the **portfolio framework** advocated by the Boston Consulting Group. This framework is also known as the BCG matrix.[32]

The BCG approach focuses on three aspects of a particular business unit: its sales, the growth of its market, and whether it absorbs or produces cash in its operations. The approach seeks to develop a balance among business units that use up cash and those that supply cash.

Figure 7-4 shows a four-square BCG matrix in which business units can be plotted according to the rate of growth of their market segment and their relative

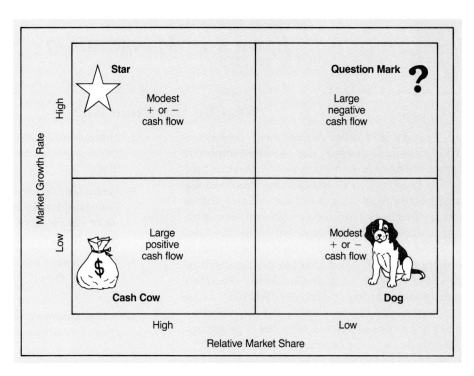

FIGURE 7-4 The BCG Matrix

Source: Reprinted by permission of Arnoldo C. Hax and Nicolas S. Majluf, "The Use of the Growth-Share Matrix in Strategic Planning," *Interfaces* 13, no. 1 (February 1983). Copyright © 1983, The Institute of Management Sciences.

A Portfolio Approach. Lacking the funds to compete in the volatile personal-care market, Gillette has cut ad budgets for these products, whose profits will be used to support Gillette's 63-percent share of the razor market.

market share. A business unit in the *question mark* category—a business with a relatively small market share in a rapidly growing market—can be an uncertain and expensive venture. The rapid growth of the market may force it to invest heavily simply to maintain its low share, even though that low market share is yielding low or perhaps negative profits and cash flow. Increasing the question mark's share of the market relative to the market leader would require still larger investments. Yet the rapid growth of the market segment offers exciting opportunities if the proper business strategy—and the funds to implement it—can be found.

A business in the *star* category—high relative market share in a rapidly growing market—should be quite profitable. However, the need to go on investing in order to keep up with the market's rapid growth may consume more cash than is currently being earned. The *cash cow*—high relative market share in a slowly growing market—is both profitable and a source of excess cash. The slow growth of the market does not require large investments to maintain market position. Finally, the *dog*—a business with low relative market share in a slowly growing or stagnant market—is seen as a moderate user or supplier of cash.

A "success sequence" in the BCG matrix involves investing cash from *cash cows* and the more successful *dogs* in selected *question marks* to enable them to become *stars* by increasing their relative market shares. When the rate of market growth slows, the *stars* will become *cash cows,* generating excess cash to invest in the next generation of promising *question marks.*

CRITIQUES OF THE BCG MATRIX. The BCG matrix was the most widely used corporate portfolio approach in the 1970s and 1980s.[33] However, it received its share of criticism[34]—not the least of which is associated with the clever and colorful names given to business units in the matrix. Since the dividing line in Figure 7-5 between high and low market growth is typically 10 percent per year in physical units, and since only the single market-share leader is classified as "high" in market share, using

the BCG matrix results in classifying about 60 to 70 percent of all business units as
"dogs." This misleading label encourages business managers to neglect the prospects
and opportunities of those businesses.[35] Similarly, the concept underlying the "cash
cow" encourages managers to milk the cow—or use its revenues to fund *other*
businesses—when the cash cow itself may be an excellent candidate for further
investment. Obviously, skillful analysis can avoid these dangers, but the BCG approach tends to encourage rather simplistic approaches to complex problems and
situations.

■ BUSINESS-UNIT STRATEGY: PORTER'S FRAMEWORK

One well-known example of business-unit strategy was developed by Michael Porter
of Harvard Business School.[36] In Porter's view, an organization's ability to compete
in a given market is determined by that organization's technical and economic resources, as well as by five environmental "forces," each of which threatens the
organization's venture into a new market. The manager of a business unit, says Porter, must analyze these forces and propose a program for influencing or defending
against them.

The Five Forces

Porter's five environmental forces are threats to entry, the bargaining power of
consumers, the bargaining power of suppliers, the threat of substitute products, and
jockeying for position in crowded markets. Figure 7-5 is a schematic view of how
these forces influence a company's competitive decisions.

FIGURE 7-5 Porter's Summary of Forces Governing Industrial Competition
Source: Michael E. Porter, "How Competitive Forces Shape Strategy," *Harvard Business Review* 57, no. 2 (March–April
1979):141. Copyright © 1979 by the President and Fellows of Harvard College, all rights reserved.

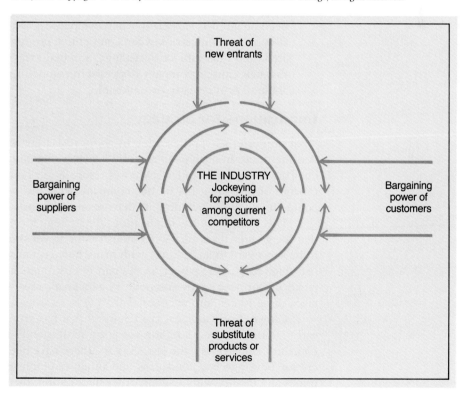

COORDINATED RESOURCE

See Samaras Case 2.3, "Barriers and the Convenience Store."

1. *The barriers to entry.* This topic is covered extensively in Exhibit 7-2.

2. *The bargaining power of customers.* As new companies enter the field and consumer options become greater, conditions of profitability can change radically. For example, when a large segment of the U.S. wine-producing industry stepped up diversification and advertising in the 1960s and 1970s, entry into the field became more difficult because consumers were aware of an already existing broad range in choice and price. Consumers also have power when products are particularly expensive or when advertising helps them realize that a range of products is relatively undifferentiated.

3. *The bargaining power of suppliers.* If an industry (say, soft-drink producers facing competition from powdered mixes and concentrated beverages) is not realistically able to raise prices to cover the cost of necessary goods and services, the power of the supplier of goods and services naturally increases. Among other things, the supplier is generally powerful if the industry is dominated by only a few competitors or if the purchasing industry is only of moderate importance to the supplier. By contrast, the buyer can exercise power if it purchases in large volume, if the low-profit performance of the product makes the buyer cost-conscious about its material or ingredients, or if the buyer can threaten to manufacture the seller's product itself. U.S. automakers, for example, have often used the threat of self-manufacture in their negotiations with suppliers.

4. *The threat of substitute products.* If a product can be upgraded or differentiated in the interest of higher profitability, buyers can substitute products normally furnished by traditional suppliers. Strategic managers must pay special attention to products with an ongoing or current history of improved price performance because of substitute products. (The sugar industry has certainly learned its lesson in an era of American weight consciousness and the availability of fructose corn syrup.)

5. *Jockeying for position.* What Porter calls "advertising slugfests" have become a staple of everyday television programming. If competitors are numerous and roughly equal in advertising energy (say, fast-food chains), competition can become intense, especially when competitors are fighting for market shares of slow-growth industries, when competitive products are relatively undifferentiated (and thus subject to raiding), or when *exit barriers*—a variety of factors that may cause a company to persist in competing despite questionable profitability—prove costly or unflexible.

Implications for Strategy

What do Porter's hypotheses tell us about the larger issue of strategy formulation? For one thing, an analysis of these five factors can contribute to an evaluation of a company's strengths and weaknesses. More importantly, the strategist should be capable of providing his or her company with the best possible position in the competitive field—including its defenses against current or potential competitors.

This framework has implications for strategy formulation. Porter hypothesizes that the greater the forces in an industry, the lower the average returns. Therefore, to be successful in an industry with many new entrants, numerous substitute products, high bargaining power on the part of customers and suppliers, and a constant jockeying for position by competitors, a company must carefully craft a strategy that takes these forces into account.

Crown, Cork and Seal is a company that has grown from $200 million in the early 1960s to over $1 billion today by understanding the forces at work in the container industry. For the last 35 years, there have been many large single customers for beverage and food cans and other can-industry products who can affect prices and quality with a single order. In addition, the suppliers to can companies

EXHIBIT 7-2 Porter's Six Barriers to Market Entry

1. *Economies of scale.* These economies deter entry by forcing the aspirant either to come in on a large scale or to accept a cost disadvantage. Scale economies in production, research, marketing, and service are probably the key barriers to entry in the mainframe computer industry, as Xerox and GE sadly discovered.

2. *Product differentiation.* Brand identification creates a barrier by forcing entrants to spend heavily to overcome customer loyalty. Advertising, customer service, being first in the industry, and product differences are among the factors fostering brand identification. For example, to create high fences around their businesses, brewers couple brand identification with economies of scale in production, distribution, and marketing.

3. *Capital requirements.* The need to invest large financial resources in order to compete creates a barrier to entry, particularly if the capital is required for unrecoverable expenditures in up-front advertising or R&D. Capital is necessary not only for fixed facilities but also for customer credit, inventories, and absorbing start-up losses. For example, an industry like mineral extraction is likely to entail immense initial capital requirements.

4. *Cost disadvantage independent of size.* Entrenched companies may have cost advantages not available to potential rivals, no matter what their size and attainable economies of scale. These advantages can stem from the effects of the learning curve (and of its first cousin, the experience curve), proprietary technology, access to the best raw material sources, assets purchased at preinflation prices, government subsidies, or favorable locations.

5. *Access to distribution channels.* The new boy on the block, must, of course, secure distribution of his product or service. A new food product, for example, must displace others from the supermarket shelf via price breaks, promotions, intense selling efforts, or some other means.

6. *Government policy.* The government can limit or even foreclose entry to industries with such controls as license requirements and limits on access to raw materials. Regulated industries like trucking, liquor retailing, and freight forwarding are noticeable examples; more subtle government restrictions operate in fields like ski-area development and coal mining.

Porter also advises that any organization desiring to compete in a new market analyze its incumbent competitors' likely reactions, especially if:

1. The incumbents possess substantial resources to fight back, including excess cash and unused borrowing power, productive capacity, or clout with distribution channels and customers.

2. The incumbents seem likely to cut prices because of a desire to keep market shares or because of industrywide excess capacity.

3. Industry growth is slow, affecting the organization's ability to absorb the new arrival and probably causing the financial performance of all the parties involved to decline.

Source: Reprinted by permission of the *Harvard Business Review.* An excerpt from "How Competitive Forces Shape Strategy" by Michael E. Porter (March–April 1979). Copyright © 1979 by the President and Fellows of Harvard College; all rights reserved.

like Crown are large integrated steel and aluminum companies, and Crown has no effect on the price of its raw materials. New technologies, such as plastics, cardboard, and new metals, threatened Crown, while large customers began to integrate backward into can-making activities. There was fierce competition among National Can, Continental Can, Crown, and others. It was only by understanding these forces and executing a focused strategy that Crown, Cork and Seal was able to survive and flourish, posting over 20 years of increased returns to shareholders.

CRITIQUE OF PORTER'S FRAMEWORK. Although Porter's framework has become widely used in the last ten years, it has been criticized from two perspectives. The first is typified by the famous case of the United States Football League, which struggled for survival against its entrenched rival, the National Football League. Critics charged that the NFL, following Porter's model, erected entry barriers against the USFL, and in general tried to influence the five forces in ways that seemed to violate the antitrust laws. Of course, this was a complex case involving unions, media, and other groups, but it does seem that Porter's approach avoids both legal and ethical analyses of the role of organizational power. The second critical perspective holds that Porter's approach ignores many of the external stakeholders we discovered in Chapter 3.[37] By focusing only on the five forces, it is possible to overlook many groups, such as consumer activists and environmentalists, that can have major effects on an organization. One possible response is that these groups are important only insofar as they can affect the competitive dynamics—the five forces—in an industry. But from a managerial point of view, it is the stakeholder relationships that must be managed, not the five forces.

■ FUNCTIONAL-LEVEL STRATEGY

In a *functional organization,* separate business functions such as marketing and finance are grouped within separate departments, each of which must develop a strategy that will help carry out higher-level strategies.

Functional strategies are more detailed than organizational strategies and have shorter time horizons. Their purpose is threefold: (1) to communicate short-term objectives, (2) to describe the actions needed to achieve short-term objectives, and (3) to create an environment that encourages their achievement. It is critical that lower-level managers participate in the development of functional strategies so that they will better understand what needs to be done and feel more committed to the plan.

Functional strategies must also be coordinated with one another to minimize inevitable conflicts and improve the chances of meeting organization goals. Each functional area has different responsibilities and therefore different priorities. Marketing, for example, is bound to want high inventories of finished goods so that customer orders can be filled quickly; finance will want to keep inventories—and hence costs—down. Such conflicts can be settled by referring to the organization's overall strategy. Typical functional units are marketing, finance, production/operations, research and development, and human resources/personnel.

Marketing

Marketing strategies match products and services with customer needs, decide where and when to sell and promote products, and set prices. The approach depends (1) on whether the company is addressing existing customers or is trying to attract new ones and (2) on whether the product is new or already established.[38]

Market penetration is an attempt to expand the organization's control of a market in which it already has a product or service. For example, the Hanes Corporation, already established in the market for men's hosiery, used innovative packaging and sales promotion, distribution through drugstores and supermarkets, discounts, and a massive ad campaign to win a larger share of the women's hosiery market with its L'eggs pantyhose offering.

Market development introduces an existing product or service to new customers. One example is the expansion of Coors Beer from the western part of the United States throughout the rest of the country. *Product development* does the reverse: It creates a new product or service for existing customers—for example, when a company specializing in frozen foods expands its product line.

Diversification marketing involves both a new product and new customers. For example, an entrepreneur might launch a new publication design and production service that relies on desktop publishing software and laser printers.

Finance

Finance strategies are concerned with the acquisition and allocation of capital and the management of working capital and dividends. Unlike other functional strategies, finance strategies must have long-term as well as short-term components. Some typical issues are record keeping, calculating financial needs, managing debt, and dealing with creditors.

Production/Operations

This functional area is concerned with the transformation of materials, labor, and capital inputs into products or services. Strategic decisions include plant size and location, the selection of equipment, inventory size and control, wages and supervision, and product design and engineering. In the mobile-home industry, for example, Winnebago has opted for a single large production center located near critical raw materials as part of its strategy to automate and integrate production. One of its competitors, Fleetwood, has decided instead on multiple production facilities located near various markets. Fleetwood rarely replaces equipment and relies on labor-intensive production techniques.[39] For more on operations, see Chapter 21.

Research and Development

Organizations engage in research and development to be sure their products, services, and production methods do not become obsolete. They may choose to carry out basic research to increase their technical knowledge, applied research to create a commercial application, or development research to develop a new or improved product or process. The research may be done in-house or contracted outside; it may be a long- or short-term program.

Human Resources/Personnel

Human resource management includes recruiting, training, and counseling employees; determining compensation; and maintaining contact with both unions and governments. Its objective is to attract, motivate, and retain those employees required by the organization. Depending on whether the organizational strategy calls for growth or retrenchment, the human resources strategy may be geared to increasing or reducing employee numbers.

ILLUSTRATIVE CASE STUDY

WRAP-UP

Planning for the Future at Federal Express

Federal Express's continued success will depend in large part on how well it understands its business and the factors that influence it. As the ZapMail experiment indicates, the information-delivery market is made up of several segments, each of which presents different competitive forces. In addition, now that Federal Express has entered the cargo business, it must learn to deal with new and different market conditions and competitors.

At the corporate level, Smith and his associates have to incorporate these various projects into a coherent strategy that will allocate resources wisely. At

the business-unit level, Federal Express managers must know the critical features and requirements of each of their information-delivery services.

Smith's effective challenge to such well-established businesses as United Parcel Service and the U.S. Postal Service provides important lessons for other corporate leaders. His bold vision and commitment to customers and service are important to Federal Express's success, but this vision and commitment would be worthless without Smith's skill in strategic planning. ■

■ SUMMARY

Peter Drucker's criteria of effectiveness and efficiency parallel the two aspects of planning: setting the "right" goals and then choosing the "right" means for attaining those goals. Goals are important because (1) they provide a sense of direction, (2) they focus our efforts, (3) they guide our plans and decisions, and (4) they help us evaluate our progress. Although planning is normally shown as just one of the four management functions, it is more appropriate to think of planning as a locomotive that drives a train of organizing, leading, and controlling activities.

Organizations use two main types of plans. Strategic plans, created by top and middle managers, aim to meet the organization's broad goals, while operational plans show how strategic plans will be implemented in day-to-day endeavors. Strategic plans and operational plans are linked by goals and objectives, which should reflect the organization's mission statement, the broad goal that justifies the organization's existence. Mission statements are based on planning premises, basic assumptions about the organization's purpose, its values, its distinctive competencies, and its place in the world. Strategic plans and operational plans differ in their time horizons, their scope, their complexity and impact, and their independence.

The formal planning process requires the manager to follow nine steps that result in the setting of goals, the identification of current objectives and strategy, an analysis of the environment and available resources, the identification of strategic opportunities and threats, the identification of performance gaps, decision making, implementation, and measurement and control of progress.

The term *strategy* is used in two ways: to refer to what an organization *actively* intends to do or to describe its *passive* reaction to environmental changes. Both anecdotal evidence and research have demonstrated the value of actively pursuing strategic management. Today's concept of strategic management grew out of the policy-formulation and initial-strategy approaches developed to cope with the many changes following World War II.

Organizations use three levels of strategy: corporate-level, business-unit level, and functional-level strategy. Corporate-level strategy can use either the values-based approach or the corporate portfolio approach. The BCG matrix is the best-known example of the portfolio approach. A well-known example of business-unit strategy is Porter's framework. Functional-level strategies, which set goals for specific functional areas, are more detailed and involve shorter time periods than higher-level strategies, which help coordinate efforts and resolve conflicts.

■ REVIEW QUESTIONS

1. What are Peter Drucker's criteria for judging managerial performance? How are they related to planning?
2. Explain the four reasons goals are important to planning.
3. What are the two types of plans and how are they related? Different?
4. Explain the nine steps that make up the formal planning process.
5. Explain the two ways the term *strategy* is used.
6. How did our current concept of strategy develop?
7. What are the three levels of strategy and how are they different?
8. How do the values-based and corporate portfolio approaches differ?
9. What is the BCG matrix and how can it guide corporate-level strategy? What are its disadvantages?
10. Describe Porter's framework for business-unit strategy.
11. How is functional-level strategy different from the other levels of strategy?
12. How can strategy help resolve conflicts between different functional areas?

CASE STUDY

Planning for Diversified Activities in a Changing Environment

John Sullivan is CEO of Diversified Conglomerate Incorporated (DCI), a leader in air compressors and basketball backboards, both low-growth industries, and coffee imports, a high-growth industry. In addition, DCI has a substantial presence in baby beds and inner-spring mattresses and has recently started ventures in biotechnology and retailing gourmet coffee; other ventures are planned. Also, there are 15 other businesses in which DCI engages to varying degrees. In short, DCI is a company with many diverse and unrelated businesses and with many diverse people involved in different projects.

John Sullivan has a problem that is solely a function of DCI's diversification. He needs to be able to allocate resources across a wide range of businesses that do not have much in common. He must compare baby beds with air compressors, and he needs a *language* of some kind to make such comparisons.

George Russell is the division manager at DCI responsible for baby beds. The business is in a difficult position. After years of flat sales, the market for baby beds has been growing for several years because baby-boom women have been starting families. However, an increasing share of that market is going to K-Mart, Wal-Mart, and Sears—the large retailers. DCI manufactures the wooden parts of the beds but buys the brackets and other metal parts. Recently, one source of supply went out of business, leaving only one U.S. firm and one Taiwanese firm capable of sup-

plying the quantity of parts that DCI needs. There are also several new companies in the industry that have more features than DCI's best bed and that command premium prices. Moreover, Russell suspects that the Taiwanese supplier is set to enter the U.S. market with two products that would compete directly with his low-end beds. To ice the cake, a recent study questioned the use of baby beds or cribs altogether, touting a new idea—the infant "sleep carousel"—as producing a happier baby.

Both John Sullivan and George Russell have strategic problems that are of the utmost importance to DCI.

Source: Adapted from R. Edward Freeman and Daniel R. Gilbert, Jr., *Corporate Strategy and the Search for Ethics* (Englewood Cliffs, N.J.: Prentice Hall, 1988).

Case Questions

1. Use the BCG approach to help John Sullivan think about the strategy for DCI. Are there obvious products that are stars, cash cows, question marks, and dogs?

2. How would Porter's model analyze George Russell's situation?

3. To what extent can the methods of strategic planning give the managers at DCI a means of talking to each other about their common problems? What are some disadvantages?

VIDEO CASE STUDY

Raiding the Redwoods

Pacific Lumber Company has been good to the town of Scotia, California, for over one hundred years. In fact, one might take the relationship Pacific Lumber has with the town as a model for employer–employee and business–environment relations. In this town of 1,100, a job with Pacific Lumber was a job for life. It included company housing, a scholarship fund for children of employees, a pension fund for retirees, and a harvest/replenish plan that would keep the redwood trees it depended on growing forever. This was particularly impressive, given the fact that many consider the redwoods a national treasure—

and an endangered one, since over 95 percent of the virgin forests have been cut down. However, recent events have changed things dramatically.

Charles Hurwitz, a well-known corporate raider, bought Pacific Lumber in 1985 for $745 million, taken mostly from high-yield junk bonds. The buyout was made much easier by the large tracts of forest land Pacific Lumber owned but sparingly harvested, along with its more than 5,000 acres of virgin redwood forests.

Pacific Lumber's strategy in taking light harvests was to ensure the long-term survival of the redwoods and thus the company. Unfortunately, this also made the company "lumber rich" and a prime target for takeover.

Under pressure to meet interest payments of $80 million per year on the high-yield junk bonds used to buy Pacific Lumber, Hurwitz soon changed the company's conservative strategy. He raided the money in the pension fund and more than doubled the harvest rates, creating working conditions many argue are unsafe. Employees, the town as a whole, and environmentalists everywhere are deeply worried by these changes, especially the stepped-up harvests, which threaten to wipe out vast segments of the forests and create gaps of several years between harvestable trees. Workers feel that Hurwitz's heavy-handed management style and his priorities—

particularly his push for short-term payoffs—are out of step with what they want and what they think is best for the company.

Case Questions

1. Given the company's huge untapped resources, was the original owners' strategy in the best interests of the environment? of the company?

2. What kind of planning and strategy techniques could the previous owners of Pacific Lumber have used to prevent the hostile takeover of Hurwitz?

3. Is there a strategy Hurwitz or his employees can adopt to prevent the apparently reckless management of the redwood forests?

■ NOTES

[1]See Peter F. Drucker, *Managing for Results* (New York: Harper & Row, 1964), and *The Effective Executive* (New York: Harper & Row, 1967).

[2]Joshua Hyatt, "Sole Survivors," *Inc.,* October 1987, pp. 115–120.

[3]Quoted in Charles H. Granger, "The Hierarchy of Objectives," *Harvard Business Review* 42, no. 3 (May–June 1964):63–74.

[4]Jeremy Main, "Waking Up AT&T: There's Life After Culture Shock," *Fortune,* December 24, 1984, pp. 66–74.

[5]Robert H. Hayes and Steven C. Wheelwright, *Restoring Our Competitive Edge Through Manufacturing* (New York: Wiley, 1984), pp. 27–28.

[6]Patricia Sellers, "Coke Gets Off Its Can in Europe," *Fortune,* August 12, 1990, pp. 67–73.

[7]Our discussion is based mainly on Charles W. Hofer, *Strategy Formulation: Issues and Concepts,* 2nd ed. (St. Paul, Minn.: West Publishing, 1986); Dan E. Schendel and Charles W. Hofer, eds., *Strategic Management: A New View of Business Policy and Planning* (Boston: Little, Brown, 1978); Kenneth R. Andrews, *The Concept of Corporate Strategy,* rev. ed. (Homewood, Ill.: Dow Jones-Irwin, 1980); and J. Kalman Cohen and Richard M. Cyert, "Strategy: Formulation, Implementation, and Monitoring," *Journal of Business* 46, no. 3 (July 1973):349–367. See also Max Richards, *Setting Strategic Goals and Objectives* (St. Paul, Minn.: West Publishing, 1986); and Glenn Boseman, Arvind Phatak, and Robert Schellenberger, *Strategic Management* (New York: Wiley, 1986).

[8]This perspective, while essentially accurate, does not emphasize the active debate concerning the proper societal roles (purposes) of business, government, and other types of organizations, and it minimizes both the ambiguity of their roles and the role changes that continue to take place today.

[9]Thomas J. Peters and Robert H. Waterman, Jr., *In Search of Excellence* (New York: Harper & Row, 1982); and Richard Tanner Pascale and Anthony G. Athos, *The Art of Japanese Management: Applications for American Executives* (New York: Simon & Schuster, 1981).

[10]Our model of the formal strategic planning process starts with the goal-formulation process, but other approaches are also used. For example, the process can start by focusing on current strategies and organizational strengths; the preexisting objectives are accepted with little or no further scrutiny. See Steven C. Wheelwright, "Strategic Planning in the Small Business," *Business Horizons* 14, no. 4 (August 1971):51–58; and Michael B. McCaskey, "A Contingency Approach to Planning: Planning with Goals and Planning without Goals," *Academy of Management Journal* 17, no. 2 (June 1974):281–291. Also see Peter Grinyer, Shawki Al-Bazzaz, and Masoud Yasai-Ardekani, "Towards a Contingency Theory of Corporate Planning," *Strategic Management Journal* 7 (1986):3–28.

[11]Hofer, *Strategy Formulation.* Henry Mintzberg also feels that managers need to be aware of the environment and the relative power of its stakeholders when setting goals; see his *Power in and Around Organizations* (Englewood Cliffs, N.J.: Prentice Hall, 1983), and "Power and Organizational Life Cycles," *Academy of Management Review* 9 (April 1984):207–224. See also Harold E. Klein and Robert E. Linneman, "Strategic Environmental Assessment: An Emergent Typology of Corporate Planning Practice," *Contribution of Theory and Research to the Practice of Management* (Proceedings of the Southern Management Association, New Orleans, November 1982):4–9.

[12]James M. Utterback, "Environmental Analysis and Forecasting," in Schendel and Hofer, eds., *Strategic Management,* p. 135. See also Utterback's article, pp. 134–144, and Harold E. Klein's commentary on it, pp. 144–151, for discussions on the use of environmental analysis in strategy formulation.

[13]Ian C. MacMillan, "Commentary," in Schendel and Hofer, eds., *Strategic Management,* p. 171.

[14]See William L. Sammon, Mark A. Kurland, and Robert Spitalnic, *Business Competitor Intelligence* (New York: Wiley, 1984); and Liam Fahey and V. K. Narayanah, *Environmental Analysis* (St. Paul, Minn.: West Publishing, 1986).

[15]Richard P. Rumelt, "Evaluation of Strategy," in Schendel and Hofer, eds., *Strategic Management.*

[16]See David A. Aaker, "How to Select a Business Strategy," *California Management Review* 26, no. 3 (Spring 1984):167–175. Aaker has suggested that the accuracy of a strategy's evaluation increases when factors beyond sales and profit forecasts are included, such as judgments of its flexibility, feasibility, consistency with the firm's mission, and responsiveness to the environment.

[17]For a history of the concept of strategy, see Roger Evered, "So What *Is* Strategy?" *Long Range Planning* 16, no. 3 (June 1983):57–72. Recent research is contributing to our understanding of organizational strategy. See Ari Ginsberg, "Operationalizing Organizational Strategy: Toward an Integrative Framework," *Academy of Management Review* 9, no. 3 (July 1984):548–557; and James W. Frederickson, "Strategic Process Research: Questions and Recommendations," *Academy of Management Review* 8, no. 4 (October 1983):565–575.

[18]Our discussion of strategy and strategic planning in this chapter draws upon Schendel and Hofer, eds., *Strategic Management.* However, our classifications and interpretations differ somewhat from theirs.

[19]For research showing the value of strategic planning to industry, see Stanley S. Thune and Robert J. House, "Where Long-Range Planning Pays Off," *Business Horizons* 13, no. 4 (August 1970):81–87; David M. Herold, "Long-Range Planning and Organizational Performance," *Academy of Management Journal* 15, no. 1 (March 1972):91–102; and Zafar A. Malik and Delmar W. Karger, "Does Long-Range Planning Improve Company Performance?" *Management Review* 64, no. 9 (September 1975):27–31. For research showing the benefits of strategic planning in the service sector, see D. Robley Wood, Jr., and R. Lawrence LaForge, "The Impact of Comprehensive Planning on Financial Performance," *Academy of Management Journal* 22, no. 3 (September 1979):516–526. Also see Lawrence C. Rhyne, "The Relationship of Strategic Planning to Financial Performance," *Strategic Management Journal* 7 (1986):423–436. In contrast, no positive relationship was found in the service sector by two other investigators: Robert M. Fulmer and Leslie W. Rue, "The Practice and Profitability of Long-Range Planning," *Managerial Planning* 22, no. 6 (May–June 1974):1–7. This may be because many of the service organizations studied had begun their planning activities too recently for the systems to begin to have an effect.

[20]Daniel Gilbert, Edwin Hartman, John Mauriel, and Edward Freeman, *A Logic for Strategy* (Boston: Ballinger Press, 1988).

[21]Quoted in Alfred D. Chandler, Jr., *Strategy and Structure: Chapters in the History of the American Industrial Enterprise* (Cambridge, Mass.: MIT Press, 1962), p. 325.

[22]Richard Rumelt, *Strategy, Structure, and Economic Performance* (Boston: Graduate School of Business Administration, Harvard University, 1974).

[23]Schendel and Hofer, eds., *Strategic Management,* pp. 7–18.

[24]Chandler, *Strategy and Structure,* p. 16.

[25]Andrews, *The Concept of Corporate Strategy;* H. Igor Ansoff, *Corporate Strategy: An Analytic Approach to Business Policy for Growth and Expansion* (New York: McGraw-Hill, 1965). See also Edmund P. Learned, C. Roland Christensen, Kenneth R. Andrews, and William D. Guth, *Business Policy: Text and Cases* (Homewood, Ill.: Irwin, 1965).

[26]Charles W. Hofer and Dan E. Schendel, *Strategy Formulation: Analytical Concepts* (St. Paul: West Publishing, 1978).

[27]This task is highly theoretical and controversial, mainly because researchers cannot agree on whether goal setting should be separate from strategy formulation. For more on this debate, see Thomas J. McNichols, *Policy Making and Executive Action: Cases on Business Policy* (New York: McGraw-Hill, 1972); Frank T. Paine and William Naumes, *Strategy and Policy Formation: An Integrative Approach* (Philadelphia: Saunders, 1974); Hugo Uyterhoeven, Robert Ackerman, and John Rosenblum, *Strategy and Organization* (Homewood, Ill.: Irwin, 1973).

[28]For a discussion of some of the finer distinctions between the formulation and implementation of strategy, see also Arthur A. Thompson, Jr., and A. J. Strickland III, *Strategy Formulation and Implementation: Tasks of the General Manager,* 3rd ed. (Dallas: Business Publications, 1986).

[29]The discussions of levels of strategy and corporate-level strategy are drawn largely from Thompson and Strickland, *Strategy Formulation and Implementation.* Also see Paul Miesing and Joseph Wolfe, "The Art and Science of Planning at the Business Unit Level," *Management Science* 31, no. 6 (June 1985):773–781.

[30]Peter F. Drucker, *The Practice of Management* (New York: Harper & Row, 1954), pp. 65–83.

[31]Steven C. Wheelwright, "Strategy, Management, and Strategic Planning Approaches," *Interfaces* 14, no. 1 (January–February 1984):19–33.

[32]See Allan Gerald, "A Note on the Boston Consulting Group Concept of Competitive Analysis and Corporate Strategy," *Intercollegiate Case Clearing House* 9 (June 1976):175; Milton Leontiades, *Strategies for Diversification and Change* (Boston: Little, Brown, 1980), p. 63; Schendel and Hofer, eds., *Strategic Management,* pp. 11–14.

[33]A survey of U.S. companies by Phillipe Haspeslagh (*Harvard Business Review* 60, no. 1 [January–February 1982]:58–73) concluded that by 1979, 36 percent of Fortune 1000 and 45 percent of Fortune 500 industrial companies had introduced this approach.

[34]For a further discussion of the BCG matrix, see Barry Hedley, "A Fundamental Approach to Strategy Development," *Long Range Planning* 9, no. 6 (December 1976):2–11. For a critique, see Thompson and Strickland, *Strategy Formulation and Implementation.*

[35]For example, "dogs" are frequently seen as providing only minimal cash flow, if any. However, recent research has concluded that the average dog has enough positive cash flow to finance one question mark. Donald C. Hambrick, Ian C. MacMillan, and Diane L. Day, "Strategic Attributes and Performance on the BCG Matrix—A PIMS-Based Analysis of Industrial Product Businesses," *Academy of Management Journal* 25, no. 3 (September 1982):510–531.

[36]Michael E. Porter, "How Competitive Forces Shape Strategy," *Harvard Business Review* 57, no. 2 (1979):137–145. See also Porter, *Competitive Strategy: Techniques for Analyzing Industries and Competitors* (New York: Free Press, 1980); and *Competitive Advantage: Creating and Sustaining Superior Performance* (New York: Free Press, 1985). See as well Gregory G. Dess and Peter S. Davis, "Porter's (1980) Generic Strategies and Performance: An Empirical Examination with American Data—Part I: Testing Porter," *Organization Studies*, no. 1 (1986):37–55; and "Porter's (1980) Generic Strategies and Performance: An Empirical Examination with American Data—Part II: Performance Implications," *Organization Studies*, no. 3 (1986):255–261.

[37]R. E. Freeman, *Strategic Management: A Stakeholder Approach* (Boston: Pitman Publishing, 1984).

[38]Lloyd L. Byars, *Concepts of Strategic Management Planning and Implementation* (New York: Harper & Row, 1984), pp. 200–202.

[39]John A. Pearce II and Richard B. Robinson, Jr., *Formulation and Implementation of Competitive Strategy* (Homewood, Ill.: Richard D. Irwin, 1985), p. 310.

CHAPTER EIGHT

STRATEGY IMPLEMENTATION

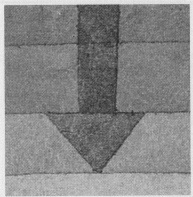

Detail from Paul Klee, *Scheidung Abends.*

Upon completing this chapter, you should be able to:

1. Explain the key aspects of strategy implementation and its relationship to strategic planning.

2. Match strategic problems with an appropriate approach to strategy implementation.

3. Describe Chandler's thesis concerning the three stages in the growth and development of an organization's strategy and structure.

4. List the seven factors in the Seven-S model and explain how they interact in strategy implementation.

5. Explain the concept of institutionalizing strategy, the role played by the CEO, and considerations in choosing key personnel.

6. Distinguish between the two basic types of operational plans.

7. List the three types of standing plans and explain why each is useful.

8. Demonstrate the effective and ineffective wording of objectives.

9. Explain the concept of management by objectives and describe its essential elements.

10. Discuss the advantages and disadvantages of various types of reward systems and explain how their effectiveness can be improved.

11. List the environmental and internal constraints that block effective strategy implementation and suggest ways that organizations can overcome them.

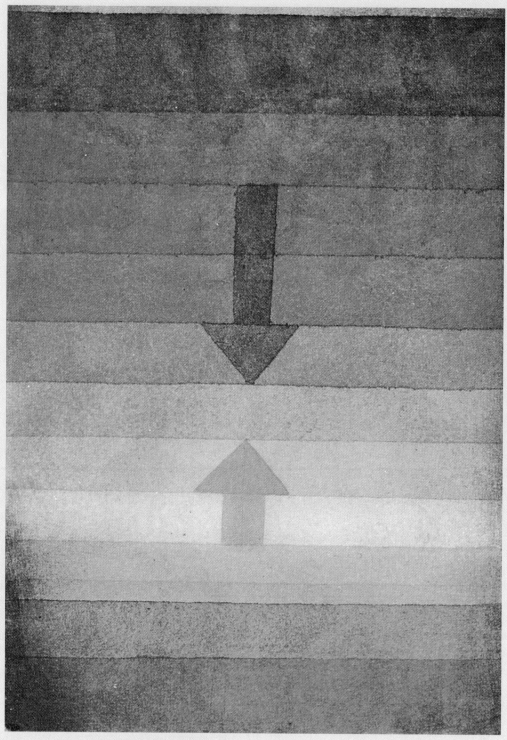

Paul Klee, *Scheidung Abends (Separated at Night),* 1922. Watercolor. 33.5 × 23.5 cm.
Copyright by COSMOPRESS, Geneva.

ILLUSTRATIVE CASE STUDY

INTRODUCTION

Maintaining the Competitive Edge at Merck & Co.

A pharmaceutical company lives and dies by new drug discoveries, primarily because drug patents last only a few years. Once a patent expires, competitors are free to duplicate the company's formula, and consumers who want to save money purchase these duplications. For the consumer, this is a boon, but for the company that spent years to develop the original formula, it signals an end of the profit stream from that drug.

New drugs are incredibly expensive to develop. First, it often takes years of basic research before even the *idea* for a drug is discovered. Then more years of research follow, as the idea is turned into a prototype drug. Next animal studies are conducted. Nine out of ten prototypes fail during this stage because they cause too many side effects or are not as effective as anticipated. If the animal studies go well, clinical human studies are initiated. Finally, after all these studies, FDA approval is sought—a process that can take one to two years. All told, it is often ten years from the time an idea for a new drug is generated until it reaches the market.

This is why pharmaceutical companies have aggressive programs for recruiting and retaining the best scientists. Merck, a leading pharmaceutical company headquartered in Rahway, New Jersey, has long been successful at this process. Merck has maintained its edge largely because it is unwilling to take anything for granted. In fact, Chairman Roy Vagelos, a former research chief, is always searching for new ways to improve the company, primarily by improving the productivity of the people who work for it.

One of his principal concerns is the atmosphere in which his scientists work. What do the scientists want and need? How can he keep them working for Merck rather than for a competitor? Both pay and benefits are liberal, and the researchers' contributions, individually and as a group, are regularly recognized. Yet, as a former researcher himself, Vagelos realizes that intellectual challenges, freedom, and supportive managers are also important to making scientists productive.

Merck's other principal concern is the time frame in which new drugs are developed. Obviously, scientists cannot be forced to invent on a schedule. But can other parts of the process be speeded up? Merck has been aggressive in implementing policies to do this.

Searching for the Formula for Success. Merck Chairman Roy Vagelos is constantly looking for ways to keep his researchers happy and speed up the process of discovering and developing new drugs.

Its record is impressive. The world's No. 1 pharmaceutical house, Merck has been hailed as the nation's most innovative company and, for the past four years, its most admired business. Sales have grown nearly $1 billion annually, and Merck has introduced 10 major new drugs in the last four years; 2, rated "megadrugs," net over $1 billion annually. Still, sales of 10 other Merck drugs are flat or declining, and of 13 drugs known to be in development, only one has the potential to be a megadrug.

Part of the problem lay with Merck's growth—40 percent in research and development (R&D) alone since 1985—and its size—Merck now has 17 research centers and 4,500 R&D employees in Europe, Japan, and North America. This has hampered the communication and brainstorming researchers thrive on. Another problem was Merck's highly centralized management of R&D, in which the head of R&D approved most major decisions. Frustrated by the bureaucracy, lack of autonomy, and slow decision making, a number of top researchers have left, jeopardizing Merck's strategy of developing a constant stream of important drugs. Now Vagelos must face the question: How can he improve the implementation of this strategy?

Sources: John A. Byrne, "The Miracle Company," *Business Week,* October 19, 1987; Gordon Bock, "Merck's Medicine Man," *Time,* February 22, 1988, pp. 44–45; Joseph Weber, "Merck Needs More Gold from the White Coats," *Business Week,* March 18, 1991, pp. 102–104.

215

*I*n large part, Merck's success can be traced to its skill at **strategy implementation,** the administrative tasks needed to put strategy into practice. For example, Merck's strategy requires that it hire—and keep—talented scientists. Accordingly, the company strives to maintain *policies* and *procedures* that will attract and reward valuable researchers. Policies and procedures are just one aspect of strategy implementation, a recently emerging subfield of strategic management.

Although the field is so new that there is no consensus about its dimensions, scholars and managers alike agree on some central ideas, which we discuss in this chapter. First, successful strategy implementation depends in part on the organization's structure. We will examine *structure* in more detail in Chapter 11, but here we will review the classic work of Alfred Chandler and his followers in tracing the relationship between *strategy* and *structure*. Second, strategy must be *institutionalized,* or incorporated into a system of values, norms, and roles that will help shape employee behavior, making it easier to reach strategic goals. Here we will study the role managers play in institutionalizing strategy. Third, strategy must be *operationalized,* or translated into specific policies, procedures, and rules that will guide planning and decision making by managers and employees. We will also look at procedures for setting short-term objectives and rewarding effective performances. Finally, the effective managers must be aware of internal and external barriers to strategy implementation.

■ *MATCHING STRATEGY IMPLEMENTATION TO STRATEGY*

The scope and pace of strategy implementation depend, in large part, on the goals of corporate strategy and the type of problems the strategy must solve. Lawrence Hrebeniak and William Joyce have described four different approaches to strategy implementation, each depending on the size of the problem facing an organization and on the time available to solve it. (See Fig. 8-1).[1] Not surprisingly, the larger and more immediate the problem, the more difficult the manager's task.

Evolutionary interventions take place when an organization's problems are small and there is relatively little pressure to solve them. These interventions consist of managers' routine decisions, often concerning personnel, made in direct response to problems or in an attempt to improve a unit's performance. They do not involve a major shift in organizational strategy or basic operating procedures and are not usually perceived as strategic changes. The process may be inefficient, but it is generally tolerated since it involves only small changes.

Minor problems that must be solved immediately call for *managerial interventions.* Since the situation is basically stable, the manager can afford to focus on the trouble spot and ignore the effects of decisions on other parts of the organization. These secondary effects are small, and thus are absorbed by the organization without difficulty.

In contrast, serious problems demand planned interventions in more than one area of the organization: Managers must recognize and preserve the interrelationships among the different areas even during the course of making changes. Given enough time, a manager can subdivide the problem and address each part in turn in a process called *sequential intervention.* Over a period of years, he or she can methodically carry out an entire series of changes.

When time is short, however, managers are forced to make large changes simultaneously according to a process called *complex intervention.* Negotiating and coordinating this web of interdependent decisions generally demands a task force or some other mechanism to bring all interested parties together. A drastic shift in the environment most commonly calls for complex intervention. Moreover, as the environment grows more turbulent, complex interventions may be needed more frequently.[2] Change can effectively destroy an organization if it is not anticipated.[3]

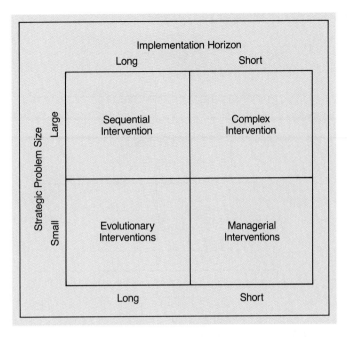

FIGURE 8-1 A Typology of Strategy Implementations

Source: Reprinted with permission of Macmillan Publishing Company from *Implementing Strategy* by Lawrence G. Hrebeniak and William F. Joyce. Copyright © 1984 by Macmillan Publishing Company, a Division of Macmillan, Inc.

■ *MATCHING STRUCTURE AND STRATEGY*

Successful implementation depends in part on how the organization's activities are divided, organized, and coordinated—in short, on the structure of the organization. Not surprisingly, the chances that an organization's strategy will succeed are far greater when its structure matches its strategy. By the same token, as its basic strategy changes over time, so must its structure.[4]

Chandler's Thesis

In his ground-breaking study of the history of large corporations, Alfred Chandler examined the growth and development of 70 of the largest businesses in the United States, including Du Pont; General Motors; Sears, Roebuck; and Standard Oil.[5] He observed a common pattern in their development. Although the organizations changed their growth strategies to suit technological, economic, and demographic changes, new strategies created administrative problems and economic inefficiencies. Structural changes were needed to solve those problems and to maximize the organization's economic performance. Chandler thus concluded that organizational structure followed and reflected the growth strategy of the firm.

According to Chandler, organizations pass through three stages of development, moving from a unit, to a functional, and then to a multidivisional structure (see Fig. 8-2). At first, organizations are small. There is usually a single location, a single product, and a single entrepreneurial decision maker. For example, when Bill Hewlett and Dave Packard founded a company to build an audio oscillator in 1939, they were personally responsible for its design, manufacture, testing, and marketing.[6] Eventually, increased volume and additional locations create new problems. The organization then becomes a unit firm, with an administrative office to handle interunit coordination, specialization, and standardization.

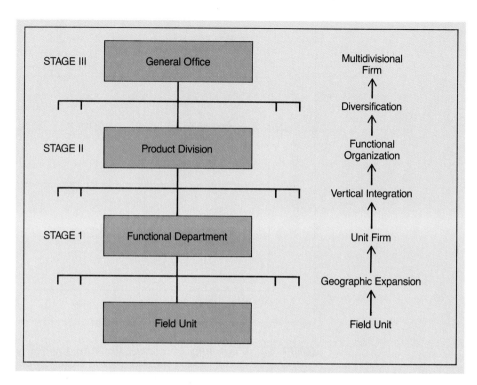

FIGURE 8-2 Strategies and Structure

Source: Reprinted by permission from *Strategy Implementation: Structure, Systems, and Process,* by J. R. Galbraith and R. K. Kazanjian. Copyright © 1986 by West Publishing Company. All rights reserved.

vertical integration
Broadening the scope of an organization's operations by buying a supplier or distributor that will contribute to efficient production of primary product or service offerings.

functional organization
A form of departmentalization in which everyone engaged in one functional activity, such as marketing or finance, is grouped into one unit.

multidivisional firm An organization that has expanded into different industries and diversified its products.

The next step is **vertical integration.** The organization keeps the original product but broadens its scope and strives for economies of scale by acquiring a supplier of raw materials and components or a distributor of finished goods. For example, the pioneers of vertical integration, the steel companies, eventually moved into mining. A manufacturer might naturally move into warehousing and wholesaling. However, vertical integration creates new problems in moving goods and materials through the organization's various functions. Therefore, the organization evolves into a **functional organization,** with finance, marketing, production, and other subdivisions and formalized budgeting and planning systems. Thus, as Hewlett-Packard's production of test equipment expanded, *functional* managers took over operating decisions.

In the third stage, an organization expands into different industries and diversifies its products. This phenomenon poses a significant new challenge: selecting products and industries in which to invest the organization's capital. The result is the **multidivisional firm,** which operates almost as a collection of smaller businesses. Semiautonomous product divisions take responsibility for short-term operating decisions, with the central office remaining responsible for strategic decisions with a longer time horizon. Hewlett-Packard, for example, has expanded horizontally by diversifying into computers, calculators, and components. (We will examine some of Hewlett-Packard's current operations in Chapter 11.)

Chandler also observed that the transition from one structure to another was often both delayed and painful. He concluded that organizations do not readily change structure because their entrepreneurial founders excel at strategy but are generally neither interested in nor knowledgeable about organizational structure. Indeed, when the organization is finally restructured, the entrepreneur often leaves. This has happened frequently in recent years in rapidly growing, technology-oriented firms like Apple Computer.[7]

A Multidivisional Firm. Van de Kamp seafood is one of the many brands owned by Pet Inc., a former division of the Whitman Corp., which began life as the Illinois Central Railroad. After a buying spree in the 1970s, the resulting conglomerate, named IC Industries Inc., sold a number of divisions in the late 1980s (including the railroad), and took a new name—the Whitman Corp., after Pet Inc.'s Whitman Sampler candies. Pet Inc. was soon made an independent company, though, leaving three main divisions—Pepsi-Cola General Bottlers Inc., Hussmann Corp. (the nation's largest maker of refrigerated display cases), and Midas International Corp.—with plans to consider further consolidations in the 1990s.

Further Research

Researchers have tried to confirm and refine Chandler's thesis. Wrigley, for example, identified four different diversification strategies among Fortune 500 companies.[8] The least diversified firms were obviously single-product businesses. Others, such as the automakers, had multiple products but allowed one business to dominate 70 to 95 percent of their sales. Still other firms, while diversified, moved primarily into businesses that shared customers, distribution channels, or technology with their main business. The most diversified firms moved into completely unrelated businesses. Wrigley found that the more diversified the strategy, the more likely the firm would have a multidivisional structure. The firms with a dominant business were sometimes hybrids, using a functional structure to manage the dominant business and a divisional structure for the rest.

In a similar study covering the years 1949–1969, Rumelt found that the number of dominant-product and single-product business firms fell, while the proportion of more-diversified firms doubled from 30 to 60 percent.[9] Over the same time period, functional structures declined from 63 to 11 percent of the sample, while multidivisional structures grew from 20 to 76 percent. This pattern continued through 1974.[10] In addition, the greater a firm's diversity, the more likely it was to have a multidivisional structure.

More recently, Raymond Miles and Charles Snow have done extensive studies analyzing the fit among an organization's strategy, structure, and management processes—that is, the balance between its alignment with its environment and its maintenance of stable internal interrelationships. They argue that successful organizations achieve strategic fit with their market environments and support their strategies with appropriately designed structures and management processes, while less successful organizations typically exhibit poor fit externally and/or internally.[11]

DISCUSSION QUESTION

How do Miles and Snow's propositions fit in with contingency theory?

OVERSEAS EXPERIENCE. Other researchers have tried to apply Chandler's thesis outside the United States, with mixed results.[12] They have found that product diversity in itself is not enough to bring about a multidivisional structure; competitive pressures are also required. For example, a study of leading Japanese firms found that the smaller domestic market in Japan caused businesses to diversify earlier and to wait much later to change to a multidivisional structure. (This delay is caused in part by the traditional clustering of companies around a major bank—a fact that effectively reduces competition.[13])

MULTINATIONAL FIRMS. Chandler's thesis has also been confirmed by the experience of U.S. multinationals. As American firms expanded abroad during the 1960s, they first added an international division to their existing product divisions.[14] Ultimately, however, firms that internationalized entire or diversified product lines adopted worldwide product divisions. By contrast, firms that competed globally only in their dominant business tended to adopt geographic divisions dividing the world into regions.

European multinationals followed a different pattern, partly because prior agreements and cartels limited competition.[15] Initially, they combined a holding company for international operations with a functional structure for domestic business. By the early 1970s, however, many had shifted to a multidivisional structure.

Today intensified global competition, greater demands by host governments, and growing participation in joint ventures are weakening the strategic control of the head offices of multinational organizations. For example, under the U.S.S.R.'s joint venture law, the Soviet government must own 51 percent of the company and appoint the top manager. Structure itself has become less important to performance. Rather than reorganize, top management may choose to upgrade personnel and implement new management systems in order to solve problems.[16]

Chandler's thesis remains a topic of active research. Some critics have argued that he reversed the relationship between strategy and structure. It may be that a company's structure is so resistant to change that it prevents the company from adopting the most feasible strategies under given circumstances. For example, the Bell System before divestiture in 1984 organized over one million employees functionally and geographically; this structure kept the company from pursuing certain areas and attempting certain strategies.

Regardless of the final verdict on Chandler's thesis, it is impossible to understand an organization's strategy without examining its structure. Indeed, one framework for organizational effectiveness goes even further in its analysis of this relationship.

The Seven-S Model

Seven-S model According to Waterman and others, framework for change identifying seven key factors that can adversely affect successful change in an organization.

COORDINATED RESOURCE

See Samaras Exercise 2.3, "Company Analysis: Compare and Contrast."

Based on discussions with consultants, academics, and business leaders, the consulting firm of McKinsey & Co. has proposed the **Seven-S model** for organizational effectiveness.[17] McKinsey's consultants found that neglecting any one of seven key factors could make the effort to change a slow, painful, and even doomed process.

As Figure 8-3 illustrates, each of these factors is equally important and interacts with all the other factors. Any number of circumstances may dictate which of the factors will be the driving force in the execution of any particular strategy.

STRUCTURE. The Seven-S model adds a contemporary perspective to the problem of organizational structure. The McKinsey consultants point out that in today's complex and ever-changing environment, a successful organization may make temporary structural changes to cope with specific strategic tasks without abandoning basic structural divisions throughout the organization. Thus, the General Motors Corporation, while holding onto its traditional divisions, incorporated additional project centers during its major downsizing effort.

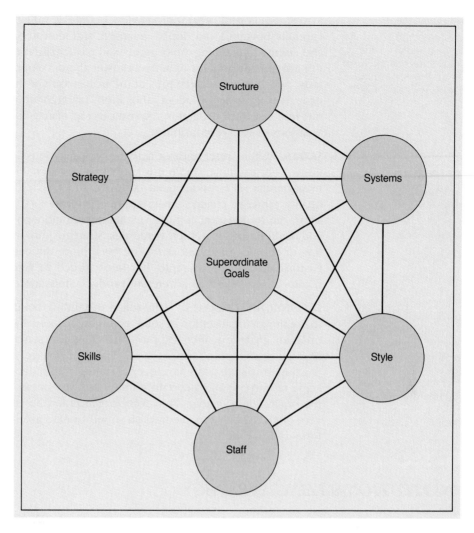

FIGURE 8-3 The Seven-S Model

Source: Robert H. Waterman, Jr., Thomas J. Peters, and Julien R. Phillips, "Structure Is Not Organization," *Business Horizons* (June 1980). Copyright © 1980 by the Foundation for the School of Business at Indiana University. Used with permission.

STRATEGY. The Seven-S model emphasizes that, in practice, the *development* of strategies poses less of a problem than their *execution.*

SYSTEMS. This category consists of all the formal and informal procedures that allow the organization to function, including capital budgeting, training, and accounting systems. Systems can overpower expressed strategies. Thus, a consumer-goods manufacturer might find it impossible to implement a new portfolio strategy if its management information system is not adjusted to produce the necessary cost data by segment, because there would be no way to compare the different segments of the business.

STYLE. "Style" refers not to personality, but to the pattern of substantive and symbolic *actions* undertaken by top managers. It communicates priorities more clearly than *words* alone, and may profoundly influence performance. For example, consultants have found that even oil- and mineral-exploration efforts—surely matters of operational skills and luck—benefit from top-management attention. Exploration is more successful in companies whose top managers spend more of their own and the board's time participating in exploration activities, articulate better reasons for exploration, recruit more people with exploration experience, fund exploration more consistently, and have exploration managers report to higher organizational levels.

STAFF. Successful organizations view people as valuable resources who should be carefully nurtured, developed, guarded, and allocated. Top managers devote time and energy to planning the progress and participation of existing managers, and use job assignment policies to actively foster the development of new managers. Similarly, new hires are given jobs in the mainstream of the organization, whether that be marketing or new-product innovation. Talented individuals are assigned mentors, put into fast-track programs, exposed to top management, and rapidly moved into positions of real responsibility.

SKILLS. "Skills" refer to those activities organizations do best and for which they are known. For example, Du Pont is known for research, Procter & Gamble for product management, ITT for financial controls, and Hewlett-Packard for innovation and quality. Strategic changes may require organizations to add one or more new skills. Thus, the termination of their U.S. telephone monopoly forced the Bell System to add marketing skills to their resources. Strategic initiatives that require the dismantling or revising of an old skill pose even more difficult implementation problems. Eastman Kodak, for example, has been forced to give up some of its traditional quality-control skills to accelerate product innovation.

SUPERORDINATE GOALS. This refers to guiding concepts, values, and aspirations that unite an organization in some common purpose. As we saw in Chapter 7, superordinate goals are often captured in a mission statement, but they can also be phrased as a simple slogan, such as "customer service" at IBM or "new products" at 3M. Superordinate goals have deep meaning within the organization. They provide a sense of purpose and a certain stability as other, more superficial characteristics of the organization change. Not every organization has superordinate goals, but it is very often the drive to accomplish superordinate goals that separates superior performers from the crowd.

■ *INSTITUTIONALIZING STRATEGY*

In emphasizing systems, style, staff, skills, and superordinate goals, the Seven-S model began to look at how strategy is institutionalized. An *institution* is a collection of values, norms, roles, and groups that develop to accomplish a certain goal. The institution of education, for example, developed to prepare children to be productive members of society. To *institutionalize* a business strategy, business leaders must also develop a system of values, norms, roles, and groups that will accomplish strategic goals.

The Role of the CEO

Because chief executive officers (CEOs) spend most of their time developing and guiding strategy, their personal goals and values inevitably shape organizational strategy. For example, Walt Disney valued family entertainment and conceived the idea of a "magical little park" that would amuse and educate both children and their parents. As a result, Disneyland opened in 1955. Although Disney died in 1966, his values and vision have continued to shape his company, as evidenced by the completion of his plans for Disney World (opened in 1971) and Epcot Center (opened in 1982). A change in CEO is usually associated with a change in strategy, though. Although current Disney CEO Michael Eisner has continued to develop the theme parks, he has moved away from Walt Disney's strategy of offering mainly G-rated films for children to create Touchstone Pictures, which offers PG and PG-13 films that appeal to wider audiences.

ILLUSTRATIVE CASE STUDY

CONTINUED

Maintaining the Competitive Edge at Merck & Co.

Faced with a slowdown in Merck's R&D, Chairman Roy Vagelos acted to replace R&D's centralized management with a more decentralized approach. Since mid-1989, research chief Edward M. Scolnick has delegated part of his decision-making authority to two executives—one responsible for basic research, the other for development. In addition, related research tasks are being grouped in certain labs, to avoid duplication of effort. For example, the Italian lab handles most research into viral diseases, while the Canadian lab concentrates on treatments for respiratory problems. Furthermore, each lab has more autonomy to discover, develop, and then market its drugs. The goal here is to make the researchers feel more involved and to increase their motivation, capturing something of the excitement of a smaller, entrepreneurial company. If this was not enough to increase motivation, Merck has also initiated a generous stock-option program to reward researchers when their

products reach the marketplace, and in 1991 increased R&D spending to $1 billion, an increase of 17 percent.

In all of these changes, we can see Vagelos making the type of adjustments characteristic of sequential intervention. The company is not in serious trouble, but it is clear changes are needed to keep it on top. Vagelos's main focus has been on structure—letting the company act more as a number of smaller, semi-autonomous units—which should improve its communication systems, increase staff satisfaction, and maintain its skills in developing new drugs. Furthermore, the decentralized changes should help Merck maintain the innovative style that made it great and allow it to continue achieving its superordinate goals.

Source: Joseph Weber, "Merck Needs More Gold from the White Coats," *Business Week,* March 18, 1991, pp. 102–104.

HERE'S AN EXAMPLE

The vice president for Lotus Development Corporation, the Cambridge, Massachusetts, software company, states that "As long as we're prudent financially, this is a great time to be stealing some advantage by being aggressive with acquisitions." (*Wall Street Journal,* 11/20/90, p. B2)

DISCUSSION QUESTION

"Line managers should make strategy." Agree or disagree and why?

COORDINATED RESOURCE

Use Transparency 43, Key Considerations in Managerial Assignments to Implement Strategy.

Their role in strategy formulation makes CEOs especially important to strategy implementation. First, they *interpret* strategy, acting as final judges when managers disagree on implementation. Second, CEOs *enact*—through their words and actions—the seriousness of an organization's commitment to a strategy. Lee Iacocca, for example, helped Chrysler's strategy succeed by preaching its virtues on television, in auto factories, and in the offices of securities analysts. Third, CEOs *motivate,* providing intangible incentives beyond pay or bonuses; by appealing to members' values, beliefs, and loyalties, CEOs can mobilize support for a strategy. Thus, a CEO's sudden death can be devastating. (See the Management Application box.)

The Role of Key Managers

In theory, of course, general managers perform better when their skills, attitudes, and practices match the competitive setting and strategy of their organization.[18] Although no one has yet developed or rigorously tested specific rules for typing managers, some corporations, including General Electric and Corning Glass Works, have tried to assess managers and match them to a particular stage of a product life cycle or a particular kind of business.

Often the central issue in choosing a key manager is deciding whether to promote from within or opt for hiring an outsider. Insiders have the advantage of knowing the organization and the important players, but they may be tied to old strategies. Outsiders can bring in needed skills, experience, and enthusiasm, but they may be difficult to find and expensive to hire. (See Fig. 8-4.)

MANAGEMENT APPLICATION

Keeping the Muppet Magic Alive

In August 1989, Walt Disney Co. announced plans to buy the licensing and publishing businesses of Jim Henson Productions and give Muppet creator Jim Henson an exclusive 15-year production arrangement. This seemed like the ultimate win-win situation. Disney would gain access to all the Muppet characters except those created for *Sesame Street*. (Henson reserved those rights for the public TV show, which depends on the income from merchandising such beloved characters as Big Bird and Cookie Monster.) In return, Henson would gain the financial support that spells artistic freedom, sophisticated distribution channels for Muppet films and videos, and the comfort of knowing that Disney could give his creations eternal life. While wags speculated affectionately about a possible love triangle between Mickey Mouse, the amorous Miss Piggy, and an ever-elusive Kermit, negotiations continued, with Disney offering a reported $150 million to $200 million.

Anticipation turned to confusion on May 16, 1990, when Jim Henson died suddenly of pneumonia. The shock waves were felt around the world, as millions of parents—many of whom had grown up with the Muppets themselves—struggled to explain that the voice of Kermit, Ernie, Rowlf, and other characters might never be heard again.

Henson's 115-person staff was devastated. To them, Henson was a father figure and they were a family united by his creativity. As Muppeteer Richard Hunt put it, "We shared the same heart."* While they contemplated a future without Henson, condolences rolled in from children and adults, including an over-size card from Disney showing Mickey Mouse comforting a grieving Kermit.

Although Disney CEO Michael Eisner expressed initial optimism that the deal would go through, he made it clear that an important part of that deal had been the creative services of Jim Henson, whose impact Eisner likened to that of Walt Disney himself. Henson's creative staff was intact and two of his children, Brian and Cheryl, had worked closely with their father, but Jim Henson, the driving force, was gone. Instead of a quick, amicable closing of the deal, Henson's heirs—his five adult children—faced increasingly nettlesome negotiations (handled by Lisa Henson, a producer at Warner Brothers, Inc., but otherwise uninvolved in Henson management).

Complicating matters further, the heirs faced estate taxes that could take as much as 55 percent of

Jim Henson and Kermit

their inheritance. Since a satisfactory deal could not be worked out, negotiations with Disney broke off in December 1990, amid plans to continue several projects already in development, including a 3-D Muppet film and live stage show for the Disney theme parks.

Less than six weeks later, Brian Henson was named president of Jim Henson Productions, and Cheryl Henson was named vice president for creative affairs, with responsibility for *Sesame Street*. (Former President David Lazer was to remain a board member and active consultant.) In Brian's words, "My father had wonderful goals and wonderful dreams. And when he died, I realized they had become mine. And I saw that in virtually everyone in the company. So I think, in some ways, he's still there in everyone. We've lost our focus temporarily, but we'll get that back right away. He's still there."* Although the Henson heirs claim the company could survive on its own, they continue to receive bids from other studios, whose funding and distribution channels could safeguard Jim Henson's legacy.

*As quoted in Stephen Harrigan, "It's Not Easy Being Blue," *Life,* July 1990, p. 96.
Sources: Stephen Harrigan, "It's Not Easy Being Blue," *Life,* July 1990, pp. 93–98; "New Post for Henson Son," *Chicago Tribune,* January 26, 1991, Sect. 2, p. 1; and Andrea Rothman, "The Henson Kids Carry On," *Business Week,* February 4, 1991, pp. 72–73.

	Advantages	Disadvantages
Using existing executives to implement a new strategy	Already know key people, practices, and conditions. Personal qualities better known and understood by associates. Have established relationships with peers, subordinates, suppliers, buyers, etc. Symbolizes organizational commitment to individual careers.	Less adaptable to major strategic changes because of knowledge, attitudes, and values. Past commitments may hamper hard decisions required in executing a new strategy. Less ability to become inspired and credibly convey the need for change.
Bringing in outsiders to implement a new strategy	Outsider may already believe in and have "lived" the new strategy. Outsider is unencumbered by internal commitments to people. Outsider comes to the new assignment with heightened commitment and enthusiasm. Bringing in an outsider can send powerful signals throughout the organization that change is expected.	Often costly, both in terms of compensation and "learning-to-work-together" time. Candidates suitable in all respects (i.e., exact experience) may not be available, leading to compromise choices. Uncertainty in selecting the right person. The "morale" costs when an outsider takes a job several insiders wanted. "What to do with poor ol' Fred" problem.

FIGURE 8-4 Key Considerations in Managerial Assignments to Implement Strategy

Source: John A. Pearce II and Richard B. Robinson, Jr., *Formulation and Implementation of Competitive Strategy* (Homewood, Ill.: Richard D. Irwin, 1985), p. 339. Copyright © 1985 by Richard D. Irwin.

According to John Pearce and Richard Robinson, four different approaches may be taken to such assignment decisions, each with its advantages and disadvantages. (See Fig. 8-5.) By and large, the relative advantages of insiders versus outsiders depends on how well the organization has already been performing and on the changes and complications entailed by the prospective strategy.[19]

turnover situation Strategy situation in which poor performance entails major changes that cannot be handled by insiders.

Outsiders are the better choice in a **turnover situation**—that is, when the organization has been performing poorly and the strategy calls for major changes. Outsiders have the experience to implement new strategies and are neither defensive about prior insufficiencies nor bound by prior commitments. In addition, employees are more likely to take the changes seriously if new people are brought in to implement them. Chrysler's near-bankruptcy is the classic example of a turnover situation. First, Lee Iacocca was brought in to serve as CEO. He, in turn, filled over 80 percent of the company's top-management positions with outsiders. These decisions went a long way toward bringing Chrysler the skills and commitment it needed to implement its new small-car strategy.

selective-blend situation Strategy situation entailing major changes in organizational strategy that blend both outsiders and insiders to perform corrective measures.

The **selective-blend situation** also requires major changes, but because of environmental fluctuations rather than poor performance. In these circumstances, the best solution seems to be to blend outsiders, who possess needed skills and experience, with insiders, who can integrate the changes into the existing system. Take IBM's move into personal computers. Most positions were filled by existing IBM employees. The firm recruited only a limited number of outsiders, mostly people with experience in direct retail outlets—the one facet of the new strategy that was totally foreign to IBM.

Changes required to implement the new strategy		Effective	Ineffective
	Many	**"Selective blend"** *Current executives* via promotion and transfer where skills match new roles; otherwise, seek skills and experience via *outsiders.*	**"Turnover"** *Outsiders* should be a high priority to provide new skills, motivation, and enthusiasm.
	Few	**"Stability"** *Current executives* and internal promotions should be a major emphasis in order to reward, retain, and develop managerial talent.	**"Reorientation"** *Outsiders* are important to replace weaknesses and "communication seriousness." *Current executives* should be a priority where possible via promotion, transfer, or role clarification.
		Assessment of past organizational performance	

FIGURE 8-5 Four Managerial Assignment Situations

Source: John A. Pearce II and Richard B. Robinson, Jr., *Formulation and Implementation of Competitive Strategy* (Homewood, Ill.: Richard D. Irwin, 1985), p. 339. Copyright © 1985 by Richard D. Irwin.

stability situation Strategy situation in which good past performance and the minor nature of needed changes make insiders the best choice for implementing.

In a **stability situation,** past performance has been fine and few changes are needed. Insiders are clearly the best choice for implementing the strategy, since they are familiar with the firm, have a network of established relationships in the industry, and have a good track record. Thus, Wendy's used internal promotions to fill its management positions during the early 1980s, when its fast-food strategy required relatively few substantive changes in its operations.

reorientation situation Strategy situation in which poor performance despite sound strategy calls for change to be implemented by outsiders.

Sometimes an organization's strategy appears to be sound even though its performance has been poor. If the organization's problems are due to bad management, such a **reorientation situation** calls for outsiders. Apple Computer found itself in this situation after IBM muscled into the personal computer market. Apple brought in a new CEO and key marketing and finance managers from outside the company to improve its competitive position. At the same time, the company transferred and clarified the role of younger product-development managers in an effort to reinvigorate its technical strengths.

Culture and Strategy

organizational culture The set of important understandings, such as norms, values, attitudes, and beliefs, shared by organizational members.

HERE'S AN EXAMPLE

One consultant has called Toyota's strategy "rapid inch-up": take enough tiny steps and pretty soon you outdistance the competition. (*Fortune,* 11/19/90, p. 66ff.)

Organizational culture is the set of shared values, beliefs, attitudes, and norms that shape the behavior and expectations of each member of the organization. Culture, while less explicit than rules and procedures, may be an even more powerful influence on the way employees and managers approach problems, serve customers, and the like. Broadly speaking, organizational culture determines what behavior is appropriate for employees and which issues should take priority. (Organizational culture is discussed in more detail in Part Four.)

When an organization's culture is consistent with its strategy, the implementation of strategy is eased considerably. For example, the organizational cultures at Delta Airlines and IBM complement their strategic emphasis on service. Because of the nature of their services, members of those companies share people-oriented values: They are eager to help and go out of their way to solve individual customer problems.[20]

It is impossible to successfully implement a strategy that contradicts the organization's culture. Thus, AT&T's traditional belief in the importance of universal

COORDINATED RESOURCE

The Distinctive Discussions for Chapter 8 found in the Lecture Extras supplement include "Bigs Acquire Smalls" and "Kaizen: Toyota's Secret."

telephone service, which dates from the days of its monopoly, has been a major stumbling block in the implementation of its new market-oriented strategy that discriminates among customers who need different services.[21] Managers faced with this type of situation must somehow change the culture to fit the new strategy. In recent years, for example, managers at Eastman Kodak have implemented a new entrepreneurial strategy designed to speed up the development of new products (recall the Illustrative Case Study in Chapter 3). This strategy has entailed replacing the old cautious, insular culture, which valued quality above all, with an aggressive, competitive culture that promotes risk taking.[22]

■ OPERATIONALIZING STRATEGY

operational plan Plan that provides the details needed to incorporate strategy into day-to-day operations.

COORDINATED RESOURCE

See Study Guide Self-Learning Exercise 8, "Operationalizing Strategy."

If strategies set the general goal and course of action for organizations, **operational plans** provide the details needed to incorporate strategic plans into the organization's day-to-day *operations*. For example, a corporate-level strategy of improving efficiency might be translated into operational plans for employee training programs.

Operational plans fall into two general classes. Single-use plans are designed to be dissolved once they have achieved specific, nonrecurring goals. Standing plans, in contrast, are standardized approaches to handling recurrent and predictable situations (see Fig. 8-6).[23]

FIGURE 8-6 The Hierarchy of Organizational Plans

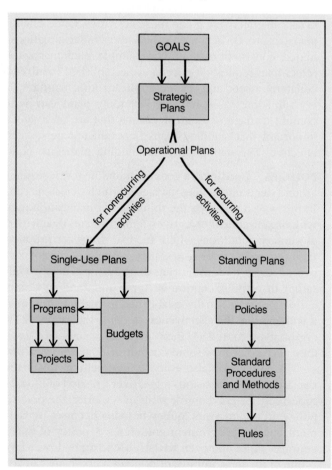

Single-Use Plans

single-use plan A detailed course of action used once or only occasionally to solve a problem that does not occur repeatedly.

Single-use plans are detailed courses of action that probably will not be repeated in the same form in the future. For example, a rapidly expanding firm planning to set up a new warehouse will need a specific single-use plan for that project. Even though it has established a number of warehouses in the past, the new warehouse presents unique requirements of location, construction costs, labor availability, zoning restrictions, and so forth. In 1982, when AT&T agreed to split itself into eight separate companies, it created a single-use plan called "The Plan for Divestiture." Many person-years of work went into creating this document, which served as a blueprint for the unique events that were to occur. The major types of single-use plans are programs, projects, and budgets.

program A single-use plan that covers a relatively large set of organizational activities and specifies major steps, their order and timing, and the unit responsible for each step.

A **program** is a single-use plan that covers a relatively large set of activities. It shows (1) the major steps required to reach an objective, (2) the organization unit or member responsible for each step, and (3) the order and timing of each step. **Projects** are smaller, separate portions of programs; they are limited in scope and contain distinct directives concerning assignments and time. If the program is to transfer inventory from one warehouse to another, one related project might be to evaluate floor space at the proposed installation. **Budgets** are statements of financial resources set aside for specific activities in a given period of time; they are primarily devices to control an organization's activities, and thus are important components of programs and projects.

project The smaller and separate portions of the programs.

budgets Formal quantitative statements of the resources allocated to specific programs or projects for a given period.

Standing Plans

standing plan An established set of decisions used by managers to deal with recurring or organizational activities; major types are policies, procedures, and rules.

Whenever organizational activities occur repeatedly, a single decision or set of decisions can effectively guide those activities. Once established, **standing plans** allow managers to conserve time because similar situations are handled in a predetermined, consistent manner. For example, bank managers can more easily approve or reject loan requests if criteria are established in advance to evaluate credit ratings, collateral assets, and related applicant information.

In some cases, however, standing plans can be a disadvantage because they commit managers to past decisions that are no longer appropriate. Therefore, it is important that standing plans be evaluated periodically to be sure they are still effective. The major types of standing plans are policies, procedures, and rules.

policy A standing plan that establishes general guidelines for decision making.

POLICIES. A **policy** is a general guideline for decision making. It sets up boundaries around decisions, telling managers which decisions can be made and which cannot. In this way, it channels the thinking of organization members so that it is consistent with organizational objectives. Some policies deal with very important matters, such as sanitary conditions where food or drugs are produced or packaged. Others concern relatively minor issues, such as the way employees dress. IBM, for example, has a strict dress code requiring dark business dress, while informal dress is the rule rather than the exception at Apple and Tandem Computers.

A policy is usually established formally by top managers because (1) they feel it will improve the effectiveness of the organization, (2) they want some aspect of the organization to reflect their personal values (for example, dress codes), or (3) they need to redress some conflict or confusion at a lower level in the organization.

whistleblowing Alerting management to decisions, policies, or practices that may be ill-advised, detrimental, or illegal; can include publicizing such matters outside the organization.

A policy may also emerge informally at lower levels because of a seemingly consistent set of decisions made over a period of time. For example, if office space is repeatedly assigned on the basis of seniority, the practice may become organization policy. In recent years, policy has also been set by factors in the external environment, such as government guidelines. A policy of open communication, which encourages input and even **whistleblowing** by lower-level managers and employees, is one of the most important policies a company can adopt. For an example of what can happen when dissent is stifled, see the Ethics in Management box.

ETHICS IN MANAGEMENT

The *Challenger* Disaster

On the crisp morning of January 28, 1986, an expectant crowd lined the beaches at Cape Canaveral, Florida, waiting for the liftoff of the space shuttle *Challenger*. Thanks to television, millions more watched across the nation, including the proud students of Christa McAuliffe, a New Hampshire high-school teacher who had won a nationwide competition to become the first teacher in space.

As the shuttle lifted off into a clear blue sky, the crowd burst into cheers. In just 73 seconds, however, the hurrahs turned to gasps of horror. After a flawless liftoff, the *Challenger* erupted in a ball of flame, broke into segments, and plunged into the ocean. McAuliffe and the six-astronaut crew were dead.

The nation was stunned. Previous shuttle flights had gone so smoothly that the launches and landings were viewed as almost routine events. All shuttle flights were immediately suspended, pending an investigation by a presidential commission, which released its report in June 1986. The immediate blame for the explosion fell on a faulty O-ring seal between segments on the solid-fuel booster rockets. Cold weather and buffeting winds during the launch further weakened the O-rings, allowing flame to leak out and trigger the explosion. This was not a surprise; millions of ordinary citizens watching slow-motion replays of the televised launch had seen the flames for themselves.

A greater surprise was the commission's criticisms of NASA's "flawed management" procedures, its overambitious schedules, and inadequate quality control systems. In fact, congressional investigators uncovered evidence that NASA had known of the O-ring problem for a long time but had not given its solution priority over planning, publicizing, and conducting a heavy schedule of missions designed to win continued support and funding for the shuttle.

Fingers were also pointed at Morton Thiokol, the company that built the rocket boosters. Engineers had long suspected something was wrong with the basic design of the O-rings, yet when they complained, wrote memos, and "blew whistles," nothing happened—until the explosion. Senior managers evidently saw the engineers' jobs as implementing policy, not questioning it.

NASA underwent sweeping management changes, the O-ring seals were redesigned, and shuttle flights were resumed in 1988. Still, the shuttle program suffered immeasurable damage. Before the

The *Challenger* Explodes.

explosion, NASA was using the shuttle to launch commercial communication satellites, hoping eventually to become financially independent. In the wake of the explosion, the shuttle program was drastically scaled back and limited to military missions and other noncommercial ventures. Worse was the damage the explosion did to the public's trust of NASA and Morton Thiokol. These huge organizations were seen as being too quick to take unacceptable risks with human lives.

How can such disasters be prevented? One way is to create built-in processes that encourage constructive disagreement and dissent among employees. To overcome the fear that dissenters will lose their jobs, employees must be guaranteed some due process and perhaps even protection under company "law." IBM has an open-door policy; other companies have employed outside ombudsmen or used confidential surveys and questionnaires. In addition, a number of states have passed laws protecting whistleblowers from retaliation, and in 1988, only President Reagan's veto kept a federal Whistleblowers Protection Act from becoming law. To be sure, some employees might abuse this protection by constantly crying wolf. Just as surely, some whistleblowers' messages will require expensive and inconvenient replanning, redesign, and delays. As the *Challenger* disaster shows, however, ignoring the whistleblower can be even more costly.

Sources: Judith H. Dobrzynski, "Morton Thiokol: Reflections on the Shuttle Disaster," *Business Week,* March 14, 1988, pp. 82–83, 86, 91; Judith Valente, "Thiokol Faces a New Shuttle Test Today," *The Wall Street Journal,* April 20, 1988, p. 6; Russell P. Boisjoly et al., "Roger Boisjoly and the *Challenger* Disaster: Ethical Dimensions," *Journal of Business Ethics* 8 (1989):217–230; Myron Peretz Glazer and Penina Migdal Glazer, *The Whistleblowers: Exposing Corruption in Government and Industry* (New York: Basic Books, 1989).

STANDARD PROCEDURES. Policies are carried out by means of more detailed guidelines called "standard procedures" or "standard methods." A **procedure** provides a detailed set of instructions for performing a sequence of actions that occurs often or regularly. For example, the refund department of a large discount store may have a policy of "refunds made, with a smile, on all merchandise returned within seven days of purchase." The procedure for all clerks might then be (1) smile at customer, (2) check receipt for purchase date, (3) check condition of merchandise . . . and so on. Such detailed instructions help ensure a consistent approach to a specific situation.

At The Limited, a specialty clothing store, standard procedure ensures that customers get an offer of assistance within the first few seconds of entering the store. At Wal-Mart, a discount merchandiser, store procedure requires that one person greet all customers and smile at them. At the Red Cross, the advent of AIDS has meant numerous changes in the standard procedure for accepting blood donations and handling blood products.

procedure A standing plan that contains detailed guidelines for handling organizational actions that occur regularly.

rules Standing plans that detail specific actions to be taken in a given situation.

RULES. **Rules** are statements that a specific action must or must not be taken in a given situation. They are the most explicit of standing plans; they are not guides to thinking or decision making, but substitutes for them. The only choice a rule leaves is whether or not to apply it to a particular set of circumstances. For example, in an office where the rule requires all employees to work until five o'clock, the manager may decide to suspend the rule on a hot day if the air-conditioning system breaks down. Rule proliferation often adversely affects employee morale.[24] This is especially true when employees have been accustomed to working without many rules, as they were at Apple Computer under its innovative founders Steven Jobs and Stephen Wozniak. When professional manager John Sculley was hired, he instituted a more traditional set of rules, from tough product-development deadlines to formal reporting procedures. The changes created quite a morale problem.

■ USING PROCEDURES TO FACILITATE IMPLEMENTATION

Although procedures can seem bureaucratic and limiting, they are powerful tools for implementing strategy and gaining greater commitment from employees. To show this, we will take a closer look at procedures for setting annual objectives, management by objectives, and reward systems.

Annual Objectives

Annual objectives lie at the very heart of strategy implementation—especially when detailed functional strategies are being implemented. They identify precisely what must be accomplished each year in order to achieve an organization's strategic goals; in the process, they also provide managers with specific targets for the coming year's performance. For example, if strategy dictates an increase in market share, annual objectives for the coming year might include a 15 percent increase in sales, the opening of a regional distribution center in a specific area of the country, and the negotiation of a certain line of credit to pay for the increased production and distribution expenses.[25]

Thus, annual objectives clarify managers' tasks and give them a better understanding of their role in the organization's strategy. Insofar as annual objectives challenge managers and give them a sense of purpose, they also increase motivation. At the same time, they furnish a quantitative basis for monitoring performance and make it easier to spot performance problems.

Well-designed annual objectives are clearly linked to the organization's long-term goals and they are measurable. It is important that they *quantify* performance

TABLE 8-1 Operationalizing Measurable Annual Objectives

EXAMPLES OF DEFICIENT ANNUAL OBJECTIVES	EXAMPLES OF ANNUAL OBJECTIVES WITH MEASURABLE CRITERIA FOR PERFORMANCE
To improve morale in the divisions (plant, department, etc.).	To reduce turnover (absenteeism, number of rejects, etc.) among sales managers by 10 percent by January 1, 1992. *Assumption:* Morale is related to measurable outcomes (i.e., high and low morale are associated with different results).
To improve support of the sales effort.	To reduce the time lapse between order date and delivery by 8 percent (two days) by June 1, 1992. To reduce the cost of goods produced by 6 percent to support a product price decrease of 2 percent by December 1, 1992. To increase the rate of before- or on-schedule delivery by 5 percent by June 1, 1992.
To develop a terminal version of the SAP computer program.	To develop a terminal version of SAP capable of processing X bits of information in time Y at cost not to exceed Z per 1,000 bits by December 1, 1992. *Assumption:* There is virtually an infinite number of "terminal" or operational versions. Greater detail of specificity defines the objective more precisely.
To enhance or improve the training effort.	To increase the number of individuals capable of performing X operation in manufacturing by 20 percent by April 15, 1992. To increase the number of functional heads capable of assuming general management responsibility at the division level by 10 percent by July 15, 1992. To provide sales training to X number of individuals, resulting in an average increase in sales of 4 percent within six months after the training session.
To improve the business's image.	To conduct a public opinion poll using random samples in the five largest U.S. metropolitan markets and determine average scores on 10 dimensions of corporate responsibility by May 15, 1992. To increase our score on those 10 items by an average of 7.5 percent by May 1, 1993.

Source: Adapted from John A. Pearce II and Richard B. Robinson, Jr., *Formulation and Implementation of Competitive Strategy* (Homewood, Ill.: Richard D. Irwin, 1985). Copyright 1985 by Richard D. Irwin.

in absolute terms, so there can be no dispute over a unit's results. Some areas, like production, naturally lend themselves to this kind of measurement. It is more difficult to create quantitative standards for personnel. The examples in Table 8-1 illustrate the difference between well- and poorly designed annual objectives.

Another important design issue is the way in which the annual objectives of different units interact with one another. Managers must *coordinate* the annual objectives of the organization, resolving their contradictions, setting priorities, and designing objectives to reinforce one another. Marketing, for example, often has a clearly defined annual objective for delivery time to customers; marketing cannot meet that objective, however, unless manufacturing has compatible objectives regarding delivery time and acceptable levels of inventory.

Managers should participate in the process of setting annual objectives to ensure that they are realistic and to screen out flaws in their design. Manager involvement has another potential benefit: It allows political conflicts to be aired and resolved before they begin interfering with strategy implementation.

Management by Objectives

management by objectives (MBO) A formal set of procedures that establishes and reviews progress toward common goals for managers and subordinates.

Management by objectives (MBO) goes beyond setting annual objectives for *organizational* units to setting performance goals for *individual* employees. The approach was first proposed by Peter Drucker in his 1954 book *The Practice of Management.*[26] Since that time, MBO has spurred a great deal of discussion, evaluation, and research, and inspired many similar programs.[27]

MBO refers to a formal, or moderately formal, set of procedures that begins with goal setting and continues through performance review. Managers and their subordinates act together to set common goals. Each person's major areas of responsibility are clearly defined in terms of measurable expected results or "objectives" used by subordinates in planning their work, and by both subordinates and superiors for monitoring progress. Performance appraisals are conducted jointly on a continuing basis, with provisions for regular periodic reviews.

The objectives, which are at the heart of MBO, spell out the individual actions needed to fulfill the unit's functional strategy and annual objectives. Thus, MBO provides a way to integrate and focus the efforts of all organization members on the goals of higher management and overall organizational strategy.

Another key to MBO is its insistence on the active involvement of managers and staff members at every organizational level. Drucker insisted that managers and staff members set their own objectives or, at the very least, be actively involved in the objective-setting process; otherwise, people might refuse to cooperate or make only half-hearted efforts to implement "someone else's" objectives. Drucker also suggested that managers at every level help set objectives for those at levels higher than their own, in the belief that this would give them a better understanding of the broader strategy of the company and how their own specific objectives relate to the overall picture.

ELEMENTS OF THE MBO SYSTEM. MBO systems vary enormously. Some are designed for use in a subunit; others for the organization as a whole. Some emphasize corporate planning, others stress individual motivation. Managers, of course, may also choose to use different methods and approaches. Nevertheless, most effective MBO programs share the following six elements:[28]

1. *Commitment to the program.* At every organizational level, managers' commitment to achieving personal and organizational objectives and to the MBO process is required for an effective program. Managers must meet with subordinates, first to set objectives and then to review progress toward these objectives.

2. *Top-level goal setting.* Effective MBO programs usually start with the top managers who determine the organization's strategy and set preliminary goals that resemble annual objectives in their content and terms (for example, "a 5 percent increase in sales next quarter" or "no increase in overhead costs this year"). This procedure gives both managers and subordinates a clearer idea of what top management hopes to accomplish and shows them how their own work directly relates to achieving the organization's goals.

3. *Individual goals.* In an effective MBO program, each manager and subordinate has clearly defined job responsibilities and objectives. The purpose of setting *objectives* in specific terms at every level is to help employees understand clearly just what they are expected to accomplish and to help each individual plan effectively to achieve his or her targeted goals. Individual objectives

should be set in consultation between that individual and his or her supervisor. Because they know best what they are capable of achieving, subordinates might well help managers develop realistic objectives; in turn, managers might help subordinates "raise their sights" toward higher objectives by showing willingness to help them overcome obstacles and confidence in their abilities.

4. *Participation.* The degree of subordinate participation in setting objectives can vary enormously. At one extreme, subordinates participate only by being present when objectives are dictated by management. At the other extreme, subordinates are completely free to set their own objectives and methods for achieving them. Neither extreme is likely to be effective. As a general rule, the greater the participation of both managers and subordinates in the setting of goals, the more likely the goals will be achieved.

5. *Autonomy in implementation of plans.* Once the objectives have been agreed upon, the individual enjoys a wide range of discretion in choosing the means for achieving them. Managers should be free, within the normal constraints of organization policies, to develop and implement programs to achieve their goals without being second-guessed by their superiors.

6. *Performance review.* Managers and subordinates periodically meet to review progress toward the objectives. During the review, they decide what problems exist and what they can each do to resolve them. If necessary, objectives may be modified for the next review period. To be fair and meaningful, review should be based on *measurable* performance results rather than on subjective criteria such as attitude or ability.

EVALUATION OF MBO. Do MBO concepts really work? The lack of studies on MBO programs makes it difficult to answer this question. Some research conducted at General Electric, Purex, the University of Kentucky, and elsewhere has indicated that MBO can improve managerial planning and performance, but that successful implementation requires considerable time and effort. Moreover, the active support of managers and their continued attention to program requirements are necessary to introduce MBO techniques effectively.

In their review of the literature on MBO research, Stephen J. Carroll and Henry L. Tosi focused on three key concepts—specific goal setting, feedback on performance, and participation—to determine whether the optimism about MBO was justified.[29] They concluded that individuals who are successful in achieving the goals they have set tend to aim for increased performance.[30] Employees who received specific and timely feedback performed better,[31] and those who participated in goal setting show higher performance levels.[32] Finally, Carroll and Tosi concluded that the very process of participation leads to increased communication and understanding between managers and subordinates.[33]

Reward Systems

Rewards and incentives contribute to strategy implementation by shaping individual and group behavior. Well-designed incentive plans are consistent with an organization's objectives and structure. They motivate employees to direct their performance toward the organization's goals.[34]

In setting up an incentive plan, the organization is faced with a series of choices: Should bonuses be in cash or stock? Current or deferred? How will performance be measured? How much discretion will managers have in awarding bonuses? How large will the bonuses be?[35] The idea is to tailor the program to the organization's objectives. Incentive plans can encourage short-term or long-term decision making, greater or lesser risk taking, more or less cooperation with other managers, and the like. Table 8-2 reviews established practice in incentive plans for top management.

TABLE 8-2 Key Aspects of Incentive Compensation

POLICY ISSUES	FINANCIAL INSTRUMENTS	PERFORMANCE MEASURES	DEGREE OF DISCRETION IN ALLOCATING BONUS AWARDS	SIZE AND FREQUENCY OF AWARDS
Short run vs. long run	Mix of current bonus awards and stock options should reflect the relevant time horizon for policy-level executives. Deferred instruments are weak reinforcers of short-term performance.	Mix of quantitative measures of performance and more qualitative measures should reflect the relevant time horizon for executives. Qualitative measures usually reflect long-run considerations more effectively than quantitative measures.	Nondiscretionary, formula-based bonuses tend to encourage a short-run point of view.	Frequent bonus awards encourage concentration on short-term performance.
Risk aversion vs. risk taking	Current bonus awards, in cash or stock, can reinforce risk-taking behavior.	Qualitative measures of performance can reinforce initiative by assuring executives that total performance will be evaluated for purposes of bonus awards.	Completely discretionary, highly personalized bonuses do not clarify the "rules of the game" and as a result can discourage risk-taking behavior.	The size of both salary and incentive awards should be commensurate with the business and personal risks involved.
Interdivisional relationships		Bonus pools can be based on divisional performance, total corporate performance, or some mix of the two. Each arrangement sends different signals in terms of interdivisional cooperation.	Nondiscretionary, formula-based bonuses for division managers are most practical in companies where little cooperation among divisions is required. Discretionary bonuses are practical when top management wants to encourage cooperation among divisions.	
Company-division relationships	Stock options can effectively link the interests of division personnel to the interests of the corporation.	Use of objective measures of performance for division managers is more meaningful where the primary role of headquarters is to allocate capital than it is in instances where the head office plays an important role in "managing the business" of the divisions.	Nondiscretionary, formula-based bonuses are most practical in companies where headquarters does not interfere in management of the profit centers. Discretionary bonuses are most useful when top management wants to exert a direct influence on decisions in the divisions.	

Source: Reprinted by permission from *Strategy Implementation: Structure, Systems, and Process,* Second Edition, by J. R. Galbraith and R. K. Kazanjian. Copyright © 1986 by West Publishing Company. All rights reserved.

Critics have pointed out four problems faced by managers with conventional incentive plans. First, incentives may be inappropriately correlated with the absolute size of the firm instead of with the rate of return.[36] Second, short-term performance may be emphasized at the expense of long-term strategic development.[37] Third, incentives may be tied to accounting measures, such as earnings per share and return on investment, which do not accurately reflect the creation of economic value for shareholders.[38] Finally, these accounting measures also ignore portfolio concepts of corporate strategy, holding managers to the same standards of performance regardless of the rate of growth of their division.[39]

In response to these criticisms, organizations have begun to make changes in their incentive plans.[40] They may use three- to five-year performance-evaluation periods and deferred stock-option plans to encourage long-term planning. They may calculate a more meaningful return on assets for current operations by separating out expenses incurred by strategic projects. They may develop new performance measures that are more meaningful than simple accounting criteria. Finally, they may adjust the incentives for managers of high- and low-growth businesses within the same corporation, giving a different weight to market share, product quality, new-product development, and the like.

■ RECOGNIZING BARRIERS TO EFFECTIVE STRATEGY IMPLEMENTATION

There are many barriers to effective strategy implementation. While some result from changes in a complex environment, others stem from internal obstacles. (To see how these barriers affect even nations, see the International Management box.)

Environmental Constraints

Peter Lorange identifies five major trends in the environment that pose particular challenges to strategy implementation and argues that organizations must actively integrate these environmental concerns into their strategy planning.[41]

SCARCITY. The first trend is the growing shortage of natural resources—energy, food, minerals—that causes the cost of raw materials to rise. In response, organizational strategies must (1) cultivate those businesses that use resources efficiently and whose profits are less vulnerable to the rising cost of raw materials and (2) forecast imminent shortages while seeking substitutes and alternative sources of supply.

POLITICS. Organizational fortunes often spin unpredictably as the globe turns according to changes in political stability, legal systems, and government attitudes toward business. Therefore, knowledge of an organization's external stakeholders (see Chapter 3) is increasingly important to its strategy, which must establish a consistent set of priorities to allow the organization to interact effectively with government, labor unions, consumer activists, and the like.

ATTITUDES. Like political realities, social values are in flux. In particular, two recent changes in social attitude may act to reduce organizational effectiveness. First is the change in attitude toward growth. Growth is devalued in the current social and economic climate, and managers' strategy must somehow counterbalance this attitude to ensure that the organization will continue to recognize and pursue growth opportunities.

Second is the challenge to traditional expectations of strong commitment and performance on the part of organization members. Organizations must respond by encouraging managers to participate in the development and implementation of strategy. The better its managers understand the organization's strategic direction and the more they feel they are contributing to its success, the greater will be their sense of commitment.

INTERNATIONAL MANAGEMENT

Planning in the U.S.S.R.: Gorbachev as CEO

In 1985, Mikhail S. Gorbachev became, at 54, the youngest leader of the Soviet Union since Stalin. Soon Gorbachev announced a sweeping program of economic reforms called *perestroika,* an essentially socialist program that included capitalist experiments, and a political policy of *glasnost,* or openness to new ideas. As the whole world anxiously watched, Gorbachev attempted to overcome the monumental barriers to implementing his bold new strategies.

To understand the enormousness of these barriers, consider the command economy the Soviet Union has used for more than 50 years. In a command economy, economic planning is centralized in the state, which owns most means of production and distribution. Quotas—not quality—are the key element in production, and profit is not a consideration in the planning process. When the centralized planning is poor—as it often is—there are costly inventory overruns or aggravating shortages. Small wonder, then, that in times of shortages black markets spring up to address demands unmet by the central planners. Consider, too, the Soviet Union's size—more than 8.5 million square miles—and its population—almost 300 million people representing over 90 national and ethnic groups.

Now imagine that you want to transform this troubled, inefficient command economy into an economically viable, quality-oriented mixed economy. You want to keep the state a central part of the economy, but you also want to leave room for such market-economy features as joint ventures, entrepreneurial firms, and the incentives of increased wages and profits. This is the task Gorbachev set himself.

Gorbachev had to walk a careful line in terms of how many market-type innovations he called for. On the one side, political conservatives pushed him to retain most of the features of the centralized economy; on the other side, political rivals like Boris Yeltsin, the elected leader of Russia, the largest of the Soviet Union's 15 republics, pushed for faster, more radical changes.

Meanwhile, the Soviet economy continued to decline, and shortages of food and consumer goods were at an all-time high. This, coupled with the political and economic reforms in the Eastern Bloc, increased ethnic and nationalist tensions in the Soviet Union, with many republics chafing at the restrictions imposed by Gorbachev's centralized approach. Given more freedom to pursue economic opportuni-

A Rare Treat. Moscow shoppers endured a three-hour wait for a chance to buy bananas from Chiquita Brands International, a welcome change from increasingly severe food shortages within the Soviet Union.

ties on its own, for example, Lithuania envisioned itself as a "European Hong Kong, where Western technology could be matched with raw materials from Russia and cheap labor in Lithuania. 'Look at the map,' says President Vytautas Landsbergis. 'We are closer to Berlin than to Moscow.'"[*]

When Gorbachev used tanks and troops to crush Lithuanian protesters early in 1991, his popularity took a sharp nosedive. Foreign investors began to have second thoughts about joint ventures in the Soviet Union, and political rivals quickly denounced Gorbachev's actions. A bitter struggle raged over whether the Soviet Union should maintain its centralized approach or give greater autonomy to the Soviet republics. Events reached a head on August 19, 1991, when Gorbachev was removed from office in a coup supported by the military and the secret police. The collapse of the coup just two days later accelerated democratic reform and the independence movement but also foreshadowed serious economic problems.

[*] As quoted in Paul Hofheinz, "Mother Russia's Freedom Fighter," *Fortune,* April 8, 1991, p. 74.

Sources: "Reforming the Soviet Economy," *Business Week,* December 7, 1987, pp. 76–80; Marshall Goldman, "Gorbachev, Turnaround CEO," *Harvard Business Review* 66, no. 3 (1988):107–113; "Can Gorbachev Control the Nationalism Glasnost Unleashed?" *Business Week,* March 28, 1988, p. 43; Gordon F. Boreham, "Gorbachev's Vision: On Hold or Rolled Back?" *Canadian Banker,* March–April 1990, pp. 14–21; Rosalind Klein Berlin, "Can the Russians Really Reform?" *Fortune,* May 7, 1990, pp. 117–118; Rose Brady et al., "The Market Is Coming! The Market Is Coming!" *Business Week,* June 4, 1990, pp. 60–61; Richard I. Kirkland, Jr., "Can Capitalism Save Perestroika?" *Fortune,* July 30, 1990, pp. 137ff; Paul Hofheinz, "Mother Russia's Freedom Fighter," *Fortune,* April 8, 1991, pp. 72–74.

HERE'S AN EXAMPLE
Pitney Bowes Inc. has had a long and close relationship with the U.S. Postal Service. Both parties have benefited from the sale of PB's postage meters, but rival competitors feel locked out of the market. (*Wall Street Journal*, 4/4/91, p. A1ff.)

HERE'S AN EXAMPLE
Sears Roebuck and Company, the giant retailing and financial services company, is described as "an organization in chaos." (*Business Week*, 2/11/91, p. 56ff.)

HERE'S AN EXAMPLE
Motorola Inc. is losing its edge in microprocessors because their obsession with technological excellence has delayed new products at critical times. Also, the company is experiencing corporate infighting between champions of a new technology and defenders of a successful older one. (*Wall Street Journal*, 3/4/91, p. A1ff.)

COORDINATED RESOURCE
See Study Guide Problem Exercise 8, "Time Management System."

POWER SHIFTS.   Interest groups and outside pressures on the organization are also constantly shifting. Organizations can monitor these trends and try to reduce their vulnerability to outside pressures by shifting their resources away from sensitive areas. Thus, many businesses have left South Africa to escape the attention of the antiapartheid movement.

TECHNOLOGY.   In the future, technical expertise may very well become the single most important strategic resource. Strategies will then have to manage technology in the same way they currently manage money. Technical knowledge will be allocated among the various parts of the organization and transferred between them as needed. In addition, methods of business departmentalization may be redefined to facilitate the transfer of knowledge. As technology increases at greater rates, product life cycles will unquestionably be affected.

Internal Constraints

Lorange also observes that some of the greatest difficulties facing managers are created by the organization itself.[42] Ideally, strategy prevents such handicaps; at the very least, it must cope with them.

INFLEXIBILITY.   All too often, functional divisions become rigidly independent fiefdoms that fail to communicate or cooperate with one another. Managers must become aware of the inherently *cross-functional* nature of the organization's major tasks. Thus Lorange proposes a dual-responsibility system that would assign managers to strategic cross-functional task forces in addition to their own functional operating responsibility.

EXECUTIVE OBSOLESCENCE.   Members of an organization may become obsolete as environmental changes make their accumulated knowledge and experience irrelevant. Therefore, the strategic planning process should be a learning process for managers, keeping them up-to-date. In addition, strategy should view human competencies as transferable resources to be shifted from problem to problem rather than hired to cope with rigidly defined problems and then fired when no longer needed.

PAROCHIALISM.   Managers often feel loyalty to their particular operation rather than to the organization as a whole. If the organizational strategy calls for a portfolio style (see Chapter 7), it must somehow develop values and attitudes that reinforce that point of view. Lorange recommends that feedback from the executive office emphasize the role each division plays within the organization—stressing the organization's portfolio perspective, not the division's relative success or failure.

VALUES, STYLES, TRADITIONS.   Organizational culture simplifies strategy implementation because it ensures that everyone involved will approach the issues from a similar point of view. But those same shared values, styles, and traditions can become vested interests that prevent managers from recognizing the significance of environmental changes and make them reluctant to modify their priorities or shift strategic resources. According to Lorange, central corporate planning must adopt a style that is responsive to strategic processes, which, in turn, must be receptive to goal modification, new-business developments, and environmental problems and opportunities.

POWER.   In many organizations, the CEO simply lacks the power to alter the firm's direction and to reallocate strategic resources. This can happen when executive power is decentralized in favor of functional managers, when the CEO is a lame duck nearing retirement, when a poor track record has undermined all confidence in the CEO, or when there is no coalition of top executives to support or supplement the CEO's efforts. The best solution is to develop a group of top managers who are able and willing to work together to develop and execute strategy.

Illustrative Case Study

Maintaining the Competitive Edge at Merck & Co.

External factors play an extremely important role in erecting barriers to successful strategy implementation. Among the external barriers faced by pharmaceutical manufacturers is the problem of securing the approval of the Food and Drug Administration (FDA) for the marketing of their products. In this respect, Merck, under Roy Vagelos's leadership, has been remarkably effective in implementing long-term—and highly costly—strategies to transform extremely expensive research-and-development commitments into profitable products.

A case in point is a product the company markets as Mevacor, which can reduce cholesterol levels in the body by up to 40 percent. Merck began preliminary research on the product back in 1956. When Roy Vagelos joined the company in 1975 as senior vice president for research, he championed Mevacor through a series of breakthroughs and setbacks in the development until, by 1986, about 25 percent of the company's $530 million R&D budget was committed to the project.

In November 1986, Merck presented the FDA with some 42,000 pages of documents supporting a request for a public review by an FDA advisory panel—a request that can take as long as a year to be granted. But Merck had started to implement its approval campaign much earlier. Since 1978, a special group for regulatory affairs had been working with the FDA, advising the agency not only of progress but of problems as well. A team of over 100 people made sure the FDA continually received the necessary information, and by February 19, 1987, the company had already met some 6,000 individual target deadlines. On that day—three months after filing its application—Merck won its hearing date. The next day, Mevacor received the panel's unanimous preliminary approval, and final approval was granted in August. Merck had accomplished in 9 months what normally takes about 30.

The next step in implementation was marketing. Merck is an industry leader in R&D, spending $1 billion in its laboratories each year; it also devotes $670 million per year to marketing and advertising, key functions in its strategy implementation. Some industry analysts estimate that Mevacor (and its improved versions) will become the leading product in a $4.5 billion market composed of cholesterol-conscious consumers.

Vagelos is openly pleased with Merck's performance, but he is quick to point out the company's weaknesses—it has only a 4.4 percent market share (half of what Vagelos wants) and its R&D efforts are not keeping pace with the amazing successes of the past few years. Meanwhile, competitors such as Bristol-Myers Squibb, SmithKline, Kodak, and Dow have merged with other companies to increase their product lines and market shares. Vagelos's dilemma was this: Could Merck's newly decentralized approach to R&D keep Merck competitive or should Merck follow suit and merge with another pharmaceutical giant to stay ahead?

Banking on the benefits of independence, Vagelos opted for an impressive alternative: He entered Merck into several joint ventures to gain access to new drugs while offering other companies Merck's experience in marketing and rushing drugs through the tedious FDA approval process. Partnerships with DuPont, Immulogic Pharmaceutical Corporation, and Johnson & Johnson, as well as a "drug-swapping" arrangement with ICI Americas, have secured the additional new drugs Merck needs without a merger and the multitude of problems mergers bring—higher operating costs, increased debt, melding corporate cultures, and so on. The DuPont deal gives Merck the lion's share of the profits on the A2 inhibitor, a promising new drug that combats heart disease—a drug DuPont has spent over $2 billion to research and develop. The deal has also brought forth a new company, DuPont Merck Pharmaceuticals, which will take over DuPont's entire pharmaceutical operation and have the foreign marketing rights on some of Merck's prescription medicines, plus some additional capital from Merck. Both companies claim that their earnings won't be diluted by the arrangement.

Some experts are uncertain how long this strategy will work. As more and more pharmaceutical giants merge, Merck will face increasing pressures to follow suit. For the time being, however, Vagelos's strategy of incremental innovation and "win-win" joint ventures is paying impressive dividends and could preserve both Merck's momentum and its independence. ■

Sources: Stephen W. Quickel, "Merck & Co.: Sheer Energy," *Business Month,* December 1988, p. 36; Sandra Friedland, "Pharmaceutical Company Shares Its Harvest of Achievement," *The New York Times,* March 5, 1989, Sect. 12, p. 1; Elizabeth S. Kiesche, "An Affair of the Heart," *Chemical Week,* October 11, 1989, pp. 6–7; Joseph Weber and Emily T. Smith, "Merck Wants to Be Alone—But with Lots of Friends," *Business Week,* October 23, 1989, p. 62; "Leaders of the Most Admired," *Fortune,* January 29, 1990, pp. 41–42; Michael Waldholz, "Merck and DuPont Ally to Form Drug Joint Venture," *The Wall Street Journal,* July 26, 1990, p. B1, Joseph Weber, "Merck Needs More Gold from the White Coats," *Business Week,* March 18, 1991, pp. 102–104.

■ SUMMARY

Strategy implementation consists of the administrative tasks needed to put strategy into practice. The scope and pace of implementation depend, in part, on the goals of corporate strategy and the problems strategy must solve. Major problems require either complex or sequential interventions, while minor problems require evolutionary or managerial interventions.

Implementation also depends on the organization's structure. Chandler's thesis was that U.S. organizations typically pass through three stages of strategic and structural development as they move from a unit, to a functional, and then to a multidivisional structure. The Seven-S model moves beyond Chandler to suggest that successful strategy implementation depends on the interaction of structure, strategy, systems, style, staff, skills, and superordinate goals.

Strategies are institutionalized when they are incorporated into a collection of values, norms, roles, and groups devoted to reaching a certain goal. Because CEOs spend so much time formulating strategy, their personal values inevitably shape strategy and corporate culture. In addition, CEOs interpret strategy, demonstrate the firm's commitment to its values, and motivate others. CEOs also try to be sure the right people are in key managerial positions. Hiring outsiders over insiders has both advantages and disadvantages, depending on whether the company is in a turnover, selective-blend, stability, or reorientation situation.

Operational plans, which provide the details of implementation, fall into two general classes: single-use plans, designed to deal with nonrecurring goals; and standing plans, designed to handle recurring and predictable situations. Standing plans include policies, procedures, and rules. Procedures such as setting annual objectives, management by objectives, and reward systems can be powerful tools for implementing strategy and increasing employee commitment to strategic goals.

Successful implementation can be blocked by environment constraints (such as scarce resources, politics, social attitudes, power shifts, and technology) and by internal constraints (such as inflexible structures, executive obsolescence, parochialism, outdated values, and lack of CEO power).

■ REVIEW QUESTIONS

1. What are the differences among evolutionary, managerial, sequential, and complex interventions?

2. Describe Chandler's thesis concerning the three stages in the growth and development of an organization's strategy and structure.

3. What are the seven factors in the Seven-S model?

4. What do we mean when we say a strategy is institutionalized? What role does the CEO play here? What factors should be considered in choosing key managers?

5. What are the two basic types of operational plans? Describe when each would be used.

6. List the three types of standing plans and explain why each is useful.

7. Give some examples of well and poorly designed annual objectives.

8. Define management by objectives. What are its strengths and weaknesses?

9. What are the weaknesses of traditional incentive plans? How can organizations improve them?

10. List some factors that can prevent effective strategy implementation. How can an organization overcome these barriers?

CASE STUDY

The Competition Chips Away at Cray Research

The world of superfast supercomputers is heating up. Although computer genius Seymour Cray pioneered the technology and his Cray Research Co. long dominated the field, American, European, and particularly Japanese challengers are threatening Cray's leadership. Supercomputers are vital to cutting-edge scientific research, military defense, and the development of numerous technologies from pharmaceuticals to aerospace engineering and high-definition TV. The international race in this field has many American politicians scrambling to aid U.S. efforts for economic and national security reasons. What happened to Cray?

Cray Research was founded in 1972 by Seymour Cray, who had started out as a key designer at Control Data. Ever since he introduced the world's first supercomputer, the Cray 1, in 1976, the firm had maintained a wide lead in the industry. Partly because of his dominance of the new technology, Cray could afford to focus his energies on what he did best—R&D and extensive exploration of risky new projects to make the fastest computers in the world.

Meanwhile, many other firms were eating away at Cray's market by concentrating on "minisupers," which were smaller and slower, but less expensive and better suited to the needs of individual companies. As the competition heated up and the demand for supercomputers declined, Cray was pressured to become more pragmatic and market-oriented.

In addition, pressures were being generated internally. In 1980, Cray had handed over the reins of the company to John Rollwagen, a man with both engineering and business degrees, and had begun to change his own focus and orientation. While Cray was working on the Cray 2, which was using a radical new technology (computer chips made of gallium arsenide rather than silicon), CEO Rollwagen was becoming concerned about putting all of Cray's eggs into one basket. He authorized a more certain project by Steve Chen, a brilliant Taiwanese computer designer, called the X-MP, which would revamp the Cray 1 to generate higher performance. The project succeeded and brought forth a model three times faster than the Cray 1. In 1986, when the Cray 2, using the older silicon technology, was finished, Rollwagen faced a difficult challenge. Seymour Cray began working on the Cray 3, another cutting-edge breakthrough, which would depend on the gallium arsenide technology, while Chen sought extensive funds for his own research project, which would rival the Cray 3. After spending more than $50 million on Chen's project, Rollwagen chose to cut funding in 1987 on the grounds that it was too risky and that money was tight. Rollwagen's decision prompted Chen to leave and start his own company, Supercomputer Systems Inc., using funding from IBM. Thus, Cray Research lost a research mind second only to Seymour Cray's and a key to the company's success.

More tough choices have come Rollwagen's way. In 1985, the company grew by 66 percent and its net profits increased by 20 percent, but sales rose only 10 percent in 1988 and profits in the first quarter of 1989 fell to $1.5 million on $116 million sales (1988 earnings were $26.4 million on $145.8 million revenues). A number of rival computers appeared on the market, the most notable being NEC's new SX-3, a silicon-based computer that is said to run faster than the Cray 3. By 1989, the Cray 3 had eaten up $120 million of research funds and its scheduling was being pushed back. Rollwagen again chose to pick a safer and cheaper alternative. He decided to stop funding the Cray 3 and to back the Y-MP16, an extension of Cray's existing silicon computers, which is projected to be as fast as the Cray 3. This choice led Seymour Cray to leave and found the Cray Computer Company, a "friendly" rival to Cray Research. Cray Research owns a 10 percent stake in the company and gave it $150 million in funds. Seymour Cray will have to seek any additional funds elsewhere.

The evolution of the market in supercomputers and minicomputers has meant a drastic shift in the landscape of Cray Research, once a company that paid little attention to the market. Now the business end of supercomputers, the dynamics of competition, and internal pressures have pushed Cray Research's leadership to adopt strategies that are moving the company farther away from its origin as a bastion for visionary, cutting-edge research in supercomputers.

Sources: "Sign of the Times: Even Cray Scales Back R&D," *Electronic Business,* August 7, 1989, pp. 61–62; David Chrubuck, "Cray versus Japan, Inc.," *Forbes,* September 4, 1989, pp. 118–119; Jim Bartimo, "Can Convex Throw the Big Boys a Curve?" *Business Week,* December 18, 1989, p. 104D; Richard Brandt et al., "The Future of Silicon Valley," *Business Week,* February 5, 1990, pp. 54–60; Thomas Donlan, "Not So Super Outlook for Cray Research, Competition Looms," *Barron's,* February 5, 1990, pp. 39–41; Russell Mitchell, "The Genius," *Business Week,* April 30, 1990, pp. 81–88.

Case Questions

1. Has Rollwagen's more pragmatic and market-oriented emphasis been the right strategy? Can you suggest a better alternative?

2. Was his decision to split the two companies the best approach?

3. What special problems come with diversification? What can Rollwagen do to integrate the minisuper and supercomputer efforts?

4. What can Cray and other U.S. companies do to compete better with the Japanese?

5. What role will people like Seymour Cray play in computer firms of the 1990s?

VIDEO CASE STUDY

Trying to Swallow a Whale When You're a Minnow

Although in 1991 Pan Am was forced to sell its assets to other airlines, in May 1989 it made an unusual bid for the parent company of Northwest Airlines, NA Corporation. What made the deal surprising was not that the size and prestige of the firms are in stark contrast, but that the relative health of the two airlines in recent years would have made one think the deal would have been working in the opposite direction.

Since 1981, Pan Am had totaled over $1.7 billion in losses, while Northwest Airlines had managed to build up over a half a billion in profits. To analysts, it appeared that the deregulation of the airline industry in the 1970s had sent Pan Am into a tailspin—one that it was still struggling to get out of. Other airlines had the means and resources to establish domestic networks and root systems, while Pan Am lagged behind and had slowly diminished into a "cash-poor minnow." Despite its poor performance, though, evidence suggested that Pan Am had solidified its base and may have been on more solid ground.

Northwest, by contrast, was a promising firm with a sound root system and a solid cash base—a "cash whale." The main negative in Northwest's situation was its relationship with its pilots; contract negotiations had been going on for more than two years with little success.

Pan Am was not the only bidder for Northwest. Other offers included that of oil man Marvin Davis, who had little experience with the airline industry and would have had to borrow most of the money. Another offer came from Alfred Checchi and Gary Wilson who seem interested in buying Northwest to break it up and sell it. Fortsman, Little & Company was also interested in buying Northwest to improve it and then sell it for a higher price.

Northwest, of course, would prefer to see the airline remain intact, but it was also interested in getting the most it can. Also, one of the major obstacles to any negotiations was the pilots' strong desire to keep the airline intact.

Case Questions

1. How would you evaluate Pan Am's strategy? What are the major impediments to implementing its strategy?

2. What can Pan Am do to make their bid more attractive to Northwest?

3. What are the biggest problems that Pan Am will face in integrating Northwest's systems, pilots, routes, planes, and so on, into Pan Am's operations.

■ *NOTES*

[1]Lawrence G. Hrebeniak and William F. Joyce, *Implementing Strategy* (New York: Macmillan, 1984), pp. 19–22.

[2]See L. J. Bourgeois, "Strategic Goals, Perceived Uncertainty, and Economic Performance in Volatile Environments," *Academy of Management Journal,* September 1985, pp. 548–573.

[3]Tom Peters, *Thriving on Chaos: Handbook for a Management Revolution* (New York: Alfred A. Knopf, 1988); Robert H. Waterman, *The Renewal Factor: How the Best Get and Keep the Competitive Edge* (New York: Bantam Books, 1987).

[4]Our discussion of structure and strategy draws heavily on Chapter 2 of *Strategy Implementation: Structure, Systems, and Process,* 2nd ed., by Jay R. Galbraith and Robert K. Kazanjian (St. Paul, Minn.: West Publishing, 1986).

[5]A. D. Chandler, *Strategy and Structure* (Cambridge, Mass.: MIT Press, 1962).

[6]This example is taken from Donald F. Harvey, *Strategic Management* (Columbus, Ohio: Merrill, 1982), pp. 269–270.

[7]R. K. Kazanjian, "The Organizational Evolution of High Technology Venture: The Impact of Stage of Growth on the Nature of Structure and Planning Process," Ph.D. dissertation, The Wharton School, University of Pennsylvania, 1983.

[8]L. Wrigley, "Divisional Autonomy and Diversification," Ph.D. dissertation, Harvard Business School, 1970.

[9]R. P. Rumelt, *Strategy, Structure, and Economic Performance* (Boston: Division of Research, Harvard Business School, 1974).

[10]R. P. Rumelt, "Diversification Strategy and Profitability," *Strategic Management Journal* 3 (1982):359–369.

[11]Raymond E. Miles and Charles E. Snow, "Fit, Failure and the Hall of Fame," *California Management Review* 26, no. 3 (1984):10–28. See also Miles and Snow, *Organizational Strategy, Structure, and Process* (New York: McGraw-Hill, 1978), and "Organizations: New Concepts for New Forms," *California Management Review* 28, no. 2 (1986):64–71; and Donald C. Hambrick, "Some Tests of the Effectiveness and Functional Attributes of Miles and Snow's Strategic Types," *Academy of Management Journal* 26 (1983):5–26.

[12]D. Channon, *The Strategy and Structure of British Enterprise* (London: Macmillan, 1973); G. Pooley-Dyas, "Strategy and Structure of French Enterprise," Ph.D. dissertation, Harvard Business School, 1972; B. R. Scott, "The Industrial State: Old Myths and New Realities," *Harvard Business Review* 51 (1973):133–148.

[13]Y. Suzuki, "The Strategy and Structure of Top 100 Japanese Industrial Enterprises 1950–1970," *Strategic Management Journal* 1 (1980):265–291.

[14]J. Stopford and L. Wells, *Managing the Multinational Enterprise* (London: Longman, 1972).

[15]L. Franko, "The Move Toward a Multi-Divisional Structure in European Organizations," *Administrative Science Quarterly* 19 (1974):493–506; L. Franko, *The European Multinationals* (Greenwich, Conn.: Greylock Press, 1976).

[16]C. A. Bartlett, "MNCs: Get Off the Reorganization Merry-Go-Round," *Harvard Business Review* 62 (March–April 1983):138–147; C. K. Prahalad and Y. L. Doz, "An Approach to Strategic Control in MNCs," *Sloan Management Review* (Summer 1981):5–13.

[17]See Robert H. Waterman, Jr., Thomas J. Peters, and Julien R. Phillips, "Structure Is Not Organization," *Business Horizons* (June 1980).

[18]A. Gupta, "Contingency Linkages Between Strategy and General Manager Characteristics," *Academy of Management Review* 27 (1984):25–41; N. M. Tichy, C. J. Fombrun, and M. A. Devanna, "Strategic Human Resource Management," *Sloan Management Review* (Winter 1982):47–61.

[19]John A. Pearce II and Richard B. Robinson, Jr., *Formulation and Implementation of Competitive Strategy* (Homewood, Ill.: Irwin, 1985), pp. 336–341.

[20]Thomas J. Peters and Robert H. Waterman, Jr., *In Search of Excellence* (New York: Harper & Row, 1982), pp. xx–xxi.

[21]"The Corporate Culture Vultures," *Fortune,* October 17, 1983, p. 66.

[22]Claudia H. Deutsch, "Kodak Pays the Price for Change," *The New York Times,* March 6, 1988, pp. F1, F7–F8.

[23]Our discussion draws on the classification and description of plans in William H. Newman, *Administrative Action: The Techniques of Organization and Management,* 2nd ed. (Englewood Cliffs, N.J.: Prentice Hall, 1963), pp. 13–54. The types of plans we include in the classification and our specific interpretation of their use differ somewhat from Newman's version.

[24]See Lloyd L. Byars, *Concepts of Strategic Management: Planning and Implementation* (New York: Harper & Row, 1984), p. 212.

[25]Pearce and Robinson, *Formulation and Implementation of Competitive Strategy,* p. 291.

[26]Peter F. Drucker, *The Practice of Management* (New York: Harper & Brothers, 1954).

[27]See Dale D. McConkey, *How to Manage by Results,* 4th ed. (New York: American Management Association, 1983), p. 3. See also Stephen J. Carroll, Jr., and Henry L. Tosi, Jr., *Management by Objectives: Applications and Research* (New York: Macmillan, 1973), p. 3. For a comprehensive review of the literature on planning in general and goal setting in particular, see Scott Armstrong, "The Value of Formal Planning for Strategic Decisions: Review of the Empirical Research," *Strategic Management Journal* 3, no. 2 (1982):197–211.

[28]See W. J. Reddin, *Effective Management by Objectives: The 3-D Method of MBO* (New York: McGraw-Hill, 1971), pp. 13–19; and George S. Odiorne, *MBO II: A System of Managerial Leadership for the 80's* (Belmont, Calif.: Fearon Pitman, 1979), pp. 127–140, 161–165, 320–321.

[29]Carroll and Tosi, *Management by Objectives,* pp. 1–19.

[30]See also John M. Ivancevich, "Different Goal-Setting Treatments and Their Effects on Performance and Satisfaction," *Academy of Management Journal* 20, no. 3 (September 1977):406–419; Gary P. Latham

and Timothy P. Steele, "The Motivational Effects of Participation versus Goal Setting on Performance," *Academy of Management Journal* 26, no. 3 (September 1983):406–417; Mark E. Tubbs, "Goal Setting: A Meta-Analytic Examination of the Empirical Evidence," *Journal of Applied Psychology,* August 1986, pp. 474–483; and Gary P. Latham and Edward A. Locke, "Goal Setting—A Motivational Technique That Works," *Organizational Dynamics* 8, no. 2 (Autumn 1979):68–80. Latham and Locke reach the conclusion that goal setting increases performance whether goals are set unilaterally by the supervisor or with the participation of the employees—as long as the goals are *accepted* by the employees. A thorough review of the effects of goal setting on performance is provided in Gary P. Latham and Gary A. Yukl, "A Review of Research on the Application of Goal Setting in Organizations," *Academy of Management Journal* 18, no. 4 (December 1975):824–845.

[31]See Jay S. Kim, "Effect of Behavior Plus Outcome Goal Setting and Feedback on Employee Satisfaction and Performance," *Academy of Management Journal* 27, no. 1 (March 1984):139–149.

[32]See Herbert H. Meyer, Emmanuel Kay, and John R. P. French, Jr., "Split Roles in Performance Appraisal," *Harvard Business Review* 43, no. 1 (January–February 1965):123–129; and Miriam Erez, P. Christopher Earley, and Charles L. Hulin, "The Impact of Participation on Goal Acceptance and Performance: A Two-Step Model," *Academy of Management Journal,* March 1985, pp. 50–66. For a thorough discussion of the literature on participation, and the ambiguities in much of the research, see Edwin A. Locke and E. M. Schweiger, "Participation in Decision-Making: One More Look," in Barry M. Staw, ed., *Research in Organizational Behavior,* Vol. 1 (Greenwich, Conn.: JAI Press, 1979), pp. 265–339.

[33]For a discussion of how satisfaction is related to setting objectives, see Thomas I. Chacko, "An Examination of the Affective Consequences of Assigned and Self-Set Goals," *Human Relations* 35, no. 9 (September 1982):771–776.

[34]Hrebeniak and Joyce, *Implementing Strategy,* p. 15.

[35]M. Salter, "Tailor Incentive Compensation to Strategy," *Harvard Business Review* 51 (1973):94–102.

[36]A. Rappaport, "Corporate Performance Standards and Shareholder Value," *Journal of Business Strategy* 3 (Spring 1983):28–38.

[37]P. Lorange, *Corporate Planning: An Executive Viewpoint* (Englewood Cliffs, N.J.: Prentice Hall, 1980).

[38]A. Rappaport, "How to Design Value—Contributing Executive Incentives," *Journal of Business Strategy* 4 (Fall 1983):49–59.

[39]D. Norburn and P. Miller, "Strategy and Executive Reward: The Mis-Match in the Strategic Process," *Journal of General Management* 6 (Summer 1981):17–27.

[40]See Rappaport, "How to Design Value"; A. Rappaport, "Selecting Strategies That Create Shareholder Value," *Harvard Business Review* 60 (May–June 1981):139–149; P. J. Stonich, "Using Rewards in Implementing Strategy," *Strategic Management Journal* 2 (1981):345–352; and P. J. Stonich and C. E. Zaragoza, "Strategic Funds Programming: The Missing Link in Corporate Planning," *Managerial Planning* (September–October 1980):3–11.

[41]Peter Lorange, "Where Do We Go from Here: Implementation Challenges for the 1980s," in *Implementation of Strategic Planning* (Englewood Cliffs, N.J.: Prentice Hall, 1982), pp. 209–226.

[42]Ibid., pp. 220–225.

DECISION MAKING

Upon completing this chapter, you should be able to:

1. Explain the principal difference between problem finding and opportunity finding and show how they are related.

2. Describe the four situations that usually alert managers to the existence of a problem.

3. Discuss the factors that affect a manager's threshold for problem recognition.

4. List and explain the questions managers can use to set decision-making priorities.

5. Explain how managers can decide to delegate a decision or refer it to a superior.

6. Compare and contrast programmed and nonprogrammed decisions.

7. Explain the differences between the decision-making states of certainty, risk, uncertainty, and turbulence.

8. List and explain the four basic stages in the rational model of decision making and problem solving.

9. Explain how the rational model differs from Simon's model of "bounded rationality."

10. Describe the three heuristics managers commonly use and explain how they can both help and hinder decision making.

11. Discuss Norman R. F. Maier's suggestions for improving the effectiveness of managerial problem solving and decision making.

Guy Billout, *Solutions*. Courtesy of the Artist.

ILLUSTRATIVE CASE STUDY

INTRODUCTION

Diplomacy and Determination in High-Level Decision Making

John McKinley, CEO of Texaco, knew he was faced with a difficult issue, both for his career and for the future of his company. Did Texaco want to become an active bidder to acquire Getty Oil? Getty and Pennzoil had already reached an "agreement in principle" for a Pennzoil takeover, so any action taken by Texaco would have to be made immediately, before the Getty-Pennzoil deal was finalized.

The situation was very complicated. It had begun when Getty Oil began searching for a buyer. Getty was largely controlled by the Getty family trust, Getty trust shares, and the shares held by the Getty Museum—a total constituting 52 percent of the outstanding shares. The remaining 48 percent were publicly held. Gordon Getty had begun by seeking a partner to buy the publicly held shares, planning to combine the family shares with those held by the museum and thus take control of the company. However, he needed to eliminate the board of directors, which represented the public, to gain his ultimate goal—total control. Pennzoil had agreed to purchase the outstanding public shares at a value of $112.50 per share.

Since the Getty Oil board of directors objected to this proposal on the grounds that the public was being cheated, they sought a company to make a counteroffer, buying the public and museum shares and thereby thwarting Gordan Getty's bid for control of Getty Oil. It was this role of "white knight" that Texaco was being asked to fill. Texaco would have to pay approximately $125 per share—a price that would assure the public shareholders of receiving full value and entice the museum to sell rather than join with Gordon Getty in taking control. Additionally, the investment bankers advising Texaco thought this price would be high enough to lure Getty into selling, rather than buying, the family shares.

The purchase of Getty could solve a number of problems for Texaco, which was currently draining its reserves much faster than it was locating new sources of oil. Although refinery modernization guaranteed efficiency in turning crude oil into marketable products, Texaco was fast losing its competitive position within the industry, as it was spending nearly double the industry standard to explore for new oil reserves and consistently coming up empty-handed. The purchase of Getty Oil would almost double Texaco's oil reserves—and at a quarter of the price Tex-

aco was presently paying for exploration. In addition, the purchase of such a large company would greatly enhance Texaco's position in an industry in which it was a large but not a key player.

However, McKinley was not entirely comfortable with the proposed deal. It had long been Texaco policy not to engage in any hostile takeovers, and the situation with Getty was so unclear that he could not tell how welcome his offer would be. Certainly the Getty Oil board members who had approached him would welcome an offer. But how would Gordon Getty respond? If he was against Texaco, then McKinley did not want to pursue the possibility any further. Unfortunately, it was not as simple as merely asking Gordon Getty. Takeover negotiations are extremely delicate, and any such overt action on Texaco's part could irrevocably disturb the process as it was currently evolving. The lawyers and investment bankers were encouraging McKinley to move forward, but their advice was suspect, since their fees would be considerably higher if the deal were pursued.

All of these considerations weighed heavily on McKinley. Any move would have to be made within the next 24 hours, and the sooner the better. Taking too long to consider all the options would be the same as deciding against pursuing the deal. Once a move was made, McKinley would be obligated to continue. Therefore, he had to be totally committed to pursuing the takeover of Getty Oil before making even preliminary moves, including the gathering of any more information.

Source: Steve Coll, *The Taking of Getty Oil* (New York: Atheneum Books, 1987).

decision making The process of identifying and selecting a course of action to solve a specific problem.

THOUGHT PROVOKER

Why did you decide to come to class today? What were your alternatives, and what consequences affected your decision?

*J*ohn McKinley faced a difficult decision. **Decision making**—identifying and selecting a course of action to deal with a specific problem or take advantage of an opportunity—is an important part of every manager's job. We have seen, for example, how decision making shapes a company's strategic and operational plans. Thus, every manager needs to develop skill in decision making and problem solving. In this chapter, we will discuss the problem- and opportunity-finding process, the nature of managerial decision making, and the rational model of decision making. We will also discuss real-world challenges to rational decision making as well as tips for improving decision making and problem solving by individuals and by organizations.

■ *PROBLEM AND OPPORTUNITY FINDING*

problem Situation that occurs when an actual state of affairs differs from a desired state of affairs.

COORDINATED RESOURCE
See Samaras Case 2.2, "Solve the Problem!"

TEACHING TIP
Have your students look at making a job choice from a problem-finding perspective and an opportunity-finding perspective.

A **problem** arises when an actual state of affairs differs from a desired state of affairs. In many cases, though, a problem may be an opportunity in disguise. The *problem* of "too many" employees, for example, could also be seen as an *opportunity* to restructure, saving jobs and improving efficiency at the same time. Because organizations face many problems and opportunities, we will begin our discussion by looking at the factors that help effective managers recognize both problems and opportunities. Then we will look at the circumstances that lead managers to act.

The Problem-Finding Process

William Pounds has argued that the problem-finding process is often informal and intuitive. Four situations usually alert managers to possible problems: when there is a deviation from past experience, when there is a deviation from a set plan, when other people present problems to the manager, and when competitors outperform the manager's organization.[1]

A *deviation from past experience* means that a previous pattern of performance in the organization has been broken. This year's sales are falling behind last year's; expenses have suddenly increased; employee turnover has risen. Events such as these are signals to the manager that a problem has developed.

A *deviation from the plan* means the manager's projections or expectations are not being met. Profit levels are lower than anticipated; a department is exceeding its budget; a project is off schedule. Such events tell the manager that something must be done to get the plan back on course.

Other people often bring problems to the manager. Customers complain about late deliveries; higher-level managers set new performance standards for the manager's department; subordinates resign. Many decisions that managers make daily involve problems presented by others.

The *performance of competitors* can also create problem-solving situations. When other companies develop new processes or improvements in operating procedures, the manager may have to reevaluate processes or procedures in his or her own organization. Competitors within the same organization may also pose problems. If a company has many plants, for example, top management may compare the performance of each plant, a problem for the manager of a plant that is performing below average.

A study by Marjorie A. Lyles and Ian I. Mitroff collected case histories from upper-level managers of major organizations. Eighty percent of these managers said they had become aware of the existence of a major problem before it showed up on financial statements or in other formal indicators—and even before it was presented to them by superiors and subordinates. "Informal communication and intuition" were described as the sources of their information.[2]

Opportunity Finding. To his leasing agents, the tiny rental-car side of Executive Leasing was a nuisance, so founder Jack Taylor turned it over to an ambitious young assistant, who carved out a market niche in "replacement cars," low-cost rentals for drivers whose cars had been stolen or damaged in accidents. Then fate intervened: A number of court decisions held insurance companies liable for the "economic loss" policyholders suffered from being without a car. In defense, insurers began to cover the cost of replacement rentals, steering policyholders toward companies that offered the lowest prices. Taylor and his managers complied, sparking off a growth momentum that led to a name change—to Enterprise Rent-A-Car—a 90,000-car fleet, and double-digit growth rates throughout the 1980s and early 1990s.

Problem finding is not always straightforward. Sara Kiesler and Lee Sproull have identified some of the more common errors managers make in sensing problems. They describe three main categories of pitfalls that managers may encounter: false association of events, false expectation of events, and false self-perceptions and social image. For example, during the 1960s and early 1970s, managers at mainframe computer manufacturers had false expectations: They believed that a significant demand for personal computers did not and probably never would exist. The reality of the market for personal computers did not fit their expectations.[3]

Opportunity Finding

It is not always clear whether a situation faced by a manager presents a problem or an opportunity. For example, missed opportunities create problems for organizations, and opportunities are often found while exploring problems.[4] David B. Gleicher, a management consultant, provides a useful distinction between the two terms. He defines a problem as something that endangers the organization's ability to *reach* its objectives, and an **opportunity** as something that offers the chance to *exceed* objectives.[5]

The **dialectical inquiry method,** sometimes called "The Devil's Advocate Method," is useful in problem solving and opportunity finding.[6] In this method, the decision maker determines possible solutions and the assumptions they are based

opportunity Situation that occurs when circumstances offer an organization the chance to exceed stated goals and objectives.

dialectical inquiry method A method of analysis in which a decision maker determines and negates his or her assumptions, and then creates "countersolutions" based on the negative assumptions.

Problem Recognition. Sears employee Catherine DiGiovanna awaits customers for a line of fashionable, but moderately priced career separates introduced when Sears managers realized the company had a performance gap in women's apparel, which can be a store's most profitable items.

on, considers the opposite of all of the assumptions, and then develops countersolutions based on the negative assumptions. This process may generate more useful alternative solutions and identify unnoticed opportunities.

An enormous amount of research has been devoted to problem solving, whereas very little concerns problem finding, and even less concerns opportunity finding. Yet, as Peter Drucker makes clear, opportunities rather than problems are the key to organizational and managerial success. Drucker observes that solving a problem merely restores normality, but results "must come from the exploitation of opportunities." Drucker links exploitation of opportunities to finding "the right things to do, and . . . [concentrating] resources and efforts on them.[7]

Deciding to Decide

The idea that managers are problem solvers may conjure up the image of managers sitting behind their desks, calmly deciding what to do about every problem that arises. In fact, managers differ widely in *what* they consider to be a problem and how they elect to deal with it.

THRESHOLDS FOR PROBLEM RECOGNITION. How big is the gap between the actual and desired state of affairs? How does this gap affect our chances of reaching or exceeding organizational goals? If this gap is a problem, how hard will it be to fix? How quickly do we need to move to fix the problem? to take advantage of an opportunity? These are the sorts of questions managers ask in defining a situation as either a problem or an opportunity. Some of these answers can be found in strategic and operational plans, which include standards for performance, or by statistical analysis of available data. Other answers depend on contingencies, or events that could not be anticipated during the planning process. To answer such questions effectively, managers must use their judgment, based on their knowledge of both the direct- and indirect-action environments for their organizations. That is why gathering information, either through formal or informal information systems, is so important to being an effective manager.

As Guth and Tagiuri have noted, though, all this information is filtered through managers' values and backgrounds, which also influence the types of problems and opportunities they choose to work on.[8] If managers are motivated primarily by economic values, they usually want to make decisions on practical matters, such as those involving marketing, production, or profits. If they have a more theoretical orientation, they may be concerned with the long-term prospects of their organization. If their orientation is political, they may be more concerned with competing with other organizations or with their own personal advancement.

The backgrounds and expertise of managers will also influence what they see as problems and opportunities. A study of executives by De Witt C. Dearborn and Herbert A. Simon found that managers from different departments will define the same problem in different terms.[9] In this study, a group of executives were presented with a complex business case and asked to describe what they saw as the most important problem facing the company. Each executive tended to be sensitive to those parts of the case that related to his or her department, defining opportunities and problems from his or her particular perspective. For example, marketing managers want inventory to be high and view low inventory as a problem situation. Finance managers, on the other hand, view a high-inventory situation as a problem, preferring low inventory in most cases.[10] If the organization is to move toward its goals, though, all managers must take a larger view of their role in the total organization. In addition, top managers must work to coordinate the actions of lower-level managers, a process we will discuss in more detail in Chapter 11.

SETTING PRIORITIES. No manager can possibly handle every problem that arises in the daily course of business. It is important, therefore, that managers learn to establish priorities and to delegate minor problems to subordinates. When managers are presented with a problem, they should ask themselves the following questions:

1. *Is the problem easy to deal with?* A manager who gives the same level of attention to every problem will get very little work done. Most problems, however, require only a small amount of the manager's attention. Even if the decision turns out to be wrong, correcting it will be relatively speedy and inexpensive. To avoid getting bogged down in trivial details, effective and efficient managers reserve formal decision-making techniques for problems that truly require them.

2. *Might the problem resolve itself?* The classic illustration of this principle concerns Napoleon, who was reputed to have let incoming mail pile up on his desk for three weeks or more. When he finally read the accumulated mail, he was pleased to find that most matters had been resolved in the interim. In like manner, managers find that an amazing number of time-wasting problems can be eliminated if they are simply ignored. Therefore, managers should rank problems in order of importance. Those at the bottom of the list usually take care of themselves or can be dealt with by others. If one of these problems worsens, it moves to a higher-priority level on the list.

COORDINATED RESOURCE
See Study Guide Problem Exercise 9, "Deciding Who Decides."

3. *Is this my decision to make?* When confronted with an important problem requiring a decision, a manager must determine if he or she is actually responsible for making the decision. Here a general rule can be of help: The closer to the origin of the problem the decision is made, the better. This rule has two corollaries: (a) pass as *few* decisions as possible to those higher up, and (b) pass as *many* as possible to those lower down. Usually, those who are closest to a problem are in the best position to decide what to do about it.

When managers refer an issue to someone higher up for a decision, they have to be sure they are not simply passing the buck instead of being properly cautious. (Referring a matter to a subordinate is not passing the buck because the manager still retains ultimate responsibility.) How can managers decide when they should pass a problem on to a superior? If our basic rule and its corollaries do not supply the answer, managers can supplement them with a few other questions: Does the issue affect other departments? Will it have a major impact on the superior's area of responsibility? Does it require information available only from a higher level? Does it involve a serious breach of our departmental budget? Is this problem outside my area of responsibility or authority? A "yes" answer to any of these questions indicates the issue should probably be referred to a superior.

■ *THE NATURE OF MANAGERIAL DECISION MAKING*

TEACHING TIP
Emphasize to your students the simplicity yet thoroughness of the decision-making process.

COORDINATED RESOURCE
Use Transparency 47, The Continuum of Decision-Making Conditions.

Different problems require different types of decision making. Routine or minor matters, such as a return of merchandise, can be handled by a procedure, a type of *programmed decision.* More important decisions, such as the location of a new retail outlet, require a *nonprogrammed decision,* a specific solution created through a less structured process of decision making and problem solving. Because most decisions involve future events, managers must also learn to analyze the certainty, risk, and uncertainty associated with alternative courses of action.

Programmed and Nonprogrammed Decisions

It is useful to distinguish between situations that call for programmed decisions and those that call for nonprogrammed decisions.[11]

PROGRAMMED DECISIONS. **Programmed decisions** are made in accordance with written or unwritten *policies, procedures,* or *rules* that simplify decision making in recurring situations by limiting or excluding alternatives. For example, managers rarely have to worry about the salary range for a newly hired employee because organizations generally establish a salary scale for all positions. Routine procedures exist for dealing with routine problems.[12]

Programmed decisions are used for dealing with complex as well as with uncomplicated issues. If a problem recurs, and if its component elements can be defined, predicted, and analyzed, then it may be a candidate for programmed decision making. For example, decisions about how much inventory of a given product to maintain can involve a great deal of fact-finding and forecasting, but careful analysis of the elements in the problem may yield a series of routine, programmed decisions.

To some extent, programmed decisions limit our freedom because the organization rather than the individual decides what to do. However, programmed decisions are intended to be liberating. The policies, rules, or procedures by which we make programmed decisions save time, allowing us to devote attention to other, more important activities. For example, deciding how to handle customer complaints on an individual basis would be time-consuming and costly, but a policy stating "exchanges will be permitted on all purchases within 14 days" simplifies matters considerably.

We should note that while effective managers lean on policy to save time, they remain alert for exceptional cases. For example, company policy may put a ceiling on the advertising budget for each product, but a particular product may need an extensive advertising campaign to counter the newly aggressive marketing strategy of a competitor. Anheuser Busch launched such a strategy to defend its market share when Miller introduced its new Miller Lite. A programmed decision—to advertise the product in accordance with budget guidelines—might have been a mistake. Ultimately, managers must use their judgment in deciding whether a situation calls for a programmed decision.

NONPROGRAMMED DECISIONS. **Nonprogrammed decisions** deal with unusual or exceptional problems. If a problem has not come up often enough to be covered by a policy or is so important that it deserves special treatment, it must be handled by a nonprogrammed decision. Such problems as how to allocate an organization's resources, what to do about a failing product line, how community relations should be improved—in fact, most of the significant problems a manager will face—usually require nonprogrammed decisions. Furthermore, as one moves up the organizational hierarchy, the ability to make nonprogrammed decisions becomes more important. For this reason, most management-development programs try to improve managers' abilities to make nonprogrammed decisions—usually by teaching them to analyze problems systematically and to make logical decisions. The rational decision-making process we describe later is used mainly for nonprogrammed decisions.

Certainty, Risk, and Uncertainty

In making decisions, all managers must weigh alternatives, many of which involve future events that are difficult to predict: a competitor's reaction to a new price list, interest rates in three years, the reliability of a new supplier. For that reason, decision-making situations are frequently categorized on a continuum ranging from *certainty* (highly predictable) to *turbulence* (highly unpredictable).[13] (See Fig. 9-1.)

CERTAINTY. Under conditions of **certainty,** we know our objective and have accurate, measurable, reliable information about the outcome of each alternative we are considering. Consider, for example, the director who must order programs for a storytelling festival. She knows the objective—get programs printed—and can easily compare representative samples from local printers and the prices they quote for printing varying quantities of programs. With this information, she can select a

Nonprogrammed Decisions. Faced with deep Pentagon spending cuts, Ball Corp. CEO Richard M. Ringoen made a series of nonprogrammed decisions. He cut back the company's aerospace division, which depended on defense spending, and pumped money back into Ball's basic business—glass and metal containers. In other nonprogrammed decisions, Ball bought back part of the business it sold in 1987 and paid $1 billion for the European packaging operations of Continental Can Co., moves meant to prepare Ball to tap a European demand for beverage cans that is growing at twice the rate of demand in the United States.

COORDINATED RESOURCE

See Samaras Exercise 2.2, "Certainty, Risk, and Uncertainty and the Reverse."

risk Decision-making condition in which managers know the probability a given alternative will lead to a desired goal or outcome.

probability A statistical measure of the chance a certain event or outcome will occur.

printer and know with certainty what the printing will cost. This information will *not* help her make a more difficult decision, though: How *many* programs should she order? In making this decision, she must consider the fact that money wasted on ordering too many programs cuts into the amount of money available for ordering high-margin souvenir items such as tee-shirts or sweatshirts, and will probably draw complaints from the other members of the festival's board of directors. The director now moves from conditions of certainty to conditions of risk, uncertainty, or even turbulence. Unfortunately, such conditions are far more common than conditions of certainty, which exist mostly for programmed and relatively simple nonprogrammed decisions.

RISK. **Risk** occurs whenever we cannot predict an alternative's outcome with certainty, but we do have enough information to predict the **probability** it will lead to desired state. (If you have ever flipped a coin to make a decision or played a roulette wheel, you have dealt with probabilities.) If this is the tenth annual storytelling festival held in this town at this time of the year, the director can analyze past attendance records and predict with reasonable certainty the number of programs needed. If this is the event's first year, though, the director faces *uncertainty*.

FIGURE 9-1 The Continuum of Decision-Making Conditions

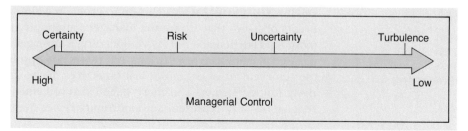

uncertainty Decision-making condition in which managers face unpredictable external conditions or lack the information needed to establish the probability of certain events.

UNCERTAINTY. Under conditions of **uncertainty**, little is known about the alternatives or their outcomes. Uncertainty arises from two possible sources. First, managers may face external conditions that are partially or entirely beyond their control, such as the weather that will occur during a three-day festival held in outdoor tents. Second and equally important, the manager may not have access to key information. If this is a new festival, perhaps the director has not formed a network with other festival directors who could share valuable information about likely attendance records. Or perhaps there is no one who can accurately predict the turnout for a new storytelling festival held in the fall, when many families are busy with school activities and attend professional football games.

turbulence Decision-making condition that occurs when objectives are unclear or when the environment is changing rapidly.

TURBULENCE. Under conditions of certainty, risk, and uncertainty, the ultimate objective is clear. Under conditions of **turbulence**, though, even this may be unclear. Perhaps the festival's board of directors are at odds with each other about their priorities—printing fancy programs, ordering both tee-shirts *and* sweatshirts, or paying well-known performers the higher fees they demand, knowing that such performers will probably attract larger crowds and make it easier to publicize the festival. Turbulence also occurs when the environment itself is rapidly changing or uncertain. If a local business lays off a significant number of workers or the government announces a recession, for example, local families may cut back on all entertainment, endangering the festival's ultimate success.

■ THE RATIONAL MODEL OF DECISION MAKING

rational model of decision making A four-step process that helps managers weigh alternatives and choose the alternative with the best chance of success.

Organizations that weigh their options and calculate optimal levels of risk are using the **rational model of decision making**.[14] This model is especially useful in making nonprogrammed decisions and in helping managers go beyond *a priori reasoning*, the assumption that the most superficially logical or obvious solution is the correct one.[15] For example, one company was plagued by a serious quality problem—too many parts were being returned because of defects. The obvious solution was to tighten quality control procedures. This did not solve the problem, however. Further investigation revealed the real culprit to be excess worker fatigue caused by a faulty ventilation system.

COORDINATED RESOURCE
See Cotter and Fritzsche's *Modern Business Decisions.*

COORDINATED RESOURCE
See the Oddou section on Organizing the Corporation, "Decision Making."

COORDINATED RESOURCE
See *Management Live!* Chapter 7 video, "Decision Making."

COORDINATED RESOURCE
Use Transparency 48, The Decision-Making Process.

COORDINATED RESOURCE
Use Transparency 50, Diagnosis of Symptoms to Find Causes.

No approach to decision making can guarantee that a manager will always make the right decision, but managers who use a rational, intelligent, and systematic approach are more likely than other managers to come up with high-quality solutions. The basic process of rational decision making involves diagnosing, defining, and determining the sources of the problem, gathering and analyzing the facts relevant to the problem, developing and evaluating alternative solutions to the problem, selecting the most satisfactory alternative, and converting this alternative into action. The model of this process consists of four major stages. (See Fig. 9-2.)[16]

Stage 1: Investigate the Situation

A thorough investigation has three aspects: problem definition, identification of objectives, and diagnosis.

DEFINE THE PROBLEM. Confusion in problem definition arises in part because the events or issues that attract the manager's attention may be symptoms of another, more fundamental and pervasive difficulty. A manager may be concerned about an upsurge in employee resignations, but this is not a problem unless it interferes with the achievement of organizational objectives. If the individuals resigning are relatively low performers and more qualified replacements can be readily found, the resignations may represent an opportunity rather than a problem. Curing the turn-

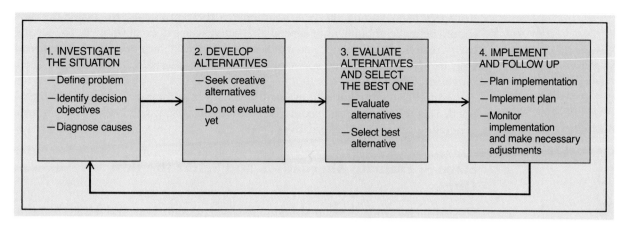

FIGURE 9-2 The Rational Decision-Making Process

over problem, then, may be the last thing the manager should do. Defining the problem in terms of the organizational objectives that are being blocked helps to avoid confusing symptoms and problems.

IDENTIFY THE DECISION OBJECTIVES. Once the problem has been defined, the next step is to decide what would constitute an effective solution. As part of this process, managers should begin to determine which parts of the problem they *must* solve and which they *should* solve. Most problems consist of several elements, and a manager is unlikely to find one solution that will work for all of them. Managers therefore need to distinguish between their "musts" and their "shoulds" so they will have a basis for proposing and evaluating alternative solutions. For example, a manager with a staff opening *must* hire someone who can do a good job in a difficult position at a certain salary and he or she *should* fit in with others in the organization. Managers can eliminate all candidates who do not meet their "musts" criteria; they will evaluate all the other candidates by how well they meet their "shoulds."

If a solution enables managers to achieve organizational objectives, it is a successful one. However, more ambitious objectives may be appropriate. The immediate problem may be an indicator of future difficulties a manager can prevent by taking early action. Or the problem may offer the opportunity to improve, rather than merely restore, organizational performance.

DIAGNOSE THE CAUSES. When managers have found a satisfactory solution, they must determine the actions that will achieve it. But first, they must obtain a solid understanding of all the sources of the problem so they can formulate hypotheses about the causes. They should ask such questions as: What changes inside or outside the organization may have contributed to the problem? What people are most involved with the problem situation? Do they have insights or perspectives that may clarify the problem? Do their actions contribute to the problem?

Causes, unlike symptoms, are seldom apparent, and managers sometimes have to rely on intuition to identify them. Different individuals, whose views of the situation are inevitably shaped by their own experiences and responsibilities, may perceive very different causes for the same problem. It is up to the manager to put all the pieces together and come up with as clear a picture as possible.

COORDINATED RESOURCE
Use Transparency 51, Nominal Group Techniques.

COORDINATED RESOURCE
Use Transparency 52, Delphi Method for Decision Making.

Stage 2: Develop Alternatives

This stage may be reasonably simple for most programmed decisions but not so simple for complex nonprogrammed decisions, especially if there are time constraints. Too often the temptation to accept the first feasible alternative prevents managers from finding the best solutions to their problems. No major decision should be made, though, until several alternatives have been developed. To increase their creativity at this task, some managers turn to individual or group **brainstorming,** in which participants spontaneously propose alternatives even if they seem unrealistic or fantastic.

Another temptation is to evaluate alternatives as they are proposed and developed. This temptation, too, should be resisted, because it will keep managers from generating other viable alternatives.

Stage 3: Evaluate Alternatives and Select the Best One

Once managers have developed a set of alternatives, they must evaluate each one on the basis of three key questions. (See Fig. 9-3.)

1. *Is this alternative feasible?* Does the organization have the money and other resources needed to carry out this alternative? Replacing all obsolete equipment might be an ideal solution but it is not feasible if the company is already near bankruptcy. Does the alternative meet all the organization's legal and ethical obligations? Closing a plant to save costs, for example, involves a complicated web of legal and ethical obligations to displaced workers. Is the alternative a reasonable one given the organization's strategy and internal politics? Any solution is only as effective as the support it wins within the organization. In evaluating an alternative, then, managers must try to anticipate what would happen if employees fail to support and implement it wholeheartedly.

2. *Is the alternative a satisfactory solution?* To answer this question, managers need to consider two additional questions. First, does the alternative meet the decision objectives—both the "musts" and the "shoulds"? Second, does the alternative have an acceptable chance of succeeding, assuming this can be calculated? (In conditions of uncertainty or turbulence, of course, this may be

FIGURE 9-3 Stage 3: Evaluating Alternatives

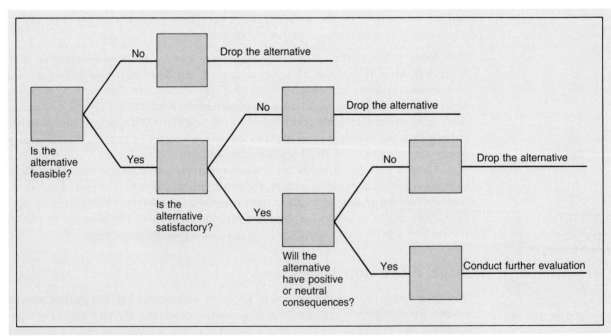

extremely difficult or impossible.) Managers should realize, too, that the definition of "acceptable" may differ from organization to organization and from person to person, depending on the organization's culture and the individual's tolerance for risk.

3. *What are the possible consequences for the rest of the organization?* Because an organization is a system of interrelated parts and exists among other systems, managers must try to anticipate how a change in one area will affect other areas—both now and in the future. Cutting back research and development, for example, might save money in the short term but it could cripple or even kill the organization when it fails to develop new products for the future. If the decision might affect other departments, they too should be consulted.[17] Competitors may also be affected by the decision and their reactions will have to be taken into account. Can competitors mount a counterattack to a new marketing strategy or a new product? If so, managers must also decide how to deal with competitors' reactions. Alternatives with negative consequences should be eliminated, of course, while alternatives with positive consequences will usually be favored over those with merely neutral consequences.

Ultimately, managers select an alternative based upon the amount of time and information available, as well as their imperfect judgment. More likely than not, the selected alternative will represent a compromise among the various factors that have been considered. (*Decision trees,* like Fig. 9-3, and other modern tools that help managers evaluate alternatives will be discussed in more detail in Chapter 10.) As we will soon see, unlimited time is an important consideration in most decision making and problem solving.

Stage 4: Implement and Monitor the Decision

HERE'S AN EXAMPLE
The new notepad computer technology will allow executives to store, cross-reference, and instantly retrieve names, addresses, phone numbers, correspondence, and calendars. The computers can be used to send and receive memos or review and mark up contracts, documents, and spreadsheets. They will also be quiet enough to be used unobtrusively during meetings. (*Fortune,* 2/11/91, p. 113ff.)

Once the best available alternative has been selected, managers are ready to make plans to cope with the requirements and problems that may be encountered in putting it into effect.[18]

Implementing a decision involves more than giving appropriate orders. Resources must be acquired and allocated as necessary. Managers set up budgets and schedules for the actions they have decided upon. This allows them to measure progress in specific terms. Next, they assign responsibility for the specific tasks involved. They also set up a procedure for progress reports and prepare to make corrections if new problems should arise. Budgets, schedules, and progress reports are all essential to performing the management functions of control.

Potential risks and uncertainties that have been identified during the earlier evaluation-of-alternatives stage must also be kept in mind. There is a natural human tendency to forget possible risks and uncertainties once a decision is made. Managers can counteract this failing by consciously taking extra time to reexamine their decision at this point and to develop detailed plans for dealing with these risks and uncertainties.

After managers have taken whatever steps are possible to deal with potential adverse consequences, actual implementation can begin. Ultimately, a decision (or a solution) is no better than the actions taken to make it a reality. A frequent error of managers is to assume that once they make a decision, action on it will automatically follow. If the decision is a good one but subordinates are unwilling or unable to carry it out, then that decision will not be effective.

Actions taken to implement a decision must be monitored. Are things working according to plan? What is happening in the internal and external environments as a result of the decision? Are subordinates performing according to expectations? What is the competition doing in response? Decision making is a continual process for managers—and a continual challenge.

ILLUSTRATIVE CASE STUDY

CONTINUED

Diplomacy and Determination in High-Level Decision Making

Using the rational model of decision making posed several problems for John McKinley, CEO of Texaco, and his advisers. He was receiving conflicting information from various sources and could not get all the information he needed to calculate the risk of his various options. In addition, he was under a severe time constraint.

The only certainty was that there were risks. In a similar case, Bendix's William Agee had made an approach to buy Martin Marietta. To his surprise, Martin Marietta launched the so-called Pac Man defense, countering with its own tender offer for Bendix. Suddenly, Bendix the *hunter* was Bendix the *hunted*. On top of the risks, the takeover of a major competitor involves proxies, regulatory filings, and other legal obstacles, plus the eventual challenge of merging two companies into a cohesive whole.

Despite its careful analysis of the known alternatives, Texaco was blindsided when Pennzoil filed a lawsuit claiming Texaco had interfered in its attempts to acquire Getty Oil. A Texas court agreed and awarded Pennzoil over $10 billion in damages. After its legal challenges failed, Texaco found itself facing bankruptcy. Rather than securing its position as an oil industry leader, Texaco was now fighting for its life in a sequence of events none of its advisers had envisioned.

Texaco's strategic mindset changed drastically. The court settlement left Texaco's shareholders with tremendous power to determine the company's future, since its breakup value far exceeded its trading value. Texaco was now "takeover bait." In addition, the Pennzoil crisis exposed and magnified some of Texaco's perennial problems: thousands of unprofitable service stations, overly centralized decision making, a sluggish corporate culture (termed by some "secretive and stodgy"), diminishing oil reserves, and the worst exploration record in the industry.

In the context of these pressing problems, Texaco's new CEO James Kinnear had to simultaneously fight off takeovers and forge a plan to transform the company and pull it back from the brink. The most serious takeover threat came in a proxy fight with Carl Icahn, then a 16.6 percent shareholder. To stave off Icahn, Kinnear had to shift from strategy master and corporate head to politician and consensus builder. Icahn's threat kept Kinnear from taking aggressive action and forced Texaco to settle with Pennzoil for close to $3 billion.

The silver lining was that this helped transform the managerial approach at Texaco. Kinnear has cut half the layers of bureaucracy between upper management and local service stations. He has tied managerial pay to performance and profit ratios and has encouraged risk taking in an effort to generate entrepreneurial zeal throughout the company. By today's business standards, this is nothing special; at Texaco, it was viewed as radical innovation.

Kinnear has also managed to trim down and reinvigorate Texaco's resources. He sold off some long-unprofitable businesses—2,500 service stations and 7 oil refineries—and cashed in other assets, including Texaco's West German subsidiary, for a total of $9 billion. In short, Kinnear has tightened Texaco's belt, cut costs, and reduced its debt ratio to one of the lowest in the oil industry, making it a "meaner, leaner" contender for the 1990s.

In perhaps his most important coup, Kinnear folded 60 percent of Texaco's U.S. refining and marketing into a joint venture with the Saudis to bring in $812 million in cash, 22.5 million barrels of crude inventories, and a steady flow of oil for the next 20 years. Texaco also signed a preliminary agreement with the Soviet Union to tap its vast oil reserves. This, along with a more conservative and studied approach to finding new oil, has converted the company's reserves from a major liability to a vital asset.

After five years and all these changes, Texaco is now worth about what it was before the Pennzoil suit. But there is a major difference: Today's Texaco is a transformed and vastly improved company that finds itself on Wall Street's "best buy" list, thanks to the ability of James Kinnear and his advisers to solve the many problems the company faced.

Sources: "Catch a Fallen Star," *Economist,* January 14, 1989, pp. 66–67; Stratford P. Sherman, "Who's in Charge at Texaco Now?" *Fortune,* January 16, 1989, pp. 69–71; Allanna Sullivan, "Icahn Raises Stake in Texaco to 16.6% and Repeats That He May Seek Firm," *The Wall Street Journal,* January 18, 1989, p. B9; Robert J. Cole, "Texaco Sets New 'Pill' to Block Takeovers," *The New York Times,* March 17, 1989, p. D4; Mark Ivey, "Jim Kinnear Is Pumping New Life into Texaco, *Business Week,* April 17, 1989, pp. 50–51; David Halpert, "Texaco: Star Crossed No Longer," *Financial World,* December 12, 1989, p. 20; Barnaby J. Feder, "The Texaco Star Rises Again," *The New York Times,* December 24, 1989, Sect. 3, p. 4; Thomas Jaffe, "Texaco Without Hype," *Forbes,* February 19, 1990, pp. 196–197; Allanna Sullivan, "Texaco Alters Exploration and Production," *The Wall Street Journal,* March 8, 1990, p. 9; Mark Potts, "Texaco, Soviets Sign Pact," *Washington Post,* August 15, 1990, p. D1.

■ CHALLENGES TO THE RATIONAL MODEL

The rational model conjures up an image of the decision maker as a super calculating machine, but we know that real human beings do not make all their decisions like this. Instead, they tend to use what Herbert Simon calls "bounded rationality" and rules of thumb called *heuristics,* and they let biases influence their decisions.

Bounded Rationality

bounded rationality The concept that managers make the most logical decisions they can within the constraints of limited information and ability.

satisfice Decision-making technique in which managers accept the first satisfactory decision they uncover.

In trying to describe the factors that affect real-life decision making, Herbert Simon, among others, has proposed a theory of **bounded rationality.** This theory points out that real-life decision makers must cope with inadequate information about the nature of the problem and its possible solutions, a lack of time or money to compile more complete information, distorted perceptions, an inability to remember large amounts of information, and the limits of their own intelligence.

Instead of searching for the perfect or ideal decision, managers frequently settle for one that will adequately serve their purposes. In Simon's terms, they **satisfice,** or accept the first satisfactory decision they uncover, rather than *maximize,* or search until they find the optimal decision.[19] It is important to try to follow the rational model when making major decisions—for example, whether or not to venture into a new line of business or to restructure an organization. But it would be foolish, and thus irrational, to put the same effort into every decision.

Heuristics

heuristic principles A method of decision making that proceeds along empirical lines, using rules of thumb, to find solutions or answers.

CLASS COMMENT
A good answer to the question "Why shouldn't we?" is no substitute for an answer to the question "Why should we?" (*Fortune,* 7/30/90, p. 247)

COORDINATED RESOURCE
See DuBose Reading #4, "Minds and Managers: On the Dual Nature of Human Information Processing and Management."

Research by Amos Tversky and Daniel Kahneman has extended Simon's ideas on bounded rationality. They have demonstrated that people rely on **heuristic principles,** or rules of thumb, to simplify decision making.[20] Loan officers, for example, may screen mortgage applicants by assuming people can afford to spend no more than 35 percent of their income on housing. Heuristics can speed up decision making, but they are fallible if individuals rely on them too heavily or taint them with their own biases.

Three heuristics show up repeatedly in human decision making.[21] These are not specific rules; rather, they are general cognitive strategies people use because they make intuitive sense.

AVAILABILITY. People sometimes judge an event's likelihood by testing it against their memories. In principle, it is easier to recall frequently occurring events. Thus, events that are more readily "available" in memory are assumed to be more likely to occur in the future. This assumption is based on the experience of a lifetime, and it seems reasonable enough. However, human memory is also affected by how *recently* an event has occurred and how *vivid* the experience was. Thus, a risk manager recently caught in a flood is likely to overestimate the importance and frequency of flooding the next time he or she procures insurance.

REPRESENTATIVENESS. People also tend to assess the likelihood of an occurrence by trying to match it with a preexisting category. For example, employers may rely on stereotypes of sexual, racial, and ethnic groups to predict an individual job candidate's performance. In a similar way, product managers may predict the performance of a new product by comparing it to other products with proven track records. In fact, however, each individual or product is a new commodity, not just the representative of a group, and should be judged accordingly.

ANCHORING AND ADJUSTMENT. People do not pull decisions out of thin air. Usually, they start with some initial value—even if it is randomly chosen—and then make adjustments to that value in order to arrive at a final decision. Salary decisions, for example, are routinely calculated by assuming last year's salary to be an initial value to which an adjustment must be made. Unfortunately, depending heavily on the single factor of initial value tends to obscure relevant criteria. In addition, different initial values lead to different decisions.

Biases in Decision Making

Each of these three heuristics leads to a number of biases that are so deeply embedded in the human thinking process that it is difficult to recognize them as illogical. (See the Management Application box, "How Biased Are You?") Even scientific training does not prevent these biases from distorting people's judgment.[22] We will describe some of the most common biases here.[23]

EASY RECALL. The more easily people can recall examples of an event, the more frequently they believe it occurs. However, both the recentness and the vividness of an event can bias this judgment. Thus, annual performance appraisals are consistently biased toward employee performance during the most recent three months, because that is what stands out in managers' memories. In another example, a purchasing agent selected a supplier because the firm's name was familiar; as it turned out, he remembered the name because the firm had recently been in the news for extorting funds from its clients!

EASY SEARCH. Our search strategies are based on our assumptions about the way the world is organized. Thus, managers may seek advice about computers from the management information systems (MIS) division of their company. If the expertise they need is elsewhere in the organization, they will not find it. Consumers work the same way. The Cadillac Cimarron, a compact car, was a marketing failure because potential small-car buyers did not associate compacts with the Cadillac name and price tag.

INSENSITIVITY TO PRIOR PROBABILITY. People tend to overrate the importance of representative information and underrate the importance of basic trends. Take an MBA student who is interested in the arts and once considered a career as a musician. Given a choice, most people would guess that the student is more likely to take a job in the management of the arts than with a management consulting firm. Why? Because the student fits a stereotyped image of a person working in the arts better than the usual image of a management consultant. People may ignore the fact that this person is an MBA student and that far more MBAs find jobs in management consulting than in the management of the arts. This basic trend is a better predictor than the personal description.

INSENSITIVITY TO SAMPLE SIZE. Few people appreciate the role of sample size when they evaluate information. Statistically, the smaller the sample, the more likely it is to stray from the mean. Consumers are regularly misled by advertising claims such as "Four out of five dentists surveyed recommend sugarless gum for their patients who chew gum." The claim is worthless without knowing how many dentists were surveyed. A sample of five or ten dentists may not reflect the opinions of the entire profession.

MISCONCEPTIONS OF CHANCE. Most people do not understand the nature of random events.[24] They often assume that multiple random events are somehow connected. In a series of coin tosses, for example, the average person believes that the odds of tails coming up is greater after heads has come up ten times in a row. In fact, each toss of the coin is an independent event with fifty-fifty odds.

INSUFFICIENT ADJUSTMENT. People sometimes arrive at final decisions by adjusting some initial value to suit a specific situation. Their adjustments, however, are usually inadequate.[25] Salaries, for example, typically consist of last year's wages plus

COORDINATED RESOURCE
The Distinctive Discussions for Chapter 9 found in the Lecture Extras supplement include "Being Smart Doesn't Mean You Can Think" and "The Ultimate Yes-Man."

COORDINATED RESOURCE
See *Management Live!* Reading 7.2, "Continuum of International Decision-Making Styles."

A Decision Anchored in a Basic Value. "You don't lose money making modest-sized loans to people who put everything on the line to start a business," says South Shore Bank VP David Shyrock (left), explaining why the bank helped Doug Jones (right) purchase this Precision Tune franchise.

MANAGEMENT APPLICATION

How Biased Are You?

Biases can be insidious. They so pervade the human thinking process that we are not even aware of them. Max Bazerman has put together the following test to illustrate some common flaws in our judgment. Try to develop logical answers to the following questions—without bias. You may be surprised by the traps you fall into.

Quiz Item 1: The following 10 corporations were ranked by *Fortune* magazine as among the 500 largest U.S.-based firms according to sales volume for 1982:

Group A: American Motors, Wang Laboratories, Lever Brothers, Kellogg, Scott Paper
Group B: Coastal, Signal Companies, Dresser Industries, Agway, McDermott
Which group (A or B) had the largest total sales volume for the total of the five organizations listed?

Quiz Item 2: The best student in the author's introductory MBA class this past semester writes poetry, is rather shy, and is small in stature. What was the student's undergraduate major: (A) Chinese studies or (B) psychology?

Quiz Item 3: Are there more words in the English language (A) that start with an *r* or (B) for which *r* is the third letter?

Quiz Item 4: Assume that two research groups sampled consumers on the driving performance of a 1991 Dodge Caravan versus a 1991 Plymouth Voyager in a blind road test (the consumers did not know when they were driving the Caravan or the Voyager). As you may know, these vans are identical; only the marketing varies. One research group (A) samples 66 consumers each day for 60 days (a large number of days to control for such factors as weather); the other research group (B) samples 22 consumers each day for 50 days. Which consumer group would observe more days in which 60 percent or more of the consumers tested would prefer the Dodge Caravan?

Quiz Item 5: You are the sales forecaster for a department store chain with nine locations. The chain depends on you for quality projections of future sales in order to make decisions on staffing, advertising, information system developments, purchasing, renovation, and so on. All stores are similar in size and merchandise selection. The main difference in their sales occurs because of location and random fluctuations. Sales for 1991 were as follows:

Store	1991	1993
1	$12,000,000	_____
2	11,500,000	_____
3	11,000,000	_____
4	10,500,000	_____
5	10,000,000	_____
6	9,500,000	_____
7	9,000,000	_____
8	8,500,000	_____
9	8,000,000	_____
TOTAL	90,000,000	99,000,000

Your economic forecasting service has convinced you that the best estimate of total sales increases between 1991 and 1993 is 10 percent (to 99,000,000). Your task is to predict 1993 sales for each store. Because your manager believes strongly in the economic forecasting service, it is imperative that your total sales be equal to $99,000,000.

Quiz Item 6: A newly hired engineer for a computer firm in the Boston metropolitan area has four years' experience and good all-around qualifications. When asked to estimate the starting salary for this employee, my secretary (knowing very little about the profession or the industry) guessed an annual salary of $17,000. What is your estimate?

Quiz Item 7: It is claimed that when a particular analyst predicts a rise in the market, the market always rises. You are to check this claim. Examine the information available about the following four events (cards):

Card 1	Card 2	Card 3	Card 4
Prediction:	Prediction:	Outcome:	Outcome:
Favorable report	Unfavorable report	Rise in the market	Fall in the market

You currently see the predictions (cards 1 and 2) *or* outcomes (cards 3 and 4) associated with four events. You are seeing one side of a card. On the other side of cards 1 and 2 is the actual outcome, whereas on the other side of cards 3 and 4 is the prediction that the analyst made. Evidence about the claim is potentially available by turning over card(s). Which cards would you turn over for the *minimum* evidence that you need to check the analyst's claim? Circle the appropriate cards.

Source: Max H. Bazerman, *Judgment in Managerial Decision Making,* pp. 15–17. Copyright © 1986 by owner. Reprinted by permission of John Wiley & Sons, Inc.

a raise. Even though last year's salary may not reflect an employee's true worth, it will bias this year's salary; thus, someone who is initially overpaid or underpaid may never be equitably paid.

OVERCONFIDENCE. People tend to be overconfident when answering questions on subjects they are unfamiliar with; overconfidence is much less likely in an individual's area of expertise. This problem can be reduced if people adjust their level of confidence to reflect their actual knowledge about a specific subject.[26] It is possible to get people to do this by providing them with feedback on their judgments or by prodding them to think about why their answer might be wrong.[27]

THE CONFIRMATION TRAP. People rarely try to discredit their tentative decisions; rather, they tend to look for evidence in their favor.[28] After employers make preliminary hiring decisions, for example, they usually follow up by seeking more information about the candidate's skills and accomplishments rather than searching for evidence of the candidate's incompetence. According to the rules of logic, however, no proof is complete without some attempt to discredit it.

HINDSIGHT. Once people know the outcome of a decision, they may start to believe they could have predicted it ahead of time.[29] They forget how uncertain the situation originally looked and remember the evidence as more clear-cut than it actually was. Unfortunately, this means that managers may be judged entirely on results even when the results are out of their control. Take a hiring decision that turns out poorly. Senior managers may claim, after the fact, that there was plenty of evidence that the new employee would not work out. Some leading researchers have suggested that a better system would reward managers for *how* they make their decisions, not how the decisions *turn out.*[30]

Some Conclusions

The use of heuristics to simplify the decision-making process has two strengths. First, heuristics have reasonable rationales, so they generally produce correct results. Second, they save enormous amounts of time for the decision maker, and often (but not always) this time savings outweighs any loss in the quality of the decisions.

Still, the most commonly employed heuristics produce systematic biases in judgment—biases of which we are not always aware. Common heuristics are not obvious rules that we choose to employ, but rather the intuitive approaches of the human mind; in a very real sense, we use them involuntarily. If managers learn how to recognize and eliminate such biases, the quality of their decisions will improve.

■ *IMPROVING THE EFFECTIVENESS OF DECISION MAKING AND PROBLEM SOLVING*

Norman Maier has isolated two criteria by which a decision's potential effectiveness can be estimated. The first is the *objective quality* of the decision; the second is its *acceptance* by those who must execute it.[31] A decision's objective quality is determined by how well the formal decision-making process is carried out; its acceptance is determined by its nature and by who makes it. In the rest of this section, we will look at these two criteria in more detail.

Improving Individual Problem Solving

Most managers realize that an apparently excellent decision may turn out poorly because of an unforeseeable event. Conversely, an unlikely and unpredictable event may turn a bad or illogical decision into a fortunate choice. Even if a decision works as well as predicted, a manager can never be completely sure another one would not have been equally effective or even better.

Most managers experience some tension in deciding how to go about solving a problem and then implementing the solution. They know they will frequently be evaluated on the success or failure of their solution, and that almost all second-guessing will be aimed at their less successful decisions. It is not unusual for people in such situations to set up barriers to problem solving or to devote time and energy to developing justifications for avoiding difficult problems, such as the "Prisoner's Dilemma" (see the Ethics in Management box). To make effective decisions, managers must first overcome the barriers that discourage them from recognizing and attacking emerging problems in their organizations.

BARRIERS TO INDIVIDUAL PROBLEM SOLVING. Irving L. Janis and Leon Mann have identified four defective problem-recognition and problem-solving approaches that can hinder people who must make important decisions in situations of conflict.[32] (See Fig. 9-4.)

1. *Relaxed avoidance.* The manager decides not to decide or act after noting that the consequences of inaction will not be very great. This might be the attitude of a manager whose superior has said a promotion will depend on improved

ETHICS IN MANAGEMENT

The Game of "Prisoner's Dilemma"

Suppose you had to make the following decision. You and an accomplice are apprehended after a crime has been committed. You are held and interrogated separately, each of you being told that if you turn state's evidence, you will get a very light sentence (one year in jail), while the other will be put away for a long time (ten years). However, if *both* of you confess, you will each get eight years. If *neither* of you confesses, you will be convicted of some more minor charge and be given two years each. The game is depicted in the following diagram. Prisoner #1's dilemma can be seen by reading from left to right; Prisoner #2's dilemma can be seen by reading from top to bottom.

best outcome for *him* and the worst for *me*." And so on.

This simple game is at the heart of many ethical dilemmas in decision making. When *each* prisoner fails to cooperate with the other in not confessing—*each* acting in accordance with *his own* self-interest—*both* prisoners fare worse. In a path-breaking book, Robert Axelrod showed that if the game is repeated an indefinite number of times, cooperation will begin to emerge as the dominant strategy adopted by each of the players. But the result is paradoxical: Sometimes when we try to be selfish, we end up faring worse. Axelrod shows that in "Prisoner's Dilemma"

		Prisoner #2	
		Confess	Don't Confess
Prisoner #1	Confess	Both get 8 years	#1 gets 1 year #2 gets 10 years
	Don't Confess	#1 gets 10 years #2 gets 1 year	Both get 2 years

#1 reasons this way: "The best outcome for me is to confess while #2 does *not* confess. But #2 will realize this and confess and we'll *both* be worse off, so I won't confess. But if I choose this route, then #2 will realize I may do this and confess—which will be the

situations, we can generally do better for *ourselves* by *cooperating*.

Sources: Robert Axelrod, *The Evolution of Cooperation* (New York: Basic Books, 1984); Anatol Rapoport and Albert Chammah, *Prisoner's Dilemma* (Ann Arbor: University of Michigan Press, 1965).

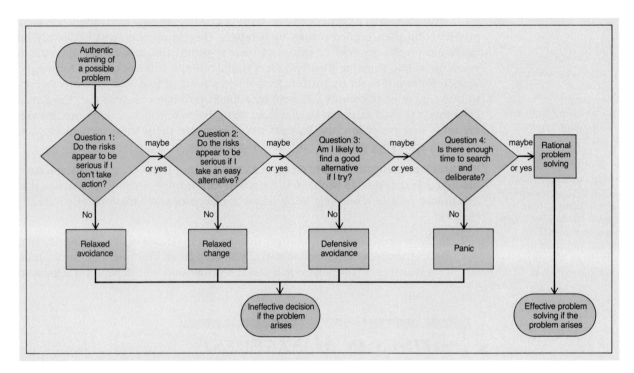

FIGURE 9-4 Effective and Ineffective Problem-Solving Approaches
This model shows the preferred management styles for various types of problems. The most "time-efficient" feasible alternative for each problem is shown in the rectangle along the bottom.

Source: Reprinted by permission of the publisher from *Organizational Dynamics,* Spring 1973. Copyright © 1973 by the American Management Association, New York. All rights reserved.

Coordinated Resource

Use Transparency 53, Effective and Ineffective Problem-Solving Approaches.

performance. Learning through the grapevine that the superior may be dismissed, the manager does nothing. Without this knowledge, the same manager would eagerly work harder and put in longer hours.

2. *Relaxed change.* The manager decides to take some action after noting that the consequences of doing nothing will be serious. However, rather than analyzing the situation, the manager takes the first available alternative that seems to involve low risk. Careful analysis is avoided.

3. *Defensive avoidance.* Faced with a problem and unable to find a good solution based on past experience, this manager seeks a way out. The manager may put off considering the consequences or may try buck passing. He or she may let someone else make the decision (and suffer the consequences) or simply ignore the risks and choose the most obvious solution. This resigned posture may prevent consideration of more viable alternatives.

4. *Panic.* The manager feels pressured not only by the problem itself but also by time. This produces a high level of stress that may manifest itself in sleeplessness, irritability, other forms of agitation, and, in extreme form, physical illness. In the panicked state, the individual may be so agitated that he or she is unable to appraise the situation realistically or to accept help from subordinates. Given inappropriate handling, the situation is likely to deteriorate.

Managers who tend to react to problems in these four ways often opt for a simplistic approach to decisions. A frequent method is **incremental adjustment**—choosing an alternative that represents only a minor change from existing policies.[33] In many instances, this is indeed the most sensible approach because it avoids extensive investigation of the problem, and thus saves time and money, and because it presents the manager with familiar, nonspeculative, and relatively stable and predictable data for analysis. But such an approach often results in inferior solutions

incremental adjustment
A method of managerial problem solving in which each successive action represents only a small change from activities.

because it prevents gathering new information and innovative thinking. When managers use incremental adjustment, it is also quite likely that long-run advantages will be sacrificed to short-term gains.

OVERCOMING BARRIERS TO INDIVIDUAL PROBLEM SOLVING.   Being familiar with the rational decision-making and problem-solving process gives managers confidence in their ability to understand and deal with difficult situations. This confidence is important for two reasons. First, it increases the likelihood that managers will actively try to locate problems—and opportunities—in their organizations. Second, it increases the likelihood that they will, in fact, find good solutions to the problems they confront.

In addition to using the rational model, there are other specific ways individuals can manage their decision making more effectively.

1. *Set priorities.* Managers are faced with many problems and tasks every day. Sometimes the sheer quantity of the workload is overwhelming. To avoid being snowed under, managers should review their priorities daily and allocate their time accordingly. (Some effective managers review their priorities and replan their work a number of times a day.)[34]

2. *Acquire relevant information.* As they work on identifying and solving a problem, managers should collect the information they will eventually need to make the final decision. This information consists of potential alternatives and their consequences, any relevant events that may occur in the future (termed *states of nature* by the management scientist), and the criteria for evaluating the eventual decision and solution.[35]

3. *Proceed methodically and carefully.* There are many forms of the rational problem-solving model outlined above, but none of them works well unless it is used well. In following a rational problem-solving model, managers should keep in mind some common mistakes. For example, in stage 1, many people tend to define a problem in terms of only one possible solution, to focus on lower-priority goals, or to diagnose the problem in terms of its symptoms instead of its underlying causes. In stage 2, when alternatives are being developed, there is a tendency to evaluate them right away, which prevents the creation of a sufficient number of alternatives. In stage 3, evaluating alternatives, people fail to use information systematically and tend to proceed in a hit-or-miss fashion. Finally (in stage 4), mistakes crop up during implementation. Managers may not motivate staff members or give them clear instructions; they sometimes do not gain acceptance of the decision, allocate appropriate resources, or provide in advance the information needed to monitor the solution program.[36] By knowing these common pitfalls, we can avoid them as we make and follow through on decisions.

4. *Be aware of heuristics and biases.* As we have seen, these rules of thumb can be both good and bad. Managers need to understand how heuristics can lead to biases, to bad decisions, and to overconfidence. Once managers are aware of their faulty assumptions, they can make a deliberate effort to avoid overrelying on them.

Deciding Who Decides

Often the first decision a manager must make is: Who will decide? In making this decision, Maier's concepts of objective quality and acceptance are useful guidelines. If a manager working alone uses the rational model effectively, the resulting decision should have high objective quality. Where the problem is largely a technical one, Maier suggests, a quality decision may be sufficient. But if other people are affected by the decision, Maier cautions, their acceptance may also be required. Often a manager faces a dilemma when "quality" considerations conflict with "acceptance" considerations.

HERE'S AN EXAMPLE
High-tech is helping salespeople to be better. For example, General Foods USA recently gave several hundred sales-account managers laptops after tests showed that the computers helped salespeople track customers, conduct presentations, and conduct paperwork. (*Wall Street Journal*, 3/6/91, p. B1)

Shared Decision Making. "The Lone Ranger solved problems and rode out. When he left in his cloud of dust, the people were no more able to solve the next problem than before he came," says Control Data Corp. Chief Operating Officer Larry Perlman, who holds weekly informal meetings with lower-level employees and supports intuitive, nonrational, and shared decision making.

ILLUSTRATIVE CASE STUDY

WRAP-UP

Diplomacy and Determination in High-Level Decision Making

The decision-making process at Texaco took a very difficult and unexpected turn for the worse. Undoubtedly, some of the heuristics that Texaco's managers used did not work in this set of unusual circumstances. Perhaps "Easy Search" and "Easy Recall" were at work. After all, who would have thought that a David like Pennzoil could bring down a Goliath like Texaco? Since the Texas court set a precedent with this case, the heuristic of availability would not have worked. In thinking through the precedents, McKinley would simply have discovered that no court had ever done what the Texas court eventually did in this case—after all, Texaco's offer was higher than Pennzoil's. In addition, a number of the actors in this large-scale drama were overconfident in their roles as parties to a major corporate takeover—though they had little expertise with "Pac Man defenses" and other exotic attacks and counterattacks. In short, what had begun as a fairly easy, nonprogrammed decision quickly became a political morass that threatened Texaco's survival, necessitating a number of new—but difficult—decisions. ■

HERE'S AN EXAMPLE
Mark Lembersky, president of Innovis Interactive Technology, boasts that employees at all levels of his company are empowered to make decisions. (*Business Month,* May 1990, p. 77ff.)

HERE'S AN EXAMPLE
The merger of Ernst & Whinney and Arthur Young & Company saw both CEOs staying on as co-chiefs. The two say they really trust each other. Personal rapport and professional respect have kept the setup functional. (*Business Month,* July 1990, p. 14ff.)

Traditionally, the final responsibility for making decisions belongs to managers, who may have to persuade or compel subordinates to obey. But this approach is not always appropriate. Sometimes subordinates have excellent reasons for resisting a decision. Perhaps they are aware of alternatives or relevant factors that were not considered in the original analysis. Then a managerial decision may fail because the manager is unable to convince subordinates to carry it out willingly or subordinates may implement a decision loyally even though they disagree with it—with poor results because the decision was poor.

One solution is to involve subordinates in decision making. When subordinates are given the responsibility for dealing with a problem, their self-esteem increases and they take pride in their demonstrated value to the organization. As a result, many companies, including corporations as large as General Foods and Burlington Industries, have initiated policies of using teams to assist management decision making at several levels. Of course, there are disadvantages as well as advantages to involving a number of individuals in the problem-solving process. Because individuals' time is valuable, we should involve them only when the benefits—quality, acceptance, morale, development—are greater than the likely costs in time, money, or the frustration of employees who feel they should not be involved.

■ SUMMARY

Decision making—the process of identifying and selecting a course of action to deal with a problem or take advantage of an opportunity—is an important part of the manager's job.

A problem, resulting whenever an actual state of affairs differs from a desired state of affairs, may also be seen as an opportunity to exceed stated objectives.

Four informal and intuitive situations usually alert managers to a problem's existence: performance deviates from past experience; performance deviates from a plan; other people express dissatisfaction; or the performance of competitors challenges an organization.

Whether managers recognize a situation as a problem depends upon their threshold for problem recognition, which is determined by their understanding of goals, plans, and acceptable standards of performance, as well as by their personal values and backgrounds. Because managers sometimes focus too narrowly on their units' needs, upper-level managers must coordinate the actions of all managers.

No manager can solve every problem. Instead, managers must learn to set priorities in deciding which decisions to handle and which ones they should delegate to subordinates or refer to superiors.

Decisions can be thought of as programmed or nonprogrammed. Programmed decisions involve routine matters and can be handled by written or unwritten policies, procedures, and rules. Nonprogrammed decisions involve unusual or exceptional problems. Because most decisions involve some element of the future, managers must be able to analyze the certainty, risk, uncertainty, or turbulence of each situation. Under conditions of certainty, managers can predict the results of each alternative. Under conditions of risk, the probable outcome of each alternative can be predicted. Under conditions of uncertainty, the outcome probabilities cannot be predicted. Under conditions of uncertainty, the probabilities cannot be predicted, and under conditions of turbulence, objectives may be unclear or the environment may be changing rapidly.

The rational model of decision making (and problem solving) assumes the most effective decisions result when managers follow a four-step process of investigating the situation, developing alternatives, evaluating alternatives and selecting the best one, and then implementing and following it up.

The rational model pictures decision makers as super calculating machines. In reality, people use bounded rationality to pick an alternative that "satisfices," given limited time and information; they use heuristics or rules of thumb; and they allow biases to slant their decisions.

Decision making and problem solving can be improved if people learn to recognize and overcome the barriers of relaxed avoidance, relaxed change, defensive avoidance, and panic. To do this, they must become more comfortable with the rational problem-solving process, set priorities, and be aware of heuristics and biases. In making decisions that require the acceptance of others, effective managers will share decision-making responsibilities with subordinates when the likely benefits in quality and morale outweigh the likely costs in time or money, realizing that managers retain the ultimate responsibility for making and carrying out decisions.

■ REVIEW QUESTIONS

1. What is the principal difference between problem finding and opportunity finding?
2. What four situations usually alert managers to the existence of a problem?
3. What factors affect a manager's threshold for problem recognition?
4. What questions can managers use to set priorities in decision making?
5. How can managers decide to delegate decisions? to refer them to superiors?
6. Contrast programmed and nonprogrammed decisions and give an example of each.
7. Explain the difference between making a decision under conditions of certainty, risk, uncertainty, and turbulence.
8. Describe the four basic stages in the rational model of decision making and problem solving.
9. How does the rational model differ from Simon's model of "bounded rationality"?
10. What three heuristics do decision makers routinely employ? How can these heuristics help or hinder the decision-making process?
11. What does Norman R. F. Maier suggest for improving the effectiveness of managerial problem solving and decision making?

CASE STUDY

Business and Political Action: To PAC or Not to PAC?

Jessica Smythe, founder and chief executive officer of a chain of 17 hardware and hobby stores in a heavily populated midwestern state, has seen her firm grow in 15 years from a single store on a neighborhood shopping street to a corporation with assets of $9 million and annual sales of $22 million. Twelve of the stores are located in larger thriving suburban shopping malls, two in urban neighborhoods undergoing a renaissance, and the remaining three, including the original store, in declining urban areas and undergoing a decrease in sales concurrent with a surge in operating expenses.

At its last meeting, the board of directors voted to leave these last three stores in their present locations rather than move them to more profitable settings, and to become involved in efforts to rejuvenate the neighborhoods. Their decision was motivated both by concern for the maintenance of urban neighborhoods and by the knowledge that renovation efforts in the two renaissance areas had produced heavy demand for hardware and other remodeling aids.

Each of the three declining areas had formed a neighborhood association at the urging of the local merchants and had sought public development funds to renovate the older buildings. Partly owing to financial entrenchment that severely limited the money available at all levels of government, and partly due to insensitivity to the communities' needs on the part of their congressional representatives, no federal funds in the form of block grants were forthcoming. It was apparent that the neighborhood associations had little political clout.

As Jessica Smythe pondered the insensitivity of locally elected officials to neighborhood interests, she was aware that the next congressional election was just six months away. Most likely, some form of political involvement was needed . . . perhaps in the form of campaign financing.

Smythe would like to see one congressman in particular defeated. Not only had Congressman X voted against the enabling legislation for neighborhood development funds, but he also had refused to discuss the matter when she visited his local office during the congressional recess.

The other two congressmen were neither antagonistic nor helpful, and Smythe felt that they would listen to reason once the political clout of their neighborhood groups was established.

Smythe reviewed the strengths and weaknesses of the neighborhoods. All three were heavily populated with middle-aged and older adults with a common ethnic origin. They had remained in the neighborhood in which they had settled and raised their children, even though many of the children had moved away, leaving a customer base of individuals on fixed incomes. Other, less affluent families had been attracted to the neighborhoods in recent years because of their proximity to the urban center and because rental and home-sales prices were reasonable.

Each neighborhood association wished to maintain the identity of the neighborhood; both the older and the more recent residents agreed about this. Furthermore, the residents cooperated with one another in keeping the neighborhood clean and in a modest state of repair. Each could point to specific improvements that had resulted from community effort: one or more homes that had been repainted using volunteer labor and paint supplied by an elderly homeowner and porch steps replaced in similar fashion. However, because of the age of the homes and the lack of financial resources, outside funding was clearly needed just to maintain the status quo.

Faced with the prospect of seeing the neighborhoods decline further, and of losing the equity they had in their properties (frequently a high percentage of their total worth), the residents and merchants involved believed that each neighborhood group would be cohesive and active. Smythe herself felt certain of this.

The city would lose property, business, sales, and personal income taxes if local merchants and residents were forced to move from the area, and these costs could be calculated. Moreover, there would be higher costs for protection services to avoid property damage, fires in empty buildings, and crime on dark streets. Also, it was doubtful that any new enterprises could be found to move into the neighborhoods to occupy empty store spaces and to create new jobs.

The best approach appeared to be immediate action directed at elected officials such as Congressman X. But for a political action committee (PAC) to be formed, several things had to occur quickly. Jessica Smythe knew that her firm could provide administrative services for a PAC associated with it, but she would need the support of the board of directors. Jessica Smythe owned 40 percent of the stock, but approval of the remaining stockholders would be critical.

Smythe knew of a firm of similar size that had raised $50,000 for a PAC, and she wondered how she might be able to accomplish such a goal. Funds could be solicited directly from stockholders and employees, but would employees from suburban areas and nearby cities where branch stores were located be willing to contribute? What type of internal network would be needed? Since PACs can solicit funds from individuals outside the parent organization twice a year, the Smythe PAC could approach merchants and residents within the area and also appeal to civic-minded individuals from a wider geographic region.

If like-minded groups could be identified, such as party committees for candidates the PAC wished to support, the League of Women Voters, and perhaps groups interested in neighborhood preservation, the efforts of the Smythe PAC could be extended. Since the election was just six months away, the PAC might not be able to qualify as a multicandidate committee; therefore, it would have to follow the dollar limitations established for individuals and other such groups acting in concert. Each candidate that was supported could receive $1,000 per election (primary, general, runoff); however, $5,000 could be given to any other committee in support of one or more candidates the PAC favored, and $20,000 could be given to a national party committee for use in congressional elections. Adding this together, the PAC could contribute $3,000 directly to the three congressional candidates it selected for the general election, as much as $20,000 to the party of the candidate opposing Congressman X, and $10,000 to two committees that lent their support to the opposing candidate. Altogether, $33,000 could be allocated for contributions, and the remaining money could be used for the preparation of leaflets and for solicitation expenses.

There were additional considerations. For the PAC to qualify eventually as a multicandidate PAC and be able to contribute $5,000 per candidate per election another time, it would have to contribute to at least five federal candidates and to obtain funds from at least 50 individuals.

Would it be wise to plan for the long term and to qualify as a multicandidate PAC? Smythe knew that the 17 stores were scattered throughout 12 congressional election districts in the state and that some employees lived in still other districts. How would five candidates be selected for support? Should small amounts be given to a large number of candidates, with larger sums reserved for the three targeted districts? The uncle of one suburban store manager was running in a "safe" election. How much money should be diverted to his campaign? Would a wider dispersal of funds to include the suburbs hinder solicitation efforts from groups interested primarily in urban neighborhood preservation? There were five stores in urban areas, each in a different congressional district.

Of course, other types of PAC organization were possible. Each neighborhood association could form a PAC, but this would prevent the Smythe firm from providing administrative services. There was a national trade association of hardware dealers, but if support was sought from this group, other firms learning of these efforts might try to acquire a large share of the block grant money for areas they served, even if they provided little support for the association PAC. On another level, the effort could boomerang through negative publicity or through retaliatory action on the part of developers interested in tearing down the buildings and creating large office or apartment buildings.

Source: This case was prepared by Carol J. Fritz. Copyright © 1982 by Pittman Press. Reprinted with permission.

Case Questions

1. What recommendations should Jessica Smythe make to the board of directors?

2. Should a PAC be formed? If not, what other alternatives should be considered, and on what criteria should decisions be made to accept or reject them?

3. If a PAC is formed, what criteria should be used in making the following decisions: The selection of candidates to be supported? The solicitation of funds from various individuals and groups? The expansion of the PAC to an organizational level beyond the firm?

4. Beyond a wealth of practical political decisions, which of Smythe's decisions have ethical ramifications for the activities of her organization and its responsibilities to its stakeholders?

VIDEO CASE STUDY

A Decision-Making Crisis at Burroughs-Wellcome

Burroughs-Wellcome, a subsidiary of Britain's Wellcome P.L.C., is one of the oldest and most respected drug companies in the world. It has also established the largest private charity in Britain, the Wellcome Trust, which funds medical libraries and research. As a company that emphasizes basic investigative research, Burroughs specializes in obscure or elusive diseases, and its researchers have won four out of eight Nobel Prizes awarded to industry scientists. So it's not surprising that Burroughs came to be involved with azidothymidine, better known as AZT, the only drug approved for fighting AIDS. What is surprising is that this highly respected company ended up being denounced by the very people AZT was designed to help.

AZT, first synthesized at the Michigan Cancer Foundation in 1964, was among the hundreds of compounds Burroughs scientists screened when the AIDS virus (human immunodeficiency virus or HIV) was identified in 1984. When they found AZT was effective in the laboratory against certain animal viruses akin to HIV, Burroughs turned to the National Cancer Institute (NCI), which had been urging drug companies to submit promising anti-AIDS drugs to them for testing against the HIV virus.

In 1985 NCI, in conjunction with Duke University, established that AZT was effective against HIV. Because the drug was thought, at that time, to have a limited market and therefore limited profitability, the Food and Drug Administration (FDA) granted it "orphan drug" status in July of that year. This special status gave Burroughs exclusive marketing privileges for seven years and generous tax incentives as an enticement to develop AZT.

In the same month, Burroughs started preclinical human studies, using people dying from AIDS. The results yielded the first good news AIDS sufferers had had. Although the drug had serious side effects and didn't cure AIDS, it slowed the reproduction of the virus, thereby lengthening and improving the quality of life for some patients.

Next came the larger studies, the human clinical trials, and Burroughs's first crisis of conscience. The standard clinical trial design uses hundreds of patients and tests an active drug (in this case, AZT) against a placebo (a "sugar pill"). The problem: If AZT proved to be effective, dozens of patients receiving the placebo might die. Prominent scientists urged Burroughs to give AZT to all patients and compare their state of health with untreated patients in previous years. But Burroughs decided to conduct placebo trials, arguing that comparing death rates from different years had led to erroneous conclusions in other drug studies. Besides, Burroughs didn't have enough drug to treat all the patients in the study.

Outraged, AIDS activists accused the company of being callous and greedy, of caring only about its bottom line. The gay community galvanized support nationwide, creating a vocal and influential lobby that Burroughs was not prepared to deal with.

The success of the clinical trials in 1987 also seems to have caught the company by surprise. The company didn't know what the demand would be, how to produce AZT in large quantities, what it would cost to manufacture the drug, or what competing drugs were on the horizon. When the FDA approved AZT for sale in March 1987 to about 50,000 seriously ill patients, the company put an enormous price on it; a year's supply would cost each AIDS sufferer $10,000 to $14,000, making AZT one of the most expensive drugs on the market.

Burroughs tried to justify its pricing on the grounds that making AZT was an expensive, complicated, and lengthy process. Although the drug had cost less than $50 million to develop, the company said, it was committed to spending tens of millions on raw materials, plant, and equipment. Burroughs also pointed out that, in the past five years, Wellcome P.L.C. had spent $726 million on R&D without producing any financially successful drugs.

Despite the fact that Burroughs's pricing rationale followed standard practice for the pharmaceutical industry, then-President Theodore Haigler and other executives almost immediately found themselves in the middle of a congressional investigation for price gouging. The ill-prepared Haigler made a poor showing, unable to justify AZT's price and unwilling to disclose development costs.

In December 1987, Burroughs cut its price by 20 percent, explaining that manufacturing costs had decreased. But the pressure for deeper cuts continued. In its own defense, Burroughs pointed to a program to provide free AZT to patients who couldn't afford it and were not eligible for other assistance. Unfortunately, the program was not publicized. In addition, the company gave scant credit to the government and university scientists who had helped to test AZT, thereby engendering further criticism from fellow scientists. In the meantime, Wellcome P.L.C. shares had quadrupled in value on the London Exchange and the stock was valued at thirty times projected (1987) earnings.

Activists and politicians kept the pricing pressure on, and in September 1989, the company cut the cost of AZT by another 20 percent. AIDS victims still claimed the company didn't care about them. Yet, no one at Burroughs emerged to take on the role of spokesperson.

For all the controversy, AZT has not proved to be a big money maker for Burroughs. Sales of AZT are expected to peak in 1993 at $460 million, with competing drugs expected on the market soon. Since its experience with AZT, Burroughs hasn't changed much. Some may argue that there is no reason to change. The company didn't make any unethical decisions, and its rational pricing decision followed industry rules. Burroughs's big mistake was that it failed to realize that AIDS was more than a disease; it was (and is) an emotional issue. As such, it involves a number of stakeholders that Burroughs did not recognize and acknowledge.

Sources: Tim Kingston, "The Unhealthy Profits of AZT," *The Nation,* October 17, 1987, pp. 408–409; Christine Gorman, "How Much for a Reprieve from AIDS?" *Time,* October 2, 1989, pp. 81–82; Brian Reilly, "The Inside Story of the AIDS Drug," *Fortune,* November 5, 1990, pp. 112–129.

Case Questions

1. Was Burroughs's pricing of AZT a programmed or nonprogrammed decision? What elements did the company weigh when setting the price? What other factors should the company have considered?

2. What opportunities did Burroughs miss when it introduced AZT? What could the company have done to improve its public image?

3. Using the rational model of decision making, discuss how Burroughs's production problems could have been avoided.

■ *NOTES*

[1] W. E. Pounds, "The Process of Problem Finding," *Industrial Management Review* (Fall 1969):1–19. See also Peter F. Drucker, *The Practice of Management* (New York: Harper & Brothers, 1954), pp. 351–354.

[2] Marjorie A. Lyles and Ian I. Mitroff, "Organizational Problem Formulation: An Empirical Study," *Administrative Science Quarterly* 25, no. 1 (March 1980):102–119. For a discussion of the use of intuition by managers, see Thomas S. Isaack, "Intuition: An Ignored Dimension of Management," *Academy of Management Review* 3, no. 4 (October 1978):917–922; W. H. Agor, "Tomorrow's Intuitive Leaders," *Futurist,* August 1983, pp. 49–53; and W. H. Agor, "The Logic of Intuition: How Top Executives Make Important Decisions," *Organizational Dynamics* 14 (Winter 1986), 5–18.

[3] Sara Kiesler and Lee Sproull, "Managerial Response to Changing Environments," *Administrative Science Quarterly* 27, no. 4 (December 1982):548–570.

[4] The author uses the phrase "the Pollyanna theory of management" to describe the belief that every problem has an opportunity embedded in it. Robert J. Graham uses the maxim that "problems are merely opportunities in disguise" in "Problem and Opportunity Identification in Management Science," *Interfaces* 6, no. 4 (August 1976):79–82.

[5] Personal communication.

[6] For a discussion of dialectical inquiry, see Richard A. Cosier, "Approaches to the Experimental Examination of the Dialectic," *Strategic Management Journal* 4, no. 1 (January–March 1983):79–84; Lyle Sussman and Richard Herden, "Dialectical Problem Solving," *Business Horizons,* January–February 1982, pp. 66–71; and David M. Schweiger and Phyllis A. Finger, "The Comparative Effectiveness of Dialectical Inquiry and Devil's Advocate: The Impact of Task Biases on Previous Research Findings," *Strategic Management Journal* 5 (1984):335–350.

[7] Peter F. Drucker, *Managing for Results* (New York: Harper & Row, 1964), p. 5. See also J. Sterling Livingston, "Myth of the Well-Educated Manager," *Harvard Business Review* 49, no. 1 (January–February 1971):79–89.

[8] See William D. Guth and Renato Tagiuri, "Personal Values and Corporate Strategy," *Harvard Business Review* 37, no. 5 (September–October 1965):123–132.

[9] De Witt C. Dearborn and Herbert A. Simon, "Selective Perception: A Note on the Departmental Identification of Executives," *Sociometry* 21, no. 2 (June 1958):140–144.

[10] Robert J. Graham, "'Give the Kid a Number': An Essay on the Folly and Consequences of Trusting Your Data," *Interfaces* 12, no. 2 (June 1982):41.

[11] These terms are from the computer field. A program provides the computer with a sequence of coded instructions for carrying out tasks. See Herbert A. Simon, *The Shape of Automation* (New York: Harper & Row, 1965), pp. 58–67. See also Simon, "Using Cognitive Science to Solve Human Problems." Paper presented at a Science and Public Policy Seminar, Washington, D.C. Sponsored by the Federation of Behavioral, Psychological, and Cognitive Sciences, 1985.

[12] See also Herbert A. Simon, *The New Science of Management Decision,* rev. ed. (Englewood Cliffs, N.J.: Prentice Hall, 1977), pp. 45–49.

[13] See F. H. Knight, *Risk, Uncertainty, and Profit* (New York: Harper & Brothers, 1920); and Stephen A. Archer, "The Structure of Management Decision Theory," *Academy of Management Journal* 7, no. 4

(December 1964):269–287. See also Samuel M. Natale, Charles F. O'Donnell, and William R. C. Osborne, Jr., "Decision Making: Managerial Perspectives," *Thought* 63, no. 248 (1990):32–51.

[14]In this section, we will use the terms *problem solving* and *decision making* more or less interchangeably because most of our discussion focuses on the decision-making portion of the total process.

[15]Francis J. Bridges, Kenneth W. Olm, and J. Allison Barnhill, *Management Decisions and Organizational Policy* (Boston: Allyn & Bacon, 1971).

[16]The discussion that follows is based on John Dewey, *How We Think* (Boston: Heath, 1933), pp. 102–118; Drucker, *The Practice of Management* (New York: Harper & Row, 1954), pp. 354–365; Charles H. Kepner and Benjamin B. Tregoe, *The Rational Manager: A Systematic Approach to Problem Solving and Decision Making* (New York: McGraw-Hill, 1965); and Ernest R. Archer, "How to Make a Business Decision: An Analysis of Theory and Practice," *Management Review* 69, no. 2 (February 1980):43–47. We have adapted and modified Archer's approach for our basic model.

[17]A "corporate devil's advocate" who would specifically search for the flaws in solutions has been suggested by Theodore T. Herbert and Ralph W. Estes in "Improving Executive Decisions by Formalizing Dissent: The Corporate Devil's Advocate," *Academy of Management Review* 2, no. 4 (October 1977):662–667.

[18]Kepner and Tregoe, *The Rational Manager: A Systematic Approach to Problem Solving and Decision Making*, pp. 190–194. See also Morgan W. McCall, Jr., and Robert E. Kaplan, *Whatever It Takes: Decision Makers at Work* (Englewood Cliffs, N.J.: Prentice Hall, 1985).

[19]Herbert A. Simon, *Models of Man: Social and Rational* (New York: Wiley, 1957). See also James G. March and Herbert A. Simon, *Organizations* (New York: Wiley, 1958); Herbert A. Simon, *Administrative Behavior,* 3rd ed. (New York: Free Press, 1976); Herbert A. Simon, *Reason in Human Affairs* (Stanford, Calif.: Stanford University Press, 1983), pp. 12–23; Anna Grandori, "A Prescriptive Contingency View of Organizational Decision Making," *Administrative Science Quarterly* 29, no. 2 (June 1984):192–209; and Neil M. Agnew and John L. Brown, "Bounded Rationality: Fallible Decisions in Unbounded Decision Space," *Behavioral Science,* July 1986, pp. 148–161.

[20]A. Tversky and D. Kahneman, "Judgment under Uncertainty: Heuristics and Biases," *Science* 18 (1974):1124–1131.

[21]Tversky and Kahneman, "Availability: A Heuristic for Judging Frequency and Probability," *Cognitive Psychology* 5 (1973):207–232.

[22]Tversky and Kahneman, "The Belief in the 'Law of Numbers,'" *Psychological Bulletin* 76 (1971):105–110.

[23]The following discussion and many of the examples cited are drawn from Chapter 2 of *Judgment in Managerial Decision Making* by Max H. Bazerman (New York: Wiley, 1988).

[24]D. Kahneman and A. Tversky, "Subjective Probability: A Judgment of Representativeness," *Cognitive Psychology* 3 (1972):430–454.

[25]P. Slovic and S. Lichtenstein, "Comparison of Bayesian and Regression Approaches in the Study of Information Processing in Judgment," *Organizational Behavior and Human Performance* 6 (1971):649–744.

[26]R. S. Nickerson and C. C. McGoldrick, "Confidence Ratings and Level of Performance on a Judgmental Task," *Perceptual and Motor Skills* 20 (1965):311–316; G. F. Pitz, "Subjective Probability Distributions for Imperfectly Known Quantities," in L. W. Gregg, ed., *Knowledge and Cognition* (New York: Wiley, 1974), pp. 29–41.

[27]A. Koriat, S. Lichtenstein, and B. Fischoff, "Reasons for Confidence," *Journal of Experimental Psychology: Human Learning and Memory* 22 (1980):107–118; S. Lichtenstein, B. Fischoff, and L. D. Phillips, "Calibration of Probabilities: State of the Art to 1980," in D. Kahneman, P. Slovic, and A. Tversky, eds., *Judgment Under Uncertainty: Heuristics and Biases* (New York: Cambridge University Press, 1982).

[28]H. J. Einhorn and R. M. Hogarth, "Confidence in Judgment: Persistence in the Illusion of Validity," *Psychological Review* 85 (1978):395–416; P. C. Wason, "On the Failure to Eliminate Hypotheses in a Conceptual Task," *Quarterly Journal of Experimental Psychology* 12 (1960):129–140; P. C. Wason, "Reason about a Rule," *Quarterly Journal of Experimental Psychology* 20 (1968):273–283.

[29]B. Fischoff, "Hindsight ≠ Foresight: The Effect of Outcome Knowledge on Judgment Under Uncertainty," *Journal of Experimental Psychology: Human Perception and Performance* 1 (1975):288–299.

[30]H. J. Einhorn and R. M. Hogarth, "Behavioral Decision Theory: Process of Judgment and Choice," *Annual Review of Psychology* 32 (1982):53–88; J. M. Feldman, "Beyond Attribution Theory: Cognitive Process in Performance Appraisal," *Journal of Applied Psychology* 66 (1981):127–148.

[31]Norman R. F. Maier, *Problem-Solving Discussions and Conferences: Leadership Methods and Skills* (New York: McGraw-Hill, 1963).

[32]Irving L. Janis and Leon Mann, *Decision Making: A Psychological Analysis of Conflict, Choice, and Commitment* (New York: Free Press, 1977). We have used a somewhat different terminology for their four approaches.

[33]Charles E. Lindblom, *The Intelligence of Democracy* (New York: Free Press, 1965), pp. 143–145.

[34]This process, known as *time management,* may be the single most important way managers can improve their overall efficiency. Some useful books are Kenneth Blanchard and Spencer Johnson, *The One-Minute Manager* (New York: Morrow, 1982), which emphasizes a process for establishing and remaining focused on a limited set of priorities ("one-minute goal setting"); and Peter Turla and Katherine Hawkins, *Time Management Made Easy* (New York: Dutton, 1984).

[35]George P. Huber, *Managerial Decision Making* (Glenview, Ill.: Scott, Foresman, 1980), pp. 30–40.

[36]Ibid., pp. 11–12.

CHAPTER TEN

PLANNING AND DECISION-MAKING TOOLS AND TECHNIQUES*

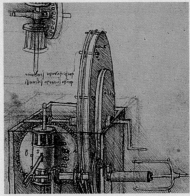

Detail from da Vinci, *Plans for a Spinning Wheel.*

Upon completing this chapter you should be able to:

1. Explain why management science is needed.
2. List and discuss the goals of management science.
3. Explain the four steps of the management science process.
4. Discuss the uses of forecasting and the importance of accuracy.
5. Describe quantitative and qualitative forecasting methods.
6. Discuss the advantages and disadvantages of a Gantt chart as a scheduling technique.
7. Explain the basic concepts of PERT and its usefulness to management.
8. Describe situations in which a payoff matrix is useful.
9. Discuss the nature and usefulness of decision trees.
10. Identify applications of certain emerging management science techniques.

*This chapter is based in part on information and research supplied by Rick Hesse, Mercer University.

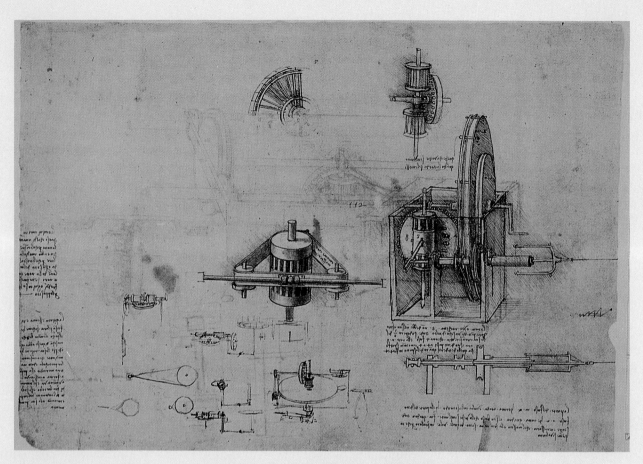

Leonardo da Vinci, *Plans for a Spinning Wheel*. 1490. Bibliotica Ambrosiana, Milan.

ILLUSTRATIVE CASE STUDY

INTRODUCTION

Reducing Logistics Costs at General Motors

General Motors (GM), one of the largest corporations in the world, fabricates and assembles roughly 13,000 different parts, varying widely in size and value. To do this, it has built a massive production and distribution network that, in the 1980s, consisted of 20,000 supplier plants, 133 GM parts plants, 31 GM assembly plants, and 11,000 dealers in the United States and Canada.

This network represents an enormous problem of *logistics,* the smooth and timely flow of materials from place to place. Logistics has three aspects: (1) the shipping of inventories from place to place; (2) the storage of inventories of raw materials, work-in-progress, and finished goods; and (3) the handling of materials throughout the network.

Each aspect of logistics represents a great expense for a multinational enterprise the size of GM. Freight transportation costs alone were $4.1 billion yearly in the 1980s, with about 60 percent for material shipment and the remainder for finished-vehicle shipments. Additionally, GM's inventory was valued at $7.4 billion. About 70 percent of this represented work-in-progress, and the remainder finished vehicles waiting for shipment to dealers. Furthermore, like all U.S. automakers in the 1980s, GM was facing intense competitive pressures from the Japanese, as well as rising costs associated with a deregulated shipping industry and high interest rates. Too much uncontrolled waste and GM would fail to meet both strategic and operational goals.

Logistics was a special concern for GM's Delco Electronics Division, which produces electronic control modules, radios, speakers, heater controls, and a variety of small plastic parts and sensors that are used on all GM vehicles. The Delco plants in Milwaukee, Wisconsin, and Matamoros, Mexico, ship finished goods to the Kokomo, Indiana, facility for product consolidation before order filling and shipping by truck directly to about 30 GM assembly plants throughout the country. As part of the campaign to reduce its product cost, Delco decided to focus both on controlling and reducing inventory costs at the plants and at the warehouse in Kokomo and on reducing inventory costs due to material handling time and transit time.

Jim Schneider, manager of material control for Delco, was given the job of finding the means of re-

ducing inventory costs. He began by analyzing the flow of materials and by looking at ways to reduce the logistics costs associated with the product-shipping network. He knew that he could lower inventory costs by shipping directly from the Delco plants to each GM assembly facility, thus avoiding the costs associated with the Kokomo component-consolidation and warehousing functions. But he also knew that this system would substantially raise shipping costs for the components because he would ship less than full loads on an irregular schedule. Jim quickly realized that before he could make any shipping decisions, he needed to understand the trade-offs in these transportation and inventory costs. He recognized that his real objective was not to control inventory costs, but to minimize the combined costs of inventory and transportation for all Delco products shipped to the GM assembly plants. Clearly, this was a problem for GM Research Laboratories, which formed a team of management scientists to help Schneider.

Source: Dennis E. Blumenfeld, Lawrence D. Burns, Carlos F. Daganzo, Michael C. Frick, and Randolph W. Hall, "Reducing Logistics Costs at General Motors," *Interfaces* 17, no. 1 (January–February 1987):26–47.

*I*n previous chapters, we explained the basics of planning and decision making in simplified, almost abstract, terms. As GM's dilemma shows, though, reality is usually far from simple. Managers at all levels face a potentially bewildering array of options and raw data. In this chapter, we will show you how management science techniques can make sense of these data and help managers make both effective and efficient plans and decisions. We begin by taking a closer look at the management science approach and the way management scientists support managers in their planning and decision making. Then we will take a quick look at some of the most popular management science tools in use today.

■ THE MANAGEMENT SCIENCE APPROACH

Management science today uses teams of experts who have mathematical, analytical, and computer-oriented skills, as well as intuition and good judgment, to support management planning and decision making. Given today's business environment, the odds are very good that almost every manager will at some time work directly with a team of management scientists or benefit from their work.

Why Management Science Is Needed

As you learned from previous chapters, the external environment of organizations is growing more complex every day. Much of this complexity can be traced to the global economy and technology. Together, these two forces are expanding the external environment of almost every organization and, at the same time, making it less stable and predictable. This means that managers face less certainty and more risk, uncertainty, and turbulence. This is one reason managers need management science: It can help them gain control over the environment by forecasting the future and calculating the probable outcomes of various what-if scenarios.

The second reason managers need management science is the size of the plans and decisions they must handle. Few organizations, plans, or decisions remain simple for very long. In today's global economy, there are simply more customers, competitors, suppliers—stakeholders of every type—to consider in making sound decisions. Thus, the number of variables that must be taken into account tends to increase exponentially. (A **variable** is simply any measure that can vary, such as number of employees or amounts of money.)

variable Any measure that can vary.

Consider the fairly routine problem of scheduling workers. Each year the American Baseball League must schedule the umpiring crews for all 14 teams over 162 games. Besides trying to minimize the travel costs for the crews, the managers must consider **constraints,** or limitations, agreed upon by the union. Crews must have one day off between games that involve flying coast to coast, no crew should umpire more than two series in a row for any team, and there must be a day off between a series that ends with a night game and one that begins with a day game. To solve this problem, league managers have to consider 8 by 8×54 or 3,456 combinations of umpiring crews and series. Since 1979, Dr. Jim Evans of the University of Cincinnati has been helping to develop a system that combines management science **algorithms** (step-by-step procedures) with human judgment and microcomputers. This system has made it possible to create better schedules in less time.[1]

constraints Limitations upon resources, usually expressed mathematically.

algorithm Step-by-step procedure for solving a problem or completing a task.

These two dimensions of decisions—predictability and size—are shown in Figure 10-1. The shaded area approximates the size and type of decisions that management science can help managers make.

The Goals of Management Science

Management science has been defined as "the use of logic, mathematics, and computers to solve complex real-world problems in such a way that it doesn't interfere

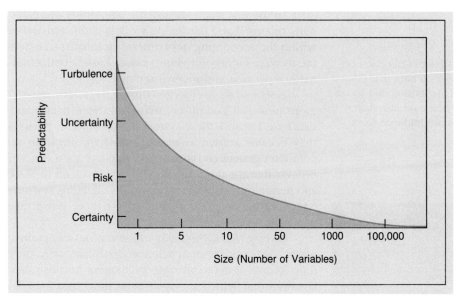

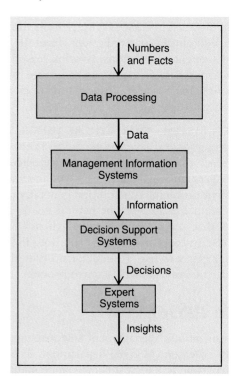

FIGURE 10-1 The Two Dimensions of Decisions
The shaded area approximates the size and types of decisions that management science can help managers make.

with common sense."[2] In practice, this is expressed as three interrelated goals: convert data into meaningful information; support the making of transferable, independent decisions; and create solution systems useful to nontechnical users.

COORDINATED RESOURCE
Use Transparency 54, The
Two Dimensions of Decisions.

CONVERT DATA INTO MEANINGFUL INFORMATION. The term *data* refers to facts (both words and numbers) about objects, people, and events; *information* refers to data that have been organized in some meaningful way. One of the basic goals of management science is to organize data into information. This parallels the goal of computer information systems, which also convert data into information. (See Fig. 10-2.)

FIGURE 10-2 The Evolution of Computer Information Systems

data base Collection of integrated data that eliminates repetition and inconsistencies; usually shared between multiple work units.

Supporting the Making of Transferable Decisions. To help the city of Barcelona, Spain, schedule the 2,000 events of the 1992 summer Olympic games, Professor Rafael Andrue of the Universidad de Navarra in Barcelona and Professor Albert Corominas of the Universitat Politécnica de Catalunya used management science techniques to develop a computerized scheduling system that could also reschedule any events canceled because of weather.

In the first stage, during the late 1950s and early 1960s, *data-processing systems* recorded and managed raw data about transactions, or business events, often within the accounting department. Gradually, transaction data from several departments were incorporated into a **data base,** a collection of integrated data that eliminates repetition and inconsistencies.

A second stage emerged during the 1960s and 1970s, with the development of more powerful computers that could manipulate and summarize data within the data base. Because these systems could produce periodic reports useful to managers, they became known as *management information systems (MIS).* (In fact, these computer-generated reports have become such an accepted part of the management process that the term *MIS* is often used to refer to the entire discipline of designing and managing computer systems for collecting, storing, and manipulating data.) And with the proper programming, these more powerful systems could also perform management science analyses.

During the 1980s, two additional developments gave management science a boost. First, management science algorithms were programmed into computer systems known as *decision support systems,* because they performed quantitative calculations that helped managers make more informed decisions. The second development was the introduction and popularity of increasingly powerful microcomputers, which helped managers gain a greater appreciation of the ways computers and management science tools could help them. Today management scientists are working with computer specialists to build *expert systems,* which incorporate rules based on an expert's accumulated knowledge of a field and use these rules to manipulate data, producing greater insight for managers.

SUPPORT THE MAKING OF TRANSFERABLE, INDEPENDENT DECISIONS. Management science is based on the scientific method and uses the rational approach to decision making. It assumes there is a logical, orderly way of making decisions that is transferable from person to person and is independent of the decision maker's emotions. Most often, management science techniques are quantitative, or number based, but this does not mean that intuition and subjective judgments have no place in decision making. As the mathematician Donald Knuth said, "The importance of computing is insight, not numbers."

In fact, numbers must be viewed with caution. Almost every set of calculations begins by making assumptions or predictions about the future, which can introduce errors into all subsequent calculations. For this reason, most management science tools include provisions for calculating an error rate, usually expressed as a $\pm$ percentage. This figure helps managers decide how much faith to put in a quantitative measure produced with management science tools.

CREATE SOLUTION SYSTEMS THAT WILL BE USEFUL TO NONTECHNICAL USERS. Few managers or employees have the technical skills needed to use management science tools themselves. Instead, a team of management scientists is often called in to work with managers and employees to understand and then create a solution for a specific management problem. This solution generally takes the form of a computer system that will seem *transparent,* or natural, to users, letting them approach a problem in ways that seem familiar, rather than forcing them to make radical changes. Often these systems present their solutions in the form of colored graphics, which makes them easier to use. To understand how these systems are developed, let's take a look at the management science process.

■ *THE MANAGEMENT SCIENCE PROCESS*

In most large organizations, management scientists are grouped in a management science/operations research (MS/OR) department. In other organizations, they are part of the MIS department, a logical choice since management science needs both

MANAGEMENT APPLICATION

Management Science Takes Flight

The Decision Technologies Division of American Airlines is typical of the MS/OR divisions found within large corporations. Its president, Thomas M. Cook, reports to American Airlines's senior vice president of planning and finance.

In 1989, Decision Technologies had approximately 100 professionals, about 70 percent of them devoted to American Airlines projects and the other 30 percent to projects for outside clients. The group is organized in a matrix style, which means that each person belongs to a department and is also assigned to one or more projects, with each project having a leader responsible for that project. Most management functions, including project performance reviews, are carried out by the individual project managers. The division has three major departments: OR/MS (65 percent), Computer Science/Artificial Intelligence (15 percent), and Industrial Engineering (20 percent).

In 1989, more than 100 projects were in development and 25 percent of resources were committed to developing prototypes. One successful project at American Airlines illustrates the value of prototyping. Daily flight plans used to be developed by trial and error, depending on wind, weather conditions, and other factors. A management science prototype tested over a wide variety of flights resulted in an estimated savings of 2.3 percent in fuel consumption. These savings translated into about $30 million per year. The prototype results were used to convince senior management to create and implement a system that could operate effectively in real time.

Scheduling Considerations. In addition to making the best use of its airplanes and fuel, American Airlines also needs to build schedules that meet the legal and contractual limits on how long its crews can work.

Most system-development projects are joint OR and Data Processing department projects. These types of projects are typically large multiyear efforts in which Decision Technologies develops the decision modules of the system and Data Processing develops the user interfaces (user-friendly screens for input and output), the necessary data bases, and the reporting modules. After the systems have been put into production, the two departments share maintenance responsibility for the system.

Source: Thomas M. Cook, "OR/MS: Alive and Flying at American Airlines," *OR/MS Today* 16, no. 3 (Summer 1989):16–18.

TEACHING TIP

Emphasize to your students that these tools and techniques do not replace the manager, but simply support the manager in his/her job.

COORDINATED RESOURCE

See Study Guide Problem Exercise 10, "Developing a Plan."

accurate data and access to high-speed computers. A few companies even have separate MS/OR *divisions* that solve in-house problems and also provide outside consulting services. McDonnell Douglas and American Airlines are examples. (See the Management Application box.) Smaller companies can turn to traditional accounting and auditing firms, which have been adding management science consulting teams.

Management scientists are rarely part of the department or division they are trying to help. Instead, they are formed into teams that act as consultants to help "client" departments solve specific problems. Once a problem is solved, the management science team is dissolved and its members are reassigned to a new team. Thus, teamwork and the ability to communicate are crucial to the management science process of determining the problem, mathematical modeling and prototyping, selecting a solution, and implementing the new system (see Fig. 10-3).

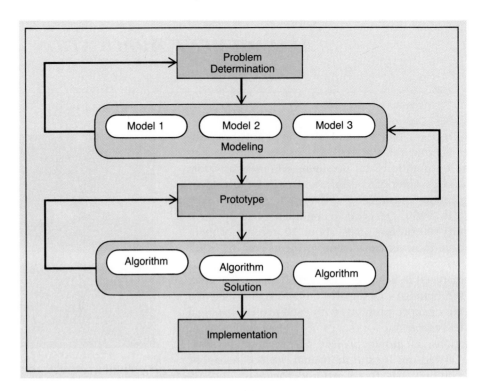

FIGURE 10-3 The Management Science Process

COORDINATED RESOURCE

Use Transparency 55, The Management Science Process.

Problem Determination

According to management expert Peter Drucker, the *wrong* answer to the *right* question at least yields some information, but the *right* answer to the *wrong* question can be disastrous.[3] Thus, the MS/OR team usually begins by playing detective— talking to people and observing them at work to determine the real problem. As Federal Express's Michael Fisher put it:

> It is very tempting to run right out and model an operation as a mathematical programming problem. Our increased operational complexity and the need for strong, effective communications between OR and our internal client groups force us to devote a lot of time and energy to two activities:
>
> 1. We must understand what the actual problem is before we model it. This entails visiting our airport ramps and our stations, and learning how we actually operate in real life. It is easy to dismiss such a simplistic thought as obvious, yet it is also easy to overlook this essential experience.
>
> 2. In the interest of our effectiveness as problem solvers and planners, we must accurately assess the needs of our clients. Often, a proper response to their requirements entails building a significant body of supporting software around the core model. In fact, the supporting software must often be designed first to enable the clients to solve their problems "manually" to begin with. The actual OR model must come later.[4]

Because problem determination is so important, many universities are teaching special courses in what Russ Ackoff terms "mess management," the process of turning a "mess" into a problem.[5]

Mathematical Modeling and Prototyping

model A simplified representation of the key properties of a real-world object, event, or relationship; can be verbal, physical, or mathematical.

As we saw in Chapter 1, a **model** is a simplified representation of the key properties of some real-world object, event, or relationship. Models can take the form of verbal descriptions ("Management is the process of planning, organizing, leading, and controlling"), physical models (a model car), or mathematical formulas that represent the relationship between key variables. Thus, the formula—Net Profit = Gross Profit − Total Costs—is a mathematical model of the relationship between net profit, gross profit, and total costs.

Management science, of course, relies on mathematical models and can draw upon many existing models, like the one above, that describe recurring situations. Because most situations are complex, the management science team typically uses a *system analysis* approach to identify key variables and then model the relationship between them. This is often a trial-and-error process, as the team double-checks and revises the assumptions of their models. Often the quickest way to do this is to create a **prototype,** or working model. Prototypes have two advantages: (1) they can be tested with representative data; and (2) they can be shown to users for their evaluation and comments.

THOUGHT PROVOKER

Can you identify some instances where prototypes would be useful? Some instances where they would not be useful?

prototype Working model of a product, a problem solution, or a computer system.

Solution Selection

Once the management science team is confident they have an accurate model, they are ready to choose a tool—an algorithm—that will solve the client's problem. Although algorithms can be nonmathematical (a recipe is a good example), most management science algorithms are mathematical.

Psychologist Abraham Maslow has been quoted as saying, "To the person whose only tool is a hammer, every problem looks like a nail." To avoid this bias, management scientists need to have a "toolbox" of algorithms. Consider an airline trying to determine where to fuel its planes. It might be able to do this by using linear programming, dynamic programming, a network representation, or assignment technique. The problem remains the same, but the perspective changes slightly with each technique. To choose the right tool, the management science team must understand the real problem and its effect on organization goals. Like modeling, this may be a trial-and-error process, as the team applies first one and then another algorithm to the prototype until it becomes clear one algorithm is more effective and efficient than others. Table 10-1 shows some of the most frequently used tools and typical problems they can solve.

TEACHING TIP

Do a quick survey of your students to find out how many of them know something about these listed techniques.

TABLE 10-1 Usage of OR/MS Techniques Among 125 Large Corporations

METHODOLOGY	FREQUENCY OF USE (% OF RESPONDENTS)		
	Never	Moderate	Frequent
Statistical analysis	1.6	38.7	59.7
Computer simulation	12.9	53.2	33.9
PERT/CPM	25.8	53.2	21.0
Linear programming	25.8	59.7	14.5
Queuing theory	40.3	50.0	9.7
Nonlinear programming	53.2	38.7	8.1
Dynamic programming	61.3	33.9	4.8
Game theory	69.4	27.4	3.2

Source: Guisseppi A. Forgionne, "Corporate Management Science Activities: An Update," *Interfaces* 13, no. 3 (May–June 1983):20–23.

Implementation

Implementation involves setting up and testing the system, preparing user manuals, training users, and then adopting the system for daily use. In this stage, the management science team passes the solution system on to the users—the department members who will use it long after the management science team has disbanded and moved on to other projects.

This is a crucial stage, as indicated by Gene Woolsey's First Law of Management Science: "Managers would rather live with a problem that can't be solved than use a technique they don't understand."[6] Because most of these solution systems are computerized, team members with experience in designing and implementing computer systems are especially important to creating systems that will actually be used.

The key factors to winning user acceptance are (1) user involvement throughout the management science process, (2) management support, (3) training, (4) mutual understanding, and (5) an evolutionary, step-wise development process that employs user feedback to modify the system to fit their needs.

■ *PLANNING FOR THE FUTURE: FORECASTING*

forecasting The process of using past events to make systematic predictions about the future.

Forecasting is the process of using past events to make systematic predictions about future outcomes or trends. An observation popular with many forecasters is that "the only thing certain about a forecast is that it will be wrong." Beneath the irony, this observation touches on an important point: Forecasts do not have to be *right* to be *useful*—they simply have to predict future events closely enough to guide present actions in a valid and purposeful way. Even though many forecasts made by meteorologists, economists, politicians, and managers prove inaccurate, we should not forget how widespread and important forecasts are.

premise Assumption that forms the basis of plans.

Their most important use is in planning, when managers use forecasts to create **premises,** or basic assumptions that become the basis of planning or decision making. Such forecasts fall into two general categories:

sales and revenue forecasting Forecasting amounts of income expected from sales and other sources of revenue.

1. *Forecasts about events that will be largely determined by what the organization does or doesn't do.* **Sales and revenue forecasting** is the most common example here, since an organization's income is vital to its survival and determines the scope and direction of almost all plans and decisions. Thus, a community college might forecast the number of additional students (and tuition income) it would gain if it expanded its courses in computer programming and systems analysis—offset, of course, by the costs of buying more computers and hiring faculty with specialized skills.

TEACHING TIP
This section would provide a good spot to review the importance of understanding the external environment and what the external environment consists of.

2. *Forecasts about changes in the basic social, economic, political, and technological variables that make up the indirect-action environment.* Often these forecasts are supplied by outside organizations or by the government. Thus, the community college administrators might look to federal or state statistics that project economic trends, long-term trends in college enrollments, and the demand for employees with certain computer skills. They might also contact professional organizations or consulting firms that project employment trends in the computer industry.

technological forecasting Forecasting how quickly technological innovations will become practical and make existing technology obsolete.

Like many organizations, the community college must also use **technological forecasting,** or predictions about how quickly technological innovations will become practical and make current technologies obsolete. Otherwise, the college may train students on equipment that will be outdated by the time the students enter the job market. Ongoing developments in such areas as lasers, jet aircraft, energy, data communications, biotechnology, and advanced plastics have made technological forecasting a priority at many organizations.

TEACHING TIP

You might want to set up a debate format for discussing quantitative and qualitative forecasting. Have teams take sides and debate the use of each of these approaches.

quantitative forecasting Forecasting based on use of mathematical rules to manipulate existing data.

time series data Data that is collected at regular intervals of time.

time series analysis Quantitative forecasting technique that predicts changes in one variable over time.

Forecasts that are affected by an organization's actions are more difficult to make, since they also involve assumptions about the direct-action and indirect-action environments. If these assumptions are inaccurate, the company may face a planning gap that needs to be corrected—quickly—by another round of planning.

In making forecasts, managers use two basic techniques. *Quantitative forecasting* is based on data from the past, while *qualitative forecasting* reflects opinions and judgments based on past experience. As we will see, both techniques are useful in different situations.

Quantitative Forecasting

Quantitative forecasting makes its predictions by using mathematical rules to manipulate existing data about certain variables. *Time series analysis* looks at changes in just one variable over time, while *causal forecasting* tries to measure the cause-and-effect relationship among a number of variables.

TIME SERIES ANALYSIS. Data that are sequenced by regular intervals of time (days, weeks, months, years, and so on) are called **time series data.** Examples are daily inventory, weekly sales, monthly profits, quarterly dividends, and yearly revenues. If you plot these data on a line graph, you might see that they form some sort of pattern. The pattern may not be clear, though, because time series data have four components.

The *trend component* refers to a long-term pattern of growth or decay, such as the sale of snowblowers. While this information has some general value for strategic planning, it is not precise enough to allow both the effective and efficient use of organization resources. Furthermore, the trend may be obscured by the *seasonal component,* a periodic fluctuation related to a certain recurring event, such as the winter snow season. In contrast, the *cyclical component* refers to fluctuations that vary in duration and amount. A sales drop during an economic recession is a good example. Even if trend, seasonal, and cyclical components could be measured accurately, the *random component,* made up of chance or unpredictable events, would still introduce errors into the forecast.

How can the confusing effects of these four components be eliminated? Enter mathematics. The basic technique of **time series analysis** is to average the last few periods of data, which produces a model that is very responsive to change.

An example of a simple time series forecasting model is weighted moving averages. The term *weighted* refers to the fact that such averages give more weight to one time period than to others in order to achieve a more accurate representation of reality. Typically, management scientists give higher weights to more recent events than to older events, which may even receive a negative weighting. In calculating an average, each period's data are multiplied by the weight assigned them and then divided by the total of the weights. The term *moving* refers to the fact that each calculation of an average "moves" to take in the most recent data available, dropping off older data.

To see how this works, let's use weighted moving averages to forecast the price of a 30-second TV commercial during the 1992 Super Bowl. (See Table 10-2.) The forecasts in this case were all based on the previous two years of data. Thus, the 1978 forecast was based on the actual prices in 1976 and 1977, the 1979 forecast was based on the 1977 and 1978 prices, and so on. In this case, the best weights are -1 for the first year and $+2$ for the second year. Thus, our forecast for 1992 would be based on the 1990 price ($775,000) and the 1991 price ($800,000). The weighted moving average is then calculated as follows:

$$\frac{[(-1)725,000 + (2)800,000]}{(-1 + 2)} = 875,000$$

Each forecast depends only on the last two periods of data and is simple to calculate.

TABLE 10-2 Actual and Forecast Prices for a 30-Second Commercial During the Super Bowl

Year	Prices	Forecast	Absolute Error
1976	$125,000		
1977	$162,000		
1978	$185,000	$199,000	$14,000
1979	$222,000	$208,000	$14,000
1980	$225,000	$259,000	$34,000
1981	$275,000	$228,000	$47,000
1982	$345,000	$325,000	$20,000
1983	$400,000	$415,000	$15,000
1984	$450,000	$455,000	$5,000
1985	$500,000	$500,000	$0
1986	$550,000	$550,000	$0
1987	$600,000	$600,000	$0
1988	$650,000	$650,000	$0
1989	$675,000	$700,000	$25,000
1990	$725,000	$700,000	$25,000
1991	$800,000	$775,000	$25,000
1992		$875,000	

M.A.D. = $16,000

Furthermore, it is quite accurate, as indicated by the absolute error column. (An absolute value ignores a plus or minus sign.) If we use statistics to calculate a mean average deviation (M.A.D.), we see that the average deviation (or error) is $16,000, which translates into an average error rate of ±2 percent.

causal forecasting Forecasting that predicts how a dependent variable is affected by changes in independent variables.

dependent variable Variable whose value depends on the value of an independent variable.

independent variable Variable whose value does not change when the value of other variables are changed.

regression analysis Statistical tool for performing causal forecasting.

CAUSAL FORECASTING. **Causal forecasting** uses past data to determine how some measurable variable, such as sales, is affected by the interaction of a number of other variables, such as marketing budget, price, competitors' actions, and economic trends. Sales in this instance is a **dependent variable,** since its value depends on the value of the **independent variables** of marketing budget, price, and so on.

Causal forecasting can be based on **regression analysis,** a statistical tool for predicting the effect various combinations of independent variables will have on a dependent variable. (In mathematics, the term *regression* refers to going backward— using old data—to project forward.) Regression analysis is especially useful for indicating long-term trends and making forecasts about the availability of resources or sales.

Possible regression models would look as follows:

$$y = a + bx_1$$
$$y = a + bx_1 + cx_2$$
$$y = a + bx_1 + cx_2 + dx_1x2$$

where the x's (x_1, x_2, and so on) are the independent variables, y is the dependent variable, and the parameters a, b, c, and d are coefficients determined by minimizing the error of the forecasting model.

Regression analysis assumes that there is some underlying trend or relationship over the range of data that can be discovered by solving the equation with various values of x for a, b, c, and so on.

Consider the case of a power company that needs to forecast the average weekly household usage of electricity (expressed as thousands of kilowatts or kilos) to be sure of having sufficient capacity during periods of peak demand. (The alterna-

TABLE 10-3 A Regression Analysis of Electricity Usage

Temperature (x_1)	Kilowatts (y)	Forecast	Squared Error
46.9	11,330	12,520	1,416,082
52.0	11,260	10,794	217,604
54.9	11,530	10,170	1,849,577
59.3	10,160	9,720	193,667
62.0	9,900	9,740	25,690
66.1	10,090	10,200	12,155
70.1	10,090	11,150	1,123,177
76.9	12,540	13,898	1,844,035
79.1	16,030	15,093	878,396
80.1	15,440	15,685	60,162
81.7	16,470	16,698	51,767
83.4	18,860	17,860	1,000,699

$$y = 66,051.94 - 1,865.54x_1 + 15.44x_1^2$$

tive is a brownout or a blackout, lost revenue, and increased complaints.) Table 10-3 compares actual electricity usage (y) at various temperatures (x_1) and determines the coefficients *a, b,* and *c* that will minimize the squared error (a measure of variance) of the forecast. (Unlike in a time series analysis, the data used in regression analysis do not need to be collected at fixed intervals.) The results are graphed in Figure 10-4.

The original data points are dots, while the curve indicates the forecast, which clearly shows electricity usage increasing most rapidly at hotter temperatures. (This makes intuitive sense, since air conditioners require electricity, while most heating uses natural gas.) Engineers can use these results to anticipate power needs at various temperatures. But how accurate are the results? As with time series analysis,

FIGURE 10-4 Electricity Usage at Various Temperatures

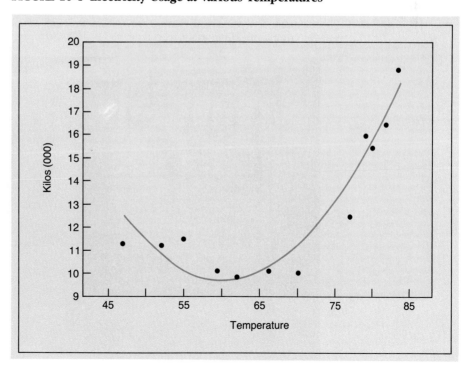

management scientists can also calculate an average error term for any forecast made with regression analysis. This helps them evaluate the forecast's accuracy and credibility.

Econometric models are also important in forecasting. They usually involve many independent variables in a simple linear relationship such as the following:

$$y = a + bx_1 + cx_2 + dx_3 + ex_4 + fx_5 + gx_6$$

A few of these independent variables are known as *leading indicators* (or *bellwethers*) since they rise or fall one, two, or three months ahead of the action of the dependent variable. Thus, a rise in housing starts might affect the GNP positively in a few months, and a rise in interest rates might affect the GNP negatively in a couple of months. The biggest problem with econometric models lies in identifying truly independent variables (factors that don't affect each other), since most economic variables *do* affect each other.

Qualitative Forecasting

Not all factors can be easily quantified, or measured, when trying to predict the future. Thus, managers also rely on **qualitative forecasting,** rating schemes that transform subjective judgments, accumulated knowledge, and opinions into quantitative estimates. Two of the more successful methods are the Delphi technique and multicriteria analysis.

DELPHI TECHNIQUE.   Named for the ancient Greek oracle at the city of Delphi, the **Delphi technique** is a method of eliciting opinions from groups of experts who brainstorm about a certain topic with the goal of gaining insight into future possibilities. For instance, the National Labor Board periodically invites leaders of industry and academia to meet in groups to speculate about what the world will be like in 25 years. After a couple of hours of brainstorming, the ideas are collected, summarized, and circulated to the members of each group. At a second meeting, each group

THOUGHT PROVOKER
What does the statement, "The importance of computing is insight, not numbers," imply?

qualitative forecasting
Forecasting technique that transforms judgments, opinions, and knowledge into quantitative estimates.

Delphi technique Qualitative forecasting technique that uses group brainstorming to reach a consensus and insight into the future.

Quantifying Subjective Criteria. To overcome the problem of measuring "quality service," Federal Express used feedback from customer satisfaction surveys to assign numbers to potential problems, ranging from 1 for a late delivery to 10 for a lost or damaged shipment. The numerical values gave Fed Ex workers a goal and helped them focus on the criteria most important to customers.

discusses ideas from the other groups. Then the results of these discussions are also summarized. At this point one or two representatives from each group form a final group that refines the ideas generated from the first two meetings.

The three critical factors in using the Delphi technique successfully are choosing people who are truly expert in the field under study, brainstorming rather than critically analyzing proposals, during the initial sessions, and limiting contact among the groups to prevent the formation of a hasty consensus and *groupthink* (the illusion that everyone agrees, which stifles dissent and the generation of fresh ideas).

A major use of the Delphi technique is in crisis-prevention management. Teams of people spend time anticipating different scenarios, assess the risks of each, and then propose appropriate responses. The purpose is to convert the ambiguous nature of a turbulent environment into a specific number of possibilities, each of which is analyzed and thus made more manageable. According to one study, Exxon's failure to integrate prevention, planning, and response clearly affected its management of the *Exxon Valdez* oil spill in Alaska.[7] Given the cost of the crisis, the authors easily showed that it would have been worth Exxon's while to investigate the linkages and trade-offs between risk reduction and contingency planning. (For more detail on the handling of the *Exxon Valdez* crisis, see the Illustrative Case Study for Chapter 4.)

IBM has formalized parts of the Delphi technique at 21 different decision centers across the country.[8] Each center contains 11 PC ATs networked to a main data base. GroupSystems, a collection of software tools developed at the University of Arizona, provides information to support parallel, anonymous, and collaborative group communication, which is displayed on a large-screen projector and used to aid planning. Recent studies have shown that brainstorming by computer in business meetings may be more effective than brainstorming face-to-face because using the computer makes people feel less inhibited about proposing ideas.[9]

MULTICRITERIA ANALYSIS. In making decisions, the natural human tendency is to fix upon one alternative that has emotional appeal, ignoring other options that have more quantitative or qualitative merit. A decision about the new site for company headquarters, for example, might be colored by upper management's desire to work in a warm climate or a metropolitan region, neglecting other important considerations, such as the size and quality of the local labor supply, tax incentives, and travel costs. To avoid this bias, many organizations use the powerful tool of **multicriteria analysis** (also known as *multiattribute analysis* and, in engineering circles, as *merit analysis*).

In multicriteria analysis, a "jury" of people is selected from the different areas that will be involved in and affected by a decision. Individually, each person is asked to list what he or she thinks are the critical success factors in a given decision. Then, in a group meeting, this list is reviewed and the factors are grouped into several major categories. Next, each participant is asked to assign weights of importance to each category; these weightings are shared with the group and again a consensus is reached. Finally, these weightings are used to evaluate different project proposals quantitatively.

Multicriteria analysis can resolve disagreements, or at least clarify their source, whether they be about facts (actual costs or time requirements) or judgments (the relative importance of various factors). This helps managers deal with the real issues. Additional insight can be gained by changing the value of the weightings assigned to different factors. If the scores are sensitive (meaning the rankings of the projects change), this may indicate that further study needs to be done before choosing between two or three projects that finished close to each other.

The Federal Aviation Administration (FAA) research division successfully used multicriteria analysis in the early 1980s.[10] Several systems for detecting bombs in luggage were under development, and the program manager had to decide which

multicriteria analysis
Qualitative forecasting technique in which a jury of experts evaluates various alternatives by assigning numerical scores to key criteria identified by consensus.

TEACHING TIP
There are several databases on the market for PCs. You might want to bring in some to show your students how useful these can be. Or you might invite a representative from a computer store to talk about databases.

TABLE 10-4 Results of a Multicriteria Analysis of Six Bomb Detection Systems

Attribute Category	Preference Weight	Candidates					
		A	B	C	D	E	F
Detection effectiveness	50	57	72	88	62	39	0
Development considerations	25	80	90	51	73	10	65
Cost to employ	20	82	91	88	87	39	70
Public acceptance	5	70	90	90	85	0	100
	Overall value	68	81	79	71	30	35

Source: Adapted from Jacob W. Ulvila and Rex V. Brown, "Decision Analysis Comes of Age," *Harvard Business Review,* September–October 1982, pp. 130–141.

ones would receive continued funding. Since none was clearly superior in all respects, a multicriteria analysis using four steps was performed:

1. The critical success factors (requirements) for the decision were defined.
2. The performance of the candidates on each requirement was assessed.
3. Trade-offs across requirements were determined.
4. Overall values for each candidate were calculated.

A team of analysts came to agree on four requirements: (1) effectiveness in detecting bombs, (2) development considerations, (3) cost of employing the system, and (4) acceptability to passengers. Each requirement was further divided into several categories and ranked according to one of two types of measures: scales with natural units (dollars, months or hours for time, and percentages for detection rates) and qualitative relative scales (from 0 to 100). The initial results (see Table 10-4) showed that of six candidates A–F, E and F should no longer be considered, candidates A and D were in the second tier of projects, and B and C should definitely be funded.

Multicriteria analysis can be used for a wide range of decisions, including selecting personnel for a job, setting water-supply policy, choosing sites for nuclear facilities, and evaluating crime-prevention programs. Even divergent groups have found that reaching a consensus is not very difficult with this technique. For example, the coastal planning commission of a California community invited private citizens, environmental groups, and builders to perform such an analysis in developing a building code for their beach area. The resulting code was hailed by all participants as fair and satisfactory.

■ PLANNING FOR THE FUTURE: SCHEDULING

Schedules are an inevitable part of life and an essential part of every plan. Without them, managers cannot be certain they are actually progressing toward their goals. In this section, we will look at two scheduling tools. We begin with the Gantt chart, an early graphic scheduling technique, and then discuss program evaluation and review technique (PERT), which is more effective for scheduling and coordinating complex projects.

The Gantt Chart

One of the earliest approaches to scheduling was developed by Henry L. Gantt (see Chapter 2). A **Gantt chart** (Fig. 10-5) is a graphic planning and control method in which a project is broken down into separate tasks and estimates are made of how much time each requires, as well as the total time needed to complete the entire project.

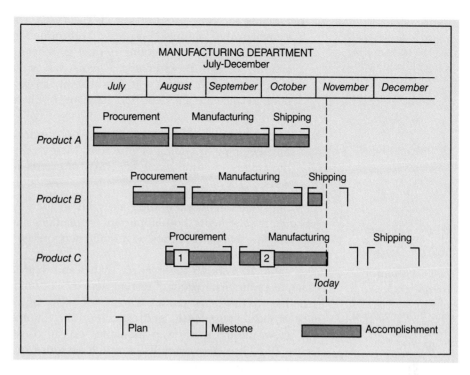

FIGURE 10-5 Gantt Chart for a Manufacturing Department

TEACHING TIP

You could invite to class a speaker from a manufacturing organization that uses Gantt charts for scheduling or, if possible, take a field trip to a facility that uses scheduling tools/techniques.

network Set of interrelated tasks or events.

COORDINATED RESOURCE

Use Transparency 56, Gantt Chart for Manufacturing Department.

program evaluation and review technique (PERT) A network analysis technique, using estimates of the time required to complete tasks, which is employed to schedule and control projects for which task-completion times cannot be predicted fairly precisely.

network analysis A technique used for scheduling complex projects that contain interrelationships between activities or events.

This information is then charted as pairs of brackets; the opening bracket indicates the task's desired starting date, and the closing bracket its desired end date. In addition, Gantt charts sometimes show *milestones,* dates on which certain intermediary approvals or goals must be achieved. By filling in the chart, the manager can get an at-a-glance idea of a project's progress. In Figure 10-5, for example, the shipping of product B is slightly behind schedule, meaning corrective action will have to be taken to meet the project's completion date.

Gantt charts are useful for tracking relatively small projects made up of tasks that are performed in a fairly straightforward sequence. However, most complex projects are made up of **networks**—interrelated tasks performed by separate departments or teams of workers. Some tasks cannot start until certain other tasks are completed, but many tasks (such as new product testing and market surveys) can occur simultaneously. The Gantt chart is not very effective at capturing these interrelationships, so it has given way to such tools as PERT.

PERT

The development of the U.S. Navy's Polaris submarine during the late 1950s was an enormous undertaking. More than 3,000 contractors and agencies were involved, many of which were performing multiple tasks that had to be coordinated. Faced with the problem of predicting with certainty the completion time for many interrelated tasks that had never been attempted before, the U.S. Navy's Special Projects Office worked with Lockheed and the consulting firm of Booz, Allen & Hamilton to develop a new method of estimating and controlling scheduling needs. The result was **PERT,** short for **program evaluation and review technique.**[11]

PERT is a type of **network analysis** that divides a project into separate tasks and then determines which must be performed in sequence and which can be performed independently. It involves four steps:

1. Determine the individual tasks, or *activities,* needed to complete the project.
2. Determine the *precedence relationships*—which activities must precede others—and identify activities that can occur simultaneously.

3. Estimate the time required for each activity. This is usually based on three estimates: the "optimistic estimate," reflecting ideal circumstances; the "most probable estimate," reflecting normal contingencies, such as routine delays; and the "pessimistic estimate," a "worst-case scenario" that assumes that anything that can go wrong will. A probability analysis of these three estimates is done to calculate an "expected estimate" of the time needed to complete the activity.

4. Draw a PERT network. In a PERT network, circles are used to represent *events,* the beginning or ending of an activity. Arrows representing activities connect the circles, creating *paths* or strings of events and activities within the network.

The PERT network is then analyzed to identify potential bottlenecks and schedule requirements, both important for planning and controlling the project. To see how this works, let's look at a PERT network for developing a new cordless vacuum cleaner.

Table 10-5 shows the major activities and their immediate predecessors. For example, preliminary product testing, activity G, cannot begin until activity D, construction of a prototype model, is completed. The table also includes the optimistic, most probable, pessimistic, and expected time estimates.

From the information in the table, we can construct the network shown in Figure 10-6. This network tells us which activities can be performed at the same time and which must wait for predecessors to be completed. For example, once the design is completed, construction and testing of the prototype, routing (manufacturing engineering), and cost estimation can go on simultaneously. But the market survey cannot be started until the market research plan and marketing brochure have been completed.

critical path The longest path through a PERT network; identifies the maximum amount of time required for essential tasks.

The longest path through the network in terms of time is called the **critical path.** The critical path is determined by totaling the amount of time required for each sequence of tasks (as opposed to those that can be performed independently). Look again at Figure 10-6. Once the path reaches 2, there are three possible routes to

TABLE 10-5 Activity List and Time Estimates for Cordless Vacuum Cleaner Project, in Weeks

Activity	Description	Immediate Predecessors	Optimistic Time Estimate	Most Probable Time Estimate	Pessimistic Time Estimate	Expected Time
A	R&D product design	—	4	5	12	6
B	Plan market research	—	1	1.5	5	2
C	Routing (manufacturing engineering)	A	2	3	4	3
D	Build prototype model	A	3	4	11	5
E	Prepare marketing brochure	A	2	3	4	3
F	Cost estimates (industrial engineering)	C	1.5	2	2.5	2
G	Preliminary product testing	D	1.5	3	4.5	3
H	Market survey	B, E	2.5	3.5	7.5	4
I	Pricing and forecast report	H	1.5	2	2.5	2
J	Final report	F, G, I	1	2	3	2
						Total 32

Source: Reprinted by permission from *Quantitative Methods for Business,* Second Edition, by Anderson et al. Copyright © 1983 by West Publishing Company. All rights reserved.

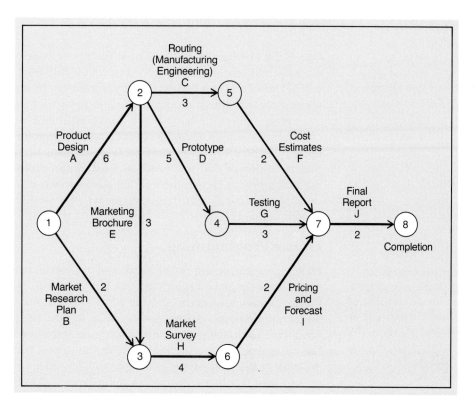

FIGURE 10-6 PERT Chart for Cordless Vacuum Cleaner Project with Expected Activity Times, in Weeks

Source: Reprinted by permission from *Quantitative Methods for Business,* Second Edition, by Anderson et al. Copyright © 1983 by West Publishing Company. All rights reserved.

8. Because we are looking for the longest route, the critical path follows 2, 3, 6, 7, and 8, since that will add the most weeks (9) to the total time required. The significance of the critical path is that it determines the total length of time, or completion date, of the entire project. If an activity on the critical path is delayed, the entire project will be delayed.

subcritical path In a PERT network, path other than the critical path; identifies opportunity to save time by reassigning slack resources to critical path.

Paths other than the critical path are called **subcritical paths.** These contain some slack, since the total time for their completion is less than that of the critical path. If these slack resources can be transferred to activities on the critical path, the total time needed to complete the project can probably be reduced. For example, transferring staff from F, cost estimates, to I, pricing and forecast report, might increase the time for F by a week, but the time needed for I might be reduced by a week. Since I is on the critical path, this reallocation of resources would reduce completion time for the whole project by a week.

PERT offers many benefits. First, it is useful for planning on both the strategic and operational level, since it indicates where resources should be allocated to reach goals efficiently. Second, it shows managers how to save time. Since time and cost are closely related, saving time usually leads to saving money. Third, it helps managers control projects by indicating which activities are critical to the timely completion of goals. Fourth, it helps managers set and communicate priorities to everyone working on a project. For these reasons, PERT is often referred to as a *project management technique* rather than just a scheduling tool. Furthermore, PERT software is available for microcomputers, making this valuable tool accessible to computer-literate managers.

■ PLANNING TO MEET GOALS WITH CERTAINTY

THOUGHT PROVOKER
Can you think of some decisions that managers might have to make that would "make the most efficient use of available resources"?

One of the manager's most important goals is to make plans and decisions that make the most efficient use of available resources. But what mix of products or services will be "most efficient"? This type of question can be answered by such management science tools as linear programming and network models.

Both of these tools are based on the assumption that managers are faced with constraints—limited amounts of time, money, equipment, personnel, materials, and other resources. However, these tools also assume there is some optimum combination of resources that will produce a maximum profit or the least waste. Because these algorithms focus on the company's known resources (as opposed to such uncertain measures as customer demand), they deal with a decision-making condition of certainty.

Linear Programming

linear programming (LP) Mathematical technique for determining the optimum combination of resources.

Linear programming (LP) can be used to determine the optimum blending of raw ingredients (to make cookies or cake, say), the mix of products that will maximize profits or minimize costs, and the most efficient way to physically distribute and assign supply points. It can also be used to plan the production and inventory of products that are subject to fluctuating demand and to determine the ideal quantities of products to be purchased at different prices. No wonder linear programming is probably the best known of all the OR/MS modeling techniques. The term *linear* refers to the fact that constraints can be expressed as equations that form a straight line when graphed. For example, if x refers to the numbers of work hours in a week,

$$x \leq 40$$

can be used to represent the fact that certain workers cannot be scheduled to work as many as but no more than 40 hours a week. The term *programming* refers to using a system of linear equations to determine the most efficient use of resources.

An easy way to understand linear programming is to look at a graphic solution. Consider the Faze Linear Company, a small manufacturer of power amplifiers and preamplifiers for fine stereo systems.[12] Table 10-6 shows information collected during problem determination—the resources required to produce each product, the total supply of each resource, and each product's contribution to profit. Given the object of maximizing profit, what mix of amps and preamps should be produced each day? To answer this question, we need to express the information gathered as a set of equations.

Let's assume x_1 represents the number of amplifiers to be produced and x_2 represents the number of preamplifiers to be produced. Our objective—to maximize profit—can be expressed as some combination of x_1 and x_2. Since the profit for each amp (x_1) is \$200, we can express its potential contribution to profit as $200x_1$; similarly, the profit potential of each preamp can be expressed as $500x_2$. Our objective function can then be stated as

$$\text{Maximize } 200x_1 + 500x_2$$

TABLE 10-6 Faze Linear Resources Needed to Produce Amplifiers and Preamplifiers

	Assembly Time (hrs.)	Inspection/ Testing (hrs.)	Transistors (units)	Profits (dollars)
Per amplifier	1.2	.5	0	200
Per preamplifier	4	1	1	500
Total available	240	81	40	

Next we express the constraints as mathematical statements. Because only preamps (x_2) require transistors and we get as many as but no more than 40 transistors a day, we create the mathematical statement

$$x_2 \leq 40$$

Assembly time for amps (1.2 hours) and preamps (4 hours) can equal but not exceed 240 hours. Mathematically, this is shown as

$$1.2x_1 + 4x_2 \leq 240$$

In a similar fashion, inspection time for amps (.5 hour) and preamps (1 hour) can equal but not exceed 81 hours, shown mathematically as

$$.5x_1 + 1x_2 \leq 81$$

And because the numbers of amps or preamps produced have to be equal to or greater than zero, we add a final constraint

$$x_1, x_2 \geq 0$$

The completed model, then, looks like this:

Maximize $200x_1 + 500x_2$ (profit)
subject to $x_2 \leq 40$ (transistor availability)
     $1.2x_1 + 4x_2 \leq 240$ (assembly time)
     $.5x_1 + 1x_2 \leq 81$ (inspection/testing time)
     $x_1, x_2 \geq 0$

If we graph the three constraints, we can identify a *feasible region,* or a set of points that satisfies all constraints. The shaded region in Figure 10-7 shows this feasible region, as well as its five extreme points—*A, B, C, D,* and *O*—created wherever two or more constraints intersect. In theory, the optimal solution of a linear programming problem must be at one of these extreme points. Maximum profit will occur at the point that is (a) furthest from the origin and (b) on a line that has only one point in common with the feasible region. Here, this point is *C,* 105 amps and 28.5 preamps. If for some reason it is impractical to leave a partially finished preamp at

FIGURE 10-7 Graph of All Three Faze Linear Constraints

Source: Thomas M. Cook and Robert A. Russell, *Introduction to Management Science,* 4th ed. (Englewood Cliffs, N.J.: Prentice Hall, 1989), p. 75. Reprinted by permission of Prentice-Hall, Inc., Englewood Cliffs, New Jersey.

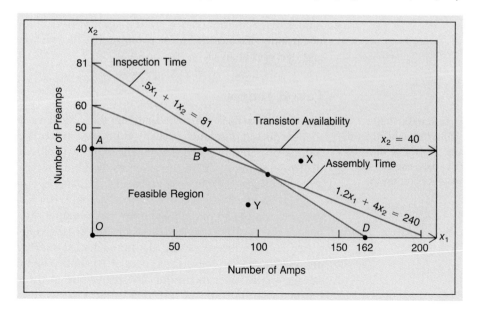

The Future of Linear Programming. This computer-generated figure was created by the Karmarkar algorithm, a linear programming technique invented by Narendra Karmarkar at AT&T Bell Laboratories to streamline the solution of such complex problems as the design of a telephone network for 21 countries in the Pacific Basin.

the end of the day, we could use a technique called *integer programming* to produce an answer that involves only whole numbers.

Solving linear problems graphically is a good way to understand how linear programming works, but it is not very practical for problems involving more than two or three variables and constraints. Most problems are rarely this simple. Small problems, such as blending different animal feeds at Ralston Purina to minimize cost, might involve 30 to 50 variables (the ingredients), subject to 20 to 25 constraints (restrictions on fat content, requirements for protein, and so forth). In contrast, an oil refinery planning its spring blend of gasolines and fuel production might have to deal with 50,000 to 500,000 variables and 10,000 to 50,000 constraints. These larger problems have to be solved mathematically, using computer programs that incorporate algorithms to eliminate all but the most feasible solutions.

Generalized Networks

An extremely powerful and visual way of representing management science models is found in the area of generalized networks. We have already seen a specialized network representation of a scheduling model with PERT. Generalized networks can also be used to determine the best layout for physical distribution systems, communications networks, airline flights, and production assembly lines. One of the classic network algorithms, the shortest-route problem, can be used to maximize the efficiency of delivery routes.

A network, made up of nodes (shown as circles) connected by branches or arcs (shown as lines), lets an analyst represent problems involving routing, shipping, and distribution of people and/or material. Interestingly, the visual model can look very similar to the problem encountered by the company, while the mathematical algorithm running on the computer may not look familiar to the user at all. Fortunately, more programs are becoming available that will take users' input, convert it into the necessary algorithms, run the model, and then give results in terms familiar to users.

■ *PLANNING TO MEET GOALS WITH UNCERTAINTY*

One way to make decisions involving change and uncertainty is to perform large surveys and then subject the resulting data to various statistical analyses. This is a costly and time-consuming method, though, so in the 1980s, managers sought techniques that required only a limited amount of data for making decisions involving uncertainty. Two of the most promising techniques developed are payoff matrices and decision analysis.

Payoff Matrix

payoff matrix Table showing the expected outcomes of various decision alternatives; used in decisions involving uncertainty.

A **payoff matrix** is a matrix, or table, that shows various decision alternatives and their expected outcomes (usually expressed in terms of money) under various conditions of risk and uncertainty. The biggest problem in using payoff matrices is determining the probabilities associated with each outcome. A classic application of a payoff matrix has become known as the *newsboy problem.*

Let us assume that a newsboy sells either 10 (50 percent of the time), 15 (20 percent), or 20 (30 percent) afternoon newspapers at a corner stand each day. Each paper costs him 17 cents and sells for 25 cents, giving him an 8-cent profit on each paper. Further, let us assume that for each customer who wants a paper but doesn't get one, there is an opportunity loss of 10 cents. The newsboy is able to get a 5-cent salvage value for each unsold newspaper late in the day on his way home at the hospital waiting room. A resulting payoff table is shown in Table 10-7.

CONTINUED

Reducing Logistics Costs at General Motors

Figure 10-8 is a network representation of the problem Delco had at GM. Delco could ship any of 300 parts from their three plants in Milwaukee, Kokomo, and Matmoros, Mexico, directly to each of 30 assembly plants (blue arrows), or ship to the warehouse (black arrows) and then on to the assembly plants. Loads could be full or partial, or products could be grouped together into families of similar products. In addition, "peddling" (deliveries made to several nearby assembly plants from the same truck) was allowed.

In its entirety, the network consisted of a large number of branches and nodes. However, by judicious use of common sense, the team was able to break the problem down into several smaller networks that could be easily solved.

Each shipment from a Delco plant to a GM assembly plant typically contained a variety of products. Modeling the trade-off between transportation and inventory costs over the entire network used to ship Delco products became the key to reducing cost. What was needed was an analytical tool that would allow convenient and quick evaluation of alternative strategies for shipping Delco's products.

Thus, the group tried to keep the models and analyses as simple as possible. This was accomplished by first studying the simplest type of network and then gradually considering more complex networks. The first step was to develop a model to analyze the trade-off between transportation and inventory costs on a single link or path in the distribution network. Sensitivity analyses were performed to see how total cost varied as a function of the demand on a link. These single-link results served as a building block for studying networks with several links.

Analysis showed that routing decisions could not be evaluated with standard mathematical programming techniques. Fortunately, the group was

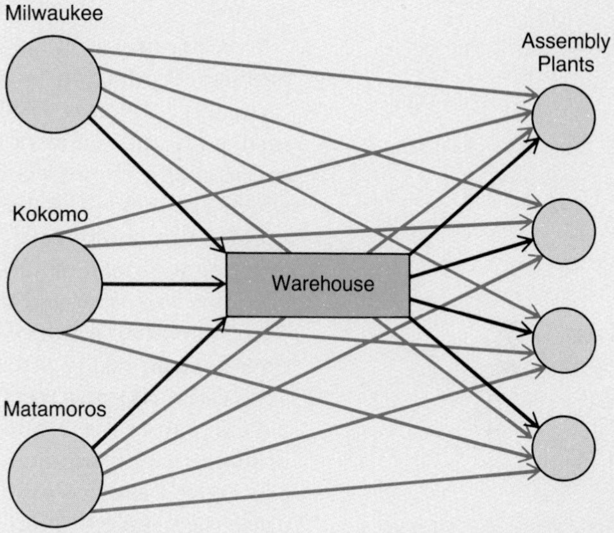

FIGURE 10-8 A Network Representation of the Problem at GM

Source: Adapted from Dennis E. Blumenfeld, Lawrence D. Burns, Carlos F. Daganzo, Michael C. Frick, and Randolph W. Hall, "Reducing Logistics Costs at General Motors," *Interfaces* 17, no. 1 (January–February 1987):32.

able to show that only two routing options had to be considered for each Delco assembly plant pair: ship all products direct, or ship all products via the warehouse. Routing options that involved shipping some products direct and some via the warehouse for the same plant pair were always more costly.

The team discovered a simple solution technique, a fast FORTRAN-based decision tool that was easily developed and named TRANSPART. This program broke the network down into smaller networks to evaluate the costs of alternative shipping strategies.

Source: Dennis E. Blumenfeld, Lawrence D. Burns, Carlos F. Daganzo, Michael C. Frick, and Randolph W. Hall, "Reducing Logistics Costs at General Motors," *Interfaces* 17, no. 1 (January–February 1987):26–47.

THOUGHT PROVOKER

Where do you think the subjective probabilities come from?

Once the table is constructed, the expected (weighted) value can be computed using the given probabilities. It can be seen that, in the long run, it would be best for the newsboy to buy 15 papers each time. We can also perform statistical analyses that will show how sensitive the individual probabilities or the various cost components are.

TABLE 10-7 A Payoff Matrix for the Newsboy Problem

	Buy 10	Buy 15	Buy 20	Prob.
10 customers	$0.80	$0.20	($0.40)	50%
15 customers	$0.55	$1.20	$0.60	20%
20 customers	$0.30	$0.95	$1.60	30%
Expected value	$0.60	$0.63	$0.40	

A payoff matrix helped Hallmark, the greeting card giant, solve an expensive problem: Production managers responsible for deciding the press run of specific cards were ordering production lots that were either too small or too large. Too small a lot, and Hallmark lost sales to potential customers. Too large a lot, and the company lost money discarding or salvaging unsold cards, such as Valentine cards, which are difficult and expensive to store from one year to the next. Hallmark decided that a simple payoff matrix could be used to illustrate the consequences of ordering too small or too large a production lot. These numbers were easily computed because costs and revenues were essentially known for each state and activity. Three important factors were incorporated into each analysis: (1) the probability of each demand taking place, (2) the salvage value, and (3) shortage costs.

Over 100 managers have been formally trained in this approach. The most difficult part of the training was teaching them to express their uncertainty in terms of subjective probability. Today the basic model is an integral part of the decision process at Hallmark—in fact, in some parts of the company, it is the "business as usual" technique.[13]

Decision Trees

decision tree Type of network used to model a progression of decisions involving uncertainty.

COORDINATED RESOURCE
Use Transparency 59, A Decision Tree for Making a TV Pilot.

Decision trees are a useful way of modeling decisions that involve a progression of decisions, each with outcomes that include uncertainty. A decision tree is a type of network, so named because it looks like a tree with branches. This representation forces the decision-maker to assign probabilities to each possible outcome and to use simple expected values to determine the best decision.

A simple example of a decision tree for deciding whether to make a TV pilot is shown in Figure 10-9. The circles represent decision points, while the squares stand for possible outcomes for which probabilities need to be assigned. The dotted lines at the top of the figure represent the outcomes shown at the bottom (Top 10, Mediocre, Bomb). By using simple expected values, users can determine the best decision at each juncture—go ahead with the pilot, do a preview, or rework the pilot if it gets a mixed review. Sensitivity analysis can be performed by changing the probabilities or the cost of previews or by obtaining better information to see how sensitive the decision is to these factors. Because the decision tree model is so visual, it is easy to explain (or defend) to others.

The United States Postal Service recently used a decision tree to help it make a very expensive decision: whether to make a capital investment of over $350 million in automated zip code readers. Besides the initial investment, annual maintenance and other costs could escalate to over $300 million per year. On the plus side was the possible, but highly uncertain, chance of saving as much as $1.5 billion from reduced clerical and carrier costs. A decision tree became the basis of an economic and technical analysis and evaluation of future operations that was presented to Congress and the Postal Service.[14]

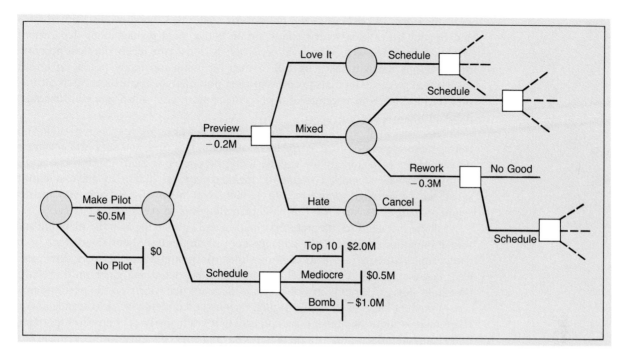

FIGURE 10-9 A Decision Tree for Making a TV Pilot

■ *EMERGING TECHNIQUES IN MANAGEMENT SCIENCE*

Management science is continuing to evolve and develop new techniques, three of which are highlighted in this section: yield management, spreadsheet models and nonlinear optimizers, and decision support and expert systems.

Yield Management

yield management
Mathematical technique for increasing revenue by pricing products to reflect either low or high demand.

Reinterpreting the simple basics of supply-and-demand pricing from microeconomics, yield management found applications in the 1980s in the airline, hotel, and car rental industries. **Yield management** is a set of mathematical techniques designed to increase revenue (yield) by discounting prices when inventory is not selling and charging premium prices when it is. These techniques are appropriate in the following circumstances:

1. A firm is operating with a relatively fixed capacity (only so many seats, rooms, or cars).
2. Demand can be segmented into clearly identified partitions (customers might be identified as time-sensitive or price-sensitive).
3. Inventory is perishable (empty seats or rooms from yesterday can't be sold).
4. The product is sold well in advance (industries with reservations systems, such as the airlines).
5. Demand fluctuates substantially (perhaps owing to holiday travel, weekday versus weekend travel, and other factors).
6. Marginal sales costs are low, but marginal production costs are high (building extra rooms or moving cars from one location to another immediately is impossible).[15]

By 1982, 75 percent of the nation's air traffic was flying on discounted fares, and by the late 1980s, every major airline had a yield management department. When an airplane takes off with empty seats, obviously the airline has lost potential revenue; but when it takes off full, it may be flying too many people at cheap, discounted prices, which also represents lost potential for the airline. Many airlines reported increases in revenue of 5 percent or more after starting a yield management program.

Essential to all yield management systems is a first-rate management information reservation system that keeps track of data in real time and supports a tremendous number of terminals for agents. Using computer systems, algorithms, and a detailed analysis of market segments, management has begun to make scientific sense out of pricing.[16] Patterns can be detected in buyer behavior, and market segments can be isolated on the basis of willingness to pay different rates.

There is a need to integrate information and knowledge into the planning and scheduling of operations. Yield management techniques have been divided into four categories: mathematical programming (linear programming or network flow models), economics-based (marginal revenue and expected marginal unit review), threshold curves (looking at booking and demand behavior), and expert systems.

Retailers have been quick to pick up on the concepts of yield management, adapting it to their own businesses and calling it "value pricing." PepsiCo Inc.'s Taco Bell chain offered a "value" menu of items for 59 cents, 79 cents, and 99 cents in late 1990 and saw its fourth quarter sales jump 15 percent and profits rise by 99 percent.[17] Of course "convenience" stores have always understood the economic concept of charging higher prices in return for convenience and availability (quick service, open at all hours, nearby).

The 1990s will see yield management practiced by other industries such as telecommunications, financial services, and utilities. Meanwhile the issues of possible customer alienation, employee training and incentive systems, and consumer behavior will provide fruitful areas for yield management to improve.

Spreadsheet Optimizers

spreadsheet optimizer
Electronic spreadsheet enhancement that automatically adjusts "what-if" cells based on user-entered data.

TEACHING TIP
Relate the use of spreadsheet optimizers to the contingency theory of managment. "What if" can be related to the "if then."

The two most powerful inventions affecting management science in the 1980s were the personal computer (PC) and the electronic spreadsheet. One of the biggest impacts in the 1990s will be **spreadsheet optimizers.** These spreadsheet add-ins allow a user to develop a model directly on the spreadsheet, and instead of manually adjusting different cells to play "what if . . . ", the spreadsheet optimizer will do it automatically. The user will identify which cells are "what if" cells (variables), which (if any) are constraints, and which single cell is to be optimized (maximized or minimized). For most optimizers, both upper and lower bounds can be given for variables and constraints. The optimizer then uses numerical calculus-based techniques to search for the nearest local optimum. (This has been likened to feeling your way around in a dense fog for the highest mountain or lowest valley.) The values of the constraints are shown, along with the marginal value (MV) for each constraint. *Marginal value* is the increase or decrease resulting from one unit of change in the constraint.

Figure 10-10 shows the results of minimizing the average total cost of a two-product constrained-inventory problem with a limit of 3,000 square feet of inventory and a capital investment limit of $1,500. The what-if cells are B6 and G6, the constraint cells are B9 and B12, and the optimizing cell is I15. Thus, 271.0 of product 1 and 205.6 of product 2 should be ordered to minimize total cost. The marginal value of an extra square foot of space is a savings of 11 cents (shown in cell E9), while the capital expenditure is not constraining (indicated by cell E12).

	A	B	C	D	E	F	G	H	I	J
1										
2		EOQ for Two Products w/Constraints								
3	Order Cost1 =	$100.00			Order Cost2 =		$150.00			
4	Carrying Cost1 =	$0.25			Carrying Cost2 =		$0.35			
5	Demand1 =	500			Demand2 =		300			
6	EOQ1 =	271.00	<==What If Cell		EOQ2 =		205.62	<==What If Cell		
7										
8	Storage < 3000:	5*Q1 + 8*Q2 ≤ 3000			Marginal Values					
9		3000.0	<==Constraint #1		− $0.111162					
10										
11	Capital < $1,500	$3*Q1 + $2*Q2 ≤ $1,500								
12		$1,224.24	<==Constraint #2		$0.000000					
13										
14	AVG TOTAL COST =	D*Co/Q	+ Cc(Q/2)			D*Co/Q	+ Cc(Q/2)		OPTIMIZE	
15	ATC =	$184.50	$33.88			$218.85	$35.98		$473.21	
16										

FIGURE 10-10 A Spreadsheet Optimizer

The advantage of this optimizer is that the model is highly visual and transparent to the user. The disadvantage is that the optimizer may find a good but not necessarily the best answer.

Decision Support and Expert Systems

In the early days of OR/MS, there was great promise that computers and artificial intelligence (computer programs that can "think") would soon revolutionize decision making. It has taken over 35 years, but with new powerful desktop work stations, mass storage devices, networking, sophisticated computer languages, and management science software, such fantasies are now becoming a reality. Now person-machine systems are developing into *decision support systems (DSS)* that let users select different management science software, data bases, and graphic displays to help them make decisions.

FOR DISCUSSION

Can you think of some ways that expert systems could be used in business organizations?

Expert systems are a type of DSS that can be programmed to emulate the decision making of a person with 20 to 30 years' experience. These systems can greatly increase an organization's productivity in two ways. First, they can bring new employees up to speed quickly. Second, they can extract new decision rules implied by expert behavior.

These systems are programmed by using special computer languages that can include qualitative rules as well as quantitative calculations to aid decision makers. Such systems have already been successfully developed for such diverse applications as medical diagnosis, real estate analysis, and flight-testing experimental aircraft. Expert systems are also being applied to such computer software as word processors to develop "smart word processors" that distinguish spelling mistakes in context (i.e., determine if "to," "too," or "two" is correct). Such systems promise to make great contributions to the practice of management science.

ILLUSTRATIVE CASE STUDY

WRAP-UP

Reducing Logistics Costs at General Motors

In its initial mathematical modeling effort, GM discovered it could save $2.9 million annually just by adjusting shipment sizes and routes. Even more important than the dollar savings, Delco no longer had to speculate about the merits of alternative strategies. It could evaluate them objectively instead.

The GM program provides as output the routes and shipment sizes that minimize total corporate cost for Delco's shipping and inventory network. It also provides a breakdown of cost by each link, which allows for separating out costs paid by Delco and by GM. Because the research team focused on trade-offs and provided graphical answers, the usefulness of the program and the merits of various strategies could be illustrated easily. Presenting trade-offs graphically was also effective in evaluating Delco's entire product-shipping network.

Another factor contributing to the project's success was that the ability to use personal computers involved potential users of the program in rapid prototyping, creating a sense of user ownership. Doing pilot tests in real settings makes it easy to refine prototypes quickly and to document real savings. As a testimony to its success and acceptance, over 40 GM facilities now use this program, with documented annual savings ranging from $35,000 to $500,000 at each site.

From this successful implementation of management science tools, the GM team discovered several important lessons about OR/MS. First, pursue results that allow the development of simple decision models and principles. Formulate models that are simple functions of a few key parameters with clear physical interpretations. This helps make decision tools transparent and meaningful to potential users. Transparency is important because decision makers want to understand the logic underlying decision tools.

Second, management science tools are more likely to be used if they require users to have only simple quantitative skills. Such tools should focus on (1) quantifying trade-offs between key variables, (2) using a minimal amount of data, (3) facilitating sensitivity analyses, and (4) presenting ranges of solutions graphically. These tools should help users evaluate several options and highlight the practical implications of various alternatives, as well as optimal solutions. Thus, the user can identify numerous options that are feasible in practice and nearly optimal in case the optimal cannot be used.

Third, to ensure successful implementation, it is imperative that users share a sense of ownership in a tool. This allows individual decision makers to (1) generate their own findings, (2) take pride in their individual accomplishments, and (3) monitor the implications of their own decisions. Thus, they are not forced to accept the findings of a central group.

Fourth, personal computers are a powerful medium for both decision tool development and implementation. They can greatly reduce the time and costs of developing systems, while increasing system benefits and enhancing the chances a system will be used.

Fifth—and this lesson pertains to management science in general—never forget that people make decisions, not models or computers. Management scientists must therefore be exceptional listeners and view potential users as their most important resource. ■

Source: Dennis E. Blumenfeld, Lawrence D. Burns, Carlos F. Daganzo, Michael C. Frick, and Randolph W. Hall, "Reducing Logistics Costs at General Motors," *Interfaces* 17, no. 1 (January–February 1987):26–47.

■ SUMMARY

Management science uses teams of experts with mathematical, analytical, and computer-oriented skills, as well as intuition and good judgment, to support management planning and decision making.

Management science is needed because decisions are complex and because the environment is changing and uncertain. Its goals are to convert data into meaningful information, to support the making of transferable, independent decisions, and to create solution systems that will be useful to nontechnical users.

The management science process is made up of problem determination, mathematical modeling and prototyping, solution selection, and implementation—the passing on of solution systems to users.

Forecasting, the process of using past events to make systematic predictions about future outcomes or trends, is used to create premises, or planning assumptions, about events that are largely determined by the organization's actions (for example, sales and revenue forecasting) and about events in the indirect-action environment (for example, technological forecasting).

Quantitative forecasting makes predictions by using mathematical rules to manipulate existing data, while quantitative analysis converts subjective judgments, knowledge, and opinions into quantitative measures.

Gantt charts are useful for analyzing and scheduling tasks within simple projects, but they are not very useful for dealing with the more complex problems typical of modern business. These problems are better scheduled and managed by PERT, a type of network analysis that determines the critical path, or maximum time required for a project, as well as the critical activities. PERT networks also identify subcritical paths, which are a source of slack resources that can be reassigned to activities on the critical path to save time.

Linear programming and network models are quantitative techniques for determining the optimum combination of limited resources.

Payoff matrices can help managers evaluate simple decisions involving uncertainty, while decision trees can help them evaluate series of interrelated decisions involving uncertainty.

Up-and-coming management science techniques include yield management, spreadsheet optimizers, and decision support and expert systems.

■ REVIEW QUESTIONS

1. Why is management science needed today?
2. What are the goals of management science?
3. What are the four steps of the management science process?
4. How is forecasting used? How important is accuracy?
5. Explain the difference between quantitative and qualitative forecasting methods. When is each useful?
6. What are the pros and cons of using Gantt charts?
7. What are the advantages of PERT?
8. What is a payoff matrix and when is it useful?
9. Explain the idea of a decision tree and when it is useful.
10. Which of the emerging techniques in management science seem to have most promise?

CASE STUDY

The $10-Million Faux Pas

Most managers would be delighted if anyone could find a way to save $10 million—unless it meant scuttling a pet project. This was the lesson one young management scientist learned the hard way.

On the surface, the situation seemed clear-cut. The 700-bed midwestern hospital had one enclosed parking garage—a necessity given the harsh midwestern winters. However, the garage was filled to capacity during peak hours. Even if hospital administrators were not concerned about the ethical implications of inconveniencing sick patients and the people who accompanied them to the hospital, there were important financial considerations: The hospital operated a number of high-volume outpatient clinics and patients were threatening to go elsewhere.

The hospital's assistant administrator turned to a junior member of the operations department, a recent graduate with a master's degree: Investigate the situation and make a recommendation. If the problem was minor, the hospital could probably make do with a new ground-level lot. If the problem was more serious, it was considering building a new $10-million multilevel parking garage. This done, the assistant administrator left for a three-week vacation.

Eager to please, the young graduate spent two weeks analyzing the time-stamped tickets issued by the parking garage. The surprising conclusion: The garage was only full because hospital employees were parking there instead of in the employees' less-convenient open lot across the freeway. The hospital didn't need a $10-million garage. It only needed to enforce its own parking rules.

Because the assistant administrator was still on vacation, the young graduate had to present his findings to the top executives at the next big meeting.

After having braced themselves for the worst, the grateful executives thanked the graduate and asked his department for further instructions.

All was well until the assistant administrator returned. Not only had his pet project—the $10-million garage—been squashed, making him look like a fool, but someone now had to enforce parking rules that were very unpopular with the hospital's blue-collar workers. The hapless graduate was rebuked by his boss, made to apologize to the assistant administrator, and given the task of finding a way to enforce the parking rules.

After considering various strategies, the graduate finally convinced a vice president and several department heads to meet him at the parking garage booth at 5:00 A.M., where bosses personally nabbed offending parkers. After just two days of these personalized parking tickets, the garage was half empty at peak demand periods.

As for the young graduate, he left the hospital for a job in private industry, taking with him some valuable lessons in the difference between being brutally frank and politically wise.

Source: Mark G. Simkin and Edward B. Daniels, "He Saved the Company $10 Million—and Apologized," *Interfaces* 19, no. 3 (May–June 1989):61–64. Names have been disguised at the request of the hospital and participants.

Case Questions

1. How would you rate the graduate on his ability to reach the goals of management science?
2. Where in the management science process did the graduate go wrong? What could he have done differently?

VIDEO CASE STUDY

Managing the Magic at L.L. Bean

L.L. Bean, Inc., a name synonymous with hunting boots, flannel shirts, and other outdoor apparel, is something of a legend among mail-order businesses. Founded in 1912, the company has just one retail outlet in Freeport, Maine. On an average, more than 3 million people visit the cavernous store, which is open 24 hours a day, 365 days a year. But most people know L.L. Bean through its catalogs; over 75 mil-

lion are mailed each year, with combined retail and catalog sales of $580 million in 1988. In a field crowded with mail-order catalogs, L.L. Bean stands out for "L.L.'s Golden Rule"—an old-fashioned approach to customer service and quality merchandise, backed up by a 100-percent guarantee. But Leon Gorman, the founder's grandson and current president, supports this business ethic with modern management practices, including the tools of management science.

Actually, the term *mail order* is a bit misleading. Only 20 percent of L.L. Bean's "mail order" business is done by mail, while 65 percent is done via toll-free (800) phone lines. In these telemarketing operations, large numbers of sales agents answer questions and take orders in a room divided into cubicles, each equipped with a telephone headset and computer terminal.

On a busy day, as many as 78,000 people call the L.L. Bean 800 number. But, if they get a busy signal or have to wait on hold too long, they tend to give up and may never call back. All this translates into lost revenue. In 1988, L.L. Bean conservatively estimated it lost $10 million in profit due to inadequate telemarketing facilities. By analyzing telephone records, its OR/MS specialists found that in some half-hours, customers were getting busy signals 80 percent of the time or had to wait 10 minutes or more for an agent. On busy days, they estimated, lost orders approached $500,000 in gross revenues. This revelation was especially sobering for L.L. Bean managers as they contemplated the three-week period before Christmas. This brief time accounted for 18 percent of annual call volume and could make or break the year for the company.

In spring 1989, senior management launched a project to use both in-house staff and two consultants from the University of Southern Maine to improve its telemarketing facilities.

After talking to users, the MS/OR team decided any system had to help managers make the following long-term decisions: (1) How many telephone lines do we need? This can vary from month to month but needs to be planned well in advance. (2) How many full-time, part-time, and temporary sales agents do we need? (3) Should we have one huge telemarketing center or several smaller ones? (4) What facilities and equipment can we afford? In the short term, the system had to help managers decided how to schedule the available staff on a 24-hour-a-day, seven-day-a-week basis and how many customers should be put on hold before the next customer hears a busy signal.

The traditional approach would try to hold costs at a minimum, but the MS/OR team decided to take a different tack. They would create a prototype that would increase resources until the cost of doing so outweighed the marginal increase in profit.

The team used the forecasting technique of regression analysis, which related the number of customers who abandoned their calls to customer service levels, and a Delphi approach to arrive at a consensus about the possibility that a caller who gets a busy signal will eventually give up. They also used queuing (waiting line) theory to determine the number of phone lines needed to achieve specific service levels during certain periods.

Even before the prototype was completed, it showed such tremendous promise that senior managers were quickly convinced that increasing resources was the way to increase profitability. The team then demonstrated the prototype to a steering committee, whose comments led to several important modifications of the model. This honest show of concern for user satisfaction eventually helped the system find wide acceptance at all levels of the corporation.

The results have been stunning. For an investment of $40,000, L.L. Bean has seen an increase of almost $14 million in revenue. When it compared the 1988 pre-Christmas period with the 1989 pre-Christmas season, the number of calls answered increased 24 percent; the number of orders taken increased 16.7 percent; and revenue grew by 16.3 percent. Abandoned calls—the people who gave up— dropped 81.3 percent, and the number of people who had to wait for an answer plunged a whopping 208 percent. The average speed of L.L. Bean's answer plummeted from 93 seconds in 1988 to just 15 seconds in 1989. Most important, perhaps, modern technology and management science helped preserve the tradition of old-fashioned service.

Sources: Bruce Andrews and Henry Parsons, "L.L. Bean Chooses a Telephone Agent Scheduling System," *Interfaces* 19, no. 6 (November–December 1989):1–9, and Phil Quinn, Bruce Andrews, and Henry Parsons, "Allocating Telecommunications Resources at L.L. Bean, Inc.," *Interfaces* 21, no. 1 (January–February 1991):75–91.

Case Questions

1. How did L.L. Bean's mission and strategic goals affect its decision to use management science techniques?

2. Which management science techniques were used during the modeling/prototyping process?

3. What did the OR/MS team do to win support throughout the company?

■ *NOTES*

[1] James R. Evans, "A Microcomputer-Based Decision Support System for Scheduling Umpires in the American Baseball League," *Interfaces* 18, no. 6 (November–December 1988):42–51.

[2] Rick Hesse and Gene Woolsey, *Applied Management Science: A Quick and Dirty Approach* (Chicago: SRA, 1980), p. 1.

[3] Peter F. Drucker, *The Effective Executive* (New York: Harper & Row, 1967), p. 130.

[4] Michael Fisher, "Operations Research at Federal Express," *OR/MS Today* 16, no. 3 (June 1989):20–21.

[5] Russell L. Ackoff, "Beyond Problem Solving," *Decision Sciences* 5, no. 2 (Spring 1974):x–xv.

[6] As quoted in Hesse and Woolsey, *Applied Management Science,* p. 5.

[7] John R. Harrald, Henry S. Marcus, William A. Wallace, "The *Exxon Valdez:* An Assessment of Crisis Prevention and Management Systems," *Interfaces* 20, no. 5 (September–October 1990):14–30.

[8] Chris McGoff, Ann Hunt, Doug Vogel, and Jay Nunmaker, "IBM's Experience with GroupSystems," *Interfaces* 20, no. 6 (November–December 1990):39–52.

[9] "Brainstorming by Modem," *The New York Times,* March 24, 1991, p. F6.

[10] Jacob W. Ulvila and Rex V. Brown, "Decision Analysis Comes of Age," *Harvard Business Review,* September–October 1982, pp. 130–141.

[11] See Harold E. Fearon, William A. Ruch, Vincent G. Reuter, C. David Wieters, and Ross R. Reck, *Fundamentals of Production/Operations Management,* 3rd ed. (St. Paul, Minn.: West, 1986); W. J. Erickson and O. P. Hall, *Computer Models for Management Science* (Reading, Mass.: Addison-Wesley, 1986).

[12] This example is from Thomas M. Cook and Robert A. Russell, *Introduction to Management Science,* 4th ed. (Englewood Cliffs, N.J.: Prentice Hall, 1989), Chap. 2 and 3. Copyright © 1989 by Prentice Hall. Adapted by permission.

[13] F. Hutton Barron, "Payoff Matrices Pay Off at Hallmark," *Interfaces* 15, no. 4 (July–August 1985):20–25.

[14] Jacob W. Ulvila, "Postal Automation (Zip+4) Technology: A Decision Analysis," *Interfaces* 17, no. 2 (March–April 1987):1–12.

[15] Sheryl E. Kimes, "Yield Management: A Tool for Capacity-Constrained Service Firms," *Journal of Operations Management* 8, no. 4 (1990):343–363.

[16] James C. Makens, "Yield Management: Pricing Strategy for the '90s?" *Mariott's Portfolio,* November/December 1989, pp. 14–18.

[17] Joseph B. White, "'Value Pricing' Is Hot as Shrewd Consumers Seek Low-Cost Quality," *The Wall Street Journal,* March 12, 1990, pp. A1, A9.

Case on Planning

THE ADAMS CORPORATION

In January 1972, the board of directors of the Adams Corp. simultaneously announced the highest sales in the company's history, the lowest after-tax profits (as a percentage of sales) of the post–World War II era, and the retirement (for personal reasons) of its long-tenured president and chief executive officer, Jerome Adams.

Founded in St. Louis in 1848, the Adams Brothers Co. had long been identified as a family firm both in name and operating philosophy. Writing in a business history journal, a former family senior manager commented:

> My grandfather wanted to lead a business organization with ethical standards. He wanted to produce a quality product and a quality working climate for both employees and managers. He thought the Holy Bible and the concept of family stewardship provided him with all the guidelines needed to lead his company. A belief in the fundamental goodness of mankind, in the power of fair play, and in the importance of personal and corporate integrity were his trademarks. Those traditions exist today in the 1960s.

In the early 1950s, two significant corporate events occurred. First, the name of the firm was changed to the Adams Corp. Second, somewhat over 50 percent of the corporation's shares were sold by various family groups to the wider public. In 1970, all branches of the family owned or influenced less than one-fifth of the outstanding shares of Adams.

The Adams Corp. was widely known and respected as a manufacturer and distributor of quality brand-name consumer products for the American, Canadian, and European (export) markets. Adams products were processed in four regional plants located near raw material sources. (No single plant processed the full line of Adams products, but each plant processed the main items in the line.) The products were stored and distributed in a series of recently constructed or renovated distribution centers located in key cities throughout North America, and they were sold by a company sales force in thousands of retail outlets—primarily supermarkets.

In explaining the original, long-term financial success of the company, a former officer commented:

> Adams led the industry in the development of unique production processes that produced a quality product at a very low cost. The company has always been production-oriented and volume-oriented and it paid off for a long time. During those decades the Adams brand was all that was needed to sell our product; we didn't do anything but a little advertising. Competition was limited and our production efficiency and raw material sources enabled us to outpace the industry in sales and profit. Our strategy was to make a quality product, distribute it, and sell it cheap.

> But that has all changed in the past 20 years. Our three major competitors have outdistanced us in net profits and market aggressiveness. One of them—a first-class marketing group—has doubled sales and profits within the past five years. Our gross sales have increased to almost $250 million, but our net profits have dropped continuously during that same period. While a consumer action group just designated us as "best value," we have fallen behind in marketing techniques; for example, our packaging is just out of date.

Structurally, Adams was organized into eight major divisions. Seven of these were regional sales divisions with responsibility for distribution and sales of the company's consumer products to retail stores in their areas. Each regional sales division was further divided into organizational units at the state, county, and/or trading-area level. Each sales division was governed by a corporate price list in the selling of company products, but each had some leeway to meet the local competitive price developments. Each sales division was also assigned (by the home office) a quota of salespeople it could hire and was given the salary ranges within which these people could be employed. All salespeople were on straight salary with an expense-reimbursement salary plan—a policy which resulted in compensation under industry averages.

A small central accounting office accumulated sales and expense information for each of the several sales divisions on a quarterly basis, and it prepared the overall company financial statements. Each sales division received, without commentary, a quarterly statement showing the following information for the overall division: number of cases processed and sold, sales revenue per case, and local expenses per case. Somewhat similar information was obtained

305

from the manufacturing division. Manufacturing division accounting was complicated by variations in the cost of obtaining and processing the basic materials used in Adams's products. These variations—particularly in procurement—were largely beyond the control of the division. The accounting office, however, did have one rough external check on manufacturing-division effectiveness: A crude market price existed for case lot goods sold by smaller firms to some large national chains.

Once every quarter, the seven senior sales vice presidents met with general management in St. Louis. Typically, management discussion focused on divisional sales results and expense control. The company's objective of being #1—the largest-selling line in its field—directed group attention to sales as compared to budget. All knew that last year's sales targets had to be exceeded, no matter what. The manufacturing division vice president sat in on these meetings to explain the product-availability situation. Because of his St. Louis office location, he frequently talked with Jerome Adams about overall manufacturing operations and specifically about large procurement decisions.

The Adams Corp., Price Millman knew, had a trade reputation for being very conservative with its compensation program. All officers were on a straight salary program. An officer might expect a modest salary increase every two or three years; these increases tended to be in the thousand-dollar range, regardless of divisional performance or company profit position. Salaries among the seven sales divisional vice presidents ranged from $40,000 to $55,000, with the higher amounts going to more senior officers. Jerome Adams's salary of $75,000 was the highest in the company. There was no corporate bonus plan. A very limited stock-option program was in operation, but the depressed price of Adams stock meant that few officers exercised their options.

The corporate climate at Adams had been of considerable pride to Jerome Adams. "We take care of our family" was his oft-repeated phrase at company banquets honoring long-service employees. "We are a team and it is a team spirit that has built Adams into its leading position in this industry." No member of first-line, middle, or senior management could be discharged (except in cases of moral crime or dishonesty) without a personal review of his case by Mr. Adams; as a matter of fact, executive turnover at Adams was very low. Executives at all levels viewed their jobs as lifetime careers. There was no compulsory retirement plan, and some managers were still active in their mid-70s.

The operational extension of this organizational philosophy was quite evident to employees and managers. For over 75 years, a private family trust provided emergency assistance to all members of the Adams organization. Adams led its industry in the granting of educational scholarships, in medical insurance for employees and managers, and in the encouragement of its members to give corporate and personal time and effort to community problems and organizations.

Jerome noted two positive aspects of this organizational philosophy:

> We have a high percentage of long-term employees—Joe Girly, a guard at East St. Louis, completes 55 years with us this year and every one of his brothers and sisters has worked here. And it is not uncommon for a vice president to retire with a blue pin—that means 40 years of service. We have led this industry in manufacturing-process innovation, quality control, and value for low price for decades. I am proud of our accomplishments and this pride is shown by everyone from janitors to directors.

Industry sources noted that there was no question that Adams was #1 in terms of manufacturing and logistic efficiency.

In December 1971, the annual Adams management conference gathered over 80 members of Adams's senior management in St. Louis. Most expected the usual formal routines—the announcement of 1971 results and 1972 budgets, the award of the "Gold Flag" to the top processing plant and sales division for exceeding targets, and the award of service pins to executives. All expected the usual social good times. It was an opportunity to meet and drink with "old buddies."

After a series of task force meetings, the managers gathered in a banquet room—good-naturedly referred to as the "Rib Room" since a local singer, Eve, was to provide entertainment. In the usual fashion, a dais with a long, elaborately decorated head table was at the front of the room. Sitting at the center of that table was Jerome Adams. Following tradition, Adams's vice presidents, in order of seniority with the company, sat on his right. On his left sat major family shareholders, corporate staff, and a newcomer soon to be introduced.

After awarding service pins and the "Gold Flags" of achievement, Adams formally announced what had been corporate secrets for several months. First, a new investing group had assumed a control position on the board of Adams. Second, Price Millman would take over as president and CEO of Adams.

Introducing Millman, Adams pointed out the outstanding record of the firm's new president: "Price got his M.B.A. in 1958, spent four years in control and marketing, and then was named as the youngest divisional president in the history of the Tenny Corporation. In the past years, he has made his division the most profitable in Tenny and the industry leader in its field. We are fortunate to have him with us. Please give him your complete support."

In a later, informal meeting with the divisional vice presidents, Millman spoke about his respect for Adams's past accomplishments and the pressing need to infuse Adams with "fighting spirit" and "competitiveness." He said, "My personal and organizational philosophy are the same—the name of the game is to fight and win. I almost drowned, but I won my first swimming race at 11 years of age! That philosophy of always winning is what enabled me to build the Ajax Division into Tenny's most profitable operation. We are going to do this at Adams."

In conclusion, Millman commented, "The new owner group wants results. They have advised me to take some time to think through a new format for Adams's operations—to get a corporate design that will improve our effectiveness. Once we get that new format, gentlemen, I have but one goal—each month must be better than the past."

Source: Copyright © 1972 by the President and Fellows of Harvard College. This case was prepared by Charles B. Weigle under the direction of C. Roland Christensen as the basis for class discussion rather than to illustrate either effective or ineffective handling of an administrative situation. Reprinted by permission of the Harvard Business School.

Case Questions

1. What are the key strengths of the company?

2. What are the weaknesses of Adams Corp.?

3. Develop a plan of action for Millman.

4. What are some important factors and potential barriers to implementing your plan?

CHAPTER ELEVEN

ORGANIZATIONAL STRUCTURE, COORDINATION, AND DESIGN

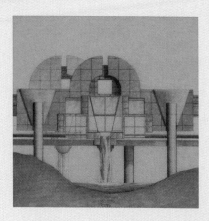

Organizational Structure
Division of Work
Departmentalization and the Span of Management
The Formal and Informal Organizational Structure

Types of Organizational Structures
Functional Organization
Product/Market Organization
Matrix Organization

Coordination
Problems in Achieving Effective Coordination
Approaches to Achieving Effective Coordination
Selecting the Appropriate Coordination Mechanisms

Organizational Design
The Classical Approach
The Neoclassical Approach
The Environmental Approach
The Task-Technology Approach
The Need to Reorganize

Upon completing this chapter, you should be able to:

1. Explain why organizational structure is important.

2. Define division of work and how it can be shown on an organization chart.

3. Discuss the key considerations in choosing an appropriate span of management and explain how span of management creates tall and flat organizational structures.

4. Give examples of how the informal organizational structure can increase efficiency.

5. Compare and contrast functional and product/market structures.

6. Explain a matrix structure and the circumstances where it would be appropriate.

7. Discuss the reasons differentiation hampers coordination and how coordination can be improved.

8. Compare and contrast the major approaches to organizational design.

9. Identify situations that indicate an organization needs to consider a reorganization.

Michael Graves, Fargo-Moorehead Cultural Center—Bridge Center. South elevation, 1977–78. Pencil and prisma-color on yellow tracing paper. 11 ⅞ × 11 ⅞″. Collection, The Museum of Modern Art, New York. Lily Auchincloss Fund.

ILLUSTRATIVE CASE STUDY

INTRODUCTION

Hewlett-Packard Reinterprets the HP Way

In the spring of 1990, Hewlett-Packard (HP) CEO John A. Young got a nasty shock: HP's Snakes project was slipping a year behind schedule, taking with it the California-based company's best chance to remain an industry leader. Snakes was the code name for a new line of workstations—one of the few segments of the computer market that was still growing.

A workstation is an enhanced microcomputer that has the same processing power and speed of a minicomputer. Workstations have two advantages over minicomputers, though. First, they are cheaper—$5,000 for a workstation versus $100,000 for an equally powerful minicomputer.

Second, workstations are more versatile. A minicomputer is a stand-alone machine, designed to be used by itself, and most are "closed systems," meaning they can use only the manufacturer's software. In contrast, a workstation can be used alone, it can be networked with other computers, or it can act as a terminal for a mainframe computer. Workstations are especially appealing for computer-aided design (CAD) and computer-integrated manufacturing (CIM), both of which need large amounts of computer memory and processing power to draw and manipulate exploded views of products. Furthermore, many workstations are "open systems," meaning they can use software from a variety of providers. Little wonder then that HP, a leader in minicomputers with closed systems, was eating the dust of giant Sun Microsystems, which favored open systems.

The threatened delay was doubly costly, given HP's risky purchase of Apollo Computer, an ailing rival and workstation pioneer, for $500 million just a year before. Young wanted Apollo to enlarge HP's customer base, buying HP the time needed to develop a new, more competitive line of workstations. Furthermore, Apollo engineers had experience with RISC microprocessors, the brains of the fastest, most powerful workstations.

The move did make HP No. 1 briefly, but Sun soon regained its lead. And, while HP was struggling to integrate Massachusetts-based Apollo into its operations, IBM announced a line of workstations. Even the best HP products would have faced an uphill battle. Now, they faced not one, but two, entrenched competitors, and the clock was still ticking.

Senior Managers at HP. CEO John A. Young (in shirtsleeves) is surrounded by the electronic images of (left) Computer Products Head Richard A. Hackborn and (right) Computer Systems Chief Lewis E. Platt.

The irony is that HP is revered for the "HP Way"—a corporate culture that typifies the innovations of California's Silicon Valley. Fancy offices, rigid chains of command, formal procedures—all were sacrificed to the single-minded pursuit of engineering excellence. Indeed, HP had topped the nation's list of best-managed companies year after year. Yet, now, when the company needed to be its most nimble, it found itself hobbled by a chain of committees.

In some ways, HP was a victim of its success. It had adopted the committee system back in the mid-1980s, when it was trying to make the transition from closed to open systems. Which features were most essential? Which projects should HP keep? Which should it drop? The committees were set up to let HP experts brainstorm answers to these questions and reach a consensus that would guide its strategy. The committees multiplied, though, like a computer virus, reports *Business Week* analyst Barbara Buell.

In the summer of 1990, he called in founder David Packard, the chairman of the board and still HP's largest shareholder, to work out a major revamping of the corporate structure that would return the company to the HP way.

Source: John W. Verity, et al., "In Computers, a Shakeout of Seismic Proportions," *Business Week,* October 15, 1990, pp. 34–36; Barbara Buell et al., "Hewlett-Packard Rethinks Itself," *Business Week,* April 1, 1991, pp. 76–79.

O rganizational structure—the way in which an organization's activities are divided, organized, and coordinated—provides a stable framework that helps organization members work together to achieve organizational goals. Some organizational structures, however, make it difficult, or even impossible, to adapt to a change in environment or strategy. This was the case at Hewlett-Packard. In these circumstances, managers usually look to restructure the organization.

In this part, we will study the process of organizing. We begin in this chapter with a discussion of the different forms of organizational structure, the task of *coordination,* and the process of *organizational design,* or choosing an organizational structure that is appropriate to a specific strategy and environment. In the next chapter, we will discuss another aspect of organizational structure and design—the way in which authority is centralized or decentralized. Chapter 13 covers *human resource management,* or how employees are selected, trained, and developed. In the last chapter in Part IV, Chapter 14, we will focus on how organizing can help an organization adapt to change and encourage innovation.

■ ORGANIZATIONAL STRUCTURE

Organizational structure refers to the way in which an organization's activities are divided, organized, and coordinated. Ernest Dale's description of organizing as a five-step process provides a good framework for our discussion.[1]

1. List the work that needs to be done to accomplish organization goals. A hospital's goal of caring for the sick, for example, would involve tasks ranging from purchasing equipment and supplies to hiring staff and applying for accreditation, or recognition, from various professional organizations.
2. Divide the total work load into tasks that can logically and comfortably be performed by individuals or groups. This is referred to as the **division of work.**
3. Combine tasks in a logical and efficient manner. The grouping of employees and tasks is generally referred to as **departmentalization.**
4. Set up mechanisms for **coordination.** This integration of individual, group, and department efforts makes it easier to achieve goals.
5. Monitor the organizational structure's effectiveness and make adjustments as needed.

Division of Work

Adam Smith's *Wealth of Nations* opens with a famous passage on the minute specialization of labor in the manufacture of pins. Describing the work in a pin factory, Smith wrote, "One man draws the wire, another straightens it, a third cuts it, a fourth points it, a fifth grinds it at the top for receiving the head." Ten men working in this fashion, he said, made 48,000 pins in one day. "But if they had all wrought separately and independently," each might at best have produced 20 pins a day. As Smith observed, the great advantage of the division of labor was that by breaking the total job down into small, simple, separate operations in which each worker could specialize, total productivity was multiplied geometrically.[2]

Today we use the term *division of work* rather than division of labor to indicate that all organizational tasks, from manufacturing to management, can be specialized. Another term for division of work is **job specialization.** Many people believe that the rise of civilization can be attributed to this specialization, which gave humanity the resources to develop art, science, and education.

Division of Work. Actors Glenn Close and John Malkovich prepare for a scene from *Dangerous Liaisons* under the watchful eye of a camera operator, just one of the hundreds of behind-the-scenes people that perform the many tasks needed to complete a modern movie.

organization chart A diagram of an organization's structure, showing the functions, departments, or positions of the organization and how they are related.

span of management (or **span of control**) The number of subordinates reporting directly to a given manager.

Why does the division of work greatly increase productivity? The answer is that no one person is physically or psychologically able to perform all the operations that make up most complex tasks—even assuming one person could acquire all the specialized skills needed to do so. In contrast, division of work creates simplified tasks that can be learned and completed relatively quickly. In addition, it creates a variety of jobs, letting people choose, or be assigned to, positions that match their talents and interests.

Job specialization also has its disadvantages. If tasks are divided into small, discrete steps, and if each worker is responsible for only one step, then *alienation*— the absence of a sense of control over one's work—may easily develop. Karl Marx built his theory of socialist economics partly on the contention that division of work causes workers to lose pride in their work. On a more practical level, boredom and absenteeism may rise when a specialized task becomes repetitive and personally unsatisfying.[3] Many techniques of *job enlargement* and *job enrichment* (to be discussed in Chapter 12) are aimed at overcoming labor alienation. For example, General Motors and Toyota decided to let work teams decide who performs what tasks and to train workers to perform multiple tasks at their Fremont, California, joint venture.

Departmentalization and the Span of Management

Most organizational structures are too complex to be conveyed verbally. For this reason, managers customarily draw up an **organization chart.** (See Figs. 11-1 through 11-6 for examples.) In an organization chart, the individual boxes represent the division of work and the way in which tasks are departmentalized. These boxes are then arranged in levels that represent the management hierarchy. The solid lines connecting certain boxes represent the *chain of command,* or "who reports to whom."

By looking at an organization chart, we can quickly assess the **span of management** (also called the **span of control**), which can be defined as the number of subordinates who report directly to a particular manager. The modern approach to span of management began with the Industrial Revolution. In the nineteenth and first half of the twentieth century, various writers tried to determine the maximum

Here's an Example
The U.S. Postal Service is the biggest civilian employer, with 740,000 people. One out of every 160 employed Americans works at the Postal Service. (*Time*, 3/4/91, p. 10ff.)

tall organizational structure Organizational structure characterized by a narrow span of management and many hierarchical levels.

flat organizational structure Organizational structure characterized by a wide span of management and few hierarchical levels.

For Discussion
What does an organization chart tell you about an organization? What does it not reveal?

number of subordinates one manager could supervise, and many concluded that the universal maximum was six. The idea that a manager can control only six subordinates regardless of circumstances seems odd today, but the earlier writers must be given credit for recognizing that there is an optimal number of subordinates, as well as a number beyond which supervision becomes less effective.[4]

Choosing an appropriate span of management is important for two reasons. First, it affects efficiency. Too wide a span may mean that managers are overextended and subordinates are receiving too little guidance or control. When this happens, managers may be pressured to ignore or condone serious errors. In contrast, too narrow a span may mean that managers are underutilized. Second, span of management is related to organizational structure. Narrow spans of management create **tall organizational structures** with many levels between the highest and lowest managers. In these organizations, a long chain of command slows decision making, a disadvantage in a rapidly changing environment. Wide spans, in contrast, create **flat organizational structures,** with fewer management levels between top and bottom. (See Fig. 11-1.) One of the most noticeable trends in recent years is toward flat organizational structures. Organizations are moving toward these flat structures to cut the costs associated with levels of middle management and to speed decision making. The risk, of course, is that the remaining managers have greater responsibilities and may be overtaxed.

Contemporary researchers agree, though, that there is no one ideal span of management. Choosing an appropriate span of management requires weighing such factors as the environment and the capabilities of both managers and subordinates. As managers and subordinates become more experienced, for example, the optimal span of management tends to increase.

If the span of management is a problem, we can fix it by adjusting either the span or the factors that influence it. Let's assume the span of management is too large and supervisors and subordinates both feel harassed and frustrated. One solution

FIGURE 11-1 Tall and Flat Organizational Structures

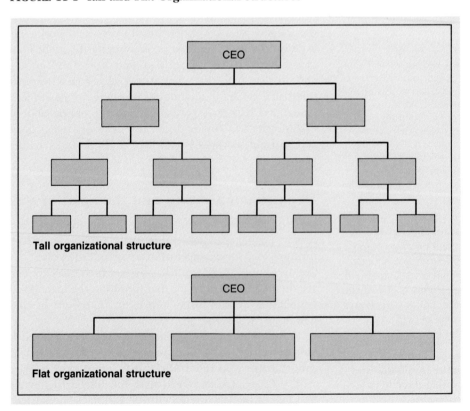

Tall organizational structure

Flat organizational structure

would be to adjust the span of management by transferring some employees or responsibilities to another manager. Another solution would be to provide additional training for managers or to add supervisory assistants to handle nonsupervisory tasks. It is only by analyzing the situation and the people involved that we can identify the best factors to adjust.[5]

The Formal and Informal Organizational Structure

Organization charts are useful for showing the formal organizational structure and who is responsible for certain tasks. In addition, just making up a chart can pinpoint organizational defects, such as duplication of effort or potential conflicts. However, organization charts tend to hide many characteristics of the organizational structure.[6] For one thing, the charts imply that managers on the same level all have the same amount of authority and responsibility, and this is not always true. For another, people often read things into organization charts that they are not intended to show. For example, employees may infer status and power on the basis of distance from the CEO's box. Robert Townsend, former president of Avis, even suggests that organization charts are demoralizing because they reinforce the idea that all authority and ability rest at the top of the organization.[7]

informal organizational structure The undocumented and officially unrecognized relationships between members of an organization that inevitably emerge out of the personal and group needs of employees.

In reality, though, the organization chart cannot begin to capture the interpersonal relationships that make up the **informal organizational structure.** Herbert A. Simon has described this as "the interpersonal relationships in the organization that affect decisions within it but either are omitted from the formal scheme or are not consistent with it."[8] These interpersonal relationships are often referred to as the dotted lines on the organization chart. For example, during a busy period, one employee may turn to another for help rather than going through a manager. Or an employee in sales may establish a working relationship with an employee in production, who can provide information about product availability faster than the formal reporting system. And anyone who has worked in an organization knows that the importance and authority of secretaries and executive assistants can never be shown on an organization chart.

One of the first scholars to recognize the importance of informal structures was Chester Barnard (discussed in Chapter 2). He noted that informal relationships help organization members satisfy their social needs *and* get things done. In fact, insisting that employees always "go through channels" can be a disadvantage. Consider the plight of Xerox, which built up so many bureaucratic layers that new-product ideas were being strangled by red tape. As a result, Xerox, once "the name" in photocopiers, let IBM and various Japanese competitors cut into its market share.

Given the pace of change in today's environment, many organizations are finding that tall structures mean slow decision making and lost opportunities. As a result, they are trying to encourage the ad hoc relationships typical of informal organizational structures and turning from tall to flat organizational structures, which have shorter chains of command.

■ *TYPES OF ORGANIZATIONAL STRUCTURES*

An organization's departments can be formally structured in three major ways: by function, by product/market, or in matrix form.

Organization by *function* brings together in one department everyone engaged in one activity or several related activities. For example, an organization divided by function might have separate manufacturing, marketing, and sales departments. A sales manager in such an organization would be responsible for the sale of *all* products manufactured by the firm.

Product or *market* organization, often referred to as organization by division, brings together in one work unit all those involved in the production and marketing of a product or a related group of products, all those in a certain geographic area, or all those dealing with a certain type of customer. For example, an organization might have separate chemical, detergent, and cosmetic divisions, with each division head responsible for the manufacturing, marketing, and sales activities of his or her entire unit. Currently, General Motors is a good example of this type of organizational structure.

In a *matrix* organization, two types of structure exist simultaneously. Permanent functional departments have authority for the performance and professional standards of their units, while project teams are created as needed to carry out specific programs. Team members are drawn from various functional departments and report to a project manager, who is responsible for the outcome of the team's work. Many aerospace companies that rely on contract work use this matrix. On the whole, however, the matrix structure is found much less frequently in organizations than the functional and product/market structures.[9]

All three types of organization design have advantages and disadvantages. Few organizations rely on any one type exclusively and most adapt and combine these general patterns to reflect their unique strategies and personnel.

Functional Organization

Functional organization is perhaps the most logical and basic form of departmentalization. (See Fig. 11-2.) It is used mainly (but not only) by smaller firms that offer a limited line of products because it makes efficient use of specialized resources. Another major advantage of a functional structure is that it makes supervision easier, since each manager must be expert in only a narrow range of skills. In addition, a functional structure makes it easier to mobilize specialized skills and bring them to bear where they are most needed.

As an organization grows, either by expanding geographically or by broadening its product line, some of the disadvantages of the functional structure begin to surface. It becomes more difficult to get quick decisions or action on a problem because functional managers have to report to central headquarters and may have to wait a long time before a request for help is acted on. In addition, it is often harder to determine accountability and judge performance in a functional structure. If a new product fails, who is to blame—research and development, production, or marketing? Finally, coordinating the functions of members of the entire organization may become a problem for top managers. Members of each department may feel isolated from (or superior to) those in other departments. It therefore becomes more difficult for employees to work in a unified way to achieve the organization's goals. For example, the manufacturing department may concentrate on meeting cost standards

FIGURE 11-2 Functional Organization Chart for a Manufacturing Company
Note: Each vice president is in charge of a major organizational function.

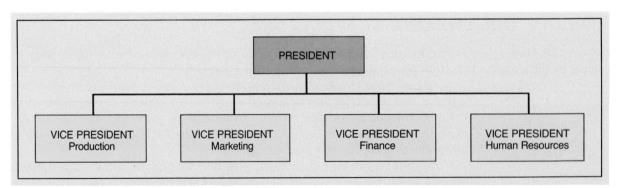

and delivery dates and neglect quality control. As a result, the service department may become flooded with complaints.

Top managers who wish to use a functional structure or add a functional department to an existing structure must weigh potential benefits against expected costs. The economic savings brought about by a functional structure may be outweighed by the additional managerial and staff salaries and other overhead costs that are required. Top managers also have to consider how often they expect to use the special skills of a functional department. In a small firm, for example, it may be more economical to retain outside legal services than to set up an in-house legal department.

Product/Market Organization

product or **market organization** The organization of a company into divisions that bring together all those involved with a certain type of product or market.

division Large organization department that resembles a separate business; may be devoted to making and selling specific products or serving a specific market.

COORDINATED RESOURCE

Use Transparency 66, Product/Market Organization Chart for a Manufacturing Company: Division by Product.

Most large, multiproduct companies, such as General Motors, have a **product** or **market organization** structure. At some point in an organization's existence, sheer size and diversity of products make servicing by functional departments too unwieldy. When a company's departmentalization become too complex for the functional structure, top management will generally create semiautonomous **divisions,** each of which designs, produces, and markets its own products.

Unlike a functional department, a division resembles a separate business. The division head focuses primarily on the operations of his or her division, is accountable for profit or loss, and may even compete with other units of the same firm. But a division is unlike a separate business in one crucial aspect: It is not an independent entity; that is, the division manager cannot make decisions as freely as the owner of a truly separate enterprise because he or she must still report to central headquarters. As a rule, a division head's authority ends at the point where his or her decisions have a significant effect on the workings of other divisions.

A product/market organization can follow one of three patterns. Most obvious is *division by product,* shown in Figure 11-3. General Foods, which has a different division for each of its major types of products, is a good example here. Setting up product divisions is logical when each product requires different manufacturing technology and marketing methods.

Service, financial, and other nonmanufacturing firms generally use *division by geography,* although mining and oil-producing companies also use geographic divi-

FIGURE 11-3 Product/Market Organization Chart for a Manufacturing Company: Division by Product

Note: Each general manager is in charge of a major category of products, and the vice presidents of the functional areas provide support services to the general managers.

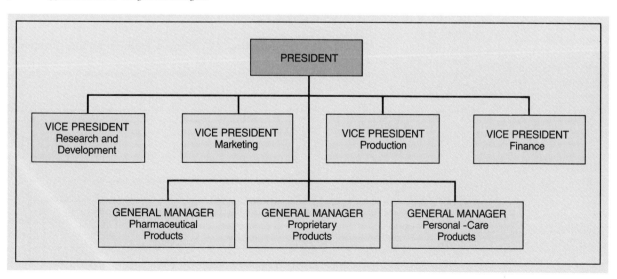

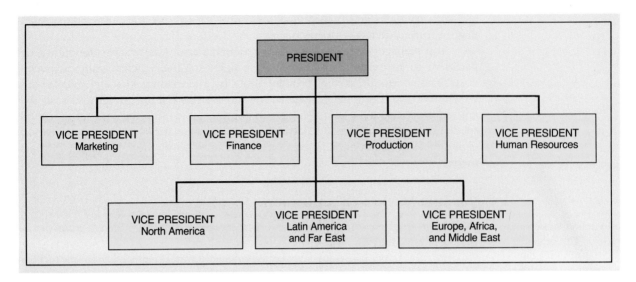

FIGURE 11-4 Product/Market Organization Chart for a Manufacturing Company: Division by Geography

Note: Each area vice president is in charge of the company's business in one geographic area. The functional vice presidents provide support services and coordination assistance for their areas of responsibility.

HERE'S AN EXAMPLE

Alcoa has set up an independent unit to create a market for its new metal. The company hopes that by freeing these workers "from the shackles of bureaucracy" and by letting them work in their own small unit, it can tap the entrepreneurial spirit. (*Wall Street Journal,* 8/1/90, p. B2)

COORDINATED RESOURCE

Use Transparency 67, Product/Market Organization Chart for a Manufacturing Company: Division by Geography.

COORDINATED RESOURCE

Use Transparency 68, Product/Market Organization Chart for a Manufacturing Company: Division by Customer.

sions. (See Fig. 11-4.) This organization is logical when a plant must be located as close as possible to sources of raw materials, to major markets, or to specialized personnel, such as the diamond-cutting operations in New York, Tel Aviv, and Amsterdam.

In *division by customer,* a division sells most or all of its products to a particular customer. (See Fig. 11-5.) An electronics firm, for example, might have separate divisions for military, industrial, and consumer customers. As a general rule, manufacturing firms with highly diversified lines of products tend to be organized either by customer or by product.

Organization by division has several advantages. Because all the activities, skills, and expertise required to produce and market particular products are grouped in one place under a single head, a whole job can be more easily coordinated and high work performance maintained. In addition, both the quality and the speed of decision making are enhanced because decisions made at the divisional level are closer to the scene of action. Conversely, the burden on central management is eased because divisional managers have greater authority. Perhaps most important, accountability is clear. The performance of divisional management can be measured in terms of that division's profit or loss.

FIGURE 11-5 Product/Market Organization Chart for a Manufacturing Company: Division by Customer

Note: Each vice president is in charge of a set of products grouped according to the type of customer to whom they will be marketed.

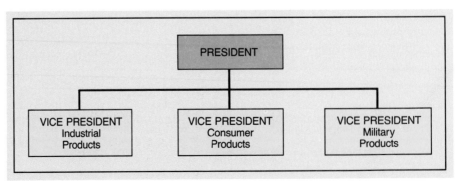

There are, however, some disadvantages to the divisional structure. The interests of the division may be placed ahead of the needs and goals of the total organization. For example, because they are vulnerable to profit-and-loss performance reviews, division heads may take short-term gains at the expense of long-range profitability. In addition, administrative expenses increase because each division has its own staff members and specialists, leading to costly duplication of skills.

Matrix Organization

Coordinated Resource
See DuBose Reading #11, "Evolution to a Matrix Organization."

matrix organization An organizational structure in which each employee reports to both a functional or division manager and to a project or group manager.

Neither of the two types of structures we have discussed meets all the needs of every organization. In a functional structure, specialized skills may become increasingly sophisticated—but coordinated production of goods may be difficult to achieve. In a divisional structure, various products may flourish while the overall technological expertise of the organization remains undeveloped. The matrix structure attempts to combine the benefits of both types of designs while avoiding their drawbacks.[10]

In a **matrix organization,** employees have in effect two bosses—that is, they are under dual authority. One chain of command is functional or divisional, diagrammed vertically in the preceding charts. The second is shown horizontally in Figure 11-6, which depicts the multidimensional structure of Dow-Corning. This lateral chain depicts a project or a business team, led by a project or group manager who is an expert in the team's assigned area of specialization. For this reason, matrix structure is often referred to as a "multiple command system." (In mathematics, a matrix is an array of vertical columns and horizontal rows.)

FIGURE 11-6 The Dow-Corning Matrix

Source: Reprinted by permission of the *Harvard Business Review.* An exhibit from "How the Multidimensional Structure Works at Dow-Corning" by William C. Goggin (January–February 1974). Copyright © 1974 by the President and Fellows of Harvard College; all rights reserved.

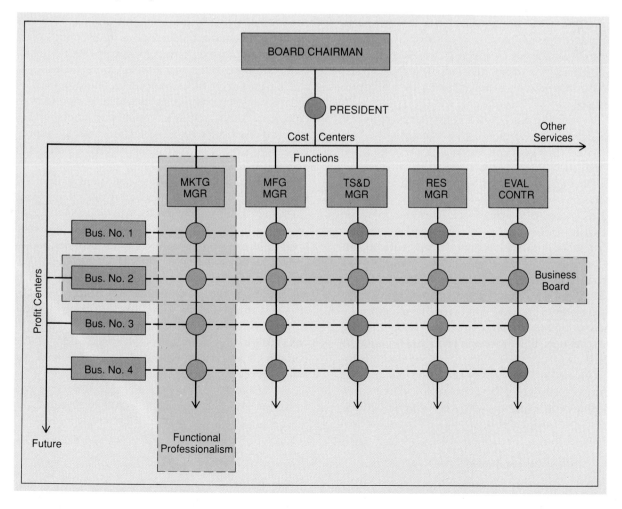

Matrix organizations were first developed in the aerospace industry by firms such as TRW. The initial impetus was a government demand for a single contact manager for each program or project who would be responsible to the government for the project's progress and performance. To meet this need, a project leader was appointed to share authority with the leaders of the preexisting technical or functional departments. This temporary arrangement then evolved into formal matrix organizations. Now matrix organization is used in the units of many major companies, in management consulting firms, and in advertising agencies, among many other types of businesses. In some companies, the matrix structure is found at all levels, while in others, it is used only in certain departments.

As organizations have become more global, many use the matrix form in their international operations. There may be product or division managers, as in a divisionalized firm, and national managers for each country in which the company does business. Thus, a division employee would report to the divisional manager on product-related issues and to the national manager on political issues or those involving international relations.

Few organizations are able to make a sudden and effective transition from functional or divisional organization to a fully functioning matrix structure. When

ILLUSTRATIVE CASE STUDY

CONTINUED

Hewlett-Packard Reinterprets the HP Way

Reorganization was not a new idea at Hewlett-Packard. In fact, the company had already undergone a major reorganization as recently as 1984. At that time, HP had two major divisions—computers and scientific instruments—each with its own separate sales force.

Because the markets for computers and instruments seemed to be merging, HP thought the two sales forces represented a wasteful duplication of effort. Indeed, HP sales reps often found themselves competing against each other to sell different HP products to the same customers. As a result, HP decided to combine its sales force. This new program successfully integrated once-independent groups from the computer side of the company with groups from the instruments side. In addition, it helped focus company attention on meeting customer needs—a plus for a company that had thrived for years simply by being one of the few companies to offer certain types of equipment. Competition had become more intense, though, and customers had a wider variety of options.

Unfortunately, this reorganization did nothing to address the fact that the computer market is made up of different segments with very different needs.

Personal computers, printers, and other peripherals are even becoming standard items in discount stores, where computer equipment from name brand manufacturers shares shelf space with clones from Korea and Japan. Given the advanced technology used in today's personal computers, as well as generous warranties and service contracts, retail customers tend to focus on price and power. To keep its prices competitive, then, a manufacturer needs to focus on efficient manufacturing operations.

Workstations, in contrast, represent a more volatile market, where sophisticated and demanding customers push manufacturers to supply a steady stream of innovative products. In addition, workstations customers often require customizing and other special services. In theory, the innovation needed to serve these customers should have been easy for HP, a pioneer among the quick-moving, entrepreneurial start-ups of Silicon Valley. Yet, by the spring of 1989, it was clear that too much of a good thing—committees and consensus—were threatening the company's survival, as indicated by the delays in the Snakes project.

CEO John A. Young's immediate response was to liberate the Snakes project's 200 engineers from

considering such a changeover, management must realize that much time and effort are required to make a matrix work.[11]

The matrix structure is often an efficient means for bringing together the diverse specialized skills required to solve a complex problem. Problems of coordination—which plague most functional designs—are minimized here because the most important personnel for a project work together as a group. This in itself produces a side benefit: By working together, people come to understand the demands faced by those who have different areas of responsibility. A report from AT&T Bell Labs, for example, indicated that systems engineers and systems developers overcame their preconceptions about each other's jobs and acquired more realistic attitudes about each other after working together as a project team. (This was not, however, in a pure matrix structure.) Indeed, the exposure to workers in other areas was so effective that some systems developers decided to move into full-time systems engineering.[12] Another advantage of the matrix structure is that it gives the organization a great deal of cost-saving flexibility: Since each project is assigned only the number of people it needs, unnecessary duplication is avoided.

A disadvantage is that not everyone adapts well to a matrix system. To be effective, team members must have good interpersonal skills and be flexible and

the burden of committee oversight. Then he and David Packard, founder and chairman of the board, went to work on a more permanent solution. The result—a major reorganization—was announced in October 1990.

HP would now have two major divisions. The Computer Products Organization would be responsible for computers, printers, and similar products sold through retail outlets, while the Computer Systems Organization would focus on the workstations. Each division would have its own sales and marketing force. In addition, Young swept away the committee system and introduced an early retirement program to reduce staff, creating a leaner, flatter organization. Young tapped Richard A. Hackborn, head of the company's thriving laser printer business, to be head of the computer products division, while Lewis E. Platt was named head of the workstation division.

In many ways, the laser printer business Hackborn had built was a model of what HP had been and needed to become again. In the early 1980s, computer users could choose between noisy daisy-wheel printers that produced "letter-quality" type slowly, noisier dot matrix printers that produced mediocre "draft-quality" type quickly, or quiet but very expensive laser printers, which produced type that looked like a photocopy of a typeset page. Hackborn and his engineers became convinced there was a potentially huge market for an *inexpensive* laser printer, especially among business users of the newly introduced IBM PC.

Because Hackborn's unit was based in Idaho, it was free of the committees that characterized the

California headquarters. This allowed it to make a number of vital decisions quickly. One, they decided to buy an existing "engine" from Japan's Canon Inc., rather than developing an HP engine. Second, they decided to market their laser printer to the entire PC market, instead of designing it to be used with only HP equipment. Third, they lined up an extensive network of retailers and put strict controls on operations, which let them introduce a steady supply of printers with more features at increasingly lower prices. Sales took off immediately and got an additional boost when Apple Computer Inc. began to promote desktop publishing in 1984. Today, HP has nearly 60 percent of the $3.6 billion market for laser printers and offers dozens of low-cost ink-jet and laser printers.

Can Hackborn repeat his success with the computer products? That remains to be seen, although it is clear he will bring his innovative approach to the problem.

Sources: "Can Morton Calm Ruffled Feathers?" *Industry Week,* August 20, 1984, p. 64; Robert L. Yeager, "Hewlett-Packard: Continuing the Search for Excellence," *Business Marketing,* November 1985, pp. 74, 76; Kathleen K. Wiegner, "John Young's New Jogging Shoes," *Forbes,* November 4, 1985, pp. 42–44; John A. Young, "The Quality Focus at Hewlett-Packard," *The Journal of Business Strategy* 5 (Winter 1985):6–9; David Finn, "Growing Up with the Founding Fathers," *Across the Board* 23 (March 1986)47–55; Wiegner, "Making the Short List Again," *Forbes,* June 15, 1987, pp. 124, 125–126; Jonathan B. Levine, "Mild-Mannered Hewlett-Packard Is Making Like Superman," *Business Week,* March 7, 1988, pp. 110–111, 114; Jim Carlton, "Hewlett-Packard Tried to Revive Share of Market by Realigning Computer Lines," *The Wall Street Journal,* October 8, 1990, p. B4; Barbara Buell et al., "Hewlett-Packard Rethinks Itself," *Business Week,* April 1, 1991, pp. 76–79.

cooperative. In addition, morale can be adversely affected when personnel are rearranged once projects are completed and new ones begun.[13] Finally, if hierarchies of authority are not firmly established and effectively communicated, there is the danger, according to some analysts, that conflicting directives and ill-defined responsibilities will plunge certain managers into a state of virtual chaos.[14] To overcome these obstacles, special training in new job skills or interpersonal relationships may be necessary when a matrix overlay is first introduced or when a temporary overlay becomes permanent. To protect individuals who function well in traditional structures but are likely to have difficulty adjusting to a matrix structure, many companies either make special efforts to retrain personnel before assigning them to project teams or select only volunteers for the teams.

■ COORDINATION

Coordination is the process of integrating the objectives and activities of separate work units (departments or functional areas) in order to realize the organization's goals effectively.[15] Without coordination, people and departments would lose sight of their roles within the organization and be tempted to pursue their own special interests, often at the expense of organizational goals.

The extent of the need for coordination depends on the nature and communication requirements of the tasks performed and the degree of interdependence of the various units performing them.[16] When these tasks require or can benefit from information flow between units, then a high degree of coordination is best. Otherwise, the work might be better completed if less time is spent interacting with members of other units. A high degree of coordination is likely to be beneficial for work that is nonroutine and unpredictable, for work in which factors in the environment are changing, and for work in which task interdependence is high (for example, if one unit cannot function without receiving information or a product component from another unit). A high level of coordination is also needed in organizations that set high performance objectives.[17]

Problems in Achieving Effective Coordination

Ironically, the more organizations need efficient coordination, the harder it is to achieve. This is especially true when tasks are highly specialized. Paul R. Lawrence and Jay W. Lorsch have noted that division of work involves more than individual work duties, such as managing a warehouse or writing advertising copy.[18] It also influences the way employees perceive the organization and their role in it, as well as the way individuals relate to others. These differences—which Lawrence and Lorsch call **differentiation**—can complicate the tasks of effectively coordinating work activities.

Lawrence and Lorsch have identified four types of differentiation. First, different work units tend to develop their own sense of the organization's goals and how to pursue them. For example, accountants may see cost control as most important to the organization's success, while marketing pushes for more varied products and improved quality. Second, work units often differ in their time orientation. Production problems, for example, are often crises that have to be dealt with immediately, while research and development may be preoccupied with problems that will take years to solve.

Time orientation affects a third type of differentiation—interpersonal styles. Production, for example, which usually needs to make fast decisions, may favor more abrupt communication and clear-cut answers; R&D may favor more easygoing communication that encourages brainstorming and consideration of many alternatives. Finally, different units may differ in their formality. Production may have strict, explicit standards of performance, while personnel has more general standards.

differentiation The principle that differences in working styles, including differences in orientation and structure, can complicate the coordination of an organization's activities.

Differentiation encourages conflict among individuals and organizational units. Various members of the organization present their viewpoints, argue them openly, and in general make certain that they get heard. In this way, they force managers to consider the special needs and knowledge of individual departments when problems exist. Constructively resolved conflict is healthy for an organization's operations. A study of managers in eight nations and four national groupings found that most managers appeared to be rewarded more for noncooperativeness, *within reasonable limits,* than for cooperativeness. Exceptions included Japan and the Scandinavian countries, where cooperativeness was more rewarded.[19]

integration The degree to which employees of various departments work together in a unified way.

In place of the term *coordination,* Lawrence and Lorsch use **integration** to designate the degree to which members of various departments work together in a unified manner. Departments should cooperate and their tasks should be integrated where necessary, without reducing the differences that contribute to task accomplishment. It may be useful for the sales department to give advice on advertisements to the graphic artists who will prepare them; however, if salespeople view themselves as adjuncts of the advertising department, then the functioning of both the sales and advertising units will be impaired. Division of work and specialization help the organization use its resources most efficiently, even though they increase the coordination burden of managers.

Approaches to Achieving Effective Coordination

Communication is the key to effective coordination. Coordination is directly dependent on the acquisition, transmission, and processing of information. The greater the uncertainty of the tasks to be coordinated, the greater the need for information. For this reason, it is useful to think of coordination as essentially an *information-processing* task.[20]

In this section, we will examine three approaches to achieving effective coordination: using basic management techniques, increasing the potential for coordination, and reducing the need for coordination. (See Fig. 11-7.)

FIGURE 11-7 Three Approaches to Effective Coordination Methods for Managers

Source: Adapted from Jay R. Galbraith, "Organization Design: An Information Processing View," *Interfaces* 4, no. 3 (May 1974). Copyright © 1974 by The Institute of Management Sciences. Reprinted by permission.

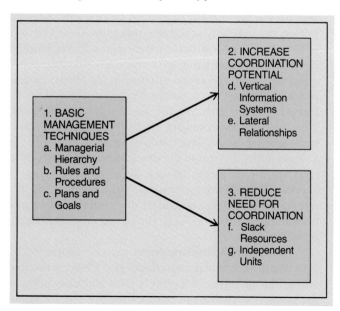

USING BASIC MANAGEMENT TECHNIQUES. Relatively modest coordination requirements can often be met through basic management mechanisms. One such mechanism is the organization's chain of command, which specifies relationships among members and units, thereby facilitating the flow of information. Another useful tool is the body of rules and procedures designed to let employees handle routine coordination tasks quickly and independently. In addition, the coordination of strategic and operational plans can be achieved by ensuring that all units are working toward the same broad goals. (These mechanisms are discussed in detail elsewhere, so we will not repeat the material here.)

INCREASING COORDINATION POTENTIAL. As an organization's various units become more interdependent or expand in size or function, more information is needed to achieve organizational objectives. Thus, coordination potential must be increased. If basic management techniques are insufficient, coordination potential may be increased through vertical information systems or through lateral relationships.

vertical information system Means through which data are transmitted up and down the managerial hierarchy.

A **vertical information system** transmits data up and down the levels of the organization. The communication may occur within or outside the chain of command. Management information systems for individual departments, as well as data bases that pool information from many departments, expand the information available for planning, coordination, and control.[21]

lateral relationship A relationship that cuts across the chain of command, allowing direct contact between members of different departments. Examples are some committees, liaison roles, and integrating roles.

Lateral relationships cut across the chain of command, permitting information to be exchanged and decisions to be made at the level where the needed information exists. There are several kinds of lateral relationships. The simplest form is **direct contact** between the individuals who must deal with the same situation or problem. Direct contact avoids the need to refer problems up the chain of command.

direct contact Simplest form of lateral relationship; communication between individuals who must deal with the same situation or problem.

When the number of contacts between departments increases dramatically, it may be best to create a permanent liaison between the departments. Such a liaison is said to fill a **boundary-spanning role.** Effective boundary-spanning employees understand their own units' needs as well as the responsibilities and concerns of the other units. Members of the engineering and marketing departments, for example, can almost be said to speak different languages. An effective, boundary-spanning employee is able to translate the customer-oriented language of marketing into the product-oriented language of engineering, and vice versa.

boundary-spanning roles Jobs in which individuals act as liaisons between departments or organizations that are in frequent contact.

Committees and task forces are often effective for pooling the expertise of different employees and channeling their efforts toward a common goal. *Committees* are usually formally organized groups with a designated membership and chairperson and regularly scheduled meetings. Generally long-lasting or permanent parts of an organization's structure, they deal with recurring problems and decisions. *Task forces,* on the other hand, are formed to deal with special problems. Each of the units concerned with the problem contributes one or more members. Once a solution is reached, the task force is dissolved. The distinctions between committees and task forces and their effective use are discussed more fully in Chapter 17.

integrating roles Roles that are established when a specific product, service, or project spans several departments and requires coordination and attention from a single individual not in the departments in question.

Integrating roles are established when a specific product, service, or project spans several departments and requires continuing coordination and attention from a single individual not in the departments in question. Integrators act like diplomats, speaking the languages of each department or group (for example, computer programmers and line supervisors). They maintain neutrality when the groups to be integrated are excited and distrustful, and they attempt to balance power differences between departments—restraining the more powerful ones and bolstering the less powerful.

managerial linking role A role that may be required if an integrating position does not coordinate a particular task effectively.

Managerial linking roles may be called for if the integrating role cannot coordinate a particular task effectively. A linking manager has *formal authority* over all the units involved in a project. This authority often takes the form of control over the budgets of all units to ensure that they work together toward organization goals.

Reducing the Need for Coordination. A Federal Express worker checks a shipment being prepared for IBM. IBM, long famous for its vertical integration, decided it was cheaper to do away with its 21 parts warehouses and farm the warehousing function out to half a dozen outside vendors, including Fed Ex.

As we have seen, a *matrix organization* has characteristics of both the managerial linking role and the task force. In a matrix structure, the managers of two areas supervise a group of employees responsible to them both, so the requirements of both areas are routinely taken into account. Like a task force, a particular matrix structure may be dissolved when a project has been completed.

REDUCING THE NEED FOR COORDINATION. When the need for coordination is so great that the previous methods are ineffective, the best approach may be to reduce the need for tight coordination. Jay Galbraith describes two ways to do this: creating slack resources and creating independent units.[22]

Providing slack (additional) resources gives units leeway in meeting each other's requirements.[23] Suppose Mercedes-Benz anticipates that it will sell 10,000 cars in a given region of the United States over a three-month period beginning January 1. The manufacturer might establish a production quota of 12,000 cars, in case demand is larger than anticipated, and a production deadline of October 1 of the previous year to give itself a three-month safety margin should production or transportation difficulties arise.

Another way to reduce the need for coordination is to create independent units that can perform all the necessary aspects of a task internally. A company that builds a variety of kitchen appliances, for example, could form an independent unit that designs, manufactures, and markets all of its food processors, thereby eliminating the need for continual consultations with centralized engineering, manufacturing, and marketing staffs. Apple Computer used this technique with Macintosh, forming an entirely new unit to design and produce the machine. Similarly, GM created a new unit to produce the Saturn car. New labor agreements were negotiated, new advertising agencies hired, and completely new plants constructed.

Selecting the Appropriate Coordination Mechanisms

The key consideration in selecting the best approach to coordination is to match the organization's *capacity* for coordination with its *need* for coordination. How much information does the organization need to perform its operations? How much information is it capable of processing? If the need is greater than the ability, the organization must make a choice: It can either increase its coordination potential (by improving its performance of the basic management techniques, by introducing or expanding vertical information systems and lateral relationships, or both) *or* it can reduce the need (by appropriating slack resources or creating independent units). As information-processing capacity increases, both complexity and cost increase as well.

In selecting appropriate coordinating mechanisms, managers in the 1990s need to recognize that organizational coordination capabilities are improving rapidly because of electronic information-processing systems, which are simple, readily available, and increasingly inexpensive. It is practical and cost-effective for even small organizations to purchase information systems that reduce bottlenecks in information processing and that can grow and change with the organization and its needs.

■ *ORGANIZATIONAL DESIGN*

organizational design
The determination of the organizational structure that is most appropriate for the strategy, people, technology, and tasks of the organization.

COORDINATED RESOURCE
See DuBose Reading #9, "Trends in Organizational Design."

HERE'S AN EXAMPLE
Bill McGowan, chairman of MCI Communications, loathes corporate bureaucracy. "The greatest handicap [in running a company] is that organizations hate to change. You're always at risk for getting chains of committees, manuals, procedures." (*Business Week*, 3/4/91, p. 46ff.)

bureaucracy Organization with a legalized formal and hierarchical structure.

COORDINATED RESOURCE
Acumen: Relate the dichotomy between bureaucratic and organic organizations to how scales on the opposite sides of the *Acumen* clock are often in conflict with each other.

Organizational design, the process of choosing an organizational structure that is appropriate to a given strategy and a given environment, can be crucial to an organization's survival. When the Pennsylvania Railroad merged with the New York Central Railroad to form Penn Central, the opportunities for a larger, more efficient operation seemed promising. Management failed to merge the two organizations into a single, sound structure, however, and the resulting rivalry and duplication of effort contributed to Penn Central's financial collapse in the early 1970s.[24] Following large losses by creditors and shareholders, Penn Central emerged from bankruptcy in 1980 with a very different organizational structure and strategy. In fact, it was no longer in the railroad business.

As we study the evolution of thinking about organizational design, it is important to realize two things. First, because both strategies and environments change over time, organizational design is an ongoing process. Second, changes in structure usually involve trial and error, accidents, and accommodations to political realities rather than purely rational approaches.[25]

The Classical Approach

Early management writers were not aware of the environment's power. Instead, they sought the "one best way"—a set of principles for creating an organizational structure that would be efficient and effective in all situations. The sociologist Max Weber[26] and management writers Frederick Taylor and Henri Fayol were major contributors to the so-called classical approach to organizational design. They believed that the most efficient and effective organizations had a hierarchical structure based on a legalized formal authority. (Weber called an organization with such a structure a **bureaucracy.**) Members of the organization were guided in their actions by a sense of duty to the organization and by a set of rational rules and regulations. When fully developed, according to Weber, such organizations were characterized by specialization of tasks, appointment by merit, provision of career opportunities for members, routinization of activities, and a rational, impersonal organizational climate.

Early management writers found much to commend in bureaucracy as an organizational design. Weber in particular praised its rationality, its establishment of rules for decision making, its clear chain of command, and its promotion of people on the basis of ability and experience rather than favoritism or whim. He also admired the bureaucracy's clear specification of authority and responsibility, which he believed made it easier to evaluate and reward performance.

The classical approach came under criticism for being too theoretical. Because

MANAGEMENT APPLICATION

Downsizing the American Management Lifestyle

Many American companies adopted bureaucratic organizational structures when times were more stable, when companies dominated their respective environments, and when assumptions about continued economic growth were regularly borne out. Thus, such companies as Xerox, Exxon, IBM, and GM developed multilayered bureaucracies that eventually became too cumbersome to make decisive responses to rapidly changing times.

The advent of increasingly complex national fiscal problems, an unprecedented wave of mergers, divestitures, and acquisitions, the deregulation of some industries, and an increasing number of new, entrepreneurial firms greatly accelerated both domestic and international competition. Far-reaching technological advances further compelled complacent, highly bureaucratic companies to become less hierarchical and more adaptive to their environments. The important new concepts are efficiency and productivity, with organizations seeking to become leaner, more flexible structures that can respond more readily to the acceleration and maneuverability of market-driven economies. The term used to describe this complex process is *downsizing.*

Although many people have been affected by the trend toward downsizing, middle managers have been particularly hurt. Once seen as fairly safe, this group has been hard hit by downsizing. Between 1984 and 1988, over 1 million management and professional workers were dismissed from their jobs. Between August 1989 and August 1990, almost another 170,000 permanent management and professional positions were eliminated entirely. The trend continues as such corporations as CBS, AT&T, GE, IBM, Exxon, and GM reorganize and restructure byzantine bureaucracies into more manageable configurations.

Once known for their paternalistic attitudes and operations, these large corporations have pro-

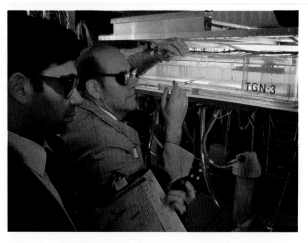

Downsizing at Pittsburgh Plate Glass. Convinced that a creeping bureaucracy was crippling PPG's ability to add new, higher-margin products and build overseas sales, PPG Industries Chairman Vince Sarne simply did not replace the vice chairman and president when they retired, wiping out an entire level of management. Additional cuts eliminated many middle- and upper-middle-level management positions and slashed the total work force by nearly 8 percent, freeing up money that was used for capital investments, acquisitions, and research and development, such as this model fiberglass furnace at PPG's research center near Pittsburgh.

duced great disillusionment among the many managers who have lost the lifetime job security they once took for granted. Many feel the corporations are neglecting their ethical obligations to employees, while others worry that all employees are less likely to feel any loyalty toward their employers. One thing seems clear: There are no guarantees in the unspoken contract between employer and employee.

Sources: Rod Willis, "What's Happening to America's Middle Managers?" *Management Review,* January 1987, pp. 24–33; "The Downside of Downsizing," *Fortune,* May 23, 1988, pp. 45–52; Michael J. Mandel, "This Time the Downturn Is Dressed in Pinstripes," *Business Week,* October 1, 1990, pp. 130–131.

COORDINATED RESOURCE
Acumen: Relate the characteristics of bureaucracies to the Power and Perfectionism scales.

the world does not currently fit the assumptions in Weber's model (if it ever did), critics claim a bureaucracy is unlikely to yield the results he described.[27] In addition, the word *bureaucracy* has come to be associated with bigness and all its problems—a bloated and costly staff, a formal impersonality that loses sight of larger goals, slow reactions to changing environments, and political infighting among individuals and work units. (See the Management Application box.)

The Neoclassical Approach

COORDINATED RESOURCE

See DuBose Reading #13, "Designing Managerial and Professional Work for High Performance: A Sociotechnical Approach."

Early human relations researchers and behavioral scientists attempted to deal with what they saw as the major inadequacy of the classical bureaucratic model: It neglected the human element. They argued that an industrial organization has two objectives: economic effectiveness *and* employee satisfaction.

As we saw in Chapter 2, the initial impetus for this point of view was provided by the Hawthorne Studies, which were thought to imply that when management showed concern for employees, productivity increased. Human relations researchers and behavioral scientists argued that the bureaucratic structure could be improved by making it less formal and by permitting subordinates greater participation in decision making. Because they did not reject the classical model but only tried to improve it, these researchers are sometimes called neoclassicists. Among them are Douglas McGregor,[28] Chris Argyris,[29] and Rensis Likert.[30]

DOUGLAS McGREGOR. Bureaucracies are characterized by a vertical division of labor in which upper levels of management make plans and decisions that are carried out by people at lower levels. Although this separation has always existed, it was sharpened by the application of scientific management principles.

McGregor believed that managers who used this vertical division of labor also accepted an underlying set of negative assumptions about workers. These included the conviction that most people have little ambition, that they desire security above all, and that they avoid work unless coerced into it. In this view, a rigid, formal organizational hierarchy is necessary to maintain managers' authority over subordinates. McGregor claimed that organizations would better meet their members' needs and use their potential more effectively by assuming that people can find satisfaction in work, that they desire achievement, and that they seek responsibility. Such assumptions would permit employees more independence, a larger role in decision making, and greater openness in communication with their managers and with one another. McGregor's view will be discussed in more detail in Chapter 15.

CHRIS ARGYRIS. Argyris was concerned that in a bureaucratic organization managers had nearly total responsibility for planning, controlling, and evaluating the work of their subordinates. He argued that such managerial domination of the workplace can make subordinates passive and dependent and decrease their sense of responsibility and self-control.

To Argyris, such conditions were incompatible with the human needs for self-reliance, self-expression, and accomplishment. He believed that members of the organization, particularly at lower levels, become dissatisfied and frustrated in their work when these needs are blocked. The results, he suggested, are increased unhappiness among organization members and more problems in meeting organizational goals. For example, dissatisfied workers may change jobs frequently, increasing staffing costs, or do their work carelessly, increasing production costs. Employees may also insist on higher wages when their work is psychologically unrewarding.

As an alternative, Argyris argued for an organizational design that would better meet human needs and raise the satisfaction of organization members. Like McGregor, he favored allowing subordinates much more independence and decision-making power and creating a more informal organizational culture.

RENSIS LIKERT. In his research on effective group performance, Likert found that traditional authoritarian managers were less able to motivate their subordinates to high standards of achievement than managers who actively supported their subordinates' feelings of self-worth and importance. Based on these findings, Likert created a model to describe different organizational designs and their effectiveness.

According to Likert's model, organizational structure is based on one of four systems. In **System 1,** the traditional organizational structure, power and authority

System 1 Traditional organizational structure where power and authority are distributed according to the manager-subordinate relationship.

Systems **2** and **3** Intermediate stages between the traditional structure and the ideal structure.

System **4** Ideal organizational structure where there is extensive group participation in supervision and decision making.

COORDINATED RESOURCE
Use Transparency 63, Organizational Types in Four Environments.

COORDINATED RESOURCE
The Distinctive Discussions for Chapter 11 found in the Lecture Extras supplement include "Hyatt's Start-Ups" and "Organizations That Learn."

HERE'S AN EXAMPLE
The company Japanese most admire for entrepreneurship and technological progress? Not Sony, not Toyota, but Kyocera Corporation. Kyocera manufactures ceramic components and is typically Japanese in the way it manages people and manufacturing, but atypically Japanese in its emphasis on innovation. (*Fortune*, 1/1/90, p. 83ff.)

are distributed strictly according to the manager-subordinate relationship. Managers at one level tell members at lower levels what to do, and so on down the chain of command. **Systems 2** and **3** are intermediate stages. **System 4** organizations represent Likert's view of how an organization should ideally be designed and managed. In this system, there is extensive group participation in both supervision and decision making. The System 4 manager's primary task is to build a group that can make decisions and carry them out. To reach System 4, Likert says, organizations must (1) accept that managers and work activities should enhance individual members' personal sense of worth and importance, (2) use group decision making where appropriate, and (3) set high performance goals.

CRITICISMS OF THE NEOCLASSICAL APPROACH. Like the classical approach, the neoclassical approach has been criticized for assuming there is "one best way" to design an organization, regardless of strategic or environmental considerations. Critics also feel that the neoclassicists oversimplify human motivation. Not everyone is motivated by nonmonetary rewards and not all work can be made intrinsically challenging and rewarding. Because people come to work with their own objectives, critics add, the neoclassicists also underestimate the challenge of coordinating fragmented work groups.

The Environmental Approach

One of the major modern approaches to organizational design holds that understanding the environment is the first and most important task in organizational design.[31]

THE STABLE ENVIRONMENT. A stable environment is one with little or no unexpected or sudden change. Product changes occur infrequently and modifications can be planned well in advance. Market demand has only minor and predictable fluctuations. Laws that affect the particular organization or product have remained the same for a long time and are unlikely to change abruptly. New technological developments are improbable, so research budgets are either minimal or nonexistent.

Because of the increasing rate of technological change, stable organizational environments are hard to find. Still, they do exist. For example, E. E. Dickinson, the major distiller of witch hazel, a topical astringent, has been operating in essentially the same way since 1866. The product, the process, and the company's way of doing business have remained viable despite the passage of more than a century.[33]

THE CHANGING ENVIRONMENT. Though environmental changes can occur in any or all of the previously mentioned areas—product, market, law, or technology—they are unlikely to take the top managers of the organization by surprise. Trends are usually apparent and predictable, so that the organization is easily able to adjust. For example, a Wall Street law firm like Willkie, Farr & Gallagher is in a changing environment because its lawyers must acquaint themselves with each new law. However, the basic body of law changes very gradually. Other organizations in changing environments include many in the service, construction, appliance, computer, financial, transportation, and energy industries. The rate of change in the environment has accelerated in some industries—such as trucking, air carrying, natural gas, and savings and loans—because of the relatively recent institution of deregulation policies. A once-stable environment has become a very competitive one, causing the downfall of banks, airlines, and other organizations, both product manufacturers and service providers. The advent of greatly increased international competition has also created a highly competitive, sometimes hostile, environment for many firms.

THE TURBULENT ENVIRONMENT. When competitors launch new, unexpected products, when laws are passed without appreciable warning, and when technologi-

CLASS COMMENT

Lots of companies are looking to multiyear, multimillion-dollar alliances with computer makers, telephone companies, and high-technology consultants to take responsibility for their communications/computer networks. This practice is called outsourcing. (*Business Week*, 10/8/90, p. 148)

cal breakthroughs revolutionize product design or production methods, the organization is in a turbulent environment.

Few organizations face a continued turbulent environment. When a rapid and radical change does occur, organizations usually pass through only a temporary period of turbulence before making an adjustment. For example, hospitals had to adjust to a sudden increase in demand for their services when Medicaid legislation was passed. Similarly, new pollution-control laws and the energy crisis created a turbulent environment for some time. Some firms, however, experience almost constant turbulence. Computer companies, for example, have been dealing with a rapid rate of technological and market change for three decades.

The rash of takeovers and leveraged buyouts in the 1980s, coupled with stock-market volatility, added another dimension of turbulence to the environment of many organizations. The Pennzoil-Getty-Texaco case discussed in Chapter 9 is the story of three companies sailing almost constantly turbulent industrial seas. Similarly, when Saul Steinberg, CEO of the acquisitive conglomerate Reliance Group Holdings, announced a hostile takeover attempt at Disney, shockwaves were felt throughout the company for some time.

International competition and the emergence of new and powerful domestic competitors have also increased environmental turbulence. Even the once stable U.S. automobile industry has experienced turbulence because of competition from Toyota, Nissan, and Honda in Japan and Hyundai in Korea. The result: a virtually complete internal redesign at both Ford and Chrysler and a rethinking of General Motors' overall organizational design.

MATCHING THE STRUCTURE TO THE ENVIRONMENT. Tom Burns and G. M. Stalker have distinguished between two organizational systems: mechanistic and organic.[33] In a **mechanistic system,** the activities of the organization are broken down into separate, specialized tasks. Objectives and authority for each individual and unit are precisely defined by higher-level managers. Power in such organizations follows the classical bureaucratic chain of command. In an **organic system,** individuals are more likely to work in a group setting than alone. There is less emphasis on taking orders from a superior or giving orders to subordinates. Instead, members communicate across all levels of the organization to obtain information and advice.

mechanistic system According to Burns and Stalker, one characterized by a bureaucratic organization.

organic system According to Burns and Stalker, one characterized by group actions and open communication.

HERE'S AN EXAMPLE

At Taco Bell, division managers used to oversee several unit managers, who were each responsible for two or three restaurants. Now each division manager directs one unit manager in charge of all restaurants in the division and spends more time on planning. (*Business Month*, July 1990, p. 20)

COORDINATED RESOURCE

Use Transparency 70, Mechanistic Versus Organic Organizations.

After studying a variety of companies, Burns and Stalker concluded that the mechanistic system was best suited to a stable environment, whereas organic systems were best suited to a turbulent one. Organizations in changing environments would probably use some combination of the two systems.

In a stable environment, each organization member is likely to continue performing the same task. Thus, skill specialization is appropriate. In a turbulent environment, however, jobs must constantly be redefined to cope with the ever-changing needs of the organization. Organization members must therefore be skilled at solving a variety of problems, not at repetitively performing a set of specialized activities. In addition, the creative problem solving and decision making required in turbulent environments are best carried out in groups in which members can communicate openly. Thus, for turbulent environments, an organic system is appropriate.

The findings of Burns and Stalker were supported and extended by the research of Paul Lawrence and Jay Lorsch discussed earlier in this chapter.[34] They examined ten companies, measuring the degree of differentiation and integration these companies exhibited in relation to the type of external environment in which they operated.

Lawrence and Lorsch hypothesized that departments in organizations operating in unstable environments, such as plastics manufacturing companies, would be more differentiated than departments in organizations operating in stable environments, such as container manufacturing companies. They further reasoned that not all departments would be affected to the same extent by an unstable environment,

An Organic System. Mary Vandehay discusses work issues with fellow members of an insurance representatives' team at Aid Association for Lutherans (AAL), a fraternal society headquartered in Appleton, Wisconsin, which operates one of the nation's largest life-insurance businesses. AAL provides extensive training to the nearly 500 employees who process applications and claims, with the goal of helping them work together in self-managed teams.

so different types of structures might be appropriate for different departments in the same organization. Last, they predicted that high-performing organizations in each type of environment would have a greater degree of integration than low-performing companies because effective cooperation and coordination within an organization would make it more successful.

The results of their study confirmed all three of their hypotheses. Of the companies studied, those operating in an unstable environment were the most highly differentiated, and those operating in a stable environment were the least differentiated. In addition, high-performing organizations in both types of environments had a higher degree of integration than did the low-performing organizations. Those successful organizations with a high degree of differentiation used a variety of integrating mechanisms such as committees and task forces.

John J. Morse and Jay W. Lorsch extended this line of research by comparing the *effectiveness* of departments that matched or failed to match their environments.[35] In their study, four departments of a large company were evaluated. Two of these departments, which manufactured containers, operated in a comparatively stable environment. Two other departments were in the unstable environment associated with communications research. In each pair, one department had been evaluated as highly effective and the other as less effective. Morse and Lorsch found that the more effective manufacturing department was structured in a mechanistic fashion, with clearly defined roles and duties, while the more effective research department was structured in an organic fashion, with roles and duties loosely defined. On the other hand, the less effective manufacturing department was structured in an organic way, while the less effective research department was mechanistically structured. In short, the structures of the most effective departments fit their environments, while the structures of the less effective departments did not.

Once an organization's business environment has been defined, it must be evaluated along two dimensions: simple-complex and static-dynamic. Simple business environments have relatively few factors; complex environments, more of them. Static environments change slowly; dynamic environments, quickly. Today's business environments are mostly complex and dynamic.

Let's begin by considering companies whose environment is simple and static. In the early 1970s, there were a number of such companies in the motor home/recreational vehicle (RV) industry. The market for their products was fairly homogenous, or uniform. In addition, demand was high and static for a number of years. In most cases, such companies should adopt the functional form of organization.

Yet an environment that is static today may become dynamic tomorrow. Change came to the RV industry after 1973, when the cost of oil began to soar. Simple but dynamic environments require a different kind of organization. They need a faster flow of information and greater closeness to markets than the pure functional form allows. A company may find that it makes sense to modify a basically functional form of organization to allow for lateral relations among employees. Such organizations could, for example, create special task forces or committees to deal with specific problems or products.

When a business environment is complex, a new factor must be taken into account: whether the company's activities can be segmented along product, market, or geographical lines. Hospitals are typical of organizations whose activities are complex and static but cannot be segmented by product or market. Here the correct form of organization will usually be functional—surgery, medicine, and so forth.

By contrast, many companies that market health-care products are complex and static, but segmentable. Such companies might segment their offerings into divisions responsible for, let's say, medical products, dental products, pharmaceuticals, and hospital products. Each of these divisions might have its own internal facilities for all functional areas, such as marketing, engineering, and production.

However, some companies that market health-care products must function in environments that are complex, segmentable, and dynamic. Suppose, for example, that the company's pharmaceuticals division has trouble introducing a new line of products. The line is directed at doctors, the province of the company's medical division, and likely to be used in hospitals, the province of the hospital division. In this case, the company might set up a task force with employees from all three divisions to study the problem.

Some companies whose environments are complex, segmentable, and dynamic want the sophistication that a specialized functional department provides. In this case, a matrix organization, with both product and functional links, is usually the most appropriate choice.

The Task-Technology Approach

COORDINATED RESOURCE
Use Transparency 62, Technological Imperatives and Organizational Structures.

COORDINATED RESOURCE
See Samaras Case 3.1, "Adias Electronics Inc."

Clearly, there is an important relationship between an organization's technological commitments and the motivation and productivity of its employees—a relationship sometimes called the organization's "task technology." Classical studies conducted in the mid-1960s by Joan Woodward and her colleagues found that an organization's task technology affected both its structure and its success.[36] Woodward's team divided about 100 British manufacturing firms into three groups according to their respective task technologies: (1) unit and small-batch production, (2) large-batch and mass production, and (3) process production.

Unit production refers to the production of individual items tailored to a customer's specifications—custom-made clothes, for example. The technology used in unit production is the least complex because the items are produced largely by individual craftspeople. *Small-batch production* refers to products made in small quantities in separate stages, such as machine parts that are later assembled. *Large-batch* and *mass production* refer to the manufacture of large quantities of products, sometimes on an assembly line (such as automobiles). *Process production* refers to the production of materials that are sold by weight or volume, such as chemicals or drugs; these materials are usually produced with highly complex equipment that operates in a continuous flow.

Woodward found a number of relationships between technological processes and organizational structure. In each category, successful firms had similar structural characteristics, which tended to cluster around the median value at each technological level. For example, if the median span of management in process firms was five, the successful process firms would have spans near that number.

Woodward's findings fall into three general classes. First, the more complex the technology—from unit to process production—the greater the number of managers and managerial levels. In other words, complex technologies lead to tall organizational structures and require more supervision and coordination. (See Fig. 11-8.)

Second, the span of management for first-line managers increases as we move from unit to mass production, but decreases when we move from mass to process production. Because lower-level employees in both unit and process production firms usually do highly skilled work, they tend to form small work groups, making a narrow span inevitable. In contrast, a large number of assembly-line workers, who perform similar tasks, can be supervised by one manager.

Third, as the firm's technological complexity increases, its clerical and administrative staffs become larger because managers need help with paperwork and non–production-related work so they can concentrate on specialized tasks. Also, complex equipment requires more maintenance and scheduling, both of which generate additional paperwork.

Woodward's research showed that *for each type of technology, specific aspects of organizational structure are associated with more successful performance.* In other words, the successful firms were those with the appropriate struc-

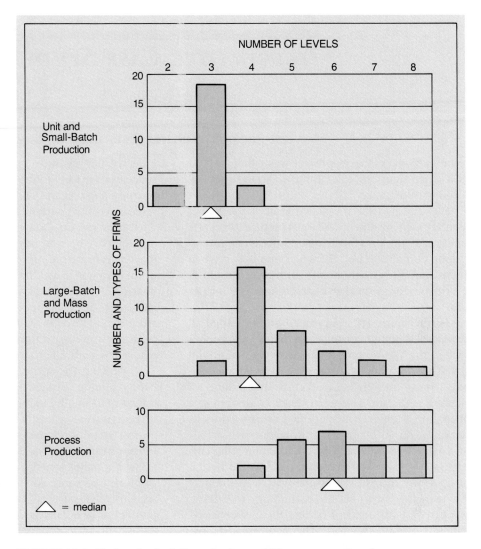

FIGURE 11-8 Technological Complexity and Management Levels
Source: Joan Woodward, *Industrial Organization.* Copyright 1965. By permission of Oxford University Press.

COORDINATED RESOURCE

See Oddou section on Organizing the Corporation, "Designing Your Company."

COORDINATED RESOURCE

See Samaras Case 3.5, "Wizard Computers, Ltd."

THOUGHT PROVOKER

A book called *Workplace 2000* says that "in the Workplace 2000 large corporation, there will be 50, 100 or more CEOs, each leading an autonomous, small business unit." What are the implications of this?

ture for their level of technology. For mass-production firms, the appropriate structure conformed to the classical management principles. In the other two types of firms, however, the appropriate structure did *not* conform to classical guidelines.

Woodward's studies provided evidence of the influence of technology on organizational structure. Other research has suggested that the impact of technology on structure is strongest in small firms (which the firms studied by Woodward tended to be). For large firms, the impact of technology seems to felt mainly at the lowest levels of the organization.[37]

The Need to Reorganize

There are several signs that a company's organizational design isn't working. Managers may consistently fail to predict changes in the business environment, or they may be unable to adapt to these changes. Perhaps, too, the right information often fails to get to the right people at the right time. When companies face such problems, it is time to rethink organizational design.

ILLUSTRATIVE CASE STUDY

WRAP-UP

Hewlett-Packard Reinterprets the HP Way

The news that the Snakes project was falling behind was a clear signal to CEO John A. Young that HP needed to reorganize.

We can also see this if we look at the fit between HP's environment and its structure. Over the years, it had built up a mechanistic system of committee upon committee. Yet, HP was trying to survive in a highly unstable environment—one better suited to the organic approach that characterized HP's early years.

Furthermore, HP's old organization lumped all computers together, despite the clear differences between the customers for various types of equipment. This grouping was convenient from an engineer's viewpoint, since the technical problems of designing a PC are similar to those of designing a workstation. However, it made it too easy to focus internally—on goals important to engineers—rather than on aggressively analyzing and then meeting customer needs. Over and over again, HP would be the first company to research an innovative technology but one of the last to get the technology to market. The open systems concept behind the Snakes workstations is a good example. The new organization, though, is based upon a clear view of the market segments and what customers want and what HP must do to be competitive in each segment.

This latest reorganization also reassured some industry analysts, who noted that there was no clear successor for CEO John A. Young, who is expected to retire in a few years. Under the reorganization, three senior executives have been given a chance to show what they can do. One is Dean Morton, chief operating officer, who was given responsibility for overseeing the reorganization. Another is Richard A. Hackborn, who was named head of the computer products division. The third is Lewis E. Platt, who will have the chance to show whether he can make Hewlett-Packard a major force in workstations. This planning for continuity is important for HP and its internal and external stakeholders.

Hewlett-Packard's approach to organizing is hardly unique. In fact, part of HP's success can be traced to its flexibility. The company has been willing to reorganize—a costly and painful process—even during times of relative strength. Too many organizations wait until a crisis is upon them before they undertake a major structural shift—which they expect to work like some sort of magic tonic. As we have seen throughout this chapter, however, reorganization is not generally an ad hoc or stop-gap measure. Rather, it is the product of long-term planning and goal-oriented strategy. ■

Source: Jim Carlton, "Hewlett-Packard Tries to Revive Share of Market by Realigning Computer Lines," *The Wall Street Journal,* October 8, 1990, p. B4.

■ SUMMARY

Organizational structure—the way in which an organization's activities are divided, organized, and coordinated—provides stability and helps organization members work together to achieve goals. Division of work, also called job specialization, is based on the observation that productivity increases when tasks are specialized, although oversimplifying tasks can lead to work alienation.

Departmentalization, the grouping of tasks, can be easily depicted on an organization chart, which also shows the levels in the management hierarchy and the chain of command. In addition, organization charts show the span of management (also called span of control), which affects the effectiveness and efficiency of decision making. Contemporary researchers agree that there is no single ideal span of management; choosing an appropriate span involves such factors as the environment and the personalities and capabilities of managers and subordinates.

As far back as Chester Barnard, management thinkers realized that the informal organization was valuable for smoothing the flow of information and coordinating organizational tasks. Today many companies are relying on informal organizational structures to adapt quickly to environmental changes.

There are three types of formal organizational structure: the functional organization, the product/market organization, and the matrix organization.

Coordination, the integration of individual and departmental tasks, is needed to overcome differentiation, the different mind-set that individual departments tend to develop. The key consideration is matching the organization's capacity for coordination with its need for coordination.

Today we realize that organizational design—the process of choosing an organizational structure that is appropriate to a given strategy and environment—is an ongoing process that involves trial and error and political considerations. The classical approach, originated by Max Weber, Frederick Taylor, and Henri Fayol, has been criticized for seeking the "one best" design for every situation.

The neoclassicists, led by McGregor, Argyris, and Likert, tried to improve the classical model by suggesting ways to give members greater independence and power. The neoclassicists have been criticized for overlooking environmental variables and for oversimplifying human motivation.

The environmental approach holds that different organizational structures will be more effective in stable, changing, and turbulent environments. Thus, the key task of organizational design is analyzing the business environment.

In the task-technology approach, managers focus on one element of the company's internal environment—the task technology it uses to produce goods. Researchers have found that certain designs are usually most effective for firms using unit and small-batch production, large-batch and mass production, or process production.

Signals that reorganization is needed: managers' consistent failure to predict and adapt to environmental changes, the failure of right information to reach the right people at the right time, and the company's being out of step.

■ *REVIEW QUESTIONS*

1. Why is organizational structure important?
2. What is division of work? What are its advantages and disadvantages?
3. What does an organization chart show?
4. What are the key considerations in choosing a span of management?
5. What do we mean by the term *informal organizational structure*? Why is it important?
6. What is a functional structure? How is it different from a product/market structure? What are the advantages and disadvantages of each?
7. Under what conditions would a matrix structure be most suitable? What are its advantages and disadvantages?
8. What is differentiation and why does it make coordination more difficult?
9. Describe the three basic approaches to achieving effective coordination.
10. What are the advantages and disadvantages of the classical approach to organizational design? The neoclassical approach?
11. What form of organizational structure is best suited to a simple, static environment? A simple, dynamic environment? A complex but static environment? A complex and dynamic environment?
12. Use Woodward's task-technology approach to explain why technologically complex firms tend to have tall organizational structures with large administrative and clerical staffs.
13. How can managers tell when it is time to rethink their organizational structure?

Options for Change at Imperial Chemical Industries

Mr. John Harvey-Jones sat at his desk and pondered the future. He had just taken over as chairman of the board at Britain's Imperial Chemical Industries (ICI), and he knew he had some serious reorganization to do.

ICI is an international firm whose major business is commodity chemicals. It consists of 11 divisions doing business in the following areas: specialty chemicals, pharmaceuticals, agricultural chemicals and fertilizers, paints, explosives, oil, fibers, petrochemicals, and plastics. It is a British firm with a large market presence in the United States and Europe and smaller markets in almost all other countries.

The Current Situation. The 1980 world recession hit ICI hard. Earnings in 1979 had been $595 million, but in 1980 ICI lost $27 million; in 1982, the company earned only $196 million. This drastic decline in earnings was the result of several factors: a poor world economy, an inflated pound, the fall of commodity-chemical prices, and a rise in operating expenses all took their toll. However, an unfocused response to these outside factors also contributed to the problems. By 1982, some of these factors were reversing: The pound was weakening and the world economic picture was brightening. However, many of the underlying problems within ICI were still present and had to be addressed by ICI's new chairman.

The Alternatives. Harvey-Jones believed that the first step was to examine the current structure and functioning of the board of directors. In doing so, he recognized three basic alternatives for structuring the future management of ICI: maintain the status quo, become a holding company, or make the company more than the sum of its parts through a restructuring of responsibilities. Each alternative offered advantages and disadvantages, but one had to be chosen.

At the time, the company was structured so that each board member was responsible for a separate division. Thus, the board member planned the future of his division and tried to persuade other members to support it. Each member, then, had a vested inter-

est in seeing his or her division receive capital expenditure funds, larger budgets, and the chance to pursue a goal that may or may not have been consistent with either the goals of another division or the company's overall goals. Each member mapped out a strategy for his or her own division, and no one oversaw the direction for the entire company. Not surprisingly, conflicting goals were likely, and self-interest was common.

One option for change was to become a holding company, whereby the board would give a minimum amount of guidance to each division. Each division would then be expected to contribute a certain amount of profit to the corporation; each would be independently responsible for meeting its profit goal. In large part, the holding-company option negated the necessity of an active board of directors.

The final option was to make the board responsible for the overall direction and performance of the entire company. Rather than overseeing one division per person, the entire board would set goals for every division, individually and corporately. Day-to-day responsibility would rest with the president of each division, but the process and decisions would be reviewed by the board.

Mr. Harvey-Jones knew he had some major decisions to make.

Note: This case was prepared by Rebecca Villa.
Sources: Graham Turner, "ICI Becomes Proactive," *Long Range Planning* 17, no. 6 (December 1984):12–16; "ICI: Changing the Shape of a Giant," *Chemical Week,* July 25, 1984, pp. 28–32; Stephanie Cooke and John P. Tarpey, "Behind the Stunning Comeback at Britain's ICI," *Business Week,* June 3, 1985, pp. 62–63.

Case Questions

1. What factors are most important in deciding the structure of the board of directors?
2. Who should make the final decision about the shape of the board of directors?
3. What should that shape be?
4. How would any changes that were necessary be implemented?

Harley-Davidson Regroups for Success

When William Harley and the Davidson brothers—Walter, Arthur, and William—used salvaged parts to build three motorized bikes in the Davidsons' Milwaukee backyard in 1903, they didn't know they were making history. By 1907, though, Harleys were used around the country as police bikes, and in both World Wars, they were used as scout bikes and dispatch vehicles. At the peak of motorcycle popularity, in the 1940s, more than 150 U.S. companies manufactured motorcycles. The Harley-Davidson name was associated with high quality, though, and by 1953, Harley-Davidson was the nation's only surviving motorcycle manufacturer.

Yet by the 1970s, this leader of the pack was facing bankruptcy as it lost more and more sales to foreign imports. What had happened? One problem was reliability. To keep a Harley in good running order, owners had to know how to fix their machines—often on the road. As American life became more hectic, most Americans lacked the time, skill, or desire to tinker with their bikes, so many sales were lost to more reliable Japanese and German imports. A second problem was the Harley's tarnished image. The aging baby-boom generation had disposable income, but they weren't inclined to spend it on a product that was linked to the Hell's Angels motorcycle gangs. How could Harley overcome these problems? This was the question that faced Chairman Vaughan L. Beals, Jr., and a group of senior executives who used a leveraged buyout to purchase Harley-Davidson from AMF in 1981.

Harley executives began their corporate soul-searching by analyzing the way Japanese companies designed, manufactured, and marketed motorcycles. According to Thomas Gelb, a senior vice president, HD discovered that the big difference between Japanese and Harley bikes had "nothing to do with culture, wage rates, or robotics. Their competitive edge came from highly efficient manufacturing techniques."

To focus their efforts, HD executives decided to concentrate on the products the company was known for—heavyweight and super-heavyweight motorcycles. Thus, HD sold off all other product lines, including lightweight motorcycles, snowmobiles, and golf carts. Next, HD hired top-level engineers and built new engineering facilities. This paid off immediately: The newly invented Evolution engine became a leading product in the motorcycle market.

However, Japanese competitors quickly copied the engine, as well as HD's ad campaigns, and once again, HD was floundering. Desperate, HD filed a petition with the International Trade Commission, and in 1983, tariffs were levied on Japanese bikes. Thus, HD had five years to turn the company around. To do this, HD implemented three fundamental concepts: employee involvement, just-in-time inventory, and statistical operator control.

Company-wide employee involvement programs were virtually unknown in this country when HD began a "quality circles program" encouraging employees to contribute ideas, solve problems, and improve the efficiency and quality of their own work. The result was dramatic increases in productivity as well as morale. The quality circles technique is still working for HD; at present, employees must be consulted in the planning of any changes in the workplace or in equipment. Employee grievances are down 20 percent, and absenteeism has been reduced by 55 percent.

To generate cash flow, HD developed a just-in-time inventory program called Materials As Needed (MAN), which reduced in-process inventory costs by $22 million. Next, HD adopted a machine setup program, which cut down manufacturing lead time, providing stable schedules and consistent daily production. Machine operators act as miniconsultants, keeping track of quotas, quality, and ways to improve the production process. Gelb says that production time has been reduced by an average of 75 percent per machine.

Production now runs in a continuous cycle at the HD plant rather than in batches. Kanban cards, a Japanese technique, act as request and authorization forms that follow units down the assembly line, reducing red tape, paperwork, and production-control man-hours. Finally, HD implemented statistical operator control (SOC). Under SOC, machine operators use statistics to analyze measurements of parts for dimensional accuracy and quality. This helps to identify the sources of problems. All employees are trained in problem solving and statistics, and are constantly retrained on the job to facilitate constant product improvement.

Once the manufacturing side was streamlined, Beals and his colleagues had to contend with the Harley's bad reputation. Because heavyweight bikes carry an equally heavy price tag (at least $15,000 apiece), HD executives knew they had to cultivate an upscale market for their bikes. HD decided to focus on niche buyers: high-income yuppies, both male and female. To banish the "bad biker" image, HD ordered dealers to light their showrooms better and issued guidelines for creating window displays of well-designed, high-quality jackets, jewelry, and other items bearing the Harley logo.

HD's niche marketing approach has been very lucrative: Today, one in three Harley buyers is a professional or a manager. Buyers' median age is 35, and their median income is $45,000. HD so thoroughly changed its image that in 1990 it was able to market clothing and accessories bearing the HD logo independently of dealers. HD plans to sell franchises for MotorClothes to department stores nationwide.

Another major challenge for HD was how to hang on to customers. To do this, it formed Harley Owners Groups (HOG). HOG holds rallies, organizes rides, and backs charity groups. Bike owners are automatically linked up with like-minded enthusiasts. At many Harley rallies, senior executives from HD show up to participate so customers can air their complaints and compliments directly.

In 1990, HD had more than 60 percent of the $600 million U.S. motorcycle market. Production goals are increasing; the company exported 20,000 bikes in 1990, and is expected to export 25,000 in 1991. HD has also acquired Holiday Rambler, a recreational vehicle company, and plans to diversify its products to the same market that buys motorcycles.

HD's turnaround was so dramatic and so thoroughgoing that HD now conducts productivity consultations for other manufacturers, which is proving to be a very lucrative sideline.

Sources: Paul Dean, "A Message from Milwaukee," *Cycle World,* October 1988, p. 7; Norman S. Mayersohn, "Motorcycles: Touring First Class," *Popular Mechanics,* April 1989, pp. 90–94; Sarah Smith, "Hogs with Wheels," *Fortune,* April 10, 1989, pp. 38–39; Steve Kichen, "More Than Motorcycles," *Forbes,* October 3, 1989, pp. 193–194; Thomas Gelb, "Overhauling Corporate Engine Drives Winning Strategy," *Journal of Business Strategy,* November–December 1989, pp. 9–14; Stephen Taub, "Vrrroom: The Battle over Harley-Davidson," *Financial World,* December 12, 1989, p. 15; Kate Fitzgerald, "Harley-Davidson Revs Up for Retail," *Advertising Age,* August 27, 1990, p. 10; Holt Hackney, "Easy Rider: While Its Fans Go Hog-Wild over Harley-Davidson, Who's Watching the Road?" *Financial World,* September 4, 1990, pp. 48–49; Kate Fitzgerald, "Kathleen Demitros Helps Spark Comeback at Harley-Davidson," *Advertising Age,* January 9, 1990, p. 32.

Case Questions

1. What did Harley-Davidson do to improve coordination and employee morale?

2. Does Harley-Davidson's redesigned manufacturing division have a mechanistic or an organic structure? Why is this design suitable for its environment?

3. How does Harley-Davidson's new design reflect neoclassical principles? Which, in your opinion, is more important—the involvement of employees or the new manufacturing techniques?

◼ *NOTES*

[1] Ernest Dale, *Organization* (New York: American Management Association, 1967), p. 9. The five-step process described here is an elaboration of Dale's original three-step process.

[2] Adam Smith, *Wealth of Nations* (New York: Modern Library, 1937; orig. pub. 1776), pp. 3–4.

[3] Gareth R. Jones, "Task Visibility, Free Riding, and Shirking: Explaining the Effect of Structure and Technology on Employee Behavior," *Academy of Management Review,* October 1984, pp. 684–695; Dan R. Dalton and Debra J. Mesch, "The Impact of Flexible Scheduling on Employee Attendance and Turnover," *Administrative Science Quarterly* 35 (June 1990):370–387; J. Barton Cunningham and Ted Eberle, "A Guide to Job Enrichment and Redesign," *Personnel,* February 1990, pp. 56–61; Benjamin Schneider and Andrea Marcus Konz, "Strategic Job Analysis," *Human Resource Management* 28, no. 1 (Spring 1989):51–63.

[4] Some early writers did, however, consider situational factors. Early in this century, for instance, F. R. Mason referred to variables that affected the span of management in *Business Principles and Organization* (Chicago: Cree Publishing, 1909). Considerably later, Lyndall F. Urwick emphasized the interdependence of the work of subordinates, and Luther Gulick mentioned a variety of important factors, such as the type of work and the variety of tasks performed. See Lyndall F. Urwick, "The Manager's Span of Control," *Harvard Business Review* 34, no. 3 (May–June 1956):39–47; and Luther Gulick, "Notes on the Theory of Organization," in Luther Gulick and L. Urwick, eds. *Papers on the Science of Administration* (New York: Institute of Public Administration, Columbia University, 1937), pp. 1–46.

[5] For subsequent research on span of management, see David Van Fleet and Arthur G. Bedeian, "A History of the Span of Management," *Academy of Management Review* 2, no. 3 (1977):356–372; and Van Fleet, "Empirically Testing Span of Management Hypotheses," *International Journal of Management* 2, no. 2 (1984):5–10.

[6] See Dale, *Organization,* p. 238; Harold Stieglitz, "What's Not on an Organization Chart," *Conference Board Record* 1, no. 11 (November 1964):7–10; and Karol K. White, *Understanding the Company Organization Chart* (New York: American Management Association, 1963), pp. 13–19.

[7]Robert Townsend, *Further Up the Organization* (New York: Alfred A. Knopf, 1984), p. 159.

[8]Herbert A. Simon, *Administrative Behavior,* 3rd ed. (New York: Macmillan, 1976). For other rich discussions of informal groups, see Chester I. Barnard, *The Functions of the Executive* (Cambridge, Mass.: Harvard University Press, 1938); F. J. Roethlisberger and William J. Dickson, *Management and the Worker* (Cambridge, Mass.: Harvard University Press, 1947); and Charles Perrow, *Complex Organizations,* 3rd ed. (New York: Random House, 1986).

[9]Robert A. Pitts and John D. Daniels, "Aftermath of the Matrix Mania," *Columbia Journal of World Business* 19, no. 2 (Summer 1984):48–54; and John R. Adams and Nicki S. Kirchof, "The Practice of Matrix Management," in David I. Cleland, ed., *Matrix Management Systems Handbook* (New York: Van Nostrand Reinhold, 1984), pp. 13–30. See also Wolf V. Heydebrand, "New Organizational Forms," *Work and Occupations* 16, no. 3 (August 1989):323–357.

[10]See John F. Mee, "Matrix Organizations," *Business Horizons* 7, no. 2 (Summary 1964):70–72; Jay R. Galbraith, "Matrix Organization Designs," *Business Horizons* 14, no. 1 (February 1971):29–40; Stanley M. Davis and Paul R. Lawrence, *Matrix* (Reading, Mass.: Addison-Wesley, 1977); and Harvey F. Kolodny, "Evolution to a Matrix Organization," *Academy of Management Review* 4, no. 4 (1979):543–553.

[11]For a discussion of the typical evolution of a matrix structure, see Davis and Lawrence, *Matrix,* pp. 39–45.

[12]R. F. Grantges, V. L. Fahrmann, T. A. Gibson, and L. M. Brown, "Central Office Equipment Reports for Stored Program and Control Systems," *Bell System Technical Journal* 62, no. 7 (September 1983):2365–2395.

[13]Christopher A. Bartlett and Sumantra Ghoshal, "Matrix Management: Not a Structure, a Frame of Mind," *Harvard Business Review,* July–August 1990, pp. 138–145.

[14]Ralph Katz and Thomas J. Allen, "Project Performance and the Locus of Influence in the R&D Matrix," *Academy of Management Journal,* March 1985, pp. 67–87.

[15]James Mooney defines coordination as "the orderly arrangement of group effort, to provide unity of action in the pursuit of a common purpose." See *The Principles of Organization,* rev. ed. (New York: Harper & Brothers, 1947), p. 5.

[16]See Joseph L. C. Cheng, "Interdependence and Coordination in Organizations: A Role-System Analysis," *Academy of Management Journal* 26, no. 1 (March 1983):156–162.

[17]James D. Thompson, *Organizations in Action: Social Sciences Bases of Administrative Theory* (New York: McGraw-Hill, 1967), pp. 54–60.

[18]Paul R. Lawrence and Jay W. Lorsch, *Organization and Environment: Managing Differentiation and Integration* (Homewood, Ill.: Irwin, 1967), p. 9.

[19]Eliezer Rosenstein, "Cooperativeness and Advancement of Managers: An International Perspective," *Human Relations* 38, no. 1 (January 1985):1–21.

[20]Our discussion of coordination is based to a large extent on Jay R. Galbraith, "Organization Design: An Information Processing View," *Interfaces* 4, no. 3 (May 1974):28–36; Jay R. Galbraith, *Organization Design* (Reading, Mass.: Addison-Wesley, 1977); and Michael L. Tushman and David A. Nadler, "Information Processing as an Integrating Concept in Organizational Design," *Academy of Management Review* 3, no. 3 (July 1978):613–624.

[21]See Richard L. Daft and Robert H. Lengel, "Information Richness: A New Approach to Managerial Behavior and Organization Design," in *Research in Organizational Behavior,* Vol. 6 (Greenwich, Conn.: JAI Press, 1984), pp. 191–233.

[22]Galbraith, *Organization Design,* pp. 50–52. Galbraith also offers a third method: managing the organization's relationship with the environment so as to reduce the need for tight coordination. We consider this part of the basic task of relating the organization to the environment through its strategy-making and planning/control systems. However, Galbraith's discussion calls attention to the open nature of the organization as a system: It can reduce the need for internal capacity by altering the ways in which it deals with the external environment.

[23]See Kenneth E. Marino and David R. Lange, "Measuring Organizational Slack: A Note on the Convergence and Divergence of Alternative Operational Definitions," *Journal of Management* 9, no. 1 (Fall 1983):81–92.

[24]Joseph R. Daughen and Peter Binzen, *The Wreck of the Penn Central* (Boston: Little, Brown, 1971).

[25]For the overall perspective in this section, the authors are indebted to Kenneth N. Wexly and Gary A. Yukl, *Organizational Behavior and Personnel Psychology,* rev. ed. (Homewood, Ill.: Irwin, 1984); Y. K. Shetty and Howard M. Carlisle, "A Contingency Model of Organizational Design," *California Management Review* 15, no. 1 (Fall 1972):38–45; and Jay R. Galbraith and Daniel A. Nathanson, "The Role of Organizational Structure and Process in Strategy Implementation," in Dan E. Schendel and Charles W. Hofer, eds., *Strategic Management: A New View of Business Policy and Planning* (Boston: Little, Brown, 1979), pp. 249–283. See also Daniel Robey, *Designing Organizations,* 2nd ed. (Homewood, Ill.: Irwin, 1986).

[26]Max Weber, *Economy and Society: An Outline of Interpretative Sociology* (New York: Bedminster Press, 1968; orig. pub. 1925), pp. 956–958.

[27]Weber addressed this criticism by defining a hypothetical "ideal" organization that incorporated every one of the characteristics of bureaucracy. He believed that the closer an actual institution approached this ideal one, the more fully it would enjoy the benefits of bureaucracy.

[28]Douglas McGregor, *The Human Side of Enterprise* (New York: McGraw-Hill, 1960), and *The Professional Manager* (New York: McGraw-Hill, 1967).

[29]Chris Argyris, *Personality and Organization* (New York: Harper Brothers, 1957), and *Integrating the Individual and the Organization* (New York: Wiley, 1964).

[30]Rensis Likert, *New Patterns of Management* (New York: McGraw-Hill, 1961), and *The Human Organization* (New York: McGraw-Hill, 1967); and Rensis Likert and Jane Gibson Likert, *New Ways of Managing Conflict* (New York: McGraw-Hill, 1976).

[31]This discussion of modern approaches to organizational design is based on Robert Duncan, "What Is the Right Organizational Structure? Decision Tree Analysis Provides the Answer," *Organizational Dynamics* 7, no. 3 (Winter 1979):447–461.

[32]Peter Kerr, "Witch Hazel Still Made in Old-Fashioned Way," *The New York Times,* May 11, 1985, pp. 27–28.

[33]Tom Burns and G. M. Stalker, *The Management of Innovation* (London: Tavistock, 1961).

[34]Lawrence and Lorsch, *Organization and Environment.*

[35]John J. Morse and Jay W. Lorsch, "Beyond Theory Y," *Harvard Business Review* 48, no. 3 (May–June 1970):61–68. See also Robert Duncan, "What Is the Right Organization Structure? Decision Tree Analysis Provides the Answer," *Organizational Dynamics* 7, no. 3 (Winter 1979):59–80. Duncan has classified environments in terms of their complexity and rate of change and offers guidelines for selecting between several forms of functional and divisional structures that vary according to the requirements of the environment.

[36]Joan Woodward, *Industrial Organization* (London: Oxford University Press, 1965). See also Karl O. Magnusen, "A Comparative Analysis of Organizations," *Organizational Dynamics* 2, no. 1 (Summer 1973):16–31; James D. Thompson, *Organizations in Action* (New York: McGraw-Hill, 1967); Charles Perrow, *Complex Organizations: A Critical Essay,* 2nd ed. (Glenview, Ill.: Scott, Foresman, 1979); and Paul D. Collins and Frank Hull, "Technology and Span of Control: Woodward Revisited," *Journal of Management Studies* 23 (1986):143–164.

[37]See, for example, David J. Hickson, D. S. Pugh, and Diana C. Pheysey, "Operations Technology and Organizational Structure: A Clinical Reappraisal," *Administrative Science Quarterly* 14, no. 3 (September 1969):378–397.

CHAPTER TWELVE

AUTHORITY, DELEGATION, AND DECENTRALIZATION

Detail from Theo. van Doesburg. *Simultaneous Counter-Composition.*

Authority, Power, and Influence

The Basis of Formal Authority: Two Views
The Sources of Power
Power in Organizations

Line and Staff Authority

Line Authority
Staff Authority
Functional Authority

Delegation

Delegation, Authority, Accountability, and Responsibility
The Advantages of Delegation
Barriers to Delegation
Guidelines for Effective Delegation

Job Design

Approaches to Job Design
Job Design and Job Satisfaction

Decentralization

Factors Influencing Decentralization
Trends in Decentralization

Upon completing this chapter, you should be able to:

1. Distinguish between authority, power, and influence.

2. Discuss the two major views of authority.

3. List and explain the five sources of power.

4. Compare and contrast line, staff, and functional authority.

5. Explain the relationship between delegation, authority, accountability, and responsibility.

6. Discuss the advantages of delegation, why managers hesitate to delegate, and the guidelines that can help them delegate effectively.

7. Describe the major approaches to job design and their effect on job satisfaction.

8. Distinguish between a centralized and decentralized approach to authority.

Theo. van Doesburg, *Simultaneous Counter-Composition* (1929–30). Oil on canvas. 19¾ × 19⅝″. Collection, The Museum of Modern Art, New York. The Sidney and Harriet Janis Collection.

ILLUSTRATIVE CASE STUDY

INTRODUCTION

Responsiveness and Restructuring at IBM

IBM had always been the leader in many segments of the computer industry, but by 1987, it seemed to have forgotten how it had gotten there. Over the years, IBM had become less responsive to consumer needs and was being perceived as a little arrogant. Consumers once tolerated this attitude because they had little choice. After all, everyone assumed IBM was the only reliable brand of computer equipment and any company contemplating a large capital expenditure for computers would naturally avoid the risk of purchasing an inferior product from an untested or less trustworthy source.

So IBM prospered. As the computer age advanced, however, more and more competition entered the market. Suddenly, IBM was no longer unchallenged. Other companies began selling trustworthy computers, and often they outperformed IBM in customer service. Some of IBM's new products did not succeed as well as expected, and older ones no longer met the needs of more demanding consumers. For three years, IBM watched earnings decline, and investors became less enthusiastic about backing a company whose traditional approaches were no longer paying off so handsomely. Clearly, it was time to make changes before IBM was knocked from its traditional place at the head of the industry.

Ultimately, chairman John Akers decided to decentralize a company that had grown over the years into a mammoth organization. IBM was structured around a central management committee that made all major decisions. As the company had expanded, new layers of management had been added, as had new policies and procedures. Akers wanted to remove many of these layers so that decisions could be made at much lower levels in the organization. First, he moved thousands of employees into sales positions in order to increase the effectiveness of IBM's selling effort. The second change—and the biggest challenge—was the program to decentralize the company's headquarters. Today, instead of a single management committee making all the decisions, there are six separate divisions organized according to product lines. The general manager of each division now functions more autonomously than any manager at IBM ever did in the past. Since IBM is such a large organization, this restructuring displaced a great many people, but by offering early-retirement

Boosting IBM's Sales Effectiveness. IBM sales representatives attend a seminar in Information Systems Investment Strategies (ISIS) software they can use to compare the estimated costs of investing in new IBM software against the benefits customers can expect.

incentives and by taking advantage of natural attrition rates, Akers managed his changes without violating the company's history of not laying off employees.

Akers reasoned that the smaller groups within IBM would be better able to meet customer needs. The large bureaucracy that had long characterized IBM had made it difficult for the company to move quickly enough to exploit market fluctuations and new market niches. IBM's critics have claimed that it was this failure that allowed Digital Equipment to capture the mid-size market and Apple to make great inroads into the personal computer market. Smaller groups seem better able to spot opportunities and to move quickly to take advantage of them. Since each manager at IBM now has fewer markets to consider, each division should be much better equipped to determine and respond to the needs of its particular consumers.

Sources: Paul B. Carroll and Michael W. Miller, "IBM to Realign Top Managers, Sources Say," *The Wall Street Journal,* January 28, 1988, p. 3; Miller and Carroll, "IBM Unveils a Sweeping Restructuring in Bid to Decentralize Decision-Making," *The Wall Street Journal,* January 29, 1988, p. 3; Larry Reibstein, "IBM's Plan to Decentralize May Set a Trend—But Imitation Has a Price," *The Wall Street Journal,* February 19, 1988, Sect. 2, p. 21; Geoff Lewis with Anne R. Field, John J. Keller, and John W. Verity, "Big Changes at Big Blue," *Business Week,* February 15, 1988, pp. 92–98.

***T**o help it become more responsive to a changing environment, IBM *decentralized* the authority to make decisions—that is, it pushed authority down the chain of command to lower and smaller work units that were in closer contact with the markets for specific product lines.*

The concept of authority is such an ingrained part of our culture that it is difficult to imagine a workable society—or organization—without clearly defined lines of authority. Yet the way we organize authority can have profound effects on both effectiveness and efficiency. In this chapter, we will begin by taking a closer look at the distinctions between authority, power, and influence, and then we will discuss line versus staff authority. Next we will look at the theory and practice of delegating authority before we conclude with a discussion of job design and decentralization.

■ *AUTHORITY, POWER, AND INFLUENCE*

COORDINATED RESOURCE

The Additional Lecture for Chapter 12 found in the Lecture Extras supplement looks at "Who Needs a Boss."

formal authority Power rooted in the general understanding that specific individuals or groups have the right to exert influence within certain limits by virtue of their position within the organization. Also called legitimate power.

power The ability to exert influence; that is, the ability to change the attitudes or behavior of individuals or groups.

influence Any actions or examples of behavior that cause a change in attitude or behavior of another person or group.

COORDINATED RESOURCE

The Distinctive Discussions for Chapter 12 found in the Lecture Extras supplement include "The Good, The Bad and The Ugly of Office Politics" and "New Faces of Power."

COORDINATED RESOURCE

Use Transparency 71, Two Views of Formal Authority.

Writers on management have defined and used the terms *authority, power,* and *influence* in a variety of conflicting ways.[1] **Formal authority** is one type of power. It is based on the recognition of the legitimacy or lawfulness of the attempt to exert influence. Individuals or groups attempting to exert influence are perceived as having the right to do so within recognized boundaries, a right that arises from their formal position in an organization.

We define **power** as the ability to exert influence. To have power is to be able to change the behavior or attitudes of other individuals. In general, those who can exert influence over others in an organization are called stakeholders, as we mentioned in Chapter 3. For example, environmental groups have the power to force companies to change products and their packaging to minimize harm to the environment.

Influence is defined here as actions or examples that, either directly or indirectly, cause a change in behavior or attitude of another person or group. For example, a hard-working person may, by setting an example, influence others to increase their productivity. This definition also takes into account those types of influence that do not lead to more tangible changes. For example, managers may use their influence to improve morale. As Chrysler's CEO, Lee Iacocca used his influence to change traditional business strategies among management personnel, the United Auto Workers, government officials, and consumers. His influence enabled Chrysler to arrange a large federal bailout loan, a new negotiated contract with the union providing for cuts, and a reduced management work force—all of which led to Chrysler's comeback as a major automobile maker.

The Basis of Formal Authority: Two Views

"What gives you the right to tell me what to do?" This familiar question bluntly suggests that before we comply with an instruction, we must be satisfied that the person issuing it has the right to do so. It is unlikely that we would ask this question of a superior in our organization, since we assume that a superior does have the right to issue instructions to us. But why is this so? Where do managers get the right to direct subordinates' activities? There are two major views on formal authority in organizations: the classical view and the acceptance view. (See Fig. 12-1.)

THE CLASSICAL VIEW. The *classical view* supposes that authority originates at some very high level of society and then is lawfully passed down from level to level. At the top of this high level may be God, the state (in the form of king, dictator, or elected president), or the collective will of the people.[2]

According to the classical view of formal authority in American organizations, management has a right to give lawful orders and subordinates have an obligation to

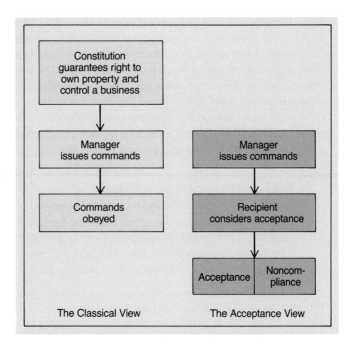

```
┌─────────────────────────────────────────────────────────┐
│   Constitution                                          │
│   guarantees right to                                   │
│   own property and                                      │
│   control a business                                    │
│          │                                              │
│          ▼                                              │
│   Manager              Manager                          │
│   issues commands      issues commands                  │
│          │                   │                          │
│          ▼                   ▼                          │
│   Commands             Recipient                        │
│   obeyed               considers acceptance             │
│                              │                          │
│                              ▼                          │
│                        Acceptance │ Noncom-             │
│                                   │ pliance             │
│                                                         │
│   The Classical View   The Acceptance View              │
└─────────────────────────────────────────────────────────┘
```

FIGURE 12-1 Two Views of Formal Authority

obey. This obligation is, in effect, self-imposed. Members of our society, in agreeing to abide by the Constitution, accept the rights of others to own private property and therefore to own and control a business. By entering and remaining in an organization, subordinates in the United States accept the authority of owners or superiors and therefore have a duty to obey lawful directives.

THE ACCEPTANCE VIEW. The second perspective on the origin of formal authority, the *acceptance view,* finds the basis of authority in the *influencee* rather than in the *influencer.* This view starts with the observation that not all legitimate laws or commands are obeyed in all circumstances. Some are accepted by the receiver of the orders, and some are not. The key point is that the *receiver* decides whether or

The Acceptance View of Authority. Most management policies, such as wearing uniforms and following assembly-line procedures in preparing food and serving customers, fall within the "area of acceptance" for employees at Wendy's Old Fashioned Hamburgers.

not to comply. According to the acceptance viewpoint, therefore, whether or not authority is present in any particular law or order is determined by the receiver, not the issuer of the order. For example, if a supervisor storms along an assembly line shouting at everyone to work harder, the subordinates may not question the supervisor's right to do so but, through anger or indifference, may choose not to comply with the order. The authority of the order will then be nullified.

This view should not suggest that insubordination and chaos are the norm in organizations; most formal authority is, in fact, accepted by organization members. Chester I. Barnard, a strong proponent of the acceptance view, has defined the conditions under which a person will comply with higher authority:

> A person can and will accept a communication as authoritative only when four conditions simultaneously occur: (a) he can and does understand the communication; (b) *at the time of his decision* he believes that it is not inconsistent with the purpose of the organization; (c) *at the time of his decision* he believes it to be compatible with his personal interest as a whole; and (d) he is able mentally and physically to comply with it.[3]

In addition to these conditions, cooperation in accepting authority is fostered by what Barnard calls the **"zone of indifference"** and Herbert A. Simon refers to, perhaps more descriptively, as the **"area of acceptance."**[4] Both expressions refer to the inclination of individuals to accept most orders given to them by their superiors, provided the orders fall within a "normal" range. Most of us, for example, will accept the need for periodic progress reports on our work and will rarely stop to consider whether or not to comply with a request for such reports from our superiors. An order that requires an illegal or unethical action, though, is an entirely different matter.

The Sources of Power

Power does not simply derive from an individual's level in the organizational hierarchy. John French and Bertram Raven have identified five sources or bases of power.[5] Each may occur at all levels.

Reward power is based on one person (the influencer) having the ability to reward another person (the influencee) for carrying out orders or meeting other requirements. One example is the power of a supervisor to assign work tasks to subordinates. The greater the attractiveness of a particular task in the eyes of the influencee, the greater the reward power of the influencer. However, rewards are best used to reinforce the desirable actions of subordinates and not as "bribes" to carry out tasks.[6]

Coercive power, based on the influencer's ability to punish the influencee for not meeting requirements, is the negative side of reward power. Punishment may range from loss of a minor privilege to loss of a job. Coercive power is generally used to maintain a minimum standard of performance or conformity among subordinates.

Legitimate power, which corresponds to our term *formal authority* (see above), exists when a subordinate or influencee acknowledges that the influencer has a "right" or is lawfully entitled to exert influence—within certain bounds. It is also implied that the influencee has an obligation to accept this power. The right of a manager to establish reasonable work schedules is an example of "downward" legitimate power. A plant guard may have the "upward" authority to require even the company president to present an identification card before being allowed onto the premises.

Expert power is based on the perception or belief that the influencer has some relevant expertise or special knowledge that the influencee does not. When we do what our doctors tell us, we are acknowledging their expert power. Expert power is usually applied to a specific, limited subject area. Although we may accept

"zone of indifference" or **"area of acceptance"** According to Barnard and Simon, respectively, inclinations conditioning individuals to accept orders that fall within a familiar range of responsibility or activity.

reward power Power derived from the fact that one person, known as an influencer, has the ability to reward another person, known as an influencee, for carrying out orders, which may be expressed or implied.

coercive power The negative side of reward power, based on the influencer's ability to punish the influencee.

legitimate power Power that exists when a subordinate or influencee acknowledges that the influencer has a "right" or is lawfully entitled to exert influence—within certain bounds. Also called *formal authority.*

expert power Power based on the belief or understanding that the influencer has specific knowledge or relevant expertise that the influencee does not.

Sources of Power. As CEO of Wisconsin Power & Light (WPL), Errol B. Davis Jr., shown here with his wife, Elaine, has legitimate and reward power, as well as expert power gained through a B.S. in electrical engineering, an M.B.A. from the University of Chicago, and finance jobs at Xerox, Ford, and WPL. Unlike his predecessor, James R. Underkofler, who was known for his coercive use of power, Davis prefers to emulate the quiet strength of his grandfather. And, as the first black to head a Business Week 1000 company, he draws on referent power when he delivers "tough-love" lectures to troubled teens about the rewards of making the right choices in their lives.

referent power Power based on the desire of the influencee to be like or identify with the influencer.

FOR DISCUSSION
Relate the sources of power to a contingency view of management.

TEACHING TIP
Stress to students the concept that *informal* power may also be used to influence behavior. Try to have them come up with some examples of informal power from organizations to which they belong.

the advertising advice of our company's marketing specialists, we may discount their recommendations on how to lower production costs.

Referent power, which may be held by a person or a group, is based on the influencee's desire to identify with or imitate the influencer. For example, popular, conscientious managers will have referent power if subordinates are motivated to emulate their work habits. Referent power also functions at the peer level—charismatic colleagues may sway us to their sides in department meetings. The strength of referent power is directly related to such factors as the amount of prestige and admiration the influencee confers upon the influencer.

These are *potential* sources of power only. They are the ways in which one person *can* influence another person. Possession of some or all of them does not guarantee the ability to influence particular individuals in specific ways. For example, a manager may have subordinates' respect and admiration as an expert in his or her field, but still may be unable to influence them to be more creative on the job or even to get to work on time. Thus, the role of the influencee in accepting or rejecting the attempted influence remains the key one.

Normally, each of the five power bases is potentially inherent in a manager's position. A specific degree of legitimate power always accompanies a manager's job and is especially important because it shapes the hierarchical relationships within which the other forms of influence and power occur. Subordinates are assumed to accept a manager's formal authority and will generally obey him or her within reasonable limits. Managers usually have the power to reward subordinates with money, privileges, or promotions and to punish them by withholding or removing these rewards. Also, managers are assumed to possess some degree of expertise, at least until they prove otherwise. Since referent power so obviously depends on an individual's style and personality, it is least likely to be an expected part of a manager's position. Many examples exist in organizations, however, such as the tendency of subordinates to model themselves after successful senior executives.

Power in Organizations

The concept of power is a difficult one for Americans to deal with objectively—perhaps because the United States was founded in opposition to an authoritarian regime and peopled by successive waves of immigrants who were fleeing oppressive governments throughout the world. A distrust of excessive power is reflected in the United States Constitution, which both establishes and limits the powers of the federal government. In addition, the Constitution's system of checks and balances was designed to keep any of the three branches of government—legislative, executive, and judicial—from accumulating too much power. Furthermore, the Bill of Rights and subsequent amendments were enacted to protect individuals' rights.

Some Americans, then, have ambivalent feelings about power, both admiring and resenting it in others. They may covet power, but are reluctant to admit it openly, since both history and scientific research have shown how easy it is to misuse and abuse power, with tragic and often horrifying consequences. (See the Ethics in Management box.) This national uneasiness about power perhaps explains why U.S. management writers neglected the subject for so long, even though the exercise of power is an obvious part of a manager's job. But, if we learn to think about power as influence, as suggested here, it will start to lose its negative meaning.

COORDINATED RESOURCE
See Study Guide Self-Learning Exercise 12, "Political Behavior."

In recent years, power and political processes in organizations have become major concerns of management writers.[7] Our realistic understanding of both the role of these factors and how they can be used constructively has been increasing rapidly. For example, David McClelland has described "two faces of power"—a negative face and a positive one.[8] The negative face is usually expressed in terms of dominance-submission: If I win, you lose. To have power implies having power over

FIGURE 12-2 Stanley Milgram's Obedience Experiment

Note: See Ethics in Management box entitled "Obedience and Conscience."

Source: Copyright 1965 by Stanley Milgram. From the film *Obedience,* distributed by the New York University Film Library.

(a) The shock generator.

(b) Electrodes are attached to the learner, who answers by pressing a switch that lights up an answer box.

(c) The subject gives the learner a shock while the experimenter watches.

(d) The subject breaks off the experiment.

ETHICS IN MANAGEMENT

Obedience and Conscience

In 1960, Stanley Milgram conducted the famous "Yale experiments" probing the conflict between personal conscience and obedience to an outside authority figure. He found that people ordered to act against their consciences entered an "agentic state." That is, they viewed themselves as merely instruments (agents) of the authority figure and felt no responsibility for their actions.

In the Yale experiment, Milgram asked a random sample of New Haven residents—excluding students—to help him test whether people learned best by negative or positive reinforcement. He asked the subjects to serve as "teachers," saying another subject would be the "learner." The teacher was to read a series of word pairs to the learner and then prompt the learner with the first word of one of the pairs.

If the learner responded correctly with the second word in the pair, the teacher would go on to another series. If, however, the learner answered incorrectly, the teacher was told to give the learner an electric shock. The strength of the shock increased with each wrong answer. A researcher, who served as an authority figure, stayed in the room with the teacher while the teacher read the word pairs and "punished" the learner.

In fact, no electric shocks were being given. The learner was an actor who, as time went on, pretended to be in extreme pain and asked to withdraw from the experiment. Milgram wanted to know how many subjects would complete the experiment and administer up to 450 volts of "electricity" to a stranger. Figure 12-2 dramatizes the experiment. In the basic experiment, depending on the proximity of the teacher to the learner, 30 to 65 percent of the subjects obeyed the experimenter to the end of the test.

In variations on the experiment, Milgram tested to see how peer pressure, the sex of the subject, the clarity of the experimenter's commands, the affiliation of the experimenter to the university, the health condition of the learner, and the physical presence of the experimenter (the authority figure) would affect its outcome. The only factor that tended to cause the teacher to stop the experiment was the absence of the authority figure.

Milgram concluded that loyalty and discipline are so highly regarded in our society that disobedience produces no satisfaction. "The price of disobedience," he said, "is the growing sense that one has been faithless." And though a cooperative, hierarchical structure is necessary for a society's or a corporation's harmonious survival, he cautioned, "Accept nothing which contradicts our basic experience merely because it comes to us from tradition or convention or authority."

Some researchers responded to Milgram's experiment with outrage because he had misled his subjects about the nature of the experiment and manipulated them in a way that was dangerous from a psychological standpoint. In fact, the American Psychological Association censured Milgram and instituted strict guidelines for the conduct of numerous types of experiments. In Milgram's defense, it must be said that he was in control of his procedure and had established a comprehensive debriefing and follow-up procedure to mitigate any potentially harmful consequences to his subjects. Milgram found out what he wanted to find out, but questions about the ethics of such experimentation and the use of power remain.

Source: Stanley Milgram, *Obedience to Authority* (London: Tavistock Publications, 1975). © 1974 by Stanley Milgram.

---

another, who is less well off for it. Leadership based on the negative face of power regards people as little more than pawns to be used or sacrificed as the need arises. This is self-defeating to the power wielder, since people who feel they are pawns tend either to resist leadership or to become passive, and in either case, their value to the manager is severely limited.

CLASS COMMENT
Note the emphasis again on goals. Also be aware that managers will have personal, as well as organizational, goals.

The positive face of power is best characterized by a concern for group goals—for helping to formulate and achieve them. It involves exerting influence on behalf of, rather than over, others. Managers who exercise their power positively encourage group members to develop the strength and competence they need to succeed as individuals and as members of the organization.

McClelland and David H. Burnham report that successful managers have a greater need to influence others for the benefit of the organization than for self-aggrandizement.[9] Managers who use their power with self-control will be more effective than those who wield power to satisfy a need to dominate others or those who refuse to use their power out of a strong need to be liked. When a manager continually eases rules and changes procedures to accommodate subordinates, subordinates will see that manager not as flexible, but as weak and indecisive. McClelland concluded that good managers exercise power with restraint on behalf of others. Such managers encourage team spirit, support subordinates, and reward their achievements, thereby raising morale. Successful managers also employ certain proven techniques to channel their power productively. John P. Kotter has argued that the external environment of organizations has contributed to the growing need for power skills among managers. Some of his key characteristics of successful power skills are listed in Exhibit 12-1.

Rosabeth Kanter has argued that power can easily become institutionalized. Those whom others believe to possess power seem to find it easier to influence the people around them—and thus to garner even more genuine power. By the same token, "powerlessness" is a difficult condition to overcome. Kanter claims, for example, that many of the real problems experienced by women and minorities can be traced to their lack of power rather than to the disadvantages of race or sex.[10]

A number of other arguments can be raised to support French and Raven's typology of the five sources of power. For example, a changing business climate can make different functions within an organization more important than others at a crucial point in time. As the amount of uncertainty faced by an organization increases, the number of potential power bases also increases. Sometimes formal authority is only the official ratification of power acquired through other means. If that base of power is not supported by actual influence, other members of the organization can secure real influence and practical power.

Kanter proposes a number of ways an organizational member can acquire power. Four of the most important means are categorized in Exhibit 12-2.

Power is not limited to managers. Lower-level members of an organization may have a great deal of informal power because of their knowledge, their skills, or the resources they control. Nurses, for example, gain influence over new doctors in a hospital when they "show them the ropes," and copy machine attendants have the power to impede or improve a manager's work flow. Likewise, subordinate employees with computer skills can exercise increasing influence over an organization's

EXHIBIT 12-1 Kotter's Key Characteristics of Successfully Handled Power

Kotter maintains that managers who handle power successfully:

1. *Are sensitive to the source of their power.* They keep their actions consistent with people's expectations. For example, they do not try to apply expert power in one field to another field.
2. *Recognize the different costs, risks, and benefits of the five bases of power.* They draw on whichever power base is appropriate to a particular situation or person.
3. *Appreciate that each of the five power bases has merit.* They try to develop their skills and credibility so they can use whichever method is best.
4. *Possess career goals that allow them to develop and use power.* They seek jobs that will build their skills, make people feel dependent on them, and employ a type of power with which they are comfortable.
5. *Act maturely and exercise self-control.* They avoid impulsive or egotistical displays of their power, and they try not to be unnecessarily harsh on others around them.
6. *Understand that power is necessary to get things done.* They feel comfortable using power.

Sources: John P. Kotter, "Power, Dependence, and Effective Management," *Harvard Business Review* 54, no. 2 (March–April 1976):100–110; *Power in Management* (New York: AMACOM, 1979); and *Power and Influence* (New York: Free Press, 1983).

EXHIBIT 12-2 Kanter's Key Means to Organizational Power

1. *Extraordinary activities.* Making changes, being the first person to occupy a position, or being successful upon taking exceptional risks can lead to greater power.
2. *Visibility.* Being noticed, gaining "exposure" in the eyes of those in power, and even making certain activities appear to be riskier than they actually are can also increase power—a fact that has led Kanter to speculate that public appearance may be a more influential factor than genuine substance.
3. *Relevance.* Solving an authentic organizational problem can be a source of power and may well lend credence to the factors of extraordinary activity and visibility.
4. *Sponsors.* Having a sponsor or mentor—someone who advises you on how to succeed in the organization—can be an informal source of power, especially if the sponsor enjoys a good deal of power. Kanter claims that sponsors are especially important for women who are inexperienced in organizational power politics.

Source: Rosabeth Moss Kanter, *Men and Women of the Corporation* (New York: Basic Books, 1977), pp. 165–205.

day-to-day activities as the organization comes to rely more and more on computer technology. To an extent, knowledge, combined with hands-on input into daily activities, is tantamount to power, and those members of an organization who possess in-demand skills are in a position to secure themselves a base of practical power.

Power, then, is an important fact of organizational life. As managers, we must not only accept and understand it as an integral part of our jobs, we must also learn how to use, and not abuse, it to further our own and our organization's goals.[11]

■ *LINE AND STAFF AUTHORITY*

TEACHING TIP

Show students a copy of your school's organization chart. Try to determine line, staff, and functional authority positions from it.

COORDINATED RESOURCE

Use Transparency 73, Line and Staff Positions.

line authority The authority of those managers directly responsible, throughout the organization's chain of command, for achieving organizational goals.

We have said that formal authority is the legitimate power associated with an organizational position. In this section, however, we will use the word *authority* to make a distinction between *line authority* and *staff authority.* Not all authors agree that this distinction is meaningful,[12] but line and staff authority are such pervasive elements in organizations that they need to be examined and understood. Figure 12-3 elaborates on the various interactions possible in line- and staff-position systems.

Line Authority

Every organization exists to achieve specific goals. Line managers may be defined as those people in the organization who are directly responsible for achieving these goals. **Line authority** is represented by the standard chain of command, starting with the board of directors and extending down through the various levels in the hierarchy to the point where the basic activities of the organization are carried out.

Since line activities are identified in terms of the company's goals, the activities classified as line will differ in each organization. For example, a manufacturing company may limit line functions to production and sales, while a department store, in which buying is a key element, will include the purchasing department as well as the sales department in its line activities.

When an organization is small, all positions may be line roles; staff roles are added as the organization grows and finds it useful to hire specialists to assist the line members in doing their primary jobs.[13]

Staff Authority

staff authority The authority of those groups of individuals who provide line managers with advice and services.

Staff authority belongs to those individuals or groups in an organization who provide services and advice to line. The concept of staff includes all elements of the organization that are not classified as line. Advisory staffs have been used by decision makers from emperors and kings to parliamentary governments and dictatorships over the course of recorded history.[14]

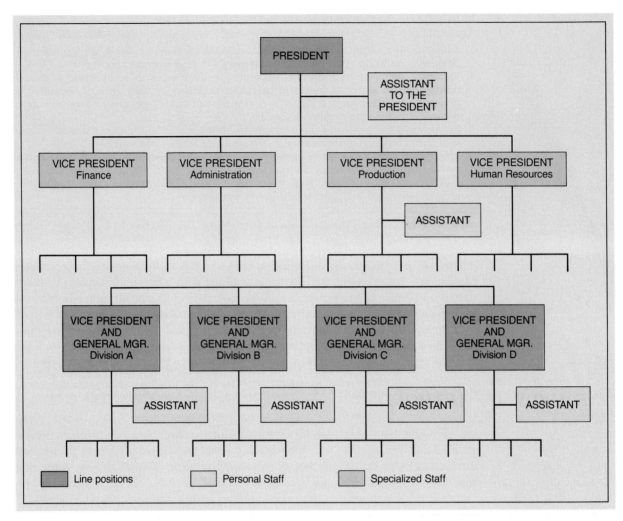

FIGURE 12-3 Line and Staff Positions

Coordinated Resource
Use Transparency 74, Three Views of Staff Assistants.

Staff provides managers with varied types of expert help and advice. Staff can offer line managers planning advice through research, analysis, and options development. Staff can also assist in policy implementation, monitoring, and control, in legal and financial matters, and in the design and operation of data-processing systems.[15]

It is sometimes difficult to distinguish between line and staff: Line managers seem to be performing staff functions, and staff members seem to have some line responsibilities. Staff personnel, however, devote most of their time to providing services and advice to line members, while line managers tend to focus directly on producing the organization's products or services.

Coordinated Resource
Use Transparency 75, Functional Authority and "Dotted-Line" Relationships.

Functional Authority

functional authority
The authority of staff department members to control the activities of other departments that are related to specific staff responsibilities.

The role of staff members to provide advice and service to line members implies that staff lacks independent, formal authority. In reality, staff departments, especially those responsible for audit functions, may have formal authority over line members within the limits of their functions. The right to control activities of other departments as they relate to specific staff responsibilities is known as **functional authority.** In Figure 12-4, the finance manager of Division A reports through the chain of command to the general manager of Division A, but is also responsible to the vice president for finance at the corporate level in a "dotted-line" relationship representing the functional authority between specialized staff and line managers.

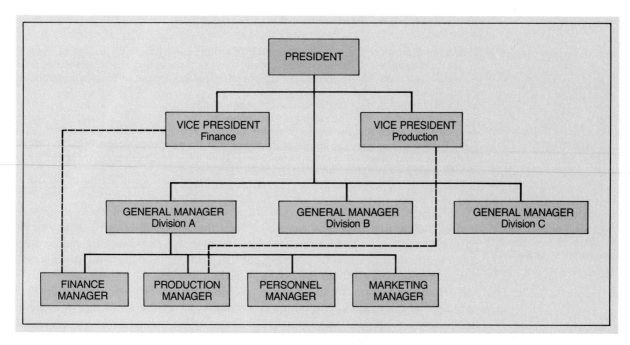

FIGURE 12-4 Functional Authority and "Dotted-Line" Relationships

The need for functional authority arises from the need for a degree of uniformity and an unhindered application of expertise in carrying out many organizational activities. For this reason, functional authority is common in organizations. The skills required to manage functional authority relationships and the problems arising from those relationships are similar to the skills required to manage dual-boss relationships in matrix organizations.

■ *DELEGATION*

delegation The act of assigning formal authority and responsibility for completion of specific activities to a subordinate.

scalar principle The concept that a clear line of authority through the organization must exist if delegation is to work successfully.

We may define **delegation** as the assignment to another person of formal authority and accountability for carrying out specific activities. The delegation of authority by superiors to subordinates is obviously necessary for the efficient functioning of any organization, since no superior can personally accomplish or completely supervise all the organization's tasks.

Delegation, Authority, Accountability, and Responsibility

Note that our definition designates precisely what can be delegated—*authority* and *accountability.* But note also that this definition implicitly raises two closely related questions: Can *authority* be delegated? Can *responsibility* be delegated? Our definition has already answered the first of these two questions: There is little debate concerning the delegation of *authority*—it can and should be delegated. This is the basis of the **scalar principle,** the idea that a clear line of authority runs step by step from the highest to the lowest level of the organization. This clear line of authority, then, is the basis for all delegation. Thus, a manager might choose to delegate the authority to subordinates to make expenditures without approval—at least up to a stipulated amount. However, considerable debate often arises with regard to the delegation of *responsibility.* A close analysis of this debate often reveals that it is more the result of semantics—of the variables occurring in the use of language in different contexts—rather than a misunderstanding of the concepts involved.

EXHIBIT 12-3 What Delegation Is Not

1. It is not abdication: It is not simply a matter of giving people jobs to do and telling them to get them done. When this approach is taken, the results the manager wants or expects are seldom achieved. The recipients of this type of delegation are put in the position of being second-guessed at the end of the job.
2. It is not abandonment of the manager's responsibility.
3. It does not mean that the manager loses control.
4. It does not mean that the manager avoids making decisions: The manager who delegates still makes decisions. The important point is that he or she can concentrate on those decisions and issues of most importance and allow subordinates to make those decisions which are best made at the point of direct contact.

COORDINATED RESOURCE
Use Transparency 77, Degrees of Delegation Along the Spectrum of Authority.

Those contending that responsibility cannot be delegated support their position by stating that managers can never shed the responsibilities of their jobs by passing them on to subordinates. Those contending that responsibility can be delegated justify their position by pointing out that managers can certainly make subordinates responsible to them for certain actions.

However, responsibility is not like an object that can be passed from individual to individual. For example, suppose a loan manager for a bank decided to delegate to his or her loan officers the responsibility for ensuring that all loans are processed within the 10-day limit stated by bank policy. The loan manager can certainly make the loan officers *accountable* regarding the matter. At the same time, the loan manager is no less *responsible* to his or her boss—that is, he or she is *responsible* for seeing that the activity is carried out, for explaining why it was not, and/or correcting any problems that are caused by the actions of his or her subordinates. In short, one does not delegate responsibility, because responsibility always remains with the delegating manager.

Perhaps we can get a better idea of what delegation *is* by looking at Exhibit 12-3, which specifies what delegation *is not*.

Although delegation is the transfer of legitimate power, it relates to the other power bases as well. When formal authority is conferred, the power to reward and punish goes with it to some extent. Expert power can also be indirectly conveyed by delegation: The subordinate who now acts in place of the superior will acquire expert power to the extent that he or she develops the necessary skills to perform the task.

The Advantages of Delegation

When used properly, delegation has several important advantages. The first and most obvious is that the more tasks managers are able to delegate, the more opportunity they have to seek and accept increased responsibilities from higher-level managers. Thus, as managers, we will try to delegate not only routine matters but also tasks requiring thought and initiative, so that we will be free to function with maximum effectiveness for our organizations.

Another advantage of delegation is that it frequently leads to better decisions, since subordinates closest to the "firing line" are likely to have a clearer view of the facts. For example, the West Coast sales manager will be in a better position than the vice president of sales to allocate the California sales territories.

Effective delegation also speeds up decision making. Valuable time is lost when subordinates must check with their superiors (who then may have to check with *their* superiors) before making a decision. This delay is eliminated when subordinates are authorized to make the necessary decision on the spot. In addition, delegation causes subordinates to accept accountability and exercise judgment. This not only helps train subordinates—an important advantage of delegation—but also improves their self-confidence and willingness to take initiative.

Delegating Authority. To carry out Alcoa CEO Paul O'Neill's strategic focus on safety, specially trained hourly workers observe fellow workers and then discuss any deviations that might cause accidents. The observers strip out worker names before making their reports to managers.

Barriers to Delegation

Despite these advantages, many managers are as reluctant to delegate authority as subordinates are to accept it. Managers often have a number of excuses for not delegating: "I can do it better myself"; "My subordinates just aren't capable enough"; "It takes too much time to explain what I want done." The real reason may be the manager is simply too disorganized or inflexible to delegate work effectively.

Other barriers to delegation are insecurity and confusion about who is ultimately responsible for a specific task—the manager or the subordinate. Managers cannot sidestep their responsibility to higher-ups simply by delegating difficult or unpleasant tasks to subordinates. They are always accountable for the action of their subordinates—a fact that makes some of them reluctant to take a chance on delegating. Others fear that delegating authority to a subordinate reduces their own authority. Still others feel threatened if their subordinate does "too good" a job. Some subordinates, on the other hand, want to avoid responsibility and risks; they prefer that their managers to make all the decisions. These barriers can be overcome if we follow certain guidelines for effective delegation.

Guidelines for Effective Delegation

Delegation was an important subject to early management writers, who created the classical guidelines shown in Exhibit 12-4. Although many of these guidelines are still valid, they are based on the classical top-to-bottom view of authority in organizations, and therefore do not recognize that it is a subordinate's acceptance of authority that largely determines the manager's effectiveness. Another limitation of the classical guidelines arises from the complexity of modern organizational structures. For instance, the matrix structure, in which employees report to two managers, violates the **unity-of-command principle**—the idea that each employee should answer to only one supervisor.[16] (See Chapter 2.)

For these reasons, the classical guidelines have been modified slightly. The most basic prerequisite to effective delegation remains the manager's willingness to give subordinates real freedom to accomplish delegated tasks. This means letting them choose different methods and solutions than the ones the manager would have chosen. It also means giving them the freedom to make mistakes and to learn from their mistakes. Subordinate mistakes are not an excuse to stop delegating, but rather an opportunity to offer training and support.

EXHIBIT 12-4 Classical Guidelines for Effective Delegation

1. *Establish a clear line of authority running from the highest to the lowest level of authority.* This rule, known as the scalar principle, helps organization members understand to whom they can delegate, who can delegate to them, and to whom they are accountable.
2. *To avoid confusion, each person should be accountable to just one superior.* This is known as the unity-of-command principle.
3. *Assign accountability for specific tasks to the lowest organizational level at which sufficient ability and information exist to carry them out completely.* Checking time cards, for example, would be delegated to lower-level supervisors rather than to division heads.
4. *Give subordinates sufficient authority to carry out delegated tasks.* A sales manager who is expected to meet a certain quota would be handicapped without the authority to assign territories, reward effective salespeople, and fire incompetents.
5. *Be sure subordinates realize they are responsible for specific results.* This does not mean the managers are no longer responsible for delegated tasks; it merely means that managers must communicate tasks and goals clearly to subordinates and influence them to accept the authority and responsibility for those tasks.

Source: Adapted from James D. Mooney and Alan C. Reiley, *The Principles of Organization* (New York: Harper & Row, 1939), pp. 14–19, 23–24; and S. Avery Raub, *Company Organization Charts* (New York: National Industrial Conference Board, 1964).

COORDINATED RESOURCE
The Application Exercise for Chapter 12 found in the Lecture Extras supplement is a role-playing exercise in delegating.

COORDINATED RESOURCE
See Samaras Case 3.2, "To Delegate or Not."

COORDINATED RESOURCE
See Samaras Reading "Delegation for Employee Development."

unity-of-command principle A guideline for delegation that states that each individual in an organization should report to only one superior.

COORDINATED RESOURCE
See Geis and Kuhn Chapter 4, "Successful Delegation—Be a Leader."

A second prerequisite for delegation is open communication between managers and subordinates. Managers who know the capabilities of their subordinates can more realistically decide which tasks can be delegated to whom. Subordinates who are encouraged to use their abilities and who feel their managers will back them up will, in turn, be more likely to accept responsibility.[17] The third prerequisite for delegation is the manager's ability to analyze such factors as the organization's culture, the task's requirements, and the subordinate's capabilities.[18] These prerequisites are all important to carrying out the following tasks of effective delegation:

1. *Decide which tasks can be delegated.* Many items can and should be delegated. Some of these are minor decisions, recurring chores, etc. However, unusually demanding and challenging assignments may often be delegated to your subordinates and will do much to develop them.

2. *Decide who should get the assignment.* Who has available time? Does the job require special competence? For whom would it be an appropriate and useful developmental experience? Ask yourself these questions when deciding which of your people should get the assignment.

3. *Delegate the assignment.* Provide all relevant information on the task. As far as possible, delegate by results expected, not by methods to be used. Cultivate a climate of free and open communication between yourself and the person to whom you have delegated the task.

4. *Establish a feedback system.* Provide for a system of checkpoints and/or feedback information so that you will remain advised of progress. Select your feedback system carefully, however, bearing in mind that the tighter your controls, the less the delegation that is actually taking place.

ILLUSTRATIVE CASE STUDY

CONTINUED

Responsiveness and Restructuring at IBM

Although IBM had often reorganized during the course of its history, this most recent change may well be its most important in several decades because it is a major attempt to delegate authority *down* in the organization. For years, most major decisions were made or reviewed by a six-person executive committee.

Now authority for a huge number of decisions has been delegated to the six divisional committees. Division heads act as if they are running their own businesses, no longer needing to seek and wait for permission to try new things that may modify or violate traditional IBM policy.

Paradoxically, Akers *relinquished* some control and authority in order to *maintain* control and authority. This notion of giving up control to gain control is not peculiar to IBM, according to Robert Waterman, who argues that one of the hallmarks of companies that have successfully renewed themselves is their ability to delegate authority to all levels in the organization. For IBM, such an extensive program of decentralization represents a major change.

■ JOB DESIGN

job design The division of an organization's work among its employees.

HERE'S AN EXAMPLE
At Rainwater Inc., a Fort Worth investment company, founder Richard E. Rainwater despises memos, bureaucracy, and big titles. (*Business Week*, 6/11/90, p. 48ff.)

FOR DISCUSSION
What are the potential negative consequences of poorly designed jobs?

The structure of authority in organizations is directly related to the ways in which jobs are designed. Some jobs are designed to afford employees wide latitude in decision making, while others permit the exercise of very little authority. There is a growing body of research on the subject of **job design,** but before we explore some of the ideas that have come out of these studies, let us recall a fateful day that affected the very idea of organizational behavior, not only in the United States, but throughout the world.

In late March 1979, the core of a nuclear reactor on Three Mile Island in Pennsylvania almost melted down. The island happens to be near Harrisburg, the state capital. If a meltdown had actually occurred, many thousands of people might have died. The problem was not the reactor. The problem was that the jobs of the people who operated the reactor were "actually (though inadvertently) designed to be error-prone—that is, designed for disaster."[19] For example, the hundreds of lights and gauges that told the operators what was happening inside the reactor were hard to see. Even when the workers could read the indicators, the equipment was hard to use because the reactor's controls were often far removed from the lights and gauges that indicated what effect the controls were having.[20]

These problems had nothing to do with the internal design of the reactor. Even if the reactor itself had been flawless, its controls—the interface between the reactor and those who ran it—made a disaster quite likely. At bottom, that disaster was a failure of perceptual/motor job design, not of equipment or people. This is just one of the approaches to job design we will discuss.

Approaches to Job Design

Experts have been thinking about job design for at least a century. We will now take a look at the four basic ways of viewing the subject: the mechanistic, motivational, biological, and perceptual/motor approaches.

MECHANISTIC JOB DESIGN.   Consider the jobs of factory workers on an assembly line. Each worker is required to do only one or two simple things, over and over again. Most of these jobs are fairly easy to learn and to do. Such jobs are suited to the mechanistic approach to job design, inspired by the turn-of-the-century researcher Frederick W. Taylor, the "father of scientific management" (see Chapter 2) who systematically attempted to make jobs simple and efficient.

Jobs designed in this way are usually rather boring. The workers who hold them tend to be dissatisfied and unmotivated and to have high rates of absenteeism and on-the-job injury. Jobs that require workers to be alert and to perform more than one function—for example, the jobs of the operators at Three Mile Island—are not suited to this approach.

COORDINATED RESOURCE
Acumen: People scoring high on the Self-Actualization scale have a wide range of interests and are knowledgeable about a variety of different areas. For those scoring low on this scale, the *Acumen* report suggests seeking out new situations both in and outside the workplace. Cross-training would be a way to do this.

COORDINATED RESOURCE
Use Transparency 78, The Job Characteristics Model.

MOTIVATIONAL JOB DESIGN.   As the limits of the mechanistic approach become clear, researchers began to seek out ways of making jobs more varied and challenging. J. Richard Hackman and others[21] who wished to motivate workers to do their jobs have come up with five core jobs dimensions: skill variety, task identity, task significance, autonomy, and feedback. Table 12-1 describes these dimensions and gives examples of them.

Hackman argues that employees who have responsible jobs they understand are more motivated and satisfied with their positions.[22] People whose jobs involve high levels of skill variety, task identity, and task significance experience work as very meaningful. A high level of autonomy makes workers more responsible and accountable for their acts. Feedback gives them a useful understanding of their specific roles and functions. The more of all five characteristics a job has, the more likely it is that the person who holds it will be highly motivated and satisfied.

TABLE 12-1 Task Characteristics

CHARACTERISTIC	DESCRIPTION	HIGH DEGREE	LOW DEGREE
Skill variety—the extent to which a variety of skills and talents are required to complete assigned tasks.	Perform different tasks that challenge the intellect and develop skills in coordination.	Dress designer	Messenger
Task identity—the extent to which the job involves completion of an identifiable unit, project, or other piece of work.	Handle an entire job function from start to finish and be able to show a tangible piece of work as the outcome.	Software designer	Assembly-line worker
Task significance—the extent to which the task affects the work or lives of others, inside or outside the organization.	Be involved in a job function that is important for the well-being, safety, and perhaps survival of others.	Air traffic controller	House painter
Autonomy—the extent of the individual's freedom on the job and discretion to schedule tasks and determine procedures for carrying them out.	Be responsible for the success or failure of a job function and be able to plan work schedule, control quality, etc.	Project manager	Cashier in a department store
Feedback—the extent to which the individual receives specific information (praise, blame, etc.) about the effectiveness with which his or her tasks are performed.	Learn about the effectiveness of one's job performance through clear and direct evaluation from a supervisor or colleagues or the results of the work itself.	Professional athlete	Security guard

Much effort has been concentrated on making routine jobs more rewarding. These efforts fall into three broad categories: job enlargement, job enrichment, and flexible work schedules.

Job enlargement stems from the thinking of industrial engineers. The idea behind it is to break up the monotony of a limited routine and work cycle by increasing a job's scope. Work functions from a horizontal slice of an organizational unit are combined, thereby giving each employee more operations to perform. For example, the work from two or more positions may be combined to restore some sense of the wholeness of the job. Or workers may be shifted routinely from job to job within the same company so they can develop a variety of skills. Job rotation of this sort motivates workers by challenging them.

Another basic strategy was inspired by motivational theory. **Job enrichment** tries to deal with dissatisfied workers by increasing the depth of their jobs. Work activities from a vertical slice of the organizational unit are combined into one position so that employees have more autonomy on the job. The idea is to develop a stronger sense of accountability by allowing workers to set their own work pace, correct their own errors, and decide the best way to perform various tasks. They may also be asked to help make decisions that affect their own subunits. As the work becomes more challenging and worker responsibility increases, motivation and enthusiasm should increase as well.[23]

Because job enrichment involves the delegation of accountability, one way to think about this mode of delegation is through the concept of **empowerment.** The manager literally gives the subordinate the power to act and accomplish his or her goals. Empowerment means autonomy, and it rests on a relationship of trust between superior and subordinate. The obvious question here is: Who is ultimately *responsible?* According to the principle of empowerment, responsibility devolves upon the subordinates but can never be abdicated by the manager. The answer to the question, then, is: *Both* the subordinate and the manager. Consider the illustration provided in the Management Application box entitled "Quality at Huffy Corporation." Huffy workers were urged to take responsibility for product quality. Authority was delegated to them and jobs were designed so that responsibility was jointly determined by workers and management.

job enlargement The combining of various operations at a similar level into one job to provide more variety for workers and thus increase their motivation and satisfaction. An increase in job scope.

job enrichment The combining of several activities from a vertical cross section of the organization into one job to provide the worker with more autonomy and responsibility. An increase in job depth.

empowerment The act of delegating power and authority to a subordinate so that the goals of the manager can be accomplished.

Job Enlargement at Corning. Like other workers at Corning's Blacksburg, Virginia, plant, Robert Hubble works on a self-managed team made up of workers with interchangeable skills, gained through company-sponsored training programs that teach employees at least three skill "modules," or families of related skills, plus interpersonal skills. Says Hubble, "We have a lot of responsibility, but that makes me feel good. . . . I'm responsible for my own job security."

MANAGEMENT APPLICATION

Quality at Huffy Corporation

Huffy Corporation, a bicycle manufacturer, was in a squeeze in 1982. Manufacturing costs had to be cut by at least 20 percent to meet the competition. Japanese imports had increased dramatically, and competition in the American market had never been so fierce. The usual way to cut costs was to increase plant automation and fire line workers, most of whom had been with Huffy all their working lives. Early in 1983, however, Huffy found it had to close a brand-new plant in Oklahoma because the automated equipment simply could not do the job.

Huffy decided to take another approach. The company enlisted the support of its employees in a radical quality and productivity program. Management made the employees responsible for product quality, delegating to them both the authority to act and the responsibility for results. In short, they were "empowered." Now all workers and production teams routinely inspect their own work and fix any defects. Only perfect products count toward their quotas. They also act as a quality control on the people or machines just before them in the production process. In this way, problems are noticed and corrected before the bikes are assembled.

Huffy's plant in Celina, Ohio, is now the most productive bicycle factory in the world. Workers there turn out bikes in a third to a quarter of the time it takes in Japan. And quality is up. Inspectors who randomly take apart finished bikes rarely find anything wrong these days. Huffy employees now collect a second check each month, worth about 5 to 8 percent of their basic wages, as part of a special gain-sharing program. The company calculates its cost savings each month by comparing the factory's output with the hours logged by employees. This money is split fifty-fifty with the employees.

Source: Ralph E. Winter, "Upgrading of Factories Replaces the Concept of Total Automation," *The Wall Street Journal,* November 30, 1987, pp. 1, 8.

Job enlargement and job enrichment attempt to make work itself more meaningful. Alternative work schedules, by contrast, try to make work hours more convenient and to enhance the quality of nonwork time. Two kinds of alternative work schedules are today being incorporated into organizational structures: the compressed workweek and flextime.

Employees whose schedules have been compressed usually exchange the traditional five-day week for a week of four or even three days. Instead of working 8 hours a day for five days (5/40), they may work 10 hours a day for four days (4/40), or 12 hours a day for three (3/36)—or any other combination that suits them and their employers. Such work schedules let employees share household responsibilities with their spouse, attend school, or pursue other activities of their own choosing.[24]

The advantage to the company of the compressed workweek is a reduction in the costs of overtime, overhead, and personal-leave time. Small manufacturing or service operations are often well suited to such a schedule—especially those that demand little or no physical work, so there is no danger that tired workers will hurt themselves. Young or newly hired workers especially like the compressed workweek because of the extra leisure time it permits. By contrast, workers who are used to the standard Monday-to-Friday, 9-to-5 routine generally take longer to adjust to a compressed workweek, and some resist it altogether.

Flextime, which is more widespread in Europe than in the United States, permits employees to arrange their daily work hours to suit their personal needs and lifestyles. One attractive aspect of flextime is that it lets workers avoid rush-hour travel.

Flextime typically requires employees to be on the job during a core period—often about 4 hours in the middle of the day—but allows them to choose their own starting and ending times. Employees are therefore responsible for coordinating their functions with other employees—which means they have more responsibility and autonomy than most workers do. Flextime is particularly suited to companies whose work loads fluctuate from hour to hour within a single day. It is not usually suited to assembly-line operations.[25]

BIOLOGICAL JOB DESIGN. We have already seen that jobs involving little physical work are suited to compressed schedules, since there is less danger that tired workers will hurt themselves. Such considerations have given rise to a whole new ap-

flextime A system that permits employees to arrange their work hours to suit their personal needs.

FOR DISCUSSION
What are the *individual* and *organizational* advantages of alternative work schedules?

Biological Job Design. Ergonomics consultant Lori Monson uses a goniometer to measure the angle of *Business Week* writer Suzanne Woolley's neck, an important factor in easing back and neck pain caused by working long hours at a terminal.

proach to job design. This biological approach, sometimes called *ergonomics,* is a systematic attempt to make work as safe as possible.

The biological approach has been used extensively in heavy industry (such as steel, mining, and construction), both to make jobs safer and to help women do the kind of physically demanding work that used to be done only by men. In offices, ergonomic techniques can reduce the back- and eyestrain suffered by employees who spend their days sitting in chairs, looking at computer screens.

PERCEPTUAL/MOTOR JOB DESIGN. Experimental psychology has suggested yet another approach to job design. Just as the biological approach tries to ensure that the physical demands of a job do not exceed the physical capabilities of the people who do it, the perceptual/motor approach seeks to ensure that the mental demands of their work do not exceed workers' mental capabilities. For example, the jobs of the people who operated the reactor at Three Mile Island had been poorly designed from the perceptual/motor point of view, since the operators had to respond to excessive amounts of information from the lights and gauges. The problem with the perceptual/motor approach, as with the mechanistic approach, is that jobs can be made so simple that they become boring.

Job Design and Job Satisfaction

COORDINATED RESOURCE

Use Transparency 79, Guidelines for Job Redesign.

As you can see in Table 12-2, each of these four ways of designing jobs has advantages and disadvantages. The mechanistic approach cuts training time and error rates, but also job motivation and satisfaction. The motivational approach promotes job motivation and satisfaction, but involves more training time and a higher risk of error and stress. The biological approach can be expensive, although it cuts the effort and fatigue of many jobs. The perceptual/motor approach, like the mechanistic one, tends to make jobs less satisfying, although (like the biological approach) it also makes them safer.

TABLE 12-2 Summary of Outcomes from the Job-Design Approaches

JOB-DESIGN APPROACH	POSITIVE OUTCOMES	NEGATIVE OUTCOMES
Mechanistic	Decreased training time Higher utilization levels Lower likelihood of error Less chance of mental overload and stress	Lower job satisfaction Lower motivation Higher absenteeism
Motivational	Higher job satisfaction Higher motivation Greater job involvement Higher job performance Lower absenteeism	Increased training time Lower utilization levels Greater likelihood of error Greater chance of mental overload and stress
Biological	Less physical effort Less physical fatigue Fewer health complaints Fewer medical incidents Lower absenteeism Higher job satisfaction	Higher financial costs because of changes in equipment or job environment
Perceptual/Motor	Lower likelihood of error Lower likelihood of accidents Less chance of mental overload and stress Lower training time Higher utilization levels	Lower job satisfaction Lower motivation

Source: Reprinted, by permission of American Management Association, from Michael A. Campion and Paul W. Thayer, "Job Design: Approaches, Outcomes, and Trade-Offs," *Organizational Dynamics,* Autumn 1973, p. 76. © 1973 American Management Association, New York. All rights reserved.

In fact, these four approaches to job design differ in degree rather than in kind. They can be thought of as a continuum. On one end of the continuum lie jobs designed with the motivational approach, maximizing the individual worker's job satisfaction and motivation, and at the other end are jobs designed with the mechanistic and perceptual/motor approaches, promoting organizational ends by limiting the scope of jobs in order to use equipment more efficiently.

The relationship between job design and job satisfaction is complex. Motivational theorists have argued that the more we use job-enrichment and job-enlargement techniques, the more satisfied individual employees will be. A study by Charles Hulin and Milton Blood concluded that satisfaction or dissatisfaction with specialized jobs depends to a great extent on employees' own attitudes.[26] Those who accept the "Protestant work ethic"—that is, who see work as important and meaningful and who strongly desire financial success—are likely to become dissatisfied in jobs that are too specialized.

Those who feel alienated, however, are likely to prefer narrower, more restricted jobs because they are easier and require little attention or commitment. Hackman, who has drawn similar conclusions, refers to a "growth need" rather than to the Protestant work ethic. His studies indicate that people with high growth needs will be more satisfied in expanded and challenging jobs than individuals with low growth needs.[27]

One group of researchers, reviewing 28 separate research studies of job satisfaction,[28] found that the relationship between job satisfaction and the characteristics of jobs themselves is higher in those employees who have high growth needs. This conclusion supports Hackman's research. In those employees with lower needs for growth and development, situational characteristics—like work group or management support for a job-enrichment program—may be more important.

Gerald Salancik and Jeffrey Pfeffer also argue that social dimensions are important to job satisfaction. Social influences may affect not only the way people value their jobs but also how they describe them. It has been shown, for example, that the extent to which a supervisor engages in "small talk" and offers advice on how to do a job affects the extent to which employees feel independent.[29] In addition, a number of researchers have concluded that workers' personality traits have a great impact on job satisfaction.

Job design is complex and often difficult. Managers must often make trade-offs between characteristics that are both good in themselves: between simplicity and motivation, for example. To make sensible choices, you must understand all four approaches, as well as the strengths and weaknesses of each.

■ DECENTRALIZATION

decentralization The delegation of power and authority from higher to lower levels of the organization, often accomplished by the creation of small, self-contained organizational units.

centralization The extent to which authority is concentrated at the top of the organization.

The delegation of authority by individual managers and the design of jobs in organizations are closely related to an organization's decentralization of authority. Delegation is the process of assigning authority or accountability from one level of management down to the next. Job design is based on the amount of authority and accountability delegated to an employee. The concepts of decentralization and centralization refer to the extent to which authority and accountability have been passed down to lower levels (**decentralization**) or have been retained at the top of the organization (**centralization**). This terminology derives from a perspective of the organization as a series of concentric circles. The chief executive of the organization is situated in the very center and a "web" of authority radiates out from him or her. The greater the amount of authority delegated throughout the organization, the more decentralized the organization is. For example, the freer lower-level managers are to spend significant sums on equipment or supplies without first checking with higher-level managers, the more decentralized the organization is.

Centralization at Delta.
Bucking the trend to de-
centralization, Delta Chairman and CEO Ronald W.
Allen insists that every
expenditure over $5,000,
with the exception of jet
fuel, be approved by top
management, saying the
system lets Delta cut costs
at the first sign of a downturn.

There is considerable confusion between the terms *decentralization* and
divisionalization. Part of this confusion stems from the tendency to refer to divisionalized firms as decentralized and to functionally structured firms as centralized.
After all, the most obvious example of an increase in decentralization is an organization that moves from a centralized functional structure to a decentralized divisional
structure. Furthermore, many of the advantages of divisionalization, as discussed in
Chapter 11, also apply to decentralization. The two, however, are not the same. Any
divisionalized organization may be relatively centralized or decentralized in its operations.

The advantages of decentralization are similar to the advantages of delegation:
unburdening of top managers; improved decision making because decisions are
made closer to the scene of action; better training, morale, and initiative at lower
levels; and more flexibility and faster decision making in rapidly changing environments. These advantages are so compelling that it is tempting to think of decentralization as "good" and centralization as "bad."

But total decentralization, with no coordination and leadership from the top,
would clearly be undesirable. The very purpose of organization—efficient integration of subunits for the good of the whole—would be defeated without some centralized control. For this reason, the question for managers is not whether an organization should be decentralized but to what extent it should be decentralized.

As we will see, the appropriate amount of decentralization will vary with time
and circumstances. It will also vary for the different subunits of the organization. For
example, production and sales departments have gained a high degree of decentralization in many companies, whereas financial departments have tended to remain
comparatively centralized.

Factors Influencing Decentralization

Decentralization has value only to the extent that it helps an organization achieve its
objectives. In determining the amount of decentralization appropriate for an organization, the following factors are usually considered: (1) environmental influences,
such as market characteristics, competitive pressures, and availability of materials;
(2) the organization's size and growth rate; and (3) other characteristics of the
organization, such as costliness of given decisions, top management preferences, the
organization's culture, and abilities of lower-level managers.[30]

The first two factors help to determine the logical degree of decentralization—
they suggest what top managers *should* do. The last factor suggests what managers
are *likely* to do. For example, a particular supermarket chain might be better off if
each store manager had some discretion in adapting purchasing and pricing policies
to local conditions, but an autocratic top management is unwilling to delegate this
authority. Either top management will have to change their attitude or they will have
to accept losses in some areas at the hands of competitors.

STRATEGY AND THE ORGANIZATION'S ENVIRONMENT. An organization's strategy
will influence the types of markets, technological environment, and competition
with which the organization must contend. These factors will, in turn, influence the
degree of decentralization that the firm finds appropriate. Alfred Chandler found that
firms, such as Westinghouse and General Electric, that developed new products
through a strategy of research and development that led to product diversification,
chose a decentralized structure. Other companies, operating in industries in which
markets were more predictable, production processes less dynamic technologically,
and competitive relationships more stable, tended to remain or become more centralized. United States Steel, for example, became more, rather than less, centralized
in the first half of this century.[31]

SIZE AND RATE OF GROWTH. It is virtually impossible to run a large organization efficiently while vesting all decision-making authority in a few top managers. Size is almost certainly the strongest single force for delegation, and hence for decentralization.

As an organization continues to grow in size and complexity, decentralization tends to increase. The faster the rate of growth, the more likely it is that upper management, bearing the weight of an ever-increasing work load, will be forced to accelerate the delegation of authority to lower levels. When the growth rate slows, however, upper management may attempt to regain decision-making authority under the guise of "tightening things up" and protecting profits.

OTHER CHARACTERISTICS OF THE ORGANIZATION. The extent to which decision-making authority is centralized is also likely to be influenced by such internal characteristics of the company as:

1. *The cost and risk associated with the decision.* Managers may be wary of delegating authority for decisions that could have a heavy impact on the performance of their own subunits or of the organization as a whole. This caution is out of consideration for both the company's welfare and their own, since the delegator retains responsibility for the results.

2. *An individual manager's preference and confidence in subordinates.* Some managers pride themselves on their detailed knowledge of everything that happens within their area of responsibility ("the good manager runs a tight ship" approach). Others take equal pride in confidently delegating everything possible to their subordinates in order to avoid getting bogged down in petty details and to save their own expertise for the unit's major objectives.

3. *The organizational culture.* The shared norms, values, and understandings (culture) of members of some organizations support tight control at the top. The culture of other organizations supports the opposite. The history of an organization helps to create its current culture. A firm that has had slow growth under a strong-willed leader may have a very centralized structure. In contrast, a firm that has grown rapidly through acquisitions will have learned to live with the greater independence of the acquired companies.

4. *The abilities of lower-level managers.* This dimension is, in part, circular. If authority is not delegated because managers lack faith in the talent below, the talent will not have much opportunity to develop. In addition, the lack of internal training will make it more difficult to find and hold talented and ambitious people, and this, in turn, will make it more difficult to decentralize.

Trends in Decentralization

The period from the end of World War II to the early 1970s was a time of great economic growth in the United States. On balance, decentralization probably increased during this period. From the 1970s to the mid-1980s, low rates of economic growth, pressure from foreign competition, and eventually the competitive disadvantages arising from the strength of the U.S. dollar encouraged centralization; many companies sought ways to increase productivity by eliminating costly duplication of functions.

The clear trend today is toward more decentralization. Many companies have "restructured," which often means simply eliminating staff jobs and pushing decision-making authority farther down the organization. GE, AT&T, and Eastman Kodak, to name but a few, have eliminated thousands of corporate staff jobs in an effort to decentralize. At the same time, advances in information technology have made centralized control systems much more sophisticated. At The Limited and other retailers, every sale feeds into an inventory system so that stores can be restocked automatically according to their own needs. Information systems allow some pro-

HERE'S AN EXAMPLE
At Sun Microsystems, a $2.5 billion workstation company, CEO Scott McNealy recently reorganized his company to give more direct responsibility for some key activities to his top managers. (*Business Week*, 2/25/91, p. 47)

THOUGHT PROVOKER
Some effective executives have chosen to operate as No. 2 at winning corporations rather than be CEO someplace else. "It's like having Ruth and Gehrig in the same line-up. You can't walk one to get to the other, so they both hit a lot of homers." Discuss the implications of this.

HERE'S AN EXAMPLE
At Daewoo, Chairman Kim Woo-Choong, once a "hands-off manager," is taking control and slashing executive ranks. (*Business Week*, 2/18/91, p. 68ff.)

CLASS COMMENT
With the flattening of the corporate pyramid in many companies, more managers are doing hands-on work in teams. An increasing number are even working in open areas so they can interact easily with employees. (*Business Month*, September 1990, p. 5)

cesses to be centrally controlled, while decentralizing decision making to the managers closest to the customer. Indeed, the issue of decentralization promises to be one of the most hotly debated topics in the years to come.

∎ *SUMMARY*

Power, influence, and authority are necessary elements of organizational life. From a classical viewpoint, formal authority is a legitimate managerial right that subordinates are obligated to recognize. From an "acceptance" viewpoint, formal authority is legitimized by subordinates.

There are five sources or bases of power: reward, coercive, legitimate, expert, and referent. In exercising their power, managers may take a dominance-submission approach toward subordinates, or they may use a more positive style based on concern for group goals and the encouragement and support of subordinates. The latter approach seems to work better, and effective managers are those who have learned to temper their use of power with maturity and self-control.

Line positions can be defined as those directly responsible for achieving the organization's goals. *Staff positions* provide expert advice and service to the line.

Effective delegation helps an organization use its resources efficiently—it frees managers for important tasks, improves decision making, and encourages initiative. Classical guidelines for effective delegation include the need to give subordinates authority and accountability and the need to follow the scalar principle and the principle of unity of command. These guidelines, however, do not apply to all situations.

The structure of authority in organizations is directly related to the organization's policies for job design. The mechanistic approach to job design seeks to make all jobs as efficient and simple as possible; jobs so designed tend to be dull. The motivational approach attempts to inspire workers by increasing the skill variety, task identity, task significance, autonomy, and feedback involved in their work; job enrichment and job enlargement are ways to enhance such task characteristics and heighten work involvement. The biological approach attempts to ensure that the physical demands of work do not exceed the physical capacities of those who do it.

Likewise, the perceptual/motor approach seeks to ensure that the mental demands of work do not exceed workers' mental capacities.

Delegation is closely related to decentralization in the sense that the greater the amount of delegation, the more decentralized the organization. The appropriate amount of decentralization for a particular organization will depend on external environmental forces, the organization's size and growth, and its culture. The current trend, fueled both by corporate restructuring and by advances in information technology, is toward decentralization.

■ *REVIEW QUESTIONS*

1. What are the two major views of authority? How do you think each view would affect a manager's attitude and behavior toward subordinates?

2. What is the "zone of indifference"?

3. What are the five bases of power described by French and Raven? Give one example of a manager's exercise of each type of power.

4. What are the "two faces of power" described by David McClelland?

5. What are the characteristics of successful power users?

6. What is the difference between line positions and staff positions? Is the difference always clear in organizations?

7. What does the phrase *functional staff authority* mean?

8. What are the advantages of delegation? Describe the key guidelines for effective delegation.

9. What are the advantages of job specialization? Why did it emerge?

10. What is the purpose of job enlargement and job enrichment?

11. How are decentralization and delegation related?

12. What factors influence the extent to which an organization is decentralized?

13. Do you believe there will be a trend toward centralization or decentralization over the next several years? Why?

CASE STUDY

The Use and Abuse of Joyce Roberts

Joyce Roberts, 29 years old, was a middle-level manager at Amalgamated Products, Inc. (API). For the last nine months, she had been on special assignment to a key marketing staff function at corporate headquarters, working directly with the Marketing Vice President, Bernard Peach, even though there were two levels of management between them. Peach had told Roberts's boss not to give her any other assignments—that she was to work directly for him. In order to communicate more closely, Peach had Roberts install a high-tech phone system in her office and gave her access to an executive secretary.

API was a staid company facing a number of changes in its external environment. It was highly centralized, and a number of key managers complained that the company was overly bureaucratic. Many older managers, like Roberts's boss (and her boss's boss) were looked upon as "dead wood" incapable of operating in the new environment. Nevertheless, change was normally a slow process at API, and on a number of matters Roberts found herself in direct conflict with her boss even though she was acting on Peach's direct orders. She was unsure how much resentment was building up beneath the surface, but she found working directly with Peach, occasionally mentioned as a future CEO, exhilarating— even though she was frustrated at being caught in the middle of larger bureaucratic struggles.

Peach and Roberts worked together closely on a high-profile revamping of API's products, and the project promised to be quite successful. Two days before the presentation to API's Executive Committee, Peach dispatched Roberts to the resort where the meeting was to be held to double- and triple-check all the arrangements. When Peach arrived, he called Roberts's room at 3 A.M., and together they checked the slide projector to be sure that the tops of the slides were straight when projected.

After the presentation, the committee adopted most of the recommendations, and two days later Bernard Peach was promoted to Group Vice President for Asia. Joyce Roberts went into her office to find two memos on her desk. The first was the announcement that Bernard Peach had been promoted and had already left for his new job. The second was a handwritten note from her boss suggesting they talk about her performance problems over the last six months. Roberts wondered what she should do.

Source: This case is based on an actual situation, but all names and some facts are disguised.

Case Questions

1. What are the sources and uses of power in this case?
2. What problems does Joyce Roberts now have?
3. What advice would you give Roberts?

VIDEO CASE STUDY

A Lesson in Downsizing: Digital Equipment Corp.

Smaller, cheaper, and more powerful: The popular computers of the 1990s range from versatile laptops and notebooks to inexpensive pocket-sized machines designed to be used on the go. What this has meant for manufacturers of larger computers, such as Digital Equipment Corp. of Maynard, Massachusetts, is hard times. In the late 1980s, Digital was growing at a rate of 20 percent yearly and was rated second only to IBM among computer manufacturers. At the time, frustration with IBM was growing; the company was perceived as overstaffed, underproductive, and insensitive to customers' needs. Digital was able to step in and offer products and services IBM could not, and

its sales and profits soared. Yet by early 1991, Digital's stock had fallen from $199 per share to $56.

Digital's hardware line traditionally emphasized large, expensive minicomputers for sophisticated office and laboratory applications. The equipment was designed for use with Digital's operating software, which interfaces between the hardware and the applications software—the minicomputer equivalent of the MS-DOS system used by PCs. With the availability of smaller, cheaper, more flexible hardware, such as work stations, and open systems thast use nonproprietary software, the market for Digital's type of equipment rapidly shrank.

Management failed to respond to the changes in demand, even when Digital's earnings began to dwindle. Executives assumed that the introduction of a new version of the company's mainframe computer—costing over $1 million—would boost sales. They did institute some cost-cutting measures, but these proved inadequate, and suddenly the company was losing money—a lot of it—for the first time in its history. Survival demanded a reorganization of the management structure and product mix, as well as staff cuts that would eventually reach 7 percent worldwide.

The reorganization of the management structure was the most radical of the changes at Digital. Like IBM, the company decentralized, but whereas IBM created five semiautonomous divisions, Digital created 18 suborganizations, each with the responsibility for servicing a specific industry and each with its own authority and profit/loss responsibility. The intent was to shift decision making away from the top of the organization and closer to the actual marketplace, where technology and consumer demand could be more closely monitored.

The management changes Digital made were not only structural, they also involved shifts in overall approach and attitude. Traditionally, Digital relied heavily on consensus building among top executives, a system that had become unwieldy and ineffectual. This was abandoned in favor of allowing decision making by individual lower-level managers. The new system changes permitted greater responsiveness to subtle shifts in the market—crucial in such a fast-changing field.

Digital also set out to develop more competitive hardware that would appeal to customers as well as software developers. The company's bread-and-butter computer, the VAX, was streamlined in size and cost, which made it more competitive in a market where profit margins are very narrow. Production time was accelerated, so that new models would appear in two years rather than five. The company also began to actively seek the attention of software manufacturers, and soon compatible Lotus and WordPerfect programs became available. In addition, Digital adapted its own operating software for use by all in-dustry-standard computers, allowing the linkage of previously incompatible Apple Macintoshes, PCs, and work stations with Digital minicomputers.

At first the layoffs associated with the company's downsizing were voluntary, with 2,500 employees accepting severance and 5,000 more being transferred and retrained. Mandatory layoffs followed, but in the attempt to make cost-cutting measures more palatable to employees, workers themselves were encouraged to contribute suggestions and participate in the streamlining process.

The lesson for management, according to Digital's vice president of operations, John F. Smith, is that during a time of companywide shakeup, employee stress and disruption can be minimized. He advises other managers to avoid obvious favoritism during restructuring and to let employees know what reorganizing the structure will involve and what its advantages will be. To the extent possible, employees also need to know what the future will hold for them, especially whether more layoffs are anticipated.

Sources: Laura Brennan, "Some Say DEC Layoffs Still Not Enough," *PC Week,* January 14, 1991, p. 4; Barbara Buell et al., "Hewlett Packard Rethinks Itself," *Business Week,* April 1, 1991, pp. 76–79; John W. Verity, "In Computers, a Shakeout of Seismic Proportions," *Business Week,* October 15, 1990, pp. 34, 36; Gary McWilliams, "Can DEC Beat the Big Blue Blues?" *Business Week,* August 13, 1990, pp. 114–115; Michael J. Mandel, "This Time, the Downturn Is Dressed in Pinstripes," *Business Week,* October 1, 1990, pp. 130–131; Stratford P. Sherman, "Digital's Daring Comeback Plan," *Fortune,* January 14, 1991, pp. 100–103; Thomas A. Stewart, "Do You Push Your People Too Hard?" *Fortune,* October 22, 1990, pp. 121–128.

Case Questions

1. What do you see as the reasons for the near-disaster at DEC? In hindsight, what preventive measures could the company have taken?

2. How did DEC's management incorporate the principles of delegation and decentralization to solve the crisis they faced? How effective were their measures?

3. What lessons about management and a rapidly changing marketplace can be learned from the experiences of IBM and DEC?

■ NOTES

[1]See, for example, Dennis H. Wrong, "Some Problems in Defining Social Power," *American Journal of Sociology* 73, no. 6 (May 1968):673–681. See also David Krackhardt, "Assessing the Political Landscape: Structure, Cognition, and Power in Organization," *Administrative Science Quarterly* 35 (1990):342–369.

[2]See Max Weber, "The Three Types of Managerial Rule," *Berkeley Journal of Sociology* 4 (1953; orig. pub. 1925):1–11; and Cyril O'Donnell, "The Source of Managerial Authority," *Political Science Quarterly* 67, no. 4 (December 1952):573–588.

[3]Chester I. Barnard, *The Functions of the Executive,* 30th anniversary ed. (Cambridge, Mass.: Harvard University Press, 1968), p. 165.

[4]Herbert A. Simon, *Administrative Behavior,* 3rd ed. (New York: Macmillan, 1976), pp. 12, 18.

[5]John R. P. French and Bertram Raven, "The Bases of Social Power," in Dorwin Cartwright, ed., *Studies in Social Power* (Ann Arbor: University of Michigan Press, 1959), pp. 150–167.

[6]Gary Yukl and Tom Taber, "The Effective Use of Managerial Power," *Personnel* 60, no. 2 (March–April 1983):37–44.

[7]Jeffrey Pfeffer has explored the basis for the contemporary unease about power and politics and has concluded that power processes are often ubiquitous and generally beneficial rather than harmful to organizations and the people who work in them. See Jeffrey Pfeffer, *Power in Organizations* (Marshfield, Mass.: Pitman, 1981); and Henry Mintzberg, *Power in and Around Organizations* (Englewood Cliffs, N.J.: Prentice Hall, 1983).

[8]David C. McClelland, "The Two Faces of Power," *Journal of International Affairs* 24, no. 1 (1970): 29–47.

[9]David C. McClelland and David H. Burnham, "Power Is the Great Motivator," *Harvard Business Review* 54, no. 2 (March–April 1976):100–110.

[10]Rosabeth Moss Kanter, *Men and Women of the Corporation* (New York: Basic Books, 1977), pp. 165–205. See also Kanter, "Men and Women of the Corporation Revisited," *Management Review,* March 1987, pp. 14–15; Kanter, *The Change Masters* (New York: Simon & Schuster, 1983), pp. 156–179; and Sharon Nelton, "Meet Your New Work Force," *Nation's Business* 76, no. 7 (1988):14–21.

[11]A key concern of current research is the integration of the various theories of power into a unified theory. See W. Graham Astley and Paramjit S. Sachdeva, "Structural Sources of Intraorganizational Power: A Theoretical Synthesis," *Academy of Management Review* 9, no. 1 (January 1984):104–113; and Anthony T. Cobb, "An Episodic Model of Power: Toward an Integration of Theory and Research," *Academy of Management Review* 9, no. 3 (July 1984):482–493.

[12]See, for example, Gerald G. Fisch, "Line-Staff Is Obsolete," *Harvard Business Review* 39, no. 5 (September–October 1961):67–79; and Vivian Nossiter, "A New Approach Toward Resolving the Line and Staff Dilemma," *Academy of Management Review* 4, no. 1 (January 1979):103–106.

[13]For a discussion of the various ways staff activities are integrated in the organizational structure, see Harold Stieglitz, "On Concepts of Corporate Structure: Economic Determinants of Organization," *Conference Board Review,* February 1974, pp. 148–150.

[14]Alfred Kieser, "Advisory Staffs for Rulers: Can They Increase Rationality of Decisions?" Unpublished paper delivered at the seminar on "Improvement of Top-Level Decision-Making" at the Institute for Advanced Study, Berlin, February 1983.

[15]For an early discussion of ways in which staff members can support line managers, see Louis A. Allen, "The Line-Staff Relationship," *Management Record* 17, no. 9 (September 1955):346–349ff.

[16]John R. Adams and Nicki S. Kirchof, "The Practice of Matrix Management," in David I. Cleland, ed., *Matrix Management Systems Handbook* (New York: Van Nostrand Reinhold, 1984), pp. 13–30.

[17]See Gerald G. Fisch, "Toward Effective Delegation," *CPA Journal* 46, no. 7 (July 1976):67; and William Newman, "Overcoming Obstacles to Effective Delegation," *Management Review* 45, no. 1 (January 1956):36–41.

[18]See Fisch, "Toward Effective Delegation," pp. 66–67.

[19]Michael A. Campion and Paul W. Thayer, "Development and Field Evaluation of an Interdisciplinary Measure of Job Design," *Journal of Applied Psychology* 70, no. 1:29–43. The following discussion of the four approaches to job design is based on this source.

[20]For a complete account of Three Mile Island, see Charles Perrow, *Normal Accidents* (New York: The Free Press, 1985).

[21]J. Richard Hackman and Edward E. Lawler, "Employee Reactions to Job Characteristics," *Journal of Applied Psychology, Monograph 55* (1971):269–286; J. Richard Hackman and Greg R. Oldham, "Development of the Job Diagnostic Survey," *Journal of Applied Psychology* 60, no. 2 (April 1975):159–170; and J. Richard Hackman and J. Lloyd Suttle, eds., *Improving Life at Work* (Santa Monica, Calif.: Goodyear, 1977), pp. 130–131.

[22]J. Richard Hackman, "Work Design," in Hackman and Suttle, eds., *Improving Life at Work,* pp. 128–130.

[23]A paper by Robert N. Ford, "Job Enrichment Lessons from AT&T," *Harvard Business Review* 51, no. 1 (January–February 1973):96–106, describes some of the techniques used by AT&T to redesign white- and blue-collar jobs in one of the most extensive job-enrichment programs in American industry.

[24]Riva Poor, *Four Days, Forty Hours* (Cambridge, Mass.: Bursk and Poor, 1970).

[25]"Flextime in the Utilities Industry," *Personnel* 61, no. 2 (March–April 1984):42–44.

[26]Charles L. Hulin and Milton R. Blood, "Job Enlargement, Individual Differences, and Worker Responses," *Psychological Bulletin* 69, no. 1 (1968):41–53.

[27]See Hackman, "Work Design," p. 118.

[28]Brian Lober, Raymond Noe, Nancy L. Moeller, and Michael Fitzgerald, "A Meta-Analysis of the Relation of Job Characteristics to Job Satisfaction," *Journal of Applied Psychology* 70, no. 2 (1985):280–289.

[29]Gerald Salancik and Jeffrey Pfeffer, "Determinants of Supervisory Behavior: A Role Set Analysis," *Human Relations* 28 (1975):139–154.

[30]See Ernest Dale, *Organization* (New York: American Management Associations, 1967), pp. 114–130.

[31]Alfred D. Chandler, Jr., *Strategy and Structure: Chapters in the History of the American Industrial Enterprise* (Cambridge, Mass.: MIT Press, 1962).

CHAPTER THIRTEEN

HUMAN RESOURCE MANAGEMENT

Detail from Max Weber, *Rush Hour, New York.*

Upon completing this chapter, you should be able to:

1. Present an overview of the HRM process.
2. Explain the need for and procedures of human resource planning.
3. List and describe the various methods of recruitment.
4. Compare and contrast the various legal considerations involved in human relations.
5. Explain the seven-step hiring sequence.
6. Discuss the pros and cons of the interview process.
7. Explain the function of the orientation process.
8. Distinguish between training and development programs and give examples of each.
9. Explain the difference between informal and formal systematic appraisals and the problems common to both methods.
10. Discuss the important issues involved in making promotion, transfer, demotion, and separation decisions.
11. Explain how HRM interacts with organization strategy.

Max Weber, *Rush Hour, New York.* 1915. Canvas 36½ × 30¼. National Gallery of Art, Washington, D.C. Gift of the Avalon Foundation.

ILLUSTRATIVE CASE STUDY

INTRODUCTION

Human Relations at Sony Corporation

Akio Morita, founder of Sony Corporation, says that there is no "magic" in the success of Japanese companies in general and Sony in particular. The secret of their success is simply the way they treat their employees. In his biography, *Made in Japan*, Morita says:

> The most important mission for a Japanese manager is to develop a healthy relationship with his employees, to create a familylike feeling within the corporation, a feeling that employees and managers share the same fate. Those companies that are most successful in Japan are those that have managed to create a shared sense of fate among all employees, what Americans call labor and management, and the shareholders.

While Morita was chairman of Sony, he made a point every year of addressing each class of college recruits, explaining his view of the differences between school and work. According to Morita, the world of work gave them an exam every day. Performance had to be continual, and mistakes resulted not in failed exams, but in costs to the company. Morita stressed that each employee had to seek happiness in his or her work and to decide personally whether to spend the rest of his or her working life at Sony.

At Sony, there are few noticeable differences between management and labor. Although management writers sometimes paint a too-rosy picture of Japanese management-labor relations, the basic management philosophy is: Employees should be treated as colleagues and helpers, not as mere means to profits. Investors are important, Morita admitted, but they establish only a *temporary* relationship with the company. Employees are *more* important because they are a *permanent* part of the company, just as much as top management.

In return for showing loyalty to employees, Morita expected loyalty from his employees. He also urged them to question management views and to use their best efforts on the company's behalf. Ironically, this emphasis on loyalty was partly inspired by Morita's experience with American managers and employees. In its early days, Sony hired many employees in the United States in an effort to keep pace with the remarkable demand for its products. Morita

Akio Morita, founder of Sony Corporation.

was stunned by an American colleague's blunt advice about a problem employee: "Fire him." Morita was equally surprised when an American employee walked into his office one day and announced he was quitting to take a job with a competitor who had offered to double his salary.

Under Morita, the whole process of recruiting, selecting, training, and appraising employees was built on the premise that employees are the most valuable part of the company. Granted, Morita's policies—especially the idea of lifetime job security—are not as typical of Japanese companies as Americans were once led to believe. In fact, a recent study conducted by the Japanese government showed that only 29 percent of all 20- to 29-year-old Japanese workers planned to stay with the same employer for their entire career. But this does not mean that American management cannot learn a great deal from Morita's philosophy. Indeed, his ideas are the basis for what management writer Tom Peters proposes as a new, more realistic pact between employer and employee: Employees will commit themselves to doing their best to help the company meet its goals, and in return, the company will give employees an opportunity to develop and hone their skills. Of course, they are free to leave and sell these skills to another employer, but ideally, the opportunity to keep learning and to do good work will keep them with the company and increase both their loyalty and their productivity.

Sources: Akio Morita, *Made in Japan* (New York: E. P. Dutton, 1986); Joel Kotkin, "Japan's New Face," *Inc.,* October 1990; Tom Peters, "Goal of Employment Security for a Lifetime Is Out of Sync with the Times," *Chicago Tribune,* October 1, 1990, Sect. 4, p. 6.

ony's success is evidence of the validity of Akio Morita's view that an organization's most important resources are the people who supply their work, talent, creativity, and drive to the organization. It seems logical, then, that among a manager's most critical tasks are the selection, training, and development of people who will best help the organization meet its goals.

In this chapter, we will look at **human resource management (HRM)**, the management function that helps managers recruit, select, train, and develop organization members. We will begin by discussing the traditional view of human resource management and how HRM can assure the organization of an adequate and constant supply of skilled employees. We will then show how environmental pressures require us to coordinate HRM and strategy.

human resource management (HRM) The management function that deals with recruitment, placement, training, and development of organization members.

■ THE HRM PROCESS: A TRADITIONAL VIEW

CLASS COMMENT

"We must find better ways to tap the creative talent and energy of American workers. This requires that we change from the concept of 'management' to 'leadership.'" (Institute of Industrial Engineers Newsletter, Winter 1991, p. 3)

FOR DISCUSSION

Why is it so important to have the right people in the right positions at the right time?

COORDINATED RESOURCE

Use Transparency 80, The HRM Process in Organizations.

COORDINATED RESOURCE

Use Transparency 81, Human Resource Management Activities.

Change is the one constant in the American work force. Effective managers are promoted or leave for better positions elsewhere; ineffective managers are demoted or even fired. Furthermore, the company may need more or fewer employees and managers from time to time. Thus, the HRM process never stops. Rather, it is an ongoing procedure that tries to keep the organization supplied with the right people in the right positions at the right time.

The HRM process, shown in Figure 13-1, includes seven basic activities:

1. *Human resource planning,* designed to ensure that personnel needs will be constantly and appropriately met, is accomplished through analysis of (a) internal factors, such as current and expected skill needs, vacancies, and departmental expansions and reductions; and (b) factors in the external environment, such as the labor market. The use of computers to build and maintain information about all employees has enabled organizations to be much more efficient in their planning of human resources.

2. *Recruitment* is concerned with developing a pool of job candidates in line with the human resource plan. Candidates are usually located through newspaper and professional journal advertisements, employment agencies, word of mouth, and visits to college and university campuses.

FIGURE 13-1 The HRM Process in Organizations

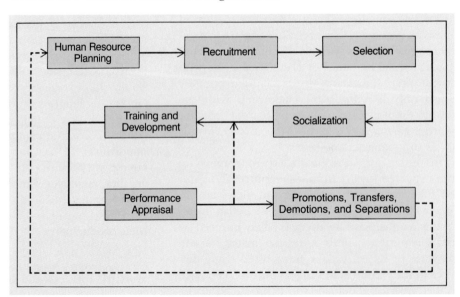

3. *Selection* involves using application forms, résumés, interviews, employment and skills tests, and reference checks to evaluate and screen job candidates for the managers who will ultimately select and hire a candidate.

4. *Socialization* is designed to help the selected individuals fit smoothly into the organization. Newcomers are introduced to their colleagues, acquainted with their responsibilities, and informed about the organization's goals, policies, and expectations regarding employee behavior.

5. *Training and development* aim to increase employees' ability to contribute to organizational effectiveness. Training is designed to improve skills in the present job; development programs are designed to prepare employees for promotion.

6. *Performance appraisal* compares an individual's job performance to standards or objectives developed for the individual's position. Low performance may prompt corrective action, such as additional training, a demotion, or separation, while high performance may merit a bonus or promotion. Although an employee's immediate supervisor will perform the appraisal, the HRM department is responsible for working with upper management to establish the policies that guide all performance appraisals.

7. *Promotions, transfers, demotions, and separations* reflect an employee's value to the organization. High performers may be promoted or transferred to help them develop their skills, while low performers may be demoted, transferred to less important positions, or even separated. Any of these options will, in turn, affect human resource planning.

■ *HUMAN RESOURCE PLANNING*

CLASS COMMENT
Unum Corporation estimates that more than 40,000 small firms will offer "flex plans" during 1991. Only 8,300 did in 1988. (*Wall Street Journal,* 3/19/91, p. A1)

human resource planning Planning for the future personnel needs of an organization, taking into account both internal activities and factors in the external environment.

COORDINATED RESOURCE
Use Transparency 82, Dimensions of Human Resource Planning.

COORDINATED RESOURCE
See DuBose Reading #14, "Increasing Organizational Effectiveness Through Better Human Resources Planning and Development."

COORDINATED RESOURCE
See *Management Live!* Reading 12.1, "For American Business: A New World of Workers."

The need for **human resource planning** may not be readily apparent. After all, one might ask: If an organization needs new people, why doesn't it simply hire them? In fact, an organization's human resource needs can hardly ever be met as quickly or as easily as this question implies. An organization that does not plan for its human resources will often find that it is not meeting either its personnel requirements or its overall goals effectively.

For example, a manufacturing company may hope to increase productivity with new automated equipment, but if the company does not start to hire and train people to operate the equipment *before* installation, the equipment may remain idle for weeks or even months. Similarly, an all-male, all-white organization that does not plan to add women and minority group members to its staff is likely to become the defendant in a civil rights lawsuit. Planning for human resources is a challenging task today, given the increasingly competitive environment, projected labor shortages, changing demographics, and pressure from government to protect both employees and the environment.[1]

Planning Procedures

Human resource planning has four basic aspects: (1) *planning for future needs* by deciding how many people with what skills the organization will need, (2) *planning for future balance* by comparing the number of needed employees to the number of present employees who can be expected to stay with the organization, which leads to (3) *planning for recruiting or laying off employees* and (4) *planning for the development of employees,* to be sure the organization has a steady supply of experienced and capable personnel.[2]

To be effective, the managers of a human resource program must consider two major factors. The primary factor is the organization's strategic plan, which defines the organization's human resource needs. For example, a strategy of internal growth means that additional employees must be hired. Acquisitions or mergers, on the other hand, probably mean the organization will need to plan for layoffs, since mergers tend to create duplicate or overlapping positions that can be handled more efficiently with fewer employees.

The second factor to consider is the external environment of the future. In a booming economy, financing might be available for expansion, which will increase the demand for employees. Unemployment will be low, however, making it harder and more expensive to attract qualified employees. Similar problems face organizations that want to expand overseas. AT&T solved this problem by forming joint ventures with Philips and Olivetti, which allowed it to use its foreign partner's human resources until it was ready to hire its own European managers.

Together, the organization's strategy and the external environment broadly define the limits within which the human resource plan must operate.[3] Forecasting and human resource audits can then determine more specific human resource needs.

Forecasting and the Human Resource Audit

The two central elements in human resource planning are forecasting and the human resource audit. These two elements give managers the information they need to plan the other steps in the HRM process, such as recruiting and training.

human resource forecasting The attempt, using specific techniques, to predict and project future personnel needs.

FORECASTING. **Human resource forecasting** attempts to determine what personnel the organization will need to maintain its growth and exploit future opportunities. Thus, forecasters try to predict the number, type, and quality of people needed in the future; specify the range of responsibilities that will have to be met; and establish what skills and knowledge organization members will need.[4]

HUMAN RESOURCE AUDIT. Once the forecasts are completed, the next step is to obtain information about the organization's present personnel. Two kinds of information are needed: Do organization members have the appropriate skills for their jobs? Are they performing effectively? The answers to these questions will enable planners to match the organization's personnel strengths and weaknesses against future requirements. Particular emphasis should be placed on finding existing skills and potential within the organization, since it is usually more economical to promote from within than to recruit, hire, and train people from outside. Promoting from within also fosters loyalty to the firm and acknowledges the possibility of career paths for personnel.

human resource audit The analysis and appraisal of the organization's current human resources.

In a **human resource audit,** the skills and performance of each individual in the organization are appraised. Within each department, individuals are ranked according to the quality of their work. The information thus obtained will give upper-level managers an idea of the effectiveness of staff in each department.

replacement chart A chart that diagrams an organization's positions, showing the incumbents, likely future candidates, and readiness of candidates to enter those positions.

For higher levels of management, the next step in the auditing process may be to develop a detailed succession plan or replacement chart. The **replacement chart** shows the positions in the organization, incumbents in those positions, likely future candidates for those positions, and the readiness of candidates to take over those positions. Detailed replacement charts such as that in Figure 13-2 are usually developed only for upper-level managers. However, the need to compare present human resources with future requirements exists at all levels of the organization. GE uses a "slate system," whereby every senior manager at a certain level has a potential replacement. Both former chairman Reg Jones and current chairman Jack Welch have attested that managing the company's slate system is among their most important tasks and highest priorities.

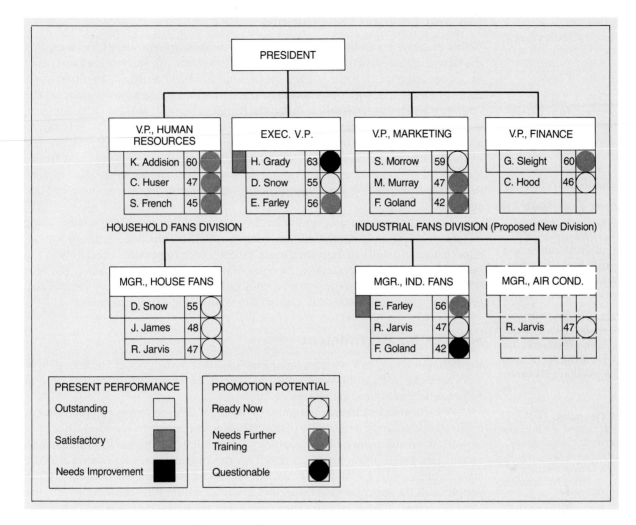

FIGURE 13-2 Management Replacement Chart

Source: Adapted from *Developing Managerial Competence* by Walter S. Wikstrom. Copyright © 1964 The Conference Board.

■ *RECRUITMENT*

recruitment The development of a pool of job candidates in accordance with a human resource plan.

COORDINATED RESOURCE

See Samaras Exercise 3.3, "Help Wanted."

The purpose of **recruitment** is to provide a group of candidates that is large enough to let the organization select the qualified employees it needs. *General recruiting,* which is most appropriate for operative employees, takes place when the organization needs a group of workers of a certain kind—for example, typists or salespeople. It follows comparatively simple, standardized procedures. *Specialized recruiting,* which is used mainly for higher-level executives or specialists, occurs when the organization wants a particular type of individual. In specialized recruiting, candidates get personalized attention over an extended period.[5]

The recruiting of college and MBA graduates falls somewhere between these two extremes. It resembles general recruiting in the sense that many candidates are screened for a given group of openings and many may be hired with only a vague idea about their initial jobs—especially if the first "job" is in a management training program. At some companies, the CEO and other top executives become directly involved in recruiting to symbolize its importance to company strategy.

CLASS COMMENT
Job analysis and writing a
job description must take
place before looking for
employees to fill jobs.

job description On the
operative level, a written
description of a job's title,
duties, and responsibilities,
including its location on
the organization chart.

position description On
the management level, a
written description of a
position's title, duties, and
responsibilities, including
its location on the organization chart.

hiring specification A
written description of the
education, experience, and
skills needed to perform a
job or position effectively.

HRM Planning. HRM
considerations are a major
factor in deciding where
to locate new facilities. In
a 1990 *Fortune* survey of
the best cities for business,
Salt Lake City ranked
No. 1 for its large pool of
skilled workers who have
a strong work ethic, which
is backed up by the sup-
port of local government,
led by Mayor Palmer
DePaulis, shown high
above the city.

Job and Position Descriptions

Before employees can be recruited, recruiters must have some clear ideas regarding
the new employees' activities and responsibilities. Thus, job analysis is an early step
in the recruitment process. Once a specific job has been analyzed, a written statement of its content and location is incorporated into the organization chart. At the
operative level, this statement is called the **job description;** at the managerial level,
it is called a **position description.** Each box on the organization chart is linked to
a description that lists the title, duties, and responsibilities for that position. For
example, a brief position description might read as follows: "Sales Manager: Duties
include hiring, training, and supervising small sales staff and administration of sales
department; responsible for performance of department; reports to Division Manager."

Once the position description has been determined, an accompanying hiring
or job specification is developed. The **hiring specification** defines the education,
experience, and skills an individual must have in order to perform effectively in the
position. The hiring specification for Sales Manager might read: "Position requires
BBA degree; five years' experience in sales and two years' supervisory experience;
energetic, motivated individual with well-developed interpersonal skills."

Sources for Recruitment

Recruitment takes place within a *labor market*—that is, the pool of available people
who have the skills to fill open positions. The labor market changes over time in
response to environmental factors.

Which sources a human resources department turns to to meet its recruitment
needs depends on the availability of the right kinds of people in the local labor pool
as well as on the nature of the positions to be filled. An organization's ability to
recruit employees often hinges as much on the organization's reputation and the
attractiveness of its location as on the attractiveness of the specific job offer. If the
people with the appropriate skills are not available within the organization or in the
local labor pool, they may have to be recruited from competing organizations and/or
from some distance away.

Some companies have enhanced the success of their recruitment policies by
establishing good reputations as places to work. According to *Fortune's* 1991 list of
"America's Most Admired Corporations," among those companies that attract, develop, and retain talented people are Merck, Wal-Mart, and Rubbermaid. Other firms
have become known for providing particularly good opportunities for women:
American Express, Hallmark, Honeywell, Pepsico, and Hewlett-Packard.[6]

OUTSIDE RECRUITMENT FOR MANAGERS AND PROFESSIONALS. Large companies
use various outside recruitment sources to fill vacancies at different levels of management. For many large companies, college and graduate school campuses are a
major source of entry-level and new managerial help. Campus recruiting, however,
has some disadvantages: The recruitment process can be quite expensive, and it is
not uncommon for hired graduates to leave an organization after two or three years.
When recruiting to fill middle-management and top-level positions, many large companies must resort to even costlier and more competitive hiring strategies. When
top-quality ability is in short supply, middle-management recruitment often requires
the services of placement agencies or the purchase of expensive ads in newspapers
and national publications. And when recruiting is done to fill top-level positions,
many corporate managements must turn to executive search firms for help in locating three or four carefully considered prospects who not only are highly qualified
but who also can be enticed from their present positions by the right offer. For
example, after the breakup in 1984, AT&T realized that its new environment would
require a better mix of talent than it had in many areas, so it immediately began

TEACHING TIP
This would be a good time to enlist a speaker from your school's job placement service to talk to students about job recruiting. This is a topic of high interest and importance to students. It also fits in well with the whole area of human resource management.

approaching a number of executives from a variety of companies. The difficulties inherent in recruiting outside the organization, however, especially for senior-level positions, argue that organizations should carefully weigh the costs against the expected benefits.

RECRUITMENT FROM WITHIN. Many firms, such as IBM, General Foods, and Procter & Gamble, have a policy of recruiting or promoting from within except in very exceptional circumstances. There are three major advantages of this policy. First, individuals recruited from within are already familiar with the organization and its members, and this knowledge increases the likelihood they will succeed. Second, a promotion-from-within policy fosters loyalty and inspires greater effort among organization members. Finally, it is usually less expensive to recruit or promote from within than to hire from outside the organization. The major disadvantages of this policy are that it limits the pool of available talent, it reduces the chance that fresh viewpoints will enter the organization, and it may encourage complacency among employees who assume seniority ensures promotion.

Legal Considerations

COORDINATED RESOURCE
See Study Guide Problem Exercise 13, "Legal Questions."

THOUGHT PROVOKER
Companies are increasingly combing through databases to find information on job applicants. What are the implications of this practice? (*Business Week*, 9/24/90, p. 128ff.)

In the early 1960s, the growing civil rights and women's movements called national attention to the discriminatory effects of existing human resource practices. Responses to these efforts began with the Equal Pay Act of 1963 and the Civil Rights Act of 1964. These early efforts were expanded by the courts and most state legislatures and through various federal amendments and executive orders. The implications of such legislation for human resource policies and practices are still evolving and being clarified by court decisions and administrative interpretations. Although the median annual earnings of women at work have increased significantly in the past quarter century, the ratio of women's to men's wages varies widely from one occupation to another. Moreover, while the increase of women in some of the higher-status, higher-paid occupations is dramatic, the proportion of women in those occupations is still low (see Table 13-1). "For example," as Janet L. Norwood, U.S. Commissioner of Labor Statistics, noted, "the number of women lawyers increased more than fivefold over the last decade, but there are still less than 100,000 in the legal profession, and they make up only 15 percent of the total."[7]

COORDINATED RESOURCE
See *Management Live!* Chapter 14 video 2, "Affirmative Action."

THE LAWS. The key legislation is Title VII of the Civil Rights Act of 1964 (amended in 1972 to establish the Equal Employment Opportunity Commission [EEOC] to enforce the provisions of Title VII), which prohibits employment discrimination on the basis of race, sex, age, religion, color, or national origin. These requirements for nondiscriminatory treatment are called *equal employment opportunity (EEO)* re-

TABLE 13-1 The Wage Gap Between the Sexes

	WOMEN AS PERCENT OF ALL WORKERS		EARNINGS RATIO, FEMALE TO MALE	
	1979	1988	1979	1988
Accountants and auditors	34%	45%	0.60	0.79
Computer programmers	28	40	0.80	0.81
Computer systems analysts	20	30	0.79	0.82
Lawyers	10	15	0.55	0.63
Managers and administrators	22	29	0.51	0.67
Sales of business services	28	34	0.58	0.79
Teachers, elementary school	61	82	0.82	0.96

Note: Figures are for full-time workers in selected occupations.
Source: Census Bureau.

TABLE 13-2 Some Differences Between EEO (Nondiscrimination) and AA

	EEO	AFFIRMATIVE ACTION
Who is affected?	Virtually everyone is covered by law	Legally applies only to certain organizations
What is required?	Employment neutrality Nondiscrimination	Systematic plan
What are the sanctions?	Legal charges can be filed Possible court action	Withdrawal of contracts or funds if noncompliant
What are some examples of compliance?	Not barring female, minority, or disabled persons from employment	Actively recruiting and hiring female, veteran, minority, or disabled persons
	Selecting, promoting, and paying people solely on the basis of bona fide job-related qualifications	Validating tests; rigorously examining company practices in selection, promotion, and benefits to eliminate non–job-related qualifications that discriminate against protected persons

Source: The Management of Affirmative Action by Francine S. Hall and Maryann H. Albrecht. Copyright © 1979 by Scott, Foresman and Company. Reprinted by permission.

THOUGHT PROVOKER

How can "comparable worth" issues ever be resolved?

comparable worth The principle that jobs requiring comparable skills and knowledge merit equal compensation even if the nature of the work activity is different.

COORDINATED RESOURCE

See Samaras Reading "Comparable Worth: An Issue of Equality."

quirements. They apply to virtually all private and public organizations. Executive Orders 11246 and 11375 of 1965 and 1968 (amended in 1977) require, in addition, that firms doing business with the federal government make special efforts to recruit, hire, and promote women and members of minority groups. These requirements are called *affirmative action (AA)*.[8] The differences between equal employment opportunity and affirmative action are summarized in Table 13-2.

The Equal Pay Act, originally introduced in 1946, prohibits discrimination in which employers pay men more than women for performing jobs requiring equal skill, effort, responsibility, and working conditions. Thus, the Equal Pay Act requires *like* pay for *like* jobs. Also, the act established the foundation for addressing concerns about **comparable worth,** the idea that different jobs that require comparable skills and knowledge deserve comparable pay. This idea arose from the observation that women tend to be segregated in certain occupations, such as nursing and teaching, that are lower paying than some male-dominated fields, despite similar educational requirements and responsibilities. In fact, some women-dominated fields require more education than better-paying men's jobs. Over and over again, statistics show that women make less than 70 cents for every dollar men earn; much of this difference is attributed to occupational segregation. By taking into account the actual skills and knowledge needed for jobs, the principle of comparable worth seeks to invalidate patterns of wage and job discrimination that have often established or influenced salary guidelines.[9]

The employment rights of persons 40 and older are protected by the Age Discrimination in Employment Act of 1967 (amended in 1986). The Vocational Rehabilitation Act of 1973 (amended in 1974) added protection for the physically and mentally disabled if they were qualified to perform job tasks with reasonable accommodation by the employer. The rights of the disabled were further protected by the Americans with Disabilities Act. (See the Management and Diversity box.) The Veterans' Readjustment Act of 1974 requires those doing business with the federal government to extend affirmative action programs to veterans of the Vietnam War era and to disabled veterans in general.

Sexual harassment (unwanted sexual requests or advances or the creation of a sexually harassing environment through sexual jokes and remarks) in hiring or pro-

The Disabled Bill of Rights

In August 1990, Congress passed the Americans with Disabilities Act, popularly known as the Disabled Bill of Rights. This hotly disputed act promises sweeping changes in the American workplace, which must now accommodate workers with physical and mental disabilities, as well as those with chronic illnesses. (In keeping with President Bush's war on drugs, the law does not protect people who are disabled by illegal drug use.)

The Disabled Bill of Rights is important because disabled Americans were not covered by the 1964 Civil Rights Act, which banned discrimination on the basis of race, sex, religion, and national origin. Now the same protections are granted to the disabled.

The first right the Disabled Bill of Rights protects is the right to employment. Employers are prohibited from discriminating against any job applicant who can perform "essential" job responsibilities; they are obliged to make "reasonable accommodations" as long as they can do so without "undue" hardship. This provision will go into effect in 1992 for employers with 25 or more employees, and in 1994 for employers with 15 or more employees.

The Disabled Bill of Rights also gives disabled persons more rights to access public facilities. Newly constructed or renovated buildings will have to comply with new federal standards; existing buildings will have to be modified for wheelchair access and so on. In addition, newly purchased transportation vehicles, such as train and subway cars and buses, will have to be accessible to the disabled, although existing vehicles do not have to be modified. The bill also requires telephone companies to provide relay services to enable people with speech and hearing disabilities to communicate. Finally, sports arenas, theaters, museums, doctors' offices, hospitals, and pharmacies will have to be made accessible.

This law remains highly controversial. For one thing, it will be very expensive to modify buildings and public transit systems. Second, many businesses are concerned about the ambiguous wording of the act, especially the "essential functions" clause, which seems to take away an employer's right to define a job's critical tasks. Could a restaurant owner be sued, for example, if the restaurant's kitchen cannot accommodate a chef in a wheelchair?

Such concerns should not blind us to the act's many benefits, however. Most importantly, this law has the potential of moving 43 million disabled Americans into the workplace and off government assistance, and this will ultimately benefit the economy.

Employing the Disabled. Paul L. Scher, manager of selective placement and rehabilitation for Sears, shown here talking to office manager Amber Ford, says that only 10 percent of Sears's 19,800 disabled employees need any type of accommodation and many of the accommodations don't cost anything.

Furthermore, many hope the law will open employers' eyes to the fact that disabled workers can perform many tasks using personal computers and "adaptive technology"—devices such as voice-recognition software, Braille keypads, and "sip-and-puff" breath sticks, which allow even quadriplegics to use a computer. With this equipment, disabled workers can perform such skilled tasks as drafting, telemarketing, research, accounting, and word processing.

Employers who want proof that this accommodation can work need look no further than the Social Security Administration's Office of Appeal and Adjudication, where word processors input decisions written by the agency's administrative law judges. These word processors are the most productive team in the national organization and their work meets the agency's highest standards—even though six out of the nine word processors are blind. To do their work, they use specially modified PCs, voice-recognition software, and Braille keypads. The cost is about $8,000 per worker versus $3,000 for a standard word processing setup. Meanwhile, IBM and other major computer manufacturers have been training the disabled as computer programmers for nearly ten years. As Tom R. Shworles, chairman of the Committee on Personal Computers and the Handicapped, puts it, "Today, if a disabled worker can get to the office, he or she can do most work."

Sources: Bradford A. McKee, "A Troubling Bill for Business," *Nation's Business,* May 1990, pp. 58–59; Helen Dewar, "Senate Approves Disabled Rights Bill," *The Washington Post,* July 14, 1990, pp. A1, A7; Len Strazewski, "PCs Level Field for Disabled," *Crain's Chicago Business,* June 11, 1990, pp. T1, T2.

HERE'S AN EXAMPLE
At Honeywell, a sexual harassment education program with role playing and films was instituted in May 1990. The company also makes visual inspections of plants and offices and gives workers a handbook detailing examples of sexual harassment. (*Business Week*, 3/18/91, p.98ff.)

HERE'S AN EXAMPLE
Johnson & Johnson supports an on-site day-care center at its headquarters in New Brunswick, New Jersey. The company subsidizes part of the cost, but employees still pay most of the cost of child care. (*Fortune*, 5/20/91, p. 38ff.)

COORDINATED RESOURCE
See *Management Live!* Reading 14.4, "Past Tokenism."

COORDINATED RESOURCE
See *Management Live!* Reading 14.1, "Minority Women Feel Racism, Sexism Are Blocking the Path to Management."

COORDINATED RESOURCE
See *Management Live!* Reading 14.2, "The New Old Boy."

THOUGHT PROVOKER
New York State's attorney general has proposed banning integrity tests as a worker-screening tool. These questionnaires are designed to predict whether someone is likely to steal or goof off on the job. Discuss the advantages and drawbacks of using integrity tests. (*Wall Street Journal*, 3/6/91, p. A3)

motion decisions or the work environment violates Title VII.[10] A 1978 amendment to Title VII, the Pregnancy Discrimination Act, prohibits dismissal of women solely because of pregnancy and protects their job security during maternity leaves.[11] Legislation in various states extends these rights to employees of very small firms and to specific groups not mentioned in federal legislation, such as homosexuals and former prison inmates.[12]

In a landmark decision on employment discrimination in 1982, the Supreme Court departed from the policy of the previous two decades and ruled that the fact that a seniority system at American Tobacco Company has a discriminatory impact is not in itself enough to make it illegal: Actual intent to discriminate must be proved.[13] Since 1981, the Justice Department has appeared to favor seniority systems over affirmative action programs.

IMPLICATIONS FOR MANAGERS. In the recruitment process, the human resources department normally has prime responsibility for ensuring compliance with the mass of legislation and subsequent legal decisions concerning discrimination. Two kinds of discrimination are of concern to managers. *Access discrimination* refers to hiring considerations and practices (different qualifying tests, lower starting salaries) that are not related in any way to present or future job performance but are based on the employee's membership in a particular population subgroup. *Treatment discrimination* involves practices unrelated to job performance (less favorable work assignments, slower promotion rates) that treat subgroup members differently from others once they are in the work force.[14]

Ultimately, however, the human resources department must instruct and educate managers in the implications of compliance for their respective departments. Even job titles can be sexist and reflect de facto discrimination. For example, the job titles *foreman* and *salesman* are now outmoded; they should be replaced by *supervisor* and *sales worker* or *salesperson*, respectively. Managers must realize that neither they nor the organization has completely free choice in the recruiting, hiring, training, and promotion of human resources. Any individual or organization that fails to comply with the law may be reported to the Equal Employment Opportunities Commission (EEOC) for investigation or become a defendant in a class action or specific lawsuit. In one widely reported class action suit, several thousand female flight attendants won $52.5 million from Northwest Airlines when the company's employment practices were found to be discriminatory. Female employees elsewhere, including clerical workers who struck at Yale University in 1984, have demanded equal pay for jobs deemed by the employer to be of comparable worth.

For practical assistance in interpreting and complying with equal employment opportunity legislation, managers can turn to the Uniform Guidelines on Employee Selection Procedures, issued in 1978. Under these guidelines, organization practices or policies that adversely affect employment opportunities for any race, sex, or ethnic group are prohibited unless the restriction is a justifiable job requirement. Thus, courts have found height and weight requirements illegal when they prevented employment of women and people of Hispanic or Asian origin and were not shown to be job-related. There are justifiable instances in which discriminatory hiring requirements are permitted—such as hiring only males to play male roles in theater productions. These are called *bona fide occupation qualifications* (BFOQs). Race and color, however, have never been judged BFOQ criteria.

In recent years, social problems are affecting both recruitment and management more and more. For example, a 1987 Supreme Court ruling held that the Vocational Rehabilitation Act of 1973 covers workers with contagious diseases, a rule with wide-ranging implications given our current concern over AIDS.[15] Another controversial and important issue is privacy. The use of drug testing, AIDS testing, computer surveillance, and even genetic screening by many companies has stirred fears among workers and others that employers are delving too far into employees' personal lives.

■ *SELECTION*

Drug testing is particularly controversial. Drug use costs U.S. industry about $50 billion a year in employee turnover and absenteeism, and countless dollars in less reliable and productive work. Lives have been lost due to accidents caused by employees under the influence of alcohol, drugs, or both. This situation has caused some companies to insist on random drug testing of employees. Such mandatory drug testing raises the issue of employee civil rights. Some experts predict that except for a small number of occupations, such as train operators and pilots, American workers will not be randomly tested. However, an increasing number of companies—IBM, American Airlines, Dupont, GE, and Kodak among them—are currently testing all job applicants.

Some companies have addressed the reality of drug and alcohol problems at all levels within the organization in a way that employees perceive as more supportive. Employee Assistance Programs (EAPs) provide confidentiality, appropriate referrals, and other support to employees whose job performance is impaired because of drug dependency.[16]

The **selection** process ideally involves mutual decision making: The organization decides whether or not to make a job offer and how attractive the offer should be, and the job candidate decides whether or not the organization and the job offer fit his or her needs and goals. In reality, the selection process is often more one-sided. When the job market is extremely tight, several candidates will be applying for each position, and the organization will use a series of screening devices to hire the candidate it feels is most suitable. When there is a shortage of qualified workers, or when the candidate is a highly qualified executive or professional who is being courted by several organizations, the organization will have to sweeten its offer and come to a quicker decision.

Steps in the Selection Process

The standard hiring sequence follows the seven-step procedure described in Table 13-3.[17] In practice, the actual selection process will vary with organizations and between levels in the same organization. For example, the selection interview for lower-level employees may be quite perfunctory; heavy emphasis may be placed instead on the initial screening interview or on tests. Although written tests designed to define a candidate's interests, aptitudes, and intelligence have long been a staple of employment screening, their use has declined over the past 25 years. Many tests have proved to be discriminatory in their design and results, and it has been difficult to establish their job relatedness when they have been subjected to judicial review.

In selecting middle- or upper-level managers, on the other hand, the interviewing may be extensive—sometimes lasting 8 hours or more—and there may be little or no formal testing. Instead of initially filling out an application, the candidate may submit a résumé. Completion of the formal application may be delayed until after the job offer has been accepted. Some organizations omit the physical examination (Step 6 in Table 13-3) for managers hired at this level.

For many positions, particularly in management, the in-depth interview is an important factor in the organization's decision to make a job offer and in the individual's decision to accept or decline the offer. The most effective interviews—those that are best able to predict the eventual performance of applicants—are usually planned carefully. Ideally, all candidates for the same position are asked the same questions.[18] Most interviews, however, tend to be far less structured and deliberate.

Inadequate interviewing can lead to poor employment decisions. Richard Nehrbass has identified three common defects in interviewing that may produce

TABLE 13-3 Steps in the Selection Process

PROCEDURES	PURPOSES	ACTIONS AND TRENDS
1. Completed job application	Indicates applicant's desired position; provides information for interviews.	Requests only information that predicts success in the job.*
2. Initial screening interview	Provides a quick evaluation of applicant's suitability.	Asks questions on experience, salary expectation, willingness to relocate, etc.
3. Testing	Measures applicant's job skills and the ability to learn on the job.	May include computer testing software, handwriting analysis, medical and physical ability.†
4. Background investigation	Checks truthfulness of applicant's résumé or application form.	Calls the applicant's previous supervisor (with permission) and confirms information from applicant.‡
5. In-depth selection interview	Finds out more about the applicant as an individual.	Conducted by the manager to whom the applicant will report.
6. Physical examination	Ensures effective performance by applicant; protects other employees against diseases; establishes health record on applicant; protects firm against unjust worker's compensation claims.	Often performed by company's medical doctor.
7. Job offer	Fills a job vacancy or position.	Offers a salary plus benefit package.

*See, for example, Robert Hershey, "The Application Form," *Personnel* 48, no. 1 (January–February 1971):38; and Irwin L. Goldstein, "The Application Blank: How Honest Are the Responses?" *Journal of Applied Psychology* 55, no. 5 (October 1971):491.
†David Tuller, "What's New in Employment Testing?" *The New York Times,* February 25, 1985, p. F17.
‡Kirk Johnson, "Why References Aren't 'Available on Request,'" *The New York Times,* June 9, 1985, pp. F8–F9.
Source: Wendell L. French, *The Personnel Management Process,* 6th ed. Copyright © 1987 by Houghton Mifflin Co. Adapted with permission.

inaccurate information about job applicants.[19] The first defect is the imbalance of power in the interview situation. The interviewer is likely to be experienced and at ease, while the interviewee is probably inexperienced in interviewing and ill at ease because the job represents a livelihood, a career, and an important part of his or her self-image.

The second defect of interviews is that they may cause the job candidate to adopt "phony" behavior in the desire to project an image that is acceptable to the interviewer. Sometimes the "act" put on by a qualified applicant is so obviously false or projects an image so contrary to the organization's style that a less qualified candidate who projects a realistic image is offered the position.

The third defect is the tendency of interviewers to ask questions that have no useful answers, such as "Tell me about yourself" or "What would you say is your greatest weakness?" Applicants, sensing the lack of skill and preparation of an interviewer who asks such open-ended questions, may feel uneasy and give superficial answers or may try to second-guess the interviewer and go off on a lengthy tangent. As Nehrbass asserts, interviews that focus on the requirements of the job and the actual skills and abilities of candidates will provide interviewers with more useful information and be better predictors of performance.

Interviewing for a Service Orientation. A management interview at Rosenbluth Travel Inc. may involve a game of catch, a drive in a car, or even a short vacation with CEO Hal F. Rosenbluth, who believes that such impromptu interactions reveal a candidate's true personality and ability to fit into the business.

The interview process may also prove unreliable because of the differing objectives of the interviewer and interviewee. The prospective employer wants to sell the organization as a good place to work and may therefore exaggerate its strengths; the prospective employee wants to be hired and may therefore exaggerate his or her qualities. Some organizations have attempted to reduce this problem through the **realistic job preview (RJP),** in which candidates are exposed to the unattractive as well as the attractive aspects of the job, and by using structured, focused interviews to acquire a more accurate picture of each interviewee's likely job performance.[20]

Manager Selection

The task of selecting managers is difficult because of the complexity of the manager's job. Since managers must use a wide variety of skills and abilities, their selection depends on an accurate assessment of candidates' proven or potential skills and abilities.

SELECTING EXPERIENCED MANAGERS. Organizations may seek to hire experienced managers for a variety of reasons. A newly created post may require a manager with experience not available within the organization; the talent to fill an established post may not be available within the organization; a key position may suddenly open up before there is time to train a replacement; or a top performer in a competing organization may be sought to improve the organization's own competitive position.

An experienced manager who is up for selection usually goes through several interviews before being hired. The interviewers are almost always higher-level managers who attempt to assess the candidate's suitability and past performance, since past performance is generally expected to predict future performance. However, interviewers often find it difficult to obtain verifiable data on a manager's past performance, so they must frequently rely on the interview process, asking questions that may reveal such desirable qualities as emotional stability, self-confidence, and good interpersonal skills. In short, interviewers try to determine how well the candidate fits their idea of what a good manager should be and how compatible the candidate's personality, past experience, personal values, and operating style are with the organization and its culture.

SELECTING POTENTIAL MANAGERS. Potential managers usually enter the organization after graduating from college. Typically, they take entry-level positions—a research or staff job or a position in a training program. Their performance in these entry-level positions will strongly influence the type of managerial job they eventually receive.

Assessing an individual's managerial potential is difficult because it involves judging the future manager on things he or she has not yet done. Such an assessment is extremely important, nonetheless, since potential managers may well determine the future success of the organization.

Most assessments of prospective managers begin with a review of college grades, even though, except for technical positions, college performance does not seem to be strongly associated with managerial performance. Other aspects of the college record can provide some insights into nonacademic abilities, such as interpersonal skills, leadership qualities, and ability to assume responsibility. For this reason, many organizations look for evidence of extracurricular managerial interest or experience—working on a campus journal, for example, or directing part of a community project.[21] Finally, like experienced managers, prospective managers may be interviewed extensively to determine whether they have what the interviewers consider an appropriate personal style for a manager.

In general, the likelihood of making good candidate choices improves when several managers interview each candidate. The resulting number of viewpoints lessens the possibility that effective managers will be lost to the organization because of one interviewer's bias.

Assessment Centers

assessment center Selection technique in which candidates are asked to participate in simulated tasks and exercises.

Another method that has proved effective in selecting qualified candidates is the **assessment center**. Originally used during World War II to select OSS (Office of Strategic Services) agents, assessment centers have since been used with considerable success to predict the future management performance of both experienced and potential managers.[22] Under this approach, candidates participate in a wide range of simulation exercises while trained observers note and assess their behavior. One common exercise is the *in-basket*, in which the candidate is informed that he or she has just been promoted to a newly vacant position and will have to leave town soon to attend an important meeting. The candidate is given one hour to deal with the memos, letters, reports, telephone messages, and other materials in the previous incumbent's in-basket. The candidate must handle each item in the most appropriate manner, and in many cases will have an opportunity to explain or discuss his or her decisions in a follow-up interview.

In the activity known as the *leaderless group discussion* exercise, participants are given a problem requiring a group decision. The way the candidates handle themselves in this situation helps to reveal their leadership qualities and interpersonal skills. Candidates may also participate in *management games* geared to the level of the job being filled, make oral presentations, and take any number of tests probing their mental ability, general knowledge, and personality.

Besides being excellent predictors of management potential; assessment centers can serve as part of a management development program. In fact, some graduate schools of business use assessment center techniques to guide an individual's self-development program. Unfortunately, only a few, relatively large, successful organizations can afford the assessment center approach, which typically involves a number of assessors working with a small group of candidates over a period of several days.[23]

Assessment centers have come under criticism on other grounds besides cost. Richard Klimoski, for example, has pointed out that the tests focus on maximum performance under certain conditions rather than *typical* performance. They prove that a person *can* perform well without evidence that he or she *will* perform well.[24]

■ *ORIENTATION OR SOCIALIZATION*

orientation or socialization A program designed to help employees fit smoothly into an organization.

Orientation or **socialization** is designed to provide a new employee with the information he or she needs to function comfortably and effectively in the organization. Typically, socialization conveys three types of information: (1) general information about the daily work routine; (2) a review of the organization's history, purpose, operations, and products or services, as well as how the employee's job contributes to the organization's needs; and (3) a detailed presentation, perhaps in a brochure, of the organization's policies, work rules, and employee benefits.

Many studies have shown that employees feel anxious on entering an organization. They worry about how well they will perform in the job; they feel inadequate compared to more experienced employees; and they are concerned about how well they will get along with their co-workers. Effective socialization programs reduce the anxiety of new employees by giving them information on the job environment and on supervisors, by introducing them to co-workers, and by encouraging them to ask questions.[25]

HERE'S AN EXAMPLE

Lotus Development is one of only a few companies to offer paid paternity leave to men. (*Business Week*, 4/15/91, p. 90ff.)

CLASS COMMENT

According to Professor Michael Crino, workplace sabotage is up and is more dangerous than ever. (*Business Month*, July 1990, p. 5)

Early job experiences—when the new employee's expectations and the organization's expectations confront each other—seem to play a critical role in the individual's career with the organization. If the expectations are not compatible, there will be dissatisfaction; turnover rates are almost always highest among an organization's new employees.[26] An important aspect of job satisfaction—for all workers—is the assurance that employees can work for the company's good without neglecting their personal obligations. One of the most pressing concerns in this area is adequate child care. (See the Ethics in Management box.)

ETHICS IN MANAGEMENT

The Issue of Corporate Day Care

Few parents can do their best work when they are worried about their children. Yet this is the plight of millions of working parents who cannot find adequate, affordable day care. Over 50 percent of mothers with infants and toddlers hold jobs outside the home, and the percentage of two-career households continues to rise. Furthermore, young professionals often live far from doting grandparents, who, in any case, are often working themselves. So the demand for reliable, affordable day care is an important issue in the workplace.

The supply of day-care centers has not kept pace with demand, and fewer women—historically, the labor pool for this service industry—are available to care for children in the home. In some areas, the shortage is so acute that good day-care centers have waiting lists of up to two years; pundits suggest that a couple enroll their child before conception. And if finding day care for the conventional workday is difficult, finding it for a night shift is all but impossible.

In theory, this is not the organization's problem, but in reality, the issue clearly affects employers. Studies have shown that parents devote a significant amount of their energy while at work to worrying about their children, and a high percentage of absenteeism can be attributed to family conflicts due to child-care failures or sick children who could not attend their day-care centers. Even if employers could downplay their ethical obligation to help employees meet their parental obligations, they must remember that children represent the future of our society and demand our care.

What employers should do about this is a matter of lively debate. Companies that believe it is in their best interest to help employees find child care have gone about it in a variety of ways. A few have set up child-care centers for their employees, either on-site or nearby. Such centers are often filled to capacity, however, with waiting lists as long as those at privately operated centers. Many larger companies sponsor information and referral centers for parents seeking day care. Small companies that cannot afford these solutions tend to institute flexible hours and/or

An Investment in Human Capital. That's how Du Pont views the $1 million it has invested in Delaware programs to expand child-care services. Here, Faith A. Wohl, director of work force partnering at Du Pont, visits a Du Pont day-care center.

flexible leave policies, which make it a little easier for employees to be parents.

Many companies have done little or nothing to help employees in this area, however, mainly because of simple economics. Corporate day-care centers can be very expensive to set up and run; some companies fear the liability involved. Even the referral center's usefulness is limited by the facilities available in the community. Other companies feel that day care is strictly an employee's responsibility.

During the 1988 presidential campaign, both Michael Dukakis and George Bush took positions on the need for federal support for day care. As of 1991, however, no action had been taken, although the demographic data suggest that this issue is not going to resolve itself or go away. Rather, it will continue to grow, becoming an important item on the human resource management agenda.

Sources: Cathy Trost, "Best Employers for Women and Parents," *The Wall Street Journal,* November 30, 1987, p. 23, and "Creative Child-Care Programs Aid Employees Who Work Odd Hours," *The Wall Street Journal,* March 18, 1988, Sect. 2, p. 29; Albert R. Carr, "Child-Care Plans Provided by 11% of Surveyed Firms," *The Wall Street Journal,* January 15, 1988, p. 12.

■ TRAINING AND DEVELOPMENT

Training programs are directed toward maintaining and improving *current* job performance, while **development programs** seek to develop skills for *future* jobs. Both managers and nonmanagers may receive help from training and development programs, but the mix of experiences is likely to vary. Nonmanagers are much more likely to be trained in the technical skills required for their current jobs, while managers frequently receive assistance in developing the skills—particularly conceptual and human relations skills—required in future jobs. In our discussion of training and development, we will cover training briefly and then focus on management development.

Training Programs

The need to train new or recently promoted employees is self-evident. Such employees have to learn new skills, and since their motivation is likely to be high, they can be acquainted relatively easily with the skills and behavior expected in their new position. On the other hand, training experienced employees can be problematic. The training needs of such employees are not always easy to determine, and when they can be, the individuals involved may resent being asked to change their established ways of doing their jobs.

Managers can use four procedures to determine the training needs of individuals in their organization or subunit:

1. *Performance appraisal.* Each employee's work is measured against the performance standards or objectives established for his or her job.
2. *Analysis of job requirements.* The skills or knowledge specified in the appro-

Training Phone Representatives at GE. In addition to a college degree and sales experience, phone reps get six weeks of hands-on training, dismantling GE appliances, before they start answering customer calls to the GE Answer Center, an 800 number that GE appliance owners can call with service questions. Considered the nation's best 800-number service network, the Answer Center costs GE more than $10 million a year to operate, but the phone reps garner suggestions that help GE improve its products.

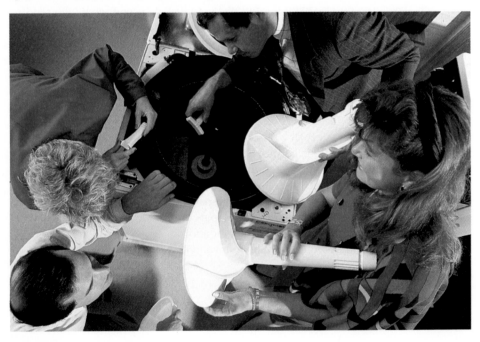

HERE'S AN EXAMPLE
Corning Glass Works sends
workers to a four-hour orientation that deals with a
diversity of issues, including sexual harassment.
Guidelines dating back to
1976 ban pin-up calendars.
(*Business Week*, 3/18/91,
p. 98ff.)

HERE'S AN EXAMPLE
Companies had to prepare
to deal with veterans re-
turning from the Gulf War.
Benefits such as adequate
counseling and reentry
programs and perhaps
low-interest loan programs
were put into place in
some companies. (*Wall
Street Journal*, 3/1/91,
p. B1ff.)

**computer-assisted in-
struction (CAI)** A training technique in which
computers are used to
lessen the time necessary
for training by instructors
and to provide additional
help to individual trainees.

CLASS COMMENT
Some common topics for
management development
programs are improving
supervisory skills, developing good communication
skills, time management
and priority setting, and
becoming an effective listener.

CLASS COMMENT
According to a survey by
consultant Towers Perrin,
almost half of employees
say they have little or no
trust in their bosses.
(*Business Month*, July
1990, p. 5)

priate job description are examined, and those employees without necessary skills or knowledge become candidates for a training program.

3. *Organizational analysis.* The effectiveness of the organization and its success in meeting its goals are analyzed to determine where differences exist. For example, members of a department with a high turnover rate or a low perfor- mance record might require additional training.

4. *Survey of human resources.* Managers as well as nonmanagers are asked to describe what problems they are experiencing in their work and what actions they believe are necessary to solve them.

Once the organization's training needs have been identified, the personnel department must initiate the appropriate training effort. Managers have available a variety of training approaches. The most common of these are *on-the-job-training* methods, including *job rotation,* in which the employee, over a period of time, works on a series of jobs, thereby learning a broad variety of skills; *internship,* in which job training is combined with related classroom instruction; and *apprentice- ship,* in which the employee is trained under the guidance of a highly skilled co- worker.

Off-the-job training takes place outside the workplace but attempts to simu- late actual working conditions. This type of training includes *vestibule training,* in which employees train on the actual equipment and in a realistic job setting but in a room different from the one in which they will be working. The object is to avoid the on-the-job pressures that might interfere with the learning process. In *behavior- ally experienced training,* some of the methods used in assessment centers— business games, in-basket simulation, problem-centered cases, and so on—are em- ployed so that the trainee can learn the behavior appropriate for the job through *role playing.* Off-the-job training may focus on the *classroom,* with seminars, lec- tures, and films, or it may involve **computer-assisted instruction (CAI)**, which can both reduce the time needed for training and provide more help for individual trainees.[27]

Management Development Programs

Management development is designed to improve the overall effectiveness of man- agers in their present positions and to prepare them for greater responsibility when they are promoted. Management development programs have become more preva- lent in recent years because of the increasingly complex demands being made on managers and because training managers through experience alone is a time- consuming and unreliable process. The investment of many companies in manage- ment development is quite large. For example, for years, IBM has required a mini- mum of 40 hours of human resource management training for all new managers;[28] similar levels of training continue after this initial involvement. Some companies, however, do not rely on costly formal training approaches. Exxon, for example, prefers to nurture its new talent by providing it with practical job experience, dis- patching executives at all levels to key positions around the world in order to broaden their outlook and hone their judgment.

Early management development activities were program-centered; that is, a program would be designed and administered to managers regardless of their indi- vidual differences. However, it is now generally recognized that managers differ in ability, experience, and personality. Thus, management development programs today are more *manager-centered*—tailored to fit the unique developmental re- quirements of the managers attending. Before a program is selected, a *needs analy- sis* is made to identify the particular needs and problems of the manager or group of managers. Then the appropriate training activities are recommended.[29]

As with training programs, there are a number of on-the-job and off-the-job approaches to management development.[30]

ON-THE-JOB METHODS. On-the-job methods are usually preferred in management development programs. The training is far more likely than off-the-job training to be tailored to the individual, to be job-related, and to be conveniently located.

There are four major formal on-the-job development methods:

CLASS COMMENT
One hallmark of a well-run business: it pays attention to employee complaints. According to a survey by the Hay Group, only about 30 percent of workers at most companies feel that management listens to them. (*Business Month,* July 1990, p. 5)

1. *Coaching*—the training of a subordinate by his or her immediate superior—is by far the most effective management development technique. Unfortunately, many managers are either unable or unwilling to coach their subordinates. To be meaningful, on-the-job coaching must be tempered by considerable restraint—subordinates cannot develop unless they are allowed to work out problems in their own way. Managers too often feel compelled to tell their subordinates exactly what to do, thereby negating the effectiveness of coaching. In addition, some managers feel threatened when asked to coach their subordinates, fearing they are creating a rival. Actually, the manager has much to gain from coaching subordinates, since a manager frequently will not be promoted unless there is a successor available to take his or her place.

   Many firms make a point of training their managers in the fine art of coaching. Conscientious managers often keep a "development file" for each subordinate, indicating what training the subordinate is receiving, what skills the subordinate is acquiring, and how well the subordinate is performing. A record of *critical incidents*—situations in which a subordinate displayed desirable or undesirable behavior—may be included. In discussing these incidents with the subordinate, managers can reinforce good habits ("You really handled that customer's complaint well"), gently point out bad habits ("Do you think you should be firmer with the supplier?"), and identify areas in which the subordinate needs further development.

COORDINATED RESOURCE
See Samaras Exercise 3.2, "To Enlarge, to Enrich, and to Compare."

2. *Job rotation* involves shifting managers from position to position so they can broaden their experience and familiarize themselves with various aspects of the firm's operations.

3. *Training positions* are a third method of developing managers. Trainees are given staff posts immediately under a manager, often with the title of "assistant to." Such assignments give trainees a chance to work with and model themselves after outstanding managers who might otherwise have little contact with them.

4. Finally, *planned work activities* involve giving trainees important work assignments to develop their experience and ability. Trainees may be asked to head a task force or participate in an important committee meeting. Such experiences help them gain insight into how organizations operate and also improve their human relations skills.

FOR DISCUSSION
What are the advantages and disadvantages of having an in-house trainer instead of an outside consultant?

OFF-THE-JOB METHODS. Off-the-job development techniques remove individuals from the stresses and ongoing demands of the workplace, enabling them to focus fully on the learning experience. In addition, they provide opportunities for meeting people from other departments or organizations. Thus, employees are exposed to useful new ideas and experiences while they make potentially useful contacts. The most common off-the-job development methods are in-house classroom instruction and management development programs sponsored by universities and organizations such as the American Management Association.

Almost every management development program includes some form of *classroom instruction* in which specialists from inside or outside the organization teach trainees a particular subject. To counteract possible passivity and boredom, classroom instruction is often supplemented with case studies, role playing, and business games or simulations. For example, managers may be asked to play roles on both sides in a simulated labor-management dispute.

Some organizations send selected employees to *university-sponsored management development programs.* Many major universities have such programs,

Off-the-Job Development Programs. Consultant Terrence C. Simmons, of Simmons Associates, center, conducts day-long diversity management workshops, designed to help mid- and upper-level managers confront their positive and negative stereotypes about minorities. Becoming more sensitive to diversity is a bottom-line issue, these consultants hold, since firms that fail to retain and promote talented minorities will incur the ongoing expense of trying to replace them.

which range in length from about a week to three months or more. Some universities (such as MIT and Stanford) also have one-year full-time study programs for middle-level managers. Usually, these managers have been slated for promotion; their organizations send them to university programs to broaden their perspectives and prepare them for movement into general (as opposed to functional) management. University programs often combine classroom instruction with case studies, role playing, and simulation.

Increasingly, large corporations are assuming many of the functions of universities with regard to advanced off-the-job training of employees. U.S. business now spends an estimated $60 billion each year on in-house education, a figure comparable to that spent by the nation's colleges and universities. By the mid-1990s, more than two dozen corporations and industry associations are expected to be offering advanced, accredited academic degrees. Xerox, RCA, Arthur Andersen, GE, and Holiday Inns have each acquired educational facilities that closely resemble university campuses. IBM, Westinghouse, and Digital Equipment Company have established the National Technological University, a "satellite university" where high-level continuing education is transmitted via satellite to classrooms throughout the country and abroad.[31]

COORDINATED RESOURCE

Acumen: *Acumen* could be used for management development programs.

CONDITIONS FOR EFFECTIVE MANAGEMENT DEVELOPMENT PROGRAMS. One of the greatest challenges to the development program takes place when the trainee returns to his or her job. If the on-the-job environment does not support the new managerial skills and knowledge, they will quickly disappear. This has been observed following human relations training, in which individuals are taught to use more democratic, participative management styles. Those whose supervisors do not favor such a style may become even more autocratic than they were before the training. Thus, the support of both top management and the trainees' supervisors is important in making a training program effective.

ILLUSTRATIVE CASE STUDY

CONTINUED

Human Relations at Sony Corporation

Sony has long been a leader in human resources management in Japan. The company has adopted such American concepts as the five-day, 40-hour work week, even though Japanese law still sanctions a maximum of 48 hours and the average in Japanese manufacturing remains 43 hours per week. Morever, Sony was one of the first Japanese firms to close its factories for one week every summer to allow all its employees to be off work at the same time.

In addition, the Japanese system enforces a different view of recruits. Morita urges managers to see recruits as rough stones and the managerial job as the task of building a strong and sturdy wall out of these rough stones. The Japanese ideal is to shape and smooth managerial recruits so that they become a cohesive part of the company.

Japanese companies, at least the large ones, also have a humane view of dealing with employees in declining industries. Most companies offer retraining—and most workers eagerly accept it. At Sony, workers are retrained when their particular jobs become obsolete.

■ PERFORMANCE APPRAISAL

COORDINATED RESOURCE
See Study Guide Self-Learning Exercise 13, "Performance Appraisal."

Performance appraisal is one of the manager's most important tasks, but most managers freely admit it gives them difficulty. It is not always easy to judge a subordinate's performance accurately, and often it is even harder to convey that judgment to the subordinate in a constructive and painless manner. This applies to both informal and formal appraisals.

Informal Appraisals

informal performance appraisal The process of continually feeding back to subordinates information regarding their work performance.

TEACHING TIP
Have students relate experiences they have had with performance appraisals—both as appraiser and appraisee.

We will use the term **informal performance appraisal** to mean the continual process of feeding back to subordinates information about how well they are doing their work for the organization. Informal appraisal is conducted on a day-to-day basis. The manager spontaneously mentions that a particular piece of work was performed well or poorly, or the subordinate stops by the manager's office to find out how a particular piece of work was received. Because of the close connection between the behavior and the feedback on it, informal appraisal quickly encourages desirable performance and discourages undesirable performance before it becomes ingrained. An organization's employees must perceive informal appraisal not merely as a casual occurrence but as an important activity, an integral part of the organization's culture.[32]

Formal Systematic Appraisals

formal systematic appraisal A formalized appraisal process for rating current subordinate performance, identifying subordinates deserving raises or promotions, and identifying subordinates in need of further training.

Formal systematic appraisal usually occurs semiannually or annually. Formal appraisal has four major purposes: (1) to let subordinates know formally how their current performance is being rated; (2) to identify subordinates who deserve merit raises; (3) to locate subordinates who need additional training; and (4) to identify candidates for promotion.

It is important for managers to differentiate between the current performance and the promotability (potential performance) of subordinates. Managers in many organizations fail to make this distinction because they assume that a person with

COORDINATED RESOURCE

Acumen: Acumen is a managerial assessment and development tool based on the belief that improving performance depends on recognizing one's thinking patterns, changing those that are counterproductive, and strengthening productive ones. It assesses and helps develop behaviorally-oriented, rather than technically-oriented, management skills.

TEACHING TIP

It would be beneficial to have examples of the different types of appraisal forms to share with students. Check in any personnel management or human resources management textbook for examples.

the skills and ability to perform well in one job will automatically perform well in a different or more responsible position. This is why people are often promoted to positions in which they cannot perform adequately.[33]

Who is responsible for formal performance appraisals? In answer to this question, four basic appraisal approaches have evolved in organizations. The first approach, *a superior's rating of subordinates,* is by far the most common. However, other approaches are becoming more popular and can be a valuable supplement to appraisal by a single superior.

A group of superiors rating subordinates is the second most frequently used appraisal approach. Subordinates are rated by a managerial committee or by a series of managers who fill out separate rating forms. Because it relies on a number of views, this approach is often more effective than appraisal by a single superior. However, it is time-consuming and often dilutes subordinates' feelings of accountability to their immediate superior.

The third appraisal approach is *a group of peers rating a colleague.* The individual is rated separately and on paper by co-workers on the same organizational level. This approach, uncommon in business organizations, is used mainly in the military, particularly in military academies, to identify leadership potential.

The fourth approach is *subordinates' rating of bosses.* This approach has a common analog in colleges, where faculty are often asked to evaluate their dean on a number of performance measures. Although it is the least common formal approach in business organizations, subordinate rating of superiors is becoming more widespread as an informal means of evaluating managers and helping them improve their performance.[34]

Traditionally, appraisals have concentrated on such personal characteristics as intelligence, decisiveness, creativity, and ability to get along with others. Today, however, appraisals are increasingly based on the individual's actual performance—that is, on how well the employee is helping the organization achieve its goals. MBO (see Chapter 8) is an example of a performance-based appraisal approach that involves establishing specific objectives and comparing performance against those objectives.

Problems of Appraisal

Probably the most influential study of performance appraisal was conducted at the General Electric Company in the early 1960s by Herbert Meyer and his associates.[35] They found that formal appraisals by managers are often ineffective in improving the performance of subordinates. Individuals who were formally criticized about their job performance once or twice a year tended to become defensive and resentful, and their performance after the appraisal interview tended to decline.

Meyer and his colleagues suggest that the goal of appraisal—to improve the future performance of subordinates—is difficult to achieve if managers act in their traditional role of judge. Instead, Meyer and his colleagues argue, a manager and an individual subordinate should set performance goals together and then evaluate progress toward those goals. Participatory appraisal, they found, leads to both greater satisfaction and higher job performance. Meyer and his co-workers also suggest the appraisal process be continual—that is, it should become part of the everyday interaction between managers and subordinates rather than be imposed on subordinates once or twice a year.

Aside from the tendency to judge subordinates, there are a number of other pitfalls managers must avoid in order to make their formal and informal appraisal programs effective:

1. *Shifting standards.* Some managers rate each subordinate by different standards and expectations. A low-performing but motivated employee, for example, might be rated higher than a top-performing but seemingly indifferent

employee. To be effective, the appraisal method must be perceived by subordinates as based on uniform, fair standards.[36]

2. *Rater bias.* Some managers allow their personal biases to distort ratings. These biases may be gross prejudices regarding sex, color, race, or religion, as well as personal characteristics, such as age, style of clothing, or political viewpoint. An increasing number of organizations try to deal with this problem by requiring documentation or explanations for rating reports.

3. *Different rater patterns.* Managers (like teachers) differ in their rating styles. Some managers rate harshly, others easily. The lack of uniform rating standards is unfair to employees, who can become confused about where they stand; it is also unfair to the organization, since it makes it difficult to decide which employees should be rewarded. Differences in rating patterns can be reduced through precise definitions of each item on the rating form.

4. *The halo effect.* There is a common tendency, known as the halo effect, to rate subordinates high or low on *all* performance measures based on *one* of their characteristics. For example, an employee who works late constantly might be rated high on productivity and quality of output as well as on motivation. Similarly, an attractive or popular employee might be given a high overall rating. Rating employees separately on each of a number of performance measures and encouraging raters to guard against the halo effect are two ways to reduce this problem.

Approximately two decades after the original study by Meyer and his colleagues, a research team headed by Edward E. Lawler, Allan M. Mohrman, and Susan M. Resnick conducted a follow-up study at GE. Their study supported many of the original findings and led to some additional recommendations.[37] First, top management should take care to integrate performance appraisal into the overall organizational culture and human resource strategy, to emphasize its importance, and to evaluate it continually. Second, the nature of an employee's job, the performance expectations attached to it, and the ways in which performance will be measured should all be made clear at the outset of employment. Third, discussions about the bases for pay increases and the relationship between pay and performance should be a natural and important part of appraisal process. Fourth, in a *separate* process, but one well integrated into the overall human resource management system, a manager should discuss an employee's career development opportunities and outline what an employee needs to do to reach his or her potential. Finally, the employee should be an equal and active partner with the manager throughout the appraisal process.

■ *PROMOTIONS, TRANSFERS, DEMOTIONS, AND SEPARATIONS*

COORDINATED RESOURCE
The Additional Lecture for Chapter 13 found in the Lecture Extras supplement is called "Requiem for Upward Mobility."

The movement of personnel within an organization—their promotion, transfer, demotion, and separation—is a major aspect of human resource management. The actual decisions about whom to promote and whom to fire can also be among the most difficult, and important, a manager has to make.

Promotions

The possibility of advancement often serves as a major incentive for superior managerial performance, and promotions are the most significant way to recognize superior performance. Therefore, it is extremely important that promotions be fair—based on merit and untainted by favoritism. Still, even fair and appropriate promotions can create a number of problems. One major problem is that organization members who are bypassed for promotion frequently feel resentful, which may affect their morale and productivity. Another major problem is discrimination. Most people accept the need, or at least the legal obligation, to avoid racial, sex, or age discrimination in the hiring process, but less attention has been paid to discrimination against women, the aged, and minority groups in promotion decisions. Consequently, affirmative action programs have been introduced to be sure typical victims of discrimination are groomed for advancement.

CLASS COMMENT
Today's managers may find that lateral moves are becoming routine and even desirable; that jobs last longer; that it's acceptable to speak out and try to reshape the organization; that success means inner fulfillment and money; that a good pay package includes an equity stake or profit sharing; and that work lasts until the job is done. (*Fortune,* 7/2/90, p. 38ff.)

Transfers

Transfers serve a number of purposes. They are used to give people broader job experiences as part of their development and to fill vacancies as they occur. Transfers are also used to keep promotion ladders open and to keep individuals interested in the work. For example, many middle managers reach a plateau simply because there is no room for all of them at the top. Such managers may be shifted to other positions to keep their job motivation and interest high. Finally, inadequately performing employees may be transferred to other jobs simply because a higher-level manager is reluctant to demote or separate them. Increasingly, however, some employees are refusing transfers because they do not want to move their families or jeopardize a spouse's career. Other employees, offered overseas transfers, are rightly concerned about unstable political situations. In these cases, employers must make plans to protect their employees overseas. (See the International Management box.)

INTERNATIONAL MANAGEMENT

Managers in the Cross-Fire

The overseas transfer: Is it a once-in-a-lifetime chance to live in another country, getting to know its culture and people intimately? Or a life-threatening risk? In some countries, American managers have been the target of terrorists and kidnappers; in others, they have been endangered by unstable political situations. This was the case in the summer of 1990, when Iraq launched a surprise invasion of tiny but wealthy Kuwait, trapping thousands of Westerners who lived and worked in Kuwait and Iraq.

In the immediate confusion, the American embassy had its hands full helping vacationing Americans and students. Communications broke down within a few days, as journalists were kicked out of Kuwait, phone lines were cut, and television studios were taken over by the invaders. While the United States and other countries tried to work through diplomatic channels, Iraqi leader Saddam Hussein dispatched hundreds of Westerners to key military and intelligence posts, where they were used as "human shields" against feared foreign retaliatory attacks. As the stalemate continued, it became clear that no nation—including the United States—could rescue its citizens from this predicament without risking their lives.

AT&T did not wait for this revelation, however. On the day of the invasion, its special situation room and crisis management center in suburban New Jersey opened at dawn. AT&T, which has 18,000 employees in 37 countries, opened the center in 1988 to maintain communications with employees during times of international turmoil and to assist in evacuation. Although the center had operated during the invasion of Panama and during a coup attempt in the Philippines, the invasion of Kuwait involved the largest number of employees trapped in a besieged country. Besides Americans, stranded AT&T employees included Britons, Canadians, Dutch, Filipinos, and Sri Lankans in Kuwait, as well as several hundred employees of more than 30 nationalities in Saudi Arabia.

Equipped with telephones, communications equipment, maps, and computers, the center made calls into and out of Kuwait, to Riyadh, the capital of Saudi Arabia, and to relatives of the trapped employees. Many of the employees who fled Kuwait were flown by AT&T to Frankfurt, Germany, where they were met by AT&T personnel and given counseling by the company's medical department.

Multinational companies are coming to realize that emergency evacuation plans are an important part of their human resource policies.

Sources: William J. Holstein, "Going Global," *Business Week,* October 29, 1988, pp. 8–10; and Cindy Skrzycki, "Phone Co. Employees Escape Gulf," *The Washington Post,* August 31, 1990, pp. A1, A21.

Discipline, Demotions, and Separations

THOUGHT PROVOKER
Alcohol is involved in 47 percent of industrial accidents. What are the implications? (*Business Week,* 3/25/91, p. 76ff.)

Discipline is generally administered when an employee violates company policy or falls short of work expectations and management must act to remedy the situation. Discipline usually progresses through a series of steps—warning, reprimand, probation, suspension, disciplinary transfer, demotion, and discharge—until the problem is solved or eliminated.[38] Some ineffective managers may be asked to go for retraining or development, others may be "promoted" to a position with a more impressive title but less responsibility.

If demotion or transfer is not feasible, separation is usually better than letting a poor performer stay on the job. No matter how agonizing the separation decision may be, the logic of human resource planning frequently requires that it be made. (Interestingly, a surprising number of poor performers at one firm become solid successes at another.) The present turbulent environment of increased competition has accelerated the trend toward restructuring, which has contributed to a growing rate of separations. As a result, some companies provide *outplacement services* to help separated employees find new positions.

HERE'S AN EXAMPLE
Most companies lavish help on laid-off employees. McDonnell Douglas Company is taking extraordinary measures to help those who remain after layoffs. (*Business Month,* September 1990, p. 5)

It has become increasingly important for companies to establish—and follow to the letter—a policy on termination. For many years, it was accepted doctrine that managers could fire at their own discretion. Through legislative and judicial action, however, employees have won an increasing number of complex rights. As a result, more and more companies are finding themselves answering charges of "wrongful termination" in courts that seem to view jobs as a form of legal contract or property, with roughly comparable rights. Judgments against employers can be costly: The average settlement in California is currently about $450,000.

■ HRM AND STRATEGY

COORDINATED RESOURCE
The Distinctive Discussions for Chapter 13 found in the Lecture Extras supplement include "What Job Skills Are Necessary?" and "Us vs. Them No More."

As Table 13-4 shows, environmental changes require a number of reactions by organizations trying to meet their strategic goals. Because so many of these reactions involve human resources, HRM is feeling the pressure.[39] In the rest of this section, we will see how HRM can analyze environmental pressures and then evaluate its effectiveness in meeting these pressures.

HRM and Environmental Pressures

CLASS COMMENT
The new American work force will be smaller, poorly educated, and no longer white and male. (*Business Month,* November 1990, p. 59ff.)

Researchers at the Harvard Business School have proposed a broad way of understanding human resources management that takes HRM beyond the narrow connotation of just planning, selecting, training, and appraising. Figure 13-3 indicates how external stakeholder interests, such as union interests, and situational factors, such as the local labor market, can influence HRM policies. These policies naturally have consequences for the organization itself—consequences that, in turn, affect both the external and internal environments.

COORDINATED RESOURCE
Use Transparency 85, Map of the HRM Territory.

COORDINATED RESOURCE
See DuBose Reading #19, "Reforming the U.S. System of Collective Bargaining."

For example, many people are forecasting a labor shortage in the United States for the 1990s. If this proves true, then business strategies must take this fact into account. Some labor-intensive activities may have to be transferred to other countries, or, alternatively, executives may have to lobby for a liberalization of immigration laws. Additionally, industries will be affected differently by a labor shortage. Companies may have to adopt a variety of new reward systems and even new ways of dividing and sharing work.

Such considerations provide clear evidence that the HRM process cannot be divorced from strategy—the overall direction of the firm. The most important point to remember, however, is that unless HRM policies are influenced by all stakeholders, the organization will fail to meet the needs of the stakeholders in the long run and will fail as an organization.

TABLE 13-4 Reactions of an Organization to Changes in Its Environment

ACTIONS	REACTIONS
Situational/Stakeholder Pressures Influencing Effectiveness	Countervailing Measures by HRM to Retain Effectiveness
Increasing international competition	Improve human productivity Increase employee commitment Ensure long-term supply of competent people
Increasing complexity and size of organizations	Reduce levels of bureaucratization Improve HRM in diverse societies
Slower growth and declining markets	Reevaluate advancement opportunities to high potential employees Reevaluate employment security to long-service employees
Greater government involvement	Reexamine HRM policies and practices Develop new HRM policies and practices
Increasing education of the work force	Reexamine employee competency
Changing values of the work force	Reexamine employee autonomy
More concern with career and life satisfaction	Reexamine employee career paths, lifestyle needs, and work schedules
Changes in work force demography	Reexamine all policies, practices, and managerial values affecting minorities

Source: Adapted with permission of The Free Press, a Division of Macmillan, Inc., from *Human Resource Management* by Michael Beer, Bert A. Spector, Paul R. Lawrence, and Richard E. Walton. Copyright © 1985 by The Free Press.

FIGURE 13-3 Map of the HRM Territory

Source: Adapted with permission of The Free Press, a Division of Macmillan, Inc., from *Human Resource Management* by Michael Beer, Bert A. Spector, Paul R. Lawrence, and Richard E. Walton. Copyright © 1985 by The Free Press.

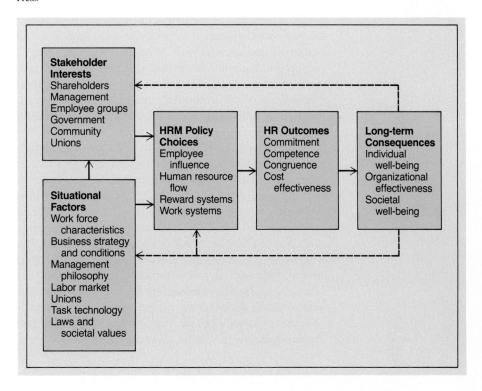

The Four C's Model for Evaluating Human Resources

COORDINATED RESOURCE

See *Management Live!* Chapter 12 video "9 to 5."

To evaluate the effectiveness of the HRM process within an organization, the Harvard researchers have proposed a four C's model for human resources outcomes: commitment, competence, congruence, and cost effectiveness. It is hoped that managers will develop creative solutions to human resource problems when they address questions related to the four C's during the HRM evaluation. Examples of questions interrelated with the four C's, as well as some methods used in measuring them, are as follows:[40]

1. *Competence.* How competent are employees in their work? Do they need additional training? Assessment centers and performance evaluations by managers can help a company determine what talent it has available. To what extent do HRM policies attract, keep, and develop employees with skills and knowledge needed now and in the future?

2. *Commitment.* How committed are employees to their work and organization? Surveys can be conducted through interviews and questionnaires to find answers to this question. Additional information can be gained from personnel records about voluntary separation, absenteeism, and grievances. To what extent do HRM policies enhance the commitment of employees to their work and organization?

THOUGHT PROVOKER

More managers are striking deals for flexible work schedules. They end up having more time for their kids, *and* their careers are prospering. Comment on the implications for human resource managers. (*Fortune,* 5/20/91, p. 60ff.)

3. *Congruence.* Is there congruence, or agreement, between the basic philosophy and goals of the company and its employees? Is there trust and common purpose between managers and employees? Incongruence can be detected in the frequency of strikes, conflicts between managers and subordinates, and grievances. A low level of congruence results in low levels of trust and common purpose; tension and stress between employees and managers may increase. What levels of congruence between management and employees do HRM policies and practices enhance or retain?

4. *Cost effectiveness.* Are HRM policies cost-effective in terms of wages, benefits, turnover, absenteeism, strikes, and similar factors?

Even more difficult than addressing and measuring the extent of the four C's within a company is the problem of assessing HRM *outcomes.* In other words, how do you make judgments about the long-term consequences of HRM policies on employee and societal well-being and organizational effectiveness? How, for example, do you go about the formidable task of assigning a value to employee commitment or to an organizational climate and culture that encourages motivation and employee growth? In the final analysis, managers need the participation of a broad range of stakeholders (including management, unions, and governmental agencies) to obtain the data needed to evaluate the impact of HRM practices and policies.

COORDINATED RESOURCE

See Samaris Case 3.3, "Placid Plastics, Inc."

By shaping HRM policies to enhance commitment, competence, congruence, and cost effectiveness, an organization increases its capacity to adapt to changes in its environment.[41] *High commitment,* for example, means better communication between employees and managers. Mutual trust is enhanced, and all stakeholders are responsive to one another's needs and concerns whenever changes in environmental demands occur. *High competence* means that employees are versatile in their skills and can take on new roles and jobs as needed. They are better able to respond to changes in environmental demands. *Cost effectiveness* means that human resource costs, such as wages, benefits, and strikes, are kept equal to or less than those of competitors. All stakeholders have undoubtedly faced the realities of the business). Finally, *higher congruence* means that all stakeholders share a common purpose and collaborate in solving problems prompted by external changes in environmental demands, a crucial capacity in an ever-changing environment.

ILLUSTRATIVE CASE STUDY

WRAP-UP

Human Relations at Sony Corporation

Clearly, Akio Morita's human resource policies accommodate Sony's overall strategy. By focusing on the shared fate of management and employees, Sony develops among its workers a sense of commitment to the overall goals of the firm. Partly because of this employee commitment, Sony has been able to stay competitive in terms of wages and benefits and to motivate highly competent people to continue to innovate.

By focusing on people as resources rather than as costs, companies like Sony are writing the book on future management theory and practice. ■

■ SUMMARY

The HRM process includes (1) human resource planning; (2) recruitment; (3) selection; (4) socialization; (5) training and development; (6) performance appraisal; (7) promotions, transfers, demotions, and separations.

Human resource planning includes planning for the future personnel needs of the organization, planning what the future balance of the organization's personnel will be, planning a recruitment-selection or layoff program, and planning a development program. Human resource plans are based on forecasting and on the human resource audit, in which the skills and performance of organization members are appraised. To be meaningful, human resource plans must consider both the strategic plan and the external environment of the organization.

General and specialized recruitment are designed to supply the organization with a sufficiently large pool of job candidates. Before recruitment can take place, a job analysis, consisting of the position description and job specification, must be made. Job recruits can be drawn from within or outside the organization.

Successive federal and state legislation, executive orders, and legal decisions since the early 1960s have mandated equal employment opportunity (EEO) regardless of race, sex, age, color, religion, or ethnic group membership. EEO legislation also covers Vietnam era and disabled veterans and the physically and mentally handicapped. Nondiscriminatory procedures must provide equal access to jobs, training, and promotion and equal treatment in the workplace. Firms doing business with the federal government are subject to affirmative action (AA) programs to add and develop women and minority-group members.

The selection process follows a seven-step procedure: completed job application, initial screening interview, testing, background investigation, in-depth selection interview, physical examination, and job offer. For managerial positions, the in-depth interview is probably the most important step. Ideally, it should be realistic and factually based. Assessment centers may also be used to select managers.

Socialization helps the new employee and the organization accommodate to each other. Giving new employees challenging assignments correlates with future success.

Training programs seek to maintain and improve current job performance, while development programs are designed to impart skills needed in future jobs. The need for training may be determined through performance appraisal, job requirements, organizational analysis, and human resource surveys. Both training and development methods can be classified as on-the-job or off-the-job. Coaching is the most important formal on-the-job development method. Other development methods include job rotation and classroom teaching. Both training and development should be reinforced in the work situation.

Performance appraisal may be informal or formal. To improve performance, appraisal should be based on goals jointly set by managers and subordinates. Problems of appraisal include shifting standards, rater bias, different rater patterns, and the halo effect.

To be useful as employee incentives, promotions must be fair. Discrimination in promotion, though illegal, has still not disappeared.

Transfers are used to broaden a manager's experience, to fill vacant positions, and to relocate employees whom the organization does not want to demote, promote, or fire. Demotion is an infrequently used option in dealing with ineffective managers. Separations, though painful, are more widely used and frequently prove beneficial to the individual as well as to the organization.

New trends call for linking HRM more closely with an organization's strategy. The Harvard researchers' four C's model is useful for evaluating how effectively an organization's human resource policy is supporting its business strategy.

■ REVIEW QUESTIONS

1. What are the steps in the HRM process? Are managers likely to be engaged in more than one step at a time? Why or why not?

2. Why is human resource planning necessary? Name the four steps in human resource planning. What factors must managers of a human resource planning program consider?

3. What methods of recruitment can managers use? What are the advantages and disadvantages of recruitment from within?

4. What changes have occurred in EEO and affirmative action in recent years? What are the implications for managers?

5. What is the standard seven-step hiring sequence? Is this sequence the same under all conditions? Why or why not?

6. What are the defects of in-depth interviews? How can they be minimized?

7. What information is socialization designed to provide?

8. What is the difference between training and development?

9. What development approaches and methods can managers use? Which method is most effective?

10. What are the basic differences between systematic and informal appraisal? What are the four basic appraisal approaches? How may formal appraisals be made more effective in improving performance? What appraisal pitfalls do managers need to avoid?

11. What are the problems associated with promotions? How may these problems be overcome?

12. When are transfers used in organizations?

13. Explain how the four C's criteria may be used to evaluate the effectiveness of a human resource management policy.

The Gannett Company: A Leader in Minority Employment

In an industry not noted for having minority employees, the Gannett Company, owner of 90 newspapers throughout the country, has placed minority employees in 20 percent of its jobs and boasts a professional, technical, managerial, and sales force consisting of 15 percent minority employees. The U.S. population is about 22 percent minorities, and the percentage of minorities in the journalism industry is 7 percent, up from 4 percent in 1978, when the American Society of Newspaper Editors first took the count. Approximately half of the 1,600 daily newspapers in this country have no minority reporters.

Currently, only two of Gannett's 90 newspapers have no minority employees. Although praise has been lavished on the company for its achievements in hiring and promoting minorities, some of its white male employees have complained that *merit* is being given short shrift in staffing decisions. Company executives have denied these charges of reverse discrimination.

On the other hand, some minorities claim that Gannett needs to do more. They say that management's concern is strictly with hiring quotas—so that, paradoxically, minorities always end up underrepresented, since once a quota is met, other minority candidates are not given a fair chance.

Gannett's hiring policy is based on aggressive recruitment and promotion programs whereby jobs may remain open until nonwhites apply for them. The company also sends recruiters to job fairs and publishes its job classifieds in magazines targeted to minorities. Managers at Gannett are trained in equal employment hiring goals, and they forward their figures in monthly or quarterly reports to keep track of their progress toward employment goals. Gannett also provides bonuses for managers who compile good records in hiring minorities. Although this kind of reward must reflect a balanced consideration of both the hiring opportunities available to a manager and his or her hiring choices, financial incentives do encourage managers to reach equal opportunity goals.

Allan Neuharth, chairman of Gannett, is fully committed to the company's program. In 1979, he began a campaign called Partners in Progress that established an agenda for the hiring and promotion of minorities and women. Now, almost ten years later, Neuharth wonders how he should evaluate the progress of the program.

Source: Adapted from Johnnie L. Roberts, "Gannett Surpasses Other Newspaper Firms in the Hiring and Promotion of Minorities," *The Wall Street Journal,* May 11, 1988, p. 11.

Case Questions

1. Why might newspapers have a substantially lower representation of minority employees?
2. Why has Gannett's program been successful in attracting minority employees?
3. What are some possible problems with this program, now and in the future?
4. What advice would you give Mr. Neuharth as he ponders the program's future?

Diversity Initiatives at Avon

By the not-so-distant year 2000 there will be striking changes in the demographics of the American workplace, according to *Workforce 2000,* a 1987 report from the Hudson Institute. Only 15 percent of people joining the work force will be native white males, 61 percent of all adult women will hold jobs, and the percentage of minorities and immigrants joining the work force will have increased sharply. It is further projected that the population and work force as a whole will grow slowly, that the average age of the work force will rise, and that the pool of young workers entering the labor market will diminish.

American corporations are facing the challenge of this increasingly heterogeneous workplace in a variety of ways. Two current trends involve (1) programs that go far beyond legally-mandated recruitment of women and minorities and (2) increasingly diversified workplaces that provide greater opportunities for the advancement of women and minorities into positions of greater influence. These diversity management programs seek to minimize stress faced by employees and management in a heterogeneous workplace and to maximize productivity for all.

Avon began adapting to the changing work force in the 1970s with affirmative action strategies. Attention was focused on hiring practices, and the Women and Minorities Committee was formed to provide a forum for issues concerning these groups. The company recruited through black and minority organizations on college campuses, as well as through employment agencies specializing in hiring minorities. Although the corporate culture at Avon is strongly female, with women holding 70 percent of management positions and enjoying generous opportunities for advancement, other minority employees became disaffected during the early days of affirmative action, seeing little chance for upward mobility.

In the 1980s, management at Avon changed their approach and began thinking in terms of multiculturalism. They began to see a competitive advantage in having a diverse work force that more closely matched the changing consumer base, a factor that was clearly important to a direct-sales company. Nationwide employee networks for black, Asian, and Hispanic employees were established to provide support and mentoring. Members of these networks elected leaders who were advised by senior management.

A Multicultural Participation Council made up of network representatives and company executives was established to improve communication between employees and management and to oversee the process of working toward multiculturalism. A director of multicultural development and design was appointed. At the same time Avon became involved with the American Institute for Managing Diversity at Morehouse College in Atlanta, where talented minority trainees underwent an executive development program.

With the beginning of the 1990s, company needs and attitudes again evolved, and multiculturalism gave way to a program of diversity initiatives. Avon wants to be the employer of choice, and to retain, not just recruit, the best pool of employees possible. Company executives stress that their program of diversity management is not just a recycled version of affirmative action. They explain that the emphasis has shifted away from affirmative action hiring and toward improving and closely tracking minority employees' progress within the company. An ambitious employee hired under affirmative action who is passed over for promotions or who hits the "glass ceiling" probably will not stay with the company. Company executives see this process as a waste of resources, and believe their program of diversity initiatives gives them a competitive advantage.

The training program at The American Institute for Managing Diversity is no longer limited to minority employees. Nonminority managers now have the opportunity to undergo intensive three-week courses to learn new approaches to dealing with communication difficulties and the more subtle aspects of cultural differences. The company also sponsors sensitivity awareness workshops to overcome negative assumptions about ethnicity and gender. Finally, a task force has been established to oversee and evaluate new initiatives for effective management in the changing workplace.

Company executives are also developing strategies for extending their diversity initiatives beyond race and gender. They are encouraging interest in alternative lifestyle and workstyle choices, and are looking at issues relating to elder care and day care. Their goal for the workplace pluralism expected in the 2000s is to provide a flexible and accommodating environment in which each employee is effective, productive, and upwardly mobile.

Sources: Workforce 2000: Work and Workers for the 21st Century (Indianapolis, Ind.: The Hudson Institute, 1987); Ronni Sandroff, "The Hiring Crisis of the '90s," *Working Woman,* February 1989, pp. 92–94; Janice Castro, "Get Set: Here They Come!" *Time,* Fall 1990 Special Issue "Women: The Road Ahead," pp. 50–52; R. Roosevelt Thomas, Jr., "From Affirmative Action to Affirming Diversity," *Harvard Business Review,* March–April 1990, pp. 107–117; Sheryl Hilliard Tucker and Kevin D. Thompson, "Will Diversity = Opportunity + Advancement for Blacks?" *Black Enterprise,* November 1990, pp. 50–60; Linda Winikow, "How Women and Minorities Are Reshaping Corporate America," *Vital Speeches,* February 1, 1991, pp. 242–244.

Case Questions

1. How will the demographic changes expected by the turn of the century affect American corporations?

2. What are the benefits—to the employer as well as the employee—of a diversified workplace?

3. How has Avon tried to reshape its attitudes in the face of a changing labor force?

4. What are the problems companies face in establishing programs of diversity management? How can these problems be overcome?

■ NOTES

[1] Cynthia A. Lengnick-Hall and Mark L. Lengnick-Hall, "Strategic Human Resources Management: A Review of the Literature and a Proposed Typology," *Academy of Management Review* 3, no. 3 (1988):454–470.

[2] See Edwin L. Miller, Elmer H. Burack, and Maryann H. Albrecht, *Management of Human Resources* (Englewood Cliffs, N.J.: Prentice Hall, 1980); and Burckhardt Wenzel, "Planning for Manpower Utilization," *Personnel Administrator* 15, no. 3 (May–June 1970):36–40. For an example, see John W. Boroski, "Putting It Together: HR Planning in '3D' at Eastman Kodak," *Human Resource Planning* 13, no. 1 (1990):45–57.

[3] Jennifer McQueen, "Integrating Human Resource Planning with Strategic Planning," *Canadian Public Administration* 27, no. 1 (Spring 1984):1–13; Judy D. Olian and Sara L. Rynes, "Organizational Staffing: Integrating Practice with Strategy," *Industrial Relations* 23, no. 2 (Spring 1984):170–183; Randall S. Schuler and Ian C. MacMillan, "Gaining Competitive Advantage Through Human Resource Management Practices," *Human Resource Management* 23, no. 3 (Fall 1984):241–255; Raymond E. Miles and Charles E. Snow, "Designing Strategic Human Resources Systems," *Organizational Dynamics* 13 (1984):36–52; and Elmer H. Burack, "Corporate Business and Human Resource Planning Practices: Strategic Issues and Concerns," *Organizational Dynamics* 15 (1986):73–87; and Dave Ulrich, "Assessing Human Resource Effectiveness: Stakeholder, Utility, and Relationship Approaches," *Human Resource Planning* 12, no. 4 (1989):301–315.

[4] For a survey of recent advances in task analysis, see Kenneth N. Wexley, "Personnel Training," *Annual Review of Psychology* 35 (1984):522–525.

[5] See John B. Miner and Mary G. Miner, *Personnel and Industrial Relations*, 3rd ed. (New York: Macmillan, 1977); Richard M. Coffina, "Management Recruitment Is a Two-Way Street," *Personnel Journal* 58, no. 2 (February 1979):86–89; and John P. Wanous, *Organizational Entry: Recruitment, Selection, and Socialization of Newcomers* (Reading, Mass.: Addison-Wesley, 1980).

[6] Ellen Schultz, "America's Most Admired Corporations," *Fortune,* January 18, 1988.

[7] William Serrin, "Experts Say Job Bias Against Women Persists," *The New York Times,* November 25, 1984, pp. A1, A32; Madeline E. Heilman, Caryn J. Block, Michael Simon, and Richard F. Martell, "Has Anything Changed? Current Characterizations of Men, Women, and Managers," *Journal of Applied Psychology* 74, no. 6 (1990):935–942.

[8] See Ann Weaver Hart, "Intent vs. Effect: Title VII Case Law That Could Affect You (Part I)," *Personnel Journal* 63 (1984):31–47; and Hart, "Intent vs. Effect: Title VII Case Law That Could Affect You (Part II)," *Personnel Journal* 63 (1984):50–58.

[9] See George Ritzer and David Walczak, *Working: Conflict and Change,* 3rd ed. (Englewood Cliffs, N.J.: Prentice Hall, 1986), pp. 104–106; John B. Golper, "The Current Legal Status of 'Comparable Worth,' in the Federal Sector, " *Labor Law Journal* 34 (1983):563–580; Golper, *Pay Equity and Comparable Worth* (Washington, D.C.: Bureau of National Affairs, 1984), pp. 13–34; and Marsha Katz, Helen Lavan, and Maura Malloy, "Comparable Worth: Analysis of Cases and Implications for Human Resource Management," *Compensation and Benefits Review,* May–June 1986, pp. 26–38.

[10] Our discussion of equal employment opportunity and affirmative action issues derives from Terry L. Leap, William H. Holley, Jr., and Hubert S. Field, "Equal Employment Opportunity and Its Implications for Personnel Practices in the 1980s," *Labor Law Journal* 31, no. 11 (November 1980):669–682; and Francine S. Hall and Maryann H. Albrecht, *The Management of Affirmative Action* (Santa Monica, Calif.: Goodyear, 1979), pp. 1–23. See also David P. Twomey, *A Concise Guide to Employment Law* (Cincinnati: South-Western, 1986).

[11] Leap, Holley, and Field, "Equal Employment Opportunity," pp. 677–679. See also Bette Ann Stead, *Women in Management* (Englewood Cliffs, N.J.: Prentice Hall, 1978). Attitudes toward women in an organization might be assessed using the MATWES scale in Peter Dubno, John Costas, Hugh Cannon, Charles Wankel, and Hussein Emin, "An Empirically Keyed Scale for Measuring Managerial Attitudes Toward Women Executives," *Psychology of Women Quarterly* 3, no. 4 (Summer, 1979):357–364.

[12] Leap, Holley, and Field, "Equal Employment Opportunity," p. 671. See also Richard A. Fear and James F. Ross, *Jobs, Dollars, and EEO* (New York: McGraw-Hill, 1983).

[13] The case was *American Tobacco* v. *Patterson,* cited in Karen Paul and George Sullivan, "Equal Employment Opportunity vs. Seniority Rights: The Emergence of a Changing Social Policy," *Business and Society* 23, no. 1 (Spring 1984):8–14, See also Philip Shenon, "U.S. Acts to Stop Quotas on Hiring It Once Supported," *The New York Times,* April 30, 1985, pp. A1, A22.

[14] Hall and Albrecht, *The Management of Affirmative Action,* pp. 9–10. See, for example, David A. Thomas, "Mentoring and Irrationality: The Role of Racial Taboos," *Human Resource Management* 28, no. 2 (Summer 1989):279–290.

[15] *School Board of Nassau County v. Airline,* No. 85–1277 (1987).

[16] See "Privacy," *Business Week,* March 28, 1988, pp. 61–68; Craig Mellon, "The Dope on Drug Testing," *Human Resource Executive* 2, no. 4 (1988):34–37; and Jeffrey Rothfeder, "Looking for a Job? You May Be Out Before You Go In," *Business Week,* September 24, 1990, pp. 128, 130.

[17] Wendell L. French, *The Personnel Management Process,* 5th ed. (Boston: Houghton Mifflin, 1982).

[18] See Robert E. Carlson, Donald P. Schwab, and Herbert G. Heneman III, "Agreement Among Selection Interview Styles," *Journal of Industrial Psychology* 5, no. 1 (March 1970):8–17.

[19] Richard G. Nehrbass, "Psychological Barriers to Effective Employment Interviewing," *Personnel Journal* 56, no. 2 (February 1977):60–64.

‍

[20]See Wanous, *Organizational Entry;* and S. L. Premack and Wanous, "A Meta-Analysis of Realistic Job Preview Experiments," *Journal of Applied Psychology* 70 (1985):706–719.

[21]See Frank Malinowski, "Job Selection Using Task Analysis," *Personnel Journal* 60, no. 4 (April 1981):288–291.

[22]See Larry D. Alexander, "An Exploratory Study of the Utilization of Assessment Center Results," *Academy of Management Journal* 22, no.1 (March 1979):152–157. An excellent description of the well-known AT&T assessment center can be found in Douglas W. Bray, Richard J. Campbell, and Donald Grant, *Formative Years in Business* (New York: Wiley, 1974).

[23]For additional information on assessment centers, see Marilee S. Niehoff, "Assessment Centers: Decision-Making Information from Non–Test-Based Methods," *Small Group Behavior* 14, no. 3 (August 1983):353–358; and Clive A. Fletcher and Victor Dulewicz, "An Empirical Study of a U.K.-Based Assessment Centre," *Journal of Management Studies* 21, no. 1 (1984):83–97.

[24]Richard Klimoski, quoted in Barbara Lovenheim, "A Test to Uncover Managerial Skills: Hopefuls Try Out, Watched by Assessors," *The New York Times,* January 21, 1979, pp. D1, D4.

[25]See, for example, Earl R. Gomersall and M. Scott Myers, "Breakthrough in On-the-Job Training," *Harvard Business Review* 44, no. 4 (July–August 1966):62–72. See also Gareth R. Jones, "Organizational Socialization as Information Processing Activity: A Life History Analysis," *Human Organization* 42, no. 4 (1983):314–320.

[26]For studies of the relationship between early job experience and subsequent job performance and career progress, see David E. Berlew and Douglas T. Hall, "The Socialization of Managers," *Administrative Science Quarterly* 11, no. 2 (September 1966):207–223; also James A. F. Stoner, John D. Aram, and Irwin M. Rubin, "Factors Associated with Effective Performance in Overseas Work Assignments, " *Personnel Psychology* 25, no. 2 (Summer 1972):303–318. See also Morgan W. McCall, Jr., "Developing Executives Through Work Experiences," *Human Resource Planning* 11, no. 1 (1988):1–11.

[27]Dennis L. Dossett and Patti R. Hulvershorn, "Increasing Technical Training Efficiency: Peer Training via Computer-Assisted Instruction," *Journal of Applied Psychology* 68, no.4 (November 1983):552–558; Stephen Schwade, "Is It Time to Consider Computer-Based Training?" *Personnel Administrator* 30, no. 2 (February 1985):25–28; and William C. Heck, "Computer-Based Training—The Choice Is Yours," *Personnel Administrator* 30, no. 2 (February 1985):39–48.

[28]George T. Milkovich and William F. Glueck, *Personnel: Human Resource Management,* 4th ed. (Plano, Tex.: Business Publications, 1985), pp. 72–73.

[29]On needs analysis, see F. L. Ulschak, *Human Resource Development: The Theory and Practice of Need Assessment* (Reston, Va.: Reston, 1983).

[30]Lynn S. Summers, "Out of the Ivory Tower: A Demand-Side Look at the Future of Management Development," *Training and Development Journal* 38, no. 1 (January 1984):97–101; and Jan Asplind, Håkan Behrendtz, and Frank Jernberg, "The Norwegian Savings Banks Case: Implementation and Consequences of a Broadly Scoped, Long-Term, System-Driven Program for Management Development," *Journal of Applied Behavioral Science* 19, no. 3 (1983):381–394.

[31]Edward B. Fiske, "Booming Corporate Education Efforts Rival College Programs, Study Says," *The New York Times,* January 28, 1985, p. A10.

[32]Edward E. Lawler III, Allan M. Mohrman, Jr., and Susan M. Resnick, "Performance Appraisal Revisited," *Organizational Dynamics* 13, no. 1 (Summer 1984):20–35; and Roy Serpa, "Why Many Organizations—Despite Good Intentions—Often Fail to Give Employees Fair and Useful Performance Review," *Management Review* 73, no. 7 (July 1984):41–45.

[33]See Laurence J. Peter and Raymond Hull, *The Peter Principle* (New York: William Morrow, 1969).

[34]In a fifth approach, the training and development section of the human resources department appraises performance and assists line managers in implementing any of the four approaches already described. See R. Bruce McAfee, "Performance Appraisal: Whose Function?" *Personnel Journal* 60, no. 4 (April 1981):298–299.

[35]Herbert H. Meyer, Emanual Kay, and John R. P. French, "Split Roles in Performance Appraisal," *Harvard Business Review* 43, no. 1 (January–February 1965):123–129. See also Douglas M. McGregor, "An Uneasy Look at Performance Appraisal," *Harvard Business Review* 35, no. 3 (May–June 1957):89–94.

[36]See Ed Yager, "A Critique of Performance Appraisal Systems," *Personnel Journal* 60, no. 4 (February 1981):129–133.

[37]See Lawler, Mohrman, and Resnick, "Performance Appraisal Revisited," pp. 31–34. See also Charles J. Fombrun and Robert L. Laud, "Strategic Issues in Performance Appraisal: Theory and Practice," *Personnel* 60, no. 6 (November–December 1983):23–31; and Donald L. Kirkpatrick, "Two Ways to Evaluate Your Performance Appraisal System," *Training and Development Journal* 38, no. 8 (August 1984):38–40.

[38]See Richard D. Arvey and Allen P. Jones, "The Use of Discipline in Organizational Settings," in L. L. Cummings and Barry M. Shaw, eds., *Research in Organizational Behavior,* Vol. 7 (Greenwich, Conn.: JAI Press, 1985).

[39]Michael Beer, Bert Spector, Paul R. Lawrence, D. Quinn Mills, and Richard E. Walton, *Human Resource Management* (New York: Free Press, 1985), pp. 4–6.

[40]Ibid., p. 20–22.

[41]Ibid., p. 37–39. For one recent trend, see Frances J. Milliken, Jane E. Dutton, and Janice M. Beyer, "Understanding Organizational Adaptation to Change: The Case of Work-Family Issues," *Human Resource Planning* 13, no. 2 (1990):91–108. See also Arlene A. Johnson, "Parental Leave—Is It the Business of Business?" *Human Resource Planning* 13, no. 2 (1990):119–131.

CHAPTER FOURTEEN

MANAGING ORGANIZATIONAL CHANGE AND INNOVATION

Upon completing this chapter, you should be able to:

1. Define the term *planned change* and identify situations in which it is appropriate.

2. List and discuss the concepts of Kurt Lewin's force-field theory.

3. Discuss the three major sources of resistance to planned change.

4. Explain Lewin's three-step process of change.

5. List and discuss some of the ways employee resistance can be addressed.

6. List the three types of planned change and give an example of each.

7. Define the term *organizational development* and explain how it differs from other approaches to planned change.

8. Discuss the ethical considerations of organizational development.

9. Describe the most widely used OD techniques.

10. Distinguish between innovation and creativity and explain how organizations can encourage both.

The art of progress is to preserve order amid change and to preserve change amid order

Alfred North Whitehead, 1861-1947   artist: herbert bayer

Great Ideas of Western Man   one of a series   [CCA] Container Corporation of America

Herbert Bayer, Poster from the Great Ideas of Western Man Series. Courtesy of the Jefferson Smurfit Corporation, St. Louis.

ILLUSTRATIVE CASE STUDY

INTRODUCTION

Organizational Trauma and Triumph at AT&T

In perhaps the most celebrated case in business history, AT&T agreed in 1983 to a consent decree with the Department of Justice to divest itself of three-quarters of its $150 billion in assets. Until that time AT&T and the associated Bell Telephone Companies were widely and highly regarded as among the most consistently profitable and best-managed companies in the world. The changes that resulted from divestiture were enormous. Each of the resulting multibillion-dollar companies had to establish new ways of planning and organizing, and AT&T itself was plunged into a brand-new competitive world.

In the early 1970s, AT&T recognized that its external environment was changing and that it was inevitably going to be more competitive. In an early effort at organizational development, AT&T took the unprecedented step of hiring Arch McGill, a fiery ex-IBM employee, to bolster its marketing expertise. Ten stormy years later, McGill left the company after having put an indelible mark on it. His style of confrontation and conflict, along with his marketing and customer orientation, began a process of change that is still going on.

Prior to 1983, AT&T was the largest private employer in the United States. It was well known for rewarding loyalty, perseverance, and hard work with responsibility and job security. The tradition of serving the public interest was deeply ingrained in AT&T employees. Under the stress of change, however, many of the company's traditions collapsed. As part of its cost-cutting efforts, AT&T eliminated 75,000 jobs, some via retirement but many more through layoffs. For a while, even top management seemed to be in shock, too paralyzed to prevent the disorganization and erosion of morale.

In the fall of 1986, a 22-year AT&T veteran killed himself when he discovered that he was probably going to be laid off—after three transfers and five jobs in two years. His suicide note wondered aloud how a company could do this to a loyal employee only a few years from retirement. According to James E. Olson, then AT&T's chairman, "Nobody's been through what this company's been through. We put our people through hell."

Olson began a move to unify the company and heal its wounds. He devised a broad new plan: to protect AT&T's core telecommunications business,

Charting a Course for the Future. Quiet and deliberate where Olson was passionate and impulsive, current AT&T CEO Robert E. Allen logs 20,000 miles a month, meeting with managers and rebuilding AT&T morale.

drive its sagging computer business out of the red, and increase AT&T's overseas revenues. Part of his strategy was to do away with the multiple payroll procedures, phone systems, and ID badges that had characterized the old divisions of the company and to forge a single new corporate culture. In addition, he set more realistic goals for the computer division. Rather than challenge IBM directly in many markets, Olson focused the division on a few products and markets.

Olson began implementing this strategy during a special meeting of his 27 top executives. After five days of hard-fought battles over the new shape of AT&T, each of the executives had to stand and publicly affirm his commitment to the plan when asked: "Are you with me?"

Still troubled by the morale problem, Olson took to the road, toured seven cities, and spoke to over 40,000 AT&T workers in an effort to explain the company's problems and his proposed solutions. Unfortunately, he died of cancer early in 1988. His successor, Robert Allen, faced a difficult job in continuing the task of organizational change.

Sources: John J. Keller, Geoff Lewis, Todd Mason, Russell Mitchell, and Thane Peterson, "AT&T: The Making of a Comeback," *Business Week,* January 18, 1988, pp. 56–62; Steve Coll, *The Deal of the Century: The Break-up of AT&T* (New York: Atheneum, 1986).

407

AT&T is only one of many organizations undergoing the tumultuous and potentially rewarding process of *planned change,* the systematic attempt to redesign an organization in a way that will help it adapt to significant changes in the external environment and achieve new goals. In this chapter, we will look at the reasons organizations embark on a course of planned change, a model of the change process, and the aspects of the organization that can be changed. Then we will end the chapter by looking at *organizational development,* one of the major approaches to changing the culture and people within an organization, with special emphasis on how managers can encourage creativity and innovation.

■ *WHY PLANNED CHANGE IS NEEDED*

Planned change has been defined as "the deliberate design and implementation of a structural innovation, a new policy or goal, or a change in operating philosophy, climate, or style."[1] Every organization makes minor structural adjustments in reaction to changes in its direct-action and indirect-action environments, of course. A sales form is revised to eliminate customer confusion, say, or the human resources department may create a training program on OSHA-mandated safety programs. What distinguishes planned change from these *reactive* changes is its scope and magnitude. Planned change aims to prepare the *entire* organization, or a major part of it, to adapt to significant changes in the organization's goals and direction.

A planned change is not simple, inexpensive, or painless, as evidenced by the suicide of the AT&T veteran. Employees are asked to surrender familiar work habits for a new organization with new policies, procedures, and expectations. Other loyal employees may lose their jobs entirely. Given the potential disruption, then, why do organizations undertake a program of planned change? There are at least three reasons.

1. *Environmental changes threaten the organization's survival.* Like any system, organizations depend on and must interact with their external environments. If an organization loses touch with its environment, it may find itself offering products or services few people want to buy, while more agile competitors eat into its market share. Often the best way to become more responsive is to restructure, as shown by the example of Kodak, profiled in the Illustrative Case Study for Chapter 3.

2. *Environmental changes offer new opportunities for prosperity.* As you learned in earlier chapters, an environmental change can represent either a problem or an opportunity, depending on one's perspective. In fact, opportunity finding is the hallmark of the successful entrepreneur and has much to do with the continued success of established organizations like Hewlett-Packard. As you saw in the Illustrative Case Study for Chapter 11, Hewlett-Packard reorganized when its managers realized its current structure was keeping it from taking advantage of an opportunity for growth (offer a better computer workstation) that also represented a survival-threatening problem (offer a better computer workstation or lose HP's position as an industry leader).

3. *The organization's structure is slowing its adaptation to environmental changes.* This is the driving force behind many planned changes today, as organizations scramble to respond to a complex and changing external environment. (Figure 14-1 will give you a good idea of how two major environmental changes—globalization and information technology—have complicated the environment of organizations.) Some of the largest, most successful, and venerable firms are victims of their own success. Over the years they have built up highly stable, bureaucratic, and tall organizational structures that are very efficient at achieving certain goals in a given environment. Decision mak-

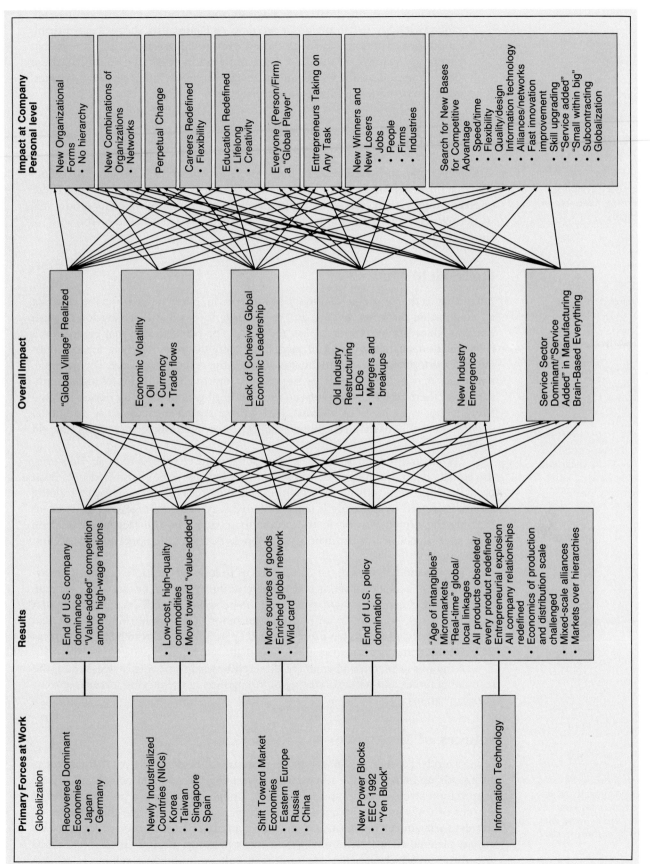

FIGURE 14-1 The Impact of Globalization and Information Technology

Source: Tom Peters, "Prometheus Barely Unbound," *Academy of Management Executive* 4, no. 4 (1990):71.

ing, though, is methodical, even sluggish, and new ideas and competitive advantages tend to get strangled by red tape. As Figure 14-1 shows, many organizations are experimenting with flatter, even no-hierarchy, organizations that encourage teamwork and faster communication, with the idea that these "leaner" organizations will be more flexible, creative, and innovative in reacting to environmental changes of every type.

■ A MODEL OF THE CHANGE PROCESS

COORDINATED RESOURCE
See Study Guide Self-Learning Exercise 14, "Openness to Change."

Although organizations are beset by many forces for change, it is important to recognize that opposing forces act to keep an organization in a state of equilibrium. These opposing forces, then, support stability or the status quo. To understand how this works, let's take a look at a model of the change process that is based on the work of Kurt Lewin.

Force-Field Analysis

COORDINATED RESOURCE
See Study Guide Problem Exercise 14, "Changing with Force Field Analysis."

CLASS COMMENT
Remove or *weaken* restraining forces. *Create* or *strengthen* driving forces.

COORDINATED RESOURCE
Use Transparency 86, Force Field Diagram.

According to the "force-field" theory of Kurt Lewin, every behavior is the result of an equilibrium between *driving* and *restraining* forces.[2] The driving forces push one way, the restraining forces push the other. The performance that emerges is a reconciliation of the two sets of forces. An increase in the driving forces might increase performance, but it might also increase the restraining forces. For example, a manager may believe that he or she can get improved results by telling subordinates that there will be absolutely no time off until productivity increases. But the likely response of hostility, distrust, and greater resistance may cause additional declines in productivity, even though the formal prohibition against taking time off is observed.

The natural tendency for most of us, if we want change, is to push. However, the equally natural tendency of whomever or whatever is being pushed is to push back: Driving forces activate their own restraining forces. Decreasing the restraining forces, therefore, is normally a more effective way to encourage change than increasing the driving forces. In the productivity example, the manager would be more likely to get results by identifying pointless bureaucratic bottlenecks and eliminating them.

Lewin's model (see Fig. 14-2) reminds us to look for multiple causes of behavior rather than a single cause. It is applicable to our purposes because it is generalized: The forces can be of many types, and the behavior or performance can be that of an individual, a group, or an entire organization. The equilibrium concept also suggests that organizations have forces that keep performance from falling too low as well as forces that keep it from rising too high.

Programs of planned change are directed toward removing or weakening the restraining forces and toward creating or strengthening the driving forces that exist in organizations.

Sources of Resistance

FOR DISCUSSION
Have there been any campus changes to which there was student resistance? What were they, and why was there resistance?

Lewin's model is useful because it makes us aware of the many factors that can act as either driving or restraining forces. The restraining forces—the ones that keep an organization stable—are of special interest, though, since they represent potential sources of resistance to planned change. If managers can change these forces or address their underlying concerns, they have a much better chance of accomplishing any planned change. For convenience, we will group these sources of resistance into three broad classes: the organizational culture, individual self-interests, and individual perceptions of organizational goals and strategies.

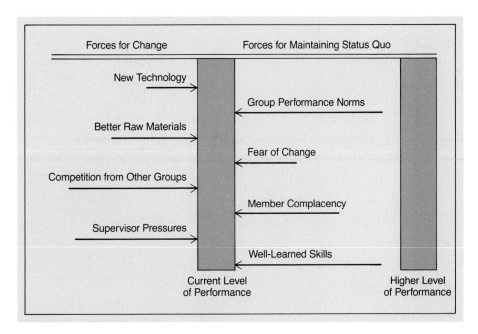

FIGURE 14-2 Force-Field Diagram

Note: Length of arrow is equal to amount of force.

Source: Adapted by permission from *Organization Development and Change,* 3rd ed. by Edgar F. Huse and Thomas G. Cummings, p. 73. Copyright © 1985 by West Publishing Company. All rights reserved.

organizational culture
The set of important understandings, such as norms, values, attitudes, and beliefs, shared by organizational members.

COORDINATED RESOURCE

See Samaras Exercise 3.4, "Resistance to Change."

COORDINATED RESOURCE

Use Transparency 89, The Iceberg of Organizational Culture.

COORDINATED RESOURCE

Acumen: Individuals with high scores on the Apprehension scale have low self-confidence, hesitate to make decisions, avoid taking responsibilities, and often feel a lack of efficacy—the ability to effect change.

ORGANIZATIONAL CULTURE. Of the three forces, this may be the most important in shaping and maintaining an organization's identity. **Organizational culture** refers to the important understandings members share, such as norms, values, attitudes, and beliefs.[3] As Figure 14-3 shows, organizational culture can be compared to an iceberg. On the surface are the overt, or open, aspects—the formally expressed organizational goals, technology, structure, policies and procedures, and financial resources. Beneath the surface lie the covert, or hidden, aspects—the informal aspects of organizational life. These include shared perceptions, attitudes, and feelings, as well as a shared set of values about human nature, the nature of human relationships, and what the organization can and will contribute to society.[4]

As a general rule, employees stay with an organization because the work helps them meet their life goals and because their personalities, attitudes, and beliefs fit into the organizational culture. Indeed, many employees identify with their organization and take its gains and losses personally. As a result, they may feel threatened by efforts to radically change the organization's culture and "the way we do things."

SELF-INTERESTS. Although employees can and do identify with their organizations, their ultimate concern is for themselves. In return for doing a good job, they expect adequate pay, satisfactory working conditions, job security, and certain amounts of appreciation, power, and prestige. Any change that threatens their individual status quo, then, becomes a source of fear and uncertainty. At best, employees may face a potentially uncomfortable period of adjustment as they settle into a new organization or a redesigned job. At worst, they may lose their job. These fears, coupled with uncertainty about their ultimate job security, create powerful barriers to change, especially if employees who share the same fears and self-interests band together.

PERCEPTIONS OF ORGANIZATIONAL GOALS AND STRATEGIES. Goals and strategies are extremely powerful for organizing and coordinating the efforts of any organization. Indeed, mission statements (such as Nordstrom's "give the customer the best service possible") can guide employee actions in the absence of formal policies and procedures. This powerful force for stability can make it difficult to change, how-

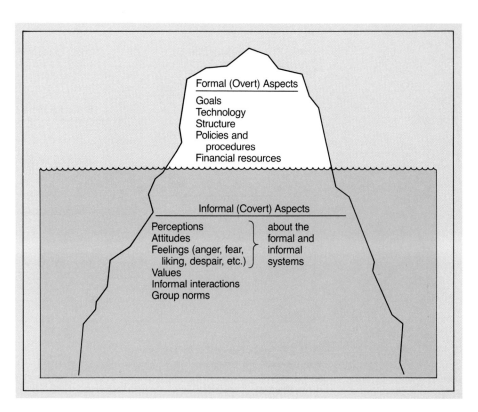

FIGURE 14-3 The Iceberg of Organizational Culture

Source: Adapted from Stanley N. Herman, "TRW Systems Group," in Wendell L. French and Cecil H. Bell, Jr., *Organization Development: Behavioral Science Interventions for Organization Improvement,* 3rd ed., p. 19. © 1984. Used by permission of Prentice Hall, Englewood Cliffs, N.J.

ever. Sometimes employees do not understand the need for a new goal because they do not have the same information their managers have. Or they may long for the "good old days." In other cases, though, employees may resist change because they have information their managers do not.

The Process of Change

Lewin also studied the process of bringing about effective change. Most efforts at change fail for two reasons, he thought. First, people are unwilling (or unable) to alter long-established attitudes and behavior. Tell a manager he or she must learn a new analytic technique and that manager will probably accept the order. Tell the same manager he or she is too aggressive and abrasive in dealing with others, though, and expect fireworks. Resentment and resistance are natural reactions to any suggestion that violates a person's self-image and implies a personality fault.

Second, even if employees are willing to change their attitudes and behavior, these changes tend to be short-lived. After a short period of trying to do things differently, individuals left on their own tend to return to their habitual patterns of behavior.

To overcome obstacles of this sort, Lewin developed a three-step sequential model of the change process. The model, later elaborated by Edgar H. Schein and others, is equally applicable to individuals, groups, and entire organizations.[5] It involves "unfreezing" the present behavior pattern, "changing" or developing a new behavior pattern, and then "refreezing" or reinforcing the new behavior.

1. **Unfreezing** involves making the need for change so obvious that the individual, group, or organization can readily see and accept it.
2. Changing involves appointing a trained **change agent,** who will lead individuals, groups, or the entire organization through the process. During this process, the change agent will foster new values, attitudes, and behavior through the processes of *identification* and *internalization.* Organization members will identify with the change agent's values, attitudes, and behavior, internalizing them, once they perceive their effectiveness in performance.
3. **Refreezing** means locking the new behavior pattern into place by means of supporting or reinforcing mechanisms, so that it becomes the new norm.

Change agents can be members of the organization or consultants brought in from the outside. For complex and lengthy change programs, hiring an outside consultant has many advantages. First, the outside consultant typically offers specialized expertise and skills. Second, the consultant will not be distracted by day-to-day operating responsibilities. Third, as an outsider, the consultant may have more prestige and influence than an insider. Fourth, because the consultant has no vested interest in the organization, he or she may be more objective than an insider and find it easier to win the confidence of employees.[6]

Overcoming Resistance to Change

Resistance to a change proposal is a signal to managers that something is wrong with the proposal or that mistakes have been made in its presentation. Managers, therefore, must determine the actual causes of resistance and then be flexible enough to overcome them in an appropriate manner.[7]

In recent years, for example, American automakers have experienced numerous forces pressing for relatively broad changes in long-standing policies and long-standing relationships with stakeholder groups that resist those changes. In at least one instance—a top-level determination to downsize at General Motors—flexible, and even innovative, measures have both lessened resistance to change and increased the likelihood that all parties involved will ultimately benefit.

One of the enduring realities of the auto business in the United States is that management has long been dealing with unions over such issues as work rules, working conditions, and wages and benefits. As a rule, labor-management relations have been characterized by adversarial stances even when all appeared to be going well for both parties. However, as automakers fell on tough times and were forced to struggle to save their commercial fortunes, they attempted to negotiate less traditional, more flexible relations with their union stakeholders. GM, which once made 52 percent of the new cars sold in the United States, is now settling for less than 40 percent. Its current management is pledged to downsize the organization considerably by the mid-1990s—a policy that could mean closing at least 4 out of 26 plants and eliminating at least 100,000 jobs. This would be in addition to the almost 60,000 United Auto Workers members already on indefinite layoff.

To help create a changed relationship in which management and workers could work together and not at cross-purposes, each GM plant formed joint union/management committees to study ways to boost productivity. GM has also worked with the union to adopt more flexible production methods such as those used in Japanese-style team systems.

While there has been some progress, there is still some reluctance on the part of the union to change. This reluctance is based not just on the dislike of changing traditional ways of doing work, but also on the fear that as productivity increases, job security will decrease. Although GM negotiated some job security, the 1987 contract stipulated that if sales continue to fall, GM could lay off more workers. Since

TABLE 14-1 Methods for Dealing with Resistance to Change

APPROACH	INVOLVES	COMMONLY USED WHEN . . .	ADVANTAGES	DISADVANTAGES
1. Education + communication	Explaining the need for and logic of change to individuals, groups, and even entire organizations.	There is a lack of information or inaccurate information and analysis.	Once persuaded, people will often help implement the change.	Can be very time-consuming if many people are involved.
2. Participation + involvement	Asking members of organization to help design the change.	The initiators do not have all the information they need to design the change, and others have considerable power to resist.	People who participate will be committed to implementing change, and any relevant information they have will be integrated into the change plan.	Can be very time-consuming if participators design an inappropriate change.
3. Facilitation + support	Offering retraining programs, time off, emotional support, and understanding to people affected by the change.	People are resisting because of adjustment problems.	No other approach works as well with adjustment problems.	Can be time-consuming, expensive, and still fail.
4. Negotiation + agreement	Negotiating with potential resisters; even soliciting written letters of understanding.	Some person or group with considerable power to resist will clearly lose out in a change.	Sometimes it is a relatively easy way to avoid major resistance.	Can be too expensive if it alerts others to negotiate for compliance.
5. Manipulation + cooptation	Giving key persons a desirable role in designing or implementing change process.	Other tactics will not work or are too expensive.	It can be a relatively quick and inexpensive solution to resistance problems.	Can lead to future problems if people feel manipulated.
6. Explicit + implicit coercion	Threatening job loss or transfer, lack of promotion, etc.	Speed is essential, and the change initiators possess considerable power.	It is speedy and can overcome any kind of resistance.	Can be risky if it leaves people angry with the initiators.

Source: Reprinted by permission of the *Harvard Business Review.* An exhibit from "Choosing Strategies for Change" by John P. Kotter and Leonard A. Schlesinger (March–April 1979). Copyright © 1979 by the President and Fellows of Harvard College; all rights reserved.

GM's plans to downsize coincide with falling sales for its products, there seem to be many barriers to successful changes in both work patterns and the union-management relationship. Yet many people, both analysts and participants, are hopeful that new approaches and strategies will increase productivity and profits for GM—and thus bring greater job security for both management and union members.[8]

John P. Kotter and Leonard A. Schlesinger have proposed six ways of overcoming resistance to change, including the two primary means adopted by GM and its union workers—namely, participation + involvement and negotiation + agreement. All six methods are summarized in Table 14-1. Each method has advantages and disadvantages, and no method is appropriate for all situations.

■ TYPES OF PLANNED CHANGE

An organization can be changed by altering its structure, its technology, its people, or some combination of these aspects.[9] (See Fig. 14-4.)

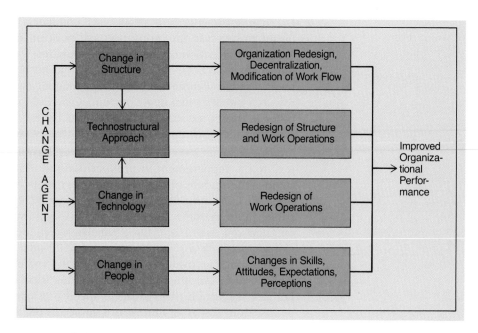

FIGURE 14-4 The Three Change Approaches

Approaches to Structural Change

COORDINATED RESOURCE

Use Transparency 90, The Three Change Approaches.

Changing an organization's structure involves rearranging its internal systems, such as the lines of communication, work flow, or management hierarchy. This can be accomplished in three ways.

1. *Classical organizational design* focuses on carefully defining job responsibilities and on creating appropriate divisions of labor and lines of performance. One of the most significant trends here is toward the flat, lean organization, in which middle layers of management are eliminated to streamline the interaction of top managers with nonmanagement employees, who are given more responsibilities. Wal-Mart, recently named the United States's leading retailer, is a good example of this trend.[10]

A "Flat" Organization. Alan Darling is a manager of Quad/Text at Quad/Graphics, Inc., a fast-growing, high-tech printing firm in Pewaukee, Wisconsin, where there are only two management levels between the lowest level workers and founder Harry Quadracci.

2. *Decentralization* creates smaller, self-contained organizational units that are meant to increase the motivation and performance of unit members and to focus their attention on high-priority activities. Decentralization also lets each unit adapt its structure and technology to its particular tasks and to its environment. Cray Research's decision to let founder Seymour Cray pursue his own research interests in a new company, Cray Computer, is a good example. Another is Disney's decision to create Touchstone Pictures, which offers more sophisticated films than the traditional Disney fare.

3. *Modification of the work flow* and careful grouping of specialties may also lead to an improvement in productivity and morale. One expression of this trend is the amount of money employees can spend without getting authorization. The consulting firm of A. T. Kearney found that the best-performing companies in the Fortune 200 let division managers spend as much as $20 million on their own signature. On a smaller scale, the WIX division of the Dana Corporation lets any employee spend $100 on a process innovation without going through a slow and potentially painful and humiliating process of getting authorization. Another expression of this idea is management writer Tom Peters's suggestion that managers speed product development by "jamming people from disparate functions together in the same room or workspace or cubby hole. . . ."[11]

Approaches to Technological Change

Changing an organization's technology involves altering its equipment, engineering processes, research techniques, or production methods. This approach goes back to the scientific management theory of Frederick W. Taylor (presented in Chapter 2).

As indicated by one of Taylor's premier achievements, the modern assembly line, production technology often has a major effect on structure. For that reason, *technostructural* or *sociotechnical* approaches attempt to improve performance by simultaneously changing aspects of an organization's structure and its technology. Job enlargement and job enrichment, discussed in Chapter 12, are examples of technostructural approaches to change.

Approaches to Changing People

Both the technical and structural approaches try to improve organizational performance by changing the work situation. The people approaches, on the other hand, try to change employee behavior by focusing on their skills, attitudes, perceptions, and expectations.

Many such efforts are known as *organizational development (OD) techniques,* to be discussed in more detail shortly. Non-OD approaches for changing people include management by objectives (discussed in Chapter 8), management development (discussed in Chapter 13), and behavior modification (to be discussed in Chapter 15).

Interdependence of the Three Approaches

Because organizations are systems made up of interacting, interdependent elements, any change program will be more effective if it acknowledges this interaction and tries to change more than one element.[12] Normally, the number of elements that need to be involved increases with the magnitude of change desired.

Let us assume, for example, that we are managers in a large company and want to increase sales in two product categories: proprietary drugs and personal-care products. To achieve our goal, we might conclude that a major structural change will be required. The sales force will have to be divided into two separate units so that the efforts of salespeople are more focused on each product line and account-

Organizational Trauma and Triumph at AT&T

The managers at AT&T could no doubt identify with all of the concepts discussed in this chapter. Both internal and external forces for change clearly existed. Even before the divestiture, AT&T had undertaken programs designed to make changes, especially under the guidance of Archie McGill; for example, the company had already negotiated a union agreement with the Communications Workers of America that included a new quality-of-work-life program to improve management-labor communications and cooperation.

Because AT&T was so large before the divestiture, overcoming the sheer inertia of over 1 million employees and $150 billion in assets required constant vigilance. Once the layoffs started, resistance to change increased among some employees in proportion to the company's own uncertainty, but it less-ened in others—those who were eager for something, almost anything, to happen.

Over the years there have been numerous reorganizations, some mandated by regulatory changes, some undertaken to align AT&T more closely with customer needs and concerns. As technology has increased in the industry, AT&T has used a variety of technological approaches, ranging from time-and-motion studies of operators to the development of electronic monitoring devices that encourage some workers to spend less time on customer premises. Throughout these efforts, AT&T has sought to give its people the skills—especially marketing and technical skills—that they need to be more productive. Although all of these approaches have been at work, no one of them can be pointed out as the sole reason for AT&T's survival in managing its historic change.

ability is easier to determine. Such a structural change may well involve technological changes. For example, new computer programs may have to be used to transfer the old marketing and sales information into more appropriate formats, or new sales techniques and procedures may have to be developed to increase the professionalism of the sales force. In addition, people changes are also likely to be required. Some new sales personnel may have to be hired and trained, and previously hired personnel will have to be retrained or reassigned. IBM, for example, instituted a no-layoff policy early in its history, and that policy has forced the company to increase the number of its personnel transfers, either because facilities were closed down or because positions were opened up at other locations. IBM insiders often refer to the company as "I've Been Moved." At IBM, as elsewhere, individuals unable to adjust to changing circumstances, whether in current locations or through transfer, may have to be replaced.

COORDINATED RESOURCE

Use Transparency 91, Linkage of Change, Conflict, and Stress.

■ *ORGANIZATIONAL DEVELOPMENT*

organizational development (OD) A long-range effort supported by top management to increase an organization's problem-solving and renewal processes through effective management of organizational culture.

Many of the approaches to planned change are appropriate for solving immediate and specific problems. **Organizational development (OD),** in contrast, is a longer-term, more encompassing, more complex, and more costly approach to change that aims to move the entire organization to a higher level of functioning while greatly improving its members' performance and satisfaction. Although OD frequently includes structural and technological changes, its primary focus is on changing people and the nature and quality of their working relationships.

Formally, OD has been defined as

a top-management–supported, long-range effort to improve an organization's problem-solving and renewal processes, particularly through a more effective

COORDINATED RESOURCE
See Samaras Case 3.4,
"Morcess Machine Company."

CLASS COMMENT
OD is more extensive and comprehensive than management development since it focuses on the entire organization.

collaborative management Management through power sharing and subordinate participation; the opposite of hierarchical imposition of authority.

action research The method through which organizational-development change agents learn what improvements are needed and how the organization can best be aided in making those improvements.

COORDINATED RESOURCE
See *Management Live!* Chapter 3 video, "David Letterman Meets GE."

COORDINATED RESOURCE
See *Management Live!* Reading 3.1, "Creating a New Company Culture."

COORDINATED RESOURCE
See *Management Live!* Chapter 18 video, "Broadcast News."

COORDINATED RESOURCE
Use Transparency 92, How Shared Things, Sayings, Actions, and Feelings Suggest Shared Cultural Understanding.

and collaborative diagnosis and management of organization culture—with special emphasis on formal work team, temporary team, and intergroup culture—with the assistance of a consultant-facilitator and the use of the theory and technology of applied behavioral science, including action research.[13]

This definition includes a number of important phrases. *Problem-solving process* refers to the organization's methods of dealing with the threats and opportunities in its environment, while *renewal process* refers to the way managers adapt their problem-solving processes to the environment. One aim of OD is to improve an organization's self-renewal process so that managers can quickly adapt their management style to new problems and opportunities.

Another aim is the sharing of management power with subordinates, a goal indicated by the phrase *collaborative management*. **Collaborative management** means that managers put aside the hierarchical authority structure and let subordinates play a greater role in decision making. To carry out this change, managers must consciously change the *organizational culture*—the members' shared attitudes, beliefs, and activities, which includes beliefs about who has the power and authority to initiate and carry out changes. Because organizational culture is so important to effective OD, we will discuss it in more detail in the next section.

A final key phrase, **action research,** refers to the way OD change agents go about learning what aspects of the organization need to be improved and how the organization can be helped to make these improvements. Briefly, action research involves (1) a preliminary diagnosis of the problem by OD change agents, (2) data gathering to support (or disprove) the diagnosis, (3) feedback of the data to organization members, (4) exploration of the data by organization members, (5) planning of appropriate action, and (6) taking appropriate action.

Organizational Culture

OD focuses on organizational culture because that is what shapes employee attitudes and determines the way the organization interacts with its environment. For example, in the U.S. banking industry, pressures unleashed by deregulation have produced a marked change in attitude among established banks from what one banker called "the old bureaucratic 'your books balance at the end of the day' culture" to a culture that is more entrepreneurial, more oriented to sales, and more attuned to competition.[14] Peters and Waterman (see Chapter 1) make the point that companies with strong cultures that are focused externally—that is, centered on service to the customer—may, in fact, be more sensitive to environmental changes and better able to adapt quickly than companies without strong cultures.[15]

Indeed, a strong, widely recognized corporate culture is frequently cited as a reason for the success of such companies as IBM and Procter & Gamble. The ceremonies, rewards, decor, and other symbolic forms of communication found in Mary Kay Cosmetics have established a corporate culture that guides the actions of organization members. Apple Computer, a company that quickly advanced to an eminent position in its industry, worked hard to maintain the informality and personal relationships characteristic of a small company, even positioning itself in its marketing as the small-company alternative to IBM and other industry giants. Hewlett-Packard (see the Illustrative Case Study for Chapter 11) maintains a culture built on the principles of its founders; Tandem Computers emphasizes a culture of employee-centered incentives; and 3M gears its corporate culture toward innovation.

Of course, a durable, efficient culture can be a liability if it makes the organization unresponsive to its environment, and a smart manager learns to stop perpetuating an unresponsive culture. Changing corporate culture is not easy, however. One difficulty is just identifying the current culture, since culture emerges out of the actions of organization members and the relationships they sustain over time. However, we can often infer the culture's true nature by looking at the things, sayings, actions, and feelings its members share. Such an inference is shown in Figure 14-5.

Preserving an Organizational Culture. Since its Depression-era founding, a bowl of apples has graced the receptionist's desk at Leo Burnett Co. advertising agency. The tradition continues today, as does a culture built on teamwork and a concern for doing "what Leo would have done." The agency is managed by an executive committee (some of whom are shown here); half are drawn from the creative side (writers and artists) and half from the account executives who work with clients on their marketing plans. Every year all creative people from mid-level up meet at Camp Leo to review the previous year's ads, with the goal of keeping the ideas fresh.

FIGURE 14-5 How Shared Things, Sayings, Actions, and Feelings Suggest Shared Cultural Understanding

Source: Adapted from Vijay Sathe, "Implications of Corporate Culture: A Manager's Guide to Action," *Organizational Dynamics* 12, no. 2 (Autumn 1983):9.

Shared Things

1. Shirt sleeves.
2. One-company town.
3. Open offices.

Shared Sayings

4. "Get out there" to understand the customer. (Belief in travel)
5. "We cannot rely on systems" to meet customer needs. (Highly responsive customer service)
6. "We don't stand on rank." (No parking privileges)

Shared Actions

7. Participate in lots of meetings.
8. Make sure organization is detail-oriented to provide quality customer service.
9. Engage in personal relationships and communications.
10. Rally to meet customer needs in a crisis.
11. Expedite jobs to deliver highly responsive service.
12. Maintain close relationship with union.

Shared Feelings

13. The company is good to me.
14. We like this place.
15. We care about this company because it cares about us as individuals.

Shared Cultural Understanding

A. Provide highly responsive, quality customer service (4, 8, 11).
B. Get things done well and quickly ("expediting") (4, 7, 10, 11).
C. Operate informally (1, 6, 9, 12).
D. Perceive company as part of the family (2, 12, 13, 14, 15).
E. Encourage constructive disagreement (3, 7).

COORDINATED RESOURCE
See *Management Live!* Reading 4.1, "Managers of Meaning: From Bob Geldof's Band Aid to Australian CEOs."

THOUGHT PROVOKER
How easy do you think it can be to change an organization's culture? How would you approach this task?

In many ways, culture resembles the well-worn sports metaphor of "momentum." Many a sports announcer, especially in football, analyzes the action in terms of which team has the momentum. Momentum, however, is not a useful concept for coaches. They cannot simply order their players to "go out there and get the momentum." Rather, they must prepare a detailed plan of action, spelling out a series of plays and instructing each member of the team how to maneuver on the field. The team gains the momentum by executing this plan.

In the same way, any efforts to change organizational culture must focus on what people *do* on a routine basis. If a manager can get the organization's members to behave differently, cultural change will follow. Take, for example, a company that, after a long history of minimal competition, wished to become more marketing oriented. Several years of memos, conferences, speeches, and videotapes preaching a new culture had no effect. It was only when senior executives acted—in this case, simply by talking more to customers—that a new marketing orientation emerged.

Types of OD Activities

Change agents have many techniques and intervention approaches available to them, not all of which will be used in a given change program. One useful way of classifying these techniques is in terms of the target groups with which they might be employed. The techniques can be used to improve the effectiveness of individu-

ETHICS IN MANAGEMENT

OD Assumptions and Values

Organizational development is not value-neutral. There are a number of ethical assumptions and values that most OD practitioners share and that determine the kinds of changes they suggest.

On the personal level, OD change agents assume that individuals have a natural desire for personal development and growth and that most employees are willing and able to make a greater contribution to the organization. They also believe that satisfying human needs and aspirations is an important purpose of organizational life. Therefore, they are concerned with individual self-fulfillment and try to overcome organizational factors discouraging personal growth.

On the group level, OD practitioners assume that it is important for people to be accepted by their work group and that most groups do not encourage the open expression of feelings. However, OD practitioners believe that hiding feelings has a negative effect on group members' willingness and ability to solve problems constructively, on job satisfaction, and on job performance. Therefore, they encourage the awareness and development of feelings as an inte-

gral part of organizational life.

On the organizational level, OD practitioners assume that the links between work groups influence their effectiveness. For example, there will be more coordination and cooperation between work groups when all group members can interact, less when just the managers communicate. A second assumption is that the policies and methods of managers of large groups will affect the way smaller groups operate. Finally, OD practitioners assume that strategies based on one group or department winning at the expense of another will not be successful in the long run. Organizations should rely instead on approaches acceptable to all the groups involved.

OD change agents also value the equalization of power within an organization, arguing that it is necessary for the long-term health of the organization. In most cases, power equalization means increasing the influence of subordinates. In some organizations, however, such as universities, hospitals, and city administrations, lower-level people may actually possess too much power. The solution then is to enhance the power of the administrators at the top.

als, the working relationship between two or three individuals, the functioning of groups, the relationship between groups, or the effectiveness of the total organization.[16] Some techniques described here are applicable to more than one target group, as indicated by the Management Application box.

Before we discuss these activities, though, we need to note the two levels of ethical issues involved in OD activities. One level involves the assumptions and values underlying OD; this level is discussed in the Ethics in Management box. The other level involves the effect OD activities have on individual employees. Many employees will be intrigued and exhilarated by the chance to examine their attitudes and interaction styles; others will be confused and frightened at first, though they may ultimately learn more effective behaviors and attitudes. Thus, the change agent needs to be sensitive to employee fears and trained to minimize their anxieties.

OD FOR THE INDIVIDUAL. **Sensitivity training** was an early and fairly widespread OD technique. In "T" ("training") groups, about ten participants are guided by a trained leader to increase their sensitivity to and skills in handling interpersonal relationships. Sensitivity training is less frequently used by organizations nowadays, and participants are usually screened to make sure they can withstand the anxiety raised by a T group. Precautions are also taken to ensure that attendance is truly voluntary.[17]

OD FOR TWO OR THREE PEOPLE. **Transaction analysis** (TA) concentrates on styles and content of communication (transactions or messages) between people. It teaches people to send messages that are clear and responsible and to give responses that are natural and reasonable. Transactional analysis attempts to reduce destructive communication habits or "games" in which the intent or full meaning of messages is obscured.[18]

OD FOR TEAMS OR GROUPS. In **process consultation,** a consultant works with organization members to help them understand the dynamics of their working relationships in group or team situations. The consultant helps the group members to change the ways they work together and to develop the diagnostic and problem-solving skills they need for more effective problem solving.[19]

Team building, a related approach, analyzes the activities, resource allocations, and relationships of a group or team to improve its effectiveness. This technique can be used, for example, to develop a sense of unity among members of a new committee.[20] Team building can be directed at two different types of teams or working groups: an existing or permanent team made up of a manager and his or her subordinates, often called a *family group;* or a new group that may have been created through a merger or other structural change in the organization or formed to solve a specific problem, which we will call the *special group.*

For both kinds of groups, team-building activities aim at diagnosing barriers to effective team performance, improving task accomplishment, improving relationships between team members, and improving processes operative in the team, such as communication and task assignment. Table 14-2 summarizes these activities for both family and special groups.

Diagnostic meetings may involve the total group or several subgroups and require only a brief time—a day or less—to identify strengths and problem areas. Actual team building requires a subsequent longer meeting, ideally held away from the workplace. The consultant interviews participants beforehand and organizes the meeting around common themes. The group proceeds to examine the issues, rank them in order of importance, study their underlying dynamics, and decide on a course of action to bring about those changes perceived as necessary. A follow-up meeting at a later time may then evaluate the success of the action steps.

sensitivity training An early personal growth technique, at one time fairly widespread in organizational development efforts, that emphasizes increased sensitivity in interpersonal relationships.

transaction analysis An approach to improving interpersonal effectiveness, sometimes used in organizational development efforts, that concentrates on the styles and content of communication.

process consultation A technique by which consultants help organization members understand and change the ways they work together.

team building A method of improving organizational effectiveness at the team level by diagnosing barriers to team performance and improving interteam relationships and task accomplishment.

Coordinated Resource
Use Transparency 93, Potential Conflict Between Individuals.

Coordinated Resource
Use Transparency 94, Potential Conflict Between Individuals and Groups.

Organizational Development at British Airways. Believing that a cold, authoritarian style of management would jeopardize the belief in warm, caring service that was key to British Airways' turnaround, the airline put 35,000 employees through a training program designed to make them more sensitive to their own needs, as well as those of co-workers and customers. In addition, it taught its 2,000 managers group decision-making techniques, held seminars with titles such as "Putting People First" and "Fit for Business," and even had junior managers play tiddlywinks as a way to develop team spirit. Volume is up 10 percent and the airline now has an outstanding reputation for service, even though employees report that they feel less busy and harried today.

COORDINATED RESOURCE
Use Transparency 95, Potential Conflict Between Groups.

OD FOR INTERGROUP RELATIONS. To permit an organization to assess its own health and to set up plans of action for improving it, the *confrontation meeting* may be used. This is a one-day meeting of all of an organization's managers in which they discuss problems, analyze the underlying causes, and plan remedial actions. The

TABLE 14-2 Team-Building Activities

ACTIVITY	FAMILY GROUPS	SPECIAL GROUPS
Diagnosis	Diagnostic meetings: "How are we doing?"	Diagnostic meetings: "Where would we like to go?"
Task accomplishment	Problem solving, decision making, role clarification, goal setting, etc.	Special problems, role and goal clarification, resource utilization, etc.
Building and maintaining relationships	Focus on effective interpersonal relationships, including boss-subordinate and peer	Focus on interpersonal or interunit conflict and underutilization of other team members as resources
Management of group processes	Focus on understanding group processes and group culture	Focus on communication, decision making, and task allocations
Role analysis and role negotiation	Techniques used for role clarification and definition	Techniques used for role clarification and definition

Source: Adapted from Wendell L. French and Cecil H. Bell, Jr., *Organization Development: Behavioral Science Interventions for Organization Improvement,* p. 104. © 1984. Used by permission of Prentice Hall, Englewood Cliffs, N.J.

Change at Southwestern Bell and Honeywell

In recent years, planned change programs have transformed Southwestern Bell and Honeywell Information Systems. Change was mandated at Southwestern Bell by the court-ordered breakup of the Bell System. The company was forced to become fully independent for the first time, taking over all the functions previously provided by AT&T. These ranged from purchasing to investor relations. Southwestern Bell, accustomed to the role of protected utility, also had to learn how to compete in order to exploit the new opportunities created by the divestiture. A new, entrepreneurial spirit was a top priority.

In contrast, Honeywell's change program came in response to the sluggish growth, poor morale, and widespread infighting plaguing the organization. While a 1982 program of cutbacks temporarily restored profits, it did not provide a basis for long-term growth. Top management decided to use organizational development to renew the business. Outside consultants used survey feedback and process consultation techniques to infuse Honeywell with a new organizational culture that incorporated basic OD values about the importance of the individual.

While the impetus for change was different at the two companies, their change programs shared a people-oriented approach. Both companies, for example, implemented mandatory retraining programs for managers. At Southwestern Bell, all mid- and upper-level managers attended a week-long Corporate Policy Seminar that focused on stimulating intrapreneurship. The Honeywell Executive Leadership Program also consisted of week-long workshops, but the focus here was on the development of team spirit (the group struggled together with physical obstacles such as a 12-foot wall) and commitment to the change process.

Participative management became the new order of the day. Honeywell systematically reeducated its managers and encouraged a participative management style by promoting those managers who employed it. Southwestern Bell rewarded its managers with bonuses. The company also created a formal "Quality of Work Life" program to encourage employee contributions to the organization. A QWL team from Kansas City, for example, successfully developed a new plan for the efficient restoration of phone service after a storm.

Communication was also a hallmark of both programs. The change team at Honeywell visited every company computer facility and produced a videotape for employees explaining their goals and the kinds of behavior they were trying to encourage. Southwestern Bell staged a satellite linkup of all 55,000 company employees and their spouses in 57 locations immediately after divestiture. This event allowed employees to vent their emotions about the change and gave management a chance to demonstrate their new leadership.

What else do the change programs at Southwestern Bell and Honeywell have in common? Both are success stories. At Southwestern Bell, intrapreneurship caught hold: Individual employees devised better ways to restore service to customers with defective lines, to monitor cellular systems, and to market the company's services. At Honeywell, the changes in information systems spread throughout the rest of the corporation. Revenues and profits went up in both organizations.

Sources: Zane E. Barnes, "Change in the Bell System," *Academy of Management Executive* 1, no. 1 (February 1987):43–46; James J. Renier, "Turnaround of Information Systems at Honeywell," *Academy of Management Executive* 1, no. 1 (February 1987):47–50.

confrontation meeting is typically used after a major organizational change, such as a merger or the introduction of a new technology.[21]

OD FOR THE TOTAL ORGANIZATION. The *survey feedback* technique can be used to improve the total organization's operations. It involves conducting attitude and other surveys and systematically reporting the results to organization members. Members then determine what actions need to be taken to solve the problems and exploit the opportunities uncovered in the surveys.

■ MANAGING CREATIVITY AND INNOVATION

HERE'S AN EXAMPLE
At General Electric Company, researchers are given wide latitude to image and invent and then "shop" the invention around GE's divisions. GE and its scientists regularly manage to transfer technology from the laboratory to the market. (*Wall Street Journal,* 6/14/90, p. A1ff.)

THOUGHT PROVOKER
Can you name some innovations available today that weren't available when you were younger?

Many management writers define *creativity* as the generation of a new idea and *innovation* as the translation of a new idea into a new company (Apple Computer), a new product (the Sony Walkman), a new service (Federal Express's overnight delivery), a new process (one waiting line for multiple services at a bank or amusement park), or a new method of production (computer-aided design and manufacturing).

Economic historian Joseph Schumpeter viewed innovation as the source of success in the market economy, a view that is reinforced by today's changing and competitive environment. The organization that is not creative and innovative may not survive. Thus, more and more organizations are looking for ways to encourage and foster creativity and innovation on both the individual and the organizational level.[22]

Individual Creativity

Individuals differ in their ability to be creative. Highly creative people tend to be more original than less creative people. If asked to suggest possible uses for automobile tires, noncreative people might say "buoys" and "tree swings"; creative people might say such things as "eyeglass frames for an elephant" or "halos for big robots." Creative people also tend to be more flexible than noncreative people—they are able and willing to shift from one approach to another when tackling a problem. They prefer complexity to simplicity and tend to be more independent than less creative people, sticking to their guns stubbornly when their ideas are challenged. Creative people also question authority quite readily and are apt to disobey orders that make no sense to them. For this reason they may be somewhat difficult to manage in most organizations. Motivated more by an interesting problem than by material reward, they will work long and hard on something that intrigues them.

Organizational Creativity and Innovation

Just as individuals differ in their ability to translate their creative talents into results, organizations differ in their ability to translate the talents of their members into new products, processes, or services. To enable their organizations to use creativity most effectively, managers need to be aware of the process of innovation in organizations and to take steps to encourage this process. The creative process in organizations involves three steps: idea generation, problem solving or idea development, and implementation.[23]

COORDINATED RESOURCE
See Samaras Reading "Tom Peters Invites Chaos for Survival."

GENERATION OF IDEAS. The generation of ideas in an organization depends first and foremost on the flow of people and information between the firm and its environment. For example, the vast majority of technological innovations have been made in response to conditions in the marketplace. If organization managers are unaware that there is potential demand for a new product or that there is dissatisfaction with already existing products, they are not likely to seek innovations.

Outside consultants and experts are important sources of information for managers, because they are frequently aware of new products, processes, or service developments in their fields. New employees may have knowledge of alternative approaches or technologies used by suppliers and competitors. Among the organization's regular members, those who constantly expose themselves to information outside their immediate work setting are valuable sources of new ideas. These people, called "technological gatekeepers" by Thomas Allen, can play a particularly

THOUGHT PROVOKER
Innovation is a precious resource that can't be bought. What are the implications of this as it relates to this chapter?

important role in stimulating creativity and innovation in research and development labs.[24]

According to Rosabeth Moss Kanter, the generation of ideas is more likely to promote innovation when those ideas issue from the grass-roots level of the organization. She argues that empowering people on the lower levels of organizations to initiate new ideas within the context of a supportive environment is a valuable means of implementing successful innovations.[25] In addition, although many new ideas challenge a company's cultural traditions, such innovative companies as Hewlett-Packard, Wang Laboratories, and Toyota nevertheless routinely encourage their employees to generate new ideas.

IDEA DEVELOPMENT.   Unlike idea generation, which is greatly stimulated by external contacts, idea development is dependent on the organizational culture and processes within the organization. Organizational characteristics, values, and processes can support or inhibit the development and use of creative ideas. Commitment to the rational problem-solving approaches discussed in Chapter 8 increases the likelihood that high-quality and creative ideas will be recognized and developed fully.

The organizational structure also plays an important role. Rigidly structured organizations that inhibit communication between departments will often keep potentially helpful people from knowing that a problem exists. By creating barriers to communication, such organizations may also prevent problem solutions from reaching managers who need them. Management information systems (MISs), decision support systems (DDSs), and expert systems store and retrieve generated ideas and aid managers in idea development.[26] Recent advances in the networking of such systems are especially helpful for integrative problem solving.

At Cray Research, which specializes in computer technology, new ideas are propelled through the organizational system by a variety of means, one of which is the policy of making external commitments to consumers even before a new computer product has actually been built. For example, Cray committed itself to the development of its innovative galium arsenide circuits before implementation of the project was actually under way. In addition, Cray has fashioned an overall organizational structure that encourages creativity and performance as instigating factors in planning and development.[27]

IMPLEMENTATION.   The implementation stage of the creative process in organizations consists of those steps that bring a solution or invention to the marketplace. For manufactured goods, these steps include engineering, tooling, manufacturing, test marketing, and promotion. While a high rate of innovation often reduces short-term profitability, it is crucial for long-term growth. For example, the Swiss watch industry, which operates by traditional practices and old-fashioned individual craftsmanship, has been in the decline since the mid-1970s, when more innovative competitors introduced new products, such as digital watches, into the market.[28] When Swiss watchmakers recently introduced new products, such as the popular, inexpensive Swatch wristwatch, they were able to regain part of a market that had appeared to be lost to them.

For innovation to be successful, a high degree of integration is required among the various units of the organization. Technical specialists, responsible for the engineering side of the new product, must work with administrative and financial specialists responsible for keeping the cost of innovation within practical limits. Production managers, helping to refine the specifications of the new product, must work with marketing managers, who are responsible for test marketing, advertising, and promoting it. Proper integration of all these groups is necessary for a quality innovation to be produced on time, on budget, and for a viable market. Organizations that are too rigidly structured may have a difficult time integrating their activities. In contrast, frequent and informal communication across an organization has been shown to have positive effects on innovation.[29] For this reason, task forces (to be discussed in Chapter 17) and matrix-type organizational structures (Chapter 11), which encourage interdepartmental communication and integration, are particularly suited for generating, developing, and implementing creative ideas and approaches.

Establishing a Climate for Organizational Creativity and Innovation

HERE'S AN EXAMPLE

3M has managed to keep its creative spirit alive by demonstrating a wide tolerance for new ideas, believing that unfettered creative thinking would pay off in the end. (*Business Week,* 4/10/89, p. 58ff.)

FOR DISCUSSION

Why is creativity best nurtured in a permissive climate? As a manager, how can I nurture creativity?

As we have seen, creativity is best nurtured in a permissive climate, one that encourages the exploration of new ideas and new ways of doing things. Many managers find it difficult to accept such a climate. They may be uncomfortable with a continuing process of change, which is the essential accompaniment of creativity. They may also be concerned that a permissive atmosphere encourages the breakdown of discipline or cost control.

Rosabeth Moss Kanter has developed a list of ten managerial attitudes—contrasted with the appropriately counterproductive behavior—that she believes ensure the stifling of innovative efforts. After studying attitudes and policies regarding innovation and creativity in a number of large organizations, Kanter was able to describe the means by which some managers regularly stifled innovation and prevented employees from generating new ideas. Chapter 3 of her book *The Change Masters* is entitled "Innovating Against the Grain: Ten Rules for Stifling Innovation," and her prescriptions for how *not* to encourage innovation are presented in Exhibit 14-1.

But what is the other side of the coin? How can managers accommodate their concerns about the effects of change and innovation to the increasing need to foster a climate that encourages creative participation by employees at various levels of the organization? Some positive steps—some possible answers to these question—are listed in Exhibit 14-2.

EXHIBIT 14-1 Kanter's "Ten Rules for Stifling Innovation"

1. Regard any new idea from below with suspicion—because it's new, and because it's from below.
2. Insist that people who need your approval to act first go through several other levels of management to get their signatures.
3. Ask departments or individuals to challenge and criticize each other's proposals. (That saves you the job of deciding; you just pick the survivor.)
4. Express your criticisms freely, and withhold your praise. (That keeps people on their toes.) Let them know they can be fired at any time.
5. Treat identification of problems as signs of failure, to discourage people from letting you know when something in their area isn't working.
6. Control everything carefully. Make sure people count anything that can be counted, frequently.
7. Make decisions to reorganize or change policies in secret, and spring them on people unexpectedly. (That also keeps people on their toes.)
8. Make sure that requests for information are fully justified, and make sure that it is not given out to managers freely. (You don't want data to fall into the wrong hands.)
9. Assign to lower-level managers, in the name of delegation and participation, responsibility for figuring out how to cut back, lay off, move people around, or otherwise implement threatening decisions you have made. And get them to do it quickly.
10. And above all, never forget that you, the higher-ups, already know everything important about this business.

Source: Rosabeth Moss Kanter, *The Change Masters* (New York: Simon & Schuster, 1983), p. 101.

EXHIBIT 14-2 Some Prescriptions for Fostering Organizational Creativity

1. *Develop an acceptance of change.* Organization members must believe that change will benefit them and the organization. This belief is more likely to arise if members participate with their managers in making decisions and if issues like job security are carefully handled when changes are planned and implemented. (See our discussion on overcoming resistance to change earlier in this chapter.)
2. *Encourage new ideas.* Organization managers, from the top to the lowest-level supervisors, must make it clear in word and deed that they welcome new approaches. To encourage creativity, managers must be willing to listen to subordinates' suggestions and to implement promising ones or convey them to higher-level managers.
3. *Permit more interaction.* A permissive, creative climate is fostered by giving individuals the opportunity to interact with members of their own and other work groups. Such interaction encourages the exchange of useful information, the free flow of ideas, and fresh perspectives on problems.
4. *Tolerate failure.* Many new ideas prove impractical or useless. Effective managers accept and allow for the fact that time and resources will be invested in experimenting with new ideas that do not work out.
5. *Provide clear objectives and the freedom to achieve them.* Organization members must have a purpose and direction for their creativity. Supplying guidelines and reasonable constraints will also give managers some control over the amount of time and money invested in creative behavior.
6. *Offer recognition.* Creative individuals are motivated to work hard on tasks that interest them. But, like all individuals, they enjoy being rewarded for a task well done. By offering recognition in such tangible forms as bonuses and salary increases, managers demonstrate that creative behavior is valued in their organizations.

ILLUSTRATIVE CASE STUDY

WRAP-UP

Organizational Trauma and Triumph at AT&T

Two important events have focused AT&T's efforts to manage change. The first is the consistent management style of CEO Robert Allen, who listens to employees and encourages them to speak out and to take pride in the new, aggressive AT&T. Allen will often go into a meeting and simply sit down and not say a word. He is committed to drawing on the substantial human resources of AT&T for a constant stream of creative ideas and innovations.

An indication of the success of AT&T's planned change program is its recent hostile takeover of NCR Corporation. Such an aggressive move would have been unthinkable in the old culture. While the jury is still out on the success of this move, AT&T is clearly looking to NCR to help its computer business and to provide yet another source of change and innovation. ■

■ *SUMMARY*

Planned change is the systematic attempt to redesign an organization in a way that will help it adapt to significant changes in the external environment and achieve new goals. As such, it is not simple, inexpensive, or painless. However, such changes are important because they help the organization respond to environmental changes that threaten its survival or present new opportunities for prosperity. Given the rapid change of the external environment, many organizations are embarking on planned change simply to improve the speed with which they adapt to new conditions.

According to Kurt Lewin's force-field theory, every behavior is the result of an equilibrium between *driving* forces, which push for change, and *restraining* forces, which resist change and strive to maintain the status quo. Forces of resistance include the existing organizational culture, individual employees' self-interests, and differing perceptions of organizational goals and strategies.

In Lewin's view, people find it difficult, if not impossible, to change long-established attitudes and behavior. Even if they do make changes, they will soon return to their old ways if the new ways are not reinforced. To prevent this, Lewin suggests a three-step process: unfreezing existing behavior patterns; using a change agent to help employees identify with and internalize new attitudes, values, and behavior; and then refreezing to lock in the new behavior patterns. In addition, Kotter and Schlesinger have proposed six ways to overcome resistance, such as combining education and communication.

Planned change can focus on organizational structure, technology, people, or some combination of these aspects. Generally, the number of organizational elements that must be addressed increases with the magnitude of change desired.

Structural change takes in classical organizational design, decentralization, and modification of the work flow. Technological change, which involves the equipment and processes used to produce goods and services, also affects structure, as shown by the technostructural or sociotechnical approaches of job enlargement and job enrichment. People approaches, in contrast, try to change employee skills, attitudes, perceptions, and expectations. Examples are management by objectives, management training programs, and the techniques of organizational development (OD).

OD is a long-range effort to improve the organization's problem-solving and renewal processes through a collaborative management of the organizational culture. It is pervasive and requires the support of top management. It focuses on organizational culture because that has a strong and lasting influence on employee attitudes, beliefs, and actions.

OD activities focus on individuals (sensitivity training), small two- or three-person groups (transaction analysis), teams or groups (process consultation or team building), intergroup relations (confrontation meetings), and the whole organization (the survey feedback technique).

Creativity is defined as the generation of new ideas, while *innovation* is defined as the translation of these ideas into new companies, products, services, processes, and methods of production. Increasingly, creativity and innovation are seen as being the key to survival in an ever-more competitive and global economy. Like individuals, organizations vary in their level of creativity and their ability to translate creativity into usable innovations. The creative process has three steps: idea generation, problem solving or idea development, and implementation. An equally important process is establishing an organizational climate that encourages creativity and innovation. Kanter gives rules for stifling innovation as well as tips for fostering creativity.

■ REVIEW QUESTIONS

1. What is planned change and why is it needed?
2. Explain the concepts involved in Kurt Lewin's force-field theory.

3. What are three major sources of resistance to planned change?
4. Describe Lewin's three-step process of change.
5. What are some of the ways employers can deal with employee resistance?
6. List the three types of planned change and give an example of each.
7. Give a good working definition of organizational development.
8. What value assumptions do OD change agents make?
9. What are three widely used OD techniques?
10. What is the difference between creativity and innovation? How can organizations encourage both?

CASE STUDY

Is There Creative Life After Post-it Notes?

Art Fry felt a little worried. Now that he had been branded an inventor, he felt some pressure to repeat his success; unfortunately, he was not quite sure he could do that. Where did *creativity* come from? Could you create because you were expected to? Could your surroundings contribute to the process? Certainly his employer thought so, but were 3M's expectations realistic?

Art had invented Post-it Notes—those small pads with an adhesive strip that are now standard equipment in every office in the country. Originally, they came only in yellow, but now they appear in a rainbow of colors and with clever sayings written on them. They have many imitations—the sincerest form of flattery. The product is definitely a success.

Art hadn't started out with the intention of fathering a revolution, even among office dwellers. He invented Post-it Notes because his bookmarks kept falling out of his hymnbook at church. In order to solve this fairly minor problem, he took an adhesive strip that was an interesting but unsuccessful product of 3M research and stuck it to scraps of paper. The adhesive had been rejected at 3M, where Fry worked as a scientist, because it stayed put only so long as you left it alone. But that was precisely the quality that is largely responsible for the success of Post-it Notes.

After concocting a design and playing with the results for a while, Art knew he had a product that people could use. However, convincing his managers at 3M was another matter—they were not sure that people would pay for adhesive-backed scrap paper. In fact, early sales results seemed to confirm their skepticism. Post-it Notes did not really start to sell until the marketing strategy was changed from a program of sending out ads and brochures to one of sending out samples of the product itself. Once people were able to play with Post-its and discover their variety of uses for themselves, sales took off Everyone who received samples, from top-level managers to mailroom gofers, soon became a loyal user.

Obviously, 3M was delighted with the success of Post-it Notes. As a company, 3M works hard to establish policies that will aid their people in creating precisely this sort of success. It sees its role as providing the tools that creative people need to turn an idea into a useful, marketable reality. An isolated individual with a "better mousetrap" may not have the expertise or the equipment to manufacture and market items like those in which 3M specializes. Even if he or she is able to do so in the early stages of the product's life, trouble commences once the competition has heated up and efficient manufacturing and lavish advertising come into play. Therefore, 3M manages the overall process, contributing the resources and the combined talents of a large corporation.

To do this, 3M needs original ideas. Therefore, the company allows—even encourages—employees to spend company time on personal or pet projects. Post-it Notes is only one example of what can result from these personal endeavors. Moreover, 3M is careful to give full credit to its salaried originators, allowing them to feel responsible for their contributions to the company.

Which brings us back to Art Fry's personal dilemma. He knew 3M expected a little more out of him now that he had proved he could come up with a good idea, champion it through the system, and create a commercial success. He also expected more out of himself. He had done it once, and he wanted to do it again. All he needed was a new idea, and it was precisely that, along with the drive to pursue and succeed with it, which no company could provide. Art Fry had solved the problem of fumbled unsung hymns. Now what other problem could he solve?

Source: "Lessons from a Successful Intrapreneur," *The Journal of Business Strategy* 9, no. 2 (March–April 1988):20–24.

Case Questions

1. Why were Post-it Notes successful?
2. Can creativity be managed at all?
3. Why is Art Fry worried and what can he do about it?
4. Suppose that Art Fry reported to you. What advice, as his manager, would you give him?

VIDEO CASE STUDY

Who's Minding the Store at Nordstrom's?

Nordstrom's, the upscale Seattle-based clothing store, built a nationwide reputation by providing exceptional service to customers, and successfully expanded at a time when other retail stores were experiencing poor sales and dwindling profits. New stores were opened in Virginia and New Jersey during 1990, and in southern California, the company reported the fastest growth in sales of any retail chain in the country.

The extraordinary personal attention that is the cornerstone of Nordstrom's reputation is, of course, a welcome relief to shoppers accustomed to service in many stores that ranges from surly to nonexistent. It is the result of an unusual, highly intensive system of employee motivation based on generous salary and commission sales. "Nordies" are encouraged to do whatever is necessary to make a sale: Customers can expect to receive a personal thank-you note after a purchase, and returns are accepted without question, even after use and without a sales slip.

The original Nordstrom's was a Seattle shoe store founded in 1901 by John W. Nordstrom, who, according to company lore, arrived from Sweden with $5 in his pocket and made his first fortune panning for gold. Management has been kept in the family for three generations, and a fourth is being groomed. This continuity has provided a strong, stable management environment, though company executives insist that they don't interfere with store operations, whose day-to-day functioning is highly decentralized. They describe the structure of the company as an inverted pyramid, with the executives on the bottom supporting the widening levels of managers and workers. Customers are at the top.

Most entry-level employees are college graduates. The average salary is $25,000, compared to a national average for retail employees of $12,000, and a few company legends earn up to $80,000. All employees start out in sales, and the company promotes only from within.

The employee environment is intensely competitive, with awards, cash prizes, and in-store discounts given for exceptional service and sales. Awards also go to individual stores having the largest scrapbooks of laudatory notes from customers. Salespeople are rated on a sales-per-hour system, and a consistently low SPH rating is grounds for dismissal.

This intense competitiveness has not been without problems, however. Some former employees say the company environment is intimidating, and report an almost cultlike atmosphere prevails in the mandatory "motivation seminars."

Serious difficulties arose for the company when the United Food and Commercial Workers Union complained that employees were being coerced into performing many nonsales duties "off-the-clock." The extra touches Nordstrom's is famous for—the personal deliveries and thank-you notes—are commonly done on the employee's time, so that no sales time is lost and the SPH rating stays high. Nordstrom management insists that it has never been company policy to illegally force employees to work without compensation, but employees report that they feel this is expected of them—and that the SPH system demands it. Early in 1990, the Washington State Department of Labor and Industries ruled that Nordstrom's was violating the state's minimum wage law, and that back wages must be paid to employees for their off-the-clock activities.

Nonetheless, competing retail stores such as Macy's and Bloomingdale's have begun imitating Nordstrom's practice of paying commissions to salespeople. An alternative approach to incentive selling that tries to avoid the more troublesome aspects of the Nordstrom system is practiced by the lower-priced Wal-Mart retail chain. At Wal-Mart, employees are stockholders in the company and earn bonuses based on the profits of their store as a whole.

Sources: Bob Baker, "The Other Nordstrom," *Los Angeles Times,* February 4, 1990, pp. D1–D8; Susan C. Faludi, "Sales Job; At Nordstrom Stores, Service Comes First—But at a Big Price," *The Wall Street Journal,* February 20, 1990, p. A1; Eva Pomice, "A Seattle Shoe Store Steps Out, Gives Rivals a Run for Their Money," *U.S. News & World Report,* December 5, 1988, p. 52; Francine Schwadel, "Courting Shoppers: Nordstrom's Push East Will Test Its Renown for the Best in Service," *The Wall Street Journal,* August 1, 1989, pp. A1–A4; Richard W. Stevenson, "Watch Out Macy's, Here Comes Nordstrom," *The New York Times Magazine,* August 27, 1989, pp. 34–40.

Case Questions

1. What is responsible for the unusual motivation found among Nordstrom's employees?

2. What aspects of the "company culture" at Nordstrom's have contributed to corporate and employee well-being? What aspects have created problems?

3. How could Nordstrom's have avoided legal problems with its employees? What measures should the company take to prevent further difficulties?

■ NOTES

[1]John M. Thomas and Warren G. Bennis, eds., *The Management of Change and Conflict* (Baltimore: Penguin, 1972), p. 209.

[2]Kurt Lewin, *Field Theory in Social Science: Selected Theoretical Papers* (New York: Harper & Brothers, 1951).

[3]Vijay Sathe, "Implications of Corporate Culture: A Manager's Guide to Action," *Organizational Dynamics* 12, no. 2 (Autumn 1983):5–23. Several books published in the early 1980s aroused great interest in corporate cultures. On the culture of Japanese organizations, see William G. Ouchi, *Theory Z: How American Business Can Meet the Japanese Challenge* (Reading, Mass.: Addison-Wesley, 1981); and Richard Tanner Pascale and Anthony G. Athos, *The Art of Japanese Management* (New York: Simon & Schuster, 1981). For discussions of successful companies and the cultures they have generated, see Thomas J. Peters and Robert H. Waterman, Jr., *In Search of Excellence* (New York: Harper & Row, 1982); and Terrence E. Deal and Allan A. Kennedy, *Corporate Cultures: The Rites and Rituals of Corporate Life* (Reading, Mass.: Addison-Wesley, 1982). Recent books exploring the concept in depth include Edgar H. Schein, *Organizational Culture and Leadership* (San Francisco: Jossey-Bass, 1985); Stanley M. Davis, *Managing Corporate Culture* (Hagerstown, Md.: Ballinger, 1985); and Ralph H. Kilman, Mary Jane Saxton, and Ray Serpa, eds., *Gaining Control of Corporate Cultures* (San Francisco: Jossey-Bass, 1985). See also Geert Hofstede, Bram Neuijen, Denise Ohayv, and Geert Sanders, "Measuring Organizational Cultures: A Qualitative and Quantitative Study across Twenty Cases," *Administrative Science Quarterly* 35 (June 1990):286–316.

[4]For a fuller discussion of the basic underlying assumptions around which cultural paradigms form, see Schein, *Organizational Culture and Leadership,* p. 86.

[5]Kurt Lewin, "Frontiers in Group Dynamics: Concept, Method, and Reality in Social Science," *Human Relations* 1, no. 1 (1947):5–41. See also Edgar H. Schein, *Organizational Psychology,* 3rd ed. (Englewood Cliffs, N.J.: Prentice Hall, 1980), pp. 243–247; and Edgar F. Huse and Thomas G. Cummings, *Organizational Development and Change,* 3rd ed. (St. Paul, Minn.: West, 1985), p. 20; William J. McGuire, "Attitudes and Attitude Change," in Gardner Lindzey and Elliot Aronson, eds., *Handbook of Social Psychology,* 3rd ed., Vol. 2 (New York: Random House, 1985), Chap. 6; and Joel Cooper and Robert T. Croyle, "Attitudes and Attitude Change," *Annual Review of Psychology* 35 (1984):395–426.

[6]For a review of the various types of change agents, see Richard N. Ottaway, "The Change Agent: A Taxonomy in Relation to the Change Process," *Human Relations* 36, no. 4 (April 1983):361–392. On the use of political skills by change agents, see Newton Margulies and Anthony P. Raia, "The Politics of Organization Development," *Training and Development Journal* 38, no. 8 (August 1984):20–23.

[7]See Paul C. Nutt, "Tactics of Implementation," *Academy of Management Journal* 29 (1986):230–261.

[8]"GM Faces Reality," *Business Week,* May 9, 1988, pp. 114–122; "GM's New 'Teams' Aren't Hitting Any Homers," *Business Week,* August 8, 1988, pp. 46–47; and Stephen Kindel, "The Designated Hitter," *Financial World* 157, no. 14 (1988):20–21.

[9]Harold J. Leavitt, "Applied Organization Change in Industry: Structural, Technical, and Human Approaches," in W. W. Cooper, H. J. Leavitt, and M. W. Shelly II, eds. *New Perspectives in Organization Research* (New York: Wiley, 1964), pp. 55–71. For an amplification of such a model, see David A. Nadler, "Managing Organizational Change: An Integrative Perspective," *Journal of Applied Behavioral Science* 17, no. 2 (April–May–June 1981):191–211. See also Ralph Kilmann, "A Completely Integrated Program for Creating and Maintaining Organizational Success," *Organizational Dynamics* 18, no. 1 (Summer 1989):4–19.

[10]Tom Peters, "Get Innovative or Get Dead," *California Management Review* 22, no. 1 (Fall 1990):9–26.

[11]Ibid., pp. 21, 24.

[12]For a more detailed description of system element interdependence, see Wendell L. French and Cecil H. Bell, Jr., *Organization Development: Behavioral Science Interventions for Organization Improvement,* 3rd ed. (Englewood Cliffs, N.J.: Prentice Hall, 1984), pp. 54–62.

[13]Ibid., p. 17.

[14]Raoul D. Edwards et al., "Marketing in a Deregulated Environment," *U.S. Banker* 95, no. 4 (April 1984):34–36ff.

[15]Peters and Waterman, *In Search of Excellence,* pp. 77–78; Ralph H. Kilmann, Mary J. Saxton, and Roy Serpa, eds., *Gaining Control of the Corporate Culture* (San Francisco: Jossey-Bass, 1985).

[16]French and Bell, *Organization Development,* p. 131. French and Bell also discuss other ways of classifying OD techniques and describe many of the techniques in detail.

[17]Morton A. Lieberman, Irvin D. Yalom, and Matthew B. Miles, *Encounter Groups: First Facts* (New York: Basic Books, 1973).

[18]See Eric Berne, *Games People Play* (New York: Ballantine, 1978); and Abe Wagner, *The Transactional Manager: How to Solve People Problems with Transactional Analysis* (Englewood Cliffs, N.J.: Prentice Hall, 1981).

[19]See Edgar H. Schein, *Process Consultation: Its Role in Organization Development* (Reading, Mass.: Addison-Wesley, 1969); and Larry Hirshhorn and James Krantz, "Unconscious Planning in a Natural Work Group: A Case Study in Process Consultation," *Human Relations* 33, no. 10 (October 1982):805–844.

[20]Examples of team-building efforts in a broadcast system and a university administration can be found in William G. Dyer, *Team Building; Issues and Alternatives* (Reading, Mass.: Addison-Wesley, 1977), pp. 64–67 and 82–83, respectively. An experiment in which this technique did not improve performance

but did generate a perceptible increase in participation is reported in Richard W. Woodman and John J. Sherwood, "Effects of Team Development Intervention: A Field Experiment," *Journal of Applied Behavioral Science* 16, no. 1 (April–May–June 1980):211–227. See also French and Bell, *Organization Development*, pp. 138–154. For a discussion of the distinctions between the interactions of a *group* and the coordination of a *team*, see H. H. Emurian, J. V. Brady, R. L. Ray, J. L. Meyerhoff, and E. H. Mougey, "Experimental Analysis of Team Performance," *Naval Research Reviews* 36 (1984):3–19.

[21]See Richard Beckhard, "The Confrontation Meeting," *Harvard Business Review* 45, no. 2 (March–April 1967):149–155.

[22]See Peters, "Get Innovative or Get Dead," pp. 9–26; and Andrew H. Van de Ven, "Findings on Innovation Development from the Minnesota Innovation Research Program," Discussion Paper # 51, University of Minnesota Strategic Management Research Center, Minneapolis, 1989. See also Dorothy Leonard-Barton, "Implementation Characteristics of Organizational Innovations," *Communication Research* 15, no. 5 (October 1988):603–631; Andrew Van de Ven and Marshall Poole, "Methods for Studying Innovation Development in the Minnesota Innovation Research Program," *Organizational Science* 1, no. 3 (August 1990):313–335.

[23]James M. Utterback, "Innovation in Industry and the Diffusion of Technology," *Science*, February 15, 1974, pp. 620–626. See also James Brian Quinn, "Managing Innovation: Controlled Chaos," *Harvard Business Review* 63 (1985):73–84.

[24]Thomas J. Allen and Stephen I. Cohen, "Information Flow in Research and Development Laboratories," *Administrative Science Quarterly* 14, no. 1 (March 1969):12–19; and Lewis A. Myers, Jr., "Information Systems in Research and Development: The Technological Gatekeeper Reconsidered," *R&D Management* 13, no. 4 (July 1983):199–206.

[25]Rosabeth Moss Kanter, *The Change Masters* (New York: Simon & Schuster, 1983); Rosabeth Moss Kanter, "Three Tiers for Innovation Research," *Communication Research* 15, no. 5 (October 1988):509–523.

[26]Stephen G. Green, Alden S. Bean, and B. Kay Snavely, "Idea Management in R&D as a Human Information Processing Analog," *Human Systems Management* 4, no. 2 (1983):98–112; Jane Howell and Christopher Higgins, "Champions of Technological Innovation," *Administrative Science Quarterly* 35 (June 1990):317–341.

[27]See Steve Gross, "Breaking Out of the Shell," *Datamation*, January 1, 1987, pp. 112–113; Kenneth Labitch, "The Shootout in Supercomputers," *Fortune*, February 29, 1988, pp. 67–70; and Gross, "Cray Designs Its Future Without Designer Steve Chen," *Electronic Business*, May 1, 1988, pp. 78–80.

[28]R. W. Roetheli, H. U. Balthasar, and R. R. Neiderer, "Productivity Increase and Innovation," an unpublished paper delivered at the TIMS/ORSA Conference, Dallas, October 17, 1984.

[29]Yar M. Ebadi and James M. Utterback, "The Effect of Communication on Technological Innovation," *Management Science* 30, no. 5 (May 1984):572–585.

CASE ON ORGANIZING

CHRIS CUNNINGHAM

Stover Industries was an amalgamation of four small companies in the electrical parts industry. The company was managed by its president, Elizabeth Stover, whose husband inherited one of the companies from his father. Stover, herself an engineer, elected to run the company while her husband pursued a separate career as a dental surgeon. Stover subsequently purchased the other three companies to form the present Stover Industries.

Stover was only 31 years old, but she was a dynamic individual, full of ideas and drive. In the space of a year, she had transformed Stover Industries into a profitable organization known for its aggressive pursuit of sales.

Stover integrated the four companies into a unified organization by welding the individual managements into one unit. Some people were let go in each organization as it was purchased and became part of Stover Industries. In several other instances, executives of the newly purchased companies resigned because of difficulties in working for such a young and driving boss. The four companies continued as individual manufacturing units of the company and together employed approximately 475 production workers. Because the original companies had been competing with one another, there were some problems in integrating the various sales staffs, so the salespeople had overlapping territories. This problem was gradually being worked out, but the salespeople were permitted to keep their own old customers, making it next to impossible to assign exclusive territories to each salesperson.

Until recently, the sales staff had included 17 salespeople and the sales director. The sales director, Bill Johnson, had been with the original Stover Company as sales manager. He knew Eliabeth Stover well and was able to work as her complacent subordinate. Most of his time and energy were devoted to routine direction and coordination of the sales team. Although a trusted lieutenant of Stover, Johnson was not much more than titular head of the sales force. Stover herself provided the active leadership.

Approximately six months before, Stover had personally hired Chris Cunningham, a college classmate, as a salesperson for the organization. Cunningham shared some of Stover's drive and enthusiasm, and in a short time had justified Stover's choice with a sensational sales record. In terms of sales performance, Chris Cunningham's record left little to be desired.

Nevertheless, Cunningham presented a thorny problem for Stover. The problem, as outlined by Stover, shaped up as follows:

I hired Chris because we knew and admired each other in our college days. Chris was always a leader on campus and we had worked well together in campus affairs. Chris was just the kind of person I wanted in this organization—a lot of drive and originality, combined with tremendous loyalty. The way I operate, I need a loyal organization of people who will pitch right in on projects we develop.

Chris has already proven to be a top-notch performer and will probably be our best salesperson in a year or two. Could one ask for anything better that that?

Here is where the rub comes in. Chris is the sort of person who has absolutely no respect for organization. A hot order will come in, for example, and Chris will go straight to the plant with it and raise hell until that order is delivered. It doesn't make any difference that our production schedule has been knocked to pieces. The order is out, and Chris has a satisfied customer. Of course, that sort of thing gets repeat business and does show well on Chris's sales record. But it has made running our plants a constant headache. It is not only the production people who have felt the impact of Cunningham on the operations. Chris gets mixed up with our engineering department on new designs and has even made the purchasing department furious by needling them to hurry supplies on special orders.

You can just imagine how the rest of the organization feels about all this. The other salespeople are pretty upset that their orders get pushed aside—and are probably a bit jealous too. The production people, the engineers, the purchasing agent, and most of the rest of the staff have constantly complained to me about how Chris gets in their hair. On a personal level, the staff say they like Chris a lot but that they just cannot work with such a troublemaker in the organization.

I have talked with Chris many times about this. I have tried raising hell over the issue, pleading for change and patient, rational discussion. Chris seems like a reformed character for maybe a week after one of these sessions, everyone relaxes a bit, and then bang—off we go again in the same old pattern.

I suppose that in many ways Chris is just like me. I must admit I would probably be inclined to act in much the same way. You see, I have a lot of sympathy for Chris's point of view.

I think you can see now what my problem is. Should I fire Chris and lose a star salesperson? That does not make too much sense. In fact, Chris is probably the person who should be our sales director, if not immediately, at least in a few years. But without the ability to get along with the organization, to understand the meaning of "channels" and "procedures," Chris is not only a valuable and talented addition to the company, but a liability as well. Should I take a chance on things eventually working out and Chris getting educated to the organization?

Should I put on a lot of pressure and force a change? What would that do to Chris's enthusiasm and sales record? If I just let things go, there is a real danger to my organization. My executives will think I have given Chris the green light, and they will transfer their antagonism to me. I certainly cannot afford that.

Source: This case was prepared by Todd D. Jick for the Harvard Business School, Boston, Massachusetts. Copyright © 1986 by the President and Fellows of Harvard College. Reprinted by permission.

Case Questions

1. What are the problems and issues in this case?
2. What factors in successful organizational behavior are suggested in this case? What possible weaknesses?
3. Where should the line be drawn between organizational control over personal initiative and the contribution of personal initiative to organizational effectiveness?
4. What should Stover do to deal with each of the variety of problems raised by this case?

CHAPTER FIFTEEN

Motivation, Performance, and Job Satisfaction

Upon completing this chapter, you should be able to:

1. Distinguish between early and contemporary views of motivation.

2. Explain and evaluate the major content theories of motivation.

3. Explain and evaluate the major process theories of motivation.

4. Discuss the underlying assumptions of reinforcement theory and explain why it is controversial in some circles.

5. Explain a systems view of motivation in organizations.

Art Direction: Tyler Smith. Illustration: Anthony Russo. Client: CCS/TOYO Printing Inks,
180 Kerry Place, Norwood, Mass.

Creating a Committed Work Force at Domino's Pizza

Why would anyone want to work hard at delivering pizzas? Tom Monaghan, founder of Domino's Pizza, Inc., found an answer to this question and became a multimillionaire. By the early 1990s, Domino's had 5,100 franchises and independent stores across the United States, as well as in Australia, Great Britain, Canada, Japan, and Germany. Each outlet had annual sales of close to $500,000.

Monaghan's own life, recounted in his autobiography, *Pizza Tiger,* reads like a proverbial rags-to-riches story. His father, a truck driver, died when Tom was only four, and his mother placed Tom and his younger brother, Jim, in a series of foster homes and Catholic orphanages while she attended nursing school, reclaiming the two boys when Tom was in sixth grade. Tom and his mother did not get along, though, and he spent the rest of his youth rebounding between his mother's home, foster homes, and even a brief stay at a seminary, where he was expelled for being too rambunctious. When he was 17, his mother had him placed in a detention home when he used her car without permission. Monaghan graduated last in his public high school class of 1955.

Frustrated in his hopes of studying architecture at the University of Michigan, he enlisted in the Marine Corps for the educational benefits, returning three years later with $2,000 he had saved for tuition at the University of Michigan—only to be swindled by a con artist. He scraped together tuition money once again by setting up a home delivery system for *The New York Times,* but dropped out twice before buying DomiNick's, a failing Ann Arbor, Michigan, pizza shop with his brother Jim for just a few hundred dollars in 1960. Jim had a full-time job, though, so Tom bought out his brother after only eight months. Giving up all hope of going back to school, Monaghan decided to commit himself "heart and soul" to being a pizza man.

It took a number of false starts and near failures before Monaghan came upon the recipe that helped him build an ever-widening network of franchises: a limited menu to hold down preparation time, free delivery guaranteed within 30 minutes, and the provision of such performance rewards and perks as trips to the Indy 500, BMWs for top executives, and visits to his retreat in Michigan's Upper Peninsula. Most importantly, Monaghan trusted his employees and gave them the freedom to try out new ideas.

In Monaghan's view of human nature, people work for challenges, to see their efforts rewarded,

Domino's Founder Tom Monaghan. Frustrated in his efforts to become an architect, Monaghan found he actually enjoyed twirling the pizza dough.

and to gain a sense of belonging and cooperation. He believes that his employees are like him and willing to work to achieve their dreams. And he gives them every opportunity to prove him right.

In terms of career development, Domino's offers employees the chance to duplicate Monaghan's own success. By starting out as a delivery person and moving up through the position of store manager, a number of Domino's employees have taken advantage of generous terms and started their own franchises, almost all of which are held by former employees.

Sources: Jeffrey A. Trachtenberg, "The Dream of a Lifetime," *Forbes 400,* October 1, 1984, pp. 250, 254; Susan Ager, "An Appetite for More Than Pizza," *Nation's Business,* February 1986, pp. 81–83; and Aimée Stern, "Domino's: A Unique Concept Pays Off," *Dun's Business Month,* May 1986, pp. 50–51; *Current Biography Yearbook* (New York: H.W. Wilson & Co., 1990):450–454.

*L*ike many entrepreneurs, Tom Monaghan had a good idea. But his success rested ultimately on his *human skills*—his ability to motivate and lead others to do a good job. This is true for any manager, who must work with and through others to achieve organizational goals. A manager can be a skilled planner, a judicious decision maker, and a farsighted student of organization—and still fail if he or she cannot make the human connection needed to motivate others. For this reason, we begin this unit on leadership with the study of *motivation*—the factors that cause, channel, and sustain human behavior. Then, in the next chapter, we will study leadership styles, followed by a chapter on using and leading groups and committees. We will end the unit with chapters on effective communication and negotiation skills and on individual career development.

■ THEORIES OF MOTIVATION: AN OVERVIEW

motivation The factors that cause, channel, and sustain an individual's behavior.

COORDINATED RESOURCE
See Oddou section on Leading the Organization, "Motivating Employees."

TEACHING TIP
This is a good time to re-emphasize how early management theory/practice contributed to the evolution of current theories and practices.

THOUGHT PROVOKER
A study by Grotta, Glassman & Hoffman found that 69 percent of the managers surveyed said their employees lacked motivation. What are the implications? (*U.S. News & World Report,* 1/28/91, p. 68)

COORDINATED RESOURCE
See *Management Live!* Reading 14.3, "The Best New Managers Will Listen, Motivate, Support."

No organization can succeed without a certain level of commitment and effort from its members. For that reason, managers and management scholars have always formed theories about **motivation**—those factors that cause, channel, and sustain behavior. These theories, in turn, affect the ways managers treat employees. As in other areas of management thought, our thinking about motivation has evolved from early approaches, which sought the one "right" model of motivating the individual, to more contemporary approaches, which realize that motivation arises from the interplay of both individual and environmental factors.[1]

Early Views of Motivation

The early theories of motivation were alike in that they tried to construct a single model of motivation that would apply to every worker in every situation. As Table 15-1 shows, however, the traditional model, the human relations model, and the human resources model each presented a different view of human beings.

THE TRADITIONAL MODEL. This model is associated with Frederick Taylor and scientific management (see Chapter 2). Managers determined the most efficient way to perform repetitive tasks and then motivated workers with a system of wage incentives—the more workers produced, the more they earned. The underlying assumption was that managers understood the work better than workers, who were essentially lazy and could be motivated only by money.

At first, the model seemed to work; output increased in many situations. As efficiency improved, however, fewer workers were needed for specific tasks. Managers tended to reduce the size of the wage incentive and layoffs became common. At that point, the model began to fail, as workers started to demand job security over temporary and minor wage increases.

THE HUMAN RELATIONS MODEL. Elton Mayo and other human relations researchers found that the boredom and repetitiveness of many tasks actually *reduced* motivation, while social contacts helped create and sustain motivation. The obvious conclusion: Managers could motivate employees by acknowledging their social needs and by making them feel useful and important.

As a result, the human relations model urged managers to give employees some freedom to make job-related decisions, as well as more information about managers' intentions and organization goals. Because the researchers discovered that employees tended to set group norms—about, say, the amount of work or the speed of work—managers also began to pay attention to informal work groups.

Under the traditional model, workers had been expected to accept management's authority in return for high wages. Under the human relations model, workers were expected to accept management's authority because supervisors treated

TABLE 15-1 Early Views of Motivation

TRADITIONAL MODEL	HUMAN RELATIONS MODEL	HUMAN RESOURCES MODEL
Assumptions		
1. Work is inherently distasteful to most people. 2. What they do is less important than what they earn for doing it. 3. Few want or can handle work that requires creativity, self-direction, or self-control.	1. People want to feel useful and important. 2. People want to belong and to be recognized as individuals. 3. These needs are more important than money in motivating people to work.	1. Work is not inherently distasteful. People want to contribute to meaningful goals that they have helped establish. 2. Most people can exercise far more creativity, self-direction, and self-control than their present jobs demand.
Policies		
1. The manager should closely supervise and control subordinates. 2. He or she must break down tasks into simple, repetitive, easily learned operations. 3. He or she must establish detailed work routines and procedures, and enforce these fairly but firmly.	1. The manager should make each worker feel useful and important. 2. He or she should keep subordinates informed and listen to their objections to his or her plans. 3. The manager should allow subordinates to exercise some self-direction and self-control on routine matters.	1. The manager should make use of underutilized human resources. 2. He or she must create an environment in which all members may contribute to the limits of their ability. 3. He or she must encourage full participation in important matters, continually broadening subordinate self-direction and self-control.
Expectations		
1. People can tolerate work if the pay is decent and the boss is fair. 2. If tasks are simple enough and people are closely controlled, they will produce up to standard.	1. Sharing information with subordinates and involving them in routine decisions will satisfy their basic needs to belong and to feel important. 2. Satisfying these needs will improve morale and reduce resistance to formal authority—subordinates will "willingly cooperate."	1. Expanding subordinate influence, self-direction, and self-control will lead to direct improvements in operating efficiency. 2. Work satisfaction may improve as a "by-product" of subordinates' making full use of their resources.

Source: Adapted from Richard M. Steers and Lyman W. Porter, eds., *Motivation and Work Behavior,* 3rd ed. (New York: McGraw-Hill, 1983), p. 14. Copyright ©1983 by McGraw-Hill, Inc., publisher of the English edition. Reproduced by permission.

them with consideration and allowed them to influence the work situation. Note that the intent of managers remained the same: to get workers to accept the work situation as established by managers.

FOR DISCUSSION
Under what conditions might Theory X assumptions be appropriate? What about Theory Y?

Theory X According to McGregor, a traditional view of motivation that holds that work is distasteful to employees, who must be motivated by force, money, or praise.

THE HUMAN RESOURCES MODEL. Douglas McGregor and other theorists criticized the human relations model as simply a more sophisticated approach to the manipulation of employees. They also charged that, like the traditional model, the human relations model oversimplified motivation by focusing on just one factor, such as money or social relations.

McGregor identified two different sets of assumptions that managers have about their subordinates. The traditional view, known as **Theory X,** holds that people have an inherent dislike of work; although they view it as a necessity, they will avoid it whenever possible. Most people, being lazy and unambitious, prefer to be directed and to avoid responsibility. As a result, the work is of secondary importance, and managers must coerce employees or motivate them with wages or a show of consideration. We can see this theory at work in both the traditional and the human relations models.

Theory Y According to McGregor, the assumption that people are inherently motivated to work and do a good job.

Theory Y is more optimistic. It assumes that work is as natural as play or rest, that, in fact, people want to work and, under the right circumstances, derive a great deal of satisfaction from work. People have the capacity to accept—even seek—responsibility and to apply imagination, ingenuity, and creativity to organizational problems.[2]

The problem, according to Theory Y, is that modern industrial life does not fully tap the potential of the average human being. To take advantage of their subordinates' innate willingness and ability to work, managers should provide a climate that gives employees scope for personal improvement. *Participative management* is the ideal way to do this.

One study found that contemporary managers often hold two models of motivation simultaneously. For their subordinates, managers favor the human relations model; they try to reduce resistance by improving morale and satisfaction. For themselves, however, managers favor the human resources model; they feel their own talents are underused and seek greater responsibility from their superiors.[3]

COORDINATED RESOURCE

The Additional Lecture for Chapter 15 found in the Lecture Extras supplement focuses on "Pushing People, but Not Too Hard."

COORDINATED RESOURCE

The Distinctive Discussions for Chapter 15 found in the Lecture Extras supplement include "Motivated to Healthy Living" and "Comic Relief."

COORDINATED RESOURCE

Use Transparency 96, The Basic Motivation Behavior Sequence.

Contemporary Views of Motivation

Contemporary views of motivation focus on a number of factors that may affect motivation. *Content theories* emphasize the "what" of motivation—the content of individual goals and aspirations. *Process theories,* in contrast, emphasize the "how" of motivation—the thought processes that go into motivation. A third approach, *reinforcement theory,* bypasses the "what" and "how" of motivation to focus on the ways in which behavior is learned. In the sections that follow, we will take a closer look at each of these theories, concluding with a systems view of motivation that considers both individual and environmental influences.

■ CONTENT THEORIES OF MOTIVATION

content theories Theories of motivation that focus on the needs that motivate behavior.

Maslow's hierarchy of needs Content theory of motivation that people are motivated to meet five types of needs, which can be ranked in a hierarchy.

Content theories of motivation focus on the inner needs that motivate behavior. In an effort to reduce or satisfy their needs, people will act in certain ways (see Fig. 15-1). This approach is associated with such thinkers as Maslow, Alderfer, McGregor, Herzberg, Atkinson, and McClelland.

Maslow's Hierarchy of Needs

Abraham **Maslow's hierarchy of needs** has probably received more attention from managers than any other theory of motivation, since it classifies human needs in a logical, convenient way—one that has important implications for managers.

FIGURE 15-1 A Content Theory Model of Motivation

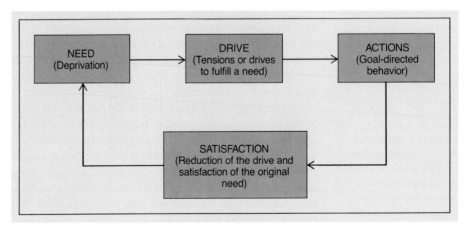

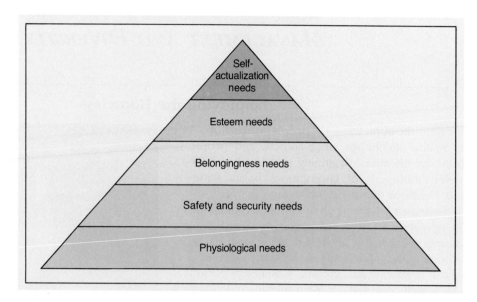

FIGURE 15-2 Pyramid Representing Maslow's Hierarchy of Needs

Maslow viewed human motivation as a hierarchy of five needs, ranging from the most basic physiological needs to the highest needs for self-actualization.[4] (See Fig. 15-2.) According to Maslow, individuals will be motivated to fulfill whichever need is *prepotent,* or most powerful, for them at a given time. The prepotency of a need depends on the individual's current situation and recent experiences. Starting with the physical needs, which are most basic, each need must be at least partially satisfied before the individual desires to satisfy a need at the next higher level. In our society, we long assumed that almost everyone can meet his or her most basic needs. In recent times, however, the number of homeless men, women, and children has grown. This is an individual tragedy, as well as a challenge to society and businesses. To see what a few innovative organizations are doing to combat this problem, see the Management and Diversity box.

An obvious conclusion of Maslow's theory is that employees need a wage sufficient to feed, shelter, and protect them and their families satisfactorily, as well as a safe working environment, before managers try to offer incentives designed to provide them with esteem, feelings of belonging, or opportunities to grow. Security needs include job security, freedom from coercion or arbitrary treatment, and clearly defined regulations.

In the modern organization, both physiological and security needs are usually (but not always) met satisfactorily. Next in the hierarchy is the need to belong and be loved. This is most strongly felt in relation to one's family, but also affects the work environment. Unless employees feel they are an integral part of the organization, they will be frustrated by an unmet need to belong and will be unlikely to respond to higher-order opportunities or incentives.

Maslow described two types of esteem needs—the desire for achievement and competence and the desire for status and recognition. In organizational terms, people want to be good at their jobs; they also want to feel they are achieving something important when they perform those jobs. As managers, we can fulfil both types of esteem needs by providing challenging work assignments, performance feedback, performance recognition, and personal encouragement, as well as by involving subordinates in goal setting and decision making. When AT&T divested itself of the Bell Operating Companies, its executives had to give careful consideration to how AT&T employees could continue to achieve important goals in their jobs. The old AT&T value of "serving the public interest" was no longer clearly operable, and some employees began to question the worth of what they were doing.

MANAGEMENT AND DIVERSITY

Employing the Homeless

At one time, the homeless—the people on Skid Row— were mainly alcoholics, drug addicts, and people with mental disorders. Beginning in the early 1980s, however, thousands of corporations began widespread layoffs at about the same time that government assistance programs were cut back. Simultaneously, upscale housing developments were reducing the supply of affordable housing in many inner cities. Now homelessness is a problem that transcends race, class, and economic background. A homeless person can be a well-educated, once-prosperous individual who has fallen on hard times; an elderly person who has run out of money because of medical bills; a family that wanders from town to town, with one or both parents looking for work; or a battered woman fleeing an abusive husband. It is estimated that between 600,000 and 4 million men, women, and children are homeless in America today.

The homeless face a special Catch-22 when it comes to regaining that most basic commodity—a roof over their head. Many are homeless because they have no job, but they cannot get a steady job without a home. They have no closet in which to store clean clothes, no shower, and no phone or fixed address. Many employers worry that people are

Employing the Homeless. A homeless street vendor sells the *Street Sheet,* a San Francisco-based imitator of Manhattan-based *Street News,* the first such paper.

ERG theory Content theory of motivation that says people strive to meet a hierarchy of existence, relatedness, and growth needs; if efforts to reach one level of needs are frustrated, individuals will regress to a lower level.

According to Maslow, when all other needs have been adequately met, employees will become motivated by the need for self-actualization. They will look for meaning and personal growth in their work and will actively seek out new responsibilities. Maslow stresses that individual differences are greatest at this level. For some individuals, producing work of high quality is a means for self-actualization, while for others, developing creative, useful ideas serves the same need. By being aware of the different self-actualization needs of their subordinates, managers can use a variety of approaches to enable subordinates to achieve personal as well as organizational goals.[5]

ERG Theory

Psychologist Clayton Alderfer agreed with Maslow that worker motivation could be gauged according to a hierarchy of needs. However, his **ERG theory** differs in two basic ways.[6]

First, Alderfer broke needs down into just three categories: *Existence* needs (Maslow's fundamental needs plus such factors as fringe benefits in the workplace), *Relatedness* needs (needs for interpersonal relations), and *Growth* needs (needs for personal creativity or productive influence). The first letters of each category form the now-familiar acronym *ERG.* Some research indicates that workers themselves tend to categorize their needs much as Alderfer does.[7]

homeless simply because they are unstable and unreliable. Beginning in the late 1980s, however, a number of organizations tried to overcome these doubts.

The first well-publicized organization to hire the homeless was *Street News,* a monthly newspaper based in Manhattan. Launched in November 1989 by Hutchinson Persons, a former rock musician, as a nonprofit, charitable venture, all of the paper's resources and office space were donated by Manhattan businesses. *Street News,* usually a 28-page tabloid, featured a mix of news stories and celebrity interviews.

Homeless vendors receive 50 cents from each 75-cent paper they sell and deposit 5 cents per paper in a mandatory apartment savings plan. Within four months, 200 homeless people had saved enough money to move into their own cheap rooms and apartments.

Unfortunately, questions arose about the management of Street Aid, the parent company, within the year. Both the New York State Attorney General and the Better Business Bureau's Philanthropic Advisory Service raised questions about the small amount of money actually going to charitable services, and the Internal Revenue Service was debating whether Street Aid qualified as a nonprofit organization. Nevertheless, *Street News*'s success inspired a number of imitators across the nation.

Days Inns of America is another organization that has a work program for what it calls "special-sector people"—the homeless, the elderly, and the disabled. The program, which uses these workers as reservation sales clerks, has been growing since 1985.

Days Inn Senior Vice President for Human Resources Richard Smith says that the decision to use special-sector people as sales agents stemmed as much from a desire for good business practices as it did from altruism. Smith explains that the company had positions to fill and saw homeless people as good candidates. Most of the homeless employees are drawn from shelters for battered women.

Because most of these women don't have job skills or previous experience in an office situation, Days Inns provides classroom instruction and on-the-job training. The corporation had to change its expectations and approach to management for its special-sector workers. Smith says that the problems encountered with homeless workers could not be solved with conventional management practices, so his managers came up with new solutions. Training lasts 8 hours a day for one to six weeks, as necessary. Usually three supervisors oversee each recruit until she feels comfortable with the reservations computers, her co-workers, and the duties she is expected to perform. Then one supervisor can handle 15 workers.

What other jobs might be filled with homeless workers? The answer depends mainly on the ingenuity of managers with jobs to fill. As the experience of both *Street News* and Days Inns shows, however, the homeless can be as motivated as any other workers, once they are given a chance.

Sources: Bill Stack, "Jobs Available: Homeless and Seniors Encouraged to Apply," *Management Review* 78 (August 1989):13–16; Leslie Whitaker, "Helping Them Help Themselves," *Time,* February 26, 1990, p. 56; Farai Chideya, "The Kindness of Strangers," *Newsweek,* August 12, 1990, p. 48.

Second, and more importantly, Alderfer stressed that when higher needs are frustrated, lower needs will return, even though they were already satisfied. Maslow, in contrast, felt that a need, once met, lost its power to motivate behavior. Where Maslow saw people moving steadily up the hierarchy of needs, Alderfer saw people moving up and down the hierarchy of needs from time to time and from situation to situation. Alderfer's theory, like Maslow's, is difficult to test, which makes it hard to evaluate its application to organizational settings, management practice, or even the personal fulfillment of employees.[8] Nevertheless, both theories offer useful insights into human needs.

The Need for Achievement

COORDINATED RESOURCE
Use Transparency 100, McClelland's Acquired Needs and Related Values.

John W. Atkinson and others hold that all healthy adults have a reservoir of useful energy. The means by which that energy is released depends on (1) the strength of the basic motive or need involved, (2) the individual's expectation of succeeding, and (3) the incentive value of the goal.[9]

Atkinson's model relates behavior and performance to three basic drives: the need for achievement, the need for power, and the need for affiliation, or close association with others. The balance between these drives varies from person to person. For example, one person might have a strong need for affiliation, while another might have a strong need for achievement.

David C. McClelland's research has indicated that a strong need for achievement—the desire to succeed or excel in competitive situations—is related to how well individuals are motivated to perform their work tasks. People with a high need for achievement like to take responsibility for solving problems; they tend to set moderately difficult goals for themselves and take calculated risks to meet those goals; and they greatly value feedback on how well they are doing.[10] Thus, those with *high achievement needs (nAch)* tend to be highly motivated by challenging and competitive work situations; people with low achievement needs tend to perform poorly in the same sort of situations.[11]

There is considerable evidence of the correlation between high achievement needs and high performance. McClelland found, for example, that people who succeeded in competitive occupations were well above average in achievement motivation. Successful managers, who presumably operated in one of the most competitive of all environments, had a higher achievement need than other professionals.[12] McClelland later reported considerable success in teaching adults to increase their achievement motivation and, in turn, to improve their work performance.[13] He also found *the need for affiliation (nAff)* an important factor in employee satisfaction.

For managers, these findings highlight the importance of matching the individual and the job. Employees with high achievement needs thrive on work that is challenging, satisfying, stimulating, and complex; they welcome autonomy, variety, and frequent feedback from supervisors. Employees with low achievement needs prefer situations of stability, security, and predictability; they respond better to considerate than to impersonal high-pressure supervision and look to the workplace and co-workers for social satisfaction. McClelland's research also suggests that managers can, to some extent, raise the achievement need level of subordinates by creating the proper work environment—permitting their subordinates a measure of independence, increasing responsibility and autonomy, gradually making tasks more challenging, and praising and rewarding high performance. McClelland characterized this aspect of managerial motivation as a *need for power (nPow)*.

High achievement needs can also be fueled by an individual's *fear of failure.*[14] Managers may be strongly motivated to take action by their fear of failing to meet personal or organizational goals and by their fear of possible public embarrassment when these failures are recognized. Conversely, for some individuals, *fear of success* can be a motive.[15] Such people fear the stress and burden of success and the envy and dislike it may awaken in others.

The Two-Factor Theory of Motivation

In the late 1950s, Frederick Herzberg and his associates conducted a study of the job attitudes of 200 engineers and accountants. As Figure 15-3 shows, Herzberg placed responses in one of 16 categories: the factors on the *right* side of the figure were consistently related to job satisfaction; those on the *left* side to job dissatisfaction. From this research, Herzberg concluded that job dissatisfaction and job satisfaction arose from two separate sets of factors. This theory was termed the **two-factor theory.**[16]

Dissatisfiers ("hygiene" factors) included salary, working conditions, and company policy—all of which affected the *context* in which work was conducted. The most important of these factors is company policy, which many individuals judge to be a major cause of inefficiency and ineffectiveness. Positive ratings for these factors did not lead to job satisfaction but merely to the absence of dissatisfaction.

Satisfiers (motivating factors) include achievement, recognition, responsibility, and advancement—all related to the job *content* and the rewards of work performance.

Herzberg's work has been criticized for his method of collecting data, which assumes that people can—and will—report their satisfying and dissatisfying experi-

COORDINATED RESOURCE

Acumen: High achievers are interested in attaining high-quality results. They often have effective planning skills.

COORDINATED RESOURCE

Acumen: Contrast what McClelland and *Acumen* say about managerial effectiveness relative to high need for affiliation.

COORDINATED RESOURCE

Acumen: Contrast *Acumen's* and McClelland's use of the word *power.*

COORDINATED RESOURCE

Acumen: Frederick Herzberg co-authored *The Motivation to Work,* which analyzes what causes employees to want to be productive members of the work team. Douglas McGregor in *The Human Side of Enterprise* outlines Theories X and Y and discusses humanistic management, leadership, team building, and development of managerial talent. Relate this to the Humanistic-Helpful scale.

two-factor theory Herzberg's theory that work dissatisfaction and satisfaction arise from two different sets of factors.

THOUGHT PROVOKER

Think of the "best" and "worst" jobs you have had. What made them good and bad? Relate these to Herzberg's satisfiers and dissatisfiers.

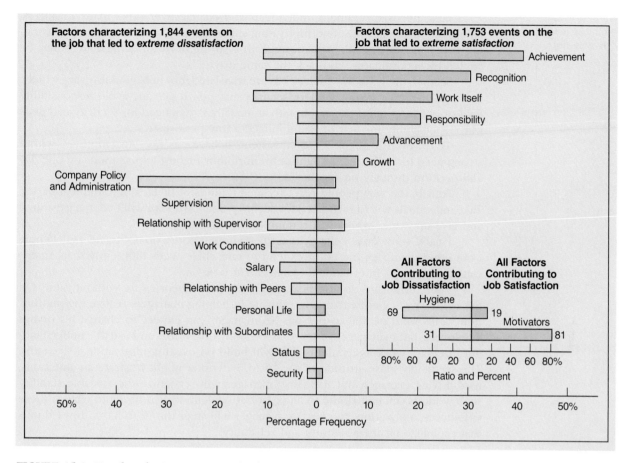

FIGURE 15-3 Herzberg's Comparison of Job-Satisfaction and Job-Dissatisfaction Factors

Source: Frederick Herzberg, "One More Time: How Do You Motivate Employees?" *Harvard Business Review* (January–February 1969):57. Copyright © 1969 by the President and Fellows of Harvard College; all rights reserved.

Confounding the Content Theories. Although Intel sales rep Aaron Evans, shown here with girlfriend Meredith Mendelsohn, appreciates his career as a way to make money, he looks forward to banking enough money so that he can "retire" from corporate life and enjoy life while he is young.

ences accurately. People are biased, however; they tend to credit themselves for successful events, while blaming outside factors for their failures. Furthermore, Herzberg's work, unlike previous research, does not take into account individual differences. A factor that causes dissatisfaction in one person may bring satisfaction to another. More importantly, subsequent research indicates that the two-factor theory oversimplifies the relationship between satisfaction and motivation. Although Herzberg *assumed* a relationship between satisfaction and productivity, he examined only satisfaction and *not* productivity or its link to satisfaction.[17]

Nevertheless, Herzberg's theory is regarded as an important contribution to our understanding of the effects of job characteristics on satisfaction, motivation, and performance. Job-enrichment programs, discussed in Chapter 11, were strongly influenced by the work of Herzberg and his colleagues.

Critique of the Content Theories

Content theory stresses understanding the factors within individuals that cause them to act in a certain way. For example, an employee who has a strong need to achieve may be motivated to work overtime to complete a difficult task on time; an employee with a strong need for self-esteem may be motivated to work carefully to produce high-quality work.

At first glance, this approach seems simple: Determine a subordinate's needs, and a manager can predict the type of task and setting that will best motivate the subordinate. In practice, motivation is far more complicated.

THOUGHT PROVOKER
Does money motivate?
Why or why not?

First, needs vary among individuals and change over time. Many managers, failing to understand this, find motivating subordinates a discouraging and frustrating task. Thus, an ambitious manager with a strong need for achievement may be baffled by subordinates who lack the same drive.

Second, the ways in which needs are translated into behavior also vary widely. One person with a strong need for security may play it safe and avoid responsibility for fear of failing; another person with an equally strong need for security may seek out responsibility for fear of being judged a low performer.

Third, even if needs were consistent, behavior is not. An employee with a strong need for self-esteem might outperform our highest expectations on one day and perform dismally on another day.

Fourth, the way people react to need fulfillment or lack of fulfillment varies. Take individuals with a high need for security. Some who fail will become frustrated and give up, while others will redouble their efforts.

Finally, some critics charge that the content theories do not travel well. People from other countries and cultures tend to rank their needs differently than Americans do. (See the International Management box.)

These criticisms do not mean that the content theories are without value. On the contrary, they are extremely valuable in helping managers realize that motivation varies from person to person. No manager can expect to change his or her employees, but managers can try to assess individual needs and use this understanding to create work assignments that will build on existing motivational strengths. The seemingly blasé attitude of the "9 to 5" worker might frustrate an ambitious, hard-driving manager, but the savvy manager will recognize the valuable stability such workers can contribute to an organization. Rather than trying to change these employees' motivation, an effective manager will steer the "9 to 5-ers" toward jobs that capitalize on their stability and reliability.

■ PROCESS THEORIES OF MOTIVATION

process theories Theories of motivation that study the thought processes by which people decide how to act.

role perception The individual's understanding of the behaviors needed to accomplish a task or perform a job.

expectancy approach A model of motivation specifying that the effort to achieve high performance is a function of the perceived likelihood that high performance can be achieved, and will be rewarded if achieved, and that the reward will be worth the effort expended.

Rather than emphasizing the content of needs and their power to motivate behavior, the **process theories** consider needs as just one element in the process by which individuals decide how to behave. Other elements are the individual's *abilities,* his or her **role perception,** or understanding of what behaviors are needed to achieve high performance, and his or her expectations concerning the results of certain behaviors. For example, someone with a high need for achievement may expect a bonus for completing a difficult project on time; the expectation of a bonus, then, will help motivate that individual's behavior. The most important process theories are expectancy theory, equity theory, and goal-setting theory.

The Expectancy Approach

The **expectancy approach** (also called the *expectancy/valence approach*) tries to overcome the criticisms directed at certain assumptions of other motivational theories—namely, that all employees are alike, that all situations are alike, and that there is one best way of motivating employees. Instead, the expectancy approach tries to account for differences among individuals and situations. Because it has received considerable support from research, and because it is easily applied in business settings, this theory has significant implications for managers.

EXPECTATIONS, OUTCOMES, AND WORK BEHAVIOR. David Nadler and Edward Lawler base the expectancy approach on four assumptions about behavior in organizations: (1) behavior is determined by a combination of factors in the individual and in the environment; (2) individuals make conscious decisions about their behavior in the organization; (3) individuals have different needs, desires, and goals; and (4)

INTERNATIONAL MANAGEMENT

Are Motivation Theories Culturally Biased?

In 1973, Geert Hofstede, a Dutch organizational consultant and scholar, studied the concepts of motivation, leadership, and organization in 72 countries to find out if American theories applied elsewhere around the globe. Using the IBM databank on international employee-attitude surveys, Hofstede was able to determine the extent to which Maslow's and other motivational theories could be applied in other nations to aid management in motivating employees.

Not surprisingly, Hofstede discovered great variation among cultures. He proposed that many of the differences in employee motivation, management styles, and organizational structures throughout the world could be traced to differences in the "collective mental programming" of people in different cultures.

Hofstede concluded that Maslow's hierarchy of needs was by no means the description of a universal human motivational process, but rather the description of a specific value system—namely, that of the American middle class to which Maslow belonged. People in cultures that have other value systems may rate security needs above social or self-esteem needs. For example, in Sweden, which has been quite successful in implementing participatory management styles, social needs are valued higher than esteem needs. In Germany, Japan, Switzerland, Italy, and Austria, security is generally valued over social and esteem needs. In France and Yugoslavia, security needs are highly valued, but so are social needs. In Canada, India, Great Britain, and the United States, Maslow's theory applied relatively well.

Findings such as Hofstede's prompt further speculation. The United States is a quite heterogeneous country—a culture formed by and composed of a diverse population from all over the world. Moreover, that culture has experienced changes in the conformation of its diverse social structure—some leading to greater homogeneity, others to new problems in cultural diversity. Just how valuable is it to apply ostensibly universal theories of work motivation to such a culture merely because it happens to be geographically identifiable?

Consider the influx of Mexican immigrants into the United States—some two million documented since the 1860s, between four and seven million undocumented between the 1920s and 1980s. Recent federal statistics give the unemployment rate for Mexican-American men at 8.5 percent, compared to about 5.5 percent for non-Hispanic white males. Mexican-American workers are sharply underrepresented in sales, managerial, and professional positions, and as of the early 1980s, median family income for Mexican-American families (one-fifth of whom live below the official poverty level) was only about 70 percent of that for Anglo-American families. It is not likely that the sociocultural influences on the thinking of Maslow and other classical theorists about work motivation will be directly applicable to such growing segments of the U.S. work force as its Mexican-American population.

Sources: Geert Hofstede, "Motivation, Leadership, and Organization: Do American Theories Apply Abroad?" *Organizational Dynamics,* Summer 1980, pp. 42–63; Hofstede and Michael Harris Bond, "The Confucius Connection: From Cultural Roots to Economic Growth," *Organizational Dynamics,* Spring 1988, pp. 5–21; Joe R. Feagin, *Racial and Ethnic Relations,* 2nd ed. (Englewood Cliffs, N.J.: Prentice Hall, 1984), Chap. 9.

---

individuals decide between alternative behaviors on the basis of their expectations that a given behavior will lead to a desired outcome.[18]

These assumptions become the basis for the so-called *expectancy model,* which has three major components:

COORDINATED RESOURCE
Use Transparency 101, The Expectancy Model of Motivation.

1. *Performance-outcome expectancy.* Individuals expect certain consequences of their behavior. These expectations, in turn, affect their decisions on how to behave. For example, a worker who is thinking about exceeding the sales quota may expect praise, a bonus, no reaction, or even hostility from colleagues.

valence The motivating power of a specific outcome of behavior; varies from individual to individual.

2. *Valence.* The outcome of a particular behavior has a specific **valence,** or power to motivate, which varies from individual to individual. For example, to a manager who values money and achievement, a transfer to a higher-paying position in another city may have high valence; to a manager who values affiliation with colleagues and friends, the same transfer would have low valence.

3. *Effort-performance expectancy.* People's expectations of how difficult it will be to perform successfully will affect their decisions about behavior. Given a choice, individuals tend to select the level of performance that seems to have the best chance of achieving an outcome they value.

We can think of these three components as three questions: "If I do this, what will be the outcome?" "Is the outcome worth the effort to me?" and "What are my chances of achieving an outcome that will be worthwhile for me?"

An individual's answers to these questions will depend, to some extent, on the types of outcome expected. Some outcomes act as **intrinsic rewards**—rewards that are experienced directly by the individual. Examples are feelings of accomplishment, increased self-esteem, and the satisfaction of developing new skills. **Extrinsic rewards,** in contrast, such as bonuses, praise, or promotions, are provided by an outside agent, such as a supervisor or work group. A single level of performance may be associated with several outcomes, each having its own valence. (If I perform better, I will receive higher pay, be noticed by my supervisor, be loved more by my spouse, and feel better about myself.) Some of these outcomes may even have valence because of the individual's expectation that they will lead to other outcomes. (If my supervisor notices the quality of my work, I may get a promotion.)

Figure 15-4 illustrates the theoretical working of the expectancy model. The value of the expected reward to the individual (1) combines with the individual's perception of the effort involved in attaining the reward and the probability of achieving it (2) to produce a certain level of effort (3). This effort combines with the individual's abilities and traits (4) and the way he or she sees the task (5) to yield a specific performance level (6). This resulting level of performance leads to intrinsic rewards (or negative consequences if the performance level is lower than expected) that are inherent in the task accomplishment (7a) and perhaps to extrinsic rewards (7b). (The wavy line in the model leading to the extrinsic rewards indicates that those rewards are not guaranteed, since they depend on how others assess the individual's performance and on the organization's willingness to reward that perfor-

Working for Intrinsic Satisfaction. Research scientist Anita Flynn, who works out of Massachusetts Institute of Technology's Artificial Intelligence Laboratory, holds "Squirt," her prototype of tiny robots that will ultimately be no bigger than a microchip. Although she envisions practical applications—repairing hair-thin fiber-optic cables or exploring distant planets—Flynn just thinks it would be "cool" to have the tiny robots living with and helping people.

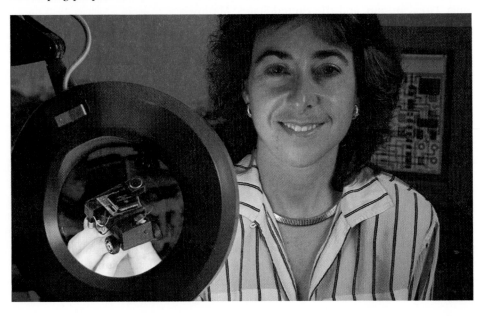

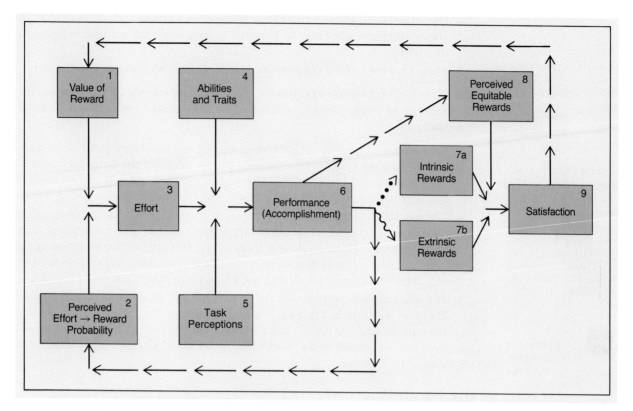

FIGURE 15-4 The Expectancy Model of Motivation
Source: Lyman W. Porter and Edward E. Lawler III, *Managerial Attitudes and Performance,* p. 165. Copyright ©1968. Used by permission of Richard D. Irwin, Inc.

HERE'S AN EXAMPLE

A single manufacturing plant of NCR Corporation has beat out even IBM as the world's leader in automated teller machines. They did it by giving employees considerable freedom to pursue the company's goals. (*Fortune,* 11/19/90, p. 165)

HERE'S AN EXAMPLE

Walt Disney Company is often touted as the "ultimate employee motivator." One thing Disney does is to communicate incessantly with cast members to get them to "buy into" the Disney culture. (*Business Month,* October 1990, p. 24)

mance.) The individual has his or her own idea about the appropriateness of the total set of rewards received (8), which, when measured against the rewards actually received, results in the level of satisfaction experienced by the individual (9). The individual's experience will then be applied to his or her future assessments of the values of rewards for further task accomplishment.[19]

IMPLICATIONS FOR MANAGERS. The expectancy model has a number of clear implications for how managers should motivate subordinates. As outlined by Nadler and Lawler, these include:

1. *Determine the rewards valued by each subordinate.* If rewards are to be motivators, they must be suitable for the individuals. Managers can determine what rewards their subordinates seek by observing their reactions in different situations and by asking them what rewards they desire.

2. *Determine the performance you desire.* Managers must identify what performance level or behavior they want so they can tell subordinates what they must do to be rewarded.

3. *Make the performance level attainable.* If subordinates feel the goal they are being asked to pursue is too difficult or impossible, their motivation will be low.

4. *Link rewards to performance.* To maintain motivation, the appropriate reward must be clearly associated within a short period of time with successful performance.

5. *Analyze what factors might counteract the effectiveness of the reward.* Conflicts between the manager's reward system and other influences in the work situation may require the manager to make some adjustments in the reward.

equity theory A theory of job motivation that emphasizes the role played by an individual's belief in the equity or fairness of rewards and punishments in determining his or her performance and satisfaction.

For example, if the subordinate's work group favors low productivity, an above-average reward may be required to motivate a subordinate to high productivity.

6. *Make sure the reward is adequate.* Minor rewards will be minor motivators.[20]

IMPLICATIONS FOR ORGANIZATIONS. The expectancy model of motivation also has a number of implications for organizations. As outlined by Nadler and Lawler, these include:

1. *Organizations usually get what they reward, not what they want.* The organization's reward system must be designed to motivate the behaviors desired. Seniority benefits, for example, reward the duration of one's employment in the organization, not the quality of one's performance.

2. *The job itself can be made intrinsically rewarding.* If jobs are designed to fulfill some of the higher needs of employees (such as independence or creativity), they can be motivating in themselves. This implication is obviously the basis of many job-enrichment programs; however, those individuals who do not desire enriched jobs should not be made to take them.[21]

3. *The immediate supervisor has an important role in the motivation process.* The supervisor is in the best position to define clear goals and to provide appropriate rewards for his or her various subordinate; the supervisor should therefore be trained in the motivation process and given enough authority to administer rewards.[22]

The Equity Approach

Another approach to job motivation, known as **equity theory,** is based on the thesis that a major factor in job motivation, performance, and satisfaction is the individual's evaluation of the equity or fairness of the reward received. Equity can be defined as a ratio between the individual's job inputs (such as effort or skill) and job rewards (such as pay or promotion) *compared with the rewards others are receiving for similar job inputs.* Equity theory holds that people's motivation, performance, and satisfaction depend on their subjective evaluation of the relationships between their effort/reward ratio and the effort/reward ratio of others in similar situations.[23]

Most discussion and research on equity theory focus on money as the most significant reward in the workplace. People compare what they are being paid for their efforts with what others in similar situations receive for theirs. When they feel inequity exists, a state of tension develops within them, which they try to resolve by appropriately adjusting their behavior. A worker who perceives that he or she is being underpaid, for example, may try to reduce the inequity by exerting less effort. Overpaid workers, on the other hand (also in a state of tension through perceived inequity), may work harder.

Recent studies have shown that an individual's reaction to an inequity is dependent on that person's history of inequity. Richard A. Cosier and Dan R. Dalton point out that work relationships are not static and that inequities are not usually isolated or one-time events.[24] They suggest that there is a threshold up to which an individual will tolerate a series of unfair events, but that once the "straw that breaks the camel's back" is added—that is, a relatively minor injustice that pushes the individual beyond his or her limit of tolerance—an extreme and seemingly inappropriate reaction will result. For example, an outstanding worker who is denied an afternoon off for no compelling reason may suddenly become enraged if he or she has experienced a string of similar petty decisions in the past.

Individuals differ, so naturally their methods of reducing inequity also differ. Some will rationalize that their efforts were greater or less than they originally perceived them to be, or that the rewards are more or less valuable. For example, one person failing to receive a promotion may "decide" that the previously desired

The Equity Approach. The equity approach can be seen in the management-by-objectives (MBO) system President David Brandon instituted at Vlassis Inserts, a Michigan-based printer of coupon inserts. Employees have a say in setting the objectives they will strive for and know what they must do to earn a bonus.

job actually involved too much responsibility. Others may try to make the co-workers with whom they are comparing themselves change their behavior; work team members receiving the same pay but exerting less effort, for example, may be persuaded to work harder, or high-performance workers may be discouraged from "making the rest of us look bad." For managers, equity theory has several implications, the most important being that, for most individuals, rewards must be perceived as fair in order to be motivating.

Pitney-Bowes, whose core business has long been mailing equipment, is one company that devotes a good deal of energy to fostering fairness among its employees. Special "jobholders" meetings, chaired by a member of the Council of Personnel Relations (CPR), are held regularly. The council's sole purpose is to make employees' concerns known to management. The CPR is responsible for functioning as a "watchdog" group so that employees who believe they have been treated unfairly or inequitably can voice their concerns outside the chain of command to which they are normally subject. Unfair bonuses, benefits, and even personal matters are among the issues addressed by CPR representatives, some of whom are elected by employees.[25]

Goal-Setting Theory

goal-setting theory A process theory of motivation that focuses on the process of setting goals.

Like the other process theories, **goal-setting theory** is a *cognitive* theory of work motivation—that is, it holds that workers are thinking creatures who strive toward goals. Goal-setting theory focuses on the process of setting goals themselves. According to psychologist Edwin Locke, the natural human inclination to set and strive for goals is useful only if the individual both understands and accepts a particular goal.[26] Furthermore, workers will not be motivated if they do not possess—and know they do not possess—the skills needed to achieve a goal.[27]

When goals are specific and challenging, they function more effectively as motivating factors in both individual and group performance.[28] Research also indicates that motivation and commitment are higher when subordinates participate in the setting of goals.[29] Employees need accurate feedback on their performance, however, to help them adjust their work methods when necessary and to encourage them to persist in working toward goals.

Critique of the Process Theories

The process theories have much to recommend them. They help explain what goes on inside the heads of employees and colleagues and can aid us to understand, and even anticipate, people's reactions to a manager's efforts to lead. The major drawback of these theories is that they are only really useful after managers have gotten to know their subordinates and their individual personalities, and this takes some time and effort. Moreover, employees who have experienced inequity in the past or who have unfulfilled security needs may be slow to trust a manager and reveal what rewards have the most valence for them.

These drawbacks can be overcome, however, if managers are careful to establish clear standards for acceptable performance and an equitable system of extrinsic rewards. They should also remember that while the valence of certain extrinsic rewards will vary from person to person, the satisfaction of doing a good job is intrinsically satisfying for almost everyone. The manager's first task, then, is to be sure employees have the resources they need to do their best.

ILLUSTRATIVE CASE STUDY

CONTINUED

Creating a Committed Work Force at Domino's Pizza

Monaghan ran Domino's according to a modification of Alderfer's model of work motivation. Clearly, he acted on the belief that people need to be rewarded for their efforts and that most of them, like him, have dreams that can be nurtured and satisfied by material wealth. Whether these dreams coincide with basic "existence needs" or the need of some people to find self-esteem through possessions is a matter of debate among psychologists. Whether they can be applied in the workplace is a question of practical managerial creativity.

Monaghan also believed that people need a sense of belonging and that they want to cooperate with others in a successful working environment. Thus, Domino's emphasizes teamwork. Even working at a somewhat routine and standardized job like pizza delivery, it is possible for a Domino's employee to be part of a group, a family, with the sense of belonging that families engender.

In addition, Domino's has a clear system of extrinsic rewards, including the opportunity to advance and become a franchise owner. Thus, employees have a clear expectation of what they must do to earn certain rewards.

Finally, we might explain Domino's success by the fact that it challenges people to use their creativity. In a business as straightforward as pizza parlors, Domino's has found that innovation and creativity can play an important role in giving people a sense of improving the company product, in enhancing their own talents in the pursuit of their own opportunities, and in making the organization successful.

COORDINATED RESOURCE
Use Transparency 102, Model of the Relationship of Performance to Satisfaction.

■ REINFORCEMENT THEORY

reinforcement theory
An approach to motivation based on the "law of effect"—the idea that behavior with positive consequences tends to be repeated, while behavior with negative consequences tends not to be repeated.

COORDINATED RESOURCE
See DuBose Reading #16, "On the Folly of Rewarding A While Hoping for B."

COORDINATED RESOURCE
Use Transparency 103, Conceptual Model of Reinforcement Factors and Motivation.

behavior modification
The use of reinforcement theory to change human behavior.

COORDINATED RESOURCE
See Samaras Exercise 4.1, "Application of Behavior Modification."

positive reinforcement
The use of positive consequences to encourage desirable behavior.

avoidance learning
Learning that occurs when individuals change behavior to avoid or escape unpleasant circumstances.

extinction The absence of reinforcement for undesirable behavior so that the behavior eventually stops recurring.

punishment The application of negative consequences to stop or correct improper behavior.

Reinforcement theory, associated with the psychologist B. F. Skinner and others, sidesteps the whole question of inner motivation and instead looks at how the consequences of past behavior affect future actions in a cyclical learning process. This process may be expressed as follows:

$$\text{Stimulus} \rightarrow \text{Response} \rightarrow \text{Consequences} \rightarrow \text{Future Response}$$

That is, the individual's own voluntary behavior (response) to a situation or event (stimulus) is the cause of specific consequences. If those consequences are positive, the individual will in the future tend to have similar responses in similar situations; if those consequences are unpleasant, the individual will tend to change his or her behavior in order to avoid them. For example, people may be likely to obey the law—and a manager's legitimate instructions—because they have learned at home and at school that disobedience leads to punishment. The other side of the coin is that people try to meet goals at work because they have learned that they stand a good chance of being rewarded. This is known as the *law of effect.*[30]

Behavior Modification

Behavior modification uses reinforcement theory to change human behavior. Thus, a manager who wishes to change employee behavior must change the consequences of that behavior. Someone who is frequently late, for example, might be motivated to come in on time (a behavior change) if the manager expresses strong approval for each on-time or early appearance (change of consequences), rather than shrugging the matter off. Lateness may also be stopped by expressing strong disapproval of the late arrival time. However, as we shall see, researchers believe that it is generally more effective to reward desired behavior than to punish undesired behavior.

There are four methods of behavior modification. In **positive reinforcement,** desirable behaviors are encouraged, or reinforced, by positive consequences, such as a raise or praise. In **avoidance learning,** employees change their behavior to avoid unpleasant consequences, such as criticism or a poor evaluation. To stop a behavior, a manager can use **extinction,** the absence of reinforcement. Suppose a manager's laxness at staff meetings has reinforced employees for coming late to the meetings and wasting time making jokes. To stop this behavior, the manager could start meetings on time and ignore jokesters. If the mere refusal to reinforce disruptive behavior does not work, a manager may resort to **punishment**—the application of negative consequences. Common examples range from criticism to docking pay and even dismissal. Of all the behavior modification methods, positive reinforcement is the most powerful.

W. Clay Hamner has developed a six-rule formula for using behavior modification, shown in Exhibit 15-1. Although these rules may seem like common sense, Hamner points out that managers often violate them.

Critique of Reinforcement Theory

Reinforcement theory may seem *too* simple. In fact, if we substitute *money* or its *lack* for *positive* or *negative* consequences, reinforcement theory may sound like the traditional model. However, reinforcement theory acknowledges the variety of consequences that can reinforce behavior and goes far beyond the traditional model in recognizing the ways in which individuals interact with their environment.

To many people, the idea of "behavior modification" is disturbing since it implies that individual behaviors can be predicted from a person's past experiences

EXHIBIT 15-1 Hamner's Rules for Using Behavior Modification Techniques

Rule 1: *Don't reward all individuals equally.* To be effective behavior reinforcers, rewards should be based on performance. Rewarding everyone equally in effect reinforces poor or average performance and ignores high performance.

Rule 2: *Be aware that failure to respond can also modify behavior.* Managers influence their subordinates by what they do not do as well as by what they do. For example, failing to praise a deserving subordinate may cause that subordinate to perform poorly the next time.

Rule 3: *Be sure to tell individuals what they can do to get reinforcement.* Setting a performance standard lets individuals know what they should do to be rewarded; they can then adjust their work pattern accordingly.

Rule 4: *Be sure to tell individuals what they are doing wrong.* If a manager withholds rewards from a subordinate without indicating why the subordinate is not being rewarded, the subordinate may be confused about what behavior the manager finds undesirable. The subordinate may also feel that he or she is being manipulated.

Rule 5: *Don't punish in front of others.* Reprimanding a subordinate might sometimes be a useful way of eliminating an undesirable behavior. Public reprimand, however, humiliates the subordinate and may cause all the members of the work group to resent the manager.

Rule 6: *Be fair.* The consequences of a behavior should be appropriate. Subordinates should be given the rewards they deserve. Failure to reward subordinates properly or over-rewarding undeserving subordinates reduces the reinforcing effect of rewards.

Source: Based on W. Clay Hamner, "Reinforcement Theory and Contingency Management in Organizational Settings," in Henry L. Tosi and W. Clay Hamner, eds., *Organizational Behavior and Management: A Contingency Approach,* rev. ed., 1977. Reprinted by permission of W. Clay Hamner.

and present environment, which seems to challenge deeply held beliefs that human beings freely choose how to act.[31] In addition, many fear that behavior modification techniques can be abused to make people behave in unethical ways. (See the Ethics in Management box.) However, one does not need to agree with all the underlying assumptions of reinforcement theory to see it in action every day. A manager praises extra effort and sees the effort continue. A division meets a deadline and the manager announces a bonus for everyone. In both cases, we assume—and, in effect, predict—that the receivers of such actions will behave in desired ways.

Furthermore, reinforcement-based approaches are sometimes more practical than approaches based on other theories of motivation. In day-to-day operations, a manager may not be able to take the time to understand the personal needs of every employee in a large unit. Setting forth clear guidelines for acceptable behavior and positive and negative consequences saves time and helps employees guide their own behavior. This may be especially useful when dealing with employees from different cultures, since needs and values vary from culture to culture. Because so much work behavior is learned behavior, reinforcement theory is also useful for training. In fact, computer-assisted instruction is based on reinforcement theory; the computer presents a small amount of information and then quizzes users on what they have just studied. The immediate feedback serves as positive or negative reinforcement.[32]

A SYSTEMS VIEW OF MOTIVATION IN ORGANIZATIONS

COORDINATED RESOURCE
See Study Guide Problem Exercise 15, "Your Motivation Theory."

COORDINATED RESOURCE
The Application Exercise for Chapter 15 found in the Lecture Extras supplement involves students in a motivation survey.

With so many different views of motivation, how can managers use current knowledge to improve their understanding of how individuals behave in organizations? Lyman Porter and Raymond Miles have suggested that a systems perspective toward motivation will be most useful to managers.[33] By *systems perspective* they mean that the entire system of forces operating on the employee must be considered before the employee's motivation and behavior can be adequately understood. Managers who adopt a systems perspective draw on the ideas put forth by content, process,

ETHICS IN MANAGEMENT

The Button Experiments

Do people really want control over their lives or do they want to be told what to do? In Chapter 12, we looked at some experiments by Stanley Milgram that suggested that most people will do as they are told when instructed by someone they perceive represents legitimate authority; specifically, they will send 450 volts of electricity through a total stranger. In Chapter 17, we will see that other experiments show people are capable of going even further.

A set of classical experiments by David Glass and Jerome Singer and their colleagues suggest that while people will do as they are told, they perform much more productively if they have some control over their situation. In one experiment, subjects were divided into two groups and told to perform a series of boring and repetitive tasks, some of which were impossible to complete. There was background noise consisting of people speaking Spanish and Armenian, machines roaring and grinding, and a clicking typewriter. One group was given a button that would shut off the noise and was told to feel free to use it—but only if the noise became too great to bear. The other group was given no button.

As expected, the group *with* the button outper-

formed the group *without* the button by a large margin: Members tried to solve five times the number of insoluble puzzles and had fewer errors in the repetitive tasks. But no one in the group even used the button; it was enough for them to know that they had control and could exercise it if need be.

In a direct application of this experiment, every worker on the assembly line at the GM-Toyota joint-venture plant in Fremont, California, enjoys the authority to stop the line. The increase in the quality of the product and the productivity of the workers has been phenomenal. It would seem that one way to motivate people is simply to give them some control over what you are asking them to do.

Sources: Herbert Lefcourt, *Locus of Control: Current Trends in Theory and Research* (Hillsdale, N.J.: Erlbaum, 1976); D. C. Glass, B. Reim, and J. E. Singer, "Behavioral Consequences of Adaptation to Controllable and Uncontrollable Noise," *Journal of Experimental Social Psychology* 7 (1971):244–257; D. C. Glass, J. E. Singer, and L. N. Friedman, "Psychic Cost of Adaptation to an Environmental Stressor," *Journal of Personality and Social Psychology* 12 (1969):200–210; D. C. Glass, J. E. Singer, H. S. Leonard, D. Krantz, S. Cohen, and H. Cummings, "Perceived Control of Aversive Stimulation and the Reduction of Stress Responses," *Journal of Personality* 41 (1973):577–595; Tom Peters and Robert Waterman, *In Search of Excellence* (New York: Harper & Row, 1982).

COORDINATED RESOURCE

See *Management Live!* Chapter 13 video, "Pat Carrigan (The Learning Allliance)."

and reinforcement theories. Porter and Miles believe that the system consists of three sets of variables affecting motivation in organizations: individual characteristics, job characteristics, and work situation characteristics. (See Table 15-2.)

Individual characteristics are the interests, attitudes, and needs that a person brings to the work situation. Obviously, people differ in these characteristics, so

TABLE 15-2 Variables Affecting Motivation in Organizational Settings

INDIVIDUAL CHARACTERISTICS	JOB CHARACTERISTICS	WORK SITUATION CHARACTERISTICS
1. Interests	Examples:	1. Immediate Work Environment
2. Attitudes (examples):	—Types of intrinsic rewards	a. Peers
—Toward self	—Degrees of autonomy	b. Supervisor(s)
—Toward job	—Amount of direct performance	2. Organizational Actions
—Toward aspects of the work situation	feedback	a. Reward practices
3. Needs (examples):	—Degree of variety in tasks	(1) Systemwide rewards
—Security		(2) Individual rewards
—Social		b. Organizational culture
—Achievement		

Note: These lists are not intended to be exhaustive; they are meant to indicate some of the more important variables influencing employee motivation.
Source: Lyman W. Porter and Raymond E. Miles, "Motivation and Management," in Joseph W. McGuire, ed., *Contemporary Management: Issues and Viewpoints*, p. 547. © 1974. Adapted by permission of Prentice Hall, Inc., Englewood Cliffs, N.J.

COORDINATED RESOURCE
See *Management Live!*
Reading 13.1, "Forever
Young."

COORDINATED RESOURCE
See Samaras Case 4.1,
"What's Wrong?"

COORDINATED RESOURCE
See Samaras Reading
"Worker's Needs: The
Same Around the World."

Motivating Employees by Changing the Work Situation. John Allegretti (center) convinced Hyatt Vice President Don DePorter (left) to let him head a recycling project. It worked out so well that Hyatt let Allegretti develop and run a new waste-consulting company for Hyatt, called ReCycleCo Inc. Allegretti has the full support of Hyatt President Thomas J. Pritzker (right), who encourages such staff suggestions.

their motivations will also differ. For example, one person may desire prestige and be motivated by a job with an impressive title; another may desire money and be motivated to earn a high salary.

Job characteristics are the attributes of the employee's tasks and include the amount of responsibility, the variety of tasks, and the extent to which the job itself has characteristics that people find satisfying. A job that is intrinsically satisfying will be more motivating for many people than a job that is not.

Work situation characteristics are factors in the work environment of the individual. Do colleagues encourage the individual to perform to a high standard or do they encourage low productivity? Do superiors reward high performance or do they ignore it? Does the organization's culture foster concern for members of the organization or does it encourage cold and indifferent formality?

Characteristics of the Individual

Each individual brings his or her own skills, interests, attitudes, and needs to the work situation. To understand this, we simply need to review the content theories of Maslow, Alderfer, McGregor, Herzberg, Atkinson, and McClelland.

Characteristics of the Job Task

The characteristics of the job and its associated tasks, the second variable influencing motivation in organizations, is the one on which managers can have the greatest impact. Researchers have tried to discover how a particular job will affect an individual's desire to perform that job well. Significant interest in this area developed because it was shown that routine assembly-line types of jobs reduced employee motivation and produced dissatisfaction. The relationship between job characteristics and motivation was better understood after Frederick Herzberg introduced his two-factor theory. Herzberg's work generated a great deal of interest in the role of motivation in the daily operations of organizations.

Characteristics of the Work Situation

The work situation, the third set of variables that can affect job motivation, consists of two categories: the actions, policies, and culture of the organization as a whole, and the immediate work environment.

ORGANIZATIONAL POLICIES, REWARD SYSTEMS, AND CULTURE.   The overall personnel policies of the organization, its methods for rewarding individual employees, and the organization's culture all translate into organizational actions that influence and motivate workers.

Personnel policies, such as wage scales and employee benefits (vacations, pensions, and the like), generally have little impact on individual performance. But these policies do affect the desire of employees to remain with or leave the organization and its ability to attract new employees. For example, a no-layoffs policy at IBM was a factor in motivating people to seek employment with the company; that policy is the result of trade-offs in other personnel matters. Similarly, bargaining between such unions as the United Auto Workers and major U.S. automobile firms at least temporarily increased workers' motivation to improve productivity; the trade-off for improved employment security was payroll and benefits concessions.

The organization's *reward system* guides its actions that have the greatest impact on the motivation and performance of individual employees. Salary increases, bonuses, and promotions can be strong motivators of individual performance—provided they are effectively administered. The reward or compensation must justify, in the employee's mind, the extra effort that improved performance requires; the reward must be directly and specifically associated with improved performance

HERE'S AN EXAMPLE
At Corning Inc., high achievers are designated "associates." (*Wall Street Journal,* 2/19/91, p. A1)

CLASS COMMENT
If worker morale is down, many companies try communication and employee input. (*Wall Street Journal,* 11/20/90, p. A1)

HERE'S AN EXAMPLE
Southern California Edison has tried to broaden employee roles by allowing decision making at lower levels. (*Wall Street Journal,* 2/19/91, p. A1)

so that it is clear why the reward has been given; and the reward must be seen as fair by others in the work group so that they will not feel resentful and retaliate by lowering their own performance levels.

The organization's *culture*—the shared norms, values, and beliefs of its members—can enhance or decrease an individual's performance. For example, a long-time employee at IBM, which is noted for its highly formal culture, might experience some difficulty in adjusting to the more informal cultures at Apple or Tandem, even though all these companies are in the same industry. In addition, certain types of cultures are likely to be more successful in motivating employees than others. Cultures that foster respect for employees, that integrate them into the decision-making process, and that give them autonomy in planning and executing tasks encourage better performance than do highly regimented cultures.

As managers, we want to motivate employees to high levels of performance, to loyalty and commitment to the organization, and to stability on the job. Money is the most obvious and frequently used incentive, but it is not the only means of motivating workers. In fact, assuming they perceive their compensation as fair, today's workers are responsive to such nonmonetary incentives as extra vacation days, flex-time arrangements, day care for their children, recreation facilities at the workplace, and company-sponsored local transportation. Financial incentives other than salary or bonuses also have a place in an incentive system; these include pension plans with early vesting, company shareholding, company contributions to further education, and auto or home loans.

Despite the obvious advantages of linking pay to performance, many organizations do not attempt to use extra compensation as a motivating factor. It can be difficult to measure the performance of individuals accurately, especially when output is not as easily measured as in most production and sales jobs. In addition, when managers do not feel capable of determining differences in individual performance, they may prefer to keep employees performing the same type of task at about the same salary level to avoid creating resentment about hard-to-justify pay differences.

According to Rosabeth Moss Kanter, however, the conventional "wisdom" of pay-motivation correlation is undergoing a revolution, albeit a quiet one.[34] It is her contention that, traditionally, pay largely reflected input rather than output. For example, pay reflected factors such as cost to hire, with adjustment for internal equity. The real basis for pay was status or the standing of one's job in the organizational hierarchy. Jobs came with an assigned pay level that remained relatively fixed regardless of how well a job was performed or the value of that performance to the organization. But with such emerging concerns as cost, productivity, and fairness, many organizations are changing their concepts of the pay-motivation correlation. Examples are pay-for-performance policies (Bank America); dollars-for-behavior policies—that is, eliminating simple across-the-board commissions in favor of an array of incentives for meeting performance targets (Merrill Lynch, GE); policies for entrepreneurial pay or partial employee ownership (AT&T, Sun Microsystems); gain-sharing policies—productivity bonuses on top of salaries (Preston Trucking, GM's new Saturn plant, Marine Systems Division at Honeywell, Inc.); and pay-for-skills policies, which provide individual incentives for employees to upgrade performance while creating teams that are virtually self-managed (General Foods). New theories of motivation will no doubt be needed to explain the evolving relationship between management and employees these new approaches to the pay-motivation correlation imply.

THE IMMEDIATE WORK ENVIRONMENT. The immediate work environment includes the attitudes and actions of peers and supervisors and the "climate" they create. Numerous studies have found that peer groups at work can have an enormous influence on people's motivation and performance. Since most people desire the friendship and approval of their peers, they will behave in accordance with the norms and values of their peer group. If the group has an "us-versus-them" approach to management and regards high producers as "rate-busters," its members will not be motivated to perform at their best level and may even be motivated to perform poorly.

Immediate supervisors strongly influence the motivation and performance of employees by example and instruction as well as by rewards and penalties ranging from praise, salary increases, and promotions to criticism, demotions, and dismissals. They also strongly affect job design and are important transmitters of the organizational culture, especially to new employees. Terrence E. Deal and Allan A. Kennedy point out that corporate "heroes" and "heroines"—managers who embody the values of the culture—provide "a pantheon of role models for managers and employees."[35] Supervisors who emulate the behavior of the organization's heroes and heroines will, in turn, transmit these same cultural values to their subordinates.

CHANGES IN WORK SITUATION VARIABLES.   The key work situation variables of organizational action, policy, and culture have begun to play a more important role in contemporary organizational practice—especially as they have become subject to a climate of change influenced by a number of internal and external factors. Let us consider one of these factors: the trend toward *downsizing,* or the reduction of an organization's work force in order to make it more competitive. Developments like downsizing are particularly interesting because they bring to light an important new issue in motivational theory and practice—namely, the need to motivate managerial personnel as well as workers at lower levels in the organization.

The motivational principles of Maslow and other theorists were developed at a time when most major U.S. corporations had a paternalistic relationship with their managers. The implicit employment contract was that if the manager followed the prescribed motivational incentives within the corporate culture, he or she would obtain lifetime tenure and assured employment security. In effect, the corporation demanded loyalty, dependability, and a fair day's work in exchange for a fair day's pay, a secure future, and a chance for advancement. Salary was based more on one's position in the organizational hierarchy than on performance. People tended to stay with a firm for their entire careers—and the organization expected them to stay to ensure hierarchical stability.

During the 1980s, the rules of the game changed drastically. Corporations of every size were under pressure from increased international competition, the mismanagement of human resources, the accelerated use of technology, and disenchantment with large bureaucratic structures. These pressures, coupled with a renewed determination to focus on the organization's core business, spawned a "lean and mean" philosophy. Thus, major corporations such as IBM, Xerox, Exxon, and USX began restructuring to eliminate overlapping layers of bureaucracy. At first, restructuring hit blue-collar workers the hardest. Then, during the second half of the 1980s, hundreds of thousands of managers also lost their jobs or were forced to take early retirement. Many once-loyal managers are now prey to distraction, disloyalty, alienation, and resentment. Their outlook on advancement has shifted from faith in top management's assurances of continued employment to a conviction they must manage their own careers.

Some argue that the traditional employee contract was doomed by corporate America's failure to foresee or plan for changes in the environment and by the swelling of managerial ranks by the vast influx of grown-up baby boomers. Whatever the causes, the new reality is that top management is now compelled to devise new motivational strategies to cope with the fallout of downsizing. When the rules of the game changed, so did the traditional employment contract that was the basis of many classic motivational theories. It is questionable whether these theories will provide appropriate guidance for motivating a new generation of managers. Thus, the problem of motivating managers promises to be one of the key issues in motivational theory and practice.[36]

ILLUSTRATIVE CASE STUDY

WRAP-UP

Creating a Committed Work Force at Domino's Pizza

Can Domino's sustain its success in motivating employees? One key, some analysts feel, will be Domino's method of clearly setting goals for improvement and giving concrete rewards. Of course, Domino's can only reward employees with new franchises if it continues to grow in the face of stiff competition from No. 1 Pizza Hut, which added delivery service as a direct attack on Domino's early in 1991.

In 1985, Monaghan announced an ambitious five-year plan that aimed to increase the number of franchises worldwide to 10,000, expand the menu, and introduce such high-tech wizardry as a special touch-tone pizza ordering device and a special fuel-efficient delivery car. The plans were unofficially abandoned sometime in 1988, though, and in 1989 Monaghan shocked the business world by turning the president's job over to former vice president P. David Black. (Monaghan still holds the titles of chairman and CEO.)

An avid philanthropist, Monaghan said he wanted to devote most of his time to charitable causes, particularly those associated with the Roman Catholic Church. One of his pet projects is a Catholic mission in a small town in Honduras, complete with a medical clinic, clothing factory, and, in the town square, a Domino's Pizza.

Others speculated, though, that Monaghan was dispirited over a number of controversies, including a protracted court battle with Amstar Corp. that claimed Domino's was infringing on its trademark for Domino sugar. (A judge ultimately ruled in Domino's favor.) A more serious problem was the charge that drivers trying to meet Domino's 30-minute delivery pledge had caused a number of accidents and deaths. The death of one Domino's driver led to the creation of People Against Dangerous Delivery in November 1989; a short time later, the Association of Trial Lawyers formed the Delivery Service Negligence Group, to coordinate the efforts of attorneys representing people killed or injured in accidents with delivery vehicles, most of which involved Domino's drivers.

In response, Black has tried to rally the forces and restore Domino's falling profits by cutting spending. He also paid more careful attention to the location of outlets to ensure maximum sales and safe deliveries. Drivers are carefully trained, the corporation says, and any and all speeding is done inside the pizza shop, not on the road. Whether Black can maintain the motivation success of Tom Monaghan remains to be seen. ■

Sources: Wendy Zellner, "Tom Monaghan: The Fun-Loving Prince of Pizza," *Business Week,* February 8, 1988, p. 90–91; Stephen J. Madden, "Pizza Pie in the Sky," *Fortune,* December 19, 1988, p. 175; "Domino's Delivery Pledge: Danger to Go?" *Newsweek,* July 10, 1989, p. 32; Wendy Zellner, "Why the Pizza King May Abdicate the Throne," *Business Week,* September 25, 1989, p. 36.

■ SUMMARY

No organization can succeed without a certain level of commitment and effort from its members. For that reason, managers need to understand motivation—the factors that cause, channel, and sustain behavior.

The early views of motivation were alike in that they tried to construct a single model of motivation that would apply to every worker in every situation. The traditional model, associated with Frederick Taylor and scientific management, assumed workers were best motivated by financial incentives, while the human relations model emphasized employees' social needs. Theorists of the human resources model criticized both these models for subscribing to what McGregor called Theory X—the idea that work itself is distasteful. In its place, McGregor proposed Theory Y—the idea that work is inherently satisfying. Contemporary views of motivation focus on a number of internal and external factors that influence motivation.

Content theories of motivation emphasize the individual's inner needs. The most influential theories here are Maslow's hierarchy of needs, ERG theory, McClelland's work on the need for achievement, and Herzberg's two-factor theory. The relative simplicity of content theories is appealing, but they have been criticized for not recognizing that needs vary among individuals and change over time, just as the behavior resulting from needs varies over time.

Process theories of motivation examine the thought processes by which people decide how to act. In the expectancy approach, this decision involves answering three questions: "If I do this, what will be the outcome?" "Is the outcome worth the effort to me?" and "What are my chances of achieving an outcome that will be worthwhile to me?" The equity approach studies how motivation is affected by expectations of equity or inequity, while goal-setting theory studies the process by which people set goals. Although process theories have many advantages, they work best when managers come to know their employees as individuals, a time-consuming and sometimes frustrating task.

Reinforcement theory, associated with the psychologist B. F. Skinner, sidesteps the question of inner motivation by looking at how the consequences of past behavior affect future actions. Behavior modification, the use of reinforcement theory to change human behavior, is controversial because it seems to threaten individual freedom. However, behavior modification can be very useful in training and in dealing with many employees who have widely varying values and levels of motivation.

To help managers apply the various theories of motivation, Porter and Miles have suggested using a systems perspective that analyzes individual characteristics, job characteristics, and work situation characteristics. At one time, managers and employees assumed they had considerable job security as long as they met corporate expectations. Beginning in the 1980s, however, this changed, as corporations of all sizes began to downsize (reduce staff size at every level). This trend has raised serious questions about the best way to motivate managers and keep their loyalty.

■ REVIEW QUESTIONS

1. What is motivation and why is it important?

2. Describe the early views of motivation. How were they alike? How were they different?

3. What is Theory X? Theory Y? How might each theory create a different management style?

4. According to content theories, what motivates people? What theorists advocated this approach? Why are content theories difficult to apply?

5. How is Maslow's hierarchy of needs related to motivation in organizations?

6. According to Atkinson, what determines the strength of an individual's motivational drive? How did McClelland relate Atkinson's work to management? What are the implications of his findings for managers?

7. What is Herzberg's two-factor approach to job satisfaction and dissatisfaction? Why has this approach been criticized?

8. What aspects of motivation do process theories emphasize? How do process theories relate the concepts of expectancy and valence to motivation?

9. On what assumptions is the expectancy approach based?

10. Define performance-outcome expectancy, valence, and effort-performance expectancy. How do they affect a worker's level of performance?

11. What does equity theory suggest about the motivation, performance, and satisfaction of individuals in the organization?

12. How do reinforcement theories explain behavior? To what extent does the process of learning play a part in reinforcement theories?

13. Why is behavior modification controversial? What do you think of behavior modification techniques?

14. In the systems perspective, what three variables affect motivation in the workplace?

15. How may an organization's culture and its personnel and reward policies affect motivation?

CASE STUDY

Idealism, Motivation, and Community Service at the Center City YWCA

After three days of interviewing for the job of director of the Center City YWCA, Harriet Bowen was having lunch with Margaret Pierce, the retiring director. When Pierce offered her the position, Bowen hesitated. "You still aren't sure?" Pierce asked. "Tell me what's bothering you."

"As I've told you," Bowen replied, "I'm looking for a job with a challenge. I would expect the YW to face financial difficulties—in today's economy, every nonprofit agency has these problems. But despite all the ideas and energy you have—not to mention the wide diversity of programs—the staff seems uninspired and worn out."

Pierce smiled. "That's true. You've hit on one of our biggest problems. As I've told you, the YWCA has undergone major changes in goals and programs over the past few decades. We no longer serve as a dormitory for young women when they first move to the city. Nor are we simply a place for a quick swim after work. At the National Convention, the YWs declared our major targets to be relevant programs for women, youth, and minorities. And yet our image in Center City—and even for some of our staff—is clearly that of a community recreation center, not a powerful force in the women's movement."

Bowen became animated. "I can see the types of programs you have: bilingual activities for Hispanics, creative skills classes, the Women's Center, the Rape Crisis Center, a battered wives program, youth programs, a nursery, as well as a health club for women, men, and children, and a small residence. The building is in pretty good shape. Where's the problem?"

Pierce paused, "As you know, a lot of our staff in the 1960s and 1970s started as volunteers and became paid staff when we got federal funding. But the fervor of the social movement waned just at the time that government grants, including CETA programs, were cut back. Although the neighborhood is much safer, thanks to urban renewal, many of our traditional big contributors have moved to the suburbs. Membership has not really increased substantially. So we've had to cut some programs, lose staff, and freeze wages. As a result, we don't have enough people to maintain the building or keep up the records, let alone reach out into the community."

"But surely you must still have some idealists around," Bowen commented.

"Yes, we do. But many have left, and most of our staff does just the minimum work required, for barely adequate wages." Pierce continued, "The morale problem is more complex. In the 1970s, we adopted the strong affirmative action program of the National YWCA; as a result, our staff today reflects the racial composition of Center City—half white, half minority. This wasn't easy. Qualified minority professionals are difficult to recruit. We lost some board members and long-term volunteers because of affirmative action. And some of the staff complained that less qualified people were being hired to meet quotas. Furthermore, we lost many white members who resisted integration. Therefore, some of our programs are unintentionally segregated. But with our limited finances, it's hard to create new programs and recruit really talented staff."

Bowen listened carefully as Pierce added, "It's very frustrating. We have the facilities and some good programs—but I haven't been able to communicate this to the staff or the community. I don't have time to institute better record keeping and an organized system of promotion and raises. So you see, we have a lot of the basic resources, but also a lot of problems."

Bowen smiled and sat back. "I think I understand the situation. It won't be easy to communicate my enthusiasm, but I'd like to try. I'll take the job."

"I'm very pleased," responded Pierce. "And remember, I intend to stay a member of the YW, so you can always call on me for help. Good luck."

Source: This case was written by Ellen Greenberg of the Columbia University Graduate School of Business. It is based on a real organization, but facts have been altered to enhance the teaching value of the material. Preparation of the case was supported by The Institute for Not-for-Profit Management of Columbia University. Parts of this case are adapted from an earlier case. © 1981 by The Institute for Not-for-Profit Management, Columbia University. All rights reserved.

Case Questions

1. What are the major problems facing Harriet Bowen?

2. If you were Herzberg, how would you advise Harriet Bowen to manage the YWCA?

3. What would Nadler and Lawler tell Harriet Bowen to assist her in leading her staff?

4. How might reinforcement theory apply to this case?

Motivation at Mary Kay: Driving the Pink Cadillac

Mary Kay Ash loves her work as head of Mary Kay Cosmetics—so much so that she rises at 5 A.M. to make productive use of the quiet early hours. She also loves her employees (all 220,000 of them) and invites them to join her in "The Five O'Clock Club." Those who become club members may be telephoned by Mary Kay herself at 5:30 any morning to discuss the employee's goals for the day. Many join.

After a frustrating career as a sales representative demonstrating various home-care products, Mary Kay opened her original cosmetics store in September 1963 in a rented storefront in Dallas. Her intention was to create a company of and for women, where there would be no barriers to their advancement and success. There were ten employees in the Dallas shop; today Mary Kay Cosmetics, with 220,000 independent sales agents, is the largest direct-sales cosmetic company in the world. Retail sales approximate $1 billion annually.

The bottom line has never been Mary Kay's primary concern, however. It may be an important consideration, but real success to her means having satisfied customers and happy, motivated employees. In Mary Kay parlance, *P* and *L* do not signify profit and loss; they stand for people and love.

The company's remarkably successful motivational approach relies on a combination of positive reinforcement ("praising to success") and a flamboyant material reward system. Mary Kay's ideal is that her employees' every transaction—both personal and business—be carried out according to the Golden Rule. She wants people to be treated as though each one wears an invisible sign saying "Make Me Feel Important," and she likes to illustrate this with a story from her youth, when she and a group of co-workers were sent by bus from Texas to Boston to be congratulated by a company executive for top-notch service. They eventually travelled back to Texas, never having met the too-busy executive—and it was a long, angry trip. In contrast, Mary Kay personally greets each new company employee.

Enthusiam is one cornerstone to the Mary Kay approach to employee motivation. The company song, "I've Got That Mary Kay Enthusiasm," is sung at all gatherings ranging from small weekly sessions to the annual company meeting. Managers are expected to be enthusiastic and to see that the mood spreads among employees. They also are expected to set an example in effort, attitude, and demeanor, and to adhere to lofty standards of dress and makeup. Mary

Kay herself will not answer her front door if she is not impeccably groomed.

Participation in the decision-making process is another important aspect of employee-management relations at Mary Kay Cosmetics. Management actively solicits ideas and suggestions from all employees on company matters. Mary Kay wants her employees to feel that they are not simply carrying out the wishes of their superiors, but that they are involved and their projects are their own. She believes that if company employees are going to love their work as much as she does, they must feel entirely responsible for their efforts and successes. An unusual example of this is that employees who attend the annual meeting in Dallas pay their own way—hotels, transportation, and the $125 fee for each seminar they attend.

The material rewards a successful Mary Kay employee can aspire to include mink coats, diamond rings, luxury vacations, and the trademark pink Cadillacs awarded to top sales representatives. There are now 5,000 of these cars on the road, and they are a much-sought-after status symbol among Mary Kay employees. The awards are presented at the annual meeting in Dallas, in a ceremony reminiscent of Miss America contests. Winners wear satin sashes and tiaras, carry bunches of roses, and are applauded by the 25,000 attendees. Mary Kay herself gives the keynote congratulatory speech.

Of more importance than the Cadillacs, fur coats, and tiaras are the applause and fanfare employees receive at the annual convention, according to Mary Kay. She believes that what most people want more than anything is recognition and the appreciation of their peers, and if these are given in plenty, employees will be happy—and successful. The company magazine, *Applause,* provides a further ongoing forum for individual recognition, and all sales directors are encouraged to send out newsletters congratulating local employees on their accomplishments.

The very highest award a Mary Kay employee can achieve—more meaningful than the pink Cadillac or membership in the Five O'Clock Club—is a diamond studded pin. Shaped like a bumblebee, the pin is the definitive reminder from Mary Kay of what enthusiasm and motivation can do, since after all, bumblebees are not supposed to be able to fly.

Sources: Jon Anderson, "In the Pink," *Chicago Tribune,* February 14, 1991, Sect. 5, pp. 1, 6; Mary Kay Ash, *Mary Kay Ash on People Management* (New York: Warner Books, 1984).

Case Questions

1. What assumptions underlie the management-employee relationship at Mary Kay Cosmetics?
2. To what do you attribute Mary Kay's success?
3. The comment is often made that the "Mary Kay approach" is specifically designed for a largely female organization. Do you agree? If so, how could such an approach be adapted to a company with a different employee base?

■ *NOTES*

[1] Any discussion of motivation, performance, and satisfaction in the workplace is in fact a discussion of *industrial/organizational (I/O) psychology*—the general study of organizational behavior with an emphasis on behavior in the workplace. This field of study was introduced by the German psychologist Hugo Münsterberg in 1913, with his book *Psychology and Industrial Efficiency.* See the following: A. Anastasi, *Fields of Applied Psychology,* 2nd ed. (New York: McGraw-Hill, 1979); B. M. Staw, "Organizational Behavior: A Review and Reformulation of the Field's Outcome Variables," *Annual Review of Psychology* 35 (1984):627–666; B. Schneider, "Organizational Behavior," *Annual Review of Psychology* 36 (1985):573–611; Frank J. Landy, *Psychology of Work Behavior,* 3rd ed. (Homewood, Ill.: Dorsey, 1985); T. Peters and N. Austin, *A Passion for Excellence: The Leadership Difference* (New York: Random House, 1985). The complex variety of principles established by I/O psychologists informs Thomas J. Peters and Robert H. Waterman's *In Search of Excellence* (New York: Harper & Row, 1982), pp. 55–57, 80–81. For a major part of our discussion on motivation, we are deeply indebted to Richard M. Steers and Lyman W. Porter, eds., *Motivation and Work Behavior,* 3rd ed. (New York: McGraw-Hill, 1983); and to Lyman W. Porter and Raymond E. Miles, "Motivation and Management," in Joseph W. McGuire, ed., *Contemporary Management: Issues and Viewpoints* (Englewood Cliffs, N.J.: Prentice Hall, 1974), pp. 545–570.

[2] Douglas McGregor, *The Human Side of Enterprise* (New York: McGraw-Hill, 1960); and *The Professional Manager* (New York: McGraw-Hill, 1967).

[3] Raymond E. Miles, "Human Relations or Human Resources," *Harvard Business Review* 43, no. 4 (July–August 1965):148–163.

[4] See Abraham H. Maslow, *Motivation and Personality,* 2nd ed. (New York: Harper & Row, 1970), pp. 35–58.

[5] See Ellen L. Betz, "Two Tests of Maslow's Theory of Need Fulfillment," *Journal of Vocational Behavior* 24, no. 2 (April 1984):204–220; and Howard S. Schwartz, "Maslow and the Hierarchical Enactment of Organizational Reality," *Human Relations* 36, no. 10 (October 1983):933–956.

[6] C. P. Alderfer, "An Empirical Test of a New Theory of Human Needs," *Organizational and Human Needs* 4 (1969):142–175, and *Existence, Relatedness, and Growth: Human Needs in Organizational Settings* (New York: Free Press, 1972).

[7] J. Rauschenberger, N. Schmitt, and J. E. Hunter, "A Test of the Need Hierarchy Concept by a Markov Model of Change in Need Strength," *Administrative Science Quarterly* 25 (1980):654–670.

[8] J. P. Wanous and A. Zwany, "A Cross-Sectional Test of the Need Hierarchy Theory," *Organizational Behavior and Human Performance* 18 (1977):78–79.

[9] John W. Atkinson and David Birch, *An Introduction to Motivation,* rev. ed. (New York: Van Nostrand Reinhold, 1978), pp. 346–348; and John W. Atkinson, *Personality, Motivation, and Action: Selected Papers* (New York: Praeger, 1983), pp. 174–188.

[10] David C. McClelland, *The Achieving Society* (Princeton, N.J.: Van Nostrand Reinhold, 1961), and "Business Drive and National Achievement," *Harvard Business Review* 40, no. 4 (July–August 1962):99–112. Also see John G. Nicholls, "Achievement Motivation: Conceptions of Ability, Subjective Experience, Task Choice, and Performance," *Psychological Review* 91, no. 3 (July 1984):328–346. For a good discussion of achievement motivation in work situations, see Edward E. Lawler III, *Motivation in Work Organizations* (Monterey, Calif.: Brooks/Cole, 1973), pp. 20–23.

[11] Danny Miller, "The Correlates of Entrepreneurship in Three Types of Firms," *Management Science* 29, no. 7 (July 1983):770–791.

[12] See McClelland, "Business Drive and National Achievement," pp. 99–112; and Michael J. Stahl, "Achievement, Power and Managerial Motivation: Selecting Managerial Talent with the Job Choice Exercise," *Personnel Psychology* 36, no. 4 (Winter 1983):775–789.

[13] David C. McClelland, "Toward a Theory of Motive Acquisition," *American Psychologist* 20, no. 5 (May 1965):321–333. Also see the interview with David C. McClelland in "As I See It," *Forbes,* June 1, 1969, pp. 53–57.

[14] See Leonard H. Chusmir, "Personnel Administrators' Perception of Six Differences in Motivation of Managers: Research-Based or Stereotyped?" *International Journal of Women's Studies* 7, no. 1 (January–February 1984):17–23; and Heinz Heckhausen, Heinz-Dieter Schmalt, and Klaus Schneider, *Achievement Motivation in Perspective* (Orlando, Fla.: Academic Press, 1985).

[15] Maureen Kearney, "A Comparison of Motivation to Avoid Success in Males and Females," *Journal of Clinical Psychology* 4, no. 4 (July 1984):1005–1007.

[16] Frederick Herzberg, Bernard Mausner, and Barbara Synderman, *The Motivation to Work* (New York: Wiley, 1959). See also Frederick Herzberg, *Work and the Nature of Man* (New York: World Publishing,

1966), and "One More Time: How Do You Motivate Employees?" *Harvard Business Review* 46, no. 1 (January–February 1968):53–62. For a critique of this and other models, see James A. Lee, *The Gold and Garbage in Management Theories* (Athens: Ohio University Press, 1980).

[17]Victor Vroom, *Work and Motivation* (New York: Wiley, 1964); Robert J. House and Lawrence A. Wigdor, "Herzberg's Dual-Factor Theory of Job Satisfaction and Motivation," *Personnel Psychology* 20, no. 4 (Winter 1967):369–389; Michael E. Gordon, Norman M. Pryor, and Bob V. Harris, "An Examination of Scaling Bias in Herzberg's Theory of Job Satisfaction," *Organizational Behavior and Human Performance* (February 1974):106–121; and Edwin A. Locke and Roman J. Whiting, "Sources of Satisfaction and Dissatisfaction Among Solid Waste Management Employees," *Journal of Applied Psychology* (April 1974):145–156.

[18]David A. Nadler and Edward E. Lawler III, "Motivation—a Diagnostic Approach," in J. Richard Hackman, Edward E. Lawler III, and Lyman W. Porter, eds., *Perspectives on Behavior in Organizations* (New York: McGraw-Hill, 1977), p. 27.

[19]Lyman W. Porter and Edward E. Lawler III, *Managerial Attitudes and Performance* (Homewood, Ill.: Irwin, 1968). See also Cynthia M. Pavett, "Evaluation of the Impact of Feedback on Performance and Motivation," *Human Relations* 36, no. 7 (July 1983):641–654; and Vida Scarpello and John P. Campbell, "Job Satisfaction and the Fit Between Individual Needs and Organizational Rewards," *Journal of Occupational Psychology* 56, no. 4 (1983):315–328.

[20]Philip M. Podsakoff, William D. Tudor, Richard A. Grover, and Vandra L. Huber, "Situational Moderators of Leader Reward and Punishment Behaviors: Fact or Fiction?" *Organizational Behavior and Human Performance* 34, no. 1 (August 1984):21–63.

[21]See J. Richard Hackman, Greg Oldham, Robert Janson, and Kenneth Purdy, "A New Strategy for Job Enrichment," *California Management Review* 17, no. 4 (Summer 1975):57–71.

[22]James C. Naylor and Daniel R. Ilgen, "Goal Settings: A Theoretical Analysis of a Motivational Technology," *Research in Organizational Behavior* 6 (1984):95–140.

[23]J. Stacey Adams, "Toward an Understanding of Inequity," *Journal of Abnormal and Social Psychology* 67, no. 5 (November 1963):422–436. See also Robert P. Vecchio, "Models of Psychological Inequity," *Organizational Behavior and Human Performance* 34, no. 2 (October 1984):266–282.

[24]Richard A. Cosier and Dan R. Dalton, "Equity Theory and Time: A Reformulation," *Academy of Management Review* 8, no. 2 (April 1983):311–319.

[25]Robert Levering, *A Great Place to Work* (New York: Random House, 1988), pp. 68–72.

[26]E. A. Locke, "Toward a Theory of Task Motivation and Incentives," *Organizational Behavior and Human Performance* 3 (1968):157–189, and "The Nature and Causes of Job Satisfaction," in M. D. Dunnette, ed., *The Handbook of Industrial and Organizational Psychology* (Chicago: Rand McNally, 1976).

[27]E. A. Locke, K. N. Shaw, L. M. Saari, and G. P. Latham, "Goal Setting and Task Performance, 1969–1980," *Psychological Bulletin* 90 (1981):125–152; and Frank J. Landy, *Psychology of Work Behavior,* 3rd ed. (Homewood, Ill.: Dorsey, 1985).

[28]James C. Naylor and Daniel R. Ilgen, "Goal Setting: A Theoretical Analysis of a Motivational Technique," in *Research in Organizational Behavior,* Vol. 6, B. M. Staw and L. L. Cummings, eds. (Greenwich, Conn.: JAI Press, 1984), pp. 95–140.

[29]Miriam Erez, P. C. Earley, and C. L. Hulin, "The Impact of Participation on Goal Acceptance and Performance: A Two-Step Model," *Academy of Management Journal* 28 (1985):50–66.

[30]The original formulation of the law of effect was based on years of animal experiments by Edward L. Thorndike and appeared in *Animal Intelligence* (New York: Macmillan, 1911), p. 244.

[31]See, for example, B. F. Skinner, *Beyond Freedom and Dignity* (New York: Alfred A. Knopf, 1971).

[32]Our discussion is based on W. Clay Hamner, "Reinforcement Theory and Contingency Management in Organizational Settings," in Henry L. Tosi and W. Clay Hamner, eds., *Organizational Behavior and Management: A Contingency Approach* (Chicago: St. Clair Press, 1974); Donald Sanzotta, *Motivational Theories and Applications for Managers* (New York: American Management Associations, 1977); and Fred Luthans and Robert Kreitner, "A Social Learning Approach to Behavioral Management: Radical Behaviorists 'Mellowing Out,'" *Organizational Dynamics* 13, no. 12 (August 1984):47–63.

[33]Porter and Miles, "Motivation and Management," pp. 546–550.

[34]Rosabeth Moss Kanter, "From Status to Contribution: Some Organizational Implications of the Changing Basis for Pay," *Personnel,* January 1987, pp. 12–37.

[35]Terrence E. Deal and Allan A. Kennedy, "Culture: A New Look Through Old Lenses," *Journal of Applied Behavioral Science* 19, no. 4 (1983):498–505.

[36]Kanter, "From Status to Contribution: Some Organizational Implications of the Changing Basis for Pay."

CHAPTER SIXTEEN

LEADERSHIP

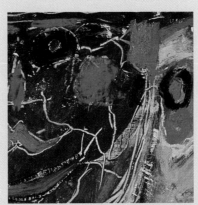

Detail from Dubuffet, *Leader in a Parade Uniform.*

Upon completing this chapter, you should be able to:

1. Define leadership and explain how it is similar to and different from management.

2. Explain the key ideas of the trait approach to leadership.

3. Discuss and evaluate the behavior approach to leadership.

4. List and explain the major contingency approaches to leadership.

5. Explain the concept of transformational or charismatic leadership and give examples.

6. Discuss some recent challenges to leadership theory.

Jean Dubuffet, *Leader in a Parade Uniform*, 1945. Oil on canvas. 36⅜ × 25⅞".
Morton G. Neumann Family Collection.

ILLUSTRATIVE CASE STUDY

INTRODUCTION

New Leadership Policies at GE

Jack Welch took over as chairman of General Electric in 1981 after an extensive and well-publicized competition. Reginald Jones, chairman before Welch, managed a carefully crafted selection process, which culminated in the selection of Welch, who has a doctorate in chemical engineering, to run the appliance business. Chosen CEO at only age 45, Welch made sweeping changes in almost every aspect of the company, shifting its business mix and corporate culture—and its vision for the future. His stated goal was to make GE number one or number two in market share in every business in which it competes. He has confronted this challenge with single-minded determination.

A competitor from boyhood sports to his adult career in business, Welch has spent his entire career at GE. His initial success was in increasing the revenues of the plastics division from a small piece to a major portion of GE's sales and profits. From his early days at GE, Welch had been frustrated by the company's bureaucracy, and he had spent a lot of time trying to find ways to get things done by working around the system. He had found that the key ingredients for accomplishing things were initiative, managerial freedom, and an intolerance for managers who did not produce. Welch still tries to apply these simple rules.

From his years of experience at the company, Welch was convinced that GE was too bureaucratic—so fat with layer upon layer of management that it was not capable of making quick decisions, let alone implementing them. By eliminating several unnecessary layers, he was able to delegate authority to the lower levels of management, where problems were first encountered and solutions were most readily available. He reduced the corporate staff from 1,700 to under 1,000 and made cuts in all parts of the company. Since 1981, GE has trimmed over 100,000 workers, earning Welch the nickname "Neutron Jack," a reference to the proposed neutron bomb, which allegedly spares buildings while destroying the enemy's human resources. Welch has also tried to instill a sense of teamwork and individual responsibility for the performance of each part of GE. He has rewarded managers who are willing to streamline, to change, to take risks.

The sailing has not been smooth. Cutting 25

GE chairman Jack F. Welch

percent of the work force has had severe effects on morale, with the work force becoming polarized: Most employees either admire or detest Jack Welch. Organized labor is an outspoken opponent of Welch's methods. Joseph F. Egan, chairman of International Union of Electronic Workers, has said, "GE has a disease—Welch-ese. It is caused by corporate greed, arrogance, and contempt for its employees."

But Welch's admirers believe he is doing an outstanding job. They claim that his vision and the often difficult changes he has made at GE are exactly what the company needed. Buying RCA and Kidder, Peabody were brilliant strategic moves, say Welch's admirers, and trimming the work force was overdue.

Jack Welch's impact on GE cannot yet be fully assessed. It is clear, however, that he has changed the direction and culture of the company. And he has produced results. Yet, while some people at GE follow Welch because they think his chosen direction is right, many others believe that they have no choice but to follow. Some say that Welch is a leader, others that he is an intimidator. Whatever the case, GE will never be the same.

Source: "Jack Welch: How Good a Manager?" Business Week, December 14, 1987, pp. 92–103.

*I*s Jack Welch an effective leader? How does he compare to such world-famous leaders as Abraham Lincoln, Franklin Delano Roosevelt, and Winston Churchill? Although managers are seldom called on to be leaders in the heroic mold of a Lincoln or a Churchill, their leadership abilities and skills play a major role in their organizations' success or failure. For this reason, thousands of scholars have studied leadership, using three major approaches—the study of *traits,* the study of leadership *behaviors*, and the study of *contingencies*, or the situations in which leaders act.

In this chapter, we will see what each of these approaches has contributed to our understanding of leadership, concluding with some current trends in our thinking about leadership. Before we do this, though, let's take a closer look at the meaning of *leadership*.

■ DEFINING LEADERSHIP

In his survey of leadership theories and research, Ralph M. Stogdill has pointed out that "there are almost as many different definitions of leadership as there are persons who have attempted to define the concept."[1] We will define managerial **leadership** as the process of directing and influencing the task-related activities of group members. There are three important implications of our definition.

First, leadership involves *other people*—subordinates or followers. By their willingness to accept directions from the leader, group members help define the leader's status and make the leadership process possible; without subordinates, all the leadership qualities of a manager would be irrelevant.

Second, leadership involves an unequal distribution of **power** between leaders and group members. Group members are not powerless; they can and do shape group activities in a number of ways. Still, the leader will usually have more power.

Where does a manager's power come from? We partially answered this question in Chapter 12 when we discussed the five bases of a manager's power: *reward power, coercive power, legitimate power, referent power,* and *expert power.*[2] The greater the number of these power sources available to the manager, the greater his or her potential for effective leadership. Yet it is a commonly observed fact of organization life that managers at the same level—with the same amount of legitimate power—differ widely in their ability to use reward, coercive, referent, or expert power.

Thus, a third aspect of leadership is the ability to use the different forms of power to **influence** followers' behaviors in a number of ways. Indeed, leaders have influenced soldiers to kill and influenced employees to make personal sacrifices for the good of the company. For this reason, many believe, leaders have a special obligation to consider the ethics of their decisions. (See the Ethics in Management box.)

Before we look at some of the specific theories of leadership, we need to make one more point about the nature of leadership. Although leadership is highly related to and important to management, leadership and management are not the same concepts. In fact, a person can be an effective manager—a good planner and a fair, organized administrator—but lack the motivational skills of a leader. Others can be effective managers—skilled at inspiring enthusiasm and devotion—but lack the managerial skills to channel the energy they arouse in others. Given the challenges presented by today's changing environment, many organizations are putting a premium on managers who also possess leadership skills. As a result, anyone who aspires to become an effective manager must also make a conscious effort to practice and develop his or her leadership skills.

Is Moral Leadership Different?

Leadership is generally considered in terms of its effectiveness or ineffectiveness, but there is another aspect to leadership—namely, ethics or morality. (Recall from Chapter 4 that, for our purposes, the distinction between *ethics* and *morality* is negligible.) How far should leaders go in trying to get others to follow them? Human history is full of leaders who used power ruthlessly to gain and solidify support. Adolf Hitler built a special army, the SS, to terrorize opposition and innocents alike. Followers are obviously more likely to follow if the penalty for going in another direction is severe enough.

In a book entitled *Leadership*, James McGregor Burns proposes a concept called "moral leadership" as a means for evaluating the ethics of leaders. According to Burns, moral leadership goes beyond power and examines the extent to which the leader-follower relationship is based on *mutual* needs and aspirations. Moral leadership obliges leaders to do the things they promised to do. For Burns, charisma, cheerleading, and enforced conformity are not sufficient criteria for evaluating effective or appropriate leadership.

Moral leadership concerns values and requires that followers be given enough knowledge of alternatives to make intelligent choices when it comes time to respond to a leader's proposal to lead. Finally, Burns says about moral leadership, "I mean the kind of leadership that can produce social change that will satisfy followers' authentic needs. I mean less the Ten Commandments than the Golden Rule. But, even the Golden Rule is inadequate, for it measures the wants

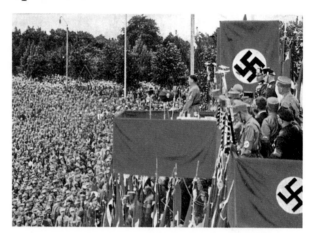

A Study in Ruthlessness. A charismatic and forceful speaker, Adolph Hitler used the Nazi-controlled radio and mass rallies of troops to convince the German people to accept his plan for world conquest.

and needs of others simply by our own."

Clearly, leadership has a moral dimension. Whether or not we focus entirely on moral leadership, as Burns does, is less important than recognizing that the relationship between leader and led has a component of morality. For Burns, the leader who ignores the moral component of his position can be successful, but may well go down in history as a scoundrel, or worse. A legacy of poor managerial performance will be the least of his posthumous worries.

Source: James MacGregor Burns, *Leadership* (New York: Harper & Row, 1978).

■ *THE TRAIT APPROACH TO LEADERSHIP*

CLASS COMMENT

According to executive recruiter John Wareham, firstborns seek power and status; middle kids are rational and democratic; and those born last want affection. (*Wall Street Journal*, 4/11/91, p. B1)

The first systematic effort by psychologists and other researchers to understand leadership was the attempt to identify the personal characteristics of leaders. The view that leaders are born, not made, is still popular among laypersons, though not among professional researchers. After a lifetime of reading popular novels and viewing films and television shows, perhaps most of us believe that there are individuals who have a predisposition to leadership—who are naturally braver, more aggressive, more decisive, and more articulate than other people.

In searching for measurable leadership traits, researchers have taken two approaches: (1) comparing the traits of those who emerged as leaders with the traits of those who did not; and (2) comparing the traits of effective leaders with those of ineffective leaders.

Most studies on leadership traits have fallen into the first category and have largely failed to uncover any traits that clearly and consistently distinguish leaders from followers.[3] Leaders as a group have been found to be brighter, more extroverted, and more self-confident than nonleaders; they also tend to be taller. But although millions of people have these traits, most of them will never attain leadership positions. And many indisputable leaders have not had these traits—Napoleon, for example, was rather short, and Abraham Lincoln was moody and introverted. It is also possible that individuals become more assertive and self-confident once they occupy a leadership position, so the traits identified may be the *results* rather than the *causes* of leadership ability. Although personality measurements may one day become exact enough to isolate leadership traits, the evidence thus far suggests that people who emerge as leaders possess no single constellation of traits that clearly distinguishes them from nonleaders.

The issue is also clouded by the question of cultural bias. For example, tallness has long been associated with American leaders. Does this mean that tallness is a leadership trait? Or does it just reflect our culture's inclination to seek its leaders from among the ranks of Caucasian males? Our assumptions about leadership traits may well change as increasing numbers of women, minorities, gays, and disabled people assume leadership positions.

Attempts to compare the characteristics of effective and ineffective leaders— the second category of leadership trait studies—are more recent and fewer in number, but they, too, have generally failed to isolate traits strongly associated with successful leadership. One study did find that intelligence, initiative, and self-assurance were associated with high managerial levels and performance.[4] However, this study also found that the single most important factor related to managerial level and performance was the manager's supervisory ability—that is, his or her skill in using supervisory methods appropriate to the particular situation. Most other studies in this area also have found that effective leadership does not depend on a particular set of traits, but rather on how well the leader's traits match the requirements of the situation.[5]

Some researchers have also found that although women are still less likely than men to emerge as leaders, they are just as effective when they do. Even though an increasing number of people believe in equality of ability and opportunity, persistent, often unconscious sexual stereotyping continues to hamper the recognition of women as potential leaders. When women do become leaders, however, they perform as well as male leaders, and are generally perceived as equally effective by their subordinates.[6]

Racial stereotyping, of course, is another problem when attempting to identify the connections between traits and leadership qualities. Although the number of blacks in managerial ranks has been growing, very few of them have made it to the highest echelons in organizational hierarchies. However, such corporations as GM, AM International, Xerox, Avon, Godfather's Pizza, IBM, and Procter & Gamble have initiated programs to enhance the placement of black men and women in leadership positions.[7]

COORDINATED RESOURCE

Acumen: The Achievement scale measures an individual's interest in effectiveness in attaining high-quality results. Those who score high on this scale encourage co-workers to set challenging yet realistic goals. They often have the potential to organize work teams efficiently and show confidence in their own judgment and ability.

THOUGHT PROVOKER

Women executives (47%) have an edge over men (39%) in leadership traits for handling profit-and-loss responsibilities, according to a Columbia University survey. (*Wall Street Journal*, 12/27/90, p. B1)

■ *THE BEHAVIORAL APPROACH TO LEADERSHIP*

COORDINATED RESOURCE

Use Transparency 105, Continuum of Leadership Behavior.

When it became evident that effective leaders did not seem to have any distinguishing traits, researchers tried to isolate the *behaviors* characteristic of effective leaders. In other words, rather than try to figure out what effective leaders *were*, researchers tried to determine what effective leaders *did*—how they delegated tasks, how they communicated with and tried to motivate their subordinates, how they

COORDINATED RESOURCE
The Additional Lecture for Chapter 16 found in the Lecture Extras supplement is called "What Leaders Really Do."

carried out their tasks, and so on. Unlike traits, behaviors can be *learned*, so it followed that individuals trained in appropriate leadership behaviors would be able to lead more effectively. These researchers have focused on two aspects of leadership behavior: leadership functions and leadership styles.

Leadership Functions

leadership functions
The group-maintenance and task-related activities that must be performed by the leader, or someone else, for a group to perform effectively.

Rather than looking at the individual, these researchers took a closer look at **leadership functions.** To operate effectively, a group needed *someone* to perform two major functions: "task-related" or problem-solving functions; and "group-maintenance" or social functions, such as mediating disputes and ensuring that individuals felt valued by the group.

An individual who is able to perform *both* roles successfully would obviously be an especially effective leader. In practice, however, a leader may have the skill or temperament or time to play only one role. This does not mean that the group is doomed, though. Studies have found that most effective groups have some form of *shared* leadership; one person (usually the manager or formal leader) performs the task function, while another member performs the social function.[8]

Leadership Styles

leadership styles The various patterns of behavior favored by leaders during the process of directing and influencing workers.

The two leadership functions—task-related and group-maintenance—tend to be expressed in two different **leadership styles.** Managers who have a *task-oriented style* closely supervise employees to be sure the task is performed satisfactorily. Getting the job done is more important to them than employees' growth or personal satisfaction. Managers with an *employee-oriented style* try to motivate rather than control subordinates. They seek friendly, trusting, and respectful relationships with employees, who are often allowed to participate in decisions that affect them.

Robert Tannenbaum and Warren H. Schmidt were among the first theorists to describe the various factors thought to influence a manager's choice of leadership style.[9] While they personally favored the employee-centered style, they suggested

A Leader for the 21st Century. As president of American Express Consumer Card Group, USA, Kenneth I. Chenault excels at task-related functions, such as analyzing competitive information and devising innovative business techniques for achieving strategic goals of providing more personalized products and services. Just as importantly, Chenault is seen as "the quarterback" of American Express, a team builder who is confident, approachable, diplomatic, and fully capable of infusing employees with his evangelical dedication to providing ever-improving service to cardholders.

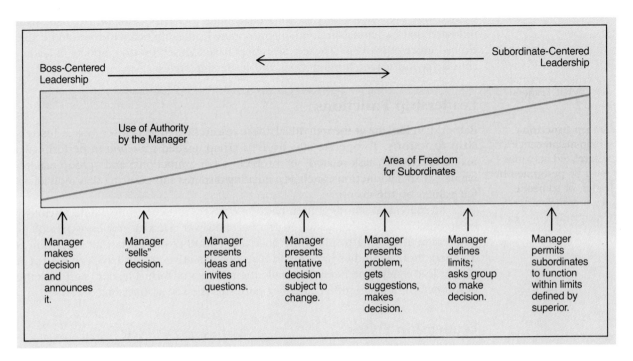

FIGURE 16-1 Continuum of Leadership Behavior

Source: Reprinted by permission of the *Harvard Business Review.* An exhibit from "How to Choose a Leadership Pattern" by Robert Tannenbaum and Warren H. Schmidt (May–June 1973). Copyright © 1973 by the President and Fellows of Harvard College, all rights reserved.

COORDINATED RESOURCE

See *Management Live!* Reading 6.3, "The End of the Big Bad Boss."

that a manager consider three sets of "forces" before choosing a leadership style: forces in the manager, forces in subordinates, and forces in the situation.

How a manager leads will undoubtedly be primarily influenced by his or background, knowledge, values, and experience (*forces in the manager*). For example, a manager who believes that the needs of the individual must come second to the needs of the organization is likely to take a very directive role in subordinates' activities. (See Fig. 16-1.)

But *characteristics of subordinates* must also be considered before managers can choose an appropriate leadership style. According to Tannenbaum and Schmidt, a manager can allow greater participation and freedom when subordinates crave independence and freedom of action, want to have decision-making responsibility, identify with the organization's goals, are knowledgeable and experienced enough to deal with the problem efficiently, and have experiences that lead them to expect participative management. Where these conditions are lacking, managers may have to lean toward an authoritarian style. They can, however, modify their behavior once subordinates gain self-confidence.

Finally, a manager's choice of leadership style must reckon with such *situational forces* as the organization's preferred style, the specific work group, the nature of the group's tasks, the pressures of time, and even environmental factors—all of which may affect organization members' attitudes toward authority. Most managers, for example, lean toward the leadership style favored by the organization's hierarchy. If top management emphasizes human relations skills, the manager will incline toward an employee-centered style; if a decisive, take-charge style seems favored, the manager will tend to be task- rather than employee-oriented.

The specific work group also affects the choice of style. A group that works well together may respond better to a free and open atmosphere than to close supervision; so will a group confident of its ability to solve problems as a unit. But if a work group is large or widely dispersed geographically, a participative management style may be difficult to use. Cultural factors will also affect the choice of leadership style. (See the International Management box.)

INTERNATIONAL MANAGEMENT

Who's in Charge Here?

American theorists tend to advocate participative management—as long as it is the manager's idea. This is just one conclusion drawn by the Dutch management scholar Geert Hofstede, who believes that many American *theories* of management cannot be applied to management *practices* abroad.

Take the idea that the manager *allows* employees to participate in management. This is compatible with the particularly American view that power in institutions and organizations is distributed unevenly. In Germany, Sweden, Norway, and Israel, however, the power distances between people are smaller. In these countries, there is more acceptance of industrial "democracy," in which subordinates take the initiative. Examples include codetermination in Germany and the cooperative management style of some Scandinavian nations. Ironically, many of these ideas were proposed by W. Edwards Deming and other U.S. management theorists, who were largely ignored by U.S. managers for many years.

Recently many American companies have tried to adopt such practices as the participative management of Sweden and the highly successful Japanese quality circles. Most of these efforts have failed to take root, however. Some evaluations blame the failures on American managers, who resist the idea of genuinely sharing power with employees.

Hofstede concludes that leaders cannot choose a style at will. Instead, they must understand the culture of their subordinates and what that culture holds about the "right" power distance between managers and subordinates. This conclusion is important for American managers who must work in other nations. It is also important for managers who never leave the country, since our work force is increasingly made up of women and minorities—who bring different cultural expectations to the workplace. It seems only

Building a Cultural Marriage. When GE bought a controlling stake in Tungsram, a Hungarian light-bulb maker, it sought to ease the culture shock by installing a 28-year GE veteran, Hungarian-born George Varga, who had fled to the United States at the time of the 1956 uprising. Bypassing some of GE's more aggressive "young tigers," Varga surrounded himself with other seasoned GE executives from the United States, such as Production Chief Kevin Gallimore (center), who possess the sensitivity to help Eastern European workers adapt to a capitalistic work ethic.

logical that their influence will help reshape our expectations of power in the workplace.

Sources: Geert Hofstede, "Motivation, Leadership, and Organization: Do American Theories Apply Abroad?" *Organizational Dynamics,* Summer 1980, pp. 42–63; and Ron Zemke, "Scandinavian Management—A Look at Our Future?" *Management Review* 77, no. 7 (1988):44–47.

The Ohio State and University of Michigan Studies

COORDINATED RESOURCE
Use Transparency 106, Two-Dimensional Leadership Model.

COORDINATED RESOURCE
Use Transparency 107, Leadership Styles Studied at Ohio State.

Tannenbaum and Schmidt, as well as other early researchers, thought leadership style was a "zero-sum" game: The more task-oriented a manager, the less relationship-oriented he or she could be. Subsequent research was undertaken to determine which of these two leadership styles produces the most effective group performance.

At Ohio State University, researchers studied the effectiveness of what they called "initiating structure" (task-oriented) and "consideration" (employee-

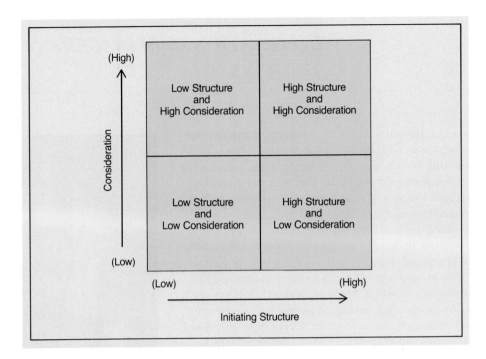

(High)

Consideration

(Low)

| Low Structure and High Consideration | High Structure and High Consideration |
| Low Structure and Low Consideration | High Structure and Low Consideration |

(Low)   (High)

Initiating Structure

FIGURE 16-2 Leadership Styles Studied at Ohio State

oriented) leadership behaviors. They found, as might be expected, that employee turnover rates were lowest and employee satisfaction highest under leaders who were rated high in consideration; conversely, leaders who were rated low in consideration and high in initiating structure had high grievance and turnover rates among their employees. (Fig. 16-2 diagrams the leadership styles studied at Ohio State.)

The researchers also found, interestingly, that subordinates' ratings of their leaders' effectiveness depended not so much on the particular *style* of the leader as on the *situation* in which the style was used. For example, Air Force commanders who rated high on consideration were rated as less effective than task-oriented commanders. It is possible that the more authoritarian environment of the military, coupled with the air crews' belief that quick, hard decisions are essential in combat situations, caused people-oriented leaders to be rated less effective. On the other hand, nonproduction supervisors and managers in large companies were rated more effective if they ranked high in consideration.

Similarly, researchers at the University of Michigan distinguished between production-centered and employee-centered managers. Production-centered managers set rigid work standards, organized tasks down to the last detail, prescribed work methods to be followed, and closely supervised subordinates' work. On the other hand, employee-centered managers encouraged subordinate participation in goal setting and other work decisions and helped ensure high performance by inspiring trust and respect. The Michigan studies found that the most productive work groups tended to have leaders who were employee-centered rather than production-centered. They also found that the most effective leaders had supportive relationships with their subordinates, tended to depend on group rather than individual decision making, and encouraged subordinates to set and achieve high performance goals.[10]

The Managerial Grid®

One conclusion from the Ohio State and Michigan studies is that leadership style may not be unidimensional: Both task orientation and employee orientation may be

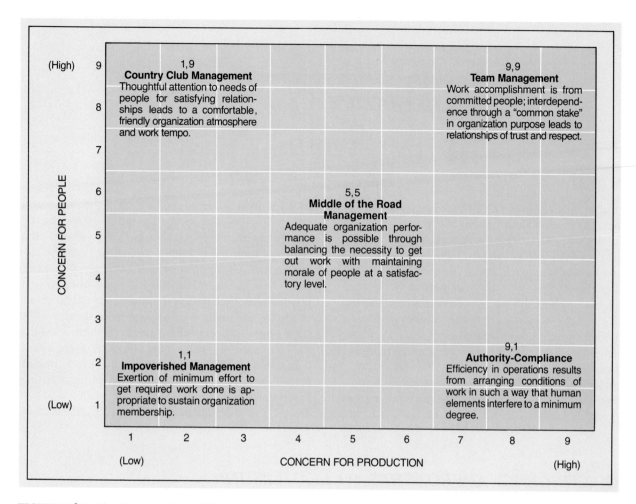

FIGURE 16-3 The Leadership Grid®

Source: The Leadership Grid® figure from *Leadership Dilemmas—Grid Solutions,* by Robert R. Blake and Anne Adams McCanse, p. 29 (Houston: Gulf Publishing Company). Copyright © 1991, by Scientific Methods, Inc. Reproduced by permission of the owners.

Managerial Grid Diagram developed by Blake and Mouton to measure a manager's relative concern for people and production.

crucial to superior performance. The **Managerial Grid,** developed by Robert Blake and Jane Mouton to help measure a manager's relative concern for people and tasks, reflects this bidimensional nature of leadership.[11]

The Managerial Grid (republished as the Leadership Grid figure in 1991 by Robert R. Blake and Anne Adams McCanse) identifies a range of management behaviors based on the various ways that task-oriented and employee-oriented styles (each expressed as a continuum on a scale of 1 to 9) can interact with each other. (See Fig. 16-3.) Thus, Style 1,1 management, at the lower left-hand corner of the grid, is *impoverished management*—low concern for people and low concern for tasks or production. This style is sometimes called *laissez-faire management* because the leader abdicates his or her leadership role.

Style 1,9 management is *country club management*—high concern for employees but low concern for production. Style 9,1 management is *task* or *authoritarian management*—high concern for production and efficiency but low concern for employees. Style 5,5 is *middle-of-the-road management*—an intermediate amount of concern for both production and employee satisfaction.

Style 9,9 management is *team* or *democratic management*—a high concern for both production and employee morale and satisfaction. Blake and Mouton argue strongly that Style 9,9 is the most effective management style. They believe this leadership approach will, in almost all situations, result in improved performance, low absenteeism and turnover, and high employee satisfaction. The Blake and Mouton Managerial Grid is widely used as a training device for managers.

ILLUSTRATIVE CASE STUDY

CONTINUED

New Leadership Policies at GE

Part of the controversy at GE has focused on Welch's style. There is no doubt about the man's intensity. Watching videotapes of his speeches, one can see the fire in his eyes and his determination to realize his vision for GE. Welch has devoted a great deal of time and energy to trying to get managers at GE to confront one another, to be more open about solving conflicts. One story goes that after a bitter argument in which Welch ripped apart one manager's ideas, Welch hugged the man for openly engaging in debate and creative conflict.

Welch wants people to focus on tasks, to bring a higher level of intensity to their jobs. He believes that such intensity is one of the keys to being a successful competitor—to achieving his goal of making GE number one or number two in every industry division in which the company is engaged. But he also knows that managing relationships is equally important—that managers accomplish tasks through people. In short, he has siezed upon Blake and Mouton's challenge and made team management the means for GE's future success. Unfortunately, some view his radical policy of streamlining the work force as evidence that Jack Welch does not really have a concern for people in any capacity other than as members of a team working toward Jack Welch's goals.

■ *CONTINGENCY APPROACHES TO LEADERSHIP*

TEACHING TIP
Ask your students to think of persons they would call "effective" or "good" leaders. What elements can be identified in their leadership situations?

contingency approach
The view that the management technique that best contributes to the attainment of organizational goals might vary in different types of situations or circumstances.

COORDINATED RESOURCE
Use Transparency 110, Personality and Situational Factors That Influence Effective Leadership.

Researchers using the trait and behavioral approaches showed that effective leadership depended on many variables, such as organizational culture and the nature of tasks. No *one* trait was common to all effective leaders; no *one* style was effective in all situations.

Therefore, researchers began trying to identify those factors in each *situation* that affected the effectiveness of a particular leadership style.[12] Taken together, the theories resulting from this research constitute the **contingency approach** to leadership. These theories focus on the following factors (see Fig. 16-4):

❑ *The leader's personality, past experiences, and expectations.* For example, a manager who has been successful exercising little supervision may be more prone to adopt an employee-oriented style of leadership. Evidence has also demonstrated that situations often work out the way we *expect* them to—a phenomenon referred to as the *self-fulfilling prophecy.* One study, for instance, found that new leaders who were told their subordinates were low performers managed in a more authoritarian way than did new leaders who were told their subordinates were high performers.[13]

❑ *The superiors' expectations and behavior.* Because they have the power to dispense such organizational rewards as bonuses and promotions, superiors clearly affect the behavior of lower-level managers. In addition, lower-level managers tend to model themselves after their superiors. One study found that supervisors who learned new behaviors in a human relations training program tended to yield those behaviors quickly if they were not consistent with their immediate superior's leadership style.[14]

Using Past Experiences. When Levi Strauss patriarch Walter A. Haas, Jr. bought the Oakland Athletics baseball team in 1980, he quickly established a team of managers, including son Wally (above) to rebuild the team, using marketing skills learned at Levi Strauss. By 1990, the Oakland A's were world champs and the team had shown a profit for three years running.

❏ *Task requirements.* The nature of subordinates' job responsibilities will also influence the leadership style a manager chooses. Jobs that require precise instructions (say, testing printed circuits) demand a more task-oriented style than do jobs whose operating procedures can be left largely to the individual employees (say, university teaching).

❏ *Peer's expectations and behavior.* The opinions and attitudes of a manager's peers often affect how effectively the manager performs. The behavior of managers influences that of their associates; for example, a hostile colleague may harm a manager by competing for resources and behaving uncooperatively. Whatever their own inclinations, managers tend to some extent to imitate the management style of their peers.

❏ *Subordinates' characteristics, expectations, and behavior.* The skills, training, and attitudes of subordinates also influence the manager's choice of style. Highly capable employees require a less directive approach, and while some employees want an authoritarian leader, others prefer taking total responsibility for their own work.

❏ *Organizational culture and policies.* Both of these shape the leader's behavior and subordinates' expectations. To make the transition from entrepreneurial start-up to stable maturity, for example, many fast-growing computer companies, such as Sun Microsystems and Apple, had to adopt different management styles.

In the sections that follow, we will review four of the more recent and well-known contingency models of leadership.

FIGURE 16-4 Personality and Situational Factors That Influence Effective Leadership

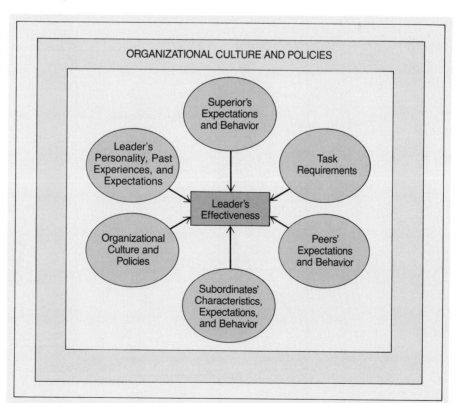

Hersey and Blanchard's Situational Leadership Theory

COORDINATED RESOURCE
Use Transparency 111, The Situational Theory of Leadership.

One of the major contingency approaches to leadership is Paul Hersey and Kenneth H. Blanchard's **situational leadership theory,**[15] which holds that the most effective leadership style varies with the "maturity" of subordinates. Hersey and Blanchard define maturity not as age or emotional stability, but as desire for achievement, willingness to accept responsibility, and task-related ability and experience. The goals and knowledge of followers are important variables in determining effective leadership style.

Hersey and Blanchard believe that the relationship between a manager and subordinates moves through four phases (a kind of life cycle) as subordinates develop and "mature," and that managers need to vary their leadership style with each phase. (See Fig. 16-5.) In the initial phase—when subordinates first enter the organization—a high task orientation by the manager is most appropriate. Subordinates must be instructed in their tasks and familiarized with the organization's rules and procedures. A nondirective manager would cause anxiety and confusion in new employees. A participatory employee relationship approach would also be inappropriate at this stage because subordinates cannot yet be regarded as colleagues.

As subordinates begin to learn their tasks, task-oriented management remains essential because subordinates are not yet willing or able to accept full responsibility. However, the manager's trust in and support of subordinates should increase as the manager becomes familiar with them and wishes to encourage further efforts on

FIGURE 16-5 The Situational Theory of Leadership

Source: Adapted from Paul Hersey and Kenneth H. Blanchard, *Management of Organizational Behavior: Utilizing Human Resources,* 5th ed., p. 173. Copyright © 1988. Reprinted by permission of Leadership Studies, Inc.

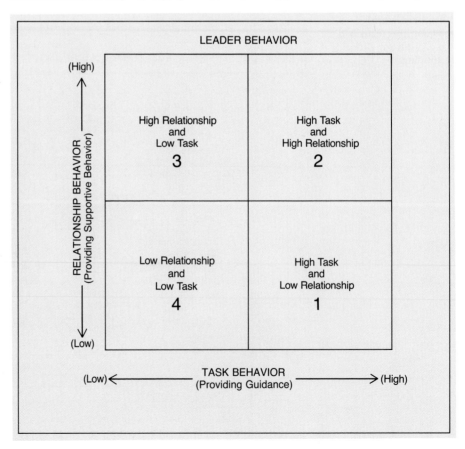

their part. Thus, the manager may choose to initiate employee-oriented behaviors in this second phase.

In the third phase, the subordinates' ability and achievement motivation are increased and they actively begin to seek greater responsibility. The manager will no longer need to be directive (indeed, close direction might be resented). However, the manager will still have to be supportive and considerate in order to strengthen the subordinates' resolve for greater responsibility. As subordinates gradually become more confident, self-directing, and experienced, the manager can reduce the amount of support and encouragement. In this fourth phase, subordinates no longer need or expect a directive relationship with their manager. They are on their own.

The situational leadership theory has generated interest because it recommends a leadership type that is dynamic and flexible rather than static. The motivation, ability, and experience of subordinates must constantly be assessed to determine which style combination is most appropriate under flexible and changing conditions. If the style is appropriate, according to Hersey and Blanchard, it will not only motivate subordinates but will also help them move toward maturity. Thus, the manager who wants to develop subordinates, increase their confidence, and help them learn their work will have to shift style constantly.[16]

Yet a practical question remains: To what extent are managers actually able to choose among leadership styles in different situations? This issue is important because it affects management selection, placement, and promotion. If managers are flexible in leadership style, or if they can be trained to vary their style, presumably they will be effective in a variety of leadership situations. If, on the other hand, managers are relatively inflexible in leadership style, they will operate effectively only in those situations that best match their style or can be adjusted to match their style. Such inflexibility would hamper the careers of individual managers and complicate the organization's task of filling its management positions effectively.

COORDINATED RESOURCE

Use Transparency 113, Hersey and Blanchard's Life Cycle Approach.

Leadership Style and the Work Situation: The Fiedler Model

The second—and most thoroughly researched—of the contingency models we will discuss was developed by Fred E. Fiedler. Fiedler's basic assumption is that it is quite difficult for managers to alter the management styles that made them successful. In fact, Fiedler believes, most managers are not very flexible, and trying to change a manager's style to fit unpredictable or fluctuating situations is inefficient or useless. Since styles are relatively inflexible, and since no one style is appropriate for every situation, effective group performance can only be achieved by matching the manager to the situation or by changing the situation to fit the manager. For example, a comparatively authoritarian manager can be selected to fill a post that requires a directive leader, or a job can be changed to give an authoritarian manager more formal authority over subordinates.

The leadership styles that Fiedler contrasts are similar to the employee-centered and task-oriented styles we discussed earlier. What differentiates his model from the others is the measuring instrument he used. Fiedler measured leadership style on a simple scale that indicated "the degree to which a man described favorably or unfavorably his **least preferred co-worker (LPC)**"—the employee with whom the person could work least well. This measure locates an individual on the leadership-style continuum. According to Fiedler's findings, "a person who describes his least preferred co-worker in a relatively favorable manner tends to be permissive, human relations–oriented, and considerate of the feelings of his men. But a person who describes his least preferred co-worker in an unfavorable manner—who has what we have come to call a low LPC rating—tends to be managing, task-controlling, and less concerned with the human relations aspects of the job."[17]

least preferred co-worker (LPC) Fiedler's measuring instrument for locating a manager on the leadership-style continuum.

According to Fiedler, then, high-LPC managers want to have warm personal relations with their co-workers and will regard close ties with subordinates as important to their overall effectiveness. Low-LPC managers, on the other hand, want to get the job done; the reactions of subordinates to their leadership style is of far lower priority than the need to maintain production. Low-LPC managers who feel that a harsh style is necessary to maintain production will not hesitate to use it.

Fiedler has identified three "leadership situations" that help determine which leadership style will be effective: leader-member relations, the task structure, and the leader's position power. (Fiedler's studies did not include such other situational variables as employee motivation and the values and experiences of leaders and group members.)

The quality of **leader-member relations** is the most important influence on the manager's power and effectiveness. If the manager gets along well with the rest of the group, if group members respect the manager for reasons of personality, character, or ability, then the manager may not have to rely on formal rank or authority. On the other hand, a manager who is disliked or distrusted may be less able to lead informally and may have to rely on directives to accomplish group tasks.

Task structure is the second most important variable in the leadership situation. A highly structured task is one for which step-by-step procedures or instructions are available; group members therefore have a very clear idea of what they are expected to do. Managers in such situations automatically have a great deal of authority: There are clear guidelines by which to measure worker performance, and the manager can back up his or her instructions by referring to a rulebook or manual—in other words, to established policy. But when tasks are unstructured, as in committee meetings, group member roles are more ambiguous. The manager's power is diminished in these situations because group members can more easily disagree with or question the manager's instructions.

The leader's **position power** is the final situational variable identified by Fiedler. Some positions, such as the presidency of a firm, carry a great deal of power and authority. The chairperson of a fund-raising drive, on the other hand, has little power over volunteer workers. Thus, high-position power simplifies the leader's task of influencing subordinates, while low-position power makes the leader's task more difficult.

Fiedler then went on to specify eight possible combinations of these three variables in the leadership situation: Leader-member relations can be good or poor, tasks may be structured or unstructured, and position power may be strong or weak.

Using these eight categories of leadership situations and his two types of leaders—high- and low-LPC—Fiedler reviewed studies of over 800 groups to see which type of leader was most effective in each situation. Among the groups he studied were basketball teams, executive training workshops, and Air Force and tank combat crews. A well-liked leader of a bomber crew, for example, would be in category 1 of Figure 16-6, while a disliked temporary committee chairperson would be in category 8. He found that low-LPC leaders—those who were task-oriented or authoritarian—were most effective in extreme situations: situations in which the leader either had a great deal of power and influence or had very little power and influence. High-LPC leaders—those who were employee-oriented—were most effective in situations where the leader had moderate power and influence.

For example, the head of a research team would have only moderate influence over team members—influence based largely on whether or not the team respects the leader. Since research tasks are relatively unstructured, the leader would have little influence over the way the work is organized and performed. In addition, the leader's position power is low because team members would be likely to regard themselves as colleagues rather than subordinates (category 4). An authoritarian style would therefore be ineffective: Team members would resent it, and it would encourage low performance by the group.

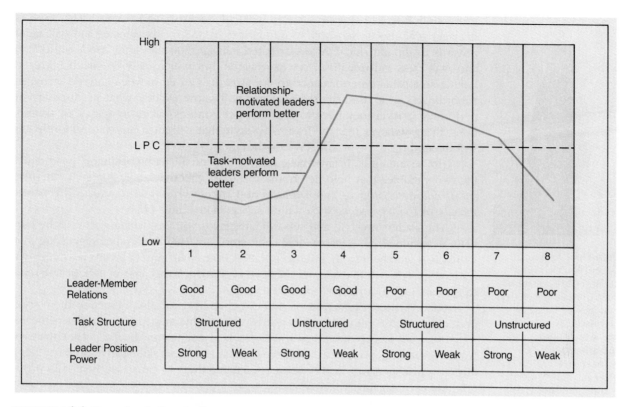

FIGURE 16-6 How the Style of Effective Leadership Varies with the Situation

Source: Fred E. Fiedler and Martin M. Chemers, *Leadership and Effective Management* (Glenview, Ill.: Scott, Foresman, 1974), p. 80. Reprinted by permission of Fred E. Fiedler.

COORDINATED RESOURCE

See Study Guide Self-Learning Exercise 16, "Determining Your Preferred Situational Leadership Style."

COORDINATED RESOURCE

See Study Guide Problem Exercise 16, "Selecting the Appropriate Situational Leadership Style."

path-goal model A leadership theory emphasizing the leader's role in clarifying for subordinates how they can achieve high performance and its associated rewards.

TEACHING TIP

Here is an opportunity once again to draw the connection between leadership and motivation.

Fiedler's model, then, suggests that an appropriate match of the leader's style (as measured by the LPC score) to the situation (as determined by the interaction of these three variables) leads to effective managerial performance. His model has been used with some success as the basis of a training program in which managers are shown how to alter the situational variables to match their leadership styles rather than their styles to fit the situation.[18]

Although the validity of Fiedler's model has been questioned,[19] it is widely agreed that he has made a significant contribution to our understanding of how leaders and situations can be matched for effective performance.

A Path-Goal Approach to Leadership

Like other contingency approaches, the **path-goal model** of leadership tries to help us understand and predict leadership effectiveness in different situations. The model, formulated by Martin G. Evans[20] and Robert J. House,[21] represents a new and evolving approach.

The path-goal approach is based on the expectancy model (described in the previous chapter), which states that an individual's motivation depends on his or her expectation of reward and the *valence,* or attractiveness of the reward. Although managers have a number of ways to influence subordinates, Evans notes, the most important is their ability to provide rewards and to specify what subordinates must do to earn them. Thus, managers determine the availability of "goals" (rewards) and the "paths" that will earn them.

Evans suggests that a manager's leadership style influences the rewards available to subordinates, as well as subordinates' perceptions of the path to those rewards. An employee-centered manager, for example, will offer not only pay and

A Path-Goal Approach.
President Richard Rose (left) and Chief Financial Officer Gordon McLenithan use money to motivate sales reps at Dataflex Corp., which outfits major corporations with PCs. Rose once bet a saleswoman his new Mercedes that she could not gross $600,000 a month for three months. She won the bet and went on to win a Rolex and diamond earrings.

promotion, but also support, encouragement, security, and respect. That type of manager will also be sensitive to differences between subordinates and will tailor rewards to the individual. A task-oriented manager, on the other hand, will offer a narrower, less individualized set of rewards, but will usually be much better at linking subordinate performance to rewards than an employee-centered manager. Subordinates of a task-oriented manager will know exactly what productivity or performance level they have to attain to get bonuses, salary increases, or promotions. Evans believes that the leadership style that will most motivate subordinates will depend on the types of rewards they most desire.

House and his colleagues have tried to expand the path-goal theory by identifying two variables that help determine the most effective leadership style: the *personal characteristics of subordinates* and the *environmental pressures and demands in the workplace* with which subordinates must cope.

The leadership style that subordinates favor will, according to House, be partially determined by their personal characteristics. He cites studies suggesting that individuals who believe their behavior affects the environment favor a participatory leadership style, while those who believe events occur because of luck or fate tend to find an authoritarian style more congenial.

Subordinates' evaluation of their own ability will also influence their style preference. Those who feel highly skilled and capable may resent an overly supervisory manager, whose directives will be seen as counterproductive rather than rewarding. On the other hand, subordinates who feel less skilled may prefer a more directive manager, who will be seen as enabling them to carry out their tasks properly and earn organizational rewards.

Environmental factors also affect the leadership styles preferred by subordinates. One such factor is the nature of the subordinates' tasks. For example, an overly directive style may seem redundant and even insulting for a highly structured task. If a task is unpleasant, however, a manager's consideration may add to the subordinate's satisfaction and motivation. Another factor is the organization's formal authority system, which clarifies which actions are likely to be met with approval (coming in *under* budget, say) and which with disapproval (coming in *over* budget). A third environmental factor is the subordinates' work group. Groups that are not very cohesive, for example, usually benefit from a supportive, understanding style. As a general rule, a leader's style will motivate subordinates to the extent that it compensates them for what they see as deficiencies in the task, authority system, or work group.

The path-goal theory of leadership is considered highly promising, especially because it attempts to explain *why* a particular leadership style is more effective in one situation than in another and because it supports the position that flexibility in responding to situatorial influences is both possible and desirable. Some research supporting the validity of path-goal theory predictions has already appeared.[22]

Deciding When to Involve Subordinates: The Vroom-Yetton and Vroom-Jago Models

In a recent book, Victor Vroom and Arthur Jago criticize the path-goal theory because it fails to take into account the situation within which managers decide to involve subordinates. As a solution, they extend the classic Vroom-Yetton model of situational leadership to include a concern for both the quality and the acceptance of decisions.[23]

The original Vroom-Yetton model was developed in 1973 to help managers decide when and to what extent they should involve subordinates in solving a particular problem. This model isolated five styles of leadership that represent a continuum from authoritarian approaches (AI, AII), to consultative (CI, CII), to a fully participative approach (GII). (See Exhibit 16-1.)[24]

EXHIBIT 16-1 Types of Leadership Styles

AI Managers solve the problem or make the decision themselves, using information available at that time.

AII Managers obtain the necessary information from subordinate(s), then decide on the solution to the problem themselves. They may or may not tell subordinates what the problem is when they request information. The role played by subordinates in making the decision is clearly one of providing the necessary information to managers rather than generating or evaluating alternative solutions.

CI Managers share the problem with relevant subordinates individually, getting their ideas and suggestions without bringing them together as a group. Then managers make the decision, which may or may not reflect subordinates' influence.

CII Managers share the problem with subordinates as a group, collectively obtaining their ideas and suggestions. Then they make the decision, which may or may not reflect subordinates' influence.

GII Managers share a problem with subordinates as a group. Managers and subordinates together generate and evaluate alternatives and attempt to reach agreement (consensus) on a solution. Managers do not try to influence the group to adopt their preferred solution, and they accept and implement any solution that has the support of the entire group.

Source: Adapted, by permission of the publisher, from "A New Look at Managerial Making," by Victor H. Vroom, *Organizational Dynamics,* Summer 1973, p. 67. © 1973 by American Management Association, New York. All rights reserved.

The authors suggest several questions that managers can ask themselves to help determine which style to use for the particular problem they are facing:

❑ Do I have enough information or skill to solve the problem on my own? If not, then AI, where I make the decision myself, would be inappropriate.

❑ Do I need to make a high-quality decision that my subordinates are likely to disagree with? If so, GII, where I seek the consensus of the group, would be inappropriate. In this case, giving up my authority to make the final decision would probably mean that the decision would not have the objective quality the problem requires.

❑ Is the problem structured? That is, do I know what information I need and where to get it? If not, then CII and GII, which allow for the greatest group interaction, would be preferable. (The other styles would either keep me from getting the information I need or supply me with information in an inefficient manner.)

❑ Is the acceptance of the group critical for the success of the decision? If so, then styles AI and AII, which involve subordinates the *least,* might not be appropriate.

❑ If acceptance of the decision is important, are my subordinates likely to disagree among themselves about which is the best solution? If so, then styles CII and GII, which involve group decision making, are preferable. Only within the group can differences between subordinates be discussed openly and ultimately resolved. The other styles might leave some subordinates dissatisfied with the decision.

Depending on the nature of the problem, more than one leadership style may be suitable. Vroom and Yetton call this suitable group the "feasible set of alternatives." (See Fig. 16-7.) Where there are feasible choices, the manager may freely choose among them because both decision quality and acceptance have been taken into account. As guidance for choosing within a feasible set, Vroom and Yetton suggest two criteria. First, when decisions must be made quickly or time must be saved, managers should choose authoritarian ("time-efficient") decision styles. The payoffs for these choices will occur in the short run, in the form of quicker, more efficient decisions. (Fig. 16-7 indicates the approaches that may be feasible in a given problem-solving situation. The most time-efficient solutions are circled.) Second,

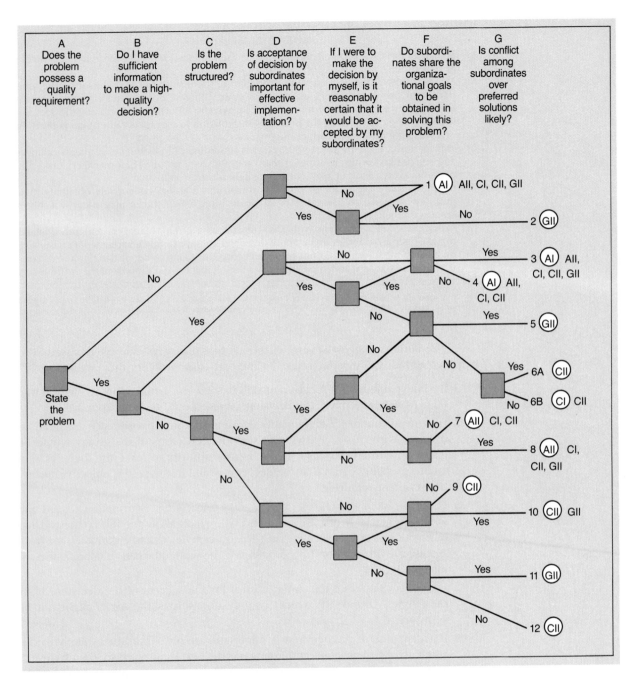

FIGURE 16-7 Decision Model Showing Feasible Set of Alternatives
This model shows the preferred management styles for various types of problems. The most "time-efficient" feasible alternative for each problem is circled; the most participative style is listed last.

Source: Adapted, by permission of the publisher, from "A New Look at Managerial Decision Making," by Victor H. Vroom, *Organizational Dynamics*, Summer 1973, p. 70. Copyright © 1973 by American Management Association, New York. All rights reserved.

when managers wish to develop their subordinates' knowledge and decision-making skills, the more participative ("time-investment") styles should be selected. The payoffs for these choices will occur in the longer run, in the form of more effective subordinates and perhaps better working relationships. (In Fig. 16-7, the most participative style is the last one in each feasible set.)

Research by Vroom and others has concluded that decisions consistent with this model tend to be successful and those inconsistent with the model are generally unsuccessful. Moreover, subordinates seem to prefer managerial decisions consistent with the model.[25]

Vroom and Jago have extended this approach by hypothesizing that the effectiveness of decisions depends on the quality of the decisions, the commitment made to the decisions, and the time expended to make the decisions. They also believe that the overall effectiveness of leadership is a function of *the effectiveness of decisions* minus *the cost of making the decisions* plus *the value realized in developing people's abilities by means of committed decision making.* It is possible to make a series of highly effective decisions, but if these decisions do little or nothing to develop the abilities of others—or if the decision-making process is cumbersome or costly—then the decisions in question will lower the overall human capital of the organization. Thus, Vroom and Jago argue that leadership styles can be time-driven or development-driven, and as in the earlier Vroom-Yetton model, each focus may be appropriate in different circumstances.

Obviously, some people find it easier than others to adjust to different life situations. Several studies on leadership imply that managers do, in fact, have a great deal of *potential* flexibility in responding to situational influences on their leadership style.[26] No reasonably alert manager whose subordinates are clearly uncooperative and whose group's performance is declining will persist in using a specific leadership style without at least questioning its effectiveness. Thus, it is possible that individuals can learn how to diagnose a leadership situation and can, at least to some extent, alter their style to make their leadership in that situation more effective. In organizations, as elsewhere in life, flexibility is desirable.

■ *THE FUTURE OF LEADERSHIP THEORY*

COORDINATED RESOURCE
See Samaras Exercise 4.2, "The Way to Lead."

FOR DISCUSSION
Why are organizations all of a sudden so interested in leadership?

Research on leadership behavior continues, but is moving in many directions. In this section, we will look at a recent area of interest—transformational or charismatic leadership. Then we will look at three challenges to our traditional ideas of leadership. One challenge casts a skeptical eye on the leader's personality, while another raises questions about the way followers see their leaders. A final challenge asks whether leaders are really necessary or whether individuals are more capable of leading themselves than we realize.

Transformational or Charismatic Leadership

One area of growing interest is individuals who have an exceptional impact on their organizations. These individuals may be called **charismatic**[27] or **transformational**[28] **leaders.**

charismatic or **transformational leaders** Leaders who, through their personal vision and energy, inspire followers and have a major impact on their organizations.

The recent interest in such transformational leaders stems from at least two sources. First, many large companies—including such giants as AT&T, IBM, and GM[29]—have recently embarked on "transformations," programs of extensive changes that must be accomplished in short periods of time. Such transformations, it has been argued, require transformational leaders.[30] Second, many feel that by concentrating on traits, behaviors, and situations, leadership theory has lost sight of the *leader.* The visibility of a business leader like Lee Iacocca of Chrysler or a military figure like General Douglas MacArthur reminds us that some leaders seem to have personal characteristics that do make a difference—but are not accounted for by existing theories.

transactional leaders Leaders who determine what subordinates need to do to achieve objectives, classify those requirements, and help subordinates become confident they can reach their objectives.

BASS'S THEORY OF TRANSFORMATIONAL LEADERSHIP. In his explorations of the concept of transformational leadership, Bernard M. Bass has contrasted two types of leadership behaviors: *transactional* and *transformational.* **Transactional leaders** determine what subordinates need to do to achieve their own and organizational objectives, classify those requirements, and help subordinates become confident

COORDINATED RESOURCE
Acumen: While there is no perfect *Acumen* profile, research shows that high scores on Humanistic-Helpful, Self-Actualization, Achievement, and Affiliation scales are associated with greater effectiveness in the managerial role.

TEACHING TIP
Emphasize the importance of these last few sentences for students learning about effective leadership.

COORDINATED RESOURCE
The Distinctive Discussions for Chapter 16 found in the Lecture Extras supplement include "Does the CEO Really Matter?" and "Modern Discipline."

A Transformational Challenge. When former Chief Financial Officer James A. Unruh became Unisys Corp. CEO in 1989, he tore down a wall separating him from other executives, symbolizing his goal of creating an open culture that will help the troubled computer maker reduce its heavy debt load and regain market share.

COORDINATED RESOURCE
See Oddou section on Leading the Organization, "Leading."

COORDINATED RESOURCE
See *Management Live!* Chapter 6 video, "Martin Luther King's 'I Have a Dream' Speech."

they can reach their objectives by expending the necessary efforts. In contrast, transformational leaders "motivate us to do more than we originally expected to do" by raising our sense of the importance and value of our tasks, by "getting us to transcend our own self-interests for the sake of the team, organization, or larger policy," and by raising our need level to the higher-order needs, such as self-actualization.[31]

Much of the leadership theory that we have discussed in this chapter fits Bass's transactional category reasonably well, and Bass argues that such theory is useful and helpful, as far as it goes. However, to be fully effective—and to have a major impact on their organizations—leaders need to use their personal vision and energy to inspire their followers.

BOYD'S REFINEMENT. Building on and modifying the theory of transformational leadership, Richard Boyd has proposed that changes in the structure and strategy of American industry have created a need for a new kind of leader who commands a range of skills different from those called for by prior management theories. These new leadership skills include: (1) anticipatory skills—foresight into a constantly changing environment; (2) visioning skills—the use of persuasion and example to induce a group to act in accord with the leader's purposes or (more likely) the shared purposes of a larger group; (3) value-congruence skills—the need to be in touch with employees' economic, safety, psychological, spiritual, sexual, aesthetic, and physical needs in order to engage people on the basis of shared motives, values, and goals; (4) empowerment skills—the willingness to share power and to do so effectively; and (5) self-understanding—introspective or self-understanding skills, as well as frameworks within which leaders understand both their own needs and goals and those of their employees.

Having argued for this new framework, Boyd poses a question raised by most classical theories of leadership. Can these skills be *taught?* He contrasts Peter Drucker, who has argued that the essential qualities of effective leadership cannot be created or promoted, taught or learned, with Gordon Lippett, who has argued that the needs, attributes, and competencies of leaders are complex but identifiable and that leaders are made, not born. Boyd recommends that we embrace Lippett's hypothesis in order to develop leadership skills in U.S. corporations as well as create conditions in which leadership can emerge. He points out that many of the highly successful computer firms of California's Silicon Valley recognize the need for leaders to develop and nurture certain sets of skills in themselves and in their work forces.[32]

HOUSE'S THEORY OF CHARISMATIC LEADERSHIP. Although the transformational leadership concept dates back at least to Max Weber's discussion of charismatic leaders in the first decades of the century,[33] the concept received relatively little research attention until recently. One of the few notable contributions to systematic analysis of the subject is Robert J. House's theory of charismatic leadership.[34]

In Chapter 12, we discussed the referent power that some managers possess. House's theory suggests that charismatic leaders have very high levels of referent power and that some of that power comes from their need to influence others. The charismatic leader has "extremely high levels of self-confidence, dominance, and a strong conviction in the moral righteousness of his/her beliefs"—or at least the ability to convince followers that he or she possesses such confidence and conviction.[35]

House suggests that charismatic leaders communicate a vision or higher-level ("transcendent") goal that captures the commitment and energies of followers. They are careful to create an image of success and competence and to exemplify in their own behavior the values they espouse. They also communicate high expectations for followers and confidence that followers will perform up to those expectations.

COORDINATED RESOURCE
See Samaras Case 4.2, "The Crisis Situation."

House's theory has not yet been extensively researched, but we can expect it will be in the near future. One aspect likely to receive careful attention is the *type* of vision transformational leaders and their followers pursue. Though the names and deeds of Winston Churchill, Mahatma Gandhi, and Martin Luther King are stirring, House and others are well aware that the ability to inspire great commitment, sacrifice, and energy is no guarantee that the cause or vision is a worthwhile one. Adolf Hitler was also known for his charisma—and for the tragedies his leadership brought to his followers and others. Transformational leaders may possess great potential for revitalizing declining institutions and helping individuals find meaning and excitement in their work and lives, but they can pose great dangers if their goals and values are opposed to the basic tenets of civilized society.

Challenges to Leadership Theory

A PSYCHOANALYTIC APPROACH TO LEADERSHIP. The example of Hitler has led some people to suggest that we question all leaders' motives. In a series of studies, theorist Manfred Kets de Vries has concluded that leadership theories are based on an oversimplified model of human nature.[36]

To understand why some people become leaders, Kets de Vries argues, we need to take a *psychoanalytic view.* This view, originated by Sigmund Freud, holds that much of human behavior is shaped by unconscious efforts to satisfy unfulfilled needs and drives. In other words, we may not know why we do what we do. Indeed, much human behavior can be traced to early childhood experiences, which are difficult to recall.

Take House's concept of the charismatic leader rallying people to a heroic vision. In reality, Kets de Vries suggests, the adult leader may be acting out a three-year-old's need to control his or her environment. The fact that this misplaced drama has positive social consequences may be of secondary importance to the leader, who is unconsciously trying to ease a personal frustration.

Kets de Vries holds that appearances can be deceiving, and that we need to return to a more basic theory of human nature if we are to understand the complex dynamics of leadership.

THE ROMANCE OF LEADERSHIP. A second challenge to traditional theories of leadership focuses on the followers—the people who look to leaders for guidance. In this view, followers have developed *romanticized,* or idealized, views of what leaders do, what they can accomplish, and how they can affect followers' lives. These romantic views have evolved because most of us find it hard to understand the workings of the large, complex systems within our society, so we turn to leaders to simplify our lives. Thus, romantic views of leadership and leaders say as much about followers as they do about leaders. It may be that people need a romanticized view of leaders to help them focus on and meet organizational goals. If this is so, a leader will be able to motivate and influence only so long as the followers retain confidence in that leader. Once that confidence is lost, the leader's effectiveness will be diminished, no matter what he or she may do.[37]

self-managed work groups Work teams organized around a particular task and composed of members who possess both the skills necessary to accomplish the task and the power to determine such factors as method of operation, assignment of responsibilities, and creation of work schedules.

SELF-MANAGED GROUPS AND SELF-LEADERSHIP. In contrast to the romantic view of leadership, which sees people as confused by too much information and craving guidance, this third challenge sees modern employees as knowing too much to need traditional leaders. Manz and Sims, for example, claim that major high-technology "change agents" have so dramatically altered the methods of production and operations that previously successful methods of management are now inadequate.[38]

Today many business organizations deploy **self-managed work groups,** which usually have responsibility for "a relatively whole task; members who each possess a variety of skills relevant to the group task; workers with the power to determine such factors as methods of work, task schedule, and assignment of mem-

COORDINATED RESOURCE

See *Management Live!* Reading 6.1, "The New Breed of Leaders: Taking Charge in a Different Way."

HERE'S AN EXAMPLE

Apple Computer's CEO John Sculley is giving up some authority over the company's new-product efforts to spend more time on a few potential breakthrough projects. (*Wall Street Journal*, 3/15/91, p. B1)

self-leadership The ability of workers to motivate themselves to perform both tasks that are naturally rewarding and those that are necessary but not appealing.

bers to different tasks; and compensation and feedback about performance for the group as a whole."[39] The presence of such groups in industry means individual strategies for completing tasks are replaced by group methods for job accomplishment.[40]

This participative approach is seen in both manufacturing and nonmanufacturing organizations within the United States. For example, in Worthington Industries and Chaparral Steel, it is routine for security guards to enter orders and run ambulances, for supervisors to hire and train their own staffs, and for supervisors to determine operating procedures for new equipment. Similarly, at the GM Delco-Remy plant in Fitzgerald, Georgia, workers generally handle all quality control, track their own time, and rotate as work team leaders. Chaparral's steel is of superb quality, and the GM Delco-Remy plant has an exceptionally good record on absenteeism, quality, and productivity.[41] (A simplified schematic of the Delco-Remy plant organization is presented in Fig. 16-8.)

Manz and Sims suggest that the new leadership roles emerging from these self-managed groups are more effective than the more formal and traditional roles.[42] They call this new leadership style **self-leadership,** which they define as the ability of workers to motivate themselves to perform both tasks that are naturally appealing to them and those that are necessary but not naturally attractive.

To understand self-leadership, Manz and Sims suggest we look at the psychological processes by which employees perceive the *organizational control system*— its structure, its goals and values, and its standards, rules, policies, and procedures, including its policies and procedures for appraisals, rewards, and punishments. This

FIGURE 16-8 Organization Chart for Participative or Self-Managed Organization
Source: From *Thriving on Chaos: Handbook for Management Revolution,* by Tom Peters. Copyright © 1987 by Excel, a California Limited Partnership. Reprinted by permission of Alfred A. Knopf, Inc.

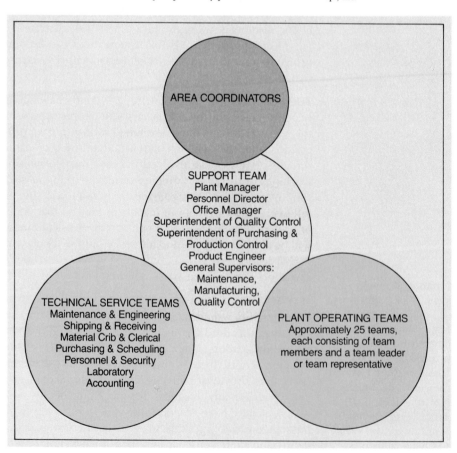

COORDINATED RESOURCE
Use Transparency 115, Organization Chart for Participative or Self-Managed Organizations.

control system provides "psychological scripts" for employees that guide their work activities. Unfortunately, these control systems only work *indirectly,* since they are filtered through the employees' own control systems—the needs, wants, goals, values, beliefs, and standards each employee brings to the organization.[43] Consciously or unconsciously, all employees measure their behavior against their own control system and reward or punish themselves accordingly.

An important element of self-leadership is the employee's ability to choose appealing work settings and to build natural rewards into tasks. For example, a manager could choose to give instructions verbally, rather than through memos, because he or she enjoys talking to people.[44] Moreover, face-to-face communication gives the manager a chance to acknowledge the employee's participation in the communication process.

Manz and Sims advocate a process that lets the individual's systems, values, and attitudes play a more active role in implementing overall management goals—what they call "superordinate standards." They also believe that when employees are allowed to invoke strategies on the basis of self-leadership and to behave on the basis of self-management, they are more likely to develop, more quickly and more consistently, behavior that does not deviate significantly from the organization's behavioral standards.[45] Conceptually, the process of this control system is schematized in Figure 16-9.

Manz and Sims studied leaders who held roles in an environment that was self-managed or self-led. They found that such leaders encouraged others to practice self-reinforcement, self-observation and evaluation; to value and act on self-expectations; to set goals for themselves; to rehearse critical procedures; and to engage in self-criticism when necessary.[46]

FIGURE 16-9 The Self-Leadership/Self-Management Control Process

Source: Reprinted by permission of *Academy of Management Review.* A figure from "Self-leadership: Toward an Expanded Theory of Self-Influence Processes in Organizations" by Charles C. Manz (Vol. 11, No. 3, 1986). Copyright © 1986; all rights reserved.

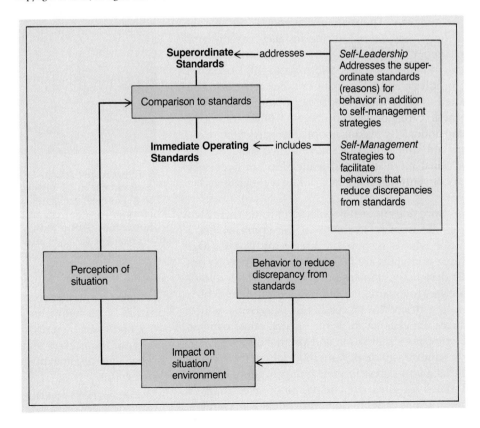

One organization encountered many pitfalls when it tried to introduce a participative or self-management approach because upper-level managers misunderstood the concept and process, while middle managers and supervisors resisted, often to the point of outright sabotage. Within the quality circles, some members became "empire builders," trying to substitute the illusion of immediate success for the long-term goal of institutionalizing the quality circle process. The quality circles were also undermined by poor and one-shot training for circle members, supervisor-leaders, and managers, as well as by inadequate information and support for members trying to solve problems. Furthermore, the organization failed to provide incentives for participating in quality circles and did not prepare to measure the impact of such participation on defect rates, productivity rates, and so on. In short, the company failed to develop and codify a set of process rules *before* forming the first quality circles. Moreover, once it started the quality circles, the organization moved too quickly—forming more circles than it could deal with adequately.[47]

Of course, one failure hardly means that the concept of self-management is faulty. It simply means that self-management, like any strategy, must be enacted with care and forethought. Even modest efforts to tap employees' potential for self-leadership can reap substantial rewards. (See the Management Application box.)

MANAGEMENT APPLICATION

Innovative Leadership at W. L. Gore and Associates

Management and leadership are different at W. L. Gore. The standard notion that people need to be motivated and led in the direction of organizational goals has largely been supplanted by a system of self-managed groups. For starters, there are no job titles at the company: There are no "workers" or "managers," only "associates." In one instance, a secretary-bookkeeper named Sarah Clifton was worried about having no business cards. She went to Bill Gore with the problem, and when he asked her what title she wanted, she replied, "Supreme Commander." Her business cards now read "Sarah Clifton, Supreme Commander." By making people feel part of the team, Gore and other companies have shown that a lot less traditional motivation and leadership are necessary than conventional wisdom would have managers believe.

Gore does not set people adrift to do their own thing—far from it. Everyone at the company has a sponsor who is responsible for seeing that its four guiding principles are followed: *fairness,* which controls destructive dissension; *freedom,* which allows associates to experience failure; *commitment,* which fuels the desire to succeed; and *discretion,* which reduces the chances for behavior that could damage the company's reputation and profitability.

Sponsors guide new members, help them progress, take an interest in their compensation, and are advocates for their well-being. Since everything is done in teams at W. L. Gore, individual achievement

A Team Approach to Leadership. Associates have ready access to Genevieve Gore (center), who founded W. L. Gore & Associates with her late husband, Wilbert, a former Du Pont chemist who vowed to avoid stifling bureaucracies. Son Robert (right) only accepts the title of president for legal reasons and aims to maintain the open culture his father created.

is hard to measure, but then no one is given assignments. With help from their sponsors, new employees find their own. By focusing on getting people to commit themselves voluntarily to the pursuit of personal and organizational goals, Bill Gore has been successful.

Source: Tom Peters and Nancy Austin, *A Passion for Excellence* (New York: Random House, 1985).

WRAP-UP

New Leadership Policies at GE

Leadership at GE is complex. As the company's environment changed from one characterized by government regulation and high inflation in the 1970s to one of intense global competition in the 1980s, Reginald Jones, until 1981 chairman of GE's board, thought that GE needed a different brand of leadership. Fully aware of the risk of making a change in managerial style that was bound to have wide-sweeping consequences for the entire organization, Jones and the board nevertheless chose young, brash, smart Jack Welch to head the company. Perhaps recent media attention has made Jack Welch a larger-than-life figure—responsible for all the good and evil that naturally befall a large organization such as GE. One thing, however, is certain: GE is not standing still. ∎

∎ *SUMMARY*

Leadership is an important subject for managers because of the critical role leaders play in group and organizational effectiveness. Leadership may be defined as the process of influencing and directing the task-related activities of group members.

Three approaches to the study of leadership have been identified: the trait, behavior, and contingency approaches. The trait approach has not proved useful, since no one combination of traits consistently distinguishes leaders from nonleaders or effective leaders from ineffective leaders.

The behavior approach has focused on leadership functions and styles. Studies have found that both task-related functions and group-maintenance functions have to be performed by one or more group members if a group is to function effectively. Studies of leadership styles have distinguished between a task-oriented, authoritarian, or initiating structure on the one hand and an employee-centered, democratic, or participative style on the other. Some studies suggest that the effectiveness of a particular style depends on the circumstances in which it is used. Tannenbaum and Schmidt, for example, maintain that a manager's choice of leadership style should be influenced by various forces in the manager, in subordinates, and in the work situation.

The difficulty of isolating universally effective leadership traits or behaviors has caused researchers to try to determine the situational variables that will cause one leadership style to be more effective than another. The major situational variables they identified are the leader's personality and past experience; the expectations and behavior of superiors; the characteristics, expectations, and behavior of subordinates; task requirements; organizational culture and policies; and the expectations and behavior of peers.

The contingency approach to leadership attempts to identify which of these situational factors is most important and to predict which leadership style will be more effective in a given situation. The Hersey-Blanchard situational theory of leadership suggests that leadership style should vary with the maturity of subordinates. The manager-subordinate relationship moves through four phases as subordinates develop achievement motivation and experience; a different leadership style is appropriate for each phase. According to the Fiedler model, leader-member relations, task structure, and the leader's position power are the most important situational variables; this model predicts which types of leaders (high-LPC or low-LPC) will be most effective in the eight possible combinations of these variables.

The path-goal approach formulated by Evans and House focuses on managers' abilities to dispense rewards. The leadership style a manager uses will affect the types of rewards offered and subordinates' perceptions of what they must do to earn those rewards. The personal characteristics of subordinates, as well as the environmental pressures and demands to which they are subjected, will affect which leadership style subordinates actually or potentially find rewarding.

The approach characterized by Fiedler suggests that leadership styles are relatively inflexible and that leaders should therefore be matched to an appropriate situation or the situation changed to match the leader. Others, however, believe that managers have a great deal of potential flexibility in their leadership styles and can therefore learn to be effective in a variety of situations.

Vroom and Yetton developed a model of situational leadership that identified five styles, ranging from authoritarian to fully participative. They also encouraged managers to seek the "feasible set of alternatives" in choosing a style to accommodate a given problem or situation. Vroom and Jago extended the Vroom-Yetton model by putting greater emphasis on the quality of the managerial decision and the nature of the manager's commitment to it. They also cautioned against otherwise good decisions that were too costly or cumbersome to implement and urged that decisions be made with the view of developing the abilities of others involved in the decision.

Another, more recent focus of leadership is the transformational or charismatic leader who has the ability to lead a company through a major transformation. Recent challenges to traditional leadership theory include the psychoanalytic approach, the romantic approach, and the concept of self-managed groups and self-leadership.

■ REVIEW QUESTIONS

1. How is leadership defined in this chapter? Discuss three implications of this definition.

2. Why was the trait approach a logical attempt to understand leadership? What two approaches did the trait researchers take? What did these trait studies reveal about leadership?

3. Describe the two basic leadership functions needed for effective group performance. Must one leader perform both these functions?

4. Outline the basic idea of the Tannenbaum and Schmidt model. What factors should influence a manager's style, according to this model? What are some of the practical considerations the model suggests managers must take into account in selecting a style?

5. What are the two basic leadership styles identified by the Ohio State and University of Michigan studies? Which style was thought to be more effective?

6. What is the "situational leadership theory"? How should the manager's style vary in each of its four phases?

7. Outline the basic theory of the Managerial Grid. Which leadership style in the grid do Blake and Mouton believe is most effective?

8. What basic assumptions underlie the Fiedler model? What is the LPC scale? What are the basic elements in the work situation that determine which leadership style will be most effective? In what situations is a high-LPC leader effective? In what situations is a low-LPC leader effective?

9. Describe the path-goal model. On what theory of motivation is the model based? According to this model, how do managers with different leadership styles differ in their ability to influence or reward subordinates? What variables, according to this theory, help determine the most effective leadership style? Why?

10. What are the five styles of managerial decision making suggested by Vroom and Yetton? What are the most important modifications made by Vroom and Jago to the Vroom-Yetton model of leadership?

11. Explain the difference between a transactional and a transformational leader. When is each type useful?

12. Why are charismatic leaders sometimes dangerous?

13. How does the psychoanalytic approach challenge traditional theories of leadership?

14. Why does the romantic approach say we follow leaders?

15. Define the terms *self-managed work groups* and *self-leadership*. What do these terms mean for traditional theories of leadership and traditional ideas about control within organizations?

CASE STUDY

Three Managerial Decisions

1. You are a manufacturing manager in a large electronics plant. At considerable expense, the company's management has recently installed new robotic assembly equipment, trimmed the work force, and put in a new simplified work system. To the surprise of everyone, yourself included, the expected increase in production has not materialized. In fact, production has begun to drop, overall quality has fallen off, and the number of voluntary employee separations has risen.

You do not believe there is anything wrong with the robots. Reports from other companies using them confirm this opinion, and representatives from the firm that built them have inspected the robots and reported they are working at peak efficiency. The robot-made assemblies are of uniformly high quality.

You suspect that the new work system may be responsible for the fall-off in production. But this view is not shared by your immediate subordinates—four first-line supervisors, each in charge of a section—and your supply manager. They variously attribute the drop in production to poor retraining of the operators, lack of adequate financial incentives, and poor worker morale due to fear of increasing automation. Clearly, this is an issue about which there is considerable depth of feeling among workers and disagreement among your subordinates.

This morning you got a phone call from your division manager. She had just received your production figures for the last six months and was calling to express her concern. She indicated that the problem was yours to solve as you thought best, but that she would like to know within a week what steps you plan to take.

You share your division manager's concern over the falling productivity and know that your workers do too. The problem is to decide what steps to take to rectify the situation.

2. You are a general supervisor in charge of a construction team laying a coal slurry pipeline and have to estimate your rate of progress in order to schedule materials deliveries to the next field site.

You know the nature of the terrain you will be crossing and have the historical data you need to compute the mean and variance in the rate of speed over that type of terrain. Given these two variables, it is a simple matter to calculate the earliest and latest times at which materials and support facilities will be needed at the next site. It is important that your estimate be reasonably accurate, for an underestimate will result in idle supervisors and workers, and an overestimate will tie up materials unnecessarily for a period of time.

Progress has been good so far, and your five supervisors and other members of the team stand to receive substantial bonuses if the project is completed ahead of schedule.

3. You are supervising the work of 12 chemical engineers. Their formal training and work experience are very similar, permitting you to use them interchangeably on projects. Yesterday your manager informed you that a request had been received from a Middle Eastern affiliate for four engineers to go abroad on extended loan for a period of six to eight months. For a number of reasons, he argued—and you agreed—that this request should be met from your group.

All your engineers are capable of handling this assignment, and from the standpoint of present and future projects, there is no particular reason why anyone should be retained over any other. The problem is somewhat complicated by the fact that the overseas assignment is in what is generally regarded as an undesirable location.

Source: Reprinted by permission of the publisher, from "A New Look at Managerial Decision Making," by Victor H. Vroom, *Organizational Dynamics.* Summer 1973, pp. 72–73. © 1973 by American Management Association, New York. All rights reserved.

Case Questions

Three managerial decision-making situations have been described. Using the five decision-making styles outlined in Exhibit 16-1, answer the following questions for each of the decision-making situations.

1. After reading about the three situations, but before analyzing them, decide which of the decision-making style alternatives (AI, AII, CI, CII, GII) you would *personally* prefer to use in making each decision. Then answer the remaining questions.

2. Which is more important in the situation, quality or acceptance of the decision?

3. How critical is time in making a decision?

4. Does the manager have the information necessary to make the decision?

5. Is the decision-making situation highly structured?

6. Choose the best decision-making style (AI, AII, CI, CII, GII) and give the reason for your choice.

7. Did your choice of the "best" style in question 6 differ from the style you would personally have chosen in question 1? If so, why do you think it differed?

NASA and the Quest for Leadership

When astronaut Neil Armstrong set foot on the moon, it was the culmination of everything the National Aeronautics and Space Administration (NASA) had worked toward for ten years. Plenty of money and strong management, along with high-level political support, guided NASA to the moon. But since then NASA's leadership has floundered.

Part of the problem is lack of money. Another problem is that one-third of NASA's top managers are of retirement age, and the agency's relatively low pay has hampered efforts to recruit younger replacements. And, since the explosion of the space shuttle *Challenger,* NASA has been plagued with launching delays and mishaps, as well as more serious problems, such as the flaws in the $1.5 billion Hubble Space Telescope.

Those problems have led to reduced political and popular support. In addition, costs consistently exceed budgets. Many of NASA's planned projects, notably the Freedom Space Station, are considered too expensive by Congress.

Bruce Murray, a former director of NASA's Jet Propulsion Laboratory, is among those who believe that NASA engineers have been ordered to cut corners to save money and maintain projects that will keep the agency alive. But leadership that encourages cost cutting, he says, simply doesn't work. "We're headed for real disasters. The plan is sin now, pay later," Murray says. "Good managers drop things they might otherwise do when money is tight," says Alton D. Slay, a retired Air Force general who led a shuttle safety inquiry after the *Challenger* disaster.

A panel of experts, established by NASA at the request of President George Bush, says that to get back on track, NASA must first control costs. Runaway costs, the panel said, cause poor management, which in turn causes low employee morale.

The panel also recommended that NASA's top management structure in Washington, D.C., be revamped and that outside contractors be hired to run NASA's regional research centers.

Originally intended to be "think-tanks," which would specialize in different aspects of research and development, the centers have become mini-fiefdoms, vying with each other for both funding and manpower. The lack of centralized planning for major projects adds to the lack of leadership.

Before the Apollo moonwalk, leadership at NASA had come directly from the top—in this case, the White House—during the administrations of Presidents John F. Kennedy and Lyndon B. Johnson. But subsequent presidents did not show the same strong support for the agency. They also did not set clear goals for NASA.

President Bush has tried to reverse the lack of White House leadership. He has called for a manned flight to Mars and further moon exploration. He has also established the National Space Council, headed by Vice President Dan Quayle. The council has been a political supporter of NASA, but has clashed with the agency over future projects.

NASA has attempted to solve some of its own problems. The agency established an Engineering Council, composed of two dozen senior executives who review new projects to keep costs in line. But the agency has been slow to consider new ways of doing things or to look at ideas suggested by those outside of NASA.

One of those suggestions is that NASA should concentrate on those projects that could pay for themselves, such as shuttle launches of commercial cargo.

To do that, NASA needs to centralize responsibility for the shuttle, which is now split between the agency and Lockheed Space Operations Co. Although it has a $1.6 billion contract with NASA, Lockheed is not responsible for making sure that parts manufactured by other companies will work. With a prime contractor overseeing the shuttle project, it would be easier to ensure performance. Says Phillip E. Culbertson, a former NASA general manager: "It's an intriguing idea to ensure greater accountability."

Lack of accountability, coupled with lack of money, were behind the major problems discovered in the Hubble Space Telescope after it was launched. The telescope's mirrors, designed to be the most technologically advanced ever, were flawed, affecting the clarity of the photographs the telescope was able to transmit.

NASA blamed the main contractor, which in turn blamed subcontractors. Ultimately, it became clear that no one had overall supervision of the project. The result was a demoralized NASA work force and a drop in political support and public confidence.

The debate over what to do about NASA is likely to continue. But without greater funding and strong leadership, it is unlikely that the agency can return to its glory days.

Sources: Seth Payne, "NASA Is Losing Altitude. Run It Like a Business," *Business Week,* July 16, 1990, p. 36; William J. Cook, "Straighten Up and Fly Right, " *U.S. News & World Report,* July 16, 1990, p. 39; "Star in the Descendant," *The Economist,* September 29, 1990, pp. 95–96, 98; "The Wisdom of Augustine," *The Economist,* December 15, 1990, pp. 81–82; Jeffrey Kluger, "Lost in Space," *Discover,* January 1991, pp. 32–34; John Carey, Seth Payne and Eric Schine, "A Disaster for NASA or a Blessing?" *Business Week,* June 3, 1991, pp. 122–123; William J. Broad, "Space Errors Share Pattern: Skipped Tests," *The New York Times,* June 11, 1991, pp. C1 and C12.

Case Questions

1. In what negative ways has NASA's management influenced employees?

2. By encouraging employees to cut corners, how has NASA management shown a lack of leadership and undermined employee morale?

3. Who could be considered the ultimate leader at NASA?

4. What style of leadership has prevailed at NASA? What style do you think would work best?

■ *NOTES*

[1] Bernard M. Bass, *Stogdill's Handbook of Leadership: A Survey of Theory and Research*, 3rd ed. (New York: Free Press, 1990), p. 7. For a thorough review of recent theory, see Gary Yukl, "Managerial Leadership: A Review of Theory and Research," *Journal of Management* 15, no. 2 (1989):251–289.

[2] John R. P. French and Bertram Raven, "The Bases of Social Power," in Dorwin Cartwright, ed., *Studies in Social Power* (Ann Arbor: University of Michigan, 1959), pp. 150–167. See also Dennis A. Gioia and Henry P. Sims, Jr., "Perceptions of Managerial Power as a Consequence of Managerial Behavior and Reputation," *Journal of Management* 9, no. 1 (Fall 1983):7–26; and Edwin P. Hollander, "Leadership and Power," in Gardner Lindzey and Elliot Aronson, eds., *Handbook of Social Psychology*, 3rd ed. (New York: Random House, 1985), Chapter 9. For a recent summary of research on leadership, see Gary Yukl, "Managerial Leadership: A Review of Theory and Research," *Journal of Management,* 15, no. 2 (1989):251–289.

[3] Robert J. House and Mary L. Baetz, "Leadership: Some Empirical Generalizations and New Research Directions," in Barry M. Staw, ed., *Research in Organizational Behavior*, Vol. 1 (Greenwich, Conn.: JAI Press, 1979), pp. 348–354; David A. Kenny and Stephen J. Zaccaro, "An Estimate of Variance Due to Traits in Leadership," *Journal of Applied Psychology* 68, no. 4 (November 1983):678–685; Ralph M. Stogdill, "Personal Factors Associated with Leadership: A Survey of the Literature," *Journal of Psychology* 25, no. 1 (January 1948):35–71; R. D. Mann, "A Review of the Relationships Between Personality and Performance in Small Groups," *Psychological Bulletin* 56, no. 4 (July 1959):241–270; and Howard M. Weiss and Seymour Adler, "Personality and Organizational Behavior," *Research in Organizational Behavior* 6 (1984):1–50.

[4] See Edwin E. Ghiselli, *Explorations in Managerial Talent* (Pacific Palisades, Calif.: Goodyear, 1971), pp. 39–56.

[5] See Dorwin Cartwright and Alvin Zander, eds., *Group Dynamics*, 3rd ed. (New York: Harper & Row, 1968).

[6] Natalie Porter, Florence Lindauer Geis, and Joyce Jennings, "Are Women Invisible Leaders?" *Sex Roles* 9, no. 10 (October 1983):1035–1049; Robert W. Rice, Debra Instone, and Jerome Adams, "Leader Sex, Leader Success, and Leadership Process: Two Field Studies," *Journal of Applied Psychology* 69, no. 1 (February 1984):12–31; and Susan M. Donnell and Jay Hall, "Men and Women as Managers: A Significant Case of No Significant Difference," *Organizational Dynamics* 8, no. 4 (Spring 1980): 60–77.

[7] Colin Leinster, "Black Executives: How They're Doing," *Fortune*, January 18, 1988, pp. 109–120.

[8] See Robert F. Bales, *Interaction Process Analysis* (Reading, Mass.: Addison-Wesley, 1951). A more recent study that found contrary evidence is C. Roger Rees and Mady Wechsler Segal, "Role Differentiation in Groups: The Relationship Between Instrumental and Expressive Leadership," *Small Group Behavior* 15, no. 1 (February 1984):109–123.

[9] Robert Tannenbaum and Warren H. Scmidt, "How to Choose a Leadership Pattern," *Harvard Business Review* 51, no. 3 (May–June 1973):162–164ff. (Reprint of March–April 1958 article.)

[10] See Victor H. Vroom, "Leadership," in Marvin D. Dunnette, ed., *Handbook of Industrial and Organizational Psychology* (New York: Wiley, 1983), pp. 1527–1551.

[11] Robert R. Blake and Jane S. Mouton, *The New Managerial Grid III* (Houston: Gulf Publishing, 1985); Robert R. Blake and Anne Adams McCanse, *Leadership Dilemmas—Grid Solutions* (Houston: Gulf Publishing, 1991). For an early classification of leadership styles into authoritarian, laissez-faire, and democratic leadership, see Kurt Lewin, Ronald Lippitt, and Ralph K. White, "Patterns of Aggressive Behavior in Experimentally Created Social Climates," *Journal of Social Psychology* 10, no. 2 (May 1939):271–299.

[12] See, for example, Martin M. Chemers, "The Social, Organizational, and Cultural Context of Effective Leadership," in Barbara Kellerman, ed., *Leadership: Multidisciplinary Perspectives* (Englewood Cliffs, N.J.: Prentice Hall, 1985), pp. 91–112.

[13] George F. Farris and Francis G. Lim, Jr., "Effects of Performance on Leadership, Cohesiveness, Satisfaction, and Subsequent Performance," *Journal of Applied Psychology* 53, no. 6 (December 1969):490–497. See also Dov Eden, "Self-Fulfilling Prophecy as a Management Tool: Harnessing Pygmalion," *Academy of Management Review* 9, no. 1 (January 1984):64–73.

[14]E. A. Fleishman, "Leadership Climate, Human Relations Training, and Supervisory Behavior," *Personnel Psychology* 6, no. 2 (Summer 1953):205–222.

[15]Paul Hersey and Kenneth H. Blanchard, *Management of Organizational Behavior,* 4th ed. (Englewood Cliffs, N.J.: Prentice Hall, 1982). See also William J. Reddin, "The 3-D Management Style Theory," *Training and Development Journal* 21, no. 4 (April 1967):8–17, on which Hersey and Blanchard base much of their work.

[16]The theory has been criticized for its inability to logically account for some actual management situations. See Claude L. Graeff, "The Situational Leadership Theory: A Critical View," *Academy of Management Review* 8, no. 2 (April 1983):285–291. Blake and Mouton also critique the situational theory and argue for the universal superiority of the 9,9 style in "A Comparative Analysis of Situationalism and 9,9 Management by Principle," *Organizational Dynamics* 10, no. 4 (Spring 1982):20–43.

[17]Fred E. Fiedler, "Engineer the Job to Fit the Manager," *Harvard Business Review* 43, no. 5 (September–October 1965):116. See also Fred E. Fiedler, "The Contingency Model," in Harold Proshansky and Bernard Seidenberg, eds., *Basic Studies in Social Psychology* (New York: Holt, Rinehart & Winston, 1965), pp. 538–551, and "Validation and Extension of the Contingency Model of Leadership Effectiveness," *Psychological Bulletin* 76, no. 2 (August 1971):128–148.

[18]Fred E. Fiedler and Linda Mahar, "A Field Experiment Validating Contingency Model Leadership Training," *Journal of Applied Psychology* 64, no. 3 (June 1979):247–254.

[19]See, for example, John E. Stinson and Lane Tracy, "The Stability and Interpretation of the LPC Score," *Proceedings of the Academy of Management* 32 (1972):182–184; George Graen, James B. Orris, and Kenneth Alvares, "Contingency Model of Leadership Effectiveness: Some Experimental Results," *Journal of Applied Psychology* 55, no. 3 (June 1971):196–201; and Walter Bungard, "Sense and Nonsense of the LPC Scale: Criticism of Fiedler's Contingency Model," *Gruppendynamik* 15, no. 1 (1984):59–74 (in German).

[20]Martin G. Evans, "Leadership and Motivation: A Core Concept," *Academy of Management Journal* 13, no. 1 (March 1970):91–102.

[21]See Robert J. House, "A Path-Goal Theory of Leader Effectiveness," *Administrative Science Quarterly* 16, no. 5 (September 1971):321–328; and Robert J. House and Terence R. Mitchell, "Path-Goal Theory of Leadership," *Journal of Contemporary Business* 3, no. 4 (Autumn 1979):81–97.

[22]Chester A. Schriesheim and Angelo S. DeNisi, "Task Dimensions as Moderators of the Effects of Instrumental Leader Behavior: A Path-Goal Approach," *Proceedings of the Academy of Management* 39 (1979):103–106.

[23]Victor H. Vroom and Arthur G. Jago, *The New Leadership: Managing Participation in Organizations* (Englewood Cliffs, N.J.: Prentice Hall, 1988).

[24]Victor H. Vroom and Philip W. Yetton, *Leadership and Decision Making* (Pittsburgh: University of Pittsburgh Press, 1973). This model has been subsequently refined by Vroom and Arthur Jago. We will refer to it throughout the text as the Vroom-Yetton model since this is now its standard title. Also see Victor H. Vroom, "Reflections on Leadership and Decision-Making," *Journal of General Management* 9, no. 3 (Spring 1984):18–36.

[25]Vroom, "Reflections on Leadership and Decision-Making." Supporters of the model and challengers have studied it extensively. See, for example, Arthur Jago, "A Test of Spuriousness in Descriptive Models of Participative Leader Behavior," *Journal of Applied Psychology* 63, no. 3 (June 1978):383–387; R. H. Field, "A Critique of the Vroom-Yetton Contingency Model of Leadership Behavior," *Academy of Management Review* 4, no. 2 (April 1979):249–257; and Victor H. Vroom and Arthur C. Jago, "An Evaluation of Two Alternatives to the Vroom-Yetton Normative Model," *Academy of Management Journal* 23, no. 2 (June 1980):347–355. In support of the model, also see Richard M. Steers, "Individual Differences in Participative Decision-Making," *Human Relations* 30, no. 9 (September 1977):837–847.

[26]Vijay Sathe, "Implications of Corporate Culture: A Manager's Guide to Action," *Organizational Dynamics* 12, no. 2 (Autumn 1983):5–23. Several books published in the early 1980s aroused great interest in corporate cultures. On the culture of Japanese organizations, see William G. Ouchi, *Theory Z: How American Business Can Meet the Japanese Challenge* (Reading, Mass.: Addison-Wesley, 1981); and Richard Tanner Pascale and Anthony G. Athos, *The Art of Japanese Management* (New York: Simon & Schuster, 1981). For discussions of successful companies and the cultures they have generated, see Thomas J. Peters and Robert H. Waterman, Jr., *In Search of Excellence* (New York: Harper & Row, 1982); and Terrence E. Deal and Allan A. Kennedy, *Corporate Cultures: The Rites and Rituals of Corporate Life* (Reading, Mass.: Addison-Wesley, 1982). Recent books exploring the concept in depth include Edgar H. Schein, *Organizational Culture and Leadership* (San Francisco: Jossey-Bass, 1985); Stanley M. Davis, *Managing Corporate Culture* (Hagerstown, Md.: Ballinger, 1985); and Ralph H. Kilman, Mary Jane Saxton, and Ray Serpa, eds., *Gaining Control of Corporate Cultures* (San Francisco: Jossey-Bass, 1985).

[27]Max Weber, *Economy and Society: An Outline of Interpretative Sociology* (New York: Bedminster Press, 1968; orig. pub. 1925), pp. 241–254; and Robert J. House, "A 1976 Theory of Charismatic Leadership," in James G. Hunt and Lars L. Larson, eds., *Leadership: The Cutting Edge* (Carbondale: Southern Illinois University Press, 1976), pp. 189–207.

[28]Bernard M. Bass, "Leadership: Good, Better, Best," *Organizational Dynamics* 13, no. 3 (Winter 1985):26–40; Bernard Bass, "From Transactional to Transformational Leadership: Learning to Share the Vision," *Organizational Dynamics* 18, no. 3 (Winter 1990):19–31; Noel M. Tichy and David O. Ulrich, "The Leadership Challenge—A Call for the Transformational Leader," *Sloan Management Review* 26, no. 1 (Fall 1984):59–68; and Bernard M. Bass, "From Transactional to Transformational Leadership: Learning to Share the Vision," *Organizational Dynamics* 18, no. 3 (Fall 1990):19–31.

[29]See Jeremy Main, "Waking Up AT&T: There's Life After Culture Shock," *Fortune,* December 24, 1984,

pp. 66ff.; David E. Sanger, "The Changing Image of IBM," *The New York Times Magazine,* July 7, 1985, pp. 13ff.; and Cary Reich, "The Innovator: The Creative Mind of GM Chairman Roger Smith," *The New York Times Magazine,* April 21, 1985, pp. 29ff.

[30]See Tichy and Ulrich, "The Leadership Challenge." Tichy and Ulrich list the following additional companies as ones undergoing major transformations: Honeywell, Ford, Burroughs, Chase Manhattan Bank, Citibank, U.S. Steel, Union Carbide, Texas Instruments, and Control Data.

[31]Bass, "Leadership: Good, Better, Best," pp. 27–28, 31.

[32]Richard E. Boyd, "Corporate Leadership Skills: A New Synthesis," *Organizational Dynamics* 16, no. 1 (1987):34–43.

[33]Weber, *Economy and Society,* pp. 241–254.

[34]House, "A 1976 Theory of Charismatic Leadership," pp. 189–207.

[35]Ibid., p. 193.

[36]M. F. R. Kets de Vries, *Prisoners of Leadership* (New York: Wiley, 1989); M. F. R. Kets de Vries and S. Perzow, *Handbook of Character* (New York: International University Press, 1990); and M. F. R. Kets de Vries, "The Organizational Fool: Balancing a Leader's Hubris," *Human Relations* 43, no. 8 (1990):751–770. See also Abraham Zaleznik, "The Leadership Gap," *Academy of Management Executive* 4, no. 1 (1990):7–22.

[37]James R. Meindle, Sandford B. Ehrlich, and Janet M. Dukerich, "The Romance of Leadership," *Administrative Science Quarterly* 30 (1985):78–102. For a different approach to the replacement of leadership, see Jan Howell, David Bowen, Peter Dorfinan, Steven Kerr, Philip Podsakoff, "Substitutes for Leadership: Effective Alternatives to Ineffective Leadership," *Organizational Dynamics* 19, no. 1 (1990):21–28; Karl Popper, "The Critical Approach versus the Mystique of Leadership," *Human Systems Management* 8 (1989):259–265.

[38]Charles C. Manz and Henry P. Sims, Jr., "Leading Workers to Lead Themselves: The External Leadership of Self-Managing Work Teams," *Administrative Science Quarterly* 32 (1987):106–107.

[39]Thomas Cummings, "Self-Regulated Work Groups: A Socio-Technical Synthesis," *Academy of Management Review* 3 (1978):625.

[40]Charles C. Manz, "Self-Leadership: Toward an Expanded Theory of Self-Influence Processes in Organizations," *Academy of Management Review* 11 (1986):589–590.

[41]Manz, "Self-Leadership," p. 593.

[42]Manz and Sims, "Leading Workers to Lead Themselves," p. 120.

[43]Ibid., p. 586.

[44]Manz, "Self-Leadership," p. 593.

[45]Ibid., pp. 590–593.

[46]Manz and Sims, "Leading Workers to Lead Themselves," p. 120.

[47]Peters, *Thriving on Chaos: Handbook for a Management Revolution.*

CHAPTER SEVENTEEN

GROUPS AND COMMITTEES

Types of Groups
Formal Groups
Informal Groups

Characteristics of Groups
Leadership Roles
Group Norms
Group Cohesiveness

Problem Solving in Groups
Advantages of Group Problem Solving
Disadvantages of Group Problem Solving
Key Factors in Group Decision Making: Assets or Liabilities

Making Formal Groups Effective
Guidelines for Committees
Special Procedures for Task Forces
Conflict Within Groups

Upon completing this chapter, you should be able to:

1. Distinguish between the two major types of groups found in organizations and the manager's role in each type.

2. List and explain the three characteristics of groups.

3. Discuss some guidelines for increasing group cohesiveness.

4. Explain the advantages and disadvantages of group problem solving.

5. Explain how key factors in group decision making can be made into assets or liabilities.

6. Provide some guidelines for making committees effective.

7. Discuss some special procedures for making task forces effective.

8. Explain how managers can deal with conflicts within groups.

Cover of Smith Barney's Mergers & Acquisitions Brochure. Design: Carbone Smolan Associates. Artist: Mark Kostabi.

ILLUSTRATIVE CASE STUDY

INTRODUCTION

The Team Taurus Approach to Management at Ford

Like the other American automakers, Ford entered the 1980s in bad shape. Japanese competition was fierce, and Ford quality was down. In fact, Ford recalled more autos in 1980 than it built. As a result, Ford's market share fell, from 23.5 percent in 1978 to just 17.2 percent in 1980. Not surprisingly, employee morale sagged. By the end of the 1980s, however, Ford had transformed itself into an industry leader—thanks to the team approach introduced on the Taurus project.

Before the Taurus project, Ford designed cars by the "tossing it over the wall" system. The design department would come up with a concept for a new model, then toss it over the wall to engineering, which would, in turn, toss it over to production. There was no feedback between department leaders, no leeway for correcting mistakes, no feeling of teamwork, and absolutely no interfunctional cooperation. No wonder Ford had to recall so many cars.

Under the direction of Lew Veraldi, Ford formed a task force to investigate ways of changing car production, beginning with the new Taurus model. With the approval of then-CEO Donald E. Petersen, Veraldi instituted a system called *parallel processing.* Instead of tossing a car over the wall, all department heads were involved in all aspects of a car's production right from the start. Work groups from design through assembly came together and contributed to all aspects of car production—from the beginning. Instead of a linear flow of information from department to department, all functional areas moved forward together. That way problems could be attended to immediately, and each department had instant access to positive or negative feedback—and thus the opportunity to repair or strengthen the product.

Employee suggestions also played an important role in the Taurus project. This may sound fundamental, but it was an innovation for Ford. In the past, assembly-line workers' suggestions were not considered while a car was being designed and built. On the Taurus project, however, workers were asked to compile a "wish list" of details they thought would improve the product and please customers. The evidence of their success: *Motor Trend* voted the Ford Taurus Car of the Year in 1986.

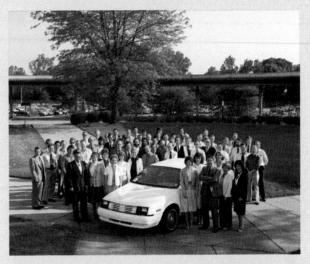

Team Taurus Celebrates. Mr. Lew Veraldi (at left, in brown suit) and Team Taurus gather around the first Ford Taurus engineering prototype in August 1984.

At about the same time, Ray A. Ablondi, Jr., Ford's head of customer research, began asking customers exactly what they wanted in a car. Now Ford surveys 2.5 million customers a year, and regularly invites car owners to meet with engineers and dealers to discuss quality problems. Customers were also asked to ride in prototypes and make suggestions on how to improve the cars—in effect, to become part of the Ford "team." For example, customers overrode plans to discontinue the Lincoln Town Car, which was revamped and won *Motor Trend*'s Car of the Year award in 1990.

Largely because of its new respect for teamwork, Ford had revenues of $5 billion, with accumulated funds of $10 billion, by 1988. In November 1990, Ford bought Jaguar, a British manufacturer of high-performance luxury cars, with plans to use the Taurus team ideas to make Ford Europe another industry leader.

Sources: "What's Creating an 'Industrial Miracle' at Ford?" *Business Week,* July 30, 1984, pp. 80–81; Robert Waterman, *The Renewal Factor* (New York: Bantam Books, 1987); Jim Harbour, "Ford, Where Quality Is Job 1," *Automotive Industries,* September 1986, p. 17; Lynn Adkins, "Such a Grand Design," *Business Month,* December 1987, pp. 30–31; Jerry Flint, "Luxury Doesn't Come Cheap," *Forbes,* January 22, 1990, pp. 72–75; and David Woodruff, "Putting Alternative Fuels in Ford Tanks," *Business Week,* July 16, 1990, p. 58.

Ford survived—to a great extent—because it adopted new ways of managing groups. Instead of clinging to a rigid hierarchy of "bosses" and "subordinates," Ford's managers created new groups that opened a floodgate of ideas from employees at every level. Like Ford, many organizations are finding that the best way to get the most out of *individual* employees is to pay closer attention to the way work *groups* are managed.[1] In this chapter, we will describe work groups and explain how they can be managed effectively.

■ TYPES OF GROUPS

A **group** is defined as two or more people who interact with and influence each other toward a common purpose.[2] Traditionally, two types of groups have existed in organizations: *formal groups* and *informal groups.*

Formal Groups

Formal groups are created deliberately by managers and charged with carrying out specific tasks to help the organization achieve its goals.[3] The most prevalent type of formal group is the **command group,** which includes a manager and the employees who report to that manager. In fact, the formal structure of organizations consists of a series of overlapping command groups. Managers belong to command groups made up of the people they manage, and also to command groups made up of their fellow managers and their own higher-level manager. In Rensis Likert's terminology, managers are the "linking pins" between the various formal work groups in their organizations. (See Fig. 17-1.)

Permanent formal groups include command groups and permanent or standing **committees,** which are generally long-lasting and deal with recurrent problems and decisions. (A planning committee is a common example.)

Temporary formal groups include **task forces** and **project teams** created to deal with a particular problem. For example, when former President Ronald Reagan appointed Hewlett-Packard CEO John Young to chair a task force on the competitiveness of American business, the task force called on a number of experts and interested parties to assemble its findings. Once a task force achieves its mission, it is usually disbanded.

FIGURE 17-1 The Manager as Linking Pin
Note: The arrows indicate the linking pin function.
Source: Rensis Likert, *New Patterns of Management* (New York: McGraw-Hill, 1961), p. 113. Copyright © 1961 by McGraw-Hill, Inc., publisher of the English edition. Reproduced by permission.

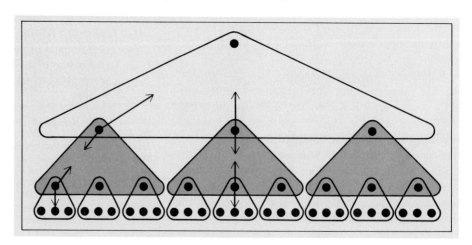

In all these formal groups, the assumption is that a manager is "in charge." However, many companies are finding they can achieve the same—or better—results with "superteams" made up of workers all at the same level. For an explanation, see the Management Application box.

Informal Groups

Informal groups emerge whenever people come together and interact regularly.[4] Such groups develop within the formal organizational structure. Members of informal groups tend to subordinate some of their individual needs to those of the group as a whole. In return, the group supports and protects them.[5] Informal groups may further the interests of the organization—Saturday morning softball games, for example, may strengthen the players' ties to the organization. They may also oppose organizational objectives, such as high performance standards, when these are considered harmful to the group.

MANAGEMENT APPLICATION

Three Cheers for the Superteams

At Federal Express, they figured out how to solve a billing problem and wound up saving the company $2.1 million a year. At one of General Mills' cereal plants in California, they run the factory during the night shift—without the help of a manager. Who are *they?* Meet the "superteams"—groups of 3 to 30 workers drawn from different areas of a corporation. Initially called "self-managed work teams," "cross-functional teams," or "high-performance teams," these kinds of teams were dubbed *superteams* by *Fortune* magazine in May 1990, and the name has stuck.

What sets them apart from other formal groups is that they ignore the traditional "chimney hierarchy"—a strict up-and-down arrangement with workers at the bottom and managers at the top—that was often too cumbersome to solve problems the workers dealt with every day. Well-run superteams manage themselves, arrange their work schedules, set their productivity quotas, order their own equipment and supplies, improve product quality, and interact with customers and other superteams.

Large corporations such as Corning, DEC, General Mills, and Federal Express all use superteams. Superteams seem to work as well in the service and finance sectors as they do in manufacturing. They can be created to work on a specific project or problems, or they can become a permanent part of the company's work force.

According to General Mills, productivity is up by 40 percent in plants that use superteams. And at Johnsonville Foods in Wisconsin, superteams of blue-collar workers helped CEO Ralph Stayer decide to proceed with a plant expansion. The workers also told Stayer they would be able to produce more sausage faster than he thought reasonable to ask. Between 1986 and 1990, productivity at Johnsonville has risen 50 percent.

Superteams are not all roses and rainbows, however. For simple problems, such as those met with in straight assembly-line production, the superteam may be overkill. Superteams make the most sense when there is a complex problem to solve or layers of progress-delaying management to cut through; the key concept here is cross-functionalism.

Superteams are not the right choice for every company. Middle managers often feel threatened by superteams because they leave fewer rungs on the corporate ladder to move up. Other important issues that need to be considered are: How can the team be kept on track? How should the team be rewarded for inventing a new product or saving the corporation money? How much spending authority should the team have? And finally, what happens when team members don't get along?

Organizing a corporation into superteams is a long, complex process that may take years. A Harvard Business School study found that it was easier to start a new plant with superteams than it was to convert an existing plant into superteams. Still, experts predict that superteams may be the most productive business innovation of the 1990s.

Source: Brian Dumaine, "Who Needs a Boss?" *Fortune,* May 7, 1990, pp. 52–62.

Informal Groups Create Harmony at Work. The 3M chorus has a budget of about $10,000 a year and travels all over the United States to perform at corporate and community events. Like the more than 50 other Fortune 500 companies that sponsor corporate choruses, 3M finds the chorus an excellent way to help employees from all ranks mingle and make friends throughout the company.

FOR DISCUSSION

Why do managers need to understand both formal and informal group behavior?

FOR DISCUSSION

Is the class you're in now a formal or informal group? Why?

reference group A group with whom individuals identify and compare themselves.

FOR DISCUSSION

Ask students to name some of their reference groups.

Informal groups serve essentially four major functions.[6] First, they maintain and strengthen the norms and values their members hold in common. Second, they give members feelings of social satisfaction, status, and security. In large corporations, where many people feel that their employers hardly know them, informal groups enable employees to share jokes and complaints, eat together, and perhaps socialize after work. Thus, informal groups satisfy the human need for friendship, support, and security.

Third, informal groups help their members communicate. Members of informal groups learn about matters that affect them by developing their own informal channels of communication to supplement more formal channels. In fact, managers often use informal networks to convey information "unofficially."

Fourth, informal groups help solve problems. They might aid a sick or tired employee or devise activities to deal with boredom. Quite often, such group problem solving helps the organization—for example, when co-workers tell nonproductive employees to "shape up." But these groups can also reduce an organization's effectiveness—for example, when they pressure new employees to reduce their efforts so the group's normal standards will not be called into question.

Beyond these four functions, informal groups may act as **reference groups**—groups that we identify with and compare ourselves to. A middle manager's reference group, for example, might be higher-level managers. Because people tend to model themselves after their reference groups, these groups have an important influence on organizational life.[7]

Informal groups can have a positive or negative influence on employees. For example, when employees are *not* informed about matters that directly affect them, the "grapevine"—the informal communication system all organizations have for circulating both true and false rumors—goes into overdrive, lowering morale among workers and causing them to set up barriers to any change that seems to threaten their job security. Many corporations, such as Ford and GM, have introduced new team-oriented approaches on the assembly line so that informal group goals might more nearly mirror formal group goals.

■ CHARACTERISTICS OF GROUPS

COORDINATED RESOURCE
See Study Guide Self-Learning Exercise 17, "Group Characteristics."

COORDINATED RESOURCE
See *Management Live!* Reading 8.3, "Who Needs a Boss?".

task role The specific role within a group performed by the leader, whether formal or informal.

group-building and -maintenance role The group leader's specific function to fulfill the group's social needs by encouraging solidarity feelings.

COORDINATED RESOURCE
Use Transparency 117, Stages of Group Development.

COORDINATED RESOURCE
The Application Exercise for Chapter 17 found in the Lecture Extras supplement asks students to read and comment on the group dynamics classic "Banana Time."

COORDINATED RESOURCE
See Samaras Case 4.3, "To Stamp Conformity."

TEACHING TIP
Ask your students if they can identify some norms of groups to which they belong.

The first step in learning to manage groups effectively is to become aware of their characteristics—that is, the way they develop leadership roles, norms, and cohesiveness.

Leadership Roles

The formal leader of a group is, of course, appointed or elected. Informal leaders, on the other hand, tend to emerge gradually as group members interact. The man or woman who speaks up more than the others, who offers more and better suggestions than anyone else, or who gives direction to the group's activities usually becomes the informal leader. Even in formal groups, such a self-confident, assertive individual may develop into a rival of the formally chosen leader, thereby weakening the leader's hold on group members.[8]

As we discussed in Chapter 16, both formal and informal leaders play two basic roles. In the **task role,** the leader directs the group toward completion of the activities it is seeking to accomplish. A sales manager's task role, for example, would include hiring and firing personnel, assigning territories, and supervising the training of new sales force members. In the **group-building and -maintenance role,** the leader tries to fulfill the group's social needs by encouraging feelings of solidarity. For example, a sales manager who helps settle some non–work-related dispute between salespeople is acting in a maintenance role. Proper exercise of this role enables the leader to keep members attached to the group over extended periods of time.

The ideal group leader plays both roles, enabling the group to perform with a high degree of effectiveness. In practice, however, few leaders are able to perform both roles equally well, so a second person is needed to close the gap by taking over the neglected function (usually the maintenance role).

Group Norms

Over time, group members form norms—expectations about how they and the other members will behave. Some of these norms are carried over from society in general, such as dressing "properly" for work or showing up on time. Others are particular to the group and its special goals, such as questioning "traditional ideas" in a task group charged with launching a new product.

When an individual breaks with group norms, the other group members will probably pressure that individual to conform. Methods of enforcing conformity range from gentle ridicule to criticism, sarcasm, ostracism, and even physical harassment for serious violations, such as being a "rate buster" on the assembly line.[9]

Conforming to norms can be extremely useful; it answers many questions about how we should behave toward one another on a day-to-day basis, and thus frees us to concentrate on other tasks. But conformity can be negative if it stifles initiative and innovation, holding back the group's performance. Solomon Asch showed this negative power in a classic set of experiments.

Asch told his subjects he was simply testing their visual judgment. People in a group were shown one card with lines of varying lengths and then asked to say out loud, one by one, which of the lines was the same length as a single line on a comparison card. The lines were in fact drawn so that the correct response was obvious. (See Fig. 17-2.) What Asch did not say was that all but one person in the group was working with him. Their task was to give the same wrong answer and then see what the one real subject said. On about 35 percent of the trials, the unwitting subject conformed and gave the wrong answer—even though the correct answer was obvious. However, if even one of Asch's confederates failed to follow the majority, the subject's tendency to conform dropped noticeably.[10]

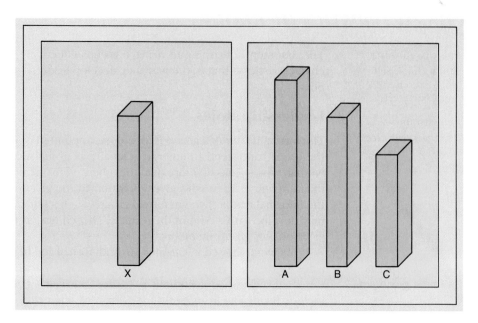

FIGURE 17-2 Cards Such as Those Used in Asch's Social Conformity Experiment

Asch's experiments are not the only ones demonstrating the power of norms and conformity pressures. Recall Stanley Milgram's "Yale Experiments," in which individuals' fear of harming a "learner" were not as strong as their need to *obey* an authority figure—an important norm in our society (see Chapter 12). For another disturbing example of conformity's negative side, see the Ethics in Management box.

What do these findings mean for the manager who wants to bring out the *best* in a work group? First, you must realize that as manager you will be in a good position to set norms that discourage too much conformity. You can do this by what you do (for example, by questioning assumptions), by what you say (perhaps you can begin each meeting by stressing the importance of independent thinking), and by rewarding innovation over conformity. You yourself can be innovative. For example, at Coloroll Inc., CEO John Ashcroft gave each employee a mug imprinted with ten cost-cutting questions they should consider in day-to-day actions.[11] Above all, the manager's goal is to communicate norms that will channel the inevitable group pressures in constructive directions.

Group Cohesiveness

cohesiveness The degree of solidarity and positive feelings held by individuals toward their group.

The solidarity, or **cohesiveness,** of a group is an important indicator of how much influence the group has over its individual members. The more cohesive the group— the more strongly members feel about belonging to it—the greater its influence. If the members of a group feel strongly attached to it, they are not likely to violate its norms.

Highly cohesive groups often have less tension and hostility and fewer misunderstandings than less cohesive groups do.[12] Studies have also found that cohesive groups tend to produce more uniform output than less cohesive groups, which often have problems with communication and cooperation.[13] When cooperation is especially vital—for instance, in meeting strategic goals—managers have four ways to improve cohesiveness: introduce competition, increase interpersonal attraction, increase interaction, and create common goals and common fates for employees.

INTRODUCE COMPETITION. As we saw in Chapter 14, conflict with outside individuals or other groups increases group cohesiveness. With this factor in mind, GE has

ETHICS IN MANAGEMENT

The "Authority of Violence"

"Torturing became a job. If the officers told you to beat, you beat. . . . You never thought you could do otherwise." Such is the recollection of a young soldier who was discharged from the army after serving a hitch as an official torturer for the Greek military regime. He had been systematically trained in the arts of obedience, desensitization, and brutality, but he had originally been selected for his job because he was judged to be psychologically and intellectually well-adjusted. By most accounts, he—and others in the elite torturer corps in which he worked—demonstrated normal, emotionally stable behavior after hours, when the workday of brutalizing other human beings was done. In 1976, when psychologist Molly Harrower presented a panel of personality assessment experts with the psychological test results of eight Nazi war criminals and eight healthy Americans, these experts could not sort them out with any certainty.

Both fact and research suggest strongly that torturers, rather than being hereditary or social deviants, are usually ordinary people who submit to what psychologists call the "authority of violence" under the right circumstances. These circumstances include the powerful norms and socialization processes that can be exercised by groups. In 1973, three psychologists at Stanford University—Craig Haney, Philip Zimbardo, and W. Curtis Banks—conducted an elaborate experiment to examine this hypothesis. Recruiting from newspaper ads, the scientists interviewed and tested numerous applicants before selecting 24 males—all between the ages of 17 and 30—whom they judged to be equally psychologically normal and socially well-adjusted. The group was *randomly* divided into "prisoners" and "guards," and all of the volunteers were informed as to the precise nature of the experiment. One Sunday morning, the "prisoners" were rounded up by local police, properly booked, and delivered to the "Stanford County Prison"—a complete and detailed prison environment built in a university building basement. They were stripped, given prison uniforms, and assigned barren steel-barred cells; the "guards" were given more comfortable quarters and a recreation area.

An experiment designed to last two weeks was terminated after just six days. "Prisoners," who were referred to only by ID numbers and dressed so as to be "deindividuated," had been stripped of most day-to-day civil rights, and although physical punishment had been prohibited, they soon began to show signs of dramatic emotional change, including "acute anxiety" and a passivity verging on complete servility; they became extremely distressed and even physically ill. Some of the "guards," meanwhile, seemed almost exhilarated by the experience. They reinforced their roles with "creative cruelty and harassment," substituting verbal aggression—threats and insults—for the prohibited physical violence.

Afterward, some "guards" expressed a combination of excitement and dismay over their experience of group authority. "It was degrading," recalled one. "They abused each other because I told them to. No one questioned my authority at all." Others reflected with distress at having witnessed the darker sides of their own personalities: "When I was doing it," said one "guard," "I didn't feel regret. . . . Only afterwards . . . did it begin to dawn on me that this was a part of me I hadn't known before."

Certainly, the researchers—and the participants—learned some disturbing things about *individual* human behavior. But they also confirmed some alarming suspicions about *group* behavior. An expressly mock situation had been established between two groups. Not only did the simulated situation rapidly become socially real in the minds of both groups—though it was totally different from situations they had known all their lives—but the members of each group readily assumed the roles expected of them as group members. Moreover, whenever anyone deviated from expected group norms, he was quickly suppressed by escalating tactics of pressure to conform. Individual inclination and a lifetime of emotional normalcy had succumbed to the pressures of authority and conformity with alarming quickness and thoroughness.

Sources: Craig Haney, Philip Zimbardo, and W. Curtis Banks, "Interpersonal Dynamics in a Simulated Prison," *International Journal of Criminology and Penology* 1 (1973):69–97; Molly Harrower, "Were Hitler's Henchmen Mad?" *Psychology Today,* July 1976, pp. 76–80; and Janice T. Gibson and Mika Haritos-Fatouros, "The Education of a Torturer," *Psychology Today,* November 1986, pp. 50–58.

Building Group Cohesiveness. Believing that special events inspire enthusiasm among his employees, Convex Computer CEO Robert Paluck complied with employee suggestions that he dive into 72 gallons of iced raspberry Jell-O at the 1990 annual summer picnic. In years past, Paluck has paid quarterly profit sharing in silver dollars—every employee gets the same amount—and provided cruises for workers designated top performers by their co-workers.

COORDINATED RESOURCE
Acumen: Note that the Approval and Affiliation scales are closely related on the *Acumen* clock.

TEACHING TIP
Ask your students to think of groups to which they belong and examples of how attractiveness and cohesiveness are enhanced or destroyed within these groups.

task interdependence
The extent to which a group's work requires its members to interact with one another.

sense of potency Collective belief of a group that it can be effective.

outcome interdependence The degree to which the work of a group has consequences felt by all its members.

developed a new program to train managers in the creation and leadership of competitive work teams.[14] Meanwhile, at Nintendo, the company that brought us Super Mario Brothers, Creative Director Shiegeru Miyamoto often encourages creativity by dividing his 200 designers into opposing teams.[15]

INCREASE INTERPERSONAL ATTRACTION. People tend to join groups whose members they identify with or admire. Thus, an organization may want to begin by trying to attract employees who share certain key values. Rosenbluth Travel, winner of a Tom Peters award as Service Company of 1990, uses its advertisements and unique interviewing techniques, such as an impromptu baseball game, to discover associates who share a concern for consideration and service. More importantly, Rosenbluth follows through with training, seminars, and policies that foster pride in meeting the common organizational goal of providing outstanding service.[16]

INCREASE INTERACTION. Obviously, we cannot like everyone we work with, but increased interaction can improve camaraderie and communication. Corporations such as Tandem Computers and Genentech, a biotechnology firm, hold regular beer parties to which all employees are invited. At Merle Norman Cosmetics, management sponsors Saturday night movies and serves ice cream at a 1920s-style movie emporium.[17] In Huntsville, Alabama, Goldstar of America, Inc., a South Korean subsidiary of Lucky-Goldstar noted for its success in encouraging parallel production teams to compete against one another, occasionally closes down its plant early for volleyball games in which employees can meet one another in a spirit of camaraderie as well as good-natured competition.[18]

CREATE COMMON GOALS AND COMMON FATES. Gregory Shea and Richard Guzzo have proposed that a group's effectiveness is a function of three variables: task interdependence, potency, and outcome interdependence. (See Fig. 17-3.)[19] **Task interdependence** is the extent to which a group's work requires its members to interact with one another. A high level of task interdependence increases the group's **sense of potency,** "the collective belief of a group that it can be effective." **Outcome interdependence** is the degree to which the consequences of the group's work are felt by all the group's members.

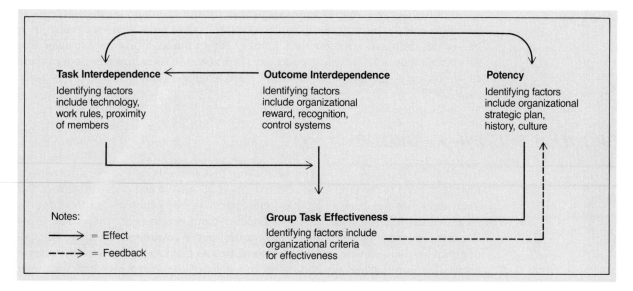

FIGURE 17-3 Determinants of Work-Group Effectiveness

Source: Gregory P. Shea and Richard A. Guzzo, "Group Effectiveness: What Really Matters?" *Sloan Management Review* 27 (Spring 1987):26. Copyright © 1987 by the Sloan Management Review Association. All rights reserved.

Shea and Guzzo further explain how astute managers can create successful groups. Managers must first give each group a "charter"—a clear and achievable set of objectives. A strategic planning group, for example, might be chartered to devise a five-year company plan. Because groups should be given flexibility in arranging their own affairs, the manager should "concentrate on getting the charter right and not on details of how a group organizes itself." The members of the group should decide how much task interdependence their work requires. However, the members must believe the organization has given them sufficient resources—skills, money, flexibility—to fulfill the charter.

In addition, managers must strive to create a sense of outcome interdependence. If the members of a group do not share some common fate, they will have little

ILLUSTRATIVE CASE STUDY

CONTINUED

The Team Taurus Approach to Management at Ford

Ford used a variety of techniques in implementing Team Taurus. First of all, there were a number of types of groups at work. The union was a formal group that had clear guidelines of its own and had to agree to any changes Ford wanted. In addition, the Taurus group was a clearly identified, formal task force with a specified leader, Lew Veraldi. Finally, and perhaps most importantly, an informal group emerged during the design and production of the car itself—because Team Taurus was really all of the peo-ple who worked on the car, from factory-maintenance people to high-powered design engineers. By setting a clear task—namely, "being better than the best"— Veraldi and other Ford managers were able to keep the attention of these various groups focused on the over-all goal of the project. By giving the groups clearly mea-surable goals, Ford let their members see results and improvements as they happened. As a result, a feel-ing of success and satisfaction, rather than failure and uncertainty, predominated throughout the project.

sense of belonging. Group bonuses or peer evaluation can help create this sense of common fate. Rewards do not have to take the form of money; in fact, recognition can be as strong or stronger than money. For example, a group of managers at Honeywell won a $100 million contract. Their reward? Their manager bought them all ice cream cones. Petty, perhaps, but many engineers still have the photo taken that day.[20]

■ PROBLEM SOLVING IN GROUPS

TEACHING TIP
Develop a problem that your class can work both as individuals and in a group. Compare the amount of time and the "creativity/effectiveness" of the solution(s). The "Lost on the Moon" or "Lost in the Desert" exercises are good examples of this.

In earlier chapters, we focused on *individual* problem solving and the sorts of skills managers need to develop to be effective problem solvers and decision makers. But many decisions are made in groups—either because the problems are too large for an individual decision or because they concern many departments within a business. We therefore need to take a closer look at the special advantages and disadvantages of group problem solving, as well as at some factors that can be assets or liabilities in group decision making, depending on the skills of the group members and their leader.

Advantages of Group Problem Solving

Group problem solving has four major advantages over individual problem solving. First, groups can suggest more approaches to problem solving. Generally, the more approaches that are presented, the better the chance of finding the best one.

Second, groups bring more knowledge to most problems than any individual could. For example, a design engineer might be the best person to develop a blueprint for a new machine, but an assembly-line worker would probably have a better idea of how co-workers would use it in production.

Third, group problem solving increases the chances of successful implementation by including all concerned parties in the decision-making process. When people

Group Problem Solving. When Mobil hired Bernard Brennan as chief executive of Montgomery Ward, they gave him three years to turn around the ailing retailer. Convinced that he needed to take quick action to overcome the stifling bureaucracy, Brennan formed an executive committee of seven trusted colleagues to re-create Ward as a chain of discount specialty stores selling name-brand goods displayed as in specialty stores like the Limited and the Gap.

help to solve a problem, they see the solution as their own and have a personal stake in making it work.

Finally, people who have helped to make a decision are more likely to know and understand that decision and its outcome. When a manager makes a decision unilaterally, it must be relayed to those who will have to carry it out, and it may become garbled in the process. When those who must execute the decision have participated in making it, the chances of communication failure are greatly reduced.

Disadvantages of Group Problem Solving

The group problem-solving process has at least three major disadvantages. First, groups tend to be too quick to limit the alternative solutions they will consider. Although members may initially toss out a number of alternatives, they tend to focus on the most traditional solutions or the ones that are presented most skillfully.[21] Other, more unconventional, but potentially better, solutions may well be ignored.

Second, groups tend to be dominated by formal or informal leaders who may or may not have good problem-solving skills. Extroverted and socially assertive people—especially those whose past successes or friendly relations have given them self-confidence—tend to dominate discussions.[22] Some of these people come into the group secretly committed to a solution that will benefit them. Or perhaps they hope to score "points" with management. In the worst case, they become committed to winning the debate rather than to finding the best solution. If their monologues are not checked, others may become frustrated and "tune out"—or start playing exactly the same game.[23]

Third, group members sometimes become victims of "groupthink"—the tendency to conform uncritically to group judgments, even when those judgments have clear dangers. Groupthink encourages committee members to give up their individual responsibility to think objectively and critically about all proposals that come before them.[24] Because no one member feels responsible for the committee's ultimate decision, everyone is less careful. Among the many historical examples of groupthink is the thinking that went into the fateful launching of the space shuttle *Challenger* on the morning of January 28, 1986.[25]

Key Factors in Group Decision Making: Assets or Liabilities

FOR DISCUSSION

What are the advantages and disadvantages of using groups instead of individuals for getting work done?

Generally speaking, five factors in group decision making can be *either* assets or liabilities to group effectiveness. First, the clash of ideas within a group can promote both creativity and innovation on the one hand and resentment and ill will on the other. Skillful leaders use disagreements to generate creative solutions, proposing, for example, that "Both ideas look good; how about a solution that incorporates both?"

The second factor is that group members often have different goals and perspectives. A group might, for example, be considering ways to increase profits from an unsuccessful product line. The sales manager, regarding the problem as a failure to break into specific markets, suggests more aggressive sales and promotion tactics; the controller, however, believes that costs are out of control and that sales commissions should be cut. Before solutions to the problem are proposed, the leader must get the members to agree on the essence of the problem and desired goals by citing evidence offered by both advocates. If the leader succeeds in doing this, the conflict is an asset; if he or she fails, the conflict may become a liability.

In the third place, despite popular assumptions to the contrary, groups often make riskier decisions than individuals do.[26] This tendency is referred to as the "risky shift" by management writers.[27]

Fourth, group decisions take longer to make (and are often more expensive) than decisions made by individuals. But because group decisions are frequently more sound than individual decisions, some experts argue that groups use their time more effectively than individuals do. When a decision has to be made quickly, however, a skillful group leader will have to prevent irrelevant or uselessly prolonged discussion. Moreover, common sense tells us there is a difference between decisions resulting from prolonged, indecisive discussion and imperfect compromise and decisions resulting from patient deliberation. The group leader must encourage the group to weigh the value of the time that they are spending.

Finally, it is rare for all members of a group to start out supporting the same solution to a problem, so it is inevitable that some people will have to change their original positions. This necessity can be an asset or a liability, depending on whose mind is changed. If those with the most creative or practical ideas are induced to change, the group winds up with a mediocre decision. It is the responsibility of the group leader to get the group to evaluate both the creativity and practicality of every proposal or position.

■MAKING FORMAL GROUPS EFFECTIVE

Making Formal Groups Effective. Compaq Computer Corp. Founder and President Joseph "Rod" Canion fosters consensus management, in which teams of people work together to make critical decisions. A team leader functions mainly to keep group members on track.

COORDINATED RESOURCE
See Study Guide Problem Exercise 17, "Task Forces and Committees."

THOUGHT PROVOKER
Could any organization or group ever function effectively without committees? Why or why not?

Many managers joke—or moan—about committees as big time-wasters. "No committee ever painted a *Mona Lisa,*" these rugged individualists grouse, "or sculpted a *Pietà.*" In reality, a committee or task force is often the best way to pool the expertise of different members of the organization and then channel their efforts toward effective problem solving and decision making. In addition, these formal groups let members learn how their work affects others, increasing all members' willingness and ability to coordinate their work for the organization's good. Also, committees can serve as "incubators" for young executives, teaching them to think beyond the needs and concerns of their own work unit. Even if formal groups did not offer these advantages, they are an inescapable part of business life. As long ago as 1960, Rollie Tillman concluded from a survey that "94 percent of the firms with more than 10,000 employees reported having formal committees." Furthermore, managers spent from 50 to 80 percent of their time serving on committees.[28] Thus, the real challenge is not to avoid formal groups. Rather, it is to learn how to use groups more effectively. (To see how some Scandinavian countries have done this, read the International Management box.)

Guidelines for Committees

Because committees differ greatly in their functions and activities, these guidelines will not be appropriate for all cases. For example, a highly directive committee responsible for communicating instructions from top management to subordinates should be managed differently from a committee whose major task is to solve complex managerial problems. The following suggestions apply to problem-solving committees, which must be managed flexibly if their members' skills are to be used most effectively.

FORMAL PROCEDURES. Several formal procedures are useful in helping committees operate effectively.[29]

❑ The committee's goals should be clearly defined, preferably in writing. This will focus the committee's activities and reduce discussion of what the committee is supposed to do.

❑ The committee's authority should be specified. Is the committee merely to investigate, advise, and recommend, or is it authorized to implement decisions?

❑ The optimum size of the committee should be determined. With fewer than 5

INTERNATIONAL MANAGEMENT

Some Lessons in Scandinavian Management

One of the challenges in making formal groups effective is ensuring that everyone has a chance to contribute and participate. After all, no one can predict who will offer the best ideas. Yet the idea of participative management is still "foreign" to many American managers.

This is not so in the Scandinavian countries, especially Sweden, where worker participation is not a temporary experiment or an ad hoc measure. Instead, corporate accomplishments are regarded as the results of the combined creative and decision-making talents of all participants. Management applications among Scandinavian businesses tend to be based on respect for individual dignity and contribution and tend to ensure tangible rewards for individual contributions to the effectiveness of the group. Some analysts suggest that this orientation is a significant factor in the ability of such companies as Scandinavian Airline System (SAS) and Volvo to gain increasing competitive edges over their international competition.

Both SAS and Volvo are models of participatory management. The central theme of SAS's management approach is a strong belief in the ability and integrity of front-line personnel, who are entrusted with a great deal of responsibility in servicing the needs of customers. The role of management is to assist the front-line people who are directly in charge of day-to-day customer relations—not to dictate top-level policy to people whose contact with customers is immediate and practical. Volvo, which during the 1960s and early 1970s shared with its American counterparts problems of employee dissatisfaction and alienation on the assembly line, has developed a successful sociotechnical-system design that eliminates the assembly-line technique dating back to Henry Ford in favor of small teams of workers who rotate assignments and perform their jobs with considerable autonomy. Through this participatory approach, management and the company's unions have come closer together in their basic values and in their ideas about how to improve overall corporate effectiveness.

Can American companies reorient themselves and successfully manage according to such models? Analysts suggest they can—if they adopt the premise that, by and large, the work force consists of intelligent people who want to do a good job. Without an acceptance of this underlying premise, they argue, American experiments in participatory management will probably continue to produce mixed results.

Sources: Ron Zemke, "Scandinavian Management—A Look to the Future," *Management Review* 77, no. 7 (1988):44–47; "Kalmar: Ten Years Later," *Via Volvo,* Vol. 6 (1984):14–19; Pehr G. Gyllenhammar, *People at Work* (Reading, Mass.: Addison-Wesley, 1977).

COORDINATED RESOURCE

See Samaras Exercise 4.3, "Commit the Committee."

members, the advantages of group work may be diminished. Potential resources increase as group size increases. While size will vary according to circumstances, the ideal number of committee members for many tasks ranges from 5 to 10. With more than 10 to 15 members, a committee usually becomes unwieldy, so that it is difficult for each member to influence the work.[30]

❑ A chairperson should be selected on the basis of his or her ability to run an efficient meeting—that is, to encourage the participation of all committee members, to keep the committee meetings from getting bogged down in irrelevancies, and to see that the necessary paperwork gets done. (Appointing a permanent secretary to handle communications is often useful.)

❑ The agenda and all supporting material for the meeting should be distributed to members before the meeting to permit them to prepare in advance. This makes it more likely they will be ready with informed contributions and will stick to the point.

❑ Meetings should start and end on time. The time when they will end should be announced at the outset.

GUIDELINES FOR LEADERS. Committee leadership is a key factor in the successful outcome of the committee's work. The leader is responsible for the membership of the committee, for the satisfactory completion of its assigned tasks, and for his or her own leadership behavior.

The leader should control not only the size of the committee but also the qualifications of its members. Are they the right people for this committee's work? Do they have the needed skills? If not, can others be added? Are some members unnecessary? Can time be saved by removing them? For many committees, the membership is fixed, so the chairperson has little control over who becomes a member. Even then, however, it may be possible to bring in special people with needed skills to provide assistance.

The leader must also screen the work assigned to the committee. Many committees are ineffective because they try to grapple with problems for which they have neither the expertise, the organizational power, the required information, nor the responsibility. The leader can save time and concentrate the committee's efforts by detecting inappropriate work at the outset and refusing it.

A committee leader should be aware of his or her own preferred decision-making style and the leadership style that is most suitable for the committee's task. Leaders should make certain that the two essential leadership roles—task and maintenance—noted earlier in this chapter are provided, either by themselves or by other committee members.

To manage discussions effectively, Anthony Jay recommends that leaders follow these seven rules: (1) control the garrulous; (2) draw out the silent; (3) protect the weak; (4) encourage the clash of ideas; (5) watch out for the suggestion-squashing reflex; (6) come to the most senior people last; and (7) close on a note of achievement.[31]

GUIDELINES FOR MEMBERS. For Jay Hall, the group decision process has one basic aim: to resolve conflicts creatively by reaching a consensus. He defines consensus not as unanimity but as a condition in which each member accepts the group's decisions because they seem most logical and feasible. Hall offers five guidelines to help group members achieve consensus.[32]

1. State your position as clearly and logically as you can—but do not argue for it. Listen to and ponder the other members' reactions before you push your point.

2. If discussion between some members gets bogged down on any one point, do not treat it as a win-or-lose proposition. Instead, seek out the next most acceptable alternative.

3. Do not yield on any point just for the sake of harmony. Accept a solution only if it is based on sound logic.

4. Shun techniques that bypass logic for the sake of reducing conflict (such as majority vote, flipping a coin, bargaining, and averaging). When a dissenting member finally agrees to go along with the group, don't make up for this by letting the yielder have his or her own way on some other point.

5. Root out differences of opinion and pull everyone into the discussion. Only by airing the widest possible range of opinions and drawing in all information can the group come up with high-quality solutions.

Working with college students and with management executives, Hall found that groups trained to apply this five-point process did consistently better in solving problems than untrained groups. A trained group frequently outperformed even its best individual member—an outcome he described as "synergy." **Synergy** may be defined as "a condition in which the whole is greater than the sum of its parts." Hall's guidelines encourage the maximum participation of group members and the search for the best possible solutions. They are most useful for committees working on a task that requires an ingenious or creative solution.

synergy A condition in which the whole is greater than the sum of its parts.

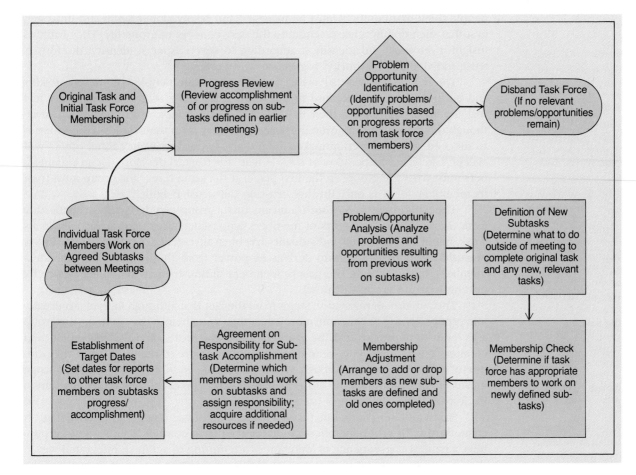

FIGURE 17-4 Task Force Work Flow

Source: Copyright © 1982 by James A. F. Stoner. Used by permission.

Special Procedures for Task Forces

Although the guidelines for committee leaders and members also apply to task forces, formal procedures may be less appropriate here. Also, much of the task force's work is done *outside* meetings, which are mainly used to define problems and opportunities and to assign subtasks to be accomplished between meetings.[33]

Figure 17-4 indicates the work flow of a task force meeting. Past progress is briefly reviewed, and then the current situation is described and analyzed in terms of its problems and opportunities. Based on this analysis, new outside-the-meeting subtasks are defined. Next, the task force membership is reviewed for its appropriateness to the current roster of subtasks, and arrangements are made to add or drop members as needed. Finally, subtask responsibility is allocated among task force members, and target dates are established for subtask completion.

This task force management procedure is well suited to complex, ambiguous problems of major scale, such as reorganizing a company's entire sales force or developing a new generation of computer terminals. There are, however, a number of other ways to manage task forces and their work.

Conflict Within Groups

Conflicts emerge not only *between* groups but also *within* them. In an important book entitled *Paradoxes of Group Life,* Kenwyn Smith and David Berg have proposed a new way to understand such intragroup (within-group) conflicts. Most

CLASS COMMENT

Executive retreats are often used to teach managers to work as a team. (*Business Month,* September 1990, p. 5)

COORDINATED RESOURCE

See *Management Live!* Reading 8.1, "Word Teams Muffle Labor's Voice."

COORDINATED RESOURCE

Use Transparency 120, Conflict and Organizational Performance.

COORDINATED RESOURCE
See Samaras Exercise 3.5,
"Identify the Conflict."

COORDINATED RESOURCE
See DuBose Reading #25,
"'Conflict Management'
and 'Conflict Resolution'
Are Not Synonymous
Terms."

HERE'S AN EXAMPLE
AT&T is trying an experiment with its salespeople, who are outfitted with a portable office (a seven-pound notebook computer, modem, portable printer, and cellular phone). AT&T is monitoring the scheme to see how workers respond to their new environment. Employees fear the loss of social relationships. (*Business Week*, 3/18/91, p. 124)

COORDINATED RESOURCE
See Samaras Reading "A Strategy for Managing Conflict in Complex Organizations."

people think that conflicts must be managed and resolved, but Smith and Berg suggest that such conflicts are essential to the very concept of group life. They call this insight a *paradox* and identify it according to seven aspects: identity, disclosure, trust, individuality, authority, regression, and creativity.[34]

The paradox of *identity* is that groups must unite people with different skills and outlooks precisely because they are different, while those people usually feel that the group diminishes their individuality. The paradox of *disclosure* is that although the members of a group must disclose what is on their minds if the group is to succeed, fear of rejection makes them disclose only what they think others will accept. Likewise, the paradox of *trust* is that "for trust to develop in a group, members must trust the group" in the first place; at the same time, "the group must trust its members, for it is only through trusting that trust is built."

The paradox of *individuality* means that a group can derive its strength only from the individual strengths of members who, when they participate fully in its work, might feel that their individuality has been threatened. Similarly, the paradox of *authority* is that the group derives its power from the power of its individual members, but in joining the group, members diminish their individual power by putting it at the group's disposal.

The paradox of *regression* stems from the fact that although individuals usually join groups hoping to "become more" than they were before they joined, "the group asks them to be less so that the group can become more." In this sense, the group counters the individual desire to progress with pressure to regress. Finally, the paradox of *creativity* is that although groups must change in order to survive, change means the destruction of the old as well as the creation of the new. Thus, any refusal to destroy limits the group's creative potential.

Smith and Berg conclude that if a group cannot use conflict to its advantage, it cannot grow: "If group members could learn to treat conflict as endemic to groupness, a natural consequence of 'differences attempting to act in an integrated way,'" they would understand that group conflict is "just in the nature of things, like the wetness of water and the warmth of sunlight."

ILLUSTRATIVE CASE STUDY

WRAP-UP

The Team Taurus Approach to Management at Ford

Even though Ford has been revitalized, the jury is still out on the Team Taurus approach. The Taurus has experienced major repair problems, and Ford has been forced to carry through on its "quality is job 1" all the way to its dealers. Are the repair problems the result of "groupthink" in the Taurus design? Or of too much change made too quickly and perhaps too optimistically? Can the Taurus approach work for Jaguar and Ford Europe? Most importantly, can the people at Ford continue to manage the paradoxes of group life? These are just a few of the questions that managers at Ford need to ask continually as they manage and modify group processes in the interest of successful organizational enterprises. ∎

■ SUMMARY

Organizations have both formal and informal groups. Formal groups are created deliberately by managers and charged with carrying out specific tasks. The most prevalent types of formal groups are command groups, committees, and task forces.

Informal groups develop whenever people come into contact regularly—with or without management's encouragement. Informal groups perform four functions: (1) they maintain and strengthen group norms and values—which may differ from management's; (2) they provide members with social satisfaction and security; (3) they help members communicate; and (4) they help members solve problems.

All groups share at least three characteristics. First, they have one or more leaders who perform task roles as well as group-building and -maintenance roles. Second, they have group norms and pressure members to conform to those norms. Third, they have some degree of cohesiveness, which can be enhanced by introducing competition, increasing interpersonal attraction, expanding the opportunities for interaction, and creating common goals and fates for all group members.

Groups are better at problem solving than individuals because they suggest more approaches than individuals can and bring more information and expertise to bear on a problem. In addition, group problem solving improves the chances a decision will be implemented successfully, since the group members helped make it. By the same token, group problem solving simplifies the task of communicating the decision to others. Disadvantages of group problem solving are that groups tend to be too quick to limit the alternatives they consider, they can be dominated by a few members, and they are prone to "groupthink." Some factors—such as the clash of ideas and the different perceptions of members—can be advantages or disadvantages, depending on how the leader handles them.

Managerial skill in guiding, but not dominating, group activities is an important factor in achieving success in group work. Suggestions for effective results include formal procedures for meetings and guidelines for group leaders and members. Although conflicts sometimes disrupt groups, Smith and Berg suggest that conflict is normal and natural when different people attempt to act in an integrated way. Groups that understand this process can use their conflicts creatively.

■ REVIEW QUESTIONS

1. What are the two basic types of groups in organizations? Which type of group do you think is more important? Why?
2. What are reference groups? Why is it important for managers to be aware of them? Can you identify your own reference groups?
3. Why do you think informal groups emerge in organizations? What organizational needs do they serve? What member needs do they serve?
4. What are the two leadership roles of formal and informal group leaders?
5. How do group members try to enforce conformity?
6. What is the relationship between group cohesiveness and group performance? How can group cohesiveness be increased?
7. On what bases would a manager decide whether to use individual or group problem solving?
8. What are the possible advantages and disadvantages of group decision making and problem solving?
9. According to Shea and Guzzo, how can managers create effective groups?
10. What formal procedures help make a committee effective? How can leaders and members help make a committee effective?
11. What are the "paradoxes of group life" as seen by Smith and Berg? Why do they feel that intragroup conflict is inevitable and basically good?

CASE STUDY

The New-Products Group

Karen Smith looked at her calendar for the day. It was Thursday, and the report she had been working on was due tomorrow. That meant the group would have to meet today to hammer out its recommendations and presentation. She was not looking forward to an afternoon spent devoted to this task.

The group had been formed to design the market introduction of the company's newest product. Since the company had never before marketed a retail product, no one was quite sure what to expect. Karen and her group were charged with producing recommendations for advertising and promotion, product distribution and rollout, and anything else they thought important. After the plan was approved, implementation would probably fall to Karen, although it could be given to another member of the Marketing Department. It was a large undertaking, and Karen and four other people had given it most of their time for the last few months.

Right from the start, the group had not worked well together. This had not surprised Karen: The personalities were strong all around, and she knew at the outset that there would be some personality conflicts. All four group members were on the same level in the company, and no one had been designated the leader. Therefore, the early meetings were mostly a struggle for leadership.

Karen realized very early that Ben had a deep-seated belief that women had no place in business—and certainly were not capable of leading men. Even though other women had warned her, the venom in some of his comments had come as a surprise. Ben clearly thought he was the only one capable of leading the group: After all, had he not just finished four years in the Navy? James was only slightly more open-minded than Ben. The two of them often formed a team, and once they had come to a joint decision, it was impossible to get them to consider anyone else's recommendations. Charles was more willing to listen to others, but he had a tendency to show up armed with so much data that the group often spent all its time trying to understand how the data had been derived rather than making decisions. All in all, Karen was quite frustrated at both the group's slow progress and the tense atmosphere that pervaded their meetings.

They were nowhere near finished with their plan, but they would have to present their recommendations tomorrow morning. She knew that senior management was expecting a full report, and she was not very confident that she could deliver one. How would the group members manage to work together well enough at today's meeting to agree on a set of recommendations? The atmosphere at past meetings had been so poor that Karen shuddered to think what would happen when the stress of a deadline was added. She wondered if she could control the show of tempers that usually marked their gatherings, the last of which had dissolved into a shouting match between herself and Ben when she had tried, as tactfully as possible, to suggest that one of his ideas for a promotional campaign was impractical. He had quickly dropped the discussion and moved to a more personal level: accusing her of undermining his authority by trying to imply that she, a mere woman, knew more than he did. He had even said she could not be a true Christian, since any Christian woman would be at home raising children. Her faith was important to her, but she never considered it related to her job performance. It certainly wasn't something she was willing to discuss in the group.

She sighed. It was going to be a very long day. Should she call the other group members to set the time, or should she let one of them call her? How should she act toward Ben? What could she do to keep things on track in preparation for tomorrow's presentation? All she really wanted to do was tell her boss she was sick and go home.

Source: Written by Rebecca Villa and R. Edward Freeman, based on actual situations. Prepared especially for this book.

Case Questions

1. Why is Karen's group having problems?
2. Can you use the Shea-Guzzo model to give Karen a better idea of why the group is dysfunctional?
3. What should Karen do now?

Building Group Spirit at Toyota

There were days when Bill Constantino didn't know if he would ever actually work at the Toyota Motor Manufacturing plant in Georgetown, Kentucky.

"At times I wondered if it would ever end," Constantino says of Toyota's eight-step employee selection process that took about 15 weeks to complete. "But as I went through the process, I began to feel a real sense of accomplishment. I recognized that Toyota was taking its work force seriously, that the company was going to end up with high-caliber, motivated people."

The application process included work simulations and group problem solving. The system was designed to cull applicants who the company thought would work well in teams. Toyota was also looking for people who could adapt to the concept of *kaizen. Kaizen* is a philosophy of gradual, continuous improvement by every employee.

By insisting on a rigorous application process, Toyota gave potential employees a sense of what it would be like to work for the company, both in terms of what Toyota expected from workers and what it was prepared to do for them. The process also created a sense of unity among applicants that carried over into the plant. And the screening weeded out many potentially unsuitable workers. As a result, employee turnover in Georgetown is less than 5 percent, compared to about 20 percent for most new plants.

The application process was just the first step in Toyota's program to foster teamwork and break down the hierarchy in its plants. Employees are referred to as team members. They work in small groups and have the primary responsibility for production quality. Leaders of these teams were trained at Toyota's plants in Japan.

There are also about 250 Japanese trainers based in Georgetown. To encourage plant team members and trainers to get acquainted, Toyota subsidizes a program of after-hours socializing. Employees participate in decision making about the plant, such as how to schedule overtime or rotate jobs. In many U.S. plants, such decisions are made solely by management.

Toyota relies on American managers in Georgetown, but doesn't offer many of the perks managers are used to in this country. For instance, there are no reserved parking spaces, and senior executives eat lunch in the same cafeteria as assembly-line workers.

Everyone wears the same type of uniform. And there are no corner offices. Instead, managers share large, open work areas. Toyota believes the homogeneity encourages team spirit and cooperation.

Toyota has sought to keep its workers from unionizing the Georgetown plant by claiming that *kaizen* would be less effective if employees were organized. This has led to charges that the company is intent on undercutting American automobile companies, all of which must deal with unionized labor.

Yet Toyota has shown that it can work with unions and still practice its management techniques. In Fremont, California, where Toyota began a joint venture with General Motors in 1984, a contract signed with the United Autoworkers specifies that the company will reduce management salaries and find alternative jobs within the plant for employees before resorting to layoffs.

Not every Japanese technique has translated well. Workers in Fremont, for instance, have criticized Toyota's insistence on publicly displaying attendance records and marking unauthorized absences in red. Despite some glitches, however, most employees say Toyota has worked hard to create a good working climate. "I'm working with a group of people who really participate and engage in creative action," says Bill Constantino, who is now a team leader in the Plastics Section. "Without question, the quality of our people is unmatched."

Sources: Chuck Cosentino, John Allen, and Richard Wellins, "Choosing the Right People," *HR Magazine,* March 1990, pp. 66–70; Louis Kraar, "Japan's Gung-Ho U.S. Car Plants," *Fortune,* January 30, 1989, pp. 98–108; Alex Taylor III, "Why Toyota Keeps Getting Better and Better and Better," *Fortune,* November 19, 1990, pp. 66–79; James B. Treece, "Just What Detroit Needs: 200,000 More Toyotas a Year," *Business Week,* December 10, 1990, p. 29; and Mark A. Fischetti, "Banishing the Necktie," *IEEE Spectrum,* October 1987, pp. 50–52.

Case Questions

1. Why did Toyota use such a strenuous application process to recruit workers for its Georgetown plant?

2. How did the process foster employee cooperation and teamwork?

3. What is the concept of *kaizen* and why is it the key to Toyota's program of employee relations?

4. Do you think Toyota can sustain the initial level of enthusiasm among its Georgetown employees? If so, how?

■ NOTES

[1]See Dorwin Cartwright and Ronald Lippitt, "Group Dynamics and the Individual," *International Journal of Group Psychotherapy* 7, no. 1 (1957):86–102; Linda N. Jewell and H. Joseph Reitz, *Group Effectiveness in Organizations* (Glenview, Ill.: Scott, Foresman, 1983); and Deborah L. Gladstein, "Groups in Context: A Model of Task Group Effectiveness," *Administrative Science Quarterly* 29 (1984):499–517.

[2]See Marvin E. Shaw, *Group Dynamics,* 3rd ed. (New York: McGraw-Hill, 1981).

[3]See Edgar H. Schein, *Organizational Psychology,* 3rd ed. (Englewood Cliffs, N.J.: Prentice Hall, 1980), pp. 146–153.

[4]George Homans, *The Human Group* (New York: Harcourt, 1950).

[5]John P. Wanous, Arnon E. Reichers, and S. D. Malik, "Organizational Socialization and Group Development: Toward an Integrative Perspective," *Academy of Management Review,* 9, no. 4 (1984):678–683.

[6]Keith Davis, *Human Relations at Work,* 2nd ed. (New York: McGraw-Hill, 1962), pp. 235–257, and *Human Behavior at Work: Organizational Behavior,* 6th ed. (New York: McGraw-Hill, 1981), pp. 331–332; and Schein, *Organizational Psychology,* pp. 150–152.

[7]See Dorwin Cartwright and Alvin Zander, eds., *Group Dynamics: Research and Theory,* 3rd ed. (New York: Harper & Row, 1968), p. 53; and Harold H. Kelley, "Two Functions of Reference Groups," in Guy E. Swanson, Theodore Newcomb, and Eugene J. Hartley, eds., *Readings in Social Psychology,* rev. ed. (New York: Holt, 1952), pp. 410–414.

[8]David O. Sears, Jonathan L. Freedman, and Letitia A. Peplau, *Social Psychology,* 5th ed. (Englewood Cliffs, N.J.: Prentice Hall, 1985), pp. 367–368.

[9]Davis C. Feldman, "The Development and Enforcement of Group Norms," *Academy of Management Review* 9, no. 2 (1984):47–53; and Kenneth Bettenhausen and J. Keith Murninghan, "The Emergence of Norms in Competitive Decision-Making Groups," *Administrative Science Quarterly* 30 (1985):350–372.

[10]Solomon E. Asch, "Effects of Group Pressure upon the Modification and Distortions of Judgments," in H. Guetzkow, ed., *Groups, Leadership, and Men* (Pittsburgh: Carnegie Press, 1951); and Asch, "Studies of Independence and Conformity: A Minority of One Against a Unanimous Majority," *Psychological Monographs* 70, no. 9 (September 1956). Subsequent experiments have found specific factors that cause individuals to succumb to group pressure and other factors that reduce conformity. See Sarah Tanford and Steven Penrod, "Social Influence Model: A Formal Integration of Research on Majority and Minority Influence Processes," *Psychological Bulletin* 95, no. 2 (1984):189–225; and Serge Moscovici, "Social Influence and Conformity," in Gardner Lindzey and Elliot Aronson, eds., *Handbook of Social Psychology,* Vol. 2, 3rd ed. (New York: Random House, 1985), Chap. 7.

[11]James A. Belasco, "Teaching the Elephant to Dance," *Success,* July–August 1990, pp. 50–51.

[12]Sears, Freedman, and Peplau, *Social Psychology,* pp. 356–357. See also Robert S. Feldman, *Social Psychology: Theories, Research, and Applications* (New York: McGraw-Hill, 1985); and Steven Penrod, *Social Psychology,* 2nd ed. (Englewood Cliffs, N.J.: Prentice Hall, 1986).

[13]John C. Whitney and Ruthu A. Smith, "Effects of Group Cohesiveness on Attitude Polarization and the Acquisition of Knowledge in a Strategic Planning Context," *Journal of Marketing Research* 20, no. 2 (1983):167–176.

[14]A. Nicholas Komanecky, "Developing New Managers at GE," *Training and Development Journal* 42, no. 6 (1988):62–64.

[15]Susan Moffat, "Can Nintendo Keep Winning?" *Fortune,* November 5, 1990, pp. 131–136.

[16]"Many Happy Returns," *Inc,* October 1990, pp. 30–43.

[17]David L. Kirp and Douglas C. Rice, "Fast Forward—Styles of California Management," *Harvard Business Review* 66, no. 1 (1988):74–83.

[18]Henry Easton, "The Corporate Immigrants," *Nation's Business,* April 1987, pp. 12–19.

[19]Gregory P. Shea and Richard A. Guzzo, "Groups as Human Resources," *Research in Personnel and Human Resources Management* 5 (1987):323–356; Shea and Guzzo, "Group Effectiveness: What Really Matters," *Sloan Management Review* 27 (Spring 1987):25–31. Shea and Guzzo's model is a natural and more modern extension of the classical work of George Homans.

[20]Belasco, "Teaching the Elephant to Dance," pp. 50–51.

[21]L. Richard Hoffman, "Applying Experimental Research on Group Problem Solving to Organizations," *Journal of Applied Behavioral Science* 15, no. 3 (July–August–September 1979):382.

[22]Ibid., pp. 377–378; Donal E. Carlston, "Effects of Pooling Order on Social Influence in Decision-Making Groups," *Sociometry* 40, no. 2 (1977):115–123; and Godfrey M. Hochbaum, "The Relation Between Group Members' Self-Confidence and Their Reactions to Group Pressures to Uniformity," *American Sociological Review* 19, no. 6 (1954):678–687.

[23]Max H. Bazerman, Toni Giuliano, and Alan Appelman, "Escalation of Commitment in Individual and Group Decision Making," *Organizational Behavior and Human Performance* 33, no. 2 (1984):141–152. See also Hoffman, "Applying Experimental Research on Group Problem Solving to Organizations," p. 378.

[24]Irving Janis, *Groupthink: Psychological Studies of Policy Decisions,* 2nd ed. (Boston: Houghton Mifflin, 1982); and Jeanne Longley and Dean G. Pruitt, "Groupthink: A Critique of Janis's Theory," in Ladd Wheeler, ed., *Review of Personality and Social Psychology,* Vol. 1 (Beverly Hills, Calif.: Sage Publications, 1980), pp. 74–93.

[25]A. W. Kruglanski, "Freeze-Think and the Challenger," *Psychology Today,* August 1986, pp. 48–49.

[26]Dorwin Cartwright, "Risk Taking by Individuals and Groups: An Assessment of Research Employing Choice Dilemmas," *Journal of Personality and Social Psychology* 20, no. 3 (1971):361–378, and "Determinants of Scientific Progress: The Case of Research on the Risky Shift," *American Psychologist* 28, no. 3 (1973):222–231.

[27]See James A. F. Stoner, "A Comparison of Individual and Group Decisions Involving Risk," Master's thesis, Massachusetts Institute of Technology, School of Industrial Management, 1961. There have been hundreds of studies published since the first "risky shifts" were demonstrated by Stoner in 1961. In spite of these extensive research efforts, the types of situations in which the phenomenon occurs and the cause and nature of the phenomenon remain a source of lively debate and research. See also James A. F. Stoner, "Risky and Cautious Shifts in Group Decisions: The Influence of Widely Held Values," *Journal of Experimental Social Psychology* 4, no. 4 (1968):442–459; and Russell D. Clark, "Group-Induced Shift toward Risk: A Critical Appraisal," *Psychological Bulletin* 76, no. 4 (1971):251–270.

[28]Rollie Tillman, Jr., "Committees on Trial," *Harvard Business Review* 48, no. 4 (1960):6–7ff.

[29]Cyril O'Donnell, "Ground Rules for Using Committees," *Management Review* 50, no. 10 (1961):63–67. See also Anthony Jay, "How to Run a Meeting."

[30]L. Richard Hoffman and M. Clark, "Participation and Influence in Problem-Solving Groups," in L. Richard Hoffman, ed., *The Group Problem-Solving Process* (New York: Praeger, 1979). See also Philip Yetton and Preston Bottger, "The Relationship Among Group Size, Member Ability, Social Decision Schemes, and Performance," *Organizational Behavior and Human Performance* 32, no. 2 (1983):145–149.

[31]Ibid., pp. 56–57.

[32]Jay Hall, "Decisions, Decisions, Decisions," *Psychology Today,* November 1971, p. 54.

[33]See, for example, Lawrence W. Bass, *Management by Task Forces* (Mount Airy, Md.: Lomond Books, 1975).

[34]Kenwyn K. Smith and David N. Berg, *Paradoxes of Group Life* (San Francisco: Jossey-Bass, 1987); and Smith and Berg, "A Paradoxical Conception of Group Dynamics," *Human Relations* 40, no. 10 (1987):633–658.

COMMUNICATION AND NEGOTIATION

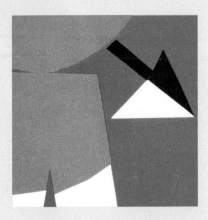

Upon completing this chapter you should be able to:

1. Identify the essential elements of the communication process.

2. Discuss the key elements in a more elaborate model of the communication process.

3. Distinguish between one-way and two-way communication and identify situations in which each is appropriate.

4. Recognize barriers to effective interpersonal communication.

5. Practice techniques for overcoming barriers to interpersonal communication.

6. Explain the four factors that influence organizational communication.

7. Discuss the advantages and disadvantages of various communication networks.

8. Discuss the role of vertical communication in organizations.

9. Discuss ways to overcome organizational barriers to communication.

10. Explain the key elements of the negotiation process and how it can be used to manage conflict.

Paul Rand. Poster for Advertising Typographers' Association of America. Courtesy of the Artist.

ILLUSTRATIVE CASE STUDY

INTRODUCTION

Communication Failures at Bhopal

All the safety features had failed—that much was abundantly clear. What Warren Anderson could not find out was *why*. As CEO of Union Carbide, he needed to know exactly what had happened in Bhopal, India, that night for a number of reasons. He knew that he would have to explain a tragic accident to employees, to government officials in both the United States and India, to the courts, and to the people. Yet he could not get answers to his own preliminary and personal questions. When telephone contact failed to yield answers, Anderson got on a plane and flew to India, where he was immediately placed under house arrest—unable to attend to the very business that had brought him there. His plant managers had also been arrested and were not allowed to talk to anyone. Indian government officials had closed the plant to Union Carbide management in order to prevent "tampering with evidence."

The basic facts that Anderson could not determine on December 3, 1984, were really quite simple. A runaway reaction had occurred in a storage tank of methylisocyanate (MIC), which was used to manufacture a pesticide. The valves on the tank had burst and a cloud of poisonous gas had escaped. Climatic conditions kept the gas from dissipating, and the winds carried it to nearby shantytowns and the populous city of Bhopal, where many people either died in their sleep or woke and died while fleeing. Those who survived suffered from burning eyes and lungs. Local medical facilities were not equipped for the disaster, and over the next few weeks thousands more died.

The Bhopal plant was operated by Union Carbide India, Ltd. (UCIL), with the parent company, Union Carbide, owning roughly 51 percent. After installing the plant and training its first staff, Union Carbide withdrew from the daily operation of the plant, as it was required to do by the Indian government. Union Carbide did participate in the inspections and responded to official questions and concerns, but no U.S. official of the company was on-site in Bhopal.

Before the accident, the plant had been under a great deal of pressure to cut costs. Because of production problems, it was unable to run at more than 50 percent capacity, and meeting its original profit predictions had become impossible. Thus, a number of shortcuts had been taken in such matters as crew

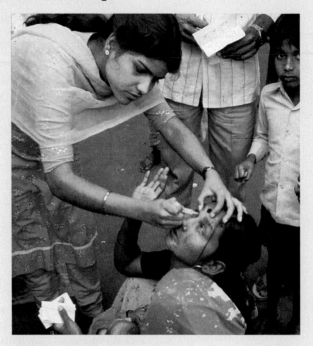

Treating Bhopal victims.

training, staffing patterns, and maintenance schedules. Although the plant had been virtually shut down for weeks for extensive maintenance and cleaning, a number of important safety features remained inoperable—and there is some doubt whether they would have been adequate even if they had been working.

Perhaps most importantly, the staff did not realize the danger of the situation—they even took a tea break after the leak had been noticed, thinking they would have plenty of time to fix it. The operator in the control room did not notify his supervisor when the temperature began to rise inside the tank, and the entire situation went untended for at least an hour. The original procedures called for up to two years of training for employees in critical superintendent capacities, but these men had received only about a month, using classroom materials developed in the United States and printed in English.

Sources: Dan Kurzman, *A Killing Wind: Inside Union Carbide and the Bhopal Catastrophe* (New York: McGraw-Hill, 1987); Arthur Sharplin, "Union Carbide of India, Ltd.," *Journal of Management Case Studies* 2 (1986):100–115; Pico Iyer, "India's Night of Death," *Time*, December 17, 1984, pp. 22–31.

O bviously, Warren Anderson, the individual, faced a severe communication problem. Even more important, Union Carbide, the organization, experienced a tragic breakdown in its ability to communicate with its internal and external stakeholders—a breakdown it tried to fix while a horrified world watched the devastation on the nightly news. Ultimately, this breakdown raised questions about ethics, technical difficulties, and cultural differences, as well as Union Carbide's strategy for communicating with the Bhopal plant.

CLASS COMMENT
Communication is the thread that binds together individuals, groups, and organizations.

Most organizational communication problems are not this severe, of course, but the tragedy at Bhopal reminds us of how important communication is to the manager's job. In fact, if you look back at the Illustrative Case Study for Chapter 1, "A *Typical* Day in the Life of Alison Reeves," you will see how much of her day was spent communicating.[1]

In this chapter, we will begin by presenting a model of interpersonal communication and note some of the barriers that hamper effective interpersonal communication. Then we will do the same thing on the organizational level. Finally, we will take a brief look at *conflict,* which arises when resources need to be shared or when communicators have different goals, and show how the communication skill of *negotiation* can be used to manage these conflicts.

■ *THE IMPORTANCE OF COMMUNICATION*

COORDINATED RESOURCE
The Additional Lecture for Chapter 18 found in the Lecture Extras supplement is "Communication: Tool for Managers."

FOR DISCUSSION
Why is good *writing* so important in business? How can good writing skills be developed?

As we have seen, effective communication is important for managers for two reasons. First, communication is the process by which managers accomplish the functions of planning, organizing, leading, and controlling. Second, communication is an activity to which managers devote an overwhelming proportion of their time. Rarely are managers alone at their desks thinking, planning, or contemplating alternatives. In fact, managerial time is spent largely in face-to-face, electronic, or telephone communication with subordinates, peers, supervisors, suppliers, or customers. When not conferring with others in person or on the telephone, managers may be writing or dictating memos, letters, or reports—or perhaps reading memos, letters, or reports sent to them. Even in those few periods when managers are alone, they are frequently interrupted by communications. For example, one study of middle and top managers found that they could work uninterrupted for a half hour or more only once every two days.[2] As Exhibit 18-1 shows, Henry Mintzberg has described the manager's job in terms of three types of roles; communication plays a vital role in each.

EXHIBIT 18-1 Mintzberg's Definition of the Role of Communication in Three Managerial Roles

1. In their *interpersonal roles,* managers act as the figurehead and leader of their organizational unit, interacting with subordinates, customers, suppliers, and peers in the organization. Mintzberg cites studies indicating that managers spend about 45 percent of their contact time with peers, about 45 percent with people outside their units, and only about 10 percent with superiors.
2. In their *informational roles,* managers seek information from peers, subordinates, and other personal contacts about anything that may affect their job and responsibilities. They also disseminate interesting or important information in return. In addition, they provide suppliers, peers, and relevant groups outside the organization with information about their unit as a whole.
3. In their *decisional roles,* managers implement new projects, handle disturbances, and allocate resources to their unit's members and departments. Some of the decisions that managers make are reached in private, but even these are based on information that has been communicated to them. Managers, in turn, have to communicate those decisions to others.

Source: Henry Mintzberg, "The Manager's Job: Folklore and Fact," *Harvard Business Review* 53, no. 4 (July–August 1975). Copyright © 1975 by the President and Fellows of Harvard College; all rights reserved.

Plumbing the Depths of Diverse Communication Styles. Thomas Kochman, president of Kochman Communication Consultants Ltd. (center), and Adrian Chan, professor of educational psychology at the University of Wisconsin at Milwaukee (right), lead a day-long seminar exploring the culturally-based behavior differences between Anglos and Asians, Hispanics, and African-Americans. Instead of the melting pot, Kochman says, today's minority groups favor the salad bowl approach—finding a common ground that allows them to communicate and work with others without losing their cultural identity. Participants were drawn from corporations, as well as from social service agencies, schools, and government programs.

COORDINATED RESOURCE
See *Management Live!* Chapter 9 video, "Hyman Rickover Interview."

Communication has been characterized as the "lifeblood" of an organization, and miscommunication has caused the equivalent of cardiovascular damage in more than one organization. Certainly, today's managers face an environment in which the issue of communications has become increasingly complex. The acceleration of technology both expedites and complicates means of communication, and an unstable environment sends rapidly changing signals reflecting shifts in social and cultural values. In addition, greater demands are being made by various "subcultures" within our larger culture, necessitating the targeting of communications to groups that respond to messages that are different from those to which the larger culture has traditionally responded. For example, Coca-Cola, Procter & Gamble, Anheuser-Busch, and McDonald's are among the many firms that have been budgeting larger sums of advertising dollars to communicate with the Hispanic market, which by 1988 was worth $130 billion and growing.[3] Within this market are an estimated 1 million Cuban Americans, according to current census statistics, and 10 to 20 percent of these Cuban Americans have annual incomes over $50,000.[4]

Moreover, the globalization of business has required managers to become acutely conscious of the communication procedures and conventions of a diverse number of cultures. For example, Americans are relatively direct in their communication style, while the Japanese tend to incorporate traditional ceremonial details into their style of communication. A renewed appreciation of languages will also be required if U.S. managers are to communicate effectively here and abroad. Although English has been termed the first truly "global language," it is the mother tongue of only about half of the 750 million people who speak it, and people who speak other native tongues still value and guard their language as expressions of themselves and their cultures.

COORDINATED RESOURCE
See *Management Live!* Reading 9.1, "Successful vs. Effective Real Managers."

Finally, the influx of more women and minorities into our organizations and their managerial ranks also increases both the potential for miscommunication and the need to be sensitive to the nuances of linguistic messages and other forms of communication.

All in all, then, communication is a much more complex factor today than it was 25 years ago. Not surprisingly, the problem of defining *communication* as a subject of study has also become increasingly difficult. One researcher uncovered as many as 95 definitions, none of them entirely feasible or widely accepted.[5] For our purposes, **communication** is defined as the process by which people attempt to share meaning via the transmission of symbolic messages.

communication The process by which people attempt to share meaning via the transmission of symbolic messages.

■ *INTERPERSONAL COMMUNICATION*

Our working definition of communication calls attention to three essential points: (1) that communication involves *people,* and that understanding communication therefore involves trying to understand how people relate to each other; (2) that communication involves *shared meaning,* which suggests that in order for people to communicate, they must agree on the definitions of the terms they are using; and (3) that communication is *symbolic*—gestures, sounds, letters, numbers, and words can only represent or approximate the ideas that they are meant to communicate.[6]

The Communication Process: Essential Elements

John Kotter has defined communication as a process consisting of "a sender transmitting a message through media to a receiver who responds."[7] In its simplest form, this model can be schematized as follows:

Sender → Message → Receiver

This model indicates there are three essential elements of communication; obviously, if one of them is missing, no communication can take place. For example, we can send a message, but if it is not heard or received by someone, no communication has occurred.

Although psychologists specializing in interpersonal communication continue to pursue the implications and nuances of this model, it must be regarded as a highly ideal model. For example, it assumes a hypothetical "common ground" between sender and receiver that is more easily conceptualized than precisely described.[8]

The Communication Process: A Workable Model

Most of us are familiar with the game of "telephone," in which one person whispers a message into the ear of another, who whispers the message to the next person, and so on. Inevitably, when the last person says the message out loud, it is quite different from what was first whispered.

"Telephone" illustrates one complexity in the communication process: The sender may send one message, but the receivers may "hear" or receive a different message. Psychologists have studied other complex variables of communication, such as the receiver's disposition toward one-sided or two-sided arguments,[9] the receiver's response to superficial as opposed to logical aspects of a message,[10] and whether women are more easily persuaded receivers than men.[11] Figure 18-1 illustrates a far more workable model of the communication process. In the discussion that follows, we will describe each of the major elements of this model.[12]

SENDER (SOURCE). The **sender,** or source of the message, initiates the communication. In an organization, the sender will be a person with information, needs, or desires and a purpose for communicating them to one or more other people. A

COORDINATED RESOURCE
Use Transparency 121, A Model of the Communication Process.

COORDINATED RESOURCE
Acumen: Acumen research indicates that the best managers are achievement-oriented and flexible rather than power-oriented and dominating. For those with an average score or lower on the Power scale, an *Acumen* report would suggest (a) listening more and talking less; (b) asking specialists and co-workers for advice and communicating that the advice will be taken seriously; (c) avoiding threatening or pushing people; instead providing co-workers with support and involving them in the decision-making process.

sender The initiator of a communication.

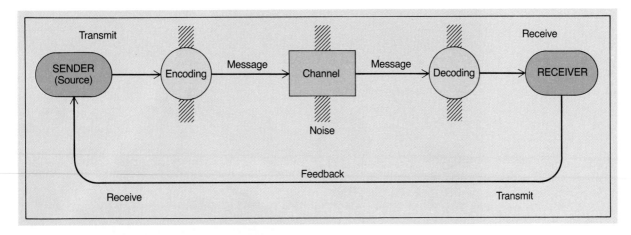

FIGURE 18-1 A Model of the Communication Process

manager wishes to communicate information about an important deadline for the purpose of motivating other members of the department. A production-line worker speaks to the shop supervisor for the purpose of requesting additional help with a project. Without a reason, purpose, or desire, the sender has no need to send a message.

encoding The translation of information into a series of symbols for communication.

ENCODING. **Encoding** takes place when the sender translates the information to be transmitted into a series of symbols. Encoding is necessary because information can only be transferred from one person to another through representations or symbols. Since communication is the object of encoding, the sender attempts to establish "mutuality" of meaning with the receiver by choosing symbols, usually in the form of words and gestures, that the sender believes to have the same meaning for the receiver.

Lack of mutuality is one of the most common causes of misunderstanding or failure of communication. In Bulgaria and some parts of India, for example, "yes" is indicated with a side-to-side shake of the head; "no" is indicated with a nod. Visiting foreigners who do not share these symbols can quickly experience or cause bewilderment when they talk with citizens of these areas. Misunderstandings may also result from subtler differences in mutuality. A manager who asks a number of subordinates to "work late" may cause a good deal of confusion as each employee decides independently what "late" means.

Gestures, too, may be subject to different interpretations. A worker in a noisy factory may convey to a co-worker that he wants a machine to be shut off by drawing his hand, palm down, across his neck in a "cutthroat" gesture.[13] If one walked up to a police officer and made the same gesture, a different reaction might result. Even raising one's eyebrows can have varying meanings, expressing surprise in one context and skepticism in another.

message The encoded information sent by the sender to the receiver.

COORDINATED RESOURCE

See Samaras Exercise 4.4, "See the Picture."

MESSAGE. The **message** is the physical form into which the sender encodes the information. The message may be in any form that can be experienced and understood by one or more of the senses of the receiver. Speech may be heard; written words may be read; gestures may be seen or felt. A touch of the hand may communicate messages ranging from comfort to menace. A wave of the hand can communicate widely diverse messages depending on the number of fingers extended. Nonverbal messages are an extremely important form of communication, since they are often more honest or meaningful than oral or written messages. For example, a manager who frowns while saying "Good morning" to a late-arriving subordinate is clearly communicating something more than a polite greeting.

A Channel of Communications. President Arthur Blank (left) and CEO Bernard Marcus of Home Depot, a fast-growing chain of home improvement stores, monitor *Breakfast with Bernie and Arthur,* a quarterly satellite broadcast geared to showing Home Depot's 20,000 employees how to help pennypinching homeowners see the wisdom of improving their property even when the housing market is soft.

channel The medium of communication between a sender and a receiver.

COORDINATED RESOURCE
See Geis and Kuhn Chapter 7, "The Power of Graphics—Making Your Point."

CHANNEL.   The **channel** is the method of transmission from one person to another (such as air for spoken words and paper for letters); it is often inseparable from the message. For communication to be effective and efficient, the channel must be appropriate for the message. While a phone conversation would be an unsuitable channel for transmitting a complex engineering diagram,[14] a fax or overnight express mail might be quite appropriate. The needs and requirements of the receiver must also be considered in selecting a channel. An extremely complicated message, for example, should be transmitted through a channel that permits the receiver to refer to it repeatedly.

Although managers have a broad array of channels available to them, they may not always use the one that is most effective. Their choices may be guided by habit or personal preference. One person may use the telephone because he or she dislikes writing; another may continue to use handwritten memos when electronic mail would be much more efficient. Both modes are appropriate in certain circumstances, so the manager must make individual decisions for each situation.

How does one choose the best channel? Written and graphic communications, such as memos, letters, reports, and blueprints, are clear and precise and provide a permanent record. The telephone and face-to-face oral communication offer the advantage of immediate feedback. In choosing the appropriate channel, then, managers must decide whether clarity or feedback is more important. Many different factors are involved in the communication process, so no single technique is always preferable to the alternatives.[15]

receiver The individual whose senses perceive the sender's message.

RECEIVER.   The **receiver** is the person whose senses perceive the sender's message. There may be a large number of receivers, as when a memo is addressed to all the members of an organization, or there may be just one, as when one discusses something privately with a colleague. The message must be crafted with the receiver's background in mind. An engineer in a microchip manufacturing company, for exam-

COORDINATED RESOURCE
See Study Guide Self-Learning Exercise 18, "Listening Skills."

decoding The interpretation and translation of a message into meaningful information.

noise Anything that confuses, disturbs, diminishes, or interferes with communication.

feedback (interpersonal) The reversal of the communication process that occurs when the receiver expresses his or her reaction to the sender's message.

COORDINATED RESOURCE
See DuBose Reading #18, "Active Listening."

ple, might have to avoid using technical terms in a communication with someone in the company's advertising department; by the same token, the person in advertising might find engineers unreceptive to communications about demographics. If the message does not reach a receiver, communication has not taken place. The situation is not much improved if the message reaches a receiver but the receiver doesn't understand it.

DECODING. **Decoding** is the process by which the receiver interprets the message and translates it into meaningful information. It is a two-step process: The receiver must first perceive the message, then interpret it.[16] Decoding is affected by the receiver's past experience, personal assessments of the symbols and gestures used, expectations (people tend to hear what they want to hear), and mutuality of meaning with the sender. In general, *the more the receiver's decoding matches the sender's intended message, the more effective the communication has been.*

One decoding problem occurred when a manager asked a subordinate if she would like to work overtime on a weekend. There were a number of other employees available to do the work, but the supervisor thought the one he singled out would appreciate an opportunity to earn extra income. The subordinate had made special plans for Saturday, but she interpreted the manager's offer as a demand, canceled her plans, and spent the weekend working. As a result of poor communication, she interpreted the manager's message differently than he intended.[17]

NOISE. **Noise** is any factor that disturbs, confuses, or otherwise interferes with communication. It may be internal (as when a receiver is not paying attention) or external (as when the message is distorted by other sounds in the environment). Noise can occur at any stage of the communication process. It may occur during passage through the channel—for example, a radio signal may be distorted by bad weather—but most interference arises in the encoding or decoding stage.[18]

The urge to make sense of a communication is so strong that a puzzling or even nonsensical communication is often decoded by the receiver into a sensible statement that may have an entirely different meaning from the originally encoded message. For example, unclear instructions on how to perform a task may cause employees to "hear" different and incorrect instructions.

Since noise can interfere with understanding, managers should attempt to restrict it to a level that permits effective communication. It can be very tiring to listen to a subordinate who speaks softly on a noisy assembly line or to try to conduct a conversation over telephone static.[19] Physical discomfort such as hunger, pain, or exhaustion can also be considered a form of noise and can interfere with effective communication. The problems are made worse, of course, by a message that is excessively complex or unclear to begin with. A clear message expressed in a straightforward fashion ("Turn off that radio!"), however, can be conveyed even in an extremely "noisy" environment.

FEEDBACK. **Feedback** is a reversal of the communication process in which a reaction to the sender's communication is expressed. Since the receiver has become the sender, feedback goes through the same steps as the original communication. Organizational feedback may be in a variety of forms, ranging from direct feedback, such as a simple spoken acknowledgment that the message has been received, to indirect feedback, expressed through actions or documentation. For example, a straightforward request for a faster rate of production may be met directly with an assenting nod of the head or indirectly with record-breaking output or a union strike.

Feedback is optional and may exist in any degree (from minimal to complete) in any given situation. In most organizational communications, the greater the feedback, the more effective the communication process is likely to be. For example, early feedback will let managers know if their instructions have been understood and accepted. Without such feedback, a manager might not know (until too late) that instructions were inaccurately received and carried out.

One-Way and Two-Way Communication

one-way communication
Any communication from the sender without feedback from the receiver.

two-way communication
Communication that occurs when the receiver provides feedback to the sender.

COORDINATED RESOURCE
Use Transparency 122, Communication Flow Between Individuals.

As our description of the communication process implies, communication may be one-way or two-way. In **one-way communication**, the sender communicates without expecting or getting feedback from the receiver. Policy statements from top managers are usually examples of one-way communication. **Two-way communication** exists when the receiver provides feedback to the sender. Making a suggestion to a subordinate and receiving a question or countersuggestion is an example of two-way communication.

How does a manager decide when to use one-way versus two-way communication? The answer depends on the *reason* for communicating. Some categories of managerial communications, such as straightforward statements of company rules and policies, require little or no feedback to ensure clarity. In those cases, one-way communication is more than adequate. But in many other cases, such as the formulation of division objectives or the implementation of a new sales strategy, two-way communication is essential to achieving clarity and the commitment of employees who must carry out the ideas communicated.[20]

■ BARRIERS TO EFFECTIVE INTERPERSONAL COMMUNICATION

COORDINATED RESOURCE
The Application Exercise for Chapter 18 found in the Lecture Extras supplement has students playing the old kids' game of "Telephone" to see how communication becomes confused.

The "telephone" game shows how easily communication can be garbled when sender and receiver begin with different perceptions. Other barriers to effective communication are language differences, noise, emotions, inconsistencies between verbal and nonverbal communications, and distrust.[21]

Communication barriers vary in their imperviousness and their significance. Total blocks are rare, so the gist of the message usually gets through. Take a mailroom clerk who understands relatively little English. As long as the clerk understands the difference between first class and express mail, all may be well. But if the clerk consistently delivers John Johnson's mail to John Jenson or hesitates to answer the phone because he or she cannot understand callers' questions, the manager may have to take corrective action. Usually this is a two-step process of identifying the barriers to communication and then taking active steps to overcome them.[22] Our discussion will help you learn to identify these barriers and then suggest ways to overcome them.

Recognizing Barriers to Effective Interpersonal Communication

The following are some of the most common barriers to effective communication.

COORDINATED RESOURCE
Acumen: The Oppositional scale is a measure of an individual's tendency to take a critical, questioning, and somewhat cynical attitude. High scorers on this scale are often dogmatic, rigid, and mistrustful of others. Even those with average scores do not always accept things at their face value and occasionally take a rigid stand, rather than being open to others' opinions and views.

DIFFERING PERCEPTIONS. This is one of the most common communication barriers. People who have different backgrounds of knowledge and experience often perceive the same phenomenon from different perspectives. Suppose that a new supervisor compliments an assembly-line worker for his or her efficiency and high-quality work. The supervisor genuinely appreciates the worker's efforts and at the same time wants to encourage the other employees to emulate his or her example. Others on the assembly line, however, may regard the worker's being singled out for praise as a sign that he or he has been "buttering up the boss"; they may react by teasing or being openly hostile. Thus, individual perceptions of the same communication differ radically.

The way a communication is perceived is influenced by the circumstances in which it occurs. A disagreement between colleagues during a planning session for a major project might be regarded by others as acceptable or even healthy. If the same disagreement broke out during the chief executive officer's annual address to employees, it would be regarded somewhat differently.

LANGUAGE DIFFERENCES. Language differences are often closely related to differences in individual perceptions. For a message to be properly communicated, the words used must mean the same thing to sender and receiver. Suppose that different departments of a company receive a memo stating that a new product is to be developed in "a short time." To people in research and development, "a short time" might mean two or three years. To people in the finance department, "a short time" might be three to six months, whereas the sales department might think of "a short time" as a few weeks. Since many different meanings can be assigned to some words—the 500 most common English words have an average of 28 definitions *each*[23]—great care must be taken that the receiver gets the message that the sender intended.

Another barrier to communication is jargon. Some corporations have their own special jargon, as the Management Application box on "Corporate Jargon" indicates. People who have special interests or knowledge often forget that not everyone is familiar with their specialized terms.

MANAGEMENT APPLICATION

Corporate Jargon

"I'm really in the weeds. Please drop a red chimi on the fly. Wait! Eighty-six that. All I need is a follower."

"That looks like a bad Mickey!"

"What a dinger on a hanging hook!"

If these statements make no sense to you, don't worry. Each is an example of just how complex and inscrutable the specific jargon of a given business can get. The first example is a waitress addressing the cooking staff in a restaurant. It translates as: "I'm very busy. Please cook this food as quickly as possible. Wait! Cancel that. All I need is someone to help me carry these plates to my table." The second is a Disney employee pointing out an unsavory fact, like a cigarette butt on the sidewalk. The third is a major-league baseball player admiring a teammate's long home run off a pitcher's hanging curve ball.

Many industries, and even individual companies, develop their own languages. Sometimes this is a ploy to keep others from understanding company secrets or to help insiders feel important. In other instances, the jargon develops out of a need for special terms to define special items or activities.

The development of a company slang can have both positive and negative aspects. On the positive side, it may help employees feel they are part of a well-defined culture. Most people like to feel they are on the inside of a group, and corporate slang can create that feeling very quickly. More importantly, an internal language can also lead to more efficiency—if the jargon has developed so that, say, 2 words take the place of 20 and are more specific at the same time. Of course, someone new to a firm may find this

practice tremendously frustrating, and some companies have gone so far as to publish dictionaries of organizational slang to help initiate newcomers.

A more serious problem is that internal codes can obscure the real meaning of language. When intracompany slang creeps into employees' telephone calls and conversations with people on the outside, communication can get quite complicated. Customers may have no idea what the person is trying to communicate or, worse, become offended by the use of the special language. To outsiders, jargon often seems like an attempt to keep them on the outside rather than an effort to resolve a problem or accomplish a goal. Employees of one company trying to communicate with employees of another company can get hopelessly confused if their languages do not coincide, almost as if a French person and a Chinese person were trying to hold a conversation in their native tongues. An external consultant coming into a firm may have to spend days just trying to understand what the problem *is* before trying to solve it.

Corporate slang usually develops in companies rich in history or occupying a unique position in their industry. Walt Disney, for example is almost as famous for having such internal lingo as "good" and "bad Mickeys" as for the images it creates. It is often comfortable—and efficient—to communicate with co-workers in a special way, but employees should be aware that not everyone they meet will be able to speak their language nor should they be expected to.

Source: Adapted from Michael W. Miller, "At Many Firms, Employees Speak a Language That's All Their Own," *The Wall Street Journal,* December 29, 1987, Sect. 2, p. 17.

Finally, the contemporary globalization of industry means dealing with major language differences—a problem that cannot be ignored.

FOR DISCUSSION
What "noise" factors are there in our classroom?

NOISE.   As we have already explained, noise is any factor that disturbs, confuses, or otherwise interferes with communication. Communication rarely occurs in totally noise-free environments, of course, so people learn to screen out many of the irrelevant messages they receive. The problem is that they sometimes also screen out the relevant information. A person talking on the phone in a busy office may not hear the message her secretary is giving her from across the room. The "boy who cried wolf" was eventually correct, but he had given the same message falsely so often that people no longer paid any attention to him. Similarly, a manager who labels every order "urgent" may find that subordinates are slow to respond when a real emergency develops.

COORDINATED RESOURCE
See Samaras Case 4.4, "The Memo."

EMOTIONAL REACTIONS.   Emotional reactions—anger, love, defensiveness, hate, jealously, fear, embarrassment—influence how we understand others' messages and how we influence others with our own messages. If, for example, we are in an atmosphere where we feel threatened with loss of power or prestige, we may lose the ability to gauge the meanings of the messages we receive and will respond defensively or aggressively.

CLASS COMMENT
Nonverbal communication can affect the intended and interpreted meanings.

INCONSISTENT VERBAL AND NONVERBAL COMMUNICATION.   We think of language as the primary medium of communication, but the messages we send and receive are strongly influenced by such nonverbal factors as body movements, clothing, the distance we stand from the person we're talking to, our posture, gestures, facial expressions, eye movements, and body contact. Even when our message is as simple as "Good morning," we can convey different intents by our nonverbal communication. A busy manager who does not want to be disturbed might respond to a subordinate's greeting without looking up from his or her work, for example.[24]

DISTRUST.   A receiver's trust or distrust of a message is, to a large extent, a function of the credibility of the sender in the mind of the receiver. A sender's credibility is determined by a variety of factors. In some cases, the fact that a message comes from a manager will enhance its credibility. In other cases, it can have the opposite effect. In negotiations between labor and management, for example, labor often regards the claims of managers with some suspicion. In this situation, as in others, the perceived character or honesty of the sender is important. In general, a manager's credibility will be high if he or she is perceived by others as knowledgeable, trustworthy, and sincerely concerned about the welfare of others.[25]

Overcoming Barriers to Effective Interpersonal Communication

OVERCOMING DIFFERING PERCEPTIONS.   To overcome differing perceptions, the message should be explained so that it can be understood by receivers with different views and experiences. Whenever possible, we should learn about the background of those with whom we will be communicating. Empathizing—seeing the situation from the other person's point of view—and delaying reactions until the relevant information is weighed will help to reduce ambiguity. When the subject is unclear, asking questions is critical.[26]

OVERCOMING DIFFERENCES IN LANGUAGE.   To overcome language differences, the meanings of unconventional or technical terms should be explained in simple, direct, natural language. To ensure that all important concepts have been understood, it is particularly helpful to ask the receiver to confirm or restate the main points of the message. When all members of an organization or group are going to be dealing

Overcoming Differences in Language. Frank Meeks, CEO and owner of Domino's Pizza Team, a chain of 42 Domino's Pizza stores in the Washington, D.C., area, thinks most employees have trouble understanding abstract language, so he puts a dollar figure on the real cost of alienating customers, many of whom order from Domino's twice a week.

TEACHING TIP
Reemphasize to students
that they are learning the
"jargon" of management in
this class.

with a new terminology, it may be worthwhile to develop a training course of instruction to acquaint them with the new topic. Receivers can be encouraged to ask questions and to seek clarification of points that are unclear.[27]

It is also helpful to remain sensitive to the various alternative ways of phrasing a message. Messages can often be restated in different terms. Sometimes even a minor change can have beneficial effects. If, for example, we are replacing an unpopular sales quota system with a new system in which reaching sales objectives is only one measure of productivity, we might do well to avoid the word "quota" entirely because of its negative association with the old system.

OVERCOMING NOISE. Noise is best dealt with by eliminating it. If noise from a machine makes talking difficult, turn off the machine or move to a new location. If you notice that your receiver is not listening closely, try to regain his or her attention. Avoid distracting environments. Alternately, when noise is unavoidable, increase the clarity and strength of the message.

OVERCOMING EMOTIONAL REACTIONS. The best approach to emotions is to accept them as part of the communication process and to seek to understand them when they cause problems. If subordinates are behaving aggressively, get them to talk about their concerns and pay careful attention to what they say. Once you understand their reactions, you may be able to improve the atmosphere by changing your own behavior. Before a crisis, try to anticipate your subordinates' emotional reactions and prepare yourself to deal with them. Also, think about your own moods and how they influence others.

OVERCOMING INCONSISTENT VERBAL AND NONVERBAL COMMUNICATION. The keys to eliminating inconsistencies in communication are being aware of them and guarding against sending false messages. Gestures, clothes, posture, facial expression, and other powerful nonverbal communications should all agree with the message. Analyzing the nonverbal communication of other people and applying what is learned to oneself and to one's dealings with others is helpful.

OVERCOMING DISTRUST. To a large extent, distrust is overcome through a process of creating trust. Credibility is the result of a long-term process in which a person's honesty, fairmindedness, and good intentions are recognized by others. There are few shortcuts to creating a trusting atmosphere; a good rapport with the people one communicates with can only be developed through consistent performance.

redundancy Repeating
or restating a message to
ensure its reception or to
reinforce its impact.

FOR DISCUSSION
Is redundancy used in
education? How? Give examples.

TEACHING TIP
Have your students "tune
in" to their communication over the next 24-hour
period. Have them note
when barriers arise and try
to identify what factors or
situations created the barrier. What did they do to
reduce the barriers?

REDUNDANCY. One additional approach is generally useful in getting one's message across. This is **redundancy**—repeating the message or restating it in a different form. Redundancy counteracts noise by reducing uncertainty in the transmission of the message.[28] The optimal level of redundancy varies with circumstances. If a message is sent in a permanent form—on paper, tape, or disk, for example—then little redundancy within the communication is called for. An exception is when the message is extremely complex. Then it may be useful to repeat key points in several different forms even in a permanent communication. Redundancy is always more important in oral and other "perishable" forms of communication. If someone is giving us a phone number and we don't have a pencil and paper, we are more likely to remember it if it is repeated several times.

Like other techniques, redundancy can be overused. Hearing the same message over and over again may leave the receiver bored or angry. Eventually, the receiver will come to treat such a message as mere noise. Furthermore, storage of redundant information can be a problem. Many libraries would like to have two copies of every book they buy, for example, but two copies cost twice as much, take up twice as much space, and take almost twice as long to catalog. The money, space, and time might better be devoted to another book.

ILLUSTRATIVE CASE STUDY

CONTINUED

Communication Failures at Bhopal

Clearly, Anderson and Union Carbide had a significant communication problem. First of all, there was a lot of confusion over the facts. Even today, no one is clear as to exactly what sequence of events led to the disaster. Second, each party has a different interpretation of the "facts" that *have* come to light. That is why, after Union Carbide settled its lawsuit with the government of India in late 1989, a number of voluntary groups claiming to represent the victims asked to have the settlement voided.

Of course, there were a number of barriers to effective communication in the immediate aftermath of the event. Various parties gave voice to differing perceptions of the "facts," and the high pitch of emotion amounted to a form of noise interfering with communications channels. In addition, Anderson had to communicate in multiple ways in the wake of the disaster—all of which were hampered by subsequent events and circumstances. The whole world was watching to see what Union Carbide would do. Anderson made the symbolic move of going to India to show his concern, but his subsequent arrest made any form of communication virtually impossible. Ultimately, he needed to have a policy of one-way communication in order to state what Union Carbide was going to do, but before that he needed to engage in multiple-party communication to determine exactly what had happened. Both channels of communication had been effectively shut down.

There was also the little-publicized, but important, issue of Anderson's communication with other Union Carbide employees. After all, some of them worked in facilities very much like the one in Bhopal.

Source: Subatra N. Chakravarty, "The Ghost Returns," *Forbes,* December 19, 1990, p. 108.

■ COMMUNICATION IN ORGANIZATIONS

Because Christmas Eve falls on a Thursday, the day has been designated a Saturday for work purposes. Factories will close all day, with stores open a half day only. Friday, December 25, has been designated a Sunday, with both factories and stores open all day. Monday, December 28, will be a Wednesday for work purposes. Wednesday, December 30, will be a business Friday. Saturday, January 2, will be a Sunday, and Sunday, January 3, will be a Monday.—*From an Associated Press report on a Prague government edict.*

As this example shows, unclear organizational communication can make a complex idea or process completely unintelligible.

FOR DISCUSSION

How are new information technologies changing organizational communication?

All the factors that we have discussed in relation to interpersonal communication also apply to communication in organizations, which also involves getting an accurate message from one person to another (or perhaps to several people). However, several factors unique to organizations influence the effectiveness of communication. In this section, we will deal specifically with how the realities of formal organizations can affect the communication process. We will begin by discussing some factors that influence the effectiveness of communication in organizations. Then we will discuss communication networks, vertical communication, and the effects of lateral and informal communication, which includes the company grapevine. We will conclude the section by discussing barriers to effective organizational communication and how to overcome them.

Factors Influencing Organizational Communication

Raymond V. Lesikar has described four factors that influence the effectiveness of organizational communication: the formal channels of communication, the organization's authority structure, job specialization, and what Lesikar calls "information ownership."[29]

FORMAL CHANNELS OF COMMUNICATION. The *formal channels of communication* influence communication effectiveness in two ways. First, the formal channels cover an ever-widening distance as organizations develop and grow. For example, effective communication is usually far more difficult to achieve in a large retail organization with widely dispersed branches than in small department store. Second, the formal channels of communication inhibit the free flow of information between organizational levels. An assembly-line worker, for example, will almost always communicate problems to a supervisor rather than to the plant manager. While this accepted restriction in the channels of communication has its advantages (such as keeping higher-level managers from getting bogged down in information), it also has its disadvantages (such as sometimes keeping higher-level managers from receiving information they should have). The formal channels of communication can have unexpected consequences, as the box below suggests.

ETHICS IN MANAGEMENT

One Memo Too Many

For years, managers have wished that employees knew when—and when *not*—to write memos. Mostly, this complaint has come from managers weary from reading too many pieces of material suitable for "circular filing." However, recent court events have revealed a new reason for people to think twice before writing another memo: That memo can become incriminating evidence in a legal battle. Such memos indicate when a company learned of a problem, what it knew, and its true ethical position.

Tobacco companies, for example, have been fighting lawsuits for years as smokers (or their relatives or their survivors) have sought to make the cigarette manufacturers responsible for their poor health. Until 1980, no one had succeeded with such a lawsuit, mainly because the tobacco companies have been adamant in claiming that there is no proof that cigarettes cause the cancer or lung problems alleged in the suits. Their other argument, of course, is that the smoker was free to choose *not* to smoke and was not compelled by an addiction.

This state of affairs has changed. Evidence in a 1988 trial indicated that the tobacco companies may have been fully aware of the consequences of smoking decades ago—or at least should have been. Internal documents of the Liggett Group, Inc., indicated that its own scientists duplicated the experiments that suggested the tar in cigarettes caused cancerous tumors to grow on mice. The documents had been in circulation as far back as 1953. Memos written by other scientists and external consultants also indicated a belief in some link between cancer and cigarette smoking.

Memos written in the early 1970s indicate that Philip Morris scientists had invented a "safer" cigarette. The company, however, killed its development, apparently because they feared the liability of suggesting their current product was less than safe. When R. J. Reynolds announced a new cigarette that produces less smoke and has fewer harmful ingredients in the late 1980s, company lawyers wrote a memo warning management that marketing the new product could increase their vulnerability to charges that they knew conventional tobacco products to be less safe than they were presently admitting. Such memos have been used in the courts to prove that the companies are fully aware of the hazards of smoking, and they will undoubtedly be used again and again.

Sources: Adapted from Patricia Bellew Gray, "Smoking Foes Cite New Evidence Emerging in Tobacco-Liability Suit," *The Wall Street Journal,* April 4, 1988, p. 19; and Ed Bean, "Memo Warns of Legal Risk of 'Smokeless' Cigarettes," *The Wall Street Journal,* April 13, 1988, p. 31.

AUTHORITY STRUCTURE. The organization's *authority structure* has a similar influence on communication effectiveness. Status and power differences in the organization help determine who will communicate comfortably with whom. The content and accuracy of the communication will also be affected by authority differences. For example, conversation between a company president and a clerical worker may well be characterized by somewhat strained politeness and formality; neither party is likely to say much of importance.

job specialization The division of work into standardized, simplified tasks.

JOB SPECIALIZATION. **Job specialization** usually facilitates communication *within* differentiated groups. Members of the same work group are likely to share the same jargon, time horizons, goals, tasks, and personal styles. Communication *between* highly differentiated groups, however, is likely to be inhibited.

information ownership The possession by certain individuals of unique information and knowledge concerning their work.

INFORMATION OWNERSHIP. The term **information ownership** means that individuals possess unique information and knowledge about their jobs. A darkroom employee, for example, may have found a particularly efficient way to develop photoprints, a department head may have a particularly effective way of handling conflict among subordinates, and a salesperson may know who the key decision makers are in his or her major accounts. Such information is a form of power for the individuals who possess it; they are able to function more effectively than their peers. Many individuals with such skills and knowledge are unwilling to share this information with others. As a result, completely open communication within the organization does not take place.

Communication Networks within the Organization

COORDINATED RESOURCE

Use Transparency 123, Types of Communication Networks.

Some very interesting research has been carried out on communication channels in organizations and their effects on communication accuracy, task performance, and group member satisfaction. This research is particularly important because managers have some influence over how communication channels develop in their units. For example, the formal authority structure that managers establish will help determine who will interact with whom. Thus, managers can design their work units to facilitate effective communication.

communication network A set of channels within an organization or group through which communication travels.

Organizations design their **communication networks,** or structures, in a variety of ways. Some communication networks are rigidly designed: Employees are discouraged from talking with anyone except their immediate supervisor. Such networks are usually intended both to keep higher-level managers from becoming overburdened with unnecessary information and to maintain the higher-level managers' power and status. Other networks are more loosely designed: Individuals are encouraged to communicate with anyone at any level. Such networks are often used wherever a free flow of information is highly desirable, as in a research department.

A series of experiments was performed to test the effect of various communication structures.[30] In a representative study in this series, five subjects were seated at a table and asked to solve different types of problems. The subjects were separated by partitions and could communicate with each other to solve the problems along communication lines controlled entirely by the researchers.

Figure 18-2 illustrates four communication networks the researchers tested. In the "circle" network, for example, subject B could communicate (through the partitions) only with subjects A and C. To communicate with subject E, subject B would have to go through subject A or through subjects C and D. Subject C in the "star" pattern, on the other hand, could communicate directly with A, B, D, and E, although these subjects could not communicate directly with each other. Each of these four networks can represent a real network in an organization. The "star" pattern, for example, might represent four salespeople (A, B, D, E) reporting to a district manager (C); the "chain" pattern might represent two subordinates (A and E) reporting to supervisors (B and D, respectively), who in turn report to the same supervisor (C).

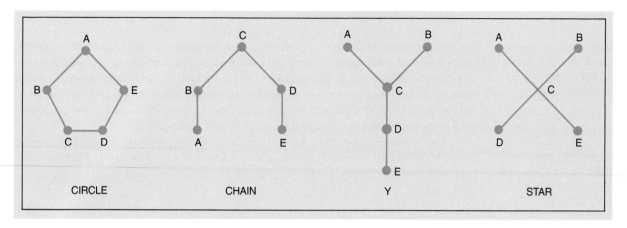

FIGURE 18-2 Types of Communication Networks

The subjects in the experiments were given both simple and complex problems to solve. The series of studies demonstrated that network centrality was the critical feature in determining whether a particular communication network was effective and/or satisfying to its members on a particular type of task. Some networks, such as the "Y" and the "star," are highly centralized, with subject C at the central position. But the "circle" and "chain" networks are decentralized, with no one member able to communicate with all the other members.

In most tests, centralized networks performed faster and more accurately than decentralized networks, *provided the tasks were comparatively simple.* For *complex* tasks, however, the decentralized networks were comparatively quicker and more accurate. The structure of communication networks is also intricately linked to larger organizational structure. Highly centralized organizational structures will inhibit the development of broad informal communications networks because most communication will be forced "through proper channels." The functioning of military units provides a good example of this principle: While a battlefield is likely to be rife with rumor, the actual deployment of troops and resources is usually centrally controlled by means of formal communications channels.

The centrality of the networks also affected leader emergence and group member satisfaction. For both simple and complex tasks, centralized groups tended to agree that person C, occupying the central position, was the leader. Obviously, C emerged as the leader in centralized networks because the other group members were so completely dependent on C for their information. In decentralized networks, however, no one position in the network emerged as the leadership position.

Group member satisfaction, on the other hand, tended to be higher in decentralized networks for all types of tasks. In fact, satisfaction was highest in the "circle," next highest in the "chain," and then in the "Y." The least satisfied group members were in the "star" network. The reason for the greater satisfaction in the decentralized networks was that members of those networks could participate in finding solutions to problems. The only highly satisfied member of the centralized networks was the person at position "C," who played an active leadership role.

These experiments have many implications for the relationships between organizational structure and communication. For example, an organization with mostly routine, simple tasks would seem to work most efficiently with a formally centralized communication network, whereas more complicated tasks seem to call for decentralization. Also, the emergence of the person in the most centralized position as the leader reinforces the idea that access to information is an important source of power in organizations.

Communication network design and implementation remains a fruitful area of research in terms of both managerial behavior and the availability of new technology. Chapter 22 will return to some of these issues in greater detail.

Vertical Communication

Vertical communication consists of communication up and down the organization's chain of command. Downward communication starts with top management and flows down through management levels to line workers and nonsupervisory personnel. The major purposes of downward communication are to advise, inform, direct, instruct, and evaluate subordinates and to provide organization members with information about organizational goals and policies.

The main function of upward communication is to supply information to the upper levels about what is happening at the lower levels. This type of communication includes progress reports, suggestions, explanations, and requests for aid or decisions.[31]

PROBLEMS OF VERTICAL COMMUNICATION. Downward communication is likely to be filtered, modified, or halted at each level as managers decide what should be passed down to their subordinates. Upward communication is likely to be filtered, condensed, or altered by middle managers who see it as part of their job to protect upper management from nonessential data originating at the lower levels.[32] In addition, middle managers may keep information that would reflect unfavorably on them from reaching their superiors. Thus, vertical communication is often at least partially inaccurate or incomplete.

The importance to an organization of vertical communication was emphasized by a survey of research conducted by Lyman W. Porter and Karlene H. Roberts, who reported that two-thirds of a manager's communications take place with superiors and subordinates.[33] The studies reviewed by Porter and Roberts also found that the accuracy of vertical communication was aided by similarities in thinking between superior and subordinate. But it was limited by status and power differences between manager and subordinate, by a subordinate's desire for upward mobility, and by a lack of trust between manager and subordinate. For example, some studies suggest that communication is likely to be less open and accurate the higher the subordinates' aspirations for upward mobility. Such subordinates are likely to be ambitious, strongly opinionated, forceful, and aggressive, and consequently more concerned with defending their self-image than with reaching an agreement or an objectively accurate appraisal of a situation. They are also less likely to communicate reports that may be interpreted as negative comments on their own performance or ability. Subordinates are also more prone to screen out problems, disagreements, or complaints when they feel that their superior has the power to punish them.

Even unambitious subordinates will be guarded in their communications if an atmosphere of distrust exists between them and their superiors. Subordinates conceal or distort information when they feel that their superiors cannot be trusted to be fair or that they may use the information against them. The net result of these communication problems is that higher-level managers frequently make decisions based on faulty or inadequate information.

Problems in downward communication exist when managers do not provide subordinates with the information they need to carry out their tasks effectively. Managers are often overly optimistic about the accuracy and completeness of their downward communication; in fact, they frequently fail to pass on important information (such as a higher-level change in policy) or to instruct subordinates adequately on how to perform their duties. This lack of communication is sometimes deliberate, as when managers withhold information to keep subordinates dependent on them. The net effect of incomplete downward communication is that subordinates may feel confused, uninformed, or powerless and may fail to carry out their tasks properly.

Lateral and Informal Communication

Lateral communication usually follows the pattern of work flow in an organization, occurring between members of work groups, between one work group and another, between members of different departments, and between line and staff. The main purpose of lateral communication is to provide a direct channel for organizational coordination and problem solving. In this way, it avoids the much slower procedure of directing communications through a common superior.[34] An added benefit of lateral communication is that it enables organization members to form relationships with their peers. These relationships are an important part of employee satisfaction.[35]

A significant amount of lateral communication takes place outside the chain of command. Such lateral communication often occurs with the knowledge, approval, and encouragement of superiors who understand that lateral communication often relieves their communication burden and also reduces inaccuracy by putting relevant people in direct contact with each other.[36]

Another type of *informal communication,* not officially sanctioned, is the grapevine. The grapevine in organizations is made up of several informal communication networks that overlap and intersect at a number of points—that is, some well-informed individuals are likely to belong to more than one informal network. Grapevines show admirable disregard for rank or authority and may link organization members in any combination of directions—horizontal, vertical, and diagonal. As Keith Davis puts it, the grapevine "flows around water coolers, down hallways, through lunch rooms, and wherever people get together in groups."[37] The grapevine should not be confused with legitimate information that management seeks to transmit by word of mouth. However, when such information is transmitted by word of mouth, people at the lowest level of the organization are least likely to receive it accurately. For this reason, managers who wish to ensure that the lowest-level employees receive certain information often communicate in writing.

In addition to its social and informal communication functions, the grapevine has several work-related functions. For example, although the grapevine is hard to control, it is often much faster in operation than formal communication channels. Managers may use it to distribute information through planned "leaks" or judiciously placed "just-between-you-and-me" remarks.

Keith Davis, who has extensively studied grapevines in organizations, has identified four possible types of **grapevine chains.**[38] (See Figure 18-3.) In the "single-strand" chain, person A tells something to person B, who tells it to person C, and so on down the line. This chain is least accurate at passing on information. (It is the equivalent of the chain in the "telephone" game we described earlier in the chapter.) In the "gossip" chain, one person seeks out and tells everyone the information he or she has obtained. This chain is often used when information of an interesting but non–job-related nature is being conveyed. In the "probability" chain, individuals are indifferent about whom they offer information to; they tell people at random, and those people in turn tell others at random. This chain is likely to be used when the information is mildly interesting but insignificant. In the "cluster" chain, person A conveys the information to a few selected individuals, some of whom then inform a few selected others.

Davis believes that the cluster chain is the dominant grapevine pattern in organizations: Usually, only a few individuals, called "liaison individuals," pass on the information they have obtained, and they are likely to do so only to people they trust or from whom they would like favors. They are most likely to pass on information that is interesting to them, job-related, and, above all, timely. People do not pass on old information for fear of advertising the fact that they are uninformed.

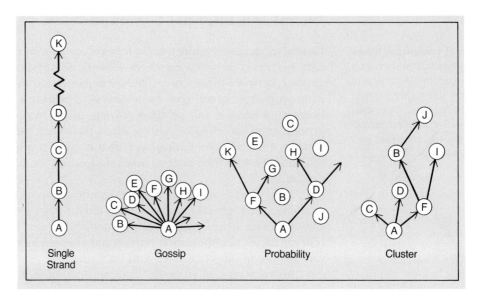

FIGURE 18-3 Types of Grapevine Chains

Source: Reprinted by permission of the *Harvard Business Review.* An exhibit from "Management Communication and the Grapevine" by Keith Davis (September–October 1953). Copyright © 1953 by the President and Fellows of Harvard College; all rights reserved.

Overcoming Organizational Barriers to Communication

In order to deal with the barriers to organizational communication, we must first recognize that communication is an inherently complex process. For one thing, the verbal and visual symbols we use to describe reality are far from precise. A simple word like "job," for example, can be applied to anything from a child's newspaper route to the presidency of the United States. Words like "achievement," "effectiveness," and "responsibility" are even more vague. This imprecision of language (and gestures) is one reason that perfect communication is difficult, if not impossible, to achieve.

Another reason that communication is inherently difficult is that human beings perceive and interpret reality according to their individual backgrounds, needs, emotions, values, and experiences. A production manager's memo to supervisors asking for figures on absenteeism will be seen as a legitimate request by one supervisor and as unnecessary meddling by another; a manager's instructions may seem coldly formal to some subordinates and appropriately polite to others; a quarterly report may be clear to one superior and confusing to another. Some writers, in fact, believe that most organizational barriers to communication are based on differences in the way people interpret the communications they receive.[39] Often these differences can be traced to cultural differences, as shown in the International Management box.

Comprehending the innate barriers to communication and taking steps to minimize them are therefore the first steps toward improving a manager's ability to communicate effectively. Making explicit as many relevant aspects of a situation as possible will probably lead to a more effective and meaningful communication: A memo to members of the quality control department about the need to adjust inspection standards, for example, will usually be better received if it states the practical reasons for the changes (such as an increased marketing emphasis on the organization's ability to deliver high-quality products). Such a memo will sound less like an autocratic directive and more like a frank request from one person to another. Similarly, the manager should not assume that information left out of a communica-

Communication in an Increasingly Global Economy

Here is a simple question that raises the issue of *cultural relativism*—the principle that it is unfair to judge the standards of one culture by those of another: Do the Japanese and the Chinese value teamwork equally as a managerial approach to encouraging productivity? One Chinese manager responded to this question in terms of the following parable: One Chinese worker can carry two buckets of water; two Chinese workers will carry one bucket; three Chinese workers will probably end up carrying no water at all. This answer has at least one clear implication for assessing the influence of cultural differences on worker motivation: The Chinese appear to be much more individually motivated than the Japanese, whose organizational structures reflect the highly group-oriented motivations of the culture as a whole.

Such differences, paradoxically, become both more pronounced and more important when we consider the interdependence of global business activities. For example, more and more countries are investing in the U.S. economy, and Americans today work not only for U.S.-based multinational corporations all over the world but for a variety of foreign interests located in this country. By 1988, approximately 3 million Americans were working for foreign-owned businesses.

Communication difficulties, both verbal and nonverbal, become a good deal more complicated as the commercial community becomes more international in scope, and awareness of other cultures' manners, languages, customs, and values—and thus of their management approaches and business priorities—is essential to effective communication in a global business environment. Unfortunately, however, sociological studies show that Americans tend to be rather *ethnocentric*—that is, prone to judge the standards of other cultures by their own—in their attitudes toward foreign business cultures. We do not communicate as well as we should in the practical interest of international cooperation, but we do tend to communicate our penchant for ethnocentric thinking, and the result is usually the loss of both prestige and business.

Consider the following situation and answer the concluding question yourself before pondering the findings of the researchers who devised it:

> On an ocean voyage, you are traveling with your spouse, your child, and your mother. The ship develops problems and begins to sink. You are the only swimmer in the family and you can save only one other person. Whom would you save?

Cultural Relativism and Communication. Cultural differences have the potential of disrupting communication at this meeting between American and Japanese managers at the Chukin Bank in New York.

This situation was presented to a sampling of American and Asian men. Of the Americans, 60 percent said that they would save the child and 40 percent chose the wife. No one selected to save his mother. Among the Asian men, no less than 100 percent said that they would save their mothers. Their rationale? Although you can marry again and have another child, you have just one mother.

Clearly, there are vast cultural differences at work here in the factors influencing decision making. Equally clear is the fact that the Americans would have just as much difficulty in communicating their rationale to the Asians as the Asians would in communicating theirs to the Americans. Regardless of the direction of the communication, it would certainly be difficult for sender and receiver to work out a "common ground" for reconciling their respective decisions.

The lesson here is quite simple: It is not a very wise practice to attribute similar repositories of values and attitudes to different cultures. Multiply the simple variables involved in this illustration by the vast and intricate number of variables that arise when international corporations attempt to conduct cooperative business and you will see why so many American firms have realized the need to initiate cross-cultural training programs for the growing number of employees who will be participating in cooperative international business ventures.

Sources: Brendan Boyd, "Americans Working for Foreign Interests: Where Are They?" *Global Trade Magazine,* February 1988, pp. 19–23; James A. McCaffrey and Craig R. Hafner, "When Two Cultures Collide: Doing Business Overseas," *Training and Development Journal,* October 1985, pp. 26–31; James O'Toole, "The Good Managers of Sichuan," *Harvard Business Review,* May–June 1981, pp. 28–40; and Mary Lenz, "Business Insecurity: Advisors Ease Culture Shock," *The Dallas Times-Herald,* July 9, 1984, pp. 1C, 2C.

tion will be known to the receiver. For example, a manager providing instructions should first check to see if the subordinates understand the specialized terms likely to be used. The manager should also remember that some words may have meanings for the receiver that are different from those the manager intends.

In recent years, the idea that the physical layout of the workplace can influence an organization's communication patterns, and in turn its culture and policies, has attracted increasing interest. An open office layout, in which everyone has direct access to everyone else, will result in one type of interpersonal interaction; linear corridors of rooms will result in a different type. Thus, the design of a company's work spaces can be used to foster or inhibit such characteristics as creativity, privacy, and direct face-to-face interactions.[40]

COORDINATED RESOURCE
See Oddou Section on Leading the Organization, "Communicating."

■ USING COMMUNICATION SKILLS: NEGOTIATING TO MANAGE CONFLICTS

conflict Disagreement about the allocation of scarce resources or clashes regarding goals, values, and so on; can occur on the interpersonal or organizational level.

negotiation The use of communication skills and bargaining to manage conflict and reach mutually satisfying outcomes.

COORDINATED RESOURCE
The Distinctive Discussion for Chapter 18 found in the Lecture Extras supplement includes "Negotiation Basics."

Both individuals and organizations must dealt with **conflict,** which involves a disagreement about the allocation of scarce resources or a clash of goals, statuses, values, perceptions, or personalities. Much of the conflict we experience arises from our communication of our wants, needs, and values to others. Sometimes we communicate clearly, but others have differing needs. Sometimes we communicate poorly, and conflict emerges because others misunderstand us. Managers can, of course, use dominance and suppression in handling conflicts with subordinates, but **negotiation** can help us manage conflicts of all types in a more effective and mutually satisfying way.[41]

Negotiating to Manage Conflicts

There are countless examples of negotiation in daily life. We negotiate with a car dealer to buy a car; we negotiate with friends about which recreational activities to pursue; and we negotiate with our boss about working hours and conditions. Organizations, in turn, negotiate with Wall Street analysts over earnings expectations, with unions over contract provisions, with environmentalists over the "best" way to prevent and clean up pollution, and with employees over particular work assignments. According to Lewicki and Litterer, all these "negotiation situations" are defined by three characteristics:

1. There is a conflict of interest between two or more parties; that is, what one wants is not necessarily what the other one wants.

2. Either there is no fixed or established set of rules or procedures for resolving the conflict or the parties prefer to work outside of a set of rules and procedures to invent their own solution to the conflict.

3. The parties, at least for the moment, prefer to search for agreement rather than to openly fight, to have one side capitulate, to permanently break off contact, or to take their dispute to a higher authority for resolution.[42]

Many factors are important to successful negotiating, as shown in Figure 18-4. The actual negotiation process—the series of offers and counteroffers that we think of as the heart of the negotiation—depends on: (1) whether or not the parties see their interests as depending on each other (regardless of whether they actually do or not); (2) the extent of trust or distrust among the parties; (3) each party's ability to clearly communicate, persuade, or coerce the other party to its point of view; (4) the personalities and idiosyncrasies of the actual people involved; and (5) the goals and interests of the parties.

Examples of each factor are easy to find in real life. Many companies like Entré Computer see their interests as dependent on their customers' interests. Thus, nego-

Initiating Negotiations. Although the computer industry is notoriously free of uniform standards, Robert C. Miller, chief executive of MIPS, a Silicon Valley maker of computer chips, invited 50 of the industry's most influential executives to a meeting, with the official goal of negotiating a software standard for machines built around MIPS's products. Because a single standard would simplify the task of developing software and give some smaller players a competitive advantage against entrenched giants, early reports indicated that most participants had reached an agreement and even enlisted more supporters.

FIGURE 18-4 Factors Important to Negotiation

Source: Roy Lewicki and Joseph Litterer, *Negotiation and Negotiator: Readings, Exercises, and Cases* (Homewood, Ill.: Irwin, 1985), p. 44. Copyright © 1985 by Richard D. Irwin, Inc. Reprinted by permission.

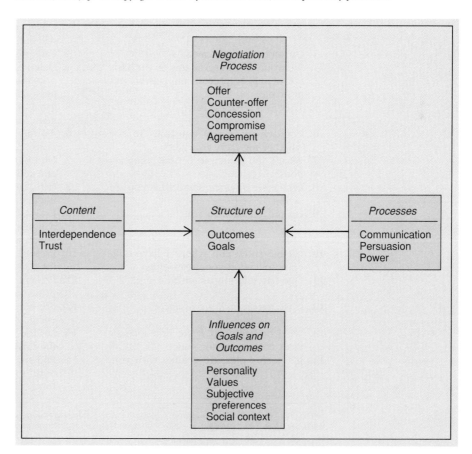

tiations often revolve around how Entré can fill a particular customer's needs and at what price. Many people distrust used car deals, so the process of offer-counteroffer on the price of a used car takes time as the parties work through this initial distrust. Sometimes third parties are involved as impartial evaluators, such as *trusted* mechanics. Salary negotiations between bosses and subordinates are driven by the options each has. Often the employee has little power, so the boss can get the employee to take any salary whatsoever, especially if he or she is a good communicator. Ronald Reagan and Mikhail Gorbachev's negotiations over nuclear arms in Iceland and James Baker's shuttle diplomacy in the Middle East during the 1991 Persian Gulf crisis illustrate the effects of personalities on the negotiating process. Sometimes, of course, negotiations are difficult because the parties have radically different interests, such as Exxon's desire to minimize its liability over the *Valdez* incident and environmentalists' desire to be sure there would be enough money for needed cleanups.

Negotiating is complex, especially when parties try to reach comprehensive and integrated agreements. In their book, based on a large-scale project at Harvard University that aimed at a comprehensive understanding of negotiation, Roger Fisher and William Ury discuss a set of stock phrases that describe the negotiation process.[43] (See Exhibit 18-2 for a summary.) Understanding the underlying concepts is critical to successful negotiating.

EXHIBIT 18-2 Stock Phrases in Negotiations

Stock Phrases	*Underlying Concepts*
1. Please correct me if I'm wrong.	1. Verify the facts so that both sides agree to them.
2. We appreciate what you've done for us.	2. Separate the people from the problem. Give personal support to the other person but not to his or her position.
3. Our concern is fairness.	3. Our position is based upon principle.
4. We would like to settle this on the basis not of selfish interest and power, but principle.	4. Defend your position based on the principle, even if the opponent tries to personalize it.
5. Trust is a separate issue.	5. Same. Return to the principle of fairness.
6. Could I ask a few questions to see whether my facts are right?	6. Ask questions rather than making assertions.
7. What's the principle behind your actions?	7. Find out the principle behind the other's actions if there is one.
8. Let me see if I understand what you are saying.	8. Use "active listening"—clarify your understanding of the other's position.
9. Let me get back to you.	9. Evaluate your position outside of the negotiation. Verify facts, think it over, check with constituency.
10. Let me show you where I have difficulty following your reasoning.	10. Present your rationale before presenting a new proposal.
11. One fair solution might be.	11. Present your proposal in context of the principle (fairness).
12. If we agree, or if we disagree.	12. Present alternative outcomes in the event of agreement or no agreement.
13. We'd be happy to settle in a manner most convenient for you.	13. Let the other have some influence on the final agreement.
14. It's been a pleasure dealing with you.	14. End the negotiation on a conciliatory note, even if you don't feel conciliatory.

Source: Roy Lewicki and Joseph Litterer, *Negotiation and Negotiator: Readings, Exercises, and Cases* (Homewood, Ill.: Irwin, 1985), p. 126. Copyright © 1985 by Richard D. Irwin, Inc. Reprinted by permission.

Negotiation in Action: Managing Management-Labor Conflict

Although unions are not as powerful as they once were, they are still an important fact of life for nonprofit, profit, and public-sector organizations such as the United States Postal Service. Furthermore, unions are actively recruiting members from nontraditional sources, such as the service sector, which will employ approximately 75 percent of the work force by the year 2000. Unions are also responding to changing work-force demographics by directing their efforts toward women and minorities.

RECOGNIZING UNION GOALS. Like their traditional counterparts, these members of the work force are looking to unions to protect a variety of job interests they feel management does not adequately guarantee:

1. *Economic*—the right to a livable wage.
2. *Job safety*—job security, freedom from arbitrary actions by management.
3. *Social affiliation*—a need to belong and to be accepted by peers.
4. *Self-esteem*—being able to have a voice in the "system."
5. *Status and self-fulfillment*—the exercise of leadership or other abilities through union service.

Of these, safety, social affiliation, and self-esteem are the major reasons why workers join unions today. Social pressure (the urgings of unionized co-workers) and job requirements ("union shops" requiring union membership as a condition of employment) also motivate workers to join unions.

In recent years, the intensification of price and technological competition, deregulation, and public-sector budget cutbacks has led managers to seek more efficient use of their organizations' work force. Efforts to improve efficiency frequently disrupt established work routines or threaten job security (for example, combining worker tasks, restricting overtime or weekend work, and laying off workers). Unions, in turn, have made work rule and job security issues a high priority. This situation, which is the source of conflict in many current management-labor interactions, shows no sign of abating and is likely to continue through this decade.

MINIMIZING NEGOTIATION CONFLICT. The success of management-labor negotiations depends a good deal on thorough preparation. The typical union contract is far too complex to leave until the last minute. It is now common, and necessary, to prepare for negotiations at least six months to a year before they are to commence.

In planning for negotiations, the manager first lists all the issues that have surfaced in previous negotiations, gathering information for this from past contracts, and then determines the overall priorities of these issues in terms of the company's financial, administrative, and productivity objectives. Next he or she reviews reports from line and staff on problem areas in the last contract, grievance statistics, morale problems, and any insights into the union climate and bargaining issues. Using this information, the manager can determine in advance the most and least preferable settlements on all of the bargaining issues.[44]

Traditionally, the union presents the company its proposed contractual changes to open the negotiations. The company replies with a counterproposal. Before entering into the negotiation process, management should be clear on its stance toward the union, its objectives and priorities on each bargaining issue, and its bargaining behavior. Either or both sides may present a proposal that contains excessive demands. This may be a negotiating ploy to obtain leverage for later trade-offs, or it may be a smoke screen to conceal the bargainer's real positions. Excessive demands by unions might also reflect the pet concerns of the rank and file or of influential officials. As the negotiations progress, flexibility becomes increasingly

EXHIBIT 18-3 Guidelines for Conducting Negotiations

❏ Have set, *clear objectives* on every bargaining item and understand the context within which the objectives are established.
❏ *Do not hurry.*
❏ When in doubt, *caucus.*
❏ Be *well prepared* with firm data support for clearly defined objectives.
❏ Maintain *flexibility* in your position.
❏ *Find* out *the motivations* for what the other party wants.
❏ *Do not get bogged down.* If there is no progress on a certain item, move on to another and come back to it later. Build the momentum for agreement.
❏ Respect the importance of *face-saving* for the other party.
❏ Be a good *listener.*
❏ Build a reputation for being *fair* but *firm.*
❏ Control your *emotions.*
❏ Be sure as you make each bargaining move that you know its *relationship* to all other moves.
❏ *Measure each move* against your *objectives.*
❏ Pay close attention to the *wording* of each clause negotiated.
❏ Remember that negotiating is by its nature a *compromise* process.
❏ Learn to *understand* people—it may pay off during negotiations.
❏ Consider the *impact of present negotiations on future ones.*

Source: Adapted from Reed C. Richardson, *Collective Bargaining by Objectives: A Positive Approach* (Englewood Cliffs, N.J.: Prentice Hall, 1985), pp. 168–169.

important. Negotiators must be able to back away from their original positions, make trade-offs, and introduce alternative solutions. Exhibit 18-3 offers some guidelines for conducting negotiations.

In the end, it is the strike deadline that often speeds up progress in the negotiations. Management may not be able to afford a strike; the union may risk losing valuable demands if it strikes. The threat of a strike can bring both parties back to reality and grant them the opportunity to reassess their positions. Each side will make major concessions in order to avert a strike that is not in their best interests.

■ *SUMMARY*

Communication may be defined as the process by which people attempt to share meanings through symbolic messages. The process of communication is important to managers because it enables them to carry on their management functions. The activity of communication, particularly oral communication, takes up a large portion of a manager's work time.

The major elements of the proposed model of communication are the sender, encoding, message, channel, receiver, decoding, noise, and feedback. Encoding is the process by which the sender converts the information to be transmitted into the appropriate symbols or gestures. Decoding is the process by which the receiver interprets the message. If the decoding matches the sender's encoding, the communication has been effective. Noise is whatever interferes with the communication. Two common types of noise are distractions and environmental noise. Feedback is the receiver's reaction to the sender's message; it repeats the communication process, with the sender and receiver roles reversed.

Communication may be one-way or two-way. In two-way communication, unlike one-way communication, feedback is provided to the sender. One-way communication is faster, but two-way communication is more accurate, and thus preferred for complex organizational tasks.

Barriers to communication include such factors as differing perceptions, language differences, noise, emotionality, inconsistent verbal and nonverbal communications, and distrust. Many of these barriers can be overcome by using simple, direct

ILLUSTRATIVE CASE STUDY

WRAP-UP

Communication Failures at Bhopal

By the time the first death tolls reached Union Carbide headquarters in Danbury, Connecticut, its formal communication channels had already been severely limited. There were only two telephone lines into the Bhopal area, so upper management had to rely on fragments of information funneled out of its Bombay subsidiary. Furthermore, the plant's supervisors had been arrested, which for all intents severed the rest of Union Carbide's formal channels of communication with the Bhopal plant. Anderson, too, was arrested when he arrived to assess the situation firsthand. Freed on bail, he was informed that the government of India expected Carbide to pay astronomical compensation damages—far beyond Carbide's $200 million insurance coverage.

Ultimately, this demand became the first offer in a long, agonizing negotiation process that, in late 1989, saw Union Carbide reaching a $470 million settlement with the government of India. In return, India's Supreme Court ordered the dismissal of all civil and criminal charges against Carbide and its officers and granted them further immunity from prosecution.

In theory, this should have ended the formal negotiations about legal liability. In the United States, certainly, the matter would have been closed, since U.S. Supreme Court decisions can only be overturned by an act of Congress. India, however, has a different system.

Under its constitution, India's Supreme Court has 26 justices, who are divided into a number of smaller benches. (Carbide's case, for example, was heard by a 5-judge bench.) Because the court is so large, any bench's decision can be reviewed by another bench, *if* anyone appeals a decision within 30 days. This is what happened in the Bhopal case: A number of voluntary organizations, claiming to represent the victims, petitioned India's Supreme Court, demanding that the settlement be voided on the grounds that it grossly underestimated the actual number of people who were severely injured.

Indian legal experts doubted that the voluntary groups had adequate grounds to reopen the case, but Carbide still faced the possibility that the long, painful negotiations might resume. Furthermore, it was bound by two critical conditions, agreed to early on in the original negotiations: It would accept the jurisdiction of the Indian courts, and it would satisfy any of their judgments—conditions that had been upheld in the U.S. Second Circuit Court of Appeals. Most troubling, perhaps, for Anderson was the provision, under Indian law, that managers could face criminal charges for organizational wrongdoing, although legal experts thought the Indian managers were more vulnerable here. In any case, Carbide's communications failures continue to haunt them and shadow their efforts to rebuild the company. Meanwhile, the money set aside for the settlement sits in a bank and cannot be used to help the real victims—the citizens of Bhopal. ■

Source: Subatra N. Chakravarty, "The Ghost Returns," *Forbes,* December 10, 1990, p. 108.

language, attempting to empathize with the receiver, avoiding distractions, being aware of one's own emotionality and nonverbal behavior, and being honest and trustworthy. Encouraging feedback and repeating one's message may also be helpful.

The effectiveness of organizational communication is influenced by the organization's formal channels of communication and authority structure, by job specialization, and by information ownership. The formal channels may be rigid and highly centralized, with individuals able to communicate with only a few persons, or they may be loose and decentralized, with individuals able to communicate with each other at any level. Experiments have found that for simple tasks, centralized networks are faster and more accurate, while for complex tasks, decentralized channels are quicker and more accurate. The most central person is most satisfied in centralized networks, while group members' satisfaction is higher in decentralized networks.

Vertical communication is communication that moves up and down the organization's chain of command. Status and power differences between manager and subordinates, a subordinate's desire for upward mobility, and a lack of trust between manager and subordinates interfere with accurate and complete vertical communication.

Lateral communication improves coordination and problem solving and fosters employee satisfaction. Informal communication occurs outside the organization's formal channels. A particularly quick and pervasive type of informal communication is the grapevine.

Overcoming the barriers to effective organizational communication requires that individual managers acknowledge the difficulties inherent in the communication process. Making relevant information explicit and remaining sensitive to how a particular communication will affect its receiver can minimize some of these difficulties.

All of a manager's communication skills come to bear in negotiations, a bargaining process that can be used to manage conflicts over the allocation of scarce resources or clashes in goals or values. The three essential elements of the negotiation situation are a conflict of interest, a lack of fixed or established rules for resolving the conflict, and a willingness to search for an agreement rather than fight or break off communication. Thus, negotiation requires a certain amount of trust and a desire to communicate. To negotiate effectively, though, managers need to learn to recognize stock phrases and understand their underlying concepts.

■ REVIEW QUESTIONS

1. Why is effective communication important to the manager?
2. List the eight elements in the expanded communication model.
3. What are some of the considerations involved in choosing the correct channel for one's message?
4. What is "noise" in a communication system?
5. Describe the common barriers to effective interpersonal communication. How may these barriers be overcome?
6. What four factors influence the effectiveness of organizational communication? How do they exert this influence?
7. What are the functions of vertical communication? How is accurate and complete vertical communication hindered?
8. What is the function of the grapevine? Why do managers sometimes use the grapevine to convey information? What are some possible grapevine chains according to Keith Davis? Which chain is most likely to be used in organizations?
9. How may the barriers to organizational communication be overcome?
10. What are the key elements in the negotiation situation? How can negotiation be used to manage conflicts?

CASE STUDY

Negotiations at Southside Electronics

Linda Muterspaugh was the manager in charge of Southside Electronics' relations with consumer groups. She had just come from a very frustrating meeting with a new group called INTACT, which was opposed to a new Southside product that could be plugged into the telephone line to reveal the number of the party making the incoming call.

Linda, on behalf of Southside, had explained that such a device would help users identify and then ignore unwelcome calls, such as the telephone salespeople who always call at suppertime. Furthermore, it could be used to trace annoying and obscene calls, a boon for many women who live alone.

She had been stunned to learn that INTACT was opposed to this device on the grounds that it was an invasion of the *caller's* privacy. INTACT's leader, a Chicago-trained lawyer named Henry Long, declared that if Southside went ahead with its plans to market the device in conjunction with local phone companies, his group was ready to marshall the support of the American Civil Liberties Union as well as local shelters for battered women. The fear motivating the latter was that abusive husbands could use the device to track down battered wives who called home to check on their children, say, or to attempt a reconciliation.

Linda had been quick to respond that she and Southside were willing to negotiate a solution, one that would resolve the conflict without resorting to the courts or a regulatory authority. However, she was unsure of how she should proceed, since she knew that Southside's managers were counting on this new product as a major source of revenue. A negotiation session was scheduled for the next week, and she needed to think through her strategy.

Source: This case is based on an actual management situation, but the names have been changed to protect the identities and interests of several parties to this very sensitive issue.

Case Questions

1. What does Linda Muterspaugh need to know about INTACT? Henry Long? Others at Southside?
2. How should Linda prepare for the upcoming meeting?
3. What factors will be important in reaching a solution?
4. What would you do if you were Linda?

VIDEO CASE STUDY

Federal Express TV

When Federal Express employees come to work in the morning, they turn on the television. But they aren't watching *The Today Show.* Instead, employees at 900 locations get 5 minutes of company news. The program, *FedEx Overnight,* features updates on delivery problems, overnight package volume, the company's closing stock price, and a national weather forecast. Employees are also recognized on the show for outstanding performance.

The programs are co-anchored by members of the company's video department and are broadcast via a private satellite network. Each program is sent out continuously for 30 minutes. It is also videotaped, so that as the company's more than 60,000 employees in the continental United States and Canada report for work during the day, they can see the shows. About 70 percent of all Federal Express employees watch the broadcast regularly. More than 90 percent watch other, special programs the company produces.

Federal Express is one of a growing number of companies that are using such networks to communicate with their employees. Before establishing FXTV in 1987, Federal Express used videotapes to reach its far-flung work force.

"We would hope people got the tape, hope they put it into the machine, and hope it would answer all their questions. But we never knew," says Tom Martin, managing director of employee communications.

Martin says television offers the advantage of simultaneously reaching large numbers of employees with the same message. "In the normal course of events, by the time a message gets repeated several times and gets to the rank and file, it can become confusing," he says. "With television, the chairman talks directly to the employees."

Federal Express uses the network for much more than the daily broadcasts. A series of televised management training sessions deals with everything from proper packaging techniques for fragile items to meeting service goals without blowing the budget or hurting employee morale. The packaging training has proved extremely successful. One month after the programs were broadcast, damage claims were down 19 percent at locations that received the show, compared with a companywide drop of 13 percent. Two months later, claims were down 31 percent at those locations compared with just 10 percent companywide.

The sales staff also watches TV. One program is exclusively for sales managers, another is aimed at the entire sales force. Both discuss new products and services as well as what the competition is doing.

Beyond this regular programming, Federal Express uses television for one-time broadcasts. Steven Priddy, vice president of personnel administration, says this may actually be the most valuable use of the network.

During one hour-long broadcast, Priddy and CEO Frederick W. Smith discussed changes in Federal Express's pay structure. After listening to an explanation of the new system, employees were able to phone in from throughout the country to ask questions and receive answers.

"If employees see the people making the decisions and hear, from them, the reasons for making those decisions, it makes the changes easier to understand," Priddy says. "Also, because we answer questions on the air during the broadcast, employees see no opportunity for propaganda. They know we haven't prepackaged the information in whatever form it's most palatable."

Often FXTV features rank-and-file employees. "When employees see their peers on the air, they are more likely to phone in questions," Martin says. "Sometimes the executives can be a bit intimidating."

Sources: Erik Calonius, "Federal Express's Battle Overseas," *Fortune,* December 3, 1990, pp. 137–140; Alan Halcrow, "FXTV Is on the Air to Employees," *Personnel Journal,* October 1988, pp. 18–20; Herb Brody, "Business TV Becomes Big Business," *High Technology Business,* May 1988, pp. 26–30; Fleming Meeks, "Live from Dallas," *Forbes,* December 26, 1988, pp. 112–113; and Virginia A. Ostendorf, "Applying Business Television," *Satellite Communications,* September 1988, pp. 19–23.

Case Questions

1. What does Federal Express's management feel are the advantages of a private satellite network over videotapes?

2. What drawbacks, if any, do you think an internal television system might have?

3. How could Federal Express expand its network to provide more information to employees?

4. How much time each day do you think employees should spend watching internal television programs?

■ NOTES

[1] Fred Luthans and Janet K. Larsen, "How Managers Really Communicate," *Human Relations* 39 (1986):161–178.

[2] Rosemary Stewart, *Managers and Their Jobs* (London: Macmillan, 1967), pp. 72–73.

[3] "Fast Times on Avenida Madison," *Business Week,* June 6, 1988, pp. 62–67.

[4] Anne Moncreiff Ararte, "Old Money, New Lifestyle," *Advertising Age,* July 9, 1990, pp. S-1, S-6.

[5] F. E. X. Dance, "The 'Concept' of Communication," *Journal of Communication* 20, no. 2 (1970): 201–210.

[6] Lyman W. Porter and Karlene H. Roberts, "Communication in Organizations," in Marvin D. Dunnette, ed., *Handbook of Industrial and Occupational Psychology,* 2nd ed. (New York: Wiley, 1983), pp. 1553–1589.

[7] John Kotter, "Power, Dependence, and Effective Management," *Harvard Business Review* 55, no. 4 (1977):125–136.

[8] H. H. Clark, "Language Use and Language Users," in *Handbook of Social Psychology,* G. Lindzey and E. Aronson, eds., 3rd ed. (Reading, Mass.: Addison-Wesley, 1984).

[9] K. Deaux and L. S. Wrightsman, *Social Psychology in the 80s,* 4th ed. (Monterey, Cal.: Brooks/Cole, 1984).

[10] R. E. Petty and J. T. Cacioppo, "The Effects of Involvement on Responses to Argument Quantity and Quality: Central and Peripheral Routes to Persuasion," *Journal of Personality and Social Psychology* 46 (1984):69–81.

[11] W. J. McGuire, "Attitudes and Attitude Change," in *Handbook of Social Psychology,* G. Lindzey and E. Aronson, eds., 3rd ed., Vol. 2 (New York: Random House, 1985).

[12] Our discussion is based on Linda M. Micheli, Frank V. Cespedes, Donald Byker, and Thomas J. C. Raymond, *Managerial Communication* (Glenview, Ill.: Scott, Foresman, 1984), pp. 186–201; and Judson Smith and Janice Orr, *Designing and Developing Business Communications Programs That Work*

(Glenview, Ill.: Scott, Foresman, 1985), pp. 4–6. See also Norman B. Sigband and Arthur H. Bell, *Communication for Management and Business* (Glenview, Ill.: Scott, Foresman, 1986); Courtland L. Bovee and John V. Thill, *Business Communications Today* (New York: Random House, 1986); and Robert W. Rasberry and Laura F. Lemoine, *Managerial Communications* (Boston: Kent, 1986).

[13]See Paul R. Timm and Christopher G. Jones, *Business Communication: Getting Results* (Englewood Cliffs, N.J.: Prentice Hall, 1983), p. 5.

[14]Larry R. Smeltzer and John L. Waltman, *Managerial Communication: A Strategic Approach* (New York: Wiley, 1984), p. 4.

[15]Ibid., p. 41.

[16]Ibid., p. 5.

[17]Ibid., p. 8.

[18]See James L. Gibson, John M. Ivancevich, and James H. Donnelly Jr., *Organizations: Behavior, Structure, Processes,* 5th ed. (Dallas: Business Publications, 1985), p. 535.

[19]Smeltzer and Waltman, *Managerial Communication,* p. 189.

[20]Harold J. Leavitt, *Managerial Psychology,* 4th ed. (Chicago: University of Chicago Press, 1978), pp. 117–126. See also John T. Samaras, "Two-Way Communication Practices for Managers," *Personnel Journal* 59, no. 8 (1980):645–648.

[21]C. Glenn Pearce, Ross Figgins, and Steven P. Golen, *Principles of Business Communication: Theory, Application, and Technology* (New York: John Wiley, 1984), p. 516.

[22]Ibid., p. 538.

[23]Ibid., p. 524.

[24]R. Buck, *The Communication of Emotion* (New York: Guilford Press, 1984). For a discussion of how nonverbal behavior communicates such messages as sympathy, threat, or status, see A. W. Siegman and S. Feldstein, *Multichannel Integrations of Nonverbal Behavior* (Hillsdale, N.J.: Erlbaum, 1985). Nonverbal cues can also contribute to turn-taking during communication; see C. L. Kleinke, "Gaze and Eye Contact: A Research Review," *Psychological Bulletin* 100 (1986):78–100.

[25]W. Charles Redding, *The Corporate Manager's Guide to Better Communication* (Glenview, Ill.: Scott, Foresman, 1984), pp. 74–75.

[26]Pearce et al., *Principles of Communication,* pp. 522–523.

[27]Ibid., pp. 522, 524.

[28]David V. Gibson and Barbara E. Mendleson, "Redundancy," *Journal of Business Communication* 21, no. 1 (1984):43–61, especially 52.

[29]See Raymond V. Lesikar, "A General Semantics Approach to Communication Barriers in Organizations," in Keith Davis, ed., *Organizational Behavior: A Book of Readings,* 5th ed. (New York: McGraw-Hill, 1977), pp. 336–337.

[30]See Harold J. Leavitt, "Some Effects of Certain Communication Patterns on Group Performance," *Journal of Abnormal and Social Psychology* 46, no. 1 (1951):38–50. Our discussion is also based on H. Joseph Reitz, *Behavior in Organizations,* rev. ed. (Homewood, Ill.: Irwin, 1981); Gibson et al., *Organizations: Behavior, Structure, Processes,* pp. 544–545; Leavitt, *Managerial Psychology;* and Marvin E. Shaw, "Communication Networks," in Leonard Berkowitz, ed., *Advances in Experimental Social Psychology,* Vol. 1 (New York: Academic Press, 1964), pp. 111–147. See also Karlene H. Roberts and Charles O'Reilly III, "Some Correlations of Communication Roles in Organizations," *Academy of Management Journal* 22, no. 1 (1979):42–57.

[31]Kenneth N. Wexley and Gary A. Yukl, *Organizational Behavior and Personnel Psychology,* rev. ed. (Homewood, Ill.: Irwin, 1984), pp. 80–83.

[32]Michael J. Glauser, "Upward Information Flow in Organizations: Review and Conceptual Analysis," *Human Relations* 37, no. 8 (1984):613–643.

[33]Porter and Roberts, "Communication in Organizations," pp. 1573–1574. See also Robert A. Snyder and James H. Morris, "Organizational Communication and Performance," *Journal of Applied Psychology* 69, no. 3 (1984):461–465.

[34]Wexley and Yukl, *Organizational Behavior and Personnel Psychology,* pp. 82–83.

[35]See also Robert E. Kaplan, "Trade Routes: The Manager's Network of Relationships," *Organizational Dynamics* 12, no. 4 (1984):38–52; and Eric M. Eisenberg, Peter R. Monge, and Katherine I. Miller, "Involvement in Communication Networks as a Predictor of Organizational Commitment," *Human Communication Research* 10, no. 2 (1983):179–201.

[36]See Richard L. Simpson, "Vertical and Horizontal Communication in Formal Organizations," *Administrative Science Quarterly* 4, no. 2 (1959):188–196.

[37]Keith Davis, "Grapevine Communication Among Lower and Middle Managers," *Personnel Journal* 48, no. 4 (1969), pp. 269–272. See also Joe Thomas and Ricky Griffin, "The Power of Social Information in the Workplace," *Organizational Dynamics* 18, no. 2 (Autumn 1989):63–75.

[38]See Keith Davis, "Management Communication and the Grapevine," *Harvard Business Review* 31, no. 5 (1953):43–49; "Communication *Within* Management," *Personnel* 31, no. 3 (November 1954):212–218; and "Cut Those Rumors Down to Size," *Supervisory Management,* June 1975, pp. 2–6.

[39]Raymond V. Lesikar, *Business Communication: Theory and Application,* 5th ed. (Homewood, Ill.: Irwin, 1984), pp. 20–22.

[40]Fritz Steele, "The Ecology of Executive Teams: A New View of the Top," *Organizational Dynamics* 11, no. 4 (1983):65–78.

[41]This section is based on Roy Lewicki and Joseph Litterer's excellent book, *Negotiation and Negotiator: Readings, Exercises, and Cases* (Homewood, Ill.: Irwin, 1985).

[42]Ibid.

[43]Roger Fisher and William Ury, with Bruce Patton, ed., *Getting to Yes* (Boston: Houghton Mifflin, 1981). See also Frank Tutzauer and Michael Roloff, "Communication Processes Leading to Integrative Agreements," *Communication Research* 15, no. 4 (August 1988):360–380.

[44]See *The Negotiating Edge* (Palo Alto, Calif.: Human Edge Software, 1985). Another program for preparing for negotiations is *The Art of Negotiating* (Berkeley, Calif.: Experience in Software, 1985). See also Robert Bies, Debra Shapiro, and Larry Cummings, "Causal Accounts and Managing Organizational Conflict," *Communication Research* 15, no. 4 (August 1988):381–399.

CHAPTER NINETEEN

INDIVIDUAL CAREER MANAGEMENT

Detail from Paul Klee, *The Timid Brute*

Upon completing this chapter, you should be able to:

Describe early career experiences and dilemmas that can make it hard for young and reentry workers to adjust to the business world.

2. Explain the importance of becoming politically sensitive to organizational life.

3. Explain the causes of work stress and how it can be relieved.

4. Compare and contrast Erikson's and Levinson's models of careers over the life cycle.

5. Explain the meaning of the terms "career concepts," "career anchors," and "career plateau."

6. Identify the key tasks of individual career management and map out a personal career plan.

7. Explain how you would handle specific career issues, such as being part of a dual-career couple or finding a mentor.

Paul Klee, *The Timid Brute*. 1938. Oil and gouache on canvas. 22¼ × 29 inches. Private
Collection, New York.

ILLUSTRATIVE CASE STUDY

INTRODUCTION

Selina Proctor: Parent and Professional

When Elizabeth screamed, Selina Proctor bolted out of bed and grabbed her bathrobe. She glanced at the clock—it was 3:30 A.M.—and at her husband, Kenneth, who had slept through the piercing wail of their 18-month-old child. Elizabeth continued to cry as Selina held her closely and tried to comfort her. Selina guessed that Elizabeth was suffering from yet another ear infection—the fourth of the winter—and would probably need medical attention.

As she stood there gazing at the whimpering child, Selina's thoughts turned abruptly to practicalities. The baby needed to see the doctor first thing in the morning, but Selina had an important meeting scheduled for 9:00 A.M. She and a senior partner in her law firm were to represent one of the firm's clients in discussions about the terms of a $20 million lawsuit brought against the client and five other defendants. Because of the number of defendants, the meeting had been difficult to arrange. At last, after delays of several weeks, it was set. Selina had prepared memoranda for the senior partner in charge and was to make a presentation to all the defendants concerning the costs if a prompt settlement were not reached. It was obvious to Selina that somehow she had to make the meeting.

Selina realized that she could not possibly take Elizabeth to the doctor and get to work in time for the meeting. The doctor's office wouldn't open until 8:00 A.M., and the earliest possible appointment was at 9:00 A.M.—and in all likelihood, that appointment would not be available.

As a lawyer, Selina could generally set her own schedule, but work still conflicted with the demands of being a parent and homemaker—and she got little help from Kenneth, who was not very flexible about his own work. She couldn't tell whether his job was really as demanding as he claimed, but she suspected it wasn't. Kenneth believed women were as fully capable as men in every aspect of the modern workaday world, but in Selina's view, he didn't fully appreciate the demands of parenthood and how these demands conflicted with a woman's career.

Selina had never missed an appointment or meeting because of child-care responsibilities. She had always been able to work things out to accommodate her clients, her employer, and her child. She

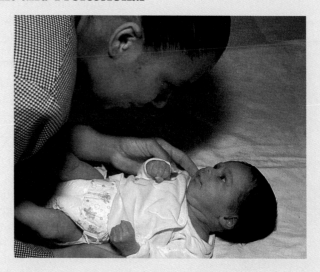

was both amused and disgusted by the lawyers who worried that part-timers were likely to miss important meetings. Busy lawyers were always missing important meetings—you can only be in one place at a time, and busy lawyers have numerous clients constantly clamoring for their attention. Scheduling seemed to become a controversial issue only when children were involved. Sometimes it seemed that tennis matches and dental appointments received more respect when offered as a scheduling constraint than a child's needs.

Nevertheless, Selina did not want to miss tomorrow's meeting. She hoped that Kenneth would be able to stay home in the morning to take Elizabeth to the doctor. If he couldn't, what would she do? She didn't want to challenge Kenneth about which commitment—his or hers—was more important. A confrontation would only lead to bigger questions: Whose career was more important? Whose contribution to the family was more valuable?

It was half past five, and Elizabeth had dozed off. Selina was starting to grow weary of her own thoughts—she had been through them so many times before. Maybe she should just quit her job and spend more time with her family.

Source: Adapted from Lynda Sharp Paine, a case prepared for The Olsson Center for Applied Ethics, The Darden School, University of Virginia, 1984.

561

TEACHING TIP
This chapter should be a
fun one to teach. Encour-
age your students to think
about their future careers.
What do they want to ac-
complish? By when? Are
they taking steps now to
meet these goals?

COORDINATED RESOURCE
See Samaras Exercise 6.2,
"Find Your Career."

THOUGHT PROVOKER
Why are careers impor-
tant?

Selina's decision is typical of the dilemmas adults face throughout their careers. They must select an employer, satisfy supervisors, handle stress on the
job, compete for promotions, decide when to change jobs, balance their
work and home lives, and so on. Fortunately, many of these events and problems are predictable, so you *can* prepare for them ahead of time. Indeed, a growing
body of research on career development has given us a better understanding of how
careers evolve and how career problems can be managed.[1]

In other chapters of this book, we have been concerned with how individuals
manage *other people's* careers or the organization's resources. In this chapter, the
emphasis is on the *individual's* own career. We will describe the influence of early
organizational experiences on the individual's future performance and satisfaction;
the early career dilemmas a young manager is likely to encounter; the stages through
which careers evolve; and finally, how you can take an active role in managing your
career and realize your career goals.

■ EARLY CAREER EXPERIENCES: EXPECTATIONS VERSUS REALITY

For many young and reentry workers who are new to the business world, the excitement of being hired quickly turns to frustration and disappointment. In their eager-
ness to get a job, applicants tend to overstate their abilities and understate their
needs, neglecting crucial research on the organization to which they are applying.
Meanwhile, recruiters and interviewers, hoping to attract a large pool of qualified
applicants, sometimes inflate the attractiveness of a job. Thus, each side offers an
assortment of truths, half-truths, and concealments.

**syndrome of unused
potential,** or **reality
shock syndrome** Ac-
cording to Hall, an individual's reaction to the difference between high job
expectations and the frustrating day-to-day realities
of the workplace.

COORDINATED RESOURCE
The Distinctive Discus-
sions for Chapter 19 found
in the Lecture Extras sup-
plement include "Baby
Busters: What Type of
Managers Are They?" and
"Glass Ceilings."

COORDINATED RESOURCE
The Application Exercise
for Chapter 19 found in
the Lecture Extras supplement is a "Job Expecta-
tions Exercise."

As a result, many new employees face what Douglas T. Hall terms the **syndrome of unused potential** or **reality shock syndrome.**[2] They may be dismayed
to find their initial assignments routine and even boring. Worse, the boss expects
them to conform to established rules and procedures, is threatened or unmoved by
their brash proposals to reform the workplace, and is usually too busy to give them
feedback on how well they are doing. The reality shock syndrome is especially
severe for young MBAs who have done particularly well in their studies or graduated
from prestigious business schools. They are used to a challenging atmosphere in
which feedback (usually favorable) is fast and regular. But once on the job, they
perceive themselves as just additional cogs on a wheel—their skills and abilities
unused and unsought.[3]

Edgar Schein found that almost 75 percent of one sample of MBA graduates
changed jobs at least once over a five-year period.[4] He also found that within five
years most companies lose over half the college graduates they hire. Schein attributes this high turnover to the clash between the graduates' expectations and the
realities of the organization. Similarly, in their study of a small group of American
business school graduates working in South America, John D. Aram and James A. F.
Stoner found that job continuation and satisfaction were related to how closely the
graduates' initial expectations matched the realities of their jobs.[5]

Obviously, this kind of turnover is a waste for both employer and employee. In
the rest of this section, we will look at three aspects of the early job experience—
the hiring process and initial job assignment, the actions of the first superior, and the
new employee's introduction to the corporate culture—with the idea of seeing how
these disappointments can be avoided.

The Hiring Process and the First Job Assignment

Many problems can be avoided if the organization is thorough and conscientious in
presenting the job and explaining the qualifications and personal characteristics

TEACHING TIP
You could have your students do a "practice" résumé.

COORDINATED RESOURCE
See Samaras Reading "Selling Yourself in the Career Market."

they seek. Organizations like IBM recruit with the utmost care, expending time, resources, and energy to screen and select potential employees. Other firms have gone out of their way to attract women and minorities as candidates for middle-management positions—among them IBM, American Express, General Mills, GTE, Hallmark, Levi-Strauss, Hewlett-Packard, Lotus, and Simon & Schuster.

One of the organization's most effective tools here is the realistic job preview (RJP), whereby the organization summarizes both the positive and negative aspects of the job. (See Chapter 13.) By creating an atmosphere of honesty with RJPs, organizations hope to increase the chances that job candidates will be honest about their skills and interests and turn down inappropriate jobs. To keep their end of the bargain, job applicants must analyze their career goals and be accurate in presenting their skills and qualifications on their résumés and in their job interviews. (See the Ethics in Management box.)

Once hired, of course, the newcomer's impression of the organization—and the world of work as a whole—will be refined by the initial job assignment. The importance of the initial job assignment has been affirmed by a number of research studies. One study of 1,000 recent college graduates hired by a large manufacturing company found that about half had left the company within a three-year period. Those who had left the company, as well as those who had remained, cited the lack of job challenge as the major cause of their disenchantment with the firm.[6] In another study, David E. Berlew and Douglas T. Hall followed the careers of 62 junior executives over the first five years of employment.[7] The researchers found that the degree of challenge the junior executives were given in their first jobs correlated closely with how successfully they performed subsequent assignments and with how rapidly their careers advanced.

Berlew and Hall suggest that the successful accomplishment of challenging tasks causes people to internalize high performance standards, which they then apply to future work tasks. In addition, individuals who accomplish their first assignment successfully increase the organization's expectations for them, so they receive more difficult and challenging assignments. Those who are given unchallenging jobs initially, on the other hand, neither internalize high standards nor receive as much recognition for their work. Yet, despite the evident importance of challenging job assignments, many organizations continue to provide their new employees with relatively routine initial assignments.

Actions of the First Supervisor

The influence of the first supervisor on a new employee's subsequent performance has also been noted by a number of researchers.[8] For the newcomer, the first supervisor embodies the virtues and defects of the organization itself. If the supervisor is found wanting by the new employee, the organization may be regarded as an undesirable place to work. Nevertheless, many companies often entrust the handling of incoming graduates to men and women who are not trained for the task and who are not especially good managers. Other companies—including Merck Pharmaceuticals and Philip Morris—are noted for their willingness and ability to recruit, develop, and retain new employees through programs designed to assist managers in the integration of newcomers.

Special training, patience, and insight are required by supervisors of new employees for a number of reasons. First, new employees are likely to make a higher-than-average number of mistakes, and if impatient supervisors overreact to those mistakes, they will weaken the new employees' self-image and enthusiasm. Second, insecure supervisors often control new employees too closely—either to keep them from making mistakes or to prevent them from appearing too successful or knowledgeable. As a result, the employees are not permitted to learn from their mistakes and may not achieve recognition for their successes.

Finally, and most important, the expectations of supervisors affect new employee's attitudes and performance, since the employees will tend to fulfill those expectations regardless of their actual ability.[9] A supervisor who looks upon newcomers as potentially outstanding performers will treat them accordingly, thereby motivating them to do their best—and the supervisor's expectation will tend to be confirmed. Conversely, a supervisor who expects newcomers to perform poorly will communicate these expectations directly or indirectly, thereby triggering the indifferent performance that fulfills the negative expectation.

How Individuals Fit into the Organizational Culture

CLASS COMMENT
According to the U.S. Department of Labor, women make up 40 percent of a loosely defined demographic category of managers and administrators. (*Fortune*, 7/30/90, p. 40ff.)

COORDINATED RESOURCE
See *Management Live!* Reading 5.2, "Women Managers Experience Special Power Failures."

Every organization has a culture—a set of shared understandings that determine its goals, style of work, and attitude toward employees. In one job, a newcomer may feel comfortable from the outset because he or she speaks the same language as co-workers and gets good responses to early efforts and initiatives. In another job, a clash of styles is evident from the beginning or soon emerges. The congruence between an individual's style and an organization's culture has an early impact that may color the individual's whole experience with the organization. It helps determine how well employees are likely to perform, how much they will enjoy working in the organization, and whether they are likely to want to stay.

A fit that is initially less than perfect does not necessarily mean that a person is in the wrong job. The individual will probably make adjustments as he or she is socialized into the organization's practices. Indeed, adjustments of this sort are likely even when the employee and the organization are very compatible. If the initial fit is good, these adjustments will tend to be small and painless for both the individual and his or her co-workers. On the other hand, attempts to make major changes can be traumatic and are not very likely to be successful. Of course, the organization may also make adjustments to accommodate the individual, but such adjustments are normally small in magnitude and slow in coming.[10]

■ *EARLY CAREER DILEMMAS*

Based on a review of the literature and on an analysis of his own interviews with hundreds of young managers, Ross A. Webber has pinpointed three classes of career problems that typically plague managers early in their working lives: political insensitivity and passivity, loyalty dilemmas, and personal anxiety, which are complicated by role conflict and stress.[11] Webber suggests that being aware of these problems may minimize their potentially damaging consequences.

COORDINATED RESOURCE
See Samaras Case, 6.2, "It's Your Career, Buddy."

COORDINATED RESOURCE
See Study Guide Self-Learning Exercise 19, "Attitudes Toward Women at Work."

Political Insensitivity and Passivity

The struggle for and exercise of power are inevitable and probably essential parts of organizational life. Managers *seek* power because it helps them achieve personal and organizational goals. Managers *exercise* power in order to influence their subordinates to perform effectively and also to protect the integrity of their units.

Of course, political power can be misused—to dominate others, say, or to treat them like pawns.[12] For this reason, young business school graduates are often repelled by the idea of "playing politics" or forming political alliances. They may be unable to distinguish between healthy organizational politics and the unhealthy manipulation of power. Furthermore, their schooling tends to create the impression that organizational problems are always solved *rationally*. In reality, supervisors tend to ignore threatening suggestions from newcomers they do not know or trust.

Confronted with these realities, Weber says, new employees often become passive or withdrawn. They concentrate on their narrow specialties and permit their

ETHICS IN MANAGEMENT

The Art of Writing a Résumé

Your résumé is important: This single page can make or break your search for a position. If it does not make a good impression, you probably won't get invited for an interview. Employers use résumés to screen hundreds of prospective employees and pare the list down to the 10 or 20 they want to interview. During this process, the average résumé is only examined for about 30 seconds—a very short time in which to make your presentation and convince a stranger that you are worthy of further consideration. Small wonder, then, that writing that résumé is an important and high-pressure start on a job search.

Regardless of the source, much of the professional advice you get will be virtually identical. Everyone says, "Use action verbs" and "Present accomplishments, not just duties." People tell you to "Use numbers to back up your assertions." Although such advice is generally solid, the process of writing a résumé is not as easy as it may first appear.

Applicants search for just the right words to describe their experience and education, trying to find the key to passing the first screen. Given the importance of the document, it is not surprising that some candidates go beyond "dressing up" résumés with overembellished prose to inserting complete falsehoods. Degrees from colleges attended only briefly, if at all, and positions never held appear more frequently than most people realize. To combat this, many employers now use certification services to check the accuracy of the résumés they receive. Obviously, discovery of inaccuracies in a résumé normally precludes further consideration. Even if the inaccurate résumé does land you the job, eventual discovery can result in charges of fraud.

But what about the vast gray area between complete honesty and blatant lies? When do action verbs and embellished accomplishments distort the real picture? How much difference is there between "*contributed to* the budget report" and "*wrote* the budget report"? Between "*part of a team* to establish a new program to . . ." and "*established* a new program to . . ."? Just when does the natural inclination and practical necessity of presenting yourself in the best possible light become dishonest? These are questions all job hunters must confront, knowing that they may be the ultimate loser if a misleading résumé wins them a job that doesn't match their actual capabilities or interests.

Source: William Bryant Logan, "Detective Story," *Venture,* September 1987, p. 124; "Certified Résumés Eliminate Hiring Fears," *Chain Store Age Executive,* June 1987, p. 68.

A Consummate Politician. Unlike many young professionals, General Colin L. Powell, chairman of the Joint Chiefs of Staff, has never shied away from the task of forming political alliances. Indeed, this holder of an M.B.A. from George Washington University lectures every new group of generals that it is not enough just to understand military doctrine; they must also understand the role that politics and public relations play in achieving military objectives.

careers to drift. This is a grave mistake. Young managers who learn to accept organizational realities develop their political awareness and begin to build effective working relationships with a broad base of people who will help them do their jobs.

Loyalty Dilemmas

FOR DISCUSSION
Ask students if they have had any of these experiences. Would they be willing to share them with the class? If you have had any of these experiences, describe it.

New employees face various legitimate demands on their loyalty. Loyalty is necessary to organizational functioning, but definitions of loyalty differ and loyalty demands often conflict with reality as perceived by a newcomer. Moreover, meeting extreme definitions of loyalty can damage both the subordinate and the organization. Webber describes five common ways that loyalty can be defined by a superior:

1. *"Obey me."* Managers have a right to expect that their legitimate directives will be obeyed because disobedience, if carried too far, will prevent the organization from reaching its objectives. However, unquestioning obedience on the part of subordinates can lead to ineffective actions. Subordinates who know, for example, that a superior's instructions are inappropriate but who proceed to obey them out of loyalty are doing both their superior and organization more harm than good. Sometimes loyalty may even call for disobedience of an order that is unethical or made in haste or anger. (Recall our discussion of Stanley Milgram's obedience experiment in a previous chapter.)

2. *"Protect me and don't make me look bad."* Because managers are responsible for and ultimately judged by the actions of their subordinates, they have a right to expect those subordinates to consider their superiors' reputation as they carry out their work activities. Sometimes, however, this loyalty demand leads subordinates to avoid taking necessary risks or to cover up mistakes.

3. *"Work hard."* In the eyes of many managers, the best proof of loyalty is the willingness to work long and hard. However, if unrealistic standards of performance are demanded, morale may drop and subordinates may feel overburdened.

4. *"Be successful."* "Get the job done no matter what" and "I don't care what you do as long as the bottom line shows a profit" are often implicit (if not explicit) in managers' instructions to their subordinates. This may cause subordinates to feel a conflict between organizational loyalty and their own ethical codes. If they disobey instructions, their careers might suffer; if they violate their ethics (or the law), guilt or scandal might result.

5. *"Tell me the truth."* It is obviously important for superiors to be told about problems in their units—not only so they can take steps to deal with the problems, but also so they can prepare to deal with their own superiors. All too often, however, reporting a problem—especially when it is in the subordinate's area of responsibility—causes the subordinate to be blamed or punished. In such situations, newcomers often learn to apply their loyalty selectively, putting self-protection before the needs of their superiors or the organization. As a consequence, failures may not be reported until it is too late to mimimize their consequences.

Personal Anxiety

COORDINATED RESOURCE
See DuBose Reading #26, "The Stress of Excellence."

As their assignments grow more challenging, and salary increases and promotions signal recognition of their efforts, young managers derive greater satisfaction from their jobs. Paradoxically, Webber suggests, they also begin to feel anxiety about their growing commitment to the organization. The independence and integrity they valued as students and as young managers sometimes conflict with the increasing demands made on them in higher-level positions. The manner in which they resolve this conflict will play an important role in determining how their careers unfold.

Edgar Schein has described three ways in which an individual can respond to the organization's efforts to enforce compliance with its values and expectations:[13]

1. *Conformity.* The individual completely accepts all the organization's norms

and values. This represents a loss for both the individual and the organization. The individual loses his or her sense of identity and initiative, while the organization loses access to the diversity of opinion and ideas that its long-term health requires.

2. *Rebellion.* The individual completely rejects the organization's values and expectations. The rebellious, extremely individualistic person either causes the organization to change or, more likely, voluntarily leaves the organization or is dismissed.

3. *Creative individualism.* The individual accepts the organization's important, constructive values and neglects those that are trivial or inappropriate. Obviously, this distinction is difficult to make. The individual's decision about which norms are important may not be accurate, and the individual may be criticized for violating even unimportant norms. Moreover, with each lateral transfer or promotion, new norms come into play while others lose their relevance. Nevertheless, the benefits of creative individualism are high: The individual maintains integrity, independence, and a personal sense of satisfaction, while the organization has access to the fresh ideas and objective viewpoints it needs.

Role Conflict

role conflict According to Katz and Kahn, a situation in which an individual is confronted by two or more incompatible demands.

TEACHING TIP
Give your students examples of each of these role conflicts. Or ask them to give examples from jobs they've had.

Daniel Katz and Robert L. Kahn have discussed the **role conflict** individuals experience when confronted with two or more incompatible demands. Katz and Kahn have identified six types of role conflict that they believe are fairly common in organizations:[14]

1. *Intrasender conflict* occurs when a single supervisor presents a subordinate with a set of incompatible orders or expectations. For example, a division manager orders a purchasing agent to buy materials immediately at a price that requires prior home office authorization and then warns the agent not to violate the rulebook regulations.

2. *Intersender conflict* arises when orders or expectations from one person or group clash with expectations or orders from other persons or groups. For example, a manager orders a supervisor to speed up production but the work crew objects.

3. *Person-role conflict* occurs when on-the-job requirements (say, to bribe a foreign official) run counter to personal values (bribery is wrong).

4. In *role overload conflict,* the individual is confronted with conflicting orders that cannot be completed within the given time and quality limits. Should quality be sacrificed in the interests of time? Or should some tasks be carried out and others ignored? If so, which tasks should get priority? Dilemmas like these are a constant part of the manager's job.

5. *Role ambiguity* occurs when the individual is provided with insufficient or unclear information about his or her responsibilities and is therefore uncertain about what to do. New managers often experience role ambiguity when they are given a set of duties and responsibilities without being told exactly how to carry them out.

6. *Inter-role conflict* occurs when the different roles played by the same person give rise to conflicting demands. The relationship between work and family, for example, has become an increasing source of tension, especially in two-career families.[15]

Jeffrey H. Greenhaus, Arthur G. Bedeian, and Kevin W. Mossholder have found that role conflict, along with other factors such as the time committed to work and the perceived supportiveness and equity of the work environment, influences the relationship between job performance and well-being.[16]

Stress

stress The tension and pressure that result when an individual views a situation as presenting a demand that threatens to exceed his or her capabilities or resources.

stressor Source of pressure and tension that creates stress.

quantitative overloading Situation that occurs when an individual is given more tasks than he or she can accomplish in a given time.

qualitative overloading Situation that occurs when an individual lacks the abilities or resources necessary to satisfactorily complete a task.

underloading Stress, resulting in boredom and monotony, produced when an individual has insufficient work to do.

COORDINATED RESOURCE
Use Transparency 130, Unremitting or Overload Stress in the Three-Stage Model.

COORDINATED RESOURCE
The Additional Lecture for Chapter 19 found in the Lecture Extras supplement looks at "Workaholics."

burnout State of emotional, mental, and physical exhaustion that results from continued exposure to high stress.

Office politics, the issue of loyalty versus personal independence, and role conflicts all create **stress** for organizational members, and some evidence indicates that young people are more vulnerable to stress than older employees.[17] Fortunately, many of the causes and effects of stress can be managed.[18]

CAUSES OF STRESS. What exactly do we mean by *stress?* One widely accepted definition is offered by Joseph E. McGrath: ". . . there is a potential for stress when an environmental situation is perceived as presenting a demand which threatens to exceed the person's capabilities and resources for meeting it."[19] The sources of pressure and tension that cause stress are known as **stressors.**

When most of us imagine a stressful environment, we envision a harried office worker, in-box overflowing with work to be done, trying simultaneously to answer the phone, explain to the boss why everything is late, and write a report. This picture is not inaccurate—role overload is a major cause of stress at work. There are two kinds of overload. **Quantitative overloading** occurs when a person has more work than he or she can complete in a given time. **Qualitative overloading** occurs when the employee lacks the skills or abilities to complete the job satisfactorily. **Underloading** can also be a problem—a person who does not have enough to do faces boredom and monotony, which are also quite stressful.

In addition to role conflicts and over- and underloading, a variety of aspects of the work environment can cause stress. These include:

❑ *Responsibility for others.* Those who must work with other people, motivate them, and make decisions that will affect their careers experience more stress than those who do not have such responsibilities.

❑ *Lack of participation in decisions.* People who feel that they are not involved in decisions that influence their jobs have relatively high levels of stress.

❑ *Performance evaluations or appraisals.* Having one's performance evaluated can be very stressful, especially when it affects one's job and income.

❑ *Working conditions.* Crowded, noisy, or otherwise uncomfortable working conditions can be a source of stress.

❑ *Change within an organization.* Stress can result from any major change within an organization—an alteration in company policy, a reorganization, or a change in leadership, for example.

Obviously, different jobs vary greatly in the amount of stress they generate. Physicians, office managers, and supervisors, for example, must endure a good deal of stress. Craft workers, farm laborers, and college professors, on the other hand, face relatively little on-the-job stress.[20]

EFFECTS OF STRESS. Many medical practitioners believe that 50 to 70 percent of all physical illnesses are related to stress. The link between stress and heart disease is well known, and high levels of stress are associated with diabetes, ulcers, high blood pressure, and arteriosclerosis. Stress can also cause depression, irritation, anxiety, fatigue, lowered self-esteem, and reduced job satisfaction and performance. Sustained over a long enough period, stress can lead to attempts to escape through the use of drugs or alcohol. It may also lead to **burnout,** a state of physical, emotional, and mental exhaustion.[21]

Salvatore R. Maddi and Suzanne C. Kobasa have investigated the factors that cause some people to become exhausted and drained by stressful events and others to be stimulated and challenged by them. The ability to handle stress, they found, is a function of four characteristics: (1) personal style and personality (how the individual tends to perceive, interpret, and respond to stressful events); (2) social sup-

COORDINATED RESOURCE
Use Transparency 131,
Emergency Adaptation and
Potential for Exhaustion.

transformational coping
According to Maddi and
Kobasa, the process
whereby commitment to
work values, a sense of
control over work vari-
ables, and the view of
problems as challenges can
turn stressful situations in
less stressful directions.

COORDINATED RESOURCE
See DuBose Reading #31,
"The Work Ethic—An Idea
Whose Time Has Gone."

COORDINATED RESOURCE
See Geis and Kuhn Chapter
1, "Time Management—
Check Your Schedule."

FOR DISCUSSION

Why should employers be
concerned with helping
employess cope with
stress? What can they do
to make the workplace
less stressful?

coping skills training
Programs that teach peo-
ple to recognize and cope
with situations in which
they feel helpless.

relaxation training Popular methods, including
meditation and biofeed-
back, by which individuals
learn to control muscle
tension and ease the experience of stress.

ports (the extent to which family, friends, co-workers, and others provide encouragement and emotional support during stressful events); (3) constitutional
predisposition (how robust and healthy the individual's body is); and (4) health
practices (the extent to which the individual stays in good physical condition
through exercise and avoiding destructive behaviors like smoking).[22] The most important factor by far, they found, was a personality dimension they called "hardiness." Individuals high in hardiness are *committed* to their work and life rather than
alienated from them, have a sense of control rather than a feeling of powerlessness
when confronted with problems, and interpret change and problems as challenges
rather than as threats.

These three characteristics—commitment, control, and challenge—lead individuals to think about stressful events in optimistic ways and to act decisively toward them, thus changing them in a less stressful direction. This **transformational
coping** process not only serves hardy individuals well in managing their organizations but also reduces the likelihood of illness in both the short and the long run.
Unhardy individuals, on the other hand, tend to think pessimistically about stressful
events and to take evasive action to avoid contact with them. This makes them less
effective managerially as well as much more likely to experience health problems.

MANAGING STRESS. If individuals are to grow and prosper in organizations, they
must learn to prevent and manage stress. Perhaps the single best way to prevent
stress is to pay more attention to the fit between oneself and the organization when
selecting a job. Thus, career management can be a primary method of reducing
stress.

Managers can also eliminate some of the overloading that causes stress by
delegating work to their subordinates, passing some tasks on to other units of the
organization, and planning carefully for periods of peak workload. In addition,
upper-level managers can reduce stress throughout the organization by decentralizing authority (to reduce feelings of helplessness among employees); by adjusting
reward systems (so that performance appraisals are viewed as fair and reasonable);
by allowing employees to participate in making decisions that will affect them; by
improving and broadening lines of communication; by enlarging jobs so that they
include more varied activities; and by enriching jobs to give employees more responsibility for planning and directing their own careers.[23]

One of the best ways to cope with stress is to develop the habit of viewing
problems optimistically and acting decisively toward them so that one experiences
commitment, control, and challenge rather than alienation, powerlessness, and
threat. Although Maddi and Kobasa refer to hardiness as a "personality" characteristic—and personality is notoriously difficult to change—they are optimistic about
people's ability to increase their hardiness and offer some specific suggestions for
doing so. Similar approaches are used in **coping skills training,** programs in which
people learn to recognize and cope with situations that cause them to feel helpless.[24]

Improving physical fitness is another way to handle stress. People who exercise to strengthen their cardiovascular systems and increase their endurance are less
susceptible to illnesses caused by stress.

Training in relaxation techniques can also diminish the effects of stress. **Relaxation training** is a popular method in which people learn how to relax their mus-
cles progressively. Deep breathing can also lower tension, as can *meditation,* in
which individuals assume a comfortable position, close their eyes, and attempt to
clear all disturbing thoughts from their minds. Finally, *biofeedback* techniques help
people learn how to detect and control physical changes (such as high blood pressure) that may be linked to stress. Occupational stress-management programs use
techniques such as these to help people handle stress on the job.

Selina Proctor: Parent and Professional

Selina Proctor is experiencing a number of early career dilemmas, not the least of which is caring for a chronically sick child. Although Selina works only part-time, she is a professional who has to meet the same high expectations as her full-time co-workers. Moreover, it is difficult to manage the expectations of others in a professional setting—meetings must occur when the schedule has been worked out. Selina had thought a great deal about her place and role in the law firm. Ignoring such warnings as fatigue and conflicting schedules, she had come to believe that with her part-time schedule she had made the culture of the firm work for her rather than against her.

Part of Selina's problem can be explained as role conflict. Being a mother, spouse, and professional is a difficult balancing act under any circumstances, and when there is a complex crisis including an important meeting, a sick baby, and a spouse who is not very helpful, the inevitable results are anxiety and stress. If Selina is to continue her success, she will have to find ways to manage the stress factors in her life. As a rule, they do not simply go away.

■ CAREERS OVER TIME

THOUGHT PROVOKER

The baby-boom generation will be sending its ranks to the CEO suites soon. Says one observer, "Those students came through a tough period—social revolution, Vietnam. Their politics were more liberal than their predecessors, their social consciousness different." (*Business Week*, 9/25/89, p. 170ff.) What are the implications?

The growing body of literature on the ways careers develop over time fascinates most of us since it helps us evaluate our own career progress and gives us a tool for understanding and managing our relationships with other people in the workplace. In this section, we will give you an overview of this literature, beginning with two influential models of how careers develop over the life cycle.[25]

Careers and the Life Cycle

THE ERIKSON MODEL. Many theorists base their analysis of career events on psychoanalyst Erik Erikson's famous theory of life stages.[26] Erikson divided the individual's life into eight stages, four in childhood and four in adulthood. The individual must successfully complete a "development task" in each stage, before going on to the next stage.

Erikson's four adult stages are adolescence, young adulthood, adulthood, and maturity. (The childhood stages are not important for our discussion.) In *adolescence*, the individual's developmental task is to achieve an ego identity. The individual tries to reconcile the differences between his or her self-perception and how he or she is perceived by others. Also, the individual attempts to select an occupation in which his or her skills and interests can be utilized. In *young adulthood*, the individual attempts to develop satisfactory relationships or intimacy with others. This intimacy may involve a mate, a work group, or supporters of a common cause. In *adulthood*, the individual is concerned with what Erikson calls generativity—the guiding of the next generation. For example, the person passes on his or her knowledge and values to children or students, or sponsors younger colleagues in the workplace. Finally, in *maturity*, the person attempts to achieve ego integrity—the feeling that life has been satisfying and meaningful.[27]

COORDINATED RESOURCE

Use Transparency 126, Careers and the Life Cycle.

THE LEVINSON MODEL. Another interesting perspective on the evolution of careers has been provided by Daniel Levinson and his colleagues.[28] Levinson studied a group of 40 men in four occupational groups (hourly workers in industry, business executives, university biologists, and novelists) between the ages of 35 and 45. He

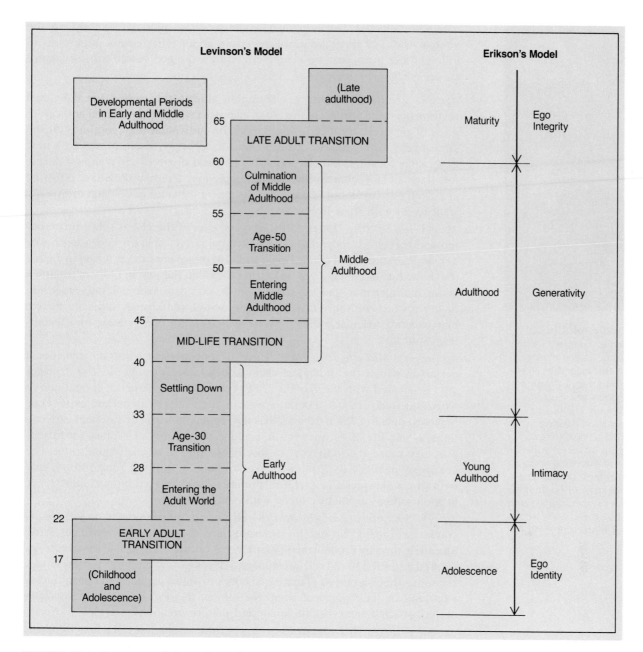

FIGURE 19-1 Careers and the Life Cycle

Sources: Levinson's Model from *The Seasons of a Man's Life,* by Daniel J. Levinson. Copyright © 1978 by Daniel J. Levinson. Reprinted by permission of Sterling Lord Literistic, Inc. Erikson's Model adapted from *Childhood and Society,* Second Edition, by Erik H. Erikson, by permission of W.W. Norton & Company, Inc. Copyright 1950, 1963 by W.W. Norton & Company, Inc. Copyright renewed 1978 by Erik H. Erikson.

suggests that adult life involves a series of personal and career-related crises or transitions that occur in a fairly predictable sequence every five to seven years. (See Fig. 19-1.)

❑ *Age 17–22: Early Adult Transition.* The individual must break away from financial and emotional dependence on parents and become his or her own person. Those who gradually assert their independence can embark on their careers with some measure of self-sufficiency and confidence. Those who prolong parental ties, according to Levinson, often underperform in their careers.

❑ *Age 22–28: Entering the Adult World.* The individual has completed his or her education and begins to make commitments for the future. A lifestyle and

A Middle Adulthood Change. Frustrated when a change in top management threatened to shunt him into a staff position at Ingersoll-Rand, Steven Sandy quit and put together the financing needed to buy Gimpel Corp., a maker of trip-and-throttle safety valves used on turbines. Besides the exhilaration of building up Gimpel's operations, Sandy relishes the chance to spend more time with his son.

career are selected. The individual becomes preoccupied with getting into the adult world. For those who are uncertain about what course they wish to follow, these years may be characterized by a dogged search for satisfactory career goals.

❑ *Age 28–33: Age-30 Transition.* Sometime during this period the individual reviews his or her progress toward previously established personal and career goals. If progress has been satisfactory, the individual may continue on the same track. If not, radical changes and turmoil may result. Moves to a new geographic location, job or career changes, and divorces are common during this stage. Even seemingly successful people may feel that they have only one last chance to break out of their established pattern and to do what they really want to do with their lives.

❑ *Age 33–40: Settling Down.* In these years, everything else is subordinated to job and career advancement. The individual strives toward becoming his or her own person. Social contacts and friendships are cut or minimized to enable the individual to concentrate on getting ahead on the job. In place of friends, a young manager may seek a "sponsor" in the company who will help steer him or her toward the top. Those who are uncomfortable with authority figures may have a particularly difficult time searching for and relating to a higher-level sponsor.

❑ *Age 40–45: Mid-life Transition.* These years represent a second transitional period in which the individual again reviews career progress. The manager who is satisfied with the way his or her career has developed will continue to work effectively. In fact, a certain pride in one's achievements and experience begins to develop. But if progress has not lived up to early dreams and expectations, a "mid-life crisis" may result. Feelings of resentment, sadness, or frustration may cause the individual to lose his or her emotional equilibrium. The crisis may manifest itself in excessive drinking, in quitting a job and possibly wrecking a managerial career, in flaunting a "middle-aged hippie" lifestyle, or in some other spectacular break with past behavior.

❑ *Age 45–50: Entering Middle Adulthood.* During this period, the reassessments conducted during the mid-life transition are consolidated. Individuals settle into their new or reconfirmed perspectives on their careers. They devote increased attention to old relationships and develop new ones more consciously. For some, this is a period of increased concern about decline and constraints at work and in their personal lives. For others, this can be a highly satisfying period—with a sense of fulfillment and mature creativity.

❑ *Age 50–55: Age-50 Transition.* In this period, issues and tasks that were not satisfactorily handled during the earlier transitions recur. Individuals who changed too little in the mid-life transition and built unsatisfactory life structures may experience crisis. Levinson believes that virtually everyone will experience a moderate crisis in either the mid-life or the age-50 transition.

❑ *Age 55–60: Culmination of Middle Adulthood.* This period is a relatively stable one, similar to the settling-down period of early adulthood. Whether or not their ambitions have been satisfied, individuals must accept the fact that their careers are coming to an end and begin to prepare for retirement. Those who have been able to rejuvenate themselves and enrich their lives can find great fulfillment in this period.

❑ *Age 60–65: Late Adult Transition.* During this period, most people retire, which has a significant effect on how they view themselves and are viewed by others. For many, it is a period of deep reflection. Some people are only too happy to leave their careers, even when they enjoyed and felt successful in them. Others find the transition painful and attempt to avoid coming to grips with it.

❑ *Age 65 and Older: Late Adulthood.* This is a period of evaluation and summing up. Freed of the responsibility of going to work, many people thoroughly enjoy their leisure and devote themselves to pursuits that they had to neglect when they were younger. Others are troubled by financial difficulties and health problems. Much remains to be learned about this period.

Levinson's work provides a valuable foundation for subsequent efforts to understand how people's lives and careers change as they get older. However, his career stages need to carefully interpreted. He conducted his interviews in the late 1960s and early 1970s, and since that time the work force and the typical career pattern have changed considerably. For one thing, Levinson and his colleagues based their stages on a sample consisting entirely of men, so it is not known how accurately these stages reflect the career development of women. In his sample, the husband tended to be the sole breadwinner and the wife a full-time homemaker and childrearer. Therefore, it is not clear how well Levinson's career and life stages will fit even men in the future, as progressively more of them become members of dual-career couples. Future research may show that the career patterns of men and women in dual-career couples more closely resemble each other than they do those of either men or women in one-earner families.

Career Patterns and Themes

Levinson's work presents a model of the career and life tasks to be addressed in different chronological periods in one's life. Michael J. Driver[29] and Edgar H. Schein[30] have suggested that careers can also be looked at in terms of broad *themes* or *patterns* that emerge over time. Their perspectives are concerned with how individuals' abilities, interests, and desires influence their subsequent career patterns.

DRIVER'S CAREER CONCEPTS. Many of us assume, first, that careers involve working in an organization; second, that an individual will attempt to move up in the organization, acquiring more influence and a larger income; and third, that the person's ultimate goal is to head the organization. However, many people—even many who have undergraduate and graduate degrees in management—do not want to become presidents of their organizations. Some do not wish to be promoted, and some try to avoid working for an organization altogether. Driver's **career concepts,** illustrated in Figure 19-2 along with two other patterns, offer several alternative ways people may perceive their careers.

The **linear career concept** most closely resembles the stereotypical view: The individual chooses a field early in life, develops a plan for upward movement in the field, and executes it. A person who has a **steady-state career concept** also selects a job or field early in life and stays with it. Although the person may continue to improve professional skills and seek a higher income, he or she does not attempt to move up the organizational hierarchy. Driver believes that individuals with linear career concepts are motivated by the need for achievement—"to move up and score according to established 'rules of the game'"—but steady-staters are motivated by security needs.[31]

Spiral career concept individuals, in contrast, are motivated by the desire for personal growth. They tend to plunge into a new job or field, work hard, and frequently perform very well—moving up in status and rank. Then, after about five to seven years, they move into another type of work or an entirely new field that offers them new challenges and opportunities to grow.

The last group, those with a **transitory career concept,** drift with no particular pattern from one job to another, never choosing a particular field and only occasionally and temporarily moving up in an organization. Driver suggests that they are driven by the need for independence and perhaps by the fear of commitment.

---

career concepts According to Driver, the four basic career patterns— linear, steady-state, spiral, and transitory—by which people perceive their careers.

linear career concept According to Driver, career concept by which an individual chooses a field, develops a plan for advancement, and executes it.

steady-state career concept According to Driver, career concept by which an individual chooses a field but, even though improving professionally and financially, does not seek to move up the organizational hierarchy.

spiral career concept According to Driver, career concept by which individuals motivated by personal growth perform well enough to advance in status and rank.

transitory career concept According to Driver, career concept by which an individual moves from one job to another with no apparent pattern or progress.

COORDINATED RESOURCE
Use Transparency 127, Career Concepts and Patterns.

Although there is no necessary connection between a person's chosen field and a particular career concept, certain fields tend to be associated with a certain concept. Semiskilled laborers and actors, for example, may follow the transitory concept, seeking work where they can find it, but rarely rising to higher levels. The steady-state career concept seems to be most common in the established professions (for example, medicine) and skilled trades (for example, carpentry). Individuals in these fields, after completing training, may become better at what they do and receive higher fees, but their day-to-day work changes relatively little. The linear concept may be most common for corporate managers and professors; they begin at the bottom rung of the organization and gradually acquire more responsibility and higher status and income. The spiral concept might predominate among consultants and writers, who may apply their skills in one area and then in another.

In addition to Driver's four career concepts, two other patterns are common in careers. A *plateaued* individual has risen to a certain level and remains there (this pattern is discussed later in the chapter). In a *declining* career, a person rises to a certain level, remains there for a time, then begins a descent back to lower levels. These two patterns are also illustrated in Figure 19-2.

career anchor According to Schein, an occupational self-concept—an individual's sense of the kind of work he or she seeks to pursue and what that work implies about the individual.

SCHEIN'S CAREER ANCHORS. A **career anchor** is an occupational self-concept—a personal sense of the type of work an individual wants to pursue and what that work implies about the individual. According to Schein, people's career anchors begin to develop early in their careers, when they and their organizations are going through a period of mutual discovery. New employees gradually come to understand how they fit into the organization and how they contribute to it, as well as how the organization meets their needs, interacts with them, and gives them feedback. As employees go through this process of adaptation, they develop a career anchor with three components: (1) self-perception of talents and abilities based on their performance in a variety of work settings; (2) self-perceived motives and needs based on both self-diagnosis and on feedback from others; and (3) self-perceived attitudes and values based on interactions with the norms and values implicit in the organization and the work setting. People need to work in an organization for a few years, Schein says, before they can develop an accurate sense of what they really want and where it can be achieved. On the basis of his research, he concluded that many people were motivated by one of the five factors categorized in Exhibit 19-1.

EXHIBIT 19-1 Schein's Five Factors in Career Motivation

1. *Technical/Functional Competence.* Some individuals "fall in love" with a particular field or function. Although they may become managers, their self-concepts are associated with their skills in their area of interest and training.
2. *Managerial Competence.* Some individuals simply want to manage. They believe their abilities lie in the area of analyzing problems, making decisions, remaining emotionally stable, and being interpersonally competent. Their early career experiences indicate to them that they will be able to rise in the management hierarchy.
3. *Security.* Some individuals seek security by tying themselves to a particular organization or geographic location. If their commitment is to a particular organization, they accept its values, norms, and definition of their career path—for example, moving geographically if they are transferred or promoted. If their commitment is to a specific geographic location, they will change employers rather than move away from the preferred location.
4. *Creativity.* Some individuals want to create something new. Their fundamental need is to start something and make it a success. They tend to take leadership roles on new projects and to become entrepreneurs.
5. *Autonomy.* Some individuals simply do not want to be in an organization. They find organizational life unpleasant or difficult in some way, and they are primarily concerned with maintaining their freedom. They seek work in realms where there will be few restrictions on their ability to pursue their interests.

Source: Edgar H. Schein, *Career Dynamics: Matching Individual and Organizational Needs* (Reading, Mass.: Addison-Wesley, 1978).

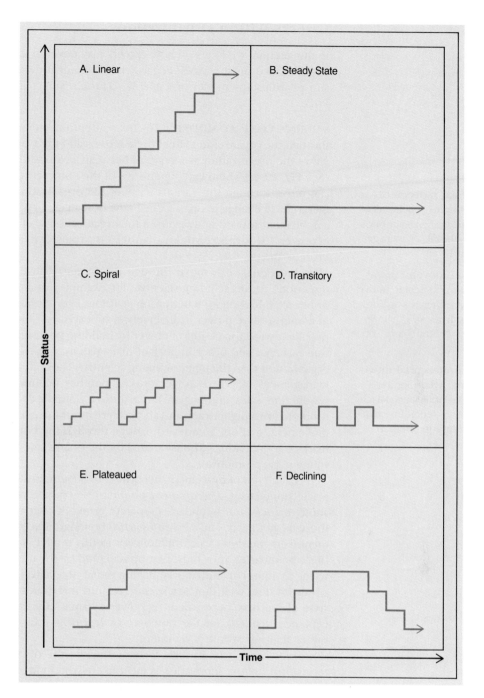

FIGURE 19-2 Career Concepts and Patterns

Source: Adapted from James G. Clawson, John P. Kotter, Victor A. Faux, and Charles C. McArthur, *Self-Assessment and Career Development,* 2nd ed. (Englewood Cliffs, N.J.: Prentice-Hall, 1985), p. 166.

People with security, technical/functional, or managerial career anchors are likely to have a comfortable relationship with the organization they work for. However, people with autonomy anchors, and some of those with creativity anchors, will probably be uncomfortable in any organization.

Although many individuals seem to feel that one or perhaps two of the career anchors fit their own self-perception fairly accurately, the five career anchors should not be considered a definitive list. Schein developed his concepts by studying the careers of only 44 graduate management school alumni, and he and other researchers have described other possible career anchors.[32]

Careers Within Organizations

COORDINATED RESOURCE
Use Transparency 128, Stages in Career Development.

In this section, we focus on how careers may develop *within* organizations. We will consider two perspectives: Edgar Schein's conical model and the sequential roles and relationships model of Gene W. Dalton, Paul H. Thompson, and Raymond L. Price.

SCHEIN'S CONICAL MODEL. To focus attention on how individuals' movements through the organization affect their actions and the way they are perceived, Schein views the organization as a cone rather than as a traditional hierarchical triangle.[33] (See Fig. 19-3.) The three dimensions of the cone represent the ways an individual can move through the various parts of the organization. **Vertical movement** is a hierarchical change in one's formal rank or management level. **Radial movement** is a movement toward or away from the organization's "central core" or "inner circle" of power. **Circumferential movement** is a transfer to a different division, function, or department.

vertical movement According to Schein, hierarchical change in one's formal rank or management level.

radial movement According to Schein, movement either toward or away from an organization's central "core" of power.

circumferential movement According to Schein, transfer from one division, function, or department to another.

Individuals can move through the organization in one or all three of these directions. An outstanding scientist, for example, might be promoted (to keep him or her from leaving for a better job) without ever coming an inch closer to the core of administrative power. Conversely, a supervisor of long standing who has moved radially toward the center of power by building good relationships with the production manager and other important managers may wield more influence within the organization than the higher-ranking scientist. Those destined for the upper levels of management may first move across a number of functional boundaries (such as production, sales, and finance) to acquire a generalist's background before they are promoted to a higher rank and allowed greater influence. Continued circumferential movement, without an upward passage through the boundaries of rank, may be the mark of an individual who is needed by the organization but who is not considered suitable for promotion.

Each type of movement, according to Schein, involves passage through appropriate boundaries. *Hierarchical* boundaries separate one management level from another, *inclusion* boundaries separate groups closer to the center of power from those farther away, and *circumferential* boundaries separate one division or department from another. A central concept in this model is that for individuals to cross these boundaries, they must first be accepted by the members of the group they are trying to join. For individuals making radial or vertical moves, this acceptance depends on how well they are *socialized* into the values, attitudes, and overall work style of the new department or power alliance. But in circumferential moves, acceptance depends on the outcome of *training*—the acquisition of new skills—rather than on attitudes or values.

Individuals can, in turn, try to influence the organization—a process Schein terms *innovation.* Innovation is most likely when individuals are in the middle of a career stage; they are fully involved then and can recommend changes with some confidence and authority. Newcomers, in contrast, have not yet been accepted, so they are relatively powerless, while people who are about to move on may be lame ducks or uninterested in making changes.

Schein also suggests that socialization, training, and innovation continue throughout a career. He believes, however, that socialization and training are more prevalent during early career stages, when the individual has not yet been fully acclimated to the organization, and that innovation is more prevalent at later career stages, when the individual has more experience and status.

FOUR CAREER ROLES AND RELATIONSHIPS. Dalton, Thompson, and Price have emphasized a different dimension of organizational activity, focusing on the se-

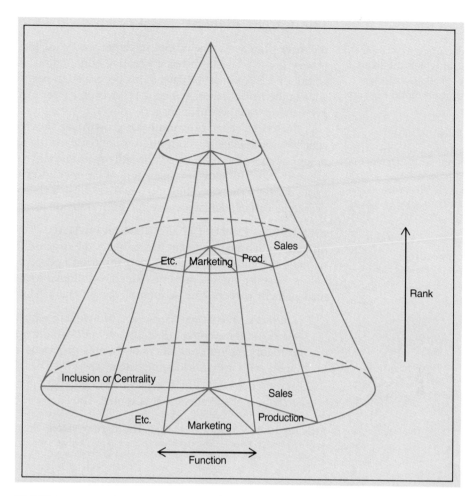

FIGURE 19-3 A Three-Dimensional Model of an Organization

Source: Adapted with permission from NTL Institute, "The Individual, the Organization, and the Career": A Conceptual Scheme by Edgar H. Schein, p. 404, *The Journal of Applied Behavioral Science,* Vol. 7, No. 4, Copyright 1971.

apprentice Starting worker who usually does routine work under a supervisor or mentor.

colleague Worker who, while still subordinate, makes independent contributions to organizational activities.

mentor Employee who develops ideas, supervises others, and assumes responsibility for the work of subordinates.

sponsor Upper-level manager involved in the major decision-making activities of the organization.

quence of roles and relationships an individual may experience.[34] When individuals start their careers, they function in the role of **apprentices.** They do mostly routine work, ideally under the supervision of mentors who will help them learn. Since they are in subordinate roles, they must accommodate themselves to a certain measure of dependence. The employee next comes to be considered a **colleague** who makes an independent contribution to the activities of the organization. Colleagues are still someone's subordinate, but they rely less on their superiors for advice and direction. Some people have trouble developing the confidence necessary for independence. At the third level, employees become **mentors** themselves. Mentors function in a number of roles. They develop ideas and manage others, and they must learn to assume some responsibility for their subordinates' work. Finally, if they continue to progress in the organization, they become **sponsors,** upper-level managers who define the direction of the entire organization or some major segment of it. Part of sponsors' influence lies in their ability to choose key people in the organization. At this level, managers must broaden their perspectives and lengthen their time horizon. Thus, at each stage, tasks change and different relationships and personal adjustments are required.[35]

The Career Plateau

career plateau Career stage in which the likelihood of additional hierarchical promotion is very low.

HERE'S AN EXAMPLE
Many mid-level executives are finding themselves unemployed. This "payroll shrinkage" has reached the executive ranks. (*Fortune*, 4/8/91, p. 36ff.)

COORDINATED RESOURCE
Use Transparency 129, A Model of Managerial Career States.

A **career plateau** is "the point in a career where the likelihood of further promotion is very low."[36] The term has a negative connotation, implying the individual lacks ability or has some other flaw. (This is derived in part from the widespread acceptance of the *linear* career concept.) However, career plateaus are normal and happen even to very successful managers.

In recent years, organizational growth has slowed while the number of management candidates has continued to increase. At the same time, mandatory retirement laws have been repealed, forcing organizations to retain plateaued workers for a longer time. In addition, managers often encounter career plateaus and mid-life crises at about the same time.[37] Together, these facts have focused attention on the problems career plateaus cause for both individuals and organizations.

IDENTIFYING EMPLOYEES AT A CAREER PLATEAU. Two variables are useful in defining an individual's current career state: the organization's evaluation of how promotable the individual is and the organization's perception of how well the individual is performing at present. Based on these variables, four basic stages in management careers can be identified (see Fig. 19-4):

1. *Learners or comers.* These are individuals who are considered to have advancement potential but are not yet performing up to par. This relatively small category includes members of training programs and recently promoted managers who are still learning their new jobs.

2. *Stars.* These individuals are seen as doing high-quality work and are considered to have high advancement potential. They are sometimes placed on "fast-track"

FIGURE 19-4 A Model of Managerial Career States

Source: Thomas P. Ference, James A. F. Stoner, and E. Kirby Warren, "Managing the Career Plateau," *Academy of Management Review,* 2, no. 4 (October 1977). Used by permission.

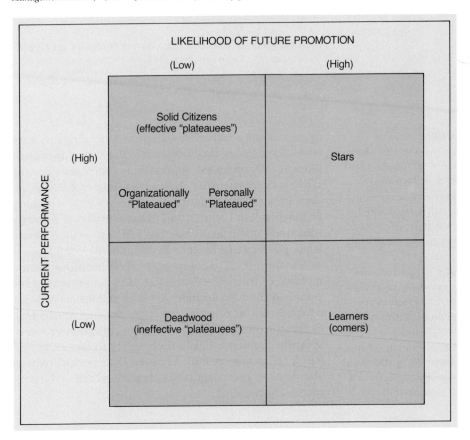

career paths and usually receive the greatest exposure to management development activities.

3. *Solid citizens.* These managers, seen as doing good or even outstanding work, have for one reason or another little, if any, chance for further advancement. They may constitute the largest group of managers in most organizations and accomplish most of their organization's work.

4. *Deadwood.* These individuals are seen as having little or no chance for advancement, and their current performance is viewed as marginal or inadequate. Often they are shunted aside to minor, dead-end posts and then forgotten, but sometimes attempts are made to rehabilitate them so that they can become solid citizens once again.

The solid citizens and deadwood have reached career plateaus; the comers and stars are still on an upward track. Since the solid citizens are effective, it might seem that management's only problems are to speed up the development of the learners and "turn around" or dismiss the deadwood. Yet solid citizens also represent a management challenge. Once they realize they have reached a career plateau, they may lose motivation and gradually drift into the deadwood category—unless management steps in. (This threat is particularly great for individuals who have a *linear* career concept or a career anchor of *managerial competence.*)

As our discussion implies, these career states change over time. Newcomers usually enter the organization as learners. If they perform well, they move into the star category and become active candidates for promotion. With each promotion, they temporarily revert to learner status, becoming stars again as they take command in their new jobs. As the years pass, however, more and more people reach career plateaus, either for *organizational* reasons (fewer job openings exist at higher levels, say) or for *personal* reasons (they lack key interpersonal skills perhaps). They then become solid citizens.

OPTIONS AT THE CAREER PLATEAU. Solid citizens can be productive and successful for many years, maintaining a sense of growth and achievement by obtaining transfers, by seeking training that qualifies them for promotions, or by pursuing new positions with other firms. Eventually, however, age, flagging motivation, or lack of new training may cause their performance to decline.[38] Indeed, in a study of middle managers at a British financial organization, Evans and Gilbert traced the decline in job satisfaction and motivation to age rather than to plateauing.[39] Older managers also had lower expectations of their future rewards (pay, benefits, and advancement) from the organization than younger managers—regardless of whether either had reached a plateau. However, older managers expressed more interest in mentoring, a potentially beneficial but underappreciated activity.

As larger organizations have come under pressure to "downsize" and "restructure," early retirement has become more common, with corporations such as AT&T and IBM offering lucrative early-retirement packages to many relatively young employees. One employee of a Fortune 500 company, for example, took early retirement at *34,* using the incentive package to fund an entrepreneurial business. This trend to start second careers after "retirement" adds a whole new dimension to career management. (See the Management and Diversity box.)

■ *INDIVIDUAL CAREER MANAGEMENT*

Although some organizations help employees manage their careers,[40] career management is ultimately the individual's responsibility. Like organizations, people who develop plans have a better chance of achieving their career goals rather than drifting from job to job. They are also less vulnerable to chance events and to having

MANAGEMENT AND DIVERSITY

Tapping the Talents of the Older Worker

When the economy weakened in the 1980s, many employers streamlined their staffs by offering employees early-retirement packages. Ironically enough, they or someone else will probably hire these same employees *back* during the 1990s, when the number of new jobs created in the United States will surpass new entrants to the labor force by at least two million.

Right now, many companies are hiring retirees because they have invaluable maturity and experience and will often work for far less than a "regular" employee. Nationwide hotel chain Days Inn hires retirees, and has saved millions of dollars because of this practice. In 1990, older workers made up 25 percent of Days Inns' 650-person reservation sales staff. The starting salary was $4.50 an hour, and the annual turnover rate for this group was about 2 percent, versus 70 percent for younger employees. The reduction in turnover rate brought down recruitment and training costs by 40 percent.

Executive retirees are also returning to the work force in large numbers. Benjamin Borne, vice president with Boyden International, a Chicago-based executive recruiting firm, thinks that the 1990s will bring a "redefinition of the workplace in which second- or third-career professionals will be the norm." Borne says that executive retirees who return to work do not bring with them the pressures of career building, and that they offer their services at reasonable rates or as unpaid volunteers. For smaller companies, the consulting services of a highly skilled retired executive can save tremendous amounts of time and money. A number of U.S. companies, such as Hewlett-Packard, often hire back their own retirees as consultants.

While many recruiting firms place executive retirees in paying jobs, a number of them match up volunteers and businesses. For example, S.C.O.R.E. (the Service Corps of Retired Executives) has 13,000 volunteers nationwide. Another group, Boston's Operation A.B.L.E. (Ability Based on Long Experience), provides candidate screening and referral for organizations, and career counseling, out-placement seminars, skills-development training, and job matching for job seekers.

But the picture for older workers isn't altogether rosy. In the 1960s, men between the ages of

A Case of Age Discrimination? Charging they were fired because of their age and the fact they were not Japanese, former Chief Financial Officer Frank B. Ensign Jr. (left), former Executive Secretary Esther M. White, and former Vice President of Marketing Terence J. Turnbull sued Fujitsu Systems of America Inc., a San Diego subsidiary of Fujitsu Ltd.

60 and 65 had 80 percent labor-pool participation; in the 1980s, that participation dropped to 55 percent. Human resource specialists say that more jobs would be available to retired workers if the federal government did not impose expensive medical and pension costs on companies that take on older workers. Another reason companies are cautious about hiring older workers is the increase in age discrimination lawsuits since the passage of the Age Discrimination in Employment Act in 1967. Having few precedents to go by, judges and juries in age discrimination cases created a whole new way of awarding damages. To avoid lengthy, costly suits, many companies began to settle out of court, whether or not they thought an employee had been discriminated against. As the labor shortage deepens during the 1990s, though, more employers will have to turn to older workers. As a result, the "new hire" may be a great-grandfather, and young managers may find themselves managing people two to three times their age.

Sources: Gary S. Becker, "What Keeps Older Workers Off the Job Rolls?" *Business Week,* March 19, 1990, p. 18; Meg Whittemore, "Retired—And Back at Work," *Nation's Business,* April 1990, pp. 37–40; Dyan Machan, "Cultivating the Gray," *Forbes,* September 4, 1989, pp. 126–129.

THOUGHT PROVOKER
What's your definition of career success?

their career decisions made for them by others. Finally, people who take an active role in managing their own careers tend to be more motivated and purposeful than others; this makes them more useful to their organizations and more likely to be successful within them.

Individual Career Planning

COORDINATED RESOURCE
See Study Guide Problem Exercise 19, "Career Plan."

FOR DISCUSSION
What are consequences of inadequate career planning?

TEACHING TIP
These career strategies are important enough to highlight individually and discuss.

To many people, career planning means developing a program for moving toward the top of the organization. Yet this linear concept is inappropriate for people who value creativity or autonomy over managerial competence. Thus, individual career planning must begin with an understanding of what you want from work, career, and life. If you are not sure, various career planning approaches can give you some insights into these matters.

REALISTIC CAREER STRATEGIES.   Individual career planning can be approached like any other type of planning, although it resembles strategic planning most closely.[41] Alan N. Schoonmaker has offered a nine-step career strategy that includes systematic career planning.[42] Some of the steps sound harsh, but his strategy is basically realistic. The steps are:

1. *Accept the fact that there are some inescapable and irreconcilable conflicts between you and your organization.* What is good for the organization is not always good for you. So, being careful not to be disloyal, you must always look out for your own interests.

2. *Accept the fact that your superiors are essentially indifferent to your career ambitions.* Your superiors are ultimately responsible only for themselves and their units; you should assume they will help you only if it helps them achieve their own objectives. If you realize this, you can avoid being manipulated by false promises and unrealistic expectations.

FOR DISCUSSION
What are the dangers in choosing a career goal that is not compatible with one's own goals or desires?

TEACHING TIP
Encourage your students to "know thyself." What are their strengths and weaknesses, their interests? What are they happiest doing?

3. *Analyze your own goals.* To get what you want, you first have to *know* what you want. Many people pursue goals they *should* want rather than those they really *do* want. As a result, they waste their lives searching for an unattainable satisfaction.

4. *Analyze your assets and liabilities.* Your career goals should let you maximize your assets and minimize your liabilities. It is unrealistic to pursue goals that require abilities you lack and foolish to neglect your natural abilities.

5. *Analyze your opportunities.* Systematically assess the positions available in your own and other firms. Published information and personal observations are useful here, as are tips gathered from a network of colleagues.

6. *Learn the rules for company politics.* Note what your company values and what behaviors it rewards. Learn which people are most crucial in accomplishing various kinds of tasks. ("If you give the parts department manager fair warning, she will help you meet your production schedule.")

7. *Plan your career.* Many managers select goals without any idea of how they are going to reach them, with the result that they drift indecisively from job to job or stay too long in one position. A plan can prevent this by helping you make better decisions at each step of your career.

CLASS COMMENT
Executives are going back to school. More than 15,000 are attending a variety of business-related programs at North American colleges in 1991, 10 percent more than in 1990. (*Fortune*, 3/25/91, p. 12)

8. *Carry out your plan.* The best plan is useless if it is not carried out. If your plan calls for you to ask for a raise, request a transfer, gain a new skill, or find another job—*do it!*

9. *Chart your progress.* Careers rarely progress without a hitch—a mentor takes early retirement, the job market changes, a new colleague becomes a star. Your goals may also change over time—a new opportunity may seem less attractive if you are satisfied in your present position. Like organizational plans, career plans have to be revised periodically to reflect current realities.

MANAGING THE WORK SITUATION.   Once you have developed a career plan and have a job in your field, you can use a number of tactics to further your career. First and most important, you can *do excellent work.*[43] People who help the organization meet its goals are more likely to garner rewards, acknowledgment, respect, and support from bosses, peers, and subordinates. Moreover, people who have proved they can do first-class work tend to be given more exciting and challenging opportunities as well as more autonomy. As a bonus, doing good work tends to be more satisfying than doing mediocre work. This list could be extended almost indefinitely.

Of course, excellent work alone does not *inevitably* lead to career success. Your efforts may be ignored or they may arouse jealousy among colleagues. First-rate work in an organization cannot be done in isolation. A person who performs brilliantly in some areas but doesn't get along with colleagues is unlikely to go very far. This suggests two other tactics for succeeding in the organization: *develop good working relationships* and *help your boss succeed.* (It is difficult to imagine how one could truly be doing excellent work without being effective in these two areas.)

Developing good working relationships is crucial to success because organizations are by their nature cooperative efforts. Ronald J. Burke notes that it's *both* what you know *and* who you know that count.[44] To accomplish tasks, you must establish a network of co-workers—superiors, peers, and subordinates—who are able and willing to help you meet your objectives. It is easier to do excellent work if you are part of such a network (and it is easier to become part of such a network if you do excellent work). Building good relationships begins early in your career. At times it may be tempting to disagree publicly with your boss, go over your supervisor's head to a superior, engage in personal criticism, hold grudges, express hostility, or seek revenge, but such actions do not advance careers. Every bad working relationship is a lost opportunity.

Helping your boss succeed is a good way to help yourself succeed. The more you help your boss—by doing good work, by suggesting new approaches to prob-

The Fruits of a Managed Career. Hellene Runtagh is president of General Electric Information Services, which sells large communication systems to the likes of Apple and Benetton. During an initial stint in employee relations at GE, Runtagh learned to think ahead, to articulate her career goals, and to enlist her bosses' help as she moved into 14 other manufacturing and cross-functional assignments, relocating six times. By the time the president's job at GE Information Services opened up, she had accumulated five years' experience in employee relations, seven years in manufacturing, three in customer service, and four years' experience running a line business.

lems, and by keeping him or her informed—the more valuable to your boss you will be. In fact, becoming indispensable to an upwardly mobile boss can help you become part of an "advancement sandwich," in which your boss, you, and the subordinate that you train move up in the organization together. Other bosses are also likely to find you an attractive subordinate if you have helped your superior become more successful.[45]

It also helps to be mobile—to be willing to move to new locations as needed—and to cultivate low-keyed ways of making your supervisors aware of your accomplishments. A short memo reporting a project's completion, for example, might praise the contributions of others, highlighting your image as a team player who can marshall the cooperation of other employees.

Specific Career Issues

FOR DISCUSSION

How can organizations help employees cope with some of these career issues?

Although we have been discussing general strategies for meeting career goals, three additional topics are of special interest to new managers. First, many new managers will be members of dual-career couples. Such couples must cooperatively plan their careers and their personal relationship more carefully than either single people or spouses in traditional marriages. Second, managers need to understand mentoring relationships. Third, women's careers in management may require especially careful planning because women often face special barriers in managerial situations and the events of their lives make some career issues more acute for them than for men.

DUAL-CAREER COUPLES. Couples in which both partners are employed full time must work hard to integrate and balance the demands and opportunities of two separate careers. Mutual accommodation on small matters is a constant necessity. When both partners return from work tired, who will make dinner? Who will stay home to take care of a child with an upset stomach? Major conflicts also arise. Suppose that one partner receives a very attractive job offer in another part of the country and the other partner is reluctant to leave his or her current job. Which one gives in? Flexibility and willingness to compromise are imperative for both the career and the relationship. Despite the extra problems faced by dual-career married couples, however, E. A. House has found that neither their marital satisfaction nor their sex-role orientations differ from those of single-provider couples.[46]

Francine Hall and Douglas T. Hall have identified four general styles of effectively managing two careers. Each is based on the spouses' differing (or similar) degree of commitment to home or to career:

❑ *Accommodators.* Couples of this type most closely resemble the traditional family. One spouse assumes major (but not total) responsibility for career roles and the other assumes major responsibility for family roles.

❑ *Adversaries.* In couples of this type, both spouses are highly involved in their careers but also value having someone take responsibility for home-related roles. There are likely to be conflicts because neither is willing or able to make the career sacrifices necessary to maintain the home.

❑ *Allies.* In this type, the two spouses are both highly involved in either their career or their home roles and place little emphasis on the other area. If both are highly involved in their careers, for example, they are likely to forgo having children and devote little attention to maintaining a well-ordered home.

❑ *Acrobats.* Couples of this sort are highly involved in all their roles. They give equal weight to family and career, but rather than attempting to get their spouses to take over, they attempt to perform both roles themselves.

As dual-career couples have become more common, organizations have become more responsive to their special needs. This may involve such changes as providing flexible work environments, revising transfer policies, offering couples career management assistance, and providing local support services, such as day care and after-school centers for children.[48]

MENTORS AND MENTORING RELATIONSHIPS. As recounted by Homer in *The Odyssey,* Mentor was the servant of Odysseus entrusted with a wide range of responsibilities in the care and training of Odysseus' son, Telemachus.[49] Today mentors are still seen as older, more experienced individuals who pass on the benefits of their experience to younger persons. Some observers believe that mentor relationships play a key role in assisting those who have successful careers. Others contend that they are less important than currently thought and that the relationships are more complex than Homer suggests.

According to Kathy E. Kram,[50] the interactions that occur in a mentoring relationship can certainly be helpful in a person's career. She divides the functions of mentoring into two broad categories: career functions and psychosocial functions. *Career functions* are those aspects of the relationship that help the younger person learn the ropes and prepare for advancement. Included in this realm are such activities as sponsoring the younger person's career through public support, helping the junior person gain exposure and visibility in the organization, coaching the younger colleague in specific strategies, protecting him or her from negative contacts, and seeing that he or she is assigned challenging, constructive work.

psychosocial function
According to Kram, aspect of a professional relationship that improves one's sense of competence, identity, and effectiveness.

Psychosocial functions are those aspects of the relationship that "enhance a sense of competence, clarity of identity, and effectiveness in a professional role."[51] The mentor's attitudes, values, and behavior provide a model for the younger person to emulate. The older person also furnishes support and encouragement for the younger colleague and helps him or her explore personal concerns that may interfere with productivity at work. Finally, the two colleagues are often friends who like and understand each other and enjoy each other's company.

Kram's studies indicate that the mentor relationship is not one-sided. In addition to the satisfaction of passing on the benefits of experience, the mentor receives technical and psychological support from a loyal subordinate and is recognized by others as someone who can effectively develop talent. Moreover, the relationship can take a number of different forms—it is not restricted to a single older person dispensing wisdom to a younger colleague. Mentor roles can be filled by a number of persons, both within the organization and outside it—one's boss, other individuals higher in the organization, co-workers, friends outside work, a spouse, and even subordinates. Attempts to identify a single individual and form a mentor relationship with him or her are frequently misdirected and unsuccessful. If one happens to find a single person with whom one feels compatible and who fulfills a variety of mentoring roles, so much the better. However, Kram says it is more important to develop a *network* of mutually supportive relationships in which a number of individuals provide a variety of mentoring functions.[52]

Overcoming Barriers.
Maria Monet, now CFO at Ogden Corp., had to change career directions—from law to investment banking—before finding an organization where she could break the "glass ceiling." Although she is married, she works out of New York and her husband works in San Francisco; they see each other once a month and have no children.

WOMEN'S CAREERS IN MANAGEMENT. Women managers must confront the same challenges and issues as men in management, but they must deal with additional issues as well. According to Yount, the division of labor along gender lines has led to sex role stereotypes and to self-images that correspond to those stereotypes.[53] Part-time work, for example, is viewed as a sign of inadequacy in a man, since he is supposed to be a breadwinner. But it is seen as appropriate for a woman, since her primary concerns are supposed to be home and family.[54] In practice, discrimination, sexual stereotyping, the conflicting demands of marriage and work life, and increased social isolation and loneliness are more likely to affect managerial women than men.[55] These factors can prevent women from entering management and may make it harder for them to do their best work when they do become managers. The problems women may face in pursuing managerial careers stem from at least three sources: (1) the woman's attitudes toward herself and her career, (2) the attitudes of the men and women with whom she works, and (3) broad organizational policies and procedures. Each source may create barriers to women's career progress and success. Circumstances in all three areas are changing, however, and the general trend is for barriers to be reduced.

CLASS COMMENT
Half of the women managers surveyed in a recent Gallup poll report frequent stress. (*Wall Street Journal,* 4/11/91, p. B1)

FOR DISCUSSION
Will prospects for women improve as more enter executive positions? Why or why not?

FOR DISCUSSION
What additional issues do you think women must cope with?

Women's Attitudes. Until recently, most women who were old enough to consider becoming managers had not been socialized to see themselves in managerial roles. This factor, combined with organizational and societal barriers to professional and managerial careers, led many women to choose other alternatives. The changes in this area have been dramatic. In 1972 and 1973, for example, less than 5 percent of all MBA graduates were female; by 1981 and 1982, the figure had risen to approximately 30 percent.[56] By 1987, 33 percent of graduating MBA students were women, and the total of women in management and administrative roles had risen to 37 percent.[57]

Nevertheless, many women's expectations remain relatively low. A study of Stanford MBAs found that women graduates had lower ultimate salary hopes and expectations than male graduates.[58] These expectations were borne out by a recent *Business Week* survey of top business schools, which showed a substantial starting salary differential between male and female MBAs from the same school.[59] In fact, on the average, women's peak salary expectations were less than 40 percent of men's.[60] Another study of educated women of all ages found that many wondered whether their achievements were worth the price.[61] These doubts and low expectations may be realistic: Women's careers often do demand sacrifices at home, and childbearing, organizational barriers, and other factors may hinder their careers. However, lower expectations may also function as a self-fulfilling prophecy, discouraging women from progressing as far as they might in their careers.

Attitudes of Co-workers. It has long been recognized that some workers are prejudiced against female professionals and managers. This prejudice is not based on the performance of women managers and professions as a group, because research shows that men and women managers are very similar in terms of attitudes, behavior, and performance.[62] More recent research indicates that the biases against women found in earlier studies are diminishing. Hazel F. Ezell, Charles A. Olewahn, and J. Daniel Sherman, for example, report that men who have been subordinates of women managers are more favorably disposed toward them than are men who have not.[63] As women become more common at all levels of management, we can expect further changes and greater acceptance.

Organizational Policies and Procedures. Although recent administrations have not been as aggressive as previous administrations in enforcing legislation for equal opportunity and affirmative action for women and minorities, there have still been dramatic reductions in the barriers holding back women and minorities in education and organizational careers since the passage of the 1964 Civil Rights Act.

Just as some men face special career barriers and members of minorities face even greater barriers, many women managers will face gender-related barriers. This is not to say that such barriers cannot be overcome with creativity and persistence—some can and some cannot. Nor is it true that being a women is never advantageous—in some circumstances it is. However, many women have to devote time and energy to dealing with issues, problems, and barriers that most men never encounter, and dealing with these issues detracts from "getting the job done."

Since the situation is changing so rapidly, it seems likely that models of women's careers and career success based on even recent experiences may prove to be poor predictors of the future. How, then, can a woman manage her own career most effectively? If we assume that most career tasks are reasonably similar for men and women and that only a few are quite different, the most fruitful approach may be to work hard at doing the best possible job with the many "general" issues and use the existing models and guidelines for handling gender-related tasks.[64]

Fortunately, there are more and more female success models for younger women to emulate as women begin to break through the glass ceiling of top manage-

ILLUSTRATIVE CASE STUDY

WRAP-UP

Selina Proctor: Parent and Professional

We can infer that Selina has entered a transitional phase of her career—she is thinking about what she must do to become a partner in the law firm and balancing that goal against other goals she has. If Selina has a linear concept of her career, it may not be compatible with working only part time. Furthermore, she faces the burden of a growing number of women—simultaneously pursuing a career and carrying out the traditional female roles of wife and primary caregiver of a small child. Unless she and Kenneth agree to modify some of their role expectations, Selina may end up wondering if working is worth the effort or whether motherhood required her to sacrifice too much of her professional ambitions. Each of these questions is complex in itself and requires outstanding problem-solving abilities. As part of charting their career progress, for example, Selina and Kenneth might decide that giving up a winter vacation to pay for a live-in housekeeper or other domestic help is a worthwhile trade-off, freeing both of them to concentrate on their priorities—building their careers and being more relaxed and loving partners and parents to their child—without needless guilt or stress. ■

ment. They include Jill Barad, division president of Mattel (1990 cash compensation $504,923); Cathleen Black, executive vice president, Gannett ($600,000); Bernice Lavin, vice president, secretary, and treasurer, Alberto-Culver ($513,746); Nina McLemore, senior vice president, Liz Claiborne ($600,000); Maria Monet, chief financial officer, Ogden Corp. ($733,617); and Marion Sandler, president and chief executive officer, Golden West Financial ($665,357).[65]

■ SUMMARY

Certain events occur with relative predictability over the course of a person's career. Understanding these events enables people to prepare for them and to take an active role in managing their own careers.

Early career experiences commonly include the formation of unrealistic expectations and reality shock when those expectations clash with frustrating on-the-job experiences. Low initial challenge and lack of performance appraisal are some organizational factors that contribute to reality shock, which realistic job previews may help prevent.

The amount of challenge in the initial job assignment, the actions of the new employee's first supervisor, and the new employee's fit with the organizational culture are particularly important career influences. Dilemmas that arise early in the individual's career relate to political insensitivity and passivity, loyalty demands, and personal anxiety about a growing commitment to the organization. The last dilemma can sometimes be resolved through "creative individualism," which permits the individual to accept only the most important values of the organization.

Stress, a part of all life, is often caused by overload. There are two kinds of overloading: quantitative, in which a person has more work than he or she has time for; and qualitative, in which the person lacks the skills to do the job. Underloading may also be a problem. Stress can have serious health consequences. A variety of techniques can be used to reduce stressful factors in the environment and to help people deal with the stress that does occur.

Several models of the career stages through which many people pass have been developed. Levinson and his colleagues, for example, devised a model that describes adult life as a series of predictable events that occur every five or seven years. The stages are called the early adult transition, entering the adult world, the age-30 transition, settling down, the mid-life transition, the beginning of middle adulthood, the age-50 transition, the second middle adult structure, the late adult transition, and the late adult era.

Driver and Schein have developed two perspectives on the patterns that careers follow. Driver has suggested that most careers follow one of four basic career concepts: linear, steady-state, spiral, or transitory. Schein developed the concept of the career anchor, a form of self-concept that develops through one's experiences in the workplace and that functions as a guide for one's entire career. Schein described five career anchors—technical or functional competence, managerial competence, security, creativity, and autonomy.

Schein has also devised a model that describes how the individual's positions within the organization change over time. The organization appears as a cone in which vertical, radial, and circumferential movement can take place across various boundaries. With each movement, the individual is socialized or trained to fit into the new position. Schein believes people are most likely to be innovative at the midpoint of their tenure in a position.

Individuals reach a career plateau when they are no longer candidates for promotion. Stars and learners are considered eligible for promotion; solid citizens and deadwood are not. Almost everyone in an organization eventually reaches a plateau, frequently because of the scarcity of positions available at higher levels of the hierarchy.

The starting point for individual career planning is to understand what one wants from one's work, career, and life. Schoonmaker has offered a nine-step career strategy that involves systematic career planning. Once one has mounted a successful job campaign and gotten a job in one's chosen field, much can be done to manage the work situation to one's advantage. The most important tasks are to do excellent work, develop good working relationships, and help your boss succeed.

Dual-career couples must work hard to integrate and balance the demands and opportunities of two separate careers. Mentors serve a variety of functions, some of them directly related to the individual's career, others more psychosocial in nature. Mentor roles can be filled by a variety of persons within and outside the organization; the employee need not attempt to form a relationship with just one person.

Women face a number of barriers to successful careers. Three major barriers are their own attitudes toward themselves and their careers, the attitudes of their co-workers, and their organization's policies and procedures. Although barriers have been reduced in recent years and will probably diminish further, women in management will face greater pressures than men for some time.

■ REVIEW QUESTIONS

1. Why do you think people develop unrealistic expectations about their first jobs? Why is this tendency especially severe among business school graduates?

2. What is reality shock? What factors contribute to it?

3. What three factors in an individual's early job experiences have an especially strong influence on subsequent job success? Why are these factors so influential?

4. Why are young business school graduates often insensitive to the political dimension of organizational life? What is the proper function of political alliances in an organization?

5. Webber describes five common ways by which superiors define loyalty. What are these five ways? What ethical and other conflicts can arise for subordinates in applying these directives?

6. In what three ways can people respond to the organization's efforts to enforce compliance with its expectations? Which way do you think is best? Why?

7. What are the six types of role conflict identified by Katz and Kahn?

8. What are the most common causes of stress? How can stress affect health? Describe the various procedures that can be used to reduce stress and help people deal with it.

9. What are the ten stages in Levinson's model of adult development?

10. Compare Driver's career concepts notion with Schein's idea of career anchors.

11. Think of some people you know who work for organizations and try to fit them into the career stages or states of the various models presented in the chapter. Can they be accurately placed?

12. According to Schein, what three types of movement are possible within organizations? What three types of organizational boundaries exist? How does the organization attempt to influence the individual who is making a position change? How can the individual most effectively influence the organization?

13. List the nine steps in Schoonmaker's career strategy. How reasonable do they sound to you?

14. What are three most important steps one can take in the work situation to further one's career?

15. What are the special issues that must be confronted by dual-career couples? Discuss the four general styles of managing two careers.

16. According to Kram, what two types of functions are served by mentors? Should one assume that it is imperative to find an individual to serve as one's mentor? Why or why not?

17. What are some of the special problems faced by women in management?

CASE STUDY

Andrew Krieger's Career Decision at Soros Fund

The last year had been a busy one, especially in terms of career moves, for Andrew Krieger. The year before, he had been a currency trader at Bankers Trust. As such, he had bought (and sold) foreign currency, betting that its value would increase (or decrease) relative to the dollar. It was a high-pressure job that demanded an ability to take huge risks in stride. His bets were usually correct, and he had done very well, earning the bank more than $300 million and a $3 million bonus for himself. Not bad for a 31-year-old who had been out of business school just five years.

However, high-volume trading created interpersonal problems on the job. Some of Krieger's coworkers were annoyed because his activities occasionally affected theirs: He worked in such large amounts of currency that the entire market would often respond to one of his trades—a fact that could catch his co-workers by surprise, frustrating their own bets on the behavior of the market. The risks he took in order to achieve his spectacular returns also worried his employer. Although his trades usually resulted in millions of dollars in profits, Krieger regularly risked many more millions in the process. His superiors tried to exert a little more control over Krieger, seeking to restrain his risk-taking impulses and to build a solid team out of the department rather than relying on a single star.

So Krieger had decided he would be happier if he left Bankers Trust, hoping to find more time for himself and a more personally rewarding job. Since Soros Fund Management was smaller, it offered him more freedom, so he had chosen to work there. But the change was not working out as he had envisioned it. When he exercised his freedom, he worried his current employer even more than he had worried Bankers Trust. In order to make the largest possible returns, he invested all the money he could find. Unfortunately, this practice often left other parts of the firm short of capital for their investments in the stock market—a fact that tended to leave a lot of people unhappy. Nor did George Soros, the president of the Soros Fund, see eye-to-eye with Krieger on strategic matters. The big-risk/big-reward strategy Krieger favored not only concerned Soros but generated publicity that Soros did not appreciate.

So, it looked as if Krieger had made a mistake. Several private investors had asked him if he would oversee their investments, and he was seriously considering going into business for himself. Maybe that way he would have the freedom he craved without having to worry about conflicts with co-workers and employers. And maybe working with an individual's money rather than an institution's would give him a greater feeling of satisfaction. However, it was a risk. He would have less capital to bet with and would be hard-pressed to take the occasionally inevitable losses.

Should he leave Soros? Or should he give the job more time, in hopes that the problems he was encountering would go away? Would he really be any happier anywhere else? Krieger could not be sure of the answers to these questions.

Sources: Adapted from Charles W. Stevens, "Andrew Krieger Made $3 Million Last Year; Why Isn't He Happy?" *The Wall Street Journal,* March 24, 1988, pp. 1, 16; Stevens and George Anders, "Options Trading Whiz Krieger Quits Again—This Time from Soros Fund," *The Wall Street Journal,* June 7, 1988, p. 28.

Case Questions

1. In what stage of his career is Andrew Krieger?

2. What are the factors that are causing stress in his life?

3. What can he do to manage this stress?

4. Should Krieger leave Soros? What advice would you give him?

Careers and Parenting: Problems and Solutions at Corning Glass

A perennial topic of conversation has emerged as one of the more controversial and frequently discussed issues of today: Should employees get time off from work to either have or take care of children? Women have been upset for years because they felt they experienced discrimination; either they did not get enough time off work to recover from childbirth or they returned to work to find their position had been filled in their absence. Now the emphasis has shifted to the issue of day care. Faced with inadequate day care centers, many parents either want to take a leave of absence or to work part time while their children are very young. Some managers see this as a problem, since employees expect the firm to hold their jobs for them. In effect, the firm has to "jog in place" or work short-handed until the parent comes back full time.

One controversial proposal (for its name if nothing else) is the "mommy track." This proposal would allow women to choose one of two tracks: career primary (women who are not likely to have children) or mommy track (career and family). Many are concerned, not only about the absurdity of the choice involved (can I see that far into the future?), but about the apparent dichotomy of choice: if I choose to be a parent, I cannot be serious about my career and vice versa. Even if someone finds the "mommy track" an unsound proposition, it does attempt to get at the complicated issue of seriously pursuing a career as well as being involved as a parent.

In the mid-1980s, Bonnie L. Milliman, 26, was a promising engineering supervisor at Corning Glass Works. She was devoted to her career and enjoyed working with Corning. Yet, a new baby forced her to reexamine her priorities and her feelings about her employers. The 50 to 70 hours per week she had to put in, combined with the "maximum devotion work ethic" at Corning, made any notion of a compromise between work and home life unrealistic. Faced with this essentially uncompromising work situation and her desire to spend time with her child, Milliman opted to quit her job, and the company lost this valued employee. Furthermore, a company survey revealed that women weren't becoming top managers and that they left the company at twice the rate of men (at a cost of over $2 million per year).

Corning obviously had to do something about this problem, and it has. Under its chairman and chief executive officer, James R. Houghton, Corning has established policies and programs designed to attract and retain both women and minorities. Committees were established to focus on compensation and promotion policies, mentors were paired with new hires to help them adapt to the company and learn new skills, and managers who were especially successful in hiring women and minorities were rewarded. As a result, the rate at which women were leaving the company was halved between 1987 and 1990, providing Corning with a larger pool of talented women who can be tapped for executive positions.

Source: Elizabeth Ehrlich, "The Mommy Track," *Business Week,* March 20, 1989, p. 29; Keith H. Hammond, "Corning's Class Act," *Business Week,* May 13, 1991, p. 68.

Case Questions

1. As a management consultant to Corning, what sort of planning provision do you suggest they offer employees who want to take time away from work to be with their children (or to have children)?

2. What factors should Corning consider in making its decision and how important ought they to be?

3 How should family fit into the value system of the corporation and what can corporations do to demonstrate that commitment to women who want to have children and parents who want to spend time at home and still pursue a "serious" career?

■ NOTES

[1]Robert B. Slaney and Joyce E. A. Russell, "Perspectives on Vocational Behavior, 1986: A Review," *Journal of Vocational Behavior* 31 (1987):111–173.

[2]Douglas T. Hall, *Careers in Organizations* (Pacific Palisades, Calif.: Goodyear, 1976). For a more recent set of articles on career development, see Douglas Hall and Associates, *Career Development in Organizations* (San Francisco: Jossey-Bass, 1986).

[3]See Lyman W. Porter, Edward E. Lawler III, and J. Richard Hackman, *Behavior in Organizations* (New York: McGraw-Hill, 1975), pp. 131–136, 172–178.

[4]Edgar H. Schein, "The First Job Dilemma," *Psychology Today,* March 1968, pp. 22–37.

[5]John D. Aram and James A. F. Stoner, "Development of an Organizational Change Role," *Journal of Applied Behavioral Science* 8, no. 4 (October–November–December 1972):438–449. See also John Paul Kotter, "The Psychological Contract: Managing the Joining-Up Process," *California Management Review* 15, no. 3 (Spring 1973):91–99. For a thorough discussion of the process of entering an organization, see John P. Wanous, *Organizational Entry: Recruitment, Selection, and Socialization of Newcomers* (Reading, Mass.: Addison-Wesley, 1980).

[6]Marvin D. Dunnette, Richard D. Arvey, and Paul A. Banas, "Why Do They Leave?" *Personnel* 50, no. 3 (May–June 1973):25–39.

[7]David E. Berlew and Douglas T. Hall, "The Socialization of Managers: Effects of Expectations on Performance," *Administrative Science Quarterly* 11, no. 2 (September 1966):207–223.

[8]See, for example, Schein, "The First Job Dilemma"; J. Sterling Livingston, "Pygmalion in Management," *Harvard Business Review* 47, no. 4 (July–August 1969):81–89; and Douglas W. Bray, Richard J. Campbell, and Donald Grant, *Formative Years in Business* (New York: Wiley, 1974), p. 73.

[9]The powerful impact of expectations on performance has been demonstrated experimentally in research review by Robert Rosenthal and Donald B. Rubin, "Interpersonal Expectancy Effects: The First 345 Studies," *Behavioral and Brain Sciences* 1, no. 3 (September 1978):377–415. See also Dov Eden, "Self-Fulfilling Prophecy as a Management Tool: Harnessing Pygmalion," *Academy of Management Review* 9, no. 1 (January 1984):64–73.

[10]For an exercise that simulates how one might assess one's fit with an organization, see James G. Clawson, John P. Kotter, Victor A. Faux, and Charles C. McArthur, *Self-Assessment and Career Development,* 2nd ed. (Englewood Cliffs, N.J.: Prentice Hall, 1985), pp. 277–287.

[11]Ross A. Webber, "The Three Dilemmas of Career Growth," *MBA* 9, no. 5 (May 1975):41–48.

[12]David C. McClelland, "The Two Faces of Power," *Journal of International Affairs* 24, no. 1 (1970): 29–47.

[13]Edgar H. Schein, "Organizational Socialization and the Profession of Management," *Industrial Management Review* 9, no. 2 (Winter 1968):1–16.

[14]Daniel Katz and Robert L. Kahn, *The Social Psychology of Organizations,* 2nd ed. (New York: Wiley, 1978). See also Robert L. Kahn, D. M. Wolfe, R. P. Quinn, J. D. Snock, and R. A. Rosenthal, *Organizational Stress: Studies in Role Conflict and Ambiguity* (New York: Wiley, 1964); and Andrew J. DuBrin, *Fundamentals of Organizational Behavior: An Applied Perspective,* 2nd ed. (Elmsford, N.Y.: Pergamon Press, 1978), Chap. 4.

[15]Francine Hall and Douglas T. Hall, *The Two-Career Couple* (Reading, Mass.: Addison-Wesley, 1978).

[16]Jeffrey H. Greenhaus, Arthur G. Bedeian, and Kevin W. Mossholder, "Work Experiences, Job Performance, and Feelings of Personal and Family Well-Being," *Journal of Vocational Behavior* 31 (1987):200–215.

[17]Saroj Parasuraman and Joseph A. Alutto, "Sources and Outcomes of Stress in Organizational Settings: Toward the Development of a Structural Model," *Academy of Management Journal* 27, no. 2 (June 1984):330–350.

[18]Our discussion is based largely on Robert A. Baron, *Understanding Human Relations: A Practical Guide to People at Work* (Boston: Allyn & Bacon, 1985), pp. 272–302. Other general sources on stress are Leonard Moss, *Management Stress* (Reading, Mass.: Addison-Wesley, 1981); James C. Quick and Jonathan D. Quick, *Organizational Stress and Preventive Management* (New York: McGraw-Hill, 1984); and Jere E. Yates, *Managing Stress: A Businessperson's Guide* (New York: AMACOM, 1979).

[19]Joseph E. McGrath, "Stress and Behavior in Organizations," in Marvin D. Dunnette, ed., *Handbook of Industrial and Organizational Psychology* (New York: Wiley, 1983), p. 1352.

[20]Based on information gathered by the National Institute for Occupational Safety and Health, U.S. Department of Health, Education, and Welfare, 1978. See Baron, *Understanding Human Relations,* p. 301.

[21]A. M. Pines, E. Aronson, and D. Kafrey, *Burnout: From Tedium to Personal Growth* (New York: Free Press, 1981).

[22]Salvatore R. Maddi and Suzanne C. Kobasa, *The Hardy Executive: Health and Stress* (Homewood, Ill.: Dow Jones-Irwin, 1984).

[23]Susan E. Jackson, "Participation in Decision Making as a Strategy for Reducing Job-Related Strain," *Journal of Applied Psychology* 68, no. 1 (1983).

[24]Lawrence R. Murphy, "Occupational Stress Management: A Review and Appraisal," *Journal of Occupational Psychology* 57, no. 1 (1984):1–15. See also Addison W. Somerville, Agnes R. Allen, Barbara A. Noble, and D. L. Sedgwick, "Effect of a Stress Management Class: One Year Later," *Teaching of Psychology* 11, no. 2 (April 1984):82–85.

[25]Much of our discussion is based on Hall, *Careers in Organizations,* pp. 47–64.

[26]See Erik H. Erikson, *Childhood and Society,* 2nd ed. (New York: Norton, 1963), pp. 247–274.

[27]Donald Super and his colleagues have divided vocational life into five stages: *growth* (birth–14), *exploration* (15–24), *establishment* (25–44), *maintenance* (45–64), and *decline* (65 and older). See Donald E. Super, John O. Crites, Raymond C. Hummel, Helen P. Moser, Phoebe L. Overstreet, and Charles F. Warnath, *Vocational Development: A Framework for Research* (New York: Teachers College Press, 1957), pp. 40–41.

[28]Daniel J. Levinson, Charlotte N. Darrow, Edward B. Kein, Maria H. Levinson, and Braxton McKee, *The Seasons of a Man's Life* (New York: Knopf, 1978). This discussion and many other parts of this chapter have benefited greatly from a review by James G. Clawson. See Clawson et al., *Self-Assessment and Career Development,* pp. 386–387; Gail Sheehy, *Passages* (New York: Dutton, 1976); and Roger L. Gould, *Transformations: Growth and Change in Adult Life* (New York: Simon & Schuster, 1978).

[29]Michael J. Driver, "Career Concepts—A New Approach to Career Research," in Ralph Katz, ed., *Career Issues in Human Resource Management* (Englewood Cliffs, N.J.: Prentice Hall, 1982), pp. 23–32; and "Career Concepts and Career Management in Organizations," in Cary L. Cooper, ed., *Behavioral Problems in Organizations* (Englewood Cliffs, N.J.: Prentice-Hall, 1979), pp. 79–139.

[30]Edgar H. Schein, *Career Dynamics: Matching Individual and Organizational Needs* (Reading, Mass.: Addison-Wesley, 1978), pp. 124–171. For a summary of these concepts, see Thomas J. DeLong, "The Career Orientations of MBA Alumni: A Multidimensional Model," in Katz, *Career Issues,* pp. 50–64.

[31]Driver, "Career Concepts—A New Approach to Career Research," p. 27.

[32]DeLong, "The Career Orientations of MBA Alumni," in Katz, *Career Issues,* p. 53. DeLong has noted three plausible possibilities: *identity,* the anchor for those who seek the status of belonging to certain companies and organizations; *service,* the anchor for those who want to use their skills to help others; and *variety,* the anchor for those who seek novelty and freshness in their work projects.

[33] Edgar H. Schein, "The Individual, the Organization, and the Career: A Conceptual Scheme," *Journal of Applied Behavioral Science* 7, no. 4 (October–November–December 1971):401–426.

[34]Gene W. Dalton, Paul H. Thompson, and Raymond L. Price, "The Four Stages of Professional Careers—A New Look at Performance by Professionals," *Organizational Dynamics* 6, no. 1 (Summer 1977):19–42.

[35]The relationship of professional and private lives of managers is dealt with by Paul Evans and Fernando Bartolomé in *Must Success Cost So Much?* (New York: Basic Books, 1980), pp. 27–41.

[36]Thomas P. Ference, James A. F. Stoner, and E. Kirby Warren, "Managing the Career Plateau," *Academy of Management Review* 2, no. 4 (October 1977):602–612. Our discussion is based on these sources: Stoner, Ference, Warren, and H. Kurt Christensen, *Managerial Career Plateaus—An Exploratory Study* (New York: Center for Research in Career Development, Columbia University, 1980); and Warren, Ference, and Stoner, "Case of the Plateaued Performer," *Harvard Business Review* 53, no. 1 (January–February 1975):30–38ff. See also John W. Slocum, Jr., William L. Cron, Richard W. Hansen, and Sallie Rawlings, "Business Strategy and the Management of Plateaued Employees," *Academy of Management Journal* 28, no. 1 (March 1985):133–154.

[37]See Harry Levinson, "On Being a Middle-Aged Manager," *Harvard Business Review* 47, no. 4 (July–August 1969):51–60.

[38]See Laurence J. Peter and Raymond Hull, *The Peter Principle* (New York: Morrow, 1969). Peter and Hull suggest that the managerial career cycle ends when managers are promoted to their "level of incompetence": a job beyond their ability. This certainly does happen, but managers probably reach plateaus more frequently while they are still performing effectively and when they then can still develop and grow.

[39]Martin G. Evans and Elizabeth Gilbert, "Plateaued Managers: Their Need Gratifications and Their Effort-Performance Expectations," *Journal of Management Studies* 21, no. 1 (1984):99–110.

[40]Many organizations have developed programs to assist individuals in managing their careers. For example, under the guidance of Walter D. Storey, General Electric has developed career planning programs and a manual entitled *Career Action Planning.* Arthur D. Little uses a manual entitled *Effective Career Management.* The point at which organizations should work with individuals to develop and manage their careers is discussed thoroughly by Manuel L. London and Stephen A. Stumpf in *Managing Careers* (Reading, Mass.: Addison-Wesley, 1982).

[41]For information on developing individual career plans, see Alan N. Schoonmaker, *Executive Career Strategy* (New York: American Management Associations, 1971); Andrew H. Souerwine, *Career Strategies: Planning for Personal Achievement* (New York: AMACOM, 1978); Richard Nelson Bolles, *What Color Is Your Parachute?* [revised annually] (Berkeley, Calif.: Ten Speed Press, 1986); and Nicholas N. Weiler, *Reality and Career Planning: A Guide to Personal Growth* (Reading, Mass.: Addison-Wesley, 1977). Detailed guidance on individual career planning can be found in London and Stumpf, *Managing Careers.* The Clawson et al. text (*Self-Assessment and Career Development*) provides detailed guidance on developing a career strategy that is especially appropriate for MBA students, but many other students have also found it useful. In addition, a growing number of college and graduate schools of business offer full-credit courses in career planning and development for their management students. Schools that have offered such courses for a number of years include the Harvard Business School, Fordham Graduate School of Business Administration, and Northeastern University.

[42]Schoonmaker, *Executive Career Strategy,* pp. 6–11.

[43]This section is based in part on Schoonmaker, *Executive Career Strategy,* and DuBrin, *Fundamentals of Organizational Behavior,* Chap. 5.

[44]Ronald J. Burke, "Relationships in and Around Organizations: It's *Both* Who You Know and What You Know That Counts," *Psychological Reports* 55, no. 1 (August 1984):293–307.

[45]See John J. Gabarro and John P. Kotter, "Managing Your Boss," *Harvard Business Review* 58, no. 1

(January–February 1980):92–100; and Lloyd Baird and Kathy Kram, "Career Dynamics: Managing the Superior/Subordinate Relationship," *Organizational Dynamics* 11, no. 4 (Spring 1983):46–64.

[46]Hall and Hall, *The Two-Career Couple,* pp. 232–235.

[47]Francine Hall and Douglas T. Hall, *The Two-Career Couple* (Reading, Mass.: Addison-Wesley, 1978).

[48]E. A. House, "Sex Role Orientation and Marital Satisfaction in Dual- and One-Provider Couples," *Sex Roles* 14 (1986):245–259.

[49]We were reminded of this fact by James G. Clawson, "Is Mentoring Necessary?" *Training and Development Journal* 39, no. 4 (April 1985):36.

[50]Kathy E. Kram, *Mentoring at Work: Developmental Relationships in Organizational Life* (Glenview, Ill.: Scott, Foresman, 1985), Chaps. 2 and 3. Also see Kathy Kram, "Mentoring in the Workplace," in Hall and Associates, *Career Development in Organizations,* pp. 160–201.

[51]Kram, *Mentoring at Work,* p. 22.

[52]See also Kathy E. Kram and Lynn A. Isabella, "Mentoring Alternatives: The Role of Peer Relationships in Career Development," *Academy of Management Journal* 28, no. 1 (March 1985):110–132.

[53]K. R. Yount, "A Theory of Productive Activity: The Relationships Among Self-Concept, Gender, Sex Role Stereotypes, and Work-Emergent Traits," *Psychology of Women Quarterly* 10 (1986):63–88.

[54]A. H. Eagly and V. J. Steffen, "Gender Stereotypes, Occupational Roles, and Beliefs About Part-Time Employees," *Psychology of Women Quarterly* 10 (1986):252–262.

[55]Debra L. Nelson and James C. Quick, "Professional Women: Are Distress and Disease Inevitable?" *Academy of Management Review* 10, no. 2 (April 1985):206–218. See also Cary L. Cooper and Marilyn J. Davidson, "The High Cost of Stress on Women Managers," *Organizational Dynamics* 10, no. 4 (Spring 1982):44–53. An excellent collection of articles on the role of women in organizations is Lynda L. Moore, ed., *Not as Far as You Think: The Realities of Working Women* (Lexington, Mass.: Lexington Books, 1986).

[56]Ruth B. Ekstrom, "Women in Management: Factors Affecting Career Entrance and Advancement," *Selection* 2, no. 1 (Spring 1985):29–32.

[57]"Corporate Women," *Business Week,* June 22, 1987, pp. 72–77.

[58]Ekstrom, "Women in Management," p. 30.

[59]Monica Roman, "Women, Beware: An MBA Doesn't Mean Equal Pay," *Business Week,* October 29, 1990, p. 57.

[60]Ekstrom, "Women in Management," p. 30.

[61]M. A. Paludi and J. Fankell-Hauser, "An Idiographic Approach to the Study of Women's Achievement Striving," *Psychology of Women Quarterly* 10 (1986):89–100.

[62]Susan M. Donnell and Jay Hall, "Men and Women as Managers: A Significant Case of No Significant Difference," *Organizational Dynamics* 8, no. 4 (Spring 1980):60–77.

[63]See, for example, Hazel F. Ezell, Charles A. Olewahn, and J. Daniel Sherman, "Women Entering Management: Differences in Perceptions of Factors Influencing Integration," *Group and Organizational Studies* 7, no. 2 (June 1982):243–253.

[64]See Eliza G. C. Collins, *"Dearest Amanda . . . " An Executive's Advice to Her Daughter* (New York: Harper & Row, 1984); and Betty Lehan Harragan, *Games Mother Never Taught You: Corporate Gamesmanship for Women* (New York: Rawson, 1977).

[65]Jaclyn Fierman, "Why Women Still Don't Hit the Top," *Fortune,* July 30, 1990, p. 46.

CASE ON LEADING

THE MERIT CORPORATION

John Kirschner, President of the Merit Corporation, was concerned about his company's new product development. The Merit Corporation was a medium-sized firm, located near Boston, which manufactured and sold children's furniture nationally. From its inception, the company had been family-owned and operated. John Kirschner's grandfather and uncle had started the company, and control eventually passed to Mr. Kirschner's father and then to him. Now, at age 54, although he was still actively involved with every aspect of the company's operations, Kirschner was considering early retirement. Kirschner decided that, before retiring, he wanted to improve the output and the operations of the New Product area. He felt that strength in this area would help to ensure the firm's continued success in its industry. The New Product area had always been especially interesting to Kirschner, particularly since it was the first place he had worked when he originally came to Merit.

New products had traditionally been developed by a series of temporary task forces. Members of existing management groups would, on a rotating basis, become members of a new product development task force. Over a six-month period, they would concentrate on developing a new product for Merit. Since Kirschner's father and grandfather had both felt it necessary for each manager to gain experience in the New Product area, this system had been used for years. The system had worked reasonably well: enough new products had been developed that the company's name was well established as a leading manufacturing of children's furniture.

Over the past ten years, however, Kirschner felt that things had changed enough to warrant a new look at this area of the company, which he felt was fundamental to Merit's success. As the population became more mobile, for example, there was an increasing need for lighter, yet more durable, furniture. As the birth rate went down, people were less willing to spend a great deal of money on juvenile furniture, and the consumers' movement had focused attention on product imperfections and poor design such as sharp corners and toxic paints, thereby prompting increased production costs. At the same time, the field had become increasingly competitive as furniture manufacturers in general began to use their excess capacity to produce children's furniture. As a result of these and other factors, it had become increasingly difficult to obtain adequate financing.

The higher cost of the company's debt had led to a price increase, which did not help to attract customers in an already highly competitive area where product differentiation was difficult. The company's sales had leveled off at approximately $120 million.

Company Background. Merit's headquarters and the largest of its three manufacturing plants were located ten miles outside of Boston, in an industrial park on a major expressway. Merit shared the building with a number of other firms, and had offices on the second and third floors of the six-story building. All employees worked a forty-hour, five-day week, although there had been some discussion a number of years earlier concerning the possibility of a four-day week because of the commuting problems in this particular area. The idea had never gone very far, however, since Kirschner felt that a four-day week would disrupt business too much. Thus, work tended to begin promptly at 8:30 and end at 4:30; coming in early or leaving late was generally considered by Kirschner to be a sign of ineffectiveness. In fact, he set the pattern himself, just as his father and grandfather had before him: his car could always be seen next to the front entrance of the building at precisely 8:30, and, with rare exception, he, too, left at 4:30.

Corporate offices were arranged quite close to one another; in fact many of the offices were divided only by a glass wall because Kirschner felt that organizing space in this manner emphasized an informal but task-oriented work atmosphere. Employee morale was high, although there tended to be little social interaction outside of the office among the corporate headquarters staff.

Merit had generous fringe benefits and a pension plan that was a model in its area. Labor disputes had never been a significant problem in any of the company's three plants, and turnover was generally low, although it was higher in the New England plants than in the southern plant. In a departure from the company's conservative philosophy and practice, Kirschner had brought in new managers from the outside, some of whom had M.B.A.'s and most of whom had extensive backgrounds either in the plastics industry or in consumer marketing. Kirschner also had begun to emphasize continuing technical and managerial education and had sent a number of his top people to Harvard's Advanced Management Program. Kirschner was also an advocate of management by committee and the Chief Executive Officer function was shared by Kirschner and two other executives, each of whom had an administrative staff.

Kirschner felt that Merit's only troubling problem was its new product development. After giving the matter considerable thought and after a number of brief discussions with his top managers, Kirschner decided that a radical change would be necessary if Merit was to continue playing a dominant role in the juvenile furniture market. He made up his mind to find six to eight young people who did not necessarily have relevant business experience or specific formal training, but who did have the enthusiasm and intelligence that he felt were necessary to develop a successful new product. Kirschner believed that if he could find these people, and give them a good deal of encouragement and freedom, the company would be able to strengthen its new product development. He began looking for young men and women with imagination and divergent viewpoints using what he described as somewhat unorthodox recruiting techniques.

The New Employees. Within six months Kirschner had hired eight young people, some of whom were already located in Boston, and some of whom were to move to Boston by the first of the year, by then three months away. Kirschner felt that the eight should start work together, so he spent the next few months finding a place for them to work and thinking through how to relate the group to the existing organization. He felt that it was important to have one person reporting directly to him, but decided against any further structuring. He decided to appoint Christopher Kane as group head, partly because he was the first to be hired, and partly because Kane had made such a good impression.

When the eight new staff members who were to make up the New Products Development group arrived at the Merit Corporation's headquarters building on January 2 and reported to Mr. Kirschner's office, they did not know each other, and they really did not know what they would be doing on a day-to-day basis. Their training and skills were also very different. In addition to what their résumés indicated

EXHIBIT 1 Members of the New Products Group at the Merit Corporation

Name; Age; Degree and Major, School; Background

Andrew Jacobson; 29; B.S. Math, M.I.T.
Systems Analyst for Mitre Corp. for one year. Founder of a Public Interest Research Group under the auspices of Ralph Nader. Heavily involved with environmental and consumer issues.

John O'Hara; 28; B.A. History, Oberlin
Sculptor and Painter. Had a one-man show at the Cleveland Art Museum. Had taught art and metal sculpting in United States and abroad.

Robert Vidreaux; 28; B.A. Social Relations, Harvard
Led two archeological digs to Iran, and has spent two years working at the Museum of Natural History in New York City. Has three patents and a variety of inventions in the area of water filtration and purification.

Suzanne Tashman; 27; B.A. English, Hollins, J.L.B., Yale
Worked for Davis, Marshall, and Polk, a law firm, for two years specializing in SEC work.

Joan Waters; 27; B.A. Chemistry, Wellesley, M.B.A., Harvard
Worked at Sloan-Kettering Laboratories in New York City for two years in the area of chromosomal aberrations and viruses. After receiving M.B.A., worked in the financial office of Lilly Laboratories on long-range planning for one year.

Matthew Kiris; 29; B.S. Chemistry, Cal Tech
Spent three years investigating the effect of high concentrations of pesticides in tidal regions both in the United States and in the Far East. Has been a consultant to the Department of Public Health both in the United States and in Japan.

Christopher Kane; 28; B.A. Math, Tufts, M.B.A. Stanford
Worked for McKinsey in a variety of areas including marketing diversification and systems analysis.

Raynor Carney; 29; B.A. Political Science, Northwestern, M.B.A. Columbia
Has had extensive political experience organizing a major gubernatorial campaign and fund raising for the state Democratic Party. Served as the primary developer and contractor for modular low-cost housing project in Maryland.

Source: Revised and reproduced with the permission of Anthony G. Athos, December 1984. Original copyright © by the President and Fellows of Harvard University, Boston, Mass. Prepared by James G. Clawson.

(see Exhibit 1), Kirschner knew a few things about each new employee from interviews.

Jacobson, for example, had worked as a systems analyst, and was also interested in consumer and environmental issues. Thus, he tended to be comfortable with large amounts of data and also tended to be concerned about the implications of the data in light of his other interests. His previous experience in a large company had led him to expect a "way of doing things," which he guessed was probably quite different from what others in the group expected, based on their backgrounds.

O'Hara, on the other hand, had never worked in a business environment at all, and although he was used to working long hours and to being committed to a project for an extended length of time, he brought with him fewer clear expectations than Jacobson.

Vidreaux was interested in inventing new ways of doing things and tended to approach a procedure by first looking at other ways in which it might be done.

The personal characteristics of the group were varied, also. Kane, who had always worn a coat and tie to work, contrasted sharply with O'Hara who was more comfortable in jeans.

Tashman had worked in a law firm before coming to Merit, and had become quite comfortable dressing formally every day; she was coming from an organizational culture where professional women tended to differentiate themselves from women on the support staff in part by the way they dressed. Waters dressed rather informally. In fact, she saw the opportunity to be even more informal as a major advantage of the job at Merit.

With regard to work style, O'Hara was extremely untidy and could only work comfortably when there were stacks of paper cluttering his desk and immediate work area. Meanwhile, Jacobson was, as he put it, "compulsively neat." Kiris felt that he worked better with low music in the room. Waters and Tashman both had strong preferences for quiet when working.

Mr. Kirschner invited the new group into his office, offered them seats, and began to speak.

Case Questions

1. What are the problems and opportunities facing the new employees at Merit?
2. What should Mr. Kirschner say to the group?

CHAPTER TWENTY

EFFECTIVE CONTROL

Detail from Jasper Johns, *Numbers in Color.*

The Meaning of Control
Steps in the Control Process
Why Control Is Needed

Types of Control Methods
Pre-Action Controls
Steering Controls
Yes/No or Screening Controls
Post-Action Controls
The Interactive Nature of Control Methods

Designing Control Systems
Identifying Key Performance Areas
Identifying Strategic Control Points

Financial Controls
Financial Statements
Ratio Analysis

Budgetary Control Methods
Responsibility Centers
The Budgeting Process

Types of Budgets
Operating Budgets
Financial Budgets
Variable versus Fixed Budgets
Zero-Base Budgeting

Auditing
External Auditing
Internal Auditing

Upon completing this chapter, you should be able to:

1. Explain why managers need control.
2. Describe the steps in the control process.
3. Identify examples of the four types of control methods.
4. Discuss the importance of key performance areas and strategic control points to the design of effective control systems.
5. Explain why financial controls are important to managers.
6. Distinguish among the three types of financial statements and explain how they are used.
7. Define ratio analysis and explain how it is used.
8. List some of the reasons budgets are used so widely.
9. Explain the main types of responsibility centers and the budget considerations associated with each.
10. Describe the budgeting process.
11. Distinguish among the four main types of budgets.
12. Explain the uses of external and internal auditing.

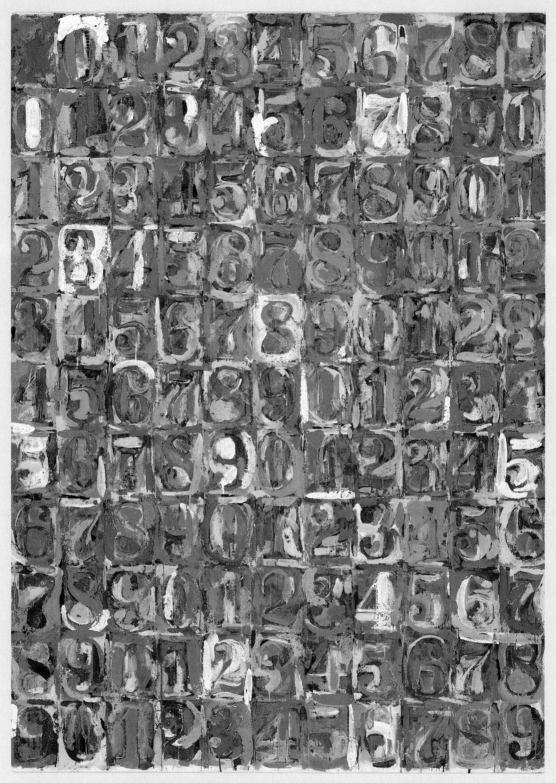

Jasper Johns, *Numbers in Color*. 1959. 66½ × 49½ inches. Encaustic and newspaper on canvas. Albright-Knox Art Gallery, Buffalo, New York. Gift of Seymour H. Knox, 1959.

ILLUSTRATIVE CASE STUDY

INTRODUCTION

Financial Resourcefulness at Deere & Co.

In the 1860s, a Vermont blacksmith named John Deere invented a plow that could turn the thick, rich soil of the vast and fertile prairies of the midwestern United States. In 1868, Deere, emphasizing a philosophy of quality products and customer service, formed a company to distribute his plows, and by 1911, that company had become a full-line manufacturer of farm equipment. In 1918, with its purchase of a gasoline engine company located in Waterloo, Iowa, Deere became one of the driving forces in the conversion of American agriculture from animal to machine power. Today Deere is the world leader in the manufacture of farm equipment and has remained a viable concern through diversification (it is also a major supplier of construction machinery), the globalization of its enterprises (it operates facilities in Mexico, Canada, Spain, France, Australia, and elsewhere), and stable leadership (between 1928 and the present, Deere has had only four CEOs).

Although Deere has built diesel engines for GM and worked with NASA on the development of metal alloys, its core business remains agricultural equipment, an industry in which Deere controls a little over 32 percent of the North American market. It is no secret, though, that American agriculture has had its ups and downs in recent years. Many farmers built up such crushing debt burdens that they were forced to sell off acreage that had been in their families for generations. Some of the land was combined into larger farms; the rest was sold to housing developers.

Even when times improved in the early 1990s, few farmers were rushing to buy new tractors, combines, or other pieces of equipment. A modest piece of equipment can cost as much as a luxury automobile, and the most sophisticated models retail for about $100,000. As a result, Deere's fortunes tend to rise and fall with those of America's farmers. For the fiscal year ending October 31, 1990, Deere posted earnings of $411 million—the best in the company's history. But in the first quarter of 1991, it posted losses of $43 million. Given this volatility, how does Deere survive?

One strategy is to help its dealers offer incentives, in the form of price cuts, sales promotions, and low-interest financing through Deere's credit subsidiary. Savvy farmers shop around and even play dealers off against one another to get the best price. Dealers

often end up selling equipment at close to cost, figuring they can make up the lost profit if they also get the farmers' parts and service business. These incentives help Deere maintain its market share.

Price incentives also help Deere create a steady demand for its goods. Under ordinary circumstances, farm equipment sales are seasonal—high in the spring and summer but low or nonexistent during the off-seasons of fall and winter. Left unchecked, this tendency might force Deere to lay off workers during the off-season and hire extra workers to meet peak demand. By using sales promotions, Deere manages to even out the highs and lows of demand and produce farm equipment at a more steady and efficient rate year round.

These price incentives are not without their costs, of course. They pare dealer profits to the bone, and they tie up Deere's operating capital, since farm equipment dealers do not pay for equipment until they sell it. As a result, as much as $3 million of John Deere's money—in the form of unsold tractors and combines—can be sitting on an average dealer's floor. No wonder Deere is fanatical about controlling costs without sacrificing the quality that keeps customers coming back generation after generation.

Sources: Adapted from Peter G. Goulet and Lynda L. Goulet, "Deere and Company," in *Strategic Management: Concepts and Applications,* Samuel C. Certo and J. Paul Peter, eds. (New York: Random House, 1988), pp. 692–714; with additional material from *Deere & Company 1990 Annual Report* and Steve Weiner, "Staying on Top in a Tough Business in a Tough Year," *Forbes,* May 27, 1991, pp. 46, 48.

Careful control has helped John Deere survive and prosper in an industry where the company must split extremely narrow profit margins with its dealers. Even organizations that enjoy more generous profit margins must use control procedures, though, to ensure they are making satisfactory progress toward their goals and using their resources efficiently. In this part of the book, we will take a closer look at the control process, beginning in this chapter with an overview of the control process and financial controls. Then, in the next chapter, we will discuss the control of *operations,* the transformation of inputs into outputs. A final chapter will show how information systems contribute to control.

■ THE MEANING OF CONTROL

control The process of ensuring that actual activities conform to planned activities.

A good definition of management **control** is the process of ensuring that actual activities conform to planned activities. From this definition we might conclude that control simply picks up where planning leaves off. However, control is a more pervasive concept, one that also helps managers monitor the effectiveness of their planning, their organizing, and their leading and take corrective actions as needed. Thus, while control is the fourth of the four management functions introduced in Chapter 1, it is certainly not last in importance. In this section, we will look at the steps in the control process, which will show how planning and control are linked, and then at the reasons control is needed.

Steps in the Control Process

The above definition suggests what control is intended to accomplish. It does not indicate what control *is.* Robert J. Mockler's definition of control points out the essential elements of the control process:

> Management control is a systematic effort to set performance standards with planning objectives, to design information feedback systems, to compare actual performance with these predetermined standards, to determine whether there are any deviations and to measure their significance, and to take any action required to assure that all corporate resources are being used in the most effective and efficient way possible in achieving corporate objectives.[1]

Mockler's definition divides control into the four steps illustrated in Figure 20-1.

FIGURE 20-1 Basic Steps in the Control Process

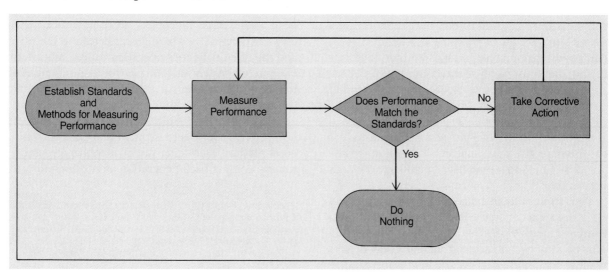

ESTABLISH STANDARDS AND METHODS FOR MEASURING PERFORMANCE. Ideally, the goals and objectives established during the planning process will already be stated in clear, *measurable* terms that include specific deadlines. This is important for a number of reasons. First, vaguely worded goals, such as "to improve employee skills," are just empty slogans until managers begin to specify what they mean by "improve" and what they intend to do to reach this goal—and when. Second, precisely worded goals (such as "improve employee skills by conducting weekly on-site seminars during the slow months of October and March") are easier to evaluate for accuracy and usefulness than empty slogans. Finally, precisely worded, measurable objectives are easy to communicate and to translate into standards and methods that can be used to measure performance. This ease of communicating precisely worded goals and objectives is especially important for control, since different people usually fulfill the planning and control roles.[2]

In service industries, standards and measurements might include the amount of time customers have to wait in line at a bank, the amount of time they have to wait before a telephone is answered, or the number of new clients attracted by a revamped advertising campaign. In an industrial enterprise, standards and measurements could include sales and production targets, work-attendance goals, and safety records.

MEASURE THE PERFORMANCE. Like all aspects of control, this is an ongoing, repetitive process, with the actual frequency of measurements being dependent on the type of activity being measured. Safe levels of gas particles in the air, for example, may be continuously monitored in a manufacturing plant, whereas progress on long-term expansion objectives may need to be reviewed by top management only once or twice a year. Similarly, the franchise owner at the local McDonald's might be required to examine customer waiting time on a continual basis. On the other hand, petitions may be put before the California Public Utility Commission only five or six times a year. Still, good managers avoid allowing extended periods to pass between performance measurements.

DETERMINE WHETHER PERFORMANCE MATCHES THE STANDARD. In many ways, this is the easiest step in the control process. The complexities presumably have been dealt with in the first two steps; now it is a matter of comparing measured results with the established targets or standards previously set. If performance matches the standards, managers may assume that "everything is under control"; as Figure 20-1 shows, they do not have to intervene actively in the organization's operations.

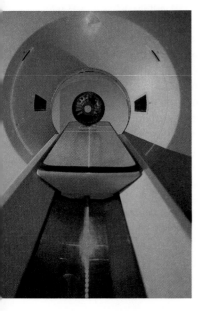

Measuring Performance. At GE, a CT scanner developed by the medical systems unit is used to inspect the integrity of parts produced by the aircraft engine division.

TAKE CORRECTIVE ACTION. This step is called for if performance falls short of standards and the analysis indicates action is required. The corrective action may involve a change in one or more activities of the organization's operations, or it may involve a change in the standards originally established. For example, the franchise owner/manager may discover that more counter workers are needed to meet the five-minute customer-waiting standard set by McDonald's. In other cases, controls can (and often do) reveal inappropriate (too high or too low) standards. Under these circumstances, the corrective action may involve a change in the original standards. Performance in GM's Buick division, for example, may cause management to raise the production target.

Figure 20-1 also illustrates another important point—namely, that control is a dynamic process. Unless managers see the control process through to its conclusion, they are merely monitoring performance rather than exercising control. The emphasis should always be on devising constructive ways to bring performance up to standard, rather than on merely identifying past failures.

FOR DISCUSSION
How many students have
had experiences with
plans not going right?
What happened? Why?
What could they have
done differently?

HERE'S AN EXAMPLE
O'Sullivan Industries of
Lamar, Missouri, puts one
out of ten workers on bi-
cycles to cut commuting
time between mainte-
nance, repair, and supervisory chores. (*Wall Street
Journal,* 11/27/90, p. A1)

HERE'S AN EXAMPLE
American Express Com-
pany now approves credit
cards in 11 days instead of
the 22 of a decade ago.
(*Business Week,* 4/29/91,
p. 52ff.)

Why Control Is Needed

One reason control is needed, obviously, is to monitor progress and correct mistakes. But control also helps managers monitor environmental changes and their
effects on the organization's progress. Given the pace of environmental change in
recent years, this aspect of control has grown steadily more important. Some of the
most pressing environmental changes are the changing nature of competition, the
need to speed up the order-to-delivery cycle, the importance of "adding value" to
products and services as a way of creating customer demand, changes in workers
and organizational cultures, and the increasing need for delegation and teamwork
within organizations.[3]

TO COPE WITH CHANGE. Change is an inevitable part of any organization's environment. Markets shift. Competitors—often from around the world—offer new products and services that capture the public imagination. New materials and technologies emerge. Government regulations are passed or amended. By helping managers
to detect changes that are affecting their organization's products and services, the
control function aids them in managing the resulting threats or opportunities.

TO CREATE FASTER CYCLES. It is one thing to recognize a customer demand for an
improved design, quality, or delivery time. It is another to speed up the cycles
involved in creating and then delivering these new products and services to customers. In fact, Steingraber has said that speed will be the standard of the 1990s, especially the speed with which orders are filled. For example, General Electric overhauled its stagnant circuit breaker business by improving cycle-time response. This
sentiment is echoed by Kazuo Morohoshi, head of Toyota's Tokyo Design Center:
"We have learned that universal mass production is not enough. In the 21st century,
you personalize things more to make them more reflective of individual needs." The
winners, predicts *Fortune's* Alex Taylor III, will be the companies that most successfully target narrow customer niches with specific models.[4]

Creating Faster Cycles. The National Bicycle Industrial Co., a Matsushita subsidiary, can
deliver a customized Panasonic bicycle within two weeks. The process begins when a
customer mounts a special frame in a Panasonic bicycle store (left), yielding measurements that are faxed to the small factory, where a DEC minicomputer and computer-
aided design software (right) produce a blueprint in about 3 minutes, along with a bar-
code label that will identify the bicycle as it moves through production. Actually, each
bike only takes three hours to make, but Koji Nishikawa, head of sales, feels the wait adds
value in the eyes of customers, who are willing to pay $545 to $3,200 for the customized bikes, vs. $250 to $510 for standard bikes.

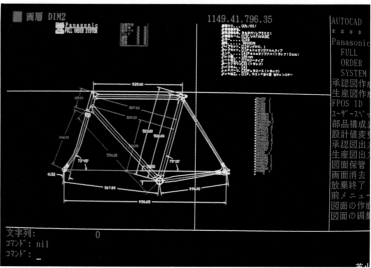

COORDINATED RESOURCE
See DuBose Reading #1, "Quality and Productivity: Challenges to Management."

HERE'S AN EXAMPLE
Sleep Inns won a hotel industry award for cost-saving steps such as locating a laundry room behind the front desk so night clerks can do laundry during slow times. (*Wall Street Journal,* 3/14/91, p. A1)

COORDINATED RESOURCE
See Geis and Kuhn Chapter 5, "Creative Inventory Management—Jumping Numbers."

COORDINATED RESOURCE
See Oddou section on Controlling the Organization, "Behavioral Control."

COORDINATED RESOURCE
The Additional Lecture for Chapter 20 found in the Lecture Extras supplement looks at "Desert Storm Logistics: Lessons for Managers."

COORDINATED RESOURCE
See *Management Live!* Chapter 11 video, "Broadcast News."

COORDINATED RESOURCE
Acumen: The Humanistic-Helpful scale measures an individual's interest in assisting others' growth and development. High scorers are usually good teachers and tend to deal with others in an empathic and considerate manner.

Effective control is essential to this process since it allows managers to monitor quality, delivery speed, order processing, and most important of all, whether customers are getting what they want when they want it.

TO ADD VALUE. Speedy cycle times are one way to gain a competitive edge. Adding value is another, advocated by the famous Japanese management guru Kenichi Ohmae. Trying to match a competitor's every move can be both expensive and counterproductive, Ohmae cautions. Instead, an organization's true objective should be to "add value" to its product or service so that customers will buy it in preference to a competitor's offering.[5] Most often, this added value takes the form of above-average quality, achieved through exacting control procedures. As a result, many Japanese goods are widely perceived to be more reliable and satisfying than U.S.-made goods. In fact, Chrysler Chairman Lee Iacocca has expressed frustration that the same automobile, made on the same assembly line, is perceived to have higher quality when it wears a Mitsubishi nameplate than when it wears a Chrysler nameplate. Chrysler, in turn, has tried to add value by increasing quality *and* offering additional safety features.

TO UNIFY WORKERS FROM DIFFERENT BACKGROUNDS AND CULTURES. Historically, U.S. firms have used fairly rigid, autocratic controls to manage workers and subordinates. Today, though, even the word *subordinate* sounds strange to many organization members, as does the idea that a manager is a *superior.* Given the better-educated work force of today, most managers believe that rigid functional controls and hierarchical structures dampen—rather than enhance—worker motivation and productivity. Furthermore, enlightened managers respect the diversity of today's work force, which takes in men and women from a variety of cultural backgrounds.

In this new workplace, control procedures help to focus the efforts of managers and employees without regard for their educational or cultural backgrounds. In fact, the clear trend is toward participative, consultative approaches to management functions, including control. Under this new approach, every employee shares responsibility for control. On Toyota's production lines, for example, workers are also quality control inspectors. By pulling a cord, any worker can warn the supervisor that he or she has received a faulty part; a second pull stops the entire line until the problem is corrected.[6]

TO FACILITATE DELEGATION AND TEAMWORK. The trend toward participative management also increases the need to delegate authority and encourage employees to work together as teams. This does not reduce the manager's ultimate responsibility, of course. Rather, it changes the nature of the control process. Under the old-fashioned, autocratic system, the manager would specify both the standards for performance and the methods for achieving them. Under the new, participative system, managers communicate the standards, but then let employees, either as individuals or as teams, use their own creativity to decide *how* to solve certain work problems. The control process, then, lets the manager monitor employees' progress without hampering their creativity or involvement with the work.

Team management programs are common in the joint ventures undertaken by GM-Toyota and Chrysler-Mitsubishi, as are efforts to adjust employees' social needs to the technological demands of efficient production. At both its GM-Toyota plant in California and its new Saturn facility in Tennessee, GM has used the team-management approach to restructure its overall approach to managing performance. Similarly, AT&T has adopted the perspective that rethinking management's approach to performance standards can be a constructive means of both raising standards and generating appropriate performance. In setting out to make its Shreveport, Louisiana, facility more competitive on a much broader international scale in 1986, AT&T overhauled not only basic plant operations but also management's approach to pro-

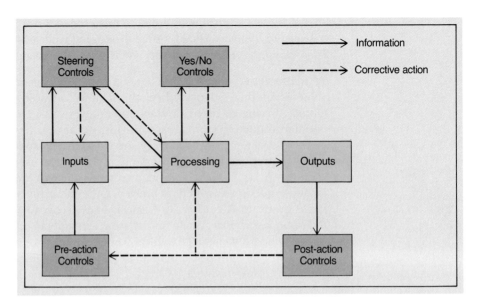

FIGURE 20-2 Flow of Information and Corrective Action for Four Types of Control

ductive performance, with managers implementing just-in-time inventory and more rigorous quality-appraisal programs. Quality improved, production costs dropped, and labor productivity doubled on some product lines.[7]

■ TYPES OF CONTROL METHODS

COORDINATED RESOURCE
See Study Guide Problem Exercise 20, "Types of Control Methods."

Most control methods can be grouped into one of four types: pre-action controls, steering controls, screening or yes/no controls, and post-action controls. As Figure 20-2 shows, each type of control affects a slightly different phase of operations—the processing of inputs into outputs.

Pre-Action Controls

pre-action controls (or precontrols) Control method ensuring that human, material, and financial resources have been budgeted.

Pre-action controls (sometimes called **precontrols**) ensure that the necessary human, material, and financial sources are set aside *before* an action is undertaken. Financial budgets (to be discussed later in this chapter) are the most common type of pre-action control, since hiring and training employees, buying equipment and supplies, and designing new products and services all require money. Schedules are another important type of pre-action control, since these preliminary activities also require an investment of time, a resource sometimes as precious as money.

COORDINATED RESOURCE
Use Transparency 135, Relationships of Types of Control to Activities.

The idea common to all pre-action controls is to *prevent* problems from occurring rather than to fix them after they happen. Thus, a budget helps an organization anticipate expenses and then set aside adequate funds for a project. A schedule helps managers identify tasks and then estimate the amount of time needed for their completion, with some extra time allowed for unforeseen events and complications.

Steering Controls

steering controls (or cybernetic or feedforward controls) Control method designed to detect deviations from some standard goal and to permit corrective measures.

Steering controls, also known as **cybernetic** or **feedforward controls,** are designed to detect deviations from some standard or goal and to allow corrections to be made before a particular sequence of actions is completed. The term *steering controls* is a simple metaphor derived from driving an automobile—the driver

A Pre-Action Control. "The Business Benchmarks," created by Chicago computer evaluator Neal Nelson, consists of 18 tests that can measure how well a computer will perform word processing, database management, accounting, programming, and computer-aided design tasks *before* it is purchased and installed.

COORDINATED RESOURCE

Use Transparency 139, Service and Use Controls.

steers the car to prevent it from going off the road or in the wrong direction. Steering controls are effective only if the manager can obtain timely and accurate information about changes in the environment or about progress toward the desired goal.

Yes/No or Screening Controls

yes/no controls (or **go/no go controls**) Control method for screening procedures that must be followed or conditions that must be met before operations continue.

Yes/no controls, or **go/no go controls,** provide a screening process in which specific aspects of a procedure must be approved or specific conditions met before operations may continue. Today many organizations, including Toyota, Ford, and Hewlett-Packard, give this type of control authority to line workers as well as to managers and supervisors. Another screening control occurs in banking, where large customer withdrawals must be approved by a senior teller and one other bank officer.

Post-Action Controls

post-action controls Method of control for measuring the results of a completed activity.

As the term suggests, **post-action controls** measure the results of a completed action. The causes of any deviation from the plan or standard are determined and the findings are applied to similar future activities. Post-action controls are also used as a basis for rewarding or encouraging service employees (for example, meeting a standard may result in a future bonus).

The Interactive Nature of Control Methods

FOR DISCUSSION
What are some externally imposed controls? Internally imposed controls? Why are both needed in organizations?

COORDINATED RESOURCE
See Samaras Case 5.1, "Is Stanley Steele Stealing?"

The four types of control—pre-action, steering, yes/no, and post-action—are not alternatives, one being the best choice that excludes the others. Rather, they complement one another, as shown by the flows of information and corrective action in Figure 20-2. Fast and accurate information flows are vital, though, since the sooner deviations are detected, the sooner they can be corrected. In most modern organizations, this information is provided by computerized information systems, to be discussed in more detail in Chapter 22.

Because steering controls provide a means for taking corrective action *while a program is still viable,* they are usually more widely used than other types of control. As a bonus, steering controls let managers take advantage of deviations from plans that represent opportunities for new sources of profit. Steering controls are rarely perfect, however. As a result, yes/no controls provide an extra margin of security when safety is a key factor, as in aircraft design, or where large expenditures are involved, as in construction programs.

■ *DESIGNING CONTROL SYSTEMS*

control system Multistep procedure applied to various types of control activities.

COORDINATED RESOURCE
See Samaras Exercise 5.1, "Appropriate Controls."

COORDINATED RESOURCE
Use Transparency 134, Open and Closed Control Systems.

On the surface, designing a **control system** is a straightforward process, as indicated by Exhibit 20-1. In practice, though, managers face a number of challenges in designing control systems that provide accurate feedback in a timely, economical fashion that is acceptable to organization members. Most of these problems can be traced back to decisions about what needs to be controlled and how often progress needs to be measured. Trying to control too many elements of operations too strictly can annoy and demoralize employees, frustrate their managers, and waste valuable time, energy, and money. Furthermore, managers may focus on easy-to-measure factors, such as the number of people served in a restaurant, and ignore

EXHIBIT 20-1 Designing a Control System

1. *Define desired results.* Ideally, these are determined during planning, when managers, alone or with their employees, establish measurable goals and objectives with realistic deadlines.
2. *Establish predictors of results.* Predictors reliably indicate whether managers need to take corrective action. Typical predictors are a change in key inputs (going over budget), the results of early steps (disappointing sales of a new ice-cream flavor), indirect symptoms (sales representatives are late in returning their sales reports, indicating they have not met their sales quotas), changes in assumed conditions (a reliable supplier fails to meet delivery dates), or past performance (the last year's sales figures). As a general rule, the greater the number of reliable and timely predictors, the more confident the manager can be in making performance predictions.
3. *Establish standards for predictors and results.* Establishing standards, or "pars," for predictors creates benchmarks that can be used to evaluate actual performance. Equally important, high but reasonable pars can help motivate employees, provided everyone concerned understands and accepts the standards as tough but fair.
4. *Establish the information and feedback network.* This step establishes the means for collecting information on predictors and for comparing predictors to pars. Feedback can be top-down, as when a manager evaluates employee performance, or bottom-up, as when employees provide information on how well a process is working. Good control systems provide both types of feedback, giving key personnel time to act on it. To focus managers' attention, feedback is often based on the *management by exception* principle—managers are only informed when the performance of predictors deviates from pars by a certain amount.
5. *Implement the system and take corrective action if needed.* Once the system is put in place, managers may find they need to make adjustments to predictors or pars to produce a more satisfactory control system.

Identifying Key Performance Areas. In managing its global operations, Levi Strauss & Co. maintains tight control where it counts—protecting the Levi's brand name by operating foreign subsidiaries, rather than granting licenses, and exporting its pioneering use of computers to track sales and manufacturing information.

COORDINATED RESOURCE

The Distinctive Discussions for Chapter 20 found in the Lecture Extras supplement include "It's a Robot's Job" and "Enemies of Efficiency."

key performance (or key result) areas Aspects of a unit or organization that must function effectively if the entire unit or organization is to succeed.

THOUGHT PROVOKER

After a decade of emphasis on improving quality in U.S. manufacturing, quality has become an issue of increased concern in office work. What are the implications? (*Business Week,* 4/29/91, p. 52ff.)

harder-to-measure factors, such as diner satisfaction. Yet diner satisfaction may be more important in the long run than the number of people served. Most of these problems can be avoided by an analysis that identifies *key performance areas* and *strategic control points.*

Identifying Key Performance Areas

Key performance or **key result areas** are those aspects of the unit or organization that *must* function effectively for the entire unit or organization to succeed. These areas usually involve major organizational activities or groups of related activities that occur throughout the organization or unit. Exhibit 20-2 shows some of the key performance areas for production, marketing, personnel management, and finance and accounting. These key performance areas, in turn, help define the more detailed control systems and standards.

Identifying Strategic Control Points

In addition to key performance areas, it is also important to determine the critical points in the system where monitoring or information collecting should occur. If

EXHIBIT 20-2 Standards Used in Functional Areas to Gauge Performance

PRODUCTION	MARKETING	PERSONNEL MANAGEMENT	FINANCE AND ACCOUNTING
Quality	Sales volume	Labor relations	Capital expenditures
Quantity	Sales expense	Labor turnover	Inventories
Cost	Advertising expenditures	Labor absenteeism	Flow of capital
Individual job performance	Individual salesperson's performance	Liquidity	

Source: Hal B. Pickle and Royce L. Abrahamson, *Small Business Management* (New York: Wiley, 1990), Chap. 8.

ILLUSTRATIVE CASE STUDY

CONTINUED

Financial Resourcefulness at Deere & Co.

Whether Deere makes or loses money often depends on its skill in controlling costs and the efficiency of its operations. As evidence of Deere's success, CEO Hans Becherer notes that Deere produced the same tonnage in 1990 as in 1980 with one-third fewer workers and that Deere has cut costs 2 to 2½ percent a year for the past five years. In this, we can see Deere controlling the input of money and using it as a gauge of efficiency.

Deere also controls its inventory, which is important because it costs money to store materials and finished equipment and because money spent to buy, make, and then store products cannot be used for other purposes. Although Deere admits its inventories may be a problem, it estimates they are only one-third of industry levels. In this, we can see Deere comparing its performance to a standard set by its industry.

Deere also works to reduce manufacturing costs, using what it calls cellular manufacturing tech-

niques—the grouping of machinery to cut manufacturing time and the cost of storing work-in-progress or partially finished goods. Under this system, the defect rate of axle spindles has dropped to zero and manufacturing costs have fallen 15 percent. (The standards used here are Deere's past performance.) Similar techniques save Deere hundreds of dollars per piece—savings that lets the company offer price incentives without going bankrupt.

This focus on controlling costs does not mean that Deere neglects quality, however. Its most recent line of combines, introduced in 1989, received more than 7,000 hours of field testing by contract harvesters before the design was finalized. This pre-action helped Deere maintain the quality that keeps farmers coming back. In fact, 85 percent of its sales are to repeat customers. In this, we can see that control has helped Deere add value to its goods.

Source: Steve Weiner, "Staying on Top in a Tough Business in a Tough Year," *Forbes,* May 27, 1991, pp. 46, 48.

---

strategic control points
Critical points in a system at which monitoring or collecting information should occur.

TEACHING TIP

Ask your students to think about what types of control measures they would need to develop to earn an A in this course.

COORDINATED RESOURCE

See Samaras Reading "Coors—Brewing a Better Controllership."

such **strategic control points** can be located, then the amount of information that has to be gathered and evaluated can be reduced considerably.

The most important and useful method of selecting strategic control points is to focus on the most significant elements in a given operation. Usually only a small percentage of the activities, events, individuals, or objects in a given operation will account for a high proportion of the expense or problems that managers will have to face. For example, 10 percent of a manufacturer's products may well yield 60 percent of its sales; 2 percent of an organization's employees may account for 80 percent of an organization's employee grievances; and 20 percent of the police precincts in a city may account for 70 percent of the city's violent crimes.

Another useful consideration is the location of operation areas in which change occurs. For example, in an organization's system for filling customer orders, a change occurs when the purchase order becomes an invoice, when an inventory item becomes an item to be shipped, or when the item to be shipped becomes part of a truckload. Since errors are more likely to be made when such changes occur, monitoring change points is usually a highly effective way to control an operation.

■ FINANCIAL CONTROLS

No single, unified method of control has ever been devised for all of an organization's activities. There are simply too many kinds of activities for any one control system to be effective. Instead, managers use a series of control methods and systems to deal with the differing problems and elements of their organization. Moreover,

COORDINATED RESOURCE
See Oddcu section on
Controlling the Organization, "Financial Control."

financial statement
Monetary analysis of the
flow of goods and services
to, within, and from the
organization.

the methods and systems can take many forms and can be intended for various groups. However, financial controls have a special prominence, since money is easy to measure and tally. In this section of the chapter, we will begin by discussing financial statements and ratio analyses, which provide insight into an organization's performance, health, and long-term chances for survival. Next we will look at budgetary control methods, which help managers control an organization's financial resources. We will end the section with a discussion of auditing, which compares an organization's performance to its budgets.

Financial Statements

Financial statements are used to track the monetary value of goods and services into and out of the organization. They provide a means for monitoring three major financial conditions of an organization:

1. *Liquidity:* the ability to convert assets into cash in order to meet current financial needs and obligations.
2. *General financial condition:* the long-term balance between debt and *equity;* the assets left after liabilities are deducted.
3. *Profitability:* the ability to earn profits steadily and over an extended period of time.

Since financial statements are usually prepared after events have occurred, they cannot be used to influence past events. This somewhat limits their value as control measures. However, they are widely used by managers, shareholders, financial institutions, investment analysts, unions, and other stakeholders to evaluate the organization's performance. Managers, for example, may compare the organization's current financial statements to past statements and to those of competitors as one measure of how well the organization is doing. Given enough information, they may be able to see trends that require corrective action. Bankers and financial analysts, on the other hand, will use the statements to decide whether they should invest in the firm.

It is important to remember that financial statements may not show all relevant financial information. Recent technological or scientific breakthroughs seldom show up on financial statements, for example. Nor do changes in the external environment, such as shifts in consumer tastes, even though these may be more crucial to the organization's success than its financial performance.[8]

Depending on the company, financial statements may cover the previous year, the previous quarter, or the previous month. The most common financial statements, used by large and small organizations alike, are income statements, balance sheets, and cash flow statements.[9]

The use of computer software for the collection and analysis of accounting and financial data is now nearly universal. About a dozen accounting software packages have achieved national prominence. When evaluating such programs for possible purchase and implementation, financial managers should make sure that they comply with the guidelines of the IRS, the FASB (Financial Accounting Standards Board), and other regulatory agencies, and that the software vendor will continue to supply updated versions.

balance sheet Description of the organization in terms of its assets, liabilities, and net worth.

BALANCE SHEET. The message of a **balance sheet** is: "Here's how this organization stacks up financially *at this particular point in time.*" The point in time covered by our sample balance sheet, Figure 20-3, is indicated by the line "As of December 31, 1992."

In its simplest form, the balance sheet describes the company in terms of its *assets, liabilities,* and *net worth.* A company's assets range from money in the bank to the goodwill value of its name in the marketplace. The left side of the balance sheet lists these assets in descending order of liquidity. A distinction is made be-

CHAPNER METALS
Consolidated Balance Sheet
As of December 31, 1992

ASSETS			LIABILITIES AND NET WORTH		
Current Assets	$ 950,000		Current Liabilities	$ 600,000	
Cash		50,000	Account Payable		475,000
Marketable Securities		350,000	Accrued Expenses		
Accounts Receivable		250,000	Payable		125,000
Inventories		300,000	Long-Term Liabilities	600,000	
			Total Liabilities	1,200,000	
Fixed Assets	1,250,000				
Land		50,000	Net Worth	1,070,000	
Plant and Equipment		1,500,000	Common Stock at Par		850,000
Less Accumulated			Accumulated Retained		
Depreciation		300,000	Earnings		220,000
Other Assets					
Patents and Goodwill	70,000				
			Total Liabilities		
Total Assets	$2,270,000		and Net Worth	$2,270,000	

FIGURE 20-3 The Balance Sheet

tween current assets and fixed assets. *Current assets* cover items such as cash, accounts receivable, marketable securities and inventories—assets that could be turned into cash at a reasonably predictable value within a relatively short time period (typically, one year). *Fixed assets* show the monetary value of the company's plant, equipment, property, patents, and other items used on a continuing basis to produce its goods or services.

Liabilities are also made up of two groups, current liabilities and long-term liabilities. *Current liabilities* are debts, such as accounts payable, short-term loans, and unpaid taxes, that will have to be paid off during the current fiscal period. *Long-term liabilities* include mortgages, bonds, and other debts that are being paid off gradually. The company's *net worth* is the residual value remaining after total liabilities have been subtracted from total assets.

The widespread use of electronic spreadsheets has made the preparation of balance sheets much easier. In addition, prewritten computer packages have been developed specifically to process accounting transactions and prepare the resulting balance sheets and other financial statements.

income statement Summary of the organization's financial performance over a given interval of time.

INCOME STATEMENT. While the balance sheet describes a company's financial condition at a given *point* in time, the **income statement** summarizes the company's financial performance over a given *interval* of time. The income statement, then, says: "Here's how much money we're making" instead of "Here's how much money we're worth."

Income statements, such as Figure 20-4, start with a figure for gross receipts or sales and then subtract all the costs involved in realizing those sales, such as the cost of goods sold, administrative expenses, taxes, interest, and other operating expenses. What is left is the net income available for stockholders' dividends or reinvestment in the business.

CASH FLOW: SOURCES AND USES-OF-FUNDS STATEMENTS. In addition to the standard balance sheet and income statement, many companies report financial data in the form of a statement of cash flow or a statement of sources and uses of funds.

```
                          CHAPNER METALS
                         Statement of Income
                    For the Year Ended December 31,1992


Gross Sales                                                        $4,298,000
Less Returns                                      $   798,000

Net Sales                                                          3,500,000

Less Cost of Sales and Operating Expenses
    Cost of Goods Sold                              2,775,000
    Depreciation                                     100,000
    Selling and Administrative Expenses                75,000    2,950,000

Operating Profit                                                   550,000

Other Income                                                        15,000

Gross Income                                                       565,000
Less Interest Expense                                 75,000

Income before Taxes                                               490,000
Less Taxes                                           196,000

Income after Taxes                                               $  294,000
```

FIGURE 20-4 The Income Statement

These statements show where cash or funds came from during the year (from operations, from reducing accounts receivable, and from the sale of investments, for example) and where they were applied (for purchase of equipment, for payment of dividends, and for reducing accounts payable, for example). They should not be confused with income statements; cash flow statements show how cash or funds were used rather than how much profit or loss was achieved.

Ratio Analysis

COORDINATED RESOURCE

The Application Exercise for Chapter 20 asks students to calculate financial ratios.

ratio analysis Reporting of key figures from the organization's financial records as percentages or fractions.

For organizations as well as for individuals, financial performance is relative. An annual salary of $30,000 will be seen as high if the average salary in the individual's field or industry is $20,000 and low if the average salary is $40,000. Similarly, company profits of $1 million might be very high for a restaurant but very low for an oil company. For the "bottom line" on a financial statement to be meaningful, it must ultimately be compared against a standard. In **ratio analysis,** key summary figures from the firm's financial statements or records are reported as percentages or fractions. Such ratios can provide quick assessments of financial performance or condition. Today, as opposed to the recent past, ratios are easily and inexpensively developed by computer from the firm's electronic records for timely use by managers.[10]

The ratio analysis comparisons can be made in one of two ways: (1) comparison over a time period—the present ratio compared with the same organization's ratio in the past (or with a future projection); or (2) comparison with ratios for similar organizations or for the industry as a whole. The first type of comparison will indicate how the organization's performance or condition has changed; the second type will suggest how well the organization is doing relative to its competitors.

There are many kinds of ratio categories and many kinds of ratios. The ratios most commonly used by organizations are profitability, liquidity, activity, and leverage; these are listed in Table 20-1. Return on investment (under profitability) is generally seen as the most important and encompassing ratio in general use; it reveals the success of the firm in employing its resources. The current ratio (under

Using Ratio Analysis. When an investment group bought Loehmann's, a women's clothing discounter, analysts judged the $182 million price at eight times cash flow to be a good one, compared to the $3.4 billion (or 9.3 times cash flow) Campeau Corp. paid for Allied Stores. Because it keeps marking down items until they sell, Loehmann's turns its inventory over 7 times a year, double the retail average.

liquidity) indicates the ability of the firm to repay its present short-term debt. Inventory turnover (under activity) is often compared to industry averages and figures from previous years to assess efficiency. Debt ratios (under leverage) are computed to assess a firm's ability to meet long-term commitments.[11]

The key to making effective *use* of ratio analysis is understanding that ratios must be *compared*. In order to compare one firm's ratios with those of a related firm or with industry-wide averages, the interested analyst needs reliable information. The Management Application box entitled "Where to Find Financial Ratios" identifies some readily available sources of such information.

TABLE 20-1 Categories of Ratios for Analysis

CATEGORY	TYPICAL RATIO	CALCULATION	MEASURES
Profitability	Return on investment	$\dfrac{\text{Profits after taxes}}{\text{Total assets}}$	The productivity of assets
Liquidity	Current ratio	$\dfrac{\text{Current assets}}{\text{Current liabilities}}$	Short-term solvency
Activity	Inventory turnover	$\dfrac{\text{Sales}}{\text{Inventory}}$	The efficiency of inventory management
Leverage	Debt ratio	$\dfrac{\text{Total debt}}{\text{Total assets}}$	The proportion of financing supplied by creditors

MANAGEMENT APPLICATION

Where to Find Financial Ratios

1. *Annual Statement Studies.* Published by Robert Morris Associates, this work includes 11 financial ratios computed annually for over 150 lines of business. Each line of business is divided into 4 size categories.

2. Dun and Bradstreet provides 14 ratios calculated annually for over 100 lines of business.

3. *The Almanac of Business and Industrial Financial Ratios.* This work, published by Prentice-Hall, Inc., lists industry averages for 22 financial ratios. Approximately 170 businesses and industries are listed.

4. *The Quarterly Financial Report for Manufacturing Corporations.* This work, published jointly by the Federal Trade Commission and the Securities and Exchange Commission, contains balance sheet and income statement information by industry groupings and by asset-size categories.

5. Trade associations and individual companies often compute ratios for their industries and make them available to analysts.

Source: James C. Van Horne, *Financial Management and Policy*, 7th ed., © 1986, pp. 767–768. Reprinted by permission of Prentice-Hall, Inc., Englewood Cliffs, New Jersey.

■ BUDGETARY CONTROL METHODS

budget Formal quantitative statement of resources allocated for planned activities over stipulated periods of time.

COORDINATED RESOURCE
See Samaras Exercise 5.2, "Budgets or Misbudgets?"

COORDINATED RESOURCE
See DuBose Reading #23, "Important Considerations in the Budgeting Process."

Budgets are formal quantitative statements of the resources set aside for carrying out planned activities over given periods of time. As such, they are the most widely used means for planning and controlling activities at every level of the organization. There are a number of good reasons for their wide usage.

First, budgets are stated in monetary terms, which are easily used as a common denominator for a wide variety of organizational activities—hiring and training personnel, purchasing equipment, manufacturing, advertising, and selling. Thus, they can be used by the organization's existing accounting system to cover all departments. Second, the monetary aspect of budgets means that they can directly convey information on a key organizational resource—capital—and on a key organizational goal—profit. They are, therefore, heavily favored by profit-oriented companies.

Third, budgets establish clear and unambiguous standards of performance for a set time period—usually a year. At stated intervals during that time period, actual performance will be compared directly with the budget. Frequently, deviations can quickly be detected and acted upon.

In addition to being a major control device, budgets are one of the major means of coordinating the activities of the organization. The interaction between managers and subordinates that takes place during the budget development process will help define and integrate the activities of organization members.

In this section, we will describe the role of budgets in a control system and the budgeting process itself.[12]

Responsibility Centers

COORDINATED RESOURCE
Use Transparency 140, Budgeting System for Controlling Functions.

Control systems can be devised to monitor organizational *functions* or organizational *projects.* Controlling a function involves making sure that a specified activity (such as production or sales) is properly carried out. Controlling a project involves making sure that a specified end result is achieved (such as the development of a new product or the completion of a building). Budgets can be used for both types of systems; our discussion will emphasize the use of budgets to control the functions illustrated in Figure 20-5.

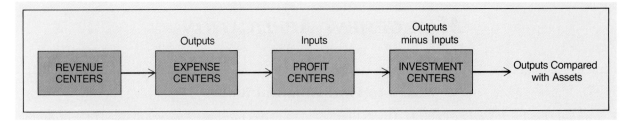

FIGURE 20-5 Budgeting System for Controlling Functions

responsibility center
Any organizational function or unit whose manager is responsible for all of its activities.

Any organizational or functional unit headed by a manager who is responsible for the activities of that unit is called a **responsibility center.** All responsibility centers use resources (inputs or costs) to produce something (outputs or revenues). Typically, responsibility is assigned to a revenue, expense, profit, and/or investment center. (See Fig. 20-5.) The decision usually depends on the activity performed by the organizational unit and on the manner in which inputs and outputs are measured by the control system. We will describe such centers briefly here.[13]

revenue center Organizational unit in which outputs measured in monetary terms are not directly compared to input costs.

REVENUE CENTERS. **Revenue centers** are those organizational units in which outputs are measured in monetary terms but are not directly compared to input costs. A sales department is an example of such a unit. The effectiveness of the center is not judged by how much revenue (in the form of sales) exceeds the cost of the center (in salaries or rent, for example). Rather, budgets (in the form of sales quotas) are prepared for the revenue center and the figures are compared with sales orders or actual sales. In this way, a useful picture of the effectiveness of individual salespeople or of the center itself can be determined.

expense center Commonly, administrative, service, and research departments where inputs are measured in monetary terms, although outputs are not.

EXPENSE CENTERS. In **expense centers,** inputs are measured by the control system in monetary terms but outputs are not. The reason is that these centers are not expected to produce revenues. Examples are maintenance, administration, service, and research departments. Budgets will be devised only for the input portion of these centers' operations.

profit center Organizational unit where performance is measured by numerical differences between revenues and expenditures.

PROFIT CENTERS. In a **profit center,** performance is measured by the numerical difference between revenues (outputs) and expenditures (inputs). Such a measure is used to determine how well the center is doing economically and how well the manager in charge of the center is performing. A profit center is created whenever an organizational unit is given responsibility for earning a profit. In a divisionalized organization, in which each of a number of divisions is completely responsible for its own product line, the separate divisions are considered profit centers.

investment center Organizational unit that not only measures the monetary value of inputs and outputs, but also compares outputs with assets used in producing them.

INVESTMENT CENTERS. In an **investment center,** the control system again measures the monetary value of inputs and outputs, but it also assesses how those outputs compare with the assets employed in producing them. Assume, for example, that a new hospital requires a capital investment of $20 million in property, buildings, equipment, and working capital. In its first year, the hospital has $2 million in labor and other input expenses and $4 million in revenue. For two reasons the hospital would *not* be considered to have earned a $2 million profit. First, an allowance must be made for the depreciation of building and equipment. Second, management must account for the interest that could have been earned from alternative investments. In this way, the company obtains a much more accurate picture of profitability.

It is important to realize that any profit center can also be considered an investment center because its activities require some form of capital investment. However, if a center's capital investment is minor (as in a consulting firm) or if its managers have no control over capital investment, it is more appropriately treated as a profit center.[14]

The Budgeting Process

COORDINATED RESOURCE
See Geis and Kuhn Chapter 8, "Family Budget Control—Taking Care."

The budgeting process usually begins when managers receive top management's economic forecasts and sales and profit objectives for the coming year, along with a timetable stating when budgets must be completed. The forecasts and objectives provided by top management represent guidelines within which other managers' budgets will be developed.

In a few organizations, the preference is for "top-down" budgeting: Budgets are imposed by top managers with little or no consultation with lower-level managers. Most companies, however, prefer the process of "bottom-up" budgeting: Budgets are prepared, at least initially, by those who must implement them. The budgets are then sent up for approval to higher-level managers.

THOUGHT PROVOKER
"Reliance on budgets is 'the fundamental flaw in American management,'" according to Donald A. Curtis, senior partner at Deloitt & Touche. (*Fortune*, 6/4/90, p. 179ff.) Discuss this statement.

Bottom-up budgeting has many advantages for many organizations. Supervisors and lower-level department heads have a more intimate view of their needs than do managers at the top, and they can provide more realistic breakdowns to support their proposals. They are also less likely to overlook some vital ingredient or hidden flaw that might subsequently impede implementation. Managers are also more strongly motivated to accept and meet budgets they have had a hand in shaping. Finally, morale and satisfaction are usually higher when individuals participate actively in making decisions that affect them. Exhibit 20-3 lists the best aspects of top-down and bottom-up budgeting.

The process by which lower-level managers participate in developing budgets is similar to the multilevel planning process described in Chapter 7. Supervisors prepare their budget proposals using the guidelines drawn up by upper management. Department heads then review the lower-level budgets and resolve any inconsistencies before compiling them into department budgets. These budgets are then submitted to higher-level managers for approval. The process continues until all budgets are completed, assembled by the controller or budget director, and submitted to the budget committee for further review. Management then uses capital budgeting techniques, such as the standard formulas presented in Table 20-2, to evaluate the budget requests. Finally, the master budget is sent to top management (the president, chief executive officer, or board of directors) for approval.

EXHIBIT 20-3 Top-Down versus Bottom-Up Budgeting

WHAT TOP-DOWN BUDGETING INCORPORATES BEST:	WHAT BOTTOM-UP BUDGETING INCORPORATES BEST:
Economic industry projections	Operational plans
Company planning parameters	Information on competition, products, and markets
Corporate goals	Alternative courses of action
Overall resource availability	Specific resource requirements

Source: Reprinted by permission of the *Harvard Business Review.* An exhibit from "Budget Choice: Planning vs. Control" by Neil C. Churchill (July–August 1984). Copyright © 1984 by the President and Fellows of Harvard College; all rights reserved.

TABLE 20-2 Capital Budgeting Techniques

TECHNIQUE	FORMULA	INFORMATION
Payback	Investment/cash flow	Time to recoup the investment
Present value	Investment—sum of discounted cash flows	Net worth of the future cash flows generated by the investment
Internal rate of return	Present value of cash outflow ÷ present value of cash inflow	Percentage return on the investment

THE ROLE OF BUDGET PERSONNEL.   Although developing budgets is the responsibility of managers, they may receive information and technical assistance from the staff of a planning group or from a formal budget department or committee. These groups are likely to exist in large, divisionalized organizations in which the division budget plays a key role in planning, coordinating, and controlling activities.[15]

The *budget department,* which generally reports to the corporate controller, provides budget information and assistance to organizational units, designs budget systems and forms, integrates the various departmental proposals into a master budget for the organization as a whole, and reports on actual performance relative to the budget.

The *budget committee*, made up of senior executives from all functional areas, reviews the individual budgets, reconciles divergent views, alerts or approves the budget proposals, and then refers the integrated package to the board of directors. Later, when the plans have been put into practice, the committee reviews the control reports that monitor progress. In most cases, the budget committee must approve any revisions made during the budget period.

SOME PROBLEMS IN BUDGET DEVELOPMENT.   During the budget-development process, when the organization's limited resources are allocated, managers may fear that they will not be given their fair share. Tension will heighten as competition with other managers increases, as will the political behavior of managers trying to find out how their budgets compare to those of other departments. Anxieties may also arise because managers know they will be judged by their ability to meet or beat budgeted standards. Hence, they are concerned about what those standards will be and may overstate their needs to create some slack. Conversely, their superiors are concerned with establishing aggressive budget objectives. As a result, the superiors will often try to trim their subordinates' expenditure requests or raise their revenue targets. The result can be an ever-widening web of distrust and anxiety, especially if employees begin to suspect the budgets will not meet their needs. Organization-wide participation in the budgeting process often minimizes these types of anxiety reactions. When all managers are involved in budget development, they are more likely to be satisfied with their resource allocations.

■ *TYPES OF BUDGETS*

operating budget Budget indicating the goods and services the organization expects to consume in a budget period.

financial budget Budget detailing the money expected to be spent during the budget period and indicating its sources.

Organization budgets are of two kinds: operating budgets and financial budgets. The **operating budgets** indicate the goods and services the organization expects to consume in the budget period; they usually list both physical quantities (such as barrels of oil) and cost figures. The **financial budgets** spell out in detail the money the organization intends to spend in the same period and where that money will come from. Figure 20-6 shows the operating and financial components of a manufacturing firm's comprehensive budget. Each rectangle in the diagram represents one or more of the types of budgets we describe below. These different types of budgets make up the firm's overall budgetary plan.[16]

Operating Budgets

The most common types of operating budgets parallel three of the responsibility centers discussed earlier—expense, revenue, and profit.[17]

EXPENSE BUDGETS.   As mentioned earlier, there are two types of expense budgets, one for each of the two types of expense centers—engineered cost budgets and discretionary cost budgets.

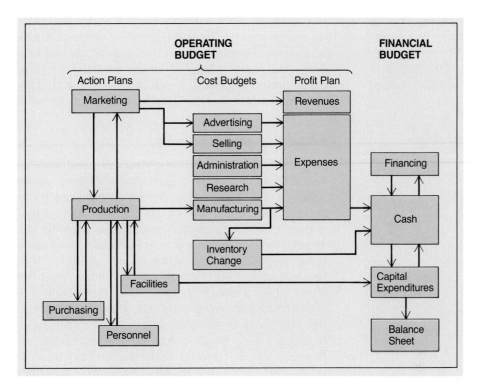

FIGURE 20-6 Budget Components

Source: Gordon Shillinglaw, *Managerial Cost Accounting,* 5th ed., p. 210. Copyright © 1982. Reproduced with permission of Richard D. Irwin, Inc.

engineered cost budget Budget describing material and labor costs of each item produced, including estimated overhead costs.

Engineered cost budgets are typically used in manufacturing plants but can be used by any organizational unit in which output can be accurately measured. These budgets usually describe the material and labor costs involved in each production item, as well as the estimated overhead costs. Hewlett-Packard, for example, has an annual budget that describes the labor, material, and overhead expenses involved in manufacturing its computer peripherals (printers, plotters, and boards). Such an engineered cost budget is designed to measure efficiency: Exceeding the budget means that operating costs were higher than they should have been.

discretionary cost budget Budget used for departments in which output cannot be accurately measured.

Discretionary cost budgets are typically used for expense centers—administrative, legal, accounting, research, and other such departments—in which output cannot be accurately measured. Discretionary cost budgets are not used to assess efficiency because performance standards for discretionary expenses are difficult to devise. For example, if Procter & Gamble's research and development department exceeds its budget, it will often be difficult for managers to determine how that department's work could have been performed more efficiently.

revenue budget Budget measuring marketing and sales effectiveness by multiplying the unit price of each product by the predicted sales quantity.

REVENUE BUDGETS. Revenue budgets are meant to measure marketing and sales effectiveness. They consist of the expected quantity of sales multiplied by the expected unit selling price of each product. The revenue budget is the most critical part of a profit budget, yet it is also one of the most uncertain because it is based on projected future sales. Companies with a large volume of back orders or companies whose sales volume is limited only by their productive capacity can make firmer revenue forecasts than can companies that must reckon with the fluctuations of an unstable or unpredictable market. However, marketing and sales managers of even the latter type of company can control the quality and quantity of their advertising, service, personnel training, and other factors that affect sales. This control gives them some influence over sales volume and frequently enables them to make reasonably accurate sales estimates.

THOUGHT PROVOKER

According to a survey by consultant Sibson & Company, one-shot cost-cutting can cause more harm than good. What are the implications? (*Wall Street Journal,* 12/27/90, p. A1)

profit budget (or **master budget**) Budget combining cost and revenue budgets in one unit.

PROFIT BUDGETS. A **profit budget** combines cost and revenue budgets in one statement. It is used by managers who have responsibility for both the expenses and revenues of their units. Such managers frequently head an entire division or company, like Corning Inc.'s technical products division. Profit budgets, sometimes called **master budgets,** consist of a set of projected financial statements and schedules for the coming year. Thus, they serve as annual profit plans.

Financial Budgets

The *capital expenditure, cash, financing,* and *balance sheet budgets* integrate the financial planning of the organization with its operational planning. These budgets, prepared with information developed from the revenue, expense, and operating budgets, serve three major purposes. First, they verify the viability of the operating budgets ("Will we generate enough cash to justify what we are planning to do?"). Second, their preparation reveals financial actions that the organization must take to make execution of its operating budgets possible ("If events conform to plans, we'll be short of cash in October and November; we'd better talk to our bankers this month about a line of credit to cover that period"). Third, they indicate how the organization's operating plans will affect its future financial actions. If these actions will be difficult or undesirable, appropriate changes in the operating plans may be required. ("In order to make our planned capital expenditures, we will have to arrange major borrowings in the capital markets in the next 12 months. But our economists say that will be poor timing; we had better rethink the expansion of our unit in Texas.") Research has found that industry is adopting increasingly sophisticated financial budgeting techniques, most of which have been developed by academics.

A Capital Decision. Although the machinery used to package Jiffy brand mixes was manufactured in the 1940s, senior managers at the family-owned Chelsea Milling Co. decided that a capital investment in newer equipment could not be cost-justified, since their strategy for selling Jiffy brand mixes calls for keeping prices low. To make repairs or expand production, they draw on spare equipment in storage.

capital expenditure budget Budget indicating future investments to be made in buildings, equipment, and other physical assets of the organization.

CAPITAL EXPENDITURE BUDGETS. **Capital expenditure budgets** indicate the future investments in new buildings, property, equipment, and other physical assets the organization is planning in order to renew and expand its productive capacity. For example, Dow Chemical annually budgets funds for innovative or additional processing plants, handling devices, and transportation equipment.

The capital expenditure budget reveals important projects the organization will undertake and significant cash requirements the organization will face in the future. Because of the long useful life of buildings and equipment and their relative inflexibility, the choices made on new capital expenditures are not easily altered. Thus, the decisions in the capital expenditure budget are frequently among the most important for the organization.

cash budget Budget combining estimates for revenues, expenses, and new capital expenditures.

CASH BUDGETS. **Cash budgets** bring together the organization's budgeted estimates for revenues, expenses, and new capital expenditures. The development of the cash budget will frequently reveal information about the *level* of funds flowing through the organization and about the *pattern* of cash disbursements and receipts. For example, preparation of the cash budget may show that the firm will be generating a great deal more cash than it will be using during the next year. This information may encourage management to move more aggressively on its capital expenditure program or even to consider additional areas of investment.

financing budget Budget that assures the organization of available funds to meet shortfalls of revenues when compared to expenses and that schedules potential borrowing needs.

FINANCING BUDGETS. **Financing budgets** are developed to assure the organization of the availability of funds to meet the shortfalls of revenues relative to expenses in the short run and to schedule medium- and longer-term borrowing or financing. These budgets are developed in conjunction with the cash budget to provide the organization with the funds it needs at the times it needs them. A local florist, for example, may establish a yearly financial budget that shows monthly revenues, as well as cash outflows for debts, labor, material, overhead, and loan payment expenses involved in operating the business. If there is a gap, the financing budget shows how the gap will be bridged.

balance sheet budget (or **pro forma balance sheet**) Budget combining all other budgets to project how the balance sheet will look at the end of the budgeting period.

BALANCE SHEET BUDGETS. The **balance sheet budget** brings together all of the other budgets to project how the balance sheet will look at the end of the period if actual results conform to planned results. This budget, also called a **pro forma balance sheet,** can be thought of as a final check on the organization's planned programs and activities. Analysis of the balance sheet budget may suggest problems or opportunities that will require managers to alter some of the other budgets. For example, the balance sheet budget may indicate that the company has planned to borrow more heavily than is prudent. This information might lead to a reduction in planned borrowing and reduced capital expenditures or—alternatively—a decision to issue additional stock to obtain some of the desired financing.

Variable versus Fixed Budgets

One difficulty with budgets is that they are often inflexible. Thus, they may seem inappropriate for situations that change in ways beyond the control of the budget makers. For example, an expense budget based on annual sales of $12 million may be completely off track if sales of $15 million are achieved. Since the expense of manufacturing almost always increases when more items are produced to meet larger demand, it would be unreasonable to expect managers to keep to the original expense budget.

To deal with this difficulty, many managers resort to a *variable* budget. (This type of budget is also referred to as a *flexible* budget, *sliding-scale* budget, and *step* budget.) Whereas *fixed* budgets express what individual costs should be at *one* specified volume, variable budgets are cost *schedules* that show how each cost should vary as the level of activity or output varies. Variable budgets are therefore useful in identifying in a fair and realistic manner how costs are affected by the amount of work being done.

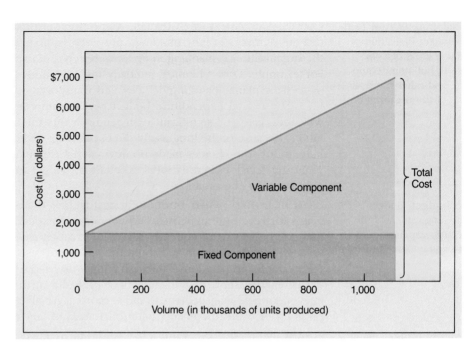

FIGURE 20-7 The Variable and Fixed Components of Total Cost

There are three types of costs that must be considered when developing variable budgets: fixed, variable, and semivariable costs, illustrated in Figure 20-7.

1. *Fixed Costs.* **Fixed costs** are those that are unaffected by the amount of work being done in the responsibility center. These costs accumulate only with the passage of time. For example, in many organizational units, monthly salaries, insurance payments, rent, and research expenditures do not vary significantly for moderate ranges of activity.

2. *Variable Costs.* **Variable costs** are expenses that vary directly with the quantity of work being performed. An example is raw materials—the more goods produced, the greater the quantity (and cost) of raw materials required.

3. *Semivariable Costs.* **Semivariable costs** are those that vary with the volume of work performed but *not* in a directly proportional way. Semivariable costs often represent a major part of an organization's expenses. For example, short-term labor costs are usually semivariable—the number of personnel hired (or laid off) is rarely based directly on day-to-day changes in production. Similarly, the cost of the total sales effort often does not vary directly with the number of products sold.

In devising their budgets, managers must try to break down their total costs into fixed and variable elements. The result will be more accurate and useful budgets, even though cost variability is often difficult to determine.

Variable budgets are used most appropriately in responsibility centers, where operations are repetitive, where there are a large number of different expenses, and where these expenses can be accurately estimated. Large-scale expense centers, such as the manufacturing facilities in the steel and toy industries, are particularly well suited for the variable budget approach. The main disadvantage of variable budgets is that they are often quite expensive to prepare.

Zero-Base Budgeting

In the normal budgeting process, the previous year's spending is used as a starting point. The task of individuals preparing the new budget is to decide what activities

COORDINATED RESOURCE
See Samaras Reading
"Whatever Happened to
Zero-Base Budgeting?"

**zero-base budgeting
(ZBB)** A budgeting ap-
proach in which managers
use cost-benefit analyses to
justify all budget decisions,
rather than using the previous year's budget as a
starting point.

and funds should be dropped and, more often, what activities and funds should be
added. Such a process creates a built-in bias toward continuing the same activities
year after year—long after their relevance and usefulness may have been lost because of environmental changes or changes in the organization's objectives.

Zero-base budgeting (ZBB), in contrast, enables the organization to look at
its activities and priorities afresh. The previous year's resource allocations are not
automatically considered the basis of this year's resource allocations. Instead, each
manager has to justify anew his or her entire budget request, using a cost-benefit
analysis of each of the organization's major activities.

In theory, zero-base budgets lead to better prioritization of budget items and
more efficient organizations. In reality, however, they can generate undue amounts
of paperwork and demoralize managers and employees who are asked to justify their
expenses—and, in essence, their existence—on a yearly basis. For those reasons,
zero-base budgets are used less often today than in the past.[18]

■ *AUDITING*

To much of the general public, the term *auditing* conjures up scenes of stern-faced
individuals scrutinizing a company's books in order to find out who is cheating the
company, how they are juggling the figures to cover it up, and how much they have
already embezzled. Although the discovery of fraud is, in fact, one important facet of
auditing, it is far from the only one. Auditing has many important uses, from validating the honesty and fairness of financial statements to providing a critical basis for
management decisions. In this section, we will discuss two types of auditing: *external auditing* and *internal auditing*.[19]

External Auditing

external audit Verification process involving the
independent appraisal of
financial accounts and
statements.

The traditional **external audit** is largely a verification process involving the independent appraisal of the organization's financial accounts and statements. Assets and
liabilities are verified, and financial reports are checked for completeness and accuracy. The audit is conducted by accounting personnel employed by an outside CPA
firm, such as Booz, Allen, and Hamilton, or by chartered accountants. The auditors'
purpose is *not* to prepare the company's financial reports; their job is to verify that
the company, in preparing its own financial statements and valuing its assets and
liabilities, has followed generally accepted accounting principles and applied them
correctly.

The external audit plays a significant role in encouraging honesty, not only in
the preparation of statements, but also in the actual operation of the organization. It
is, in fact, a major systematic check against fraud within the organization. For people
outside the organization, such as bankers and potential investors, the external audit
provides the major assurance that publicly available statements are accurate.

The external audit takes place after the organization's operating period is finished and its financial statements are completed. For this reason, and also because it
generally focuses on a comparatively limited set of financial statements and transactions, the external audit does not usually make a major contribution to control of the
ongoing operations of the organization. However, knowing that the audit will inevitably occur is a strong deterrent against actions that may lead to embarrassment (or
an uncomfortable prison term) if they are discovered during or after the audit.

Internal Auditing

internal audit Audit performed by the organization
to ensure that its assets
are properly safeguarded
and its financial records
reliably kept.

The **internal audit** is carried out by members of the organization. Its objectives are
to provide reasonable assurance that the assets of the organization are being prop-

ILLUSTRATIVE CASE STUDY

WRAP-UP

Financial Resourcefulness at Deere & Co.

According to *Forbes*'s Steve Weiner, Deere & Co. has one extremely valuable asset that will never show up on any financial statement—a loyal group of customers who wouldn't think of buying a tractor or combine that wasn't painted Deere green.

Deere's financial statements do show some disquieting facts, however. One is the 36 percent drop in the company's industrial equipment business for the first quarter of 1991. Sales of Deere bulldozers, excavators, and so on are expected to sag until the housing and general construction markets pick up. Another troubling entry reflects labor costs. About 70 percent of Deere's workers are represented by the United Auto Workers; current union contracts require Deere to pay employees about 60 percent of their regular wages even when factories are shut down, and contract negotiations are a regular event.

Even so, CEO Becherer expects Deere to show a profit in 1991. Analysts note that Deere's stock was selling for around $50 a share at a time when earnings were estimated to be between $2 and $2.25 per share. A ratio analysis might indicate that Deere's stock, priced at about 22 times earnings, is unusually high. Most analysts believe this indicates that the stock market shares Becherer's confidence in Deere & Co. ■

Source: Steve Weiner, "Staying on Top in a Tough Business in a Tough Year," *Forbes*, May 27, 1991, pp. 46, 48.

HERE'S AN EXAMPLE

Just-in-time shipping procedures adversely affected Penthouse Furniture of Springfield, Missouri. When one of Penthouse's largest customers went to a JIT system, Penthouse, to be ready to fill an order at any time, would have been forced to stockpile furniture within limited space. The company felt it could not meet these demands and closed down. (*Springfield News Leader*, 11/15/90, p. 6Bff.)

erly safeguarded and that financial records are being kept reliably and accurately enough for the preparation of financial statements. Internal audits also assist managers in evaluating the organization's operational efficiency and the performance of its control systems. Because it concentrates on the operations of the organization, this process is also known as *operational auditing*.

The internal audit may be carried out as a separate project by assigned members of the financial department or, in larger organizations, by a full-time internal auditing staff. The range and depth of the audit will also vary, depending on company size and policy, from a relatively narrow survey to a broad, comprehensive analysis that goes beyond appraising the control systems to look at policies, procedures, the use of authority, and the overall quality and effectiveness of the managerial methods being used. In this role, then, we can see that the management process is self-correcting.

■ SUMMARY

Although control is the process through which managers ensure that actual activities conform to plans, control also can be used to evaluate the effectiveness of planning, organizing, and leading. The control process consists of (1) establishing standards and methods for measuring performance; (2) measuring the performance; (3) determining if performance matches the standards; and if needed, (4) taking corrective action.

Control is important because it lets managers correct mistakes. More importantly, it helps them cope with change, creates faster cycles, adds value to the organization's products and services, unifies workers from different backgrounds and cultures, and facilitates delegation and teamwork.

There are four main types of control methods: pre-action controls, steering controls, yes/no controls, and post-action controls. Steering controls are the most important type of control, but yes/no controls provide a valuable double-check where safety or large amounts of money are involved.

Designing effective control systems can be difficult. If managers try to control too many elements in a rigid way, morale will probably suffer and valuable time, money, and energy will be wasted. These problems can be minimized if managers focus on controlling key performance areas at strategic control points.

Financial controls are important because money is one of the most prominent and easily measured inputs and outputs for most organizations. Financial statements, which include balance sheets, income statements, and cash flow statements, provide snapshots of an organization's liquidity, its general financial condition, and its profitability. This information is useful for managers and for outsiders who need to evaluate the organization's performance. Ratio analyses are used to compare an organization's financial performance in a specific area, such as return on equity, to that of similar organizations or a given industry.

Budgets, formal quantitative statements of resources set aside for a given activity and time period, are the most widely used means for planning and controlling. Because they are stated in monetary terms, budgets make it easy to compare dissimilar activities and their profit-loss potential; they establish clear standards of performance; and the interaction their creation requires helps coordinate activities within the organization.

Although budgets can be established for specific projects, most budgets are devised for responsibility centers. The four types of responsibility centers are revenue centers, expense centers, profit centers, and investment centers.

The budgeting process begins when top managers give lower-level managers their economic forecasts and objectives for the coming year. A few organizations use top-down budgeting, in which top management also completes the budgets, but most use bottom-up budgeting, in which lower-level managers, often with the help of their employees, create budgets and submit them to higher-level managers for approval on a specific timetable.

Operating budgets, which indicate the goods and services the organization expects to consume in the budget period, include the budgets created for expense, revenue, and profit centers. Financial budgets integrate the organization's financial planning with its operational planning. The main goals are to (1) verify the viability of the operating budgets; (2) indicate financial actions needed to execute operational budgets; and (3) indicate how operational plans will affect future financial actions.

Variable budgets are cost schedules that indicate how operating costs would vary with different levels of output. Although they are expensive to prepare, they are extremely useful for large-scale expense centers, such as manufacturing facilities, where demand, and therefore expenses, may vary from plans.

In most budgets, the previous period's spending is used as a starting point in calculating a new budget. Zero-base budgeting, in contrast, asks each manager to use a cost-benefit analysis to examine each activity and determine whether it should be funded and at what level. Although it can be useful for taking a fresh look at activities and priorities, zero-base budgeting generates a great deal of paperwork and can demoralize managers and their employees.

Auditing compares actual performance to budgets. External auditing, conducted by outside CPA firms, examines an organization's financial reports to verify that the organization has used generally accepted accounting principles in a proper way. As such, it can be used to detect fraud and encourage honesty and accuracy.

Internal auditing, carried out by specially appointed members of the financial department or by an internal auditing staff, helps managers evaluate the organization's operational efficiency, as well as the effectiveness of its policies, procedures, use of authority, and other managerial methods.

■ *REVIEW QUESTIONS*

1. Why is control needed?
2. Discuss the steps in the control process. What are the elements in each step?
3. Explain the four types of control methods and list the advantages of each.
4. Explain why key performance areas and strategic control points are important to designing control systems.
5. What three major conditions of an organization do financial statements indicate?
6. What are the major types of financial statements? What information does each type provide?
7. What is ratio analysis? How is it used?
8. Why are budgets so widely used by organizations?
9. What are responsibility centers and how are they used in the control process?
10. How are budgets drawn up and approved?
11. What are the elements of operating budgets? What are they used for?
12. What are the several types of financial budgets and how are they used?
13. What is the purpose of auditing and how is it achieved?

CASE STUDY

The Audit Report

Jay O'Malley was supervisor of general accounting for Mitan Mines in Butte, Montana. One of his responsibilities was to make monthly estimates of the firm's workers' compensation costs. Jay handled the estimate in a standardized manner. Every six months, Mitan Mines would get a billing from the state's Workers' Compensation Commission for costs charged against Mitan during the previous six months. Jay would take this figure, divide it by six, and charge this amount against each of the next six months. In this way, Mitan hoped to accrue the approximate amount to pay the next semiannual bill.

The bill for the last half of 1983 arrived in February 1984. To the surprise of Jay, his boss, the mine's controller, and the mine's general manager, the bill was for nearly double the amount Jay had set aside. Mitan had been charged with several large compensation cases during the latter half of 1983, resulting in a bill for $487,000. Jay had accrued only $264,000.

Standard accounting practices required Jay to charge the underaccrual—$223,000—to February 1984's operations. Jay made the appropriate entry. Jay's boss concurred. But when the preliminary February figures were worked out, the mine's forecasted profit of approximately $150,000 became a $75,000 loss. When the general manager was advised why February's profit had disappeared, he exploded: "No way. I've told head office that we'll make money this month. I understand what the accounting rules are, but I've got to placate my bosses at head office. Adjust the entry you've made. Take the $223,000 and spread it out over three months!"

Jay and the controller explained to the general manager that this was an improper practice and would certainly be uncovered when the internal auditors eventually reviewed the records. The general manager was unmoved. "Just do it the way I tell you.

Remember, you work for me, not the accounting profession!"

In July 1984, the company's internal audit group arrived at the plant, unannounced. The four-person team spent three weeks reviewing the mine's financial status and operating practices. Upon completion of their work, they submitted an audit report to the mine's general manager. Copies were also sent to the company's corporate controller, vice president of mining operations, director of corporate auditing, and chairman of the board. Among the comments made by the audit group was that the mine's controller had disregarded proper accounting practices by not charging the $223,000 workers' compensation underaccrual to the mine's operation in February of 1984. The findings of the audit report resulted in letters from the vice president of mining operations to the mine's general manager and from the corporate controller to the mine's controller. In effect, the letters said Mitan mines personnel should follow standard accounting practices and refrain from future financial manipulations.

Source: Stephen P. Robbins, *Management: Concepts and Practices,* © 1984, pp. 469–471. Reprinted by permission of Prentice Hall, Inc., Englewood Cliffs, New Jersey.

Case Questions

1. Who is at fault here?
2. Do you think the audit and resulting letters will achieve their purpose?
3. How would you have handled this situation if you had been the mine's controller?
4. How would you have handled this situation if you had been the vice president for mining operations?

At the Controls for Ben & Jerry's Homemade Inc.

Few small businesses have more appeal to the American public than the Vermont-based superpremium ice cream company, Ben & Jerry's Homemade Inc., founded in 1978 by Ben Cohen and his best friend, Jerry Greenfield. They took a $5 correspondence course in ice cream making and then set up business in a converted gas station in the college town of Burlington, where they began by offering twelve flavors. Their image was "grass roots" with T-shirts the norm; few ties are seen even 13 years later. Their approach to business was uninformed at best; once they even closed for a day to figure out the books.

There was, however, real commitment to employees and to the community. "Early on," says Greenfield, "we knew that if we stayed in the business, it was because of the support of a lot of people, so it seemed natural to want to return that support." B & J's commitment to the welfare of their employees is evidenced by free health-club memberships (to work off the three free pints of ice cream a day), affordable day care, and other distinctive perks.

Moreover, there is broad appeal in Ben & Jerry's superpremium ice cream, which features such exotic flavors as Oreo Mint, Heath Bar Crunch, Dastardly Mash, New York Super Fudge Chunk, and Cherry Garcia (named after the spiritual father of the Grateful Dead rock group, guitarist Jerry Garcia). Laden with rich, creamy ingredients, a finished gallon weighs about 7 pounds and sells at upscale prices. Even so, sales growth has been remarkable and at times frightening to the two hippies-turned-entrepreneurs. In fact, Jerry Greenfield "retired" in 1982, citing the pressures of business, although he returned in 1985. Today the company has more than 350 employees and about 90 franchised shops and enjoys sales revenues in the neighborhood of $60 million annually. In 1990, it was ranked as the number two producer of superpremium ice cream in the country, up from number three in 1987.

Although well known for the excellence of their product and their willingness to compete with the likes of Pillsbury-owned Häagen-Dazs, they also derive much of their notoriety from their approach to doing business. In 1982, Fred "'Chico" Lager sold his nightclub in Burlington and joined them as chief operating officer to assist in business operations. Still, as the cover story of the July 1988 issue of *Inc.* magazine pointed out, Ben and Jerry are widely perceived

as "The Bad Boys of American Business," whose ice cream company is not the normal kind of growth company, but rather a company founded on "funk and adventure" plus a strong interest in social change. It has become successful due to the dedication of the work force, many excitingly bold marketing maneuvers, and some good luck.

For one thing, the company has used its image of being unusual and dedicated to social change to woo the press into giving it lots of free publicity, although some writers have begun to question the pureness of B & J's motives. Consider the press conference to introduce Rain Forest Crunch and announce the lofty goal of using much of its profits from the new flavor to help save the Amazon. Some 70 people were in attendance and reportedly around 40 of them were from the media. B & J even received a lot of publicity from a "proposal" to sell their ice cream in the U.S.S.R. in the spirit of *glasnost.*

While B & J insist their motives are well meant and they keep on producing quality products, their corporate financial approach appears to be quite unique. For example, no employee (including Ben and Jerry) can earn more than five times the salary of the lowest-paid employee, according to company policy. Additionally, B & J commits a full 7.5 percent of pretax profits to a nonprofit foundation that aids various causes and charities.

Part of Ben & Jerry's distinctiveness is that they continue to focus on projects and causes outside of business. Examples are the "1% for Peace" project founded to, among other things, bring about a reduction in the U.S. defense budget. They also made the effort to help save the Amazon by producing the aforementioned Rain Forest Crunch.

Still, B & J have had some flops. They brought out the Peace Pop in 1989, an ice cream bar on a stick, which was to provide funds for their "1% for Peace" project. The bar had problems from the time of its introduction, including a lack of quality control, an ineffective, low-budget, low-key marketing strategy, and heavy marketing blitzes from the competition, which offered less expensive treats. Greenfield is quoted as saying, "We learned that a product doesn't sell just because you're trying to do good in the world. You still have to have a healthy distribution strategy, a good marketing strategy, and price the product properly."

Additionally, some key people, including the marketing director, have apparently become disgruntled with the salary cap, the 60-hour weeks, and other B & J policies. Fred Lager, age 35, who had moved up the ladder to become CEO, retired in 1990, saying he wanted some time off. Even the search for a female chief financial officer was unsuccessful, partly because female CFOs can write their own tickets. In the interim, B & J hired Fran Rathke, a young female recruit from Coopers & Lybrand accounting firm, to serve as controller.

Sources: Eric Larson, "Forever Young," *Inc.,* July 1988, pp. 50–62; Joe Queeman, "Purveying Yuppie Porn," *Forbes,* November 13, 1989, pp. 60, 64; "The Peace Pop Puzzle," *Inc.,* March 1990, p. 25; Alan Deutschman, "Inside Scoop," *Fortune,* March 12, 1990, p. 130; Kim Hubbard, "For New Age Ice-Cream Moguls Ben and Jerry, Making 'Cherry Garcia' and 'Chunky Monkey' Is a Labor of Love," *People Weekly,* September 10, 1990, pp. 73–75.

Case Questions

1. Chapter 20 discusses several types of controls that can be used by organizations. Discuss what types of control process seems to be a part of the Ben & Jerry's way of doing business.

2. Explain the apparent links between the planning and control processes at B & J.

3. Review what types of financial and marketing control concepts could have been used to evaluate the effectiveness of the Peace Pop before it was introduced to the market.

4. What do you think caused B & J to have difficulty in hiring a female chief financial officer? What solutions would you recommend?

5. Explain how you might recommend B & J use controls to cope with future growth.

■ NOTES

[1]Robert J. Mockler, *The Management Control Process* (Englewood Cliffs, N.J.: Prentice Hall, 1984), p. 2.

[2]Vijay Sathe, "The Controller's Role in Management," *Organizational Dynamics* 11, no. 3 (Winter 1983):31–48.

[3]Fred G. Steingraber, "Managing in the 1990s," *Business Horizons,* January–February 1990; and Kenichi Ohmae, "Getting Back to Strategy," *Harvard Business Review,* November–December 1988, pp. 149–156.

[4]Alex Taylor III, "Why Toyota Keeps Getting Better and Better," *Fortune,* November 19, 1990, pp. 66–79.

[5]Ohmae, "Getting Back to Strategy."

[6]Taylor, "Why Toyota Keeps Getting Better and Better," p. 74.

[7]On AT&T's strategies at its Shreveport facility, see Hank Johansson and Dan McArthur, "Rediscovering the Fundamentals," *Management Review* 77, no. 1 (1988): 34–37.

[8]Michael H. Granof, *Financial Accounting,* 3rd ed. (Englewood Cliffs, N.J.: Prentice Hall, 1985).

[9]Dan Steinhoff and John F. Burgess, *Small Business Management Fundamentals* (New York: McGraw-Hill, 1989), Chap. 7.

[10]George E. Pinches, *Essentials of Financial Management,* 3rd ed. (New York: Harper & Row, 1990), Chap. 3.

[11]Steinhoff and Burgess, *Small Business Management Fundamentals,* pp. 103–105.

[12]Jack L. Smith, Robert M. Keith, and William L. Stephens, *Accounting Principles* (New York: McGraw-Hill, 1989), Chap. 24.

[13]This discussion of budgets is based on Robert N. Anthony, John Dearden, and Norton M. Bedford, *Management Control Systems,* 5th ed. (Homewood, Ill.: Irwin, 1984), especially Chaps. 5, 6, and 7.

[14]Roger H. Hermanson, James Don Edwards, and R. F. Salmonson, *Accounting Principles* (Homewood, Ill.: Irwin, 1989), Chap. 25.

[15]Kenneth A. Merchant, "Influence on Departmental Budgeting: An Empirical Examination of a Contingency Model," *Accounting, Organizations and Society* 9, nos. 3/4 (1984): 291–307.

[16]See Gordon Shillinglaw, *Managerial Cost Accounting: Analysis and Control,* 5th ed. (Homewood, Ill., Irwin, 1982), pp. 209–210.

[17]Anthony, Dearden, and Bedford, *Management Control Systems.*

[18]Hermanson, Edwards, and Salmonson, *Accounting Principles,* Chap. 27.

[19]See Alvin A. Arens and James K. Loebbecke, *Auditing: An Integrated Approach* (Englewood Cliffs, N.J.: Prentice Hall, 1984), Chap. 1.

CHAPTER TWENTY-ONE

OPERATIONS MANAGEMENT*

Detail from Gerald Murphy, *Watch*.

Upon completing this chapter, you should be able to:

1. Describe operations as a system in both production and service organizations.

2. Discuss the relationship between operations management, productivity, and efficiency.

3. Explain how operations management lets organizations meet competitive priorities.

4. Describe operations management's role in product and service design.

5. Discuss the major considerations in capacity planning, process selection, facility-location planning, and layout planning.

6. Explain why job-design issues are important to operations management.

7. Describe the use of production plans and detailed schedules in operations planning and control.

8. Discuss the evolution of the concept of quality control.

*This chapter is based in part on information supplied by Rick Hesse, Mercer University.

Gerald Murphy, *Watch*, 1925. Oil on canvas. 78½ × 78⅞″. Dallas Museum of Art, Foundation for the Arts Collection, gift of the Artist.

ILLUSTRATIVE CASE STUDY

INTRODUCTION

At Ford, Quality Is Job One

Between 1980 and 1987, Ford Motor Company's market share rose 3 points to 20 percent. Meanwhile, the market share of General Motors, Ford's biggest and most powerful domestic rival, shriveled 9 points to 37 percent. In the first nine months of 1987, Ford earned more money than GM and Chrysler combined. The company's profits for the year totaled $3.3 billion, compared with GM's $2.9 billion. It was the first time that Ford had surpassed GM in profits since 1924. Clearly, Ford was moving forward while GM was spinning its wheels: Ford's 1986 sales were roughly the same as GM's 1981 sales.

Ford has become the comeback player of the automotive industry—after having lost over $3 billion during the early 1980s. How did such a dramatic turnaround happen? In order to answer this question, we must look at a little history. During the late 1970s and early 1980s, American automobile manufacturers increasingly lost sales to foreign competition. According to most industry analysts, the reason was relatively simple: the inferior quality of American-made cars. The symptoms were especially prominent at Ford; at one point, losses were $1 billion a quarter. Then in 1980, Henry Ford II stepped down as chairman. Philip Caldwell took over as chairman, and Donald Petersen became president and later chief operating officer. Together, they undertook one of the most dramatic restructuring programs in the annals of American corporate history.

Interestingly enough, their inspiration came from a television documentary called "If Japan Can . . . Why Can't We?" which identified W. Edwards Deming, an American business consultant, as the father of the Japanese economic miracle. Petersen arranged a meeting with Deming and soon was sending senior managers to take Deming's seminar and learn the techniques he had taught the Japanese.

Sweeping changes were in the wind, changes that struck at the very culture of the company created by the autocratic Henry Ford. Petersen's first target was the "cult of personality"—a competitive, one-man-rule style of management introduced by Ford and carried on by his grandson and the likes of Robert McNamara, who later became secretary of

Pride of workmanship. J.C. Phillips, chairman of UAW Local 882, comes to work each day at the Ford Atlanta plant determined to eliminate "no-value" work that adds nothing to product quality.

defense, and Lee Iacocca, who went on to take the helm at Chrysler. To escape the demanding, almost punitive standards of Ford's fast track, Petersen himself had transferred at midcareer to the less demanding truck division, where he stumbled upon a revelation—the pleasure of teamwork in an informal atmosphere where everyone focused on solving problems rather than competing.

Encouraged by Deming's dictums about the destructiveness of internal competition, Petersen set out to build an operations system based on teamwork and an integrated approach to creating quality products equal to any produced by the Japanese. More than just an advertising slogan, "At Ford, Quality Is Job One" became the corporate mission.

Sources: Robert E. Petersen, "How Ford Became #1," *Motor Trend* 39, no. 12 (1987): 4, 6–7; Robert E. Petersen and H. A. Poling, "The U.S.: Team at the Top of No. 2," *Fortune,* November 9, 1987, p. 82; J. S. Treece, "Donald Petersen," *Business Week,* April 15, 1988, pp. 131–134; Brian Dumaine, "A Humble Hero Drives Ford to the Top," *Fortune,* January 4, 1988, 22–24; Donald R. Katz, "Coming Home," *Business Month,* October 1988, pp. 56–62; Jerry Flint, "We Need Manufacturing People at the Top," *Forbes,* August 20, 1990, pp. 58–60, and "Banzai with a Georgia Accent," *Forbes,* February 4, 1991, pp. 58–62.

*I*n this chapter, we will learn how an advertising slogan became the guiding force for a rejuvenated Ford Motor Co. To do this, we will look at *operations,* the day-to-day activities needed to accomplish organizational goals, and the importance of *operations management.* Then we will look at some of the key elements involved in designing an effective *operations system* as well as operational planning and control decisions—all of which affect the quality of an organization's goods and services.

■ *THE NATURE OF OPERATIONS*

operations The production activities of an organization.

THOUGHT PROVOKER

At many companies, manufacturing is often a "second-class citizen." What are the implications of this, and what would you suggest be done about it? (*Fortune,* 4/23/90, p. 128ff.)

COORDINATED RESOURCE

Use Transparency 143, Conceptual Model of an Operations System.

In its simplest terms, **operations** refers to the way an organization transforms inputs—labor, money, supplies, equipment, and so on—into outputs—goods or services, ranging from computers to computerized billing services. The actual practice of operations is more complex, of course, for it takes in all the nitty-gritty, day-to-day activities by which the members of an organization strive to reach its goals. As such, operations is an all-encompassing process that shapes the quality of work life as well as the organization's efficiency and effectiveness. To see how all this works, we will first look at operations as a system. Then we will look at some of the similarities and differences between production and service organizations.

The Operations System: A Model

As we saw in Chapter 2, any organization can be viewed as a *system,* a set of related and interacting subsystems that perform functions directed at reaching a common goal. These subsystems can, in turn, be viewed as separate systems. This idea is the basis for Figure 21-1.

As the diagram shows, inputs include human labor, capital (money needed to acquire land, equipment, and so on), technology, and information. These are the resources that will be transformed into outputs that reflect the organization's goals. For Ford Motor Co., desired outputs are cars, trucks, and parts of a certain quality; for the Red Cross, desired outputs are safe supplies of blood and emergency aid to disaster victims; for a hospital, desired outputs would be patient care and perhaps preventive health care through free lectures and screening medical tests. Outputs may include both positive and negative byproducts, such as new jobs and air pollu-

FIGURE 21-1 Conceptual Model of an Operations System

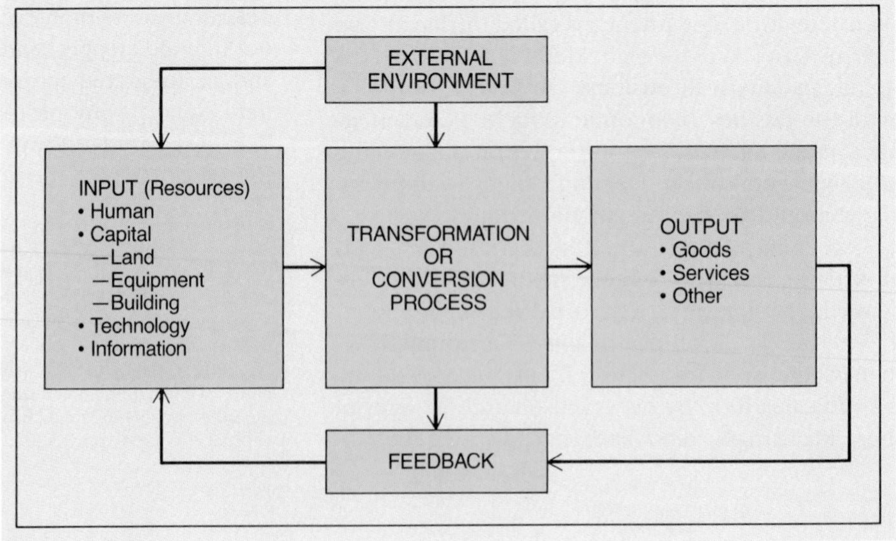

tion, which affect other subsystems as well as the external environment. If the human resources subsystem declares a six-month moratorium on hiring, the operations subsystem—and the surrounding community—will certainly feel the effects when workers who leave are not replaced.

The transformation process from input to output varies from organization to organization. *Physical transformations* of raw materials into finished goods occur mainly in production organizations, although service organizations also transform materials (forms and writing equipment) into finished goods (completed tax forms). Transportation involves *locational transformations,* while retailing involves *exchange transformations* (money for goods). In warehousing, the transformation involves *storage,* often at a certain temperature and humidity. In legal and accounting firms, *information* is usually transformed from one form into another, while in entertainment, *emotions* are transformed from boredom, say, to laughter or tears.

The external environment means any or all of the elements of the direct-action and indirect-action environments, including government regulations, inflation, suppliers, social values, and the weather. The feedback loop in Figure 21-1 reflects the information gained during the entire process, making it possible to monitor the system's performance and decide whether corrective changes are needed. As you learned in the previous chapter, this feedback loop represents the essence of the control function.

Operations in Production and Service Organizations

COORDINATED RESOURCE
See Samaras Exercise 5.3, "To Produce or Not to Produce."

production organization Organization that produces tangible goods that can be mass-produced and stored for later consumption.

Figure 21-1 and our examples indicate that production and service organizations are alike in that they both use operations. Beyond this basic similarity, though, there are some major differences in the nature of their outputs and their transformation processes, as shown in Exhibit 21-1.

A **production organization** is primarily concerned with producing physical goods, such as cars, computers, plastic bottles, or paint. These goods can be stored in a warehouse and consumed over time. Some customizing is available, of course—customers can order extra-cost options on cars or request special tinting of paint, for example—but the overall emphasis is on making uniform, mass-produced goods. As a result, there is little customer contact or participation in the production of individual products, although many progressive companies do seek customer advice when designing mass-produced goods. Ford Motor Co., for example, used a customer advisory committee in designing the Ford Taurus, and Chrysler used customer feedback in revising its successful minivans. To evaluate production performance, managers use sophisticated techniques to measure components and finished goods; these measurements are then compared to preestablished standards.

service organization Organization that produces intangible goods that require consumer participation and cannot be stored.

A **service organization,** in contrast, produces largely intangible goods that cannot be stored. Doctors, lawyers, accountants, and barbers, for example, produce customized labor in the form of advice and services that reflect the needs of individ-

EXHIBIT 21-1 Characteristics of Products and Services

	PRODUCT	SERVICE
Output	Tangible	Intangible
Output consumption	Over time; can be stored	Immediate; cannot be stored
Nature of work	Product intensive	Labor intensive
Customer contact	Minimal, indirect	Direct
Customer participation	Little or none	Essential
Performance measurement	Sophisticated	Elementary

Source: Adapted from Everett E. Adam, Jr., and Ronald J. Ebert, *Production and Operations Management,* 4th ed. (Englewood Cliffs, N.J.: Prentice Hall, 1989), p. 7.

ual consumers. A telephone company provides communication services. An airline provides transportation. Services cannot be performed without customer contact and participation; neither can they be stored. Furthermore, the measurement of service performance tends to be simpler than performance measurements for products. Service providers may ask for feedback, conduct periodic surveys, or measure arbitrary standards deemed to indicate satisfactory performance. McDonald's, for example, might specify that no customer should have to wait more than 5 minutes to give an order. L. L. Bean measures the performance of its telemarketing operations by determining how long callers have to wait to reach a sales clerk.

One of the most significant changes in the U.S. economy in recent years has been the growth of the service sector and the shrinking of the production sector. This trend actually began in the 1950s, and promises to continue well into the next century. In fact, the Hudson Institute predicts that "Despite its international comeback, U.S. manufacturing will be a much smaller share of the economy in the year 2000 than it is today."[1] Of the estimated 21 million new jobs that will be created between 1986 and the year 2000, the Bureau of Labor estimates that about 20 million will be in the service sector. Manufacturing jobs, in contrast, will employ just 14 percent of all workers by the turn of the century.[2] Such changes have made most managers aware that skillful *operations management* is essential for both production and service organizations.

■ THE IMPORTANCE OF OPERATIONS MANAGEMENT

operations management Complex management activity that includes planning production, organizing resources, directing operations and personnel, and monitoring system performance.

Operations management refers to the complex set of management activities involved in planning, organizing, directing, and controlling an organization's operations. At one time, operations management was considered the backwater of management activities—a dirty, drab necessity. This view changed in the 1970s, when the U.S. economy received a one-two punch in the form of rising energy costs and mounting competition from foreign organizations that offered high-quality products at highly competitive prices. That experience gave managers a new appreciation of operations management. Many now see it as the key to revitalizing U.S. organizations and ensuring their place in the global economy.

Operations management is important for at least two reasons. First, it can improve *productivity,* which improves an organization's health, as well as the health of the economy. Second, it can help organizations meet consumers' *competitive priorities.*

To Improve Productivity: A Measure of Efficiency

productivity Measure of how well an operations system functions and indicator of the efficiency and competitiveness of a single firm or department.

Coordinated Resource
The Distinctive Discussions for Chapter 21 found in the Lecture Extras supplement include "The Role of Employee Involvement" and "The Sweet Smell of Higher Productivity."

Productivity, the ratio of output to input, is a measure of a manager's efficiency in using the organization's scarce resources to produce goods and services. The higher the numerical value of this ratio, the greater the efficiency. (The underlying assumption, of course, is that the majority of the goods meet preestablished standards for quality because quality control systems have detected errors and allowed for their correction.)

To understand the connection between productivity and efficiency, look back at Figure 21-1 and try to visualize it as a series of strategic control points. This concept, introduced in the previous chapter, refers to junctures at which a major change occurs. In filling a customer order, for example, strategic control points would occur when the purchase order becomes an invoice, when an inventory item becomes an item to be shipped, and when an item to be shipped becomes part of a truckload of goods to be delivered. Any of these strategic control points is a potential source of confusion, as work is passed from one set of workers to another. An unclear form or a confusing policy—say, for handling out-of-stock items—creates the risk that orders will be lost or mishandled, wasting valuable time, money, or

COORDINATED RESOURCE
See Samaras Case 5.3, "A Case of Productivity."

energy. From this vantage point, the operations system looks like a sieve that can leak valuable resources unless it is managed efficiently. Productivity offers one measure of this efficiency.

For example, assume that a legal clinic with eight lawyers (the input) produces output consisting of 100 client consultations per day. Productivity would equal 100/8 or 12.50. Assume that a second legal clinic next door has 15 lawyers handling 125 consultations per day. The productivity ratio would be 125/15 or 8.33. The smaller clinic has a higher productivity ratio on a *quantitative* basis, which may or may not reflect anything about the *quality* of its output.

TEACHING TIP
Emphasize the ratio of outputs to inputs—the effort to produce more outputs with fewer inputs.

TYPES OF PRODUCTIVITY RATIOS.   There are two types of productivity ratios. The first, *total productivity,* relates the value of all output to the value of all input, using the ratio total output/total input. The second, *partial productivity,* relates the value of all output to the value of major categories of input, using the ratio total output/partial input.

COORDINATED RESOURCE
See Study Guide Problem Exercise 21, "Measuring Productivity."

The legal clinic is an example of a partial productivity ratio called a *labor productivity index* or output per work-hour ratio. Most productivity measures quoted by economists and business executives are, in fact, labor productivity indexes, since labor is one of the greatest ongoing costs for most organizations. Other partial productivity ratios measure the amount of scrap (wasted materials); the number of units that have to be reworked or fixed before they meet quality standards; and downtime, the unproductive time spent retooling a production line or waiting for customers to serve. Any of these measures gives an indication of whether resources are being used to good advantage or wasted.

USES AND ABUSES OF PRODUCTIVITY RATIOS.   Productivity ratios can be calculated for a specific time period, which measures the efficiency of operations at that time, or they can be compared with other ratios over time, as a measure of gains or losses in productivity. For example, between 1982 and 1990, the 500 largest manufactur-

TEACHING TIP
Point out the figures (indicators) given weekly in the *Business Week* index.

Reevaluating Productivity Ratios. In an effort to increase productivity, Federal Express began electronically monitoring its 2,500 customer-service agents. Holding each call to 140 seconds counted for 50 percent of an agent's evaluation. Two years later, faced with mounting complaints about stress and having to cut customers off, Fed Ex adopted a new system. Agents like Paula Biffle (left) are monitored only twice a year, and follow-up talks with manager Tish Montesi (right) focus on quality. As a result, service improved and the average call actually dropped to 135 seconds.

ers posted a 27 percent improvement in productivity, based on inflation-adjusted average sales per employee. During the same period, the service industry posted a 1 percent decline in productivity.[3]

In recent years, U.S. manufacturers have boosted productivity by closing plants (Chrysler, GM, IBM, Levi Strauss), downsizing (IBM, Xerox), laying off production workers (USX and Chrysler), and selling off failing or unwanted businesses (Exxon, Alcoa, Xerox). Still, the United States lags behind Japan, South Korea, Great Britain, Norway, Sweden, France, and other countries in productivity *growth*. What is the problem?

Many experts say the problem is the emphasis on productivity itself. They charge that, in trying to improve "the numbers"—quantitative measures of productivity—too many U.S. managers have focused on capital investment in automation as a way to reduce labor costs. This short-term focus has caused them to overlook the benefits of investing in the organization's **human capital**—employees and their skills—and improving quality.

This emphasis is changing as more organizations toss out work quotas and concentrate on finding the right mix of capital investment and human investment. One of the most important trends in operations management today—and management in general, in fact—is the focus on increasing **work-force literacy,** knowledge and skills that relate directly to job performance. Another is the trend to participative management and the use of self-managed work teams to improve productivity and quality simultaneously.

Corning Inc.'s experience at its Blacksburg, Virginia, plant illustrates both these trends. Rather than force workers to do repetitive, restricted jobs, plant managers decided to use a combination of automation and a multiskilled, team-based production to challenge employees. Out of 8,000 people who applied for jobs, Corning selected the 150 who performed the best on tests of problem-solving skills and showed a willingness to work in a team setting. In the first year of production, 25 percent of all work hours were devoted to extensive training in technical and interpersonal skills, at a cost of $750,000.

The rewards were well worth the expense. A Blacksburg team can retool a line in just 10 minutes, six times faster than the norm in traditionally managed plants. As a result, the Blacksburg plant earned $2 million in profits during an eight-month startup period, though it had been projected to lose $2.3 million. As additional bonuses, morale is high and productivity, product quality, and Corning profits have all increased. Buoyed by this success, Corning is planning to convert its 27 other plants to a team-managed approach, using on-the-job training to improve worker skills.[4] Corning's experience is just one indication of how creative operations management can help an organization meet consumers' *competitive priorities*.

To Meet Competitive Priorities: A Key to Effectiveness

Most companies develop competitive problems when they lose sight of operations' primary reason for being: to produce quality products and services consumers want at prices that seem reasonable. This relates back to measures of organizational effectiveness: the ability to set the "right" goals, ones that build on organizational strengths *and* meet the needs and wants of potential consumers. Of course, individual needs and wants vary widely, as do price perceptions. Rather than try to be all things to all consumers, effective managers make strategic decisions about how their organizations can best meet their customers' **competitive priorities,** and then adjust their operations accordingly. The four major competitive priorities are pricing, quality level, quality reliability, and flexibility.

PRICING. For many consumers, price is a major consideration, either because their funds are limited or because the differences between a higher-priced item and a

Meeting Multiple Priorities. In the face of Medicare cuts and mounting pressures on health care costs, Hospital Corp. of America's chief administrator William Arnold set about sweeping out inefficiencies. Given the goal of providing quality care at lower costs, the contracts department is working with its major supplier of medical products to reduce invoice discrepancies that cost millions to resolve, and quality programs at one of Hospital Corp's hospitals are cutting the average age of accounts receivables from 78 to 49 days.

lower-priced item do not seem justified. One task of the operations manager is to keep costs down so that the organization can offer "good" prices and still make a profit.

Earl Scheib, Inc., of Beverly Hills, which operates a nationwide chain of discount car-repair shops offering low-priced paint jobs, is an example of an organization that has built high sales volume through low prices. Scheib's low prices have resulted in annual sales increases of 15 percent and earnings increases of almost 50 percent. At the same time, Scheib protects its profit margins by careful cost accounting. This same concern for cost accounting can be seen in retail stores, since a name-brand good offers the same quality and warranty whether it is bought in a luxurious department store or a discount warehouse.

Although pricing considerations are usually associated with for-profit organizations, they are also a concern of nonprofit organizations, such as charities and professional associations, and government agencies, which charge "prices" in the form of dues, donations, taxes, and user fees. To increase consumer satisfaction and avoid complaints, these organizations need to use operations management to keep prices down while still providing high-quality service.

QUALITY LEVEL. Quality level has two components: high-performance design and fast delivery time. Characteristics of high-performance design are superior features, close tolerances, and greater durability of the product or service. An example is Maytag washers and dryers. In an industry marked by highly competitive products and prices, Maytag has been able to charge premium prices because customers believe in the superior capability and the expected longer life of its washers and dryers. Customers also expect efficient repair schedules if anything does go wrong with a Maytag product. Quality level is also exemplified by Domino's Pizza, which offers a limited menu of high-quality pizzas and 30-minute deliveries.

QUALITY RELIABILITY. Quality reliability means consistent quality and on-time delivery. Consistent quality measures the frequency with which the design specifications are met. McDonald's restaurants are world-renowned for uniformly achieving their design specifications; although you may not experience the same delights as those offered at five-star restaurants, you can expect the same quality standards whether you eat at a McDonald's in Charlotte, New York, or Paris. Toyota's small cars are not noted for the ability to compete with Cadillacs on quality *level* (consequently, Toyota's price is much lower), but they are world-renowned for their quality *reliability*—they are highly consistent in quality from one car to another.

FLEXIBILITY. Flexibility refers to both product and volume flexibility. *Product flexibility* means that product designs are in a state of flux and that the firm emphasizes specialization—that is, it customizes its products to individual preference. The level of output for an individual product is necessarily low because the firm competes primarily on its ability to produce difficult, one-of-a-kind products. This is the exact opposite of mass production, where standardization of the product has occurred and the producer makes large quantities of one item. Product flexibility is illustrated by National Semiconductor Corporation's decision to enter the growing market for custom-designed computer chips when the company was hit by a slump in the mass-production sector of the semiconductor industry. It made quick design changes and introduced new products fast in order to take advantage of an inadequate supply of custom-designed chips. Some of its custom chips sell for as much as $1 million apiece.

Volume flexibility is the ability to quickly accelerate or decelerate the rate of production as the demand for a firm's product changes. McDonald's is a good example; it increases or decreases its work force from hour to hour in order to meet changes in customer demands. McDonald's uses a certain number of employees for an 8-hour shift and supplements them by adding part-time employees at noon and 6 P.M. These part-time employees are usually housewives or elderly citizens supplementing their Social Security benefits by working a few hours each week.

MEETING MULTIPLE PRIORITIES. The primary problem with trying to meet competitive priorities is that they often conflict. Consumers want reasonable prices, but they also want high quality levels, reliability, and flexible, feature-laden products and services. At one time, meeting all these expectations would have been impossible, since such goods have traditionally been expensive to produce.

In recent years, though, creative operations managers from Japan, Europe, and the United States have shown that organizations can offer high quality and flexible goods and services at competitive prices. Toyota, for example, was once known primarily for its reliable economy models; few people associated Toyota with luxury cars. To overcome this barrier, the company launched the Lexus Division in 1989 to create and market luxury autos. Since then, Lexus models have swept all the major automotive awards and in some periods outsold both Mercedes-Benz and BMW. Convinced that Toyota's Lexus models met their needs for luxury, prestige, safety, quality, and performance, many drivers traded in $70,000 cars for Lexus models that cost about half as much.[5] Such standard-setting examples have managers around the world striving to design operations systems that will enable them to meet rising consumer expectations.

■ *DESIGNING OPERATIONS SYSTEMS*

For Discussion

Can these production and operations management topics be applied to service sector organizations? How?

Becoming aware of competitive priorities is just one way that managers can match operational plans to strategic plans. These operational plans, in turn, affect the design of operations systems. Designing an operations system involves making decisions about *what* and *how many* products or services will be produced, *how* and *where* they will be produced, and by *whom.*

computer-aided design (CAD) Design and drafting performed interactively on a computer.

bill of materials Listing of the type and number of parts needed to produce a given product.

capacity planning Operations decision concerned with the quantity of goods or services to be produced.

Product/Service Planning and Design

Planning products and services is a strategic process that involves three basic steps: (1) generating product/service ideas; (2) selecting the ideas that seem technologically feasible, marketable, and compatible with the organization's overall strategy; and (3) producing a final design of the product or service.

Although research and development, marketing, finance, and human resources all provide important input, operations managers have the primary role in deciding whether a product or service is actually feasible. To do this, they weigh the product or service's *producibility* against what is known about competitive priorities of quality level, quality reliability, and pricing.

Taken literally, the question of *producibility* simply asks: Can a product or service be produced economically and at acceptable levels of quality and reliability within the existing operations system; and if not, what kind of adjustments must be made to so produce it? These adjustments may involve the existing operations system or the new product or service's design.

DESIGN FOR MANUFACTURE (DFM). One of the most promising trends in this area is *design for manufacture (DFM),* which streamlines design to simplify assembly. Bell Labs successfully used this technique to design a new digital loop carrier, a device that transmits phone signals through fiber-optic cable. Instead of ironing out production problems on the factory floor, design engineers and production engineers worked together to select plastics that could stand up to the heat of manufacture and to identify and eliminate potentially costly engineering mistakes before production began. The result: The 1990 version had 60 percent fewer errors than the 1986 version.[6]

CAD. At one time, product design was a time-consuming multistep process that involved the creation and testing of prototypes, or working models. Today this process is faster and cheaper thanks to **computer-aided design (CAD),** which allows product design, drafting, and testing to be performed interactively on a computer.

Because 80 percent of a product's cost is determined by its design, most manufacturers are turning to simultaneous engineering, where design and manufacturing engineers work together to simplify a design. General Motors now uses CAD to design the metal-stamping dies for its new cars. Car bodies are made from sheet metal that is stamped in large presses that use different dies, or stamping forms, to bend the metal into hoods, fenders, and so on. These dies must be carefully designed to prevent wrinkling or tearing the sheet metal during the process. With CAD, GM designers can create and test computer models of proposed dies early in the design process. Before CAD, it took about 27 months to create the tooling for new car models. With CAD, GM officials estimated, the time has been cut by up to 7 months.[7]

The benefits of CAD do not stop there. Because the design is stored in the computer system, it can be "exploded" to create a **bill of materials,** a listing of the type and number of parts needed to make each unit. As we will see later, this information is crucial for ensuring that the organization has adequate supplies of the right materials on hand when needed. And as we will soon see, the computer-generated design can be used to automate and control the entire operations process.

Capacity Planning

The second decision in designing the operations system is *how many* products—or *how much* service—will be produced. This is called **capacity planning,** a process of forecasting demand and then deciding what resources will be needed to meet that demand. This process is summed up in Exhibit 21-2.

Long-range technological forecasting—which can extend five or ten years into the future—may be needed to anticipate or forecast future capacity demands. Unforeseeable events—new technological discoveries, wars, recessions, embargoes,

EXHIBIT 21-2 The Complex Process of Capacity Planning

❏ Forecast future demand, including, insofar as possible, the likely impact of technology, competition, and other events.
❏ Translate these forecasts into actual physical capacity requirements.
❏ Generate alternative capacity plans to meet the requirements.
❏ Analyze and compare the economic effects of the alternative plans.
❏ Identify and compare the risks and strategic effects of the alternative plans.

Sources: Everett E. Adam, Jr., and Ronald J. Ebert, *Production and Operations Management: Concepts, Models, and Behavior,* 5th ed. (Englewood Cliffs, N.J.: Prentice Hall, 1986); E. S. Buffa, *Modern Production/Operations Management,* 6th ed. (New York: Wiley, 1980).

COORDINATED RESOURCE
Use Transparency 146, Production and Purchasing Decisions Contrasted for Materials Control.

and the effects of an unknown inflation rate—cannot always be factored into forecasting equations. Although planning demand well into the future is complicated and risky, organizations often properly expend considerable effort in doing so. (See Chapter 10.)

Completed forecasts must be translated into capacity requirements. This implies that existing capacity must be measured. In some cases, measuring capacity is easy enough; for example, gauging the number of tons of steel produced by a steel mill. For a system with a diverse and less readily classified product or service—such as a legal office—measuring capacity is less straightforward. Input measures are generally used for such systems; that is, capacity may be defined as the number of lawyers in the legal office.

Capacity Planning. Because unpredictable events—from OPEC price-fixing to new restrictions on sulfur emissions—routinely sabotaged their long-range capacity planning, Southern California Edison's managers took a new tack. Under "scenario planning," they looked ahead ten years to envision 12 alternative futures—from a Mideast oil crisis to an economic boom—which showed they would need to generate from 5,000 megawatts more to 5,000 megawatts less than the 15,000 megawatts the utility was then producing. With this information, they set about building the right amount of flexibility into their system. To meet fluctuating demand, they can repower or shut down generating plants, buy power from other utilities, and step up or relax programs urging consumers to reduce their electricity consumption.

The forecasted physical capacity requirements may compel the organization to change its operations system to meet future demand. Capacity changes may be brought about by short-run and/or long-run modifications. *Short-run capacity changes* include overtime work, shifting existing personnel, subcontracting, and using inventories or back orders. *Long-run capacity changes* involve adding or removing capacity by physical facility expansion (more press hammers, more lawyers) or contraction (fewer press hammers, fewer lawyers).

Alternative capacity plans, each of which fits the required demand but through different means (more press hammers, subcontracting), should be analyzed. The costs of each and all of their strategic effects should be weighed and compared. The alternative with the lowest cost could turn out to result in lost sales and lost market share, which may (or may not) be inconsistent with organizational strategy. (A subcontracting slowdown may cause delays in delivery and thus loss of market to a competitor.) Costs, risks, and strategic effects must be thoughtfully weighed by managers.

Process Selection

Process selection, which determines *how* the product or service will be produced, involves four technological decisions.

MAJOR TECHNOLOGICAL CHOICE. Does technology exist to produce the product? Are there competing technologies among which we should choose? Should innovations be licensed from elsewhere, such as foreign countries, or should an internal effort be made to develop the needed technology? The importance of the major technological choice phase is highlighted by such recent developments as microchips and gene splicing. Although the major technological choice is largely the province of engineers, chemists, biogeneticists, and other technical specialists, top managers should comprehend as fully as possible the technology, its likely evolution, and the alternatives.

MINOR TECHNOLOGICAL CHOICE. Once the major technological choice is made, there may be a number of minor technological *process alternatives* available. The operations manager should be involved in evaluating alternative transformation processes for costs and for consistency with the desired product and capacity plans. Should the process be continuous? A continuous process, which is carried out 24 hours a day to avoid expensive startups and shutdowns, is used by the steel and chemical industries, among others. An assembly-line process follows the same series of steps to mass-produce each item, but need not run 24 hours a day; examples are the automobile and ready-to-wear clothing industries. Job-shop processes produce items in small lots, perhaps custom-made for a given market or customer; examples are lumberyards and aircraft manufacturers.

Even if the continuous versus job-shop choice can be easily made, the alternatives do not end there. For example, in a factory, the fabrication, joining together, and finishing of two pieces of metal may represent only a minuscule part of creating a finished product, but there may be numerous ways of casting and molding, several ways of cutting, forming, assembling, and finishing. A simple hardware operation could thus involve choosing among 46 process alternatives and numerous combinations. Deciding on the best combination of processes in terms of costs and the total operations process can be difficult.

SPECIFIC-COMPONENT CHOICE. What type of equipment (and degree of automation) should be used? Should the equipment be dedicated (tied to a specific purpose) or general purpose (leaving open the possibility of using it to make other products)? To what degree should machines replace people in performing and controlling the work? Increasingly, human workers are being used to program and monitor automated equipment, rather than doing the work themselves.

This trend began in the early 1960s, when numerically controlled (NC) lathes, milling machines, and drill presses began to invade the shop floor. These were *dedicated machines,* meaning they performed a specific task according to instructions contained in a program written on plastic mylar tape. (There was no memory, as in a computer.) The strength of NC machines is that they perform operations with a consistency and reliability that far exceeds those of the normal machinist. Their weakness is the downtime and expense involved in changing their setup—the task they are ready to perform.

This barrier was overcome, to some extent, when newly developed microcomputer chips were used to create computerized numerical control (CNC) machines. These machines are easier to reprogram and set up for another task, but they cost anywhere from $50,000 to $500,000, depending on their size and the complexity of the operations they can perform. Obviously, such a capital investment cannot be taken lightly; it requires good planning and operations management. The same is true of flexible manufacturing systems (FMS), which combine CNC machines in flexible systems of production that can be easily and efficiently set up to produce batches of different products.

CAD/CAM (computer-aided design and computer-automated manufacturing) is an integrated approach in which the computer software that is used to design a product can be used to translate the design into a computer program that will operate the NC or CNC machine. Obviously, only companies that have high-volume production can afford to invest in such a system.

CIM (computer-integrated manufacturing) is an even more integrated approach that incorporates CAD/CAM, robots, and materials-requirement planning (MRP)—a computerized approach to managing *inventory,* the supply of raw materials, partially finished goods, and completed goods needed to meet an organization's operational needs. We'll discuss inventory soon, but first we will take a closer look at the way robots are being used, since they represent a major capital investment and a significant part of many operations systems.

Integrating Computer-Aided Tools. Joseph W. Piteo, manager of engineering automation at the Sikorsky Aircraft Division of United Technologies Corp., leans on a bust of helicopter pioneer and company founder Igor Sikorsky. A computer system named after Igor integrates the division's various computer-aided design, engineering, and manufacturing tools, allowing team members to collaborate on design and production in real time. As a bonus, Igor eliminates engineering "busywork"—the hundreds of minor revisions that used to be required simply because product designers did not know what engineers were doing and vice versa.

CAD/CAM (computer-aided design and computer-automated manufacturing) Integrated approach in which the software used in designing products is also used to write a computer program to control the machinery.

CIM (computer-integrated manufacturing) Integrated approach that combines CAD/CAM with the use of robots and computerized inventory management techniques.

The Future of Robotics. Robot engineers around the world are working to design field robots, such as this Aqua Robot, which inspects undersea building sites for Japan's Transport Ministry. Unlike factory robots, field robots are equipped with wheels, tracks, legs, and even wings that let them move about outside the structured environment of the factory, as well as artificial vision (to prevent robotic pratfalls), and expert-systems software to make fairly quick and independent decisions about inspections, cleaning up nuclear waste sites, fighting fires, and other hazardous tasks.

Most industrial robots are basically computer-controlled mechanical arms that can be equipped with grippers, vacuum cups, painting guns, welding torches, or other tools. As such, they are good choices for moving and handling hazardous materials (hot ingots, radioactive rods) or for performing tasks that require precision under hazardous conditions (spray painting and welding). Robots, for example, can paint for hours without suffering ill effects from breathing the fumes; as a bonus, they use 50 percent less paint than human workers. In the future, more sophisticated robots will be equipped with video imaging systems, allowing them to "see" their work, and onboard computers, allowing them to independently perform certain tasks.

PROCESS-FLOW CHOICE. How should the product or service flow through the operations system? The final process-selection step determines how materials and products will move through the system. Assembly drawings, assembly charts, route sheets, and process flow charts are used to analyze process flow. Analysis may lead to resequencing, combining, or eliminating operations to reduce materials-handling and storage costs. In general, the less storage and delay involved in the process, the better.

In recent years, greater use has been made of automated guided vehicle systems (AGVS), which employ driverless battery-operated vehicles to move back and forth between pickup and delivery points. Currently, this is achieved by placing a wire guide path in the floor that can be sensed by the vehicles' antennas. Research is now in process to do away with the wire and to combine AGVS with robotics to create mobile robots.[8] Some organizations have extended this approach to automate their warehouse and loading facilities.

The four phases of process selection are closely interrelated. In each phase, choices should be made to minimize the process operations costs.

INTERNATIONAL MANAGEMENT

Inching Toward a Free Trade Agreement with Mexico

Carlos Salinas de Gotari, the president of Mexico, is a Harvard-trained economist with a mission: to raise the standard of living for his people and stem the tide of money, technology, and jobs streaming into other Third World nations in Asia and Eastern Europe. His most daring proposal to date is a free trade agreement with the United States, which would eliminate many of Mexico's barriers to imports and pave the way to creating a North American common market 25 percent larger than the European Community. (The United States already has a similar free trade agreement with Canada.)

The plan, proposed in 1990, has the support of the Bush administration, which sees it as a way to stabilize the troubled Mexican economy and reinforce Salinas's pro–United States stance. In addition, the free trade agreement could provide a needed boost to the U.S. economy, since Mexico has a large educated middle class that would be likely customers for U.S. goods. (U.S. trade with Mexico tripled between 1986 and 1990.) The plan is controversial, though, and faces stiff opposition from U.S. labor leaders, workers, and environmentalists.

The most obvious fear is that hundreds of thousands of U.S. workers would lose their jobs. The rea-

Will Mexico's Gain Be Detroit's Loss? Under the proposed free trade agreement, more U.S. factories may join this Chrysler factory "south of the border."

In service systems, process selection depends on the nature of the system. Service systems with low customer contact, such as the check-clearing operation of a bank, can carry out process selection by following the four phases outlined above. In systems with high customer contact, such as retail establishments, the processes or procedures for interacting with the customer must also be selected. For a standardized service, these processes can be specific and allow for little variability—for example, the cash-dispensing function of an automated teller machine (ATM) at a bank. For customized services, variable procedures must be designed—for example, the evaluation of a personal loan application at the same bank. There are specialized computer systems designed to assist bank, department store, and other service industry managers in performing customized evaluations.[9] Large banks, like the Bank of America and Chase Manhattan, use such systems to assist their officers in evaluating loan applications from traders and companies dealing in less developed countries.

Facility-Location Planning

Choosing where to locate the production facility is one of the most important design decisions. The bigger the mistake in locating a factory, a department, or a machine,

son? Under a free trade agreement, all import duties are waived. This means that a product made in Mexico can be imported into the United States without penalty, freeing manufacturers to move production to wherever they can find the cheapest source of acceptable labor. This is not a new threat, of course. For the past 25 years, U.S. manufacturers have been building *maquiladora* plants just across the border in Mexico, where workers assemble products for as little as $5 a day. (The average U.S. worker makes over $14 an *hour*.) Today there are more than 1,500 *maquiladoras* clustered along the 2,000-mile border between the two nations.

Many major corporations are moving beyond the "screwdriver" approach of the *maquiladoras,* however, to set up more sophisticated plants deeper inside Mexico. IBM, Hewlett-Packard, Wang, and others have created a Mexican Silicon Valley in Guadalajara, and many of their suppliers are following suit. Meanwhile, other corporations, such as Ford Motor Co., Bayer, and Kodak, are setting up training schools within Mexico and even sending Mexican workers to the United States for training. These more skilled jobs will command higher wages, a key to improving Mexico's overall standard of living. Eventually, Mexican wages may approach those in the United States, a pattern that has occurred in South Korea and other Third World nations. In the meantime, though, many U.S. workers envision this trend as exerting more pressure to keep their own wages down.

Environmentalists are protesting Mexico's lax enforcement of environmental standards. Mexico City is cloaked in a haze of smog, and the lower Rio Grande enters the United States as a cesspool of chemical wastes and raw sewage. Add the burden of *more* industrialization, coupled with the desire to minimize the costs associated with environmental constraints, experts say, and environmental standards for the entire continent might suffer. Salinas is not insensitive to these concerns. Under pressure from environmentalists, he has used his powers as president to close a number of Mexican and foreign-owned plants for violating environmental standards.

It will not be easy to clean up the existing pollution or to improve Mexico's infrastructure—the physical facilities needed to support more extensive industrialization. The electrical supply is unreliable in Mexico, the roads are bumpy, and the telephones don't always work—a nightmare for far-flung multinationals that need to keep in constant contact with their foreign operations. Still, many managers, economists, and government officials take the long view. Given the events of the past decade, they say, some sort of free trade agreement is inevitable. The only unknowns are *when* the agreement will be formalized and *what* measures will be required to ease the transition.

Sources: Stephen Baker et al., "Mexico: A New Economic Era," *Business Week,* November 12, 1990, pp. 102–110; William J. Holstein, "Is Free Trade with Mexico Good or Bad for the U.S.?" *Business Week,* November 12, 1990, pp. 112–113; Paul Magnusson et al., "The Mexico Pact: Worth the Price?" *Business Week,* May 27, 1991, pp. 32–35.

the more costly it will be, the less likely it will be changed, and the longer it will affect the operation.

The objective of location planning is to position the capacity of the system in a way that minimizes total production and distribution costs. For every new or additional facility, *fixed capital costs* for construction, land, and equipment, as well as *variable operations costs,* such as wages, taxes, energy and materials acquisition, and distribution, are incurred. The location decision requires balancing all of these costs, effects on potential revenues, and qualitative factors such as labor availability, union activity, quality of life, and community attitudes.

Location analysis proceeds by determining location requirements and then evaluating alternative regions, communities, and specific sites, using traditional financial models, linear programming, statistical models, computer simulation models, and location factor rating models. For many manufacturing firms, labor costs are a primary consideration in selecting a location. Many labor-intensive operations have already moved to Mexico, a trend that may accelerate if a free trade agreement with Mexico becomes a reality. (See the International Management box.) For many service organizations—particularly convenience services—nearness to the customer is often the chief consideration in the selection process because the location strongly affects demand and revenue.

Layout Planning

Layout planning involves decisions about *how* to arrange the physical facilities spatially. This is the integrative phase of designing the operations system. In layout planning, process and equipment decisions are translated into physical arrangements for production.

Space must be provided for:

❑ *Productive facilities,* such as work stations and materials-handling equipment.
❑ *Nonproductive facilities,* such as storage areas and maintenance facilities.
❑ *Support facilities,* such as offices, restrooms, waiting rooms, cafeterias, and parking lots.

Space must also be provided for materials and additional capacity. Any location-related requirements, such as docking facilities or heating units, must also be planned.

A good layout minimizes materials handling, maximizes worker and equipment efficiency, and satisfies a host of other factors, such as minimizing worker exposure to hazardous fumes. Layouts can be characterized by work flow or by the function of the operations system.

work-flow layout Layout planning concerned with product layouts (for the sequential steps in production), process layouts (for arranging production according to task), and fixed-position layouts (for handling such large or heavy products as ships).

Work-flow layouts include:

❑ *Product layouts,* arranged for the sequential steps used in producing the product or rendering the service. Such a layout is appropriate for continuous or repetitive operations, such as mass-producing air conditioners or serving food in a cafeteria. (Figure 21-2 depicts a simple product layout in a small factory.)
❑ *Process layouts,* arranged according to task. Such a layout is appropriate for job-shop operations systems, such as universities and automotive repair shops, where there is no one route through the system for all products or services.
❑ *Fixed-position layouts,* where a large or heavy production itself—such as a ship—stays in one location, with people, tools, materials, and equipment moved to the product as needed.

FIGURE 21-2 A Simple Product Layout
Source: Production and Operations Management, Third Edition, by Arthur C. Laufer. Published by South-Western Publishing Co., Cincinnati, Ohio. Reprinted by permission of the author.

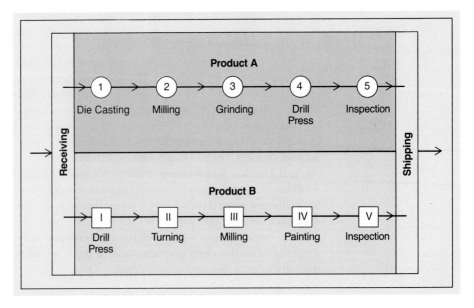

Layout Planning via Computer. Alan B. Pritsker displays some of the animated simulation software Pritsker & Association Inc. created to help managers plan a layout and see how it will function at various levels of capacity. A similar system at Polaroid is generating savings 150 percent greater than the cost of the system.

Function layouts include:

❏ *Storage layouts,* designed to minimize inventory and storage costs, as in warehouses.

❏ *Marketing layouts,* designed to maximize product exposure and sales. Supermarkets are an example.

❏ *Project layouts,* established to build projects or one-of-a-kind products, such as dams or buildings. This differs from the fixed-position layout described earlier in that the latter is designed to turn out more than one unit of a large product.

In practice, most operations systems use a combination of layouts appropriate to the needs of different stages of product or service creation.

Job Design

The final decision in designing the operations system concerns the structure of individual jobs—*how* the work will be done and *who* will do it, a process discussed in Chapter 12. Because job design is reflected in labor expenses, any inefficiencies or mistakes here will ultimately affect operating costs. In recent years, two issues have become especially important for job design: the level of skills and attitudes employees bring to the workplace and their safety once they are there.

WORKER SKILLS AND ATTITUDES. Employers have always expected to provide some on-the-job training for new employees. The problem today is that many U.S. job applicants lack even basic reading and math skills, partly because of inadequate education systems. For example, one international fastener manufacturer in the United States has applicants fill out application forms in person to be sure they know how to read and write. This "skills shortage" is expected to get worse as computers and other sophisticated technology become more commonplace. Clearly the days of the unskilled blue-collar worker are numbered.

Motivation is also a problem, especially in the low-paying jobs that characterize the growing service sector. One study reported that more than 80 percent of employers had as their primary concern finding workers with a good work ethic and appropriate social behavior and attitudes. They simply could not find enough applicants who were reliable and pleasant.[10]

As a result, some regions with inadequate school systems are losing businesses or finding it hard to attract new ones. In response, some school systems are offering to certify their students—in effect, to offer a warranty that their graduates have a certain level of skills. Other experts are suggesting that the United States adopt such a policy on a national level, perhaps through a standardized testing program. On a smaller scale, the state of Georgia is implementing a mandatory pass/fail work ethic program through its Department of Technical and Adult Education. Graduates who are willing to show up on time, dress properly, and try to meet or exceed work quotas are seen as essential to providing a viable work force for the state.

Another option is some sort of government-sponsored apprenticeship project wherein youths who drop out of high school are enrolled in programs that combine work experience with targeted classroom time to prepare them to be skilled craftsmen, such as plumbers and electricians. Such programs are common in Europe.

Traditional job training and employment programs by themselves are unlikely to have a profound impact on the future success of minority youths, though. Consider the $4 billion Job Training Partnership Act (JTPA) system, a partnership between the federal government and private industry created to place such youths in decent-paying jobs with a future.[11] A jet engine manufacturer in the Southeast was unable to fill the quota for a JTPA program for machinists because there weren't enough applicants who could do arithmetic with fractions, a skill that is supposed to be learned in elementary school.

As a result, many organizations are adding on-site training programs intended to increase work-force literacy. If workers are weak in reading or math, for instance, they are taught remedial skills, using the types of reading materials and calculations essential to their jobs. Like Corning, these firms are finding the expense pays off in improved productivity and quality.

WORKER SAFETY. Job design must also take into account health and safety requirements set forth in the Occupational Safety and Health Act of 1970 (OSHA) and subsequent federal, state, and local regulations.

One of the most serious issues is repetitive motion injuries—potentially crippling tendonitis or nerve damage in the hands and wrists that results from performing the same motions over and over again. Such injuries are most common among production workers, who often perform the same task thousands of times on an 8-hour shift, but white-collar workers who type at computers for long periods of time are also vulnerable.

Ergonomics, the biological design of jobs to reduce such hazards, is receiving new respect. OSHA recently prepared guidelines to prevent repetitive motion injuries. It forced Ford Motor Co. to institute company-wide programs to cut down on such injuries, sometimes by simply repositioning materials.[12] Tendonitis was also a hazard at a zipper company, where workers tested zippers by hand. At first, the company introduced job rotation to minimize the risk, but eventually it decided to turn the testing over to robots.

■ OPERATIONAL PLANNING AND CONTROL DECISIONS

COORDINATED RESOURCE
Use Transparency 145, Model of an Operations Planning and Control System.

Even after the operations system has been successfully designed and placed into actual operation, much of the managerial challenge remains. That is because decisions on a shorter-term basis—month to month, day to day, even hour to hour— must be made as to how the system will be operated and controlled. As Figure 21-3

ILLUSTRATIVE CASE STUDY

CONTINUED

At Ford, Quality Is Job One

Cost cutting became a priority in the early 1980s, as Caldwell and Petersen initiated a plan to trim Ford's worldwide labor force of 380,000 by some 50,000 jobs. In so doing, they sent out a clear message to the organization. Cooperation with the new culture at Ford was necessary for everyone who wished to participate in the company's rebirth. By the same token, new avenues for active participation were opened up. A firm believer in participative management, Petersen welcomed input from individuals at every level of the organization, from vice presidents to assembly-line workers. "I want you to remember one thing," he was proud of saying. "The credit goes here to my team, not me."

Second, Ford embarked on an unprecedented program of quality control that went hand-in-hand with its new policy of participative management. "We stopped shipping products," recalls Caldwell, now a senior director at Shearson Lehman Brothers, "if an employee on the floor said they weren't right, and we stopped penalizing people if they didn't make their quotas because of worries about quality. That was a radical departure for Ford." Having concurred with the industry-wide analysis that *quality* was the key to rejuvenation, Ford management undertook an ambitious program to improve quality control procedures.

During the initial stages of the quality control program, Ford managers discovered that many of the company's materials and component parts were inferior, making it necessary to rework many assembled vehicles in order to satisfy factory inspection standards. Not surprisingly, the process of reworking slowed down the production process considerably. After more stringent quality control measures were imposed, Ford encountered additional problems. Although plant layouts were generally well designed, there was poor coordination of work effort. Frequently, materials or assemblies failed to arrive at designated work centers when they were needed to keep the overall production process at full-activity levels. In addition, despite heavy expenditures on market research designed to forecast consumer demand, Ford often found itself with large stockpiles of finished cars sitting in storage areas awaiting delivery to franchise operators. Moreover, franchise dealers across the country continued to report a high incidence of consumer complaints and repairs having to be made during warranty periods.

To overcome these problems, Ford management made *preventive* quality control a high priority throughout the organization. Materials and parts were procured only from reliable suppliers, inspected upon delivery, and placed in service only when deemed acceptable. Millions of dollars were invested in robots and other specialized equipment to ensure precision assembly. Perhaps most importantly, in keeping with Petersen's philosophy of participative management, the company formed employee groups that incorporated workers into the quality control effort. An extensive system was established to monitor operations continually, and the resultant data were used to compare system performance against production input, processing, and output standards. New statistical techniques were adopted throughout the process.

Even these measures did not satisfy Petersen. Too often, he told *Forbes's* Jerry Flint, U.S. manufacturers ran into "whoops"—significant design mistakes that were not discovered until plant layouts were fixed and expensive equipment ordered or set up. Should the managers try to fix the original problem or just push on? Both options were costly and risky. To avoid this excruciating dilemma, Ford used "design for manufacture" to create the Ford Taurus.

Five years before the first year of production, plant workers at Ford's plant in Atlanta, Georgia, were asked to critique drawings and clay models of the new car. According to plant manager Robert Anderson, workers made over 400 suggestions that simplified the design and increased the economy and quality of production. The Taurus front bumper, for example, has just 10 parts; the bumper on a comparable GM model has 100. Fewer parts means fewer fasteners, fewer attachment and adjustment points—and fewer chances for things to go wrong.

Productivity and quality have both increased at Ford Atlanta. Where there were once 150 cars in the area set aside for repairing cars damaged during the manufacture process, there are now fewer than two dozen. Another measure of productivity is the number of labor hours required to build each Taurus—17.6, down from the 25.8 hours needed in 1986 and just slightly more than the 17 used in a typical Japanese plant. By comparison, a typical GM model takes around 27 labor hours and a representative European model uses about 35 hours.

None of these measures captures one of the most impressive gains made at Ford—the spirit that has even veteran workers looking for the little things that help Ford make quality job one. As we will soon see, this passion for continuous improvements is the essence of the world's new respect for quality.

Sources: Robert E. Petersen, "How Ford Became #1," *Motor Trend* 39, no. 12 (1987): 4, 6–7; Robert E. Petersen and H. A. Poling, "The U.S.: Team at the Top of No. 2," *Fortune,* November 9, 1987, p. 82; J. S. Treece, "Donald Petersen," *Business Week,* April 15, 1988, pp. 131–134; Brian Dumaine, "A Humble Hero Drives Ford to the Top," *Fortune,* January 4, 1988, 22–24; and Donald R. Katz, "Coming Home," *Business Month,* October 1988, pp. 56–62; Jerry Flint, "We Need Manufacturing People at the Top," *Forbes,* August 20, 1990, pp. 58–60; and "Banzai with a Georgia Accent," *Forbes,* February 4, 1991, pp. 58–62.

FIGURE 21-3 Model of Operations Planning and Control System
Source: Adapted from Elwood S. Buffa, *Modern Production/Operations Management,* 6th ed., p. 159. Copyright © 1980 by John Wiley & Sons. Used by permission.

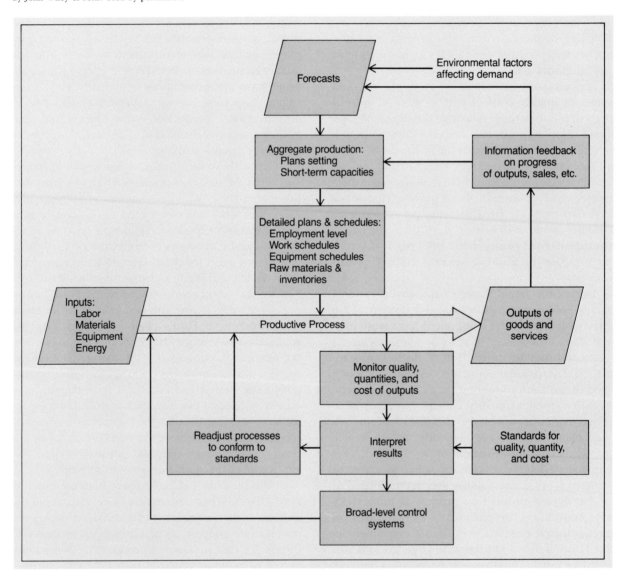

HERE'S AN EXAMPLE
At Westinghouse's Electronic Systems Group, both design and manufacturing are under one manager. (*Business Week,* 4/30/90, p. 110ff.)

illustrates, operational planning and control decisions involve scheduling and control of labor, materials, and capital input to produce the desired quantity and quality of output most efficiently.

Operational planning and control are based on forecasts of future demand for the output of the system, but even with the best possible forecasting and the most finely tuned operations system, demand cannot always be met with existing system capacity in a given time period. Unexpected market trends, new-product developments, or competitors' actions can throw the forecasts off, and problems in the operations system can reduce capacity. At these times, shorter-term managerial decisions must be made to allocate system capacity to meet demand.

Operations Planning and Control

COORDINATED RESOURCE
See Oddou section on Controlling the Organization, "Production and Operations Control."

COORDINATED RESOURCE
See Study Guide Self-Learning Exercise 21, "Operational Control."

COORDINATED RESOURCE
Use Transparency 147, Break-Even Graph.

Operations managers typically formulate plans that range from daily or weekly to yearly in outlook. The objectives of operations planning and control are to maximize customer service, minimize inventory investment, and maximize system operating efficiency. Often these three objectives conflict, and plans must be made to obtain the best balance. For example, if operations managers focus too rigidly on minimizing inventory investment, a sudden increase in sales will make it difficult to meet customer service requirements.

To some extent, completely meeting any one of the objectives means sacrificing the other two. A system may operate with the greatest efficiency when it is put into operation only after sufficient orders have been received to require a large batch of output. In meeting the third objective, then, management will definitely have failed to meet the first, since customers will have to wait for some time for service. The second objective has also been slighted because our large-batch philosophy demands a large available stock of input materials in inventory. By keeping enough output in inventory to satisfy some orders, management could achieve a higher degree of customer service and still maintain operating efficiency. However, that policy would require a larger inventory investment than the large-batch philosophy.

And so it goes . . . the trade-off calculations are endless. Achieving a balance in operations objectives is one of the most delicate jobs within an organization.

PRODUCTION PLANS. Production plans are based on forecasts. First, overall plans are made for a 6- to 18-month period. These aggregate production plans specify how operations system capacity will be used to meet anticipated output demands. The variables in the operations system that can be controlled are aggregate production rates, employment levels, and inventory levels. Next, the aggregate operations plans must be translated into master production schedules that specify the quantity and short-term timing of specific end products.[13]

DETAILED SCHEDULING WITH PROJECT MANAGEMENT (PM) SOFTWARE. Detailed or short-term scheduling specifies the quantity and type of items to be produced and how, when, and where they should be produced for the next day or week. One of the most impressive innovations in production scheduling is project management (PM) software for personal computers. These programs range in price from under $500 to about $6,000 and provide, in addition to detailed schedules of people and material resources, 11 to 16 types of standard reports. Unlike the simpler Gantt or PERT charts, PM software provides continuous updating and lets managers experiment with what-if scenarios to find the fastest and cheapest way to accomplish assignments involving hundreds or even thousands of related subtasks.[14]

Inventory Management

inventory Supply of raw materials, work in progress, and finished goods an organization maintains to meet its operational needs.

work in progress Partially finished goods; also called *work in process.*

COORDINATED RESOURCE
Use Transparency 148, Determining the Most Economic Order Quantity.

materials-requirements planning (MRP) Operational planning system whereby end products are analyzed to determine the materials needed to produce them.

materials-resource planning (MRP II) Compares MRP needs to known resources and calculates unit costs; can also be used with other computer programs to handle order entry, invoicing, and other operations tasks.

just-in-time (JIT) inventory system Inventory system in which production quantities are ideally equal to delivery quantities, with materials purchased and finished goods delivered "just in time for usage."

Inventory is the supply of raw materials, partially finished goods—called **work in progress**—and finished goods an organization maintains to meet its operational needs. As such, it represents a sizable investment and a potential source of waste that needs to be carefully controlled. If an organization keeps too much inventory on hand, it will waste money storing it and lose money if inventories are damaged or stolen. On the other hand, an organization that runs out of inventory may have to stop production until the necessary materials are supplied, wasting time and labor. To minimize these costs and maintain inventories at optimum levels, numerous mathematical and computer-based inventory models have been developed to help operations managers decide when and how much inventory to order. The three most important methods are materials-requirements planning (MRP), materials-resource planning (MRP II), and just-in-time inventory (JIT).

MATERIALS-REQUIREMENTS PLANNING AND MATERIALS-RESOURCE PLANNING. **Materials-requirements planning (MRP)** was a first attempt to look at a product and, by working backward, determine all the materials, labor and other resources required to produce it. This helps managers see the impact of late deliveries, low-quality raw materials, and so forth on the production system. This degree of control would not be possible without computer systems able to process the massive amounts of information needed to describe typically complex products and production systems.

Materials-resource planning (MRP II) goes beyond MRP to include input from the finance and marketing departments. Whereas MRP focuses merely on planning requirements, MRP II also focuses on available resources. Labor hours and other costs can be integrated into the decision making as per unit costs. MRP II programs can also interface with other programs in the computer system, such as order entry, invoicing, billing, purchasing, capacity planning, and warehouse management. As such, MRP II provides better and more comprehensive control over materials than MRP.

JUST-IN-TIME INVENTORY. Traditionally, operations managers set inventory levels by using formulas that balance the average fixed costs of buying raw materials with the variable costs of storing them. In the mid-1970s, though, the world took notice of the Japanese *kanban,* or **just-in-time (JIT) inventory system.** *Kanban* strives toward an ideal state in which production quantities are equal to delivery quantities. This minimizes carrying costs, the expense of storing and moving inventories from storage to the production floor. Materials are bought more frequently and in smaller amounts, "just in time" to be used, and finished goods are produced and delivered "just in time" to be sold. At one time, an automaker would order a truckload of spark plugs to be delivered within a two- or three-day window. Now that same firm will order a one-quarter load to be delivered within a 2- to 3-*hour* window. The Nissan plant in Smyrna, Tennessee, allows trucks a 1-hour window for delivery. In place of a warehouse, it uses a few trailers across the street from the plant for temporary storage. Trucks are loaded in order of need, with a fork lift coming right off the assembly line to pick up the parts.

JIT savings can be impressive, but the system requires clockwork timing and coordination within the operations system and between the organization and its suppliers to be effective. Even this requirement is seen as a benefit, though, since it can reveal problems in the operation system's design whose correction can yield dramatic improvements in both productivity and quality.

DATA INPUT RECORDERS. One type of data input recorder is the computer-readable bar code ("zebra stripes") that records price and other product information. It is invaluable to retailers, since it speeds up purchases and allows retailers to capture valuable marketing information. But bar codes and similar data input recorders are becoming equally important for operations management.

In many situations, these devices become the process technology. Banks have long used optical character readers (OCRs) and magnetic character readers (MCRs) to automate the sorting and processing of thousands of checks. The U.S. Postal Service also uses OCRs to read and route mail.

In other situations, data input recorders allow operations managers to track work-in-progress inventory, which is useful for a number of reasons. One benefit is that many inventory items, such as car radios and computer disk drives, are valuable; the bar codes let managers track the number of units that are lost, damaged, or stolen. Agents at Avis Rent A Car, for example, use portable hand-held computers to check in rented cars and produce a printed receipt for the customer on the spot. This not only helps Avis's inventory management but also increases the quality level of its services.

A second benefit of bar codes is that they make it easy to identify items produced in a specific batch or lot of goods. If the items are later found to be faulty, the company can use the bar-coded information to issue a targeted recall and protect consumers. As the Ethics in Management box shows, managers cannot predict when this capability will be needed—and quickly.

ETHICS IN MANAGEMENT

Recalling Fords—Just to Be Sure

In 1991, Ford learned an expensive lesson in the value of bar codes. The problem arose when Ford found out that some airbags in its cars might leak burning gases as they unfurled during an accident, endangering the drivers they were meant to save.

The airbags, supplied by TRW Inc., demonstrate the hazards of converting an experimental technology into a mass-produced good. An airbag is a complex system made up of sensors that detect an impact and then explode a small canister of gas, which temporarily inflates a parachutelike balloon to cushion the auto occupant's impact. It is also one of the most in-demand safety features on new cars today. To meet the demand, TRW tried to accelerate production by using robots to automate tasks previously performed by hand. But an out-of-tolerance machine damaged the threading on a joint in the airbag module, which *might* have allowed a few bags to spill their gases. No injuries have occurred because of the defect, and TRW stressed that few airbags had the defect.

The only problem was no one knew *which* airbags had the defect, for neither TRW nor Ford had used bar coding or any other system to identify individual airbags or the production lots they came from. What should Ford managers do? If they ignored the defect, someone might eventually be hurt, either from the gases or from an improperly cushioned impact. Furthermore, the company would be legally liable for ignoring a known product hazard.

TRW workers cut out airbags by hand.

To play it safe, Ford issued a multimillion-dollar recall of 165,000 cars, even though the best estimates indicated that little more than 3,000 cars had the defective airbags. Ford also announced that it expected TRW to share in the expense. At the same time, it canceled its exclusive contract with TRW, assigning 20 percent of its airbag business to TRW competitors, with plans to routinely buy airbags from multiple sources by the mid-1990s. This was a major blow to TRW and left industry observers shaking their heads over the hidden expense of not using bar codes.

Source: Dana Milbank, "Airbag Woes Knock Wind Out of TRW," *The Wall Street Journal,* March 12, 1991, p. A4.

A third benefit of bar codes is that they can be used to track the progress of items though an operations systems. This provides an accurate and timely measure of how smoothly and efficiently the system is functioning. Some railroads now use bar codes or transponders to track shipments as they pass sensors at specific points. This information is then fed into a computerized tracking system.

FUTURE TRENDS. A number of interesting developments promise to improve inventory management for both service and production organizations in the coming decade.

One such development is the electronic pen, which United Parcel Service (UPS) has been testing since 1990. An electronic pen is a nylon stylus that can be used to write on a sensitive membrane embedded in a handheld computer. In UPS's case, the computer is built into the top of the driver's clipboard. Instead of signing a piece of paper with a pen, recipients use the electronic pen, which creates an electronic image of the signature and stores it with information about the delivery, entered either by keyboard or bar code scanner. UPS's goal is to do away with the mass of paper it now uses to document its millions of deliveries and to provide computer access to delivery information. Although the system is not expected to save much money, it will improve customer service, letting UPS respond more promptly to the 250,000 calls it receives each day from customers asking about the status of their deliveries.[15] State Farm Mutual Automobile Insurance of Bloomington, Illinois, is experimenting with a notepad computer from IBM that would allow agents to use an electronic pen to enter claims information on the site of accidents and natural disasters. The advantage of these notepad computers is that they can be carried into areas where laptops would be too heavy or clumsy to transport.[16]

■ *QUALITY CONTROL*

quality control Strategy for managing each stage of production so as to minimize or eliminate errors.

COORDINATED RESOURCE
See *Management Live!* Reading 11.1, "Making It Right the First Time."

FOR DISCUSSION
Why is quality such a popular topic?

Many people see **quality control** as *the* competitive issue of today and the future. In fact, quality may be one of the most important ways to "add value" to products and services and set them apart from competitors. Therefore, instead of being seen as a mere inspection task, quality control is now being viewed as an integral part of company strategy. One result is that quality control is consciously considered at each stage of the operations process, with the goal of identifying and correcting mistakes as soon as possible, rather than waiting until the end of the operations process to discard or rework flawed goods.

At one time, managers thought there was an inevitable trade-off between productivity and quality: To get more of one, you had to give up some of the other. Today, though, effective managers see productivity and quality as two sides of the same coin—one that can increase profits and build customer loyalty. Following the Japanese lead, Lee Iacocca turned the phrase "quality and productivity—they go together" into one of his major reform measures when he assumed the helm of the troubled Chrysler Corporation in 1978.[17] He foresaw that improved quality meant lower costs for repairs, inspection, scrap, and product warranties—a realization now common in most leading organizations. We can see why and how management views of quality changed by tracing the concept's evolution.

Traditional Quality Control

Traditional quality control focuses on identifying mistakes rather than on preventing them. Its two main techniques are *acceptance sampling* and *process control.* These techniques were developed during the 1930s at Bell Telephone Labs by Dr. Walter Shewart, one of the pioneers of quality control. Together, they are sometimes referred to as *statistical quality control,* since they involve sampling a statistically significant portion of a production lot rather than testing every item.

process-control procedure Quality control procedure for monitoring quality during production of the product or rendering of the service.

acceptance-sampling procedure Quality control procedure to determine if the finished product conforms to design specifications.

A Pioneer in Total Quality Management. W. Edwards Deming found fame teaching the Japanese about quality.

quality circles Work groups that meet to discuss ways to improve quality and solve production problems.

total quality management (TQM) Strategic commitment to improving quality by combining statistical quality control methods with a cultural commitment to seeking incremental improvements that increase productivity and lower costs.

Process-control procedures determine if a process is in control by measuring output and comparing it to preestablished standards. For example, canned soups need to remain within certain temperature guidelines during processing. If the temperature becomes too high, the soup might taste burned; if it falls too low, dangerous bacteria will not be killed. If process-control procedures detect a shift beyond an accepted temperature range, corrective action can be taken.

Acceptance-sampling procedures, in contrast, test a small sample of a batch to see if the batch as a whole should be accepted, rejected, or undergo further tests. This is a go/no go measure, and statistical charts determine the size of the lot to be sampled and how many units have to be "bad" before the lot is rejected or tested further.

Quality Assurance

Rather than dwell on the negative, quality assurance programs, introduced in the late 1960s, seek to check for quality in a positive way. The premise here is that people, not the process, are the key to quality, and workers are urged to strive for "zero defects." Over the long run, this approach has not proved very effective, though, because it assumes that workers can prevent defects that in all likelihood result from poorly designed operations systems.

Total Quality Management (TQM)

Meanwhile, the quality revolution was being launched in Japan by two Americans, W. Edwards Deming and J. M. Juran, whose lectures inspired a nation intent on rebuilding an economy devastated by World War II.[18]

One of Juran's key ideas was to define quality as "fitness for use," a phrase that referred to how well a product or service satisfied a customer's real needs. By focusing on these real needs, Juran felt, managers and workers could concentrate their effort where it really mattered. Deming, perhaps the most widely recognized American in Japanese manufacturing circles, questioned the basic assumption that high quality meant higher prices. He felt that "constancy of purpose"—an unwavering focus on an organization's mission—combined with statistical quality control, would lead to ever-improving quality at lower costs. Moreover, Deming believed the manager's job is to seek out and correct the *causes* of failure, rather than merely identify failures after they occur. Under the influence of these two men, the Japanese spent their money on designing operations systems that produced products with extremely small margins of error and mistakes.

Commitment to quality became a part of every plant's culture instead of just a slogan or an afterthought. The commitment was reinforced by the introduction of **quality circles,** work groups that meet to discuss ways to improve quality and solve production problems. This deeply embedded strategic commitment to quality has become known as **total quality management (TQM).**

The new GM Saturn plant in Tennessee represents GM's all-out effort to outdo Japanese competitors on quality performance. Decisions are made by teams of people who will be affected by the decision. Every decision must be supported by at least 70 percent of the members; failing this, all parties must bring additional facts to the meeting. If the company does not meet its quality goals, all members, including managers, can lose up to 20 percent of their pay. People can also receive rewards by exceeding company goals.[19]

Quality Awards

In appreciation for all that W. Edwards Deming did to rebuild its postwar production system, Japan named its highest quality award for him. The prestigious Deming Prize, created in 1951, is seen as an indication of Japan's commitment to quality.

The much more recent commitment to quality in the United States is honored by the Malcolm Baldrige National Quality Award. This award, named after a former secretary of commerce, was created in 1987 to acknowledge manufacturers, services, and small businesses that have made outstanding improvements in their quality. Applicants are judged on leadership, effectiveness in collecting and analyzing information, planning, human resource utilization, quality assurance, quality assurance results, and customer satisfaction. Applicants are screened on the basis of a written application and then inspected by a team of examiners who observe operations and interview employees and managers at all levels. At the Cadillac division of GM, a 1990 winner, the focus on quality has led to more open communication between management, workers, and their customers. Managers periodically work on the production line, and workers call customers to ask them if they are satisfied with their cars. In addition, production workers building prototypes have identified hundreds of potential problems, as well as ways to simplify designs and reduce costs. As a result, the front bumpers of 1992 Cadillac Eldorados will have just 139 parts, instead of 249.[20]

Many nonprofit firms that have adopted total quality management are asking that a category be added for them, and health-care and education organizations are also lobbying for their own categories.[21] Clearly, total quality management has become a driving force for U.S. organizations and will remain a force well into the future.

ILLUSTRATIVE CASE STUDY

WRAP-UP

At Ford, Quality Is Job One

One of Deming's main ideas is that a "constancy of purpose"—a shared goal—will translate into a number of tiny step-by-step improvements that eventually will create large gains in productivity and quality. This unity of purpose can be seen at the Ford Atlanta plant.

Ford Atlanta manager Jerry Anderson credits the plant's success to hard work, attention to details, and an attitude—shared by the union, workers, and management—that any obstacle can be overcome. The goal, says the local union chairman, is to realize which actions add value to the cars and eliminate wasted steps or motions that do not add value. The pace is demanding, but not grueling, as workers think about their work and look for improvements that will save money and add quality.

Some of the improvements have come from the traditional "waste not, want not" approach to manufacture. For example, a new tool for applying the proper amount of window glass sealant saved 5 gallons of $28-a-gallon sealant a day, plus the time needed to clean off the excess. Metal drums of chemicals that used to be carted away for disposal as hazardous waste when they were emptied were fitted with disposable liners so only the liners have to be discarded and the metal drums can be used again. Other ideas for savings are more elaborate. The inside of auto hoods, which do not need the same protection as the car body, receive only one coat of body-colored primer today, rather than a coat of primer and a coat of body paint. This saves money and the labor of two workers per shift.

Although Ford Atlanta does not use a team approach per se, it relies on committees of hourly workers to solve problems. The Bump and Ding Committee, for example, finally tracked down—and corrected—the source of a tiny scratch on some car hoods. Little steps like these, taken together, add up to savings of 5 to 6 percent every year—savings that are helping Ford meet its competitive priorities. ■

Sources: Robert E. Petersen, "How Ford Became #1," *Motor Trend* 39, no. 12 (1987): 4, 6–7; Robert E. Petersen and H. A. Poling, "The U.S.: Team at the Top of No. 2," *Fortune,* November 9, 1987, p. 82; J. S. Treece, "Donald Petersen," *Business Week,* April 15, 1988, pp. 131–134; Brian Dumaine, "A Humble Hero Drives Ford to the Top," *Fortune,* January 4, 1988, 22–24; Donald R. Katz, "Coming Home," *Business Month,* October 1988, pp. 56–62; Jerry Flint, "We Need Manufacturing People at the Top," *Forbes,* August 20, 1990, pp. 58–60, and "Banzai with a Georgia Accent," *Forbes,* February 4, 1991, pp. 58–62.

The term *operations* refers to the day-to-day activities an organization uses to transform inputs into outputs. As such, operations can be viewed as a system.

Production organizations are primarily concerned with producing physical goods that can be mass-produced and stored for later consumption. Service organizations, in contrast, produce largely intangible goods that require customer participation and cannot be stored.

Operations management is important because it is a way to improve efficiency, as measured by productivity, and increase effectiveness, as measured by an organization's ability to meet customers' competitive priorities of pricing, quality level, quality reliability, and flexibility. In recent years, the traditional focus on purely quantitative measures of productivity has been replaced by a concern for quality and increasing the value of an organization's human capital—its employees.

Designing an operations system is a multistep process that begins with product or service design, which affects capacity-planning, facility-location planning, layout planning, process selection, and job design. One of the most significant changes in recent years is the emphasis on design for manufacture, in which operations managers work with design engineers to simplify designs in order to make them easier to produce and more reliable. Another significant change is the use of computer-aided design. Such designs can be used to generate a bill of materials used in managing inventory and to create the instructions that operate computerized production equipment, a process known as CAD/CAM. Computer-integrated manufacturing (CIM) combines CAD/CAD with robots and computerized inventory management.

Two of the most important issues for job design at the operations level are worker skills and attitudes, which in some cases require remedial training to increase work-force literacy, and worker safety, which can be increased through ergonomics.

Once the operations system is designed, managers must make operational planning and control decisions about production plans, detailed scheduling, and inventory levels. Increasingly, managers are using project management (PM) software for personal computers to track and update schedules involving hundreds and thousands of interrelated tasks.

The term *inventory* refers to the supply of raw materials, work in progress, and finished goods an organization keeps on hand to meet its operational needs. Because it represents an expense, operations managers try to keep inventory levels at optimum levels. Materials-requirements planning (MRP) uses a computerized diagram of products to work backward to determine all materials that will be needed. Materials-resource planning (MRP (II) is a refinement of MRP that factors in unit costs for labor and other resources. Most organizations today are striving for *kanban* or just-in-time (JIT) inventory, which minimizes the expense of storing inactive inventories. Data input recorders, usually in the form of bar code readers, are also being used to record and track information concerning inventory. Electronic pens and notepad computers are other promising developments.

Quality control is *the* competitive issue of today and one of the best ways to add value to products. Although managers once thought that productivity and quality were incompatible, nowadays most managers see them as two sides of the same coin. Traditional quality control methods are sometimes called *statistical quality control,* since they involve sampling statistically significant portions of production lots. These techniques, as well as quality assurance programs, focus on discovering, rather than preventing, errors. Total quality management, in contrast, focuses on designing operations systems that prevent errors. Its leading proponents are J. M. Juran and W. Edwards Deming, whose lectures guided the rebuilding of Japan's industrial base after World War II. Japan showed its gratitude by creating the Deming Award, which also represents a national commitment to improving operations quality. This commitment was echoed in the United States by the creation of the Malcolm Baldrige Award.

1. What are operations and why can they be considered a system?
2. List some of the major differences between products and services.
3. Why is operations management important to efficiency?
4. How does operations management help organizations meet competitive priorities?
5. Why is product or service design important to operations management?
6. How do operations managers perform capacity planning?
7. What are the major considerations in process selection? In facility-location planning?
8. Describe the main types of layouts used in operations.
9. What is involved in operational planning and control?
10. What are the three types of inventory management and why are they important?
11. Describe MRP, MRP II, and JIT inventory.
12. Compare and contrast traditional methods of quality control with total quality management.

CASE STUDY

Operations Management at the U.S. Postal Service

The United States Postal Service (USPS) is the nation's largest employer. Its 760,000 employees handle 160 billion pieces of mail each year—40 percent of the world total. With 180,000 vehicles, 40,000 locations, 300,000 collection points, and 200 "factories" for sorting and routing mail, it is imperative that this huge service organization be run in a cost-effective manner. Mail volume, which has been doubling every 20 years, reached 550 million pieces daily in 1991. In 1981, the average mail carrier spent 33 percent of the workday sorting mail for her or his route; by 1991, this figure was 47 percent and rising.

Currently, mail is taken from collection points, and some of it is manually sorted at the local post office, then sent to a "factory" for further sorting and routing. In 1990, one-third of a sample of 1 million pieces of mail at a factory was incorrectly addressed and needed some intervention. Studies showed that the processing and intervention costs per 1,000 pieces of flat mail were:

❏ *Manual* (hand sort): $40.00/thousand.

❏ *Mechanical* (operators key in information and push buttons for sorting): $18.00/thousand.

❏ *Automated* (optical character readers): $3.50/thousand.

It was determined that if USPS did not completely automate sorting and routing procedures, it would need 1 million employees by the year 2000. Since union rules require that 90 percent of the work force be full time, USPS does not have many options for flexibility by using large numbers of part-timers. Thus, complete automation seemed to be the appropriate response to this situation, though it would require the most radical change in USPS's history.

The critical questions were to determine where to put temporary delivery distribution centers as the old facilities were phased out and new ones inaugurated and in what order should this occur. The goal was to keep costs at a minimum while reaping the benefits of automated equipment such as optical character readers (OCR) and advanced bar code readers (ABCR). Thus, USPS needed a way to evaluate and plan the introduction of these laborsaving devices. To help proceed with the $12 billion automation project, which projected a savings of 100,000 worker-years per year by 1995, when it would be fully implemented, USPS developed a computerized mathematical programming system named M.E.T.A. M.E.T.A. is currently being used by all 73 field managers to determine how best to automate and upgrade their facilities, based on analyses of local space constraints and savings opportunities.

Within two years (1989–1990), with only 20 percent of the equipment installed, USPS had 35,000 fewer employees, even though mail volume had increased by 5 billion pieces yearly. The new technology is capable of reducing in-office sorting time by almost 50 percent. For the first time in the history of USPS, operating costs were below the rate of inflation. In fact, the reason the current stamp has the rather odd price of 29 cents is that the Postal Rate Commission chopped one cent off the USPS's request for 30 cents because the savings from automation were so dramatic.

Still, all is not smooth sailing for USPS. The automation changes require radical changes in the number of employees and what they do. Hours, or jobs, or even workers' locations have to be altered—all of which will cause thorny personnel problems. In addition, the union is asking for a share of the savings in the form of an 8 percent raise and a cutback in work hours to a 35-hour week.

Source: F. Anura H. de Silva and Fred J. DiLisio, "Automating Post Office Operations Economically: Facility and Equipment Planning in the United States Postal Service," *Interfaces* 22, no. 1 (January–February 1992).

Case Questions

1. From your own perspective, who are the main competitors of the U.S. Postal Service?

2. What pressures required USPS to go to automation?

3. What devices are being used by USPS to automate the mail sorting system?

4. What human factors complicate this automation?

VIDEO CASE STUDY

Automation at General Motors of Canada

General Motors of Canada has made a major commitment to automating its plants using robots and automated guided vehicles (AGVs) by committing over $2 billion (Canadian) to the project. The Oshawa, Ontario, plant is involved in the GM10 program to make a new car line for the 1990s, and part of the production process is making car frames. The modernization strategy is to maximize productivity and quality through the use of improved management technology.

The plant in Oshawa will produce hundreds of cars per shift using over 600 industrial robots. It will perform various welding, loading, sealing, and assembly tasks. Cars and parts will be transported through various phases of assembly by 1,100 automatic guided vehicles (AGVs). A special study was done to analyze one segment of the plant—the AGV body-framing system. These AGVs can handle a wide variety of loads through a path selected by the user. They are controlled by a microprocessor and receive commands through a network of antennae and receivers embedded in the floor. The company had dropped the conveyor belt approach so the line could be broken into small work groups, each with the ability to control its own work speed.

The implementation of such an automated, integrated assembly system is very complicated. Each component must be tested first in isolation, and then together with other components as a working unit. Changes at this level are very costly and time-consuming. For this reason the system needed an inexpensive, quick, valid way to evaluate different work configurations. A computer simulation program was written to help determine the number of AGVs required to meet minimum production quotas.

The basic layout has 100 stations, each of which includes 10 process automation cells, 2 major areas where the underbody and sidebody come in, and a final unloading station. These 100 stations can work independently and perform three kinds of functions: process (28 stations), transfer (4 stations), and queueing (68 stations). Only 3 of the 28 process stations are operated by human workers. AGVs are used to deliver heavy parts to one of two machines in each cell. The finished product is a fully welded framed body without the doors, hood, front fenders, and trunk lid.

The computer simulation investigated the following aspects of the system:

1. Could a reliable system throughput of 525 cars per shift be achieved? What is the system's maximum rate?

2. What is the number of AGVs needed to make the production quota? Too few carriers can starve the system; too many can choke it. AGVs are also a major expense since each costs $50,000 (Canadian).

3. Where in the layout could idle "parking" spots be most effectively put? Altering the arrangement of queueing stations can eliminate bottlenecks encountered in simulation.

4. The ten automated work cells have two or three lanes. What selection rule should be used to properly utilize the equipment?

5. What is the sensitivity of the system to increased equipment failure or faster machine cycle time?

The main objective of the simulation was to determine the minimum number of carriers required to meet the desired throughput. It was found that the required throughput of 525 cars per shift could be attained with as few as 44 AGVs at least 99 percent of the time. The maximum achievable throughput was about 630 cars per shift using 74 AGVs. Thus, GM was able to determine the maximum capacity of this system and the attendant cost. There were four configurations that produced more than 600 cars per shift, and these were further investigated by making more simulation runs, which simply confirmed that 74 AGVs produced the maximum throughput. Statistical analysis showed that these configurations were significantly better than the others.

Also investigated was the sensitivity of the failure rate of the three most important cells and the cycle time of the automated processes. When the failure rate was increased by a factor of 10, throughput declined by only 2 percent. Decreasing the cycle time of the automation cells by 10 percent increased throughput by only 1.6 percent. Thus, this system was shown to be fairly stable and robust.

Source: James H. Bookbinder and Terrence R. Kotwa, "Modeling an AGV Automobile Body-Framing System," *Interfaces,* 16, no. 6 (November–December 1987), pp. 41–50.

Case Questions

1. Contrast the new and old assembly lines at GM Canada.

2. What factors did GM managers need to investigate before they set up the new assembly lines?

3. What are the three types of functions the 100 work stations can perform?

4. Why is it important for the simulation to produce a robust design?

5. Give two of the five important considerations examined by the computer simulation program and describe what they mean to GM.

■ *NOTES*

[1]*Workforce 2000: Work and Workers for the 21st Century* (Indianapolis, Ind.: Hudson Institute, 1987), p. xiii.

[2]Stephen G. Minter, "Soft Jobs?" *Occupational Hazards,* October 1989, pp. 127–135.

[3]Anthony J. Michels and Tricia Welsh, "Slouching into the 1990s," *Fortune,* June 3, 1991, pp. 254–258.

[4]John Hoerr, "Sharpening Minds for a Competitive Edge," *Business Week,* December 17, 1990, pp. 72–78.

[5]Solomon J. Herbert, "The Making of a New Classic," *Black Enterprise,* November 1990, pp. 64–68.

[6]Aaron Bernstein, "Quality Is Becoming Job One in the Office, Too," *Business Week,* April 29, 1991, pp. 52–56.

[7]John Holusha, "Metal Forming by Computer," *The New York Times,* November 22, 1984, p. D2.

[8]Gunnar K. Lofgren, "Automatic Guide Vehicle Systems," *Production and Inventory Management Review* 3, no. 2 (February 1983): 28–29.

[9]Efraim Turban, *Decision Support and Expert Systems* (New York: Macmillan, 1988), Chaps. 3 and 7, provides a description and some applications of such systems.

[10]*America's Choice: High Skills or Low Wages!* The Report of the Commission on the Skills of the American Workforce (Washington, D.C.: The National Center on Education and the Economy, 1990), Executive Summary, p. 2.

[11]*Workforce 2000: Work and Workers for the 21st Century,* p. 115.

[12]Susan B. Garland, "A New Chief Has OSHA Growling Again," *Business Week,* August 20, 1990, p. 57.

[13]Jay Heizer and Barry Render, *Production and Operations Management: Strategies and Tactics* (Boston: Allyn & Bacon, 1988), part four, discuss some of the appropriate methodologies. Barry Render and R. M. Starr, *Micro-computer Software for Management Science and Operations Management* (Boston: Allyn & Bacon, 1986), present a relevant computer system.

[14]Edward A. Wasil and Arang A. Assad, "Project Management on the PC: Software, Applications, and Trends," *Interfaces* 18, no. 2 (March–April 1988): 75–84.

[15]"Computer Deals Pen Another Setback," *The New York Times,* March 27, 1991, p. C8.

[16]Brenton R. Schlender, "Hot New PCs That Read Your Writing," *Fortune,* February 11, 1991, pp. 113–123.

[17]Al Fleming, "Chrysler Quality and Productivity VP George Butts," *Automotive News,* February 28, 1983, p. E10.

[18]Heizer and Render, *Production and Operations Management,* p. 742.

[19]"Teamwork Puts Saturn into Orbit," *The Atlanta Journal-Constitution,* April 8, 1991, p. B8.

[20]John Lipper, "Cadillac Celebrates Quality Turnaround," *The Chicago Tribune,* November 18, 1990, Sect. 17, p. 5.

[21]Gilbert Fuchsberg, "Nonprofits May Get Own Baldrige Prizes," *The Wall Street Journal,* March 14, 1991, p. B1.

CHAPTER TWENTY-TWO

INFORMATION SYSTEMS

Detail from Stuart Davis, *Blips and Ifs.*

Upon completing this chapter you should be able to:

1. Explain the relationship between data, information, and control.

2. Describe the components of a computer system.

3. Explain why managers at different levels of the organization have different information needs.

4. List and describe the four stages involved in designing a computer-based MIS.

5. Present some guidelines for effective design of MIS.

6. Discuss the reasons potential users may resist the implementation of a computer system and give some suggestions for overcoming their resistance.

7. Describe some of the issues involved in maintaining security in a computer system.

8. Define the term *end-user computing* and explain why it has occurred.

9. Describe how decision support systems and expert systems differ from conventional management information systems.

10. Discuss some of the main issues involved in managing end-user computing.

Stuart Davis, *Blips and Ifs.* Oil on canvas. 1963–1964. 71⅛ × 73⅛″. Amon Carter Museum, Fort Worth, Texas

ILLUSTRATIVE CASE STUDY

INTRODUCTION

Using Technology at Sears for Strategic Advantage

"Attention, shoppers, today we have a number of clothing specials that can be found under the revolving blue light" is the sort of announcement that can be heard daily in retail stores throughout the country. As Carl Johnson makes a dash for the special display in his local Sears store, he tries to remember how much credit he has left on his Sears charge account. His shopping companion, Bill Calkins, is trying to keep up, but the store is jammed with merchandise, and it is difficult to squeeze through the aisles. Carl turns to Bill and says, "I hope they have my size—I've been waiting for this sale on summer suits for weeks." The year is 1965, and retailing is just beginning to discover the benefits of computerization.

Carl finds several items to purchase and brings them to the sales counter. "Will this be cash or charge?" asks the sales clerk. "Charge it to my Sears account," responds Carl. The clerk rings up the merchandise, picks up the charge card, and phones the credit office. After checking a printout, the credit office approves the charge purchase, and Carl is on his way. As they are leaving the store, Carl turns to Bill and says, "Why don't you get a Sears charge so you can take advantage of the sales whenever you want? It beats running all over town to find a power drill or a sports coat." The scene, from a television commercial, ends with the announcer reminding viewers how easy it is to qualify for a Sears charge account.

Sears has been a leader in using computers to support its retail operations, and Charles Carlson, vice president of information systems and data processing for the $40 billion retailing giant, smiles as he reruns the film of the above episode. He is reviewing advertising copy from the past 25 years to get a sense of how important computers have been in the success of the Sears retail operations. In 1965, comput-

Capturing a Competitive Advantage. Giving shoppers the option of using a Sears charge card helped the company increase sales during the mid-1960s.

ers were being used for back-room functions such as accounts receivable, but they had very little impact on the rest of retailing operations. Carlson finds it hard to believe that Sears gained a strategic advantage from so simple an application as computerized credit. But in those days of large, cumbersome mainframe computers operating in a centralized environment, Sears had enjoyed the resources to develop the system and get a jump on the competition.

Sources: Catherine L. Harris, "Information Power," *Business Week,* October 14, 1985, pp. 107–114; Glenn Rifkin, "Computers in Retailing: Shopping for Strategic Advantage," *Computerworld,* November 24, 1986, pp. 39, 42, 47–48, 51, 54–55; Rifkin, "Large, Small Stores Seek High-Tech Edge," *Computerworld,* November 24, 1986, pp. 42, 44; Peter Cohen, "Retail Cashes in on PCs," *Computerworld,* November 24, 1986, pp. 50–51.

TEACHING TIP
Have your students inter-
view managers to find out
how they obtain and use
information.

COORDINATED RESOURCE
See *Management Live!*
Chapter 10 video, "The
Knowledge Navigator
(Apple Computer)."

FOR DISCUSSION
How is information tech-
nology changing the pro-
cess of education at your
school?

**management informa-
tion system (MIS)** Com-
puter-based information
system for more effective
planning, decision making,
and control.

All the managerial functions—planning, organizing, leading, and controlling—are necessary for successful organizational performance. To support these functions, especially planning and controlling, systems for supplying information to managers are of special importance. Only with accurate and timely information can managers monitor progress toward their goals and turn plans into reality. If managers cannot stay "on track," anticipating potential corrections, developing the skills to recognize when corrections are necessary, and then making appropriate corrections or adjustments as they progress, their work may be both fruitless and costly.

Information systems are being used to produce more than routine business reports. If you were to look at a new Toyota in a showroom, you would find the car has a computer-generated sticker attached to the window to display the pricing and EPA information. The Toyota dealer probably has a computerized inventory system to tell you if he has a car with the options that you want—perhaps even the color that you have dreamed about. Finally, should you need financing, the bank computer can quickly check your credit and help the salesperson close the sale. From the largest corporation to the modest home-town auto dealer, the computer plays a vital part in the control of business operations.

Managers at all levels are finding that computer-based information systems provide the information necessary for effective operation. These **management information systems (MIS)** are rapidly becoming indispensable for planning, decision making, and control. How quickly and accurately managers receive information about what is going right and what is going wrong—how well the information system functions—largely determines how effective the control system will be.[1] In addition, organizational information and decision support systems (DSS) are undergoing major changes as a result of dramatic increases in computer capabilities and use. For example, as we discuss later in this chapter, in less than a decade MIS has evolved into DSS, and artificial intelligence and expert systems are providing managers with the means to leverage expertise, improve service quality, control costs, enhance products, and gain a competitive edge. With information systems playing such an important role in managing organizations, it has become crucial for managers to understand how these systems should be designed, implemented, and managed. We begin this chapter by taking a closer look at the nature of information, the components of a management information system, the issues involved in managing such systems, and future trends in computer usage.

■ *INFORMATION AND CONTROL*

CLASS COMMENT
Information is the life-
blood of any systems, and
particularly an organiza-
tion.

FOR DISCUSSION
What gives information
value? How can the value
of information be mea-
sured?

To appreciate the central role played by information in making control effective, consider a modest-sized manufacturer of automobile replacement parts with annual sales of $10 million. Every year, the firm's 350 employees service 20,000 customer orders. These orders must be processed, billed, assembled, packed, and shipped—adding up to some 400,000 transactions that must be controlled.

And that is only the beginning. The firm writes 25,000 checks annually. Half of these cover wages; most of the others pay for the 5,000 purchase orders issued every year. Costs are assembled from 17,000 time cards, 6,000 job orders, and 20,000 materials requisitions. Each year, that small $10 million firm is processing almost a million pieces of information related to its activities—and that figure does not include all the other pieces of information related to inventory and quality control. Nor does it include the market analyses and other information an organization collects as part of its strategic planning. Increasingly, information is being seen as a key factor in helping managers respond to the complex and turbulent environment.[2]

Small wonder, then, that more and more managers view information itself as a valuable asset—one that needs to be carefully managed and protected.[3] To understand this view, we need to take a closer look at the nature of information and the differing types of information needed by operational, middle, and top managers. With this background, we will be ready to understand the role of computers.

The Nature of Information

data Raw, unanalyzed numbers and facts.

information Data that have been organized or analyzed in some meaningful way.

HERE'S AN EXAMPLE
Citicorp's POS (for point-of-sale) Information Services unit is turning out to be a nightmare. Their idea, a grocery shopper's ID card that would combine with electronic scanners at the checkout line to tell marketers exactly who bought what, seemed like a good one. But the point-of-sale unit irritated retailers and shoppers. (*Wall Street Journal,* 4/3/91, p. A1ff.)

Although we tend to use the terms *data* and *information* interchangeably, there is a very real distinction between the two concepts. **Data** are raw, unanalyzed numbers and facts about events, such as the number of computer disks produced per week or the inventory of computer disks at a local office supply store. **Information,** in contrast, results when data are organized or analyzed in some meaningful way. Thus, the operations manager at the disk manufacturer might compare one week's output to the previous week's or to production quotas as one way of monitoring and controlling performance. Similarly, managers at the software store could compare their inventory levels of disks to industry standards as one way of assessing their performance.

Though they have different operations and objectives, both the disk manufacturer and the office supply store will evaluate the information they receive on four factors: its quality, timeliness, quantity, and relevance to management.

1. *Information quality.* The more accurate the information, the higher its quality and the more securely managers can rely on it when making decisions. In general, however, the cost of obtaining information increases as the quality desired becomes higher. If information of a higher quality does not add materially to a manager's decision-making capability, it is not worth the added cost.

2. *Information timeliness.* For effective control, corrective action must be applied before there has been too great a deviation from the plan or standard. Thus, the information provided by an information system must be available to the right person at the right time for the appropriate action to be taken.

Data vs. Information. Presented with the seismic survey on the left, several geophysicists failed to spot the distinctive "bright spots" that signal potential oil and natural-gas traps in the Beaufort Sea off Alaska. But after the printout was enhanced with computer-aided exploration technology from Landmark Graphics Corp., it is much easier to see the red and yellow spots indicating promising traps (right).

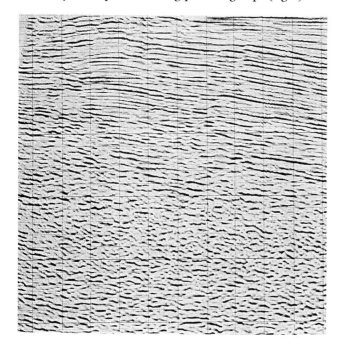
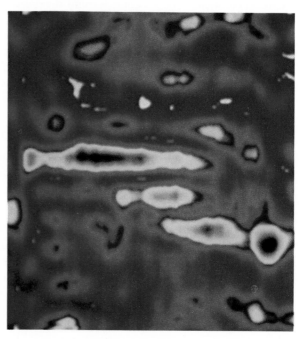

THOUGHT PROVOKER
Information is a "strategic asset." Discuss the implications. (*Wall Street Journal*, 3/19/90, p. A14)

3. *Information quantity.* Managers can hardly make accurate and timely decisions without sufficient information. However, managers are often inundated with irrelevant and useless information. If they receive more information than they can productively use, they may overlook information on serious problems.

4. *Information relevance.* Similarly, the information that managers receive must have relevance to their responsibilities and tasks. The personnel manager does not need to know inventory levels—and the manager in charge of reordering inventory does not need to know about the status of staff members in other departments.

The Role of Computers

COORDINATED RESOURCE
See Study Guide Self-Learning Exercise "Computers."

CLASS COMMENT
According to a survey by Andersen Consulting and ComputerWorld, more than half of the top executives in the nation's 1,000 largest companies are dissatisfied with their companies' computer systems. (*Wall Street Journal*, 4/29/91, p. B4)

THOUGHT PROVOKER
"Corporations aren't getting the most from their computer systems because they don't implement them properly"—Bill Laberis. (*Wall Street Journal*, 4/29/91, p. B4) What are the implications?

Before the widespread use of computers, many organizations simply found it too expensive and time-consuming to gather, store, organize, and distribute large amounts of data and information. The computer revolution changed this. Today's managers have at their command a wide range of information tools, ranging from supercomputers that can model geological surveys used to search for oil deposits to laptop computers that sales agents can carry with them to record orders and check inventory levels. Even a neighborhood retailer or a home-based business can use a desktop computer to manage records of sales, billing, and inventory, and, with the right software, produce newsletters and advertising flyers. In fact, the computer may be even more important to these small firms, since they cannot afford to pay the salaries of the people needed to perform such tasks manually.

Some experts estimate that more than 50 percent of managers already use computers daily—a trend that is expected to continue into the next century, when even routine office jobs will be fully computerized. Thus, current and future managers alike need to become effective at, and comfortable with, the use of computers and the ways they can: (1) facilitate the collection, management, and communication of information up and down the management hierarchy, as well as between workers on the same level; (2) automate operations, both in the factory and in the office; (3) support decision making and planning at all levels, a fact we explored in detail in Chapter 10; and (4) simplify management control, our focus in this chapter. Moreover, the adroit use of computers has given many companies a competitive edge, a trend described in the Management Application box.

Computer systems are particularly useful and cost-effective (1) when there is a large volume of routine data to be processed; (2) when tasks and activities are repetitive; (3) when it is necessary to store and have quick access to a large volume of data and information; (4) when speedy processing and up-to-the-minute business records are essential; and (5) when there is a need to perform complex computations.[4]

Components of Computer Systems

computer system An integrated collection of hardware, software, procedures, data, and people used to produce information.

So far we have been using the term *computer* in a general way, but we need to realize that a "computer" is actually a **computer system,** an integrated collection of hardware, software, procedures, data, and people that can be used to produce information.

HARDWARE. The term *hardware* refers to the machinery used within the computer system. Input devices, such as keyboards, bar-code readers, scanners, and mice, are used to capture data and issue instructions to the system, while the system's "brain," the central processing unit, processes data and instructions to produce information. This information can be saved on a storage device, such as a floppy disk, or it can be displayed with an output device, such as a terminal screen or a printer. In addition, telecommunications equipment can be used to send data and information from one computer system to another.

Information Power—How Companies Are Using New Technologies to Gain a Competitive Edge

The ability to use computers creatively to collect, organize, distribute, and control information is spelling the difference between success and mediocrity in industries ranging from banking to women's clothing. Computers are changing the way we do business, fast becoming indispensable allies in marketing, customer service, product development, human resource management, and even strategic planning. Consider the following:

Dun and Bradstreet may be the premier firm in the data-transformation business, processing streams of data generated by 3,000 reporters following more than 2 million firms. D&B searches out technology that lets it meet its customers' needs for low-cost credit information, and has moved from a paper-generating organization into the world of high-speed computers and communications. Today more than 75 percent of D&B's credit reports are sent from the D&B computer to a customer computer, providing almost instant service, avoiding mail delays, and saving paper and postage costs. With credit information at their fingertips, managers can quickly assess a situation and provide customers with immediate credit and order acceptance.

Security Pacific Automation Co., a subsidiary of Security Pacific Bank, sells its services both to Security Pacific and to other banks. Banking requires an immense investment in technology and considers the application of computers a competitive weapon. By putting terminals into car dealerships to link them with Security Pacific Credit Corp., the bank can provide credit-checking services and calculate loan payments immediately, helping dealers to close the sale much more efficiently. The company also generates lending business for the bank.

Benetton fashions has moved from being a street vendor of sweaters to a global business with thousands of franchised clothing shops throughout the world. A key to their growth and financial success is a sophisticated information system, especially their order-entry system. When an order is placed, the system interfaces with the factory to initiate production and with management to provide data for future production planning. Customers can query the system and obtain an order status report, finding out in just a few seconds whether their order has been shipped, is in the warehouse, or is still in production. By closely tying production to actual orders, Benetton is able to minimize inventory, focus production on popular

items, and give customers fast service—delivery of merchandise usually takes place within two weeks of when the order was placed.

American Airlines, through its Sabre reservation system, lists the flight schedules of every major airline in the world for over 10,000 automated travel agents throughout the country. American gains in two ways: It obtains increased airline travel business because it has control over the display of flight information (American can list its flights first), and it charges agents a modest fee for every reservation made through the system.

As computers, telecommunications, and video technology become more entwined, the potentials of each multiply. With the computer in mind, business is beginning to reconfigure things from the ground up. This process leads to entirely different approaches to existing markets and whole new product lines that did not previously seem a logical extension of business. Technology is changing the way we do business by providing better customer service, market intelligence, and financial and cash management.

Source: Based on Catherine L. Harris, "Information Power: How Companies Are Using New Technologies to Gain a Competitive Edge," *Business Week,* October 14, 1985; "Information Merchandisers," *Information Week,* October 31, 1988; and Lory Zottola, "The United Systems of Benetton," *Computerworld,* April 2, 1990, p. 658.

SOFTWARE. The term *software* refers to the information-processing instructions, or programs, needed to operate the information system. Software falls into two classes. The more familiar is *applications software*—software that performs specific tasks, such as word processing or accounting tasks. *Systems software,* in contrast, translates the instructions of applications software into instructions that direct the hardware itself. As such, systems software acts as a buffer between system users and the hardware. Software also includes documentation, a written narrative describing the software's capabilities, and user manuals, which contain operating instructions and reference materials, such as explanations of error codes.

DATA. As previously explained, data are the unevaluated facts and figures that will be converted into information. Data can take many forms, ranging from alphanumerical, a combination of letters and numbers, to images, such as a piece of art, a photograph, or a satellite image of a city that can be used as the basis of a computer-generated map.

An Innovation in Input Devices. Thanks to the DragonDictate System from Boston-based Dragon Systems Inc., government attorney David Bristol can write legal briefs and other documents himself, despite his cerebral palsy. Although users must pause between words, the voice-recognition system can recognize 30,000 spoken words and works so well that IBM based its first dictation product on Dragon's technology.

PEOPLE. People, the lifeblood of any computer system, fall into two classes. *Technical specialists* include the systems analysts, programmers, computer operators, communications specialists, and data-entry clerks responsible for creating and operating the computer system. Like managers, these technical specialists, especially the systems analysts and programmers, need a mix of technical and interpersonal skills that will let them translate user needs into effective, easy-to-use information systems. Increasingly, these technical specialists are coming from a variety of cultural backgrounds, which puts a greater emphasis on communication skills. (See the Management and Diversity box.)

End users are the people who use the outputs the information system produces. They may or may not have technical skills, but the information system only exists to fulfill their needs for the "right" amounts of accurate, timely, and relevant information.

PROCEDURES. Procedures are the preplanned rules and policies that govern the computer system's operation and the way end users interact with the system. Some of the most important procedures are designed to maintain security, that is, to protect the information system and its data from theft or damage.

■ *MANAGEMENT INFORMATION SYSTEMS*

COORDINATED RESOURCE
See Samaras Case 5.4, "What and How of MIS."

COORDINATED RESOURCE
See Study Guide Problem Exercise "MIS."

COORDINATED RESOURCE
See Samaras Case 5.4, "What and How of MIS."

THOUGHT PROVOKER
Do formal information systems pose any dangers to organizations? Why or why not?

One of the difficulties in discussing management information systems is that there are so many definitions of MIS. For our purposes, we will define an MIS as *a formal method of making available to management the accurate and timely information necessary to facilitate the decision-making process and enable the organization's planning, control, and operational functions to be carried out effectively.* The system provides information on the past, present, and projected future and on relevant events inside and outside the organization.

The use of the word "formal" in our definition is not intended to negate the importance of the informal communication network in the organization's control mechanism. In fact, managers often detect problems *before* they show up in formal control reports because they are tuned in to the grapevine. The ability of managers to maintain effective informal communication channels, to sense the implications of the information those channels transmit, and to evaluate, decide, and act quickly on such information extends the usefulness of the MIS enormously.

The Evolution of MIS

Organizations have always had some kind of management information system, even if it was not recognized as such.[5] In the past, these systems were highly informal in setup and utilization. Not until the advent of computers, with their ability to process

Where Will the Information Systems Professionals of Tomorrow Come From?

Computers manipulate symbols and perform logical operations, and we communicate with them using carefully structured programs. Ronald Reagan, "The Great Communicator," would find few of his skills helpful in talking to a computer. Bright individuals from a variety of cultures and backgrounds have noticed that English language skills are not necessary to pursue a formal education in computer technology. In some U.S. colleges and universities, as many as half the graduate students have limited verbal skills in English, although they are very skilled in "computerese." They work hard, study long hours, and generally graduate successfully from their programs. These highly trained people will be among the information systems (IS) professionals and leaders of tomorrow.

What are the implications for managers of this multicultural IS staff? Surely, there are many, but two are particularly important to keep in mind. First, it is critical that effective communication take place.

Managers should not assume that everyone can read between the lines when they make a request for new information resources. The English language is very complex, and we need to be sure that our requirements are expressed in a straightforward manner in order to prevent problems later on. Second, managers need to be sensitive to cultural differences in humor, motivation, rewards, and success. Don't assume that what motivates you will automatically motivate a systems professional from India. Learn the differences between the two cultures, and be sensitive to those differences.

Our educational institutions are graduating many skilled foreigners who wish to work in the United States. They are making an important contribution to MIS development efforts, and managers will get maximum performance from these systems professionals if they develop good communication skills and become sensitive to cultural differences.

COORDINATED RESOURCE
Use Transparency 150, Evolution of Information Systems.

electronic data processing (EDP) Computerized data-processing and information management, including report standardization for operating managers.

computer-based information system (CBIS) (or computer-based MIS) Information system that goes beyond the mere standardization of data to aid in the planning process.

decision support system (DSS) Computer system accessible to nonspecialists to assist in planning and decision making.

and condense large quantities of data, did the design of management information systems become a formal process and a field of study. Attempts to use computers effectively led to the identification and study of information systems and to the planning, implementation, and review of new ones.

EDP. When computers were first introduced into organizations, they were used mainly to process data for a few organizational functions—usually accounting and billing. Because of the specialized skills required to operate the expensive, complex, and sometimes temperamental equipment, computers were located in **electronic data-processing (EDP)** departments. As the speed and ease of processing data grew, other data-processing and information-management tasks were computerized. To cope with these new tasks, EDP departments developed standardized reports for the use of operating managers.

MIS. The growth of EDP departments spurred managers to focus more on planning their organizations' information systems. These efforts led to the emergence of the concept of **computer-based information systems (CBIS)**, which became better known as computer-based MIS—or simply MIS. As the EDP departments' functions expanded beyond routine processing of masses of standardized data, they began to be called MIS departments.

DSS. A **decision support system (DDS)** is an interactive computer system that is easily accessible to, and operated by, noncomputer specialists, who use the DSS to help them plan and make decisions. (Many of the information systems created by management scientists are, in fact, decision-support systems). The use of DSSs is expanding, as recent advances in computer hardware and software allow managers to gain "on-line" or "real-time" access to the data bases in CBISs. The widespread use of microcomputers has enabled managers to create their own data bases and elec-

TABLE 22-1 Information Requirements by Decision Category

CHARACTERISTICS OF INFORMATION	OPERATIONAL CONTROL (FIRST LINE)	MANAGEMENT CONTROL (TOP AND MIDDLE LEVEL)	STRATEGIC PLANNING (TOP LEVEL)
Source	Largely internal	⟷	Largely external
Scope	Well defined, narrow	⟷	Very wide
Level of aggregation	Detailed	⟷	Aggregate
Time horizon	Historical	⟷	Future
Currency	Highly current	⟷	Less current
Required accuracy	High	⟷	Low
Frequency of use	Very frequent	⟷	Less frequent

Source: Adapted from G. Anthony Gorry and Michael S. Scott Morton, "A Framework for Management Information Systems," *Sloan Management Review* 13, no. 1 (Fall 1971):59. Copyright © 1971 by the Sloan Management Review Association. All rights reserved.

tronically manipulate information as needed rather than waiting for reports to be issued by the EDP/MIS department. While MIS reports are still necessary for monitoring ongoing operations, DSS permits less structured use of data bases as special decision needs arise.[6]

ARTIFICIAL INTELLIGENCE. One of the fastest-growing areas of information technology, artificial intelligence uses the computer to simulate some of the characteristics of human thought.[7] Expert systems use artificial-intelligence techniques to diagnose problems, recommend strategies to avert or solve those problems, and offer a rationale for the recommendations. In effect, the expert system acts like a human "expert" in analyzing unstructured situations. (We discuss artificial intelligence and expert systems in more detail later in this chapter.)

Differing Information for Different Management Levels

COORDINATED RESOURCE
See Samaras Case 5.2, "What's Going On?"

G. Anthony Gorry and M. S. Scott Morton have pointed out that an organization's information system must provide information to managers with three levels of responsibilities: operational control, management control, and strategic planning.[8] We can think of these three categories in terms of the activities that take place at different levels of the managerial hierarchy (first-line, middle, and top). The design of the MIS must take into account the information needs of the various managerial levels, as well as the routine transaction-processing needs of the total organization. For example, as shown in Table 22-1, the information sources for operational control are found largely within the organization, while the information sources for strategic planning tend to be outside the organization.

HERE'S AN EXAMPLE
At Frito-Lay Inc., the delivery force uses hand-held computers to manage orders and feed daily inventory and sales to management.

OPERATIONAL CONTROL. An MIS for operational control must provide highly accurate and detailed information on a daily or weekly basis. A production supervisor has to know if materials wastage is excessive, if costly overruns are about to occur, or if the machine time for a job has expired. The MIS must provide a high volume of timely and detailed information derived from daily operations.

HERE'S AN EXAMPLE
Otis Elevator Company's servicemen learn of emergency calls and query service files with their radio-powered, hand-held computers.

MIDDLE MANAGEMENT. Middle-level managers, such as division heads, are concerned with the current and future performance of their units. They therefore need information on important matters that will affect those units—large-scale problems with suppliers, abrupt sales declines, or increased consumer demand for a particular product line. Thus, the type of information middle-level managers require consists of aggregate (summarized) data from within the organization as well as from sources outside the organization.

Providing Different Information to Different Management Levels. Williams-Sonoma, Inc. operates a number of successful retail stores, like the flagship store Chairman W. Howard Lester vists here, but a major part of its growth comes from its five mail-order catalogs. What sets Williams-Sonoma apart from other catalog merchandisers is its extensive database, which tracks up to 150 pieces of information about each of its 4.5 million customers. With a few keystrokes, marketing managers can create highly targeted mailing lists, based on what various customers bought at different times of the year. At the operational level, statisticians can use the database to project each mailing's sales (± 5 percent), while upper managers can use the database to make strategic decisions about the most promising location for new stores.

TOP MANAGEMENT.   For top managers, the MIS must provide information for strategic planning and management control. For strategic planning, the external sources of information—on economic conditions, technological developments, the actions of competitors—assume paramount importance.[9] This information is hard to computerize because supporting data are generally beyond the control of the organization.

For the *management control* functions of top managers, however, the sources of information must be both internal and external. Top managers are typically concerned about the overall financial performance of their organizations. They therefore need information on quarterly sales and profits, on the other relevant indicators of financial performance (such as stock value), and on the performance of competitors. Internal control reports for top managers come in at monthly, quarterly, and sometimes even annual intervals. At the headquarters of Mrs. Field's Cookies, computer-based reports are reviewed hour by hour.

How may the various needs of different managerial levels be translated into a management information system? One major company designed the manufacturing component of its MIS this way: *Supervisors* receive daily reports on direct and indirect labor, materials usage, scrap, production counts, and machine downtime; *superintendents* and *department heads* receive weekly departmental cost summaries and product-cost reports; *plant managers* receive weekly and monthly financial statements and analyses, analyses of important costs, and summarized product-cost reports; *divisional managers* receive monthly plant comparisons, financial planning reports, product-cost summaries, and plant-cost control reports; and, finally, *top managers* receive overall monthly and quarterly financial reviews, financial analyses, and summarized comparisons of divisional performance.

THOUGHT PROVOKER

The chief information officer, once deemed indispensable to the organization, is becoming an endangered species. (*Business Week,* 2/26/90, p. 78ff.) What are the implications?

The Role of the Chief Information Officer (CIO)

The chief information officer (CIO) is the human link between top management and information. As the architect of the firm's computerized information systems, the CIO is responsible for overseeing the preparation and dissemination of policies and

ILLUSTRATIVE CASE STUDY

CONTINUED

Using Technology at Sears for Strategic Advantage

Carl Johnson stands under the revolving blue light, with an armful of clothing bargains. "Come on, Bill," he says, "let's check out so we can get home in time to catch the rest of the game." The clerk smiles as he runs a light pen over the specially prepared pricing tag on each garment, waiting for the point-of-sale (POS) terminal to search the mainframe computer, ring up the sale price, and record the transaction details for later reporting to management. Sears has had POS for several years now, and individual store systems are linked with both headquarters and regional distribution centers to gain processing power and save on paperwork.

Carl hands his charge card to the clerk, watches him key the account number into the POS terminal, and in a few seconds sees his credit approval stamped on the sales ticket. The clerk packs the purchases, and Bill and Carl are on their way out the door. Bill still does not have a Sears charge, but he is thinking about getting one. "Carl," he muses, "it's amazing how much change there has been in the Sears store this past ten years. Here we are in 1975, in the age of computers, and the clerk doesn't even have to know the price of the item to ring it up. The POS terminal does it all. Will wonders never cease?"

Charles Carlson is still viewing films that Sears used for various advertising campaigns and remembers well the first stores that installed POS systems. Managers fell in love with them. "We were able to manage credit, gather merchandise information, calculate our inventory, and monitor staffing requirements through this single system," recalls Carlson. "It revolutionized the retailing business." It would seem that in most markets Sears was able to keep a competitive advantage by applying advanced computer technology to address a variety of retailing problems.

---

procedures for new and existing systems. The CIO also acts as a change agent who is responsible for the introduction of such technologies as telecommunications, office automation, MISs, DSSs, expert systems, and related activities. Unlike traditional data processing managers, who focus on day-to-day operations, the CIO focuses on planning and developing creative and innovative ways to meet managers' growing information needs.

■ DESIGNING A COMPUTER-BASED MIS

COORDINATED RESOURCE
See Samaras Reading "Planning and Creating an Information-Processing View."

FOR DISCUSSION
How might organizational culture affect the choice of an MIS?

COORDINATED RESOURCE
See DuBose Reading #12, "Organizational Design: An Information-Processing View."

Many articles and books have described the systematic steps that should be followed in designing and implementing an MIS.[10] Robert G. Murdick reviewed a number of these sources and adapted them to form his own model of how an MIS should be developed.[11] For the sake of simplicity, Murdick's model can be broken down into four stages.

1. *A preliminary survey and problem definition stage.* With the formation of a task force charged with the design of an MIS, there should be a thorough assessment of the organization's capabilities and strategic goals, as well as an assessment of any external factors relevant to the organization's functions. From this assessment, a definition of the information system the organization needs can be decided on, and the determination of informational, operational, and functional objectives can be accomplished.

2. *A conceptual design stage.* Through an analysis of the current information system, alternative MIS designs with specific performance requirements can be developed. These alternatives are then weighed against organization objec-

FOR DISCUSSION

Is quality of information important? Why? How would you ensure receiving high-quality information?

tives, capabilities, and needs. This examination leads to an initial selected project plan. At this point, tasks are delegated, information on the task force's study are communicated to employees, and the plan for a training program is conceived.

3. *A detailed design stage.* Once the conceptual plan is decided on, performance specifications of the new MIS can be established. Components, programming, flowcharting, and data bases (including specifications for personnel interaction with the system) can be designed. A model of the system is created, tested, refined, and reviewed until it meets the specified level of performance.

4. *A final implementation stage.* The formal requirements for the new MIS are determined. The logistics of space allocations, equipment additions, and forms design are worked out and enacted. The training program commences. Design and testing of software for the MIS are completed, and the organization's data bases are entered into the system. After a series of final checks, the MIS is ready for implementation.

It should be emphasized that creation of an MIS is a long-term task that requires the skills of a variety of specialists. In fact, the design and implementation of an MIS such as that shown in Murdick's model might well require a major team effort by managers and information systems analysts over a period of two or three years.

Guidelines for Effective Design

HERE'S AN EXAMPLE

Dillard's Department Stores of Arkansas is a highly successful company. An important factor in its success is its near-fanatical focus on computer technology. (*Fortune,* 10/23/89, p. 167ff.)

FOR DISCUSSION

Are there any management situations in which a formal MIS might not be helpful? Describe.

How can these steps in the MIS development process be carried out effectively? For our purposes, we can focus on six guidelines for effective MIS design: (1) make users part of the design team; (2) carefully consider the costs of the system; (3) consider alternatives to in-house software development; (4) favor relevance and selectivity of information over sheer quantity; (5) pretest the system before installation; and (6) train the operators and users of the system carefully.

1. *Include users on the design team.* It is widely agreed that cooperation between the operating managers (who use the information) and systems designers is not only desirable but necessary. Users know what information they need, when they need it, and how they will use it for managerial action and decision making. Unless operating managers have a decisive voice in the design of the MIS, the information system may fail to provide needed information while simultaneously overloading them with useless information.[12]

2. *Weigh the money and time costs of the system.* To keep the MIS on track and on budget, designers need to specify how the system will be developed—and this includes schedules of time required for different steps, milestones to be reached, and budgeted costs. If managers justify the design and installation of a new system on a cost-benefit basis, cost overruns are less likely to occur. It should be noted that the greater portion of MIS operating costs go for the maintenance of existing software.[13]

3. *Consider alternatives to in-house software development.* The high cost of software development has led management to look outside the organization when developing and implementing new systems. Some organizations may find that their data-processing requirements are very similar to those of other businesses and that suitable software is available from hardware manufacturers or software suppliers. In recent years, the wide acceptance of commercial software by both large and small organizations has brought down costs and increased availability.

4. *Favor relevance and selectivity of information over sheer quantity.* As we have seen, a manager needs enough information to make an informed decision; more information is not necessarily better, although many managers prefer to have too much rather than too little information.[14] In one study, decision makers who perceived themselves as experiencing information overload had a lower performance

Pretesting a System. In an effort to manage the time and paperwork associated with insurance claims, State Farm Mutual Automobile Insurance has launched a pilot project to test notepad computers, demonstrated here by computer expert Jack Kocher. Instead of a keyboard, a notepad computer has an electronic pen that adjusters can use to fill out insurance forms and mark damage on an exploded-view diagram. The computer then uses a stored parts and price list to calculate the damage and stores the information, along with digitized versions of all signatures, until they can be transmitted to the central computer at the end of the day. If the project works out, about 25,000 State Farm employees may receive notepad computers.

level but a higher satisfaction level than decision makers who perceived information underload.[15] A properly designed MIS does not supply middle- or top-level managers with the routine details of an organization's daily activities.[16] The MIS *filters* or evaluates information so that only the most relevant information is supplied to the appropriate manager. In addition, the effective MIS *condenses* information so that what is relevant can be absorbed quickly. The information system should also provide top-level managers with data on critical factors and changes related to organizational effectiveness.[17]

5. *Pretest the system before installation.* Even when managers and system designers cooperate in the system's development, important factors may be overlooked. Omissions and problems should show up during the test period. If they do not become apparent until the system is finally implemented, costly problems may arise and expensive changes may be necessary.

There are four basic approaches to installing a new MIS that have some bearing on the length and extensiveness of the pretest stage.[18] In *crash* or *direct installation,* the new system replaces the old one entirely. The switch is effected all at once, and there is total dependence on the new system. In this case, extensive pretesting should be done, since the organization will not be able to fall back on the old system if the new one fails or has major operational problems.[19]

With *parallel installation,* the new system is implemented and operated side by side with the old system. This approach allows comparison of outputs between systems so that adjustments can be made before the old system is removed.

Pilot installation offers the organization the opportunity to test the new MIS in operation as it is used by a small part of the organization—for example, by the sales management of one division—so that problems can be discovered and corrected before total installation.

In *phased installation,* the new MIS is implemented segment by segment, allowing for operational testing and problem solution before moving on to the next segment.

6. Provide adequate training and written documentation for the operators and users of the system. A training program for managers and MIS operators is important for two major reasons. Without training and written instructions for the operation and use of the MIS, the organization will be at a loss when experienced personnel leave. Also, operators must understand the information needs of managers at different levels so that they know what they are doing, for whom they are doing it, and why. Perhaps most important, managers need to understand how the MIS operates so they can control it, rather than letting it control them.

Even a carefully designed and implemented MIS may not fit the needs of users as closely as desired, either because it is difficult to use or because it does not supply all the information asked for. As each new system is developed, it should be made plain how it will change the organizational structure and task responsibilities and how it will affect the job of each employee.[20]

■ *IMPLEMENTING A COMPUTER-BASED MIS*

The use of computers to address many organizational concerns has grown rapidly, despite the problems involved in implementing a computerized MIS. Managers should be aware of the technological problems of systems design and installation, although these are, strictly speaking, the concern of information-system and data-processing personnel and are obviously beyond the scope of an introductory management text. Our discussion, therefore, focuses on the "people concerns," which are more important for most managers to understand, are at least as difficult to address, and are no less likely to inhibit successful implementation of a computerized information system. The primary responsibility for addressing such concerns will fall upon managers.[21]

Problems in Implementing a Computer-Based MIS

COORDINATED RESOURCE

See *Management Live!*
Reading 10.2, "At These
Shouting Matches, No One
Says a Word."

ORGANIZATIONAL RESISTANCE. G. W. Dickson and John K. Simmons note five major factors that determine whether and to what extent the implementation of a new MIS will be resisted.[22]

1. *Does the MIS disrupt established departmental boundaries?* The establishment of a new MIS often results in changes in several organizational units. For example, inventory and purchasing departments may be merged to make more efficient use of the MIS. Such disruptions may be resisted by department members, who may resent having to change the way they do things or the people with whom they work.

2. *Does the MIS disrupt the informal system?* The informal communication network may be disrupted as a new MIS alters communication patterns. If organization members prefer some of the earlier, informal mechanisms for gathering and distributing information, they may resist the more formal channels set up for the new system.

3. *Does the MIS challenge specific individual characteristics?* People with many years of service with the organization have "learned the ropes" and know how to get things done in the existing system. They may resist change more tenaciously than newer people who have been with the organization for a comparatively short period of time and do not have as large an investment in organizational know-how and relationships.

4. *Is the MIS supported by the organizational culture?* If top management maintains open communication, deals with grievances, and, in general, establishes a culture with high trust throughout the organization, there is likely to be less resistance to the installation of a new MIS. However, if top managers are isolated or aloof from other organization members, or if the organizational culture supports inflexible behavior, then effective implementation of the MIS is likely to be hindered.

5. *Do employees have a say in how the change is implemented?* As we have seen repeatedly in earlier chapters, the manner in which changes are designed and implemented affects the amount of resistance those changes will encounter. In general, when managers and subordinates make change decisions together, there is a greater likelihood that the changes will be accepted.

Dickson and Simmons have observed that the frustrations associated with the implementation of a new MIS can manifest themselves in three ways:

❑ *Aggression* is manifested when individuals hit back at the object (or person) frustrating them. Aggression against a computer-based MIS has gone as far as sabotage—by using equipment incorrectly, by putting incomplete or inadequate information into the system, or by actual destruction of hardware or software.

❑ *Projection* is the psychological mechanism of blaming difficulties on someone or something else. When managers (or other individuals) blame the computer system for problems caused by human error or other factors unrelated to the system itself, projection is taking place.

❑ *Avoidance* is manifested when individuals defend themselves by withdrawing from or avoiding a frustrating situation. Managers may exhibit avoidance behavior by ignoring output of an MIS in favor of their own information sources.

Because people at different levels of the organization are affected by a computer-based MIS in different ways, the frequency with which each type of behavior is manifested will depend on the hierarchical level of the individuals and managers affected by the MIS change. (See Table 22-2.) Among lower-level nonclerical personnel, for example, the installation of a new MIS may increase job complexity. Unless they fear the new system will reduce the total number of available jobs, clerical workers (like data-entry operators) who will be working directly with the new system are less likely to manifest aggression toward it. After all, the MIS represents a major part of their job. They may, however, resist changes in the system through projection—for example, by making remarks about the new system's failings and inadequacies relative to the old system.

Operating managers—including both first-line and middle managers—generally experience the greatest impact from a new MIS, since the information

TABLE 22-2 Work Groups, Their Relation to MIS, and Their Possible Dysfunctional Behaviors

ORGANIZATIONAL SUBGROUP	RELATION TO MIS	DYSFUNCTIONAL BEHAVIOR
Top management	Generally unaffected and unconcerned with systems	Avoidance
Technical staff	Systems designers and agents of systems change	None
Operating management	Controlled from above by systems; job content and context modified by new systems	Aggression, avoidance, and projection
Operating personnel: Clerical	Particularly affected by clerical systems; jobs eliminated; job patterns changed	Projection
Nonclerical	Provide system inputs	Aggression

Source: Adapted from G. W. Dickson and John K. Simmons, "The Behavioral Side of MIS," *Business Horizons* 13, no. 4 (August 1970):63.

supplied by the MIS to top management will help determine how they are evaluated. The problem for operating managers is that the MIS leaves them less control over how and when this information is filtered, interpreted, and presented to their superiors. Instead of supplying it directly to top managers, they supply it to the MIS, which is operated by staff specialists. This loss of control can be a source of anxiety.

Another source of anxiety for managers is the fact that a computerized MIS allows more centralized decision making, which makes it easier for top managers to increase their control over operating managers. In addition, there is always the possibility that a computer-based MIS will eliminate or substantially alter some first-line and middle-management jobs. Thus, the resistance of operating managers to the MIS may encompass all three types of psychological reactions: They may fight the system (aggression); they may ignore it, sticking to their old communication channels (avoidance); or they may blame the system for failures caused by other factors (projection).

In many organizations, top managers are relatively unaffected by the implementation of an MIS. They require extensive external information, and the MIS will meet only a portion of their needs. If, however, the MIS has been oversold to top management, leading to significant unrealized expectations, there will be disappointments once the MIS is operational.

The design of the MIS takes place within the political system of the organization, and nonrational considerations of MIS designers and subgroups of users can have an impact on the eventual design, implementation, use, and organizational reaction and behavior toward the new MIS.[23] For example, divisional requirements for information by middle management might differ from the overall organizational requirements for information by top management. The information most useful to top managers might also facilitate the evaluation of divisional performance, and this might be perceived by middle managers as a threat to their security. Both groups may jockey for position and try to protect their interests. After the design is completed, winners and losers of the political battle may take different stances toward the new MIS.

COORDINATED RESOURCE

The Distinctive Discussions for Chapter 22 found in the Lecture Extras supplement include "Privacy: Not What You Think" and "Coming Soon: Company TV."

SECURITY. Security of the new system is a control issue that must be addressed in the design and implementation stages—for example, by placing equipment in safe and supervised areas and by constructing password and read-only files. Table 22-3 outlines some important security concerns and the degree of risk associated with two major MIS configurations: mainframe computers and micro- or personal computers. While the protection of mainframe configurations is usually adequate, security for microcomputer systems is sorely lacking in many organizations, which tend to be ignorant of the risks involved and often neglect appropriate security measures.[24]

Organizations using microcomputer-based information systems have experienced increased control problems, such as theft and vandalism, the destruction or alteration of data, and the unauthorized dissemination of restricted or sensitive information.[25] Theft and vandalism can be limited by placing equipment in secure areas or by making existing facilities more secure. Software or program piracy can be prevented by copyguarding important programs and by securely storing authorized originals and backup copies. Data can be protected by making alterations to on-line data files impossible without the correct password or by making backup copies of disks to preserve the originals from intentional or accidental erasure. (However, duplicating software and data files creates more copies to be stolen.) Managers who need the data files on a timely basis can each be issued a disk copy under tight reporting procedures and schedules. The Ethics in Management box entitled "Security Issues and the Computer" explores additional dimensions of the security of control systems.

TABLE 22-3 Computer Security Concerns

CONCERN	MAINFRAME COMPUTERS	MICROCOMPUTERS
Physical Security Fire damage Water damage Deliberate destruction Wind damage	Greater exposure per occurrence because of cost factors.	Possibility of more frequent occurrence because of the working environment.
Theft of computer	Not a concern due to the size of the central processing unit (CPU).	Greater concern due to size and locations.
Theft of terminals, other peripherals	Size, location, general building security, and other factors are similar for both.	
Loss or destruction of storage media	Maximum exposure, but mitigated by hardware/software controls, better storage facilities, tighter security.	Maximum exposure due to physical characteristics of media (floppy disk) and physical location of computers, lack of secure storage areas.
Software Security Theft of licensed software	Some exposure, but less likely because of limited market for material.	Significant exposure due to open market for pirated material.
Programs Written In-house Accuracy of new programs	Considerable exposure, but mitigated by quality of data-processing personnel and by testing requirements.	Greater exposure because (1) users are not programmers; and (2) testing and review are incomplete.
Program changes	Considerable exposure in either case, but there are generally tighter controls in large installations. Micro users are not subject to the same constraints.	
Program loss or destruction	Exposure mitigated by software controls and by backup/recovery procedures generally in place.	Greater exposure for some configurations: may not have adequate facilities for making backup copies.
Inability to continue processing due to lack of documentation	Minimal exposure; runs generally not dependent on documentation. Also, mitigated by quality assurance reviews and turnover requirements.	Greater exposure (if the person running the job leaves, the job may have to be reprogrammed) due to user independence, lack of documentation requirements.
Data security (integrity)	Moderate exposure, but mitigated by run-to-run balancing capabilities, machine/software checks.	Greater exposure to loss due to ease of erasing files. If data are down-loaded from mainframe, some may not be received. Also, if similar data are downloaded to various micros and processed independently, the data can lose integrity.
Release of privileged data	Considerable exposure, but mitigated by locking devices and/or password protection, personnel controls.	Greater exposure due to lack of separation of duties, user-controlled security.
Inappropriate Use of Corporate Assets Initial justification for installation	Minor exposure because of required review and approval procedures.	Greater exposure, cost not considered substantial.
Processing data not required by business (game playing, use of facilities for moonlighting, duplication of effort, and so on)	Some exposure, but mitigated by console logs, review capabilities, and monitoring by management. Chargeback systems also tend to reduce exposure.	Greater exposure because the controls listed under Mainframe heading are lacking.

Source: Adapted from Edwin B. Opliger, "Identifying Microcomputer Concerns," *EDP Journal* (1985):43–44.

Security Issues and the Computer

To say that the financial community has become dependent on the computer is an understatement. With more than $500 billion transferred daily, most of it by electronic signals generated and collected by computers, it is not surprising that bank robbers no longer resemble Bonnie and Clyde. The terminal has replaced the gun, coaxial cable serves as the tunnel or ladder, and the combination to the safe is a few simple passwords keyed into the computer system. Moreover, when the computer criminal is caught, banks are often hesitant to prosecute and publicly reveal just how vulnerable they are, judges are reluctant to put white-collar criminals in jail with murderers and armed robbers, and bank managers fear personal liability for letting the crime take place. Besides, we all know that the bank is insured and nobody really gets hurt!

As an instrument for mischief, the computer is a most seductive toy—part of a game to be played by those clever enough to master its subtleties and outwit their opponents. The film *War Games* provides a good illustration of how fun can cross the boundary into much more serious territory. Computers are used in all sorts of illegal and unethical capers. Teenage "hackers" broke into medical records at the Sloan-Kettering Cancer Center in New York and "mucked around" with the data. Fortunately, no serious injury to any of the patients resulted, but invaluable medical research data were lost. Any company or organization that uses telecommunications and remote terminals is vulnerable to this kind of mischief.

The computer is a seductive temptress. For starters, the sense of anonymity and secrecy in manipulating the computer—through terminals, personal computers, or other means—undermines the fear of getting caught—which, for many of us, is unfortunately the most powerful deterrent to misbehaving. Besides, the corporate victim of a computer crime is often perceived as greedy, careless, even deserving of its fate. The crime may begin as a small manipulation, often by a trusted employee, just "to see if it works." A company that has limited safeguards, lax policies, and easy access to its computer may even be inviting computer crime, for when a company fails to provide effective security, some people feel it deserves to be taken—"the unlocked door asks to be opened," as the saying goes. Also, both the public and the media often applaud the computer criminal's ingenuity in "cracking the system."

Perhaps the most publicly acceptable unethical behavior is the copying of proprietary (copyrighted) software. It is estimated that for every legal copy of software, there are between five and ten illegal copies floating around. Most of this copying has come about since the introduction of personal computers with software that can be physically carried on a diskette from one machine to another. Software developers insist that a purchaser acquires only the right to use the software, not the right to make duplicate copies for sharing with others. However, enforcement of software ownership rights is very difficult, and in only a few cases have software developers gone after those who use bootlegged copies of their products. Lotus Development Co., marketer of the widely used spreadsheet package *Lotus 1-2-3,* has been the most aggressive in rooting out illegal copies and calling offending organizations to task.

The laws relevant to computer use are still somewhat unclear and misunderstood. The Computer Fraud and Abuse Act of 1986 and the Electronic Communications Privacy Act of 1986 have put some teeth in the laws and provided the courts with some basic guidelines. For example, since 1968, it has been illegal to intercept telephone conversations without court authorization (wiretap), but until recently, no laws prohibited the interception of electronic digital signals such as those computers use to send messages to terminals and to each other. Because many organizations have computers at different sites that communicate directly with one another, potentially vital data are being transmitted constantly. Until 1986, a competitor could literally steal all of the business information being transmitted without fear of legal recourse. The new laws made such interception illegal. However, federal legislation is generally limited to interstate activities, leaving the states to deal with their internal problems as best they can. At the state level, we do not even have agreement on how to define computer crime, and only 35 states have enacted significant legislation to make various computer activities criminal offenses. Penalties vary greatly from state to state, and some states have legislation that covers only one specific instance of computer crime.

The increasing popularity of computer crime may be a reflection of the value system in our society. We may not even care if the computer criminal gets away with his or her scheme so long as it does not hurt us. This is a short-sighted view, however, since our society is becoming increasingly dependent on computers and their security. In the long run, computer crime endangers us all.

Source: Based on William P. Haas, "The Temptress Computer," *Ocean State Business,* July 6, 1987.

Overcoming Implementation Problems

COORDINATED RESOURCE
See Oddou section on Controlling the Organization, "Information Control."

HERE'S AN EXAMPLE
Federal Express's elaborate telecommunications network is geared toward making the customer feel comfortable and relaxed. (*Wall Street Journal,* 3/19/90, p. A14)

No single approach will overcome all the implementation problems we have identified. Each situation must be separately diagnosed and its own individual "cure" prescribed. However, some implementation problems can be mitigated if the MIS design process follows the guidelines we mentioned above. Dickson and Simmons have described a number of factors that they consider important in helping managers overcome implementation problems.

1. *User orientation.* Perhaps the most critical step in overcoming implementation problems is to ensure that the MIS is user-oriented in both design and implementation. If the system's output fails to meet the users' needs, users will stick firmly, and logically, to their own systems, thereby reducing the chances that the MIS will eventually become useful to them. MIS design staff should be rewarded by fulfilling user needs as well as for meeting project deadlines.[26]

2. *Participation.* Many implementation problems can be overcome (or avoided) if future users are made members of the MIS team. Operating managers in particular should have a major say in the items to be included, the disposition of information, and possible job modifications. If the entire design and implementation process is taken over by technologists, serious line-staff conflicts may develop.[27]

3. *Communication.* The aims and characteristics of the system should be clearly defined and communicated to all members of the MIS team as well as to users. What makes this particularly difficult is that the character of an MIS evolves as it is being designed and implemented, so the final nature of the MIS cannot be known with precision at the outset. But unless they have a clear understanding of the system's basic objectives and characteristics, team members and users will have constant differences of opinion and the installed MIS will probably not satisfy the needs of users.

4. *Redefinition of performance measurements.* A new MIS may modify a manager's job to the point where old methods of performance evaluation no longer apply. For this reason, an MIS that calls for new evaluation procedures and/or criteria must be accompanied by incentives to encourage both high performance and acceptance of the system. The new methods must also be clearly explained so that managers will know how their accomplishments will be measured and rewarded.

5. *New challenges.* The notion that a computer can do many of the things that a manager can do—only faster and perhaps more thoroughly—has a lot to do with the insecurity a computer-based MIS often arouses in managers. One way to reduce this sense of insecurity is to publicize the challenges made possible by the computer system. A new MIS may liberate middle managers from many boring and routine tasks and may also give them the opportunity to use information provided by the system in more creative and productive ways.

■ END-USER COMPUTING

end-user computing
The creative use of computers by those who are not experts in data processing.

For the past decade or more, organizations have experienced a pent-up demand for computing and information resources, coupled with long lead times for MIS systems development, testing, and installation.[28] At the same time, information technology has advanced to the point where computer support permeates all the functional units and users are becoming more responsible and accountable for the information systems in their organizations.[29] With the development of problem-solving software that can be easily learned and used, **end-user computing**—the creative use of computers by employees who are not data-processing experts—is growing at the rate of 50–90 percent per year.[30]

The information center, which contains personal computers and terminals for the larger mainframe computers, has evolved as a means for assisting end users throughout the organization with educational and operational services related to

THOUGHT PROVOKER
New hardware and soft-
ware are making computer
networks the fastest growing part of the computer
industry. What are the
advantages and drawbacks
of computer networks?
(*Business Week,* 6/5/89,
p. 120ff.)

THOUGHT PROVOKER
Will artificial intelligence
or expert systems ever
replace managers? Why or
why not?

acquiring and using computers. In many cases, information centers are becoming partners with traditional system-development staffs.[31] To remain vital and viable, an information-center staff must be capable of introducing new technology and tools to the organization, and they must be able to guide and support end users who will learn to use and apply these tools.[32]

Decision support systems and artificial-intelligence techniques are becoming more useful to managers. As with MIS, DSS and artificial intelligence offer managers the ability to receive filtered, condensed, and analyzed information that can enhance their job performance and, in the case of artificial intelligence, provide them with an information system that can keep pace with their own knowledge and sophistication.

Decision Support Systems

A decision support system (DSS) is an interactive computer system that is easily accessible to, and operated by, noncomputer specialists to assist them in planning and decision-making functions. While DSSs may differ in their emphases on data-access and modeling functions, there is an overriding emphasis in all such systems on user accessibility to data for decision making.[33] This decision-making applicability permits managers to simulate problems using formal mathematical models and to test the outcomes of various alternatives for reaching the best possible decisions.[34]

DECISIONS BETWEEN DSS AND MIS. Since the DSS is an outgrowth of the MIS, there are basic similarities between them: They are both computer-based and designed to supply information to managers. However, there are some important advantages to a DSS. First of all, a DSS is geared to information *manipulation* and not essentially to data storage and retrieval, as are many MISs.[35] A DSS is operated directly by its users; when they need access to information, they can immediately consult their own on-line system without having to wait days or weeks for results from the MIS department. Once managers call up the required data through a DSS, they can manipulate it directly, asking questions and reformatting the data to meet their specific needs without having to explain what they want to the EDP/MIS staff.[36] Managers can thus be certain that they will get the information they need when they need it. In addition, direct manipulation of data has the advantage of greater security for sensitive information.

Another key difference between an MIS and a DSS is that a DSS helps managers make nonroutine decisions in unstructured situations.[37] An MIS, on the other hand, emphasizes standard, periodic reports and cannot respond well to nonroutine, unstructured, or ad hoc situations.[38] MIS departments may be unfamiliar with the decisions made in such situations; because they often have a tremendous backlog of requests for data, they may be unable to respond quickly to additional special requests. Conversely, some managers who have no difficulty manipulating the data themselves may have difficulty explaining their information requirements to MIS staff.

The ability of DSS users to access data directly and perform some of their own data-management chores has reduced one kind of intraorganizational conflict. In the early stages of computer-based MIS development, conflict and stresses between MIS users—managers and others—and EDP/MIS department personnel arose for a number of reasons, including the dependence of users on DP experts; the differing personal styles, backgrounds, values, and objectives of users and experts; and the evolving nature of information systems as new technologies and concepts appeared almost overnight.[39] The introduction of DSSs and on-line access to data has reduced the friction between people from various organizational subcultures and EDP/MIS staff, who often constitute a subculture of their own.

USING DSS. At Pet Foods in St. Louis, the sales-forecasting department performs a large percentage of its own data-processing tasks. Using readily available DSS appli-

artificial intelligence (AI) Development of computational approaches to simulate intelligent human thought or behavior.

expert system Application of artificial intelligence denoting the technology entailed by the development of computational approaches to human functioning.

cations software, users can project sales demand by units per territory and region and translate that information into a financial forecast. Through this process, the department can determine the effects of closing a particular warehouse in a matter of days, where the same task might take the MIS department weeks or months.[40] This is but one example of the successful application of DSS.

The ideal DSS solicits input data from the user and then prompts the user to consider all key-decision points.[41] Many software applications on the market can perform these functions. Among the more popular DSS applications software are spreadsheet packages such as *Lotus 1-2-3,* data-management packages such as *dBase III* and *Powerbase,* project-management software such as *Total Project Manager,* integrated software packages such as *Symphony, Framework,* and *Jazz,* and assorted financial analysis and planning packages. DSS software can support such organizational functions as marketing, production, and finance, as well as many other decision-making areas.[42]

DSS VS. EDP/MIS. The proliferation of microcomputers, off-the-shelf DSS software, and fourth-generation programming languages that boost programmer productivity has reduced the demand for MIS programmers, who generally specialize in the writing of programs for minicomputers and mainframes.[43] Thus, the reduction in user-MIS department conflicts brought about by the introduction of a DSS may be replaced by the fears of EDP/MIS staff that they are losing influence and control over information resources. Companies still need the massive data-processing and storage capacities of mainframe computers, however, and mainframes require EDP/MIS staff to operate and maintain them. Organizations are best served by an information system that integrates both DSS and MIS functions and activities.[44]

Another concern of EDP/MIS staff is that with every manager using his or her own DSS, there will be a proliferation of unauthorized and incompatible private files.[45] Some MIS staff may fear that data will become an individual resource rather than an organizational one—that is, that data will become the proprietary concern of individuals who might hold it for "ransom"—or that confusion will be created over which data files are correct. However, this possible problem is more than compensated for by the real advantages of a DSS, which are, on the whole, advantages to the organization as well as to the individual manager. The extra cost and duplication of computing resources and the lack of control over data in DSSs are outweighed by the more effective decisions that these systems make possible.[46] Centralized control of data, the aim of an MIS, should be supplanted by decentralized controls for the sharing of accurate DSS data.[47]

Expert Systems and Artificial Intelligence

Even as DSSs are being widely adopted, it seems likely that expert systems (ESs) will take their place in the near future as tools for improving organizational decision making and control.[48] Expert systems are also called "knowledge-based" systems since they are built on a framework of known facts and responses to situations. They may also be called **artificial intelligence (AI).**[49] Artificial intelligence refers to the use of the computer to simulate characteristics of human thought by developing computational approaches to intelligent behavior. Although the exact terminology for this new technology has not been totally agreed upon, we have used the term **expert systems** in our discussion to differentiate such systems from AI, of which they are more appropriately considered an application.[50] The other application of AI is natural-language processing.[51]

The potential importance to managers of artificial-intelligence research—the effort to make machines smarter—cannot be overstated. According to Patrick H. Winston and Karen A. Prendergast, "Some people believe artificial intelligence is the most exciting scientific and commercial enterprise of the century."[52] Sales of AI technology exceeded $700 million in 1985, an increase of 60 percent over 1984.

Promoting Knowledge-Based Systems. Concerned that the term *expert systems* made users fear computers would replace humans, Amoco Corp. systems analyst Steven Kleinman uses the "80 percent" figure to explain the value of knowledge-based systems: If such systems can provide useful advice on handling 80 percent of the relatively routine calls that experts get, they will free the human experts to deal with the 20 percent of the calls that are really difficult.

Projected sales are $50 billion–$120 billion by the year 2000. Hundreds of small companies, many bankrolled by industrial giants such as Lockheed, GM, and Control Data, are entering the field with specialized AI software and expert systems.[53] Expert systems are designed to apply the fruits of AI research to scientific, technological, and business problems by emulating the abilities and judgments of human experts and by making the experts' point of view available to nonexperts.

Typically, a human expert has specialized knowledge that he or she uses to solve specific problems. Expert systems perform like human experts: They can diagnose problems, recommend alternative solutions and strategies, offer rationales for their diagnoses and recommendations, and in some instances learn from previous experiences by adding information developed in solving problems to their current base of knowledge.[54] The expert systems developed in the 1980s now function productively in diverse areas, such as medical diagnosis, mineral and oil exploration, and equipment-fault locating.[55]

An expert system guides users through problems by asking them an orderly set of questions about the situation and drawing conclusions based on the answers it has been given. Its problem-solving abilities are guided by a set of programmed rules modeled on the actual reasoning processes of human experts in the field.[56] Expert systems are particularly relevant for unstructured problems and are more tolerant of errors and imperfect knowledge than conventional programs are.[57]

Because of their advanced capabilities, expert systems may supplant many kinds of DSSs. Users will no longer have to develop alternatives from information supplied by a DSS, but instead will be readily able to evaluate the alternatives and explanations offered by expert systems. Expert systems can provide expertise when human experts are not available and in many cases reach conclusions more rapidly even when they are. Human experts may find expert systems useful when making decisions involving complex, interdependent elements.

USES OF EXPERT SYSTEMS. The implementation of the first expert systems occurred at the end of the 1970s. One of the first business applications of expert

INTERNATIONAL MANAGEMENT

Information-System Strategies

A few years ago when Toyota was a pioneer among Japanese companies for its expansion efforts in the United States, it had some lessons to learn about managing information American-style. Just what makes the American style of information management so different? First, American companies purchase packaged software rather than develop each application from scratch. The Japanese style is typically to search for a best solution and then to develop software to accomplish the processing necessary to meet the best-solution requirements. Almost as important are the hardware and software standards maintained by American companies. By contrast, Japanese firms allow their work groups to acquire the hardware that they believe will be best for their processing needs, with no thought to what other work groups are doing. Finally, American companies develop voice- and data-communications expertise within the organization rather than relying on outside support, as Japanese firms generally do. It is interesting to note that many Japanese companies with American operations are standardizing their equipment by purchasing U.S.-made hardware rather than by importing NEC, Fujitsu, and other Japanese-made equipment. This practice provides compatibility with much of the American business environment, which would not be the case with imported hardware.

Business has been good and Toyota has been investing more in its U.S. operations, adding both manufacturing and distribution capabilities. Toyota has brought with it the Japanese management style, which is a management-by-consensus system, requiring a great deal of management participation in all decision making. This style calls for increasingly complex communications, especially between the American operations and the headquarters in Japan. Toyota solved this problem by implementing a private satellite-based network called Toyonet. The need for communications expertise within the organization is now very clear, as this communication network is critical to the success of Toyota's U.S. operations.

Hitachi is another Japanese firm that found out the hard way that the traditional Japanese management system does not work especially well in its U.S. operations. The company organization had been based on individual profit centers, with each division having a high degree of autonomy. This setup meant that each division was free to acquire the hardware and software that it thought would address its specific needs, without regard for what other divisions were doing. With 14 divisions in its U.S. operations, Hitachi ended up with several incompatible systems, including some of its own Hydac systems shipped in from Japan. The problem surfaced when the president of the company wanted to track certain large customers through several divisions of the company and was told that this was impossible because of hardware and software incompatibilities.

Developing custom-computer programs presents an especially difficult problem for Japanese companies. Hiring American programmers to meet their needs has proved very expensive, and the shortage of technical people in the United States makes it almost impossible to find enough staff anyway. The Americans they do hire often find it frustrating to work with the Japanese management style, which requires waiting for a consensus and exercising a great deal of patience while decisions are being made. With U.S. work visas in limited supply, Japanese software engineers and programmers cannot be relocated to America in sufficient numbers to meet system-development requirements, so Japanese companies are looking more to packaged software to satisfy their processing needs.

Although they have been slow to embrace American information systems or techniques, many Japanese firms have shown that they are willing to learn. While maintaining the long-term, pragmatic Japanese view, they are incorporating American standards and conventions into their information systems operations. Their hope is that the lessons they learn will make them more competitive on both sides of the Pacific. With the Department of Commerce reporting Japanese investment in the United States to be $23.4 billion for 1986—an increase of 142 percent from 1984—it is clear that large Japanese companies are making major commitments to their U.S. operations. A merging of Japanese and American information-system styles seems to be working for many of them. This would not be the first time that the Japanese have learned something from American business and then improved upon it.

Source: Based on Jeff Moad, "Japanese Pledge Allegiance to U.S. Information Systems Strategies," *Datamation,* February 15, 1988.

systems was developed by Schlumberger Ltd.; its system evaluates potential oil sites by using an amount of data far exceeding what human experts could interpret in a timely fashion.[58]

A task is generally more suitable for an expert system when there is a large discrepancy between the best and worst performers of the task. Whether ESs are far enough along in development to bring most organizations strategic benefits is questionable. About half of the Fortune 500 companies are developing ESs, yet few success stories have come to the attention of the business community.[59] Managers must be careful to avoid unrealistic expectations about this new technology. Nevertheless, some business-oriented expert-system software is already available. Odyssey is a scheduling system that permits users to resolve any conflicts in scheduling business trips, Nudge helps users schedule business meetings, and Omega performs personnel-assignment functions by matching job requirements to personnel characteristics.[60]

NATURAL-LANGUAGE PROCESSING. Communicating with a computer has thus far been a tedious and difficult task, requiring special codes and structure for instructions to be understood. **Natural-language processing** uses everyday language to communicate with the computer system, eliminating the need for technical training of the end user. Current systems have limited vocabularies, but they are able to deal with many of the ambiguities inherent in the English language.

natural-language processing Use of everyday language instead of special codes or instructions to communicate with a computer system.

Another benefit of natural-language processing is its ability to eliminate the keyboard. Voice-recognition systems are being marketed that utilize AI techniques to route all communication with the computer through a microphone. The user has only to speak clearly and slowly for applications as wide-ranging as word processing and circuit design. This leaves hands free to manipulate other equipment, such as a mouse, or provides communication capability for those who do not have the full use of their hands.

THE FUTURE OF EXPERT SYSTEMS. American organizations are currently investing much effort and resources in the development of artificial intelligence for expert systems and other applications.[61] The Japanese are also devoting a great deal of energy to AI in their "fifth-generation" computer project. The expectation is that a qualitative advantage in computer technology will translate into a national economic advantage.[62] Along with limited computer hardware capabilities, a principal challenge for ES designers is the effective filtering out of knowledge-base biases that are imparted by the particular, unique views and values of the experts who are the sources of the knowledge that constitutes the system's knowledge base. New expert systems will be developed rapidly as a result of these efforts, although these systems may be very expensive for some time to come.

Managing End-User Computing

End-user computing presents opportunities for improved performance, but it also entails risks for the organization. A critical starting point for effective management is the development of a strategy for end-user computing. It is important to have a vision of how end-user computing will contribute to the competitive positioning of the firm. This view will lead to enhanced productivity of white-collar workers, and by having the user initiate and control his or her own processing requests, it may help to overcome the shortage of information-system professionals experienced by most organizations. If we were to investigate a purchasing department that has moved from transaction processing to end-user computing and follow a machine tool order through the system, we would find that using the computer to access vendor and price information is only the starting point. With end-user computing, instead of being just a processor of the purchase request, the purchasing agent can check the data base and determine if the organization has existing machine tools

Standardizing Desktop Systems. Frustrated by a mishmash of incompatible desktop systems that could not share information, John D. Lowenberg, CIO of Aetna Life and Casualty, set out to define a standard, dubbed Aetna Information Technology Architecture, for the corporation's 40,000 desktop computers and the software they run—a massive project that may take as long as five years to phase in. Although employees and managers will need to be retrained to use and maintain their new systems, they will need such training just once in their career at Aetna.

similar to the one being requested. If one or more is found, the agent can interrogate the data base to determine if excess capacity exists and, if it does, can recommend that the requestor use the installed equipment.[63]

The risks associated with end-user computing include increased exposure of both data and software, leading to threats of data security and integrity. In conjunction with this problem, we also find that the end user often does not show adequate concern for data validation and quality assurance. In the MIS, the systems professional is responsible for the entire process and can control data-collection and -entry activities. End users have also been accused of making ineffective use of resources, failing to properly document their software, and practicing overanalysis.[64]

Software concerns include the responsibility for development and continued ownership of the software. Without some central control, there is sure to be duplication of effort throughout the organization. Once the end user has an operating system, he or she is often unwilling to assume responsibility for compatibility with other systems throughout the organization (for file sharing and networking). Also, if the user leaves the organization, who has ownership of any systems he or she developed while an employee? Management must establish policies to address these issues. When purchased software is used, such as *Lotus 1-2-3* or *dBASE III+,* software piracy becomes a concern. Making copies of software to share with others in the organization is illegal in most instances, and organizations can be held liable for their copying activities.

■ THE IMPACT OF COMPUTERS AND MIS ON MANAGERS AND ORGANIZATIONS

HERE'S AN EXAMPLE

The achnowledged leader in information distribution is Wal-Mart. Its satellite communication network and computer power allow it instant access to sales information. The company also broadcasts training and merchandising programs over the network. (*Fortune*, 5/6/91, p. 58ff.)

COORDINATED RESOURCE

See *Management Live!* Reading 10.1, "The Coming of the New Organization."

THOUGHT PROVOKER

A computer-integrated business is described as an enterprise whose major functions exchange operating information quickly and constantly via computer. (*Fortune*, 9/24/90, p. 114ff.) What are the implications?

The application of computer technology to management information and decision support systems has certainly had an effect on how managers perform their tasks and on how organizations behave. An early study of the impact of computerization suggested that there would be an increased structuring of middle management, higher status for some middle-management positions, more differences between top and middle management, and a recentralization of the organization.[65]

As it turns out, the chief effect of computerization on organizations has been the ability to process (and create) paperwork with ever-greater accuracy and speed; it has had little effect on the roles of managers and the structure of organizations.[66] The segregation of middle managers into "functionary" and "programmer" roles has not taken place. In fact, Paul Attewell and James Rule cite evidence that computerization may lead to an increase in the number of management levels.[67] They have also found that access to information can strengthen the positions of subordinates.

The formation of an elite and aloof top level of management has also not come to pass. The amount of use that top managers make of computer-based information and computers themselves varies from organization to organization and is a matter of contention among management authors.[68] And top management is not necessarily in control of the computerization of the organization. For example, individual departments can often purchase microcomputers and powerful DSS software directly without getting a corporate EDP/MIS decision on their purchases.[69] Thus, middle managers are determining their information and systems needs for themselves and not having systems imposed on them from above. At the same time, information-systems departments in organizations are undergoing changes. They are becoming more sensitive to the needs and management styles of the information-systems users, and are no longer considered only a back-room and behind-the-scenes activity. In many organizations, the information-systems department has become proactive to meet the needs of today's information-intensive businesses. The challenge for management is to exploit these new technologies, to question the status quo of the organization, and to manage for change rather than to work to prevent or restrict it.[70]

The Continuing Computer Revolution

COORDINATED RESOURCE

The Additional Lecture for Chapter 22 found in the Lecture Extras supplement is called "Electronic Mail: Bane or Boon?"

THOUGHT PROVOKER

How will advanced information technologies change our society?

To say that we are rapidly moving from an industrial-based society to an information-based one is not an overstatement. For the foreseeable future, managers will have to keep abreast of, and anticipate, further advancements and applications from the continuing computer revolution. In addition, managers will need to evaluate new developments and determine their effects on their organizations.

The expansion of computer capabilities and further developments in artificial intelligence may prompt major adjustments in the way managers work and in the way organizations act. Even today it is not unusual to see, for example, a manager using a pocket computer that organizes messages and schedules meetings. Robots and robot-vision systems for manufacturing control will become normal parts of the production process. One day we may truly create an information-based society whose members will have the leisure time to enjoy the fruits of its key industries: knowledge, communications, and computer-based consumer products.

ILLUSTRATIVE CASE STUDY

WRAP-UP

Using Technology at Sears for Strategic Advantage

Charles Carlson is reviewing the 1990 merchandising year, and is not happy. Sears has lost critical market shares to up-and-coming merchandisers such as Wal-Mart and K Mart, and some financial analysts are criticizing Sears' cumbersome and costly bureaucratic organization and its inability to quickly respond to customers, markets, and technology. Carlson would not have been bothered a few years ago, when Sears was riding high and installing automated information-processing systems at a record rate. Profits were also at an all-time high during the mid-1980s. Today, however, profits are down, investor confidence in the company is shaken, and senior management is struggling to develop a strategy to counter the competition and put Sears in the forefront of retailing once again.

Examining the differences between Sears' and Wal-Mart's operations, Carlson notes that Wal-Mart runs a very lean administrative headquarters staff with less than half the employees of Sears, yet Wal-Mart is able to support a retail operation almost as large. Using computer and communications technology to leverage the work of their people, Wal-Mart's staff is able to keep costs down while maintaining operational efficiency. The Wal-Mart satellite communication system and information network provides management with instant access to sales and marketing information from all of Wal-Mart's retail operations throughout the country. This has allowed management to establish agreements with suppliers for computer-to-computer ordering, which speeds up the process and keeps costs down. Also, by instantly collecting and processing sales information with their satellite system and headquarters computers, Wal-Mart can tell suppliers what merchandise is moving, at what price, how fast, and in which stores. Suppliers are willing to give price concessions if they have up-to-the-minute marketing information be-cause they can better plan their production runs. This lets Wal-Mart sell the merchandise at a lower price than their competition, giving them a competitive edge in the marketplace.

Carlson realizes that over the past several years Sears has fallen behind the competition in utilizing technology. The company does not currently have a fully integrated inventory control, ordering, and receiving system in its stores, though a plan is in place to ship merchandise with premarked prices and bar codes that can be scanned to enter the merchandise into store inventory records, which will reduce receiving room staff and cut personnel costs at each location. Sears does not, however, have the instant transmission and processing capabilities that make Wal-Mart so formidable a foe. Also, Sears still maintains a large charge card and service contract operation, requiring customer service and clerical support in each location, even if the volume does not justify the cost. They are currently unable to handle most of the credit and service tasks through the normal registers, which means they must maintain a separate operation and data-processing system. Carlson knows that Sears needs to utilize technology a good deal more, and needs to do this fast if it is to survive as one of the world's largest retailers. He also recognizes that computer technology has come full circle: starting in the 1950s and 1960s as an economical replacement for people, moving in the 1970s and 1980s into management support and decision making, and once again offering economies by replacing people with machines in the 1990s. ■

Sources: Marianne Taylor, "Sears Work Force to Be Slashed by 7% by Midyear," *Chicago Tribune,* January 4, 1991, Sect. 1, pp. 1, 15; Taylor, "Can Ed Brennan Salvage the Sears He Designed?," *Business Week,* August 27, 1990, p. 34; Taylor, "Are the Lights Dimming for Ed Brennan?," *Business Week,* February 11, 1991, pp. 56–57; and Bill Saporito, "Is Wal-Mart Unstoppable?," *Fortune,* May 6, 1991, pp. 50–59.

■ SUMMARY

Effective planning, decision making, and control all depend on the effective management of information through management information systems, a general term for any computer-based information system that is used to collect, store, organize, and distribute information that is useful to managers.

The term *data* refers to raw, unanalyzed numbers and facts, while *information* refers to data that have been organized or analyzed in some way. Increasingly, an organization's information is seen as one of its most valuable assets. Information's usefulness is evaluated on the basis of its quality, timeliness, quantity, and relevance to management. Today computers are seen as one of the most effective and efficient ways of gathering, storing, organizing, and distributing large amounts of information.

A computer system is an integrated collection of hardware, software, procedures, data, and people that interact to produce information. Over the years, MIS has evolved from the earlier electronic data-processing systems to MIS systems that produce reports useful for managers, then to DSS and artificial intelligence, which help managers plan and make decisions.

The information needs of managers depend on their place in the management hierarchy. Lower-level managers, who are concerned with operational control, require frequent, highly detailed, and accurate information—predominantly from internal sources. Middle managers require summarized information that may come from both external and internal sources. Top managers are primarily concerned with strategic planning and control, so they need information that is highly summarized and focused on identifying general trends and overall performance.

Guidelines for an effective MIS include: (1) making users part of the design team; (2) carefully considering the costs of the system; (3) considering alternatives to in-house software development; (4) favoring relevance and selectivity over sheer quantity; (5) pretesting the system before installation; and (6) training the operators and users of the system carefully.

A number of people problems can arise when a computer-based MIS is being implemented. These problems are likely to develop if the MIS disrupts established departmental boundaries, if it disrupts the informal communication system, if individuals resist the system, if the organizational culture is not supportive, and if the change is implemented without manager-subordinate participation. The reactions of organization members to a computer-based MIS may include aggression, projection, and avoidance, depending on their organizational level and how the MIS will affect them.

End-user computing, the creative use of computers by nontechnical users, emerged when the availability of personal computers and easy-to-use software combined with a pent-up demand for computer and information resources. Two of the most promising trends in end-user computing involve decision support systems and expert systems, including the development of natural-language processing. Although end-user computing presents opportunities for improved performance, it also presents threats to security and data integrity.

Computerization has had a number of effects on organizations, chief among them the ability to process and create paperwork with increased accuracy and speed. Although end-user computing represents a trend toward decentralization, most researchers have found that computer systems do not change an organization's existing structures—they simply make it easier to get certain tasks done. This is a trend that should parallel the ongoing computer revolution.

1. What is information and why is it important to effective managerial planning, decision making, and control?

2. What four factors determine the value of information?

3. What are the five components of an information system?

4. Compare and contrast the information needs of operational, middle-level, and upper-level managers.

5. What are the four stages in designing an MIS? How may they be carried out effectively?

6. Why do employees sometimes resist the implementation of a new computer system? How can their resistance be overcome?

7. What are the major security concerns associated with computer systems and how can they be resolved?

8. Why is end-user computing a strong trend in many of today's organizations?

9. Compare and contrast decision support systems, expert systems, and conventional management information systems.

10. What are some of the main issues involved in managing end-user computing?

The Human Edge in Software: Electronic Advisors

Gary Chapman ordinarily suffers fools patiently, if not gladly. But today, when a fellow employee at EEV, Inc., an electronic parts manufacturer in Elmsford, New York, pokes his head into Chapman's office, interrupting the sales manager's telephone conversation for the third time, Chapman says firmly, "I'm busy. I'm on the phone."

The tactic works. His colleague retreats—once and for all.

Chapman is both surprised and delighted by the outcome. To learn how best to handle his nettlesome co-worker, he sought advice from neither friend, how-to book, consultant, nor shrink. Instead he turned to *The Management Edge,* a software package from Human Edge Software Corporation in Palo Alto, California, a new company whose computer programs promise frazzled managers sound advice on handling subordinates, superiors, customers—indeed, anyone they might encounter during the business day.

Although using the computer to juggle people—rather than words or numbers—may have the ring of Orwellian fantasy, the concept is catching on among software developers. Resource 1, Inc., in San Diego, for example, is introducing computer programs based on the work of noted management experts and best-selling authors such as Alec Mackenzie (*The Time Trap*) and Kenneth Blanchard and Robert Lorber (*Putting the One Minute Manager to Work,* their sequel to *The One Minute Manager*). The software, claims Mona Williams, a company spokeswoman, will help managers change their behavior while simultaneously teaching them computer skills.

Human Edge's business-strategy software is by far the most sophisticated attempt yet to tackle the vagaries of human behavior. Founded by psychologist Jim Johnson, who also started Psych Systems, Inc., developer and seller of the first on-line automated psychological testing service, the company has five products—*The Sales Edge, The Management Edge, The Negotiation Edge, The Communications Edge,* and *The Leadership Edge*—that are all expert, or knowledge-based, systems, a type of artificial intelligence.

Writing this kind of software requires collecting a number of "rules" that are culled either from experts or from the existing research on a subject. Using the rules, a computer can figure out what the best course of action is in any given situation. To develop *The Sales Edge,* for example, Johnson and his staff went through stacks of sales-oriented business literature, gleaning, he says, "every piece of advice that any expert has ever offered." Then they structured the recommendations according to their appropriateness for individual personality types.

All the programs work similarly: First you agree or disagree with 70 to 100 statements, such as, "I often have trouble going to sleep because of worries about the job," "I like to attend parties related to my job," and "A good manager has total control." From your responses the computer develops a personality profile.

Then, whenever you need tips on dealing with a specific individual, you assess his or her character by checking off adjectives: "self-protecting," "simple-minded," "smart," or "prestige-oriented," for instance. (With *The Management Edge* you also describe the work environment; *The Negotiation Edge,* which used decision-making theory based on mathematical formulas, requires that you enter your expectations.)

With the profiles loaded, the computer will search through its huge store of information—the packages contain 300,000 to 400,000 words of text on two or three disks—and produce a report giving you specific pointers on how to act most effectively toward the targeted individual. *The Sales Edge,* which walks you through preparation, presentation, and opening and closing ploys, tells you what to expect from your quarry and how to succeed. *The Management Edge* covers such areas as motivating employees, finding the right niche for a worker, firing, and improving communications.

When Gary Chapman plugged in *The Management Edge,* he was told that his co-worker, whose irritating habits he had chalked up to overenthusiasm, belongs to that troublesome class of individuals who don't recognize other people's responsibilities and obligations. And, the report admonished Chapman, "you too easily forgive those things." On the second or third occasion, point your view out to him, the report continued, then go about your business—advice Chapman followed with good effect.

Chapman has also tried *The Management Edge* with customers and managers of the corporation's parent company in England. As a technical person, he says, he tends to be "very meticulous about numbers" and usually gets "right down to the details." But the computer informed him that several of his frequent business contacts become overwhelmed by too many specifics. So Chapman forced himself to concentrate on the larger picture by putting a big sign on his desk that read "No details." "It was fantastic," he says. "People were more receptive to the things I wanted to do."

"I hope nobody else gets [*The Management Edge*]," Chapman adds, "because it's like a secret weapon, like being able to hear somebody's dreams. You can plan the whole strategy before you go see [anyone], and you know you're right."

Although some users consider the programs the next best thing to an ever-vigilant personal consultant, detractors argue that this type of software is, by its nature, limited. "It's a nice game, and it might be reasonably accurate," says Murray Weiner, a consultant with Rohrer, Hibler & Replogle, Inc., an international industrial psychology and management consulting firm. "But it can't possibly get into all of the conceivable interactions."

Even Jim Johnson, who developed the business-strategy software, admits that it isn't a total solution to life's tribulations. When he wanted to fire an employee of his Palo Alto firm who had become a morale problem, he ran the outplacement section of *The*

Management Edge on him. Proceed with caution, the report advised, this employee tends to be litigious. So Johnson hired a labor lawyer to ensure that the procedure was carried out in strict accordance with California law. "Sure enough," says Johnson, "he sued."

Source: Reprinted with permission, *Business Month* magazine, March 1984. Copyright © 1984 by Goldhirsh Group, Inc., 38 Commercial Wharf, Boston, MA 02110.

Case Questions

1. How is Gary Chapman using *The Management Edge* to make decisions?

2. What are the limitations of the program? What are the advantages?

3. Do you agree with Murray Weiner that *The Management Edge* and other such programs are no more than "games"?

4. In your opinion, will most managers be using an information system like *The Management Edge* in the future? Explain. Would you be comfortable with such a system? Discuss why or why not.

VIDEO CASE STUDY

Telecommuting at Apple Computer, Inc.

Andy Harris works in the early morning. He works in the evening. In between, he might go for a walk, attend an acting class, or lunch with a friend.

Harris, a full-time senior technical writer for Apple Computer, Inc., is a telecommuter. He works at home and communicates with his office via fax machine, computer, and telephone. He almost never makes the 28-mile round trip to Apple's offices in Cupertino, California.

California has led the way in telecommuting. The state's stringent antipollution laws have required employers to reduce the number of car trips made by employees, and cities such as Los Angeles and San Francisco see telecommuting as a way to reduce road congestion.

For some workers, such as Andy Harris, telecommuting has been liberating. Instead of spending 12 to 14 hours a day on the job, he has been able to cut the number of hours he works while increasing his productivity fivefold because he has been freed from the minutia of office politics. He has also revived a moribund social life and resumed his acting hobby.

"I felt like I'd gotten a $150,000 raise, because now I could integrate two parts of myself, which had previously been impossible to do," Harris says. "It was an absolutely life-changing fantastic experience."

Telecommuting offers other advantages besides helping to decrease pollution and traffic jams. One is that it permits more flexible work schedules. Workers who find it hard to get to the office because of a disability, family emergency, or illness now can manage to work from home.

Another advantage of telecommuting is that it frequently increases productivity, perhaps as much as 15 to 30 percent, because it cuts down on interruptions and time-consuming meetings. "I did a business plan in one day at home," says Bill White, a product marketing manager for Apple. "In the office, with all the interruptions, the very same thing may have taken three days or more to accomplish."

Other advantages for home-based workers are the elimination of the stress of commuting and savings on restaurant lunches and clothes for the office.

But there are some drawbacks to telecommuting. Home-based workers can become isolated and miss out on the fruitful intellectual give-and-take that goes on among employees who work together in the same office. And office-based employees may resent those who have the "luxury" of staying home.

At Apple, for instance, where six of Harris's eight-member writing group work from home, not everyone is pleased. "I find that I'm happiest with the group when they all happen to come in [to the office] at the same time and we have an interaction going," says Armi Costello, one of the two members who works at Apple headquarters.

Even Harris admits that telecommuters sometimes feel shut out of important office decisions. They may also crave the kind of recognition for their work that's difficult to get when a manager isn't nearby.

Telecommuting also presents challenges for managers. Many are accustomed to watching their employees work and tend to equate physical presence with productivity. Telecommuting forces them to measure productivity in terms of results rather than hours spent on the job. Managers must also overcome the suspicion that employees who aren't continually supervised won't complete the job. Says David Flemming, a telecommuting consultant for the State of California: "You [learn] to start managing by results, not surveillance."

Telecommuting is often suggested as the ideal work situation for pregnant women, mothers with young children, and, especially, the disabled. Certainly, the technology allows severely disabled workers to perform complicated jobs without the inconvenience of going to an office. But specially designed equipment for the disabled is sometimes unavailable and, when it is, usually quite expensive. Apple, along with other computer companies, has been working with groups for the disabled to make computers easier to use. Some advocates for the disabled also worry that telecommuting is a convenient way for companies to comply with handicapped-access laws without actually making their buildings accessible to the handicapped.

Other concerns have been voiced by labor unions, notably the AFL-CIO. The unions are worried that telecommuting could prompt a return to substandard home working conditions. This has happened already in some industries, where telecommuters are designated "independent contractors," paid low wages, and denied benefits—a practice that has led to several lawsuits.

Despite the drawbacks, however, workers such as Andy Harris predict that the number of telecommuters will continue to grow because it is a style of working that suits so many people.

Sources: Frank Bowe, "Making Computers Accessible to Disabled People," *Technology Review,* January 1987, pp. 52–59, 72; Geoff Lewis, Jeffrey Rothfeder, Resa W. King, Mark Maremont, and Thane Peterson, "The Portable Executive," *Business Week,* October 10, 1988, pp. 102–111; Jiri Weiss, "Earthquake Shakes Telecommuting Sense into Corporations," *Home-Office Computing,* June 1989, p. 104; David Weddle, "Aren't You Going to Work?", *California,* May 1990, pp. 65–71, 148–150; Jonathan N. Goodrich, "Telecommuting in America," *Business Horizons,* July–August 1990, pp. 31–37; Lloyd Gite, "The Home-Based Executive," *Black Enterprise,* January 1991, pp. 63–65; Maryrose Wood, "Phoning It In," *Desktop,* April 1991, pp. 44–48; and Fred Davis, "Telecommuting Aids Economy, Ecology, Firm and Employee," *PC Week,* April 1, 1991, p. 138.

Case Questions

1. How has the technology revolution fueled the growth of telecommuting?
2. In what ways might telecommuting be a barrier to effective management?
3. How would an organization's culture bear on the effectiveness of telecommuting?
4. What types of employees do you think would work most effectively as telecommuters?
5. What safeguards could be created to ensure the rights of workers who telecommute?

■ NOTES

[1] For a discussion of information systems corporate issues and opportunities, see Robert K. Wysocki and James Young, *Information Systems Management Principles in Action* (New York: Wiley, 1990), pp. 123–134.

[2] Philip D. Olson, "Choices for Innovation-Minded Corporations," *The Journal of Business Strategy* 11, no. 1 (January–February 1990):42–46.

[3] Paul L. Tom, *Managing Information as a Corporate Resource* (Glenview, Ill.: Scott, Foresman, 1987), p. 4.

[4] Robert Behling, *Computers and Information Processing* (Boston: Kent Publishing, 1986), pp. 82–83.

[5] This discussion is drawn, in part, from Michael S. Scott Morton and John F. Rockart, "Implications of Changes in Information Technology for Corporate Strategy," *Interfaces* 14, no. 1 (January–February 1984):84–95.

[6] For further discussion of the differences between and the evolution of MIS and DSS, see Ralph H. Sprague, Jr., "A Framework for the Development of Decision Support Systems," in Hugh J. Watson and

Archie B. Carroll, eds., *Computers for Business* (Plano, Tex.: Business Publications, 1984), pp. 197–226.

[7]Barry Shore, *Introduction to Computer Information Systems* (New York: Holt, Rinehart & Winston, 1988), pp. 304–313.

[8]G. Anthony Gorry and Michael S. Scott Morton, "A Framework for Management Information Systems," *Sloan Management Review* 13, no. 1 (Fall 1971):55–70. Gorry and Scott Morton based their framework on the three-part division of managerial activities described by Robert N. Anthony in *Planning and Control Systems* (Boston: Harvard University Graduate School of Business Administration, 1965), pp. 15–21.

[9]Charles R. Litecky, "Corporate Strategy and MIS Planning," *Journal of Systems Management* 32, no. 1 (January 1981):36–39.

[10]See, for example, John C. Carter and Fred N. Silverman, "Establishing an MIS," *Journal of Systems Management* 31, no. 1 (January 1980):15–21; and W. L. Harrison, *Computers and Information Processing* (St. Paul: West, 1986).

[11]Robert G. Murdick, "MIS Development Procedures," *Journal of Systems Management* 21, no. 12 (December 1970):22–26.

[12]See Arnold Barnett, "Preparing Management for MIS," *Journal of Systems Management* 23, no. 1 (January 1972):40–43. For further discussion of introducing new technology into organizations, see Wallace A. Wood and Robert Behling, "Managing the Introduction of Information Systems Technology: The Case of Desktop Publishing as an Organization Wide Resource," *Journal of Microcomputer Systems Management* 2, no. 3 (Summer 1990):1–7. For a more complete discussion of developing systems to provide essential information for managers, see Harold A. Records and Michael F. Glennie, "Service Management and Quality Assurance," *The Cornell H.R.A. Quarterly* 32, no. 1 (May 1991):2–11.

[13]Michael Potter and Robin McNeill, "The New Programmer—The Next Wave of Computer Innovation in North American Business," *Business Quarterly* 48, no. 4 (Winter 1983):132–134.

[14]See Russell L. Ackoff, "Management Misinformation Systems," *Management Science* (December 1967):147–156.

[15]Charles A. O'Reilly III, "Individuals and Information Overload in Organizations: Is More Necessarily Better?" *Academy of Management Journal* 23, no. 4 (December 1980):684–696.

[16]John P. Murray, *Managing Information Systems as a Corporate Resource* (Homewood, Ill.: Dow Jones-Irwin, 1984).

[17]John F. Rockart, "Chief Executives Define Their Own Data Needs," *Harvard Business Review* 57, no. 2 (March–April 1979):81–93, describes a process for determining the factors CEOs consider critical for their organizations' success ("critical success factors").

[18]See H. L. Capron and Brian K. Williams, *Computers and Data Processing*, 3rd ed. (Menlo Park, Cal.: Benjamin/Cummings Publishing, 1990), p. 313; and Steven L. Mandell, *Computers and Data Processing: Concepts and Applications*, 2nd ed. (St. Paul, Minn.: West Publishing, 1982), p. 34.

[19]A case study from the Harvard Business School, "First National City Bank Operating Group (A), 474–165, 1975, and (B), 474–166, 1975," describes the direct installation approach used by John Reed—currently CEO of Citicorp—to mechanize the "back office" operations (routine check and other paper processing) of Citibank when he was senior vice president of the Operating Group in 1970. Though this mechanization effort was not a purely MIS installation, it is an example of the direct approach to a complex operations systems conversion that used computers and related equipment and that contained facets of Citibank's MIS.

[20]F. Warren Benton, *Execucomp: Maximum Management with the New Computers* (New York: Wiley, 1983), p. 238.

[21]Our discussion in this section is based on G. W. Dickson and John K. Simmons, "The Behavioral Side of MIS," *Business Horizons* 13, no. 4 (August 1970):59–71.

[22]Dickson and Simmons, "The Behavioral Side of MIS," pp. 59–71.

[23]Daniel Robey and M. Lynne Markus, "Rituals in Information System Design," *MIS Quarterly* 8, no. 1 (March 1984):5–15.

[24]Edwin B. Opliger, "Identifying Microcomputer Concerns," *EDP Journal*, no. 1 (1985):42–67.

[25]Paul E. Dascher and W. Ken Harmon, "The Dark Side of Small Business Computers," *Management Account* 65, no. 11 (May 1984):62–67.

[26]Michael Newman, "User Involvement—Does It Exist, Is It Enough?" *Journal of Systems Management* 35, no. 5 (1984):34–38.

[27]Blake Ives and Margrethe H. Olson, "User Involvement and MIS Success: A Review of Research," *Management Science* 30, no. 5 (May 1984):586–603. Ives and Olson note there is a lack of research demonstrating the benefits of user participation, but they do suggest that participation is useful in unstructured situations and also in situations where user acceptance is important for MIS success.

[28]John F. Rockart and Lauren S. Flannery, "The Management of End-User Computing," *Communications of the ACM* 26, no. 10 (October 1983):776–784.

[29]Thomas E. Gallo, *Strategic Information Management Planning* (Englewood Cliffs, N.J.: Prentice Hall, 1988), p. 18.

[30]Rockhart and Flannery, "The Management of End-User Computing."

[31]Ralph H. Sprague, Jr., and Barbara C. McNurlin, *Information Systems Management in Practice* (Englewood Cliffs, N.J.: Prentice Hall, 1986), pp. 311–333.

[32]John N. Oglesby, "How to Shop for Your Information Center," *Datamation* 33, no. 11 (June 1, 1987):70–76.

[33]Steven Alter, in "A Taxonomy of Decision Support Systems," *Sloan Management Review* 19, no. 1 (Fall 1977):39–59, describes seven different types of DSS, from systems that are heavily data-oriented to those that are heavily model-oriented. His taxonomy is based on the extent to which the system's outputs bear on decision making.

[34]Bernard C. Reinmann and Allan D. Waren, "User-Oriented Criteria for the Selection of DSS Software," *Communications of the ACM* 28, no. 2 (February 1985):166–179. See also Reinmann, "Decision Support Systems: Strategic Management Tools for the Eighties," *Business Horizons,* September–October 1985, pp. 71–77.

[35]"Fourth-Generation Languages Make DSS Feasible for All Managers," *Management Review* 73, no. 4 (April 1984):4–5.

[36]Donald R. Wood, "The Personal Computer: How It Can Increase Management Productivity," *Financial Executive* 52, no. 2 (February 1984):15.

[37]Andrew T. Masland, "Integrators and Decision Support System Success in Higher Education," *Research in Higher Education* 20, no. 2 (1984):211–233.

[38]Hugh J. Watson and Marianne M. Hill, "Decision Support Systems or What Didn't Happen with MIS," *Interfaces* 13, no. 5 (October 1983):81–88.

[39]These initial conflicts and stresses are described in Chris Argyris, "Management Information Systems: The Challenge to Rationality and Emotionality," *Management Science* 17, no. 6 (February 1971):B275–292.

[40]Jennifer E. Beaver, "Bend or Be Broken," *Computer Decisions* 16, no. 6 (1984):43.

[41]Andrew P. Sage, Bernard Galing, and Adolpho Langomasi, "The Methodologies for Determination of Information Requirements for Decision Support Systems," *Large Scale Systems* 5, no. 2 (October 1983):158.

[42]"What's Happening with DSS?" *EDP Analyzer* 22, no. 7 (July 1984):1–16.

[43]Potter and McNeill, "The New Programmer—The Next Wave of Computer Innovation in North American Business," p. 132.

[44]See Harry Katzan, Jr., *Management Support Systems: A Pragmatic Approach* (New York: Van Nostrand Reinhold, 1984), pp. 2–3.

[45]Beaver, "Bend or Be Broken," p. 132.

[46]"What's Happening with DSS?" *EDP Analyzer,* pp. 1–16.

[47]Wood, "The Personal Computer: How It Can Increase Management Productivity," pp. 17–18.

[48]"What's Happening with DSS?" *EDP Analyzer.*

[49]The discussion of expert systems is drawn mainly from Robert W. Blanning, "Knowledge Acquisition and System Validation in Expert Systems for Management," *Human Systems Management* 4, no. 4 (Autumn 1984):280–285; Robert W. Blanning, "Expert Systems for Management: Possible Application Areas," *Institute for Advancement of Decision Support Systems DSS-84 Transactions* (1984):69–77; and Robert W. Blanning, "Issues in the Design for Expert Systems for Management," *Proceedings of the National Computer Conference* (1984):489–495.

[50]Walter Reitman, "Artificial Intelligence Applications for Business: Getting Acquainted," in Walter Reitman, ed., *Artificial Intelligence Applications for Business* (Norwood, N.J.: Ablex Publishing, 1984), pp. 1–9. For an excellent discussion of AI, see Jeffrey Rothfelder, *Minds Over Matter: A New Look at Artificial Intelligence* (New York: Simon & Schuster, 1985). See also Karl W. Wiig, "AI: Management's Newest Tool," *Management Review* (August 1986):24–28; and R. Kurzweil, "What Is Artificial Intelligence Anyway?" *American Scientist* 73 (1985):258–264.

[51]Shore, *Introduction to Computer Information Systems,* pp. 304–313.

[52]Patrick H. Winston and Karen A. Prendergast, eds., *The AI Business: The Commercial Uses of Artificial Intelligence* (Cambridge, Mass.: MIT Press, 1985), preface.

[53]See Emily T. Smith, "A High-Tech Market That's Not Feeling the Pinch," *Business Week,* July 1, 1985, p. 78.

[54]Michael W. Davis, "Anatomy of Decision Support," *Datamation,* June 15, 1985, pp. 201ff.

[55]Kenneth Fordyce, Peter Norden, and Gerald Sullivan, "Review of Expert Systems for the Management Science Practitioner," *Interfaces* 17, no. 2 (March–April 1987):64–77.

[56]Robert C. Schank with Peter G. Childers, *The Cognitive Computer: On Language, Learning, and Artificial Intelligence* (Reading, Mass.: Addison-Wesley, 1985), p. 33.

[57]Jay Liebowitz, *Introduction to Expert Systems* (Santa Cruz, Cal.: Mitchell Publishing, 1988), pp. 3–21.

[58]Howard Austin, "Market Trends in Artificial Intelligence," in Reitman, ed., *Artificial Intelligence Applications for Business,* pp. 267–286.

[59]Hugh J. Watson, Archie B. Carroll, and Robert I. Mann, *Information Systems for Management* (Plano, Tex.: Business Publications, 1987), pp. 170–181.

[60]Blanning, "Knowledge Acquisition and System Validation in Expert Systems for Management," p. 282. See also Fred L. Luconi, Thomas W. Malone, and Michael S. Morton, "Expert Systems: The Next Challenge for Managers," *Sloan Management Review* (Summer 1986):3–14; and Efraim Turban and Paul R. Watkins, "Integrating Expert Systems and Decision Support Systems, *MIS Quarterly* 10 (1986):121–138.

[61]"What's Happening with DSS?" *EDP Analyzer.*

[62]Winston and Prendergast, eds., *The AI Business.* For discussions of Japanese and American efforts in AI, see also Edward A. Feigenbaum and Pamela McCorduck, *The Fifth Generation: Artificial Intelligence and Japan's Computer Challenge to the World* (New York: New American Library, 1984); and Frank Rose, *Into the Heart of the Mind: An American Quest for Artificial Intelligence* (New York: Harper & Row, 1984).

[63]Sprague and McNurlin, *Information Systems Management in Practice,* p. 307.

[64]Rockart and Flannery, "The Management of End-User Computing."

[65]See Jerome Kanter, *Management Information Systems* (Englewood Cliffs, N.J.: Prentice Hall, 1984), pp. 289–316.

[66]Scott Morton and Rockart, "Implications of Changes in Information Technology for Corporate Strategy," pp. 84–95.

[67]Paul Attewell and James Rule, "Computing and Organizations: What We Know and What We Don't Know," *Communications of the ACM* 27, no. 12 (December 1984):1184–1192.

[68]For a lively debate on the use and impact of computers on top management, see John Dearden, "Will the Computer Change the Job of Top Management?" *Sloan Management Review* 25, no. 1 (Fall 1983):57–60; and David Davis, "Computers and Top Management," *Sloan Management Review* 25, no. 3 (Spring 1984):63–67.

[69]Erik Sandberg-Diment, "Macintosh Marketing Overcomes Its Drawbacks," *The New York Times,* March 26, 1985, p. C4.

[70]Fred G. Steingraber, "Managing in the 1990s," *Business Horizons* (January–February 1990):50–61.

CASE ON CONTROLLING

CONTROLLING INFORMATION AT FRITO-LAY, INC.

BACKGROUND. In 1990, estimated retail sales for the U.S. snack-food industry—chips, candy, cookies, crackers, nuts, and other items—passed $37 billion, representing an annual growth rate of 5 percent. Per capita consumption of snack chips has been increasingly steadily in recent years: In 1985, annual per capita consumption was under 12 pounds; in 1990, consumption was nearly 14 pounds per person.

Frito-Lay, Inc., headquartered in Plano, Texas (north of Dallas), is the leading manufacturer of snack chips, in the United States, with nearly half the sales in the category. Eight of the company's products are among the top ten snack chip brands in this country. Frito-Lay is also the largest producer of snack chips internationally. Doritos brand tortilla chips and Ruffles brand potato chips are the only snack chips with $1 billion in retail sales in the international market.

Frito-Lay accounts for about 13 percent of sales in the total U.S. snack-food industry, which includes candy, cookies, and crackers as well as snack chips. A division of PepsiCo, Inc., Frito-Lay has been Pepsi's fastest-growing section during the past three years, mainly through acquisitions and volume growth. Sales have quadrupled and profits have increased eightfold.

COMPETITION. Like much of U.S. industry, Frito-Lay faces intense competition and a sophisticated, fragmented market. Management has had to learn to move fast and in a number of different directions at once. "We face both very strong national and regional competition," says Allen Dickinson, Frito-Lay's director of systems development. "What we realized is that regional companies are very strong, very focused. In order to compete in that market, we had to have information." Adds Charles Feld, Frito-Lay's vice president of management services: "This is really a bag-by-bag kind of business. It's 10,000 people doing thousands of things a day."

THE NEED FOR INFORMATION. Scanners at supermarket checkout counters have been collecting data about what products are being bought at what price for over a decade, but for half that time the software did not exist to present the information in a form that marketing managers could really use. By the mid-1980s, however, A. C. Nielsen Co. and others had developed systems to sort out data by brand, and the amount of scanner information increased about 500-fold. In order to manage this rising tide of data, Nielsen and other software makers, such as Information Resources and Metaphor Computer Systems, developed computer systems known as "quasi-expert systems" that automatically break down brand performance within regions and detail how competing products are doing, which promotions work, and whether specific store displays are attracting customers. These systems also generate summary reports that highlight unusual product performance.

INFORMATION SYSTEMS AT FRITO-LAY. One of the most significant breakthroughs for Frito-Lay operations came in 1988, when the company supplied its sales force with hand-held computer terminals called "bricks" that connect to a central data base. The bricks are used by drivers to gather information on sales throughout their routes and are updated daily. At each stop, the driver casts an experienced eye on the display shelves. He doesn't need to count, for he knows how many bags of Doritos or Ruffles will fill the space. He simply keys that number into the hand-held computer, and when he has finished the call, the computer prints out an itemized sales ticket, factoring in promotional allowances for the retailer. There are 10,000 Frito-Lay sales distributors who key in information on 100 Frito product lines in 400,000 stores, and that information appears on the company computer screens in easy-to-read charts. Red means a sales drop, yellow a slowdown, and green an uptick.

Also in 1988 Frito-Lay installed a sophisticated decision support system that gathers data daily from supermarkets, scans it for important clues about local trends, and flags executives about problems and opportunities in all of Frito-Lay's markets. Because the hardware and software that Frito-Lay wanted were not available on the market, the company decided to form a partnership with IBM and Comshare, Inc., to create the system. Later, Banyon, Inc., a specialist in local-area networks, and Scientific Atlanta, Inc., were added to the partnership. Frito-Lay now has what is probably the most powerful information-gathering system in the industry. The company credits its new system, an initial $40 million investment, with saving $39 million a year on returned products, or "stales."

The system also provides sales support to managers. Consider just these two examples:

In 1990, Frito-Lay had a problem in San Antonio and Houston. Sales were slumping in that area's supermarkets. CEO Robert H. Beeby turned to his computer, called up the data for south Texas, and quickly determined the cause of the problem. A regional competitor had just introduced El Galindo, a white-corn tortilla chip that was doing so well it had acquired more supermarket shelf space than Frito's traditional Tostitos tortilla chips. Within three months, Beeby had Frito-Lay producing a white-corn version of Tostitos that matched the competition and won back the lost market share.

On August 19, 1990, in the Dallas division of Frito-Lay, Managing Director Paul Davis noticed the beginnings of a disturbing trend in the weekly sales data: Sales of the company's Lay's and Ruffles potato chips were headed down. Within minutes after the offending numbers showed up in red on his computer screen, Davis was able to determine the cause of the problem—a competitor was making inroads by discounting its product and getting key display space in a leading grocery chain. Davis and his regional managers reacted quickly. They pulled comparative data from the retailer's sales and used the data to convince the retailer that the deep discounts were hurting the store's bottom line. By showing that it would be more profitable for the supermarket to reallocate space in Frito-Lay's favor, Frito-Lay won more retail space and resumed a good market position in that area.

The company intends to develop an improved system that will gather a wider range of information, including data on the performance of competitors. One benefit of the improved system is that it will let salespeople making presentations at grocery stores access data on Frito-Lay's selling position as well as on competitors' positions. Local managers like David Bugg, Frito-Lay's manager of sales marketing planning, already use the system in one-on-one meetings with regional managers to determine what goals have been met and what improvements can be made.

Ever since Frito-Lay started using its decision support system to improve local promotions and expand its share of shelf space, Tri-Sum, a competitor of Frito-Lay, has found it harder to compete. The president of Tri-Sum, Dick Dushesneau, admits that "we don't have the resources that they do. . . ."

No matter how sophisticated they become, marketing systems will never replace human decision making. Even if the sales data are only one day old, relying on them is like driving a car while looking only through the rearview mirror. Computer systems may fail to pick up certain factors that affect sales, such as the economic health of a certain target area. Still, the new information system seems to be a powerful weapon, placing Frito-Lay ahead of the competition in using scanner data. Frito's research and development department plans to integrate manufacturing, logistical, and marketing data into the system by mid-1991. At that point, about 120 managers should be on-line with executive information, and the hope is that the number will increase to 600 by 1992.

Sources: Jeffrey Rothfeder and Jim Bartimo, "How Software Is Making Food Sales a Piece of Cake," *Business Week,* July 2, 1990, pp. 54–55; Diana Kunde, "Computer Use Stacks the Chips in Frito-Lay's Favor," *The Chicago Tribune,* August 19, 1990, Sect. 7, p. 10A; and *Pepsico, Inc. Annual Report,* 1990.

Case Questions

1. Explain how management information is collected and organized by Frito-Lay and how top management uses these data.

2. Describe some of the production/operations management problems evident in this case.

3. Discuss the ways control is important to Frito-Lay and how is it integrated into the operation.

4. How does Frito-Lay use computers to stay competitive and retain market share?

GLOSSARY

acceptance-sampling procedure Quality control procedure to determine if the finished product conforms to design specifications.

action research The method through which organizational-development change agents learn what improvements are needed and how the organization can best be aided in making those improvements.

administration The performance of tasks needed to achieve predetermined goals.

administrative culture According to Stevenson and Gumpert, corporate culture focusing on existing opportunities, organizational structures, and control procedures.

algorithm Step-by-step procedure for solving a problem or completing a task.

apprentice Starting worker who usually does routine work under a supervisor or mentor.

artificial intelligence (AI) Development of computational approaches to simulate intelligent human thought or behavior.

assessment center Selection technique in which candidates are asked to participate in simulated tasks and exercises.

avoidance learning Learning that occurs when individuals change behavior to avoid or escape unpleasant circumstances.

balance sheet Description of the organization in terms of its assets, liabilities, and net worth.

balance sheet budget (or **pro forma balance sheet**) Budget combining all other budgets to project how the balance sheet will look at the end of the budgeting period.

behavior modification The use of reinforcement theory to change human behavior.

behavioral school A group of management scholars trained in sociology, psychology, and related fields, who use their diverse knowledge to understand and more effectively manage people in organizations.

bill of materials Listing of the type and number of parts needed to produce a given product.

boundary-spanning roles Jobs in which individuals act as liaisons between departments or organizations that are in frequent contact.

bounded rationality The concept that managers make the most logical decisions they can within the constraints of limited information and ability.

brainstorming Decision-making/problem-solving technique in which individuals or group members try to improve creativity by spontaneously proposing alternatives without concern for reality or tradition.

budget Formal quantitative statement of resources allocated for planned activities over stipulated periods of time.

budgets Formal quantitative statements of the resources allocated to specific programs or projects for a given period.

bureaucracy Organization with a legalized formal and hierarchical structure.

bureaucratic control Method of control that employs strict regulations to ensure desired behavior by organizational units—often used by multinational enterprises to control subsidiaries.

burnout State of emotional, mental, and physical exhaustion that results from continued exposure to high stress.

business plan Formal document containing a mission statement, description of the firm's goods or services, a market analysis, financial projections, and a description of management strategies for attaining goals.

business-unit strategy Strategy formulated to meet the goals of a particular business.

CAD/CAM (computer-aided design and computer-automated manufacturing) Integrated approach in which the software used in designing products is also used to write a computer program to control the machinery.

capacity planning Operations decision concerned with the quantity of goods or services to be produced.

capital expenditure budget Budget indicating future investments to be made in buildings, equipment, and other physical assets of the organization.

career anchor According to Schein, an occupational self-concept—an individual's sense of the kind of work he or she seeks to pursue and what that work implies about the individual.

career concepts According to Driver, the four basic career patterns—linear, steady-state, spiral, and transitory—by which people perceive their careers.

career plateau Career stage in which the likelihood of additional hierarchical promotion is very low.

cash budget Budget combining estimates for revenues, expenses, and new capital expenditures.

causal forecasting Forecasting that predicts how a dependent variable is affected by changes in independent variables.

centralization The extent to which authority is concentrated at the top of the organization.

certainty Decision-making condition in which managers have accurate, measurable, and reliable information about the outcome of various alternatives under consideration.

change agent The individual leading or guiding the process of change in an organizational situation.

channel The medium of communication between a sender and a receiver.

charismatic or **transformational leaders** Leaders who, through their personal vision and energy, inspire followers and have a major impact on their organizations.

charity principle Doctrine of social responsibility requiring more fortunate individuals to assist less fortunate members of society.

CIM (computer-integrated manufacturing) Integrated approach that combines CAD/CAM with the use of robots and computerized inventory management techniques.

circumferential movement According to Schein, transfer from one division, function, or department to another.

classical organization theory An early attempt, pioneered by Henri Fayol, to identify the principles and skills that underlie effective management.

closed system A system that does not interact with its environment.

coercive power The negative side of reward power, based on the influencer's ability to punish the influencee.

cohesiveness The degree of solidarity and positive feelings held by individuals toward their group.

collaborative management Management through power sharing and subordinate participation; the opposite of hierarchical imposition of authority.

colleague Worker who, while still subordinate, makes independent contributions to organizational activities.

collective bargaining The process of negotiating and administering agreements between labor and management concerning wages, working conditions, and other aspects of the work environment.

command group A group composed of a manager and the employees that report to that manager.

committee A formal organizational group, usually relatively long-lived, created to carry out specific organizational tasks.

common morality The body of moral rules governing ordinary ethical problems.

communication The process by which people attempt to share meaning via the transmission of symbolic messages.

communication network A set of channels within an organization or group through which communication travels.

comparable worth The principle that jobs requiring comparable skills and knowledge merit equal compensation even if the nature of the work activity is different.

competitive priorities Four major criteria, including pricing, quality levels, quality reliability, and flexibility, on which products and services are evaluated.

computer system An integrated collection of hardware, software, procedures, data, and people used to produce information.

computer-aided design (CAD) Design and drafting performed interactively on a computer.

computer-assisted instruction (CAI) A training technique in which computers are used to lessen the time necessary for training by instructors and to provide additional help to individual trainees.

computer-based information system (CBIS) (or computer-based MIS) Information system that goes beyond the mere standardization of data to aid in the planning process.

conflict Disagreement about the allocation of scarce resources or clashes regarding goals, values, and so on; can occur on the interpersonal or organizational level.

constraints Limitations upon resources, usually expressed mathematically.

content theories Theories of motivation that focus on the needs that motivate behavior.

contingency approach The view that the management technique that best contributes to the attainment of organizational goals might vary in different types of situations or circumstances.

control The process of ensuring that actual activities conform to planned activities.

control system Multistep procedure applied to various types of control activities.

coordination The integration of the activities of the separate parts of an organization to accomplish organizational goals.

coping skills training Programs that teach people to recognize and cope with situations in which they feel helpless.

corporate social performance A single theory of corporate social action encompassing social principles, processes, and policies.

corporate social responsiveness A theory of social responsibility that focuses on how companies respond to issues, rather than trying to determine their ultimate social responsibility.

corporate-level strategy Strategy formulated by top management to oversee the interests and operations of multiline corporations.

critical path The longest path through a PERT network; identifies the maximum amount of time required for essential tasks.

cultural relativism The idea that morality is relative to a particular culture, society, or community.

culture control Method of control, often associated with large Japanese companies, that emphasizes implicit and informal direction based on a broad company culture.

data Raw, unanalyzed numbers and facts.

data base Collection of integrated data that eliminates repetition and inconsistencies; usually shared between multiple work units.

decentralization The delegation of power and authority from higher to lower levels of the organization, often accomplished by the creation of small, self-contained organizational units.

decision making The process of identifying and selecting a course of action to solve a specific problem.

decision support system (DSS) Computer system accessible to nonspecialists to assist in planning and decision making.

decision tree Type of network used to model a progression of decisions involving uncertainty.

decoding The interpretation and translation of a message into meaningful information.

delegation The act of assigning formal authority and responsibility for completion of specific activities to a subordinate.

Delphi technique Qualitative forecasting technique that uses group brainstorming to reach a consensus and insight into the future.

departmentalization The grouping into departments of work activities that are similar and logically connected.

dependence According to Hannan and Freeman, the theoretical problem faced by an organization because of its need for vital resources from outside sources.

dependent variable Variable whose value depends on the value of an independent variable.

development program A process designed to develop skills necessary for future work activities.

dialectical inquiry method A method of analysis in which a decision maker determines and negates his or her assumptions, and then creates "countersolutions" based on the negative assumptions.

differential rate system Frederick W. Taylor's compensation system involving the payment of higher wages to more efficient workers.

differentiation The principle that differences in working styles, including differences in orientation and structure, can complicate the coordination of an organization's activities.

direct contact Simplest form of lateral relationship; communication between individuals who must deal with the same situation or problem.

direct investment Investment in foreign assets whereby a company purchases assets that it manages directly.

direct-action elements Elements of the environment that directly influence an organization's activities.

discretionary cost budget Budget used for departments in which output cannot be accurately measured.

distinctive competence Entrepreneurial desire to start a business coupled with the ability or experience to compete effectively once the enterprise is initiated.

division Large organization department that resembles a separate business; may be devoted to making and selling specific products or serving a specific market.

division of work The breakdown of a complex task into components so that individuals are responsible for a limited set of activities instead of the task as a whole.

duties Obligations to take specific steps or obey the law.

economic variables General economic conditions and trends that may be factors in an organization's activities.

effectiveness The ability to determine appropriate objectives: "doing the right things."

efficiency The ability to minimize the use of resources in achieving organizational objectives: "doing things right."

electronic data processing (EDP) Computerized data-processing and information management, including report standardization for operating managers.

empowerment The act of delegating power and authority to a subordinate so that the goals of the manager can be accomplished.

encoding The translation of information into a series of symbols for communication.

end-user computing The creative use of computers by those who are not experts in data processing.

engineered cost budget Budget describing material and labor costs of each item produced, including estimated overhead costs.

entrepreneur Either the originator of a new business venture or a manager who tries to improve an organizational unit by initiating productive changes.

entrepreneurial culture According to Stevenson and Gumpert, corporate culture focusing on the emergence of new opportunities, the means of capitalizing on them, and the creation of the structure appropriate for pursuing them.

entrepreneurship The seemingly discontinuous process of combining resources to produce new goods or services.

equity theory A theory of job motivation that emphasizes the role played by an individual's belief in the equity or fairness of rewards and punishments in determining his or her performance and satisfaction.

ERG theory Content theory of motivation that says people strive to meet a hierarchy of existence, relatedness, and growth needs; if efforts to reach one level of needs are frustrated, individuals will regress to a lower level.

ethics The study of rights and of who is—or should be—benefited or harmed by an action.

ethnocentric management Attitude that the home country's management practices are superior to those of other countries and can be exported along with the organization's goods and services.

expectancy approach A model of motivation specifying that the effort to achieve high performance is a function of the perceived likelihood that high performance can be achieved, and will be rewarded if achieved, and that the reward will be worth the effort expended.

expense center Commonly, administrative, service, and research departments where inputs are measured in monetary terms, although outputs are not.

expert power Power based on the belief or understanding that the influencer has specific knowledge or relevant expertise that the influencee does not.

expert system Application of artificial intelligence denoting the technology entailed by the development of computational approaches to human functioning.

external audit Verification process involving the independent appraisal of financial accounts and statements.

external environment All elements outside an organization that are relevant to its operation; includes direct-action and indirect-action elements.

external stakeholders Groups or individuals in an organization's external environment that affect the activities.

extinction The absence of reinforcement for undesirable behavior so that the behavior eventually stops recurring.

extrinsic reward Reward that is provided by an outside agent, such as a supervisor or work group.

feedback (interpersonal) The reversal of the communication process that occurs when the receiver expresses his or her reaction to the sender's message.

feedback (job-based) The part of system control in which the results of actions are returned to the individual, allowing work procedures to be analyzed and corrected.

financial budget Budget detailing the money expected to be spent during the budget period and indicating its sources.

financial statement Monetary analysis of the flow of goods and services to, within, and from the organization.

financing budget Budget that assures the organization of available funds to meet shortfalls of revenues when compared to expenses and that schedules potential borrowing needs.

first-line (or first-level) managers Managers who are responsible for the work of operating employees only and do not supervise other managers; they are the "first" or lowest level of managers in the organizational hierarchy.

fixed costs Those unaffected by the amount of work accumulated in the responsibility center.

flat organizational structure Organizational structure characterized by a wide span of management and few hierarchical levels.

flextime A system that permits employees to arrange their work hours to suit their personal needs.

flows Components such as information, material, and energy that enter and leave a system.

forecasting The process of using past events to make systematic predictions about the future.

formal authority Power rooted in the general understanding that specific individuals or groups have the right to exert influence within certain limits by virtue of their position within the organization. Also called legitimate power.

formal or systematic appraisal A formalized appraisal process for rating current subordinate performance, identifying subordinates deserving raises or promotions, and identifying subordinates in need of further training.

franchise A type of licensing arrangement in which a company sells a package containing a trademark, equipment, materials, and managerial guidelines.

function layout Layout planning concerned with storage layouts (for minimizing inventory and storage costs), marketing layouts (for maximizing product exposure and sales), and project layouts (for building such one-of-a-kind products as a dam).

functional authority The authority of staff department members to control the activities of other departments that are related to specific staff responsibilities.

functional manager A manager responsible for just one organizational activity, such as finance or human resource management.

functional organization A form of departmentalization in which everyone engaged in one functional activity, such as marketing or finance, is grouped into one unit.

functional-level strategy Strategy formulated by a specific functional area in an effort to carry out business-unit strategy.

Gantt chart A graphic method of planning and control that allows a manager to view the starting and ending dates for various tasks.

general manager The individual responsible for all activities, such as production, sales, marketing, and finance, for an organization like a company or a subsidiary.

geocentric management Attitude that accepts both similarities and differences between domestic and foreign management policies and so attempts to strike a balance between those that are most effective.

global strategic partnership Alliance formed by an organization with one or more foreign countries, generally with an eye toward exploiting the other countries' opportunities and toward assuming leadership in either supply or production.

goal-setting theory A process theory of motivation that focuses on the process of setting goals.

grapevine chains The various paths through which informal communication is passed through an organization; the four types are the "single-strand," "gossip," "probability," and "cluster" chains.

group Two or more people who interact with and influence each other toward a common purpose.

group-building and -maintenance role The group leader's specific function to fulfill the group's social needs by encouraging solidarity feelings.

Hawthorne effect The possibility that workers who receive special attention will perform better simply because they received that attention: one interpretation of studies by Elton Mayo and his colleagues.

heuristic principles A method of decision making that proceeds along empirical lines, using rules of thumb, to find solutions or answers.

hiring specification A written description of the education, experience, and skills needed to perform a job or position effectively.

human capital An organization's investment in the training and development of its members.

human resource audit The analysis and appraisal of the organization's current human resources.

human resource forecasting The attempt, using specific techniques, to predict and project future personnel needs.

human resource management (HRM) The management function that deals with recruitment, placement, training, and development of organization members.

human resource planning Planning for the future personnel needs of an organization, taking into account both internal activities and factors in the external environment.

income statement Summary of the organization's financial performance over a given interval of time.

incremental adjustment A method of managerial problem solving in which each successive action represents only a small change from activities.

independent variable Variable whose value does not change when the value of other variables are changed.

indirect-action elements Elements of the external environment that affect the climate in which an organization's activities take place, but do not affect the organization directly.

influence Any actions or examples of behavior that cause a change in attitude or behavior of another person or group.

informal organizational structure The undocumented and officially unrecognized relationships between members of an organization that inevitably emerge out of the personal and group needs of employees.

informal performance appraisal The process of continually feeding back to subordinates information regarding their work performance.

information Data that have been organized or analyzed in some meaningful way.

information ownership The possession by certain individuals of unique information and knowledge concerning their work.

infrastructure Physical facilities needed to support economic activity; includes transportation and communication systems, schools, hospitals, power plants, and sanitary facilities.

initial-strategy approach According to Alfred D. Chandler, "The determination of the basic long-term goals and objectives of an enterprise, and the adoption of courses of action and the allocation of resources necessary for carrying out these goals."

inputs Resources from the environment, such as raw materials and labor, that may enter any organizational system.

integrating roles Roles that are established when a specific product, service, or project spans several departments and requires coordination and attention from a single individual not in the departments in question.

integration The degree to which employees of various departments work together in a unified way.

internal audit Audit performed by the organization to ensure that its assets are properly safeguarded and its financial records reliably kept.

internal stakeholders Groups or individuals, such as employees, that are not strictly part of an organization's environment but for whom an individual manager remains responsible.

intrapreneuring Corporate entrepreneurship, whereby an organization seeks to expand by exploring new opportunities through new combinations of its existing resources.

intrinsic reward Psychological reward that is experienced directly by an individual.

inventory Supply of raw materials, work in progress, and finished goods an organization maintains to meet its operational needs.

investment center Organizational unit that not only measures the monetary value of inputs and outputs, but also compares outputs with assets used in producing them.

job description On the operative level, a written description of a job's title, duties, and responsibilities, including its location on the organization chart.

job design The division of an organization's work among its employees.

job enlargement The combining of various operations at a similar level into one job to provide more variety for workers and thus increase their motivation and satisfaction. An increase in job scope.

job enrichment The combining of several activities from a vertical cross section of the organization into one job to provide the worker with more autonomy and responsibility. An increase in job depth.

job specialization The division of work into standardized, relatively simple tasks.

joint venture Business undertaking in which foreign and domestic companies share the costs of building production or research facilities in foreign countries.

just-in-time (JIT) inventory system Inventory system in which production quantities are ideally equal to delivery quantities, with materials purchased and finished goods delivered "just in time for usage."

key performance (or key result) areas Aspects of a unit or organization that must function effectively if the entire unit or organization is to succeed.

lateral communication Communication between departments of an organization that generally follows the work flow, thus providing a direct channel for coordination and problem solving.

lateral relationship A relationship that cuts across the chain of command, allowing direct contact between members of different departments. Examples are some committees, liaison roles, and integrating roles.

leader-member relations The quality of the interaction between a leader and his or her subordinates; according to Fiedler, the most important influence on the manager's power.

leadership The process of directing and influencing the task-related activities of group members.

leadership functions The group-maintenance and task-related activities that must be performed by the leader, or someone else, for a group to perform effectively.

leadership styles The various patterns of behavior favored by leaders during the process of directing and influencing workers.

least preferred co-worker (LPC) Fiedler's measuring instrument for locating a manager on the leadership-style continuum.

legitimate power Power that exists when a subordinate or influencee acknowledges that the influencer has a "right" or is lawfully entitled to exert influence—within certain bounds. Also called *formal authority.*

licensing The selling of rights to market brand-name products or to use patented processes or copyrighted materials.

line authority The authority of those managers directly responsible, throughout the organization's chain of command, for achieving organizational goals.

linear career concept According to Driver, career concept by which an indi-

vidual chooses a field, develops a plan for advancement, and executes it.

linear programming (LP) Mathematical technique for determining the optimum combination of resources.

macroeconomic policy Decisions concerning such factors as taxation, development costs, regulatory control, and other external factors that might affect the development of a new product.

management The process of planning, organizing, leading, and controlling the work of organization members and of using all available organizational resources to reach stated organizational goals.

management by objectives (MBO) A formal set of procedures that establishes and reviews progress toward common goals for managers and subordinates.

management information system (MIS) Computer-based information system for more effective planning, decision making, and control.

management science (MS) Mathematical techniques for the modeling, analysis, and solution of management problems. Also called *operations research (OR).*

Managerial Grid Diagram developed by Blake and Mouton to measure a manager's relative concern for people and production.

managerial linking role A role that may be required if an integrating position does not coordinate a particular task effectively.

managerial performance The measure of how efficient and effective a manager is—how well he or she determines and achieves appropriate objectives.

Maslow's hierarchy of needs Content theory of motivation that people are motivated to meet five types of needs, which can be ranked in a hierarchy.

materials-requirements planning (MRP) Operational planning system whereby end products are analyzed to determine the materials needed to produce them.

materials-resource planning (MRP II) Compares MRP needs to known resources and calculates unit costs; can also be used with other computer programs to handle order entry, invoicing, and other operations tasks.

matrix organization An organizational structure in which each employee reports to both a functional or division manager and to a project or group manager.

mechanistic system According to Burns and Stalker, one characterized by a bureaucratic organization.

mentor Employee who develops ideas, supervises others, and assumes responsibility for the work of subordinates.

message The encoded information sent by the sender to the receiver.

middle managers Managers in the mid-range of the organizational hierarchy; they are responsible for other managers and sometimes for some operating employees.

mission statement Broad organizational goal, based on planning premises, which justifies an organization's existence.

model A simplified representation of the key properties of a real-world object, event, or relationship; can be verbal, physical, or mathematical.

moral rules Rules for behavior that often become internalized as moral values.

motivation The factors that cause, channel, and sustain an individual's behavior.

multicriteria analysis Qualitative forecasting technique in which a jury of experts evaluates various alternatives by assigning numerical scores to key criteria identified by consensus.

multidivisional firm An organization that has expanded into different industries and diversified its products.

multinational enterprise (MNE) Large corporations with operations and divisions spread over several countries but controlled by a central headquarters.

naive relativism The idea that all human beings are themselves the standard by which their actions should be judged.

natural-language processing Use of everyday language instead of special codes or instructions to communicate with a computer system.

need-achievement According to McClelland, a social motive to excel that tends to characterize successful entrepreneurs, especially when reinforced by cultural factors.

negotiation The use of communication skills and bargaining to manage conflict and reach mutually satisfying outcomes.

neo-human relations movement An integrative approach to management theory that combines a positive view of human nature with the scientific study of organizations to prescribe how effective managers should act in most circumstances.

network Set of interrelated tasks or events.

network analysis A technique used for scheduling complex projects that contain interrelationships between activities or events.

noise Anything that confuses, disturbs, diminishes, or interferes with communication.

nonprogrammed decisions Specific solutions created through an unstructured process to deal with nonroutine problems.

objective A goal characterized by a comparatively short time span and specific, measurable achievements.

one-way communication Any communication from the sender without feedback from the receiver.

open system A system that interacts with its environment.

operating budget Budget indicating the goods and services the organization expects to consume in a budget period.

operational plan Plan that provides the details needed to incorporate strategy into day-to-day operations.

operations The production activities of an organization.

operations management Complex management activity that includes planning production, organizing resources, directing operations and personnel, and monitoring system performance.

opportunity Situation that occurs when circumstances offer an organization the chance to exceed stated goals and objectives.

organic system According to Burns and

Stalker, one characterized by group actions and open communication.

organization Two or more people who work together in a structured way to achieve a specific goal or set of goals.

organization chart A diagram of an organization's structure, showing the functions, departments, or positions of the organization and how they are related.

organizational culture The set of important understandings, such as norms, values, attitudes, and beliefs, shared by organizational members.

organizational design The determination of the organizational structure that is most appropriate for the strategy, people, technology, and tasks of the organization.

organizational development (OD) A long-range effort supported by top management to increase an organization's problem-solving and renewal processes through effective management of organizational culture.

organizational structure The way in which an organization's activities are divided, organized, and coordinated.

orientation or socialization A program designed to help employees fit smoothly into an organization.

outcome interdependence The degree to which the work of a group has consequences felt by all its members.

outputs Transformed inputs that are returned to the external environment as products or services.

path-goal model A leadership theory emphasizing the leader's role in clarifying for subordinates how they can achieve high performance and its associated rewards.

payoff matrix Table showing the expected outcomes of various decision alternatives; used in decisions involving uncertainty.

performance gaps The difference between the objectives established in the goal-formulation process and the results likely to be achieved if the existing strategy is continued.

planned change The systematic attempt to redesign an organization in a way that will help it adapt to changes in the external environment or to achieve new goals.

planning The process of establishing goals and suitable courses of action for achieving those goals.

planning premises Basic assumptions about an organization's purpose, its values, distinctive competencies, and place in the world.

policy A standing plan that establishes general guidelines for decision making.

policy-formulation approach The concept of implementing day-to-day rules that puts boundaries around what a functional area can and cannot do.

political risk Possibility that political changes, either in the short or long run, will affect the activities of an organization doing business in foreign countries.

political variables Factors that may influence an organization's activities as a result of the political process or climate.

polycentric management Attitude that since a foreign country's management poli-

cies are best understood by its own management personnel, the home organization should rely on foreign offices.

portfolio framework An approach to corporate-level strategy advocated by the Boston Consulting Group; also known as the BCG matrix.

portfolio investment Investment in foreign assets whereby a company purchases shares in companies that own those assets.

position description On the management level, a written description of a position's title, duties, and responsibilities, including its location on the organization chart.

position power The power, according to Fiedler, that is inherent in the formal position the leader holds. This power may be great or small, depending on the specific position.

positive reinforcement The use of positive consequences to encourage desirable behavior.

post-action controls Method of control for measuring the results of a completed activity.

power The ability to exert influence; that is, the ability to change the attitudes or behavior of individuals or groups.

pre-action controls (or precontrols) Control method ensuring that human, material, and financial resources have been budgeted.

premise Assumption that forms the basis of plans.

primary relations Interaction between a business and market-oriented groups, such as customers, employees, shareholders, and creditors.

probability A statistical measure of the chance a certain event or outcome will occur.

problem Situation that occurs when an actual state of affairs differs from a desired state of affairs.

procedure A standing plan that contains detailed guidelines for handling organizational actions that occur regularly.

process consultation A technique by which consultants help organization members understand and change the ways they work together.

process theories Theories of motivation that study the thought processes by which people decide how to act.

process-control procedure Quality control procedure for monitoring quality during production of the product or rendering of the service.

product or market organization The organization of a company into divisions that bring together all those involved with a certain type of product or market.

product-cycle theory According to Vernon, the process whereby products originally developed for home markets earn enough foreign demand to justify direct foreign investment in their production.

production organization Organization that produces tangible goods that can be mass-produced and stored for later consumption.

productivity Measure of how well an operations system functions and indicator of the efficiency and competitiveness of a single firm or department.

profit budget (or master budget)

Budget combining cost and revenue budgets in one unit.

profit center Organizational unit where performance is measured by numerical differences between revenues and expenditures.

program A single-use plan that covers a relatively large set of organizational activities and specifies major steps, their order and timing, and the unit responsible for each step.

program evaluation and review technique (PERT) A network analysis technique, using estimates of the time required to complete tasks, which is employed to schedule and control projects for which task-completion times cannot be predicted fairly precisely.

programmed decisions Solutions to routine problems determined by rule, procedure, or habit.

project The smaller and separate portions of the programs.

prototype Working model of a product, a problem solution, or a computer system.

psychosocial function According to Kram, aspect of a professional relationship that improves one's sense of competence, identity, and effectiveness.

punishment The application of negative consequences to stop or correct improper behavior.

qualitative forecasting Forecasting technique that transforms judgments, opinions, and knowledge into quantitative estimates.

qualitative overloading Situation that occurs when an individual lacks the abilities or resources necessary to satisfactorily complete a task.

quality circles Work groups that meet to discuss ways to improve quality and solve production problems.

quality control Strategy for managing each stage of production so as to minimize or eliminate errors.

quantitative forecasting Forecasting based on use of mathematical rules to manipulate existing data.

quantitative overloading Situation that occurs when an individual is given more tasks than he or she can accomplish in a given time.

radial movement According to Schein, movement either toward or away from an organization's central "core" of power.

ratio analysis Reporting of key figures from the organization's financial records as percentages or fractions.

rational method of decision making A four-step process that helps managers weigh alternatives and choose the alternative with the best chance of success.

realistic job preview (RJP) A description provided by the organization to applicants and new employees that gives both the positive and negative aspects of a job.

receiver The individual whose senses perceive the sender's message.

recruitment The development of a pool of job candidates in accordance with a human resource plan.

redundancy Repeating or restating a message to ensure its reception or to reinforce its impact.

reference group A group with whom individuals identify and compare themselves.

referent power Power based on the desire of the influencee to be like or identify with the influencer.

refreezing Transforming a new behavioral pattern into the norm through reinforcement and supporting mechanisms.

regression analysis Statistical tool for performing causal forecasting.

reinforcement theory An approach to motivation based on the "law of effect"—the idea that behavior with positive consequences tends to be repeated, while behavior with negative consequences tends not to be repeated.

relaxation training Popular methods, including meditation and biofeedback, by which individuals learn to control muscle tension and ease the experience of stress.

reorientation situation Strategy situation in which poor performance despite sound strategy calls for change to be implemented by outsiders.

replacement chart A chart that diagrams an organization's positions, showing the incumbents, likely future candidates, and readiness of candidates to enter those positions.

research and development (R&D) Entrepreneurial function devoting organizational assets to the design, testing, and production of new products.

responsibility center Any organizational function or unit whose manager is responsible for all of its activities.

revenue budget Budget measuring marketing and sales effectiveness by multiplying the unit price of each product by the predicted sales quantity.

revenue center Organizational unit in which outputs measured in monetary terms are not directly compared to input costs.

reward power Power derived from the fact that one person, known as an influencer, has the ability to reward another person, known as an influencee, for carrying out orders, which may be expressed or implied.

rights Claims that entitle a person to take a particular action.

risk Decision-making condition in which managers know the probability a given alternative will lead to a desired goal or outcome.

role conflict According to Katz and Kahn, a situation in which an individual is confronted by two or more incompatible demands.

role perception The individual's understanding of the behaviors needed to accomplish a task or perform a job.

rules Standing plans that detail specific actions to be taken in a given situation.

sales and revenue forecasting Forecasting amounts of income expected from sales and other sources of revenue.

satisfice Decision-making technique in which managers accept the first satisfactory decision they uncover.

scalar principle The concept that a clear line of authority through the organization must exist if delegation is to work successfully.

scientific management theory A management approach, formulated by Frederick W. Taylor and others between 1890 and 1930, that sought to determine scientifically the best methods for performing any task, and for selecting, training, and motivating workers.

secondary relations Interaction between a business and non–market-oriented segments of society, such as the law and moral forces.

selection The mutual process whereby the organization decides whether or not to make a job offer and the candidate decides whether or not to accept it.

selective-blend situation Strategy situation entailing major changes in organizational strategy that blend both outsiders and insiders to perform corrective measures.

self-leadership The ability of workers to motivate themselves to perform both tasks that are naturally rewarding and those that are necessary but not appealing.

self-managed work groups Work teams organized around a particular task and composed of members who possess both the skills necessary to accomplish the task and the power to determine such factors as method of operation, assignment of responsibilities, and creation of work schedules.

semivariable costs Those, like short-term labor costs, that vary with the amount of work performed but not in a proportional way.

sender The initiator of a communication.

sense of potency Collective belief of a group that it can be effective.

sensitivity training An early personal growth technique, at one time fairly widespread in organizational development efforts, that emphasizes increased sensitivity in interpersonal relationships.

service organization Organization that produces intangible goods that require consumer participation and cannot be stored.

Seven-S model According to Waterman and others, framework for change identifying seven key factors that can adversely affect successful change in an organization.

single-use plan A detailed course of action used once or only occasionally to solve a problem that does not occur repeatedly.

situational leadership theory An approach to leadership developed by Hersey and Blanchard that describes how leaders should adjust their leadership style in response to their subordinates' evolving desire for achievement, experience, ability, and willingness to accept responsibility.

social audit Report describing a company's activities in a given area of social interest, such as environmental protection, workplace safety, or community involvement.

social variables Factors, such as demographics, lifestyle, and social values, that may influence an organization from its external environment.

span of management (or **span of control**) The number of subordinates reporting directly to a given manager.

spiral career concept According to Driver, career concept by which individuals motivated by personal growth perform well enough to advance in status and rank.

sponsor Upper-level manager involved in the major decision-making activities of the organization.

spreadsheet optimizer Electronic spreadsheet enhancement that automatically adjusts "what-if" cells based on user-entered data.

stability situation Strategy situation in which good past performance and the minor nature of needed changes make insiders the best choice for implementing.

staff authority The authority of those groups of individuals who provide line managers with advice and services.

stakeholders Those groups or individuals who are directly or indirectly affected by an organization's pursuit of its goals.

standing plan An established set of decisions used by managers to deal with recurring or organizational activities; major types are policies, procedures, and rules.

start-up Business founded by individuals intending to change the environment of a given industry by the introduction of either a new product or a new production process.

steady-state career concept According to Driver, career concept by which an individual chooses a field but, even though improving professionally and financially, does not seek to move up the organizational hierarchy.

steering controls (or **cybernetic** or **feedforward controls**) Control method designed to detect deviations from some standard goal and to permit corrective measures.

stewardship principle Biblical doctrine that requires businesses and wealthy individuals to view themselves as stewards, or caretakers, holding their property in trust for the benefit of the whole society.

strategic business-unit (SBU) planning Grouping business activities within a multibusiness corporation because they generate closely related products or services.

strategic control The process of checking strategy implementation progress against the strategic plan at periodic or critical intervals to determine if the corporation is moving toward its strategic objectives.

strategic control points Critical points in a system at which monitoring or collecting information should occur.

strategic management approach A pattern based on the principle that the overall design of the organization can be described only if the attainment of objectives is added to policy and strategy as one of the key factors in management's operation of the organization's activities.

strategic plans Plans designed to meet an organization's broad goals.

strategy The broad program for defining and achieving an organization's objectives; the organization's response to its environment over time.

strategy implementation The basically administrative tasks needed to put strategy into practice.

strategy-formulation task A model of strategy formulation that takes into account the organization's goals and its strategy.

stress The tension and pressure that result when an individual views a situation as presenting a demand that threatens to exceed his or her capabilities or resources.

stressor Source of pressure and tension that creates stress.

subcritical path In a PERT network, path other than the critical path; identifies opportunity to save time by reassigning slack resources to critical path.

subsystems Those parts making up the whole system.

syndrome of unused potential, or reality shock syndrome According to Hall, an individual's reaction to the difference between high job expectations and the frustrating day-to-day realities of the workplace.

synergy The situation in which the whole is greater than its parts. In organizational terms, synergy means that departments that interact cooperatively are more productive than they would be if they operated in isolation.

System 1 Traditional organizational structure where power and authority are distributed according to the manager-subordinate relationship.

System 4 Ideal organizational structure where there is extensive group participation in supervision and decision making.

system boundary The boundary that separates each system from its environment. It is rigid in a closed system, flexible in an open system.

systems approach View of the organization as a unified, directed system of interrelated parts.

Systems 2 and 3 Intermediate stages between the traditional structure and the ideal structure.

tall organizational structure Organizational structure characterized by a narrow span of management and many hierarchical levels.

task force or project team A temporary group formed to address a specific problem.

task interdependence The extent to which a group's work requires its members to interact with one another.

task role The specific role within a group performed by the leader, whether formal or informal.

task structure A work situation variable that, according to Fiedler, helps determine a manager's power. In structured tasks, managers automatically have high power; in unstructured tasks, their power is diminished.

team building A method of improving organizational effectiveness at the team level by diagnosing barriers to team performance and improving interteam relationships and task accomplishment.

technological forecasting Forecasting how quickly technological innovations will become practical and make existing technology obsolete.

technological variables New developments in products or processes, as well as advances in science, that may affect an organization's activities.

theory Coherent group of assumptions put forth to explain the relationship between two or more observable facts and to provide a sound basis for predicting future events.

Theory X According to McGregor, a traditional view of motivation that holds that work is distasteful to employees, who must be motivated by force, money, or praise.

Theory Y According to McGregor, the assumption that people are inherently motivated to work and do a good job.

time series analysis Quantitative forecasting technique that predicts changes in one variable over time.

time series data Data that is collected at regular intervals of time.

top management Managers responsible for the overall management of the organization. They establish operating policies and guide the organization's interactions with its environment.

total quality management (TQM) Strategic commitment to improving quality by combining statistical quality control methods with a cultural commitment to seeking incremental improvements that increase productivity and lower costs.

training program A process designed to maintain or improve current job performance.

transaction analysis An approach to improving interpersonal effectiveness, sometimes used in organizational development efforts, that concentrates on the styles and content of communication.

transactional leaders Leaders who determine what subordinates need to do to achieve objectives, classify those requirements, and help subordinates become confident they can reach their objectives.

transformational coping According to Maddi and Kobasa, the process whereby commitment to work values, a sense of control over work variables, and the view of problems as challenges can turn stressful situations in less stressful directions.

transitory career concept According to Driver, career concept by which an individual moves from one job to another with no apparent pattern or progress.

turbulence Decision-making condition that occurs when objectives are unclear or when the environment is changing rapidly.

turnover situation Strategy situation in which poor performance entails major changes that cannot be handled by insiders.

two-factor theory Herzberg's theory that work dissatisfaction and satisfaction arise from two different sets of factors.

two-way communication Communication that occurs when the receiver provides feedback to the sender.

uncertainty Decision-making condition in which managers face unpredictable external conditions or lack the information needed to establish the probability of certain events.

underloading Stress, resulting in boredom and monotony, produced when an individual has insufficient work to do.

unfreezing Making the need for change so obvious that the individual, group, or organization can readily see and accept that change must occur.

unity of command principle A guideline for delegation that states that each individual in an organization should report to only one superior.

valence The motivating power of a specific outcome of behavior; varies from individual to individual.

values Relatively permanent desires that seem to be good in themselves.

variable Any measure that can vary.

variable costs Expenses that vary directly with the amount of work being performed.

vertical communication Any communication that moves up or down the chain of command.

vertical information system Means through which data are transmitted up and down the managerial hierarchy.

vertical integration Broadening the scope of an organization's operations by buying a supplier or distributor that will contribute to efficient production of primary product or service offerings.

vertical movement According to Schein, hierarchical change in one's formal rank or management level.

whistleblowing Alerting management to decisions, policies, or practices that may be ill-advised, detrimental, or illegal; can include publicizing such matters outside the organization.

work in progress Partially finished goods; also called *work in process.*

work-flow layout Layout planning concerned with product layouts (for the sequential steps in production), process layouts (for arranging production according to task), and fixed-position layouts (for handling such large or heavy products as ships).

work-force literacy Knowledge and skills directly related to job performance.

yes/no controls (or go/no go controls) Control method for screening procedures that must be followed or conditions that must be met before operations continue.

yield management Mathematical technique for increasing revenue by pricing products to reflect either low or high demand.

zero-base budgeting (ZBB) A budgeting approach in which managers use cost-benefit analyses to justify all budget decisions, rather than using the previous year's budget as a starting point.

"zone of indifference" or "area of acceptance" According to Barnard and Simon, respectively, inclinations conditioning individuals to accept orders that fall within a familiar range of responsibility or activity.

PHOTO CREDITS

CHAPTER 17

page 505—Courtesy of Ford Motor Co.; page 508—Steve Woit; page 512—Steven Pumphrey; page 514—Tom Napper/Montgomery Ward; page 516—Danny Turner.

CHAPTER 18

page 529—Baldev/Sygma; page 531—Chuck Berman/*Chicago Tribune*; page 534—Rob Kinmonth; page 538—Tim Redel/Onyx; page 547—Sepp Seitz/Woodfin Camp; page 549—Gerry Gropp.

CHAPTER 19

page 561—Arlene Collins/Monkmeyer Press; page 565—Mathieson/Sygma; page 572—Bob Sacha; page 580—Alan Levinson; page 582—Walter P. Calahan; page 584—Antonin Kratochvil/Dot Pictures.

CHAPTER 20

page 599—Jonathan Kirn/Picture Group; page 601—Will and Deni McIntyre; page 602—Louis Psihoyos; page 605—Michael L. Abramson; page 607—Marc Chaumeil; page 612—Richard Bowditch; page 618—James Schnepf.

CHAPTER 21

page 631—Ann States/SABA; page 635—David Smart; page 637—Will and Deni McIntyre; page 640—Philip Saltonstall; page 642—Steve Boljonis; page 643—Hasimoto/Sygma; page 644—Alex Quesada/Matrix; page 647—Michael Abramson; page 653—Kevin Cruff; page 655—Shonna Valeska.

CHAPTER 22

page 665—Valrie Massey/Photo 20-20; page 667—Landmark Graphics Corp.; page 669—Valrie Massey/Photo 20-20; page 670—Katherine Lambert; page 673—John Storey; page 676—David Walbert; page 685—Mary Herlehy/Crain Communications; page 688—John S. Abbott.

COMPANY INDEX

SUBJECT INDEX

case study on (W.L. Gore), 494
case study on (NASA), 499–500
case study on (new products group), 594–96
case study on (three decisions), 498
challenges to theory of, 491–94
in committees, 518
contingency approach to, 480–89
of groups, 509
as managerial role or function, 9, 13
moral leadership, 473
trait approach to, 473–74
transformational or charismatic, 489–91
Leading indicators, 286
"Lean and mean" philosophy, 460
"Learners," 578, 579
Least preferred co-worker (LPC), 483–84
Legal environment
age discrimination suits, 580
multinational, 137
and recruitment, 379–83
and termination, 396
and tobacco company memos, 541
Legislation, on meat and food industry, 35
Legitimate power, 346, 472
Leverage, in ratio analysis, 612
Levinson career model, 570–73
Liabilities, 610
Liaison individuals, 545
Liaison role, 13–14
Licensing, 134
international, 124, 134
Life cycles, 79–80
Lifestyles, 76–77
Linear career concept, 573
Linear programming (LP), 292–94
Line authority, 351
Liquidity, 609
in ratio analysis, 612
Lithuania, 236
Locational transformations, 633
Locus of control, 164
Logistics, 275
at General Motors, 275, 295, 300
Loyalty dilemmas, 566

Macroeconomic policy, 160
Magnetic character readers (MCRs), 653
Malcolm Baldrige National Quality Award, 7, 194, 656
Management, 4
case study in (apology from superior), 21
case study in (Will-Burt), 22–23
challenge of, 15–19
collaborative, 418
and command economy, 236
decision-making approach of, 278
vs. entrepreneurship, 156–57
participative, 492–94 (see also Participative management)
skills in, 12
team (democratic), 479, 480, 603–4, 631, 636
(See also Managers)
Management by exception, 606
Management by objectives (MBO), 232–33
as equity approach, 453

Management development, 389–91
in Seven-S model, 222
Management games, 386
Management information systems (MIS), 278, 666, 670–73
case study on, 669
case study on (Frito-Lay), 699–700
case study on (Japanese firms), 686
case study on (Sears), 665, 674, 690
and chief information officer, 673–74
and cultural differences among professionals, 671
and decentralization, 364–65
and decision support systems, 671, 683
design of, 674–77
and end-user computing, 682–88
decision support systems, 683–84
expert systems and artificial intelligence, 684–85, 687
and idea development, 425
impact of, 689
implementing of, 675, 677–82
intraorganizational conflict over, 683
Management process, 6, 8–10
Management replacement chart, 376, 377
Management science (MS), 16, 43–44, 276
case study on (American Airlines), 279
case study on (L.L. Bean), 302–3
case study on (General Motors), 275, 295, 300
emerging techniques in, 297–99
goals of, 276–78
lessons learned about (GM), 300
process of, 278–82
Management style (see Leadership and leadership style; Style, management)
Management theory, 28–29
behavioral school of, 40–43
case study in (Ford), 27, 39, 50
case study on (strike/shutdown), 52
case study on (U.S. Postal Service), 53
classical, 30–38, 44–45
classical organization theory, 35–37
contingency approach to, 47–48, 141
evolution of, 44–45
management science school of, 43–44
neoclassical approach to, 28
neo-human relations movement, 48–49
and new kind of leader, 490
scientific, 28, 31–33
systems approach to, 45–47
Managerial Grid, 478–79
Managerial interventions, 216
Managerial linking role, 324
Managerial performance, 6
short-term insisted on, 73
Managerial prerogative E-Strategy, 201
Managers
Japanese, 133
and management information systems, 678–79
in MNEs, 140–41
and power, 350, 564
reactive vs. proactive, 92n.34
roles of, 12–15
communication in, 530

selection of, 383, 385
as stakeholders, 74
and strategic situation, 223, 225–26
types of
first-level, 10, 364
functional, 11
general, 11
middle, 10 (see also Middle management)
top, 10, 673, 678, 679
women as, 77, 584–86
(See also Management)
Maquiladora plants, 645
Marginal value, 298
Marine Spill Response Corporation, 103
Market development, 206
Marketing layouts, 647
Marketing strategies, 206
by Harley-Davidson, 337–38
Market penetration, 206
Masculinity vs. femininity, as Hofstede variable, 141
Maslow's hierarchy of needs, 43, 442–44, 449
Mass production
and Ford, 39
in task-technology approach, 332
Master budgets, 618
Materials as Needed (MAN), 337
Materials-requirement planning (MRP), 642, 652
Materials-resource planning (MRP II), 652
Matrix, payoff, 294–96
Matrix organization, 316, 319–22
of American Airlines Decision Technologies Division, 279
and task force/managerial linking role, 325
vs. unity-of-command principle, 355
Mechanistic job design, 357, 361
Mechanistic system, 330–31
Media, as stakeholders, 69
Meditation, 569
Memos, and legal liability, 541
Mentor, 577, 584
as power source, 351
Mergers, 73
Merit analysis, 287
Message, 533
and decoding, 535
Mexican-American workers, 449
Mexico
currency measures of (1984), 77
free trade agreement with, 644
Middle management, 10
and downsizing, 327
and flat organizational structure, 314
information-system needs of, 672
and management information systems, 679
study programs for, 391
and superteams, 507
Mid-life crisis, 572, 578
Milestones, 289
Minorities
and communication, 531–32
and cultural diversity, 16–18
and future employment policies, 401–2
at Gannett Company, 401
and leadership style, 477
(See also Blacks; Hispanics)

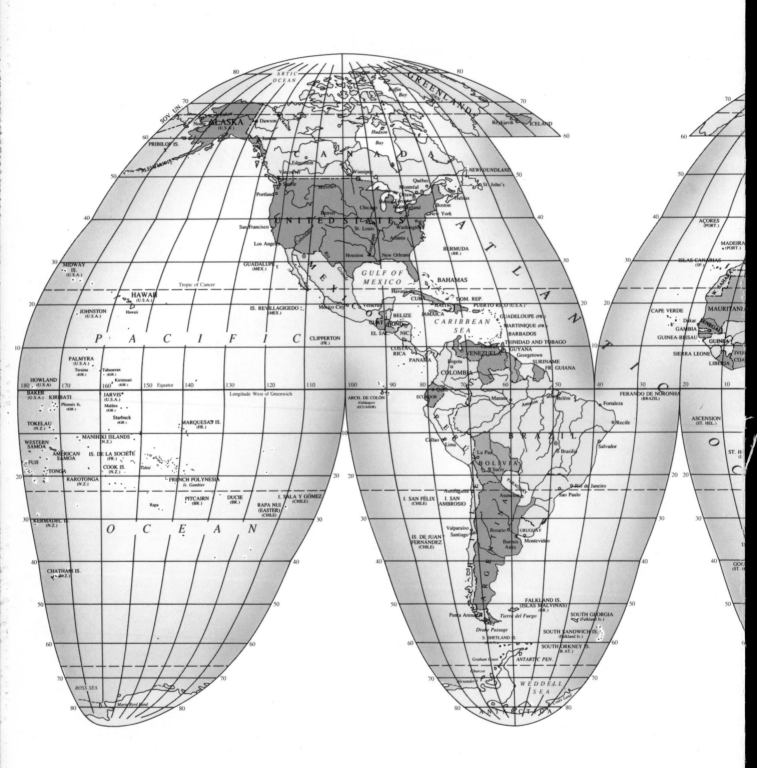